"I am truly delighted to welcome the *Routledge Handbook of European Elections,* which represents an important step forward in overcoming the gap of public knowledge and participation that has characterized the European Parliament's electoral contests over the last years. Donatella M. Viola's ground-breaking volume, targeted not just at an academic but at a wider audience, is built on a meticulous research on the organization and functioning of the European Parliament. It presents crucial insights and detailed analysis at national and EU level that may help reviving the old principles of European integration and hopefully lead to forging a common European identity."

David-Maria Sassoli, Vice-President of the European Parliament

"No student or practitioner will work on the European Parliament in the future without using this Handbook as an essential source of data and information both on the electorates in the national Member States and at the European level. No scholar will analyze the European integration process ignoring the suggestions of this volume on the necessary remedies to the EU current shortcomings, based, first of all, on the passage from initial permissive consensus to real popular legitimacy, which is the oxygen of any democratic institution of our time."

Giuliano Amato, Former Prime Minister of Italy and Professor Emeritus at the European University Institute, Florence, Italy

"The community of political scientists – be they involved in the study of EU, legislatures or elections – was awaiting for a book proposing an inclusive and fully documented view on the EP elections. Donatella M. Viola's volume proposes, for the first time, a longitudinal and comparative approach of this event in all the EU Member States since 1979. It is based on an in-depth empirical comparative research – combining the qualitative and the quantitative methods – shaped by a robust theoretical framework. This Handbook proposes a novel and refreshing exploration of the EP elections. It constitutes a major contribution to the understanding of political life, at both national and European levels, and to the study of the institutional evolutions that affect the EU regime."

Olivier Costa, Director of European Political and Administrative Studies, College of Europe, Bruges, Belgium and Research Professor, Sciences Po Bordeaux, France

"This is the definitive Handbook on European Parliament elections. The chapters paint a picture of growing heterogeneity in how these elections work: with declining turnout and legitimacy in many Central and Eastern European countries, yet the seeds of a new engagement with the 2014 *Spitzenkandidaten* process in some of the Original Six Member States. This heterogeneity is a challenge to both existing theories of these elections as well as ongoing EU democratic reform."

Simon Hix, Professor of European and Comparative Politics, London School of Economics, UK and Fellow of the British Academy

"In its combination of broad scope and close attention to detail, Donatella M. Viola's ambitious Handbook would be hard to beat as a reference of first resort for those studying the EU's democratic credentials, electoral processes or the linkage between electoral behaviour and election outcomes at national and EU level. I am confident that it will prove an essential source and important reference tool for students and scholars alike."

Mark N. Franklin, inaugural Stein Rokkan Professor of Comparative Politics, European University Institute, Florence, Italy and Fellow at the Massachusetts Institute of Technology, Cambridge, USA

"Handbooks have become an essential resource for researchers in political science as they provide a 'state of the art' on important scholarly topics. This 800-page volume entitled the *Routledge Handbook of European Elections* offers those interested in the politics of the European Union, comparative politics and electoral studies with a treasure trove of data and analysis on the largest transnational elections in the world since the inception of direct elections in 1979. Donatella M. Viola is to be congratulated on the achievement of such a Herculean task."

Brigid Laffan, Director of the Robert Schuman Centre for
Advanced Studies, European University Institute, Florence, Italy

"Donatella M. Viola has produced in this Handbook an excellent survey of the different aspects of elections to the European Parliament. It provides a broad theoretical framework for understanding and evaluating these elections as well as a rich fund of empirical data on all the elections held in each of the Member States. As the most complete and up-to-date volume of European elections in an enlarged Europe, I strongly recommend it to scholars and students of European Union politics."

John Loughlin, Professor of European Politics and Director of the Von
Hügel Institute, St Edmund's College, University of Cambridge, UK

"The European Parliament deserves a big book because it is the only institution of the European Union that is directly elected by European citizens. Donatella M. Viola's Handbook gives the subject the full coverage it deserves by combining a European overview with detailed accounts of how national parties and electorates behave in each of the EU Member States."

Richard Rose, Professor of Politics and Director of the Centre for the
Study of Public Policy, University of Strathclyde, Glasgow, UK

"It is increasingly rare to see scholars venturing upon ambitious projects aimed at writing and editing large books since it is widely recognized that what counts are just articles in highly ranking journals. Donatella M. Viola proves that this is a false and erroneous conception. There is indeed room and, what is more, a sustained need for comprehensive overviews. I am therefore very pleased to welcome this excellent and up-to-date account of theoretical and empirical efforts to understand European Parliament elections."

Hermann Schmitt, Professor of Political Science,
University of Manchester, UK and
University of Mannheim, Germany

"The *Routledge Handbook of European Elections*, comprehensive in its scope, provides an excellent reference source for students of comparative and EU politics who are looking for wide-ranging information on the political and party landscape, electoral systems, European Parliament and national elections in EU Member States since 1979. The volume will also be extremely valuable to scholars and practitioners who wish to expand their empirical and theoretical knowledge on EP contests across the European Union."

Aleks Szczerbiak, Professor of Politics and Contemporary European
Studies, University of Sussex, UK and Co-convenor of the European
Parties Elections and Referendums Network (EPERN)

ROUTLEDGE HANDBOOK OF EUROPEAN ELECTIONS

The *Routledge Handbook of European Elections* explores the multifaceted dimensions of the European Parliament's (EP) electoral contests across the European Community and European Union since 1979.

After setting a general empirical and theoretical framework, this collaborative project presents original contributions from leading experts from virtually all the corners of the European Union. Each case study adheres to a common template that makes it easy to compare data, methodology, and outcomes.

Every country chapter includes:

- a brief geopolitical profile and historical background of the Member State;
- a glance at the national political landscape;
- a short account of the main political parties, including their attitude toward the European Union;
- a section on public opinion and European integration;
- a summary of electoral systems;
- an overview of all EP and national elections;
- an in-depth analysis of the 2009 EP electoral race;
- an overall theoretical interpretation of European elections.

A comparative chapter closes the Handbook followed by an Epilogue focussing on the 2014 EP contest with a detailed analysis of the newly elected European Assembly in terms of political group and gender composition.

The volume aims to enhance readers' understanding of the European Parliament and revive their interest in the European integration process. By providing a wide range of national and European facts and figures, this investigation represents a comprehensive reference guide for scholars, practitioners, and students of the European Parliament, European elections, political parties, European Union and comparative politics.

Donatella M. Viola, PhD London School of Economics, is Assistant Professor in Politics and International Relations at the University of Calabria, Italy.

ROUTLEDGE HANDBOOK OF EUROPEAN ELECTIONS

Edited by Donatella M. Viola

LONDON AND NEW YORK

First published 2016
by Routledge
2 Park Square, Milton Park, Abingdon, Oxon OX14 4RN

and by Routledge
711 Third Avenue, New York, NY 10017

Routledge is an imprint of the Taylor & Francis Group, an informa business

© 2016 Donatella M. Viola

The right of Donatella M. Viola to be identified as the author of the editorial material, and of the authors for their individual chapters, has been asserted in accordance with sections 77 and 78 of the Copyright, Designs and Patents Act 1988.

All rights reserved. No part of this book may be reprinted or reproduced or utilised in any form or by any electronic, mechanical, or other means, now known or hereafter invented, including photocopying and recording, or in any information storage or retrieval system, without permission in writing from the publishers.

Trademark notice: Product or corporate names may be trademarks or registered trademarks, and are used only for identification and explanation without intent to infringe.

British Library Cataloguing in Publication Data
A catalogue record for this book is available from the British Library

Library of Congress Cataloging in Publication Data
Routledge handbook of European elections / edited by Donatella M. Viola.
pages cm
1. European Parliament–Elections–History. 2. Elections–European Union countries–History. I. Viola, Donatella M., editor of compilation. II. Title: Handbook of European elections.
JN45.R68 2015
324.94′05–dc23
2014040252

ISBN: 978-0-415-59203-1 (hbk)
ISBN: 978-1-315-71531-5 (ebk)

Typeset in Bembo Std
by Swales & Willis Ltd, Exeter, Devon, UK

Printed and bound in the United States of America by Publishers Graphics, LLC on sustainably sourced paper.

CONTENTS

Dedication — ix
List of figures — x
List of tables — xii
Contributors — xviii
Preface by Donatella M. Viola — xxvi
Foreword by J.H.H. Weiler — xxviii
Prologue by Donatella M. Viola — xxxiii
Acknowledgements — xxxvi

PART I
General framework — 1

1 The genesis of the European Parliament: from appointed Consultative Assembly to directly elected legislative body — 3
   Donatella M. Viola

2 European Parliament's internal composition and organization — 17
   Donatella M. Viola

3 European Parliament elections theories — 39
   Donatella M. Viola

PART II
Country reviews   **49**
The Old Member States   **49**
The founding members   *49*

  4   France   51
        Julien Navarro

  5   Germany   76
        Siegfried Schieder and José M. Magone

  6   Italy   109
        Donatella M. Viola

  7   Belgium   147
        Nathalie Brack and Jean-Benoit Pilet

  8   The Netherlands   167
        Hans Vollaard, Gerrit Voerman, and Nelleke van de Walle

  9   Luxembourg   189
        Patrick Dumont, Raphaël Kies, and Philippe Poirier

The first enlargement countries   **211**

10   The United Kingdom   213
        Julie Smith

11   Ireland   243
        Richard Dunphy

12   Denmark   267
        Carina Bischoff and Marlene Wind

The second and third enlargement countries   **289**

13   Greece   291
        Maria M. Mendrinou

14   Spain   321
        José M. Magone

15   Portugal   351
        José M. Magone

The fourth enlargement countries — **375**

16 Austria — 377
    Sylvia Kritzinger and Karin Liebhart

17 Finland — 396
    Tapio Raunio

18 Sweden — 414
    Carina Bischoff and Marlene Wind

The New Member States — **431**
The fifth enlargement countries — *431*
Southern Mediterranean countries — *431*

19 Malta — 433
    Roderick Pace

20 Cyprus — 448
    Kalliope Agapiou-Josephides

Central and Eastern European countries — 469

21 Slovenia — 471
    Danica Fink-Hafner and Tomaž Deželan

22 Estonia — 491
    Piret Ehin

23 Latvia — 507
    Jānis Ikstens

24 Lithuania — 527
    Irmina Matonytė

25 Czech Republic — 549
    Michal Klíma

26 Slovakia — 568
    Marek Rybář

27 Hungary — 589
    Attila Ágh and Sándor Kurtán

28	Poland *Jerzy Jaskiernia*	608
29	Bulgaria *Dobrin Kanev and Katia Hristova-Valtcheva*	633
30	Romania *Gabriela Borz*	653
31	Final remarks: comparative analysis of European elections *Donatella M. Viola*	674
32	Epilogue: old and new trends in the 2014 European election *Donatella M. Viola*	700

Appendix   *736*
Index   *760*

To my dearest mother Natalina Scambia

In loving memory of my father Francesco Viola

Never to forget the heroism and courage of our fathers who fought for peace, freedom and democracy . . .

*"Libertà va cercando, ch'è sì cara,
Come sa chi per lei vita rifiuta."*

*"In the search of liberty he journeys: that how dear
They know, who for her sake have life refus'd."*

Dante Alighieri, *Purgatorio*, Canto I, 71–72
(English translation by Henry Francis Cary)

FIGURES

2.1a	EP composition by nationality: July 2009	24
2.1b	EP composition by nationality: July 2013	26
2.2a	EP composition by political group: July 2009	29
2.2b	EP composition by political group: July 2013	30
4.1	Map of France	51
4.2	French attitude to the European Union	56
4.3	Map of EP electoral constituencies in France	57
5.1	Map of Germany	76
5.2	German attitude to the European Union: 1979–2009	84
5.3	National and EP election campaign expenditure in Germany: 1984–2009	103
6.1	Map of Italy	109
6.2	Map of EP electoral constituencies in Italy	120
7.1	Map of Belgium	147
7.2	Map of EP electoral constituencies in Belgium	154
8.1	Map of the Netherlands	167
9.1	Map of Luxembourg	189
10.1	Map of the United Kingdom	213
10.2	Map of EP electoral constituencies in the United Kingdom	219
11.1	Map of Ireland	243
11.2	Map of EP electoral constituencies in Ireland	251
11.3	National and EP election campaign expenditure in Ireland	264
12.1	Map of Denmark	267
12.2	Eurosceptic party performance at EP and national elections in Denmark: 1979–2009	273
12.3	Danish attitude to the European Union: 1973–2009	276
13.1	Map of Greece	291
14.1	Map of Spain	321
15.1	Map of Portugal	351
16.1	Map of Austria	377
16.2	Austrian attitude to the European Union	383
16.3	Perceived benefit of EU membership in Austria	383

Figures

16.4	Public funding at national and EP elections in Austria: 2002–2009	393
17.1	Map of Finland	396
18.1	Map of Sweden	414
18.2	Support for hard Eurosceptic parties at EP and national elections in Sweden	419
18.3	Swedish attitude to the European Union	420
19.1	Map of Malta	433
20.1	Map of Cyprus	448
20.2	Cypriot attitude to the European Union	454
20.3	Perceived benefits of EU membership in Cyprus	455
21.1	Map of Slovenia	471
22.1	Map of Estonia	491
23.1	Map of Latvia	507
23.2	Latvian attitude to the European Union	513
24.1	Map of Lithuania	527
25.1	Map of Czech Republic	549
26.1	Map of Slovakia	568
27.1	Map of Hungary	589
28.1	Map of Poland	608
28.2	Map of EP electoral constituencies in Poland	616
29.1	Map of Bulgaria	633
30.1	Map of Romania	653
32.1	Map of the European Union: May 2014	701
32.2	Map of the European Union with EP electoral constituencies: May 2014	702
32.3	EP composition by nationality: May 2014	710
32.4	EP composition by political group: July 2014	711

TABLES

2.1	EP composition: 1958–2014	25
2.2	Women in the European Parliament: 1979–2009	26
2.3a	EP composition by political group and nationality: July 2009	31
2.3b	EP composition by political group and nationality: December 2011	32
2.3c	EP composition by political group and nationality: July 2013	32
2.4	EP committees: seventh legislature	35
2.5	EP delegations: seventh legislature	36
4.1	France profile	52
4.2	List of political parties in France	54
4.3	National election results in France: 1978–2007	59
4.4	EP election results in France: 1979–2004	60
4.5	EP election abstention in France: 1979–2004	61
4.6	EP election results in France: 2004–2009	66
4.7	EP election results by constituency in France: 2009	68
4.8	List of French MEPs: seventh legislature	70
4.9	Comparison of EP and national election results in France: 1979–2004	74
5.1	Germany profile	77
5.2	List of political parties in Germany	81
5.3	National election results in Germany: 1976–2009	87
5.4	EP election results in Germany: 1979–2004	88
5.5	Euromanifestos of non-parliamentary parties	93
5.6	EP election results in Germany: 2009	97
5.7	The German MEPs' affiliation to the European parliamentary groups	98
5.8	List of German MEPs: seventh legislature	99
6.1	Italy profile	110
6.2	List of political parties in Italy	115
6.3	National election results in Italy: 1979–1992	123
6.4	EP election results in Italy: 1979–1989	123
6.5	National election results in Italy: 1994–2008	124
6.6	EP election results in Italy: 1994–2004	126
6.7	Turnout at national and EP elections in Italy: 1979–2009	128

6.8	EP election campaign issues in Italy: 2009	130
6.9	EP election results in Italy: 2009	133
6.10	Seat distribution of the Italian delegation in the EP: 2009	135
6.11	Age and gender of Italian MEPs: 2009	135
6.12	Political background of Italian MEPs: 2009	135
6.13	Tenure of the Italian delegation in the EP: 2009	136
6.14	Italian committee Chairs and Vice-Chairs: 2009	136
6.15	List of Italian MEPs: seventh legislature	137
6.16	Parties eligible for electoral reimbursement in Italy: 2009	139
6.17	EP election campaign expenditure in Italy: 2009	140
6.18	Public funding for political parties in Italy: 2009–2013	140
7.1	Belgium profile	148
7.2	List of political parties in Belgium	151
7.3	Belgian attitude to the European Union	153
7.4	Perceived benefit of EU membership in Belgium	153
7.5	Turnout at national and EP elections in Belgium: 1978–2010	155
7.6	National elections results of Flemish parties in Belgium: 1978–2010	155
7.7	EP election results of Flemish parties in Belgium: 1979–2009	156
7.8	National election results of Francophone parties in Belgium: 1978–2010	156
7.9	EP election results of Francophone parties in Belgium: 1979–2009	156
7.10	Distribution of Belgian MEPs in the European Parliament: 2009–2014	159
7.11	List of Belgian MEPs: seventh legislature	160
7.12	EP election results in the Dutch-speaking college in Belgium: 2009	162
7.13	EP election results in the French-speaking college in Belgium: 2009	162
7.14	EP election results in the German-speaking college in Belgium: 2009	163
8.1	The Netherlands profile	168
8.2	List of political parties in the Netherlands	171
8.3	National election results in the Netherlands: 1977–2012	176
8.4	EP election results in the Netherlands: 1979–2009	177
8.5	EP detailed election results in the Netherlands: 2009	182
8.6	List of Dutch MEPs in the Netherlands: seventh legislature	183
9.1	Luxembourg profile	190
9.2	List of political parties in Luxembourg	193
9.3	National elections in Luxembourg: 1979–2009	197
9.4	Sources of information at the 2004 and 2009 EP elections in Luxembourg	202
9.5	The 2009 electoral campaigning tools in Luxembourg	203
9.6	EP election results in Luxembourg: 1979–2009	204
9.7	Differences between EP and national elections in Luxembourg: 1979–2009	205
9.8	Abstention at EP and national elections in Luxembourg: 1979–2009	205
9.9	List of Luxembourg MEPs: seventh legislature	206
10.1	United Kingdom profile	214
10.2	National election results in the UK: 1979–2010	221
10.3a	EP election results in Great Britain: 1979–1994	222
10.3b	EP election results in Northern Ireland: 1979–1994	223
10.3c	EP election results in Great Britain: 1999–2009	223
10.3d	EP election results in Northern Ireland: 1999–2009	223
10.4	EP electoral lists in the United Kingdom: 2009	224
10.5	Allocation of EP seats to regions in the UK	228

10.6	British MEPs according to electoral constituencies	228
10.7	EP detailed election results in the UK: 2009	230
10.8	List of British MEPs: seventh legislature	231
11.1	Ireland profile	244
11.2	List of Irish political parties and their European alignments	247
11.3	European referendum results: 1972–2009	250
11.4	EP election results in Ireland: 1979–2004	253
11.5	National election results in Ireland: 1977–2011	256
11.6	EP election results in Ireland: 2009	262
11.7	List of Irish MEPs: seventh legislature	263
12.1	Denmark profile	268
12.2	List of political parties in Denmark	270
12.3	Referenda on Europe in Denmark	277
12.4	EP election results and turnout in Denmark: 1979–2004	278
12.5	National election results in Denmark: 1979–2011	279
12.6	EP election results in Denmark: 2009	282
12.7	List of Danish MEPs: seventh legislature	283
13.1	Greece profile	292
13.2	List of political parties in Greece	296
13.3	EP election results in Greece: 1981–2004	303
13.4	National election results in Greece: 1981–2012	305
13.5	Turnout at national and EP elections in Greece: 1981–2012	307
13.6	EP electoral lists in Greece: 2009	308
13.7	EP election results in Greece: 2009	310
13.8	List of Greek MEPs: seventh legislature	311
13.9	Re-election of Greek MEPs: 1981–2009	315
13.10	Greek MEPs by gender: 1981–2009	315
13.11	Models examining the difference between EP and national election results in Greece	318
14.1	Spain profile	322
14.2	List of political parties in Spain	326
14.3	Spanish attitude to the European Union	327
14.4	Perceived benefit of EU membership in Spain	328
14.5	Turnout at EP elections in Spain: 1987–2009	329
14.6	National election results in Spain: 1986–2011	333
14.7	EP election results in Spain: 1987–2004	333
14.8	EP election results in Spain: 2009	338
14.9	List of Spanish MEPs: seventh legislature	339
14.10	National and EP election campaign expenditure in Spain	347
15.1	Portugal profile	352
15.2	List of political parties in Portugal	355
15.3	Portuguese attitude to the European Union	356
15.4	Perceived benefit of EU membership in Portugal	356
15.5	Turnout at EP elections in Portugal: 1987–2009	357
15.6	National election results in Portugal: 1985–2011	360
15.7	EP election results in Portugal: 1987–2004	361
15.8	EP election results in Portugal: 2009	366
15.9	List of Portuguese MEPS: seventh legislature	368

Tables

15.10	National and EP election campaign expenditure in Portugal: 2009	371
16.1	Austria profile	378
16.2	List of political parties in Austria	381
16.3	EP and national election results in Austria: 1994–2009	384
16.4	Turnout at EP and national elections in Austria: 1994–2009	385
16.5	EP election results in Austria: 2009	388
16.6	Austrian MEPs' affiliation to EP political groups	390
16.7	List of Austrian MEPs: seventh legislature	391
17.1	Finland profile	397
17.2	List of political parties in Finland	399
17.3	National election results in Finland: 1995–2011	403
17.4	EP election results in Finland: 1996–2009	403
17.5	EP election results in Finland: 2009	408
17.6	List of Finnish MEPs: seventh legislature	410
18.1	Sweden profile	415
18.2	List of political parties in Sweden	418
18.3	National election results in Sweden: 1994–2010	422
18.4	EP election results in Sweden: 1995–2009	422
18.5	List of Swedish MEPs: seventh legislature	426
19.1	Malta profile	434
19.2	List of political parties in Malta	436
19.3	National and EP election results in Malta: 2003–2009	438
19.4	Turnout at national and EP elections in Malta: 2003–2009	438
19.5	EP election results in Malta: 2009	443
19.6	List of Maltese MEPs: seventh legislature	445
20.1	Cyprus profile	449
20.2a	List of Greek Cypriot political parties in Cyprus	451
20.2b	List of Turkish Cypriot political parties in Cyprus	452
20.3	National and EP election results in Cyprus: 2001–2009	458
20.4	National election results in Cyprus: 2001, 2006 and 2011	459
20.5	EP election results in Cyprus: 2009	463
20.6	List of Cypriot MEPs: seventh legislature	464
21.1	Slovenia profile	472
21.2	List of Slovenian political parties	476
21.3	List of Slovenian political parties and their European affiliations	477
21.4	EP election results in Slovenia: 2004	479
21.5	National election results in Slovenia: 2000–2011	479
21.6	EP election results in Slovenia: 2009	483
21.7	List of Slovenian MEPs: sixth and seventh legislatures	485
22.1	Estonia Profile	492
22.2	List of political parties in Estonia	495
22.3	National election results in Estonia: 2007–2011	498
22.4	EP election results in Estonia: 2004	498
22.5	EP election results in Estonia: 2009	502
22.6	List of Estonian MEPs: seventh legislature	503
23.1	Latvia profile	508
23.2	Number of slates and parties at national elections in Latvia: 2002–2010	510
23.3	List of political parties in Latvia	511

23.4	National Parliament election results in Latvia: 2002–2006	516
23.5	Turnout at national elections in Latvia: 2002–2006	516
23.6	Turnout at EP elections in Latvia: 2009	521
23.7	EP election results in Latvia: 2009	521
23.8	EP election results of major parties in Latvia: 2004–2009	521
23.9	List of Latvian MEPs: seventh legislature	523
24.1	Lithuania profile	528
24.2	List of political parties in Lithuania	530
24.3	National election results in Lithuania: 2000	533
24.4	EP election results in Lithuania: 2004	533
24.5	EP electoral lists in Lithuania: 2009	535
24.6	EP election campaign issues in Lithuania: 2009	539
24.7a	National and EP election results: 2008–2009	541
24.7b	EP election results in Lithuania: 2009	542
24.8	List of Lithuanian MEPs: seventh legislature	543
25.1	Czech Republic profile	550
25.2	List of political parties in the Czech Republic	552
25.3	National election results in the Czech Republic: 2002–2010	557
25.4	EP election results in the Czech Republic: 2004–2009	562
25.5	Czech elected MEPs in 2009: number of preferences	563
25.6	List of Czech MEPs: seventh legislature	564
26.1	Slovakia profile	569
26.2	List of political parties in Slovakia	572
26.3	National election results in Slovakia: 2002 and 2006	579
26.4	EP election results in Slovakia: 2004	579
26.5	EP election results in Slovakia: 2009	585
26.6	List of Slovak MEPs: seventh legislature	586
27.1	Hungary profile	590
27.2	List of political parties in Hungary	592
27.3	National election results in Hungary: 2002–2010	597
27.4	EP Election Results in Hungary: 2004–2009	600
27.5	List of Hungarian MEPs: seventh legislature	601
28.1	Poland profile	609
28.2a	List of political parties in Poland	612
28.2b	Parliamentary political parties in Poland	613
28.3	National election results in Poland: 2001–2007	617
28.4	Turnout at national and EP elections in Poland	618
28.5	EP election results in Poland: 2004	618
28.6	EP election results in Poland: 2009	623
28.7	Polish MEPs' affiliation to EP political group: 2004–2009	625
28.8	List of Polish MEPs: seventh legislature	626
29.1	Bulgaria profile	634
29.2	List of political parties in Bulgaria	637
29.3	National election results in Bulgaria: 2005	642
29.4	EP election results in Bulgaria: 2007	642
29.5	Importance for Bulgarians of the 2009 EP elections	646
29.6	Electoral turnout in Bulgaria: 2005–2013	647
29.7	EP election results in Bulgaria: 2009	647

29.8	List of Bulgarian MEPs: seventh legislature	648
30.1	Romania profile	654
30.2a	List of political parties in Romania	656
30.2b	List of Romanian political parties and their European alignments	658
30.3	Issue salience before and after the 2009 elections in Romania and the EU-27	659
30.4	EP election results in Romania: 2007	661
30.5	National election results in Romania: 2004–2012	661
30.6	EP election results in Romania: 2009	665
30.7	List of Romanian MEPs: seventh legislature	667
31.1	EU Member State key features	676
31.2	European Parliament election campaign issues: 1979–2009	678
31.3a	Second-Order Election theory: Old EU Member States	681
31.3b	Second-Order Election theory: New EU Member States	682
31.3c	Europe Salience theory: Old EU Member States	684
31.3d	Europe Salience theory: New EU Member States	685
31.4a	Eurosceptic/Eurocritical parties in the original six countries: 1979–2009	687
31.4b	Eurosceptic/Eurocritical parties in Old EU enlargement countries: 1979–2009	690
31.4c	Eurosceptic/Eurocritical parties in New EU enlargement countries: 2004–2009	691
31.5a	Turnout at EP elections in all EU Member States: 1979–2009	693
31.5b	National election turnout in Old EU Member States: 1973–2009	694
31.5c	National election turnout in New EU Member States: 2000–2010	695
32.1a	Turnout at EP elections in aggregate countries: 2009/2013–2014	705
32.1b	Turnout at EP elections in EU Member States: 2009/2013–2014	708
32.2a	EP composition by political group: 2009, 2011, 2013 and 2014	712
32.2b	EP composition by nationality and political group: July 2014	719
32.3a	Gender MEP ratio in aggregate countries: 2014	721
32.3b	European Parliament composition by nationality and gender: July 2014	722
32.3c	EP composition by political group, nationality and gender: July 2014	723
32.3d	Political group breakdown by gender in aggregate countries: July 2014	725
32.3e	Female representation by political group in aggregate countries: July 2014	727
32.4a	EP election winners in Old EU Member States: May 2014	728
32.4b	EP election winners in New EU Member States: May 2014	729
33.1	EP electoral systems in EU Member States	736
33.2a	EP composition by nationality, political group, and political party: 1979	737
33.2b	EP composition by nationality, political group, and political party: 1984	738
33.2c	EP composition by nationality, political group, and political party: 1989	739
33.2d	EP composition by nationality, political group, and political party: 1994	741
33.2e	EP composition by nationality, political group, and political party: 1999	743
33.2f	EP composition by nationality, political group, and political party: 2004	745
33.2g	EP composition by nationality, political group, and political party: 2009	748
33.2h	EP composition by nationality, political group, and political party: 2014	751
33.3	Political group Chair and Co-Chair: July 2014	755
33.4	List of Eurosceptic/Eurocritical parties in EU Member States: 1979–2009	756
33.5a	List of political parties in Croatia	758
33.5b	List of Croatian MEPs: seventh legislature	759

CONTRIBUTORS

Kalliope Agapiou-Josephides, PhD in Political Science from Paris I Panthéon-Sorbonne University, France, is Jean Monnet Chair in European Political Integration and Assistant Professor at the Department of Social and Political Sciences, University of Cyprus. She is Deputy President of the European Inter-University Centre for Human Rights and Democratization and Board Member of the European Gender Equality Institute. Her most recent publications include: 'Changing Patterns of Euroscepticism in Cyprus: European Discourse in a Divided Polity and Society', *South European Society and Politics*, 2011; 'Women's Suffrage in Cyprus', in Blanca Rodriquez-Ruiz and Ruth Rubio-Marin (eds) *The Struggle for Female Suffrage in Europe*, Brill (2012); with Jean Rossetto (eds) *La singularité de Chypre dans l'Union européenne: La diversité des droits et des status*, Mare & Martin (2012); with Florence Benoit-Rohmer et al., *Women's Rights During Democratic Transitions*, European Parliament (2012).

Attila Ágh, PhD in Political Science from the Centre Européen Universitaire de Nancy, France, is Professor of Political Sciences and Head of the PhD School at the Budapest Corvinus University, Hungary. He has been Visiting Professor in several universities in Moscow, Dar es-Salaam, New Delhi, Los Angeles, Vienna, Aarhus, Mexico City, Pretoria and Sidney. His research interests focus on comparative politics, especially East-Central European Democratization and Europeanization. He has published about 100 articles in international journals and 20 books including *Eastern Enlargement and the Future of the EU27: EU Foreign Policy in a Global World* (2013) and *Progress Report on the New Member States: Twenty Years of Social and Political Developments* (2013).

Carina Bischoff, PhD in Political Science from the European University Institute, Florence, Italy, is Assistant Professor at the Institute of Society and Globalization at Roskilde University. Her research interests focus on the European Union as well as national-level comparative politics, in particular on parties and party systems, electoral systems and voter behaviour, parliaments, and governments. Her recent publications include: *Changing Rule of Delegation: A Contest for Power in Comitology*, Adrienne Heritier and Catherine Moury (eds), Oxford University Press (2013); *Party Patronage and Party Government in European Democracies,* Petr Kopecky, Peter Mair and Maria Spirova (eds), Oxford University Press (2012); articles on voter volatility in *Public Choice* (2012) and on electoral thresholds in *Electoral Studies* (2009).

Contributors

Gabriela Borz, PhD in Political Science from CEU, Budapest, Hungary, is Lecturer at the University of Strathclyde, Glasgow, UK. Her research interests include representation, comparative parties and party systems, party organization, parliamentary activity, and constitutionalism. Her articles, including 'Models of Party Democracy: Patterns of Party Regulation in Postwar European Constitutions'; 'Aggregation and Representation in European Parliament Party Groups'; 'Institutional Stimuli and Individual Response as Explanations of Turnout: The 2009 EP Election', have appeared in *European Political Science Review, West European Politics, Journal of Elections* and *Public Opinion and Parties*.

Nathalie Brack, PhD in Political Science from the Université libre de Bruxelles, Belgium, is currently Post-doctoral Fellow at the University of Oxford, UK (Wiener Anspach Foundation Grant) and Université libre de Bruxelles (CEVIPOL). Her research interests include Euroscepticism, the European Parliament, political representation, parliamentary and legislative studies, as well as political opposition. She published 'Euroscepticism at the Supranational Level: the Case of the "Untidy Right" in the European Parliament' in the *Journal of Common Market Studies* (2012), co-authored 'The Challenges of Territorial Representation at the Supranational Level: The Case of French MEPs' in *French Politics* (2013), and with Oliver Costa, the book entitled *How the EU Really Works*, Ashgate (2014). She also edited a special issue of the *Journal of European Integration* (2012) on the diverging views of Europe within EU institutions.

Tomaž Deželan, PhD in Political Science from the University of Ljubljana, Slovenia, is Assistant Professor of Political Science at the Faculty of Social Sciences at the same university. His research interests include political communication, citizenship concepts, parliamentary cohesion, electoral studies, sociology of the profession, youth, gender and civil society. He has authored and co-authored more than 20 peer-reviewed articles in international journals and scientific volumes and several scientific monographs. His research has been published in the following journals: *Citizenship Studies, International Journal of Manpower, Communication, Politics & Culture, Lex Localis, Balkanistica, Teorija in Praksa*, and *Politička misao*.

Patrick Dumont, PhD in Political Science from the University of Geneva, Switzerland, is a Researcher at the University of Luxembourg. He is co-founder of the Selection and Deselection of Political Elites international network and series editor of Routledge Research in Social and Political Elites. He is member of the editorial board of the *Revue Internationale de Politique Comparée*. He has published on his main topics of interest such as coalition theory, political elites, parties and party systems, and Europeanization processes in international journals such as the *European Journal of Political Research, European Union Politics, Journal of European Public Policy, Public Choice* and won the Vincent Wright award for best article in 2007 in West European Politics. His most recent publications include two co-edited books: *European Integration and Consensus Politics in the Low Countries* and *The Selection of Ministers Around the World: A Comparative Study*, Routledge (2014).

Richard Dunphy, PhD in Political Science from the European University Institute, Florence, Italy, is Senior Lecturer in Politics at the University of Dundee, UK. His specialist areas of research are Irish and European politics, the politics of gender and sexuality, and the politics of the radical left. In recent years, he has published many papers on the problems of the radical left in Europe, especially those problems associated with coalition government formation and participation. His book, *The European Left Party: A Case Study in Transnational Party-building*, co-written with Luke March, is a study of the transnational European Left Party and will be published by Manchester University Press in 2016.

Contributors

Piret Ehin, PhD in Political Science from the University of Arizona, USA, is Senior Researcher at the Institute of Government and Politics and Director of the Centre for EU-Russia Studies at the University of Tartu, Estonia. She worked as Deputy Director of EuroCollege at the University of Tartu from from 2002 to 2004, was Chair of the Executive Board of the Open Estonia Foundation in 2008–2009, and has been affiliated with the Estonian Foreign Policy Institute since 2005. Her main research interests include legitimacy, political support, and electoral behaviour both at the national and European level, and international relations (IR) in the Baltic Sea region. Her work has been published in the *Journal of Common Market Studies, Cooperation and Conflict,* and the *Journal of Baltic Studies,* among others. She is the Estonian country collaborator for cross-national survey projects such as the European Election Studies (EES) and the Comparative Study of Electoral Systems (CSES).

Danica Fink-Hafner, PhD in Political Science from the University of Ljubljana, Slovenia, is Professor of Political Parties, Interest Groups and Policy Analysis and Head of the Centre for Political Science Research at the Faculty of Social Sciences at the same university. Her research interests include policy analysis, interest groups and lobbying, parties and party systems, democracy, gender, and Europeanization and political science. Her articles have appeared in journals such as *Public Administration,* the *Journal of Communist Studies,* the *Journal of European Public Policy, Canadian Slavonic Studies,* the *Journal of Southern Europe and the Balkans,* the *Czech Sociological Review,* the *International Journal of Manpower,* and the *European Journal of Political Research – Political Data Yearbook.*

Katia Hristova-Valtcheva, PhD in Political Science from Sofia University, Bulgaria, is Senior Assistant Professor in Political Science at New Bulgarian University, Jean Monnet Lecturer at Sofia University, St. Kl. Ohridski, and Acting Secretary General of the Bulgarian European Community Studies Association. Her research interests focus on Europeanization, civil society and civic action, and post-Communist transformations. Her most recent publications include: 'Bulgarien', in Werner Reutter (ed.), *Verbände und Interessengruppen in den Ländern der Europäischen Union,* Springer Fachmedien Wiesbaden (2012); 'Construire la citoyenneté européenne par l'initiative législative des citoyens: limites de l'approche', in Gilles Rouet (ed.), *Citoyennetés et Nationalités en Europe,* l'Harmattan (2011); and 'The "Europeanisation" of the 2009 EP Elections in Bulgaria', in Anna Krasteva and Antonii Todorov (eds), *Elections 2009 in Bulgaria: European, National and Local,* New Bulgarian University (2010).

Jānis Ikstens, PhD in Political Science from the University of Latvia, Rīga, Latvia, is Professor of Comparative Politics at the University of Latvia. He has co-edited a volume on party finance in post-Communist countries, 2008 and authored a number of articles on parties and elections in Latvia. He has written a chapter on Latvian Social Democrats in the book edited by Jean-Michel de Waele, Fabien Escalona and Mathieu Vieira, *The Palgrave Handbook of Social Democracy in the European Union,* Palgrave Macmillan (2013).

Jerzy Jaskiernia, PhD in Legal Science from Jagiellonian University, Poland, is Professor of Constitutional Law and Comparative Governments, Director of the Institute of Economy and Administration and Chair of the Department of Administration and Legal Sciences at the Jan Kochanowski University of Kielce, Poland. His main books include: *Position of the States in U.S. Federal System,* Warszawa (1979); *The United States and Contemporary Processes and Conceptions of European Integration,* Warszawa (1992); *Idea of Equity in U.S. Election Law,* Warszawa (1992); *Parliamentary Assembly of the Council of Europe,* Warszawa (2000); *Council of Europe and Democratic Transition in the States of Central and Eastern Europe 1989–2009,* Toruń (2010); *Transformation of* *the Judicial Systems*, vols I and II, Toruń (2011); *Effectiveness of the European System of Protection of Human Rights*, vols I–III, Toruń (2012).

Dobrin Kanev, PhD in Philosophy from the Bulgarian Academy of Science, Sofia, is Associate Professor in Political Science and European Studies at the New Bulgarian University in Sofia, Bulgaria. Since 2001 he has held a Jean Monnet permanent course on the European political system. He is a Permanent Senior Fellow of the Centre for European Integration Studies, Bonn University, Germany. He is a member of the Editorial Board of *SEER, Journal for Labour and Social Affairs in Eastern Europe*, Brussels. He was Secretary, Political Advisor, to the President of the Republic of Bulgaria from 2002 to 2012, responsible for research and analysis. He was also the founder and first Director of the Research Service of the Bulgarian Parliament between 1995 and 1997. His numerous publications focus on democratic transition, institution-building, and elections in contemporary Bulgaria as well as political parties in European countries and in Bulgaria.

Raphaël Kies, PhD in Political Science from the European University Institute, Florence, Italy, is Researcher in Political Science at the University of Luxembourg. He is co-responsible for the national and European electoral studies programme and for the introduction and evaluation of innovative methods of political participation at the national and European level. He has published several articles and books on e-democracy, local democracy, and deliberative democracy. His publications include *Promises and Limits of Web-Deliberation*, Palgrave (2010) and an edited book, with Patrizia Nanz, *European Citizens Deliberation: A Promising Path for EU Governance?*, Ashgate (2014).

Michal Klíma, PhD in Political Science from Taras Sevcenko University, Kiev, Ukraine, is the Rector of Metropolitan University Prague and Professor in Political Science. His areas of specialization and research interests gravitate around comparative government, European integration, party and electoral systems as well as clientelism and corruption. Michal Klima is a frequent commentator on Czech television and has authored many works on issues related to political life in the country. His publications include monographs, such as *Elections and Political Parties in Modern Democracies, Quality of Democracy in the Czech Republic and Electoral Engineering*, and scholarly articles, such as 'Conceptualising the Clientelistic Party: The Case Study of the Czech Republic', in *the Czech Journal of Political Science*.

Sylvia Kritzinger, PhD in Political Science from the University of Vienna, Austria, is Professor for Methods in the Social Sciences at the University of Vienna. Her main research interests focus on political behaviour, electoral research, democratic representation, and quantitative social science methods. Her most recent publications include: *The Austrian Voter*, with Eva Zeglovits, Michael S. Lewis-Beck and Richard Nadeau, Vienna University Press (2013); 'The Structure of Issue Attitudes Revisited: A Dimensional Analysis of Austrian Voters and Party Elites', with Martin Dolezal, Nikolaus Eder, and Eva Zeglovits, in *Journal of Elections, Public Opinion and Parties* (2013); 'How Has Radical Right Support Transformed Established Political Conflicts? The Case of Austria', with Julian Aichholzer, Markus Wagner, and Eva Zeglovits, in *West European Politics* (2014); 'Voting at 16: Turnout and the Quality of Vote Choice' with Markus Wagner and David Johann, in *Electoral Studies* (2012).

Sándor Kurtán, PhD from Eötvös Roland University, Budapest, Hungary, is Assistant Professor, at the Institute of Political Science, Corvinus University of Budapest. His main research interests focus on the Hungarian Parliament and Hungarian political elites and intelligence services. His publications include, 'The Role of National Parliament in EU affairs: A Comparative View on

Austria and Hungary', with Leile Hadj-Abdou, in Attila Ágh (ed.), *Post-Accession in East Central Europe: The Emergence of the EU 25*, Hungarian Centre for Democracy Studies (2004); and 'Hungary', with Gabriella Ilonszki, in the *European Journal of Political Research* (2004).

Karin Liebhart, PhD in Political Science from the University of Vienna, Austria, is Senior Lecturer in Political Science at the University of Vienna and Visiting Professor at the Nationalism Studies Programme/CEU Budapest, Hungary, as well as at the Institute of European Studies and International Relations, Comenius University Bratislava, Slovakia. Her main research interests focus on visual representations of politics, political cultures, memory politics, EU enlargement and European neighbourhood policy, and political, economic, social and cultural processes of transformation. Her main publications include: 'Discursive and Visual Representations of EU Presidencies: Austria, Slovenia, Czech Republic, Hungary and Poland in Comparison', in Olga Gyarfasova and Karin Liebhart (eds), *Cultural Patterns of Politics*, LIT Berlin-Münster-Vienna (2013); and 'The CEE and SEE Expansion of Austrian Banks. A Showcase Analysis of Relating Media Coverage' in Attila Ágh *et al.* (eds), *European Futures: The Perspectives of the New Member States in the New Europe*, Sage (2014).

José M. Magone, DPhil in Political Science from the University of Vienna, Austria, is Professor in Regional and Global Governance at the Berlin School of Economics and Law, Germany. His main research interests are comparative European politics, Southern European politics, European Union politics, and regional and global governance. He has published ten books, over 40 chapters in contributed books, and 14 articles. His latest publications include: *The New World Architecture: The Role of the European Union in the Making of Global Governance*, New Brunswick, Transaction (2006); *Contemporary Spanish Politics*, Routledge (2009); *Contemporary European Politics: A Comparative Introduction*, Routledge (2011); and *The Politics of Contemporary Portugal: Evolving Democracy*, Lynne Rienner (2014).

Irmina Matonytė, PhD in Political Science from Vytautas Magnus University, Kaunas, Lithuania, is Professor of Political Science at the ISM University of Management and Economics, Vilnius, Lithuania. She is a former Chair of the Lithuanian Political Science Association and former member of the Executive Committee of the International Political Science Association (IPSA). Her research interests include transformations of post-Communist elites, Europeanization, coalition governance, civil society, women in politics, and political communication. She has authored or co-authored more than 40 peer-reviewed articles in national and international journals, and ten scientific monographs. Her recent publications include: 'The Elite's Games in the Field of Memory: Insights from Lithuania', in Georges Mink and Laure Neumayer (eds), *History, Memory and Politics in Central and Eastern Europe: Memory Games*, Palgrave Macmillan (2013). Some of her academic projects have been funded by the EC FP6 framework, the European Science Foundation, and Norwegian, Austrian, and Swedish research agencies.

Maria M. Mendrinou, PhD in Government from the University of Manchester, UK, is Associate Professor of European Political Economy and European Integration at the Department of International and European Studies of the University of Piraeus, Greece. She holds degrees in Political Science from the University of Athens, Greece, and an MA in Politics from Brandeis University, USA. She has attended international conferences in Europe and the USA and has participated in numerous research projects. She has published extensively in Greek and English. Her English publications include the book *Politics, Subsidies and Competition: The New Politics of State Intervention in the European Union*, with Kostas A. Lavdas, Edward Elgar (1999), and articles in international journals such as the *European Journal of Political Research* and the *Journal of European Public Policy*, together with numerous contributions in edited volumes.

Julien Navarro, PhD in Political Science from the Bordeaux Institute of Political Studies, France, is Assistant Professor of Political Science at the Lille Catholic University, France. His research interests within the field of comparative politics include political elites, parliamentary institutions and electoral studies. He is the author of several articles and of a book entitled *Les députés européens et leur rôle. Sociologie interprétative des pratiques parlementaires*, Editions de l'Université de Bruxelles (2009). His articles have appeared in *French Politics*, *Revue Française de Science Politique*, the *Journal of Legislative Studies* and *Revue Internationale de Politique Comparée*.

Roderick Pace, PhD in Politics from the University of Reading, UK, is Director of the Institute for European Studies and Jean Monnet Chair at the University of Malta. He is a member of the editorial Board of the *Journal of South European Society and Politics*. His main research interests focus on Malta in the EU, Euro-Mediterranean relations, small states in world politics, and theories of European integration. Some of his most recent publications include: 'Malta', in Heiko Biehl, Bastian Giegerich, and Alexandra Jonas (eds), *Strategic Cultures in Europe: Security and Defence Policies Across the Continent*, Springer (2013) and 'Malta: A Lilliputian's Struggle for Security and Peace' in Michael Baun, and Dan Marek (eds), *The New Member States and the European Union: Foreign Policy and Europeanization*, Routledge (2013).

Jean-Benoit Pilet, PhD in Political Science from the Université libre de Bruxelles, Belgium, is Professor of Political Science at the Université libre de Bruxelles and is currently Director of the CEVIPOL. His main research interests focus on electoral reforms, electoral systems, candidate selection, parliamentary careers, local politics, and Belgium and party politics. He is the author of several books and articles on local politics, elections, Belgian politics and electoral reforms. He recently published 'Executive-Legislative Relations without a Government' in *European Political Science* (2012), and co-edited a special issue of *Representation, the Journal of Representative Democracy*, entitled 'Political Representation in Belgium, France and Portugal'. He currently works on a research project on electoral system changes in Europe since 1945 and, with A. Renwick, will publish a book entitled *Faces on the Ballot: The Personalization of Electoral Systems in Europe*, Oxford University Press (forthcoming).

Philippe Poirier, PhD in Political Science from the University of Rennes I, France and University of Ottawa, Canada, is Associate Professor of Political Science, holder of the Chair in Legislative Studies of Chambre des Députés du Luxembourg, coordinator of the European governance research programme at the University of Luxembourg, Visiting Professor at the University of Paris Sorbonne and Collège des Bernardins, and Director of the Parliamentary Studies Collection, éditions Larcier. He has published several articles and books on comparative politics, European Union politics and religion and politics in Europe. He has recently edited two books for the Collège des Bernardins Series, Bayard Editions, *Gouvernance mondiale et éthique au XXIème siècle*, January 2013 and *Liberté(s), Démocratie(s) et Religion(s)* (December 2013).

Tapio Raunio, PhD in Political Science from the University of Tampere, Finland, is Professor of Political Science at the same university. His research interests include the role of national legislatures and parties in European integration, the European Parliament and Euro-parties, Nordic legislatures, and the Finnish political system. He has published articles in journals such as *Comparative European Politics*, the *European Journal of Political Research*, *European Union Politics*, the

Journal of Common Market Studies, the *Journal of European Public Policy*, *Party Politics*, *Scandinavian Political Studies*, and *West European Politics*. Raunio is the co-editor of *National Parliaments within the Enlarged European Union: From 'Victims' of Integration to Competitive Actors?* with John O'Brennan, Routledge (2007) and *Connecting with the Electorate? Parliamentary Communication in EU Affairs* with Katrin Auel, Routledge (2014). Along with David Arter, he is currently leading a research project that examines the links between Nordic parliaments, MPs and their electorates.

Marek Rybář, PhD Political Science from Comenius University Bratislava, Slovakia, is an Associate Professor of Political Science at the Faculty of Philosophy, Comenius University, Bratislava. His research focusses on political parties and party competition in Central and Eastern Europe, and on the influence of European integration on domestic politics of the EU Member States. He has published numerous chapters in edited volumes and studies in several journals, including the *Journal of Communist Studies and Transition Politics*, *Communist and Post-Communist Studies*, the *Slovak Sociological Review* and *Electoral Studies*. Currently he is working on a research project examining institutional performance in the new democracies of Central and Eastern Europe.

Siegfried Schieder, PhD in Political Science from the University of Trier, Germany, is currently Professor in International Relations and Foreign Policy at the University of Trier, Germany and Visiting Professor at Fudan University, Shanghai. He has been Lecturer in International Relations at the University of Dresden, Visiting Lecturer in International Relations at the Free University of Berlin, and Assistant Professor in International Relations and German European Policy at the University of Heidelberg. In 2009–2010, he was a Jean Monnet Postdoctoral Fellow at the European University Institute in Florence, Italy. His most recent books include *Theories of International Relations*, Routledge (2014); *Die Außenpolitik der europäischen Länder*, Springer VS (2015); *Grenzen der deutschen Europapolitik*, Springer VS (2013); and *Solidarität und internationale Gemeinschaftsbildung*, Campus Verlag (2009). Among his publications are articles appearing in the *European Journal of International Relations*, the *European Journal of International Law*, the *Journal of International Relations and Development*, *Zeitschrift für Internationale Beziehungen* and *Leviathan, Zeitschrift für politikwissenschaft*.

Julie Smith, DPhil in Politics, Oxford, UK, is Director of the European Centre at Cambridge University, Fellow in Politics at Robinson College and Member of the House of Lords. She was Head of the European Programme at Chatham House, the Royal Institute of International Affairs from 1999 to 2003. Her research interests include European elections, EU enlargement, the UK's relations within the EU and migration. Her publications include: *Reinvigorating European Elections: The Implications of Electing the European Commission*, Chatham House (2005); *The Palgrave Handbook on National Parliaments and the European Union*, Palgrave (2015) and several other works on European elections.

Nelleke van de Walle works as a Diplomat at the Ministry of Foreign Affairs. She studied Contemporary History and International Relations at the University of Groningen, the Netherlands, where she worked as a Lecturer in International Relations and as a Research Assistant at the Documentation Centre on Dutch Political Parties (DNPP). In cooperation with Gerrit Voerman, she has published *Met het oog op Europa. Affiches voor de Europese verkiezingen, 1979–2009*, on the European elections, Dutch political parties and election posters, Boom (2009).

Donatella M. Viola, PhD in International Relations from the London School of Economics and Political Science, London, UK, is Assistant Professor in Politics and International Relations at the University of Calabria, Italy. Formerly Robert Schuman Scholar at the Directorate-General of the Secretariat of the European Parliament in Luxembourg and Marie Curie Fellow at the London School of Economics, she has also researched and lectured in the UK at the Universities of Bristol, Cardiff, Leeds, London, Plymouth, Regent's College and the Richmond American International University in London. Her main research interests revolve around the international relations of the European Union, the European Parliament and its transnational party groups. She is the author of the book *European Foreign Policy and the European Parliament in the 1990s,* Ashgate (2000). Her other publications cover: elections to the European Parliament; national parliaments; enlargement of the European Union; conflicts in the Gulf; the European Constitution, EU immigration and environmental policies.

Gerrit Voerman, PhD in History from the University of Groningen, the Netherlands, is Professor of Development and Functioning of the Dutch and European party systems and Director of the Documentation Centre on Dutch Political Parties (DNPP) of the University of Groningen. He is editor of the *Yearbook of the Documentation Centre* and of a series of volumes on Dutch political parties. He has published widely on various aspects of Dutch political parties and of European parties. His publications on the European elections in the Netherlands include: 'Les élections européennes aux Pays-Bas', in Pascal Delwit and Philippe Poirier (eds), *Parlement puissant, électeurs absents? Les élections européennes de juin 2004,* Editions de l'Université de Bruxelles (2005); and *Met het oog op Europa: Affiches voor de Europese verkiezingen, 1979–2009* with Nelleke van de Walle, Boom (2009).

Hans Vollaard, PhD in Political Science from Leiden University, the Netherlands, is Lecturer in Dutch and European Politics in the Department of Political Science at Leiden University. He recently published on Christianity in Dutch politics in the *Journal of Politics and Religion* and health politics in the *Journal of Health Politics, Policy and Law* and *Health Policy*. He has also co-edited the volumes *Euroscepticism in the Netherlands,* with Bartho Boer, Lemma (2005); *State Territoriality and European Integration* with Michael Burgess, Routledge (2006); and *European Integration and Consensus Politics in the Netherlands,* with Jan Beyers and Patrick Dumont, Routledge (2014).

J.H.H. Weiler is President of the European University Institute (EUI), Florence, Italy. Previously he worked as Professor of Law and Jean Monnet Chair at Harvard Law School, USA, and subsequently as Director of the Jean Monnet Center at New York University (NYU) School of Law, USA. He served for many years as Member of the Committee of Jurists of the Institutional Affairs Committee of the European Parliament. Professor Weiler is Editor-in-Chief of the *European Journal of International Law* (EJIL) and the *International Journal of Constitutional Law* (ICON). Weiler is also Honorary Professor at University College London, UK, and the University of Copenhagen, Denmark and Co-Director of the Academy of International Trade Law in Macao, China. He holds a PhD in European Law from the EUI and honorary degrees from various European universities. He is the author of several books and articles in the field of European integration, notably *The Constitution of Europe: "Do the New Clothes Have an Emperor?"* Cambridge University Press (1999).

Marlene Wind, PhD in Political Science from the European University Institute, Florence, Italy, is Professor and Director of the Centre for European Politics at the Department of Political Science, the University of Copenhagen, Denmark. She is also co-founder of the Research Centre of Excellence Courts at the Faculty of Law, the University of Copenhagen, and Professor in Law at Oslo University, Norway. She has a long publication record and is one of Denmark's leading experts on the European Union, frequently contributing to the Danish EU debate and commenting on EU affairs in the national and international media.

PREFACE

Donatella M. Viola

The inspiration for this book came from my dear father, Francesco Viola, to whom it is dedicated. He passed away in Reggio Calabria, Italy, suddenly on 31 March 2010.

At the beginning of this volume, I would like to commemorate his extraordinary life: he was a true example of how moral strength, religious faith, political and social ideals can survive the horrors of war. His story also reminds us of the concrete and terrible circumstances in which the European integration project was born and which must never again be repeated in the Old Continent.

In October 1943, soon after the signing of the Armistice, which triggered a civil war in Italy, my father was arrested in Milan, where at the time he was studying and working. The police of the puppet Fascist regime of the *Repubblica di Salò*, established in northern Italy by the Third Reich, harshly beat him for refusing to join the Black Brigades in their fight against the Allies and the Italian Partisans.

For this reason, he also underwent a rather far-fetched and ludicrous trial with no defence lawyer to represent him, resulting in his being condemned to detention in the Nazi concentration camp at Bitz in the Tübingen region in Baden-Württemberg, Germany. He remained there for a year and a half until the spring of 1945 when, along with a group of fellow prisoners, he was taken to the Brenner Pass to help remove debris to clear a route for retreating Nazi troops.

One day, while undertaking this work, as a German horse division passed by, my father – amongst others – managed to escape on horseback, not before being shot in the head, hand and thigh. On hearing the gunfire, partisans came to the fugitives' aid by taking my father, who was seriously wounded, to their shelter.

By a wonderful twist of fate, his rescuer was someone whom my father had forgotten having helped in the past, when he had persuaded an Austrian officer to find the man some warm clothes and shoes when he had arrived, ragged and shivering, at the Bitz concentration camp. As if this were not coincidence enough, this man turned out to be a shepherd from the small village of pietrapinnata in the Calabrian Aspromonte Mountains, not far from Reggio Calabria, my father's native city.

After regaining consciousness and a little strength, he travelled with the partisans for ten days to reach the city of Parma. Although weak and exhausted, he decided to continue his long journey back home alone, by train. Several days later, he barely managed to walk to his uncle's house, near Reggio Calabria main railway station. When his aunt opened the door, she hardly recognized him as he was so terribly thin, pale and emaciated: this man, who stood six feet tall, now weighed just over six stones.

Such a dreadful and painful experience left the most profound mark on my father's body and soul, yet he never let the seeds of resentment thrive. On the contrary, he taught me that life, love and compassion are the only true antidotes to the poisonous spiral of death, hatred and annihilation.

Indeed, my father's legacy has led me to believe that European unification, which has brought peace and prosperity for over half a century to all its Members, must not be jeopardized by recent and current hurdles. It is of the utmost importance, instead, to recall and revive the original principles that, in the midst of the maelstrom of the Second World War, inspired a number of visionary men and women to lay the foundations for a united Europe. Only in this way will it be possible to counteract the destructive force of extreme nationalism and resist the old temptations of intolerance, xenophobia and violence.

FOREWORD

J.H.H. Weiler

1 Why should one care about European Parliament elections?

This volume comes at an opportune time. The story of direct elections to the European Parliament has, after all, been a sorry narrative, with continued decline of voter interest, however brave a face one tries to put on it.

The elections to the European Parliament in 2014 have, however, the potential to be a watershed in the evolution of European democracy – so this is a suitable moment to take stock of European elections so far – a task admirably accomplished in this volume. The importance of these elections will be tested in the 2019 elections. The seeds sown this time round may begin to bear fruit then.

It is a virtue of this project that it understands that Europe in general, and the machinations of European democracy in particular, can only be understood by close attention to the specificities of the national Member State context. In this respect Europe is more federal, in the true sense of the word, than many federal states properly so called. In fact, the focus on the national context of European elections, up to and including the 2014 elections, helps to highlight the deepest pathologies of European democracy.

How so? At the heart of democracy there is choice: the people get to choose a 'who' and a 'how'. Who will govern? He from the Left or, perhaps She from the Right? And how will one be governed, with austerity or growth? One-party democracy, even with free elections, is no democracy at all, since there is no choice.

But likewise, a Parliament such as the EP with full legislative powers embedded, however, in a governance structure which does not allow this primordial choice will be a very flawed democracy. The result will be a Parliament with considerable legislative and supervisory powers and little political authority.

After many 'ostrich years', the European head is finally coming out of the sand: there really is a problem with the legitimacy – or rather, the perception of legitimacy – of the European construct. It is not a mere 'bee in the bonnet' of some irritating academics disconnected from reality. Eurobarometer indications are at present at their lowest and the results of a highly respected Pew Center survey, too, show a remarkable fall in support for Europe among its citizens. Political differences on how to tackle the euro-crisis are, worryingly, both reflective and constitutive of what one may call a solidarity deficit.

Foreword

Even if the EU manages to make substantive and substantial strides in the construction of the much-vaunted Banking Union, or the new buzzword the 'Securities Market Union', it is not expected that any of the above will change significantly. The dramatic increase in the anti-European vote and the mainstreaming effect it has had on general politics are a sharp reminder of this.

It used to be denied, in both political and academic circles, that Europe still suffered from a democracy deficit. The usual trope that was trotted out to defend the democratic credentials of the Union was the historic increase in the powers of the European Parliament, which, even before the Lisbon Treaty, could credibly be called a veritable co-legislator with the Council. However, even the most devout Europhiles in the 'Amen Corner' of the Union cannot wish away another historical trend establishing an ironic parallel with the development of the European Parliament: the more powers it has gained, the greater popular indifference toward it seems to have developed, as is evidenced in this volume. The decline is in voter support as measured in voter participation to EP elections. The turnout rate has declined persistently from election to election ever since 1979, by reaching historical lows in many Member States, as well as for the Union as a whole, at the 2009 elections. The decline seems to have been arrested in 2014, but paradoxically that might be a result of anti-Europe mobilization. The figures are even more depressing if one excludes from the calculus those Member States in which there is obligatory voting.

The classic historical explanation – voter indifference to a chamber without powers – naturally has no longer any purchase and has disappeared. The alternative explanation usually dished out by hard-working if anguished MEPs, who are both humiliated and flummoxed by this historical trend, is to say in a million different ways that 'we have to explain Europe better' to European citizens. This was the initial line which the Commission also took after the debacle of the Constitution. It is a morally repugnant argument, a crass resurrection in all but name of Marxist false consciousness. Maybe we should change the stupid people who do not understand – as Bertolt Brecht famously and viciously quipped? To say that people do not turn out to vote for the EP because they do not understand how important such a vote is, is both wrong and contemptuous of the very democracy on which these elections are predicated.

But in fact the people are as wise as their elected representatives in the European Parliament and elsewhere. For they intuit the truth: with all its increased powers it still makes little systemic difference to Europe, and in Europe, whether and how the people vote for the European Parliament. The problem is not the quality of parliamentarians – which is the same as in national politics, ranging from the superb to the laughable – nor scandals or gravy trains or anything of the sort. It is, I believe, and as I have argued *ad nauseam*, structural, deriving from the very design of governance in the EU.

In essence, the two primordial features of any functioning democracy are missing: the grand principles of accountability and representation.

As regards accountability, even the basic condition of representative democracy – that at election time the citizens can choose their governors – does not operate in Europe. Neither does the concomitant power to have one's vote, if part of the majority party, have a decisive influence on who will govern.

In a similar vein, it is impossible to link – in any meaningful, *systematic* way – the results of elections to the European Parliament to the performance of the political groups within the preceding parliamentary session, in the way that is part of the mainstay of political accountability within Member States. Structurally, dissatisfaction with 'Europe' has no channel to affect, at the European level, the agents of European governance.

Likewise, at the most primitive level of democracy, there is simply no moment in the civic calendar of Europe when the citizen can influence directly the outcome of any policy choice facing the Community and Union in the way that citizens can when choosing between parties which offer more or less sharply distinct programmes at the national level. The political colour of the European Parliament only very weakly gets translated into the legislative and administrative output of the Union. The regular gentlemanly habit of switching EP Presidents and governance of Parliament midway is a mockery of politics and democracy.

The 'political deficit', to use the felicitous phrase of Renaud Dehousse, is at the core of the democracy deficit. The Commission, by its self-understanding, linked to its very ontology, can not be 'partisan' in a right–left sense; nor can the Council, by virtue of the haphazard political nature of its composition.

Democracy surely must have some meaningful mechanism for expression of voter preference predicated on choice among options, typically informed by stronger or weaker ideological orientation. That is an indispensable component of politics. Democracy without politics is an oxymoron. And yet, that is not only Europe, but also a defining feature of Europe, the 'non-partisan' nature of the Commission, that is celebrated. The stock phrase that the supranational Commission vindicates the European interest, whereas the intergovernmental Council is a clearing house for Member State interests, is, at best, naïve. Does the 'European interest' not necessarily involve political and ideological choices?

The two most primordial norms of democracy, the principle of accountability and the principle of representation are compromised in the very structure and process of the Union.

Against these structural defects in European accountability and representation it should surprise no one, least of all Members of the European Parliament, that voter turnout is in decline, reaching historical lows. European citizens are not stupid after all.

2 Europe's historic choice and risk

The political outcome of the 2014 elections offers for the very first time the prospect of meaningful change. The idea had been in the books for decades, but good ideas that remain in books are just such. They collect dust together with the books which contain them. So credit must go to the outgoing and incoming President of Parliament and others alongside him who had taken the bold step to transform the recent elections.

The idea was simple: at the elections to the European Parliament voters will effectively choose the next President of the Commission. It would be impossible – it was argued – with a measure of hope and defiance, for the European Council to override such choice 'by the people' and impose one of their back-room, non-transparent, rabbit-out-of-the-hat choices on Europe. And so it turned out!

The potential importance for European democracy of this development is as great or greater than anything proposed in the defunct Constitution. Interestingly and significantly, this happened without any changes to the current treaties, demonstrating, yet again, the primacy of politics over law.

Parliament vastly overplayed the strength of its legal and political arguments for this change. The argument based on Article 17 that the European Council is *obligated* to follow the parliamentary choice was overstated both as a matter of law and as a matter of politics. This Article allows the Parliament to block all proposals by the Council, but not to impose its candidate. It allows, likewise, the Council to propose but not to impose.

In effect, it recognizes that the European Council and the European Parliament represent, as is common in many federal states, two different forms of democratic legitimation and creates a design which requires the consent of both institutions in the choice of the President. Either institution has the legal power to block the process, but not to impose its choice. It is not a flawless formulation. One could imagine a composition of Parliament in which no candidate proposed by the Council receives the necessary majority. There is no express 'fall back position' but, on the whole, one can see a certain political wisdom in the procedure of Article 17: the President of the Commission requires legitimation and authority deriving from both 'houses of democracy' which make up the European Union.

In exercising its role of submitting a name to the Parliament, the European Council must take into account the results of the elections. Yet this cannot plausibly be interpreted as 'must follow.' It is clear that by speaking of consultations, and providing for majority voting, the Council is meant to be a deliberative body and not a mere rubber stamp. 'Taking into account' is a soft term and it could, for example, be credibly claimed that simply by nominating someone from the winning party due account has been taken of the elections.

There is certainly no legal duty on the European Council to follow the choice of Parliament, indeed, to suggest such would be to run against what I consider the letter and spirit of the law. Neither institution is meant to be a rubber stamp to the other.

If there was an imperative of the Council to accept the choice of Parliament, it must be a political imperative rather than a legal one. Nonetheless here, too, the issue is not straightforward.

The argument that in the current circumstance of European politics, the Heads of State and government speak with no less democratic legitimacy than the European Parliament is not a specious argument. Given that the leading candidate had an outright victory in only 12 of the Member States and in two others shared the podium with his rival adds poignancy to this point.

Equally, it is a stretch to claim that, other than in a highly formal sense, the European peoples had really indicated any one of the five lead candidates as their choice for the presidency of the Commission. The polls we had at the time these observations are being written are sketchy. However, the common observation that in most jurisdictions the elections remained 'national' and that few electors were casting their vote with a view to who would emerge as President of the Commission must hold a lot of truth. All this compromised the ability of the successful candidate to claim with credibility and with authority 'I was elected by the Peoples of Europe.'

In my opinion, there was no legal imperative but the reality of the electoral results. A clear victory in less than half the Member States, a low turnout in all except those countries where voting is obligatory, and a sense that the electors had not really turned their mind to the presidential issue, all suggested that no compelling political imperative was dictated by these results.

So what was the European Council to do? The principled and correct approach was in fact followed and, paradoxically, the opposition of the British Prime Minister David Cameron was instrumental in creating procedural propriety. The European Council had the constitutional right and the duty to consult, take into account the results of the elections, and propose a candidate who enjoyed the support of at least a majority of Council Members, even if that necessitated a formal vote.

The selection of the President of the Commission should be the result of the voice of the peoples speaking through their two channels as provided by the treaty.

That is what they did by following the outcome of the elections and proposing the winning candidate as agreed by Parliament. It was prudent because to do otherwise would inflict huge damage to the image of the European Union, particularly at this moment.

But even more importantly, to follow the *Spitzenkandidaten* exercise logic was a great investment in the future of European democracy. Establishing this precedent will have the potential of transforming the next elections. It will help galvanize moves towards truer pan-European parties and it will create a new dynamic for the choice of future candidates. Above all, it will help Parliament match its formidable legislative powers with appropriate political authority, since the lesson of this outcome will most likely have a significant impact on voter behaviour in five years from now.

It is wise to invest in the economic future of Europe as well as in its democratic future and promise and no one can deny the vast experience that Jean-Claude Juncker will bring to these tasks ahead.

However, the European Union faces a far more consequential choice: is the logic of the *Spitzenkandidaten* to lead to a Commission which is 'political' but not 'partisan' in an ideological sense, as the outgoing President of the European Commission José Manuel Barroso maintains? Or if the people are to be heard and the political choice is to be real, should a 'partisan' Commission no longer be a dirty word? To be sure 'political' is good in the sense of the Commission not allowing itself to descend further into the role of super-secretariat of the other political institutions, but 'partisan'?

In my view, the whole exercise would be nullified if there is no movement, even if subtle or cautious, in that direction. At the heart of democracy there must be choice, not only as to whom should govern us, but as to how we should be governed. The lead candidate exercise, if it is to succeed, can not be perceived as a mere beauty contest. Part of the 'investment in the future' thesis is that, in moving to the next elections, voters must be put in a position whereby their choice is not only directed to the 'who', but also to the 'how' Europe should be governed. Their vote should have an impact on political and ideological programmes. And for that to happen, it must be seen, even if cautiously and prudently, that it makes a difference that the President belongs to the European People's Party rather than the Socialist family. For a Europe habituated to a result-based legitimacy, the adjustment will not be easy and not without costs. Different legitimacy issues will arise, but veritable democracy is political and requires courage. Let's not be afraid.

PROLOGUE

Donatella M. Viola

Since the introduction of direct and universal elections to the European Parliament (EP) in 1979, the number of Member States in the European Community (EC)/European Union (EU) has tripled from nine to 28. In June 2009, for the first time, Old and New partners chose together their own representatives to send to Strasbourg and Brussels. Such a memorable event, meant to symbolize the reunification of the Old Continent, turned out to mirror, instead, public apathy and indifference towards the European Union, highlighting the distance between political elites and the people.

In fact, the seventh and later the eighth EP electoral contests overtly challenged the dream of a European Federation by witnessing the surge of new extreme forms of nationalism. Also, over the years, the EU average turnout has fallen steadily from 62 per cent in 1979, to 43 per cent in 2009, and to its lowest historical record of 42.4 per cent in 2014. It plummeted to the shocking nadir of 13 per cent in Slovakia, where only 575,876 out of 4,414,433 voters actually went to the polls (Slovak Central Election Commission, 2014). These rates appear all the more paradoxical, as they emerged at a time when the European Parliament had never been so powerful.

Hitherto, this institution has failed to capture public imagination and mobilize political forces, whilst the European Parliament's long and strenuous fight to gain more powers and its metamorphosis from a mere consultative forum to a real law-making body have been virtually ignored. There is hardly any common understanding of the role played by the EP to promote European integration and to improve people's daily lives through its vibrant legislative activity. This reflects a great deal of misinformation and prejudice regarding the European Parliament, which goes well beyond the manifestation of political alienation common to modern democracies, as well as disillusionment over politics and the political establishment. Such a low level of general interest and awareness, truly bewildering in an era characterized by a ubiquity of media and web communications, can be due to the leaders' failure to shape a 'European demos', whilst pursuing an economic, monetary, and political integration.

Despite this gloomy portrait, it cannot be denied that the EP represents the world's first international parliamentary assembly that aims at performing a truly democratic political representation through its direct elections and deserves, as such, greater attention by voters as well as politicians. Interestingly, it has become a source of inspiration as well as a model to the Central American Parliament, which has introduced direct elections as a way to select its own representatives. Most importantly, it should not be overlooked that just few decades ago, even by giving rein to the greatest fancy, it would have been simply inconceivable to envisage the creation of a transnational assembly where former historical foes would sit peacefully side-by-side.

The thrust of this research is to explore, both in a longitudinal and comparative way, the multifaceted dimension of EP electoral contests across all EC/EU countries since 1979. In particular, the book intends to sketch out the broader meaning of the seventh Euro-election in the various EU Member States, by gathering, analysing, comparing, and interpreting general background information and specific data on all previous EP and national electoral races. As a result, it will endeavour to carry out an in-depth empirical comparative investigation within a comprehensive theoretical framework. Overall, through a combined qualitative and quantitative methodological approach, the volume is expected to increase understanding of the polyhedral nature of European elections.

Part I of the book, which entails a general framework, opens with the genesis of the European Parliament by tracing its path towards direct elections. It then turns to outline the EP internal organization and ends by setting out the various hypotheses of the two major theories on Euro-elections: Second-Order Elections (SOE) and Europe Salience (ES) models.

Part II, which embodies the heart of this research, consists of 27 original country surveys of European elections, cunningly undertaken by native scholars. Each of these chapters will include a geopolitical profile of the Member State, along with its historical background, a glance at the national political landscape, a brief account of the political parties, including their attitude toward the European Union, a section on public opinion and European integration, a summary of the electoral system, and an overview of all EP and national contests prior to focussing on the 2009 Euro-election. Such a detailed picture will be necessary for testing the above-mentioned theoretical models, thus attempting to uncover the complex interactions between domestic and European Union politics and to capture the real essence of this event.

On the basis of the information gathered, each chapter will finally attempt to craft a theoretical interpretation of Euro-elections, by ascertaining whether citizens' dissatisfaction of their government's performance in the EU has led to a loss of electoral support or whether EU policies have actually influenced voting behaviour.

Building on the work proficiently carried out in the country chapters, a comparison of all Euro-elections in the EU Member States will be eventually undertaken by highlighting similarities or differences in the voting behaviour of European citizens. To this end, summary tables will be sketched out on the basis of the data collected and the interpretation presented by national experts, precisely on the electoral outcome, the character of the EP electoral campaigns across the EU, public attitudes towards the European Union, the emergence of Eurosceptic parties, and the impact of the main variables of the SOE and ES models to the various case studies. The volume will close with an Epilogue focussing on the most recent European Parliament contest, which took place in the 28 Member States of the European Union between 22 and 25 May 2014.

By providing such a wide range of contextual data, national, and EP electoral results, coupled with turnout percentages, and details on elected MEPs respectively taken from Eurostat, European Parliament, national parliament and government official websites, the handbook will be a useful reference to students of political science and a guide to practitioners working in public administrations. Indeed, this investigation may serve as a teaching tool for courses on the European Union. Furthermore, students of comparative political behaviour are likely to draw some interesting insights, since Euro-elections represent a unique opportunity to assess, by means of a single survey, voters' choices of the same office in elections held simultaneously across all the EU countries. Indeed, these contests also offer the chance to understand party performance over domestic as well as European issues set in different contests at various stages of the national electoral cycle.

Yet, this book is not targeted strictly at scholars and students. It is addressed more generally to a wider audience in order to increase public knowledge of the function and workings of the EP, whilst recalling the ultimate scope of European integration.

Nowadays, in the wake of the crisis triggered by the 2008 financial earthquake, a dark shadow seems to have fallen on the unification project, thus confirming Altiero Spinelli's metaphor taken from Ernest Hemingway's famous masterpiece, *The Old Man and the Sea*. Although 'Europe has captured the biggest fish of its life, it will have to bring it ashore, because there will always be sharks trying to devour it' (Altiero Spinelli, Address to European Parliament, 14 September 1983).

Finally, I wish to highlight the symbolism behind the image I have humbly chosen for the cover of this handbook. The beautiful oil painting of the Tower of Babel, realized by the Flemish artist Pieter Bruegel the Elder in 1563, strongly inspired the Anglo-Italian architect Richard Rogers in his design of the European Parliament's building in Strasbourg. As a matter of fact, its unfinished and incomplete look allegorically mirrors the project of European integration, which is slowly taking shape, but it is still far from being accomplished.

By paraphrasing Joseph H.H. Weiler, the original biblical design of the Tower of Babel was considered as an act of hubris, an unbounded belief in the prowess of Man. The punishment, dispersal, and creation of a multilingual and multinational humankind was at once a curse, yet a potential blessing too (Weiler, 2002). The curse was, at its best, misunderstanding whilst, at its worst, national and cultural arrogance, pride, antagonism, and disrespect of the 'other', leading to fratricide as well as genocide. The blessing was the richness and originality that cultural diversity breeds and the challenge, which the essence of the European integration project embodies, of founding a community united in its diversity.

Let us hope that, rather than fulfilling the ancient, utopian desire of raising a tower reaching up to heaven, our current dream of establishing a fully-fledged European Union may be achieved, quietly and unpretentiously, in the twenty-first century. Only through a construct rooted firmly in the ground, always aware of the temptations and frailty of the human condition, will it be possible to bring together all the people of the Old Continent under the universal principles of peace, freedom, democracy, and social justice, finally turning the curse of the Tower into a blessing.

References

Slovak Central Election Commission (2014) *Elections to the European Parliament, May 2014: Results of Voting*, Statistical Office of the Slovak Republic, http://volby.statistics.sk/ep/ep2014/EP-dv/Tabulka1_en.html (accessed 30 May 2014).

Weiler, J.H.H. (2002) 'Babel – One Language and One Speech', in von Bogdandy, A., Mavroidis, P.C. and Móny Y. (eds), *European Integration and International Co-ordination: Studies in Transnational Economic Law in Honour of Claus-Dieter Ehlermann*, The Hague, New York, Kluwer Law International, 479–84.

ACKNOWLEDGEMENTS

This volume is the result of a meticulous research, writing and editing work that I have undertaken over the last five years. Yet, such an ambitious enterprise could not have been realized without the support of Routledge and the contribution of leading experts from virtually all the corners of the European Union.

I am delighted to acknowledge the patronage of the 'Robert Schuman' Centre for Advanced Studies (RSCAS) of the European University Institute in Florence, Italy. For such a privilege and honour, I am very grateful to Professor Giuliano Amato, Professor Stefano Bartolini and Professor Brigid Laffan. I also wish to convey my most sincere appreciation to the Kunsthistorisches Museum Wien, especially to Ilse Jung, for generously granting permission of reproducing the marvelous painting *The Tower of Babel* by Pieter Bruegel.

While the following list is not complete, I would like to thank several officials of the European Parliament, the European Commission, the Italian Parliament and the Italian Court of Auditors for their assistance with data acquisition, notably Roberto Ceselli, Giuseppe Cogliandro, Jana Chlupová, Mario Di Napoli, Michelle Flood, Jesús Gómez, Thomas Grunert, Paolo Iosue, Francis Jacobs, Jasenko Jašarević, Wolfgang Leonhardt, Roberta Quadrini, Daniel Ractliffe, Peter Schiffauer, Doriz Stolz, Stefano Tabacchi, Tereza Wennerholm and Sietse Wijnsma.

I extend my deepest gratitude to Professor Mark N. Franklin and Professor Joseph H.H. Weiler who have generously offered invaluable and inspiring comments. I am also indebted to Dr Andrew Glencross, Professor Fulco Lanchester, Professor John Loughlin, Professor Leonardo Morlino, Dr Simon Murden, Professor Francesco Raniolo, and Professor Richard Rose for their precious advice.

Furthermore, I have been the fortunate recipient of extensive help and encouragement from friends and relatives, in particular Ettore Bonadio, Stephanie Boylan Katavolos, Karl Davies, Nikolaos Karanasios, Paolo Lalli, Stefan Samodumov and Raffaella Viola.

Finally, I take this opportunity to pay tribute to Peter David, a brilliant journalist of *The Economist* who died suddenly and prematurely on 10 May 2012. Over the years, we had engaged in stimulating conversations on international and European politics that I will always cherish in my memories.

PART I

General framework

1	The genesis of the European Parliament: from appointed Consultative Assembly to directly elected legislative body	3
2	European Parliament's internal composition and organization	17
3	European Parliament elections theories	39

1
THE GENESIS OF THE EUROPEAN PARLIAMENT

From appointed Consultative Assembly to directly elected legislative body

Donatella M. Viola

Introduction

The project of European integration has been pivotal in establishing an area of peace, stability, and prosperity on the historically war-ravaged Old Continent, by enabling previous enemies to overcome their hostility, transcend their national barriers, and cooperate together.

To begin with, the first chapter of this book intends to trace the long and winding path towards direct elections to the European Parliament (EP) by also drawing attention to the attempts, which were repeatedly disdained, to establish a uniform electoral procedure, a 'vexed question' which is still far from being solved.

Indeed, one of the dilemmas connected to the European Parliament was whether granting more rights to an unelected assembly should precede the convening of direct elections to a frail parliamentary institution. In the words of the Dutch Socialist politician Schelto Patijn:

> for too long . . . opponents of direct elections have claimed that the European Parliament [should] be given wider powers before such an election could take place, while ironically denying Parliament these powers on the grounds that it [was] not directly elected.
>
> *(Patijn, 1974)*

Eventually, Members of the European Parliament (MEPs) broke out of this absurd vicious circle by stressing that once they drew genuine democratic authority from a direct link with European electors, their claim for greater involvement in the decision-making process would become automatically more justifiable and legitimate.

As such, this chapter tells the story of the EP's struggle to make an impact on the major political and institutional decisions of the European Community/Union through its successful transformation from an unelected consultative assembly to a directly elected, fully-fledged parliamentary forum.

1 Towards direct election of the European Parliament

The idea of a European forum elected by direct universal suffrage first saw the light of day at The Hague Conference in 1948, paving the way to the foundation of a parliamentary archetype, the Council of Europe Consultative Assembly in 1949 (Smith, 1999). From the very beginning, the European federalists Altiero Spinelli and Henrik Brugmans were wholeheartedly committed to achieving this goal, which would confer full democratic legitimacy to the European integration process. As the former President of the European Parliament, Emilio Colombo argued, 'although frequently disparaged and held up to derision, [this enduring aspiration for a truly popular institution] could never be completely stifled and never lost its attraction' (Colombo, 1977, 5). In fact, as long ago as 1951, the European Coal and Steel Community (ECSC) Treaty contemplated the creation of an 'Assembly consisting of representatives of the peoples of the States' that 'would draw up proposals for elections by direct universal suffrage in accordance with a uniform procedure in all Member States' (Articles 20 and 21.3 ECSC). In the meantime, but only as a provisional measure, this Assembly would consist of delegates designated once a year by their respective national parliaments (Article 21.1 ECSC).

Already in 1954, the Common Assembly of the ECSC urged implementation of direct election and this need was later reiterated in Article 138(3) of the European Economic Community (EEC) Treaty in 1957. However, it was not until May 1960 that a convention on the introduction of direct elections was adopted at last. The *Dehousse Report*, after the name of its author, argued that 'what [was] largely wanting in the European Communities [was] popular support, recognition by the European peoples of their solidarity'. On the other hand, aware of the great challenge to attain at once a uniform electoral procedure, the report realistically clarified that 'uniform' was not synonymous with 'identical', suggesting, by way of a compromise, that Member States could follow, in the first instance, their own respective electoral rules (Smith, 1999). Despite its amenable character, the proposal, forwarded to the Council in June 1960, did not meet with unanimous consensus and consequently, for almost a decade, the question fell into oblivion. At last, in December 1969, the heads of state and of government meeting in The Hague put the item back on the agenda by devoting a short but significant line in their final communiqué, whereby they promised that '[t]he problem of the method of direct elections [would have been] studied by the Council of Ministers' (The Hague Summit Final Communiqué, 1969). As a matter of fact, such a statement proved to be true and durable as it took another decade, several proposals, and lengthy negotiations before the first direct election to the European Parliament could be run. Yet, The Hague Conference had the merit of breaking the impasse, leading to the establishment of a working group chaired by the French MEP George Vedel with the task to lay down a report on this issue. The final text, which saw the light of day in 1972, stressed that the European Parliament, as by then the Assembly had named itself, could slowly move towards a single electoral law once it had won true legitimacy on the grounds of its first direct election. Once again, Member States were reassured that the term 'uniform electoral procedure' did not mean immediate and homogeneous standardization of electoral systems. Moreover, Vedel subtly acknowledged the close link between direct European elections and enhanced parliamentary powers but rejected the idea that the former should precede the latter, since

> in this way, two equally desirable objectives [would make] each other's implementation impossible. The only way to break the vicious circle [would be] to refuse to let one of the two objectives depend on the achievement of the other one first.
>
> *(Vedel, 1972,59; Smith, 1999)*

In September 1973, Schelto Patijn was appointed as rapporteur for a new Convention project which turned out to be less ambitious than that previously initiated by his colleague, the Belgian MEP Fernand Dehousse, requiring a higher level of electoral uniformity. On this basis, at the Paris Summit held in December 1974 under the chairmanship of the French President Valéry Giscard d'Estaing, the heads of state and of government took the solemn decision to convene direct elections as early as possible. Almost two years later, in September 1976, the Council issued the Act concerning the direct election of representatives of the European Parliament, whilst reaffirming the need for a future uniform electoral procedure but without fixing a clear schedule for its accomplishment. Due to the delay in the ratification process by Westminster, the first election to the European Parliament could not be conducted until June 1979 (Smith, 1999). The failure to agree on a uniform electoral procedure was, at the time, a cause of great frustration amongst the federalists, although they also had to recognize that it was right to concentrate initially on getting direct universal elections off the ground and to postpone the perfection of the system until later.

In February 1982, the first elected Parliament adopted the Seitlinger Report, which addressed the sensitive question concerning the introduction of a uniform electoral procedure. Its key proposals aimed at extending proportional representation in multi-member constituencies of between 3 and 15 MEPs, with seats allocated by the d'Hondt system, and the possibility of preferential voting. Nevertheless, a deviation from the norm on the grounds of 'special geographical or ethnic factors' could be allowed. Interestingly, the report envisaged that nationals of one Member State living in another one for more than five years be given the right to vote in their country of residence. Finally, elections were planned to be held on two days – more precisely on Sunday and Monday. However, due to the impossibility of reaching an agreement amongst the Member States, the Council decided to postpone the discussion and vote over this complex matter. Alas, the Seitlinger proposal was never re-examined and a similar fate awaited the Bocklet Report, drafted in 1985, which sank under the UK's adamant refusal to introduce proportional representation. Only after the 1989 elections, were some new attempts made by the Flemish MEP Karel De Gucht, who produced two interim reports. The first reiterated the application of the d'Hondt method and highlighted how campaigns for EP elections should be run and financed. The second recommended that the number of seats allocated to a united Germany would rise to 99, leaving France, Italy, and the UK with 87 each. It also expected that two-thirds of the British seats would be elected by simple majority in single-member constituencies, with the remaining third distributed proportionately. Like the previous reports, despite their looser requirements and more flexible approach, the De Gucht drafts failed to obtain the necessary support (Duff, 2011).

Eventually, the 1992 Maastricht Treaty on European Union (TEU) endorsed one of the key points raised ten years before by the Seitlinger Report by conferring upon all European citizens residing in another EU Member State of which they were not nationals the right to vote and the possibility to stand as candidates in EP elections (Article 8b, 2, TEU). The TEU also gave Parliament the right of assent to the Council's proposal for a uniform electoral procedure (Article 138, TEU). Unable to overcome the insurmountable hurdles to turn national election rules into a single formula, as these are deep-rooted in conventional practices and long-established traditions, it was agreed to take a step back. As Fulvio Attinà stressed, governments and parties, especially those belonging to the majority, are unlikely to support such a principle if this would mean introducing major differences between the electoral systems for national parliaments and the EP Parliament on the grounds that these disparities may cause strain to domestic politics and to some, or all, political parties (Attinà, 1995).

The 1997 Treaty of Amsterdam (ToA) sanctioned this change of route by introducing the easier alternative of applying common principles. To this avail, it entrusted Parliament with the task of identifying or defining these terms in order to reduce the discrepancies existing among the various national electoral procedures.

In particular, Article 190, 4 of the Treaty establishing the European Community (EC) in its consolidated version, contemplated that 'The European Parliament w[ould] draw up a proposal for elections by direct universal suffrage in accordance with a uniform procedure in all Member States or in accordance with principles common to all Member States.'

At last, the UK Labour government, under the leadership of Tony Blair, broke the impasse caused by the House of Lords' stark opposition to any amendments to the procedure for EP elections by invoking the Parliament Act. This exceptional move paved the way for the adoption of a closed list system of regional proportional representation as from the 1999 election (Smith, 1999). Subsequently, electoral changes were also yielded in France in time for the 2004 European vote. These two events helped to revive the political atmosphere so that the prospect of achieving a uniform electoral procedure, by way of a gradual harmonization of national electoral systems, seemed to be within reach.

On 15 July 1998, the European Parliament adopted, by 355 votes to 146 with 39 abstentions, the *Anastassopoulos Report* which put forward a number of common principles for Euro-elections. More strikingly, the text advanced, for the first time, the rather bold proposal of electing 10 per cent of MEPs from transnational and gender balanced lists. This was intended to awaken a genuine European political awareness, galvanize European political parties, and confer upon the electoral campaign a more European dimension, less focussed on national political issues (Anastassopoulos, 1998).

Whilst such an audacious idea was promptly discarded by the Council, some of the other less daring novelties contained in the report were instead endorsed in June 2002. This extensive and influential report laid down the basis for amending the original 1976 Act, eventually undertaken by the Council in 2002. The text codified the introduction of proportional representation, explicitly allowed single transferable voting and preferential voting, catered for territorial constituencies, fixed a 5 per cent threshold, phased out the dual mandate, and let national laws be applied for filling vacancies in case of withdrawal of mandates. This electoral reform, far from setting a really uniform procedure, nevertheless embedded a series of common principles by which all representatives would be elected to the EP chamber (Farrell and Scully, 2010). Finally, elections would take place over a maximum of two days and would be convened in May rather than June, so that they would not coincide with summer holidays in northern states (Anastassopoulos, 1998).

Since then, the European Parliament, which enjoys the sole right to initiate a revision of its electoral procedure, has tried to make progress on this matter by taking into account EU geographic and demographic changes and, above all, by trying to find useful ways to mobilize reluctant voters.

On 21 July 2009, the Constitutional Affairs Committee assigned the British Liberal MEP Andrew Duff the task of preparing a proposal for a modification of the Act of 20 September 1976 concerning the election of MEPs by direct universal suffrage.

Almost one year later, on 12 July 2010, following a brief debate within the Constitutional Affairs Committee, it was decided that Duff's draft required further work. Nine months later, on 19 April 2011, the committee finally adopted the text by 20 votes to 4. By contrast, after a lengthy and heated debate, no consensus was reached at the plenary of 7 July 2011, so that the report was referred back to the committee. A new version, known as the *Duff Report II*, was published two months later and endorsed by the Committee on 26 January 2012 by 16 votes in favour and 7 against. However, on 8 March 2012 – when it became clear that the largest EP political group, the centre-right European People's Party (EPP) would not support the proposal – in order to avoid the humiliation of seeing it officially rejected by the House, the report was inexorably, yet disappointingly, withdrawn. This rather cautious and wise move was also motivated by widespread concern that a rejection of the overall package would jeopardize a future debate and approval of some of its less contentious points. It was agreed to elaborate a new proposal which would set aside the crucial question, and which definitively embodied the subject of utmost controversy amongst the political groups, relating to the possibility of electing 25 MEPs from an EU-wide list, in addition to those traditionally selected within national lists, thus granting voters two ballots to cast. The advocates for this radical reform believed that the creation of this additional single EU-wide constituency would upgrade the electoral procedure of the EP by breaking the monopoly of national political parties, conferring a more direct influence to European political parties and allowing candidates from small states to reach positions of prominence in the transnational lists (Brand, 2012).

And yet, as agreed, such a controversial point no longer appeared in the far less ambitious text of the third *Duff Report*, adopted by the plenary on 4 July 2013 with 507 votes for, 120 against, and 18 abstentions. Indeed, the resolution merely aimed at improving the practical organization of the European elections to be held between 22 and 25 May 2014.

To this end, it called on the national political parties to ensure that the names of their candidates would be made public at least six weeks prior to polling day, by also stressing that the candidates should commit themselves, if elected, to taking up their European mandate. Furthermore, the need to press for a higher proportion of women on the candidate lists was reiterated.

The most groundbreaking point in the report focusses on the early nomination of the candidate for the presidency of the Commission by European political parties. This should have contributed to stimulate a truly Europe-wide electoral campaign by drawing attention to the direct and indirect implications of the EP contest, and by ultimately galvanizing voters at this critical stage of European integration.

2 The historical development of the European Parliament

2.1 The original treaties

On 9 May 1950, the French Foreign Minister Robert Schuman launched an initiative to place coal and steel production in France and Germany under a common High Authority, within an organization also open to other European countries. The so-called Schuman Plan, fundamentally conceived in order to make war between the two historical foes 'not merely unthinkable but materially impossible', did not foresee the creation of an *ad hoc* parliamentary assembly, as it originally envisaged the involvement of the Assembly of the Council of Europe (Schuman Declaration, 9 May 1950). However, since this idea was discarded due to the UK government's fierce opposition during the negotiations for the European Coal and Steel Community (ECSC), the French political economist and diplomat Jean Monnet advanced a proposal to set up a sort of parliamentary forum, tasked with monitoring the activities of the collegial executive body. The ECSC Treaty – signed in Paris on 18 April 1951 by France, Germany, Italy, the Netherlands, Belgium, as well as Luxembourg and entered into effect on 24 July 1952 with a validity of 50 years – sanctioned the official birth of the ECSC Common Assembly, gathering 78:

> delegates whom the Parliaments of each of the Member States [should] be called upon to appoint once a year from among their own membership, or who [should] be elected by direct universal suffrage, according to the procedure determined by each respective High Contracting Party.
>
> *(Articles 20 and 21, ECSC)*

Meeting for the first time in September 1952, these delegates – along with nine additional representatives, notably three from Germany, France, and Italy respectively – were entrusted with the delicate task of laying the bases of the Draft Treaty to establish a European Political Community (Dinan, 2004). This text was adopted by the ECSC Assembly in March 1953, but was rejected by the six Member States in November 1953. Likewise, the plan for a European Defence Community failed on a procedural motion in the French Parliament on 28 August 1954 (Pinder, 1998).

It became clear, therefore, that the Assembly's approval was by far insufficient to affect any decision of the nascent ECSC, since its power was strictly confined to controlling the High Authority without any effective involvement in law-making. Subsequently, within the European Economic Community (EEC) and the Atomic Energy Community (Euratom) Treaties, signed in Rome on 25 March 1957 and entered into force on 1 January 1958, the ECSC Assembly became a common institution under the label of 'European Parliamentary Assembly'. Yet its role, eclipsed by the Council of Ministers and the Commission, remained somewhat negligible. In fact, its intervention was limited to mere consultation in the legislative process and in the formulation of international agreements (Dupagny, 1992). The only important prerogative of the Assembly was, under especially serious circumstances, to dismiss the Commission following a vote of censure by two-thirds of its members.

It was not until the mid-1970s that the EP's right of consultation was extended to almost all legislation and, occasionally, even to Commission memoranda or Council resolutions. Most importantly, in accordance with the Council Decision of 21 April 1970, the European Parliament's budgetary competence gradually increased, shifting from national contributions, through which the Member States could control the policies undertaken by the Communities, to an independent system of financing by traditional own resources, such as agricultural levies, customs duties, as well as value added tax (VAT) (see http://europa.eu/legislation_summaries/budget/l34011_en.htm, accessed 21 December 2014).

Pursuant to the 1970 Treaty amending Certain Budgetary Provisions of the Treaties establishing the European Communities and the 1975 Treaty amending Certain Financial Provisions of the Treaties, the European Parliament could propose changes to compulsory expenditure, mainly referring to agriculture, and to non-compulsory expenditure subject to the ceilings set by the financial perspective, and it could reject the draft budget by a majority of its members and two-thirds of the votes cast. The budgetary authority was therefore shared by the Council and the European Parliament, with the former ultimately taking decisions on compulsory spending and the latter gaining the final word on non-compulsory ones. Nevertheless, Parliament's effective space for intervention remained rather constrained due to inter-institutional and even intra-institutional conflicts.

Under the aforementioned 1975 Treaty, the EP also acquired the so-called power of 'discharge' over the implementation of previous budgets, on the basis of the annual report presented by the European Court of Auditors. Yet, it is noteworthy that the European Parliament has hitherto refused to approve the budget only twice, in November 1984 and in December 1998. The first case did not hit the headlines since the Commission, already at the end of its term of office, fortuitously quit a few weeks later. By contrast, the second case, which highlighted serious allegations of financial mismanagement and nepotism amongst members of the Commission, triggered a major crisis that was widely reported by the media and inevitably led, in March 1999, to the resignation of the whole collegial body chaired by President Jacques Santer (Jones, 2001; Corbett et al., 2007).

2.2 The Single European Act

The desire to foster European integration inspired the Italian federalist MEP Altiero Spinelli's Draft Treaty establishing the European Union. This text, which was widely endorsed by the plenary on 14 February 1984, offered the basis for an intergovernmental debate over the reform of the original treaties. It eventually led to the signing of the Single European Act (SEA) on 17 and 28 February 1986 by all 12 Member States, which by then also incorporated Greece, Spain, and Portugal. After the EP's approval, ratification by national parliaments, and popular referenda in Denmark and Ireland held respectively on 26 February 1986 and 26 May 1987, the SEA came into force on 1 July 1987. Its main objectives were the completion of the single market by 31 December 1992 and the institutionalization of the European Political Cooperation's (EPC) forum, which remained outside the EC framework as it retained its purely intergovernmental character.

A two-reading cooperation procedure was introduced, requiring the Council's position to be referred back to the EP which, within a three-month period, would have to decide whether to approve or reject it. The legislative process would be deemed concluded unless the Council unanimously overruled Parliament or pressed for amendments that, upon the Commission's endorsement, could be discarded only following the Council's unanimous decision (Corbett *et al.*, 2007). The new procedure was generally applied to matters relating to social and environmental policy, regional and structural funds, research and technological development programmes and, above all, the implementation of the single market. As a consequence, the EP's ability to influence EC legislation was enhanced but without solving the problem of policy-making effectiveness, primarily due to the risk that the Council could forever delay the adoption of a decision in the first reading.

As George Tsebelis highlighted, the cooperation procedure conferred on Parliament a 'conditional agenda-setting power', since it could put forward proposals that were easier for the Council to adopt than to amend (Tsebelis, 1994, 128). And yet, the EP amendments were subject to the Commission's approval so that, therefore, it remained the sole institution entitled to initiate legislation. Whilst generally referring to the consultation procedure as the basic parliamentary instrument to intervene in the area of external economic relations, the SEA also established the EP's right of assent, by an absolute majority of its members, over both association and accession treaties. As far as trade agreements were concerned, the EP's opinion continued, instead, not to be required, giving the Commission, upon the Council's authorization, exclusive power over their negotiation and implementation. In addition, an important issue was left unresolved concerning the EP's right to request the European Court of Justice (ECJ) to deliver its opinion on the compatibility of concluded international agreements under EC Law (Article 228, 6 EC). Within the EPC context, Parliament was entitled to be associated with its proceedings, to observe the actions of national foreign ministers and officials, to be informed, and to have its views duly taken into account. Against this background, the creation of an EPC Secretariat in Brussels contributed to improved communication between the EP and foreign ministries.

Even if the SEA represented a step forward in the path towards a united Europe, it did not satisfy Parliament's federal aspiration (EP Resolution, 11/12/1986).

By comparing the 1984 Draft Treaty with the texts of all successive EC/EU constitutional reforms up until now, it is striking to realize the extent of Spinelli's far-sighted and innovative vision that has left an indelible imprint on the evolution of European integration. Over the years, some of his ideas have been gradually incorporated into the EC/EU structure, whilst his brainchild continues to feed the discussion on the future revision of the treaties (Trechsel, 2010).

Already in November 1989, in order to redress some of its most serious institutional and political shortcomings, the EP started a campaign to promote reforms and, a long time before any national government's proposal, it launched a Conference on Political Union. To this aim, the European Parliament undertook an intense dialogue with the Commission and the Council, by also exchanging information with Member State parliaments and fostering contacts between its transnational political groups and their national counterparts. In particular, it adopted historic resolutions on the Intergovernmental Conference on European Monetary Union and Political Union, on the Constitutional Basis of Political Union, and on the principle of subsidiarity, as outlined in David Martin's, Emilio Colombo's, and Valéry Giscard d'Estaing's reports, respectively.

In June 1988, the Inter-institutional Agreement on Budgetary Discipline and Improvement of the budgetary procedure conferred a greater parliamentary influence over compulsory expenditure by requiring its approval for any upward movement of the ceiling. Besides, as the EP had been pressing for years, the Agreement provided for an increase in non-compulsory expenditures and a decrease in compulsory ones.

2.3 The Treaty on European Union

On 7 February 1992, the Twelve meeting in the Dutch town of Maastricht decided to sign the Treaty on European Union (TEU), where 'the old-fashioned "Community" was upgraded to First with a term redolent with gravitas: "Union"' (Weiler, 2012, 825).

The Treaty represented a significant step in the integration process by laying the ground for a fully-fledged economic and monetary union, for a Common Foreign and Security Policy (CFSP), for Cooperation in Justice and Home Affairs (JHA), and by expanding the EP powers.

However, as Joseph H.H. Weiler has aptly observed, 'Maastricht was greeted by the typical indifference with which the elite-driven European construct was habitually met' (Weiler, 2012, 826). The Danes, who were consulted by way of a popular referendum held on 2 June 1992, rejected the treaty by a slim majority of 50.7 to 49.3 per cent. Only after reaching an agreement at the Edinburgh European Council – entailing four Danish exceptions over Economic and Monetary Union, Common Defence Policy, Justice and Home Affairs, and European Citizenship – on 18 May 1993, did a second popular consultation in Denmark endorse the TEU. In France, the ratification process required a constitutional revision, which was undertaken by the national parliament on 25 June 1992, as well as a referendum which was convened on 20 September 1992, upon the initiative of President François Mitterrand who, certain about its positive outcome, hoped in this way to turn the tide against the increasing Eurosceptic wave (Dinan, 2004, 259). Yet his high expectations were not fully met, since French citizens did not show great enthusiasm towards the treaty – narrowly endorsing it by just 51 per cent (Criddle, 1993). In Britain, a lengthy and thorny debate in the House of Commons risked reversing all the efforts made by the Conservative Prime Minister John Major who, after replacing Margaret Thatcher in October 1990, had unwearyingly sought and obtained for his own country special concessions regarding monetary union and social policy provisions (Jones, 2001: 25). More specifically, the government was challenged by the Labour and Liberal Democrat opposition parties – especially critical about the British opt-out on the social chapter – and even by some of his own party members, the so-called Tory rebels, who vigorously rejected the whole text. Finally, in Germany, despite the early parliamentary endorsement of the TEU in December 1992, the federal President, under the pressure of several political groups, postponed the signature of the statute until October 1993 when the *Bundesverfassungsgericht*, the Federal Constitutional Court, finally declared the compatibility of the new treaty with the *Grundgesetz*, which embodies the Constitution of the German Federal Republic (Pinder, 2001).

Under the new provisions, the EP acquired the prerogative to request the Commission to enact appropriate proposals on matters which it considered to be of great relevance. Certainly, one of the main novelties of the TEU was the setting up of a new legislative procedure, known as 'codecision', which included a third reading and the possibility of a formal conciliation committee tasked with reaching a compromise between the Council and Parliament. Codecision initially applied to 15 areas of Community action, relating to most internal market legislation, free movement of workers, consumer protection, public health, education, the equivalence of qualifications, research, and trans-European networks (Corbett et al., 2007). As a result, the EP secured additional powers in law-making although arguably, as stressed by George Tsebelis, due to the complexity of the new decision-making process, its role appeared weakened (Tsebelis, 1997).

Parliamentary powers were enhanced in the first or Community 'pillar', whilst they remained rather marginal over CFSP and JHA issues, as no supervision or political initiative was foreseen. Finally, the EP secured the right to approve the appointment of the President of the European Commission and the European Commission as a whole, whilst maintaining the power to censure it. In addition, the EP was entitled to be consulted on the membership of the European Court of Auditors as well as on the President and other members of the board of the European Central Bank. The EP itself could choose the European Ombudsman and had a more direct, albeit non-binding, role in the selection of both the management board and the executive director of the European Food Safety Authority (EFSA).

2.4 The Treaty of Amsterdam

On 2 October 1997 in Amsterdam, all 15 Member States, including the newcomers Austria, Finland, and Sweden, signed the amended Treaty on European Union, which came into effect on 1 May 1999, after national parliamentary ratifications and two referenda held in Ireland and Denmark on 22 and 28 May 1998, respectively. The new text increased the EP's legislative weight, since codecision was extended to most issues previously under the cooperation procedure, such as transport and the environment, thus covering 32 policy areas in total. Moreover, in order to prevent paralysis arising from the vetoing of an individual state or a small group of states unwilling to be part of a political initiative, the ToA introduced the possibility for Member States to work more closely together on aspects falling within the EC and JHA pillars. This option could be pursued under the 'closer cooperation procedure', better known as the 'enhanced cooperation procedure' (Jones, 2001). Over international matters, Parliament was just granted a mere advisory function over the Council's annual document relating to the main aspects and basic choices of the CFSP. Lastly, the EP's right to approve the candidate for Commission President was made legally binding.

2.5 The Treaty of Nice

Another attempt to pursue the path of institutional reforms in the European Union was made by the Fifteen in Nice in February 2001, but it was necessary to wait almost two years before the new treaty entered into force following a slow and cumbersome ratification process, which also entailed two referenda in Ireland on 7 June 2001 and 19 October 2002 (see http://europa.eu/eu-law/decision-making/treaties/index_en.htm; http://electionsireland.org/results/referendum, accessed on 20 February 2015).

Codecision was adopted for most legislation which required the Council to act by qualified majority (QM), such as transport, social policy, the internal market, and its four freedoms of circulation of goods, services, capital, and persons. Nevertheless, unanimity was required for questions relating to social security for migrant workers. By virtue of the new treaty, 'enhanced cooperation' could be broadened to CFSP, except for defence matters.

Furthermore, like the other major EU institutions, Parliament was entitled to seek the European Court of Justice's opinion on the compatibility of an international agreement with the legal order of the European Union (Article 300, 6).

Under the Treaty of Nice, regulations and general conditions governing the status of MEPs, excluding aspects relating to taxation, were finally to be adopted upon the EP's approval.

Aware of the limits and imperfections of the Treaty of Nice, its signatories annexed a declaration on the future of the Union, paving the way for further reforms, originally scheduled for 2004, to be discussed with all interested parties, representatives of national parliaments, and civil society (Declaration No. 23, OJ C80/2001, 85–6).

2.6 *The European Constitution*

In December 2001, at the Laeken European Council, it was agreed to entrust a convention with the task of drawing up a preliminary draft constitution. With Valéry Giscard d'Estaing as chairman and Giuliano Amato and Jean-Luc Dehaene as Vice-Chairmen, the convention was also composed of 2 representatives from every national parliament from all Member States and candidate countries including Turkey, 16 MEPs, 2 representatives of the European Commission, and a representative of each national government. Completed in June 2003, the draft was adopted with some minor changes as the final text of the Treaty Establishing a Constitution for Europe (TECE) and signed by the representatives of all Member States gathered in Rome on 29 October 2004 (Corbett *et al.*, 2007). Notwithstanding the approval of a very large majority of MEPs, the endorsement of 18 national parliaments, and 2 non-binding popular consultations in Spain on 20 February 2005 and in Luxembourg on 10 July 2005, the ratification process was inexorably halted by the negative outcome of the French and Dutch referenda held respectively on 29 May and 1 June 2005. Once it became clear that overall consent could never be attained, the ambitious constitutional project was abandoned in favour of the conventional and more pragmatic option of amending the pre-existing treaties.

2.7 *The Treaty of Lisbon*

From the outset, the European Parliament was involved in the preliminary talks on EU institutional reforms and, at the opening of the Intergovernmental Conference in July 2007, amongst the representatives of the 27 EU countries, there were also three Members of the European Parliament (MEPs), the Dutch Christian Democrat Elmar Brok, the Spanish Socialist Enrique Barón Crespo, and the British Liberal Andrew Duff.

Two core issues were under the spotlight: the definition of qualified majority voting (QMV) in the Council and the EP's composition. With regard to the second question, the Italian government overtly criticized the initial proposal of shifting the basis of parliamentary representation from that of population size to that of citizenship, given that these elements did not always coincide, as in the Italian case, due to strict legislation over the naturalization of migrants.

On 19 October 2007, a compromise was reached on the above matters whilst the British and Irish opt-outs/opt-ins, related to subjects originally falling within the third pillar, had been previously sorted out and the EP's right to appoint the Vice-President/High Representative for Foreign Affairs and Security Policy was maintained. Indeed, the boldest features previously advocated in the Constitution were dismissed, whilst various measures addressed to specific countries were added (Corbett and Méndez de Vigo, 2008).

On 13 December 2007, the heads of state and government of all the 27 Member States of the European Union, including the ten countries from Central and Eastern Europe, signed the Treaty of Lisbon (ToL) which entered into force almost two years later, on 1 December 2009, after the ratification of national parliaments and two popular referenda in Ireland held in June 2008 and October 2009 (http://europa.eu/lisbon_treaty/countries/, accessed on 21 December 2014).

Under the new provisions, the EP – along with all national legislative bodies across the European Union – has gained a wider and better involvement in EU decision-making, so that the ToL can be rightly defined as the 'Treaty of Parliaments' (Lenaerts and Cambien, 2009, 207). Indeed, by broadening the application of 'codecision', elevated to the rank of 'ordinary legislative procedure', the European Parliament has finally reached equal status with the Council of the European Union as a law-making body (Corbett et al., 2011).

The EP's role as a co-legislator is fully recognized in virtually all fields of EU action, and more specifically in 85 policy areas including agriculture, energy, security, asylum and immigration, justice and home affairs, public health as well as structural funds (see www.europarl.europa.eu/external/appendix/legislativeprocedure/europarl_ordinarylegislativeprocedure_glossary_en.pdf, accessed on 21 December 2014).

The European Parliament shares with the Council the prerogative to adopt European laws, thus accepting, amending, or rejecting the content of directives and regulations. Besides, the EP may examine the Commission's annual programme of work by pointing out which laws it would like to see adopted. Moreover, in accordance with Article 48 of the TEU, Parliament can exert the new power to propose treaty amendments and has the final say over the decision of setting up a convention with the task of laying the basis for further institutional reforms (Article 48, 2–3 TEU).

The Treaty envisages the possibility for the legislative body to delegate part of its own power to the Commission, although this delegated power can only consist in supplementing or amending parts of a legislative act which are not considered essential (Article 290, TFEU). Democratic control is reinforced through a new system of supervision in which the European Parliament or the Council may either call back the Commission's decisions or revoke the delegation of such powers (EP Resolution 5/5/2010).

In the area of EU finance, the artificial distinction between 'compulsory' and 'non-compulsory' expenditure is abolished and replaced by a new, simpler and more transparent budgetary procedure with a single reading. This ensures full parity between Parliament and the Council as regards the approval of the whole EU annual budget (see www.europarl.europa.eu/ftu/pdf/en/FTU_1.4.3.pdf, accessed on 21 December 2014).

In Lisbon, it was agreed to give Parliament greater access to meetings and documentation through a process of question time with commissioners and even with the Vice-President for External Relations/High-Representative for Foreign Affairs. The EP may ask the President of the Commission to withdraw confidence in one of the members of his or her team. By virtue of the new treaty, the EP does not simply endorse but elects, by a majority of its component members, the President of the Commission on the proposal of the European Council, taking into account the results of the Euro-elections (Article 17.7, TEU). The designation of the Vice-President of the Commission/High Representative of the Union for Foreign Affairs and Security Policy, together with the other members of the Commission, as a body, are also subject to a vote of consent by Parliament, as well as to a vote of censure. As to its relations with the European Council, which has acquired the status of an EU institution, the EP has the right to be informed about the preparations and the results of its meetings. Lastly, parliamentary consent is required for the conclusion of a wide range of international agreements, including those falling within the framework of ordinary legislative procedures. The inclusion of the European

Development Fund in the EU budget enhances the democratic legitimacy of the European Union's international relations with developing countries.

In brief, each of the above-mentioned treaties marked a gradual step towards the construction of a European political union. Some revolutionary elements were successfully put forward in Lisbon, but without incorporating all the institutional reforms necessary for the effective and democratic functioning of an enlarged European Union.

Conclusion

During its half-century history, the European Parliament has succeeded in becoming a directly elected institution which has carved out a greater role for itself by also evoking solutions for the development of the European Community and later of the European Union, ever more necessary in the aftermath of its numerous enlargements. The EP has gradually mutated its status from a merely consultative assembly, under the original treaties, to a fully-fledged co-legislative body, under the Treaty of Lisbon. This implies that EU legislation is now subject to a level of parliamentary approval that exists in no other supranational or international environment and that, finally, Altiero Spinelli's vision of Europe, long ago outlined in the Draft Treaty, is slowly taking shape.

Under the new provisions agreed upon in the Portuguese capital, the democratic deficit appears to have lost its intensity but does not seem to have been utterly overcome. In fact, despite being directly elected and having acquired remarkable powers, the European Parliament suffers from remoteness and obscurity, ironically remaining distant and unknown to most European citizens.

The reasons behind this paradox can be found in the failure of connecting Parliament to the people, due to the several inconsistencies inherent to the modalities for electing its members highlighted in this chapter. Electoral systems stand as core factors of democracy since they affect the nature of the trilateral relationship between representatives, voters, and political parties. In this perspective, the quest for a common electoral law is aimed at reinforcing links, bolstering the political legitimacy of the European Parliament, and fostering a greater sense of European identity.

Yet, other features contribute to perpetuate the infamous democratic deficit which more commonly arises from the current location, organization, and composition of the European Parliament, which will be unveiled in the next chapter.

The EP's claim to be representative of the European people rests on its ability to fill this gap, to mend this generalized absence of trust between the people and political elites, and to improve its public image. By way of its old and new powers, the Assembly may play a key role in enhancing the rather blurred picture of the European Union, generally and often erroneously seen exclusively through national lenses. In fact, MEPs can choose and support the election of charismatic figures as Head of Parliament and Head of Commission, able to speak on behalf of Europe with authority to Member State national governments (cf. Franklin, 2010). Only by achieving these objectives will the European Parliament raise its popular legitimacy, by preventing the revival of extreme nationalism, so tempting at times of economic turmoil and social uncertainty, in the belief that European integration is the only sensible response to globalization.

References

Primary sources

Official declarations and treaties

Declaration No. 23, Treaty of Nice (2001) *Official Journal of the European Communities* C80/2001, 10 March, 85–6.

European Coal and Steel Community Treaty (1951) http://eur-lex.europa.eu/LexUriServ/LexUriServ.do?uri=CELEX:11951K:EN:PDF (accessed on 21 December 2014).

European Economic Community (EEC) Treaty (1957) http://ec.europa.eu/economy_finance/emu_history/documents/treaties/rometreaty2.pdf (accessed on 21 December 2014).

Final Communiqué of the Conference of Heads of State or Government, The Hague Summit (2 December 1969) http://ec.europa.eu/economy_finance/emu_history/documentation/compendia/19691202fr02finalcommuniqueofsummitconference.pdf (accessed on 21 December 2014).

Referenda in Ireland on 7 June 2001 and 19 October 2002, http://electionsireland.org/results/referedum/ (accessed on 21 December 2014).

Schuman Declaration (9 May 1950) www.eurotreaties.com/schuman.pdf (accessed on 21 December 2014).

Single European Act (SEA) (1986) *Official Journal of the European Communities*, L 169, 29 June 1987.

Treaty establishing a Constitution for Europe (TECE) (2004) *Official Journal of the European Union*, C 310, 16 December.

Treaty establishing the European Community (EC) (2006) in its consolidated version, *Official Journal of the European Union*, C 321 E/132, 29 December.

Treaty of Amsterdam (1997) *Official Journal of the European Communities* C 340, 10 November.

Treaty of Lisbon (2007) *Official Journal of the European Union*, C 306, 17 December.

Treaty of Nice (2001) *Official Journal of the European Communities* C 80, 10 March.

Treaty on European Union (TEU) (1992) *Official Journal of the European Communities* C 224, 31 August.

Treaty on the Functioning of the European Union (TFEU) (2007) Official Journal of the European Communities, C 306/211, 17 December.

European Parliament reports and resolutions

Act Concerning the Election of the Representatives of the Assembly by Direct Universal Suffrage, *Official Journal of the European Communities*, L 278/1, 8 October 1976.

Anastassopoulos (1998) Report on a Proposal for an Electoral Procedure Incorporating Common Principles for the Election of Members of the European Parliament. Committee on Institutional Affairs, EP document A4-0212/98, 2 June.

Corbett and Méndez de Vigo (2008) Report on the Treaty of Lisbon, A6-0013/2008, 29 January.

Dehousse (1960) Report on the Election of the European Parliamentary Assembly by Universal Direct Elections, *Official Journal of the European Communities*, C 37, 2 June.

Duff (2011) Report Regarding the Modification of the Act Concerning the Election of the Members of the European Parliament by Direct Universal Suffrage of 20 September 1976, 28 April, A7-0176/2011.

Inter-institutional Agreement on Budgetary Discipline and Improvement of the Budgetary Procedure, 29 June 1988, *Official Journal of the European Communities*, L 185, 15 July 1988.

Legislative Resolution on the Draft Council Directive Amending Directive 93/109/EC of 6 December 1993 as Regards Certain Detailed Arrangements for the Exercise of the Right to Stand as a Candidate in Elections to the European Parliament for Citizens of the Union Residing in a Member State of Which They Are Not Nationals, 20 November 2012 (13634/2012 – C7-0293/2012 – 2006/0277(CNS)).

Patijn (1974) Report on General Elections to the European Parliament, *Official Journal of the European Communities*, No. C32, 11 February.

Resolution on a Draft Uniform Electoral Procedure for the Election of Members of the European Parliament, *Official Journal of the European Communities*, C87/61, 5 April 1982.

Resolution on Guidelines for the Draft Uniform Electoral Procedure, *Official Journal of the European Communities*, C280/141, 28 October 1991.

Resolution on the Adoption of a Draft Convention Introducing Elections to the European Parliament by Direct Universal Suffrage, *Official Journal of the European Communities*, C 32/15, 11 February 1975.

Resolution on the Draft Uniform Electoral Procedure for the Election of Members of the European Parliament, *Official Journal of the European Communities*, C115/121, 26 April 1993.

Resolution on the Single European Act of 11 December 1986, *Official Journal of the European Communities*, C07, 12 January 1987.

Resolution on Legislative Delegation, 5 May 2010, A7-0110/2010.

Seitlinger (1982) Report on a Draft Uniform Electoral Procedure for the Election of Members of the European Parliament, EP document 1–988/81/A of 10 February 1982 and 1–988/81/B-C of 26 February 1982, PE 64.569/A+B+C/fin.

Spinelli (1984) Draft Treaty Establishing the European Union, *Official Journal of the European Communities*, C 77/33, 14 February.
Vedel (1972) Report of the Working Party Examining the Problem of the Enlargement of the Powers of the European Parliament, *Bulletin EC Supplement*, 4/72.

Secondary sources

Attinà, F. (1995) *Identità, Partiti ed Elezioni nell'Unione europea*, Bari, Cacucci.
Brand, C. (2012) 'MEPs Delay Vote on Trans-National List', *European Voice*, 11 March.
Colombo, E. (1977) 'Preface', European Parliament, *Elections to the European Parliament by Direct Universal Suffrage*, Secretariat, Directorate-General for Research and Documentation, Office for Official Publications of the European Communities, Luxembourg.
Corbett, R., Jacobs, F. and Shackleton, M. (2007) *The European Parliament*, London, John Harper.
Corbett, R., Jacobs, F. and Shackleton, M. (2011) *The European Parliament*, London, John Harper.
Criddle, B. (1993) 'The French Referendum on the Maastricht Treaty September 1992', *Parliamentary Affairs*, 46(2), 228–38.
Dinan, D. (2004) *Europe Recast: A History of European Union*, Basingstoke, Palgrave.
Duff, A. (2012) 'Why Do MEPs Fear Electoral Reform?' *EU Observer*, 14 March.
Dupagny, S. (1992) 'Les compétences du Parlement européen relatives à la Politique extérieure', Mémoire pour le DEA de Droit Communautaire, Université de Droit, d'Economie et de Sciences Sociales de Paris (Paris II), 1–2.
Farrell, D. M. and Scully, R. (2010) 'The European Parliament: One Parliament, Several Modes of Political Representation on the Ground?' *Journal of European Public Policy*, 17(1), January, 36–54.
Franklin, M.N. (2010) 'The European Malaise and the Failure of Leadership', *Recon Newsletter*, 2(2), June, 5.
Jones, R. A. (2001) *The Politics and Economics of the European Union: An Introductory Text*, Cheltenham, Edward Elgar.
Lenaerts, K. and Cambien, N. (2009) 'Democratic Legitimacy of the EU after the Treaty of Lisbon', in Wouters, J., Verhey L., Kiiver Ph. (eds), *European Constitutionalism Beyond Lisbon*, Antwerp, Intersentia.
Pinder, J. (1998) *The Building of the European Union*, Oxford, Oxford University Press.
Pinder, J. (2001) *The European Union: A Very Short Introduction*, Oxford, Oxford University Press.
Smith, J. (1999) *Europe's Elected Parliament*, Sheffield, Sheffield Academic Press.
Trechsel, A. H. (2010) 'Introduction', in Glencross, A. and Trechsel, A. H. (eds), *EU Federalism and Constitutionalism: the Legacy of Altiero Spinelli*, Lanham, MD, Lexington Books.
Tsebelis, G. (1997) 'Maastricht and the Democratic Deficit', *Aussenwirtschaft*, 52, 29–56.
Tsebelis, G. (1994) 'The Power of the European Parliament as a Conditional Agenda Setter', *American Political Science Review*, 88(1), 129–42.
Weiler, J. H. H. (2012) 'In the Face of Crisis: Input Legitimacy, Output Legitimacy and the Political Messianism of European Integration', *European Integration*, 34(7), 825–41.

2

EUROPEAN PARLIAMENT'S INTERNAL COMPOSITION AND ORGANIZATION

Donatella M. Viola

Introduction

The present chapter intends to shed some light on the *sui generis* Euro-parliamentary environment by underscoring both its relevant innovative features and the striking flaws of its vibrant and complex organization. Emphasis will be conferred on sensitive questions concerning the EP's official location and languages, as well as seat allotment amongst Member States. Far from being complete and exhaustive, this brief institutional portrait is, nevertheless, useful and necessary prior to embarking on our theoretical and empirical exploratory journey into European elections, which are skilfully and meticulously depicted by national specialists in Part II of this handbook.

Over the years, the literature on the European Parliament has liberally flourished to encompass books, pamphlets, and journal articles. Amongst these, the volume written by Richard Corbett, Francis Jacobs, and Michael Shackleton, which has already reached its eighth edition in 2011, stands out as the most authoritative and comprehensive reference text on the EP by combining academic rigor with a practitioners' insight (Corbett *et al.*, 2011). Another noteworthy investigation has been undertaken by the French anthropologist Marc Abélès who, in his captivating tale *La vie quotidienne au Parlement européen*, paints a picture of the daily customs and rituals of the Euro-parliamentary nomadic tribe, portraying its inherent contradictions, anomalies, and follies (Abélès, 1992).

Moreover, a welter of general publications and background studies have been produced by the institution itself, including official documentation and updated information on the composition, organization, and activities of the European Parliament and its constituent bodies. This material has been made available either online through their dedicated multi-language website (www.europarl.europa.eu, accessed on 21 December 2014), from the EP Information Offices in the various countries, or from the Directorates-General of the Secretariat of the European Parliament headquartered in Brussels and Luxembourg.

1 Location of the European Parliament

From its outset in 1952, the Common Assembly of the European Coal and Steel Community used to meet, for practical reasons, in the same facilities as the Parliamentary Assembly of the Council of Europe in Strasbourg. This historical city, which was for a long time the subject of a ferocious and violent dispute between France and Germany, was chosen as the authentic emblem of their reconciliation and of European unification. The 1957 Treaty of Rome formally granted Member States the competence to determine the location of Community institutions, but they could only agree on 'provisional working places', which in the case of the European Parliament were located in Luxembourg, Strasbourg, and Brussels (Guizzi, 2003).

Ironically, half a century later, such a 'temporary' three-site arrangement continues to endure whilst a definitive, more suitable solution has not been found despite the EP's early recommendation on 21 June 1958 and its subsequent numerous requests that it should be situated beside the Council and the Commission. By virtue of the agreement reached at the Edinburgh Summit in December 1992, also incorporated in the Treaty of Amsterdam of 1997, and confirmed in Protocol 6 of the Lisbon Treaty of 2007:

> The European Parliament shall have its seat in Strasbourg where the twelve periods of monthly plenary sessions, including the budget session, shall be held. The periods of additional plenary sessions shall be held in Brussels. The committees of the European Parliament shall meet in Brussels. The General Secretariat of the European Parliament and its departments shall remain in Luxembourg.

In fact, the European Parliament has two main meeting places, namely the Louise Weiss building in Strasbourg, which represents its official seat, inaugurated in 1999 with a view to accommodating the increased number of representatives after successive EU enlargements, and the Espace Léopold complex in Brussels, completed in 1995 and later expanded in 2008. It consists of a number of buildings, the oldest one of which is named after the former EP President and Belgian politician Paul-Henri Spaak, that houses the hemicycle for plenary sessions; the largest one is dedicated to the former Italian MEP and Commissioner Altiero Spinelli (www.europarl.europa.eu).

Twelve plenary part-sessions, including the budget session, take place every year, two of them traditionally in October to compensate for the parliamentary summer recess in August. In accordance with the EP's practice, these four-day sessions are held in Strasbourg whilst additional two-day mini-sessions are convened in Brussels. Members of standing committees generally caucus in the Belgian capital the week following the plenary session. Additionally, the political groups usually gather in Brussels, albeit seldom in other cities, upon the invitation of one of the constituent parties, in order to discuss the plenary agenda scheduled for the subsequent week. Finally, although the EP Secretariat's official seat is located in Luxembourg, almost half of its staff is actually based in Brussels (Corbett *et al.*, 2011).

The proliferation of Euro-parliamentary sites across three cities keeps adding to the public's confusion and disorientation over this 'nomadic institution' (Palayret, 2009, 30). This issue has inevitably attracted the attention of European citizens who have so far deposited seven petitions, all – except one – requesting the discontinuation of the status quo. In 2006, the Swedish Liberal MEP Cecilia Malmström launched an online petition calling for a single seat for the European Parliament in Brussels. This campaign succeeded in collecting approximately 1.3 million signatures, thus exceeding the number required for a formal European Citizens' Initiative. An oral question and a draft resolution, tabled for May 2008, were rejected by the Conference of Presidents, which preferred, instead, to entrust the EP President with the task of writing to the Member States in order to urge them to face this thorny issue (Fox and Häfner, 2013a).

Over the years, whilst respecting the underlying historic and symbolic reasons for calling EP plenary sessions in Strasbourg, several Euro-deputies have criticized, by way of letters, recommendations, oral questions and resolutions, the European Council's decision, which obliges them to perpetuate a three-site working arrangement that is no longer sustainable.

In their capacity as directly elected representatives who have gradually accrued greater powers, MEPs feel entitled to claim the legitimate right to choose their own headquarters, in line with fundamental democratic principles. However, since EU Member States continue to reserve for themselves this privilege, hitherto it has been impossible to erase such an anomalous and costly system, especially due to the obstinate refusal of France and, to a minor extent, of Luxembourg (McCormick, 2008, 84).

In fact, any decision relating to the location of EU institutions is subject to treaty reform and can, therefore, be exclusively achieved by the unanimous consent of all EU national governments. In case number C-237-11, *France* v. *Parliament*, the European Court of Justice acknowledged the disadvantages and the costs engendered by such a plurality of working places, but reiterated that 'it [was] not for the Parliament or the Court to remedy the situation, rather it [was] for the Member States to do so, if appropriate in the exercise of their competence to determine the seats of the institutions' (ECJ, 13 December 2012).

As a last resort, under Article 48 of the TEU, Parliament may exert its new prerogative to propose a treaty modification if national governments keep omitting action in this regard. Yet, an early attempt to initiate such a procedure was blocked by the leaders of the political groups, especially by the EPP Chair, the French MEP Joseph Daul, originally from Strasbourg (Vogel, 2013a).

Hence, on 18 February 2013, an alternative course of action was pursued by the European Parliament, which appointed the British Conservative MEP Ashley Fox and the German Green MEP Gerald Häfner as draftsmen of a report on the location of the seats of the European institutions, upon the belief that, although this text would carry no binding value, it would certainly bear a strong political meaning. The report, endorsed by the Constitutional Affairs Committee on 23 October 2013 with 22 in favour and four against, was finally adopted by the plenary on 20 November 2013, after nine roll-call votes on various paragraphs and one final roll-call vote on the whole text which saw 483 MEPs in favour, 141 against, and 34 abstentions (Fox and Häfner, 2013b).

The resolution highlights the negative effects arising from the perpetuation of this monthly migration between Brussels and Strasbourg, detrimental to the European Union's image, especially at a time when the financial crisis requires serious expenditure cuts. According to the 2012 joint working group report of the Bureau and Budget Committee, the additional annual costs of the EP's geographic dispersion are estimated at between €156–€204 million, equivalent to approximately 10 per cent of Parliament's annual budget (Fox and Häfner, 2013a).

Furthermore, the physical distance between the official seats of the co-legislative bodies contributes towards the isolation of the European Parliament not simply from the Council and the Commission, but also from Member State representations, non-governmental organizations (NGOs), and civil society organizations. Hence, most MEPs support the idea that the European Parliament should cease to be a 'travelling circus' and follow the example of the Council of the European Union, more commonly known as the Council of Ministers, and the European Council of the European Union and European Council, which now meet almost exclusively in Brussels (Fox and Häfner, 2013c).

Moreover, as Fox and Häfner have emphasized, the European Parliament's enhanced competences under the Lisbon provisions are no longer compatible with the existing multiple seat arrangement:

> Questions of inner organisation such as the EP's calendar are *de jure* linked to the seat by the inflexible formulation in Protocol 6. And the court decisions on changes in the EP's calendar in 2012 show that the EP has exhausted its manoeuvrability within the current legal framework.
>
> *(Fox and Häfner, 2013a, 8)*

At the same time, given the European Parliament's higher negotiating power vis-à-vis the Council, national capitals cannot continue to ignore its demands for a single working location.

The tacit but adamant message of the resolution rests on the EP's commitment to initiate an ordinary treaty revision procedure, which is necessary to allow a more efficient work organization. This should induce EU Member States to launch a debate on a single parliamentary seat in Brussels, despite the fierce opposition of the French government.

As Fox suggests, a way to persuade the latter to give up its claim that Strasbourg should remain the official seat of the European Parliament could be to propose setting up a 'University of Europe' within the Louise Weiss building or moving the European Court of Justice to the Alsacian city (Vogel, 2013a).

In brief, by calling for an end to such an '*anacronistica inefficienza*' (anachronistic inefficiency), as defined by the Brussels-based EU correspondent for the Italian daily *Il Sole/24 Ore* Beda Romano (Romano, 2013), the November 2013 resolution will inevitably trigger a harsh confrontation between the European Parliament and the Council.

Oddly, up until now, this single-seat campaign has not involved the EP's administration. On a contrary, in an official ceremony held in September 2013, the EP Vice-President Alejo Vidal-Quadras and Luxembourg Minister for Sustainable Development and Infrastructure Claude Wiseler laid the foundation stone for the new Konrad Adenauer building in the capital of the Grand Duchy of Luxembourg (www.europarl.europa.eu).

It goes without saying that this ancillary question relating to the location of the administrative staff of the Secretariat of the European Parliament will also need to be formally addressed and sorted out sooner or later.

2 The European Parliament language mosaic

Besides its rather atypical multiple-site working organization, the European Parliament distinguishes itself for its truly pluri-linguistic character. In this sense, no other international forum features such a complex make-up, including the United Nations General Assembly that, notwithstanding the larger number of representatives worldwide, operates only in six languages.

From the beginning, the Member States have adopted multilingualism as a way to safeguard their own cultural identities and, after each EC/EU enlargement, this principle has been reiterated, based on the deep belief that if the European Parliament would not recognize equally the languages spoken in all countries, even the smallest one, it would be likely that citizens would not recognize it as being their Parliament (EP Bureau Report, 2001).

Firmly rooted in the original treaties, this peculiar trait is the reflection of Europe's rich historical and cultural heritage that the European Parliament wishes to perpetuate by allowing its members to express themselves in their mother tongues, according to the principle that lies at the heart of its democratic legitimacy (ibid.). The purpose of multilingualism is also founded on the desire to confer upon the European Parliament greater public accessibility and transparency as guarantees for the success of the EU democratic system. More specifically, it is intended to ensure that all European citizens may easily follow its activities, understand new legislation, ask questions, and receive replies in their respective native languages.

Already in 1958, a regulation sanctioned French, German, Italian, and Dutch, spoken in the six original Member States, as the four official working languages of the European Community. In the last four decades, after seven waves of enlargement, this range has gradually broadened. English and Danish were introduced in 1973, whilst Irish obtained a special status as a 'treaty language', meaning that the Act of Accession and the basic texts relating to Ireland would be translated. Subsequently, Greek entered in 1981, followed by Portuguese and Spanish in 1986 as well as Finnish and Swedish in 1995. In the lapse of nine years, in 2004, Czech, Estonian, Hungarian, Latvian, Lithuanian, Maltese, Polish, Slovak, and Slovene were added along with Romanian and Bulgarian in 2008, whilst since July 2013, Croatian has become the twenty-fourth official language of the European Union. As a result, the European Parliament offers a total of 552 possible combinations, provided that each written text or speech delivered in one language has to be translated into 23 others (www.europarl.europa.eu).

Faced with this challenge, the European Parliament has carved out impressively large interpreting, translation, and legal text verification structures. Irrefutably, these facilities involve huge direct and indirect costs, not simply economic ones, but also in terms of efficiency, inevitably affecting the timing for the submission of documents and causing considerable delays in the EP's proceedings.

Whilst recognizing the democratic value and symbolic meaning of multilingualism, its negative impact on the EP's timetable cannot be denied. Against this backdrop, the need to preserve a pluri-language institutional system has been questioned, especially considering that outside official meetings and away from the podium, MEPs and their staff easily communicate between themselves in English, which nowadays represents *de facto* the *lingua franca* par excellence.

3 The European Parliament's composition

Throughout history, international fora have traditionally gathered national delegations nominated by their respective Member States. Among these, it is worth mentioning the United Nations General Assembly born in 1945, the Council of Europe Consultative Assembly founded in 1949, the Nordic Council set up in 1952 along with the North Atlantic Assembly, later superseded by the NATO Parliamentary Assembly, as well as the now defunct Western European Union, both established in 1955. Likewise, the 1952 Common Assembly of the European Coal and Steel Community and later the 1957 European Parliamentary Assembly – as the European Parliament was called prior to 1962 – consisted of deputies from national parliaments (Guizzi, 2003). However, since 1979 its representatives have been directly elected by the citizens of the European Community/Union and their number increased to 766 by the end the seventh legislature in 2013.

Based on the experience common to most Western democracies, whereby a maximum ceiling of representatives is set in order to ensure the smooth and effective running of parliamentary work, the 1976 Brussels Act concerning the introduction of direct election by universal suffrage already prefigured the ideal number of members of the European Parliament between 600 and 700 by also sketching out the criteria of seat apportionment (OJ L 278/1, 8 October 1976). Within the early European Community, embracing just nine countries, the issue relating to the EP's composition did not raise great concern. Conversely, in the wake of continuing EC/EU enlargements, it gradually fostered an animated, and occasionally heated, debate amongst the increasingly numerous Member States.

Whilst recognizing the difference between the first appointed forum and the directly elected Assembly, both adopted the geographical criterion of seat distribution, enabling countries with the same dimensions to feature equal numbers of representatives in the EP arena (Costa *et al.*, 2009).

As described in the previous chapter, European pioneers' intrepid fight to convene direct universal election to the European Parliament was rather long. What motivated them to pursue this ambitious goal was the certainty that it would have highlighted the EP's utmost symbolic and effective democratic legitimacy. To this avail, it is worth pointing out some of the anomalies arising from the early procedure of nominating delegates from amongst members of national legislatures, which conferred on the Assembly the character of a second-degree representative body. In reality, the appointment of these deputies was based solely upon the discretion of the national political establishments rather than on a fixed set of fair, proportional democratic rules. As a result, parties not represented in national parliaments, even if they embodied an important segment of civil society, could not find a home in Strasbourg and not all Member State political parties could be reflected into the Euro-parliamentary kaleidoscope. One of the most serious limitations of this system rested on the tendency of some national parliamentary chambers, especially in France and Italy, not to designate representatives from opposition parties. This meant that the Italian and French Communists could not enter the assembly until 1969 and 1973 respectively (Costa et al., 2009). Likewise, the Italian Socialists were left out and inexplicably their exclusion was not ended even when their party became a member of a coalition government. By contrast, representatives of the extreme right-wing *Movimento Sociale Italiano* MSI (Italian Social Movement), belonging to the opposition, were appointed as Euro-deputies (Guizzi, 2003). This apparently random choice could be presumably ascribed to the anti-European attitude initially taken by both the Italian Socialists and Communists, who were not willing or interested in sitting in such a forum. Indeed, since Eurosceptics were generally reluctant to be nominated, virtually all delegates were pro-integrationist, hence altering the genuine representativeness of the institution. Another feature of the Assembly, which could be considered a hurdle to the successful development of its activities, stemmed from the so-called dual mandate, which prevented members from devoting sufficient time to their European responsibilities (Nugent, 2003).

Lastly, the non-renewal of the Italian delegation led to a rather irregular political setting due to the presence of non-incumbent members who, therefore, were lacking fully-fledged popular legitimacy. This anomaly forced the European Parliament to intervene in March 1969 by establishing that those delegates who had lost their national mandate could remain in office until substitutes were nominated but not beyond a six-month period, as stated in the EP rules (Guizzi, 2003). The limits and flaws of this appointment procedure, introduced provisionally in any case, persuaded national political leaders to follow the rough trail leading to direct election by universal suffrage.

Between 1958 and 1973, within the appointed 142-member Assembly, three categories of big, medium, and small countries could be found: the first embracing France, Germany, and Italy which had 36 representatives each, the second incorporating Belgium and the Netherlands with 14 delegates, and the third referring to Luxembourg, with only 6 deputies.

Under the first EC widening in 1973, the total number of deputies went up to 198, as it incorporated 36 seats for the UK, like the original three big countries, and 10 seats each for Denmark and Ireland, crafting a new category. The direct election to the European Parliament in 1979 marked a sensible increase in the number of representatives, which soared to 410 with the then four big countries – France, Germany, Italy, and the United Kingdom – being allocated 81 seats each, Belgium and the Netherlands 25 seats, Ireland and Denmark 15, and Luxembourg confirming its 6 seats. This apportionment was not satisfactory for Denmark, which demanded an additional seat. In order to sort out the question, with an overly generous conciliatory gesture, Belgium gave up one of its seats so that 16 Danish and 24 Belgian representatives were eventually elected (Costa et al., 2009).

In the mid-1980s, a fifth 'medium-to-large' category was created following the entry of Spain, which was awarded 60 seats, whilst Portugal and Greece joined Belgium with 24 members. During the 2004 enlargement, the quota of Polish MEPs was aligned with Spain, which at that time had reduced its number of seats to 54.

Subsequent enlargements, which involved the accession of 28 new countries, witnessed the genuine effort to combine the traditional method of seat apportionment connected to the size of the country, with a fairer ratio to population (Costa et al., 2009).

Since the entry into force of the Treaty of Lisbon, the European Parliament has become more powerful than ever, thus requiring an internal organization that is commensurate with its new role.

The amended text did not state how parliamentary seats were to be allocated between nationalities, but instructed the European Council – acting on the EP's initiative and with its assent – to decide over the composition of the Strasbourg assembly on the basis of the principle of 'degressively proportional' representation.

In particular, Article 14 of the Treaty on European Union, as revised in Lisbon, contemplated that:

> The European Parliament shall be composed of representatives of the Union's citizens. They shall not exceed seven hundred and fifty in number, plus the President. Representation of citizens shall be degressively proportional, with a minimum threshold of six members per Member State. No Member State shall be allocated more than ninety-six seats.

On 11 October 2007, the plenary adopted the *Lamassoure-Séverin Report*, which clarified the aforementioned principle of 'degressive proportionality' as:

> the ratio between the population and the number of seats of each Member State must vary in relation to their respective populations in such a way that each Member from a more populous [EU country] represents more citizens than each Member from a less populous [one] and that no less populous [country] has more seats than a more populous [one].
>
> *(Lamassoure-Séverin, 2007)*

Yet, due to the delay in treaty ratification by various Member States, further accentuated by the negative outcome of the Irish referendum, the 2009 Euro-elections were fought over 736 seats – under the rules previously agreed at the 2001 Nice Summit – instead of 751, as later established in Lisbon.

On 1 December 2009, upon completion of the long ratification process, transitional provisions were introduced in order to increase the number of seats temporarily to 754. Nevertheless, it was necessary to wait two years before the 18 new MEPs from 12 EU countries could effectively join the assembly. More specifically amongst them, there were four from Spain, two from Austria, France and Sweden, respectively, and one each from Italy, Netherlands, the UK, Slovenia, Malta, Latvia, Poland, and Bulgaria. Exceptionally, the three additional German MEPs elected in 2009 were allowed to continue their mandate until the end of the five-year term.

As depicted in Figure 2.1b, in July 2013, with the entry of 12 Croatian members, the number of MEPs has exceptionally reached 766. In fact, this represented only a temporary derogation to Article 13(2) of the Treaty on European Union, which was valid until the end of the seventh legislature. In June 2013, in view of the 2014 European election, the European Council decided that Germany's quota would drop from 99 to 96, as already foreseen in the amended TEU, and that Austria, Belgium, Bulgaria, Croatia, the Czech Republic, Greece, Hungary, Ireland, Latvia, Lithuania, Portugal, and Romania would lose one representative each (OJ L 181/57, 29/6/2013). This decision mirrors the European Parliament resolution on the composition of the European Parliament adopted in March 2013 and based on the *Gualtieri and Trzaskowski Report*, which was endorsed by the Constitutional Affairs Committee on 19 February 2013 (Gualtieri and Trzaskowski, 2013a).

D.M. Viola

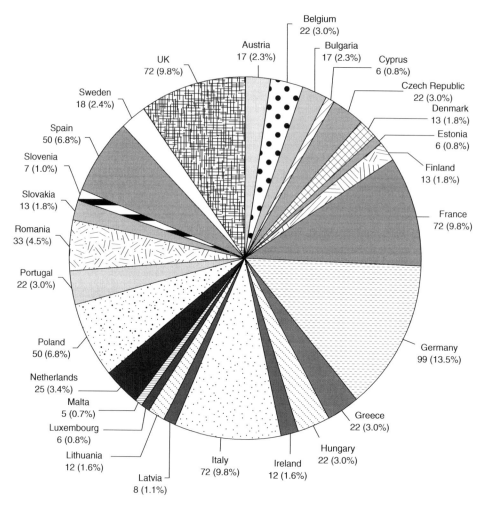

Figure 2.1a EP composition by nationality: July 2009, seats and (%)

Source: Author's figure drawn from the data of EP website: www.europarl.europa.eu

Yet, the question remains open and the European Parliament is expected to submit a new proposal to the European Council before the end of 2016 with the aim of establishing prior to each EP election a clear and durable system to allocate the seats between Member States, capable of translating the principle of 'degressive proportionality', taking account of any variation in their number and demographic trends in their population (OJ L 181/57, 29 June 2013).

The need to guarantee an efficient institution requires setting a limit to the maximum number of MEPs, whilst bearing in mind the sacrosanct basic rules of equal treatment between the big countries and over-representation of the small ones.

Finally, in order to complete this picture, it seems appropriate to add a brief note on the gender composition of the European Parliament. As Table 2.2 illustrates, the percentage of women MEPs has risen from merely 16 in 1979 to 35 in 2009, marking a slow but steady progress. In the seventh Euro-election, the overall gender rate increased by 4 per cent compared to the previous legislature, confirming the presence of over one third of women in Strasbourg.

Table 2.1 EP composition: 1958–2014

Country	1958	1973	1979	1984	1987	1994	1995	2004	2007	2009	Lisbon	2011	July 2013	June 2014
Austria	—	—	—	—	—	—	21	18	18	17	*19*	19	19	**18**
Belgium	14	14	24	24	24	25	25	24	24	22	*22*	22	22	**21**
Bulgaria	—	—	—	—	—	—	—	—	18	17	*18*	18	18	**17**
Croatia	—	—	—	—	—	—	—	—	—	—	—	—	12	**11**
Cyprus	—	—	—	—	—	—	—	6	6	6	*6*	6	6	6
Czech Republic	—	—	—	—	—	—	—	24	24	22	*22*	22	22	**21**
Denmark	—	10	16	16	16	16	16	14	14	13	*13*	13	13	13
Estonia	—	—	—	—	—	—	—	6	6	6	*6*	6	6	6
Finland	—	—	—	—	—	—	16	14	14	13	*13*	13	13	13
France	36	36	81	81	81	87	87	78	78	72	*74*	74	74	74
Germany	36	36	81	81	81	99	99	99	99	99	*96*	99	99	**96**
Greece	—	—	—	24	24	25	25	24	24	22	*22*	22	22	**21**
Hungary	—	—	—	—	—	—	—	24	24	22	*22*	22	22	**21**
Ireland	—	10	15	15	15	15	15	13	13	12	*12*	12	12	**11**
Italy	36	36	81	81	81	87	87	78	78	72	*73*	73	73	73
Latvia	—	—	—	—	—	—	—	9	9	8	*9*	9	9	**8**
Lithuania	—	—	—	—	—	—	—	13	13	12	*12*	12	12	**11**
Luxembourg	6	6	6	6	6	6	6	6	6	6	*6*	6	6	6
Malta	—	—	—	—	—	—	—	5	5	5	*6*	6	6	6
Netherlands	14	14	25	25	25	31	31	27	27	25	*26*	26	26	26
Poland	—	—	—	—	—	—	—	54	54	50	*51*	51	51	51
Portugal	—	—	—	—	24	25	25	24	24	22	*22*	22	22	**21**
Romania	—	—	—	—	—	—	—	—	35	33	*33*	33	33	**32**
Slovakia	—	—	—	—	—	—	—	14	14	13	*13*	13	13	13
Slovenia	—	—	—	—	—	—	—	7	7	7	*8*	8	8	8
Spain	—	—	—	—	60	64	64	54	54	50	*54*	54	54	54
Sweden	—	—	—	—	—	—	22	19	19	18	*20*	20	20	20
UK	—	36	81	81	81	87	87	78	78	72	*73*	73	73	73
Total EU	**142**	**198**	**410**	**434**	**518**	**567**	**626**	**732**	**785**	**736**	***751***	**754**	**766**	**751**

Source: Author's table based on information drawn from EP website: www.europarl

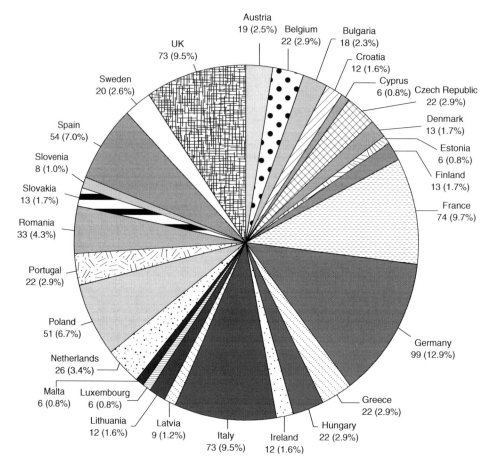

Figure 2.1b EP composition by nationality: July 2013, seats and (%)

Source: Author's figure drawn from the data of EP website: www.europarl.europa.eu

Table 2.2 Women in the European Parliament: 1979–2009

Country	1979	1984	1989	1994	1999	2004	2009
	%	%	%	%	%	%	%
Austria	—	—	—	—	38	28	41
Belgium	8	17	17	32	28	33	36
Bulgaria	—	—	—	—	—	44 (2007)	47
Croatia	—	—	—	—	—	—	50 (2013)
Cyprus	—	—	—	—	—	0	33
Czech Republic	—	—	—	—	—	21	18
Denmark	31	38	38	44	38	43	46
Estonia	—	—	—	—	—	50	50
Finland	—	—	—	—	44	43	62
France	22	21	23	30	40	45	44
Germany	15	20	31	35	37	33	37

Greece	—	8	4	16	16	29	32
Hungary	—	—	—	—	—	38	36
Ireland	13	13	7	27	33	38	25
Italy	14	10	12	13	11	21	22
Latvia	—	—	—	—	—	33	38
Lithuania	—	—	—	—	—	38	25
Luxembourg	17	50	50	50	33	50	33
Malta	—	—	—	—	—	0	0
Netherlands	20	28	28	32	35	48	48
Poland	—	—	—	—	—	15	22
Portugal	—	—	13	8	20	25	36
Romania	—	—	—	—	—	29 (2007)	36
Slovakia	—	—	—	—	—	36	38
Slovenia	—	—	—	—	—	43	29
Spain	—	—	15	33	34	26	36
Sweden	—	—	—	—	41	47	56
UK	14	15	15	18	24	26	33
Total EU	16	18	19	26	30	31	35

Source: Author's table based on data from the EP website: www.europarl.europa.eu.

Against this background, it clearly appears that a problem of female under-representation still affects the European Parliament, although some distinctions need to be made. The proportion of women elected is 7 per cent lower in the new EU-12 countries than in the old EU-15 countries. In addition, as regards two Nordic countries, Finland and Sweden, the proportion of female representation in the EP even exceeds the male one. In three other cases, Estonia, Denmark, and the Netherlands, the share of men and women reaches almost parity, with the rest of the countries attaining variable rates and only Malta unable to secure even one 'pink' seat.

3.1 Political groups

As already stated, one of the peculiarities of the EP, when compared to other international assemblies, is the adoption of a group system based on political rather than national allegiance. The unifying factor of most groups stems from an ideological identification that, regardless of the inherent traditional differences underpinning the various national parties from the same political family, naturally draws MEPs together (Nugent, 2003). This institutionalized coordination of policy positions within the European Parliament represents a significant catalyzing factor for the integration process and a step forward in the search for a solution to the democratic deficit of the European Union (Pridham and Pridham, 1981).

Initially set up within the ECSC Common Assembly in June 1953, the group structure has been further elaborated following the 1973 first enlargement of the European Communities and, more importantly, after the 1979 direct election to the European Parliament. However, it is worth mentioning that originally no official reference on the existence of the political groups (PGs) appeared either in the texts of the Paris and Rome Treaties or in the Single European Act. The proposal of including such a note was put forward in 1992, just prior to the conclusion of the Maastricht negotiations, by the three chairmen of the European party political federations, notably the former Belgian Prime Minister Wilfried Martens for the European People's Party, Guy Spitaels for the Socialist Parties of the European Community, and Willy de Clercq for the European Liberal, Democrat and Reformist Parties (Corbett, 1994, 218).

The first political groups to be founded within the European Parliament were the Socialists, the Liberals, and the Christian Democrats, although their number, size, and composition has varied meanwhile to reflect the changes that occurred within the European Community and later the European Union, especially after the accession of new partners.

The European Parliament vetoes the organization of political groups along strictly national lines by preventing, at the same time, the proliferation of small groups (Palayret, 2009). Rule 30 of the 'Rules of Procedures of the European Parliament', as amended in January 2012, stipulates that:

> Members may form themselves into groups according to their political affinities. [. . .] A political group shall comprise Members elected in at least one quarter of the Member States. The minimum number of Members required to form a political group shall be 25.

As shown in Figure 2.2, the 2009–2014 EP has been populated by seven PGs, besides the independent or non-attached members, spanning the entire left–right parliamentary spectrum and occupying distinct sections of the policy space (McElroy and Benoit, 2011).

From the outset until 1975, and then again since 1999, the European People's Party (EPP) has embodied the strongest political force within the European Parliament, comprising approximately 36 per cent of MEPs by the end of the 2009–2014 legislature. Founded in 1953 as the Christian Democrat Group, it changed to its current name after the first direct elections in 1979. Historically dominated by the German *Christlich Demokratische Union* (Christian Democratic Union) and *Christlich-Soziale Union* (Christian-Social Union), the EPP also includes Italy's *Popolo della Libertà* (People of Freedom), France's *Union pour un Mouvement Populaire* (Union for a Popular Movement), Spain's *Partido Popular* (People's Party), Poland's *Platforma Obywatelska* (Civic Platform), and numerous other Christian Democratic and centre-right parties from all Member States except for the UK (see www.europarl.europa.eu/aboutparliament/en/009cd2034d/In-the-past.html).

In terms of size, the Socialist group follows, having enjoyed a long supremacy within the Strasbourg arena from 1975 until 1999. In the aftermath of the 2009 Euro-elections, in order to reflect the entry of the Italian *Partito Democratico* (Democratic Party), the group has acquired the new name of Progressive Alliance of Socialists and Democrats in the European Parliament (S&D). Chaired by the Austrian politician Hannes Swoboda, the S&D gathers MEPs of all EU nationalities from far-left state interventionist to more moderate social democrat parties, occupying 25 per cent of the assembly.

The Alliance of Liberals and Democrats for Europe (ALDE) stands as the third largest group, yet is considerably smaller than the previous two, attracting over 11 per cent of MEPs from 19 distinct countries. Led by the Belgian MEP Guy Verhofstadt, ALDE is ideologically rather heterogeneous, with a combination of members from the UK Liberal Democrat Party, Germany's *Freie Demokratische Partei* (Free Democratic Party), and Ireland's *Fianna Fáil*. Subsequently, there is the group of the Greens/European Free Alliance (Greens/EFA), assembling members of 14 different nationalities from ecological and regionalist movements. In the light of its policy heterogeneity, the group appears rather difficult to situate within the conventional left–right spectrum. In fact it seems in tune with the left-wing tradition over social issues, but more inclined to resist further European integration in line with the typical right-wing trend of the last decades. Another distinctive feature of the group can be ascribed to the well-rooted custom of adopting a double chair with one man and one woman, usually from different countries. Since July 2009, the co-Presidents have been Daniel Cohn-Bendit, elected MEP alternatively in Germany and in France since 1994, and the German MEP Rebecca Harms. Concurrently, the EFA components of the group have chosen the Welsh MEP Jill Evans from *Plaid Cymru* as their own President.

EP internal composition and organization

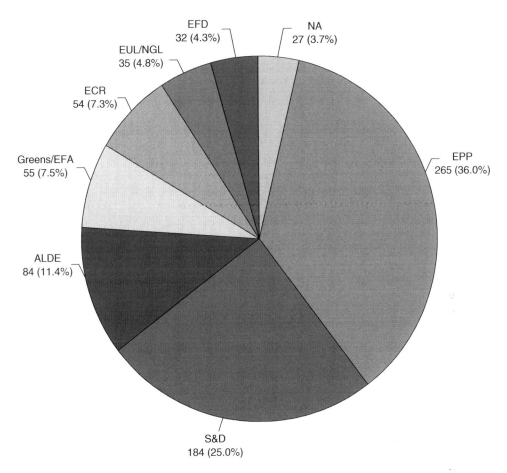

Figure 2.2a EP composition by political group: July 2009, seats and (%)

Source: Author's figure drawn from the data of EP website: www.europarl.europa.eu

On the far-right side of the policy scale, two groups can be found: the European Conservatives and Reformists (ECR) and the Europe of Freedom and Democracy (EFD), both founded in July 2009.

The creation of the former mainly stemmed from the decision of the members of the UK Conservative Party to leave the EPP, after 17 years of affiliation, in the midst of disagreements over the perspective of a federal Europe. Besides the above-mentioned MEPs, the ECR consists of representatives of the UK Ulster Unionist Party, the Czech *Obcanska democraticka strana* (Civic Democratic Party), and Poland's *Prawo i Sprawiedliwość* (Law and Justice Party), along with members from another five countries in July 2009, whilst counting MEPs of ten different nationalities by the end of the legislature.

Like their predecessors, who chose to gather together under the Europe of Democracies and Diversities Group (EDD) and the Independence and Democracy Group (IND/DEM), in July 2009 Eurosceptics decided to join together in order to forge a new group which took the name Europe of Freedom and Democracy (EFD). Dominated by the UK Independence Party (UKIP), supporting the British withdrawal from the EU, and Italy's regionalist *Lega Nord*

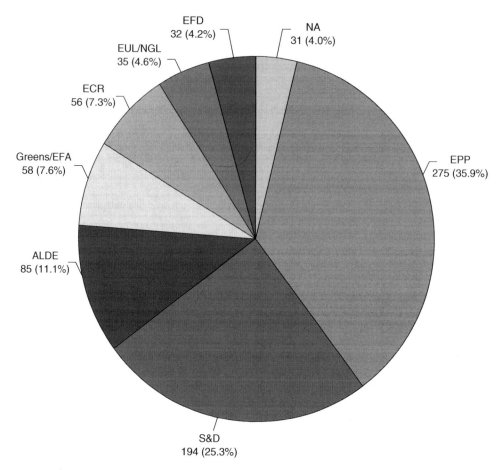

Figure 2.2b EP composition by political group: July 2013, seats and (%)

Source: Author's figure drawn from the data of EP website: www.europarl.europa.eu

(Northern League), hostile to further European integration, the EFD leadership is shared by the British MEP Nigel Farage and the Italian MEP Francesco Enrico Speroni. By the end of the seventh term, the group slightly increased its membership by attracting deputies from ten different countries.

Finally, the extreme left wing of the European Parliament is represented by the Confederal Group of the European United Left/Nordic Green Left (EUL/NGL). Chaired by the German MEP Lothar Bisky, the group caucuses members of 14 nationalities from Communist, Socialist, and other left-wing parties, including Germany's *Die Linke* (the Left), and Ireland's *Sinn Féin* (Corbett et al., 2011). Finally, since July 2013, a Croatian MEP from the *Hrvatski Laburisti–tranka Rada* (Croatian Labourists–Labour Party) has joined the EUL/NGL.

In the space of three decades, a high level of turnover and great fluidity have characterized the EP structure, with members and even national party delegations frequently shifting allegiances. At times, this has required EP party groups to modify their names and even their policy stances. Group switching, often generated by internal divergences, may also arise out of domestic political concerns (McElroy and Benoit, 2011). The partisan structure of the EP is still more fluid and less cohesive than that of most national legislative institutions. Heavily subordinate to national political developments, EP representation largely varies from one Euro-electoral contest to another (Palayret, 2009).

As shown in detail in Tables 2.3a, 2.3b, and 2.3c, the size and composition of each political group has varied during the seventh legislature, in particular upon the ratification of the Treaty of Lisbon, in accordance with Article 9 A(2) of the TEU and after the accession of Croatia to the European Union.

Since the 1960s and 1970s, extreme party polarization has been strongly discouraged and avoided, based on the assumption that the European Parliament should become more cohesive in order to assert itself vis-à-vis the other EC/EU institutions and to gain credibility in the eyes of third countries. Accordingly, the two largest groups, the Socialists and the Christian Democrats, decided to cease their ideological battle by agreeing to work jointly to shape EP policy. Whilst such a 'grand coalition' has not been seen positively by the other groups for fear of remaining at the margins of political debate, the danger has also arisen that this consensus-seeking approach would make politics within the EP rather stale and dull (Viola, 2000). Given that national parties

Table 2.3a EP composition by political group and nationality: July 2009

Country	EPP	S&D	ALDE	Greens/EFA	ECR	EUL/NGL	EFD	NA	Tot. seats	% seats
Austria	6	4	—	2	—	—	—	5	17	2.3
Belgium	5	5	5	4	1	—	—	2	22	3.0
Bulgaria	6	4	5	—	—	—	—	2	17	2.3
Cyprus	2	2	—	—	—	2	—	—	6	0.8
Czech Republic	2	7	—	—	9	4	—	—	22	3.0
Denmark	1	4	3	2	—	1	2	—	13	1.8
Estonia	1	1	3	1	—	—	—	—	6	0.8
Finland	4	2	4	2	—	—	1	—	13	1.8
France	29	14	6	14	—	5	1	3	72	9.8
Germany	42	23	12	14	—	8	—	—	99	13.5
Greece	8	8	—	1	—	3	2	—	22	3.0
Hungary	14	4	—	—	1	—	—	3	22	3.0
Ireland	4	3	4	—	—	1	—	—	12	1.6
Italy	35	21	7	—	—	—	9	—	72	9.8
Latvia	3	1	1	1	1	1	—	—	8	1.1
Lithuania	4	3	2	—	1	—	2	—	12	1.6
Luxembourg	3	1	1	1	—	—	—	—	6	0.8
Malta	2	3	—	—	—	—	—	—	5	0.7
Netherlands	5	3	6	3	1	2	1	4	25	3.4
Poland	28	7	—	—	15	—	—	—	50	6.8
Portugal	10	7	—	—	—	5	—	—	22	3.0
Romania	14	11	5	—	—	—	—	3	33	4.5
Slovakia	6	5	1	—	—	—	1	—	13	1.8
Slovenia	3	2	2	—	—	—	—	—	7	1.0
Spain	23	21	2	2	—	1	—	1	50	6.8
Sweden	5	5	4	3	—	1	—	—	18	2.4
UK	—	13	11	5	25	1	13	4	72	9.8
Total Seats	265	184	84	55	54	35	32	27	736	—
%	36.0	25.0	11.4	7.5	7.3	4.8	4.3	3.7	—	—

Sources: www.europarl.europa.eu/parliament/archive/elections2009/en/index_en.html; www.europarl.europa.eu/meps/eu/search.html.

Table 2.3b EP composition by political group and nationality: December 2011

Country	EPP	S&D	ALDE	Greens/EFA	ECR	EFD	EUL/NGL	NA	Tot. seats	% seats
Austria	6	5	—	2	—	—	—	6	19	2.5
Belgium	5	5	5	4	1	1	—	1	22	2.9
Bulgaria	7	4	5	—	—	1	—	1	18	2.4
Cyprus	2	2	—	—	—	—	2	—	6	0.8
Czech Republic	2	7	—	—	9	—	4	—	22	2.9
Denmark	1	5	3	1	1	1	1	—	13	1.7
Estonia	1	1	3	1	—	—	—	—	6	0.8
Finland	4	2	4	2	—	1	—	—	13	1.7
France	30	13	6	16	—	1	5	3	74	9.8
Germany	42	23	12	14	—	—	8	—	99	13.1
Greece	7	8	1	1	—	2	3	—	22	2.9
Hungary	14	4	—	—	1	—	—	3	22	2.9
Ireland	4	3	4	—	—	—	1	—	12	1.6
Italy	34	23	6	—	—	10	—	—	73	9.7
Latvia	4	1	1	1	1	—	1	—	9	1.2
Lithuania	4	3	2	—	1	2	—	—	12	1.6
Luxembourg	3	1	1	1	—	—	—	—	6	0.8
Malta	2	4	—	—	—	—	—	—	6	0.8
Netherlands	5	3	6	3	1	1	2	5	26	3.4
Poland	29	7	—	—	11	4	—	—	51	6.8
Portugal	10	7	—	1	—	—	4	—	22	2.9
Romania	14	11	5	—	—	—	—	3	33	4.4
Slovakia	6	5	1	—	—	1	—	—	13	1.7
Slovenia	4	2	2	—	—	—	—	—	8	1.1
Spain	25	23	2	2	—	—	1	1	54	7.2
Sweden	5	6	4	4	—	—	1	—	20	2.7
UK	—	13	12	5	27	10	1	5	73	9.7
Total	**270**	**191**	**85**	**58**	**53**	**35**	**34**	**28**	**754**	—
%	**35.8**	**25.3**	**11.3**	**7.7**	**7.0**	**4.6**	**4.5**	**3.7**	—	—

Sources: www.europarl.europa.eu/parliament/archive/elections2009/en/index_en.html; www.europarl.europa.eu/meps/eu/search.html.

Table 2.3c EP composition by political group and nationality: July 2013

Country	EPP	S&D	ALDE	Greens/EFA	ECR	EUL/NGL	EFD	NA	Tot. seats	% seats
Austria	6	5	1	2	—	—	—	5	19	2.5
Belgium	5	5	5	4	1	—	1	1	22	2.9
Bulgaria	7	4	5	—	—	—	1	1	18	2.3
Croatia	5	5	—	—	1	1	—	—	12	1.6
Cyprus	2	2	—	—	—	2	—	—	6	0.8
Czech Republic	2	7	—	—	9	4	—	—	22	2.9
Denmark	1	5	3	1	1	1	1	—	13	1.7
Estonia	1	1	3	1	—	—	—	—	6	0.8
Finland	4	2	4	2	—	—	1	—	13	1.7
France	30	13	6	16	—	5	1	3	74	9.7
Germany	42	23	12	14	—	8	—	—	99	12.9

Greece	7	8	1	1	—	3	2	—	22	2.9
Hungary	14	4	—	—	1	—	—	3	22	2.9
Ireland	4	2	4	—	—	1	—	1	12	1.6
Italy	34	22	5	—	2	—	8	2	73	9.5
Latvia	4	1	1	1	1	1	—	—	9	1.2
Lithuania	4	3	2	—	1	—	2	—	12	1.6
Luxembourg	3	1	1	1	—	—	—	—	6	0.8
Malta	2	4	—	—	—	—	—	—	6	0.8
Netherlands	5	3	6	3	1	2	1	5	26	3.4
Poland	29	7	—	—	11	—	4	—	51	6.7
Portugal	10	7	—	1	—	4	—	—	22	2.9
Romania	14	11	5	—	—	—	—	3	33	4.3
Slovakia	6	5	1	—	—	—	1	—	13	1.7
Slovenia	4	2	2	—	—	—	—	—	8	1.0
Spain	25	23	2	2	—	1	—	1	54	7.0
Sweden	5	6	4	4	—	1	—	—	20	2.6
UK	—	13	12	5	27	1	9	6	73	9.5
Total	**275**	**194**	**85**	**58**	**56**	**35**	**32**	**31**	**766**	—
%	35.9	25.3	11.1	7.6	7.3	4.6	4.2	4.0	—	—

Sources: www.europarl.europa.eu/parliament/archive/elections2009/en/index_en.html; www.europarl.europa.eu/meps/eu/search.html.

rather than EP political groups draft the lists of candidates to the EP elections, it is natural that MEPs' main constraints and allegiances rest on their home parties (Attinà, 1995).

On the other hand, compared to their national counterparts, MEPs enjoy greater freedom since a less rigid whipping system is adopted at EU level in order to check on their attendance and monitor their voting behaviour. This is mainly due to the fact that no government emerges from the EP and its existence is not reliant on the systematic support of a parliamentary majority. Furthermore, the wide range of regional, national party, and sectoral preferences that converge within the groups makes it virtually impossible to reach a common line over sensitive issues, requiring a certain degree of flexibility and open-mindedness. As such, individual members, or the whole national party delegation, may decide not to participate in a vote, abstain, or exceptionally even support the opposite stance. Political groups have less sanctioning tools against disloyal members, merely consisting in a less favourable committee membership or delegation allocation, rejection of new rapporteurships and speaking time in plenary for debates since they cannot exert the ultimate sanction of deselecting candidates in subsequent electoral races, which remains the exclusive privilege of national political leaders (Corbett et al., 2007). As matter of fact, MEPs find themselves in a rather awkward position in depending on their national parties for their nominations and on the European political groups for their career advancement. In the words of Gail McElroy and Kenneth Benoit, 'Members of the European Parliament [...] thus answer to both national- and EP-level principals, giving rise to a dual agent problem, with the associated difficulties of maintaining discipline and cohesion' (McElroy and Benoit, 2011, 150–1).

Hence, MEPs are faced with distinct and, at times, conflicting needs, between freedom of individual conscience, attention to the opinion of constituents, commitment to the national party, and loyalty to the political group (Viola, 2000).

Rule 2 of the 'Rules of Procedure of the European Parliament' proclaims that:

> Members of the European Parliament shall exercise their mandate independently. They shall not be bound by any instructions and shall not receive a binding mandate.

Prior to the opening of the part-session, the President, in agreement with the chairmen of the political groups, allocates a fixed speaking time for debates. A first share is divided among the political groups, whilst the most substantial fraction is allocated, proportionally to their size, to all PGs and attached members (Corbett *et al.*, 2011). As an essential sinew of democracy, political groups not only articulate and moderate people's aspirations by putting forward proposals before the house, but also play a decisive role in shaping the EP internal composition. Privileges of the political groups include the appointment of members to key positions as Presidents or Vice-Presidents, as well as to committees and delegations, to ensure a fair and balanced representation of all political views.

Economic and organizational benefits offer further inducement to the shaping of, and membership of, political groups. In particular, in order to cover secretarial, administrative, and research costs, funding is granted to groups on the basis of a rather complex formula which takes into account their size and number of languages (Nugent, 2003). In fact, in order to assist political groups in their multiple activities, some administrative posts are reserved to them, with a small percentage assigned to them regardless of their dimension and the largest allocation is distributed roughly on a proportional basis according to their size (Corbett *et al.*, 2011).

As a final point, it is noteworthy to look at the presence of women in the various political groups. During the seventh legislative period, the Greens/EFA achieved the highest female percentage of 47.6, followed by the S&D with 41.2 per cent, ALDE with 40.4 per cent, and the EPP/ED with a mere 24 per cent. Aware of the highly positive effects of women's political representation, and in order to increase their presence in the Strasbourg arena, the EP has called national parties to introduce gender quotas in their electoral lists (www.europarl.europa.eu).

3.2 Committees and delegations

Following the national legislative archetype, the Common Assembly, and later the European Parliament, have been shaped not only into political groups but also into committees. In principle, all MEPs sit as full members on at least one committee and as substitute members on another. The EP's enhanced legislative competence has paralleled the growing specialization of its representatives, thus favouring their prolonged stay in the same committee. As listed in Table 2.4, within the 2009–2014 European Parliament there were 20 standing committees, among which the most prestigious and numerous is the Committee on Foreign Affairs, which also features two subcommittees, on human rights as well as security and defence.

Over the years, special temporary committees have also been created in order to address topical issues, such as that on the impact of German reunification on the European Community in 1990, the Special Committee on the Financial, Economic and Social Crisis which fulfilled its function on 31 July 2011, the Special Committee on Policy Challenges which completed its task on 30 June 2011, and finally that on organized crime, corruption and money laundering (www.europarl.europa.eu/activities/committees).

The main role of the committees consists in analysing policy, budgetary, and agenda-setting issues and in adopting reports and opinions prior to their submission to the plenary (Corbett, 2007, 135). Since the introduction of direct elections, committees on employment and social affairs, the environment, women's rights and gender equality have allowed the public to attend their meetings and this well-established practice is now pursued by all the others.

Finally, from the early 1970s the Strasbourg arena has accommodated parliamentary delegations which, by acting as the 'eyes and ears of the European Parliament', have embodied the ideal interlocutor to liaise with third country parliaments (Millar, 1991, 148). Their delicate and complex task is, indeed, to keep ongoing contacts with parliamentary bodies of third countries or regional organizations. Delegations also exchange information on current topics, provide

Table 2.4 EP committees: seventh legislature

Standing committees
Foreign Affairs AFET
    Human Rights DROI
    Security and Defence SEDE
Development DEVE
International Trade INTA
Budgets BUDG
Budgetary Control CONT
Economic and Monetary Affairs ECON
Employment and Social Affairs EMPL
Environment, Public Health, and Food Safety ENVI
Industry, Research, and Energy ITRE
Internal Market and Consumer Protection IMCO
Transport and Tourism TRAN
Regional Development REGI
Agriculture and Rural Development AGRI
Fisheries PECH
Culture and Education CULT
Legal Affairs JURI
Civil Liberties, Justice and Home Affairs LIBE
Constitutional Affairs AFCO
Women's Rights and Gender Equality FEMM
Petitions PETI

Special committees
Organized Crime, Corruption, and Money Laundering CRIM

Former special committees
Financial, Economic, and Social Crisis CRIS (until 31 July 2011)
Policy Challenges Committee SURE (until 30 June 2011)

Source: Author's table based on information drawn from the EP website: www.europarl.europa.eu.

parliamentary support on EU external policies, and generally balance the work of the Commission and the Council in this area. One of their priorities is to monitor the observance of human and minority rights in the world. This implies, whenever necessary, urging partner countries to comply with universal principles and EU fundamental values, and insisting that any violation should be promptly rectified.

Every year inter-parliamentary delegations gather in turn in the European Union and in the partner country. However, in the case of the US delegation, these meetings are held twice a year: once in the United States and once in Europe. Special temporary delegations may be occasionally set up for a maximum duration of 12 months. As illustrated in Table 2.5, within the seventh legislature there are 41 delegations, each consisting of between 10 and 78 members. These may be distinguished into four types:

1. delegations to joint parliamentary committees (JPC), in charge of relations with parliaments of EU candidate countries as well as parliaments of states that have signed association agreements with the EU;
2. delegations to parliamentary cooperation committees (PCC), established after the signing of partnership and cooperation agreements between the European Union and relevant third countries;

Table 2.5 EP delegations: seventh legislature

Delegations to parliamentary assemblies
1. Delegation to the ACP–EU Joint Parliamentary Assembly
2. Delegation to the Parliamentary Assembly of the Union for the Mediterranean
3. Delegation to the Euronest Parliamentary Assembly
4. Delegation to the Euro-Latin American Parliamentary Assembly
5. Delegation for Relations with the NATO Parliamentary Assembly

Joint parliamentary committees (JPC)
6. Delegation for Relations with the Maghreb Countries and the Arab Maghreb Union
7. Delegation for Relations with Switzerland and Norway and to the EU–Iceland Joint Parliamentary Committee and the European Economic Area (EEA) Joint Parliamentary Committee
8. Delegation to the EU–Croatia Joint Parliamentary Committee
9. Delegation to the EU–Former Yugoslav Republic of Macedonia Joint Parliamentary Committee
10. Delegation to the EU–Turkey Joint Parliamentary Committee
11. Delegation to the EU–Chile Joint Parliamentary Committee
12. Delegation to the EU–Mexico Joint Parliamentary Committee
13. Delegation to the Cariforum–EU Parliamentary Committee

Parliamentary cooperation committees (PCC)
14. Delegation to the EU–Armenia, EU–Azerbaijan and EU–Georgia Parliamentary Cooperation Committees
15. Delegation to the EU–Moldova Parliamentary Cooperation Committee
16. Delegation to the EU–Russia Parliamentary Cooperation Committee
17. Delegation to the EU–Ukraine Parliamentary Cooperation Committee
18. Delegation to the EU–Kazakhstan, EU–Kyrgyzstan, and EU–Uzbekistan Parliamentary Cooperation Committees, and for Relations with Tajikistan, Turkmenistan, and Mongolia

Other inter-parliamentary delegations
19. Delegation for Relations with South Africa
20. Delegation for Relations with Iraq
21. Delegation for Relations with Israel
22. Delegation for Relations with the Arab peninsula
23. Delegation for Relations with the Palestinian Legislative Council
24. Delegation for Relations with the Mashreq countries
25. Delegation for Relations with the Pan-African Parliament
26. Delegation for Relations with Albania, Bosnia and Herzegovina, Serbia, Montenegro, and Kosovo
27. Delegation for Relations with Belarus
28. Delegation for Relations with Canada
29. Delegation for Relations with the United States
30. Delegation for Relations with Afghanistan
31. Delegation for Relations with the countries of Southeast Asia and the Association of Southeast Asian Nations (ASEAN)
32. Delegation for Relations with Australia and New Zealand
33. Delegation for Relations with India
34. Delegation for Relations with Iran
35. Delegation for Relations with the Korean peninsula
36. Delegation for Relations with the People's Republic of China
37. Delegation for Relations with Japan
38. Delegation for Relations with the Countries of South Asia
39. Delegation for Relations with the Countries of Central America
40. Delegation for Relations with the Countries of the Andean Community
41. Delegation for Relations with the Mercosur Countries

Source: Author's table based on information drawn from the EP website: www.europarl.europa.eu.

3. inter-parliamentary delegations, involving parliaments of non-EU countries that are neither EU candidate countries nor under partnership and cooperation agreements;
4. delegations to multilateral parliamentary assemblies, such as the Joint Parliamentary Assembly of the countries of Africa, Caribbean, and Pacific (ACP) and the European Union, the Euro-Latin American Parliamentary Assembly (EUROLAT), the EU's Eastern neighbouring countries (EURONEST) Parliamentary Assembly, the Euro-Mediterranean Parliamentary Assembly (EMPA), and the NATO Parliamentary Assembly (see www.europarl.europa.eu/delegations/en/home.html).

Conclusion

Nowadays, the European Parliament, whose members caucus according to political groups based on political affinity rather than nationality, represents the most far-reaching transnational democratic experiment (Corbett, 2011). With its 500 million eligible voters, it also serves one of the widest electorates in the world.

The European Parliament reflects a unique, dynamic body that combines original characteristics with elements common to international assemblies and traditions belonging to national parliamentary democracies. It is a three-sited institution that displays an increasingly articulated internal organization, a party structure, fairly transparent activities, and plenary sessions. It also rigorously operates through committees, whilst its delegations play a major role in the development of relationships with third countries. Similar to and even more than other international assemblies, it embodies a polyglot microcosm which, due to being directly elected by way of a proportional representation system, accommodates virtually all political ideologies and national parties across the 28 EU countries.

Despite all this, the European Parliament has failed to elicit wholehearted public support and to attract the desirable levels of loyalty and identification by EU citizens, who continue to perceive it as distant from their everyday lives. Regardless of the tremendous developments in information technology and communication channels, poor mass media coverage of its activities continues to conceal the European Parliament's visibility.

In fact, the EU Newsroom and EuroparlTV represent valuable, if rudimentary, information tools. There is no EU press corps as such, being still primarily national in focus, and there is no terrestrial or satellite television channel focusing on European issues. Furthermore, the EP has unsuccessfully resorted to online social networks in the vain hope of attracting younger generations.

Inexorably, the real or apparent remoteness of the Strasbourg and Brussels Assembly has continued to prompt misunderstandings, nourish sentiments of distrust, and accentuate people's feelings of powerlessness.

Although during its lifespan the EP has strongly promoted European integration, in order to succeed in forging a fully-fledged European Union, it will have to turn into a well-celebrated democratic institution, widely recognized and appreciated first of all by EU citizens.

References

Primary sources

Act concerning the election of the representatives of the Assembly by direct universal suffrage of 20 September 1976, *Official Journal of the European Communities OJEC,* Series L 278, 8 October 1976, 5.
European Parliament website,
www.europarl.europa.eu (accessed on 4 September 2012);
www.europarl.europa.eu/delegations/en/home.html (accessed on 4 September 2012);
www.europarl.europa.eu/parliament/archive/elections2009/en/index_en.html (accessed on 10 March 2010);
www.europarl.europa.eu/meps/eu/search.html (accessed on 10 March 2010);

www.europarl.europa.eu/activities/committees (accessed on 6 September 2012 and on 10 August 2013); www.europarl.europa.eu/aboutparliament/en/009cd2034d/In-the-past.html (accessed on 5 January 2015).
Draft European Council Decision Establishing the Composition of the European Parliament, 11 June 2013.
European Court of Justice, Case C-237-11, *France v. Parliament*, 13 December 2012.
European Parliament Bureau (2001) 'Preparing for the Parliament of the Enlarged European Union', PE 305/209/BUR/fin, 3 September.
European Parliament Rules of Procedure, January 2012.
Protocol 6, Treaty of Lisbon, 2007, *Official Journal of the European Union*, C 306, 17 December 2007.

European Parliament reports and resolutions

European Council Decision establishing the composition of the European Parliament (2013) *Official Journal of the European Union*, Series L 181/57, 29 June 2013.
Fox and Häfner (2013a) Report on the Location of the Seats of the European Union's Institutions, 'Explanatory Statement', A7-0350, 23 October.
Fox and Häfner (2013b) Report on the Location of the Seats of the European Union's Institutions, 'Procedure file', A7-0350, 23 October.
Fox and Häfner (2013c) Report on the Location of the Seats of the European Union's Institutions, A7-0350, 23 October.
Gualtieri and Trzaskowski (2013) Recommendation on the Draft European Council Decision Establishing the Composition of the European Parliament in view of the 2014 Elections, A7-0213, 10 June.
Lamassoure-Séverin (2007) Report on the Composition of the European Parliament, 3 October, A6-0351.

Secondary sources

Abélès, M. (1992) *La vie quotidienne au Parlement européen*, Paris, Hachette.
Attinà, F. (1995) *Identità, Partiti ed Elezioni nell'Unione europea*, Bari, Cacucci.
Corbett, R. (1994) 'Representing the People' in Duff, A., Pinder, J., Pryce R. (eds) *Maastricht and Beyond: Building the European Union*, London, Routledge.
Corbett, R., Jacobs, F. and Shackleton, M. (2007) *The European Parliament*, London, John Harper Publishing, 7th edn.
Corbett, R., Jacobs, F. and Shackleton, M. (2011) *The European Parliament*, London, John Harper Publishing, 8th edn.
Costa O. (coordinator), Bardi L., Beligh N. and Sio-López C. (2009) 'The European Parliament Reaffirms its Legitimacy', in Mény, Y. (ed.) *Building Parliament: 50 Years of European Parliament History 1958–2008*, European Parliament and European University Institute, Luxembourg, Office for Official Publications of the European Communities, 33–85.
Guizzi, V. (2003) *Manuale di diritto e politica dell'Unione europea*, Napoli, Editoriale Scientifica.
McCormick, J. (2008) *Understanding the European Union: A Concise Introduction*, London, Palgrave.
McElroy, G. (2007) 'Legislative Politics', in Jørgensen, K. E., Pollack M. A. and Rosamond B. (eds) *Handbook of European Union Politics*, London, Sage, 175–94.
McElroy, G. and Benoit, K. (2011) 'Policy Positioning in the European Parliament', *European Union Politics*, 13(1), 150–67.
Millar, D. (1991) 'European Political Co-operation', in Carstairs, C. and Ware, R. (eds) *Parliaments and International Relations*, Buckingham and Bristol USA, Open University Press, 140–59.
Nugent, N. (2003) *The Government and Politics of the European Union*, Basingstoke, Palgrave Macmillan.
Palayret, J. M. (2009) 'Introduction', in Mény, Y. (ed.) *Building Parliament: 50 Years of European Parliament History 1958–2008*, European Parliament and European University Institute, Luxembourg, Office for Official Publications of the European Communities, 13–30.
Pridham, G. and Pridham, P. (1981) *Transnational Party Co-operation and European Integration*, London, Allen & Unwin.
Romano, B. (2013) 'L'Europarlamento propone il trasloco da Strasburgo a Bruxelles: risparmi fino a 200 milioni di euro sulle trasferte', *Il Sole/24 Ore*, 20 Novembre.
Viola, D. M. (2000) *European Foreign Policy and the European Parliament in the 1990s*, Aldershot, Ashgate.
Vogel, T. (2013) 'Anti-Strasbourg Campaigners Set Up Challenge to Status Quo', *European Voice*, 26 September.

3
EUROPEAN PARLIAMENT ELECTIONS THEORIES

Donatella M. Viola

Introduction

The objective of this chapter is to offer a concise overview on the state of the art of the European Parliament election literature. This will provide readers with the necessary conceptual tools to interpret the multifaceted aspects of the still rather hazy and unknown process of selecting representatives to the Parliamentary Assembly in Strasbourg and Brussels.

We will draw a brief outline of the two main theoretical frameworks on European elections that have hitherto emerged, notably the so-called Second-Order Election (SOE) and Europe Salience (ES) models. Pioneered by Karlheinz Reif and Hermann Schmitt, in their far-sighted article entitled 'Nine Second-Order National Elections' and published in 1980, a theoretical analysis of Euro-elections has been sketched out and later carried forward, developed, and tested by an increasing number of scholars (Reif and Schmitt, 1980).

During the last three decades, research on European Union elections has steadily grown and matured by trying to detect the core features of the EP electoral campaigns and contests, to unveil their complexity, and to explain voting behaviour in EU Member States. Comparative empirical appraisals of the EP contests have been undertaken by a transnational group of experts, under the coordination of the University of Mannheim, leading to the creation of the European Elections Studies (EES) series. Although Reif can be certainly regarded as its founder and promoter, he did not become an official member of this research team. Initiated in 1979, the project does not just focus on the dynamics of voters' choices, but also extends to the evolution of the European Community/Union and to an assessment of its political performance.

In April 1987, at the Joint Sessions of Workshops of the European Consortium for Political Research in Amsterdam, Roland Cayrol, Cees van der Eijk, Mark N. Franklin, Manfred Kuechler, Renato Mannheimer, and Hermann Schmitt agreed to draft the 1989 European Election Study. Subsequently, other academics joined the project, such as Colette Ysmal, Pilar del Castillo, Erik Oppenhuis, and Michael Marsh.

Unlike the previous cases, the 2004 European Election Study was carried out and sponsored by national study directors and was partially supported by CONNEX, a network of excellence financed by the European Commission under the Sixth Framework Programme. Finally, in 2009 the European University Institute coordinated the European Election Study by framing it within a wider pilot project known as PIREDEU 'Providing an Infrastructure for Research on

Electoral Democracy in the European Union', under the Seventh Framework Programme. Its results offer a comprehensive empirical database regarding voters, candidates, media coverage, party manifestos, and contextual data relevant to EP elections.

The three-year investigation largely drew on and benefitted from the model provided by the American National Election Study (ANES), a permanent research infrastructure that since 1948 has collected survey data on all US presidential and most mid-term congressional elections.

Alongside the wide-ranging European Election Studies, it is *de rigueur* to mention Juliet Lodge's six successive edited volumes that offer excellent empirical country reviews on the EP electoral contests held from 1984 to 2009 (Lodge, 1986, 1990, 1995, 2001, 2005, 2010). The contents of these books have mainly revolved around party strategies in political campaigns, key electoral issues as well as final polling results which, after each election, have translated into a different number of parliamentary seats for the various national political parties, determined a new balance between political forces, and shaped a novel and distinctive European Parliament.

Further studies have tried to shed some light on specific aspects of the multifarious and compound mechanisms behind the EP ballot. In particular, Mikko Mattila has focussed on the effects of the timing of the EP electoral race within the national cycle and on whether it entailed weekend or compulsory voting, or voter participation (Mattila, 2003). Sara B. Hobolt, Jae-Jae Spoon and James R. Tilley have looked at age, social class, party identification, and policy distances of the electorate as factors capable of significantly affecting the likelihood of abstaining (Hobolt *et al.*, 2009).

Yet, even in these predominantly empirical studies, the concept of 'Second-Order Election', which will be outlined below, has inevitably appeared, if only in the background. Thirty-four years after writing their seminal article, Reif and Schmitt's theoretical interpretation remains pivotal and dominant in any academic debates as well as major investigations on European elections.

1 The Second-Order Election model

In 1971 Michael Steed anticipated that convening an election to a relatively powerless European Parliament would be the equivalent of organizing a sort of plebiscite on the performance of national governments (Steed, 1971). Four years later, the French MEP Christian de la Malène warned that issues raised during the campaign for the European elections would be based on domestic policy, and that these contests would not depend on European Union affairs. He also expressed his concern about citizens' participation in an electoral race where the representatives were perceived as very distant figures without a distinct ideological identity (de la Malène, 1975). Similarly, the British peer Lord Watson, sceptical about the idea that direct elections to the EP would promote a Europe-wide debate, predicted a low turnout, even lower than that achieved in local elections, and in terms of outcome envisaged a protest vote against any sitting government, with the result that the majority of MEPs would belong to parties in opposition to their national governments (Watson, 1975).

As Reif and Schmitt stressed, the first direct Euro-elections by universal suffrage – held in June 1979 – proved that such predictions were, to a large extent, true and accurate (Reif and Schmitt, 1980). These electoral contests appeared to be rather different from the national legislative ones, mostly due to the subordination of the European Parliament to other institutions within the European Community and the irrelevance of the choice of MEPs to the distribution of power amongst political parties within the Member States. For the purpose of their analysis, Reif and Schmitt drew an important distinction between what they named *Hauptwahlen,* first-order elections, referring to general elections in parliamentary systems and elections of the head of state in presidential systems and *Nebenwahlen*, second-order elections, corresponding to less influential electoral contests at regional, municipal, and local levels in parliamentary systems as well as to legislative elections in presidential systems, especially congressional mid-term elections in the United States, and more blatantly to all by-elections (Reif and Schmitt, 1980).

In this context, EP electoral races seemed to fit rather well within the second category by displaying the following features: (1) low turnout; (2) a focus on national rather than European issues; (3) the defeat of government parties; (4) losses by major parties; and (5) the impact of timing of EP contests within the domestic electoral cycle on the results for ruling and big parties. We will discuss each of these features in turn.

First, Euro-elections are strongly marked by high defection rates, partly based on citizens' perceptions that less is at stake, although this tendency is deemed to affect the supporters of government parties more than those of the opposition. On the other hand, low turnout could also be ascribed to a party mobilization deficit. In fact, despite the growing influence exercised by the European Parliament on EU policy-making, these electoral contests remain out of the central mechanisms of distribution of political offices at the national level, and thus are inevitably labelled as 'second-rate' (Weber, 2007, 531). This is an evident sign of the institutional failure to provide individuals with real political power, especially among voters who have not had the opportunity to gain partisan loyalties, either because they are young or because they live in countries where party systems have been in flux, making creation of such loyalties a difficult matter (Franklin, 2014).

The second aspect foresees that citizens vote with an eye to the national political arena rather than to express a true choice for the candidates they believe to be most suited to represent their views on the EP stage. As such, parties enter the electoral campaign by trying to mobilize voters through the refinement of their usual national policy strategies. They do not draft alternative manifestos over EU policies, but prefer to mitigate their differences on these matters. Questions inherent to the future construction and organization of the European Union play a very limited role in either the strategies adopted by political parties or citizens' voting behaviour. By and large, EP elections are characterized by a lack of European content and political parties regard these contests as valuable only to the extent that they serve as indicators of their national strength. Since the polling results largely stem from the popularity of national parties, EP elections appear more 'national' than 'European' (Oppenhuis et al., 1996; Ferrara and Weishaupt, 2004).

The third feature closely relates to the decline in popular support for government parties competing for the EP electoral podium, which echoes the losses seen by presidential parties in congressional mid-term elections in the US. According to the 'surge and decline' theory, this phenomenon is believed to occur because, during presidential election years, voters are usually more prone to back the congressional candidate who is affiliated to their preferred candidate for the White House (Campbell, 1960). By contrast, two years later at mid term, when such a link no longer exists, partisanship prevails with people favouring the candidate closer to their own personal political views and, as a result, presidential parties suffer a remarkable setback. At the EU level, the 'decline' of national government parties – and the 'surge' of their rivals sitting on the opposition benches – offers a provisional shelter for those disaffected by their respective cabinet's political performance in the various Member States (Norris, 1997, 112).

The fourth variable affects major parties, whether in government or opposition, which tend to lose votes to the benefit of minor ones. In this perspective, party size seems to be inversely proportional to the gain achieved in Euro-elections (Ferrara and Weishaupt, 2004). Subsequently, as Reif has cunningly noticed, citizens do not just privilege small parties but also radical, protest, and populist movements, which do particularly well in less crucial elections such as those of the European Parliament. Undeniably, the ability of these parties to attract a larger number of supporters can be ascribed, to a certain extent, to the greater visibility that they often achieve through media coverage (Reif, 1984, 1997).

The fifth tenet underlines that the political weight of an EP electoral contest is partially determined by its temporal location in the national electoral cycle. If this occurs immediately after a legislative election, the governing party, which is in its 'honeymoon' period, is still very popular in voters' eyes. On the contrary, if it takes place at the mid-point of the national election cycle, according to Karlheinz Reif (1984), or rather at its end, according to Erik Oppenhuis, Cees van der Eijk, and Mark N. Franklin (1996), it reaches the lowest level of public support for the governing party. EP electoral campaigns held shortly before legislative elections are expected to be more intense than those that follow just on the trail of general electoral races when a sort of 'euphoria' prevails. In cyclical patterns, governing parties experience a fall in support as voters treat Euro-elections as battlefields to win national government office and as opportunities to reward or punish political parties on the basis of their performance. As a result, a different composition is likely to distinguish the European Parliament from the Council of Ministers, with an ever-increasing number of members from peripheral parties – including radicals and Eurosceptics – sitting in the Strasbourg and Brussels Assembly in contrast to their rather limited presence amongst the representatives in EU Member States' governments.

Mark N. Franklin and Till Weber agree that the extent of vote-switching between national and EU elections depends on their actual timing (Franklin and Weber, 2010). Whilst EP electoral contests are regularly held every five years, national parliamentary elections do not follow the same cycle in all Member States, except in Luxembourg. Indeed, general elections usually take place more often, as prescribed by law or convention, and may even be convened prior to the completion of the legislature as result of political instability.

Based on the assumption that Euro-elections exert a limited impact on the national political arena, citizens may choose to vote sincerely rather than strategically by supporting opposition parties or single-issue movements, which focus their attention on topical questions such as the environment or immigration. And yet, it should not be overlooked or ignored that, in most cases, this decision stems from people's growing disaffection and disappointment with government.

Against this background, three types of voting can be detected: (1) strategic, instrumental, or 'voting with the head', when citizens choose parties or candidates with a better chance of winning rather than their preferred ones for fear of wasting their vote (Cox, 1997; Pasquino, 2003; Koepke and Ringe, 2006); (2) sincere, expressive, or 'voting with the heart', when individuals support the party that reflects their own genuine ideological preference (Reif and Schmitt, 1980; Marsh, 1998; Reif, 1984, 1985; van der Eijk and Franklin, 1991, 1996; Pasquino, 2003; Carrubba and Timpone, 2005); and (3) protest or 'voting with the boot', when citizens convey their temporary discontent with the government party at the national level, by sending a warning message to their politicians without altering the cabinet's composition (Oppenhuis *et al.*, 1996).

The distinction between 'sincere' and 'protest' voting still appears rather blurred, perhaps due to the fact that, in their original article, Reif and Schmitt had failed to address it clearly. Jason R. Koepke and Nils Ringe have tried to fill this lacuna by spelling out the nuances between these two concepts. In their eyes, 'protest voting' is commonly directed against incumbent governing parties or, more rarely, in defiance of whatever party citizens would opt for if national political power were at stake. Conversely, 'sincere voting' mainly affects large parties, which do not benefit from the wasted-vote mentality, thus leading to a sort of redistribution of consensus between parties that had been less successful in the previous national election (Koepke and Ringe, 2006). Oppenhuis, van der Eijk, and Franklin have introduced another classification between 'marker-setting' and 'throw-away' elections (Oppenhuis *et al.*, 1996). The former takes place far from the preceding first-order election, when citizens engage in expressive or protest voting and such contests represent a real test of the level of popularity of parties once the indicator set by the earlier national election has faded away. As a result, 'marker-setting' elections allow people to voice their relative support for the governing party, whilst the attention paid by politicians and the media is high, but without actually altering the composition of the cabinet. By contrast, 'throw-away' elections run parallel to – or immediately after – first-order elections, when contests appear insignificant as a source of information about the position of national parties and the people's vote is sincere. Nevertheless, as Koepke and Ringe sharply observe, the term 'throw-away election' inevitably carries a rather negative connotation that does not appear justified, considering that voters truly back their favourite party. They therefore propose the alternative expression 'pure preference election', which instead maintains the essence of the above concept without any implicit normative judgement (Koepke and Ringe, 2006, 326).

Political parties may bring into play EP election results to seize crucial information about public preferences. In the case of an electoral demise they can, hence, adjust their policy strategies accordingly prior to the subsequent national electoral contest. In their empirical survey, based on the results of 14 EU Member States, Zeynep Somer-Topcu and Michelle E. Zar reveal that opposition parties draw on the EP vote to change their positions, more than ever if the turnout levels in both electoral contests are similar and when European elections are close in time to the upcoming national ones (Somer-Topcu and Zar, 2013).

2 Europe Salience theory

Whereas there is strong evidence of a national character in EP elections, new research shows that European integration is becoming a contentious issue in the unfolding of Euro-campaigns, and in the formulation of party strategies provided that, in a specific environment, it may well affect their final results. This literature does not repudiate the SOE model, but reveals that these elections have become more salient over the past decade (de Vries, 2007, 2010; de Vries *et al.*, 2011; Gabel, 2000; Hobolt and Spoon, 2012; Hobolt *et al.*, 2009; Hobolt and Wittrock, 2011; Tillman, 2004).

In his case study investigation focussed on Austria, Finland, and Sweden, Erik R. Tillman demonstrates that public attitudes towards the EU have affected voting behaviour in national elections before and after accession to the European Union, by highlighting a close link between people and parties over European matters (Tillman, 2004).

Cees van der Eijk and Mark N. Franklin noticeably address the interface between domestic and European elections in their book entitled *Choosing Europe? The European Electorate and National Politics in the Face of Union* (van der Eijk and Franklin, 1996). National underpinnings as well as the effects of European integration on such elections are further elaborated by Catherine de Vries, who defines the last variable as 'European Union (EU) issue voting' (de Vries, 2007). Subsequently, Sara B. Hobolt and Jill Wittrock examine the power of information on voting behaviour in Europe-wide elections. Their findings clearly confirm that citizens usually build their choices on domestic preferences, but after receiving further communication on European integration matters, they generally become more inclined to cast their votes also on these grounds (Hobolt and Wittrock, 2011).

In fact, on the basis of their analysis in all 27 EU countries in the 2009 EP elections, Hobolt and Spoon (2012) demonstrate that the degree of politicization of the European Union in the national debate shapes the extent to which electors rely on European rather than domestic issues. Somer-Topcu and Zar explore the bearing of European Parliament election results on national party strategies. In particular, they focus on how opposition parties draw on these electoral outcomes in order to discern public opinion and change their left–right positions accordingly in their national election manifestos (Somer-Topcu and Zar, 2013).

Certainly, voters have started to take these contests more seriously and, as a result, political parties have to devote greater attention to the EP campaign by also investing additional financial resources. Although political parties still care less about their EP electoral manifestos and campaigns, these elections are gradually becoming more salient. To this avail, parties may even resort to their national-level information on public preferences to change their positions in their EU manifestos with the hope of increasing their vote shares in European elections. Moreover, if the polling outcome unambiguously denotes that public preferences have extensively diverged from parties' policy positions, in order to narrow such a gap and reduce consequential losses, political parties have to decide whether or not they need to adjust their national policy stance. What is important to note is that shifting away from their traditional standpoint always represents a rather hazardous move for political parties, as they may lose supporters and donors who could accuse them of being opportunistic or even deceitful. Aware of these risks, political leaders are usually reluctant to undertake drastic policy changes, unless required for the sake of the party and only after a truly harsh electoral defeat. According to Somer-Topcu and Zar, the extent of the losses by parties in the European election, compared with the previous national one, reflects proportionally their willingness to change their left–right manifesto positions at the upcoming national electoral race (Somer-Topcu and Zar, 2013).

Although EP elections do not seem to offer a real platform over alternative approaches to European integration, nor do most voters care about expressing such a preference, EU-related issues increasingly have some bearing on the performance of political parties in this electoral contest.

Indeed, studies carried out by John Curtice in 1989, Michael Marsh and Mark N. Franklin in 1996, Jean Blondel, Richard Sinnot, and Palle Svensson in 1997 and, finally, Simon Hix and Michael Marsh in 2007 and 2011, have shown that these elections are also about Europe and European issues.

As such, an alternative to the SOE model has been put forward, commonly referred to as Europe Salience (ES) theory, which entails the following predictions between the last national general election and the subsequent European election:

1. better performance of Green parties;
2. gain of extreme parties, either on the left or on the right of the political spectrum;
3. success of anti-European parties.

As to the first hypothesis regarding the increased voting share of the Greens, this may be due to the negative externalities of different environmental policies in the various Member States that trigger citizens' decisions to support a common European action in this sensitive sector, based on the belief that these issues could only be tackled efficiently at the EU level (Hix and Marsh, 2007). Cliff Carrubba and Richard Timpone claim that this new Green politics dimension, overriding the traditional, authoritarian, and nationalist outlooks, represents the most powerful source of variation in voting behaviour (Carrubba and Timpone, 2005). As such, advocates of further European integration, who are also keen on environmental issues, tend to shift to Green parties.

Turning to the second hypothesis of the ES theory, voters who believe that the pace of European integration has advanced too quickly are likely to defect from mainstream ruling parties to extreme right-wing or left-wing lists which are critical towards the European Union project. In fact, it cannot be ignored that there is often a strong nexus between the party positioning on European integration and the conventional left–right division.

Federico Ferrara and Timo J. Weishaupt suggest that all parties with a well-defined and cohesive stance on the European Union, and which address European issues, usually fare better in EP electoral contests (Ferrara and Weishaupt, 2004). By contrast, parties that face lacerating 'Euro-divisions' suffer large desertions at the EP ballot, to the extent that any ambivalence or ambiguity on European integration may well lead to significant vote losses. Even if citizens do not reward a specific position on the EU unification process, they systematically punish parties that do not have a clear vision on this matter. By using Ferrara and Weishaupt's informal expression, those parties that have not 'got their act together' on Europe are deemed to perform worse in EP elections.

Furthermore, in their opinion, this pattern is slightly more pronounced for governing than opposition forces, whilst it is especially evident in countries where the European project is strongly polarized (Ferrara and Weishaupt, 2004). From an ES perspective, Euro-elections held in the new Member States from Central and Eastern Europe differ from those which take place in the old 15. Such idiosyncrasies may also be due to the high level of electoral volatility, embodying a typical feature of new democratic party systems that require time to reach a certain degree of stability.

Based on a survey undertaken in 21 countries, Joost van Spanje and Claes de Vreese argue that voting behaviour may be influenced by concerns about the 'democratic deficit' of the European Union, the absence of a European identity, the perceived low benefits of EU membership, or even by fierce opposition to European integration (van Spanje and de Vreese, 2011). Overall, parties that give salience to European Union politics, whether negative or positive, attract consensus. Nevertheless, it is widely recognized that Eurosceptic parties are due to outperform their opponents in Euro-elections, in accordance with the third tenet of the ES model.

In addition to the three above-mentioned predictions of the Europe Salience theory, a final aspect deserves some attention. This concerns the strict correlation between citizens' propensity to go to the polls, their personal knowledge of EU institutions, and their country's attitude towards European integration (Mattila, 2003; Ferrara and Weishaupt, 2004; Stockemer, 2011). According to Studlar *et al.* (2003), three main factors account for a higher turnout in EP elections, notably: (1) hosting a European institution; (2) a feeling of European identity; and (3) the presence of agricultural workers. In fact, citizens' willingness to go to the electoral booth may depend, to a great extent, on their trust in the European Union and on their perception that the EU represents a 'good thing' (Blondel *et al.*, 1998; Flickinger and Studlar, 2007). Voting would become 'a symbolic act of showing one's support for the idea of European integration' (Irwin, 1995, 198).

This view implies the complementary proposition that abstention may be interpreted as an indication that voters are not really keen and driven to participate in the democratic governance of Europe, being either indifferent or disaffected towards the European project (Blondel *et al.*, 1998). Hence, deserting the ballot box may well signify distrust of or dissatisfaction with the European Parliament whilst generally reflecting the rise of voters' apathy and frustration with the inadequate functioning of the European Union (Sinnott, 2000). And yet, Mark N. Franklin and Sara B. Hobolt have criticized this specific tenet of the Europe Salience model, arguing and demonstrating empirically that it is the very nature of EP elections that is to blame for such a popular unconcern and detachment rather than the opposite (Franklin and Hobolt, 2011).

The next part of this volume offers a rich empirical picture, mostly drawn by native experts, on the Euro-elections in all EU Member States held since 1979 and in particular on the 2009 contest. This will be complemented by a short overview on the national parliamentary elections convened within the same time frame, thus enabling the authors to uncover the complex interface between domestic and European Union politics.

Each country chapter will include brief preliminary sections on the geographical position, historical background, geopolitical profile, political landscape, and political parties of the various Member States, combined with their respective attitudes to the European Union, as well as public opinion on European integration, and will end with a brief account of the national and EP electoral systems.

Such an empirical picture will be instrumental in order to test the above-mentioned themes framed within either the SOE or SE models. Against this background, the authors will endeavour to recognize whether and which of these theories actually fits better with their own case and if any of the respective hypotheses of the two models may be either validated or refuted in all EP electoral waves, thus identifying constant as well as common trends.

Ultimately, the case studies will wind up by shedding some light on the complex conceptual dynamics of Euro-elections. They will try to detect and situate the key features outlined in this chapter by unveiling whether such electoral platforms continue to be dominated by the search for domestic political advantage or whether 'European' issues increasingly come to the fore.

Building on the work aptly carried out by the various authors, the last chapter of this handbook will be devoted to a cross-country comparison of all Euro-elections in the EU Member States, by also drawing some theoretical conclusions. To this end, tables will be sketched out on the basis of information collected as well as interpretations advanced by national experts, in particular on the character of the EP electoral campaigns across the EU as well as on the main hypotheses of the SOE and ES models. In fact, the authors' perceptions on the applicability of the two theoretical models to the EP elections across the European Union will be summarized in tables in order to shed some light on this still rather overlooked, snubbed, or simply ignored political event.

In conclusion, the last chapter will draw an overall comparative framework where similarities and differences in the voting behaviour of European citizens across the European Union are highlighted. Set against this backdrop, it will therefore be possible as well as appropriate to assess whether EP elections have effectively attained some sort of mandate from EU citizens, by unveiling the principles that can open the door to democratic legitimacy.

References

Primary sources

de la Malène, C. (1975) Report of Proceedings from 13 to 17 January 1975, Debates of the European Parliament, *Official Journal of the European Communities*.

Secondary sources

Blondel, J., Sinnott, R. and Svensson, P. (1997) 'Representation and Voter Participation', *European Journal of Political Research*, 32(2), 243–72.
Blondel, J., Sinnott R. and Svensson P. (1998) *People and Parliaments in the European Union: Participation, Democracy and Legitimacy*, Oxford, Oxford University Press.
Campbell, A. (1960) 'Surge and Decline: A Study of Electoral Change', *Public Opinion Quarterly*, 24(3), 397–418.
Carrubba, C. and Timpone, R. J. (2005) 'Explaining Vote Switching across First- and Second-Order Elections: Evidence From Europe', *Comparative Political Studies*, 38(3), 260–81.
Cox, G.W. (1996) *Making Votes Count: Strategic Coordination in the World's Electoral Systems*, Cambridge, Cambridge University Press.
Curtice, J. (1989) 'The 1989 European Election: Protest or Green Tide', *Electoral Studies*, 8(3), 217–30.
de Vries, C. E. (2007) 'Sleeping Giant: Fact or Fairytale? Examining the Impact of European Integration on National Elections in Denmark and the Netherlands', *European Union Politics*, 8(3), 363–85.
de Vries, C. E. (2009) 'The Impact of EU Referenda on National Electoral Politics: Evidence from the Dutch Case', *West European Politics*, 32(1), 142–71.

de Vries, C. E. (2010) 'EU Issue Voting: Asset or Liability? How European Integration Affects Parties' Electoral Fortunes', *European Union Politics*, 11 (1), 89–117.

de Vries C. E., van der Brug W., and van Egmond M. H., *et al.* (2011) 'Individual and Contextual Variation in EU Issue Voting: The Role of Political Information', *Electoral Studies*, 30(1) 16–28.

European Election Series EES 1979–EES 1984 Study; EES 1989 Study–EES 1994 Study; EES 1999 Study–EES 2004 Study; EES 2009 Study, http://eeshomepage.net/ (accessed on 5 January 2015).

Ferrara, F. and Weishaupt, J. T. (2004) 'Get Your Act Together: Party Performance in European Parliament Elections', *European Union Politics*, 5(3), 283–306.

Flickinger, R. S. and Studlar, D. T. (2007) 'One Europe, Many Electorates? Models of Turnout in European Parliament Elections after 2004', *Comparative Political Studies*, 40(4), 383–404.

Franklin, M. N. (2014) 'Why Vote at an Election with No Apparent Purpose? Voter Turnout at Elections to the European Parliament', *European Political Analysis* (April), 1–12.

Franklin, M. N. and Hobolt S. B. (2011) 'The Legacy of Lethargy: How Elections to the European Parliament Depress Turnout', *Electoral Studies*, 30(1), 67–76.

Franklin, M. N., van der Eijk, C. and Oppenhus, E. (1996) 'The Institutional Context: Turnout', van der Eijk, C. and Franklin, M. N. (eds) *Choosing Europe? The European Electorate and National Politics in the Face of Union*, University of Michigan Press, 306–332.

Franklin, M. N. and Weber, T. (2010) 'The Structuring Effect of First Order Elections', Paper prepared for the Annual Meeting of the American Political Science Association, Washington DC, September.

Gabel, M. (2000) 'European Integration, Voters and National Politics', *West European Politics*, 23, 52–72.

Hix, S. and Marsh, M. (2007) 'Punishment or Protest? Understanding European Parliament Elections', *Journal of Politics*, 69(2), 495–510.

Hix, S. and Marsh, M. (2011) 'Second-Order Effects plus Pan-European Political Wings: An Analysis of European Parliament Elections across Time', *Electoral Studies*, 30, 4–15.

Hobolt, S. B. and Spoon, J.-J. (2012) 'Motivating the European Voter: Parties, Issues, and Campaigns in European Parliament Elections', *European Journal of Political Research*, 51, 701–27.

Hobolt S. B. and Wittrock, J. (2011) 'The Second-Order Election Model Revisited: An Experimental Test of Vote Choices in European Parliament Elections', *Electoral Studies*, 30(1), 29–40.

Hobolt, S. B., Spoon, J.-J. and Tilley, J. R. (2009) 'A Vote against Europe? Explaining Defection at the 1999 and 2004 European Parliament Elections, *British Journal of Political Science*, 39(1), 93–115.

Irwin, G. (1995) 'Second-Order or Third-Rate? Issues in the Campaign for the Elections for the European Parliament 1994', *Electoral Studies*, 14(2), 183–98. Koepke J. R. and Ringe N. (2006) 'The Second-Order Election Model in an Enlarged Europe', *European Union Politics*, 7(3), 321–46.

Lodge, J. (ed.) (1986) *Direct Elections to the European Parliament 1984*, Basingstoke, Macmillan.

Lodge, J. (ed.) (1990) *The 1989 Elections to the European Parliament*, Basingstoke, Macmillan.

Lodge, J. (ed.) (1995) *The 1994 Elections to the European Parliament*, London, Pinter.

Lodge, J. (ed.) (2001) *The 1999 Elections to the European Parliament*, London, Palgrave, Macmillan.

Lodge, J. (ed.) (2005) *The 2004 Elections to the European Parliament*, London, Palgrave, Macmillan.

Lodge, J. (ed.) (2010) *The 2009 Elections to the European Parliament*, London, Palgrave, Macmillan.

Marsh, M. (1998) 'Testing the Second-Order Election Model after Four European Elections', *British Journal of Political Science*, 28(4), 591–607.

Marsh, M. and Franklin M. N. (1996) 'The Foundations. Unanswered Questions from the Study of European Elections, 1979–1994', in van der Eijk, C., and Franklin, M. N. (eds) *Choosing Europe? The European Electorate and National Politics in the Face of Union*, Ann Arbor, University of Michigan Press, 11–32.

Marsh, M. and Hix, S. (2007) 'European Parliament Elections and Losses by Governing Parties', in van der Brug, W. and van der Eijk, C. (eds) *European Elections and Domestic Politics: Lessons from the Past and Scenarios for the Future*, University of Notre Dame Press, 51–73.

Mattila, M. (2003) 'Why bother? Determinants of Turnout in the European Elections', *Electoral Studies*, 22(3), 449–68.

Norris, P. (1997) 'Second-Order Elections Revisited', *European Journal of Political Research*, 30(1), 109–14.

Oppenhuis, E., van der Eijk, C. and Franklin, M. N. (1996) 'The Party Context: Outcomes', in van der Eijk, C., and Franklin, M. N. (eds) *Choosing Europe? The European Electorate and National Politics in the Face of Union*, University of Michigan Press, 287–306.

Pasquino, G. (2003) 'Comportamenti elettorali: voto sincere e voto strategico', *Sistemi politici comparati*, cap. 2, Bologna, Bononia University Press.

Reif, K. H. (1984) 'National Electoral Cycles and European Elections 1979 and 1984', *Electoral Studies* 3 (3), 244–255.

Reif, K. H. (1985) 'Ten Second-Order National Elections', in Reif, K. (ed.) *Ten European Elections: Campaigns and Results of the 1979/81 First Direct Elections to the European Parliament*, Gower, Aldershot, 10–44.

Reif, K. H. (1997) 'European Elections as Member State Second-Order Elections Revisited', *European Journal of Political Research*, 31(1–2), 115–24.

Reif, K. H. and Schmitt, H. (1980) 'Nine Second-Order National Elections – A Conceptual Framework for the Analysis of European Election Results', *European Journal of Political Research*, 8(1), 3–44.

Sinnott, R. (2000) 'European Parliament Elections: Institutions, Attitudes and Participation', in Angé, H. et al., (eds) *Citizens' Participation in European Politics*, Statens Offentliga Utredningar.

Somer-Topcu, Z. and Zar, M. E. (2013) 'European Parliamentary Elections and National Party Policy Change', *Comparative Political Studies*, May, XX(X), 1–25.

Steed, M. (1971) 'The European Parliament: The Significance of Direct Elections', *Government and Opposition*, 6, October, 462–76.

Stockemer, D. (2011) 'Citizens' Support for the European Union and Participation in European Parliament Elections', *European Union Politics*, 13(1), 26–46.

Studlar, D., Flickinger, R. S. and Bennett, S. E. (2003) 'Turnout in European Parliament Elections: Towards a European-centred Model', *Journal of Elections, Public Opinion and Parties*, 13(1), 195–209.

Tillman, E. R. (2004) 'The European Union at the Ballot Box? European Integration and Voting Behavior in the New Member States', *Comparative Political Studies*, 37(5), 590–610.

van der Eijk, C. and Franklin, M. N. (1991) 'European Community Politics and Electoral Representation: Evidence From the 1989 European Elections Study', *European Journal of Political Research*, 19(1), 105–27.

van der Eijk, C. and Franklin, M. N. (1996) 'The Research: Studying the Elections of 1989 and 1994' , in van der Eijk, C. and Franklin, M. N. (eds) *Choosing Europe? The European Electorate and National Politics in the Face of Union*, Michigan, University of Michigan Press, 33–59.

van Spanje, J. and de Vreese, C. (2011) 'So What's Wrong with the EU? Motivations Underlying the Eurosceptic Vote in the 2009 European Elections', *European Union Politics*, 12(3), 405–29.

Watson, L. (1975) 'Letters to the Editor, 12 November 1975', *The Times*.

Weber, T. (2007) 'Campaign Effect and Second-Order Cycles: A Top-Down Approach to European Parliament Elections', *European Union Politics*, 8(4), 509–36.

PART II

Country reviews

The Old Member States

The founding members

4	France	51
5	Germany	76
6	Italy	109
7	Belgium	147
8	The Netherlands	167
9	Luxembourg	189

The first enlargement countries

10	The United Kingdom	213
11	Ireland	243
12	Denmark	267

The second and third enlargement countries

13	Greece	291
14	Spain	321
15	Portugal	351

The fourth enlargement countries

16	Austria	377
17	Finland	396
18	Sweden	414

The New Member States

The fifth enlargement countries
Southern Mediterranean countries

19	Malta	433
20	Cyprus	448

Central and Eastern European Countries

21	Slovenia	471
22	Estonia	491
23	Latvia	507
24	Lithuania	527
25	Czech Republic	549
26	Slovakia	568
27	Hungary	589
28	Poland	608
29	Bulgaria	633
30	Romania	653

4
FRANCE

Julien Navarro

Figure 4.1 Map of France

Table 4.1 France profile

EU entry year	1952 ECSC; 1958 EEC and Euratom founding member
Schengen entry year	1985 original signatory
MEPs elected in 2009	72
MEPs under Lisbon Treaty	74 since 1 December 2011
	Two additional seats allocated to Jean Roatta (EPP) and to Yves Cochet (Green)
Capital	Paris
Area	632,833 km^2
Population	65,835,579
	63,378,545 Metropolitan France
Population density	103.8/km^2
Median age of population	40.8
Political system	Semi-presidential Republic
Head of state	Nicolas Sarkozy, Union for a Popular Movement (UMP) (May 2007–May 2012);
	François Hollande, Socialist Party (PS) (May 2012–)
Head of government	François Fillon, Union for a Popular Movement (UMP) (May 2007–May 2012);
	Jean-Marc Ayrault, Socialist Party (PS) (May 2012–March 2014);
	Manuel Valls, Socialist Party (PS) (March 2014–)
Political majority	Union for a Popular Movement (UMP) (May 2007–May 2012);
	Socialist Party (PS) Europe, Ecologie Les Verts (EELV), Left Radical Party (PRG) Coalition Government (May 2012)
Currency	Euro (€) since 1999
Prohead GDP in PPS	32,200 €

Source: Eurostat, 2013, 2014, http://epp.eurostat.ec.europa.eu/.

1 Geographical position

France is the largest Member State in the EU, stretching from the North Sea to the Mediterranean. Bordered to the north and east by Belgium, Luxembourg, Germany, Switzerland, and Italy and to the south by Spain, it is at once an Atlantic, continental, and Mediterranean country. Apart from its metropolitan territory, France covers over 120,000 square kilometres, at tropical as well as polar latitudes and is divided administratively into 26 regions, 99 departments, and 36,681 municipalities.

2 Historical background

France is one of the oldest nation-states in Europe. The 1789 Revolution marked a milestone in the history of the whole continent, beginning an era of political turmoil. Less than a century following the abolition of the monarchy, France experienced more than ten different political regimes, including several republics, the Napoleonic adventure, as well as the return of the monarchy and the Second Empire. It was only with the Third Republic, which lasted from 1875 to 1940, that the representative form of government was durably entrenched.

In the first half of the twentieth century, France was deeply affected by the two world wars, suffering agonizing losses at Verdun in 1916 and enduring the trauma of Nazi occupation from 1940 to 1944. The Fourth Republic, established in 1946, was characterized by its very high level of instability and ministerial turnover. Nevertheless, it succeeded in launching significant modernization programmes and was instrumental in the foundation of the European Coal and Steel Community in 1951. However, it stumbled against the challenge of decolonization. The defeat of the French army at the Battle of Dien Bien Phu in 1954 led to the loss of Indochina in the same year. Only months later, the country faced a new uprising in Algeria, then home to more than one million European settlers. The debate on whether or not to keep control of Algeria overwhelmed the country and nearly led to a civil war, marking the end of the fragile Fourth Republic and paving the way to the Fifth Republic in 1958.

3 Geopolitical profile

General Charles de Gaulle, the founder of the Fifth Republic, was especially eager to re-establish France's international status and authority. He brought to an end the Algerian War by granting independence to the former colony in 1962, although he had initially supported French rule. De Gaulle oversaw the development of national atomic weapons and promoted a foreign policy outside the US sphere of influence. In 1966, whilst remaining a member of NATO, France's armed forces were removed from the integrated military command. The President, who was a fierce defender of an intergovernmental Europe, vetoed the entry of the United Kingdom into the European Community, accusing the UK of being a Trojan Horse for the United States.

President Georges Pompidou agreed on British membership in 1969, opening a new era for French foreign policy which was later pursued by his successors, Valéry Giscard d'Estaing, François Mitterrand, and Jacques Chirac. All of them adopted more pro-European stances yet proclaimed their attachment to de Gaulle's '*politique de grandeur*'.

Finally in 2009, under Nicolas Sarkozy's presidency, the return of France into NATO's integrated military command led to the normalization of French foreign policy.

In the 1950s, France promoted the European integration process by contributing to the setting-up of the European Coal and Steel Community, the European Economic Community, and the European Atomic Energy Community. Today, it hosts the Council of Europe and the European Parliament in Strasbourg. In addition, France has a permanent seat on the UN Security Council and is a member of the G8.

4 Overview of the political landscape

The current French Constitution dates back to 1958, although it has undergone several revisions since then. It sets out a semi-presidential regime, which ushers in a balance of power between the President, who is elected by direct popular vote for a five-year period, and the Parliament, which consists of the *Assemblée Nationale* (National Assembly), directly elected every five years, and the *Sénat* (Senate), whose members are chosen by an electoral college.

The President appoints the prime minister and a cabinet of around 30 members, which is accountable to the bicameral Parliament. Executive power is vested in the President, who embodies the most powerful head of state in Western Europe. His main tasks consist of 'presiding' over the Council of Ministers and, under specified circumstances, dismissing its members, accepting the prime minister's resignation, submitting a bill to a referendum, declaring emergency powers, and dissolving the National Assembly.

At the end of Jacques Chirac's presidency in 2007, the Conservative Nicolas Sarkozy took over for the following five years, winning over his Socialist opponent, Ségolène Royal. However, he lost against his Socialist rival, François Hollande, in May 2012.

On the eve of the 2009 Euro-election, the thirteenth National Assembly elected in June 2007 was ruled by Sarkozy's party, the *Union pour un Mouvement Populaire*, UMP (Union for a Popular Movement), which had retained its majority since 2002, despite losing some 40 seats to the Socialist Party.

5 Brief account of the political parties

The French political scene changed dramatically after the adoption of the 1958 Constitution inaugurating the Fifth Republic. A reference to political parties was introduced for the first time in the new fundamental law. During the first years of the Fifth Republic, an initially fragmented party system evolved into a bipolar system of two main blocs of parties on the centre-right and centre-left (Bréchon, 2011a). Each bloc comprises many parties that frequently split and merge. There were 295 parties officially registered in France in 2009. However, the number of effective parties is much smaller: 19 parties have elected representatives in the National Assembly, Senate, or European Parliament. Major political parties with nationwide support are discussed below.

The *Union pour un Mouvement Populaire*, UMP (Union for a Popular Movement), originally named the Union for a Presidential Majority, is a French right-wing, Conservative political party (Bréchon, 2011b). It was founded in 2002 from the merger of the Rally for the Republic (RPR) and a sizeable portion of the Union for French Democracy. The UMP is a member of the European People's Party and the International Democrat Union.

Table 4.2 List of political parties in France

Original name	Abbreviation	English translation
Parti Communiste Français	PCF	French Communist Party
Parti Radical de Gauche	PRG	Left Radical Party
Parti Socialiste	PS	Socialist Party
Mouvement Républicain et Citoyen	MRC	Citizen and Republican Movement
Parti de Gauche	PG	Left Party
Les Verts	Verts	The Greens
Mouvement Démocrate	MoDem	Democratic Movement
Le Nouveau Centre	NC	New Centre
Union pour un Mouvement Populaire	UMP	Union for a Popular Movement
Mouvement Pour la France	MPF	Movement for France
Front National	FN	National Front
La Gauche moderne	LGM	Modern Left
Citoyenneté Action Participation pour le 21ème siècle	CAP 21	Citizenship Action Participation for the 21st Century
Partitu di a Nazione Corsa	PNC	Party of the Corsican Nation
Parti Communiste Réunionnais	PCR	Communist Party of Réunion
Debout La République	DLR	Arise the Republic
Nouveau Parti Anticapitaliste	NPA	New Anticapitalist Party
Lutte Ouvrière	LO	Workers' Struggle
Chasse, Pêche, Nature, Traditions	CPNT	Hunting, Fishing, Nature, and Traditions

The *Mouvement démocrate*, MoDem (Democratic Movement) was founded in 2007 by the part of the UDF that had opposed the merger with the RPR in 2002 and that maintained its hostility towards any automatic alignment with the UMP (Abrial, 2011). Under the leadership of François Bayrou, the party has maintained the usual centrist, liberal, and pro-European position of the former UDF. The MoDem is a founding member of the European Democrat Party.

Founded in 1905, the *Parti Socialiste*, PS (Socialist Party) was transformed in the early 1970s under the leadership of Francois Mitterrand, who instigated a coalition with the Communist Party (Bachelot, 2011). Their programme appealed not only to blue-collar workers, but also to middle-class voters who supported Socialist principles. The Socialist Party belongs to the Socialist International.

Founded in 1920 by the French section of the Workers' International, who supported the Bolshevik Revolution in Russia, the *Parti Communiste Français*, PCF (Communist Party) has remained true to its Marxist roots (Greffet, 2011). Until the 1970s, the PCF was a major force in French politics, although it never exercised significant government responsibilities. In the last two decades, the PCF suffered from competition from the FN (Front National) within its traditional working-class electorate.

Since 1974, the environmentalist movement has been a permanent feature of the French political landscape (Villalba, 2011). However, it was only in 1982, after the merger of the Ecologist Party with the Ecologist Confederation, that *Les Verts* (Greens) were established as a durable political party. Until 1994, the party maintained a position of non-alignment; afterwards, the Greens decided to adopt a markedly left-wing stance.

The *Front National*, FN (National Front) is a far-right party founded in 1972 by Jean-Marie Le Pen (Ivaldi, 2011). It remained relatively obscure until the 1980s, but it has gained growing electoral support. In the first round of the 2002 presidential election, Le Pen polled the second highest number of votes and contested Jacques Chirac in the second round. The party opposes immigration; it favours a return to traditional values, and is strongly opposed to European integration. It remains isolated on the political stage and cut off from office because the mainstream right-wing parties have effectively banned local and national deals with it.

On the eve of the 2009 Euro-election, the majority was dominated by the UMP founded in 2002 by Jacques Chirac as a merger of several centre-right parties, including the former Gaullist *Rassemblement pour la République*, RPR (Rally for the Republic) and the pro-European *Union pour la Democratie Française*, UDF (Union for French Democracy). As a member of the European People's Party (EPP), the UMP has evolved towards a globally pro-European approach. The party receives the support of several small pro-European parties, *Le Nouveau Centre*, NC (New Centre) and *La Gauche moderne*, GM (Modern left), as well as the implicit support of right-wing anti-European forces such as the *Mouvement pour la France*, MPF (Movement for France) or *Débout la République*, DLR (Arise the Republic).

In 2009, the Socialist Party, the first opposition party in terms of voters and MPs, had failed to prevail in a national election since 1997, but it had remained strong locally by controlling most French regions and departments. As member of the Party of European Socialists (PES) in the European Parliament, it had to cohabit with a myriad of political organizations that were both potential coalition partners and competitors.

The *Parti Communiste Français*, which had gone through an almost uninterrupted electoral decline since the 1960s, is a member of the European left. It was seriously challenged by the Greens as the main ally of the Socialist Party. A centrist party with a secular tradition, *Mouvement républicain et citoyen*, MRC (Citizen and Republican Movement) along with other small left-wing parties such as the *Parti Radical de Gauche*, PRG (Radical Left Party), and the *Parti de Gauche*, PG (Left Party), founded by the dissident Socialist Jean-Luc Mélenchon, complete the French political party picture on the left.

Other significant parties are the moderate and pro-European MoDem, a young party created after the 2007 presidential elections by UDF members who did not join the UMP, the anti-immigrant and anti-European *Front National* and two Trotskyite parties called the *Nouveau Parti Anticapitaliste*, NPA (New Anti-capitalist Party), which was formerly the *Ligue communiste révolutionnaire* (Communist Revolutionary League), and *Lutte Ouvrière*, LO (Workers' Struggle).

6 Public opinion and the European Union

Over the years, French public opinion has varied greatly on the benefits of EU membership. During the first half of the 1980s the positive response, that the European Union was 'a good thing', ranged from 48 to 58 per cent. This followed a period of Euro-optimism, with a peak of 74 per cent of positive responses in November 1987. The 1990s marked the end of the 'permissive consensus' on the EU. In 1992, the Maastricht Treaty was approved by just over 51 per cent of the voters in a referendum that was preceded by a highly disputed political campaign. Since 1991, negative responses on public opinion polls, where the EU is seen as 'a bad thing', have been consistently above 10 per cent and positive opinions range from 43 to 60 per cent.

According to the Spring 2009 Eurobarometer, 54 per cent of the French people thought that their country had benefitted from EU membership, whilst 34 per cent felt the opposite. On the other hand, the level of trust in the EU was declining, with negative opinions being the majority.

By June 2009, half of the French people thought that EU membership was a good thing, 17 per cent a bad thing, and 30 per cent neither a good nor a bad thing (Eurobarometer, 71).

7 National and EP electoral systems

Deputies to the National Assembly are elected by direct, universal suffrage using a uninominal majority system in two rounds (*Law no. 825*, 11 July 1986). There are 577 constituencies, and

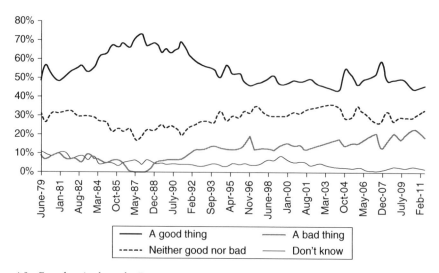

Figure 4.2 French attitude to the European Union

Source: Eurobarometer, http://ec.europa.eu/public_opinion/index_en.htm.

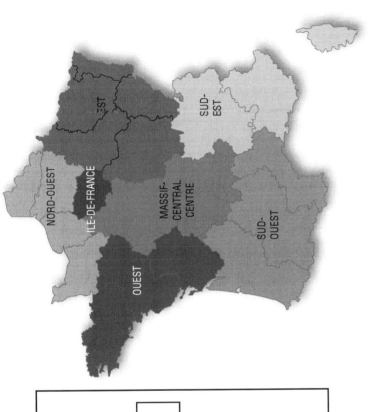
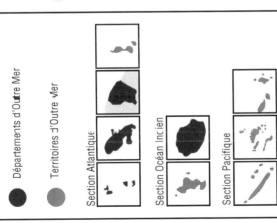

Figure 4.3 Map of EP electoral constituencies in France

more specifically 555 in metropolitan France and 22 overseas. The electoral procedure is a mixture of first-past-the-post and run-off systems. Candidates who obtain both an absolute majority of valid votes cast and a vote total equal to at least 25 per cent of all registered voters are elected in the first round. Otherwise, a run-off election is held amongst candidates polling a number of votes greater than or equal to 12.5 per cent of the electorate. If fewer than two candidates meet this requirement, the run-off is held between the top two candidates. In the second round, only a simple majority is needed to win.

The President is elected by direct universal suffrage via a two-round majority system (Articles 6-7 of the Constitution). If no candidate obtains an absolute majority on the first ballot, a second one takes place. Only the two candidates polling the greatest number of votes in the first ballot, after any withdrawal of better placed candidates, may stand in the second ballot. This ensures that the elected President always obtains an absolute majority of votes cast.

The EP electoral system differs completely from that generally relied upon for French national ballots. Since 1979, French MEPs have been elected with a party-list proportional system relying on the d'Hondt formula for the calculation and distribution of seats (*Law no. 729*, 7 July 1977). The lists are ordered with no preferential voting possible and electoral law imposes a minimum threshold of 5 per cent of the valid votes for a party list to participate in the distribution of EP seats. Several important changes were enforced for the first time in 2004 that also applied in the 2009 French Euro-election. As a consequence of French electoral law adopted in 2003, EP electoral districts were created to replace the historic single national constituency (*Law no. 327*, 11 April 2003). France is thus divided into eight so-called EP 'interregional constituencies' formed by the regrouping of metropolitan administrative regions and overseas territories.

Although the official rationale for this new organization was to allow MEPs to have closer contacts with their electors, its real aim was to reduce the scattering of votes and the dispersion of seats amongst small political forces. There are seven electoral districts for continental France, amongst which only the Ile-de-France corresponds to an administrative region. A special rule applies for the distribution of seats in the overseas constituencies: the three MEPs have to come from three represented geographic areas in the Pacific, Atlantic, and Indian Oceans. Globally, these constituencies have no other existence and identity than that of serving as electoral constituencies for the EP; they have failed almost completely to make the electorate more aware of their MEPs.

In 2004, other significant reforms were implemented for the first time, including the Law on Gender Parity requiring an equal presence of men and women on party lists that should put forward twice as many candidates as the number of seats to be filled. (*Law no. 493*, 6 June 2000).

After going from 87 MEPs to only 78 in 2004, the number of French MEPs was reduced again to 72 by the Treaty of Nice in order to accommodate the representatives of the new Member States. Subsequently, the Treaty of Lisbon, which entered into force only on 1 December 2009, established a new distribution of parliamentary seats amongst Member States, with France receiving two additional seats.

Anticipating that the Treaty of Lisbon would not be ratified before the EP elections of 7 June 2009, the European Council of 11 and 12 December 2008 decided that, in this event, the additional seats would be filled by the concerned countries during the course of the parliamentary term, without waiting for the 2014 EP elections. Whereas several countries announced in advance their chosen procedures to select the additional MEPs with a statute of observer, the French authorities did not make any specific provisions. At the time of the election, French voters were therefore completely uninformed on how these supplementary seats would be attributed. The problem was all the more complex since France is divided into eight electoral districts. Although contested by the opposition, an *ad hoc* law was voted on 26 May 2011, which established that the two additional MEPs would be chosen by the National Assembly from members within its own ranks. On 6 December 2011, Jean Roatta from UMP and Yves Cochet from the Greens were elected to represent France within the Strasbourg arena.

8 A glance at the EP and national elections

Over time, French politics has been characterized by a high level of instability which has influenced both European and national electoral outcomes. From 1978 to 2009, five presidential elections and seven legislative elections have taken place: with the exception of the 2007 election, all legislative elections resulted in the defeat of the incumbent majority.

The year 1981 marked a turning point in French political history, with the election of François Mitterrand as the first Socialist President. Mitterrand immediately used his prerogative to dissolve the National Assembly elected in 1978 to obtain a parliamentary majority. Nevertheless, the subsequent legislative election of 1986 did not confirm the victory of the Socialists, instead bringing to power a centre-right coalition of RPR and UDF parliamentarians led by Jacques Chirac. This victory led to the first period of 'cohabitation' between the President of one party and the government of another. Two years later, President Mitterrand's re-election once again caused an anticipated legislative election, which gave him only a relative and divided majority. The 1993 legislative electoral contest represented a harsh defeat for the left, which received only 31 per cent of the votes in the first round. This started the second period of 'cohabitation' between the Socialist President Mitterrand and the Conservative Prime Minister Edouard Balladur and preceded Chirac's election as President of the Republic in 1995. Two years later, Chirac dissolved the National Assembly in an attempt to give new momentum to his presidency. Contrary to his plans, the polls returned a majority from the left with a coalition made of Socialist, Communist, and Green MPs. This resulted in a five-year 'cohabitation' period between the Gaullist President Chirac and the Socialist Prime Minister Lionel Jospin. During the first round of the 2002 presidential election, Jospin was beaten by Chirac and, against all odds, by the extreme right-wing leader Jean-Marie Le Pen, this allowed

Table 4.3 National election results in France: 1978–2007

	1978	1981	1986	1988	1993	1997	2002	2007
Abstention ★	16.7	29.1	21.5	33.9	30.7	31.5	39.6	39.6
Blanked and spoiled ★	1.6	1.0	3.4	1.4	3.6	3.4	1.9	1.1
Extreme left	3.3	1.2	1.5	0.4	1.8	2.2	2.8	3.5
PCF	20.6	16.1	9.7	11.2	9.1	9.9	4.8	4.4
PS-MRG	24.9	37.4	31.6	37.5	19.0	25.7	25.6	26.4
Other left	1.4	0.9	1.2	—	1.1	2.0	2.3	1.4
Ecologists	2.0	1.1	1.2	0.3	11.1	6.4	4.5	4.1
Non-Gaullist right/UDF	19.6	20.4	41.8	18.8	20.1	14.9	5.3	7.7
Gaullists/RPR/UMP	22.8	21.2		19.2	19.8	16.5	33.3	43.5
Other right	4.3	1.3	2.7	2.5	4.2	4.4	4.8	2.2
Extreme right	0.7	0.3	10.0	9.9	12.9	15.4	12.7	4.8
Other	0.3	0.1	0.1	0.1	0.1	1.6	3.9	2.0
Total	100%	100%	100%	100%	100%	100%	100%	100%

Source: Ministère de l'Intérieur and Perrineau, 1997; Centre de Données Socio-Politiques (CDSP), 'Les élections en France', http://cdsp.sciences-po.fr/AE.php.

Note:
★ Percentage of registered voters.

Chirac to be re-elected with 82 per cent of the votes at the second round. The outgoing *gauche plurielle* majority was then defeated by the newly created UMP in the following parliamentary election, which opened a new phase of domination by the right, which received a large but reduced parliamentary majority in the National Assembly.

The instability of French politics can be also perceived through the outcomes of EP elections. The 1979 election was characterized by the good performance of both the Communist and Socialist parties, on the left, and the competition between the pro-European UDF and the Gaullist RPR within the governing centre-right coalition.

On the contrary, in 1984, the opposition was united and received 42.7 per cent of the votes, as compared to 32 per cent for the government parties. This electoral competition also saw the emergence of new political forces such as the National Front of Jean-Marie Le Pen, which received 11.1 per cent of the votes, and the Ecologists, which achieved 6.7 per cent of the votes. This result was confirmed and even strengthened five years later, when the National Front got 11.8 per cent and the Greens got 10.7 per cent. For the first time, the majority of voters were more concerned about European than national political issues when casting their ballot (Perrineau, 1989, 24). This phenomenon can be explained by the timing of the contest within the electoral cycle, which took place immediately after the French general election, and thus there were no direct national stakes. The Socialist list realized a disappointing result of 23.6 per cent of the vote, whilst the UDF-RPR list headed by former President Valéry Giscard d'Estaing was perceived as the real winner with a remarkable percentage of 28.7.

The dispersion of votes, which was already self-evident in the three first European elections, was even more accentuated in 1994. This vote, which followed the majority shift of 1993, confirmed the dynamism of the right whilst the Socialist Party realized its worst result ever, obtaining only 15.5 per cent of the vote. The party suffered badly from its direct rivalry with the '*Energie radicale*' list conducted by former minister and businessman Bernard Tapie,

Table 4.4 EP election results in France: 1979–2004

	1979	1984	1989	1994	1999	2004
Abstention ★	38.8	42.8	50.4	46.3	52.2	57.2
Blanked and spoiled ★	3.1	2.1	1.4	2.9	2.8	1.4
Extreme Left	3.1	3.7	2.0	2.7	5.2	3.3
PCF	20.6	11.2	7.7	6.9	6.8	5.2
PS-MRG	23.7	20.8	23.6	14.5	21.9	28.9
Other Left	—	—	—	16.2 ★★	1.0	—
Ecologists	4.5	6.7	10.7	5.0	11.3	7.4
Non-Gaullist Right/UDF	29.3	—	8.4	12.4	9.2	12.0
Gaullists/RPR	16.1	42.7 ★★★	28.7 ★★★	25.4 ★★★	12.5	16.6
Other Right	1.4	3.8	1.3	1.0	14.9	8.8
Extreme Right	1.3	11.1	11.8	10.9	9.1	9.8
Others	0	—	5.4	4.9	7.3	7.9
Total	100%	100%	100 %	100%	100%	100%

Source: Centre de Données Socio-Politiques (CDSP), 'Les élections en France', http://cdsp.sciences-po.fr/AE.php.

Notes:
★ Percentage of registered voters.
★★ Including MRG list conducted by Bernard Tapie.
★★★ RPR-UDF coalition.

Table 4.5 EP election abstention in France: 1979–2004

	1979	1984	1989	1994	1999	2004
Abstainers	13,823,571	15,961,916	19,606,804	18,452,817	21,364,521	23,765,992
Registered voters %	39.3	43.3	51.2	47.3	53.2	57.2

Source: Ministère de l'Intérieur and Perrineau, 1997; Centre de Données Socio-Politiques (CDSP), 'Les élections en France', http://cdsp.sciences-po.fr/AE.php.

who benefitted from Mitterrand's unofficial support and attracted 12 per cent of the vote. The Communists continued their inexorable electoral decline, confirmed at the national level, whilst the Greens toppled due to competition with the Radical list. The 1999 Euro-election saw an all-time record in abstentions of 52.2 per cent, despite a very large and diverse political offer.

Unsurprisingly, the government parties of the *'majorité plurielle'* received a smaller share of the votes compared to the previous legislative elections, equivalent to 21.9 per cent for the Socialist Party and 6.8 per cent for the Communists, but the divisions between right-wing parties had a very high cost, too. The RPR-DL list headed by Nicolas Sarkozy and Alain Madelin came second to the *Rassemblement pour la France et l'indépendance de l'Europe*, a coalition of dissident RPR leaders, including party founder Charles Pasqua, and Eurosceptic Conservative Philippe de Villiers. The extreme right suffered from a split within the National Front and the two competing lists totalled only 9.1 per cent of the votes as compared to 10.9 per cent in 1994. The amazing performance of the Hunting and Fishing list, which gathered 6.9 per cent of the votes, allowed this movement to send six representatives to Strasbourg. Finally, the successful results of pro-European parties, such as the UDF with its 9.2 per cent and the Greens with their 9.8 per cent, highlighted the *European* dimension of the EP contest in France.

9 The 2009 European elections

All in all, the themes that emerged during the campaign were not sufficient to fuel any genuine debate or controversy that could have captured the attention of the larger public. In a country where politics is dominated by the executive, it is difficult to fight an electoral campaign on the composition of the parliament and not the government. The only opportunity to raise an interesting debate on Europe on the public broadcasting Channel France 2, three days before the election on Thursday 4 June, was spoiled by personal rivalries. The programme ended up devolving into an exchange of insults and accusations between the leaders of the eight most important parties, most notably Xavier Bertrand from UMP, Martine Aubry from the PS, François Bayrou from MoDem, Daniel Cohn-Bendit from *Europe Ecologie*, Jean-Luc Mélenchon from *Front de Gauche*, Olivier Besancenot from NPA, Philippe de Villiers from MPF, and Marine Le Pen from FN.

9.1 Party lists and manifestos

By the deadline of 22 May 2009, 160 lists were officially registered, nine less than in 2004 and an average of 20 lists per constituency with a maximum of 27 lists in Ile-de-France and a minimum of 11 overseas. The decision to establish an autonomous list or to form an electoral coalition resulted from a combination of ideological and strategic considerations.

The Greens were the first to elaborate their strategy for the EP elections. During the summer of 2008, incumbent MEP Daniel Cohn-Bendit, who had been elected in France in 1999 and in

Germany in 2004, offered to form a large coalition of environmentalists and activists from beyond the traditional remit of the Green Party (*Les Verts*). Considering the disappointing percentage of 1.57 reached by the Green politician Dominique Voynet at the 2007 presidential election, his proposal was accepted by the party's congress in September 2008. Under Cohn-Bendit's leadership, the *Europe Ecologie* lists thus gathered traditional party militants and non-professional politicians, such as former head of Greenpeace France Yannick Jadot, anti-globalization activist José Bové, and anti-corruption judge Eva Joly. By doing this, the Ecologists managed to overcome the divisions between supporters and opponents to the European Constitutional Treaty, which had plagued the party since 2005. The main objective of *Europe Ecologie,* an ecological and social transformation of Europe, represented a radical version of the *Green New Deal for Europe*, which was promoted by the European Green Party but initially rejected, because of its moderate character, by the French Greens in January 2009.

Due to inner divisions in Europe following the 2005 referendum, and after the 2007 electoral defeat, the Socialist Party appeared to have lost its momentum under a rather weak leadership. The great number of incumbent Socialist MEPs, the conflicting interests of the various factions, and the low expectations for this election made the selection of candidates really difficult. According to internal rules, the lists drafted by the party leadership in Paris had to be ratified by local party activists in each electoral district. Following the negative vote of the activists, the candidate list in the Centre district was reshuffled and eventually 19 out of 31 incumbent members were reselected, with six as chief candidates. The electoral programme of the French Socialists, which was greatly inspired by the manifesto adopted by the Party of European Socialist in December 2008, called for an ambitious European recovery plan and for a European social progress pact, by emphasizing the need for tax harmonization and an increase in the EU budget. This in part reflected the new, more pro-European stance of the party in accordance with its fifth declaration of principles adopted in 2008.

Further to the left, the Communist Party and the Left Party formed an electoral coalition called the *Front de Gauche*. Under the motto '*Pour changer d'Europe*' ('To change Europe'), their two most emblematic proposals were to establish a European minimum wage and to prevent redundancies in profit-making enterprises. As for the two small Trotskyite formations *Lutte ouvrière* and *Nouveau Parti Anticapitaliste* (NPA), which had joined their forces in 1999 and 2004 but failed to gain seats in the latter election, they presented separate lists in the seven metropolitan constituencies.

The EP elections were seen as an important test for MoDem. The lists, reserved a large number of places for well-known civil society activists, such as the journalist Jean-François Kahn and the President of the European Movement France Sylvie Goulard, as well as independent politicians, such as former Environment Minister Corinne Lepage and former Green national leader Jean-Luc Bennahmias. The MoDem programme focussed on the economic crisis, agriculture, territorial policy, social issues, sustainable development, and the external policy of the EU. Like other French mainstream parties, MoDem wanted the EU to play a greater role in solving the financial and economic crisis. In institutional terms, it adopted the traditional pro-European stance of the French centrists by pleading for public consultations three months ahead of all important EU decisions, the establishment of a European military headquarters, and the creation of a European carbon tax.

On the right, the ruling majority formed coalition lists, bringing together the UMP and small satellite parties, such as *Nouveau Centre* and *Gauche moderne* as well as the Progressives of the Socialist defector Eric Besson. Although the lists were decided in a centralized fashion under the direct authority of Nicolas Sarkozy, it proved difficult to satisfy the contradictory interests of coalition partners and to attract high profile candidates such as Justice Minister Rachida Dati, who had publicly expressed her lack of interest. The UMP was the last important party to announce its lists of candidates and its electoral programme on 7 May, just one month ahead of the election. The government majority tried to take advantage of the media profile of its main national leaders. Finally, several ministers agreed to stand as MEP candidates, including Minister of Agriculture and former European Commissioner Michel Barnier, who stood as the chief candidate for Ile-de-France and national coordinator of the UMP campaign, Minister of Interior Brice Hortefeux, as well as the reluctant Rachida Dati.

President Sarkozy and German Chancellor Angela Merkel published an article entitled 'For a Europe that protects', which became the catchphrase of the UMP during the campaign (*Le Journal du Dimanche* and *Die Welt*, 31 May 2009). Based on the idea that Europe should learn from the French, the UMP raised three major electoral issues: the fight against illegal immigration and insecurity, repeated hostility to Turkish enlargement, and opposition to tax increases.

The establishment of party lists was also a source of tension and division within the National Front. The rise to power of Marine Le Pen, daughter of the historical party leader, met some strong resistance from other party figures. In the North-West district incumbent MEP Carl Lang refused to stand second on the list and thus established his own competing list. The same happened in the South-West district, where incumbent MEP Jean-Claude Martinez presented his own list against the official party list headed by one of Marine Le Pen's close assistants. In the National Front's programme, priority was given to 'economic patriotism' and the 'return of nations' as the most efficient responses to the economic crisis. In contrast to the UMP, the party of Jean-Marie Le Pen reiterated its opposition to any additional transfer of competence to EU institutions, especially in the fields of immigration and defence.

Hostility to European integration was the main convergence point between *Chasse Pêche Nature et Tradition*, CPNT (Hunting, Fishing, Nature and Traditions) and the *Mouvement pour la France*, MPF (Movement for France) of incumbent MEP Philippe de Villiers. However, it was more certainly the regionalization of the electoral system that forced these two parties to ally after the failure of CPNT to renew its success of 1999 at the 2004 EP elections. Paradoxically, MPF-CPNT was the only French party to clearly mention its pan-European affiliation due to the financial support of *Libertas*, the pan-European political party founded by the Irish businessman Declan Ganley and well-known advocate of the 'No' vote for the Irish referendum on the Lisbon Treaty held on 12 June 2008. During the campaign, the CPNT-MPF candidates hammered their traditional anti-elite, anti-establishment rhetoric. They presented themselves as the defenders of national traditions and territories against the prospect of Turkish membership and pleaded for some degree of trade protectionism.

One other striking feature of the pre-electoral period was the personalization around national figures, despite the fact that lists are drafted at regional level. On several lists the name of the national leader appeared along with that of the party, most notably Olivier Besancenot for the NPA, Jean-Marie Le Pen for the National Front, François Bayrou for MoDem, Nicolas Dupont Aignan for *Debout la République*, Philippe de Villiers and Frédéric Nihous for *Libertas*, and Daniel Cohn-Bendit, Eva Joly and José Bové for *Europe Ecologie*. This proved that personal considerations were sometimes more important than political projects or even the past performance of incumbent MEPs.

9.2 Electoral campaign

The European Parliament Information Office in France organized a series of public debates and exhibitions that nevertheless remained unknown and invisible to the public at large. As a consequence, 76 per cent of voters declared on election day that they had not been interested in the electoral campaign (*Sondage TNS Sofres Logica*). This disinterest must be taken into consideration in explaining the electoral results.

During the campaign, media coverage of European themes was particularly weak. In the six months preceding the 2009 election, from January until June, the daily newspaper *Le Monde* published only 458 articles dealing with European issues, equivalent to a mere 3.06 per cent of the total number of articles, as compared to 647 articles, corresponding to 3.87 per cent, in the first half of 2004 and 1464 articles, equal to 7.06 per cent, in the first six months of 1999. More anecdotally, journalist Jean Quatremer pointed out the media's silence on comments made by Ségolène Royale, the Socialist candidate in the 2007 French presidential election, during a meeting on 27 May in which she discussed the 'United States of Europe'. By contrast, by devoting more time and column-inches on predicting a large number of absentee voters, the press could be deemed partially responsible for the lack of citizens' interest in the Euro-election (Martin, 2009, 739).

This media deficit was not rectified by the official information campaign, which is organized during each election in France to ensure that parties have fair access to media coverage. In 2009 each of the parties forming groups in the National Assembly or the Senate, and notably the UMP, PS, MoDem, PRG, PCF, and *Nouveau Centre*, was allowed 20 minutes on public television channels (France 2, France 3, France 4, France 5) and public radio channels (France Inter and RFI and RFO), whilst other lists of candidates were entitled only to three minutes and 32 seconds of public airtime. Although it is difficult to evaluate objectively, the benefit the candidates received from these programmes was probably limited by the fact that the programmes were rather static and the rules regarding the allocation of time between parties were absurd. As a matter of fact, all parties represented at the national level were entitled to public airtime even when not presenting candidates lists. On the contrary, parties with incumbent MEPs but no representative at the national level, such as the *Front National*, were treated on an equal footing with other smaller groupings.

Four years after the referendum on the European Constitutional Treaty, which was rejected by 54.6 per cent of French voters, and two years after the election of Nicolas Sarkozy as President and the subsequent victory of the UMP at the legislative elections, the 2009 EP contest was both a national test for the Conservative majority and an opportunity to evaluate the depth of the European cleavage. The referendum campaign on the Constitutional Treaty had seen a rare popular mobilization around European affairs and intensive media coverage. This contrasted firmly with the idea that ordinary citizens were not interested in European and international questions.

On paper, at least, European issues were high on the French political agenda at the beginning of 2009. The French presidency of the Council during the second half of 2008 was perceived as a remarkable success for French diplomacy and for President Sarkozy, who was credited with solving the Georgian crisis and for prompting a swift response to the financial crisis. The UMP majority was also quick to highlight that the adoption and ratification of the Lisbon Treaty constituted a great achievement for Sarkozy. The adoption of a new 'lighter' constitutional treaty was indeed one of Sarkozy's electoral promises in 2007, although he had remained unspecific about its content, as well as how to negotiate and ratify it. The French election allowed the deadlock on European institutional reform to be lifted and the Treaty of Lisbon, which superseded the Constitutional Treaty, was eventually signed on 28 October 2007. In France the decision to ratify the Treaty through parliamentary procedure rather than by referendum, which was done in the first half of 2008, received sharp criticism from Eurosceptics who sought to use it against the government during the European electoral campaign.

In 2009, however, domestic problems remained the most salient, due in particular to social unrest that was fuelled by growing unemployment, which attained a record rate of 9.1 per cent, and by unpopular government measures. Reforms of the judicial system, hospital management, and university professors' statutes generated the most vigorous resistance. In addition, the return of France to NATO's central command as well as new internet regulations (*Loi HADOPI*) generated some criticism from within the majority's own ranks. Workers' unions organized demonstrations on 29 January, 19 March, and 1 May 2009, which along with a 44-day general strike in the overseas territory of Guadeloupe manifested the level of discontent with the government's policies.

In this context, the EP electoral campaign remained generally apathetic in two senses: (1) it received limited media attention, and (2) most parties did not invest much energy in it. Although the parties' programmes featured some proposals that were clearly connected to European integration, the mainstream parties were distracted from the EP elections by power struggles. As a consequence of the late publication of the party lists, voters were little aware of the proximity of the election and the campaign really took off only a few weeks before the election. At the beginning of 2009, only 27 per cent of the French, as compared to 32 per cent for the rest of the EU, could rightly state that the EP elections would take place that year; what is more, only a minority of the interviewees, equivalent to 45 per cent, declared themselves interested in these elections (Eurobarometer, 71).

The official campaign was planned to begin on 25 May and to finish on 6 June, but the European elections were actually brought to the fore by a speech delivered by President Sarkozy in Nimes on 5 May. Although officially non-partisan the presidential address clearly aimed at helping the UMP in a mid-term contest that promised to be difficult for the presidential party. As already noted, the majority tried to capitalize on the supposed successes of the French presidency of the European Council in the second half of 2009. It also strove to put forward issues, such as security, which usually attract voters from the right (*Le Monde*, 13 April 2009). At the same time, however, the UMP was careful to distance itself from an increasingly unpopular president.

Several opposition parties wanted to use this contest as an opportunity for the voters to punish the President and his government. To give only one example '*Sanctionner Sarkozy*' ('Sanction Sarkozy') was one of the slogans of the Left Front. Yet, it would be wrong to consider that the pre-electoral period was exclusively dominated by national considerations. Hostility to President Sarkozy was explicitly connected to resistance to the renewal of European Commission President José Manuel Barroso's mandate, which appeared as one of the crucial points carried forward by the opposition. *Europe Ecologie* supported the 'Stop Barroso' internet campaign and so did the MoDem, despite some hesitation on the part of its European partners within the ELDR Group. As for the French Socialists, they campaigned for Poul Nyrup Rasmussen, the President of the PES, as an alternative to the Portuguese incumbent.

In other words, if national issues and personalities kept their prominence, there were more efforts to 'Europeanize' the campaign than had been the case in the previous elections. Key to this was the will of some opposition parties to propose alternatives to Barroso as the 'natural' candidate for another term as President of the European Commission. The French Socialist Party's proposal to designate Poul Nyrup Rasmussen was not shared by its allies in the United Kingdom, Spain, and Portugal, who instead openly supported Barroso. As to MoDem, it backed the former Belgian Prime Minister Guy Verhofstadt, who participated in a debate organized in Montpellier which did not receive much media attention.

Substantively, the French pre-electoral period was dominated by questions related to the need for better economic regulation, environmental protection, and potential enlargement of the EU to include Turkey (Belot and Pina, 2009). In an article published in *Le Monde* on 14 November 2008, the Socialist MEP and Chair of the EP's Committee on Economic and Monetary Affairs Pervenche Bérès criticized the weakness of the European response to the financial crisis and pointed out the responsibility of the European Commission. The Commission's proposal to permit blended rosé wine in Europe triggered some angry reactions from traditional wine producers and forced Agriculture Minister and Leader of the UMP campaign Michel Barnier to go back to the Commission to ask for the overturning of the very legislation he had previously backed. The controversy eventually came to a close when the European Commission announced on 8 June 2009 that it had abandoned its plans to allow European winemakers to make cheap rosé wine by mixing red and white wines together.

J. Navarro

On the other hand, the campaign was animated by controversies surrounding the ranking of incumbent MEPs according to their activities in the EP (*Le Monde*, 23 April 2009). A former parliamentary assistant in the EP launched a website (blog.parlorama.eu) which had to be closed down after receiving protests from MEPs (*Le Monde*, 26 April 2009).

9.3 Electoral results

Polls opened on Sunday 7 June, with the exception of overseas territories, where they were convened one day earlier. Voter abstention was once more the real 'winner' of the EP elections in France, with an all-time record of 59.4 per cent of citizens who did not cast their vote. This represented a two-point increase in the rate of abstention relative to the 2004 election and a 20-point increase relative to the first-round of the 2007 legislative election. However, 2.5 million more people voted in 2009 as compared to 2004. This reflects an exceptional increase in the number of registered voters in the year preceding the presidential and legislative elections of 2007.

Turnout was above average in the more rural constituencies of West, South-West, and Massif Central-Centre as well as in Ile-de-France, where the stakes were probably higher, whilst it was particularly weak in the overseas constituency attaining only 23 per cent. Beyond these geographical variations, social factors were amongst the most significant in explaining the level of participation, which was for instance particularly weak amongst the younger, low-waged, and less educated population. This sociological gap had a substantial impact on the electoral

Table 4.6 EP election results in France: 2004–2009

	2004			2009		
	Votes	Registered votes %	Votes %	Votes	Registered votes %	Votes %
Registered voters	41,518,225	—	—	44,282,823	—	—
Abstentions	23,754,576	57.2	—	26,290,662	59.4	—
Vote cast	17,763,649	42.8	—	17,992,161	40.6	—
Blank and spoilt ballot papers	594,968	1.4	3.4	773,547	1.8	4.3
Valid votes	17,168,681	41.4	96.7	17,218,614	38.9	95.7
National party	Votes	Valid votes %	Number of seats	Votes	Valid votes %	Number of seats
UMP	2,856,218	16.6	17	4,798,921	27.9	29
PS	4,960,426	28.9	31	2,837,674	16.5	14
Europe Ecologie	1,271,134	7.4	6	2,802,950	16.3	14
MoDem (UDF)	2,051,453	12.0	11	1,455,225	8.5	6
Front National	1,684,868	9.8	7	1,091,681	6.3	3
Front de Gauche (PCF)	900,293	5.2	2	1,041,755	6.0	4
NPA (LO-LCR)	571,550	3.3	0	840,713	4.9	0
MPF-CPNT (MPF)	1,516,645	8.8	3	826,269	4.8	1
Others	—	—	—	1,523,786	8.8	0
Total			78	17,218,974		72

Source: Centre de Données Socio-Politiques (CDSP), 'Les élections en France', http://cdsp.sciences-po.fr/AE.php.

outcomes, since it favoured the government majority and the Greens to the detriment of the extreme right and the extreme left.

Unsurprisingly, for such an election, votes were scattered between a large number of parties. Of the 160 officially registered lists, 67 reached the 3 per cent threshold of valid votes and were, therefore, entitled to public funding, confirming the victory of smaller and more marginal parties.

By contrast, the 2009 contest sanctioned the declining support for the two main parties, the UMP and the PS, which jointly totalled only 44.3 per cent of the votes as compared to 45.5 per cent in 2004 and 64.2 per cent for the first round of the 2007 legislative elections.

Nevertheless, it is necessary to point out that the UMP, despite being in government, was able to outperform its main rival, the Socialist Party, by gaining two million votes more than at the 2004 Euro-election, reaching 27.9 per cent of the vote, and thus increasing the number of its representatives from 17 to 29.

Such a good outcome for the UMP must, however, be put into perspective, as it remained significantly worse than the result it had achieved at the first round of the presidential election and at the 2007 legislative election. It also should be kept in mind that the UMP significantly underperformed in the 2004 EP election, where it won the equivalent of only 16.6 per cent of the vote.

As for the Socialists, regardless of their status as the largest opposition party in France, they did not benefit from the 2009 mid-term election, by receiving only 2,837,674 votes – equivalent to 16.5 per cent – and thus losing 17 of the 31 seats they had held previously. This was largely due to the fierce competition posed by the Greens, whose performance went beyond any expectations, exceeding by far the initial objective set by Daniel Cohn-Bendit at the beginning of the campaign – to win a 10 per cent share of the vote (*Le Monde*, 20 October 2008). In particular, the Greens were particularly successful in the Ile-de-France and the South-East areas, where they outperformed the Socialists. With its 2,802,950 votes nationwide, corresponding to 16.3 per cent of the vote, *Europe Ecologie* doubled its electoral score of 2004, by almost obtaining the same results as the Socialists, and managed to send 14 MEPs to Strasbourg.

MoDem came in fourth place with a disappointing 8.4 per cent of ballots cast, far below the ambitions of its national leader François Bayrou, who had received 18.6 per cent of the vote in the first round of the 2007 presidential election. This result, however, represented an increase in comparison to the previous legislative election, where MoDem candidates gathered only 7.6 per cent of the vote, allowing the party to return six representatives to Strasbourg, despite the defection of several of its incumbent MEPs to the UMP.

This Euro-election proved particularly harsh for those parties that had opposed the ratification of the Constitutional Treaty in 2005. It notably saw an under performance on the part of the *Front National*, a party that achieved better results at the EP election rather than in the national election. Its voting share dropped by almost three-and-a-half percentage points, from 9.8 to 6.3, with a loss of 4 of its 7 seats previously held up to 2009.

As to the MPF-CPNT coalition, it barely reached 4.8 per cent with a loss of 3.6 per cent of the combined votes attained by MPF and CPNT at the 2004 Euro-election.

As such, only the seat for Philippe de Villiers could be secured in Strasbourg, inexorably marking the decline of the French sovereignty movement. The results were slightly better for the far left and, in particular for the *Front de Gauche*, which got 6.0 per cent of the votes and 3 seats, doing better than the Communist Party in 2004 when it obtained only 5.2 per cent and 2 seats. The extreme left also improved its score with the NPA by achieving 4.9 per cent in 2009 as compared to 3.3 per cent of the LO-LCR coalition in 2004, but remained unable to get a seat. The rest of the votes were spread out between other smaller parties such as the Independent Ecological Alliance, *Debout la République*, and *Lutte Ouvrière*.

Table 4.7 EP election results by constituency in France: 2009

Political party	Chief candidate	Votes (%)	Seats
North–West	18 lists 6,568,936 registered voters	Turnout: 39.8 %	
UMP	Dominique Riquet	24.2	4
PS	Gilles Pargneaux	18.1	2
Europe Ecologie	Hélène Flautre★	12.1	1
MoDem	Corinne Lepage	8.7	1
Front National	Marine Le Pen★	10.2	1
Front de Gauche	Jacky Hénin★	6.8	1
NPA	Christine Poupin	5.8	0
MPF-CPNT	Frédéric Nihous	4.3	0
West	20 lists	Turnout: 42.4%	
	6,177,375 registered voters		
UMP	Christophe Béchu	27.2	3
PS	Bernadette Vergnaud★	17.3	2
Europe Ecologie	Yannick Jadot	16.7	2
MoDem	Sylvie Goulard	8.5	1
Front National	Brigitte Neveux	3.1	0
Front de Gauche	Jacques Généreux	4.6	0
Libertas	Philippe de Villiers★	10.3	1
NPA	Laurence de Bouard	5.1	0
East	19 lists	Turnout: 39.1%	
	5,854,577 registered voters		
UMP	Joseph Daul★	29.2	4
PS	Catherine Trautmann★	17.2	2
Europe Ecologie	Sandrine Belier	14.3	1
MoDem	Jean-François Kahn	9.4	1
Front National	Bruno Gollnisch★★	7.6	1
Front de Gauche	Hélène Franco	3.9	0
MPF-CPNT	Christophe Beaudouin	4.1	0
NPA	Yvan Zimmermann	5.6	0
South–West	24 lists	Turnout: 44.5%	
	6,200,794 registered voters		
UMP	Dominique Baudis	26.9	4
PS	Kader Arif★	17.7	2
Europe Ecologie	José Bové	15.8	2
MoDem	Robert Rochefort	8.6	1
Front National	Louis Aliot	5.9	0
Front de Gauche	Jean-Luc Mélenchon	8.2	1
MPF-CPNT	Eddie Puyjalon	3.1	0
NPA	Myriam Martin	5.6	0
South–East	21 lists	Turnout: 39.6%	
	7,679,850 registered voters		
UMP	Françoise Grossetête★	29.3	5
PS	Vincent Peillon★★	14.5	2
Europe Ecologie	Michèle Rivasi	18.3	3
MoDem	Jean-Luc Bennahmias★	7.4	1
Front National	Jean-Marie Le Pen★	8.5	1
Front de Gauche	Marie-Christine Vergiat	5.9	1
MPF-CPNT	Patrick Louis★	4.3	0
NPA	Raoul Jennar	4.3	0

Massif-Central	20 lists	Turnout: 42.6%	
Centre	3,342,417 registered voters		
UMP	Jean-Pierre Audy★	28.5	3
PS	Henri Weber★★	17.8	1
Europe Ecologie	Jean-Paul Besset	13.6	1
MoDem	Jean-Marie Beaupuy★★	8.2	0
Front National	Patrick Bourson	5.1	0
Front de Gauche	Marie-France Beaufils	8.1	0
MPF-CPNT	Véronique Goncalves	4.9	0
NPA	Christian Nguyen	5.5	0
Ile-de-France	27 lists	Turnout: 42.1%	
	6,823,189 registered voters		
UMP	Michel Barnier	29.6	5
PS	Harlem Désir★	13.6	2
Europe Ecologie	Daniel Cohn-Bendit★★★	20.9	4
MoDem	Marielle de Sarnez★	8.5	1
Front National	Jean-Michel Dubois	4.4	0
Front de Gauche	Patrick Le Hyaric	6.3	1
MPF-CPNT	Jérôme Rivière	3.3	0
NPA	Omar Slaouti	3.5	0
Outre-Mer	11 lists	Turnout: 23%	
	1,635,705 registered voters		
UMP	Marie-Luce Penchard	29.7	1
PS	Ericka Bareigts	20.3	1
Europe Ecologie	Harry Durimel	16.2	0
Outre-Mer solidaire (MoDem)	Gino Ponin-Ballom	9.3	0
Alliance des Outre-Mers (Front de Gauche)	Elie Hoarau	21	1
MPF-CPNT	Erika Kuttner-Perreau	2.9	0

Source: Centre de Données Socio-Politiques (CDSP), 'Les élections en France', http://cdsp.sciences-po.fr/AE.php.

Notes:
★ Incumbent.
★★ Incumbent from different constituency.
★★★ Incumbent from another country.

At the 2009 Euro-election, only 30 incumbent French MEPs, representing 41.7 per cent of the new delegation, were re-elected. With its rate of incumbent re-election below the European average of 49.6 per cent, France ranked nineteenth amongst all EU delegations in returning incumbents. However, in the new parliamentary arena, French MEPs were slightly less dispersed across party groups, with the first four parties totalling 87.5 per cent of the seats, as compared to 83.3 per cent achieved before.

Finally, the French delegation was one of the most gender balanced, sending 33 women out of a total of 72 French MEPs, equivalent to 46 per cent of the delegation, to Strasbourg, a result just behind that achieved by the three Scandinavian countries of Finland, Sweden, and Denmark. This was clearly a consequence of the French law on parity, which requires political parties to alternate men and women on their candidate lists.

Although it is a practice that is now in decline compared to the past, the presence of politicians who simultaneously hold a local elected office along with an EP seat is another peculiarity

Table 4.8 List of French MEPs: seventh legislature

Surname	Name	Gender	Year of birth	Professional background	National party	Political group	First election	Committee/Chair
Constituency 1								
Bélier	Sandrine	Female	1973	Environment activist	Greens	Greens	2009	ENVI
Danjean	Arnaud	Male	1971	Civil servant – French Ministry of Defence	UMP	EPP	2009	SEDE (Chair)
Daul	Joseph	Male	1947	Farmer	UMP	EPP	1999	na
Gollnisch	Bruno	Male	1950	Lawyer and university professor	FN	NA	1989	TRAN
Griesbeck	Nathalie	Female	1956	University lecturer	MoDem	ALDE	2004	LIBE
Hoang-Ngoc	Liêm	Male	1964	CNRS research fellow	PS	S&D	2009	ECO
Mathieu	Véronique	Female	1955	Dental assistant	UMP	EPP	1999	LIBE
Striffler	Michèle	Female	1957	Sales officer	Modern left	EPP	2009	DEVE (Vice-Chair)
Trautmann	Catherine	Female	1951	Politician	PS	S&D	1989	PECH
Constituency 2								
Berès	Pervenche	Female	1957	Administrator at the National Assembly	PS	S&D	1994	EMPL (Chair)
Canfin	Pascal	Male	1974	Journalist	Greens	Greens	2009	ECO
Cavada	Jean-Marie	Male	1940	Journalist	NC	EPP	2004	CULT
Cohn-Bendit	Daniel	Male	1945	Political activist	Greens	Greens	1994	BUDG
Dati	Rachida	Female	1965	Accountant	UMP	EPP	2009	ECO
de Sarnez	Marielle	Female	1951	Parliamentary assistant	MoDem	ALDE	1999	INTA
Delli	Karima	Female	1979	Parliamentary assistant	Greens	Greens	2009	EMPL
Désir	Harlem	Male	1957	Political activist	PS	S&D	1999	INTA
Gallo	Marielle	Female	1949	Lawyer	Modern left	EPP	2009	JURI
Joly	Eva	Female	1943	Magistrate	Greens	Greens	2009	DEVE (Chair)
Juvin	Philippe	Male	1964	Medical doctor	UMP	EPP	2009	IMCO
Le Grip	Constance	Female	1960	Parliamentary adviser	UMP	EPP	2009	CONSTI
Le Hyaric	Patrick	Male	1957	Parliamentary assistant	PCF	EUL/NGL	2009	EMPL
Constituency 3								
Auconie	Sophie	Female	1963	Civil servant	NC	EPP	2009	REGI
Audy	Jean-Pierre	Male	1952	Chartered accountant	UMP	EPP	2005	BUDG (Vice-Chair)
Besset	Jean-Paul	Male	1946	Journalist	Greens	Greens	2009	REGI
Soullie	Catherine	Female	1954	Politician	UMP	EPP	2009	ENVI
Weber	Henri	Male	1944	Politician	PS	S&D	2004	ITRE

Constituency 4

Boulland	Philippe	Male	1955	Medical doctor	UMP	EPP	2010	na
Flautre	Hélène	Female	1958	Mathematics professor	Greens	Greens	1999	LIBE
Gauzès	Jean-Paul	Male	1947	Senior civil servant	UMP	EPP	2004	ECO
Grelier	Estelle	Female	1974	Parliamentary assistant	PS	S&D	2009	BUDG
Hénin	Jacky	Male	1960	Shopkeeper	PCF	EUL/NGL	2004	ITRE
Le Pen	Marine	Female	1968	Lawyer	FN	NI	2004	EMPL
Lepage	Corinne	Female	1951	Lawyer	CAP21	ALDE	2009	ENVI (Vice-Chair)
Pargneaux	Gilles	Male	1957	Parliamentary assistant	PS	S&D	2009	ENVI
Riquet	Dominique	Male	1946	Senior hospital doctor	UMP	EPP	2009	BUDG
Saïfi	Tokia	Female	1959	Manager of non-profit organizations	UMP	EPP	1999	INTA

Constituency 5

Cadec	Alain	Male	1954	General insurance agent	UMP	EPP	2009	PECH (Vice-Chair)
de Villiers	Philippe	Male	1949	Senior civil servant	MPF	EFD	1994	DEVE
Goulard	Sylvie	Female	1964	Diplomat	MoDem	ALDE	2009	ECO
Jadot	Yannick	Male	1967	Environment activist	Greens	Greens	2009	INTA (Vice-Chair)
Kiil-Nielsen	Nicole	Female	1949	Senior education adviser	Greens	Greens	2009	AFET
Le Brun	Agnès	Female	1961	Secondary school teacher	UMP	EPP	2011	na
Le Foll	Stéphane	Male	1960	Economics teacher	PS	S&D	2004	AGRI
Morin-Chartier	Elisabeth	Female	1947	Secondary school teacher	UMP	EPP	2007	FEMM (Vice-Chair)
Vergnaud	Bernadette	Female	1950	Secondary school bursar	PS	S&D	2004	IMCO (Vice-Chair)

Constituency 6

Hoarau	Elie	Male	1938	CNRS senior researcher	PCR	EUL/NGL	2009	REGI
Ponga	Maurice	Male	1947	School teacher	UMP	EPP	2009	DEVE
Tirolien	Patrice	Male	1946	Secondary school teacher	PS	S&D	2009	DEVE

Constituency 7

Abad	Damien	Male	1980	Parliamentary assistant	UMP	EPP	2009	BUDG
Alfonsi	François	Male	1953	na	PNC	Greens	2009	REGI
Benarab-Attou	Malika	Female	1963	Civil servant	Greens	Greens	2009	CULT

(continued)

Table 4.8 (continued)

Surname	Name	Gender	Year of birth	Professional background	National party	Political group	First election	Committee/Chair
Bennahmias	Jean-Luc	Male	1954	Journalist	MoDem	ALDE	2004	EMPL
Dantin	Michel	Male	1960	Farmers' organization manager	UMP	EPP	2009	AGRI
Franco	Gaston	Male	1944	Director-General of the Nice Tourist Board	UMP	EPP	2009	ITRE
Grossetête	Françoise	Female	1946	University lecturer	UMP	EPP	1999	ENVI
Guillaume	Sylvie	Female	1962	Civil Servant	PS	S&D	2009	LIBE
Le Pen	Jean-Marie	Male	1928	Politician	FN	NI	1984	PECH
Peillon	Vincent	Male	1960	University lecturer	PS	S&D	2004	AFET
Rivasi	Michèle	Female	1953	Secondary school teacher	Greens	Greens	2009	ITRE
Vergiat	Marie-Christine	Female	1956	Parliamentary assistant	PCF	EUL/NGL	2009	CULT
Vlasto	Dominique	Female	1946	Management assistant	UMP	EPP	2000	TRAN
Constituency 8								
Arif	Kader	Male	1959	na	PS	S&D	2004	INTA
Baudis	Dominique	Male	1947	Journalist	UMP	EPP	1984	AFET (Vice-Chair)
Bové	José	Male	1953	Farmer	Greens	Greens	2009	AGRI (Vice-Chair)
Castex	Françoise	Female	1956	Adult and youth education adviser	PS	S&D	2004	JURI
de Veyrac	Christine	Female	1959	na	UMP	EPP	1999	TRAN
Grèze	Catherine	Female	1960	Sales officer	Greens	Greens	2009	DEVE
Lamassoure	Alain	Male	1944	Senior civil servant	UMP	EPP	1989	BUDG (Chair)
Mélenchon	Jean-Luc	Male	1951	Secondary school teacher	FG	EUL/NGL	2009	AFET (Vice-Chair)
Rochefort	Robert	Male	1955	Researcher	MoDem	ALDE	2009	IMCO
Sanchez-Schmid	Marie-Thérèse	Female	1957	Secondary school teacher	UMP	EPP	2009	CULT
Appointed by national assembly								
Roatta	Jean	Male	1941	Politician	UMP	EPP	2011	DEVE
Cochet	Yves	Male	1946	Environmentalist	Greens	Greens	2011	ENVI

Source: www.europarl.europa.eu/meps/en/search.html?country=FR.

Note:

★ List of committees: Foreign Affairs (AFET); Security and Defence (SEDE); Development (DEVE); International Trade (INTA); Budgets (BUDG); Economic and Monetary Affairs (ECO); Employment and Social Affairs (EMPL); Environment, Public Health and Food Safety (ENVI); Industry, Research and Energy (ITRE); Internal Market and Consumer Protection (IMCO); Transport and Tourism (TRAN); Regional Development (REGI); Agriculture and Rural Development (AGRI); Fisheries (PECH); Civil Liberties, Justice and Home Affairs (LIBE); Constitutional Affairs (AFCO); Women's Right and Gender Equality (FE).

of the French delegation. In fact, 35 French MEPs, nearly 50 per cent as compared to 61.5 per cent before the election, hold an additional office, mostly at the local level (Rozenberg, 2010). This reveals the lack of consideration and interest in the EP that many French politicians have. An extreme example of this disdainful attitude was given by the, then, Minister for Work Brice Hortefeux, who was elected to the EP but announced right after the EP election that he would not take up his seat in Strasbourg. Nevertheless, some of Hortefeux's colleagues such as Rachida Dati and Michel Barnier were more respectful of the voters and took their seats in Strasbourg, although the latter was rapidly nominated to become French Commissioner.

9.4 Campaign finance

On the whole, neither the parties nor the media succeeded in activating the electoral campaign. The total amount of expenses declared by the candidates without including the 'official campaign' was 33,011,746 euros, as compared to 33,045,065 euros declared in the previous election. Despite the fact that the legal spending ceiling was increased by 10 per cent from 1,150,000 to 1,265,000 euros, overall expenses including staffing, stationery, postage, and campaign communications therefore declined slightly.

10 Theoretical interpretation of Euro-elections

10.1 Second-Order Election theory

An analysis of EP elections in France since 1979 seems to support most of the hypotheses set within the Second-Order Election model. The abstention rate was systematically higher for European ballots than at the first round of the preceding national legislative elections, the difference ranging from approximately 12.5 per cent in 1984 and 1994, compared to legislative elections in 1981 and 1993 respectively, to 21 per cent in 1999 and 2004, compared to legislative elections in 1997 and 2002.

In addition, with the exception of 1994, voter turnout declined faster at the European rather than at national level. On the other hand, the timing of the Euro-elections in the national cycle did not produce the envisaged effect. Whereas turnout was expected to be lower if a European election was held shortly after a national election and higher in the build-up to a new national ballot, in the French case, the electoral timing accounted neither for the absolute abstention level nor for the difference with the previous national election (Magni Berton, 2008). Yet, it should be stressed that no European election was ever held in the year immediately prior to a national contest.

The greater dispersion of votes across parties in European elections than in national elections also finds evidence from the French data. For all seven European elections, the aggregate score of the three top parties was smaller than the aggregate score of the three top parties in national legislative elections.

Additionally, with the partial exception of the first direct Euro-election in 1979, the poor performance of government parties compared to the preceding legislative ballot also went in the direction predicted by the SOE model. This gap ranged from 3.25 percentage points in 1999 to 18.4 percentage points in 1984, whilst no 'honeymoon' effect could be discerned in the EP contests of 1989 and 1994 that came one year after a national legislative ballot and a shift in majority. The interpretation of the electoral outcome of 1979 is more debatable, since the government then was comprised only of UDF members, but enjoyed the external support of the RPR: the UDF gained 6.1 percentage points in 1979 as compared to 1978, but the aggregate score of the UDF and RPR was 0.2 percentage point lower in 1979 than in 1978.

Table 4.9 Comparison of EP and national election results in France: 1979–2004

EP election	Previous national election	Abstention differential	Score of government parties★	Total percentage of votes top 3 parties	FN★★	Greens★★★	Anti-European parties
1979	1978	20.4	6.1 (−0.2)	−5.0	1.3	na	
1984	1981	12.6	−18.4	−2.5	10.6	2.3	
1989	1988	15.6	−12.3	−8.3	2.0	10.2	CPNT (4.1%)
1994	1993	12.6	−13.9	−6.3	−1.9	−14.2	De Villiers + CPNT (16.3%)
1999	1997	21.2	−3.3	−6.1	−6.0	2.9	Pasqua/De Villiers + CPNT (19.8%)
2004	2002	21.7	−16.7	−11.3	−1.5	2.9	MPF + CPNT + RPF (11.6%)
2009	2007	19.8	−11.6	−11.2	2.2	13.0	Libertas + DLR (6.6%)

Source: Centre de Données Socio-Politiques (CDSP), 'Les élections en France', http://cdsp.sciences-po.fr/AE.php.

Notes:
★ Not including (and including) the RPR in 1979.
★★ PFN in 1979 (not standing in the preceding legislative election); FN+MNR in 1999.
★★★ No Green list in 1979; Verts + Génération écologie in 1994.

In sum, European elections were less mobilizing for the electorate than national elections, parties in government were sanctioned by the voters, and small parties performed better than larger ones. This, however, does not mean that European elections were entirely subordinated to national stakes.

10.2 Europe Salience theory

The French data offer limited evidence to support the hypotheses of the Europe Salience theory. Although European elections used to offer an excellent platform for *ad hoc* anti-European parties, which achieved their best electoral results in the 1990s, their success started to wane to the point that, by 2009, they seemed to have lost their appeal.

As to the hypothesis related to extreme parties, it can best be tested through the case of the extreme right-wing *Front National*, although Trotskyites also benefitted in European elections, notably in 1999. The comparative electoral results of the FN at national and European levels revealed that whilst EP elections represented a privileged moment for the party to emerge on the political stage, particularly in 1984, three out of seven Euro-elections in 1994, 1999, and 2004 have brought the party worse results than in the preceding national election.

These results can, nevertheless, be explained by the party's competition with successful right-wing anti-European lists. Finally, the Greens managed to improve their performance in all EP elections except for those in 1994; this was perhaps also due to divisions between the environmentalists at the ballot box.

Finally, with regard to the high level of voter abstention, it could be stated that this reflects neither the subordination of European elections to national considerations, nor voter hostility to the European project, but simply the 'cognitive deficit' of uninformed citizens (Muxel, 2009, 581).

References

Primary sources

Centre de Données Socio-Politiques (CDSP), 'Les élections en France', http://cdsp.sciences-po.fr/AE.php (accessed on 29 March 2011).
Eurobarometer (2009) *Standard Eurobarometer 71: Public Opinion in the European Union, Autumn 2009* Brussels, European Commission.
Eurobarometer (various) http://ec.europa.eu/public_opinion/index_en.htm (accessed on 29 September 2011).
European Parliament website, www.europarl.europa.eu/ (accessed on 13 December 2013).
Eurostat (2013, 2014) http://epp.eurostat.ec.europa.eu (accessed on 5 June 2015).
Loi N. 77-729 du 7 juillet 1977 relative à l'élection des représentants à l'Assemblée des 'communautés européennes, *Journal officiel de la République française*, 8 July 1977, 3579.
Loi N.86-825 du 11 juillet 1986 relative à l'élection des députés et autorisant le gouvernement à délimiter par ordonnance les circonscriptions électorales, *Journal officiel de la République française*, 12 July 1986, 8700.
Loi N. 2000-493 du 6 juin 2000 tendant à favoriser l'égal accès des femmes et des hommes aux mandats électoraux et fonctions électives, *Journal officiel de la République française*, 7 June 2000, 8560.
Loi N. 2003-327 du 11 avril 2003 relative à l'élection des conseillers régionaux et des représentants au Parlement européen ainsi qu'à l'aide publique aux partis politiques, *Journal officiel de la République française*, 12 April 2003, 6488.
Ministère de l'Intérieur (1997) Centre de Données Socio-Politiques (CDSP), 'Les élections en France', http://cdsp.sciences-po.fr/AE.php (accessed on 29 March 2011).
TNS Sofres Logica (2009) *Sondage Jour du vote Elections européennes 2009* (résultats détaillés), Paris.

Secondary sources

Abrial, S. (2011) 'Les partis au centre de l'échiquier', Bréchon, P. (ed.) *Les partis politiques français*, Paris, La documentation française, 77–102.
Bachelot, C. (2011) 'Le Parti socialiste, la longue marche de la présidentialisation', in Bréchon, P. (ed.) *Les partis politiques français*, Paris, La documentation française, 103–28.
Belot, C. and Pina, C. (2009) 'Des campagnes européennes non disputées et sous contraintes', *Revue Politique et Parlementaire*, 2052, 62-72.
Bréchon, P. (ed.) (2011a) *Les partis politiques français*, Paris, La documentation française.
Bréchon, P. (2011b) 'La droite, entre tradition gaulliste et recomposition unitaire', in Bréchon, P. (ed.) *Les partis politiques français*, Paris, La documentation française, 45–76.
Greffet, F. (2011) 'Le Parti communiste français : l'espoir du retour', in Bréchon, P. (ed.) *Les partis politiques français*, Paris, La documentation française, 155–80.
Ivaldi, G. (2011), 'Le Front national : sortir de l'isolement politique', in Bréchon, P. (ed.) *Les partis politiques français*, Paris, La documentation française, 17–44.
Journal du Dimanche (31 May 2009) Angel Merkel and Nicolas Sarkozy, 'Pour une Europe qui protège'.
Le Monde (20 October 2008) Besse Desmoulières, R., 'Cohn-Bendit veut un "green new deal"'.
Le Monde (13 April 2009) 'Les élections européennes menaces d'une abstention record'.
Le Monde (23 April 2009a) Ricard, P., 'L'activité des eurodéputés passée au crible avant les élections du 7 juin'.
Le Monde (26 April 2009b) Ricard, P., 'De nombreux eurodéputés contestent l'évaluation de leur assiduité'.
Magni Berton, R. (2008) 'Pourquoi les partis gouvernementaux perdent-ils les élections intermédiaires? Enquête Eurobaromètre 2004 et élections européennes', *Revue Française de Science Politique,* 58(4), 643–56.
Muxel, A. (2009) 'La participation électorale: un déficit inégalé', *Revue Internationale de Politique Comparée*, 16(4), 569–81.
Perrineau, P. (1997) 'Le premier tour des élections législatives de 1997', *Revue Française de Science Politique,* 47(3–4), 405–15.
Rozenberg, O. (2010) 'Peu de bruit pour beaucoup: les élections européennes de 2009 en France', *Annuaire Français des Relations Internationales*, XI, 417–34.
Villalba, B. (2011) 'La transmutation d'Europe Écologie-Les Verts', in Bréchon, P. (ed.) *Les partis politiques français*, Paris, La documentation française, 129–54.

5
GERMANY

Siegfried Schieder and José M. Magone

Figure 5.1 Map of Germany

Table 5.1 Germany profile

EU entry year	1952 ECSC; 1958 EEC and Euratom founding member
Schengen entry year	1985 original signatory
MEPs elected in 2009	99
MEPs under Lisbon Treaty	96
Capital	Berlin
Total area★	357,340 km^2
Population	80,767,463
	Ethnic minorities:
	• 60,000 Sorben and Wenden
	• 50,000 Danes
	• 12,000 Friesen
	• 70,000 Sinti and Roma
Population density★★	230.0/km^2
Median age of population	45.6
Political system	Federal Republic
Head of state	Horst Köhler, Christian Democratic Union (CDU) (July 2004–May 2010); Christian Wulff, Christian Democratic Union (CDU) (July 2010–Feb 2012); Joachim Gauck, Independent (March 2012–)
Head of government	Chancellor Angela Merkel, Christian Democratic Union (CDU) (November 2005–).
Political majority	Christian Democratic Union (CDU)/Christian Social Union of Bavaria (CSU) and Social Democratic Party of Germany (SPD) Grand Coalition (November 2005–October 2009); Christian Democratic Union (CDU)/Christian Social Union of Bavaria (CSU) and Free Democratic Party (FDP) Government Coalition (October 2009–December 2013); Christian Democratic Union (CDU)/Christian Social Union of Bavaria (CSU) and Social Democratic Party of Germany (SPD) Grand Coalition (December 2013–).
Currency	Euro (€) since 1999
Prohead GDP in PPS	35,200 €

Source: Eurostat, 2013, 2014, http://epp.eurostat.ec.europa.eu/.

Notes:
★ Total area including inland waters.
★★ Density: the ratio of the annual average population of a region to the land area of the region.

1 Geographical position

Germany is located in west central Europe, bordered by nine countries: Denmark, Poland, the Czech Republic, Austria, Switzerland, France, Luxembourg, Belgium, and the Netherlands. Its territory, the fourth largest in the European Union, stretches from the North Sea and the Baltic Sea in the north to the Alps in the south. Germany boasts the largest population amongst the EU Member States, with almost 82 million inhabitants, although this figure is declining faster than in other European countries due to the low birth rate (Eurostat, 2012).

There are four recognized ethnic or cultural minorities which enjoy special political rights under the *Grundgesetz* (Basic Law), the European Convention on Human Rights and the International Covenant on Civil and Political Rights: the Sorbian people in Brandenburg and Saxony, the Danish minority in Schleswig-Holstein, the Frisians in the northern part of the country, and the Sinti and Roma, estimated at about 70,000, mainly settled in the western part of the country and in Berlin (Federal Ministry of the Interior, 2010). Germany hosts about 6.6 million immigrants, corresponding to 8.2 per cent of the overall population concentrated in the Berlin, Hamburg, and Bremen areas, although it is worth underlining that the immigration flux has been stagnating and even declining over the last few years (*Statistisches Bundesamt*, 2013).

2 Historical background

The defeat of Germany in World War II and the subsequent occupation by the Allied Forces made the country vulnerable to the emerging East–West conflict, which started after 1947. The 'Cold War' inevitably led to the division between the Federal Republic of Germany (FRG), under the sphere of influence of the Western allies, and the German Democratic Republic (GDR), under Soviet control. This situation shaped the European foreign policy of the FRG until the fall of the *Berliner Mauer* (Berlin Wall) on 9 November 1989, which had been erected in 1961 by the GDR in order to prevent their citizens fleeing to the West. William Patterson has categorized the early years after the foundation of the FRG as 'pre-sovereign' due to the relevance of the occupying Allied Forces in West Germany (Paterson, 2005, 261). Only after the *Deutschlandvertrag* in 1955, did Germany gain what Peter Katzenstein defined as 'semi-sovereignty' given that the Cold War and the European integration process were major factors limiting the choices of the country (Katzenstein, 1987; Paterson, 2005, 261–5).

On 9 May 1950, under pressure from the United States, the French Foreign Minister Robert Schuman announced the establishment of the European Coal and Steel Community (ECSC), which envisaged reconciliation with West Germany as a key objective in order to realize the process of European integration. West Germany's status as a founding member of the European Community remained an important factor of the identity of the country (Clemens *et al.*, 2008, 97–108). The project also allowed the rebuilding of a new culture within the country, including the so-called 'politics of remembrance' aimed at confronting as well as overcoming the past (*Vergangenheitsbewältigung*). Although the German Constitution was seen as a sort of democratic re-education, it was by no means clear that the West German population was able to match its democratic aspirations (Almond and Verba, 1963). After the fall of the Berlin Wall in 1989, German reunification was deemed possible only within the European integration process, thus creating the conditions for the reunification of the European continent. Article 23 of the Basic Law states that:

> With a view to establishing a united Europe, the Federal Republic of Germany shall participate in the development of the European Union that is committed to democratic, social, and federal principles, to the rule of law, and to the principle of subsidiarity, and that guarantees a level of protection of basic rights essentially comparable to that afforded by this Basic Law. To this end the Federation may transfer sovereign powers by a law with the consent of the *Bundesrat*. The establishment of the European Union, as well as changes in its treaty foundations and comparable regulations that amend or supplement this Basic Law, or make such amendments or supplements possible, shall be subject to paragraphs (2) and (3) of Article 79.

3 Geopolitical profile

Defeat in World War II represented a major turning point for the foreign policy of Germany and its subsequent division into a Western Federal Republic and an Eastern Democratic Republic after 1949 was a traumatic experience. Until 1989, both were at the forefront of the Cold War between the United States and the Soviet Union. Whilst the former became a member of the North Atlantic Treaty Organization (NATO) in 1955, the latter joined the Warsaw Pact in 1956. Only after inter-German relations were normalized in the wake of the Basic Treaty of 1972, was the path opened for both German states to enter the United Nations on 18 September 1973.

The fall of the Berlin Wall leading up to reunification allowed the changing of the geopolitical position of the country. Although the new reunified Federal Republic of Germany was very keen to emphasize allegiance to NATO, the Soviet Union was no longer the common enemy after 1991. The reorientation of NATO and the upgrading of the European Union's Common Foreign and Security Policy led to a change in German foreign policy towards a peace policy approach (*Friedenspolitik*). Although German troops were deployed in Kosovo, Macedonia, Afghanistan, and Somalia, their main task was to restore and keep the peace. The self-confidence of German foreign policy became clear when, along with France, former Foreign Minister Joschka Fischer refused to take part in the invasion of Iraq that was proposed and then carried out by the US Bush Administration in 2003 with the 'coalition of the willing' yet without an explicit mandate from the UN Security Council. One of the main reasons for this disagreement stemmed from Germany's socialized and internalized policy of peace and multilateralism, which was widely supported by its population (Bulmahn et al., 2010). This attitude, in line with the mission and vocation of the United Nations, was also appreciated by Third World countries and emerging economies, because it upholds human rights and international law, and contributes to peaceful solutions within a global governance framework. The vigour of German foreign policy has been backed up by its strong economy, giving the country a strong say at the World Bank, the International Monetary Fund, and in the European Union (Guérot and Leonard, 2011, 2). Finally, Germany can be considered as the most prominent member of the euro-zone, thus bearing an enhanced responsibility towards its stability.

4 Overview of the political landscape

Germany is a Federal Republic comprised of 16 constituent states, the so-called *Bundesländer*. The Basic Law stipulates in great detail which issues fall within the competence of the federal government and which devolve to the regional states. Most policies are implemented by so-called 'executive federalism', which means that the federal level sets framework laws that are then implemented by the government of the *Bundesländer*. Although federalist elements dominate the states' administration, formulations such as 'unitarian' are used to characterize the German federal state (Hesse, 1962).

The President has only formal representative powers and is elected for a five-year period by a federal assembly consisting of the two chambers of parliament, the lower chamber, *Bundestag*, and the upper chamber, *Bundesrat*, along with selected representatives of society. The *Bundestag*, which represents a 'working parliament' (*Arbeitsparlament*) rather than a 'talking shop' (*Redeparlament*), is the central institution in the German political system. On the eve of the 2009 Euro-election, the President was Horst Köhler, later replaced by Christian Wulff in June 2010 and since 18 March 2012 by Joachim Gauck, a former GDR civil rights activist.

Federal power lies in the hands of the German Chancellor, who has been the Christian Democrat Angela Merkel since 2005. The federal government is accountable to the *Bundestag*, which can issue a motion of censure against it. In this case, however, the opposition has to find not only grounds for denying confidence to the executive, but also to nominate an alternative candidate to replace the Chancellor. The federal government has to take into account the rulings of the Federal Constitutional Court and change legislation accordingly. In the context of the European Union, constitutional complaints (*Verfassungsklagen*) about issues of sovereignty are addressed regularly at the German Federal Constitutional Court. Before the *Bundestag* and *Bundesrat* could finally approve the Lisbon Treaty, it was necessary to wait for the ruling of the Federal Constitutional Court (*Bundesverfassungsgericht*, 2009). Although Germany's highest court established that the treaty was not fundamentally incompatible with the German Basic Law, it called for a halt to the ratification process until the German Parliament changed domestic law to strengthen the role of the country's legislative bodies in implementing European Union laws. Finally, on 8 September 2009, after the court ruling and the parliamentary adjustment of legislation, the text of the Lisbon Treaty was approved (Müller-Graff, 2010).

5 Brief account of the political parties

Prior to 1983, the Federal Republic of Germany had only a two-and-a-half party system: the *Christlich Demokratische Union/Christlich-Soziale Union,* CDU/CSU (Christian Democratic Union/Christian Social Union), the *Sozialdemokratische Partei Deutschlands,* SPD (Social Democratic Party of Germany) and the *Freie Demokratische Partei,* FDP (Free Democratic Party). The negative perception of the very fragmented party system during the Weimar Republic and the consequences leading up to Nazi rule set a high value for political stability and moderation of party politics. The Basic Law introduced the principle of a preventive defence of democracy, should any anti-systemic extreme right-wing or left-wing political party try to enter the political stage. A body called 'Defence of the Constitution' (*Verfassungsschutz*) publishes regular reports on extreme parties and movements at federal and regional levels (Rudzio, 2006, 97).

On 13 January 1980, the foundation of *Die Grünen* (The Green Party) contributed towards the changing of the traditional political landscape. Emerging in the 1970s out of social movements, the Greens were critical of established politics and wanted a new orientation in terms of economic growth. In 1993, they merged with *Bündnis 90* (Alliance '90/The Green Party), consisting of three non-Communist political groups from former East Germany. Over two decades, the Greens gained an increasing popular consensus, winning at the regional level and entering a coalition government at the federal level together with the Social Democrats under Chancellor Gerhard Schröder between 1998 and 2005 (Viola, 2010).

After the fall of the Berlin Wall, a fifth party loomed on the political horizon, the *Partei des Demokratischen Sozialismus,* PDS (Party of Democratic Socialism), which was the direct heir to the former *Sozialistische Einheitspartei Deutschlands,* SED (Socialist Unity Party), the ruling party in East Germany that had changed its name in the last days of the GDR. Between 1990 and 2006, the party remained exclusively at the regional level and was particularly strong in the new *Bundesländer* of Mecklenburg-Vorpommern, Brandenburg, Thuringia, Saxony, Saxony-Anhalt, and Berlin whilst it was non-existent in the old *Bundesländer*.

In January 2005, a new party called *Arbeit und soziale Gerechtigkeit-Die Wahlalternative,* WASG (Labour and Social Justice-The Electoral Alternative) emerged, comprising of more radical trade union representatives unhappy with the SPD, and small extreme left parties along with members of the German Communist Party, under the leadership of former SPD President and former Minister of Finance, Oskar Lafontaine (Viola, 2010). One of the main grievances

Table 5.2 List of political parties in Germany

Original name	Abbreviation	English translation
Christlich Demokratische Union Deutschlands	CDU	Christian Democratic Union
Sozialdemokratische Partei Deutschlands	SPD	Social Democratic Party of Germany
Bündnis 90/Die Grünen	Grünen	Alliance '90/The Green Party
Freie Demokratische Partei	FDP	Free Democratic Party
Die Linke	Linke	Left Party
Christlich-Soziale Union in Bayern	CSU	Christian Social Union of Bavaria
Freie Wähler	FW	Free Voters
Die Republikaner	REP	The Republicans
Mensch-Umwelt-Tierschutz	MUT	Man, Environment, and Animal Protection
Familien-Partei Deutschlands	Familie	Family Party of Germany
Piratenpartei Deutschland	Piraten	German Pirate Party
Rentner Partei Deutschlands	RENTNER	Pensioners' Party of Germany
Ökologische-Demokratische Partei	ÖDP	Ecological Democratic Party
Deutsche Volksunion	DVU	German People's Union
Rentnerinnen Und Rentner Partei	RPP	Female and Male Pensioners' Party
Feministische Partei-Die Frauen	Die Frauen	Feminist Party – The Women
Partei Bibeltreuer Christen	PBC	Party of Bible-abiding Christians
Ab Jetzt ... Bündnis für Deutschland, für Demokratie durch Volksabstimmung		Association for Germany, for Democracy through Referenda from Now
Das Generationen-Bündnis 50 Plus	50 Plus	Alliance of Generations 50 Plus
Die Grauen-Generationspartei	Grauen	The Greys
Bayernpartei	BP	Bavaria Party
Die Violetten: für Spirituelle Politik	Violetten	The Violets: for Spiritual Policy
Für Volksentscheide Gerechtigkeit braucht Bürgerrechte – Wir Danken für Ihr Vertrauen!	Wählergemeinschaft	Justice Needs Citizens' Rights – Thanks for your Trust! For People's Decision-Making
Christliche Mitte: Für ein Deutschland nach Gottes Geboten	CM	Christian Centre: for a Germany according to God's Commandments
Partei für Arbeit, Umwelt und Familie, Christen für Deutschland	AUF	Party for Labour, Environment and Family Christians for Germany
Aufbruch für Bürgerrechte, Freiheit und Gesundheit	AUFBRUCH	New Beginning for Civil Rights, Freedom and Health
Freie Bürger Initiative	FBI	Free Citizens' Initiative
Deutsche Kommunistische Partei	DKP	German Communist Party
Europa-Demokratie-Esperanto	EDE	Europe-Democracy-Esperanto
Bürgerrechtsbewegung Solidarität	BüSo	Civic Rights Movement Solidarity
Partei der Sozialen Gleichheit-Sektion der Vierten Internationale	PSG	Party of Social Equality-Section of the Fourth International
Deutsche Partei	DP	The German Party
Kommunistische Partei Deutschlands	KPD	Communist Party of Germany
Nationaldemokratische Partei Deutschlands	NPD	National Democratic Party of Germany
Partei des Demokratischen Sozialismus	PDS	Party of Democratic Socialism
Arbeit und soziale Gerechtigkeit – Die Wahlalternative	WASG	Labour and Social Justice – The Electoral Alternative

was the introduction of labour market reforms called Hartz IV, but also Germany's military engagement in Afghanistan (Jesse and Lang, 2008, 75–81; Hough and Olsen, 2007). The charismatic former SPD politician Oskar Lafontaine, who also joined the WASG, contributed to the achievement of its official representation in regional and national Parliaments. In 2007, a merger between the PDS and the WASG led to the formation of a new political party, which briefly took the name of *Die Linke* (The Left).

This party became a major challenge for the left wing of the SPD. At the 2009 federal elections, the SPD had its worst result ever, declining from 34.2 per cent to 23 per cent, whilst *Die Linke* was able to improve from 8.7 to 11.9 per cent by becoming the fourth largest party in the *Bundestag*, even if it was still ostracized from national government. The party is still ostracized from national government politics.

According to Oskar Niedermayer, the two main conflict cleavages in the German party system are socio-economic and socio-cultural. The former is based on the growing divergence of views on the future of the welfare state and labour market reform. The latter is related to 'survival' materialist values versus 'self-expressive' post-materialist values (Niedermayer, 2007, 118). Traditional cleavages related to religion and class have eroded and a more volatile electorate has emerged, which is difficult for parties to encapsulate. This volatility also led to the considerable electoral decline of the two '*Volksparteien*', the CDU/CSU and the SPD (Saalfeld, 2005, 70).

5.1 Party attitudes towards the European Union

European integration has not been a major dividing line between German political parties. No general disagreement exists about the merits of a project that has been consistently supported by the political elite over the years (Schieder, 2011, 40–7; Bulmer and Paterson, 2010). All political parties can be considered more or less pro-European, even if there are some differences.

The CDU presents itself as the European party *par excellence* in Germany and its approach is moderate in all policy dimensions, although economic efficiency and competitiveness are quite central. In spite of this, the concept of a 'social market economy' based on economic competitiveness remains a crucial foundation. The CDU sets limits to EU enlargement by offering a 'privileged partnership' with Turkey. Its Bavarian sister party, the CSU, places more emphasis on the 'Europe of Fatherlands' discourse, like the Gaullists in France, and wants an upgrading of the subnational regions within the EU multilevel governance system. In its view, there should be not only geographical limits to EU enlargements, but also limits on the scope of European integration in terms of the transfer of powers to the supranational level.

By contrast, the SPD stresses the international role of the European Union, the need for coordination in employment policy and the strengthening of social Europe, whilst the FDP puts a greater emphasis on political and economic liberalism as well as the protection of civic and political rights. The Green Party highlights the EU's potential to take a leadership role in a new global ecological paradigm and the need for the European Union to become a force for peace, far from the war logic perpetuated by the United States. Finally, *Die Linke* wants a change of direction in the European Union, from neo-liberal to more socially friendly policies, with particular attention to gender equality issues.

6 Public opinion and the European Union

As already discussed, the origin of the FRG is intrinsically linked to the process of European integration (Anderson and Goodman, 1993). From its outset, the Germans have vigorously supported the European project, which represented an opportunity to regain their shattered identity in the eyes of the world after the catastrophic totalitarian period of the Third Reich (Schild, 2003, 32). The constellation of domestic and European developments set specific parameters for the symbiotic relationship between the FRG and Europe, so that the European integration design transformed the 'relationship between Germany and Europe to one of Germany in Europe' (Katzenstein, 1997, 19; Bulmer et al., 2000, 2010). All German parliamentary parties supported this Europeanized state identity, which regarded the EEC after 1958 as an emergent 'civil power', interested in shaping world politics towards multilateralism and peace (Maull, 1990). However, since the 1990s, such unconditional support has given way to a more sceptical agenda (Schieder, 2011, 34) and its strong European vocation 'is no longer securely anchored in public opinion' (Paterson, 2010, 41).

Although Germans have been in favour of EU membership for more than three decades, as shown in Figure 5.2, which refers to the Eurobarometer surveys between 1979 and 1989, after German reunification this position changed, especially in East Germany (Scheuer and Schmitt, 2009, 580). By the late 1990s, most people believed that EU membership had brought more disadvantages than advantages. Only in the new millennium did the perception that the EU was of benefit pick up again, particularly after 2005 (Eurobarometer, 2009). This was particularly the case under the leadership of Chancellor Merkel, when a considerable improvement in the economic situation was registered, with unemployment declining from five million to slightly above three million even during the financial crisis in 2008–2009.

However, an overall air of scepticism pervades the minds of the German public towards specific aspects of EU membership. Whilst support for a common security and defence policy and for a European Constitution are high and even above the EU average, the level of trust in the EU as a whole is below average, and EU enlargement is even rejected outright by the majority of the German public (Schieder, 2011, 36). Given the shift in German attitudes towards the EU, the political parties represented in the German parliament had incentives to exploit this scepticism in the public sphere. According to Andreas Wilkens, although support for European integration may decline in the short term, it is deemed to remain intact in the long term, being extremely connected to the identity of post-war Germany (Wilkens, 2004, 76).

7 National and EP electoral systems

After the adoption of the absolute-majority two round system (TRS) in the German Empire (*Kaiserreich*) between 1871 and 1918 and the negative experience of the pure proportional representation system in the Weimar Republic, the Parliamentary Council forged a new electoral system in 1949 as a result of inter-party bargaining between democratic forces in West Germany. Whereas originally it was considered to be provisional, this system has remained virtually unchanged.

In accordance with Article 38 of the Basic Law of the Federal Republic of Germany, the members of the *Bundestag* are elected with a general, direct, free, equal, and secret vote. Whilst these five principles of voting are laid out in the Basic Law, the Federal Electoral Act regulates the German electoral system for national elections. German elections follow what is commonly known as a personalized proportional system (*Personalisiertes Verhältniswahlrecht*) or as a mixed member proportional (MMP) system that combines a personal vote in single-member districts with the principle of proportional representation.

As the MMP system has not so far unveiled any great negative effects, it therefore enjoys a high level of institutionalized legitimacy in Germany. As a result, its basic rules have remained unaltered and just some minor changes have been introduced. Since 1953, a switch to a dual-vote system has occurred, allowing citizens to cast two ballots in order to choose their representatives

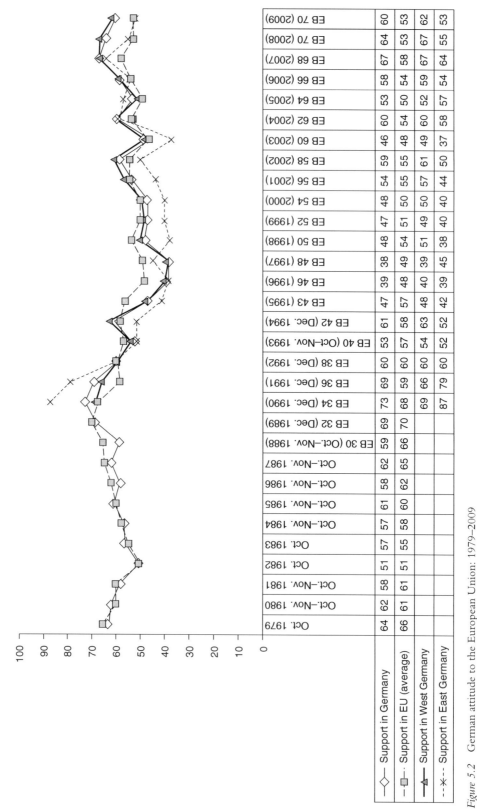

Figure 5.2 German attitude to the European Union: 1979–2009

Source: Eurobarometer (2011) http://ec.europa.eu/public_opinion/archives/eb_arch_en.htm

in Parliament. Whereas the first vote, *Erststimme*, is personal as it is conferred to a particular candidate in one of the nowadays 299 single-member constituencies, *Bundestagswahlkreise*, the second, *Zweitstimme,* is a party vote, awarded to an electoral list at the federal state level (*Landesliste*). This determines the relative strengths of the parties in the *Bundestag* and, more importantly, it may establish which parliamentary group or coalition of parties will reach the majority and, as a consequence, who will become Chancellor.

Moreover, a 5 per cent threshold for the election of members of Parliament was introduced in three constituencies in order to prevent the fragmentation of the party system, one of the major problems during the Weimar Republic. If a party fails to gain more than 5 per cent of all votes, it is not represented in the *Bundestag*, unless the party is able to win in at least three constituencies. Until 2009, the distribution of seats was calculated according to the so-called Hare-Niemeyer method, which reflects the strength of the smaller parties better than any others. Yet, since the *Bundestag* election in 2009, the so-called Sainte-Laguë/Schepers method has been introduced, whereby seats are distributed first amongst those candidates who gained more votes in the constituencies, whilst the remaining seats are then allocated to the candidates on the party list.

The number of constituency seats is crucial since it can affect the composition of the German *Bundestag*. If a party gains more constituency seats through the first vote than it is entitled according to its proportion of seats through the second vote, it nonetheless keeps these so-called 'overhang' seats (*Überhangmandate*). Hence, the *Bundestag* may exceed the number of 598 seats, such as after the 2009 general elections when it reached 622. It is worth mentioning that in July 2008, Germany's highest court ruled that the effect known as 'negative vote weight', arising in connection with 'overhang' mandates, is unconstitutional (Bundesverfassungsgericht, 2008).

The 99 German Members of the European Parliament are elected in a general, direct, free, equal, and secret ballot. The electoral system is proportional, with 'closed' lists of nominated candidates, meaning that voters do not have influence on the choice of candidates. Whilst in the past the Hare-Niemeyer method was used with a 5 per cent legal threshold, since 2009 the Sainte-Laguë/Schepers method has been introduced in Germany, allowing a high level of proportionality. Political parties can submit either a federal list or lists at the level of the *Bundesländer*. All parties field national lists, with the exception of the Christian Democrats (CDU) and the Bavarian Christian Socials (CSU). Whilst the latter present their list only in Bavaria, where their constituency is concentrated, the Christian Democrats do it in all other *Bundesländer*. There is only one national electoral district for these elections, and in order to avoid fragmentation of the party system and to reduce the chances of extreme parties, a 5 per cent threshold was imposed, as in the case of the general elections. This clause, however, was held to be unconstitutional in November 2011 by the Federal Constitutional Court, which argued that it violates the principle of equal opportunities for all political parties (Bundesverfassungsgericht, 2011).

8 A glance at the EP and national elections

The first European Parliament elections took place in Germany on 10 June 1979, following two regional elections in Rhineland-Palatinate on 18 March 1979 and Schleswig-Holstein on 29 April 1979, after the elections for the Federal President on 23 May 1979, and in conjunction with two local elections in Saarland and Rhineland-Palatinate. This explained the higher turnout rates of 81.1 and 81.5 per cent in Saarland and Rhineland-Palatinate, respectively, against the average national figure of 65.7 per cent (Menke, 1985, 80). Apart from the innovative nature of the EP elections, political parties were faced with the general phenomenon of the public's lack of awareness of and indifference to European Parliament elections. In this sense, the main political parties, the CDU/CSU, SPD, and FDP, had to turn their political campaigns into educational seminars in order to fill this gap. An electoral system based on proportional representation allowed for national or regional closed lists. Moreover, unlike other elections, citizens had only one vote, meaning that the campaign, which was usually carried out based on the personalization of candidates, was replaced by a more programmatic approach.

In terms of the campaign, the CDU and FDP adjusted their manifestos to those drafted by their respective transnational party groups. In particular, the FDP adopted entirely the European Liberal and Democrats group's 'Programme for Europe', adding to it a two-page national appeal. Although the FDP did not agree with all policy proposals, it clearly emphasized a European electoral strategy under the slogan 'A Liberal Europe' (Menke, 1985, 72, 74).

As to the CDU, its role was instrumental in formulating the European People's Party manifesto. However, pressure from its sister party CSU, headed by Prime Minister of Bavaria, Franz Joseph Strauß, led to a more polarizing national programme and campaign approach. The main slogan of the CDU changed from '*Politik für die Freiheit – Glück für die Menschen – CDU für Europa*' ('A policy for freedom – happiness for the people – CDU for Europe') to '*Deutsche wählt das freie und soziale Europa. Gegen ein sozialistisches Europa*' ('Germans vote for a free and Social Europe. Against a Socialist Europe') (Menke, 1985, 72–3).

The CSU was even more polarized than the CDU with its slogan '*Mut zur Freiheit – Chance für Europa*' ('The Courage of Freedom – a Chance for Europe') (Menke, 1985, 72). However, Franz Josef Strauß had to deal with inner party dissent in relation to the nomination of the quite conservative candidate Otto von Habsburg as head of list of the CSU. In particular, the new Secretary General Edmund Stoiber regarded the latter as a reactionary and preferred Count von Stauffenberg, the son of the former officer who took part in the assassination attempt of Hitler on 20 July 1944 (Menke, 1985, 71). Although supportive of the EU, the CSU differed from the other parliamentary parties in their position towards European integration. The CSU presented a 'Europe of Fatherlands' discourse, in which the national interest was at the forefront. Moreover, it emphasized the need to strengthen the position of the *Bundesländer* at the European level (Menke, 1985).

As to the SPD, traditionally more on the right of the political spectrum compared to other European Socialist parties, it moved slightly to the left in its electoral programme and during the campaign in order to be more consistent with the Euro-manifesto of the Socialist Group of the European Parliament. The main slogans were '*Sprecher für Deutschland – geachtet in Europa: Die Sozialdemokraten Willy Brandt and Helmut Schmidt – SPD*' ('Spokesmen for Germany – respected throughout Europe; The Social Democrats Willy Brandt and Helmut Schmidt – SPD') and '*Für ein Europa der Arbeitnehmer*' ('For a Workers' Europe') (Menke, 1985, 71). The SPD obtained 40.8 per cent of the vote and secured 35 seats in the Strasbourg arena.

Although the CDU/CSU used a polarization strategy, the overall difference in terms of share of the vote was about 2 per cent between the 1976 general election and the 1979 European Parliament election. Subsequently, the victory of the SPD/FDP coalition government and the defeat of CDU/CSU Chancellor candidate Franz Josef Strauß proved that the Euro-election was not a mere dress rehearsal for the 1980 federal electoral contest. The CDU achieved 39.1 per cent and 34 seats, whilst the CSU got 10.1 per cent and 8 seats. The FDP attracted 6 per cent of votes and managed to send seven representatives to the European Parliament.

Moreover, the first direct EP election was a key factor in structuring the highly diverse Green movement towards a fully-fledged political party. The Greens achieved 3.2 per cent nationwide and thus were entitled to benefit from 4.8 million DM of public funding (Menke, 1985, 79).

At the 1983 general elections, a change of power took place, which led to a new coalition government between the CDU/CSU and the FDP under the leadership of Chancellor Helmut

Table 5.3 National election results in Germany: 1976–2009

Political party	1976	1980	1983	1987	1990	1994	1998	2002	2005	2009
CDU/CSU	48.6	44.5	48.8	44.3	43.8	41.5	35.1	38.5	35.2	33.8
SPD	42.6	42.9	38.2	37.0	33.5	36.4	40.9	38.5	34.2	23.0
FDP	7.9	10.6	7.0	9.1	11.0	6.9	6.2	7.4	9.8	14.6
Grüne[1]	—	1.5	5.6	8.3	3.8[4] / 1.2[5]	7.4	6.7	8.6	8.1	10.7
PDS/*Linke*[2]	—	—	—	—	2.4	4.4	5.1	4.0	8.7	11.9
NPD	0.3	0.2	0.2	0.6	0.3	—	0.3	0.4	1.6	1.5
DP	—	—	—	—	—	—	—	—	—	—
KPD/DKP[3]	0.3	0.2	0.2	—	—	—	—	—	—	—
Others	0.3	0.1	0.0	0.7	4.0	3.4	5.7	2.6	2.4	4.5
Total	100.0	100.0	100.0	100.0	100.0	100.0	100.0	100.0	100.0	100.0
Turnout	**90.7**	**88.6**	**89.1**	**84.3**	**77.8**	**79.0**	**82.2**	**79.1**	**77.7**	**70.8**

Source: Bundeswahlleiter (2009) www.bundeswahlleiter.de/de/bundestagswahlen.

Notes:
[1] 1980–1990: *Die Grünen*; 1990: *Die Grünen/Bündnis 90*; 1994–today: *Bündnis 90/Die Grünen*.
[2] 1990–2004: *Partei des Demokratischen Sozialismus*; 2005: *Partei des Demokratischen Sozialismus + Die Wahlalternative Arbeit und soziale Gerechtigkeit = Die Linke*.
[3] 1949–1953: *Deutsche Kommunistische Partei* (afterwards illegal); 1972–today: *Kommunistische Partei Deutschlands*.
[4] *Grüne*.
[5] *Bündnis 90*.

Kohl. Moreover, for the first time the Greens achieved parliamentary representation one year and three months after the general elections, when the executive was still enjoying its honeymoon. As such, the opposition did not register substantial gains.

The 1984 European Parliament election sanctioned the rise of the Greens as a new party, in spite of the prejudices of the other established political parties, due to their links to more extreme left-wing elements, particularly in the terror scene of the 1980s (Bulmer *et al.*, 1986, 197–8).

As previously, the CDU presented itself as the European party in Germany. It worked closely with the EPP to coordinate its national manifesto with the transnational one. The main slogan was devised around the new Kohl government and was '*Aufwärts mit Deutschland Mit uns für Europa*' (Germany's getting better with us for Europe.') The campaign took a more Nationalist orientation, emphasizing the role of the *Bundesländer*, particularly Bavaria, within a 'Europe of nation-states'. The party was also under pressure due to the growing protests of farmers and the cutbacks in agricultural subsidies introduced by the agriculture minister in accordance with the CSU portfolio (Bulmer *et al.*, 1986, 199).

Following bribery scandals involving key figures of the FDP, such as Count Otto Lambsdorff, Hans-Dietrich Genscher decided to step down as leader and many left-wing Liberals left the party. In terms of the electoral campaign, the FDP relied on the European Liberal and Democratic parliamentary group's Euro-manifesto and did not invest very much in the campaign (Bulmer *et al.*, 1986, 200).

As to the SPD, despite the slogan '*Macht Europa stark*' ('Make Europe strong'), its campaign mainly focussed on national issues, failing nevertheless to transform the EP electoral contest into a test for the ruling centre-right coalition. In the background, European issues were raised during the campaign, especially with regard to the relevance of the Franco-German friendship for

European integration, Europe's role in international affairs, and the development of European defence policy, particularly in relation to NATO. Finally, the active participation of women was addressed with regard to the introduction of female candidates in the SPD list, although their names appeared mostly at the bottom, so that they had only a few chances to be elected (Bulmer et al., 1986, 201).

Under the main slogan 'think globally, act locally', the Greens introduced new themes into the European campaign, criticizing the Common Agricultural Policy (CAP) and its detrimental effects on the environment, warning against the rise of a superpower Europe, and calling for equal opportunities for women (Bulmer et al., 1986, 203).

The CDU obtained 34 seats by achieving 37.5 per cent of the vote, thus losing 1.6 per cent in comparison to 1979; the SPD got 33 seats with its 37.4 per cent, 3.4 per cent less than in the previous election; and the CSU secured 7 seats with its 8.5 per cent of the vote, 1.6 per cent less. In addition, there were the 3 seats nominated by the Berlin Chamber of Deputies, two for the CDU and one for the SPD. The Greens appeared as the real winners with their 8.2 per cent of the vote, five points more than in 1979, and secured 7 seats in the EP arena. By contrast, the FDP with its 4.8 per cent of the vote, 1.2 less than in the previous election, failed to meet the required threshold by a whisker and thus any representation in Strasbourg.

The subsequent EP election held in 1989 at the end of the national electoral cycle registered the lowest turnout in the German history of all national, local, and regional elections. In spite of a booming economy combined with a low unemployment rate, the coalition government led by Christian Democrat Chancellor Helmut Kohl suffered from a downturn in terms of support. The CDU campaign coordinated by Secretary-General Heiner Geißler used a polarization strategy with its provocative slogan '*Radikale und SPD – Zukunft und Wohlstand ade*' ('Radicals and SPD – Goodbye to the Future and Wealth') that raised considerable dissent within the party (*Der Spiegel*, 12 June 1989a, 25–7). The CDU strategy was nationally oriented, although its electoral manifesto was intertwined with that of the European People's Party (EPP). After the death of Franz Josef Strauß in October 1988, the CSU struggled to find another charismatic politician who could achieve the same mobilizing effects as his predecessor. Amongst the coalition government parties, with only 8.2 per cent of the vote and 8 seats, the CSU appeared as the great loser, challenged by the new opposition party *Republikaner* that coined an ironic slogan '*Nur Bayern können CSU wählen*' ('Only Bavarians can vote for the CSU') (*Der Spiegel*, 26 June 1989b, 25).

Table 5.4 EP election results in Germany: 1979–2004

Political party	1979 %	Seats	1984 %	Seats	1989 %	Seats	1994 %	Seats	1999 %	Seats	2004 %	Seats
CDU	39.1	34	37.5	34	29.5	25	32.1	39	39.3	40	36.5	40
SPD	40.8	35	37.4	33	37.3	31	32.2	40	30.7	33	21.5	23
FDP	6.0	4	4.8	—	5.6	4	4.1	—	3.0	—	6.1	7
CSU	10.1	8	8.5	7	8.2	7	6.8	8	9.4	10	8.0	9
Greens	—	—	8.2	7	8.4	8	10.1	12	6.4	7	11.9	13
PDS/*Linke*	—	—	—	—	—	—	4.7	—	5.8	6	6.1	7
Republikaner	—	—	—	—	7.1	6	3.9	—	1.7	—	1.9	—
Others	4.0	—	3.6	—	3.9	—	6.1	—	3.7	—	8.0	—
Total	100.0	100	100.0	100	100.0	100	100.0	100	100.0	100	100.0	100
Turnout	**65.7**	—	**56.7**	—	**62.3**	—	**60.0**	—	**45.3**	—	**43.0**	—

Source: Bundeswahlleiter (2009) www.bundeswahlleiter.de/de/europawahlen.

Under the leadership of the charismatic Franz Schönhuber, the *Republikaner* presented a more critical approach towards the EC, with a mix of law and order issues, anti-immigration discourse, and nationalism, which were instrumental in paving the way for its victory at the expense of the CDU/CSU.

Under the motto '*Wir sind Europa*' ('We are Europe'), the main opposition party, the SPD, tried to develop a long-term strategy in order to gain power at the federal level. The party achieved 37.3 per cent of the votes cast, 0.1 less in relation to the 1984 European election, thus losing two of its 33 seats.

By contrast, amongst the opposition parties, the more left-wing Greens appeared as the winners with their 8.4 of the vote. This outcome was favoured by the Greens' dynamic campaign, that under the slogan '*Europa: Geschäfte ohne Grenzen*' ('Europe: Business without Borders'), criticized the capitalist nature of the European project, and by the controversial nomination of Rudko Kawczynski, a stateless Roma, who according to the law was not entitled to run elections (*Der Spiegel*, 12 June 1989c, 124). Finally, the FDP was able again to achieve representation in the European parliamentary arena in Strasbourg.

The 1994 European elections were the first contested within the framework of Germany's post-reunification. Although no dramatic changes had occurred in the political landscape, the successor party of the 'Socialist Unity Party of Germany', the Party of Democratic Socialism, PDS (*Partei des Demokratischen Sozialismus*) was very keen to establish itself beyond its traditional constituencies in the eastern *Bundesländer*. Moreover, Euro-elections took place in a super election year (*Superwahljahr*), when 19 elections were scheduled, culminating in the national elections in October. By representing a crucial rehearsal for the federal electoral contests, EP elections gained more significance as a trendsetter. In total, 24 political parties and groups ran the race. In 1994, after a period of recession, the economy started to pick up again and Chancellor Helmut Kohl exploited this growth as a tool against the opposition parties.

The Christian Democrats pursued a pro-European campaign, albeit mainly dominated by domestic issues. Their main poster, 'Against War, Violence and Terrorism in Europe: Peace for Everybody!' appeared dull, disclosing an undefined and utopian approach to European elections (Paterson *et al.*, 1996, 76). Yet, the party eventually managed to perform better than expected by scoring 32 per cent of the vote, thus gaining 2.5 points more than in 1989. In contrast, the CSU shifted more to the right by conducting a sort of 'Europe of the Fatherlands' campaign, centred on the need to carry forward the interests of Bavaria. This strategy allowed the party to get 6.8 per cent of the vote, thus limiting its loss by 1.4 per cent compared to the previous Euro-election.

Due to its declining fortunes at previous elections, the FDP was especially concerned about its 'survival' and decided to pursue a pro European approach. However, due to the need to renew its internal organization, after Hans-Dietrich Genscher stepped down, it was unable to focus on the election and attract enough votes to gain representation in Strasbourg. Regarding the election as a mere electoral test, the SPD resorted to some posters – 'The Mafia in Europe must be shattered!' or 'Security instead of fear!' – that emphasized topics that were discussed at the European level (Paterson *et al.*, 1996, 77). In spite of a promising outlook at the beginning of 1994, the SPD's performance was rather disappointing: it lost over 5 per cent of the vote gained in 1989, yet at 32.2 per cent of the vote, it registered the highest score amongst all the other political parties in this contest.

The Greens, who followed a critical approach to the Treaty of the European Union, particularly in relation to the democratic process, the environment, trade, and environment policy, obtained 10.1 per cent of the vote, 1.7 points more than in the previous Euro-elections, thus securing 12 seats (Paterson *et al.*, 1996, 75–6). The reformist Communist PDS, unable to become a party with representation in the western regions of Germany, had difficulty gaining a seat at the national and European levels. The PDS supported a supranational European Union, which would offer more protection to workers through the reinforcement of European social policy.

The 1999 European Parliament election took place nine months after the setting up of an SPD/Green coalition government led by Chancellor Gerhard Schröder. Although still in their honeymoon period, the government parties did not perform well at the Euro-elections. Tensions and disagreements between the coalition partners over the Kosovo War, as well as social policy issues, contributed to undermine the image of the executive. In the end, the EP contest became an opportunity for the citizens to protest against the direction of the red–green coalition.

Overall, parties devoted less attention to the international dimension in their electoral programmes. The three traditional parties, the CDU, SPD, and FDP, emphasized both economic and foreign policy issues, whilst the smaller parties revealed a different profile in this matter. In particular, whereas the CSU highlighted international cooperation as well as the role of the regions in the EU, the Greens stressed the question of the environment and the position of women in society; the PDS underlined issues related to social justice; and the *Republikaner* called for law and order, emphasizing the importance of political leadership (Binder and Wüst, 2004, 42–3).

The 1999 Euro-election led to the victory of the CDU and CSU, with their 39.3 per cent and 9.4 per cent of vote, respectively, as well as to the defeat of the SPD and, in particular, the Greens with their 30.7 per cent and 6.4 per cent, respectively. The electoral results also sanctioned the PDS' first entry to the Strasbourg arena, whilst confirming the FDP's exclusion.

Being held one-and-a-half years after the federal general elections, the 2004 European elections could be regarded as 'mid-term'. The CDU/CSU used the European Parliament electoral race to criticize the red–green government. National issues dominated the campaign, especially the mismanagement of tax and labour market reform (Niedermayer, 2005, 56). The CDU remained loyal to its main slogan of being the European party in Germany and developing a party manifesto that was close to that of the EPP. The CSU particularly emphasized the 'Europe of the regions' theme by using the slogan 'For a strong Bavaria in Europe' (*'Für ein starkes Bayern in Europa'*).

For the FDP, under Guido Westerwelle's new leadership, it was crucial to perform well in the European elections. Silvana Koch-Mehrin became the head of the list and was instrumental in changing the image of the FDP. Her dynamism was fundamental in attracting younger voters. The party manifesto, *'Wir können Europa besser! Für ein freies und besseres Europa'* ('We can do Europe better! For a free and fair Europe'), contained a more optimistic and constructive approach of the FDP. The PDS developed a manifesto entitled *'Alternativen sind machbar: Für ein soziales, demokratisches und friedliches Europa'* ('Alternatives are possible: For a social, democratic and peaceful Europe'), whereby it presented itself as an alternative to the more established political parties (Niedermayer, 2005, 46–7).

Whilst the CDU, CSU, and SPD concentrated their campaigns on national issues, smaller parties conducted a campaign about European issues. The results of the 2004 elections led to the success of the CDU and CSU, with their respective 36.5 per cent and 8 per cent of the vote, against the government parties. The SPD faced its worse defeat in the history of Euro-elections by receiving only 21.5 per cent of vote. On the contrary, the Green Party and the FDP almost doubled their respective scores compared to the previous EU contest. Accordingly, the former succeeded in sending 13 members to Strasbourg, six more than in 1999, whilst the latter, with its seven members, finally achieved representation in the European Parliament again.

In sum, the German political parties did not invest very much in the EP contests, but rather attempted to make a profit out of the generous public funding system. Electoral manifestos did not change to a great extent over the years, whilst the vast majority of citizens did not appear very interested in such elections.

9 The 2009 European election

9.1 Party lists and manifestos

Overall, 32 political parties ran in the 2009 EP electoral race which was strongly dominated by the impact of the financial crisis triggered by the collapse of Lehman Brothers and the real estate market in the United States. In spite of the lack of a genuine discussion about European issues, most German parties being supportive of the European integration process, one of the most aggressive campaigns occurred, mainly due to the narrow window between the European Parliament and German general elections scheduled for September 2009.

In line with the manifesto of the Party of European Socialists (PES), the SPD programme was entitled 'For Europe: strong and social' ('*Für Europa: stark und sozial!*') clearly stressing the need to reinforce a social Europe against the financial crisis caused by the banking sector (*Sozialdemokratische Partei Deutschlands*, 2009). Great emphasis was put on an enhanced employment policy, achieved by an infrastructure programme financed by the European Union, and on investments in the field of education, research, and vocational training. The Social Democrats advocated a coordination of social policy at the European level rather than the harmonization of social policy, because of national differences. The SPD called for a change of the financial architecture by reinforcing regulatory and control institutions. It also urged the setting up of a credit line for small and medium-sized enterprises, so that business across the EU could be supported especially during the financial crisis. Immigration was regarded as positive; however, the Social Democrats advocated an integrated approach that involved the cooperation of migrants' countries of origin. (*Sozialdemokratische Partei Deutschlands*, 2009, 12).

The Euro-manifesto of the CDU, entitled 'Strong Europe-Secure Future' ('*Starkes Europa-Sichere Zukunft*'), aimed at strengthening and securing the social market economy in Germany and the European Union (*Christlich Demokratische Union*, 2009, 4). It spelt out the party opposition to the harmonization of social policy in Europe, as this would contribute to a damping down of the generous and strong German welfare state. The manifesto emphasized particularly the need to improve the EU economic competitiveness by adopting the successful German export-oriented model and calling for a new financial architecture to protect particularly small investors and stakeholders. The new Freedom and Security Space introduced under the Schengen Treaty put in evidence the need to strengthen judicial cooperation (*Christlich Demokratische Union*, 2009, 10–12).

Amongst the four smaller political parties, the CSU was the most conservative. It raised the importance of a 'Europe of regions' in accordance with the principle of subsidiarity. Its identity as a Christian Democratic party became clear throughout the document in which references to family and religious values were included. The Euro-manifesto also emphasized the importance of parliamentary participation in the EU decision-making process (*Christlich-Soziale Union*, 2009). The CSU Euro-manifesto devoted great space to agricultural issues, calling for the devolution of agricultural competences to the regional level.

Whilst the SPD, CDU, and CSU produced relatively short manifestos, the FDP, *Die Linke* and the Greens drafted lengthy and detailed documents to present their policy proposals. The Liberal Party's Euro-manifesto entitled 'Freedom in Europe in the World of the Twenty-first Century' ('*Freiheit in Europa in der Welt des 21. Jahrhunderts*') used several catchwords, 'freedom', 'subsidiarity', 'competitiveness', and 'responsibility', to attract the electorate. The Liberal Party, albeit strongly pro-European, regarded the need to set limits to the European Union, and in particular a cap on the budget. The Euro-manifesto claimed that the European Union had enough financial resources that were not used efficiently. In particular, funding for the CAP and for the structural funds could be reduced in order to finance other more future-oriented policies (*Freie Demokratische Partei*, 2009). Another element that was sketched out in the manifesto was the reduction of an overwhelming bureaucracy in the EU. The liberalization of markets through the reduction of red tape was also a major theme amongst the Liberals. The FDP stated that it wanted to bring more market to the European economy and cut back on those subsidies distorting competition. Finally, innovation and education were the two key aspects capable of preserving competitiveness worldwide. Like the SPD and CDU, the FDP also rejected a harmonization of social policy due to the differences between the various countries (*Freie Demokratische Partei*, 2009).

At the beginning of 2009, the German Greens launched their 170-page manifesto, entitled '*Volles Programm mit WUMS. Für ein besseres Europa!*' ('Full programme with WUMS. For a better Europe') with Rebecca Harms and Reinhard Bütikofer at the top of the electoral list (*Bündnis 90/Die Grünen*, 2009, 16). In their view, Europe was a 'matter of the heart' and should not be allowed to become a project of the elite. The core message of the Green Party was what they labelled the 'New Green Deal for Europe', which aimed at restructuring the European economy towards sustainable green technologies, including following principles of social justice between the Northern and Southern Hemispheres. According to the Greens, climate change policy was interlinked with all other policies such as energy, transport, economy, as well as foreign and development policy. The Green Party supported the Treaty of Lisbon; however, it regarded it as a transition towards a slimmed down constitution (*Bündnis 90/Die Grünen*, 2009, 3).

The Greens were very close both to the SPD and the Left Party in their conception of 'social Europe'. The protection of the working population and solidarity with less developed regions were emphasized. Moreover, the Euro-manifesto stressed the need to decentralize possible public services as much as possible in order to provide an optimal delivery to citizens. An open and welcoming Europe for minorities, particularly Roma, as well as migrants was strenuously advocated. Internationally, the EU should be engaged in reforming international institutions and contribute to the development of world peace (*Bündnis 90/Die Grünen*, 2009).

Die Linke was the only party that put forward what could be defined as 'transformative Euro-criticism', reflecting a constructive approach towards a new direction to the EU, rather than an attitude of rejection of the European project (Harmsen, 2007, 208–12). Its Euro-manifesto, entitled '*Solidarität, Demokratie und Frieden – Gemeinsam für den Wechsel in Europa*' ('Solidarity, Democracy and Peace – Together for Change in Europe') condemned EU neo-liberal and capitalist policies by calling for an increase in funding in favour of weaker economies and by promoting more radical legislation in order to prevent the recurrence of the dramatic events that led to the breakdown of the financial sector (*Die Linke*, 2009).

Under Oskar Lafontaine's leadership, *Die Linke* was the only German party to oppose the ratification of the Lisbon Treaty since it perpetuated a policy of liberalization reducing the rights of workers across Europe and allowed for the further militarization of EU foreign and security policy. Last but not least, the treaty was unfavourable as it was conceived through a top-down process without consulting the population by way of a referendum (*Die Linke*, 2009, 1–3, 23).

Besides the six parliamentary parties, another 26 lists took part in the elections, including two extreme right-wing parties, two extreme left-wing parties, three Christian-Conservative parties, two ecological movements, three pensioners' parties, three single-issue parties, and even eight citizens' lists, clearly revealing increasingly popular anti-party feelings (Saalfeld, 2005, 49–54).

The far-right-wing DVU and *Die Republikaner* expressed their opposition to the EU's centripetal tendencies and to Turkey's prospective membership. Finally, the Christian '*Partei für Arbeit, Umwelt und Familie*', AUF (Party for Labour, Environment and Family) ran the electoral race as the German representative of the transnational movement 'Libertas', financed by the Irish Tycoon Declan Ganley, but failed in the end to get representation in Strasbourg (Euractiv.com, 8 June 2009).

Table 5.5 Euromanifestos of non-parliamentary parties

Ideological origins	Political party	Main campaign points
Transnational European parties	*Europa-Demokratie-Esperanto* – EDE (Europe-Democracy-Esperanto)	• Democratization of EU • Introduction of Esperanto as main working language in EU
	Newropeans	• European government • Reinforced European integration
Citizens' groups	*Das Generationen-Bündnis* – 50 plus (50 Plus-Alliance of Generations) *Ab Jetzt . . . Bündnis für Deutschland, für Demokratie durch Volksabstimmung* (From Now) *Freie Wähler* – FW (Free Voters) *Gerechtigkeit braucht Bürgerrechte-Wir danken für Ihr Vertrauen! – Für Volksentscheide (Wählergemeinschaft):* (For People's Decision-Making [Voters' Community]. Justice Needs Citizens' Rights – Thanks for your Trust!) *Bürgerrechtsbewegung Solidarität* – BüSo (Civic Rights Movement Solidarity) *Freie Bürger Initiative* – FBI (Free Citizens' Initiative) *Aufbruch für Bürgerrechte, Freiheit und Gesundheit* – Aufbruch (New Beginning for Civil Rights, Freedom and Health)	• Anti-party movement • Direct democracy • Local democracy • Choice in the health sector • Critical of health sector being dominated by economic interests in Germany and European Union
Single-issue parties	*Bayernpartei* – BP (Bavaria Party)	• Regionalist issues • Independence of Bavaria • Against centralistic tendencies in EU
	Die Violetten: für Spirituelle Politik (The Violets: for Spiritual Policy)	• Spiritual dimension of politics • Non-violent, holistic policies • Humanistic ideology • No clear message about Europe; very abstract
	Familienpartei Deutschlands – Familie (Family Party of Germany) *Feministische Partei-Die Frauen*-Die Frauen – (Feminist Party – The Women)	• Support for family friendly policies in Germany and at EU level • Equality between men and women (gender mainstreaming) • More women in top positions of EU • Non-violent approach to politics
	Piratenpartei Deutschlands – Piraten (Pirate Party of Germany)	• Against censorship on the internet • Against patents and copyright as major obstacle to knowledge society

(continued)

Table 5.5 (continued)

Ideological origins	Political party	Main campaign points
Pensioners' parties	*Die Grauen-Generationspartei-Die Grauen* (The Grays-Generation Party)	• Better welfare conditions for pensioners
	Rentnerinnen und Rentner Partei – RRP (Female and Male Pensioners' Party)	• Better pensions for pensioners
	Rentner Partei Deutschlands – *Rentner* (Pensioners' Party of Germany)	
Extreme right-wing parties	*Deutsche Volksunion* – DVU (German People's Union)	• Against the European Union • For 'Europe of fatherlands' • Against membership of Turkey
	Die Republikaner – REP (Republican Party/Republicans)	• For a Christian defined European Union • For 'Europe of fatherlands' • Against membership of Turkey
Extreme left-wing parties	*Deutsche Kommunistische Partei* – DKP (German Communist Party)	• Against Europe of monopoly capitalism • Against capitalist Europe
	Partei der Sozialen Gleichheit-Sektion der Vierten Internationale – PSG (Party of Social Equality-Section of the Fourth International)	• For a United Europe of Socialist states • Against capitalist European Union
Christian-Conservative parties	*Partei für Arbeit, Umwelt und Familie-Christen für Deutschland* – AUF (Party for Labour, Environment, and Family, Christians for Germany)	• For subsidiarity and decentralization in EU • Christian values should be enshrined in treaties • Against abortion
	Partei Bibeltreuer Christen – PBC (Party of Bible-Abiding Christians)	
	Christliche Mitte: Für ein Deutschland nach Gottes Geboten – CM (Christian Centre: for a Germany According to God's Commandments)	
Ecological parties	*Mensch-Umwelt-Tierschutz* – MUT (Man, Environment, and Animal Protection)	• Not specific about European Union • General statements about holistic integration of environment and animal protection in overall life-style of man
	Ökologisch-Demokratische Partei – ÖDP (Ecological Democratic Party)	

Sources: Authors' table based on data from *Europa-Demokratie-Esperanto* (2009); *Newropeans* (2009); 50 plus – *Das Generationen-Bindnis* (2009); *Ab Jetzt … Bündnis für Deutschland, für Demokratie durch Volksabstimmung* (2009); *Freie Wähler* (2009); *Für Volksentscheide* (2009); *Bürgerrechtsbewegung Solidarität* (2009); *Freie Bürger Initiative* (2009); *Aufbruch Für Bürgerrechte, Freiheit und Gesundheit* (2009); *Bayernpartei* (2009); *Die Violetten* (2009); *Familienpartei Deutschlands* (2009); *Feministische Partei-Die Frauen* (2009); *Piratenpartei Deutschlands* (2009); *Die Grauen-Generationspartei* (2009); *Rentnerinnen und Rentner Partei* (2009); *Rentner Partei Deutschlands* (2009); *Deutsche Volksunion* (2009); *Die Republikaner* (2009); *Deutsche Kommunistische Partei* (2009); *Partei der Sozialen Gleichheit* (2009); *Partei für Arbeit, Umwelt und Familie-Christen für Deutschland* (2009); *Partei Bibeltreuer Christen* (2009); *Christliche Mitte* (2009); *Mensch-Umwelt-Tierschutz* (2009); *Ökologisch-Demokratische Partei* (2009).

9.2 Electoral campaign

The European Parliament's offices in Berlin and Munich launched a campaign to mobilize voters to go to the polls, reminding them that if they did not cast their ballot, others would decide for them. The campaign '*European elections 2009 – Your decision*' was coordinated with all the other 26 countries of the European Union. In particular, the European Parliament, which was very keen to attract young voters, even resorted to social networks such as Facebook and YouTube in order to reach them (Gagatek *et al.*, 2010).

Given that there was no official opening of electoral campaigns in Germany, the process started with European conferences organized by the various political parties. The SPD was the first to convene such a meeting on 8 December 2008, thus nominating Martin Schulz, Chairman of the Socialist Group in the European Parliament as *Spitzenkandidat*. The SPD appeared split between a right-centre wing around its leader Franz Müntefering and a left wing around other chief members, Kurt Beck and Sigmar Gabriel. The main dividing position was over labour market legislation known as the 'Hartz IV' reform, introduced by the Schröder government and implemented between 2002 and 2005.

There was widespread fear amongst the Social Democrats that such internal disagreement would seriously damage the party and affect its electoral outcome. The European party conference was characterized by a half-empty hall in Berlin (*Süddeutsche Zeitung*, 8 December 2008) grounded on the common feeling that the SPD was losing out as a junior partner in the Grand Coalition. Moreover, Vice-Chancellor Frank-Walter Steinmeier was not regarded as a charismatic personality capable of taking the party forward. On 11 March 2009, the CDU organized its *Europakongress* to present its programme, which mainly focussed on economic issues related to the financial crisis urging the adoption of the German model of social market economy at the European and global levels. European Parliament President Hans-Gert Pöttering campaigned under the motto '*Für Schutz durch Gemeinschaft: Wir in Europa*' ('For protection through the community: We in Europe') whilst Chancellor Merkel featured as a pillar of stability and trustworthiness in television spots (*Frankfurter Allgemeine Zeitung*, 17 March 2009).

At the European conference held on 8 May 2009, the CSU, faced with domestic problems in Bavaria and concerned about the constant low turnout at the EP elections, called for the unity of the party in order to gather sufficient consensus and exceed the 5 per cent threshold at the forthcoming Euro-elections (*Die Welt*, 9 May 2009a). The CSU ran its campaign under the slogan '*Für ein Europa der Werte*' ('For a Europe of values'), thus distancing itself programmatically from the CDU (*Christlich-Soziale Union*, 2009). After Edmund Stoiber's resignation, the party kept a dual leadership with the Prime Minister of the Regional Government, Günther Beckstein, and Party Chairman Erwin Huber. However, in September 2008, the CSU won the regional elections, yet dropped from an absolute majority of 60 per cent to a relative one of 43.3 per cent. Horst Seehofer, who became the new Leader and Regional Prime Minister, had therefore the difficult task of preparing and relaunching the party for the elections to the European Parliament.

As to the FDP, the new young and dynamic head of list Silvana Koch-Mehrin, whose smiling face graced numerous posters, contributed to the upward trend of the party through an intense campaign that focussed on 'the EU as a success story' (*Freie Demokratische Partei*, 2009). The European party conference held on 17 January 2009 was quite pragmatic and dominated by domestic questions, such as Guido Westerwelle's official announcement that the FDP would support the grand coalition government, whilst European issues were sidelined (*Freie Demokratische Partei*, 2009).

The Greens ran an optimistic and self-confident campaign based on their 'New Green Deal' socio-economic plan. Probably the most divided European party conference was that of *Die*

Linke. Almost all eight Members of the European Parliament elected in 2004 were deselected in the European party conference in Essen on 1 March 2009. A radicalization of the party took place, in which an anti-capitalist position and a total rejection of the Lisbon Treaty were approved. The overall approach was not only directed against the liberal policies of the Barroso Commission, but also against the CDU/CSU/SPD coalition. The financial crisis was regarded as a favourable background to exercise strategic opposition against the policies of the German government (*Der Spiegel*, 27 February 2009a). Two incumbent MEPs, Sylvia-Yvonne Kaufmann and André Brie were excluded from the list, presumably for their positions regarding human rights abuses in Cuba and, in the latter's case, for her support for the Lisbon Treaty, against the official party line (*Die Zeit*, 26 February 2009a; *Der Spiegel*, 14 May 2009b). The main candidate became one of the co-founders and long-standing leader, Lothar Bisky.

The CDU campaign started in mid-April 2009 with a series of slogans related to the importance of the European Union for Germany. One of its characteristics was the lack of personalization of the campaign around its chief candidate Hans-Gert Pöttering (*Der Spiegel*, 16 March 2009c; CDU.TV, 2009). This was done on purpose, given that he was hardly known at the national level even if he was at the head of the European Parliament in the previous legislature between January 2007 and June 2009 (Viola, 2010). By contrast, Chancellor Merkel featured as a key element in electoral posters and videos.

The SPD carried out an aggressive campaign against virtually all other political parties, by producing a series of provocative posters, such as 'Hot air would vote for Die Linke', 'Finance sharks vote for the FDP', and 'Wage dumpers vote for the CDU', referring to the reluctance of the Chancellor's party to adopt a national minimum wage (*Die Welt*, 29 May 2009b). Only the Green Party was spared from CDU attacks. This was interpreted as a strategic move beyond the European elections, geared towards a potential federal government coalition (*Die Zeit*, 13 June 2009b). The main Socialist candidate Martin Schulz was almost invisible in the Euro-campaign (*Die Zeit*, 4 May 2009c).

Unlike the other German parliamentary parties, the FDP centred its campaign on chief candidate Silvana Koch-Mehrin, who called herself a 'Eurofighter' in her own blog. The campaign was also combined with other local, regional, and general election campaigns. The Green Party used its detailed programme 'New Green Deal' to target issues that were common to the European Union and Germany. The slogan 'WUMS for a better Europe' was employed in all posters along with themes against nuclear energy, genetically modified food, and economic and social injustice (*Bündnis 90/Die Grünen*, 2009). Finally, *Die Linke*'s campaign was rather populist, with radical slogans in its posters and television spots against the bank bailouts by the German and other governments across Europe, such as 'Millionaires to the till' and 'Europe-wide minimum wage'.

In sum, the campaign was dominated by national issues, which were, however, connected to the European level. The lacklustre campaign was just a rehearsal for the more important general elections on 27 September 2009.

9.3 Electoral results

At the 2009 EP contest in Germany, turnout reached its lowest level of 43.3 per cent. The ruling CDU obtained 30.7 per cent of the votes cast and 34 seats, thus losing 5.9 percentage points and 6 seats. Its sister party, the CSU, also registered a slight decline of 0.8 per cent, reducing its representation in Strasbourg to seven members. Yet, the big loser in the Euro-elections was the CDU/CSU junior government partner, the SPD, which achieved its worst record of 20.8 per cent of the vote, yet kept the same number of 23 seats as before. By contrast, the Green Party was able to improve by 0.2 percentage points and one seat compared to the 2004 electoral score by achieving 12.1 per cent and 14 seats. This confirmed the Greens as the third strongest political force after the Christian Democrats and the Social Democrats.

However, the most spectacular rise was registered by the FDP, which almost doubled its electoral share from 6.1 per cent to 11 per cent, and went from 7 to 12 seats. This was certainly due to the dynamic and vibrant campaign undertaken by its head of list, Silvana Koch-Mehrin. *Die Linke*'s electoral outcome increased from 6.1 per cent to 7.5 per cent, thus assigning the party 8 seats in the European Parliament, one more than in 2004.

Table 5.6 EP election results in Germany: 2009

Political party	%	Seats
Christlich Demokratische Union Deutschlands – CDU	30.7	34
Sozialdemokratische Partei Deutschlands – SPD	20.8	23
Bündnis 90/Die Grünen	12.1	14
Freie Demokratische Partei – FDP	11.0	12
Die Linke	7.2	8
Christlich-Soziale Union in Bayern – CSU	7.2	8
Freie Wähler – FW	1.7	—
Die Republikaner – REP	1.3	—
Mensch-Umwelt-Tierschutz – MUT	1.1	—
Familien-Partei Deutschlands Familie	1.0	—
Piratenpartei Deutschland – Piraten	0.9	—
Rentner Partei Deutschlands – RENTNER	0.8	—
Ökologisch-Demokratische Partei – ÖDP	0.5	—
Deutsche Volksunion – DVU	0.4	—
Rentnerinnen und Rentner Partei – RPP	0.4	—
Feministische Partei-Die Frauen – Die Frauen	0.3	—
Partei Bibeltreuer Christen – PBC	0.3	—
Ab Jetzt ... Bündnis für Deutschland, für Demokratie durch Volksabstimmung (Volksabstimmung)	0.3	—
Das Generationen-Bündnis – 50Plus	0.3	—
Die GRAUEN-Generationspartei – Die Grauen	0.2	—
Bayernpartei – BP	0.2	—
Die Violetten: für Spirituelle Politik – Die Violetten	0.2	—
(Wählergemeinschaft): Gerechtigkeit Braucht Bürgerrechte – Wir Danken für Ihr Vertrauen! FÜR VOLKSENTSCHEIDE	0.2	—
Christliche Mitte: für Ein Deutschland nach Gottes Geboten – CM	0.2	—
Partei Für Arbeit, Umwelt und Familie-Christen für Deutschland – AUF	0.1	—
Aufbruch für Bürgerrechte, Freiheit und Gesundheit – AUFBRUCH	0.1	—
Freie Bürger-Initiative – FBI	0.1	—
Deutsche Kommunistische Partei – DKP	0.1	—
Newropeans	0.1	—
Europa-Demokratie-Esperanto – EDE	0.04	—
Bürgerrechtsbewegung Solidarität – BüSo	0.04	—
Partei der Sozialen Gleichheit-Sektion der Vierten Internationale – PSG	0.03	—
Total	100.0	

Source: *Bundeswahlleiter* (2009) www.bundeswahlleiter.de/de/europawahlen/.

Table 5.7 The German MEPs' affiliation to the European parliamentary groups

Political party	%	Seats	EPP	S&D	ALDE	Greens/EFA	ECR	EUL/NGL	EFD	NA
CDU	30.7	42	42	—	—	—	—	—	—	—
SPD	20.8	23	—	23	—	—	—	—	—	—
Bündnis 90/Grünen	12.1	14	—	—	—	14	—	—	—	—
FDP	11.0	12	—	—	12	—	—	—	—	—
Linke	7.5	8	—	—	—	—	—	8	—	—
CSU	7.2	9	9	—	—	—	—	—	—	—
Others	10.7	0	—	—	—	—	—	—	—	—
Total	100.0	108	51	23	12	14	—	8	—	—

Source: European Parliament (2009) website: www.europarl.eu.

The remaining 26 parties failed to achieve representation, as they together attained a mere 10.8 per cent of the vote, with 7 of them scoring more than 0.5 per cent and 4 over 1 per cent, notably the citizens' list *Freie Wähler* (FW) with 1.7 per cent, the *Republikaner* with 1.3 per cent, the *Tierschutzpartei* with 1.1 per cent and the *Familienpartei* with 1 per cent (*Bundeswahlleiter*, 2009).

9.4 Campaign finance

Germany boasts a generous public party financing system, which clearly shows the tendency towards a cartelization of politics and the institutionalization of a party state (Katz and Mair, 1995). For the first four million voters, a party gets €0.85, afterwards €0.70. The main condition is that the party achieves at least 0.5 per cent of the vote. Moreover, the parties get an additional €0.38 for each euro donated or each euro membership fee paid every year. The annual ceiling for public party financing is €133 million and payment is undertaken after the submission of an accountability report on 1 December of each year (Korte, 2009).

The costs of the 2009 EP campaign amounted to €10 million for the CDU, €9 million for the SPD, €1.4 million for the FDP, €1 million for the Greens, and about €3.4 million for *Die Linke* (*Landeszentrale für politische Bildung Baden-Württemberg*, 2009).

German political parties invested less funding in European elections – a large part coming from the public purse – in comparison to federal elections. All parties, except the Left Party and the CSU, devoted about half of the resources they would employ in federal elections. As shown in Figure 5.3, in the case of the SPD three times less funding was disbursed at Euro-elections.

Since 1979 a declining spending trend has been detected over Euro-campaigning in order to make a profit out of the generous public funding system. Figure 5.3 shows that similar costs were registered at the EP and national elections held in 1983 and 1984, yet over time a difference emerged. On average, in Euro-elections, the parliamentary parties disbursed just one-third of what they would normally have disbursed at general elections. Finally, parties did not resort to external marketing agencies in order to organize their Euro-campaigns and considerably reduced the costs of consulting experts (Niedermayer, 2005, 47–50).

10 Theoretical interpretation of Euro-elections

10.1 Second-Order Election theory

The German case seems to validate the hypothesis of the Second-Order Election theory relating to the lower participation of citizens in EP elections in comparison with federal general elections, even if this aspect did not become more prominent in 2009.

Table 5.8 List of German MEPs: seventh legislature

Name	National party	Political group	Professional background	Year of birth	Gender	Committee/Chair
Balz, Burkhard	CDU	EPP	Banking salesmen	1969	Male	
Böge, Reimer			Farmer, agronomy engineer	1951	Male	
Brok, Elmar			Journalist, professional politician	1946	Male	Delegation relations with USA
Caspary, Daniel			Economist	1976	Male	
Ehler, Christian			Manager	1963	Male	Delegation relations with Korean peninsula
Ferber, Markus			Engineer	1965	Male	
Florenz, Karl-Heinz			Salesman	1947	Male	
Gahler, Michael			Diplomat	1960	Male	Delegation Panafrican Parliament
Grässle, Inge			Journalist	1961	Female	
Jahr, Dieter Peter			Economist	1959	Male	
Elisabeth, Jeggle			Farmer	1947	Female	
Klaß, Christa			Rural enterprise manager	1951	Female	
Koch, Dieter Lebrecht			Architect	1953	Male	
Kuhn, Werner			Entrepreneur	1941	Male	
Langen, Werner			Economist	1949	Male	Delegation for relations with the countries of Southeast Asia and the Association of Southeast Asian Nations (ASEAN)
Lechner, Kurt			Notary	1942	Male	
Lehne, Klaus Heiner			Lawyer	1957	Male	Conference of Committee Chairs and Committee on Legal Affairs
Liese, Peter			Physician	1965	Male	
Mann, Thomas			Industrial salesman	1946	Male	
Mayer, Hans-Peter			Lawyer	1944	Male	
Pack, Doris			Local councillor	1942	Female	Culture and education
Pieper, Markus			Manager	1963	Male	
Pöttering, Hans-Gert			Lawyer	1945	Male	Vice-president regional development
Quisthoudt-Rowohlt, Godelieve			Chemist	1947	Female	
Reul, Herbert			School teacher	1957	Male	Industry, research, and energy

(continued)

Table 5.8 (continued)

Name	National party	Political group	Professional background	Year of birth	Gender	Committee/Chair
Schnellhard, Horst			Veterinarian	1946	Male	
Schmieber-Jastram, Birgit			Publishing house editor	1946	Female	
Schwab, Andreas			Civil servant	1973	Male	
Sommer, Renate			Agricultural engineer	1958	Female	
Ulmer, Thomas			Physician	1956	Male	
Verheyen, Sabine			Local councillor, Mayor of Aaachen	1964	Female	
Voss, Axel			Lawyer	1963	Male	
Wieland, Rainer			Lawyer	1957	Male	
Winkler, Herman			Engineer, local councillor	1963	Male	
Zeller, Joachim			Librarian	1952	Male	
Deß, Albert	CSU		Farmer	1947	Male	
Ferber, Markus			Engineer	1965	Male	
Hohlmeier, Monika			Hotelier	1962	Female	
Kastler, Martin			Journalist	1974	Male	
Niebler, Angelika			Lawyer	1963	Female	Delegation of relations with Arabic peninsula
Posselt, Bernd			Journalist	1956	Male	
Weber, Manfred			Engineer	1972	Male	
Weisgerber, Anja			Professional politician	1976	Female	
Bullmann, Udo	SPD	S&D	University lecturer	1956	Male	
Ertug, Ismail			Health insurance consultant, Local councillor	1975	Male	
Fleckenstein, Knut			Manager	1953	Male	Delegation EU-Russian Parliamentary Cooperation Committee
Gebhardt, Evelyne			Lecturer	1954	Male	
Geier, Jens			Party functionary	1961	Male	
Glante, Norbert			Electronic engineer	1952	Male	Vice-president of Delegation to the Euro-Latin American Parliamentary Assembly
Groote, Matthias			Industrial engineer	1973	Male	

Haug, Jutta		Local councillor, professional politician	1951	Female	Special Committee on the Policy Challenges and Budgetary Resources for a Sustainable European Union after 2013 Vice-president budgets
Kammerevert, Petra		Professional politician	1966	Female	
Krehl, Constanze Angela		IT specialist	1956	Female	
Kreissl-dorfler, Wolfgang		Farmer, qualified social science teacher	1950	Male	
Lange, Bernd		School teacher	1955	Male	
Leinen, Jo		Professional politician	1948	Male	
Neuser, Norbert		Head school teacher	1949	Male	
Rapkay, Bernhard		Public relations officer	1951	Male	
Rodust, Ulrike		Business administrator	1949	Female	Environment, public health and food safety
Roth-Behrendt, Dagmar		Civil servant	1953	Female	Vice-president European Parliament
Schulz, Martin		Bookshop owner	1955	Male	
Simon, Peter		Lawyer, civil servant	1967	Male	
Sippel, Birgit		Trade union officer	1960	Female	
Steinruck, Jutta		Personnel manager	1962	Female	
Weiler, Barbara		Industrial manager	1946	Female	
Westphal, Kerstin		Nursery teacher	1962	Female	
Albrecht, Jan Philip	*Bündnis 90/Die Grünen* Greens/European Free Alliance	Student	1982	Male	
Brantner, Franziska		University lecturer	1979	Female	
Bütikofer, Reinhard		Professional politician	1953	Male	
Cramer, Michael		School teacher	1949	Male	
Giegold, Sven		Professional politician	1969	Male	
Häfner, Gerald		Journalist	1956	Male	
Harms, Rebecca		Landscape gardener	1956	Female	Vice-president Delegation Korean peninsula
Häusling, Martin		Farmer	1961	Male	
Keller, Franziska		Professional politician	1981	Female	
Lochbihler, Barbara		Social worker	1959	Female	Delegation with relations with Iran
Rühle, Heide		Psychologist	1948	Female	
Schroedter, Elisabeth		Business director	1959	Female	Vice-president employment and social affairs

(continued)

Table 5.8 (continued)

Name	National party	Political group	Professional background	Year of birth	Gender	Committee/Chair
Schulz, Werner			Engineer	1950	Male	Vice-president delegation to the EU–Russia Parliamentary Cooperation Committee
Trüpel, Helga			Politician	1958	Female	Vice-president culture and education and Special Committee on the Policy Challenges and Budgetary Resources for a Sustainable European Union after 2013
Alvaro, Alexander	FDP	ALDE	Banking salesman	1975	Male	Vice-president budget
Chatzimarkakis, Georgios			Civil servant, manager	1966	Male	Delegation to the EU-Former Yugoslav Republic of Macedonia Joint Parliamentary Committee
Creutzmann, Jürgen			Chartered accountant	1945	Male	
Hirsch, Nadja			Business mediator	1978	Female	
Klinz, Wolf			Business administrator	1941	Male	Special Committee on the Financial, Economic and Social Crisis
Koch-mehrin, Silvana			Business consultant	1970	Female	Vice-president European Parliament
Krahmer, Holger			Banking salesman	1970	Male	Vice-president delegation of relations with Arabic peninsula
Lambsdorff, Alexander Graf			Diplomat	1966	Male	
Meissner, Gesine			Communication instructor	1952	Female	
Reimers, Britta			Farmer	1971	Female	
Thein, Alexandra			Lawyer	1963	Female	
Theurer, Michael			Newspaper editor	1967	Male	
Bisky, Lothar	Die Linke	EUL/NGL	University lecturer	1941	Male	
Ernst, Cornelia			Instructor	1956	Female	
Händel, Thomas			Electrician	1953	Male	
Klute, Jürgen			Pastor	1953	Male	
Lösing, Sabine			Social worker	1955	Female	
Scholz, Helmut			Diplomat	1954	Male	
Wils, Sabine			Midwife	1959	Female	Vice-president culture and education
Zimmer, Gabriele			Translator	1955	Female	Vice-president delegation of relations with Iran

Source: European Parliament (2009) website: www.europarl.europa.eu/meps/en/search.html?country=DE.

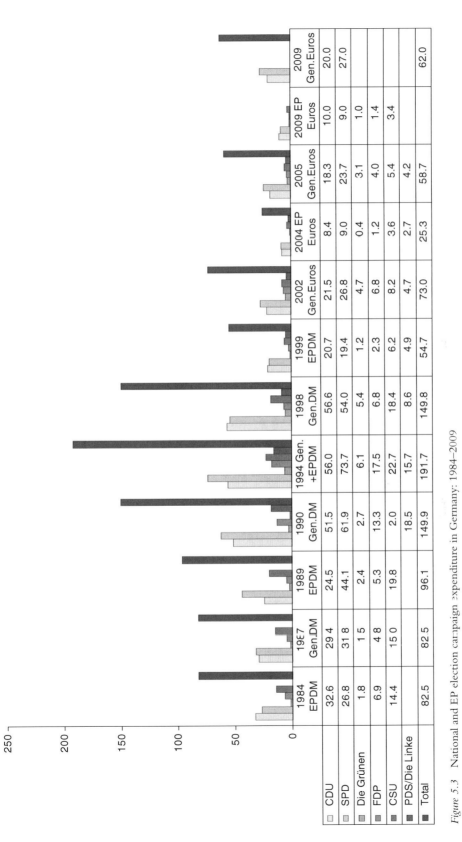

Figure 5.3 National and EP election campaign expenditure in Germany: 1984–2009

Source: *Deutscher Bundestag* 1984; 1985; 1988; 1990; 1992; 1995; 2000a; 2000b; 2004; 2006; 2007; and 2010.

A higher voting share of small and new political parties at the cost of the larger established parties was also corroborated (Treschel, 2010). In addition, the defeat of governing parties could be generally registered in Euro-elections. In particular in 2009, the most dramatic result was the loss of over 1.3 million voters by the CDU that went in a large part to the FDP (Infratest Dimap, 2009, 8; Treschel, 2010). The SPD's performance was even worse than in the 2004 European election and in the 2005 general election, which at the time was seen as an expression of protest against the government led by Chancellor Schröder and the so-called 'Agenda 2010'. The SPD did not manage to mobilize its former voters and had to face an all-time low in elections for the second time in a row.

The effects of the timing of the EP contest in the national electoral cycle could also be noticed. Euro-elections in Germany, held at the end of the electoral cycle starting in 2005, were quite a dress rehearsal for the subsequent general elections that took place on 27 September 2009. This meant that the results reached at the European elections were almost the same as those of the federal elections. The two largest parties were punished in the European elections, whilst the smaller parliamentary parties were able to improve their score.

However, the Second-Order Election theory cannot really explain the poor performance of the German Social Democrats, the junior partner of the then coalition government, which had an even worse result than the abysmal one in 2004 and reiterated its low score in the general elections.

As Simon Hix has argued, the loss of the mainstream parties on the centre-left stemmed from their adoption of economic mainstays, such as high public spending, similar to those proposed by their political rivals. As a result, 'voters cannot tell the difference between the centre-right and centre-left, and centre-right leaders in many countries look younger, fresher and more competent than centre-left leaders' (Hix, 2009, 5).

10.2 Europe Salience theory

Although 'Europe matters' in the German debates, overtly such questions were never likely to play a very prominent role in the agenda of political parties or in influencing voters' choices, with the exception of the FDP and the Greens. These parties, which actually put greater emphasis on the European Union in their manifestos, increased their voting share at the 2009 European election in relation to the 2005 legislative election. As a result, it could be argued that empirical evidence for the Europe Salience theory appears rather mixed.

Moreover, the hypothesis that anti-EU parties perform better in European elections could not be confirmed. In 2009, *Die Linke*, commonly regarded as the most German Eurosceptic party and long seen as likely to profit from the economic crisis due to its fierce criticism of the EU model, lost votes compared to the previous election. The two right-wing extreme parties which were strongly against the European integration project, the DVU and the *Republikaner*, failed to reach the nationwide 5 per cent threshold at the 2009 Euro-election.

Even if a more sceptical agenda for European integration has emerged (Harnisch and Schieder, 2006), there is no radical right-wing extreme party supporting a Eurosceptic agenda with a chance of being represented in the *Bundestag* or in the European Parliament in the short term (Lees, 2008). The most plausible working hypothesis to understand the German Euro-elections from the perspective of Europe Salience theory is that Green parties receive a greater increase in their vote share compared to other parties and in relation to previous national elections. The Greens represent a well-established party and are usually successful in European elections. German voters, concerned about environmental issues and aware of the importance of the European Parliament in the EU institutional framework, are likely to switch their vote to the Green party in a European election.

Over the years, whereas all political parties in Germany have been supportive of the European integration process, the population has become less pro-European. As a result, turnout in EP elections has been consistently lower than that at national elections. Overall, Germany seems to fit more in the Second-Order Election theory than in the Europe Salience model for the following reasons. Although European issues are raised at European Parliament elections, they are framed through national lenses. In addition, political parties spend less of their funding on such electoral contests and they even gain a profit out of the generous public funding system, in order to finance national elections that are considered to be far more important. Finally, political parties regard EP elections as a dress rehearsal for the forthcoming legislative elections. Against this background, it has to be pointed out that Euro-elections have become quite established in the multilevel governance electoral system in Germany, thus playing a crucial role as the trendsetter within the national electoral cycle.

References

Primary sources

50Plus-Das Generationen-Bündnis (2009) http:// 50plus-bund.de (accessed on 7 September 2010).
Ab jetzt. Bündnis für Deutschland, für Demokratie durch Volksabstimmung (2009) http://blog.demokratie-durch-volksabstimmung.de (accessed on 4 September 2010).
AUF – Arbeit, Umwelt, Familie-Christen für Deutschland (2009) www.auf – partei.de (accessed on 4 September 2010).
Aufbruch für Bürgerrechte, Freiheit und Gesundheit (2009) http://www.partei-aufbruch.de (accessed on 20 August 2013).
Bayernpartei (2009) www.bayernpartei.de (accessed on 4 September 2010).
Bundesamt für Statistik (2010) www.destatis.de (accessed on 4 September 2010).
Bundesverfassungsgericht (2008) Judgment of 3 July 2008 – 2 BvC 1/07, 2 BvC 7/07 – 'Provisions of the Federal Electoral Act from which the effect of negative voting weight emerges unconstitutional', www.bundesverfassungsgericht.de/en/ (accessed on 28 August 2013).
Bundesverfassungsgericht (2009) Urteil vom 30. Juni 2009: www.bundesverfassungsgericht.de/entscheidungen/es20090630_2bve000208.html (accessed on 28 February 2010).
Bundesverfassungsgericht (2011) Judgment of 9 November 2011 – 2 BvC 4/10, 2 BvC 6/10, 2 BvC 8/10 – 'Five per cent barrier clause in the law governing the European elections held unconstitutional', www.bundesverfassungs-gericht.de/en/ (accessed on 28 August 2013).
Bundeswahlleiter (2009) Europawahl 2009. Ergebnisse in Deutschland. 30 Jahre Direktwahl des Europäischen Parlaments. Informationen des Bundeswahlleiters. Flyer. Wiesbaden, Büro des Bundeswahlleiters, www.bundeswahlleiter.de/de/europawahlen/EU_BUND_09/ergebnisse/faltblatt_ergebnisse_ew2009.pdf (accessed on 7 September 2010).
Bundeszentrale für politische Bildung (2012) *Grundgesetz für die Bundesrepublik Deutschland*. Bonn: Bundeszentrale für politische Bildung.
Bündnis 90/Die Grünen (2009) Volles Programm mit WUMS für ein Besseres Europa. Berlin, Bündnis 90/Die Grünen.
Bürgerrechtsbewegung Solidarität (2009) www.bueso.de (accessed on 4 September 2010).
CDU.tv(2009) www.youtube.com/cdutv?gl=DE&hl=de (accessed on 7 September 2010).
Christlich-Demokratische Union (CDU) (2009) Wir in Europa. Starkeres Europa – sichere Zukunft. Programm der Christlich-Demokratischen Partei zur Europawahl 2009, Berlin, CDU.
Christliche Mitte (2009) www.christliche-mitte.de (accessed on 4 September 2010).
Christlich-Soziale Union (CSU) (2009) CSU-Europawahlprogramm 2009. Beschluss des CSU Parteiausschusses vom 9.Mai 2009, www.csu.de (accessed on 4 September 2010).
Deutscher Bundestag 1984; 1985; 1988; 1990; 1992; 1995; 2000a; 2000b; 2004; 2006; 2007; 2010. Campaign Expenditure for Federal and European Parliament elections, www.bundestag.de/bundestag/parteienfinanzierung/rechenschaftsberichte/rechenschaftsberichte/202446 (accessed on 4 September 2010).
Deutsche Kommunistische Partei (2009) Website, http://www.dkp.de (accessed on 29 August 2013).

Deutsche Volksunion (2009) http://www.dvu-berlin.info/index.html (accessed on 29 August 2013).
Die Grauen-Generationspartei (2009) http://www.diegrauen-generationspartei.com (accessed on 29 August 2013).
Die Linke (2009) 'Solidarität, Demokratie, Frieden – Gemeinsam für den Wechsel in Europa! Europawahlprogramm 2009 der Partei DIE LINKE'. Online. Available at: http://die-linke.de (accessed 29 August 2013).
Die Republikaner (2009) http://www.rep.de (accessed on 29 August 2013).
Die Violetten: für spirituelle Politik (2009) http://die-violetten.de (accessed on 29 August 2013).
Europa-Demokratie-Esperanto (EDE) (2009) www.e-d-e.eu (accessed on 4 September 2010).
European Parliament (2009) www.europarl.europa.eu/parliament/archive/elections2009/en/index_en.html (accessed on 7 December 2013).
Eurobarometer (2009) Europawahlen 2009, Spezialbarometer EBS 299, http://ec.europa.eu/public_opinion/archives/ebs/ebs_299_de.pdf (accessed on 10 January 2012).
Eurobarometer (2011) Eurobarometer Surveys 1979–2011, Public Opinion in the European Union, Brussels, European Commission, http://ec.europa.eu/public_opinion/archives/eb_arch_en.htm (accessed on 8 January 2011).
Eurostat (2013, 2014) http://epp.eurostat.ec.europa.eu (accessed on 5 June 2015).
Familienpartei Deutschlands (2009) www.familienpartei.de (accessed on 4 September 2010).
Federal Ministry of the Interior (2010) 'National Minorities in Germany', www.bmi.bund.de/SharedDocs/Downloads/EN/Broschueren/2010/nat_minderheiten.pdf?__blob=publicationFile (accessed 10 January 2012).
Feministische Partei-Die Frauen (2009) Website, www.feministischepartei.de (accessed on 4 September 2010).
Freie Bürger Initiative (2009) www.fbi-europawahl.de (accessed on 4 September 2010).
Freie Demokratische Partei (FDP) (2009) *Eine Europa der Freiheit für die Welt des 21.Jahrhunderts. Programm der Freien Demokratischen Partei für den Wahl zum VII. Europäischen Parlament 2009*. Beschluss des Europaparteitags der FDP, Berlin, 17 Januar 2009, www.fdp.de (accessed on 3 September 2010).
Freie Wähler (2009) http://freie-wähler-deutschland.de (accessed on 4 September 2010).
Für Volksentscheide (2009) www.fuervolksentscheide.de (accessed on 4 September 2010).
Infratest dimap (2009) Wahl zum Europäischen Parlament 7 Juni 2009, www.infratestdimap.de/uploads/media/EU_0906_Wahlreport_II_Leseprobe.pdf (accessed on 4 September 2009).
Mensch-Umwelt-Tierschutz (2009) www.tierschutzpartei.de (accessed on 4 September 2010).
Newropeans (2009) www.newropeans.eu (accessed 4 September 2010).
Ökologisch-Demokratische Partei (ÖDP) (2009) www.ödp.de (accessed on 4 September 2010).
Partei Bibeltreuer Christen (2009) www.pbc.de (accessed on 4 September 2010).
Partei der Sozialen Gleichheit (2009) www.gleichheit.de (accessed on 4 September 2010).
Partei für Arbeit, Umwelt, Familie – Christen für Deutschland (2009) http://www.auf-partei.de (accessed on 4 September 2010).
Piratenpartei Deutschlands (2009) www.piratenpartei.de (accessed on 4 September 2010).
Renterinnen und Rentner Partei (2009) www.rrp-bund.de (accessed on 4 September 2010).
Rentner Partei Deutschlands (2009) www.rentner-partei.com (accessed on 4 September 2010).
Sozialdemokratische Partei Deutschlands (SPD) (2009) Europamanifest der Sozialdemokratischen Partei Deutschlands für den Wahl zum Europäischen Parlament 2009. Berlin, SPD.
Statistisches Bundesamt (2013) Demografischer Wandel in Deutschland, Heft 1: Bevölkerungs-und Haushaltsentwicklung im Bund und in den Ländern, Wiesbaden: Statistisches Bundesamt, www.destatis.de (accessed on 28 August 2013).

Secondary sources

Almond G. and Verba S. (1963) *The Civic Culture. Political Attitudes and Democracy in Five Nations*, Princeton, Princeton University Press.
Anderson, J. J. and Goodman, John B. (1993) 'Mars or Minerva? A United Germany in a Post-Cold War Europe', in Keohane, Robert O. et al. (eds) *After the Cold War. International Institutions and State Strategies in Europe, 1989–1991*, Cambridge, MA, Harvard University Press, 23–62.
Binder, T. and Wüst, A. M. (2004) 'Inhalte der Europawahlprogramme deutscher Parteien 1979–1999', *Aus Politik und Zeitgeschichte*, B17/2004, 38–45.
Bulmahn, T., Fiebig, R. and Hilpert, C. (2010) *Sicherheits-und verteidigungspolitisches Meinungsklima in der Bundesrepublik Deutschland. Ergebnisse der Bevölkerungsbefragung 2010 des Sozialwissenschaftlichen*, Strausberg, Institut der Bundeswehr.

Bulmer, S. and Paterson, W. E. (2010) 'Germany and the European Union: From "Tamed Power" to Normalized Power?' *International Affairs*, 86(5), 1051–73.

Bulmer, S., Jeffery, C. and Padgett, S. (2010) 'Democracy and Diplomacy, Germany and Europe', in Bulmer, S. et al. (eds) *Rethinking Germany and Europe. Democracy and Diplomacy in a Semi-Sovereign State*, Basingstoke, Palgrave, 1–25.

Bulmer, S., Jeffery, C. and Paterson, W. E. (1986) 'The Federal Republic of Germany', in Lodge, J. (ed.) *Direct Elections to the European Parliament 1984*, Basingstoke, Macmillan, 190–210.

Bulmer, S., Jeffery, C. and Paterson, W. E. (2000) *Germany's European Diplomacy: Shaping the Regional Milieu*, Manchester, Manchester University Press.

Clemens, G., Reinfeldt, A. and Wille, G. (2008) *Geschichte der europäischen Integration*, Paderborn, Ferdinand Schöningh/UTB.

Die Welt (2009a) Seehofer warnt CSU vor weiteren Verlusten, 9 May. Online. Available at: www.welt.de/politik/article3708021/Seehofer-warnt-CSU-vor-weiteren-Verlusten.html (accessed on 29 August 2013).

Die Welt (2009b) 'Was uns die Wahlwerbung über die Parteien sagt', 29 May. Online. Available at: www.welt.de/politik/article3829211/Was-uns-die-Wahlwerbung-ueber-die-Parteien-sagt.html (accessed on 29 August 2013).

Die Zeit (2009a) 'Rote Front gegen Europa', 26 February. Online. Available at: www.zeit.de/online/2009/09/linke-europa-lafontaine-brie (accessed on 29 August 2013).

Die Zeit (2009b) 'SPD setzt auf sinnlose Polemik', 13 June. Online. Available at: www.zeit.de/online/2009/18/spd-wahlkampf (accessed on 29 August 2013).

Die Zeit (2009c) 'Auf ihrem Europaparteitag schwört der Kanzlerkandidat die SPD auf Krise und Superwahljahr 2009 ein', 4 May. Online. Available at: www.zeit.de/online/2008/50/spd-krise-steinmeier (accessed on 29 August 2013).

Der Spiegel (1989a) 'Schmierfinken und andere', 12 June. Online. Available at: http://magazin.spiegel.de/EpubDelivery/spiegel/pdf/13493708 (accessed on 28 August 2013).

Der Spiegel (1989b) 'Dröhnendes Geschwätz', 26 June. Online. Available at: http://magazin.spiegel.de/EpubDelivery/spiegel/pdf/13507094 (accessed on 28 August 2013).

Der Spiegel (1989c) 'Die EG liegt für die meisten eben weit ab', 12 June. Online. Available at: http://magazin.spiegel.de/EpubDelivery/spiegel/pdf/13493930 (accessed on 28 August 2013).

Der Spiegel (2009a) 'Überraschendes Strategiepapier: Steinmeier und Steinbrück wollen Finanzmärkte zähmen', 27 February. Online. Available at: www.spiegel.de/politik/deutschland/ueberraschendes-strategiepapier-steinmeier-und-steinbrueck-wollen-finanzmaerkte-zaehmen-a-610370.html (accessed on 29 August 2013).

Der Spiegel (2009b) 'Sektierer-Vorwurf: Linke EU-Abgeordnete Kaufmann wechselt zur SPD', 14 May. Online. Available at: www.spiegel.de/politik/deutschland/sektierer-vorwurf-linke-eu-abgeordnete-kaufmann-wechselt-zur-spd-a-624834.html (accessed on 29 August 2013).

Der Spiegel (2009c) 'Europawahl: CDU kürt Pöttering zum Spitzenkandidaten', 16 March. Online. Available at: www.spiegel.de/politik/deutschland/europawahl-cdu-kuert-poettering-zum-spitzenkandidaten-a-613594.html (accessed on 29 August 2013).

Euractive (2009) 'Ist London eine Gefahr für Lissabon?' 8 June 2009, http://www.euractiv.de/wahlen-und-macht/artikel/proeuropaische-parteien-der-mitte-unter-druck-001636 (accessed on 28 August 2013).

Frankfurter Allgemeine Zeitung (2009) CDU spricht sich für weitere Amtszeit Barrosos aus – Präsidium verabschiedet Programm für Europawahl, 17 March, 4.

Gagatek, W., Trechsel A. H. and Breuer, F. (2010) 'Bringing the European Parliament Election Results Closer to the Citizens', in Gagatek, W. (ed.) *The 2009 Elections to the European Parliament. Country Reports*, Florence, European University Institute, xi–xiii.

Guérot, U. and Leonard M. (2011) *The New German Question: How Europe Can Get the Germany It Needs*. Policy Brief, European Council on Foreign Relations, http://www.ecfr.eu/page//ECFR30_GERMANY_AW.pdf (accessed on 15 February 2012).

Harmsen, R. (2007) 'Euroscepticism', in Déloye, Y. and Bruter, M. (eds) *Encyclopaedia of European Elections*, Basingstoke, Palgrave, 207–12.

Harnisch, S. and Schieder, S. (2006) 'Germany's New European Policy. Weaker, Leaner, Meaner', in Maull, H. W. (ed.) *Germany's Uncertain Power: Foreign Policy of the Berlin Republic*, New York, Palgrave, 95–108.

Hesse, K. (1962) *Der unitarische Bundesstaat*, Karlsruhe, C. F. Müller.

Hix, S. (2009) 'The 2009 European Parliament Elections: A Disaster for Social Democrats', *EUSA Review*, 22(4), 3–5.
Hough, D. and Olsen J. (2007) *The Left Party in Contemporary German Politics*, Basingstoke, Palgrave.
Jesse, E. and Lang, J. (2008) *Die Linke. Der smarte Extremismus einer deutschen Partei*, München, Olzog.
Katz, R. and Mair, P. S. (1995) 'Changing Models of Party Organization and Party Democracy', *Party Politics*, 1 (1), 5–28.
Katzenstein, P. J. (1987) *Policy and Politics in West Germany: The Growth of the Semi-Sovereign Polity*, Philadelphia, Temple University Press.
Katzenstein, P. J. (1997) 'United Germany in an Integrating Europe', in Katzenstein P. J. (ed.) *Tamed Power: Germany in Europe*, Ithaca, Cornell University Press, 1–47.
Korte, K. R. (2009) Wahlkampfkosten, Dossier Bundestagswahlen. Online. Available at: www.bpb.de/themen/UZRZTH,0,Wahlkampfkosten.html (accessed on 8 September 2010).
Landeszentrale für politische Bildung Baden-Württemberg (2009) 'Europawahl 2009', Baden-Württemberg. Online. Available at: www.europawahl-bw.de/2765.html (accessed on 7 September 2010).
Lees, C. (2008) 'The Limits of Party-Based Euroscepticism in Germany', in Szczerbiak, A. and Taggart, P. (eds), *Opposing Europe? The Comparative Party Politics of Euroscepticism*, Vol. 1, Oxford, Oxford University Press, 16–37.
Maull, H. W. (1990) 'Germany and Japan: The New Civilian Powers', *Foreign Affairs*, 69(5), 91–106.
Menke, K. (1985) 'Germany' in Reif, K. H. (ed.) *Ten European Elections. Campaigns and Results of the 1979/81 First Direct Elections to the European Parliament*, Aldershot, Gower, 67–84.
Müller-Graff, P. (2010) Das Lissabon-Urteil: Implikationen für die Europapolitik, *Aus Politik und Zeitgeschichte*, B18, 22–9.
Niedermayer, O. (2005) 'Europa als Randthema: Der Wahlkampf und die Wahlkampfstrategien der Parteien?' in Niedermayer O. and Schmitt H. (eds) *Europawahl 2004*, Wiesbaden, Verlag Sozialwissenschaften, 39–75.
Niedermayer, O. (2007) 'Das Parteiensystem Deutschlands' in Niedermayer O., Stöss R. and Haas, M. (eds) *Die Parteiensysteme Westeuropas*, Wiesbaden, Verlag für Sozialwissenschaften, 109–33.
Paterson, W. E. (2005) 'European Policy-making: Between Associated Sovereignty and Semi-sovereignty' in Patterson W. E. and Green S. (eds) *Governance in Contemporary Germany. The Semi-Sovereign State Revisited*, Cambridge, Cambridge University Press, 261–82.
Paterson, W. E. (2010) 'Does Germany Still Have a European Vocation?' *German Politics*, 19(1), 41–52.
Paterson, W. E., Lee, Ch. and Green, Simon (1996) 'The Federal Republic of Germany', in Lodge, J. (ed.) *The 1994 Elections to the European Parliament*, London, Pinter, 66–83.
Rudzio, W. (2006) *Das politische System der Bundesrepublik Deutschland*, 7. Auflage. Wiesbaden, Verlag der Sozialwissenschaften.
Saalfeld, T. (2005) 'Political Parties', in Green, S. and Patterson, W. E. (eds) *Governance in Contemporary Germany. The Semisovereign State Revisited,* Cambridge, Cambridge University Press, 46–77.
Scheuer, A. and Schmitt, H. (2009) 'Sources of EU Support: The Case of Germany', *German Politics* 18(4), 577–90.
Schieder, S. (2011) 'Problematizing Europe, or Evidence of an Emergent Euroscepticism?' in Harmsen, R. and Schild, J. (eds) *Debating Europe: The 2009 European Parliament Elections and Beyond*, Baden-Baden, Nomos, 33–51.
Schild, J. (2003) 'Die Europäisierung nationaler politischer Identität in Deutschland und Frankreich', *Aus Politik und Zeitgeschichte*, B3-4, 31–49.
Süddeutsche Zeitung (2008) 'Eine Abstimmung mit hohem Symbolwert', 8, December 2008, 6.
Trechsel, A. H. (2010) 'How Much "Second-Order" Were the European Parliament Elections 2009?', in Gagatek, W. (ed.) *The 2009 Elections to the European Parliament. Country Reports*, Florence, European University Institute, 3–13.
Viola, D. M. (2010) 'Le elezioni europee del 2009 in Germania fra crisi dei partiti e indifferenza popolare'. Online. Available at: www.officinadellastoria.it (accessed on 5 December 2013).
Wilkens, A. (2004) 'Désir d´Europe et réalités nationales: l´opinion publique allemande et la construction européenne', in Dunphy, A. and Manigand, C. (eds) *Public Opinion and Europe. National Identities and the European Integration Process*, Berne, Peter Lang, 63–77.

6
ITALY

Donatella M. Viola

Figure 6.1 Map of Italy

Table 6.1 Italy profile

EU entry year	1952 ECSC; 1958 EEC and Euratom founding member
Schengen entry year	1990
MEPs elected in 2009	72 of whom:
	21 North-West Constituency
	14 North-East Constituency (lost one seat in favour of Southern Constituency in June 2011)
	15 MEPs Centre Constituency
	16 South Constituency (gained one seat after Giuseppe Gargani's appeal in June 2011)
	6 Islands Constituency
MEPs under Lisbon Treaty	73 since 1 December 2011, one additional seat within the South Constituency allocated to Gino Trematerra (EPP)
Capital	Rome
Total area★	302,073 km²
Population	60,782,668
	93.52% Italians
	German, French, Slovene, and Ladin-speaking minorities
	Foreigners:1.32% Romanians and 1.01% North Africans
Population density ★★	199.4/km²
Median age of population	44.7
Political system	Parliamentary Republic
Head of state	Giorgio Napolitano (May 2006–January 2015), Sergio Mattarella (February 2015–)
Head of government	Silvio Berlusconi, People of Freedom (PdL) (May 2008–November 2011);
	Mario Monti, Independent (November 2011–February 2013);
	Enrico Letta, Democratic Party (PD) (April 2013–February 2014);
	Matteo Renzi, Democratic Party (PD) (February 2014–)
Political majority	Party of Freedom (PdL) and Northern League (LN) Coalition (May 2008–November 2011);
	Technocratic Cabinet (November 2011–February 2013);
	Democratic Party (PD), Party of Freedom (PdL)/New Centre-Right (NCD), Civic Choice (SC), For Italy (PI) and Radicals' Grand Coalition (April 2013–February 2014);
	Democratic Party (PD), New Centre-Right (NCD), Union of the Centre (UdC) and Independents' Coalition (February 2014–)
Currency	Euro (€) since 1999
Prohead GDP in PPS	26,600 €

Source: Eurostat, 2013, 2014, http://epp.eurostat.ec.europa.eu/.

Notes:
★ Total area including inland waters.
★★ Population density: the ratio of the annual average population of a region to the land area of the region.

1 Geographical position

Italy lies in southern Europe, at the heart of the Mediterranean Sea, at the geographical coordinates of 42 degrees 49 minutes north and 12 degrees and 49 minutes east. It comprises a long, boot-shaped peninsula which features over 27 per cent of the whole Alpine mountain range as well as approximately 350 sea islands, amongst which Sicily and Sardinia are the largest. As far as Corsica is concerned, although closer geographically to Italy and originally belonging to the Republic of Genoa, the island has been under French rule since 1764. Whereas the northern border of the peninsula follows the Alpine arc, touching from west to east on France, Switzerland, Austria, and Slovenia, the remaining territorial limits are maritime including the Adriatic, Ionian, Tyrrhenian, and Ligurian Seas. Italy covers a surface area of 302,073 square kilometres, thus representing the seventh largest country in the European Union. It is the twenty-third most populous country in the world, with over 60 million inhabitants.

2 Historical background

In 1861, in the wake of the Italian *Risorgimento* (Rising Again) Movement – which resulted in three wars of independence and the historical enterprise led by Giuseppe Garibaldi – the various kingdoms, grand duchies, and small states on the peninsula were finally united under the monarchy of Vittorio Emanuele II. Sixty years later, on 28 October 1922, the era of parliamentary regime came to a close, after the 'March on Rome' that brought Benito Mussolini to power. Having obtained a parliamentary majority in the 1924 general election, his authority increased as head of government the following year, but it was not until 1926 that the Fascist dictatorship officially began. The *Dux*, as Mussolini was usually called, sought prestige through further colonial expansion, by undertaking a military campaign in Ethiopia, which started in October 1935 and ended with the official conquest of the country in May 1936, after the fall of Addis Ababa. In order to increase Italy's status as a military power, to expand its political influence in the Mediterranean, and to export its Fascist ideological model by preventing, at the same time, the spread of Communism, Mussolini decided to intervene in the Spanish Civil War between 1936 and 1939 by contributing to the victory of General Francisco Franco's Nationalist forces. Gradually, Italy's good relations with Britain, France, and the Soviet Union started to deteriorate, whilst its links with Adolf Hitler's Nazi Germany were reinforced under the so-called 'Rome–Berlin Axis', sealed on 25 and 26 October 1936. After an initially non-belligerent phase, the Pact of Steel with Germany inevitably pushed Italy to declare war on France and Britain on 10 June 1940; on the Soviet Union on 22 June 1941; and on the United States on 11 December 1941 (Spini, 1963). The tragic events of the Second World War (WWII) inexorably brought Italy to its final defeat. Mussolini's summary execution by members of the resistance near Lake Como on 28 April 1946 marked the end of the Facist era. With an outrageous act of violence and hatred, the partisans hanged his brutalized body upside down in Milan's Piazza Loreto for public viewing. The Treaty of Peace, which was signed in Paris on 10 February 1947, imposed severe territorial restrictions. Italy ceded to France several areas in the Alps; to Yugoslavia the city of Zara together with the islands off the Dalmatian coast; and to Greece the Dodecanese Islands in the Aegean Sea. Italy also had to give up all its rights in Libya, Eritrea, and Somalia whilst recognizing the independence of Albania and Ethiopia. In the aftermath of the conflict, the country had to face the great challenge of its material, political, and moral reconstruction. On 2 June 1946, after a popular referendum that abolished the monarchy by a slender majority, the country became a republic, opening a new page in its history (Spini, 1963).

3 Geopolitical profile

In the post-war period, Italy's main international objectives were to enfranchise itself after more than 20 years of isolation from the Western world under Fascism and to restore its political reputation by regaining the trust and respect of the world community. As a result, it sought and obtained membership of the United Nations (UN) in 1945, including its various agencies, most notably the Food and Agriculture Organization (FAO) headquartered in Rome. On 5 May 1949, the Italian government, along with those of Belgium, Denmark, France, Ireland, Luxembourg, the Netherlands, Norway, Sweden, and the UK, signed the Treaty of London establishing the Council of Europe with the aim of promoting European cooperation in the areas of human rights, democratic development, and the rule of law.

Italy also joined defence and military organizations, such as the North Atlantic Treaty Organization (NATO) in 1949 and the Western European Union (WEU) in 1955, under the Paris Agreements, which expanded the 1948 Brussels Treaty. As one of the beneficiaries of the Marshall Plan, the country became a member of the Organization for European Economic Cooperation (OEEC), which had the task of administering US aid for the reconstruction of Europe after WWII, and later of the Organization for Economic Cooperation and Development (OECD), which officially superseded it in September 1961. Fourteen years later, on 1 August 1975, with the aim of bringing together the two Cold War rivals, the US and the USSR, the Italian prime minister, along with the representatives of 34 other nations signed the Final Act of the Conference on Security and Cooperation in Europe (CSCE) in Helsinki.

On 30 May 1950, Italy also joined the General Agreement on Tariffs and Trade (GATT), replaced on 1 January 1995 by the World Trade Organization (WTO), and today takes part in the process of consultation between the main industrialized countries known as the Group of Eight (G8) that the Italian government chaired in 2001 and 2009. Furthermore, the Italian political class has been at the forefront of the European economic and political integration project since its outset. Indeed, Italy was one of the founding members of the European Economic Community (EEC), as well as one of the first countries to join the Economic and Monetary Union and to adopt the euro as its official currency.

In sum, European Union membership and transatlantic cooperation noticeably represent the two main pillars that have characterized Italian foreign policy since the early 1950s. By virtue of its strategic geographical position, which seems naturally to divide the west and east of Europe, Italy has had contact with the main ethnic and cultural groups of the neo-Latin, Germanic, and Slavic-Balkan civilizations. Furthermore, as a bridge between Europe and Africa, with the island of Pantelleria and, above all, the Pelagie archipelago, including Lampedusa, Linosa, and Lampione, almost reaching the coast of Tunisia, Italy has shared historical events and cultural influences with North African countries and, more widely, with the Arab-Islamic world.

Nowadays, within an increasingly more complex global economic and political framework, Italy has a crucial role to play as a promoter of peace, moderation, and stability in this strategic geopolitical area.

The country, which represents one of the natural southern gates of the European Union, is one of the preferred first destinations for a flood of clandestine migrants from Africa, attempting to escape from poverty and pursuing their 'European or Western dreams'. In addition, after the upheavals of the so-called 'Arab Spring' and the outbreak of civil wars in Libya and in Syria in 2011, the number of political refugees forced to flee from their countries, where they risked certain death, has increased remarkably. Yet, for some of them the journey has ended tragically, such as on 3 April 2013, when over 300 people drowned after a boat caught fire and sank off Lampedusa. Italy, along with its EU partners, will have to face this emergency by adopting new, efficient migration and refugee policies.

4 Overview of the political landscape

The 1948 Italian Constitution established a bicameral multiparty parliamentary system, consisting of a lower chamber, the *Camera dei Deputati* (Chamber of Deputies) with 630 deputies and an upper chamber, the *Senato della Repubblica* (Senate of the Republic), with 315 senators. According to the principle of 'perfect bicameralism', the two houses enjoy the same powers and perform equal functions: they approve legislation, steer and monitor the activities of the executive, enquire into matters of public interest, and grant and revoke motions of confidence in government. In a special joint session, representatives of both chambers, along with regional delegates, elect the President of the Republic (Article 83).

In addition, Parliament in a joint sitting elects one-third of the judges of the Constitutional Court from among judges, including those retired, of the ordinary and administrative higher courts, university full professors in law, and lawyers with at least 20 years of practice (Article 135). Finally, jointly, deputies and senators choose one-third of the members of the Higher Council of the Judiciary from amongst university full professors of law and lawyers with at least 15 years of experience (Article 104).

Both houses are elected for a five-year period, but their membership and election rules vary to a great extent. Whereas deputies must be at least 25 years old and are chosen by all Italian citizens over 18, senators have to reach at least the age of 40 and are voted for by citizens older than 25. The upper chamber also includes life senators, who are appointed by the President 'for outstanding achievements in the social, scientific, artistic or literary fields' (Article 59). In addition, Article 59 of the Italian Constitution foresees that all former Presidents of the Republic may sit as life members in the Senate. Executive power is exercised collectively by the Council of Ministers, led by a President.

On the eve of the 2009 Euro-election, Italy was ruled by a coalition government led by the *Popolo della Libertà*, PdL (The People of Freedom) party, with two regionalist movements, the *Lega Nord*, LN (Northern League) and the *Movimento per l'Autonomia, MpA* (Movement for Autonomy) as partners, after a remarkable victory at the general election in April 2008, which had secured 344 out of 630 seats in the *Camera dei Deputati* and 174 out of 315 seats in the *Senato della Repubblica*.

However, in the wake of the most serious economic crisis since WWII, Prime Minister Silvio Berlusconi's popularity started to wane and, under strong pressure from the international financial and political community, the *Cavaliere* had no alternative but to resign in November 2011, after more than 17 years in power.

By the end of the year, an emergency technocratic cabinet was installed, with bipartisan support under the guidance of Mario Monti. His government ended in December 2012 in the wake of popular discontent with economic austerity and recession. Early elections were therefore convened in February 2013, bringing about a huge protest vote, sanctioned by the resounding success of the populist and anti establishment Five Star Movement, led by former comedian Beppe Grillo. His novel party won over 25.5 per cent of the vote, creating a three-way division in the Italian Parliament, with no group able to govern alone. After a two-month impasse, at the end of April 2013, a Grand Coalition government saw the light under Enrico Letta's premiership, initially supported by the PD, PdL, *Scelta Civica* (Civic Choice), and UdC.

The new government risked collapse on a no-confidence vote in the Senate in early October 2013, after Silvio Berlusconi had sparked a crisis by calling his ministers out of Letta's Cabinet. In the wake of a flaming debate within the upper house, where severe accusations were launched against the *Cavaliere* of sowing chaos in order to avoid expulsion from the Italian Parliament over a tax fraud conviction, Berlusconi unexpectedly decided to support the government (Bondi, 2 October 2013). Yet, on 13 February 2014, after a meeting of his own party, PD, which passed a motion of no confidence in his administration, Letta decided reluctantly to resign as prime minister in favour of the young new party leader and former mayor of Florence, Matteo Renzi, who had been strongly critical about his performance. Renzi's government faces the challenges of shaking the country out of its economic malaise, introducing institutional reforms and adopting a new electoral bill. Italian democracy appears to be held hostage to a fragile compromise between parties. In view of the fact that Italy represents the third largest member of the eurozone, its political situation is deemed to have profound repercussions on the whole European Union and, by implication, on the world economy.

5 Brief account of the political parties

The early years of the political history of the Kingdom of Italy were dominated by the so-called 'social and economic notables', using Max Weber's terminology (Weber, 1922). The '*Destra storica*' (historical right), led by Count Camillo Benso di Cavour, and the '*Sinistra storica*' (historical left), inspired by Giuseppe Mazzini, faced each other as rival groups within the parliamentary assembly, but never really achieved the status of fully-fledged parties (Spini, 1963). The Great War remarkably changed Italian society, highlighting aspirations for social redemption and popular revolutionary myths of peasants, workers, and the bourgeoisie. In the aftermath of the conflict, the introduction of universal suffrage for men over 21 years old who could read and write, marked the sunset of the elitist political circles and of 'parties of the notables' and the rise of the so-called mass political parties with national scope and a modern democratic organization. The birth of these parties dates back to the late nineteenth and the early twentieth centuries. More precisely, in August 1892 in Genoa, the *Partito dei Lavoratori Italiani* (Italian Workers' Party), which later adopted the name *Partito Socialista Italiano*, PSI (Italian Socialist Party), was founded by Filippo Turati, attracting members from trade unions, Socialist circles, and cooperative organizations. An intense struggle for power started within the PSI between left-wing members, known as 'maximalists', and the so-called 'reformists'. At the 1919 Bologna Congress, the left faction prevailed, and thus the party entered the Communist International (Comintern), but the PSI was defeated by Fascist squads and, most importantly, by its own inability to foment a revolution or even to undertake effective reform. Two years later, at the Livorno Congress, further internal disputes sanctioned the official and definitive party split with the departure of the extreme left-wingers who laid the grounds for the *Partito Comunista Italiano*, PCI (Italian Communist Party).

Set on the opposite side of the political spectrum, the extreme right-wing *Fasci italiani di combattimento* (Italian Fasci of Combat) surfaced in March 1919, on the initiative of a former member of the Italian Socialist Party, Benito Mussolini. The movement, which soon started to gain wide popular support and secured 35 seats in the Chamber of Deputies in the 1921 general election, eventually turned into the omnipotent *Partito Nazionale Fascista* (National Fascist Party) (Spini, 1963).

Meanwhile, in January 1919, based on Christian roots, the *Partito Popolare Italiano*, PPI (the Italian People's Party) was founded by Luigi Sturzo. As Federico Chabod emphasized, the birth of the PPI represented one of the most remarkable events in the history of the first half of the twentieth century in Italy (Chabod, 2002). In fact, it marked the official entry of the Catholics into national political life, thus healing the historical rift between the secular liberal state and the Catholic Church. This conflict had stemmed from the annexation of the papal state to the Kingdom of Piedmont, renamed as the Kingdom of Italy, and the proclamation of Rome as its capital city in February 1871. After the fall of Fascism at the end of WWII the newly refounded *Partito popolare,* under the charismatic leadership of Alcide De Gasperi, was renamed *Democrazia Cristiana*, DC (Christian Democracy).

Table 6.2 List of political parties in Italy

Original name	Abbreviation	English translation
Alleanza Nazionale	AN	National Alliance
Centro Cristiano Democratico	CCD	Christian Democratic Centre
Cristiani Democratici Uniti	CDU	United Christian Democrats
Democrazia Cristiana	DC	Christian Democracy
Democrazia europea	DE	European Democracy
Democrazia è Libertà – La Margherita	DL	Democracy is Freedom – The Daisy
Democratici di Sinistra/Partito Democratico della Sinistra	DS/PDS	Democrats of the Left/Democratic Party of the Left
Democrazia Proletaria	DP	Proletarian Democracy
Forza Italia	FI	Forward Italy
Italia dei Valori	IdV	Italy of Values
Fiamma Tricolore (Movimento Sociale – Fiamma Tricolore)	FT (MSFT)	Tricolour Flame (Social Movement – Tricolour Flame)
Fratelli d'Italia	FdI	Brothers of Italy
Futuro e Libertà per l'Italia	FLI	Future and Freedom for Italy
Lega d'Azione meridionale	LAM	Southern Action League
La Destra	LD	The Right
Lega Nord	LN	Northern League
Liberal Democratici	LD	Liberal Democrats
Movimento per l'Autonomia	MPA	Movement for Autonomy
Movimento Repubblicani Europei	MRE	European Republicans Movement
Movimento Cinque Stelle	M5S	Five-Star Movement
Movimento Sociale Italiano/Destra Nazionale	MSI/DN	Italian Social Movement/National Right
Partito Comunista Italiano	PCI	Italian Communist Party
Partito Democratico	PD	Democratic Party
Partito dei Comunisti italiani	PDCI	Party of the Italian Communists
Popolo della Libertà	PdL	Party of Freedom
Partito Liberale Italiano	PLI	Italian Liberal Party
Partito Popolare Italiano	PPI	Italian Popular Party
(Partito di) Rifondazione Comunista	(P)RC	(Party of) Communist Refoundation
Partito Repubblicano Italiano	PRI	Italian Republican Party
Partito Socialista Democratico Italiano	PSDI	Italian Socialist Democratic Party
Partito Socialista Italiano	PSI	Italian Socialist Party
Nuovo Partito Socialista Italiano	NPSI	New Italian Socialist Party
Partito Radicale	PR	Radical Party
Rinnovamento Italiano	RI	Italian Renewal
Scelta Civica	SC	Civic Choice
Sinistra Arcobaleno	SA	Rainbow Left
Sinistra Ecologia e Libertà	SEL	Left, Ecology and Freedom
Südtirolervolkspartei	SVP	South Tyrol People's Party
Ulivo		Olive
Unione Democratica	UD	Democratic Union
Unione di Centro/Unione dei Democratici Cristiani e di Centro	UDC	Union of the Centre/Union of Christian Democrats and Centrists
Unione Democratici per l'Europa	UDEUR	Democrats' Union for Europe
Union Valdotaine	UV	Valdotanian Union
Verdi	V	Greens
Verdi Arcobaleno	V-ARC	Rainbow Greens

The post-war national political system followed a model of 'extreme multipolar and polarized pluralism' involving a wide range of parties (Sartori, 1982). Beyond their position on the left–right continuum clearly defining their ideological identity, another important party cleavage could be found in religion. This involved a confrontation between all political forces, especially between the DC and PCI, with the former promoting Christian values and the latter supporting secular principles.

After the fall of the Berlin Wall and the end of totalitarian regimes in Eastern Europe, the PCI leadership realized that the era of Eurocommunism was over and that it was necessary to transform the party into a progressive left-wing political force. At the end of its twentieth Congress on 3 February 1991, it was agreed to dissolve the Italian Communist Party and replace it with a new formation, the *Partito Democratico della Sinistra*, PDS (Democratic Party of the Left). However, a significant minority from the Stalinist left rejected such a radical transformation and, in order to maintain its orthodox roots, decided to leave the PDS and establish a new party called the *Rifondazione Comunista* (Communist Refoundation).

The First Italian Republic, characterized by pro-American and pro-European coalition governments led by the Christian Democrats, lasted until the beginning of the 1990s, when the so-called '*Tangentopoli*' bribery scandal broke out involving a welter of politicians, administrators, and businessmen. As a result, the historic and invincible DC dissolved, leaving behind a huge vacuum in Italy's political landscape that was contested by new movements: the populist and free-market oriented *Forza Italia*, FI (Forward Italy), founded the *Cavaliere*, and the separatist *Lega Nord*, LN (Northern League) under the leadership of Umberto Bossi, as well as 'reshaped' parties such as *Alleanza Nazionale*, AN (National Alliance) that split from the neo-Fascist *Movimento Sociale Italiano*, MSI (Italian Social Movement).

The Second Republic portrayed what Ilvo Diamanti defined as a 'personalized bipolarism' between a centre-right coalition dominated by Silvio Berlusconi's charismatic leadership and a centre-left alliance headed by Romano Prodi (Diamanti, 2007, 735). It was a model based on the mixed and somewhat anomalous majoritarian system introduced in 1993, which appeared to be useful for winning elections, but that inevitably became an obstacle when governing and even organizing the opposition in Parliament.

The new millennium opened to reveal a highly fragmented Italian political scene, witnessing the rise of two main rival parties. On the centre-left there was the *Partito Democratico*, PD (Democratic Party), born in October 2007 from the fusion of the former PDS, renamed as *Democratici di Sinistra*, DS (Left Democrats), and *Democrazia è Libertà – La Margherita*, DL (Democracy is Freedom – the Daisy) along with some Republicans, Social Democrats, and Greens. On the centre-right there was the *Popolo della Libertà*, PdL (People of Freedom), founded on 29 March 2009 from the merger of *Forza Italia* and *Alleanza Nazionale* as well as other members from the *Nuovo Partito Socialista Italiano* (New Italian Socialist Party), *Partito Repubblicano* (Republican Party), *Popolari Liberali* (Popular Liberals), and the far-right-wing *Azione Sociale* (Social Action). However, continuing disputes within the PdL led to the departure of Gianfranco Fini and his followers, who, in the summer of 2010, set up a new parliamentary group called *Futuro e Libertà per l'Italia*, FLI (Future and Freedom for Italy) that eventually turned into a new political party in February 2011. Just over four years after the official birth of the *Popolo della Libertà*, its fragile internal balance broke down, setting off the revival of *Forza Italia* in September 2013.

5.1 Party attitudes towards the European Union

It is widely recognized that the European integration process has not generated a new cleavage in Italy, replacing or opposing previous normative orientations. Political preferences over the

European Union have been traditionally shaped along a left–right divide being, as Nicolò Conti and Vincenzo Memoli have pointed out, 'largely subsumed by historically rooted ideologies' (Conti and Memoli, 2011, 2). Over the years, party attitudes towards the EU have therefore evolved together with their own ideological lines.

In the past, the Italian political class has fervently supported and promoted further European integration, highlighting the need for direct universal elections to the European Parliament (EP). In particular, after the initial hostility of the PCI to the European Common Market, based on its anti-capitalist principles, Italy's policy towards the EC/EU became bipartisan.

In the 1950s and 1960s the question of the European integration process divided parties along their ideological *continuum*, which saw a pro-European centre challenging anti-European Socialist and Communist parties and, albeit only to a limited extent, right-wing movements (Bellucci and Conti, 2012).

Whilst *Democrazia Cristiana* and other smaller lay parties, including the *Partito Social Democratico italiano*, PSDI (Italian Social Democratic Party), *Partito Liberale italiano*, PLI, (Italian Liberal Party) and *Partito Repubblicano italiano*, PRI (Italian Republican Party), have boasted deep-rooted and long-standing pro-European positions, the *Partito Socialista italiano* as well as the *Partito Comunista italiano* tardily converted to the European project in the 1970s.

In the last two decades of the First Republic, ideological support was combined with a utilitarian approach to Europe, seen as a vehicle to modernize Italy's political *landscape* and reinforce its economy, hence resulting into a sort of 'depoliticization' of the grand issue relating to European integration (Cotta, 2005).

After more than 50 years of generalized passive support for the EU, the Italian parties of the Second Republic have begun to challenge what Lucia Quaglia and Claudio Radaelli have referred to as 'the European orthodoxy', hence abandoning this long political tradition (Quaglia and Radaelli, 2007). Three anti-European parties, albeit to a different degree, have started to loom on the Italian political horizon. Based on the overall distinction between hard and soft Euroscepticism, *Lega Nord* has seemed to fall within the first category, embodying a principled and outright rejection of the European unification process including EU membership, whilst the neo-Fascist *Alleanza Nazionale* and the left-wing *Rifondazione Comunista* could be framed within the second one, respectively mirroring national or social concerns on one or several EU policy areas, leading to qualified opposition to the European Union (Taggart and Szczerbiak, 2002). Finally, it is worth mentioning that the post-Communist *Sinistra Ecologia Libertà*, SEL (Left Ecology and Freedom) and the Liberal-Conservative *Popolo della Libertà* have taken a more critical stance on the EU and a more pragmatic approach towards the integration process, but definitely cannot be labelled as Eurosceptic.

6 Public opinion and the European Union

For a long time, Italians have been described as the most 'Europhile' amongst the citizens of the European Union. According to Leon N. Lindberg and Stuart A. Scheingold, this attitude was based on little knowledge of European issues, coupled with a process of substantial delegation to political elites, defined as 'permissive consensus' (Lindberg and Scheingold, 1971). In addition, as Geoffrey Pridham has stressed, a low attachment to the idea of the nation state may have also provided a cultural basis for their strong support for European integration. Possibly connected to this aspect has been Italians' widespread frustration with their own governments' performances, combined with an utter disenchantment with domestic politics.

For over two decades, between the 1970s and the ratification of the Maastricht Treaty in 1993, a strong consensus emerged between political parties and public opinion over European integration, with the latter taking the lead in order to influence attitude changes amongst those parties originally hostile to this process (Isernia and Ammendola, 2005).

Since the mid-1990s, Italian enthusiasm towards Europe has started to wane. Despite the general state of apathy in the political debate over the EU, Italian public opinion still has seemed to show a certain interest in the European integration project and a fairly good level of awareness, if compared to other Member States.

This picture seemed to be confirmed in a pre-electoral survey conducted across the European Union in January–February 2009. Forty-one per cent of Italian respondents claimed to be aware that the European Parliament elections would take place in 2009, compared to a disappointing EU average of 32 per cent. Approximately 44 per cent of Italian interviewees declared themselves to be interested in the coming EP electoral contest, against 50 per cent who confirmed their total indifference. In addition, 23 per cent confirmed they would turn up at the Euro-election, 5 per cent less than the EU average, whilst only 8 per cent of them, corresponding to almost half of the EU sample of 15, said that they would not cast their ballot (Eurobarometer 71.1, 2009).

Lastly, the survey showed that Italian women were slightly less keen to participate, with 10 per cent of them declaring that they definitely would not vote. Age also emerged as a key factor, with younger cohorts up to 24 years old being overwhelmingly the most apathetic group, and 15 per cent of them were even adamantly unwilling to go to the polls.

The concerns of the Italian people appeared to be in line with European trends. According to 50 per cent of Italian respondents, the electoral campaign should raise the question of unemployment and 49 per cent stressed the need to deal with economic growth. Moreover, 44 per cent of interviewees highlighted inflation and purchasing power as the main issues; 27 per cent thought that the future of pensions should be addressed, whilst, respectively, 37 and 36 per cent of the Italians mostly feared crime and terrorism. By contrast, the question of immigration represented a sort of exception, as it emerged in Italy as one of the most crucial topics, being mentioned 38 per cent of the time, compared to the EU average of 29 per cent (Eurobarometer 71.1, 2009).

Overall, public trust in both national and European political institutions fell sharply. Despite this, most Italians still remained in favour of a European economic and monetary union. They saw the EU as the best actor to address the global economic turmoil. In particular, 53 per cent believed that the adoption of the euro had helped to prevent the worst effects of the still ongoing financial downturn (Eurobarometer 72, 2009).

Indeed, the economic crisis has boosted the 'demand' for Europe as a tool to regulate and temper the negative effects of globalization. The last decade has witnessed a change in the Italian approach to the European project, which cannot be defined as purely Eurosceptic but which discloses ever more hesitation and doubts. The evolution of Italian public opinion vis-à-vis the European Union relies, to a great extent, on the ability of European institutions to respond efficiently to such demand (Bellucci and Serricchio, 2012).

7 National and EP electoral systems

Electoral systems, which aim to convert votes into parliamentary seats, may be inaccurate and lead to considerable distortions, as has often occurred in the Italian case. The need to reform Italian electoral legislation is of great topicality and urgency, but it has so far not found a suitable solution. Parliamentary elections in Italy are regulated by Consolidated Text No. 361 of 30 March 1957. It has undergone various amendments, such as Law No. 270 of 21 December 2005, universally known as the '*Porcellum*' Bill. Interestingly, even before the new electoral legislation had entered into force, its draftsman, Roberto Calderoli from *Lega Nord*, either shamelessly or carelessly labelled it as '*porcata*', which may be translated into English as 'crap'. Subsequently, following the tradition of conferring Latin monikers upon electoral laws, Giovanni Sartori sarcastically renamed it '*Porcellum*'. Under its provisions, the highly proportional Italian election system, which has traditionally aimed at safeguarding democracy and pluralism, especially after the totalitarian experience of Fascism, was substantially altered. Hence, a nationwide majority prize would be awarded to the coalition in the lead that automatically gained 340 out of 630 seats in the Chamber. Preference for a specific candidate could not be indicated on the ballot. This froze the system and reinforced the powers of the political parties, since they exclusively compile the electoral lists by choosing the order of the candidates.

Moreover, an additional constituency was introduced for elections to both Houses of Parliament in order to allow Italian citizens residing abroad to exercise their right to vote (Legge costituzionale n.1, 2000). The Overseas constituency, covering four geographical areas – Europe, South America, North and Central America, as well as Africa, Asia, Oceania, and Antarctica – would be entitled to 12 representatives in the *Camera dei Deputati* and six in the *Senato della Repubblica*.

The elections to the Chamber are based on closed lists in 26 multi-member constituencies for 617 seats and one single-member constituency in Valle d'Aosta. The proportional representation system is applied to 629 out of 630 seats, whilst the 'first-past-the-post' system is used for the single-member constituency in Valle d'Aosta. The minimum requirements to qualify for a seat in the *Camera* are to attain 10 per cent of total valid votes for a political coalition; 2 per cent for a political party or list within a coalition; 4 per cent for a political party which is not affiliated with any political coalition; and 20 per cent of the vote within their constituency for language minority lists.

As for the Senate, seats are allocated respectively to individual parties that grasp at least 8 per cent of the vote and to coalitions that cross the 20 per cent threshold in each of the 20 regions and the Overseas constituency. In addition, within the coalitions, seats are distributed amongst those parties that have received at least 3 per cent of the preferences. If the coalition achieving a majority of votes in a given region fails to capture 55 per cent, it is nevertheless awarded a bonus to attain this percentage and the remaining seats are assigned to the other qualifying coalitions and individual lists. A proportional representation system applying the d'Hondt method to regional voting is followed in all regions, excluding Valle d'Aosta and Trentino Alto-Adige, which enjoy special autonomous status by virtue of the presence of language minority groups, where the 'first past the post' system is preferred.

One of the main criticisms of the *Porcellum* Bill is that it privileges and rewards party loyalty and obedience over ethics, and even fosters corruption. Finally, former President of the Italian Constitutional Court Gustavo Zagrebelsky (2011) has defined the law as 'absurd' because it transforms a minority of electors into a very large parliamentary majority, thus 'overthrow[ing] democracy into oligarchy' (Milella, 2010). Until now, all efforts to overturn this unfortunate law have failed; even a popular referendum held in June 2009 flopped due to insufficient participation.

European elections in Italy are regulated by national legislation, notably Law No. 18 of 24 January 1979, later amended by Decree-Law No. 408 of 24 June 1994, Law No. 78 of 27 March 2004, Law No. 90 of 8 April 2004, Decree-Law No. 3 of 27 January 2009, and Law No. 10 of 20 February 2009. For this purpose, the country is divided into five constituencies: the North-West, which incorporates Piedmont, Valle d'Aosta, Liguria, and Lombardy; the North-East, which consists of Veneto, Trentino-Alto Adige, Friuli-Venezia Giulia, and

Figure 6.2 Map of EP electoral constituencies in Italy

Emilia-Romagna; the Centre, which gathers Tuscany, Umbria, Marche, and Lazio; the South, which includes Abruzzo, Molise, Campania, Apulia, Basilicata, and Calabria, and finally the Islands, embracing Sicily and Sardinia.

In January 2008, a comprehensive bill was tabled in order to bring legislation on European elections in line with that adopted in 2005 regarding general elections. The original proposal involved three essential points: a 5 per cent vote threshold for the allocation of seats, an increase from 5 to 15 constituencies and the abolition of preferential voting. Yet, the fierce opposition of centre-left parties compelled the governing majority to abandon this proposal (Sandri, 2009, 150).

In January 2009, an agreement was finally reached between the two main parties, the *Popolo della Libertà* and the *Partito Democratico,* to reform the EP election process. The primary objective of the 2009 reform was to organize and improve the European representation of Italian parties, by reducing their number in order to fight the endemic fragmentation that has historically characterized the Italian EP delegation. As a result, a more severe threshold, equivalent to 4 per cent of the vote for party lists, was included in order to obtain seats, replacing the old 'natural' threshold, which used to oscillate between 0.7 and 0.8 per cent.

The new law entailed the withdrawal of the closed list option and of any changes in the constituency system, thus allowing up to three preference votes in the first constituency, two in the second, third, and fourth, respectively, and only a single preference in the fifth.

Yet, in order to guarantee the representation of language minorities living in Italy at the EU level, some special conditions were applied. In particular, the 4 per cent threshold was not imposed on the lists of the French-speaking region of Valle d'Aosta, the German-speaking province of Bolzano, and the Slovenian-speaking towns in the provinces of Trieste, Gorizia, and Udine in Friuli-Venezia Giulia. Moreover, the so-called language minority lists could choose to be linked, for the allocation of seats, to another political party within the same constituency which puts up candidates nationwide (Article 12, Legge n. 18/1979). In particular, as stated in Article 22 Paragraph 3 of Law No. 18 of 24 January 1979, if none of the contestants belonging to a language minority are included on the linked list, the candidate who has obtained the largest number of preferences could nevertheless be elected, provided that he or she got at least 50,000 votes.

In accordance with Article 48 of the Italian Constitution, 'All citizens, male and female, who have attained their majority age, are voters. The vote is personal and equal, free and secret. Its exercise thereof is a civic duty.' Under the First Republic, within 60 days of polling day, abstainers had to address their reasons for failing to vote to the mayor who, after due consideration, drafted a list of unjustified absentees. This list used to be published and displayed on the municipal register for a month, whilst citizens' electoral abstention would also be marked in their 'certificate of good conduct' over the subsequent five years (Articles 4–75 and 115 of DPR 361/1957, quoted in Cordini, 1988). Whereas these provisions were not foreseen for administrative elections or public referenda, they were applied, albeit rarely, in the other cases and only were totally removed after the 1993 Electoral Reform (Article 1 Law 277/1993 modifying Article 4 and deleting Article 115 of DPR 361/1957).

8 A glance at the EP and national elections

From 1979 to 1992, Italian politics, whilst still dominated by the *Democrazia Cristiana* (DC), was characterized by a sequence of short and unstable multiparty coalition governments. Within this time frame, four sets of general elections in 1979, 1983, 1987, and 1992 were held due to the premature dissolution of Parliament before its natural five-year term, whilst only three waves of European elections took place in 1979, 1984, and 1989.

The first direct universal elections to the EP were convened on 10 June 1979, just a week after the Italian legislative elections, and this was the only occasion when the two contests coincided temporally in the history of the First Republic, underscoring the relevance of the national dimension (Zincone, 1985). The pre-campaign period witnessed a quarrel between those who wished to hold domestic elections after the European ones, or at least simultaneously, and those who preferred to convene general elections prior to the European ones or a reasonable time afterwards. The supporters of the first option hoped that the European outcome would influence the national electoral platform. On the contrary, the champions of the other alternative preferred to distance the two contests so that disloyal voters would have time to rethink and return to their traditional party. In the end, the former prevailed with the EP elections following shortly after general elections.

The two main rival parties, facing each other in the political arena, registered a slight drop in popular consensus, with the governing DC decreasing from 38.3 to 36.4 per cent of the vote and the opposing PCI falling from 30.4 to 29.6 per cent. The latter's electoral loss might have been due to its external support of the government, by virtue of the so-called '*Compromesso storico*' ('historical compromise') with the Christian Democrats.

By contrast, the *Partito Liberale italiano*, PLI (Italian Liberal Party) grabbed an additional one-and-a-half percentage points, going from 1.9 to 3.5 per cent, whilst the *Partito Socialista italiano* (PSI) conquered over an additional point, from 9.8 to 11. The first Euro-elections in Italy were held in a diffuse pro-European climate shared by all political parties. The early 1980s saw a partial decline of the DC's political supremacy on the Italian political stage. As a result in June 1981, for the first time since the end of WWII, a non-Christian Democrat politician, Giovanni Spadolini, leader of the Italian Republican Party (PRI), was given the task of building a coalition government comprising of the DC, PSI, PSDI, PRI, and PLI, the so-called '*Pentapartito*' ('Five-Party Alliance'). After two years of failed attempts to run the country, first by Spadolini and later by the Christian Democrat Amintore Fanfani, early elections were convened in June 1983. On polling day, the DC registered a major setback, with a loss of almost 5.5 percentage points, whilst its main rival the PCI saw a slight decrease in public consensus, all to the benefit of small right-wing and centrist movements as well as the PSI. This led to the historic appointment of Bettino Craxi as Italy's first Socialist Prime Minister at the head of the *Pentapartito*.

On 17 June 1984, at the end of the first five-year term of the European Parliament, new elections took place in all ten countries, including Greece, which in the meantime had joined the Community. In Italy, the campaign mainly focussed on domestic political themes, but it became increasingly hard and artificial to make a clear-cut distinction between EC and national platforms (Pridham, 1985).

On this occasion, with their 33.3 per cent of the preferences and 27 seats, the Communists performed better than in the previous European election, when they obtained 29.6 per cent and 24 seats, as well as in the 1983 general elections, when they achieved 29.9 per cent. The PCI also emerged as the best-scoring party, by triumphing over even the ruling Christian Democrats for the first time in history. The sudden death of the charismatic Communist leader Enrico Berlinguer, just a few days earlier on 11 June 1984, may well have contributed to influencing this outcome by bringing forth deep emotional sympathy amongst the electorate and boosting the level of backing for his party as a tribute to his memory.

On 27 April 1987, one year ahead of schedule, early national elections were held, witnessing the victory of the PSI and DC, the defeat of the PCI, which nevertheless remained the second largest party, as well as the entry of the Greens into the Italian Parliament.

A new *Pentapartito* coalition government was forged under the leadership of the Christian Democrat Giovanni Goria. Yet, intra-party rifts within the DC and the deterioration of inter-party relationships between the Christian Democrats and the Socialists led to the withdrawal of the latter from the executive, triggering one of the longest and most serious domestic political and institutional crises.

Within this context, on 18 June 1989, the third Euro-elections were organized, taking up the dimension of a 'surrogate' for general elections all over the country. Neither the historical

Table 6.3 National election results in Italy: 1979–1992 (%)

Political party	1979	1983	1987	1992
DC	38.3	32.9	34.3	29.7
PCI (PDS)	30.4	29.9	26.6	16.1
PSI	9.8	11.4	14.3	13.6
LN	—	—	0.5	8.7
PRC	—	—	—	5.6
MSI-DN	5.3	6.8	5.9	5.4
PRI	3.0	5.1	3.7	4.4
PLI	1.9	2.9	2.1	2.8
V	—	—	2.5	2.8
PSDI	3.8	4.1	2.9	2.7
RETE (Net)	—	—	—	1.9
PR	3.5	2.2	2.6	1.2
SVP	0.6	0.5	0.5	0.5
UV	0.1	0.1	0.1	0.1
DP	1.4	1.5	1.7	—
Others	1.9	2.6	2.3	4.5

Sources: Ministero dell'Interno, http://elezioni.interno.it; Parties and Elections, www.parties-and-elections.eu/italy2b.html.

Table 6.4 EP election results in Italy: 1979–1989 (%)

Political party	1979	1984	1989
DC	36.5	33.0	32.9
PCI	29.6	33.3	27.6
PSI	11.0	11.2	14.8
MSI-DN	5.5	6.5	5.5
PLI-PRI	6.2	6.0	4.4
V	0.0	0.0	3.8
V Arc	0.0	0.0	2.4
PSDI	4.3	3.5	2.7
Lega Lombarda (Liga Veneta)	0.0	0.5	1.8
DP	0.7	1.4	1.3
PR	3.7	3.4	1.2
FFD (UV-PSdA)	0.5	0.6	0.6
SVP	0.6	0.6	0.5
Others	1.6	0.0	0.5

Source: www.parties-and-elections.eu/italy2b.html.

step taken by the EC Member States to adopt a single market, nor the decision by the Italian political elite to hold simultaneously a referendum on transforming the European Community into a true Union conferred a more European character to the EP election.

Government parties lost voters' support, but not as much as the main opposition party the PCI lost to the benefit of the PSI as well as to new small movements and lists which ran in the EP contest for the first time, including *Lista Verde* (Green List), *Verdi Arcobaleno* (Rainbow Greens), *Lega Lombarda* (Lombard League), and the Anti-Prohibitionists. According to Renato Mannheimer, the erosion of support for the government majority and other traditional parties, to the benefit of small and new political forces, were factors that had been prefigured in the 1987 general election (Mannheimer, 1996).

On 5 and 6 February 1992, national electoral contests were held, after one of the longest uninterrupted parliamentary terms since the end of WWII, mainly due to the rare political skills of the Christian Democrat Prime Minister Giulio Andreotti. The polling results mirrored a highly fragmented political scene, marking the decline of the two main political parties, the DC and PDS, the former Communist Party, as well as the success of the regionalist *Lega Nord* and the emergence of new political movements in the Italian Parliament.

Two years later, new elections were called after the resignation of Carlo Azeglio Ciampi's technocratic cabinet, which had fulfilled its main objectives of budget austerity and electoral

Table 6.5 National election results in Italy: 1994–2008 (%)

Political party	1994	1996	2001	2006	2008
PDL	—	—	—	—	37.4
PD (ULIVO)	—	—	—	31.3	33.2
LN	8.4	10.1	3.9	4.6	8.3
UDC (CCD-CDU)	(FI)	5.8	3.2	6.8	6.8
IdV	—	—	3.9	2.3	4.4
SA	—	—	—	—	3.1
LD-FT (MSFT)	—	0.9	0.4	0.6	2.4
MPA	—	—	—	LN	1.1
PS (PSI)	2.2	(DINI)	2.2	2.6	1.0
SVP	0.6	(PRODI)	0.5	0.5	0.4
PR	3.5	1.9	2.2	PS	(PD)
RB	—	—	—	—	(UDC)
PRI	(SEGNI)	(PRODI)	(FI)	(FI)	(PDL)
PRC	6.0	8.6	5.0	5.8	(SA)
PDCI	—	—	1.7	2.3	(SA)
VERDI	2.7	2.5	GS	2.1	(SA)
SD	—	—	—	—	(SA)
FI	21.0	20.6	29.4	23.7	—
AN	13.5	15.7	12.0	12.3	—
UDEUR	—	—	(DL)	1.4	—
DE	—	—	2.4	—	—
NPSI-DCA (SL. PS)	0.5	0.4	1.0	0.8	—
DS (PDS)	20.4	21.1	16.6	(ULIVO)	—
DL	—	—	14.5	(ULIVO)	—
MRE	—	—	—	(ULIVO)	—
PPI (PRODI)	11.1	6.8	(DL)	—	—
DEM	—	—	(DL)	—	—
RI (DINI)	—	4.3	(DL)	—	—
LAM	0.2	0.2	0.1	—	—
UD (AD)	1.2	(PRODI)	—	—	—
SEGNI	4.6	(DINI)	—	—	—
RETE	1.9	—	—	—	—
Others	2.2	1.1	1.0	2.9	3.1

Sources: Ministero dell'Interno: http://elezioni.interno.it; Parties and Elections, www.parties-and-elections.eu/italy2b.html.

reform at both the national and local levels, but not at the European one where the proportional representation (PR) system was retained.

The year 1994 marked a watershed in Italian history between the First and the Second Republic, with the public repudiation of the old dominating political elites against the background of corruption scandals, which had plagued the DC and PSI in particular. The shift towards a mixed electoral system, whereby 75 per cent of the seats were allocated according to majoritarian principles and the remainder by PR, encouraged and even required electoral coalition building. As a result, three rival alliances representing 15 party lists competed:

1. the conservative *Polo delle Libertà* (Pole of Freedoms) – gathering *Forza Italia* (FI) and *Lega Nord* along with *Alleanza Nazionale*, Pannella List, and *Centro Cristiano Democratico*, CCD (Christian Democratic Centre);
2. the Centrist *Patto per l'Italia* (Pact for Italy) – consisting of *Partito Popolare Italiano* (PPI), and *Patto Segni* (Segni Pact);
3. the left-wing *Alleanza Progressiva* (Progressive Alliance) – made up of the *Partito dei Democratici di Sinistra* (PDS), *Rifondazione Comunista* (RC), *Verdi*, and *Partito Socialista Italiano* (PSI).

The general election ushered in the victory of *Polo delle Libertà and*, above all, of *Forza Italia*, beginning the so-called Berlusconi era.

Less than two and a half months later, Italian citizens went back to the polls to choose their representatives in the European Parliament. As in 1979, but for the first time in the Second Republic, the two electoral contests ran almost in parallel. This novel political scenario, along with the temporal proximity of the two elections, contributed to the radical mutation of the Italian representation in the EP, with an exceptionally high turnover of MEPs. It also entailed a bigger fragmentation of the Italian delegation, thus affecting the overall composition of EP political groups. The 1994 European contest failed to attract public and press interest, mainly due to voter fatigue with politics, especially after the long national election campaign, coupled with a declining enthusiasm for the European project (Daniels, 1996).

After a highly internalized campaign and the decision of both the government and opposition coalition partners to present separate lists, reassured by the continued use of PR, the Euro-election sanctioned the triumph of FI, which obtained a remarkable 30.6 per cent, increasing its voting share by 9.5 percentage points compared with 21 per cent in the general election. In just 11 weeks between the two electoral contests, Berlusconi managed to attract two million new supporters who switched their allegiance in his favour. This double domestic and European electoral success demonstrated the extent of FI's political power, which could be mainly ascribed to its leader's strategic communication skills (Diamanti, 2007, 737). Nevertheless, a few months later, in January 1995, continuing frictions within the governing coalition, especially between the federalist LN and the far-right AN, eventually led to the departure of the former, causing the fall of the first Berlusconi cabinet. This event revealed the fragility of the Italian centre-right as capable of winning elections but not yet ready to rule the country.

After a brief interim caretaker administration that failed to obtain sufficient parliamentary support, which was headed by Lamberto Dini, new general elections were called again, three years ahead of schedule. On 21 April 1996, polling results gave Romano Prodi's *Ulivo* (Olive Tree) coalition a clear victory in both the Chamber of Deputies and the Senate. This marked a truly important historical moment in Italian politics, since the left had taken power for the first time since WWII, thus reinforcing the trend towards bipolarization. Prodi pledged a strong fiscal policy to comply with European monetary union (EMU) requirements. This step was presented to citizens as essential in order to enable Italy to enter the euro-zone and cross the magic threshold of Europe (Quaglia and Radaelli, 2007, 929).

Prodi's government remained in power until October 1998, when it narrowly lost a vote of confidence, due to the withdrawal of *Rifondazione Comunista's* external support. It was then replaced by a new government headed by Massimo D'Alema, the leader of *Democratici di Sinistra*, DS (Democrats of the Left), the new party founded on 13 February 1998 as a reshaped version of the PDS.

Against this background, the 1999 European election clearly appeared as a mid-term contest, with increased fragmentation between party lists, from ten to 18. The ruling DS went down from 19.1 to 17.3 per cent of the vote, losing one of its 16 seats whilst the main opposition party *Forza Italia* reasserted itself as the largest single group with 25.2 per cent of the vote, although it suffered a setback of 5.4 per cent compared to previous EP elections. The *Partito Popolare italiano* (PPI), descendent of the once-mighty DC, saw its vote share reduced by more than half, falling from 10 to 4.2 per cent, clearly revealing the ill-fated choice of their new name. The other centre parties, CCD, CDU, and *Unione Democratici per l'Europa*, UDEUR (*Union of Democrats for Europe*), obtained 2.6, 2.1, and 1.6 per cent of preferences, respectively. On the left of the political spectrum, *Rifondazione Comunista* got 4.3 per cent of the vote and 4 seats, whilst the Communists of PdCI and the Greens grasped only 2 and 1.8 per cent, respectively, securing each of them only two representatives in Brussels and Strasbourg. Finally, the far-right Nationalist *Fiamma Tricolore* got over 1.6 per cent, enough to gain access to the EP.

Table 6.6 EP election results in Italy: 1994–2004 (%)

Political party	1994	1999	2004
PPI	10.0	4.2	0.0
CCD-CDU/UDC	0.0	4.7	5.9
UDEUR	0.0	1.6	1.3
FI-AN/PDL	43.1	35.5	32.4
DS & Democratici/ULIVO/PD	19.1	25.0	31.1
LN	6.6	4.5	5.0
IdV	0.0	0.0	2.1
PRC-CI	6.1	6.3	8.5
PR	2.1	8.5	2.2
MS-FT	0.0	1.6	0.7
SVP	0.6	0.5	0.4
UV	0.4	0.1	0.1
V/SEL	3.2	1.8	2.5
PS (PSI)	1.8	2.2	2.0
Pensionati (Pensioners)	0.0	0.7	1.2
PRI	0.9	0.5	0.7
SEGNI	3.3	0.0	0.5
PSDI/SDI	0.7	2.2	0.0
Others	2.3	0.6	3.9

Sources: Ministero dell'Interno: http://elezioni.interno.it; Parties and Elections, www.parties-and-elections.eu/italy2b.html.

The disappointing outcome of the 1999 Euro-election, followed by a poor showing in the regional elections, induced Prime Minister D'Alema to resign in April 2000. The subsequent centre-left government, led by Giuliano Amato, which gathered together most of the same partner parties, only lasted until May 2001 when Berlusconi returned to power at the head of a refashioned centre-right alliance known as *Casa delle Libertà* (House of Freedoms) (Pridham, 1985). This consisted of his own party *Forza Italia* along with *Alleanza nazionale*, *Lega Nord*, *Centro Cristiano Democratico/Cristiani Democratici Uniti*, CCD/CDU (Christian Democratic Centre/United Christian Democrats), and *Nuovo Partito Socialista italiano*, NPSI. By obtaining an overwhelming victory in the 2001 general elections, Berlusconi's coalition enjoyed one of the largest parliamentary majorities in post-war history and formed a government, which unusually lasted for its entire five-year term (Conti, 2004).

In spite of that, the neo-liberal agenda set by the premier found resistance from some of the coalition partners and, primarily, AN. Italy's economic situation created great concern both at the domestic and European levels to the point that, on the eve of the 2004 Euro-elections, the European Commission almost issued an early warning to the Italian authorities to comply with the parameters imposed by EMU (Conti, 2004). Another sensitive issue that influenced the electoral campaign was the controversial government's endorsement of US military intervention in Iraq, especially after the national shock caused by the tragic events of November 2003, when 19 Italian soldiers were killed in the town of Nasiriyah.

In the middle of the national electoral cycle, at a time when there was increasing public disillusionment with the government's capability to fulfill its past promises and when the domestic political balance was slowly changing, Italian citizens were called to choose their representatives for the 2004–2009 EP assembly. In this climate, Berlusconi's *Forza Italia* lost ground. His party's popularity dropped by 4 per cent compared to previous European elections. In the national race, FI lost almost 8.5 per cent of its support, but it remained the single list with the highest share of the vote. Yet, on the whole, the *Casa delle Libertà* coalition did not register a substantial change in its results, due to the rebalancing quota carried by its partners, the AN, UdC, and LN. On the other hand, the main opposition parties gathered under the *Ulivo* coalition slightly improved their performance by securing up to 31 per cent of the vote.

At the general election of 9 and 10 April 2006, Berlusconi's coalition was defeated by Romano Prodi's centre-left *Union* coalition that remained in power until January 2008, when the small partner UDEUR withdrew its support. A few months later, on 13–14 April, early elections were convened, leading to a new centre-right coalition government headed by the *Cavaliere*. Historically, the results excluded the extreme left-wing *Sinistra l'Arcobaleno* (Rainbow Left) led by Fausto Bertinotti, the Socialist Party directed by Enrico Boselli, and the extreme right-wing *La Destra*, guided by Daniela Santanchè from the parliamentary arena.

As shown in Table 6.7, a constant decline in participation was a striking feature of both the EP and general elections held in Italy from 1979 to 2009. The only exception occurred in 2004, when turnout grew to 71.7 per cent if including Italians abroad, or 73.1 per cent if restricting the data only to residents in the country.

Italy has historically been characterized by high levels of electoral participation but, under the Second Republic, abstentionism started to increase, until reaching its peak in 2009. It may be reassuring to think that this is not an unrelenting process, but rather a trend merely connected to the specific and provisional circumstances triggered by citizens' feelings of frustration and anger for being subject to a sort of 'permanent' electoral campaign.

Table 6.7 Turnout at national and EP Elections in Italy: 1979–2009

Turnout	National elections	EP elections
3 June 1979 NE	90.6	
10 June 1979 EE		85.6 (Italy + abroad)
		86.1 (Italy)
26 June 1983	88.0	
17 June 1984		82.5 (Italy + abroad)
		83 (Italy)
14 June 1987	88.8	
18 June 1989		81.1 (Italy + abroad)
		81.7 (Italy)
5 April 1992	87.3	
27 March 1994	86.3	
12 June 1994		73.6 (Italy + abroad)
		74.6 (Italy)
21 April 1996	82.9	
13 June 1999		69.7 (Italy + abroad)
		70.8 (Italy)
13 May 2001	81.4 PR; 81.5 Majoritarian	
12 June 2004		71.7 (Italy + abroad)
		73.1 (Italy)
9 April 2006	83.6,* 83.4,** 38.9***	
13 April 2008	80.5,* 79.2,** 39.5***	
7 June 2009		65.0 (Italy + abroad)
		66.5 (Italy)

Source: http://elezionistorico.interno.it/.

Notes:
* Italy excluding Valle d'Aosta.
** Valle d'Aosta.
*** Abroad.

9 The 2009 European election

9.1 Party lists and manifestos

In the pre-campaign period, attention converged on the choice of PD candidates and the remonstrations of those who had been left out. The new Party Secretary, Dario Franceschini, accused the leaders of the other main political alignments – who stood as frontrunners in more than one constituency – of deceiving their voters, given that certainly none of them, if elected, would be likely to take up their seats in Strasbourg (Viola, 2005).

Questions over candidate selection found an even greater echo in the media, following Berlusconi's decision to include a number of showgirls on the list, arguably based on their looks rather than their intellectual and political skills. In an attempt to highlight the premier's questionable approach, the centre-left parties put forward the names of highly qualified professionals, including television news reporter David Sassoli, trade unionist Sergio Cofferati, and Rita Borsellino, sister of the heroic judge Paolo Borsellino, who was killed in Palermo by the mafia. Certainly the leadership of national parties played a key role in the 2009 EP campaign, reiterating the marginal European dimension of the electoral contest. Generally, the use of leaders' multiple candidatures in several or even all constituencies, along with the resort to 'amateurs', may be ascribed to the phenomenon of 'presidentialization' of the European elections that shifts the focus from the candidate to the leader (Braghiroli and Verzichelli, 2009).

Despite the need for an alliance after new electoral regulations, extreme left parties were unable to come to an agreement and, therefore, presented three competing lists to the public. The first list was the *Rifondazione Comunista-Sinistra Europea-Comunisti Italiani*, R-SE-CI, which was still tied to its Marxist ideological heritage. The second list, the *Sinistra Ecologia Libertà*, SEL, which included post-Communists, leftist Socialists and Greens, was headed by the charismatic governor of Apulia, Nichi Vendola, and reflected a post-materialist radical left approach. The third list was represented by the *Partito Comunista dei Lavoratori*, founded on a Trotskyist Communist tradition. Other competing lists included the small Liberal Democratic party and *Lista Pannella-Bonino*, also known as the Radical Party, the far-right lists *La Destra-MPA*, *Fiamma Tricolore*, *Forza Nuova*, along with a few more parties representing French and German linguistic minorities. In total, 18 lists ran in the European electoral contest, even if some parties, including the PdL, did not even bother to develop and publish their own electoral programmes until a few days prior to voting.

In their electoral programmes, the Italian political parties dealt with a combination of European and domestic questions, although from different angles. The financial crisis, climate change, immigration, EU enlargement, including Turkey's controversial application, were all addressed whilst alternative visions of Europe were outlined.

By using strong conservative rhetoric, the PdL stressed that its position was distinctly far from the Socialists' ideological leftist approach or the Liberals' view that markets alone should rule the world. With the slogan 'To count more in Europe', Berlusconi voiced his ambition to make the PdL the first force within the EPP and to give Italy a bigger weight in European affairs whilst preserving its national identity. The party outlined its main objectives in a succinct way: to rebuild the Abruzzo region after a terrible earthquake occurred on 6 April 2009, by using the resources of the European Union Solidarity Fund (EUSF); to generate prosperity for all by promising new jobs; to establish, along with the G8, better regulation of the financial markets; and to deal with climate change.

Lastly, it focussed on the issue of illegal immigration and the international role of the European Union, which should act as a 'bridge' between the US and Russia.

Unlike the PdL, its main rival the PD wrote a long and detailed programme entitled 'A Europe which suits you: stronger us, stronger you', whereby – metaphorically holding high the European flag – it placed great emphasis on the EU as the only chance for preventing economic collapse in the various Member States. In particular, the party proposed the introduction of a system of financial and banking rules monitored by the European Central Bank (ECB) in cooperation with national institutions. Moreover, it supported employment policies aimed at levelling out social inequalities. Finally, it was keen to promote a green economy, investment in research, higher education, and technological innovation by respecting economic, agricultural, environmental, and social heritage. Whilst doing this, it did not miss the opportunity to criticize the policies implemented by the Italian centre-right government.

The *Lega Nord* programme blatantly expressed its Eurosceptical views, warning about the need to maintain regional traditions and safeguard local autonomy under the subsidiarity principle. For example, Umberto Bossi stressed that questions regarding hunting should be dealt with at the local level and blamed the EU for having damaged local food and agricultural traditions under the pretext of the principle of the free market. LN argued that environmental protection should be subject to the principle of sustainable development in order to meet economic, production, and employment needs. As expected, the party fiercely opposed Turkey's accession to the EU, not only for its violation of human rights, its refusal to recognize the Armenian genocide, its repression of minorities, and its military occupation of the northern part of Cyprus, but simply because it did not belong geographically, culturally, and socially to Europe. As to the other Balkan applicant countries, LN argued that their entry should be subject to full compliance with all the Copenhagen political, democratic, and economic criteria. The party directed its attention to the crucial question of illegal immigration and the need to improve agreements and coordinate actions with border countries. Finally, LN asserted its support of traditional families and refused to endorse the legality of homosexual unions or polygamy.

Whilst sharing LN's traditional family values, the UDC totally distanced itself from the latter with regard to the question of immigration by rejecting xenophobic and racist attitudes and by promoting human solidarity. Following the Laura Englaro euthanasia case, which divided Italian public opinion, the party felt the need to address this sensitive ethical issue by reaffirming the absolute principle of life. UDC also argued that the Abruzzo earthquake raised the need for anti-seismic and energy-saving housing.

With its slogan 'Let's go back to Europe with an Italy of values', the *Italia dei Valori-Di Pietro* list devoted its programme to justice, law and order, full compliance with European legislation, and transparency in EU funding. More specifically, the party pointed out that those who had been found guilty in criminal trials should by no means be eligible as members of Parliament. A proposal was put forward to draft a Charter of European Knowledge Rights in order to enable citizens to access information, as well as a European Charter on Civil Liberties, which would include the rights of unmarried *de facto* couples and the right to a biological will.

The IdV endorsed the establishment of European consortia for developing renewable energy instead of nuclear technology, as well as increased European cooperation in university research. In addition, it proposed the creation of a European authority with the task of protecting savers by monitoring the activities of all European banks included the ECB. Above all, the IdV argued that intra- and extra-Community immigration should be regulated in accordance with the principle of solidarity and respect for human rights. Finally, the creation of a fully-fledged European army should be promoted with the aim of optimizing military expenses, financing missions abroad, and fostering the role of the EU in the world.

Under the slogan, 'Another Europe is possible', *Rifondazione comunista Sinistra europea* and *Comunisti italiani* put forward an alternative to the neo-liberal socio-economic model for Europe, by supporting a free, secular, and democratic society with an ecologically sound economy and a fair fiscal model. In their view, some basic steps should be introduced, such as an equal minimum salary for men and women, unemployment subsidies, and adequate pensions. The chief mission of the EU should consist of promoting peace in the world by reducing military expenditure, withdrawing

Table 6.8 EP election campaign issues in Italy: 2009

	PD	PdL	LN	IdV	UDC
Economic crisis	4	3	3	4	4
European integration	3	3	3	2	3
EU enlargement	2	2	4	2	2
Immigration and xenophobia	3	4	4	3	2
Foreign affairs	4	4	3	3	4
Terrorism	3	3	4	2	2
Environment/climate change	3	2	2	3	2

Note:

1 = Issue neither included in the programme, nor raised during the campaign; 2 = Issue missing in the programme, but addressed in the electoral campaign; 3 = Issue presented in the programme and/or debated in the electoral campaign; 4 = Issue examined in the programme and thoroughly addressed in the electoral campaign.

contingents from Iraq and Afghanistan, and dissolving NATO. Furthermore, the RC-SE-CI list strongly endorsed the creation of a Palestinian state and a peaceful solution to the Kurdish question. Finally, it stressed the need to cancel all debts to poor countries, to lift the economic embargo against Cuba, and to realize a common immigration policy preventing the creation of a Fortress Europe.

The other left-wing list, *Sinistra Ecologia Libertà*, which also incorporated the Greens, proposed a new social, environmental, and technological model, which – they argued – would lead to full employment and an equal-opportunity society. In particular, a truly federalist Europe should be realized, with the objective of defending the values of democracy and peace. Public investments in infrastructure, education, and renewable energy should be made, eluding the danger of reopening nuclear plants in Italy. In order to face economic, monetary, and financial problems, the European Union should call for an international conference under the aegis of the United Nations. Furthermore, the EU should hold a seat in the UN Security Council, implement a European foreign policy, promote a peaceful solution to the Israeli–Palestinian conflict, and as fight against famine and poverty in the world. Lastly, a common EU immigration policy should be implemented, with the aim of protecting migrants and refugees and integrating them in local communities.

The 88-page programme drafted by the Radicals was not a platform to compete over European issues, but rather an opportunity to protest against Italian and global political authorities. In their view, the new electoral law had technically deprived the EP vote of any democratic features, reserving the contest exclusively for government parties and their chosen official opposition.

9.2 Electoral campaign

In 2009, the EP unified its institutional action across the European Union in order promote a truly pan-European information campaign. In Italy, like in all Member States, a five-pointed star logo was adopted, whilst the widespread EU slogan 'It's your choice' was replaced by the Italian message 'Use your vote.' The same promotional materials, including billboards, posters, banners, and postcards on topical issues, were circulated by occasionally introducing some slightly different elements, whilst a range of 'choice boxes' were installed in the main Italian cities.

Andrea Ronchi, in his capacity of Italian Minister of European Affairs, discarded a rather unusual television spot produced by the German Communications Agency, officially appointed by the EP, and replaced it with some more traditional advertisements. Finally, the campaign saw the unprecedented use of the internet and social networking sites – including MySpace, YouTube, Facebook, and Flickr – by the European Parliament, as well as the homepages of individual candidates.

As to the political debate in the Italian media over the EP elections, there was no mention of those points relating to the European Union indicated in the electoral programmes or references to the Euro-manifestos drafted by the EP political groups. In this way Italian parties tried to neutralize their liabilities over unpopular issues and exploit their assets by putting forward issues that would attract voters. This meant, however, that the themes brought up in the national party programmes did not coincide with the issues that shaped the political run for election.

Parties mounted much lower profile campaigns and devoted fewer resources to the organization of European elections. The debates predominantly revolved around Italian domestic issues and Berlusconi's private life, especially when the news of his alleged affair with an 18-year-old girl broke, triggering the Prime Minister's wife to demand a divorce. Soon after another scandal risked damaging the *Cavaliere*, when British lawyer David Mills received a guilty sentence for having given false evidence in court in favour of the premier after receiving a bribe.

The dramatic earthquake in the Abruzzo region represented one of the most sensitive topics raised during the electoral campaign. The decision to convene a Council of Ministers and to organize the G8 Summit in the city of L'Aquila was highly appreciated by public opinion, increasing the premier's popularity. The rubbish emergency in Naples was also at the centre of a hot debate between the government, which claimed to have successfully solved the problem, and the opposition, which instead strongly criticized Berlusconi's inadequate measures.

The referendum on electoral law reform was intentionally disregarded, being mentioned only occasionally in connection with its economic implications rather than its political aspects. In the end, mainly due to *Lega Nord*'s pressures, the government decided to postpone a popular consultation on this matter to 21 and 22 June. Ultimately, as a result of the increasing flux of desperate people from Northern Africa, all political alignments addressed, albeit differently, the topical issue of illegal immigration. As expected, *Lega Nord* took the hardest position in this matter, with Bossi even launching demagogic appeals against a bureaucratic and centralist Europe that had been unable and unwilling to support Italy in facing this emergency. Both the government and the opposition addressed questions related to the global recession, blaming each other for Italy's poor economic performance.

During the campaign, public and private television networks, such as Rai, Mediaset, La7, and Sky, presented debates between top ranking national politicians and, on election night, featured special programmes. Yet the Italian media certainly devoted less attention to the 2009 EP vote than to the previous Italian general election held in 2008, with a lower level of coverage and a highly 'domesticized' approach.

9.3 Electoral results

On the first weekend of June 2009, almost 50 million Italian citizens were called to the polls to choose their 72 representatives in Strasbourg. During the Lisbon intergovernmental negotiations, the number of Italian MEPs had been strongly contested. The initial proposal, based on the *Lamassoure-Séverin Report* of 2007, assigned 72, 73, and 74 seats respectively to Italy, the UK, and France, according to the principle of 'degressive proportionality'. The Italian government rejected it on the grounds that it substantially altered the previous numeric equilibrium between these countries and, after threating to veto the full package, struck a deal with its EU partners that attributed 73 seats to both Italy and the UK and 74 to France.

The Euro-election took place along with local races in 62 provinces and 4,821 municipalities. The possibility of voting on Saturday afternoon, already introduced in 2004, was designed to promote greater public mobilization. However, turnout only reached 65 per cent, the lowest in Italy since the introduction of direct elections to the EP in 1979. This phenomenon was particularly noted in southern Italy and the main islands, where participation reached only 62 per cent and 44.7 per cent respectively, showing how subnational dynamics may have wide repercussions and influence the national average remarkably.

However, it is worth noting that this abstention trend affected the whole Italian electorate, including those living abroad, also in line with an overall decline in turnout throughout the EU. What is exceptional about decreasing voter participation in Italy is its extent, as can be noted by comparing turnout figures for the previous European and national parliamentary elections. On the other hand, falling turnout may certainly be due to a growing sense of frustration and exasperation that the Italian people feel about politics, being compelled to live in a 'permanent electoral campaign'. Indeed, in the *quinquennium* from 2004 to 2009, Italians went to the polls six times to choose their representatives at the EU, regional, and national levels (Diamanti, 2011).

By and large, Italy stood out as one of the countries with the most committed voters, coming just behind Luxembourg, Belgium – where compulsory voting applies – and Malta. On the whole, the difference in terms of participation between the Italian and the European averages amounted to almost 20 percentage points. The newly born *Popolo della Libertà* totalled the highest number of preferences equivalent to 35.3 per cent, thus securing 29 representatives in Strasbourg, 4 more than in 2004 when *Forza Italia* and *Alleanza Nazionale* obtained 16 and 9 seats, respectively. Nevertheless, it did not echo the overwhelming success achieved at the 1994 Euro-elections, as Berlusconi had so proudly predicted, losing over three million votes compared to the April 2008 general election.

Likewise, in relation to the previous national election, its main rival, the *Partito Democratico*, received only 26.1 per cent, losing almost 4.5 million votes, equivalent to more than one-third of its electorate. This sharp decline can be also confirmed when looking back at the 2004 Euro-elections, although it is necessary to highlight that on that occasion the PD had run in the contest within the left-wing *Ulivo* coalition that captured a higher share of the vote – 31.1 per cent. Many left-wing voters, frustrated about the lack of unity of their political leaders and the absence of a real alternative to centre-right policies, did not bother to go to the polls, whilst others showed their discontent by casting a protest vote in favour of the *Italia dei Valori*, the Radicals or extreme left-wing parties.

The main electoral winners were undoubtedly Umberto Bossi's *Lega Nord* and Antonio Di Pietro's IdV list. With its 10.2 per cent vote share, the former obtained 9 seats in the EP, more than double those acquired in 2004. As to the latter, by capturing 8 per cent of votes, it increased its share by just under 6 per cent compared with the preceding Euro-elections and by almost 3.5 per cent compared with the previous general election, securing 7 seats in Strasbourg, five more than in the earlier legislature. In addition, the small opposition centrist party UdC

Table 6.9 EP election results in Italy: 2009

Lists	Votes	%	Seats
Popolo della Libertà (PdL)	10,797,296	35.3	29
Partito Democratico (PD)	7,999,476	26.1	9
Lega Nord (LN)	3,126,181	10.2	7
Di Pietro – Italia Dei Valori (IdV)	2,450,643	8.0	5
Unione Di Centro (UDC)	1,995,021	6.5	—
Rifondazione Comunista – Sinistra Europea – Comunisti Italiani (RC-SE-CI)	1,037,862	3.4	—
Sinistra Ecologia Libertà (SEL)	957,822	3.1	—
Lista Marco Pannella/Emma Bonino	743,284	2.4	—
La Destra-MPA-Pensionati – Alleanza di Centro	681,290	2.2	—
Fiamma Tricolore	246,403	0.8	—
Partito Comunista Dei Lavoratori	166,531	0.5	—
Forza Nuova	147,343	0.5	—
Südtirolervolkspartei (SVP)	143,509	0.5	1
Liberal Democratici – Maie	71,067	0.2	—
Vallée D'aoste	32,913	0.1	—
Autonomie Liberté Democratie	27,199	0.1	—
Total	30,623,840	—	72

Source: Ministero dell'Interno: http://elezioni.interno.it.

performed well, increasing its vote share slightly from 5.9 to 6.5 per cent, thus retaining the same 5 seats as before.

The new electoral 4 per cent hurdle strongly penalized smaller parties. For example, the Radicals did not succeed in reaching the required threshold, achieving only 2.4 per cent of the votes, with a barely discernible increase compared to 2004. This was a far cry from their historical record of 8.5 per cent of the vote in the 1999 Euro-election. As a result, the party lost the 2 seats belonging to its historical leaders, human rights activist and long-standing MEP Marco Pannella and former European Commissioner Emma Bonino, despite their remarkable number of personal preferences (Ministero dell'Interno, 6/2009).

Likewise, even though *Sinistra Ecologia Libertà,* which included the Greens amongst its members, slightly improved its voting share by going from 2.5 per cent to 3.1 per cent of the vote, the party failed to retain its 2 seats. The joint RC-SE-CI list only reached 3.4 per cent against the 6.1 per cent achieved separately by the *Rifondazione Comunista* and the 2.4 per cent by *Comunisti italiani* at the 2004 European election. By and large, few voters shifted from the right to the left or vice versa, and those who switched their party preference remained nevertheless faithful to their respective coalition, casting their ballot for either the government or opposition parties (Viola, 2010).

One of the striking anomalies which clearly emerged was that party leaders and top-ranking members who had officially run the electoral race did not take their EP seats; instead, unknown candidates down the party lists who only had a handful of votes took the EP seats, whilst candidates who were on party lists that did not cross the electoral barrier failed to secure their seat in the Strasbourg assembly, even after having obtained thousands of personal preferences by voters.

At the first plenary session, MEPs were called to form or join a political group, as foreseen by the new EP regulations, which stipulated that from July 2009 all political groups would have to include members from at least seven countries and that the minimum number of members in each group would be 25. Thirty-five Italian MEPs including 29 from PdL, five from UdC as well as Herbert Dorfmann from the *Südtirolervolkspartei* joined the European People's Party (EPP). The Italian contingent, being the largest after the German one, gathered MEPs who were paradoxically opposed to each other at the domestic level. The PdL affiliation was unenthusiastically accepted by the group, considering its atypical character and origin, so different from the European Christian Democratic parties and closer to the Spanish Conservatives or the 'New Europe' group. By contrast, the five representatives of the small Christian party UdC seemed to fit perfectly within the EPP context (Braghiroli and Verzichelli, 2009, 755).

After a long internal debate, the PD decided that its 21 MEPs would adhere to the Socialist Group, which changed its name to the Group of the Progressive Alliance of Socialists and Democrats (S&D), in order to reflect the widening of its ideological extent. The Italian MEPs, like their Spanish colleagues, formed the second largest contingent after the 23 German MEPs.

Consistent with their Eurosceptic principles, like their four predecessors in 2004, the nine LN members opted for an affiliation with the Europe of Freedom and Democracy Group (EFD), with Francesco Speroni appointed as co-president. Within the 32-member EFD, the Italian representation was the largest after the British one. Finally, the seven IdV MEPs found their home within the Group of the Alliance of Liberals and Democrats for Europe (ALDE), as the second largest national contingent after the 12-member German delegation.

Against this background, it is evident that the purpose of the recent electoral reform to reduce the number of Italian parties within the EP from 15 to 6 had been achieved, thus mirroring the domestic parliamentary outlook.

With regard to the Italian presence in Strasbourg, some characteristics are worth noting. Against a 35 per cent European average, only 22.2 per cent are women, confirming that gender

Table 6.10 Seat distribution of the Italian delegation in the EP: 2009

EPP Party	Seats	%	S&D Party	Seats	%	ALDE Party	Seats	%	EFD Party	Seats	%
PdL	29	3.9	PD	21	2.9	IdV Lista Di Pietro	7	1.0	LN	9	1.2
UDC	5	0.7	—								
SVP	1	0.1									
Total Ital. Parties	35	36.0	—	21	25.0		7	1.0		9	1.2
Total EU Nat. Parties	265	36.0	—	184	25.0		84	11.4		32	4.4

Source: www.europarl.europa.eu.

is still an extremely delicate issue, which has not been properly addressed by the Italian parties. Compared to 2004, the percentage of Italian female MEPs has increased by three percentage points, gaining 16 of Italy's 72 seats: 9 for the PdL, 5 for the PD, 1 for the LN, and 1 for the IdV.

Although this upward trend may sound encouraging, given that only six women had served in the previous legislature whilst ten were elected for the first time, Italian female MEPs continue to be under-represented in the EP. Indeed, Italy comes fourth last out of the 27 EU countries, after Malta with 0 per cent, Luxembourg with 16.6 per cent, and the Czech Republic with 18.2 per cent. As such, Italian female participation lags almost 15 percentage points behind the EP average. Additionally, in terms of differences between the various Italian parties, the PdL boasts the highest rate of elected women, equivalent to 28 per cent, followed by the PD with 23 per cent, whilst the *Lega Nord* and IdV include only one female MEP, reaching 11 and 14 per cent, respectively. The UdC has no elected women MEPs (Braghiroli, 2010).

The Italian EP delegation incorporates the highest number of newcomers, with an impressive turnover of 71 per cent, whilst the incumbent members with three or more mandates account for less than 20 per cent of the Italian cohort.

Looking at the profiles of the newly elected MEPs, a 55 per cent majority had gained political experience at the local or regional levels, followed by 25 per cent at the national level, and 20 per cent with no political background.

Table 6.11 Age and gender of Italian MEPs: 2009

	Italian Delegation	EP 27
Age average	53	55
Women percentage	21%	35%

Source: Antenna Europarlamentare, 2010.

Table 6.12 Political background of Italian MEPs: 2009

Political background	Number of MEPs (%)
National/European background	36 (50%)
Regional/local background	27 (38%)
No political background	9 (13%)

Source: Antenna Europarlamentare, 2010.

Table 6.13 Tenure of the Italian delegation in the EP: 2009

EP tenure	Number of MEPs (%)
1st mandate	49 (68%)
2nd mandate	11 (15%)
3rd mandate	8 (11%)
4th mandate	2 (3%)
5th mandate	2 (3%)

Source: Antenna Europarlamentare, 2010.

Against the *Cavaliere*'s expectations 'to count more in Europe', his proposal regarding Mario Mauro's candidature for the European Parliament presidency was ignored. After the latter's resentful refusal, in return, to chair the Foreign Affairs Committee, the former mayor of Milan from PdL, Gabriele Albertini, secured this prestigious position, whilst Carlo Casini from UdC obtained the Chair of the Constitutional Affairs Committee, Paolo Castro from PD became Chair of the Agriculture Committee, and former judge Luigi De Magistris (IdV) became Chair of the Budget Committee. Ten committee Vice-Chairs were allocated to MEPs from three of the five Italian political parties in the EP, in particular six from PdL, three from PD, and one from LN. Finally, Gianni Pittella, former head of the Italian PD delegation, and Roberta Angelilli, former head of the Italian AN delegation and PdL member, were elected Vice-Presidents of the European Parliament.

Finally, it is necessary to emphasize that although most Italian MEPs profess to be Europhiles, their attendance at plenary sessions is infrequent and their participation in EP political life is rather disappointing. Their initiatives within the parliamentary arena are also sporadic, so that their re-appointment rates as Chair or Vice-Chair of committees or political groups remains fairly low (Braghiroli and Verzichelli, 2009).

Table 6.14 Italian committee Chairs and Vice-Chairs: 2009

Committee	Chair	Vice-Chair	National party	Political group
Foreign affairs	Gabriele Albertini		PdL	EPP
		Fiorello Provera	LN	EFD
Development		Iva Zanicchi	PdL	EPP
International trade		Cristiana Muscardini	PdL	EPP
Budgetary control	Luigi De Magistris		IdV	ALDE
Industry, research, energy		Patrizia Toia	PD	S&D
Internal market and consumer protection		Lara Comi	PdL	EPP
Agriculture	Paolo De Castro		PD	S&D
Fisheries		Guido Milana	PD	S&D
Legal affairs		Luigi Berlinguer,	PD	S&D
		Raffaele Baldassare	PdL	EPP
Civil liberties, justice, and home affairs		Salvatore Iacolino	PdL	EPP
Constitutional affairs	Carlo Casini		UDC	EPP
Women's rights and gender equality		Barbara Matera	PdL	EPP
Petitions	Erminia Mazzoni		PdL	EPP

Source: www.europarl.europa.eu/meps/it/performsearch.html.

Italy

Following the ratification of the Lisbon Treaty, the number of Italian MEPs increased by one, in accordance with Article 9 A(2) of the TEU. As a result, the Italian electoral office selected former Senator Gino Trematerra from UdC as the first within the list of non-elected candidates who had achieved the highest number of votes within the Southern constituency. The Italian Parliament officially approved the selection procedure in December 2010 and Trematerra took up his seat in Strasbourg on 1 December 2011 by also joining the EPP Group.

Table 6.15 List of Italian MEPs: seventh legislature

Name	Date of birth	Gender	Constituency	National party	Political group	Previous legislature
Gabriele Albertini	06/07/1950	Male	North-West	PdL	EPP	6th and 7th (until March 2013 when elected MP)
Sonia Alfano	15/10/1971	Female	North-West	IdV	ALDE	None
Magdi Cristiano Allam	22/04/1952	Male	North-West	Io Amo l'Italia	EFD	None
Roberta Angelilli	01/02/1965	Female	Centre	PdL	EPP	5th, 6th, 7th
Antonello Antinoro	03/08/1960	Male	Islands	UDC	EPP	None
Alfredo Antoniozzi	18/03/1956	Male	Centre	PdL	EPP	6th
Pino Arlacchi	21/02/1951	Male	South	PD	S&D	None
Raffaele Baldassarre	23/09/1956	Male	South	PdL	EPP	None
Francesca Balzani	31/10/1966	Female	North-West	PD	S&D	None
Paolo Bartolozzi	12/09/1957	Male	Centre	PdL	EPP	None
Sergio Berlato	27/07/1959	Male	North-East	PdL	EPP	5th, 6th
Luigi Berlinguer	25/07/1932	Male	North-East	PD	S&D	None
Mara Bizzotto	03/06/1952	Female	North-East	LN	EFD	None
Vito Bonsignore	03/07/1943	Male	North-West	PdL	EPP	5th, 6th
Mario Borghezio	03/12/1947	Male	North-West	LN	EFD	5th, 6th
Rita Borsellino	02/06/1945	Female	Islands	PD	S&D	None
Antonio Cancian	02/07/1951	Male	North-East	PdL	EPP	None
Salvatore Caronna	05/03/1964	Male	North-East	PD	S&D	None
Carlo Casini	04/03/1935	Male	Centre	UDC	EPP	4th, 5th, 6th
Sergio Gaetano Cofferati	30/01/1948	Male	North-West	PD	S&D	None
Lara Comi	18/03/1983	Female	North-West	PdL	EPP	None
Silvia Costa	12/06/1949	Female	Centre	PD	S&D	None
Andrea Cozzolino	03/08/1962	Male	South	PD	S&D	None
Rosario Crocetta	08/02/1951	Male	Islands	PD	S&D	None (up to December 2012 when elected President of Sicily Region)
Francesco De Angelis	04/10/1959	Male	Centre	PD	S&D	None
Paolo De Castro	02/02/1958	Male	South	PD	S&D	None
Ciriaco De Mita	02/02/1928	Male	South	UDC	EPP	5th
Leonardo Domenici	12/07/1955	Male	Centre	PD	S&D	None
Herbert Dorfmann	04/03/1969	Male	North-West	SVP	EPP	None
Carlo Fidanza	21/09/1976	Male	North-West	PdL	EPP	None
Lorenzo Fontana	10/04/1980	Male	North-East	LN	EFD	None
Elisabetta Gardini	03/06/1956	Female	North-East	PdL	EPP	None
Giuseppe Gargani	23/04/1935	Male	South	UDC	EPP	5th, 6th
Roberto Gualtieri	19/07/1966	Male	Centre	PD	S&D	None
Salvatore Iacolino	18/11/1963	Male	Islands	PdL	EPP	None

(continued)

Table 6.15 (continued)

Name	Date of birth	Gender	Constituency	National party	Political group	Previous legislature
Vincenzo Iovine	28/12/1955	Male	South	IdV (2009–2012) PD (2012–)	ALDE (2009–2012) S&D (2012)	None
Giovanni La Via	28/03/1963	Male	Islands	PDL	EPP	None
Clemente Mastella	05/02/1947	Male	South	UDEUR	EPP	5th
Barbara Matera	09/12/1981	Female	South	PdL	EPP	None
Mario Mauro	24/07/1961	Male	North-West	PdL	EPP	5th, 6th
Erminia Mazzoni	24/04/1965	Female	South	UDC	EPP	None
Guido Milana	02/03/1954	Male	Centre	PD	S&D	None
Claudio Morganti	14/04/1973	Male	Centre	LN	EFD	None
Tiziano Motti	07/02/1966	Male	Centre	UDC	EPP	None
Cristiana Muscardini	06/11/1948	Female	Centre	FLI	EPP	3rd, 4th, 5th, 6th
Alfredo Pallone	13/09/1947	Male	Centre	PdL	EPP	None
Antonio Panzeri	06/06/1955	Male	Centre	PD	S&D	6th
Aldo Patriciello	27/09/1957	Male	South	PdL	EPP	6th (2006–2009)
Mario Pirillo	11/09/1945	Male	South	PD	S&D	None
Gianni Pittella	19/11/1958	Male	South	PD	S&D	5th, 6th
Vittorio Prodi	19/05/1937	Male	North-East	PD	S&D	6th
Fiorello Provera	31/03/1956	Male	North-East	LN	EFD	None
Niccolò Rinaldi	03/12/1962	Male	Centre	IdV	ALDE	None
Crescenzio Rivellini	09/07/1955	Male	South	PdL	EPP	None
Licia Ronzulli	14/06/1975	Female	North-West	PdL	EPP	None
Oreste Rossi	24/03/1964	Male	North-West	LN	EFD	None
Potito Salatto	22/01/1942	Male	Centre	PdL	EPP	None
Matteo Salvini	09/03/1973	Male	North-West	LN	EFD	None
Amalia Sartori	02/08/1947	Female	North-East	PdL	EPP	None
David-Maria Sassoli	30/05/1956	Male	Centre	PD	S&D	None
Giancarlo Scottà	11/04/1953	Male	North-East	LN	EFD	None
Marco Scurria	18/05/1967	Male	Centre	PdL	EPP	None
Debora Serracchiani	10/11/1970	Female	North-East	PD	S&D	None (up to April 2013 when elected President of Friuli-Venezia Giulia Region)
Sergio Paolo Francesco Silvestris	22/12/1973	Male	South	PdL	EPP	None
Francesco Enrico Speroni	04/10/1946	Male	North-West	LN	EFD	3rd, 5th, 6th
Gianluca Susta	10/04/1956	Male	North-West	PD	S&D	None
Salvatore Tatarella	11/10/1947	Male	South	FLI	EPP	6th
Patrizia Toia	17/03/1950	Female	North-West	PD	S&D	6th
Gino Trematerra	03/09/1940	Male	South	CCD-UDC	EPP	None
Giammaria Uggias	29/03/1961	Male	Islands	IdV	ALDE	None
Gianni Vattimo	04/01/1936	Male	North-West	IdV	ALDE	5th
Iva Zanicchi	18/01/1940	Female	North-West	PdL	EPP	None
Andrea Zanoni	26/08/1965	Male	North-East	IdV	ALDE	None

Source: www.europarl.europa.eu/meps/en/search.html?country=IT.

Italy

9.4 Campaign finance

In the 1970s, in the wake of a series of corruption scandals, it was deemed necessary to lay down rules over party funding for the Chamber of Deputies and the Senate that were subsequently extended to the EP. Law No. 195 of 2 May 1974, known as the *Piccoli* Bill, allowed ordinary contributions to be granted annually to political parties as well as reimbursements for electoral campaign spending. On 18 and 19 April 1993, a referendum repealed, by a 90.3 per cent majority, Articles 3 and 9 of the above-mentioned legislation regarding any regular yearly subsidy, yet retained the section over electoral refunds.

In order to counterbalance or at least reduce the negative effects of this popular consultation the Italian Parliament has, over the years, approved a series of laws providing for a substantial increase in such reimbursements. It was agreed that parties would be refunded by way of annual instalments throughout the entire legislature, even in case of early dissolution of the chambers (Legge n. 157/1999). Subsequently, it was established that the sum originally allocated would be halved for lists failing to ensure a balanced composition between men and women and to account for one-third of candidates of the least-represented gender (Article 3 Legge n. 90/2004).

Under new electoral legislation approved on 20 February 2009, only those lists obtaining at least one seat in the European Parliament would be entitled to have their election expenses refunded. In the run up to the 2009 Euro-election, amongst the six parties that eventually succeeded in obtaining at least one seat, the PD was the top spender, spending over €17 million on the campaign, equivalent to 42.61 per cent of total campaign spending. In comparison, the UdC devoted less money to the organization of the Euro-elections, spending just over €8.2 million, corresponding to 20.53 per cent. The IdV came in third, with campaign expenses exceeding €7 million, accounting for 17.56 per cent. The LN followed with just over €4 million euro, equivalent to 10 per cent of the total spending of the six most successful parties in the EP contest. Strikingly, the largest Italian party, the PdL, bequeathed fewer resources to the campaign than its main rival parties as well as its allies, failing to reach €3.5 million.

Finally, the small regionalist SVP spent just above €200,000 for the 2009 Euro-election. By capturing 4.7 per cent of the voter preferences in the North-East constituency, and regardless of its 0.5 percentage of the nationwide and overseas vote, the party had been included amongst the recipients in compliance with the regulations to safeguard and represent ethnic minorities.

Table 6.16 Parties eligible for electoral reimbursement in Italy: 2009

Political party	Votes	%	Seats
PdL	10,797,296	35.26	29
PD	7,999,476	26.12	21
LN	3,126,181	10.21	9
IdV	2,450,643	8.00	7
UdC	1,995,021	6.51	5
SVP	143,509	4.71/0.47§	1
Total	30,623,840*	100.00	72**

Source: GU 7/ 2009, 2010, 2011, 2012.

Notes:
§ These percentages refer respectively to: North-West Constituency/Italy + Overseas Constituency.
* These figures refer to the sum of the votes attributed to all 18 lists within the 5 constituencies and the Overseas Constituency.
** Total number of Italian seats in the EP.

Table 6.17 EP election campaign expenditure in Italy: 2009

Political party	Declared/reported expenditure	%*	Incurred and ascertained expenditure	%*
PdL	4,270,420.38	10.67	3,495,092.13	8.71
PD	16,014,463.43	40.01	17,083,834.72	42.61
LN	4,019,845.82	10.05	4,040,407.74	10.08
IdV	7,010,282.56	17.52	7,043,018.68	17.56
UdC	8,500,210.18	21.23	8,231,394.24	20.53
SVP	208,078.19	0.52	204,373.13	0.51
Total	40,023,300.56	100.00	40,098,120.64	100.00

Source: Author's table based on data drawn from the Italian Court of Auditors, *Corte dei Conte* (2010).

Note: * Author's own calculations.

Table 6.18 Public funding for political parties in Italy: 2009–2013

Political party	Reimbursement 2009	Reimbursement 2010	Reimbursement 2011	Reimbursement 2012–2013	Total	%
PdL	17,644,530.02	18,978,773.52	18,291,428.89	9,226,027.64	64,140,760.07	40.7
PD	13,072,439.10	14,060,950.38	13,551,712.06	6,835,358.28	47,520,459.82	30.2
LN	5,108,685.96	5,494,994.41	5,295,984.98	2,671,245.87	18,570,911.22	11.8
IdV	4,004,747.48	4,307,578.35	4,151,572.97	2,094,015.02	14,557,913.82	9.2
UdC	3,260,187.36	3,506,716.10	3,379,715.14	1,704,697.07	11,851,315.67	7.5
SVP	234,516.95	252,250.65	243,115.01	122,624.97	852,507.58	0.5
Total	43,325,106.87	46,601,263.41	44,913,529.05	22,653,968.85	157,493,868.18	100.0

Source: Author's own calculations based on data from GU 7/2009, 2010, 2011, 2012.

Against this background, it is indeed worth noting that the PdL, despite its low campaign spending, obtained 35.26 per cent of the vote, thus becoming the major beneficiary of public funds. Paradoxically, its first instalment, equivalent to over €17.6 million and therefore 40.7 per cent of the total destined to the six parties in 2009, exceeded almost six times the amount of the expenses incurred. In reality, as shown in Tables 6.17 and 6.18, the annual refunds assigned to the six parties from 2009 to 2013 did not match the share of their total expenditure and hardly bore any relationship to the percentage of the votes gained.

According to calculations made by the Italian news agency ANSA in 2009, over €251.7 million would be awarded to political parties in five annual instalments up to 2013, inevitably raising public protests, shocked by such an outrageous waste of public money. In the eyes of the Italian taxpayers, electoral reimbursements represent nothing else but a 'disguised form of ordinary contribution' granted to parties, riddled with fraud and corruption, making political elites, if possible, even more unpopular (Pacini, 2009, 185).

10 Theoretical interpretation of Euro-elections

Prior to testing the two main conceptual frameworks on European elections outlined in the second chapter of this volume against the 1979–2009 Italian empirical evidence, it seems necessary to highlight that the complexity of the domestic political system cannot be easily examined in the light of some of the hypotheses inherent to either Second-Order Election or Europe

Salience models. These assumptions, which are suited to net bipolar structures with a genuine alternation of parties in government, are often incompatible and irreconcilable with the highly fragmented and volatile Italian political landscape.

More specifically, the first difficulty stems from the lack of party rotation in government in post-war Italian history, characterized by a kind of 'monopoly' by the DC and a *de facto* veto imposed by the second largest political party, the PCI. In the mid-1990s, with the advent of the Second Republic, new partisan actors arose from the ashes of the old parties. Indeed, this exceptional metamorphosis makes it hard to carry out comparative research due to the disappearance of some of the traditional political actors and the arrival of a welter of new political entities. Furthermore, such a proliferation of parties sometimes makes it tricky to identify their position on the political spectrum and even whether they fall within the government or the opposition sphere. This brings us to the last and most common research hurdle caused by the high number of brief and unstable multiparty coalition cabinets within the 1979–2009 time frame. The failure of these governments to complete their full terms makes it virtually impossible to detect any change in voter behaviour in the various phases of the national electoral cycle.

Bearing in mind such obstacles and within these limits, we will try to uncover whether any of the core factors of the two main theoretical approaches can be duly applied to the Italian case.

10.1 Second-Order Election theory

The analysis of all seven waves of Euro-elections in Italy reveals a wide range of features that seem to fit with the Second-Order Election (SOE) model. Overall, the campaign was largely suffocated by constant public concerns over domestic politics, which diverted attention from the European issues, turning EP elections into a kind of rehearsal for the next, more important national electoral contest.

Parties did not invest a great deal of time or resources in drafting and divulging their electoral manifestos and hardly any public debates took place on European issues. As a result, voters were mostly unaware of any specific differences between party programmes, if they existed at all, on this matter. More generally, citizens simply received scanty information, with the consequence being that votes were distributed more randomly across parties.

In line with the SOE logic, Italians were often inclined to 'punish' the governing party or coalition, which registered losses in virtually all seven sets of Euro-elections. The timing certainly influenced the extent of this outcome, reaching its maximum effect around mid-term, when EP elections represented a true experiment for the government, whilst voting losses tended to even out or decrease as the cycle went on (Marsh, 1998, 606).

A comparative analysis of all EP election results with the closest Italian parliamentary election results reveals in particular the case of the PCI in 1984, when it obtained a higher number of votes and, therefore, more seats in the European Parliament, than the governing DC. In the other circumstances, the best performing party in the national elections never lost its primacy in the European ones, even if its level of support decreased in favour of the opposition parties. The only exception occurred in the 1994 Euro-elections that sanctioned Berlusconi's triumph in the wake of the so-called 'post-electoral euphoria' or second-order election 'overconfirmation' of the general electoral outcomes achieved a few months earlier. On this occasion, the EP contest simply amplified *Forza Italia*'s success, by marking an increase in its voting share of over ten percentage points.

European elections have been an interesting test for minor parties that scored better in EP elections than in general elections. The polling results confirmed the hypothesis that minor parties were generally favoured at the Euro-elections, particularly those that were smaller at the national level than their federation was at the EU level. This was the case for the PRI, PLI, and both Socialist parties, the PSI and PSDI, as well as the Greens and the Radicals.

Consistent with one of the SOE hypotheses underlining the increasing weight of minor parties in the EP contest, the aggregate vote for the major political formations decreased whilst the share of small and new parties increased through the first five waves of European elections. By contrast, the opposite trend was registered in the last two rounds where the combined percentage of the two main centre-right and centre-left political formations, FI and *Ulivo*, amounted to 52.1 per cent in 2004 and the PdL and PD even reached 61.4 per cent in 2009.

Whereas the proportional system used to give an advantage to smaller parties, the introduction of a 4 per cent electoral threshold, prevented their representation in the European Parliament, regardless of their better performance.

Certainly, one of the key factors validating SOE can be found in low turnout at the EP electoral contests in Italy. However, when comparing abstention rates in both electoral races, it is necessary to point out that, during the first rounds of European elections, polling stations in Italy used to be open only on Sunday, whilst for general elections they stayed open until the following Monday morning. Furthermore, it should be stressed that the decline in participation does not represent an exclusive feature of European elections but, rather, a general trend, increasingly affecting all electoral races, which mirrors a wider phenomenon stemming from people's indifference and disillusionment with politics. To a lesser extent, abstention may have also been favoured by the official abolition in 1993 of any lingering repremanding provisions against non-voters, albeit virtually never implemented. On the other hand, it cannot be denied that European electoral contests in Italy presented higher percentages of invalid and blank votes, except in 1979 and 1984, hence confirming voter perception of their secondary nature.

The last feature that arises from a comparative assessment is the growing gap in terms of turnout between national and European elections, from 4.5 percentage points in 1979 to over 14 points in 2009, or even from 5 percentage points in 1979 to almost 15 points in 2009, when considering Italians voting abroad. Differential turnout rather than vote switching had a great impact, in particular in the last Euro-elections when not only the governing PdL but, even more, the opposing PD lost a large share of supporters who did not bother to go to the polls. The widening difference in rates of turnout between national and EP elections seems to corroborate the hypothesis that the latter are perceived as less important.

10.2 Europe Salience theory

The above analysis of European electoral dynamics in Italy has captured some of the tenets of the SOE model and displayed appealing arguments to support most of the original features of this theory. Nevertheless, it is worth highlighting that European issues, albeit to a minor degree, are increasingly relevant to voters' choices and cannot be regarded as trivial.

During the first four sets of Euro-elections, there has not been real inter-party conflict over EC/EU issues. The initial resistance to the Community, put forward by the two extreme right- and left-wing parties, the MSI and PCI, faded away in 1989. This change of attitude could be ascribed to reasons of international strategy, involving the development of an independent neutral area between the superpowers along with a tactic of alliances between the other political forces in Europe. Whereas, within the Socialist camp a number of Member States used to display a fairly diffident, if not negative, approach to the EC, the PSI has always shown a pro-European attitude.

In addition, as already highlighted, the positive outcome of the 1989 referendum, endorsed by over 88.1 per cent of citizens, signalled a desire for proceeding towards a closer European Union.

Conversely, from 1994, the Italian political outlook changed astonishingly with the centre-left parties displaying a more pro-European stance than their centre-right counterparts. Furthermore, mainstream parties, as opposed to the peripheral ones, expressed the strongest support for the European project (Conti, 2009, 213). The variable 'Europe', in terms of people's sentiments towards the EU, may have affected citizens' decisions not to turn up to the polling stations or to express their indifference and discontent towards the EU by invalidating their vote. And yet Mark N. Franklin and Sara B. Hobolt (2011) have established a reverse causal effect.

As to the results, there was relatively modest vote switching between national and EP elections and this shift could also be partially explained by parties' stances on European issues. Citizens who held more Eurosceptic views than their own respective parties did turn to anti-integration movements, notably the *Lega Nord*.

Over the years, parties belonging to a European or international federation, including the Socialists, Liberals, and the Greens, or presenting a cosmopolitan image such as the Radicals, were favoured in EP elections, showing that party position was one of the criteria considered by the electors in casting their ballot. Most significantly, as already mentioned, this could be confirmed by the increasingly better performance of anti-European movements.

According to the 'Europe Salience' theory, voter turnout in EP elections is fundamental in order to assess the legitimacy and success of the European Union; the increasing higher abstention rate is certainly a warning signal that cannot be ignored by political elites. The increasing gap between national and EP elections, combined with a declining participation rate in Euro-elections since 1979, mirrors a progressive disenchantment towards Europe felt by Italian citizens.

Nevertheless, as shown by public opinion polls, European integration remains a pivotal element in Italian politics, acting as a safe harbour against domestic problems and international financial turbulence.

All in all, elections to the European Parliament in Italy were influenced by a series of factors, first identified by Giovanna Zincone with regard to the first case in 1979, but easily applicable to all the other Euro-electoral races. More specifically, these factors entailed: the complex Italian political background, its often thorny inter- and intra-party relations, its electoral law, its European cultural tradition, its relationship to the electoral cycle and, above all, the widespread perception of these elections as a Second-Order event.

Undeniably, the above elements pervaded the various stages of the campaign trail, from the choice of the electoral system to the selection of candidates and the range of topics discussed (Zincone, 1985, 119). Italian electors were constant in their focus on domestic themes that continued to influence their voting behaviour, whereas European issues played only a minor role.

By applying Albert O. Hirschman's typology of 'exit/voice/loyalty' to the Italian case, it is possible to notice that voters hardly resorted to the so-called 'exit' by shifting from one party to another in the left–right political spectrum. Consequently, it is possible to conclude that this factor did not affect the domestic balance and the coalition system. Voters even made some use of 'voice' to exert pressure on the party without leaving it. This occurred, in particular, over the selection of candidates. Finally, Italian voting behaviour expressed, to a large extent, 'loyalty' towards the party by remaining at least within the same political coalition (Hirschman, 1970 quoted by G. Zincone, 1985, 130–1; Weber, 2011).

Euro-elections have been treated by all concerned as an 'oracle' predicting the likely results of national elections, should they have been held instead (Mannheimer, 1996). Finally, the EP electoral contests have been perceived as a way to gauge and test the political mood of the country, a sort of 'dress rehearsal' prior to the first public performance.

References

Primary Sources

http://elezionistorico.interno.it/ (accessed on 15 December 2012).
http://elezioni.interno.it/europee/euro090607/prefET1.htm (accessed on 10 June 2009).
http://europa.eu/abc/maps/members/italy_en.htm (accessed on 31 January 2012).
www.g8italia2009.it (accessed on 2 February 2011).
Corte dei Conti (2010) 'Referto al Presidente della Camera dei deputati sui consuntivi presentati dalle formazioni politiche rappresentate nel Parlamento europeo a seguito delle elezioni del 6 e 7 giugno 2009', 5 luglio 2010.
Costituzione della Repubblica italiana (1948) www.governo.it/Governo/Costituzione/CostituzioneRepubblicaItaliana.pdf (accessed on 10 January 2015).
Decreto Legge n. 408, 24 giugno 1994, convertito in Legge 3 agosto 1994, n. 483, 'Disposizioni urgenti in materia di elezioni al Parlamento europeo', *Gazzetta Ufficiale della Repubblica italiana*, n. 148, 27 giugno 1994.
Electoral System, Chamber of Deputies Elections, 1979, 1983, 1987, 1992, 1994, 1996, 2001, 2006, IPU's PARLINE Database, www.ipu.org (accessed on 18 October 2011).
Eurobarometer 71.1 (2009) European Parliament and Elections, Economic Crisis, Climate Change, and Chemical Products, January–February 2009, Brussels, European Commission.
Eurobarometer 72 (2009) Public Opinion in the European Union, Italy', autumn 2009, http://ec.europa.eu/public_opinion/archives/eb/eb72/eb72_it_en_exec.pdf (accessed on 10 January 2015).
European Parliament Directorate-General for Internal Policies, Policy Department, Citizens' Rights and Constitutional Affairs (2009) *The Selection of Candidates for the European Parliament by National Parties and the Impact of European Political Parties*, March, PE 410.683
European Parliament website, www.europarl.europa.eu/meps/it/performsearch.html (accessed on 10 January 2015).
Eurostat (2013, 2014) http://epp.eurostat.ec.europa.eu/ (accessed on 5 June 2015).
Gazzetta Ufficiale della Repubblica italiana (GU) Serie Generale n. 175, 30 luglio 2009, Allegato alla Deliberazione Ufficio di Presidenza n. 71, 28 luglio 2009.
Gazzetta Ufficiale della Repubblica italiana (GU) Serie Generale n. 175, 29 luglio 2010, Allegato 11 alla Deliberazione Ufficio di Presidenza n. 110, 27 luglio 2010.
Gazzetta Ufficiale della Repubblica italiana (GU) Serie Generale n. 174, 28 luglio 2011, Allegato 9 alla Deliberazione dell'Ufficio di Presidenza n. 151, 21 luglio 2011.
Gazzetta Ufficiale della Repubblica italiana (GU) Serie Generale n. 175, 28 luglio 2012, Allegato 8 alla Deliberazione dell'Ufficio di Presidenza n. 207, 25 luglio 2012.
Lamassoure-Séverin (2007) Report on the Composition of the European Parliament, 3 October, A6-0351.
Legge n. 18, 24 gennaio 1979, 'Elezione dei membri del Parlamento europeo spettanti all'Italia', *Gazzetta Ufficiale della Repubblica italiana*, n. 29, 30 gennaio 1979.
Legge n. 157, 3 giugno 1999, 'Nuove norme in materia di rimborso delle spese per consultazioni elettorali e referendarie e abrogazione delle disposizioni concernenti la contribuzione volontaria ai movimenti e partiti politici', *Gazzetta Ufficiale della Repubblica italiana*, n. 129, 4 giugno 1999.
Legge Costituzionale n. 1, 17 gennaio 2000, 'Modifica all'articolo 48 della Costituzione concernente l'istituzione della circoscrizione Estero per l'esercizio del diritto di voto dei cittadini italiani residenti all'estero' *Gazzetta Ufficiale (GU) della Repubblica Italiana*, Serie Generale n. 15, 20 gennaio 2000.
Legge n. 78, 27 marzo 2004, 'Disposizioni concernenti i membri del Parlamento europeo eletti in Italia, in attuazione della decisione 2002/772/CE, del Consiglio', *Gazzetta Ufficiale della Repubblica italiana*, n. 74, 29 marzo 2004.
Legge n. 90, 8 aprile 2004, 'Norme in materia di elezioni dei membri del Parlamento europeo e altre disposizioni inerenti ad elezioni da svolgersi nell'anno 2004', *Gazzetta Ufficiale della Repubblica italiana*, n. 84, 9 aprile 2004.
Legge 20 febbraio 2009, n. 10, 'Modifiche alla legge 24 gennaio 1979, n. 18, concernente l'elezione dei membri del Parlamento europeo spettanti all'Italia', *Gazzetta Ufficiale della Repubblica italiana*, n. 44, 23 febbraio 2009.
Ministero dell'Interno, http://elezioni.interno.it (accessed on 15 February 2015).
Parties and Elections, www.parties-and-elections.eu/italy2b.html (accessed on 15 February 2015).

Special Eurobarometer 303 (2009) 'The 2009 European Elections Report', April, http://ec.europa.eu/public_opinion/archives/ebs/ebs_303_en.pdf (accessed on 10 January 2015).
Special Eurobarometer 308 (2009) 'Europeans and the 2009 European Elections', Eurobarometer 71, 'Results for Italy', http://ec.europa.eu/public_opinion/archives/eb_special_320_300_en.htm#308 (accessed on 10 January 2015).
The Newsletter of the European Parliament Legal Affairs Committee, June 2011, Juri Report.

Secondary Sources

Books and articles

Bellucci, P. and Conti, N., (2012) 'Introduzione: europeismo, euroscetticismo', in Bellucci, P. and Conti, N. (eds) *Gli italiani e l'Europa: opinione pubblica, élite politiche e media*, Roma, Carocci.
Bellucci, P. and Serricchio F. (2012) 'Cosa pensano i cittadini dell'Europa?' in Bellucci, P. and Conti, N. (eds) *Gli italiani e l'Europa: opinione pubblica, élite politiche e media*, Roma, Carocci.
Biondi, P. (2013) 'Berlusconi U-turn secures Italian government's survival', *Reuters*, 2 October. Online. Available at: http://uk.reuters.com/article/2013/10/02/uk-italy-politics-idUKBRE9910AX20131002 (accessed on 10 January 2015).
Braghiroli, S. and Verzichelli, L. (2009) *Parlamentari a Strasburgo*, Bologna, Il Mulino, 5/2009, 753–62.
Braghiroli, S. (2010) *Antenna Europarlamentare: L'Attività dei rappresentanti italiani in Europa (Rapporto 2010)*, Siena, CIRCaP.
Braghiroli, S. and Verzichelli, L. (2009) *Parlamentari a Strasburgo*, Bologna, Il Mulino, 5/2009, 753–62.
Chabod, F. (2002) *L'Italia contemporanea 1918–1948*, Torino, Einaudi.
Conti, N. (2004) 'The European Parliament Election in Italy, June 12–13, 2004', European Parliament Election Briefing no. 20 EPERN.
Conti, N. (2009) 'Tied hands? Italian Political Parties and Europe, *Modern Italy*, 14(2), May, 203–16.
Conti, N. and Memoli, V. (2011) 'The multi-faced nature of party-based Euroscepticism', *Acta Politica*, 1–22.
Cordini, G. (1988) *Il voto obbligatorio*, Roma, Bulzoni.
Cotta, M. (2005) 'Conclusioni', in Cotta, M., Isernia P. and Verzichelli, L. (eds) *L'Europa in Italia: élite, opinione pubblica e decisioni*, Bologna, Il Mulino.
Daniels, P. A. (1996) 'Italy', in Lodge, J. (ed.) *The 1994 Elections to the European Parliament*, London, Pinter, 134–46.
Diamanti, I. (2007) 'The Italian Centre-Right and Centre-Left: Between Parties and the Party', *West European Politics*, 30(4) September, 733–62.
Diamanti, I. (2011) 'La democrazia provvisoria', *La Repubblica*, 10 gennaio.
Hirschman, A. O. (1970) *Exit, Voice, and Loyalty: Responses to Decline in Firms, Organizations, and States*, Cambridge, MA, Harvard University Press.
Isernia, P. and Ammendola T. (2005) 'L'Europa vista dagli italiani, i primi vent'anni', in Cotta, M., Isernia P. and Verzichelli, L. (eds) *L'Europa in Italia: élite, opinione pubblica e decisioni*, Bologna, Il Mulino
Lindberg, L. N. and Scheingold, S. A. (1971) *Regional Integration: Theory and Research*, Cambridge MA, Harvard University Press.
Mannheimer, R. (1996) 'Italy: Consulting the Oracle', in van der Eijk, C. and Franklin, M. N. (eds) *Choosing Europe: The European Electorate and National Politics in the Face of Union*, Michigan, The University of Michigan Press.
Marsh, M. (1998) 'Testing the Second-Order Election Model after Four European Elections', *British Journal of Political Science*, 28(4), 591–607
Pacini, M. C. (2009) 'Public Funding of Political Parties in Italy', *Modern Italy*, 14(2) May, 183–202.
Quaglia, L. and Radaelli, C. (2007) 'Italian Politics and the European Union: A Tale of Two Research Designs', *West European Politics*, 30(4), September, 924–43.
Sandri, G. (2009) 'Italy', European Parliament Directorate-General for Internal Policies, Policy Department, Citizens' Rights and Constitutional Affairs, *The Selection of Candidates for the European Parliament by National Parties and the Impact of European Political Parties*, March, PE 410.683, 145–62.
Sartori, G. (1982), Teoria dei partiti e caso italiano, Milan, SugarCo.
Spini, G. (1963) *Disegno storico della civiltà*, vol. 3, Roma, Cremonese.
Taggart, P. and Szczerbiak, A. (2002) 'The Party Politics of Euroscepticism in EU Member and Candidate States', SEI Working Paper 51, Sussex European Institute.

Viola, D. M. (2005) 'Italy', in Lodge, J. (ed.) *The 2004 Elections to the European Parliament*, Basingstoke, Palgrave, 155–72.

Viola, D. M. (2010) 'Italy', in Lodge, J. (ed.) *The 2009 Elections to the European Parliament*, Basingstoke, Palgrave, 160–8.

Weber, M. [1922] (1978) (Wirtschaft und Gesellschaft) in Roth, Guenther R. and Wittich, C. (eds) *Economy and Society*, Berkeley, University of California Press.

Weber, T. (2011) 'Exit, Voice, and Cyclicality: A Micrologic of Midterm Effects in European Parliament Elections', *American Journal of Political Science*, 55(4), 907–22.

Zincone, G. (1985) 'Italy', in Reif, K. H. (ed.) *The European Elections, Campaigns and Results of the 1979/81 First Direct Elections to the European Parliament*, Aldershot, Gower, 118–35.

Newspapers

Milella, L. (2010) 'Intervista a Gustavo Zagrebelsky: Grazie al Porcellum è oligarchia cancelliamo questa aberrazione', *La Repubblica*, 8 settembre.

Zagrebelsky, G. (2009) 'Per gli eletti arrivano i rimborsi', *Avvenire*, 9 giugno.

Zagrebelsky, G. (2011) 'Per cambiare davvero. Elezioni, partiti, partecipazione', *Libertà e Giustizia*, 12 luglio. Online. Available at: http://www.libertaegiustizia.it/2011/07/12/per-cambiare-davvero.

7
BELGIUM

Nathalie Brack and Jean-Benoit Pilet

Figure 7.1 Map of Belgium

Table 7.1 Belgium profile

EU entry year	1952 ECSC; 1958 EEC and founding member
Schengen entry year	1985
MEPs elected in 2009	22
MEPs under Lisbon Treaty	22
Capital	Brussels
Total area*	30,528 km²
Population	11,203,992
	58% Flemish, 31% Walloon, 11% Others
Population density**	368.8/km²
Median age of population	42.8
Political system	Constitutional Monarchy
Head of state	King Albert II (August 1993–July 2013);
	King Philippe VI (July 2013–)
Head of government	Yves Leterme, Flemish Christian Democratic Party (CD&V) (November 2009–December 2011);
	Elio Di Rupo, Socialist Party (PS) (December 2011–May 2014)
Political majority	Christian Democrats (CD&V-CDH), Liberals (Open VLD-MR) and Francophone Socialists (PS) Coalition Government (June 2009–December 2011);
	Socialist Party (PS), Flemish Christian Democratic Party(CD&V), Socialist Party Different (SPA), Liberals (Open VLD), Reformist Movement (MR), Humanist Democratic Centre (CDH) Coalition Government
	(December 2011–May 2014)
Currency	Euro (€) since 1999
Prohead GDP in PPS	36,000 €

Source: Eurostat, 2013, 2014, http://epp.eurostat.ec.europa.eu/.

Notes:
* Total area including inland waters.
** Population density: the ratio of the annual average population of a region to the land area of the region.

1 Geographical position

Belgium is located in north-west Europe, bordering the Netherlands to the north, Germany and the Grand Duchy of Luxembourg to the east, France to the south and west and the North Sea to the north-west. It is a small country, with a surface area of 30,528 square kilometres, but its geographical location has made it one of the economic and urban nerve centres of Europe.

Indeed, Belgium is at the heart of one of the most highly industrialized regions in the world. As one of the first countries to undergo an industrial revolution in Europe in the early nineteenth century, it developed an excellent transportation infrastructure including ports, canals, railways, and highways in order to integrate its industry with that of its neighbours. Most traditional industrial sectors, such as steel, textiles, chemicals, food processing, pharmaceuticals, automobiles, and machinery fabrication are represented in the Belgian economy, which strongly depends on world trade due to a scarcity of domestic natural resources.

2 Historical background

Belgium became independent in 1830 after popular uprisings led to its secession from the Netherlands. On 21 July 1831, under the kingship of Leopold I, Belgium became a constitutional monarchy and a parliamentary democracy with a secular constitution based on the Napoleonic Code. Universal suffrage for men was introduced after a major strike in 1893, whilst women obtained their right to vote only in 1949.

Belgium owned several colonies in Africa: the 1885 Berlin Conference gave control of the Congo Free State to King Leopold II, but as his private possession. However, due to growing international concerns for the savage treatment of the Congolese people under his rule, the Belgian state decided to take full responsibility for the colony, which was officially renamed as the Belgian Congo in 1908.

During both world wars, the neutrality of Belgium in international politics was violated by Germany. After World War I (WWI), the Prussian districts of Eupen and Malmedy were annexed to Belgium in 1925, leading to the presence of a German-speaking minority in the country. In addition, the League of Nations conferred to Belgium a mandate to take over the German colonies of Rwanda and Burundi. In the aftermath of WWII, a general strike forced King Leopold III to abdicate, mainly because of his positions and attitudes during the conflict, the so-called '*Question royale*'.

At the crossroads of Germanic and Latin Europe, Belgium is home to three language groups: Flemish, French and, to a lesser extent, German. Such linguistic diversity has led to political and cultural conflicts, as reflected in the political history of the country and its complex system of government. The second half of the twentieth century was characterized by the rise of conflicts between Flemings and Francophones, fuelled by cultural differences and asymmetric economic evolution between the two main regions of Flanders and Wallonia. These ongoing confrontations led to several state reforms, through which Belgium was transformed into a federal state.

3 Geopolitical profile

Tragic war experiences led to a rethinking of Belgium's neutral position. The country became one of the foremost advocates for collective security and started to play an active role in establishing international organizations. In particular, Belgium joined the following international organizations as a founding member: NATO in 1949; the European Coal and Steel Community in 1951; the European Atomic Energy Community in 1957; and the European Economic Community in 1957.

The international activism of Belgium has widely been recognized and Brussels was chosen both to host NATO headquarters and to be the capital of the European Union. Finally, it supported the accession of the new democracies from Central and Eastern Europe to NATO and the EU. Belgium is actively engaged in the Organization for Security and Cooperation in Europe (OSCE). It served as Chair of the OSCE in 2006 and was a member of the United Nations Security Council in 2007–2008. Nowadays, many Belgian politicians hold key international positions; for example the President of the European Union and the Deputy Secretary-General of the Organization for Economic Cooperation and Development (OECD) are Belgian.

4 Overview of the political landscape

Belgium is a constitutional monarchy where the king, who is the head of state, only has some formal powers. The bicameral federal Parliament consists of the lower chamber or the Chamber of Representatives, gathering 150 MPs elected every four years in 11 constituencies, and of the upper chamber, or Senate, made up of 50 directly-elected members, 25 from Flanders and 25 from Wallonia, of 21 senators appointed by the three community assemblies and of ten appointed senators. The bicameral system is asymmetric, since the Chamber of Representatives holds all legislative powers and controls the government whilst the Senate is only associated with questions regarding the budget, international treaties, and constitutional acts. The Belgian executive is the federal government, which is appointed by the king with the support of a majority in Parliament. The Belgian Constitution stipulates that the federal government has to be balanced linguistically, with a cabinet consisting of seven Dutch-speaking and seven French-speaking ministers in addition to the Prime Minister, who is said to be linguistically neutral. With only one exception since 1945, there have always been bilingual coalition governments in Belgium.

Below the federal level, there are three regions – Flanders, Wallonia, and Brussels-Capital – and three communities – Flemish, French, and German – which have their own directly-elected assembly and their own executive. At the local level, Belgium is divided into 11 provinces and 589 municipalities. A governor appointed by the king presides over each province, which represents a politically weak administrative unit, and is supported by an elected provincial council. Municipal governments, on the contrary, are important political entities with significant powers over local affairs.

5 Brief account of the political parties

From the outset, two opposing political camps emerged in Belgium: the clerical Catholics and the anti-clerical Liberals, although they avoided major clashes before certain stability was reached. From the 1840s, the two groups started fighting each other within the newly established parliamentary institutions. The former promoted the intervention of Catholic organizations in education, health care and social welfare, and the respect of Christian values in state action, whilst the latter strongly opposed it by supporting, instead, a religiously neutral state. The two parties dominated Belgian politics up to the end of the nineteenth century and alternated in power. At the turn of the twentieth century, the socio-economic cleavage between the working class and the *patronat* became salient. Politically, it led to the division of the anti-clerical camp, between the more right-wing Liberals and the left-wing Socialists of the POB (Belgian workers' party). This evolution, along with the shift to proportional representation in 1899, laid the basis for the three-party system that characterized Belgian politics up to the 1960s.

By this time, the linguistic cleavage acquired a new status as the only major dispute that had not yet been solved. Whilst it is often referred to as a 'linguistic' cleavage, the divisions between the Flemish and the Francophones also cover economic and political differences. Whilst the French-speaking part of the country was an early industrial boom area, one that was affluent and politically dominant in the nineteenth century and at the beginning of the twentieth century, the last 60 years have marked the rapid economic development of Flanders and the sharp decline of the coal and steel sectors in Wallonia. This has led to a corresponding shift of economic power, together with claims for more political power for Flanders. This 'ethnicization' process gradually transformed the Belgian political and institutional landscape. As such, the three traditional parties split into Flemish and French-speaking units.

The party system is highly fragmented along both political and linguistic lines. Whilst Flemish parties run for election exclusively in Dutch-speaking constituencies and in bilingual Brussels, Francophone parties compete only in the Walloon districts and in Brussels, including its suburbs, for EP elections.

On the eve of the 2009 Euro-elections in Flanders, there were eight parties represented at the federal or regional level: the Flemish Christian Democratic Party (CD&V), Flemish Liberal and Democratic Party, the Socialist Party Different, the extreme-right Flemish Interest (VB), Green!, the neo-liberal populist Dedecker List, the Conservative Nationalist New Flemish Alliance (NV-A), and the left-wing libertarian nationalist Social Liberal Party. On the French-speaking side there were five parties which enjoyed parliamentary representation: the Liberal Reformist Movement, the Socialist Party, the Humanist Democratic Centre, Ecolo, and the extreme right-wing National Front (FN). Lastly, there were six parties represented within the German-speaking community assembly: the Christian Social Party, the Party for Freedom and Progress-Reformist Movement, the Social Democratic Party, Ecolo, the Party of the German-speaking Belgians, and the neo-liberal Vivant.

What made the political landscape even more complex was that many of these parties were involved with the executive at different levels. The Flemish Christian Democratic Party and the Humanist Democratic Centre, the Flemish Liberal and Democratic Party, and the French-speaking Socialist Party were in power at all levels. The Flemish Socialists were in power in Flanders and in Brussels. Finally, whereas the French-speaking Reformist Movement was present at the federal level, Ecolo was only part of the Brussels regional executive.

The Christian-Democratic parties have developed a centrist party platform, trying to combine market economics with state intervention. They are also attached to traditional Christian values, especially CD&V, and support the principle of subsidiarity. The Socialists belong to centre-left parties, which insist on the need for strong public services, state intervention to regulate the market economy, and a redistributive welfare state system. The Liberals are a centre-right party defending the market economy. The Greens are to the centre-left on economic issues; however, they are clearly post-materialist and libertarian when it comes to cultural values, and they campaign for the implementation of the core principles of sustainable development in all policy domains. The other smaller parties often intervene in the political debate insisting on single issues, such as Flemish autonomy for the regionalists of the N-VA, immigration for the radical right VB and FN, and lower taxation for the populist Libertarian, Direct, Democratic Party (LDD).

Table 7.2 List of political parties in Belgium

Original name	Abbreviation	English translation
Vlaamse christendemocratische partij	CD&V	Flemish Christian Democratic Party
Centre Démocrate Humaniste	CDH	Humanist Democratic Centre
Christlich Soziale Partei	CSP	Christian Social Party
Nieuw-Vlaamse Alliantie	N-VA	New Flemish Alliance
Open Vlaamse Liberalen en Democraten	Open VLD	Open Flemish Liberal and Democratic Party
Mouvement réformateur	MR	Reformist Movement
Partei für Freiheit und Fortschritt	PFF	Party for Freedom and Progress
Écologistes Confédérés pour l'Organisation de Luttes Originales	Ecolo	Confederated ecologists for the organisation of original struggles
Groen!		Green!
Socialistische Partij Anders	SP.A	Socialist Party Different
Parti socialiste	PS	Socialist Party
Vlaams Belang	VB	Flemish Interest
Lijst Dedecker	LDD	Dedecker List
Front National	FN	National Front

Source: Centre d'étude de la vie politique (Cevipol), ULB.

5.1 Party attitudes towards the European Union

There are no dividing lines amongst or within all mainstream parties on European integration. They all stress the importance of Europe, promote a further deepening of the integration process, and globally support EU policies and institutions, even if some parties, such as the Greens and the Socialists, address some criticisms to specific EU policies. For instance, the Greens call for more attention – at the supranational level – to environmental issues and the Socialists stress the need for a more social Europe. Overall, all Belgian parties are pro-European and have supported the various EU amending treaties which were seen as steps forward in the European integration process, even if this had to be done at the expense of future enlargement. Within the European Parliament, Belgian MEPs sit in pro-integration groups. More specifically, the Flemish Christian Democratic Party, the Humanist Democratic Centre, and the Christian Social Party joined the EPP; the Francophone Socialist Party and the Flemish Socialist Party Different entered the S&D; the Reformist Movement and the Flemish Liberal and Democratic Party joined the ALDE; and the New Flemish Alliance, Ecolo, and Greens sit in the Greens/EFA. Overall, there is high party cohesion over the EU amongst Belgian political parties, leading to the low visibility of EP elections. The EU or European issues have never been the reason for any appreciable split in the Belgian political arena.

There are two exceptions in the Belgian political arena: the extreme right-wing regionalist Flemish Interest and the newcomer, Dedecker List. The former is the only party that rejects the Lisbon Treaty and the idea of a federal Europe whilst defending cooperation between the peoples of Europe as well as the strict application of the subsidiarity principle. Nevertheless, Flemish Interest does not overtly advocate Belgium's withdrawal from the EU and it recognized the EU's positive role in fostering peace and welfare on the continent. It also favours the common market and acknowledges its benefits for Belgium. Flemish Interest incorporates Eurosceptic positions into its traditional anti-establishment and radical right-wing stances. As such, the party can be considered as Eurosceptic, but in the sense of a 'touchstone of dissent' (Taggart, 1998).

Dedecker List considers itself as a Euro-realist party that advocates a European confederation that should tackle concrete problems, cut red tape and bureaucracy, and increase its efficiency. It also criticizes the EU as a vector for immigration: more particularly, the party accused southern European states – such as Spain and Italy – of being too tolerant towards illegal immigration. However, it never questioned the European integration project or EU supranationalism so that the 'Euro-realism' of the Dedecker List could be considered as an expression of its populist style.

Finally, radical left parties, including the Workers' Party of Belgium (PVDA) and the Communists, display rather critical or negative stances towards the European Union (Pilet and Brack, 2009).

6 Public opinion and the European Union

There is a consistency between political parties and the electorate's views on the European Union. Indeed, the Belgian population has remained very Europhile over time and its positive opinion about EU membership has always been above the EU average, fluctuating from 57 per cent to 66 per cent between 1973 and 2008 (Eurobarometer 70, autumn 2008).

Belgian citizens generally consider that their country has largely benefitted from being an EU member.

Belgians shared the views of the main political parties on the European Constitution, as more than 80 per cent were strongly in favour of it (Eurobarometer 66 and 67, winter 2006 and spring 2007). Moreover, according to the 2010 Eurobarometer polls, 57 per cent tend to

Table 7.3 Belgian attitude to the European Union

	EB 65	EB 66	EB 70	EB 72	EB 73
A good thing	65	69	65	64	64
A bad thing	10	10	12	11	12
Neither good nor bad	25	21	22	24	23
Don't know	0	0	1	1	1

Source: Eurobarometer, http://ec.europa.eu/public_opinion/archives/eb_arch_en.htm.

Table 7.4 Perceived benefit of EU membership in Belgium

Taking everything into account, would you say that Belgium has benefited or not from being a member of the EU?

	EB 68	EB 70	EB 72	EB 73
Benefitted	75	68	65	66
Not benefitted	19	28	29	29
Don't know	6	4	6	5

Source: Eurobarometer, http://ec.europa.eu/public_opinion/archives/eb_arch_en.htm.

trust the EU (Eurobarometer 73, spring 2010) and 69 per cent are optimistic about the future of the EU (Eurobarometer 72, autumn 2009). Even in the context of the economic and financial crisis, Belgians have remained in favour of a stronger EU: 96 per cent supported a closer coordination between Member States in order to find a solution for the economic crisis and 93 per cent called for a stronger role of the EU in the financial markets regulation (Eurobarometer 74, autumn 2010). Finally, as regards enlargement, the views of the population were less positive than those of the political parties: 53 per cent were against further EU membership in 2007 (Eurobarometer 67).

7 National and EP electoral systems

Overall, most Belgian election rules apply to all regional, federal, and EU elections and only a few, mostly related to district boundaries and magnitude, are different (Pilet, 2007).

The first common election rule is compulsory voting, which stipulates that citizens who do not go to the polls may be fined. Therefore turnout is generally not a serious concern, and whilst legal sanctions against absentee voters are very rarely applied, the vast majority of voters turn out on election day.

The second common feature is proportional representation, with the application of the d'Hondt method for the allocation of seats amongst parties. Since 2003, a district-level 5 per cent threshold has been introduced. Within a semi-open list, candidates are elected, taking into account both their score in terms of preference votes and their position on party lists. About 65 per cent of voters generally decide to cast a preferential vote (Wauters *et al.*, 2004).

The last common feature is the introduction of a gender parity clause, which requires a perfect balance between 50 per cent of men and 50 per cent of women. Even the top two positions on the list have to be shared between one male and one female candidate. However, whereas for federal elections the country is divided into 11 constituencies, for the election of Belgium's 22 MEPs, the Belgian territory is divided into three colleges.

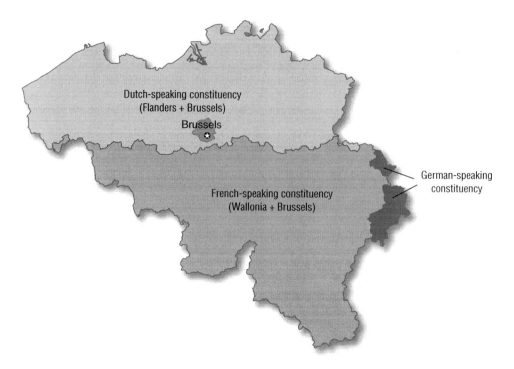

Figure 7.2 Map of EP electoral constituencies in Belgium

Since 1993, in addition to the two Dutch-speaking and one French-speaking electoral colleges, there is a German-speaking district corresponding to the German-speaking community. Whereas the Dutch-speaking college elects 13 representatives to the EP, the French-speaking college chooses 8 MEPs, and the German-speaking district selects only 1 MEP. In Wallonia and Flanders, voters can only choose amongst lists from one college. However, in the bilingual constituency of Brussels-Hal-Vilvoorde, voters have a choice between lists from both colleges.

For regional elections, Flanders is divided into five electoral constituencies and Wallonia into 13 electoral constituencies. The Brussels region is the only region where the two linguistic communities overlap. Therefore, there are Flemish and Francophone electoral colleges. Finally, the German-speaking community of about 60,000 inhabitants represents an electoral district for its own Parliament, with 25 elected members.

8 A glance at the EP and national elections

The history of European parliamentary elections in Belgium can be divided into two periods. The first one, going from 1979 to 1994 when the EP contest was not held at the same time with other elections, and the second one since 1999, when EP elections took place jointly with regional, and sometimes federal, elections. From 1999 it became compulsory to hold regional and EP elections concurrently. This strongly reinforced the lack of public debate on EU issues and the greater attention to regional matters during the campaign. When national and EP elections were held separately, EP elections were an occasion for political parties not only to compete for votes, but also to talk about their vision of what the European Union should do, and of how the EU democratic system should work. Nevertheless, campaigns for EP elections in Belgium were rather dull and dominated by domestic concerns (Claeys et al., 1985, 1986). There was no public debate on Europe, on supra-nationality, or the participation of Belgium in the construction of Europe, although some parties made some efforts to talk about Europe in the campaigns. The media did not pay much more attention to Euro-elections and most voters were primarily focussed on the other electoral contest, be it federal or regional. As recently shown by Peter Van Aelst and Jonas Lefevere (2012), only a few Belgian voters in EP elections were motivated by EU-related issues when casting their ballot. For that minority, such a contest mattered only either when the party had a prominent candidate to lead its list, like former Prime ministers Guy Verhofstadt and Jean-Luc Dehaene in 2009, or were holding positions on Europe that diverged from the mainstream consensus, like the Greens for a stronger Europe, or Flemish Interest for a much more limited Union.

By looking at EP electoral results in Belgium from a historical perspective, two elements stand out. First, turnout has been rather constant over the years, as shown in Table 7.5.

Although compulsory voting explains – for most part – the high levels of electoral participation, what is remarkable is that turnout for EP elections in Belgium is more stable than for federal elections. In 1979 there was a 5 per cent gap between elections for the two levels, with a lower turnout for EP elections. Gradually, this gap faded away, and by the late 2000s participation reached the same level for elections at both levels, somewhere around 90 per cent.

The second element concerns the evolution of electoral races. Within the Dutch-speaking community, this development has been rather similar in national and EP elections. The party system has become much more competitive over the years.

In 1979, the Christian Democrats, CVP-CD&V, were clearly the dominant force, but they steadily lost support. Subsequently, the Liberals (VLD) became the leading party in 1999, whilst the Socialist Party Different (Spa) and the extreme right, *Vlaams Belang*, became serious contenders from the late 1990s. The three traditional parties, CVP-CD&V, VLD-PVV and Spa that were dominant in 1979 are now facing three significant competitors: the regionalist (VU, N/VA), the Greens (Agalev-*Groen*) and the extreme right (*Vlaams Blok/Belang*). If we compare

Table 7.5 Turnout at national and EP elections in Belgium: 1978–2010

National elections	2010	2007	2003	1999	1995	1991	1987	1985	1981	1978
	89.3	91.3	91.9	91.0	91.2	92.7	93.4	93.6	94.5	94.9
EP elections	2009	2004	1999	1994	1989	1984	1979			
	90.4	90.8	91.1	90.7	90.7	92.1	91.4			

Source: Belgium's Ministry of Home Affairs, www.ibzdgip.fgov.be/result/fr/search.php.

Table 7.6 National election results of Flemish parties in Belgium: 1978–2010

	1978	1981	1985	1987	1991	1995	1999	2003	2007	2010
CD&V	36.3	25.8	29.2	27.5	24.6	24.9	20.0	18.7	24.6	16.4
SPA	24.8	24.5	28.3	30.5	25.5	24.4	19.7	27.9	21.1	22.9
Open VLD	15.0	20.9	21.0	21.0	20.1	23.4	24.4	26.8	24.4	17.9
Groen	0.5	4.5	6.3	7.1	9.9	8.4	14.4	5.5	9.1	9.2
VU/NVA	11.7	14.0	9.1	9.2	7.4	4.7	5.6	3.1	—	17.4
VB	1.4	1.1	1.5	2.0	7.6	10.1	11.3	13.6	14.0	8.3
Others	10.3	9.2	4.6	2.7	4.9	4.1	4.6	4.4	6.8	7.9

Source: Belgium's Ministry of Home Affairs, www.ibzdgip.fgov.be/result/fr/search.php.

Table 7.7 EP election results of Flemish parties in Belgium: 1979–2009

	1979	1984	1989	1994	1999	2004	2009
CD&V	40.1	32.5	34.1	27.4	21.7	28.2	23.3
SPA	20.9	28.1	20.0	17.6	14.2	17.8	13.2
Open VLD	15.3	14.2	17.1	18.4	21.9	21.9	20.6
Groen	2.3	7.1	12.2	10.7	12.0	8.0	7.9
VU/NVA	9.7	13.9	8.7	7.1	12.2	—	9.9
VB	0.0	2.1	6.6	12.6	15.1	23.2	15.9
Others	11.7	2.1	1.3	6.2	2.9	0.9	9.2

Source: Belgium's Ministry of Home Affairs, www.ibzdgip.fgov.be/result/fr/search.php.

federal and EP elections in Flanders, the first observation is that general trends are basically the same, with the Christian Democrats steadily reducing their vote share. The major differences are the higher number of competing lists and the relatively better performance of the Greens in EP elections.

Amongst French-speaking parties, the general trend for EP elections shows the reduction of the gap between the historically largest party, in this case the Socialists (PS), and its competitors. In particular, the Liberals (MR-PRL) were able to compete for leadership from the mid-1990s and they even became the largest party in 1999.

Table 7.8 National election results of Francophone parties in Belgium: 1978–2010

Political party	1978	1981	1985	1987	1991	1995	1999	2003	2007	2010
CDH	10.1	6.5	8.0	8.0	7.7	7.7	5.9	5.5	6.1	5.5
PS	12.5	12.2	13.8	15.6	13.5	11.9	10.2	13.0	10.9	13.7
MR	4.6	8.0	10.2	9.4	8.1	10.3	10.1	11.4	12.5	9.3
Ecolo	0.4	2.2	2.5	2.6	5.1	4.0	7.4	3.1	5.1	4.8
FDF	4.7	4.2	1.2	1.2	1.5	—	—	—	—	—
FN	—	—	—	—	1.1	2.3	1.5	2.0	2.0	0.2

Source: Belgium's Ministry of Home Affairs, www.ibzdgip.fgov.be/result/fr/search.php.

Note: Since 1992, the regionalists (FDF) formed a federation with the Liberals and, since 2002, the regionalists and the French-speaking Liberals and the German-speaking Liberals and the MCC formed a single political party: the MR (*Mouvement réformateur*).

Table 7.9 EP election results of Francophone parties in Belgium: 1979–2009

Political party	1979	1984	1989	1994	1999	2004	2009
CDH	8.2	7.6	8.1	7.0	5.0	5.7	5.0
PS	10.6	13.3	14.5	11.4	9.6	13.5	10.9
MR	6.9	9.5	7.2	9.1	10.0	10.4	9.7
Ecolo	2.0	3.9	6.3	4.9	8.4	3.7	8.6
FDF	7.6	2.5	1.5	—	—	—	—
FN	0.0	0.0	0.0	3.0	1.5	2.8	1.3

Source: Belgium's Ministry of Home Affairs, www.ibzdgip.fgov.be/result/fr/search.php.

The other contest was between the Christian Democrats and the Greens for third place. The Christian Democrats (CDH-PSC) were on a historical downward trend. Until the early 1990s, they were competing with the Liberals for second place, whilst later they fought with the Greens (Ecolo) for third place. As for the other players, the Regionalists disappeared in the late 1980s and the extreme right-wing *Front National* never consolidated its results and was always much below the performance of the Extreme Right in Flanders. A comparison between electoral performance in European and federal elections highlighted one difference: the relatively better performance of the Greens.

Finally, in order to complete this brief overview of the electoral history of Belgium since 1979, it is necessary to mention that Eurosceptic parties have never been able to secure a significant share of the vote. Neither the Flemish extreme right-wing *Vlaams Belang* nor the populist radical right-wing party *Lijst Dedecker*, which have emerged since the 1990s, have gained support on the basis of their anti-European stance (Deschouwer and Van Assche, 2008).

9 The 2009 European election

9.1 Party lists and manifestos

At the 2009 EP Election only six political parties, and most specifically NV-A, LDD, PS, Green!, Ecolo, and MR, drafted specific manifestos. By contrast, the CDH, *Vlaams Belang*, FN and CD&V developed only a section on Europe in a broader manifesto, mainly dedicated to the regional elections, whilst the Flemish Liberals (Open VLD) and Socialists (Spa) simply referred to the common manifesto of their respective political group in the European Parliament.

Moreover, traces of Euroscepticism are not to be found in any manifestos, except from the populist LDD and the radical right *Vlaams Belang*. Yet, some negative references to the European Union were present in the other parties' manifestos, such as the denunciation of the democratic deficit, the poor implementation of the subsidiarity principle, as well as the critique of EU over-regulation and bureaucracy.

If we look more into the details of the EP manifestos presented to voters on the occasion of the 2009 EP elections in Belgium, we can observe that the main differences lie in what facets of Europe parties, or more precisely party families, put forward. Christian Democrats (CD&V and CDH) insisted on the need for a more integrated EU that would eventually move towards a federal Europe. Their core argument was that more integration would help solve major political problems more efficiently. What policies in particular should be reformed was less clear though. On the contrary, the Socialists (PS-Spa) and the Liberals (VLD-MR) put more emphasis on policies rather than on institutional design. Socialists called for a more social Europe and emphasized the risk of extreme liberalization. On the contrary, the Liberals pointed out the merits of the free market and called for moving further in that direction in order to boost economic prosperity. The Greens promoted a common environmental policy as they deemed the EU to be the most appropriate level to tackle these issues. They also urged the European Union to play a more active role in international negotiations on climate change. Finally, the Greens highlighted the need for a more democratic and transparent Europe, which would favour citizens' participation, directly or through the European Parliament.

The other party families devoted much less attention to developing specific and detailed positions on the EU. The extreme right tried to associate EU politics with its traditional core concerns: immigration and anti-establishment politics. The *Vlaams Belang* in particular presented the EU as a threat in opening borders and in facilitating immigration. The party also portrayed the EU as an elitist body that was highly bureaucratic and out of touch with citizens. For *Lijst Dedecker*, EP elections represented another opportunity to diffuse its populist appeal. The party's manifesto concentrated its attacks against the elitist and bureaucratic character of the EU, as well as its tendency to over-regulate. Lastly, the rather pro-European Flemish nationalists of N-VA wanted, however, the European Union to be more in touch with the regions rather than with Member States only.

9.2 Electoral campaign

In 2009, due to the simultaneity of the EP and regional elections, European issues were largely overshadowed by the regional agenda. (Crespy, 2011; Van Aelst and Lefevere, 2012). There was no extensive media coverage on the EP elections or EU policies, as regional issues made the headlines. Nevertheless, some European themes received some attention from the quality press, such as the global economic and financial crisis and how Europe should tackle it. The importance of the EU in citizens' lives through specific policies such as energy and consumer protection was also raised. Some articles dealt more particularly with the concrete functioning of the EU and the EP, but the outgoing candidates failed to explain in the media the activities carried out during the past legislature. As noted by Amandine Crespy (2011, 25), 'it seems that the Belgian quality press tried to counter the lack of interest for Europe by means of an editorial strategy aimed at informing the public about Europe'. Media coverage also focussed on the expected low turnout in Europe as well as on the rise of Eurosceptic and radical right parties, especially in the Netherlands and the United Kingdom (Dandoy and Pauwels, 2009).

Candidates for the EP were generally less present in the media than their regional counterparts. They tended to be either well-known personalities or party leaders, such as former Prime Minister Guy Verhofstadt and the outgoing MEP and former Prime Minister Jean-Luc Dehaene, or on the other hand low-profile candidates hardly known by voters.

As far as the French-speaking media arena was concerned, the EP elections went by almost unnoticed; all the attention was focussed on good governance, on which party would be the largest one in Wallonia and Brussels and finally, on personal attacks between Liberals and Socialists.

EP elections remained largely overlooked and have not succeeded in creating any political debate or in attracting much attention from the media. Europe was not politicized in the Belgian political arena during the campaign. This can be explained on the one hand by the Europhilia of the Belgian population, and on the other by the simultaneity of EP and regional elections, where the centre of attention was the composition of the new regional executives and their impact on the relationship between Flemings and Francophones (Brack and Pilet, 2010).

Given that voting is compulsory in Belgium, the EP office did not dedicate much time and energy to this campaign. The only exception was the 'choice box action', which was undertaken in all 27 Member States. This initiative allowed citizens to express their views on European integration and ask questions about what the EU should do in the future and those recorded messages were shown on large television screens in Brussels.

9.3 Electoral results

During the 2009 EP elections, 22 MEPs were elected in Belgium. Moreover, given that the Lisbon Treaty had not altered the number of Belgian representatives in the EP, which previously had been reduced by 2 seats under the Nice provisions, no change occurred with the Belgian delegation after the ratification of the Treaty.

Table 7.10 Distribution of Belgian MEPs in the European Parliament: seventh legislature

Political group	Number of Belgian MEPs
EPP	5
S&D	5
ALDE	5
Greens/EFA	4
ECR	1
Non-attached	2

Source: European Parliament, www.europarl.europa.eu/aboutparliament/en/00082fcd21/Results-by-country-(2009).html?tab=01#result_group.

In the 2009 European Parliament, only a few Belgian MEPs were newcomers. Indeed, 13 of them, almost 60 per cent, were incumbent at the time of the elections and were thus re-elected. This was especially the case for the Flemish-speaking MEPs, as nine of them, equivalent to 69.2 per cent, were incumbent. This was further reinforced by the fact that even those that were not incumbent had, nevertheless, previous experience as MEPs. Only seven representatives, corresponding to 31 per cent, did not have any previous involvement within the EP. It seems that having been an MEP helped with either their reselection or their re-election in Belgium, despite the fact that MEPs lacked the ability to highlight their activities and achievements during the campaign.

Moreover, the elected candidates had gained, in any case, political experience at the national level, be it as MP, MRP, mayor, or even regional or federal Ministers. The only exception was Lamberts, who had never occupied any elected position before his entry into the EP although he had been in politics for some time. In terms of age, Belgian MEPs had a mean age of 51.8 years. That seems to confirm the notion that they either tended to have some political experience before entering the EP or were incumbents at the time of the election.

Finally, although electoral lists should be perfectly gender-balanced, the 2009–2014 Belgian delegation was composed of eight women, corresponding to 36.4 per cent of Belgian MEPs. This figure represents an improvement in comparison with the previous legislature, in which only 29 per cent of Belgian MEPs were female. On the other hand, we can note that whilst the French-speaking delegation was perfectly gender-balanced, the Flemish delegation was slightly less than 70 per cent male. This can result from the higher fragmentation of the party system in Flanders, with more small parties competing and gaining fewer seats, which usually affects gender balance in a negative manner (Tremblay, 2008).

Due to compulsory voting, Belgium is, along with Luxembourg, the Member State showing the highest participation rate at the 2009 EP elections, with 90.4 per cent of voters actually going to the polling station. Logically, for the other elections organized on the same day, the figures were approximately the same, albeit slightly higher in Flanders, which had a 93 per cent turnout.

Yet, about 10 per cent of the electorate decided not to vote, even though it is a legal obligation. On the morning of 7 June 2009, the Belgian Federal Minister of Justice, Stefaan De Clerck, publicly admitted on the radio that there was almost no risk of being sanctioned in case of non-voting and that solutions to this situation were currently under study. In other words, compulsory voting in Belgium is more a moral duty than a legal obligation.

A last element to point out is the significant proportion of voters casting a blank or an invalid vote, ranging from 5.5 per cent in Flanders to 11.4 per cent in the German-speaking community elections. If we add these figures to the actual turnout, we end up with 84.7 per cent of the electorate casting a valid vote for EP elections, not very much for a system of compulsory voting.

Table 7.11 List of Belgian MEPs: seventh legislature

Name	Surname	National party	Political group	Professional background	Age	Gender	Committee	Committee Chairs first half of the EP term
Belet	Ivo	CD&V	EPP	Journalist	50	Male	Industry, research and energy	Vice-Chair Delegation for relations with the countries of Southeast Asia and the Association of Southeast Asian Nations
Dehaene	Jean-Luc	CD&V	EPP	Politician	69	Male	Budgets	Vice-Chair committee on budgets
Thyssen	Marianne	CD&V	EPP	Politician	53	Female	Economic and monetary affairs	None
Brepoels	Frieda	NV-A	Greens/EFA	Politician	54	Female	Foreign affairs	None
El Khadraoui	Saïd	SP.a	S&D	Politician	34	Male	Transport and tourism	Vice-Chair Delegation for relations with Mashreq countries
van Brempt	Kathleen	SP.A	S&D	Politician	40	Female	Industry, research and energy	None
Eppink	Derk Jan	LDD	ECR	Journalist and former European civil servant	51	Male	Economic and monetary affairs	None
Sterckx	Dirk	Open VLD	ALDE	Journalist	63	Male	Transport and tourism	None
Verhofstadt	Guy	Open VLD	ALDE	Politician	56	Male	Constitutional affairs and Conference of the Presidents	None
Neyts–Uyttebroeck	Annemie	Open VLD	ALDE	Politician	63	Female	Foreign affairs and security and defence	None
Staes	Bart	Groen	Greens/EFA	Politician	51	Male	Budgets	Vice-chairman of the Committee on Budgetary Control Vice-chairman of the Delegation to the EU-Kazakhstan, EU-Kyrgyzstan and EU-Uzbekistan Parliamentary Cooperation Committees, and for relations with Tajikistan, Turkmenistan and Mongolia

Vanhecke	Franck	VB	Non-attached	Politician	50	Male	Development and human rights	None
Claeys	Philip	VB	Non-attached	Politician	44	Male	Civil liberties, justice and home affairs	None
Grosch	Mathieu	CSP	EPP	Politician	59	Male	Transport and tourism	None
Daerden	Frédéric	PS	S&D	Politician	39	Male	Employment and social affairs	None
De Keyser	Véronique	PS	S&D	Professor	64	Female	Development and human rights	None
Tarabella	Marc	PS	S&D	Politician	46	Male	Agriculture and rural development and women's rights and gender equality	None
Delvaux	Anne	CDh	EPP	Journalist	39	Female	Environment, public health and food safety	None
Durant	Isabelle	Ecolo	Greens/EFA	Politician	55	Female	Budgets and bureau of the EP	Vice-president of the EP
Lamberts	Philippe	Ecolo	Greens/EFA	Engineer and firm owner	46	Male	Industry, research and energy	None
Michel	Louis	MR	ALDE	Politician and former commissioner	62	Male	Civil liberties, justice and home affairs and conference of delegation chairs	Co-president of the Delegation to the ACP-EU Joint Parliamentary Assembly
Ries	Frédérique	MR	ALDE	Journalist	50	Female	ENVI and FEMM	None

Source: Belgium's Ministry of Home Affairs, http://elections2009.belgium.be/.

In the Dutch-speaking electoral college, the electoral results revealed two winners: the Flemish Christian Democratic Party and the Flemish Liberal and Democratic Party, with 3 seats each and more than 20 per cent of the vote.

These were the only two Flemish parties in power at both the federal and regional levels. At the 2009 Euro-elections, their lists were led by two former Prime Ministers, Jean-Luc Dehaene for the Christian Democrat and Flemish Party and Guy Verhofstadt for the Flemish Liberal and Democratic Party. The latter's performance was impressive, since he helped the Liberals to secure more than 20 per cent of the vote for EP elections, whilst for regional elections held the same day, the party only received 15 per cent of the vote. All other Flemish parties, except the New Flemish Alliance, recorded comparable results for both the EP and Flemish regional elections.

Flemish Interest and Socialist Party Different scored 15.9 per cent and 13.2 per cent, respectively, and secured 2 seats each. This result represented a severe loss for the former, down by 7.3 percentage points in comparison with 2004, when it achieved its best performance ever. Finally, three parties, the New Flemish Alliance, Dedecker List, and Green!, fell slightly below 10 per cent of the vote and each of them sent only one MEP to Strasbourg/Brussels. The most striking performance was that of the New Flemish Alliance, which ran alone for the first time in 2009.

Table 7.12 EP election results in the Dutch-speaking college in Belgium: 2009

Political party	2009 (votes)	2009 (seats)
Flemish Christian Democratic Party	23.3[a]	3 (−1)
Flemish Liberal and Democratic Party	20.6 (−1.35)	3 (0)
Socialist Party Different	13.2[b]	2 (−1)
Flemish Interest	15.9 (−7.28)	2 (−1)
New Flemish Alliance	9.9[a]	1 (+1)
Green!	7.9 (−0.08)	1 (0)
Dedecker List	7.3 (+7.28)	1 (+1)
Others	2.0	0 (0)
Total	100.0	13 (−1)

Source: Belgium's Ministry of Home Affairs, http://elections2009.belgium.be/.

Notes:
a The Christian Democrat and Flemish Party and the New Flemish Alliance (regionalists) formed a joint list in 2004. For the EP 2004 elections, the list Christian Democrat and Flemish Party–New Flemish Alliance received 28.15 of the votes and gained 4 seats.
b The Socialist Party Different formed a joint list with Spirit in 2004. For the EP 2004 elections, the list Socialist Party Different–Spirit received 17.83 of the votes and gained 3 seats.

Table 7.13 EP election results in the French-speaking college in Belgium: 2009

Political party	2009 (votes)	2009 (seats)
Socialist Party	29.1 (−6.99)	3 (−1)
Reformist Movement	26.1 (−1.53)	2 (−1)
Ecolo	22.9 (+13.03)	2 (+1)
Humanist Democratic Centre	13.3 (−1.80)	1 (0)
National Front	3.6 (−3.88)	0 (0)
Others	5.1	0 (0)
Total	100.0	8 (−1)

Source: Belgium's Ministry of Home Affairs, http://elections2009.belgium.be/.

Table 7.14 EP election results in the German-speaking college in Belgium: 2009

Political party	2009 (votes)	2009 (seats)
Christian Social Party	32.3 (−10.23)	1 (0)
Social Party	14.6 (−0.31)	0 (0)
Party for Freedom and Progress–Reformist Movement	20.4 (−2.42)	0 (0)
Ecolo	15.6 (+5.09)	0 (0)
Party of German-speaking Belgians (ProDG)	10.1 (+0.77)	0 (0)
Vivant	6.3 (+6.25)	0 (0)
Europa de Weirte	0.9 (+0.85)	0 (0)
Total	100.0	1 (0)

Source: Belgium's Ministry of Home Affairs, http://elections2009.belgium.be/.

Within the French-speaking electoral college, the party system is less fragmented.

Four parties shared the eight-seat mandate, thus losing seven percentage points compared to 2004. The Socialist Party remained the largest party, receiving 29.1 per cent of the vote and gaining 3 seats. Then came two parties: the Reformist Movement and Ecolo, which both achieved more than 20 per cent of the vote and secured 2 seats each. The performance of the Francophone Greens was particularly remarkable as they more than doubled their score compared to 2004.

The Humanist Democratic Centre almost maintained its 2004 performance with less than 15 per cent of the vote and one representative.

Finally, the last Belgian MEP was elected within the German-speaking electoral college.

Traditionally, the seat belongs to the largest party, the Christian Democrats (Christian Social Party), which, although having lost 10.2 percentage points compared to its performance in 2004, remained by far the dominant party in 2009 and sent incumbent Mathieu Grosch to Strasbourg/Brussels for the fourth time.

9.4 Campaign finance

The Law of 4 July 1989 established the financial aspects of the EP campaign by setting a maximum of €1,000,000 that parties could spend for posters, leaflets, advertisements in newspapers and publicity on the internet, except for television adverts, which were not admitted. Indeed, the bill specified where the money could come from, what types of expenses were allowed, and how candidates and parties should report their spending to state authorities.

Each party that has gained at least one seat in the Belgian federal Parliament receives €125,000 plus €1.25 per vote at the previous federal elections. Regional Parliaments have also recently introduced systems of public funding, but the amounts are not as important as for the federal level. Other sources of funding are limited. Donations from individual citizens are limited to a maximum of €500 per year. Donations from private companies are prohibited.

In order to verify their compliance with campaign finance law, political parties have to hand out a detailed report 45 days after the elections. One peculiarity of EU elections in Belgium is that election campaigns are mostly animated by parties and by candidates. Governments do not take any initiative in inviting Belgian citizens to be involved in EU elections, mainly due to compulsory voting.

10 Theoretical interpretation of Euro-elections

10.1 Second-Order Election theory

Second-Order Election theory seems to fit relatively well with the Belgian case. However, with regard to turnout, this has not been significantly lower in EP elections, largely due to compulsory voting and to the concurrence of European and regional elections since 1999.

In fact, people's participation has not been systematically lower at EP elections than at federal elections. Before 1995, the abstention rate was around 2 per cent higher at Euro-elections, but since then the gap has been reduced to almost nothing. In any case, both before and after 1995 the differences were marginal, with the largest abstention rate of 3.5 per cent registered in 1978 and 1979.

In addition, the hypothesis which relates to the electoral losses of governing parties that are punished by dissatisfied voters is difficult to evaluate, since most parties are in power either at federal or regional level. The incongruence of ruling coalitions led to a situation where not less than seven parties were in power in 2009 at both the regional and federal level (Deschouwer, 2009). However, if we leave aside the parties that are only members of regional governments, we can analyse the performance of parties in federal government between 1979 and 2009 in order to evaluate whether they have been systematically sanctioned by voters at EU elections. Parties in power at the federal level did worse in EU elections than in the previous legislative elections, with the only exception being the first direct election of the European Parliament in 1979. The situation in 1999 was also peculiar, since both federal and European elections were held on the same day. But for the rest, federal governing parties were clearly losing votes in subsequent EU elections, in the range of 3.5 to 6.5 percentage points.

In line with the Second-Order Election paradigm, Belgian voters used their vote in EU elections not so much to renew the European Parliament, but to express discontent against their governing parties. Yet, such a conclusion should be taken with caution in the Belgian case for elections from 1999 onwards. Since then, European elections have been organized concurrently with regional elections, including federal elections in 1999, and no strong differences between the results of both electoral contests could be observed. Moreover, it is difficult to understand whether the outcome of such elections could be interpreted as a sanction against the federal government or as an evaluation of the performance of the regional administrations. These questions are to be left open, but the systematic losses of federal governing parties in European elections remains clear.

The indicator of SOE, relating to the better performance of smaller parties, is also not easy to detect given that Belgium portrays a highly fragmented multiparty system and, to a certain extent, all parties are small – with the exception of the CD&V. By contrast, another distinction could be made between, on the one hand, traditional parties, such as the Christian Democrats, the Liberals, and the Socialists, that have been in existence since the nineteenth century, and, on the other hand, new parties which incorporate the Regionalists, the Greens, and the radical right.

Against this background, the hypothesis of Second-Order Election theory predicts that new parties would perform better in EP elections than in the previous federal elections. Since 1989, Belgian citizens have tended to switch from traditional parties, such as the Christian Democrats, Socialists, and Liberals to new parties which have gained between 3.0 and 6.6 percentage points.

10.2 Europe Salience theory

In line with the Europe Salience model, in most cases in Belgium, EU-awkward parties, especially the *Lijst Dedecker,* tend to score better in EP contests than at federal elections.

The second hypothesis focussed on the good performance of extreme parties, both on the far right – the *Vlaams Blok/Belang* and the *Front National* – as well as those on the radical left. However, studying the performances of the latter is very difficult due to its high fragmentation and the marginal impact of its parties.

Extreme parties fared better in most EP elections than in the previous federal elections. The only drastic exception occurred in the 2009 elections, with a significant loss compared to the 2007 federal elections, mostly due to the above-mentioned recent decline of *Vlaams Belang*.

And finally, the third hypothesis that suggests that Green parties perform better at EU elections was strongly confirmed in the Belgian case.

To sum up, it appears that for the most part the three hypotheses of the Europe Salience approach were verified in the Belgian case. That meant that citizens did care about Europe when they voted in EP elections. Yet there was only indirect evidence of the impact of Europe on voting behaviour. More direct elements taken from voter surveys would be needed to confirm those results.

References

Primary sources

Belgium's Ministry of Home Affairs website: www.ibzdgip.fgov.be/result/fr/search.php (accessed on 12 February 2012);
http://elections2009.belgium.be/. (accessed on 21 December 2014).
Eurobarometer 66, Winter 2006, Luxembourg, European Commission.
Eurobarometer 67, Spring 2007, Luxembourg, European Commission.
Eurobarometer 70, Autumn 2008, Luxembourg, European Commission.
Eurobarometer 72, Autumn 2009, Luxembourg, European Commission.
Eurobarometer 73, Spring 2010, Luxembourg, European Commission.
Eurobarometer 74, Autumn 2010, Luxembourg, European Commission.
European Parliament website: www.europarl.europa.eu/parliament/archive/elections2009/en/index_en.html (accessed on 7 December 2013).
Eurostat (2013, 2014) http://epp.eurostat.ec.europa.eu (accessed on 5 June 2015).

Party manifestos

Centre Humaniste Democratique (CDH) (2009) EP Election Programme: www.lecdh.be/nous-et-vous/elections#tab-europe/listbyterm/15794 (accessed on 12 October 2011).
Christen Democraat en Vlaams (Flemish Christian Democratic Party – CD&V) (2009) EP Election Programme: www.cdenv.be/inhoud/verkiezingsprogramma/2009 (accessed on 12 October 2011).
Ecolo (2009), EP Election Programme: http://web4.ecolo.be/IMG/pdf/Livre_VI_-_Chapitre_1_-_Europe.pdf) (accessed on 12 October 2011).
Front National (*National Front* FN) (2009) EP Election Programme: www.fn.be/europe.html (accessed on 12 October 2011).
Groen! (2009) EP Election Programme: www.groen.be/uploads/programma/09/Europees_Programma.pdf (accessed on 12 October 2011).
List Dedecker (LDD), EP Election Programme: www3.lijstdedecker.com/docs/LDD_EUROPEES_PROGRAMMA.pdf (accessed on 12 October 2011).
Movement Reformiste (Reformist Movement MR)(2009) EP Election Programme: www.mr.be/media/pdf/programmes2009/ProgramCompletMR_EUR.pdf (accessed on 12 October 2011).
New Flemish Alliance (N-VA), EP Election Programme: www.n-va.be/verkiezingen/programma/europees programma.asp (accessed on 12 October 2011).
Partei der deutschsprechenden Belgier (Party of the German-speaking Belgians (PDB) (EFA Observer Status), EP Election Programme: http://prodg.be/ziele/wahlprogramme/europawahlprogram/ (accessed on 12 October 2011).

Parti Socialiste (Socialist Party–PS) (2009) EP Election Programme: www.ps.be/Source/PageContent. aspx?MenID=16977&EntID=1 (accessed on 12 October 2011).

Socialist Partien.anders (Socialist Party Different–SP.a) (2009) EP Election Programme: http://elections2009. pes.org/en/your-manifesto/manifesto (accessed on 12 October 2011).

Vivant (2009) EP Election Programme, www.vivant.org/fr/programma.html (accessed on 12 October 2011).

Vlaams, B. (Flemish Interest–VB) (2009), EP Election Programme: www.vlaamsbelang.org/21 (accessed on 12 October 2011).

Vlaams Liberal en Democraat (Flemish Liberal and Democratic Party (Open VLD) (2009) EP Election Programme: www.eldr.eu/pdf/manifeste/eldr-manifeste-electoral-en.pdf?IdTis=XTC-DU6A-SITLR-DD-67G-AG4 (accessed on 12 October 2011).

Secondary sources

Brack, N. and Pilet, J.-B. (2010) 'One Country, Two Different Party Systems. The 2009 Regional Elections in Belgium', *Regional and Federal Studies*, 20(4–5), 549–59.

Claeys, E., Lob-Mayer, N. and van den Bergh, G. (1986), 'Belgium', in Lodge, J. (ed.) *Direct Elections to the European Parliament 1984*, Basingstoke, Macmillan, 51–72.

Claeys, P.-H., de Graeve-Lismont, E. and Loeb-Mayer, N. (1985) 'Belgium', in Reif K. H. (ed.), *Ten European Elections. Campaigns and Results of the 1979/81 First Direct Elections to the European Parliament*, Aldershot, Gower, 37–50.

Crespy, A. (2011) 'Europe and Euroscepticism: "Non-Issues" in Belgian Politics', in Harmsen, R. and Schild, J. (eds) *Debating Europe. The 2009 European Parliament Elections and Beyond*, Baden-Baden, Nomos, 17–32.

Dandoy, R. and Pauwels, T. (2009) 'Belgique', in Brack, N., Rittelmeyer, Y. S. and Stanculescu, C. 'Les élections européennes de 2009: entre national et européen. Une analyse des campagnes électorales dans 22 Etats membres', *Les Cahiers du Cevipol*, 3, 20–1.

Deschouwer, K. (2009) 'Coalition Formation and Congruence in a Multi-Level Setting, Belgium 1995–2008', *Regional and Federal Studies*, 19(1), 13–35.

Deschouwer, K. and Van Assche, M. (2008) 'Hard but Hardly Relevant. Party-Based Euroscepticism in Belgium', in Szczerbiak, A. and Taggart, P. *Opposing Europe. The Comparative Party Politics of Eurosceptics*, Oxford, Oxford University Press, 75–92.

Magnette, P. and Pilet, J.-B. (2008) 'La Belgique', in de Waele, J.-M. and Magnette, P. (eds) *Les démocraties européennes*, Paris, Armand Colin, 51–68.

Pilet, J.-B. (2007) *Changer pour gagner? Les réformes des lois électorales en Belgique*, Brussels, Editions de l'Université de Bruxelles.

Pilet, J.-B. and Brack, N. (2009) 'The European and Regional Elections of 7 June 2009 in Belgium', *EPERN European Parliament Election Briefings*, 33, 1–26.

Taggart, P. (1998) 'A Touchstone of Dissent: Euroscepticism in Contemporary Western European Party Systems', *European Journal of Political Research*, 33(3), 363–88.

Tremblay, M. (2008) *Women and Legislative Representation: Electoral Systems, Political Parties, and Sex Quotas*, New York, Palgrave-Macmillan.

Van Aelst, P. and Lefevere, J. (2012) 'Has Europe Anything to Do with the European Elections? A Study of Split-Ticket Voting in the Belgian Regional and European Elections of 2009', *European Union Politics*, 13(1), 3–25.

Vanmaercke, L. (1993) 'Vers une nouvelle démocratie', *Cahiers du CEPESS*, 5.

Wauters, B., Weekers, K. and Pilet, J.-B. (2004) 'Het gebruik van de voorkeurstem bij de regionale en Europese parlements-verkiezingen van 13 juni 2004', *Res Publica*, 46 (2–3), 377–411.

8
THE NETHERLANDS

Hans Vollaard, Gerrit Voerman, and Nelleke van de Walle

Figure 8.1 Map of the Netherlands

Table 8.1 The Netherlands profile

EU entry	1952 ECSC; 1958 EEC founding member
Schengen entry year	1985 original signatory
MEPs elected in 2009	25
MEPs under Lisbon Treaty	26 since 15 December 2011
	One additional seat allocated to Daniël van der Stoep, non-attached
Capital	Amsterdam
Total area★	41,540 km²
Population	16,829,289
	79.1% Dutch descent, 9.4% Western, 2.3% Turkish descent, 2.2% Moroccan descent, 2.1% Surinamese descent, 0.9% Netherlands Antilles' and Aruban descent, 4.1% Non-Western
Population density★★	498.4/km²
Median age of population	42.0
Political system	Constitutional Monarchy
Head of state	Queen Beatrix (April 1980–April 2013)
	King Willem Alexander (April 2013–)
Head of government	Jan Peter Balkenende, Christian Democratic Appeal (CDA), (July 2002–October 2010);
	Mark Rutte, The Free-Market Liberal (VVD) (October 2010–)
Political majority	Christian Democratic (CDA), Social Democratic (PvdA) and Orthodox-Protestant (CU) Coalition Government (2007–2010);
	People's Party for Freedom and Democracy (VVD) and the Christian Democratic (CDA) Minority Government (October 2010–April 2012);
	People's Party for Freedom and Democracy (VVD) and Social Democratic (PvdA) (also known as Cabinet Rutte II) Coalition Government (November 2012–)
Currency	Euro (€) since 1999
Prohead GDP in PPS	38,900 €

Source: Eurostat, 2013, 2014, http://epp.eurostat.ec.europa.eu/.

Notes:
★ Total area including inland waters.
★★ Population density: the ratio of the annual average population of a region to the land area of the region.

1 Geographical position

The Netherlands is located in north-western Europe around the Rhine–Meuse–Scheldt estuary and borders the North Sea, Germany, and Belgium. The country, which has a surface area of 41,526 square kilometres, is the most densely populated in Europe, with an average of about 490 people per square kilometre. The Dutch are famous for their struggle against the sea, since a large part of their territory is located below sea level. By means of a highly sophisticated system of dikes and polders, land area has been gained and preserved for agriculture, in particular livestock farming. Due to its location, the Netherlands represents a crucial transportation hub, with the port of Rotterdam and Schiphol Airport as important transit points for international trade.

2 Historical background

The First Dutch Republic, which was founded in 1588 and lasted until 1795, was a confederation of provinces, which emerged from an uprising against the taxation and religious policies of the Habsburg Empire. Decisions in the confederation were usually compromises reached after complicated negotiations, in which the province of Holland and its cities, and, in times of emergency, the princes of Orange-Nassau, dominated. During the so-called French period, from 1795 to 1813, the Netherlands evolved into a fairly centralized constitutional monarchy. Subsequently, out of fear of widespread revolution in Europe, the king granted a liberal revision of the constitution in 1848, including ministerial responsibility and direct parliamentary elections. Since the late nineteenth century, the dominating Liberal Protestants faced increasing competition from orthodox Calvinists, the Catholic minority, and – soon after – the Socialists. The Calvinists, Catholics and, to a lesser extent, the Socialists set up organizational networks, involving newspapers, parties, universities, schools, trade unions, hospitals, and employers federations, which became known as pillars. In everyday life, contacts between Liberals, Calvinists, Catholics, and Socialists remained limited. Reflecting the continuing political culture of negotiated bargaining, the leaders of the various subcultures concluded a major compromise in 1917, resulting in the equal public funding of state and private religious schools, the introduction of universal suffrage, and an electoral system of proportional representation.

3 Geopolitical profile

The book title *Peace, Profits, and Principles* aptly summarizes the key factors in Dutch foreign policy until World War II (Voorhoeve, 1979). In the late sixteenth century, soon after becoming an independent entity, the Dutch Republic was subject to military attacks on its home territory by the French and the Prussians, and on its colonies by the British. The Republic relied on counter-balancing strategies and a 'policy of non-involvement' towards continental powers to prevent military invasions (ibid., 25). A tacit agreement with the British Empire provided access to the colonies and to the sea for its large trading fleet. The policy of non-involvement also served Dutch commercial interests, because peace allowed for the smooth flow of goods and capital. Due to the importance of sea trade, Dutch foreign policy reflected a preference for worldwide free trade and a rather maritime, non-continental orientation. Its strategic location and economic interests explained Dutch support for international law and organizations, since these can prevent larger states from dominating smaller ones. This support has sometimes been linked with the Dutch self-conception of being a moral model for the entire world; as a small, non-threatening nation, it could show others how to behave rightly according to international rules.

After the protectionism of the 1930s and the disaster of World War II, Dutch foreign policy elites felt that international cooperation was both necessary and inevitable. Nevertheless, peace, profits, and principles still marked Dutch foreign policy. In the aftermath of WWII, the Netherlands abandoned its neutral stance by joining international military organizations such as the North Atlantic Treaty Organization (NATO). The country also entered the United Nations (UN) and became a founding member of the European Coal and Steel Community (ECSC) and the European Economic Community (EEC). Particularly from the 1970s until the 1990s, the Netherlands presented itself as a progressive, cosmopolitan model nation for the entire world, pursuing an active role in the UN in order to support the poor in the Third World and to promote human rights in non-democratic countries. The end of the Cold War and the emergence of Islamic terrorism in the West required a recalibration of the transatlantic orientation of Dutch security policy, but the government seemed to privilege its security and defence cooperation with the US under NATO rather than the EU. Due to intensifying discussions about Dutch national culture within a larger Europe and globalization since the 1990s, a new progressive and cosmopolitan orientation has been added, with a pragmatic and also Nationalist focus on the defence of national interests (Vollaard, 2010).

4 Overview of the political landscape

The Netherlands is a decentralized unitary state, in which the budgetary and legislative constraints of the national government considerably limit the discretion of the 12 provinces and 431 municipalities. The national political system is a constitutional monarchy with a bicameral parliamentary system. The 75 members of the First Chamber (*Eerste Kamer*) or Senate are elected every four years by the representatives of the 12 provincial Parliaments, who are elected by the citizens of the provinces at the same interval. The 150 members of the Second Chamber (*Tweede Kamer*), which is in fact the most powerful one, are elected directly by all citizens, in principle every four years or soon after a cabinet loses the confidence of this chamber.

As a result of pillarization as well as an electoral system based on proportional representation with a low threshold, the Dutch party system has become rather fragmented. Since the introduction of universal suffrage, no party has ever won an absolute majority of seats (Andeweg and Irwin, 2009). A relatively high number of parties have been represented in Parliament, fluctuating between seven and 14 since 1946. After the general elections in November 2006, following the fall of the cabinet earlier that year, ten parties held seats in the Second Chamber. Ideological distances on socio-economic as well as ethical issues between the existing parties diminished, particularly in the 1980s and 1990s. As a result, more parties became a potential coalition partner in government, strengthening their attractiveness to voters, thus enhancing electoral volatility. In addition, this ideological 'rapprochement' offered an opportunity for populist parties from both right and left to mobilize support against a fairly uniform political establishment, which once more fostered electoral volatility (Lucardie, 2008a).

The growing strong support for populist parties came at the expense of the large established parties, which made building coalition governments more difficult. At the beginning of 2007, the Social Democratic PvdA and the Christian Democratic CDA required the small orthodox Protestant *ChristenUnie* to form a majority coalition, led by the Christian Democrat Prime Minister Jan-Peter Balkenende (Lucardie, 2008b). Between 2007 and 2010, in addition to the Socialist Party and the Freedom Party, the opposition comprised the Liberal Party and the social-liberal D66, the Green Left, the Animal Rights Party, and the orthodox Protestant Reformed Political Party, the SGP. In February 2010, the Cabinet fell, because no agreement could be reached on the extension of a Dutch military mission in Afghanistan. After the elections of June 2010, a minority government of the free market-liberal VVD and Christian Democratic CDA concluded an agreement to obtain a majority in the Second Chamber with the Freedom Party (PVV), which obtained 24 seats after a campaign against the 'Islamization' of the Netherlands and in favour of the Dutch welfare state.

5 Brief account of the political parties

For a long time, between 1917 and 1967, the larger Christian parties, and particularly the Catholic one, played a pivotal role in the Dutch political system. They held a majority of seats in Parliament. Their religious principles and social-economic centre-right position largely determined the formation of government coalitions. This Christian hegemony declined in the 1960s and 1970s due to secularization, the erosion of the pillars, and individualism. The Social Democratic PvdA and the free market-liberals of the VVD attempted to divide the Christian Democratic electorate between each other. In response to their decline, Calvinists and Catholics decided to merge into one Christian Democratic party (CDA) by 1980. Meanwhile, new parties of post-materialist inclination entered Parliament, namely the social-liberal D66 and predecessors of the left-wing and environmentalist *GroenLinks* party. As recently as 1994, the Social Democrats, free market-liberals, and social-liberals created the first government without Christian Democrats since 1917. They pursued a liberal policy with respect to socio-cultural issues such as prostitution and same-sex marriage, and continued the liberalizing socio-economic policies of previous governments.

Growing popular concerns about the declining quality of public services and the increasing number of Islamic migrants contributed to the rise of populist parties both from left and right in the early twenty-first century. The Nationalist *List Pim Fortuyn* (LPF), which heavily criticized the political establishment for neglecting issues of migration, integration, and criminality, became the second largest party at the 2002 national elections (Lucardie, 2008a). The anti-neo-liberal Socialist Party (SP) increased its electoral support at the expenses of the Social Democratic PvdA, which had promoted by and large the reform of the welfare state and the introduction of liberalizing policies in the public sector. The LPF quickly dissolved after a short interval in government, but the Nationalist-populist and anti-Islam Freedom Party (PVV) that entered Parliament in 2006 became the third largest party by 2010. After a decade of electoral decline, the Christian Democratic party became the largest party between 2002 and 2010 and led four government coalitions, none of which served a full four-year term.

The Dutch multiparty system can be divided along different lines. A dominant dividing line is socio-economic in nature, with an enhanced role for a free market and greater government intervention at the opposite poles, reflecting the classic left–right division. Within the political spectrum, the most left-wing party is the Socialist Party, founded by Maoists in 1971, which has gradually transformed into a Social Democratic party with populist inclinations. Until now, it never took part in any coalition governments. The Labour Party (PvdA) is the traditional Social Democratic party, which was founded in 1946. In the last ten years, it faced competition from the SP as well as more post-materialist parties, such as D66 and *GroenLinks*. The former, established in 1966, with a radical-democratic programme, adopted a centre-left position on social-economic issues, and took part regularly in coalition governments from 1973. The latter resulted from a merger of Communists, Pacifists, and religious progressives in 1990 that never managed to join any government. On the right side of the political spectrum, it is possible to find the centre-right Christian Democratic CDA, which competes with the more right-wing free-market liberal VVD party, founded in 1948.

Since the Christian Democrats accepted by and large the individualization of ethical principles in 2002, this dimension has largely lost its significance in Dutch politics. Only the

Table 8.2 List of political parties in the Netherlands

Original name	Abbreviation	English translation
Christen-Democratisch Appèl	CDA	Christian Democratic Appeal
ChristenUnie	CU	Christian Union
Democraten 66	D66	Democrats 66
GroenLinks	GL	Green Left
Partij van de Arbeid	PvdA	Labour Party
Partij voor de Dieren	PvdD	Animal Rights Party
Partij voor de Vrijheid	PVV	Freedom Party
Socialistische Partij	SP	Socialist Party
Staatkundig Gereformeerde Partij	SGP	Political Reformed Party
Volkspartij voor Vrijheid en Democratie	VVD	People's Party for Freedom and Democracy
50PLUS partij	50PLUS	50PLUS Party

two small orthodox Protestant parties, the *ChristenUnie* and the SGP, insist on the introduction of Christian ethical issues. The former, resulting from a merger of two smaller parties in 2000, takes a more left-leaning position on social-economic issues. The latter, founded in 1918, adopts a more conservative stance on ethics and a right-wing position on social-economic issues. In recent years, there has been evidence of a different socio-cultural dimension, in which multiculturalism, libertarianism, and cosmopolitanism contrast with monoculturalism, law and order, as well as nationalism (Pellikaan *et al.*, 2003). The positive or negative appraisal of European integration and its implications have also become part of this. A prime example of a monocultural party is the secular Freedom Party (PVV), founded in 2006, which fears that Islam would threaten Dutch power and identity. Although the multiculturalist and libertarian Green Left and D66 share the PVV's desire to maintain individual freedoms in ethical issues, such as homosexuality and women's emancipation, they also wish to protect the rights of Muslim citizens and foster cultural cooperation. In turn, the Socialist SP supports international solidarity, but fears the neo-liberal pressures of globalization on the Dutch welfare state, democracy, and identity. During the 2002 election campaign, the Liberal VVD adopted a more conservative, monocultural position, whilst the Christian Democratic CDA declared multiculturalism to be no longer desirable, but rather a fact of life and increasingly leaned towards monoculturalism. The Social Democratic PvdA faced many internal discussions on the cultural dimension, but still positions itself on the multiculturalist side of the spectrum. Somewhat apart from the dividing lines marking the Dutch party-political landscape, the Animal Rights Party (PvdD), founded in 2002, mainly focusses on the single issue relating to animal well-being.

5.1 Party attitudes towards the European Union

In the initial phase of the European integration process, Dutch governments, dominated by Social Democrats and Catholics, adopted a rather anti-supranational position (Harryvan, 2009). They reluctantly accepted supranational cooperation on the condition that it would serve narrowly-defined commercial interests, whilst preferring the intergovernmental NATO for cooperation on security. Although only involved in international and European affairs in a limited way, Social Democrats and particularly the Catholics in Parliament much more warmly endorsed supranationalism. The free-market liberal VVD and the larger Protestant parties shed their initial reluctance towards a federal Europe in the 1960s, when trade within the European Economic Community grew considerably and a new progressive discourse emerged. According to this widespread discourse, the Netherlands should not just accept international cooperation as necessary and inevitable in an increasingly interdependent world, but it should also be at the forefront of the developments as a progressive and cosmopolitan model nation (Vollaard, 2010). Renewed attention to the Dutch treatment of Jews in WWII resulted in a growing sensitivity to nationalism, racism, and xenophobia, which made explicit loyalty to the nation-state something that was not just considered outdated, but also increasingly reprehensible. As a result, all major parties with the potential to form a governing coalition became at least rhetorically warm supporters of European federalism (Voerman, 2005a). Only small pockets of orthodox Protestants, Pacifists, and Communists opposed European integration for a variety of ideological reasons. However, left-wing parties particularly criticized the then EEC for not being sufficiently progressive in terms of its international solidarity, democratic nature, and social policy.

The 1990s brought a degree of change in the pro-European consensus amongst the major parties, when the Liberal Party leader Frits Bolkestein started to criticize the idea of a federal Europe. He argued that any further transfer of sovereignty to Brussels would widen the gap between mainly nationally-oriented citizens and the political elites. Bolkestein wanted to limit European integration to an efficiently, and if necessary supranationally, run liberalized Common Market, which included the Economic and Monetary Union. He wanted to see a drastic reduction in expenditure on agricultural policy and structural funds. He also argued that the Netherlands, a net contributor to the EU, should no longer be expected to pay an ever larger sum (Harmsen, 2004a, 103–9).

Initially, Bolkestein's criticism did not prompt an immediate, fundamental change amongst the major parties, including his own. The major parties with the potential to form a governing coalition, Labour, the Christian Democrats and the Liberals, all agreed on ratification of the Treaty of Maastricht in 1992. However, publicists both from left and right started to argue that the nation was not outdated, but valuable to maintain for reasons of internal cohesion, viable democracy, moral guidance, or welfare solidarity (Vollaard, 2010). Meanwhile, the Dutch government dropped its federal rhetoric, and increasingly emphasized the need to defend national interests in what it perceived as a largely completed European integration process. In addition, major parties began to criticize the inefficiency, costs, and undemocratic nature of the EU more emphatically. And yet in 1997, all the major parties endorsed the Treaty of Amsterdam, followed in 2000 by the Treaty of Nice, which provided for several institutional modifications in view of EU enlargement. The social-liberal D66, which saw itself as the most pro-European party in the Netherlands, heartily endorsed these Treaties. Consensus within Dutch politics gained still more ground when the Green Left party gradually traded its critical stance on this issue for a more positive one. The party recognized that it would not be able to realize its democratic, social, and environmental ambitions unless the EU's supranational character was bolstered. Whilst in the past, it had rejected the Treaties of Maastricht and Amsterdam, it decided to endorse the Treaty of Nice. The smaller orthodox-Christian parties also abandoned their anti-European stance. The Christian Union and the SGP accepted the Treaty of Nice because it brought with it the EU enlargement they desired without a concomitant transfer of sovereignty. Both parties also soothed their rejection of a supranational Europe of independent states rather than a fully-fledged federation, the desirable end goal of European integration (Vollaard, 2006).

At the beginning of the twenty-first century, the Socialists were almost the only party in the Dutch Parliament that continued to oppose further European integration. They believed that transnational companies and large countries would call the shots in the EU, which would lead to democracy and the welfare state being sacrificed to increased economic competitiveness. The party was willing to cooperate with others at the European level, but it was opposed to federalism. From 2001 the Nationalistic populist Pim Fortuyn castigated the political establishment for squandering the Dutch interests, democracy, and identity to a 'heartless' European bureaucracy (Harmsen, 2008). The free-market liberal VVD Party adopted an increasingly conservative and critical stance towards European Union policies and prospective enlargement. The latest Nationalistic populist offspring, the Freedom Party, totally rejected the European Union in its existing form. The party revolved around Geert Wilders, who for many years represented the VVD party in Parliament. He established his own breakaway party in 2004 out of disagreement with the VVD's refusal to halt Turkey's accession to the EU.

The new millennium opened with a growing reluctance to the 'deepening' and 'widening' of the European Union, as confirmed by the Referendum on the draft European Constitutional Treaty on 1 June 2005 (Voerman, 2005a). The then governing parties, the Christian Democrats, the social-liberal D66 and the free-market liberals, together with the Opposition Labour Party and Green Left, were in favour of the Constitutional Treaty. However, it was the opponents of the Constitution who seized the initiative during the referendum campaign. The Christian Union, the Reformed Political Party, the Pim Fortuyn List, and the Socialist Party feared that the Constitutional Treaty would result in a federal European 'super state', in which the Netherlands would no longer be a distinct political entity. Although about 85 per cent of Dutch

MPs backed the new treaty, eventually only 38 per cent of voters shared that view. In particular, the Social Democrats, the Green Left, and the free-market liberals faced divided constituencies. This discrepancy triggered a discussion about the extent to which parliamentarians and their parties had succeeded in accurately representing voter opinion on Europe (ibid.).

After the Dutch and also the French 'No' vote, the European Council eventually decided to replace it with a 'Reform Treaty', which was signed in Lisbon in December 2007. According to opponents of the Lisbon Treaty, it differed little from the rejected European Constitution. The constitutional rhetoric and the symbolism of the European anthem and flag had been removed, as well as the charter of fundamental rights, given that there was just a single reference to it. The coalition of the Christian Democrats, Labour, and the Christian Union saw the Lisbon Treaty as no more than a slight modification, without implications for the Dutch Constitution, and felt that another referendum would be superfluous. Despite the backing of the Green Left and D66 for the Lisbon Treaty, the Socialists, Freedom Party, and Animal Rights Party campaigned unsuccessfully to win a parliamentary majority for holding a referendum. In June 2008, the Second Chamber ratified the treaty by 111 votes to 39, with the Socialists, the Freedom, Animal Rights, and Political Reformed parties voting against. On the other hand, the Christian Union was the only party in favour of the Lisbon Treaty that had previously voted against the European Constitution. Despite the growing political salience of European integration in the last 20 years, party cohesion has remained sufficiently strong to have no MP deviating from the party line in ratifying the European Treaties since the 1980s.

6 Public opinion and the European Union

From the outset of European integration, European issues barely, if at all, mattered for electoral behaviour in national and, later, EP elections. According to Eurobarometer surveys, most Dutch citizens appear to be in favour of the European Union, although their support for EU membership has dropped since 1991 (CPB/SCP, 2005). The referendum on the European Constitution offered people the opportunity to talk about the European Union as never before. Declining trust in EU democracy was registered, whilst a growing number of citizens felt that the European unification process had moved too far (Thomassen, 2005). Nevertheless, Dutch opinion on European integration remained relatively positive in comparison with public opinion elsewhere in the EU. Turnout at the referendum was high, equivalent to 63 per cent, whilst the 'No' vote reached 61.5 per cent – by far the majority. It was clear that broad parliamentary support for the treaty did not reflect public opinion. Dissatisfaction with the incumbent Cabinet prompted this negative outcome, but concerns regarding ongoing European integration and enlargement threatening Dutch influence and identity played a much larger role (Aarts and Van der Kolk, 2005; Lubbers, 2008).

Interestingly, after the referendum, the large-scale public debate on European integration vanished almost completely. Both before and after the referendum, the Dutch remained relatively positive about European integration, even though a certain reluctance persisted over *further* European integration and especially enlargement. Nevertheless, in autumn 2008, Dutch support for EU membership reached about 80 per cent, its highest point since 1994 (European Commission, 2010). Reflecting a rather utilitarian attitude, the Dutch public mostly associated the EU with ease of travel, payment, studying, and working within Europe as well as with greater influence in the world, peace, and economic wealth (European Commission, 2010). European unity is considered potentially useful for dealing with the global financial, environmental, political, and economic issues (European Commission, 2010). In principle, the Dutch accepted the EU as a positive thing and they also expressed above-average trust in European institutions (European Commission, 2010). Nevertheless, many Dutch also blamed the EU for its inefficiency, associating it with bureaucracy and waste of tax money (TNS NIPO, 2009).

Widespread criticism over the EU's non-transparent bureaucracy was often followed with calls for democratic control and national freedom of decision-making. This reflected a desire to keep control of Europe, linked to concerns about declining Dutch power. Nowhere else in the EU did so many people fear that their country would lose influence in the EU in the near future (European Commission, 2008). About half of Dutch respondents believed the EU would weaken Dutch power, the welfare state, and national identity (21minuten, 2009). In addition, EU enlargement could not count on the support of a majority of the Dutch (SCP, 2009). More recently, the sovereign debt crisis in the EU fostered doubts about its effectiveness amongst the Dutch public, whilst the economic downturn made the Dutch less willing to express international and European financial solidarity (European Commission, 2011; SCP, 2011).

Despite their relatively positive assessment of the EU, within the 2002–2006 period, supporters of the five major political parties in the Netherlands increasingly came to feel that their party was more in favour of further European integration than they were themselves (Dekker, 2009, 48). This discrepancy between voters and parties is not surprising, since European issues were barely salient in national elections even after the referendum and the Dutch debate on European integration had to wait for the 2009 European election campaign to be resumed.

7 National and EP electoral systems

The 150 members of the Second Chamber of Parliament are elected every four years or after a cabinet loses the confidence of the Second Chamber. The country is divided into 19 districts for purely administrative purposes, whilst for the distribution of seats it forms a single electoral district. The electoral system is based on list-proportional representation, with a low threshold of just 0.67 per cent of the votes, approximately 65,000 votes. In order to participate, new parties have to register at the Electoral Board (*Kiesraad*), pay a deposit and persuade 30 citizens in every electoral district to sign a declaration of support at a city hall (Lucardie, 2008a). Voting during weekends is avoided for reasons of religion and convenience.

European Parliament elections follow almost the same rules. Parties have to register only once rather than in 19 districts, whilst the threshold for preferential voting is lower: 10 instead of 25 per cent of the electoral quotient. By contrast, due to the lower number of seats to be distributed, the electoral threshold is higher, meaning that small parties have to take part in European elections with combined lists, as has occurred for the predecessors of the Green Left Party and the Christian Union. Because the Lisbon Treaty had not yet been ratified by all Member States in 2009, European elections were still held in accordance with the Treaty of Nice. As a result, the number of Dutch seats in the European Parliament fell by 2, from 27 to 25, bringing the electoral threshold to 4 per cent. When the Lisbon Treaty came to force, the number of seats for the Netherlands rose to 26. As previously agreed in April 2009, this additional seat would be allocated to the first party to qualify on the basis of the 4 June election result, in accordance with the d'Hondt method. In 2009, Dutch citizens from the Netherlands' Antilles and Aruba could also participate in the European elections for the first time. Due to growing concerns about digital security, paper ballots were re-introduced.

8 A glance at the EP and national elections

After the abolition of compulsory voting in the Netherlands in 1970, participation in national elections remained relatively high, whilst it declined considerably in local, provincial, and particularly European elections. Despite a costly public awareness campaign, turnout in the first European elections in 1979 reached a relatively meagre 58.1 per cent. After a steady decline, turnout reached its lowest point in 1999, when only 29.9 per cent of the electorate showed up. This did not come as a surprise. As in previous European elections, major parties did not offer much choice regarding European integration (Kok et al., 1985; Lipschits, 1986; Oppenhuis, 1996; Van der Kolk, 2001). Many voters also found it difficult to determine and differentiate parties' positions on Europe (Oppenhuis, 1996; Irwin, 1995; Van Holsteyn and Den Ridder, 2005). If Europe gained some attention during the EP campaigns, this largely concerned questions about the European Parliament's lack of power, particularly an issue in 1979, or about low turnout and fraudulent behaviour within EU institutions, especially in 1999.

National issues did not provide much choice for voters either in 1999, since too many parties were involved with the near collapse of the 'purple' government just before the European elections, and the ramifications of a widely published parliamentary report on the government's handling of an aeroplane crash in 1992 (Van der Kolk, 2001).

Municipal and national elections in March and May, respectively, as well as the formation of a new government involving parties of the left (PvdA) and right (VVD), overshadowed the European elections in June 1994. Before this, the oppositional PvdA attempted to make the European elections of 1979, 1984, and 1989 a test of the respective centre-right governments' popularity, criticizing them for their positions on nuclear armament, employment, or welfare retrenchment. This was to little avail, since turnout in European elections remained much lower than in national elections, whilst the PvdA in particular suffered from voters staying at home more than other major parties (Oppenhuis, 1996). European Parliament election campaigns varied from dull to extremely dull up until 1999 (Voerman and Van der Walle, 2009). Both the greater public and party members hardly showed up at party rallies with national figureheads, who supported the often unknown leading candidates of the European party lists (Kok et al., 1985; Lipschits, 1986). European integration could thus not count on much

Table 8.3 National election results in the Netherlands: 1977–2012

Political party	1977	1981	1982	1986	1989	1994	1998	2002	2003	2006	2010	2012
CDA	31.9	30.8	29.4	34.6	35.3	22.2	18.4	27.9	28.6	26.5	13.6	8.5
PvdA	33.8	28.3	30.4	33.3	31.9	24.0	29.0	15.1	27.3	21.2	19.6	24.8
VVD	17.9	17.3	23.1	17.4	14.6	20.0	24.7	15.4	17.9	14.7	20.5	26.8
D66	5.4	11.1	4.3	6.1	7.9	15.5	9.0	5.1	4.1	2.0	6.9	8.0
GL★	4.3	6.7	6.5	3.3	4.1	3.5	7.3	7.0	5.1	4.6	6.7	2.3
CU★	1.0	2.0	2.3	1.9	2.2	3.1	3.3	2.5	2.1	4.0	3.3	3.1
SGP	2.1	2.0	1.9	1.7	1.9	1.7	1.8	1.7	1.7	1.6	1.7	2.1
SP	—	—	0.5	0.4	0.4	1.3	3.5	5.9	6.3	16.6	9.8	9.7
LPF	—	—	—	—	—	—	—	17.0	5.7	—	—	—
PVV	—	—	—	—	—	—	—	—	—	5.9	15.5	10.1
PvdD	—	—	—	—	—	—	—	—	0.5	1.8	1.3	1.9
50PLUS	—	—	—	—	—	—	—	—	—	—	—	1.9
Others	2.6	1.9	1.7	1.3	1.8	8.8	2.5	2.4	1.2	2.9	1.2	2.7
Total	100.0	100.0	100.0	100.0	100.0	100.0	100.0	100.0	100.0	100.0	100.0	100.0
Turnout	**88.0**	**87.0**	**81.0**	**85.8**	**80.3**	**78.7**	**73.3**	**78.9**	**79.9**	**80.4**	**75.3**	**74.6**

Source: www.parlement.com.

Note:
★ Including results of predecessors.

interest from the greater public. Dutch voters were also not very knowledgeable about the European project (Irwin, 1995).

The 2004 European elections showed, however, a recovery of electoral turnout towards almost 40 per cent, mainly due to an intense government campaign to raise public awareness of the elections, and a more lively political debate on European issues, including Turkish EU accession and the European Constitutional Treaty (Voerman and van der Walle, 2009). The pro-European D66 and the more critical VVD emphasized their mutual differences, even though they shared the same manifesto as the European Liberals (ibid.). Internal party divisions on European integration remained a largely unseen affair with the notable exception of the PvdA in 1979, when its youth wing called for voters to abstain from voting because of the undemocratic and capitalist nature of Europe (Kok et al., 1985). However, the VVD showed some internal tensions from the 1990s, when party leader Bolkestein started to criticize European integration more emphatically. A member of the party's governing board eventually left the party to compete, albeit unsuccessfully, with a separate Liberal Democratic list in the 2004 European elections. Domestic issues continued to feature more prominently in the 2004 campaign, with left-wing parties criticizing the centre-right government for its political support for the Iraq invasion and its pension reforms.

Table 8.4 EP election results in the Netherlands: 1979–2009

Political party	1979	1984	1989	1994	1999	2004	2009
CDA	10	8	10	10	9	7	5
	35.6%	30.0%	34.6%	30.8%	26.9%	24.4%	20.0%
PvdA	9	9	8	8	6	7	3
	30.4%	33.7%	30.7%	22.9%	20.1%	23.6%	12.0%
VVD	4	5	3	6	6	4	3
	16.1%	18.9%	13.6%	17.9%	19.7%	13.2%	11.4%
D66	2	0	1	4	2	1	3
	9.0%	2.3%	6.0%	11.7%	5.8%	4.2%	11.3%
GL★	0	2	2	1	4	2	3
	5.1%	5.6%	7.0%	3.7%	11.8%	7.4%	8.8%
CU/SGP	0	1	1	2	3	2	2
	3.3%	5.2%	5.9%	7.8%	8.7%	5.9%	6.8%
SP	—	—	0	0	1	2	2
			0.7%	1.3%	5.0%	7.0%	7.3%
Europa Transparant	—	—	—	—	—	2	—
						7.3%	
PVV★★	—	—	—	—	—	—	4 (5)★★
							17.0%
Others	0	0	0	0	0	0	0
	0.4%	4.2%	0.8%	3.9%	1.8%	7.0%	4.9%
Total	25	25	25	31	31	27	25 (26)
	100.0%	100.0%	100.0%	100.0%	100.0%	100.0%	100.0%
Turnout	**58.1%**	**50.9%**	**47.5%**	**35.7%**	**30.0%**	**39.1%**	**36.8%**

Source: www.parlement.com.

Notes:
★ Including results of predecessors, which participated with separate lists in the 1979 elections and with a combined list in 1984, albeit under another name.
★★ The PVV received the additional seat following the modification of national shares of seats in the European Parliament according to the Lisbon Treaty.

Until 1994, European elections did not show a clear pattern of governing or large parties losing because of sincere voting or disappointment about the incumbent government's policies (Oppenhuis, 1996). The rise of smaller and new parties started in the 1999 European elections, favouring electoral volatility and party fragmentation. In the first decade of the twenty-first century, both national and European elections in the Netherlands were marked by an antithesis between the traditional, established governing parties, on the one hand, and their populist challengers, on the other. Moreover, the overlapping antithesis between the multicultural, cosmopolitan Europhile parties and the Nationalistic Eurosceptic parties left its imprint on national as well as EP elections. As a result, the political centre has started shrinking and the wings have started growing. The subsequent fragmentation and levelling of the party landscape has also been clearly visible at the European level. Whereas in 1979, the Christian Democrats, Labour and the Liberals together won over 82 per cent of the votes, in 2004 they obtained only 64 per cent. The number of Dutch parties represented in the European Parliament doubled from four to eight within the 1979–2004 time frame. Voters rejected the Constitutional Treaty by a large majority, based on concerns about European issues such as enlargement and the Euro but they had no chance to express their views on the Treaty of Lisbon in another referendum, and had to wait for the 2009 European election for that purpose: 'This cabinet won't dare let you vote on the Lisbon Treaty. So we'll hold our own referendum on 4 June, during the European parliamentary elections.' These were the words of the populist, Nationalist and anti-Islamic Freedom Party (PVV), headed by Geert Wilders. The left-populist Socialist Party (SP, 2009) also left no doubts as to its position in the upcoming European elections:

> The fourth of June 2009 will be a historic day for Europe. On that day you'll be able to use the European Parliament elections as a referendum. You'll decide how we should go ahead on Europe. On 4 June 2009, you'll vote for or against the transfer of still more Dutch sovereignty to Brussels.

Although poles apart on many issues, the two parties were in complete agreement on one thing: the Lisbon Treaty had to be placed before the Dutch public in a referendum.

9 The 2009 European election

9.1 Party lists and manifestos

It is not customary for Dutch political parties to include key political figures in their lists for the EP elections. The flip side of this practice is that often those at the head of the lists are not well known. At the 2009 EP Elections, 56 per cent of Dutch voters knew none of the candidates on the top of the party lists (TNS NIPO, 2009). The leaders of parties that already had seats in the European Parliament were a very different group in 2009 than in 2004. The social-liberal D66 was the only party that contested the election with the same person, Sophie in 't Veld, at the helm, whilst all other parties appointed new leaders. The Christian Democrats and Liberals both chose national MPs. The Christian Democrats chose Wim van de Camp, who had served in the national Parliament since 1982, whilst the Liberals proposed Hans van Baalen, former MP and Vice-President of Liberal International. Their national political background meant that they were known by the electorate. As to Labour, the list was headed by Thijs Berman, who had been an MEP since 2004. Green Left appointed a city councillor from Amsterdam, whilst the Socialist Party and the orthodox Protestant parties each selected a civil servant. Lastly, Freedom Party leader Wilders appointed the MP Barry Madlener to head the list (TNS NIPO, 2009).

Europe featured prominently in the Dutch parties' electoral manifestos, even though references to the ideal of a federalizing Europe were largely replaced by reluctance towards further European integration. Most manifestos consisted of long lists of policy preferences on issues such as climate change, agriculture, social policy, economy, justice and home affairs, finance, animal welfare, asylum and migration, energy as well as external policies (Pellikaan and Van Holsteyn, 2010).

The progressive and cosmopolitan D66 ran a campaign under the slogan 'Yes to Europe.' It warned against a knee-jerk Nationalist and protectionist response, claiming that 'European cooperation offer[ed] the best guarantee for peace, sustainability and welfare.' The party wanted to see the Netherlands once again in the vanguard of Europe: 'Too often in recent years [the country] has stood on the sideline and put its foot on the brake' (D66, 2009, 6). The Green Left, affiliated with the European Green Party, drafted a pro-European programme whereby the European Parliament was described as 'the place to be' for an environmental party. They also enthusiastically embraced the Lisbon Treaty, their main proviso being that this should not be 'the end of the line', and called for EU democratization whilst advocating European referenda and transnational candidate lists at the EP elections. Both D66 and Green Left felt that Turkey could join the EU once it complied with the criteria.

The traditional governing parties, Labour, Christian Democrats and Liberals, pragmatically perceived European cooperation on certain cross-border issues as necessary and inevitable for a small state such as the Netherlands (Vollaard, 2010). In particular, after the rise of the Eurosceptic Pim Fortuyn List, they defined themselves as 'Euro-realistic' by placing greater emphasis on the defence of national interests and on the principle of subsidiarity to limit European bureaucratic interference. These traditional governing parties thus shifted from a principled discourse on European federalism towards a pragmatic view of the European Union as an instrument to serve Dutch interests. They also became more cautious about EU enlargement in general and the accession of Turkey in particular (De Beus and Mak, 2009). This position, partly designed to take the wind out of the sails of Eurosceptic parties, set them apart from the pro-European, cosmopolitan D66 and Green Left. This 'Euro-realist' approach, which had already emerged in the European elections of 2004, became more evident in 2009 (Voerman, 2005b; Vollaard, 2010). The Labour Party, affiliated to the Party of European Social Democrats (PES), elected a pro-Europe leader with a narrow majority over a candidate who was highly critical towards Europe. In its election programme, presented alongside the PES manifesto, Labour emphasized the positive elements of European cooperation, but it also showed considerable sympathy for the 'growing scepticism and uncertainty about the European Union'. The Social Democrats declared themselves against 'the continuing transfer of national sovereignty to Brussels', by also stressing the need to safeguard national identity (PvdA, 2009, 6–7 and 27).

The Christian Democrats, allied to the European People's Party (EPP), traditionally in favour of a strong, federal Europe, gradually became more concerned with preserving Dutch identity. Their programme envisaged 'a powerful Netherlands in a strong and stable European Union' (CDA, 2009). For this purpose, they wished to see the Lisbon Treaty come into force as quickly as possible as this would make the EU more decisive and more democratic (ibid., 3 and 6).

The Liberal VVD party, like D66 a member of the ELDR, also used to belong to the federalist camp, but the party became more critical after the Bolkestein period. The Liberal party leader's priorities were quite clear in 2009: 'I'm not going to Brussels to become a European, but to remain a Dutchman and to champion Dutch interests' (*Liber*, 2008). The party's election programme also made this crystal clear. Although European integration scored 'very favourably' on the balance sheet, the party emphatically distanced itself from federalism. The Liberals opted 'for a powerful Europe with core responsibilities' that had an added value, and which would preserve Dutch identity (VVD, 2009, 2). The VVD's conservative stance on international cooperation as well as domestic cultural issues led to the defection of Joris Voorhoeve, former national party leader, and Gijs de Vries, former European party leader, to the social-liberal D66.

All the progressive-cosmopolitan and pragmatic, Euro-realistic parties perceiving the European Union acceptable or desirable have the potential to form a government. Of the five, only Green Left has never been in government, although it aspires to taking on the responsibilities of government. As mentioned above, the small, orthodox Protestant Christian Union was part of the governing coalition between 2007 and 2010. Like its predecessors, it had always expressed opposition towards European federalism, but it voted in favour of the Lisbon Treaty in 2008 (Vollaard, 2006). This almost led to an immediate end of its membership of the Independence/Democracy Group (IND/DEM) in the European Parliament. The Christian Union had already planned to leave this group, in part because what had unified them, opposition to the European Constitutional Treaty, was in fact no longer true. The Reformed Political Party (SGP) went along with the Christian Union's constructive, critical approach, partly to continue its electoral alliance with that party, which dated back to 1984. Both parties also adopted a 'constructive and critical' approach in their joint election programme for 2009, expressing a wish to work together on 'a solid Europe that focusses on its core responsibilities'; they nonetheless flatly rejected a 'super state' (CU-SGP, 2009, 6). For Turkey, they envisaged no more than a 'privileged partnership'.

The remaining parties, with the exception of the more ambivalent Reformed Political Party, are highly critical if not outright sceptical about European integration. The Socialist Party, which is a member of the Confederal Group of the European United Left/Nordic Green Left, once again rejected the establishment of a 'neo-liberal European super state'. The party opposed the Lisbon Treaty and any further transfer of national sovereignty from The Hague to Brussels. The possibility of Turkey joining the EU was not ruled out.

The Eurosceptic Animal Rights' Party, which entered the Dutch Parliament in November 2006, ran the EP contest for the first time in 2004, to no avail. It rejected the Lisbon Treaty, which it believed made animal rights subordinate to non-animal-friendly cultural and religious customs and traditions, and which did little to make the EU more democratic. The party was opposed to Turkey joining the EU because the accession of Ankara would 'result in lowered standards for other EU Member States' (PvdD, 2009).

The Freedom Party, which made its debut in 2009, was adamantly opposed to the EU in its existing form and led a campaign under the banner 'For the Netherlands'. In its brief programme, the party demanded that the Netherlands would not surrender its right of veto, especially with regard to immigration in order to stop 'the Islamization of the Netherlands and Europe' and Turkey's accession to the EU, to support the ousting of 'corrupt states' like Romania and Bulgaria, and to reject the 'dreadful Lisbon Treaty' (PVV, 2009).

Besides the above-mentioned parliamentary parties, another seven lists took part in the June 2009 contest, ranging from supporters of European integration to those who unequivocally opposed it. They included Libertas, set up by Irish businessman Declan Ganley, which believed that the European Union had limitless possibilities, but that it needed to become more open and democratic (Libertas, 2009).

9.2 Electoral campaign

The European election campaign slowly started in spring 2009 with party meetings devoted to Europe, in which their manifestos were presented. The decision of the Freedom Party to participate in the EP contest was welcomed by the other parties, which felt it would enliven the election battle. Despite the large use of internet applications and social networking, along with television debates – which remained the main source of voters' information – and press articles, the EP election campaign never really got off the ground. Between early May and early June 2009, the Ministry of the Interior spent €441,000 on television, radio, advertisements, and websites in order to raise public awareness about the EP elections (Van den Berg et al., 2010). As part of a pan-European project, the European Parliament's office launched an information campaign to show the choices citizens can make with respect to borders, food, security, and consumer protection, using social media, website, television and radio. In the three weeks prior to the polling day, no major newspaper or television channel mentioned the EP's campaign; it remained by and large invisible (Kristensen, 2010).

More than in the past, most national party leaders preferred to keep themselves in the background (Voerman and Van de Walle, 2009, 132). A hot air balloon featured the face of the Christian Democratic Prime Minister Jan-Peter Balkenende. With the elections just a few days away, the national Liberal leader Mark Rutte caused a political furore by arguing that Holocaust deniers should not always be punished (Doorduyn, 2009). As to the PVV, the Euro-elections were perceived as a test of its electoral strength.

Despite the dominance of national politics in the 2009 European elections campaign, European issues received some attention. A limited number of newspaper editorials were devoted to the EP contest, in particular to the expected low voter turnout. When the EU was discussed by parties in the campaign, criticism of its bureaucratism and inefficiency featured prominently (Vollaard, 2010). Reflecting the perceived European threat to the Netherlands, the television programme *Europa in 10 Ergernissen* (Europe in 10 Annoyances) dealt with crucial political, economic, and social questions.

More than in previous years, voters were offered a clear choice between the rather pro-European and cosmopolitan D66 and the Green Left on the one hand, and the Nationalistic, Eurosceptic Freedom Party and, to a lesser extent, the Socialist Party, which resisted any further cession of sovereignty, on the other.

Notwithstanding the European contents of the party manifestos, the European issues discussed, and this clear choice between parties, national politics continued to dominate a rather lacklustre campaign, in which parties spent fewer resources than in national elections.

9.3 Electoral results

Overall, the election results showed a further fragmentation of the political landscape, which was considered a complicating factor in future coalition formation processes at the national level, as previously occurred in 2010.

Never before had so many parties run in the EP race as in 2009. Amongst the 17 lists, 11 – including all 10 parties represented in the Dutch Parliament and the Animal Rights' Party – managed to cross the electoral barrier and obtain seats in Strasbourg.

The number of invalid votes increased, most probably because of the re-introduction of the paper ballot. In addition, 0.2 per cent of the electorate cast an abstention vote. Out of the total number of 4,573,743 votes, 16,206 were cast by Dutch citizens in the Netherlands' Antilles and Aruba. Electoral turnout fell to 36.8 per cent, marking the lowest voter turnout amongst the six founding EU members, and was also well below the European average of 43 per cent. The participation rate also remained well below the 80.4 per cent seen in the 2006 national elections.

The traditional governing parties CDA, PvdA, and VVD lost heavily, gathering together only 43.6 per cent of the vote. As in the 2004 EP elections and the 2006 Dutch National elections, the Christian Democrats remained the largest party, but at 20 per cent their share of

Table 8.5 EP detailed election results in the Netherlands: 2009

Political party	Seats	Votes	Vote share (%)
CDA★	5	913,233	20.0
PvdA★★	3	548,691	12.0
ChristenUnie	1	310,540	6.8
SGP★★★	1		
PVV	4 (5)	772,746	17.0
D66 ★★★★	3	515,422	11.3
GroenLinks	3	404,020	8.9
VVD	3	518,643	11.4
SP	2	323,269	7.1
PvdD	0	157,735	3.5
Others	0	89,565	1.5
Invalid votes		19,879	0.4
Total Seats	25 (26)		
Votes/turnout		**4,573,743**	**36.7**

Source: www.kiesraad.nl, accessed on 21 August 2011.

Notes: Parties in national government in italics.
★ Combined its list with CU/SGP for the distribution of seats.
★★ Combined its list with GL in the distribution of seats.
★★★ Fully integrated list in EP elections, but separate lists in national elections.
★★★★ Combined its list with VVD in the distribution of seats.

the vote was the lowest since the first direct European elections in 1979. In comparison with the 2006 general elections in November 2006, they lost 6.5 per cent of the vote. Likewise, Labour recorded a mere 12 per cent, representing its worst result by far since 1979, whilst losing heavily compared with the 2006 national elections. With 7.3 per cent of the vote, the Eurosceptic Socialist Party remained fairly stable in comparison with the previous European elections. And yet, the party did not reap the benefits of Labour's losses as it had done previously in 2006, when it achieved its record score of 16.6 per cent of the vote. By contrast, the cosmopolitan Green Left and D66 grew at the expense of Labour (Synovate, 2009). Facing competition from both the Nationalistic Freedom Party and the cosmopolitan D66, the largest opposition party, the free-market Liberals, also lost *vis-à-vis* the previous European and national elections, by recording their worst 'European' result ever. The combined list of the governing party, the small orthodox Protestant Christian Union, and the other small orthodox Protestant Reformed Political Party, gained 0.9 per cent in comparison to the previous European elections.

The 2009 contest marked the breakthrough of the Nationalist populist Freedom Party, which became the second largest party, with no less than 17 per cent of the vote, 11.1 per cent more than in the last national election. Paradoxically, the Freedom Party, which had abhorred the Lisbon Treaty, benefitted from the treaty entering into force by acquiring an additional seat in Strasbourg, which became available in December 2011. This twenty-sixth seat was taken by former PVV MEP Daniel van der Stoep, who nevertheless decided to sit as an independent MEP, keeping the PVV delegation at 4 seats.

Dutch MEPs belonging to parties represented in the European Parliament remained within their respective groups, except for the orthodox Protestant CU/SGP combination. The British Conservative Party refused the entry of the SGP into a new group called the European Conservatives and Reformists (ECR) because of the latter's exclusion of women from its party

Table 8.6 List of Dutch MEPs in the Netherlands: seventh legislature

Name	Date of birth	Gender	National party	Political group	Mandate	Professional background
Baalen, J.C. van	17/06/1960	Male	VVD	ALDE	1	Member of parliament
Hennis-Plasschaert*, J.A	07/04/1973	Female	VVD	ALDE	2	Political assistant
Manders, A.J.M.	14/03/1956	Male	VVD	ALDE	3	Member of the Provincial Council Noord-Brabant
Schaake, M.R.	28/10/1978	Female	D66	ALDE	1	Self-employed adviser
Veld, S.H. in 't	13/09/1963	Female	D66	ALDE	2	Secretary of the ELDR group Committee of the Regions
Gerbrandy, G.J.M.	28/06/1967	Male	D66	ALDE	1	Senior political adviser at the Ministry of Agriculture
Camp, W. van de	27/07/1953	Male	CDA	EPP	1	Member of Parliament
Lange, E.M.R. de	19/02/1975	Female	CDA	EPP	2	Policy adviser of the CDA-delegation at the European Parliament
Nistelrooij, L.J.J. van	05/03/1953	Male	CDA	EPP	2	Member of the provincial executive Noord-Brabant
Oomen-Ruijten, M.G.H.C.	06/09/1950	Female	CDA	EPP	5	Member of Parliament
Wortmann-Kool, C.M.	27/06/1959	Female	CDA	EPP	2	Employed at the Ministry of Transport and Public Works
Bontes, L.**	28/02/1956	Male	PVV	ni	1	Chief of police, Rotterdam
Madlener, B.***	06/01/1969	Male	PVV	ni	1	Member of Parliament
Stassen, L.J.A.J.	08/02/1971	Female	PVV	ni	1	Presenter at a local station, TV Limburg
Stoep****, D.T. van der	12/09/1980	Male	PVV	ni	1	Policy adviser of the PVV-group in the Parliament
Berman, M.	26/09/1957	Male	PvdA	S&D	2	Correspondent, presenter and journalist
Bozkurt, E.	09/08/1967	Female	PvdA	S&D	2	Senior consultant social issues
Merkies, J.A.	28/09/1966	Female	PvdA	S&D	1	Programme manager at the European Commission (EACEA)
Cornelissen, M.	09/03/1974	Female	*Groen Links*	Greens/EFA	1	Chair of the District Council Amsterdam-Zuideramstel

(continued)

Table 8.6 (continued)

Name	Date of birth	Gender	National party	Political group	Mandate	Professional background
Eickhout, B.	08/10/1976	Male	*GroenLinks*	Greens/EFA	1	Senior researcher at Netherlands Environmental Assessment Agency
Sargentini, J.	13/03/1974	Female	*GroenLinks*	Greens/EFA	1	Consultant Eurostep
Jong, C.D. de	22/05/1955	Male	SP	EUL/NGL	1	Adviser foreign affairs
Liotard*****, K.T.	20/06/1971	Female	SP	EUL/NGL	2	Civil servant LASER
Dalen, P. van	03/09/1958	Male	*Christen Unie*	ECR	1	Principal ship surveyor, Ministry of Transport and Public Works
Belder, B.	25/10/1946	Male	SGP	EFD	3	Editor/correspondent at Reformatorisch Dagblad

Source: http://www.europarl.europa.eu/meps/en/search.html?country=NL.

Notes:
* Hennis-Plasschaert left the EP for the Dutch Parliament in 2010. Jan Mulder replaced her.
** Bontes was replaced by Lucas Hartong in 2010.
*** Madlener was replaced by Patricia van der Kammen in 2012.
**** After his resignation, Van der Stoop was replaced by A. Zijlstra but returned as an independent MEP in December 2011, taking the twenty-sixth seat for the Netherlands in the European Parliament.
***** Liotard left her party in 2010 after conflicts within the SP EP delegation, and became an independent member of the EUL/NGL.

lists. Whereas the *ChristenUnie* joined the ECR, the SGP ended up in the Europe of Freedom and Democracy group. The Freedom Party did not join any of the EP groups, and remained non-attached. The volatility of the Dutch electorate resulted in a replacement of more than half of the Dutch MEPs. MEP candidate Geert Wilders, the national party leader, declined to take his seat, despite receiving enough votes. As a result, the percentage of female Dutch MEPs reached 46 per cent.

9.4 Campaign finance

Until a few years ago, Dutch political parties largely depended on dues and gifts from party members to finance their electoral campaigns (Andeweg and Irwin, 2009). Since 2005, parties have also been allowed to spend government subsidies on campaign activities, which have remained a relatively inexpensive affair given that parties can largely rely on free publicity such as television debates and voting advice applications on the internet. Party campaign budgets have increased over the years, rising to an estimated €8,850,000 in 2006 spent by the parties that obtained seats in the Second Chamber (Van Praag and Brants, 2008). The lack of transparency in Dutch party budgets complicates meaningful comparisons of campaign expenditures, including those in the 2009 European election.

The annual budget reports of several parties seem to indicate that in EP elections, they spent one-half to one-third of the amount they spent in the last national elections. In 2006, the SP spent an estimated €1,100,000 on campaigning, whilst the 2009 budget report indicated that expenses for the European as well as a few local elections were about €675,000. According to budget reports, the CDA and D66 spent respectively €467,217 and €188,132. The figures available thus suggest that parties pursued a low-budget campaign in 2009.

10 Theoretical interpretation of Euro-elections

10.1 Second-Order Election theory

Since 1979, European elections in the Netherlands have maintained their secondary character. Overall, parties invested less time and resources in the EP campaigns, which remained rather dull and dominated by domestic themes, whilst polling stations were increasingly deserted by voters who preferred to stay at home.

Between 1979 and 1994, electoral outcomes did not reflect a clear pattern. Whereas some large parties won, others lost, being either in opposition or in government. In particular in 1989 and 1994, this was partly due to the timing of the EP contest.

In 1999, parties at the fringes started to make significant gains by supporting the hypotheses related to the punishment of governing parties or sincere voting. Yet, the 2004 Euro-elections could be regarded not so much as a second-order contest following a distinctive electoral logic, but rather as a secondary confirmation of the national political trends manifested in the 2002 and 2003 legislative elections (Harmsen, 2004b). The rise of small and new parties confirmed the tendencies of electoral volatility and fragmentation of the political landscape, more than reflecting voting behaviour specific to EP elections.

The 2009 EP electoral contest did not deviate from the continuing series of second-order elections, as turnout remained low, national politics dominated a lacklustre campaign, and the ruling Christian Democrats and, above all, Social Democrats, lost considerably. Only their tiny orthodox Protestant coalition partner avoided this ill fate. As in the past, their loyal constituencies provided the orthodox Protestant parties with a higher share of the vote when overall turnout was low. Also a newcomer and several smaller parties won, whereas the opposition conservative Liberals faced a steep decline in electoral support. The shift away from this larger party may be explained because of sincere voting. However, it is worth pointing out that in the Netherlands both larger and smaller parties can take part easily in national governments, thus weakening the need to vote strategically in legislative elections.

Over time, European elections in the Netherlands have remained by and large a national second-order affair. National politics continued to control the EP campaign and the interpretation of the electoral results. Voters' interest in the European elections was limited and the turnout remained low. Those citizens who went to the ballot box seemed to do so largely because of a sense of civic duty. Public perception of parties' ideological profile, mainly based on their performance in national politics, in which Europe barely played any role, has led voters' choices.

10.2 Europe Salience theory

In line with the Europe Salience theory, in the Netherlands, low turnout in European elections compared with other elections may be partially ascribed to an anti-European position amongst the Dutch people.

Voters' attempts to seek out the extremes on the European political *continuum* may also be due to the fact that traditional governing parties had adopted a less clear stance towards the European Union. Already in 1999, a wider choice of party positions on EU issues led to higher gains for anti-European and Green parties. Subsequently, the 2004 EP campaign appeared a bit less dull, whilst electoral interest over Europe and voter turnout barely increased. Support for European integration did not have an effect on voter participation.

In 2004, European issues such as the Stability and Growth Pact and Turkish accession to the EU received more attention. One year later, many people turned out to vote on the European Constitutional Treaty. However, the Freedom Party and the Socialists tried in vain to convert the 2009 European election into a new referendum on the Lisbon Treaty, even though a clear choice between Eurosceptic and pro-European parties was offered and the media neglected Europe less than before. A combination of populism, electoral volatility, and the fragmentation of the political landscape marked the European elections, as it has done in national elections in the twenty-first century.

The 2009 elections reflected the emerging dividing line in Dutch politics between cosmopolitan and Nationalist parties and voters, of which Europe is just one aspect. Even though European policies did not dominate the elections, the large victory of the Eurosceptic Freedom Party resulted in a better reflection of popular opinion on European integration.

The fact that pro-European, cosmopolitan parties had a substantial win in 2009, as did the Eurosceptic Freedom Party, suggests, however, that Europe was not an entirely negligible factor in these elections. D66 also climbed out of its electoral trough, achieving the second-best result in the European elections in 30 years, as did the Green Left. Voters who had lower trust in EU institutions, and who were less permissive towards European integration, were more inclined to vote for the Socialist Party and the Freedom Party, or to stay at home, than to vote for the Christian Democrats.

Despite the prominence of European issues in the manifestos and the larger attention given by the media, Europe thus remained secondary in the 2009 EP elections. The rise of a Eurosceptic and pro-European party, including a Green party, rather reflected the prominence of a dividing line between cosmopolitan and Nationalist parties rather than of Europe itself.

In conclusion, it could be said that EP contests in the Netherlands confirmed most elements of the Second-Order Elections theory rather than those underlying the Europe Salience model. All European elections in the Netherlands have been of a national and secondary nature, as is reflected in large-scale public apathy and low party activism in the political campaigns. Moreover, even though the traditional governing parties have largely dropped their federalist rhetoric, a majority of parties still endorse EU membership, including previously Eurosceptic orthodox Protestant and left-wing parties.

References

Primary sources

www.kiesraad.nl (2009), 'Verkiezingsuitslagen Europees Parlement' (accessed on 6 February 2015).
www.parlement.com (accessed on 15 February 2015)..
www.verkiezingsuitslagen.nl/Na1918/Verkiezingsuitslagen.aspx?VerkiezingsTypeId=5 (accessed on 6 February 2015).
21Minuten (2009) 'Editie 2009 Tussenrapportage: De Europese Resultaten': www.21minuten.nl (accessed on 24 September 2010).
CDA (2009) 'Kracht en ambitie! Verkiezingsprogramma 2009–2014'.
ChristenUnie-SGP (2009) 'Samenwerken ja, superstaat nee'.

D66 (2009) 'Europa gaat om mensen! Verkiezingsprogramma D66 voor het Europees Parlement'.
EenVandaag (2009) 'Uitslag Onderzoek Europese Verkiezingen 2009', http://opinie.eenvandaag.nl/uitslagen/34773/pvv_grootste_bij_europese-verkiezingen (accessed on 24 September 2010).
Eurobarometer (2008) Eurobarometer 68, Luxembourg, European Commission.
Eurobarometer (2010) Standard Eurobarometer 72, Luxembourg, European Commission.
Eurobarometer (2011) Standard Eurobarometer 75, Luxembourg, European Commission.
European Parliament website, www.europarl.europa.eu/parliament/archive/elections2009/en/index_en.html (accessed on 7 December 2013).
Eurostat (2013, 2014) http://epp.eurostat.ec.europa.eu (accessed on 5 June 2015).
GroenLinks (2009) 'Nieuwe energie voor Europa: Verkiezingsprogramma Europees Parlement 2009–2014'.
Liber: Ledenmagazine van de VVD (2008) 'De slag om Brussel begint nu! Hans van Baalen lijsttrekker', 3(7),5.
Libertas (2009) www.libertas.eu/nl/about-us (accessed on 17 May 2009).
Partij voor de Dieren (2009) 'EU verkiezingsprogramma 2009'.
Partij voor de Vrijheid (2009) 'Kies voor Nederland, Kies PVV'.
PvdA (2009) Verkiezingsprogramma Europees Parlement 2009–2014.
SP (2009) 'Een beter Europa begint in Nederland'.
TNS NIPO (2009) 'Overgrote meerderheid op hoogte Europese verkiezingen', www.tns-nipo.com/pages/nieuws-pers-politiek.asp?file=persvannipo\rtl_europese_verkiezingen_0609.htm (accessed on 28 April 2010).
VVD (2009) 'Voor een werkend Europa'.

Secondary sources

Aarts, K. and Van der Kolk, H. (2005) 'Understanding the Dutch "No": The Euro, the East, and the Elite', *PS Online*, April, 243–46.
Andeweg, R. B. and Irwin, G. A. (2009) *Governance and Politics of the Netherlands*, Basingstoke, Palgrave Macmillan.
Beus, J. de and Mak. J. (2009) *De kwestie Europa. Hoe de EU tot de Nederlandse politiek doordringt*, Amsterdam, Amsterdam University Press.
CPB/SCP (2005) *Europese Tijden: De Publieke Opinie over Europa & Arbeidstijden, vergeleken en verklaard*, Den Haag, CPB/SCP.
CPB/SCP (2009) *Strategisch Europa*, Den Haag, CPB/SCP.
Dekker, P. (2009) *Strategisch Europa: Markten en Macht in 2030 en de Publieke Opinie over de Europese Unie*, Den Haag, Sociaal en Cultureel Planbureau.
Doorduyn, Y. (2009) '"In mijn voorstel staat niets over de Holocaust", interview Mark Rutte', *de Volkskrant*, 30 May.
Harmsen, R. (2004a) 'Euroscepticism in the Netherlands: Stirrings of Dissent', *European Studies*, 20, 99–126.
Harmsen, R. (2004b) *The European Parliament Election in the Netherlands, June 10, 2004*, European Parliament Election Briefing 17, Belfast, School of Politics and International Studies.
Harmsen, R. (2008) 'The Evolution of the Dutch European Discourse: Defining the "Limits of Europe"', *Perspectives on European Politics and Society*, 9(2).
Harryvan, A. G. (2009), *In Pursuit of Influence: The Netherlands' European Policy during the Formative Years of the European Union, 1952–1973*, P.I.E. Peter Lang, Brussels.
Irwin, G. (1995) 'Second Order or Third Rate: Issues in the Campaign of the Elections for the European Parliament 1994', *Election Studies*, 14(2), 183–98.
Kok, W. J. P., Lipschits, I. and Van Praag, P. H. (1985) 'The Netherlands', in Reif, K. H. (ed.) *Ten European Elections: Campaigns and Results of the 1979/1981 First Direct Elections to the European Parliament*, Brookfield (VT), Gower, 153–65.
Kristensen, P. (2010) *Communicating Europe in Partnership: Getting the Message Across* (MA thesis), Amsterdam, University of Amsterdam.
Lipschits, I. (1986) 'The Netherlands', in Lodge, J. (ed.) *Direct Elections to the European Parliament 1984*, Basingstoke, Macmillan. 211–27.
Lubbers, M. (2008) 'Regarding the Dutch "nee" to the European Constitution', *European Union Politics*, 9(10), 59–86.
Lucardie, P. (2008a) 'The Netherlands: Populism versus Pillarization', in Albertazzi, D. and McDonnell, D. (eds) *Twenty-First Century Populism: The Spectre of Western European Democracy*, New York, Palgrave Macmillan, 151–65.

Lucardie, P. (2008b) 'The Netherlands', *European Journal of Political Research, Political Data Yearbook 2007*, 47(7–8), 1074–78.

Oppenhuis, E. (1996) 'The Netherlands: Small Party Evolution', in Van der Eijk, C. and Franklin, M. N. (eds) *Choosing Europe? The European Electorate and National Politics in the Face of Union*, Ann Arbor, University of Michigan Press, 209–26.

Pellikaan, H. and Van Holsteyn, J. (2010) *Verkiezing van het Europees Parlement*, Amsterdam, Rozenburg.

Pellikaan, H., van der Meer T. and de Lange S. (2003) 'The Road From a Depoliticized to a Centrifugal Democracy', *Acta Politica*, 38 (1), 23–50.

SCP (2011) *Burgerperspectieven: Kwartaalbericht 2011–2*, Den Haag, SCP.

Synovate (2009), 'Nadere Analyse Europese Verkiezingen 2009', Press release 15 June 2009. Online. Available at: www.synovate.nl (accessed on 20 June 2009).

Thomassen, J. (2005) 'Nederlanders en Europa: Een Bekoelde Liefde?' in Aarts, K. and Van der Kolk, H. (eds) *Nederlanders en Europa: Het Referendum over de Europese Grondwet*, Amsterdam, Bert Bakker, 64–86.

Van den Berg, P., Borkus, B., Burggraaff, Loef, J., Van der Noort, W., Rothengatter, E., Sonck, N., and Wennekers, C. (2010) *Jaarevaluatie Postbus 51-Campagnes 2009*, Den Haag, Rijksvoorlichtingsdienst.

Van der Kolk, H. (2001) 'The Netherlands', in Lodge, J. (ed.) *The 1999 Elections to the European Parliament*, New York, St Martin's Press, 160–70.

Van Holsteyn, J. and den Ridder, J. (2005) 'Een reus in de polder? Nederlandse kiezers en het electorale belang van Europese integratie', in Vollaard, H. and Boer, B. (eds) *Euroscepsis in Nederland*, Utrecht, Lemma, 23–44.

Van Praag, Ph. and Brants, K. (2008) 'Professioneler, harder en populistischer: veranderingen in de campagnecultuur na 2002', *Bestuurskunde*, 3, 22–9.

Voerman, G. (2005a) 'De Nederlandse politieke partijen en de Europese integratie', in Aarts, K. and Van der Kolk, H. (eds) *Nederlanders en Europa. Het referendum over de Europese grondwet*, Amsterdam, Bert Bakker, 44–63.

Voerman, G. (2005b) 'Les élections européennes aux Pays-Bas', in Delwit, P. and Poirier, P. (eds) *Parlement puissant, électeurs absents? Les elections européennes de juin 2004*, Brussels, Editions de l'Université de Bruxelles, 115–30.

Voerman, G. and van der Walle, N. (2009) *Met het Oog op Europa: Affiches voor de Europese Verkiezingen 1979–2009*, Amsterdam, Boom.

Vollaard, H. (2006) 'Euro-scepticism and Protestantism in the Netherlands', *Perspectives on European Politics and Society*, 7(3), 276–97.

Vollaard, H. (2010), 'The Dutch Discourses of a Small Nation in an Inefficient Europe: Cosmopolitanism, Pragmatism, and Nationalism', in Harmsen, R. and Schild, J. (eds) *Debating Europe: The 2009 European Parliament Elections and Beyond*, Baden-Baden: Nomos, 85–103.

Voorhoeve, J. (1979) *Peace, Profits, and Principles: A Study of Dutch Foreign Policy*, Den Haag, Martinus Nijhoff.

9
LUXEMBOURG

Patrick Dumont, Raphaël Kies and Philippe Poirier

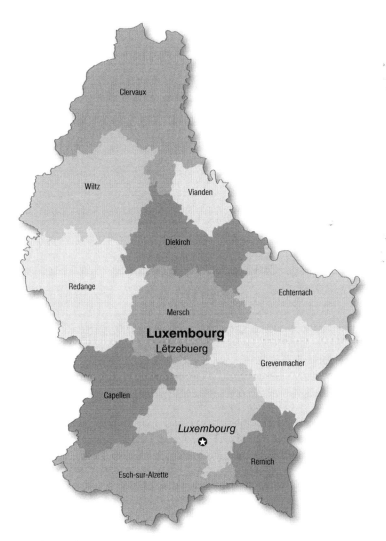

Figure 9.1 Map of Luxembourg

Table 9.1 Luxembourg profile

EU entry year	1952 ECSC; 1958 EEC founding member
Schengen entry year	1985 original signatory
MEPs elected in 2009	6
MEPs under Lisbon Treaty	6
Capital	Luxembourg
Total area★	2,586 km²
Population	549,680
	43.1% of foreigners including 37% Portuguese, 13% French, 9% Italians, 8% Belgians and 5.5% Germans
Population density★★	210.1/km²
Median age of population	39.2
Political system	Constitutional Monarchy
Head of state	Grand Duke Henri (October 2000–)
Head of government	Jean-Claude Juncker, Christian Democrats (CSV) (January 1995–July 2013); Xavier Bettel, Democratic Party (DP) (December 2013–)
Political majority	Christian Democrats (CSV) and Socialists (LSAP) Government Coalition, (July 2009–December 2013); Democratic Party (DP) Luxembourg Socialist Workers Party (LSAP) and The Green (*Gréng*) Government Coalition (December 2013–)
Currency	Euro (€) since 1999
Prohead GDP in PPS	83,200 € (2013)

Source: Eurostat, 2013, 2014, http://epp.eurostat.ec.europa.eu/.

Notes:
★ Total area including inland waters.
★★ Population density: the ratio of the annual average population of a region to the land area of the region.

1 Geographical position

Situated in north-western Europe, Luxembourg is a landlocked country bordered by Belgium to its north-west, Germany to its north-east and France to its south. With a territory of 2,586 square kilometres, Luxembourg represented the smallest EU Member State until Cyprus joined the European Union in 2004. The population of foreign residents increased from 17.1 per cent in 1981 to more than 43 per cent in 2009. This phenomenon raises an increasingly salient problem of democratic legitimacy, the most visible aspect of which is the limited participation of foreigners in the national public space and in local and EU elections.

2 Historical background

The Grand Duchy of Luxembourg was created by the Great Powers in Vienna in 1815, as a state distinct from the Kingdom of Netherlands, yet in personal union with the Dutch crown, and as a member of the German Confederation, after having been a French department from 1795, and having shared Belgium's institutional fate for several centuries. Between 1830 and 1839, after the Belgian Revolution, the Grand Duchy of Luxembourg, with the exception of its capital city, was integrated into the new Kingdom of Belgium. Under the Kingdom of William II, Luxembourg turned into a unified constitutional parliamentary monarchy and adopted its first liberal constitution in 1848 (Poirier, 2008, 134). At the London Conference in 1867, full political independence was obtained after the demise of the German Confederation, which made Luxembourg a neutral state guaranteed by the Great Powers. In 1890 a new era started with the end of the personal union with the Dutch crown and the ascent of the new Nassau dynasty to the throne. During the WW1 and WWII, Luxembourg's territorial integrity was violated by the Germans. Yet, the aftermath of WWII was much less problematic for Luxembourg on the international scene, as the legal government had fought the war from London with the allies.

3 Geopolitical profile

Mainly due to its size and its dependency on foreign markets, Luxembourg has traditionally favoured participation and loyalty to larger political and economic settings. It was therefore a founding member of all the major international organizations that promote economic, military, and political integration, including the European Coal and Steel Community (ECSC), the European Economic Community (EEC), and Euratom along with NATO, OECD, and the United Nations. Its sheer size – as compared to its powerful French and German neighbours – also largely accounts for the decision to establish in Luxembourg the executive of the ECSC, the High Authority, and, later, other EEC institutions such as the European Court of Justice, the European Investment Bank, and the European Court of Auditors, along with the General Secretariat of the European Parliament and several services of the Commission.

4 Overview of the political landscape

Luxembourg is a constitutional monarchy with a parliamentary democratic regime. Both the Chamber of Deputies and the monarch, represented in practice by the government, have the right to initiate legislation, whilst parliamentary assent is required to pass bills. Until 2009 the Grand Duke approved (with the counter-signature of a Cabinet Minister) and promulgated all bills. A revision of Article 34 of the Constitution withdrew the Grand Duke's prerogative to approve (*sanctionner*) legislation, following his refusal to endorse the law on euthanasia voted for by Parliament. Other bodies intervene in the legislative process, like the Council of State, designed in 1856 as the legal advisor to the government. The latter must issue an opinion on each bill or amendment before a final vote is taken in the Chamber and, since 1868, it may use its right to ask for a second 'constitutional' vote at least three months after the first parliamentary vote. This provision was introduced as a proxy for a second legislative chamber, which was felt inappropriate for a small country, as it provided for a period of reflection among deputies and a wider national debate among the population, before a legislative decision could be formally taken. In addition, from 1924, the elected professional chambers have to issue a non-binding opinion before the Chamber of Deputies can hold a final vote on bills relating to particular professional interests. Finally, the 1977 government bill created the 'tripartite committee' for crisis management, with the task of advising over key policies by issuing compulsory and binding recommendations. The Chamber of Deputies does not take part in this interchange between labour, employers and workers, and government representatives. This neo-corporatist device is of utmost importance and is therefore highly respected in Luxembourg (Hirsch, 1986). However, the failure to reach an agreement over the recent economic crisis has raised some doubts about its efficiency (Clément, 2011). Finally, other institutions controlling or supplementing the activity of elected politicians have been created: a Constitutional Court in 1996, a Court of Auditors in 1999, and the office of the Ombudsman in 2004.

5 Brief account of the political parties

From the end of WWI, the *Chrëschtlech Sozial Vollekspartei*, CSV (Christian Social People's Party) dominated the Grand Duchy's political landscape, always leading national cabinets except for the 1925–1926 and 1974–1979 periods. Founded in 1914 as the *Parti de la Droite/Partei der Rechten* in order to balance the power of the liberal political elites of the newly independent state, it adopted its present name in December 1944. Originally drawing most of its electorate from rural areas, it soon extended its influence to the working class through the development of a Catholic trade union. Stemming from the Liberal–Conservative cleavage, yet inspired by Catholic social doctrine, the party increasingly put emphasis on socio-economic questions, while keeping rather conservative views of society that guaranteed the support of the traditional rural and Christian population. The party relies on its traditional 'pillar' organization, based on local elites covering the whole territory, and an important presence in all layers of the national civil service allowed by its almost continuous leadership of the cabinets. Overall it claims about 10,000 members.

The second largest party, the *Lëtzebuerger Sozialistesch Arbechterpartei*, LSAP (the Socialist Party), which adopted its present name after WWII, was founded in 1902 as the Social Democratic Party and renamed in 1924 as the Workers' Party to reflect its role as political branch of the workers' movement. Over the years, the LSAP has most often been the junior party of the CSV in government.

The Socialist Party had to live through the 1921 breakaway of members forming the Communist Party on its left, and the formation in the early 1970s of a splinter party, the Social Democratic Party, on its right. The Socialists entered government in 1937 and contributed with the CSV to the establishment of a strong welfare system. From 1974 to 1979, they governed with the *Demokratesch Partei* (DP) and initiated more liberal legislation, for instance on abortion. The LSAP's electoral strongholds are situated in the highly populated and historically industrial southern constituency bordering France, but the party also represents the most powerful party at the local level. Even though formal links with the powerful Socialist trade union have decreased in the last decades, effective collaboration nevertheless remains visible for a political organization that retains the characteristics of a mass party, relying nowadays on about 6,000 members.

The DP (The Liberal Party) is the third largest party in the country and also the leading one in the capital city. It has improved its membership rate since the 2011 local elections and the emergence of popular new figures such as the new mayor of Luxembourg city, thus claiming about 6,000 members. Founded in 1904 as the Liberal League, the party adopted its present name in 1955. The Liberals used to dominate parliamentary politics as long as universal suffrage was not implemented, defending a liberal state rather than the maintenance of Catholic Church prerogatives, and modernization through industrialization rather than rural and agricultural interests. Successive and sometimes parallel movements and parties organized the Liberal camp around notabilities, making the DP the political force for which voters cast most preferential votes. Although the DP has long balanced between socially liberal and more conservative factions, it has generally favoured minimal state intervention in the economy and taken liberal views of society.

Like their sister parties in neighbouring countries, the Greens emerged as a new social movement, later becoming the fourth largest party in Luxembourg. The first Green Party organization was founded in 1983 but competition between purely environmentalist and new left tendencies, combined with personal ambitions, led to the creation of separate parties until the 1990s. Since the 2000s, the *Gréng* have positioned themselves as centrist on socio-economic issues and libertarian on social issues but have not yet managed to enter national government. The *Alternativ*

Table 9.2 List of political parties in Luxembourg

Original name	Abbreviation	English translation
Alternativ Demokratesch Reformpartei	ADR	Alternative Democratic Reform Party
Chrëschtlech Sozial Vollekspartei	CSV	Christian Social People Party
Lëtzebuerger Sozialistesch Arbechterpartei	LSAP	Luxembourg Socialist Workers Party
Déi Lénk	*Lénk*	The Left
Déi Gréng	*Gréng*	The Greens
Demokratesch Partei	DP	Democratic Party
Kommunistesch Partei Lëtzebuerg	KPL	Communist Party of Luxembourg
Biergerlëscht	*Biergerlëscht*	Citizens' List

Demokratesch Reformpartei, ADR (Alternative Democratic Reform Party) created in 1987 as the Five-Sixths Action Committee, initially focussed on the single issue of universal entitlement to pensions worth five-sixths of final salary. The party, placed on the Conservative right of the political spectrum, is led by notables adopting anti-consociational democracy and anti-corruption discourse, and finds its support mainly in the rural north but also among craftsmen, small businessmen, and qualified workers in the south.

Finally, the *Kommunistesch Partei Lëtzebuerg*, KPL (Communist Party of Luxembourg), founded in 1921, took part in the first post-war national unity coalition cabinet in 1945. Its peak of electoral support, mainly due to its stronghold in the southern, industrial constituency, dates back to the late 1960s. The party remained aligned to the Soviets throughout the Cold War, rather than engaging in Eurocommunism. It also did not change many of its policy positions after the collapse of the Iron Curtain and lost representation in the Chamber of Deputies in 1994. This ideological rigidity led some members to found the *Néi Lénk* Movement, which became the *Lénk* (The Left), gathering former Socialists, Greens, Trotskyists, and trade unionists who aimed at offering a modern alternative to the KPL.

5.1 Party attitudes towards the European Union

Since the 1950s, the main parties in Luxembourg have been strong supporters of EU integration. The Christian Democrats (CSV) were, together with their counterparts in the founding Member States, crucial in the setting up of the European integration process and are still nowadays strong defenders of the Community method. Even though their attitude is genuinely Euro-enthusiastic, the subtle discourse of their party leaders, who have also been almost permanently responsible for defending the country's national interests, can sometimes take a somewhat sovereignist tone. Over the years, prominent CSV figures emerged, such as Pierre Werner, who was decisive in solving the 'empty chair crisis' of 1965 and who drafted the blueprint for an economic and monetary union, as well as Jacques Santer, who was the President of the European Commission from 1995 to 1999, and Prime Minister Jean-Claude Juncker, who has been President of the Euro-group since the creation of a semi-permanent position in 2005.

Although the Socialist Party LSAP and the Liberal DP have at times shown signs of a declining Euro-optimism, they remain in favour of European integration for different reasons. The Greens, starting with a less enthusiastic view of European integration, have increasingly come to support it. Overall then, amongst the above-mentioned four main parties, there is no real cleavage and certainly no polarization at the party political level on European issues. The other parties, which can be defined as Eurosceptical, bear only marginal electoral weight. On the one hand, the sovereignist Conservative party ADR, and on the other, the radical left parties KPL and the *Lénk,* have distinctive critiques on European integration and varying degrees of opposition to the way this process is taking place, but only the Communists plead for the dissolution of the European Union, which they argue should be replaced by another organization forged by a European Constitutional Assembly.

6 Public opinion and the European Union

According to the Autumn 2009 Eurobarometer (Eurobarometer 72), Luxembourg's public opinion comes first amongst the 27 EU countries in considering EU membership positively, at 74 per cent, against the EU average of 53 per cent, and in believing that their national interests are well taken care of by the European Union, at 65 per cent, against the EU average of 39 per cent. Also in terms of subjective knowledge, Luxembourg stands out from all other Member States, since 63 per cent of its population claims to be well aware of the functioning of the European Union, against the EU average of 44 per cent. Luxembourg's residents are also far more likely than the EU average to trust the European Parliament and the European Commission, and to be satisfied with the level of democracy in Europe, at 75 per cent, against the EU average of 54 per cent. They also are more likely to consider the euro to be a good thing, at 80 per cent, against the EU average of 60 per cent. The only issue on which Luxembourg's population is clearly more critical than the EU average concerns enlargement: 74 per cent consider that the EU has expanded too rapidly and only 39 per cent are in favour of including new countries in the EU, putting the country amongst the most reluctant Member States on the issue. This has generally been the picture of Luxembourg's public opinion, although nuances have gradually appeared in recent decades.

Luxembourg was one of the first countries to ratify the Maastricht Treaty, which was adopted on 27 July 1992 by a large majority in parliament, including its unconstitutional provisions after the three traditional parties agreed that the relevant articles would be declared open for revision in 1994. This episode marked one of the first breaches in the general political consensus shared by the political class, the social forces of the country, and its population on EU integration. Questions of European citizenship and the right of EU residents to vote in local elections divided the population, as some saw these as potential threats to national sovereignty and identity in a country where, at the time, about 30 per cent of residents were foreigners.

And yet, only the 2005 referendum on the Constitutional Treaty unveiled a major gap between the political elites and citizens on the issue of EU integration in Luxembourg. Comparative analyses on data from the 2004 European Election Study had already showed that the Grand Duchy was amongst the Member States in which the distance between citizens and parties on EU integration was the greatest, with the former considering the latter to be 'too' EU supportive (Mattila and Raunio, 2006, 438). In 2005, whilst political elites were expecting massive backing of the treaty, only 56.5 per cent of the voting population supported its adoption. The lack of congruence between citizens and their representatives was blatant, as the proportion of MPs belonging to parties that campaigned against the European Constitution in 2005 was only 8.3 per cent, compared with 43.5 per cent of 'No' votes. Unlike France and the Netherlands, the key element determining people's negative responses did not stem from concerns over the socio-economic situation of the country, but rather from their opinion on the European Constitutional Treaty itself. The question of national identity and Turkey's application to enter the European Union also ranked high on the list of negative motivations. On the other hand, those who supported the adoption of the Constitution above all voted according to their general opinion on the EU (Dumont *et al.,* 2007). Despite the highest per capita GDP and a low level of unemployment – just above 4 per cent – the economic situation was perceived at the time as bad by almost one-third of Luxembourgers, as the rate of unemployment literally doubled in the preceding four years. Luxembourgers became among the most pessimistic Europeans about the evolution of unemployment. They were also increasingly concerned about the arrival of refugees, which started in the 1990s with the Balkan crisis and illegal immigration. A correlation was made in the minds of many inhabitants between these phenomena and increased criminality, with the European Union as the ultimate authority responsible for these problems. The 'No' Movement in Luxembourg, initially fuelled by the 'No' campaigns in France and the Netherlands, gained momentum in July 2004 with the setting up of a committee gathering civil society associations and the extreme left party (the *Lénk*). At the end of the campaign, the strong personal involvement of key politicians, and in particular of the popular Prime Minister Jean-Claude Juncker, persuaded Luxembourg citizens to back the European Constitution.

7 National and EP electoral systems

Luxembourg citizens aged between 18 and 75 are obliged to vote for the election of the 60 deputies for a five-year term. Proportional representation is based on four electoral constituencies: the South elects 23 deputies, the Centre 21, the North nine and the East seven. In each of the constituencies, citizens have the same number of votes as there are seats to be filled and may cast them for a single party list, the so-called list vote, or they may vote for candidates of one or more than one party, referred to as inter-party *panachage*.

In the 2004 general elections, at least half of the citizens expressed a preferential vote for candidates of one or several lists rather than a list vote (Dumont *et al.*, 2006, 2011). This result was confirmed in 2009, when no less than 52.8 per cent of citizens expressed such a vote, with a 2 per cent increase compared to 2004. This proportion is only somewhat lower for the EP elections, at 48.8 per cent, and the gap shrank in 2009, since the proportion of citizens choosing to vote for candidates instead of expressing simply a list vote increased by 4 per cent more than that of the national elections. In addition, for both types of elections, the proportion of votes given through inter-party *panachage* has doubled in 30 years: in 2009 four out of ten voters expressed a preference for candidates of different parties, confirming people's inclination to vote for personalities rather than parties and ideologies. Electoral studies since the 1970s show that parties that used to be of a 'cadre' type and still present well-known politicians, such as the Liberals, usually benefit from inter-party *panachage*, whereas those traditionally relying on a well-defined ideology and newer parties, such as the radical left parties and the sovereignist ADR, have more disciplined electorates expressing list votes.

Luxembourg's proportional electoral system has led to the constant need to form coalition governments in order to gain a majority in Parliament, except for the 1921–1925 period. Such a need and the proximity between voters and their representatives in a small society has constrained political competition, with parties aggregating the social demands of their electorate but refraining from claiming radical policy changes in order to remain 'coalitionable' (Dumont and De Winter, 2000). As a result, the political system as a whole can be seen as an ideal-typical consensus democracy. Nevertheless, since 1979 the pivotal Christian-Social party (CSV) has dominated the government formation process in this consensus democracy (Dumont *et al.*, 2010, 1076).

Traditionally, elections to the European Parliament are fought on the same day as national elections. Yet, contrary to the latter, there is only a single constituency that elects the six Luxembourg representatives. Up until 2004, party lists consisted of 12 candidates. This led to the practice of putting party heavyweights on both the national list, where they could fight the elections in their own constituency, and the European list, where they could attract votes from all over the country. As government formation negotiations at the national level usually start before the first meeting of the EP, those heavyweights had the time to choose between the two mandates, and if their party made it to government they resigned from their EP seat to be appointed as cabinet ministers. As a result, MEPs from the Luxembourg delegation were mostly non-elected, low profile figures. This was, for instance, the case for all three CSV members in the preceding EP term. The 2008 reform, which reduced the number of candidates running for the European elections from 12 to 6, encouraged parties to present candidates actually committed to taking up their seats in Strasbourg and Brussels. Legislation forbidding double candidatures would have been a potential alternative, but Luxembourg parties preferred to keep this possibility open. The four parties with representation in the EP reached an agreement on this issue in the second part of 2008. Only the smaller parties did not commit themselves to presenting separate lists, due to their lack of popular figures. Note also that a majority of candidates on EP lists should have Luxembourg nationality. On the other hand, no legally specified quota for gender was introduced. The 2008 reform also allowed citizens to cast up to two personal votes for the same candidate, a possibility that already existed for national elections. This evolution towards the same system as the one used for national elections made the European contest more competitive.

Finally, it is worth recalling that voting is compulsory in Luxembourg for all kinds of elections and in the case of EP elections, this obligation therefore extends to EU residents. The time gap between the electoral registration of EU citizens and the date of these EP elections has been reduced from almost a year to roughly three months in accordance with the December 2008 Electoral Reform. The residency requirement for EU citizens to be allowed to vote in these elections has also been reduced from five to two years. As a result, the proportion of registered foreign voters almost quadrupled in four elections and in 2009 accounted for 11.5 per cent of the electorate.

8 A glance at EP and national elections

Ever since 1958, regardless of the change from indirect to direct elections, the successive enlargements, and corresponding increases in size of the Assembly, the Grand Duchy of Luxembourg sends six MEPs to the European Parliament. The CSV has always been the strongest European party in the country, usually delivering three of the six representatives, except for the 1994–1999 and 1999–2004 terms, when only two returned to the Strasbourg arena. Up until 1994, the remaining EP seats were divided between Socialists and Liberals, but since then the Greens have managed to secure one seat as well. On the other hand, none of the smaller and less EU-enthusiastic parties ever reached representation in the Euro-parliamentary Assembly. In 1979, the first EP direct elections took place in a specific context, both by European and Luxembourg standards. Compared to other Member States, the Grand Duchy was the only country in which these elections were held at the same time as the national ones. For the first time since 1926, the Christian Democrats were excluded from governing office. The incumbent coalition had sought to modernize the country's legislation on ethical issues, such as abortion and divorce, and introduced the 'tripartite' mechanism of dialogue with social partners to deal with an iron and steel industry severely hit by crisis and in need of restructuring. Eight lists competed for the EP election, three of them being of negligible importance, resulting from the internal splits of the radical left and the Liberals, and carrying varied stances against capitalist or anti-democratic Europe as well as against the privileges of 'Eurocrats'. Three other lists, among which a dissident Socialist one, that proved a bit more successful in the concurrent national contests, did not present candidates for the EP, enhancing differences in party results across elections. This was especially the case in the EP elections of the Liberals, benefitting from a highly personalized combat between their leader, incumbent Prime Minister Gaston Thorn and his predecessor Pierre Werner. These two well-known political figures at both national and European levels successfully overshadowed Socialist candidates. Despite their party's attempt to bring a more regional dimension to the EP campaign, the Luxembourg Socialists – along with their counterparts in the neighbouring German and French regions – drafted a common manifesto outlining the common economic problems of these industrial areas in crisis. Yet, this gave the impression that the Socialists only cared about their stronghold in the south of the country (Hirsch, 1986, 146). The only relevant anti-European party in competition, the KPL, also brought the issue of the dismantling of industry in the transnational region, together with German and French comrades, to the heart of its campaign. According to this party, German hegemony, under US influence, in the conduct of European affairs threatened Luxembourg's sovereignty through the restructuring of the industrial backbone of the country's economy and employment.

The main issue of the 1984 EP electoral campaign was again the fate of the steel industry, with the reunited Socialist party in the opposition blaming, together with the Communists, the cuts in production demanded by the European Commission's Davignon Plan as well as the consequences of the Belgian government's unilateral decision in 1982 to devaluate the Belgian and Luxembourgish franc. Other European-related questions that concerned Luxembourg were the European Parliament's seat and EC enlargement.

As to the former, the Grand Duchy was penalized by decisions to hold EP meetings only in Brussels and Strasbourg, although it retained the EP General Secretariat and limited transfers of staff to the other seats. The latter was due to the fact that Portugal, which already represented about half of the foreigners living in Luxembourg, was about to become a Member State, thereby potentially involving further massive immigration under the context of free movement of labour. Again, some European or transnational party campaign activities were organized, but as in 1979 the campaign was mostly national for both parties and the media. The EP electoral results largely mirrored those in the Chamber of Deputies, with the LSAP winning an additional seat at the expense of the DP. All outgoing members took back their seats in Strasbourg, but only one for his own electoral achievements, the other two being substitutes for those elected MEPs who resigned after being appointed as national ministers.

Table 9.3 National elections in Luxembourg: 1979–2009 (%)

Political party	1979	1984	1989	1994	1999	2004	2009
CSV	36.4	36.7	32.4	30.3	30.1	36.1	38.0
LSAP	22.5	31.8	26.2	25.4	22.3	23.4	21.6
DP	21.9	20.4	17.2	19.3	22.4	16.1	15.0
Gréng	—	4.2	8.6	9.9	9.1	11.6	11.7
ADR	—	—	7.9	9.0	11.3	10.0	8.1
KPL	4.9	4.4	4.4	2.4	—	0.9	1.5
Lénk	—	—	—	—	3.3	1.9	3.3
BL	—	—	—	—	—	—	0.8
SDP	6.4	—	—	—	—	—	—
Others	8.0	2.6	3.3	3.7	1.6	0.1	—
Total	100.0	100.0	100.0	100.0	100.0	100.0	100.0

Source: Election Reports, CRISP 1979–1994; ELECT, University of Luxembourg, 1999–2009.

The three large parties lost heavily in the 1989 national election, due to the breakthrough of the Green lists and the direct success of the ADR, which ran for the first time – albeit only for the Chamber of Deputies. This absence in the EP contest enabled the CSV, contrary to the LSAP and DP, to maintain its 1984 electoral result. The three parties kept their EP seats despite the aggregate gains of the Greens, who ran on separate tickets. The failure of the Liberals to benefit from their opposition status was largely due to a lack of cohesion that affected the party after the departure of its leader, Thorn, to head the European Commission. Therefore, the DP adopted a more radical approach during the next term, for instance by taking neo-liberal stances on the economy and taking fewer Euro-enthusiast positions than usual during the debates over the ratification of the Maastricht Treaty, due to the latter's provisions on political rights and European citizenship. The Liberals called for a referendum or at least a constitutional revision in order to implement the treaty in the Grand Duchy, before its ratification in Parliament. Next to a profoundly divided DP, the debates over the Maastricht Treaty saw the opposition of the ADR coasting on potential threats to national sovereignty and identity, and that of the Greens and Communist MPs on the lack of social and environmental measures. The opening of the EP elections to European residents and memories of the 1992 debates were reflected in the composition of the lists in 1994, as all of the main parties, except for the DP and the ADR, comprised one foreign candidate. A still divided DP claimed equality of treatment among Member States, a preference for enlargement rather than the deepening of the EU, and the importance of the subsidiarity principle. The united Greens criticized the Maastricht Treaty for its convergence criteria, whilst the ADR insisted on the subsidiarity principle to safeguard Luxembourg's sovereignty and identity. Small, extreme right-wing lists raised the issue of safeguarding national identity. The LSAP – as the junior government party in charge of the Foreign Affairs Ministry – defended the achievements of Luxembourg's negotiators but nevertheless mentioned its will to safeguard national sovereignty within the EU, while the party of the PM Jacques Santer clearly appeared the most integrationist party in the political landscape.

In January 1995, Santer left the leadership of the coalition government to take the presidency of the European Commission. Civil service reform led to massive opposition by the latter's trade union and a large demonstration at the end of the term. At stake was the question of pensions, but also access to public sector employment in the context of the opening of some jobs to competition between nationals and European citizens. Despite their previous neo-liberal positions on the civil service and the welfare system, the Liberals seized the opportunity to contest a governmental reform that appeared to endanger the monopoly of public jobs for nationals, and therefore voters. This strategic move as the defender of national identity on this issue also allowed them to demarcate their position from that of the ADR, which originally defended private sector employees and denounced the advantages of the public sector. The resignation of the Santer Commission provided another potential problem close to the elections, which was, however, not exploited by the opposition and the press, as one would have expected, since the former PM appeared more like a victim than guilty of any kind of fraud. He even led the list of his party for the EP election, whereas his former Vice-Prime Minister, Poos, who wished to end his national career, led the Socialist one. The Greens had to fight to gain back their seat, as their incumbent MEP left the party to create another. They managed to win it but left the seat to a candidate with poor electoral support, all more successful candidates having resigned to sit in the national Parliament instead. The composition of Luxembourg's delegation to the EP did not change, although Viviane Reding replaced Juncker when the latter renewed his position as Prime Minister, and resigned in turn when she became a member of the European Commission, leaving her seat to Astrid Lulling.

In 2004, once again, the main political parties focussed their campaign on national issues such as economic growth and unemployment, education, and transport. The outgoing government appeared to have preserved Luxembourg's main national economic interest, the competitiveness of its financial centre, mainly ensured by its banking secrecy laws. Another issue on which Juncker led the game was that of granting double nationality, under certain conditions, to residents working in Luxembourg. Juncker's electoral success on the single constituency brought his party to over 37 per cent, a level never reached in the EP elections, allowing it to gain back the third seat it had lost during the two previous terms. By contrast, the Socialists lost for the fourth time in a row in the European races, but managed to get back in power thanks to their slightly better score in the national elections. This change of coalition government was facilitated by the heavy defeat of the CSV's junior partner, the Liberals even being bypassed by the Greens in votes in the EP election.

9 The 2009 European election

9.1 Party lists and manifestos

Drawing on the work of Patrick Dumont and Astrid Spreitzer (2010), we note that opposition parties, especially smaller and less Euro-enthusiastic ones, were the first to engage in the 2009 EP campaign portraying the European elections as a new referendum on the Lisbon Treaty. Parties of the radical left published their platforms for the European elections as early as January 2009, by asserting that voting for them could contribute towards punishing the 'ultraliberal Europe' of the Lisbon Treaty, the globalization of markets and the dominance of the financial sector on the economy. The Communists (KPL) called for a pure and simple dissolution of the EU, which always served the purposes of the free market, whilst the *Lénk* sought to re-establish a new European Union, which would be more interventionist in the economy and also more democratic. As a result, the EP would have more powers, the European Commission should be elected by citizens, and referenda would be held for treaty changes.

In June 2008, the ADR announced its agreement with the British Conservatives to form a common group in the European Parliament with other MEPs from the new Member States. Such an alliance was considered by the party leadership both as a political resource in the forthcoming electoral battle in Luxembourg and as an extension of the campaign on the European Constitutional Treaty. The ADR wanted to appear as the sole champion of liberal sovereignism and supported a 'Europe of Nations'. It campaigned against the entry of other Member States to the European Union, especially Turkey, and called for referenda in case of any envisaged enlargements. It insisted on the defence of national identity through the promotion of the Luxembourgish language and the non-opening of civil service jobs to non-nationals.

The newcomer *Biergerlëscht*, created by a former ADR national MP, opposed the adoption of the Lisbon Treaty by claiming to represent the 43 per cent of Luxembourg's population who voted against the European Constitutional Treaty. It campaigned for a more social Europe, but also adopted similar views to the ADR on the need to recognize Luxembourgish as one of the official EU languages and the advent of a Europe of independent nations, where small countries would keep their veto rights.

In autumn 2008, the Liberals and Greens nominated their leaders and announced their priorities for European Union policies. They were more pro-integration than the smaller opposition parties, both pointing at the international role of the EU in promoting human rights and development, with the *Gréng* naturally insisting on the need to cooperate in order to fight climate change. They nevertheless diverged regarding the liberalization policies of the EU that were promoted by the DP and criticized by the Greens for becoming ends rather than means. They broadly agreed on the inefficiency of European economic governance and called for a more dynamic Europe and the need for further European integration on environmental, migration, and ethical issues.

In January 2009, the government parties CSV and LSAP officially launched their campaigns for the European elections and presented their lists two months later in March 2009. Both parties stressed the importance of the Lisbon Treaty as an adequate response to the challenges of a social Europe and considered EP elections to be a good opportunity to explain the functioning of European governance. The two parties differed in the importance given to the platforms of their European political parties. Although the CSV was the only one with the DP to issue a specific programme for the European elections, its campaign remained primarily a national one. It claimed to be the *Luxemburgische Europapartei* (Luxembourgish Party for Europe), but considered that since Europe was rooted in the heart of the country, the electoral campaign should explain the interdependence between national and European interests. From a socio-economic perspective, Europe was considered to be the best answer to the challenge of globalization in terms of economic stability and negotiation power on the world scene, as well as regarding development policy. The Socialist Party (LSAP) was the only party that referred explicitly to the European manifesto in its general programme for national and EP elections. The party presented the European elections as a referendum against the majority of European governments dominated by the Conservatives, depicted as co-responsible actors of the deviancies of European capitalism. The LSAP considered that European integration was not a threat to national identity and proposed setting European symbols, by introducing, for instance, 9 May as a holiday across the EU, in order to promote European identity.

In sum, all programmes except the Communist one, described Luxembourg's membership in the EU as a necessity for the Grand Duchy, and only varied in terms of the evaluation of the benefits it provided or threats it represented to the country and its inhabitants, as well as the reforms to be undertaken. In addition, it is interesting to note that some candidates drafted separate manifestos. In his personal electoral platform, Charles Goerens, the leader of the Liberal list adopted a more critical stance than that of his party regarding the political functioning of the European Union. He insisted on the principle of equality between Member States and rejected the *de facto* creation of a German, British, and French directorate in Europe. Most parties rejected this 'directorate' on the grounds that it would endanger the community method or even threaten Luxembourg's national interests. In addition, Goerens was concerned about the lack of action by the European Commission and the European Central Bank since the economic and financial crisis emerged in autumn 2008.

Only a third of all candidates were already on EP lists in 2004, a reproduction rate well below the national level of 46.5 per cent. In addition, the percentage of candidates holding a political mandate, either local, national or European, decreased to 35.4, half of that achieved in 2004. This vertiginous drop was largely due to a decision by the major parties to ban dual candidatures on both the European and national lists and to their strategy of positioning their most well-known candidates for national election and draft lists of new or unknown candidates pulled by a leader with recognized EU competence for the EP contest. The average age of EP candidates was 51, a decrease compared with 2004, with a particularly young Green list of 42, compared to the LSAP's average age of 57. The 2009 Euro-elections witnessed the highest number of female candidates, corresponding to 35.4 per cent, since the first EP elections in 1979. A similar trend could be observed concerning the participation of foreign candidates whose presence increased steadily, from 6.8 per cent in 1994 to 8.3 per cent in 1999 and 11.9 per cent in 2004, to

16.7 per cent, with 7 out of 42 in 2009. Four of the seven foreign candidates were Portuguese, one was Italian, one French, and one German.

9.2 Electoral campaign

As in all other Member States, a multimedia 'choice box' was installed for about a month, from mid-April to mid-May, in Luxembourg city centre in order to let citizens record their questions through video messages. In addition, there were posters at bus stops and on buses raising themes discussed in European arenas that were likely to affect the everyday lives of European citizens. This topic was also the subject of a conference organized in January by the Luxembourg Office of the European Parliament (OEP), together with the Luxembourg representation of the Commission, the European Movement of Luxembourg, and the European Consumer Centre. In March, the OEP also jointly co-organized another conference that punctuated efforts at informing and encouraging European citizens to register for elections, through the issuing of multilingual folders and posters, made together with the Luxembourg representation of the Commission, the national government, and foreigners' associations. Finally, the most well-known sports champions of the country, cyclists Andy and Frank Schleck, also participated in a European-wide video campaign, visible on the internet and encouraging young citizens to go to vote for European elections.

Even though the interest for the European elections and campaign was comparatively strong in Luxembourg, data from the 2009 post-electoral survey among national citizens showed that it did not reach the level of the national and local elections.

Concerning the political campaign, 70.5 per cent of voters were interested in the national legislative campaign, while only 51.6 per cent were interested in the European elections. As a result, whereas 77.5 per cent of respondents declared that they would still always participate in national elections if voting was not compulsory, for the European elections this proportion was only 63.7 per cent. As could be expected, the efforts of the European Parliament in its transnational campaign to increase turnout in the elections went almost unnoticed in Luxembourg, where voting is compulsory.

From 1979, the European election campaign was less visible in the media than the national one. An analysis of media reporting showed that the four main national newspapers devoted about 73 per cent of their election campaign reports to the national elections only, those covering the European elections amounted to less than 19 per cent, and the rest mixed the two (Huberty, 2009). Another way of assessing the coverage of the EP campaign is to compare it with such media reporting in the other Member States. According to the Piredeu research programme (www.piredeu.eu), media coverage of EU news including the EP election increased in 2009 in Luxembourg as it did in most Member States.

Both television newscasts and newspaper front pages contained a higher proportion of EU-related items than during the campaigns of the previous EP elections (Schuck et al., 2011). In particular, by comparing the proportions of newspaper front pages dedicated to EU affairs to the 2009 figures, it is possible to see a steady increase from less than 4 per cent in 1994 to almost 10 per cent in 2009, the proportion was about 6.5 per cent in 2004 (de Vreese et al., 2006, 488; Schuck et al., 2011). Another noticeable evolution is the increase in the visibility of EU actors vis-à-vis domestic actors within EU-related news, from about 12 per cent in 2004 to more than 40 per cent in 2009, putting Luxembourg in this regard amongst the most 'Europeanized' countries (de Vreese et al., 2004, 492; Schuck et al., 2011, 48). This change could partly be due to the change in the electoral system, as most candidates for the EP election are neither candidates for the simultaneously held national ones anymore, nor incumbent national figures. Notice also that RTL, Luxembourg's radio and television company, did broadcast the results of an opinion survey revealing that Europe was clearly not one of the main concerns for Luxembourg citizens, but that, as indeed in most other member countries, the economy was the most salient issue for the 2009 EP election.

The party campaign looked similar to that of previous EP elections, with each party organizing either one or a couple of meetings exclusively on European issues, even though candidates for the EP elections often appeared in more general meetings. There were no signs that the parties spent more than the 10–15 per cent of the general campaign budget that they declared to have devoted to the EP election in 2004 (Dumont et al., 2006). Note, however, that by comparative standards, candidates for the EP elections in Luxembourg spend on average 2.5 times more money than the EU average and only Ireland comes close to Luxembourg in these terms (Giebler and Wüst, 2011). On the other hand, Luxembourg candidates appear to engage less time in campaigning than the EU average, 25 hours instead of an EU average of 37 hours. The electoral survey conducted in 2009 further shows that the campaigning instruments were much less effective at reaching the electorate for the EP elections than for the national ones. More than half of respondents, 56.6 per cent, declared having received election flyers, but parties reached less than one voter out of ten with all other modes of outreach. In addition to flyers, Facebook was the most effective way to contact voters. In particular, 8.5 per cent of respondents were contacted by an EP candidate through the social network. This relatively high score of Facebook is explained by the fact that more than half, 54.2 per cent, of the Euro-candidates had a profile on that social network. These results corroborate the findings of the Piredeu candidate survey revealing that Luxembourg candidates relied more on 'post-modern' campaign tools, involving the use of the internet, and less on the 'pre-modern' ones of canvassing, flyers, posters, or public debates than the EU average.

The sources of information that the electors used *sometimes* or *often* for making their choice on the European elections were primarily the press, 70.5 per cent, which also remains the most influential source according to respondents; discussions among friends and family, 67.2 per cent; television, 66 per cent; and radio, 52.6 per cent, with the latter two coming second and third in terms of influential sources. While all these sources appear to have been used more often than in 2004, the internet – 21 per cent – no less than tripled its score. Online 'Voting Advice Applications' (VAAs), which in Luxembourg was *EU-profiler*, contributed to the information on EP elections for one respondent out of ten, a similar proportion to those who participated in electoral meetings. These findings suggest that there was more interest by the electorate than in the preceding European campaign. This greater interest in the European elections may derive from both the 2008 electoral reform and an agreement by the major parties, aimed at rendering these elections more visible and competitive.

Table 9.4 Sources of information at the 2004 and 2009 EP elections in Luxembourg (%)

	2009 EP election	2004 EP election	Difference
Press	70.5	59.8	+10.7
Discussion	67.2	62.3	+4.9
Television	66.0	49.8	+16.2
Radio	52.6	—	—
Internet	21.0	7.0	+14.0
Meetings	11.0	3.5	+7.5
VAA (EU-profiler)	10.5	—	—

Source: ELECT 2004 and 2009 post-electoral survey (N respectively=1,335 and 1,267).

Table 9.5 The 2009 electoral campaigning tools in Luxembourg (%)

	EP elections	National elections	Difference
Flyers	56.6	88.4	−31.8
Facebook	8.5	23.0	−14.5
Meet in market/street	8.2	36.0	−27.8
Newsletter	7.7	34.2	−26.5
Public meetings	5.8	27.0	−21.2
Email	3.5	17.8	−14.3
Work	1.5	10.0	−8.5
Home	0.5	4.8	−4.3
Phone	0.1	1.5	−1.4
SMS	0.1	2.6	−2.5

Source: ELECT 2009 post-electoral survey (N=1,267).

Aside from the fact that citizens, the media, and political parties have a stronger interest in national elections that take place at the same time, there are other reasons that can explain the lack of visibility of European issues. First, the lower number of European candidates compared to national ones, 48 versus 452, makes the individual action of candidates less effective and noticeable. Another reason is that despite increases in the politicization of the issue in the 1990s and 2005, the European dimension remains far from being a political cleavage opposing two camps of equally balanced weight in Luxembourg.

The economic and financial crisis was high on the agenda throughout 2008 and clearly during the 2009 electoral campaign. In one year the unemployment rate rose from 5 per cent in December 2008 to 6.3 per cent in December 2009, a level the country had never reached in the last few decades. The massive increase in youth unemployment, the hiring decline in the financial sectors, the strong decrease in the agricultural economy, its 2009 income down by 25 per cent according to Eurostat, as well as the decline in temporary work, were all elements that confirmed the severe character of the crisis. For the national elections all political parties were able to position themselves on these crisis issues, from the need to diversify Luxembourg's economy rather than concentrating on the financial sector (CSV), for a greater role for the state in the economy (LSAP and radical left parties), to a criticism of the international financial system in a global economy (DP), and the need for cuts in underperforming areas of the public sector (ADR). In addition to the social crisis, several events influenced, at least indirectly, the EP electoral campaign.

In April, Luxembourg was placed by the OECD on the 'grey list' of countries that do not respect international standards against fiscal evasion and money laundering. This was a particularly sensitive issue, not only because it could lead to a further weakening of the financial sector that represents 34 per cent of state revenues but also because it could provoke the weakening of Luxembourg at the European level, particularly during negotiations on the economic governance of the European Union. This event led to an important debate in the country opposing, on the one hand, those supporting strong protection of national economic interests and privacy over personal financial data, including banking secrecy, and, on the other hand, those promoting greater moralization of the financial system. Critics of the German and French governments characterizing Luxembourg as a 'tax haven' to be eliminated in the fight against the global crisis were in any case badly received by both the political elite and the population. As a result, whether they were 'federalists' or more Eurosceptic, Luxembourg's candidates for the EP elections campaigned together against the growing threat of a 'directorate of the big Member States' in the EU. Further, let us note that the declarations of Prime Minister Juncker during the campaign also fuelled some discussions within and outside Luxembourg. First, in January, he was the main guest of the twenty-ninth conference of *Bündnis 90/Die Grünen* in Dortmund. In his introduction, the co-chairman of the German Green Party, Cem Özdemir, declared that their invitation to a Christian Democrat statesman to speak at their convention for the first time was due to the fact that they shared with him a vision that all political parties were invited to share in making the European project more attractive for all citizens. The acceptance of such an invitation was, however, diversely appreciated among the European People's Party and especially the German Christian Democratic ranks. In the Grand Duchy, several parties invited well-known figures from neighbouring countries who belonged to their European party, such as Daniel Cohn-Bendit for the *Gréng*, Martin Schulz for the LSAP, and Alain Krivine for the *Lénk*. Second, at the end of the electoral campaign Juncker declared that he would no longer keep the Ministry of Finance in the next government, leaving it to Luc Frieden, at that time Minister of Justice and Budget. This brought into question his chairmanship of the Eurogroup, which he had chaired since 2005 and was expected to chair until December 2010. Finally, in the last months of the legislative term, when the campaign intensified, controversies became more personalized: candidate MEP Goebbels of the LSAP criticized EU Commissioner Reding (CSV) for starting her EP elections campaign whilst still in place as commissioner.

9.3 Electoral results

The CSV lost nearly six percentage points of the votes in the EP elections, while at the same time reaching one of its top historic records at the national elections. This loss was mainly due to the absence of Prime Minister Juncker and other key politicians on the European list. However, the party managed to keep its three MEPs. Three other parties gained one seat, as in 2004. The LSAP did so despite scoring less than 20 per cent, its worst result since 1979, whilst, unlike in national elections, the DP gained votes thanks to its popular front-runner Goerens. The DP returned to its previous third position in the hierarchy of parties in European elections, which it had lost to the Greens in 2004. Regardless of this change in ranking, the Greens continued their impressive progression in the European election: from 6.1 per cent in 1984 to 16.8 per cent in 2009. Compared to 2004, the Greens gained almost two percentage points of support, largely due to an increase in personal votes, going mainly to their incumbent MEP Claude Turmes.

Table 9.6 EP election results in Luxembourg: 1979–2009 (%)

Political party	1979	1984	1989	1994	1999	2004	2009
CSV	36.1	34.9	34.8	31.5	31.7	37.1	31.4
LSAP	21.7	29.9	25.5	24.8	23.6	22.1	19.5
DP	28.1	22.1	20.0	18.8	20.5	14.9	18.7
Gréng	—	6.1	10.5	10.9	10.7	15.0	16.8
ADR	—	—	—	7.0	9.0	8.0	7.4
KPL	5.0	4.1	4.7	1.6	—	1.2	1.5
Lénk	—	—	—	—	2.8	1.7	3.4
BL	—	—	—	—	—	—	1.4
SDP	7.0	—	—	—	—	—	—
Others	2.1	2.9	4.6	5.4	1.8	0.0	0.0
Total	100.0	100.0	100.0	100.0	100.0	100.0	100.0

Source: Election reports, CRISP 1979–1994; ELECT, University of Luxembourg, 1999–2009.

Table 9.7 Differences between EP and national elections in Luxembourg: 1979–2009 (%)*

Political party	1979	1984	1989	1994	1999	2004	2009
CSV	−0.3	−1.8	2.4	1.2	1.6	1.0	**−6.7**
LSAP	−0.9	−1.9	−0.8	−0.6	1.3	−1.3	−2.1
DP	**6.3**	1.7	2.8	−0.5	−1.9	−1.2	**3.7**
Gréng	—	1.9	1.9	1.0	1.6	**3.4**	**5.1**
ADR	—	—	**−7.9**	−2.0	−2.3	−1.9	−0.8
KPL	0.1	−0.3	0.3	−0.8	—	0.3	0.1
Lénk	—	—	—	—	−0.5	−0.2	0.1
BL	—	—	—	—	—	—	0.6

Note:
* A positive (negative) figure indicates that the party's result at the EP election was better (worse) than the result at the national election held simultaneously. Bold figures indicate differences greater than 3 per cent points.

Table 9.8 Abstention at EP and national elections in Luxembourg: 1979–2009 (%)

	EP elections	National elections	Difference
1979	10.7	10.7	0.0
1984	11.2	11.2	0.0
1989	12.6	12.6	0.0
1994	13.0	13.3	−0.3
1999	12.7	13.5	−0.8
2004	8.6	8.0	+0.6
2009	9.2	9.1	+0.1

Source: Election reports, CRISP 1979–1994; ELECT, University of Luxembourg, 1999–2009.

As was the case since 1979, none of the more Eurosceptic parties won a single seat. The ADR obtained 7.4 per cent, 0.6 per cent less than in 2004, while the two radical left parties gained votes, reaching about 5 per cent overall. The newly created *Biergerlëscht* came close to the KPL, reaching 1.4 per cent of the vote. As Table 9.7 shows, for the first time since the 1979 EP election, the differences between voting results in the national and European elections for three parties were more than three percentage points. Prior to 2009, this phenomenon had only occurred for one party at a time, in 2004 for the Greens and in 1979 for the Liberals. In the 2009 election, the CSV recorded the highest vote share difference ever reached, scoring 6.7 percentage points lower in the European elections than in the national ones, followed by the Greens with a 5.1 percentage point gap in favour of their results in the EP election, and the Liberals with a European vote share that was 3.7 points higher than in the general elections.

From the viewpoint of the personal electoral scores, we note that foreign candidates were the weakest candidates in all the electoral lists, with the exception of one the *Lénk* foreign candidate, who arrived third out of six. It is, however, likely that the number of foreign candidates and their popularity will grow with the increase in EU residents registering to become voters. CVS member Viviane Reding was elected, but preferred to take back her seat in the Commission and was therefore replaced by Georges Bach, who had no previous political experience. Yet, it was the first time since 1979 that most elected MEPs effectively took up their seats. Five out of six of the elected MEPs had some prior EU experience, four as MEPs and one as commissioner, and two of the candidates elected were women. The average age of the Luxembourg EP delegation is 45.5 years, the youngest being 34 and the oldest 80, both belonging to the CSV.

Table 9.9 List of Luxembourg MEPs: seventh legislature

Name	National party	Mandates before 2009	Professional background	Year of birth	Gender	Committee/Chair
Astrid Lulling	CSV/EPP	5	Secretary and editor at the *Lëtzebueger Arbechter-Verband*, the Socialist trade union which became the OGB-L (1949–1963). Worked at the miners' and metalworkers' ECSC liaison office, Luxembourg (1950–1958). Member of the LSAP until 1969, for which she was MEP, then national MP for the LSAP's splinter SDP	1929	Female	Quaestor member of : Committee on Economic and Monetary Affairs; Committee on Women's Rights and Gender Equality.
Georges Bach	CSV/EPP	0	Steel industry employee (1973–1974), then railwayman at Luxembourg Railways (SNCFL). Head of SYPROLUX Christian trade union (railways and transports) since 2003.	1955	Male	Member of : Committee on Transport and Tourism.
Frank Engel	CSV/EPP	0	Secretary of the CSV parliamentary group in the Chamber of Deputies.	1975	Male	Member of: Committee on the Internal Market and Consumer Protection.
Robert Goebbels	LSAP/S&D	2	Journalist for the *Tageblatt* (Socialist newspaper) in the 1970s. Party executive functions, national MP, junior minister and minister since then.	1944	Male	Member of: Committee on Industry, Research and Energy; Special Committee on the Financial, Economic and Social Crisis.
Claude Turmes	Gréng/Greens/EFA	2	Physical education and sports teacher (1986–1999). Yoga instructor (1999).	1960	Male	Vice-Chair of the Group of the Greens/European Free Alliance. Member of: Committee on Industry, Research and Energy.

Source: www.europarl.europa.eu/meps/en/search.html?country=LU.

10 Theoretical interpretation of Euro-elections

10.1 Second-Order Election theory

With its compulsory voting system and simultaneous EP and national elections, Luxembourg is clearly a special case when it comes to testing the classical hypotheses of Second-Order Election (SOE) theory. The question of turnout effect is bound not to materialize with participation rates generally oscillating around 90 per cent for both national and European elections, as shown in Table 9.5.

Since 1979, there have been only marginal changes between national and EP elections. Rather than suggesting a decrease of interest through time in Euro-elections in comparison with national ones, these variations could stem from the introduction of voting rights for EU residents and the consequent changes in the composition of the voting population.

Finally, it is worth noticing that both null and blank votes were systematically higher in EP elections than in national ones. This phenomenon could reflect voters' lower interest in these elections in the context of a compulsory voting system. The decision to ban double candidatures could also explain this result. Paradoxically, a decision that was intended to make EP elections less dependent on domestic politics put in evidence the SOE character of this contest.

In addition, from 1979 it is possible to see that governmental losses were greater in national than EP elections on four occasions and that the differences were almost equal on two occasions. The Second-Order Election hypothesis, operationalized in the classical way without adapting to the case of simultaneous elections, was verified only in 2009, with greater losses by governmental parties in the EP contest. Losses by ruling parties mainly reflect, albeit in a smoothed way, the decreasing popularity of incumbents, from one national election to another (Narud and Valen, 2009). This is the empirical confirmation of the logical consequence of holding both elections at the same time in Luxembourg: voters did not perceive EP elections to be an instrument for sanctioning governmental parties on national issues, as they may punish incumbents in the 'first-order' election.

Some lessons may be drawn by looking at the differences between the outcome of concurrent national and EP elections. Their respective results generally match with the positive or negative evolution of party scores in national elections also reflected in the EP contest. Most likely due to the electoral reform that abolished dual mandates and increased recourse to preferential votes, in 2009 the evolution of the scores for the PM's party and that of the main opposition party clearly diverged at both levels. As a result, the former lost heavily and the latter gained in the EP election, leading to what could be perceived as proof of an increasing second-order reflex. In addition to some degree of EU voting, the absence of the popular figure of the Prime Minister on the EP list largely accounted for the poor performance of the CSV in 2009.

Finally, although the Greens had constantly fared better in EP elections compared to national ones, smaller parties generally did not do better in EP elections than at the national level, and this was once more confirmed in 2009. The limited number of MEPs to be elected probably explains a certain degree of strategic voting behaviour, citizens preferring to support parties or candidates that had a chance to gain a seat in the European Parliament.

10.2 Europe Salience theory

Ever since 1979, the simultaneity of elections has made EP campaigns less visible than national ones. Political parties had only on a minority of occasions drafted separate manifestos for EP elections. References to the manifestos of European political parties generally did not abound.

Yet, the section devoted to 'Europe' in the general electoral programme was simply copied from that of the European party.

Debates over EU issues have often been influenced by events or positions taken by political actors in Germany, France, and Belgium, thus depriving the Grand Duchy's political elite of a distinctive position. Added to the overall lack of a clear cleavage on EU integration in a population still displaying a high level of utilitarian support and a lower interest in EP elections than for the concurrent national electoral contest, these factors have contributed to the dominance of domestic issues in European election party campaigns and media coverage.

However, different trends, that may at first seem antagonistic, could be detected. During the EP campaigns, parties increasingly stressed the linkage between national and European elections by reinforcing the tendency of domestic issues to prevail. On the other hand, the 2009 elections have changed a number of parameters since, for the first time, the Euro-candidates were generally unknown or inexperienced, aside from the front-runners. The 2009 campaign was more visible and competitive. The media also reflected a clearer distinction between domestic issues handled by national actors and EU issues dealt with by EU actors, due in part to the ban on double candidatures. Several factors could account for this 'light' Europeanization of the campaign that in turn contributed to the increase in the saliency of EU issues in voters' choices in the EP elections. First, greater popular awareness of EU questions may have grown out of the 2005 referendum. Second, the main theme of both national and European elections, the international financial and economic crisis, was transnational in essence. Third, the campaign strategies of the major party front-runners in general, and of some other candidates who issued separate, personal manifestos over EU issues. The latter was certainly enhanced by the previously mentioned changes in electoral rules and practices, and probably accounts for why Luxembourg voters declared themselves to be much more informed about the EU campaign in 2009 than they were during the preceding elections.

Some studies have shown that Luxembourg displayed a comparatively low level of congruence between the positions of voters and the parties they vote for in EP elections. A certain level of 'sincere vote' on EU positions, however, appeared to materialize in the 2009 elections; the vote switching behaviour of CSV and Green Party supporters was especially noticeable. The former were much less enthusiastic about European integration than what they perceived the party to stand for, thereby leading some of them in 2004 and 2009 to switch to another party closer to their positions on Europe (Dumont et al., 2006, 2011). And yet, despite some potential support in the population for less Europhile positions, the most Eurosceptic parties in Luxembourg's political landscape continued to fare very modestly in EP elections.

The specific and evolving institutional context of Luxembourg's EP elections, that are fought concurrently with national ones, and where voting is compulsory, can only partially validate either the traditional Second-Order Election theory or the Europe Salience model. A variety of different and sometimes countervailing influences have been recorded, the combined effect of which, as already suggested by van der Eijk and Schmitt (1996), may be as dependent on the idiosyncrasies of each particular situation as on the structural features and merits of these respective theories.

For instance, whereas the changes in the 2009 EP election's institutional context and political offer were intended as a modest, but important, step for affirming the identity and specificity of European elections, they also led to results that at first sight better matched the expectations of the SOE model. However, at the micro-level, the motives for expressing a different vote than the one cast in the national elections were not, as suggested by Second-Order election, the willingness to express a sincere vote and/or to sanction the governmental parties on national matters. Those who voted differently in both elections did so essentially because they lacked the national heavyweights they used to have on their EP ballot or because of their preferences over European issues. Others strategically switched to a party that, contrary to the one they voted for in the national elections, had a chance to win a seat in Strasbourg. Under such conditions, the addition of occurrences of EP elections and potential further institutional changes may not help us much in drawing firmer conclusions on the respective merits of existing hypotheses that have developed from theoretical premises and empirical contexts that hardly apply to the case of the Grand Duchy.

References

Primary sources

CRISP (1980) *Les Elections du 10 juin 1979 au Grand-Duché de Luxembourg: Systèmes et comportements électoraux, étude réalisée pour la Chambre des Députés du Grand-Duché du Luxembourg*, Luxembourg, Service Central des Imprimés de l'Etat.

CRISP (1987) *Grand-Duché de Luxembourg, Systèmes et comportements électoraux, Analyse et synthèse des scrutins de 1974, 1979 et 1984*, Bruxelles, CRISP Editions.

CRISP (1995) *Les Elections au Grand-Duché de Luxembourg: Données sur les scrutins de 1974, 1979, 1984, 1989 et 1994. Résultats et Comportements', Les élections Législatives, vol. I*, Luxembourg, Service Central des Imprimés de l'Etat.

CRISP (1995) *Les Elections au Grand-Duché de Luxembourg: Données sur les scrutins de 1974, 1979, 1984, 1989 et 1994. Résultats et Comportements vol. II, Les élections européennes*, Luxembourg, Service Central des Imprimés de l'Etat.

CRISP (1994) *Les Elections au Grand-Duché de Luxembourg: Rapport sur les élections législatives et européennes de juin 1994*, Luxembourg, Service Central des Imprimés de l'Etat, 1995.

ELECT (1999) Fehlen, F., Piroth, I. and Poirier, Ph. (2000), *Les Elections Législatives au Grand-Duché du Luxembourg*, Luxembourg, Chambre des Députés du Luxembourg, octobre 2000.

ELECT (2004) Dumont, P., Fehlen, F., Kies, R. and Poirier, Ph. (2006) *Les Elections Législatives et Européennes de 2004 au Grand-Duché de Luxembourg*, Luxembourg, Service Central des Imprimés de l'Etat.

ELECT (2009) Dumont, P., Kies, R. Spreitzer, A., Bozinis, M. and Poirier, Ph. (2011) *Les élections législatives et européennes de 2009 au Grand-Duché de Luxembourg. Rapport élaboré pour la Chambre des Députés*, Luxembourg, Service Central des Imprimés de l'Etat.

Eurobarometer Flash 168 (2005) *The European Constitution: Post-referendum Survey in Spain*, Luxembourg, Eurostat.

Eurobarometer Flash 171 (2005) *The European Constitution: Post-referendum Survey in Luxembourg*, Luxembourg, Eurostat.

Eurobarometer Flash 172 (2005) *The European Constitution: Post-referendum Survey in The Netherlands*, Luxembourg, Eurostat.

Eurobarometer Flash 173 (2005) *The European Constitution: Post-referendum Survey in Luxembourg*, Luxembourg, Eurostat.

Eurobarometer Standard Survey 72 (2009) *National Report for Luxembourg*. Luxembourg, Eurostat.

European Parliament website, www.europarl.europa.eu/parliament/archive/elections2009/en/index en.html (accessed on 7 December 2013).

Eurostat (2013, 2014) http://epp.eurostat.ec.europa.eu (accessed on 5 June 2015).

Secondary sources

Clément, F. (2011) *Les relations professionnelles tripartites. Le cas du Grand-Duché de Luxembourg*, Paris, Conservatoire National des Arts et Métiers.

De Vreese C. H., Banducci, S. A., Semetko, H. A. and Boomgaarden, H. G. (2006) 'The News Coverage of the 2004 European Parliamentary Election Campaign in 25 Countries', *European Union Politics*, 7(4), 477–504.

Dumont, P. and De Winter, L. (2000) 'Luxembourg: Stable Coalitions in Pivotal Party System', in Strøm, K. and Müller, W. (eds) *Coalition Government in Western Europe*, Oxford, Oxford University Press, 399–432.

Dumont, P. and Spreitzer, A.(2010). 'Luxembourg', in Gagatek, W. (ed.) *The 2009 Elections to the European Parliament. Country Reports*, Florence, European University Institute.

Dumont, P., Kies, R. and Poirier, P. (2010) 'Luxembourg: The Challenge of Inclusive Democracy in a "Local State"', in Loughlin, J., Hendriks, F. and Lidström, A. (eds) *The Oxford Handbook of Local and Regional Democracy in Europe*, Oxford, Oxford University Press, 123–45.

Dumont, P., Fehlen, F., Kies, R. and Poirier, P. (2006) *Les élections législatives et européennes de 2004 au Grand-Duché de Luxembourg. Synthèse du rapport élaboré pour la Chambre des Député*, Luxembourg, Service Central des Imprimés de l'Etat.

Dumont, P., Fehlen , F., Kies, R. and Poirier, P. (2007) *Le référendum du 10 juillet 2005 sur le Traité établissant une constitution pour l'Europe: Rapport élaboré pour la Chambre des Députés*, Luxembourg, Service Central des Imprimés de l'Etat.

Dumont, P., Kies, R., Spreitzer A., Bozinis, M. and Poirier, P. (2011). *Les élections législatives et européennes de 2009 au Grand-Duché de Luxembourg. Synthèse du rapport élaboré pour la Chambre des Députés*, Luxembourg, Service Central des Imprimés de l'Etat.

Giebler, H. and Wüst, A. (2011)'Campaigning on an Upper Level? Individual Campaigning in the 2009 European Parliament Elections in its Determinants', *Electoral Studies* 30(1), 53–66.

Hirsch, M. (1986) 'Tripartism in Luxembourg: The Limits of Social Concertation', *West European Politics* 9(1), 54–66.

Huberty, M. (2009) 'The National Legislative and European Parliament Elections in Luxembourg, 7 June 2009', *EPERN Election Briefings Series*, University of Sussex.

Mattila, M. and Raunio, T. (2006) 'Cautious Voters – Supportive Parties. Opinion Congruence between Voters and Parties on the EU Dimension', *European Union Politics*, 7(4), 427–49.

Narud, H.-M. and Valen, H. (2008) 'Coalition Membership and Electoral Performance' in Strøm, K., Müller, W. C. and Bergman, T. (eds) *Cabinets and Coalition Bargaining: The Democratic Life Cycle in Western Europe*, Oxford, Oxford University Press, 369–402.

Poirier, P. (2008) 'Luxembourg', Horst, D. (ed.) *Constitutions of the World from the Late 18th Century to the Middle of the 19th Century: Sources on the Rise of Modern Constitutionalism*, 7, *Europe*, Munich, Saur Verlag, K. G.

Schuck, A. R. T., Xezonakis, G., Elenbaas, M., Banducci, S. A. and de Vreese, C. H. (2011) 'Party Contestation and Europe on the News Agenda: The 2009 European Parliamentary Elections', *Electoral Studies*, 30 (1), 41–52.

van der Eijk, C. and Franklin, M. N. (eds) (1996) *Choosing Europe? The European Electorate and National Politics in the Face of the Union*, Ann Arbor, University of Michigan Press.

Country reviews

The Old Member States

The first enlargement countries

10	The United Kingdom	213
11	Ireland	243
12	Denmark	267

10
UNITED KINGDOM

Julie Smith

Figure 10.1 Map of the United Kingdom

Table 10.1 United Kingdom profile

EU entry year	1973 ECSC, EEC and Euratom
Schengen entry year	Non-member
MEPs elected in 2009	72
MEPs under Lisbon Treaty	73 since 1 December 2011
	One additional seat allocated to Anthea McIntyre, ECR (West Midland constituency)
Capital	London
Total area★	248,527 km^2
Population	64,308,261
	92% white, 7.9% other ethnic groups, including 2% Asian/Asian British; 2% Black/Black British
Population density★★	264.3/km^2
Median age of population	39.9
Political system	Constitutional Monarchy
Head of state	Queen Elizabeth II (February1952–)
Head of government	Gordon Brown, Labour Party (Lab.) (June 2007–May 2010); David Cameron, Conservative (Cons.) (May 2010 –)
Political majority	Labour government (Lab.) (June 1997–May 2010); Conservative (Cons.)/Liberal Democrat (LD) Coalition government (May 2010–May 2015); Conservative government (May 2015–)
Currency	Pound sterling
Prohead GDP in PPS	34,400 €

Source: Eurostat, 2013, 2014, http://epp.eurostat.ec.europa.eu/.
Notes:
★ Total area including inland waters.
★★ Population density: the ratio of the annual population of a region to the land area of the region.

1 Geographical position

The United Kingdom of Great Britain and Northern Ireland is situated to the north-west of the European landmass. Geographically separate from the rest of the European Union, apart from the Republic of Ireland, it comprises four states: England, which is the most populated part of the UK, with about 81 per cent of its 42 million inhabitants living in urban areas, Scotland, Wales and Northern Ireland, each enjoying a different degree of devolution (Pateman, 2011 and ONS, 2011). London is the capital of England, Edinburgh is the capital of Scotland, which has a relatively small population of about five million. Cardiff is the capital of Wales, while Belfast is the main city in Northern Ireland.

2 Historical background

The United Kingdom (UK) is a monarchy, with the king or queen serving as both head of state and head of the established Church of England. The relationship between England and Wales was established in the sixteenth century and that between Scotland and England was codified in the 1707 Act of Union, which has laid the basis for the UK's constitutional order. During the Victorian Era, between 1837 and 1901, Britain's global ambitions led to the acquisition of an Empire upon which 'the sun never set'. Yet the borders of the United Kingdom itself were only finally settled in 1922 with the secession of the Republic of Ireland, leaving the six, predominantly Protestant, counties of Northern Ireland (Ulster) within the Union. After the end of the WWII, Britain lost most of its colonial empire.

3 Geopolitical profile

The UK's geographical location and political history help explain its semi-detached relationship with the European Union. Having come out of WWII as one of the few European states to be neither invaded nor defeated, the UK remained aloof from the integration process until the 1960s, initially assuming that the process would be doomed to failure and preferring to focus on relations with the United States and the nascent Commonwealth, the successor to the declining Empire. Economic and political realities led to a changed stance by 1961 when the UK first applied, but France twice blocked British membership of the 'European club'. Repeated attempts to join the then European Economic Community (EEC) eventually culminated in accession on 1 January 1973. Once a member, the UK sought at various times to play a leading role while simultaneously distancing itself from key initiatives, notably from economic and monetary union (EMU) and Schengen. By contrast, the UK, a nuclear power and permanent member of the United Nations Security Council, has been an active member of the North Atlantic Treaty Organization (NATO) since its foundation and a firm ally of the United States. Indeed, the relationship with the US led France to veto British entry to the EEC, perceiving the UK to be a Trojan Horse for the Americans. With hindsight, such a view might appear to have been vindicated, as most of the subsequent British governments have placed greater weight on the so-called 'special relationship' with the US than on Europe. Over the years, however, both the US and Commonwealth links have become relatively less significant to the UK, while the EU has become important in terms of trade and, to a lesser extent, foreign policy cooperation, even if it has not attracted great enthusiasm.

4 Overview of the political landscape

The United Kingdom of Great Britain and Northern Ireland is a constitutional monarchy whereby the head of state enjoys virtually no powers, but is required to give formal consent to legislation. Renowned for its lack of a codified constitution, the UK legislative tradition is enshrined in a wealth of primary and statute law along with custom and practice, some dating back over 800 years. Its Parliament, typically referred to as 'Westminster', consists of a lower chamber, the House of Commons, including 650 elected members, and an unelected upper chamber, the House of Lords. Originating in the aristocracy of the Middle Ages, until 1958 membership of the House of Lords was solely on the basis of the hereditary principle. Since then, most members have been appointed as 'life peers', typically for party political reasons. Currently the Lords comprises 92 hereditary members, Bishops of the Anglican Church, Law Lords, some 'people's peers' and a large number of political appointees, including many former MPs. Some members, usually chosen for their professional eminence, do not take the whip of any established party and are known as 'cross-benchers'.

Scotland has a separate Parliament enjoying legislative and revenue-raising powers, while Wales and Northern Ireland have assemblies which enjoy rather fewer powers. However, in a referendum held on 3 March 2011, the Welsh voted for a substantial increase of their Assembly's powers. By contrast, England does not have its own Parliament, so its central or 'national' legislation is made in Westminster. Within the four states that comprise the UK, there are also various levels of local government. Each of these layers of government from the EU down to local has a core of political parties alongside other less nationally significant parties, which emerge or disappear according to context.

5 Brief account of the political parties

The British political parties discussed here are parties in the three states comprising Great Britain, unless explicitly stated otherwise. Northern Irish political parties are divided essentially along Nationalist lines, which do not translate easily to the rest of the British system and are hence listed separately in the tables.

Three British political parties date back over 100 years: the Conservative, or Tory, Party is a centre-right party based on pragmatism rather than any deep ideology. It has been in government for long periods ever since the eighteenth century, evolving to meet the challenges to *bourgeois* parties at the time of mass suffrage in the late nineteenth century in a way that its great rival, the Liberal Party, previously known as Whigs, failed to do. Having obtained a landslide victory in 1906, the progressive Liberals declined rapidly and were overtaken as the second main party by Labour, representing the newly enfranchised working classes. From the end of WWII until 2010, the centre-left Labour Party and the centre-right Conservatives alternated in government as the pendulum of electoral politics swung left then right, then left again. Long considered a two-party polity, in practice the UK featured a three-party system until the end of the wartime coalition and again from the 1970s, when the Liberals were called in to support a weak minority Labour government. Subsequently, as a result of rising Nationalist tendencies, the Scottish Nationalist Party (SNP) and *Plaid Cymru* (Party of Wales) have managed to secure representation in Westminster.

Since devolution to Scotland and Wales in 1999, the British political system has become increasingly complicated as elections under party list proportional representation (PR) have resulted in coalition governments of varying hues, sometimes including Scottish and Welsh Nationalists as well as Liberal Democrats and Labour politicians. Northern Ireland has a distinctive party system, its main parties mirroring the Unionist/Nationalist division arising from the 'home rule' issue prior to 1922, reinforced by the religious cleavage, with on the one hand, Catholic Nationalists represented by *Sinn Féin* and the more moderate Social Democratic and Labour Party (SDLP) favouring the unification of Ireland and, on the other hand, Protestant Unionists – the Official Unionist Party and the Democratic Unionist Party – seeking ongoing union with Great Britain.

Since the mid-1980s, the left-of-centre Green Party has gained prominence and, eventually, parliamentary representation, in the European Parliament since 1999 and in Westminster in 2010. By contrast, the far right has enjoyed relatively little support in the UK although the British National Party (BNP) has had some electoral success, initially in local elections and since 2004 in EP elections, securing two MEPS in 2009, thereby causing serious anxieties amongst mainstream politicians. Since the mid-1990s, parties whose *raison d'être* is to oppose EU membership, initially the Referendum Party and later the UK Independence Party (UKIP) have gained significant electoral support and representation in the EP, although until 2014 not in Westminster where they could actually influence governmental decisions about closer cooperation within the EU.

5.1 Party attitudes towards the European Union

British political parties have been amongst the most Eurosceptic in the Union. However, none of them has been wholly consistent in its stance on Europe. Initially, the Labour Party was the most Eurosceptic as it considered the European Communities to be a 'capitalist club'. By contrast, the Conservatives took a positive, albeit pragmatic, approach towards European integration and it was under the leadership of Tory Prime Minister Edward Heath that the UK eventually joined the EC in 1973. The Liberals unambiguously supported membership of the European Community, displaying the most pro-European approach, while the Scottish and Welsh Nationalists appeared initially hostile to integration.

The position of British parties has changed dramatically over the years, with the Conservatives shifting to broad Euroscepticism, initially as a result of Jacques Delors's attempts to create a social Europe, followed by the Maastricht Treaty of 1992. The Labour position was a mirror image of the Tories', as the party, seemingly condemned to opposition in the domestic arena, realized that it was able to wield influence in the European Parliament. The party also saw the European agenda beginning to shift in a more social democratic direction better suited to its own policies (Smith, 2005b). Likewise, the Scottish and Welsh Nationalists gradually adopted a more positive stance towards the European Union, which seemed to offer significant opportunities to pursue their independence agendas. Meanwhile the Liberal Democrats became rather more cautious about advocating further integration as they gained more support at the national level, although they remained more positive about Europe than the other main parties.

The situation became more complex in the mid-1990s when Eurosceptic parties, initially the Referendum Party and then UKIP, emerged to advocate Britain's withdrawal from the European Union. UKIP took votes predominantly from the Conservative Party, which in turn sought to stiffen its opposition to the European Union. This was most notable in the 2001 general election, when the Conservatives fervently campaigned to 'save the pound', a reference to concerns that the Labour Party would take the UK into the single European currency. While that approach brought the Tories little electoral success, it highlighted how far the party had shifted from its pro-integration stance. This was reconfirmed a few years later when David Cameron pledged to withdraw the Conservatives from the European People's Party Group in the European Parliament if he was elected party leader. Having secured the leadership in 2005, he duly fulfilled his promise in the run-up to the 2009 EP elections, causing considerable frustration within the EPP and derision from Liberal Democrats and Labour. Meanwhile, Labour confirmed their by now broadly pro-European stance, although the Iraq War ensured that Labour's links to the US appeared to be stronger from 2003 onwards, and the advent of Gordon Brown as Prime Minister to replace Tony Blair brought a somewhat more cautious approach to the EU.

Not only have parties changed their attitudes towards European integration, they have also frequently been divided over EU questions. In 1983, a breakaway group of pro-European Labour members established the Social Democratic Party (SDP), which later merged with the pro-European Liberals. In the early 1990s, Tories were split over the ratification of the Maastricht Treaty and from May 2010 onwards divisions were strongly evident in the Conservative-Liberal Coalition Government, as many backbenchers sought a referendum on the UK's ongoing membership of the EU.

6 Public opinion and the European Union

British citizens have been amongst the most Eurosceptic in all EU Member States, certainly until the 2004 enlargement, as reflected in Eurobarometer surveys. In one of the surveys undertaken in 2008, 20 per cent of UK respondents spontaneously said they did not wish to be EU citizens compared with an EU-27 average of 5 per cent (European Commission, 2009, 30). Moreover, British voters appeared to be amongst the least well informed on European matters, at least in terms of self-placement on the issue (European Commission, 2009, 84; European Parliament, 2009, 8), least interested in European elections, and most distrustful of the EP (European Commission, 2009, 93 and 106).

While political parties of whatever hue frequently expressed concerns over the development of the Union, until the late 1990s there was scant opportunity for British voters to demonstrate their views for or against integration, as the main political parties tended to be internally divided over Europe and were thus reluctant to discuss European issues in any depth, believing there were few votes to be won on the issue, and there was little scope for fringe parties to emerge under the first-past-the-post electoral system. Thus voters could not opt to vote for a particular party in order to demonstrate their support or otherwise for the integration process *per se*, although in some constituencies they could select an individual candidate whose views for or against integration were clear. This situation altered with the emergence of anti-EU parties in the 1990s, which gave Eurosceptic voters a clear option to express their dissatisfaction with the integration process. This opening up of the party system for European elections was facilitated by a significant change to the electoral system in 1999.

7 National and EP electoral systems

Great Britain, comprising England, Scotland, and Wales, uses a majoritarian electoral system, commonly known as first-past-the-post (FPTP), in single-member constituencies for national general elections and local elections. Under this system, the electoral threshold is very high and parties that enjoy significant but diffuse support across the country find it difficult to secure representation, although regionally- or nationally-based parties are able to gain seats on a small percentage of the total votes. The same system was used for European elections until 1999, when an EU-level agreement introduced the requirement that all Member States use some form of proportional representation. As shown in Figure 10.2, Great Britain adopted a closed regional list system, with England divided into nine regions, while Scotland, Wales, and Northern Ireland were separate units.

The precise allocation of seats to regions was altered under the terms of the 2011 EU Act, which granted the additional seat given to the UK under the Lisbon Treaty to the West Midlands. In contrast to the rest of the UK, Northern Ireland has used the Single Transferable Vote form of proportional representation for both national and European elections for many years. The Local Elections Order 2008 ensured that EP and local elections would be held on the same day in 2009 (Ordinary Day of Elections in 2009).

The upshot of the change in electoral law has been profound: the two-party stranglehold on EP representation discussed below has been replaced by a multi-party system in which a new Eurosceptic party, UKIP, became the second largest in terms of seats in the European Parliament and the Liberal Democrats, which had previously struggled to gain any EP seats moved into double figures in terms of seats, even though their percentage share of the vote did not increase markedly.

8 A glance at EP and national elections

The first EP elections fell just weeks after the Conservatives had swept to power under the UK's first female Prime Minister, Margaret Thatcher, in May 1979. Thus, despite their innovative nature, little attention was paid to this event in the UK as party activists at least as much as voters were suffering from election fatigue, and the political parties had few resources to fight another campaign so soon after the vital general election. Posters of nine ballot boxes, reflecting the simultaneous elections in all nine Member States went up on advertising hoardings in an attempt to raise awareness amongst voters, but the elections were characterized by second-order syndrome. Turnout was lower than in any of the other Member States, at just 32.3 per cent. The Conservatives enjoyed an electoral honeymoon, despite doing little campaigning; they secured 48.4 per cent of the popular vote and, thanks in large part to the first-past-the-post electoral

Figure 10.2 Map of EP electoral constituencies in the United Kingdom

system, 60 of the available 81 seats, with Labour winning just 17 seats. Outside of Northern Ireland, only one seat went to a party outside the big two, notably to a Scottish Nationalist.

Turnout in the EP elections in the UK remained low in comparison to the other Member States in 1984, 1989, and 1994, albeit it rising marginally to 36.2 per cent in 1989. The main opposition Labour Party saw its support rise in EP elections, so that by 1994 it enjoyed the levels of support the Tories had seen in their electoral honeymoon of 1979, securing 42.7 per cent of the vote and 62 seats. Although the Labour vote went up in every EP election, with their numbers in the European Parliament kept artificially high thanks to the electoral system, the party lost the subsequent national elections of 1987 and 1992.

Third parties failed to make a significant impact in the UK until the changes to the electoral system in 1999. In particular, the SDP/Liberal Alliance, with 19.5 per cent of the vote in 1984, the Greens, with 15 per cent in 1989, and the newly created Liberal Democrats, with 6.4 per cent that same year all failed to secure representation in the EP. By 1994 the Greens, whose support dropped to 3 per cent, could not field candidates in all seats (Smith, 1994, 55; Smith, 1995a, 53). Only the 1994 Euro-elections saw a slight deviation in the pattern of Labour and the Conservatives sweeping all the seats, as two Liberal Democrats managed to breach the threshold to get elected.

Europe was initially a divisive issue within the Labour Party, which campaigned to withdraw from the European Community in the 1983 general election, while from the early 1990s the Conservatives found themselves bitterly split on the matter, as Labour's opposition to integration softened. Nonetheless, it featured little in the first sets of European elections, which in the UK as elsewhere were characterized by a focus on national politicians and national questions. This situation gradually altered in the 1990s as the Conservatives began to feel that Europe was a platform on which they should fight, despite being internally divided on the issue. In 1994, Tory candidates were keen to run a pro-European campaign, but this did not occur, largely because the Party at home was far less wedded to the European cause. Labour fought a far more pro-European campaign on the basis of the Party of European Socialists' manifesto (Smith, 1995a). However, the 1994 elections were in any case overshadowed by John Smith's death and the ensuing party leadership campaign. Despite this turn of events, Labour secured a massive victory in the 1994 elections at the mid-term of a fourth consecutive Conservative government, becoming the largest single party within the European Parliament from 1994 to 1999. Meantime, the Liberal Democrats obtained 2 seats in the South-west region, the only time they managed to do so in European elections under first-past-the-post.

The nature of European elections altered in 1999 with the introduction of proportional representation. Labour and the Conservatives were no longer so heavily over-represented in terms of the ratio of their votes to seats, the Greens gained their first two MEPs, the Liberal Democrats saw their seats soar from 2 to 10 and the new Eurosceptic UK Independence Party secured three MEPs (House of Commons, 1999b).

The Conservatives were in the ascendant in the European elections that took place two years after a landslide Labour victory in national elections; like Labour earlier, benefitting from opposition at home to see their vote increase in European elections, albeit on the basis of historically low turnout. British membership of the euro-zone was an issue but, as in the past, the elections were quite low-key and the European dimension remained limited (Mather, 2001). By contrast, the Conservatives under William Hague opted to focus on Europe in the ensuing general election of 2001, which the leader used as a countdown to loss of the British pound, given Labour's more positive attitude towards both the EU and membership of the common currency. The campaign was not successful, as Labour won a landslide victory, but it did indicate the significance a major mainstream political party now placed on Europe.

By 2004, Euroscepticism had become more ingrained in the British debate and UKIP got the third largest number of votes, pushing the pro-European Liberal Democrats into third place.

Table 10.2 National election results in the UK: 1979–2010

	Turnout		Conservative	Labour	Lib. Dem.	Total (incl. others)
1979	75.9 %	No. of votes	13.7 million	11.5 million	4.31 million	31.22 million
		% vote	43.9	36.9	13.8	100
		Seats	339	268	11	635
1983	72.5%	No. of votes	13.01 million	8.46 million	7.78 million	30.67 million
		% vote	42.4	27.6	25.4	100
		Seats	397	209	23	650
1987	75.4%	No. of votes	13.74 million	10.03 million	7.34 million	32.53 million
		% vote	42.2	30.8	22.6	100
		Seats	375	229	22	650
1992	78.0%	No. of votes	14.09 million	11.56 million	6 million	33.61 million
		% vote	41.9	34.4	17.8	100
		Seats	336	271	20	651
1997	71.4%	No. of votes	9.6 million	13.52 million	5.24 million	31.29 million
		% vote	30.7	43.2	16.8	100
		Seats	165	418	46	659
2001	59.38%	No. of votes	8.36 million	10.72 million	4.81 million	26.37 million
		% vote	31.7	40.68	18.26	100
		Seats	166	412	51	646
2005	61.4%	No. of votes	8.78 million	9.55 million	5.96 million	27.15 million
		% vote	32.4	35.2	22.0	100
		Seats	198	355	62	646
2010	65.1%	No. of votes	10.7 million	8.6 million	6.8 million	29.7 million
		% vote	36.1	29	23	100
		Seats	306	258	57	650

Source: House of Commons Library, 2001; 2006; 2011.

UKIP was assisted perhaps in 2004 by fielding a daytime television personality, and former Labour MP, Robert Kilroy Silk as the lead candidate in the East Midlands region, while veteran actress Joan Collins announced her support for the Eurosceptic cause as well (House of Commons, 2004, 17). Finally, British voters could indicate their feelings towards Europe in EP elections and many were willing to do so. The opposition Conservatives failed to garner the level of success they might have anticipated mid-term as UKIP took away more right-wing voters, as did the British National Party in some areas, although that party did not secure representation in 2004. Low and declining turnout was finally reversed as four English regions used all postal ballots, which significantly increased turnout compared with 1999.

9 The 2009 European election

9.1 Party lists and manifestos

The 2009 elections highlighted the extent to which the UK has moved beyond a two-party system. Thirty-three parties put forward lists in one or more states or regions of the UK. Sixteen separate parties fielded candidates in the south-west of England alone, and fourteen in London as well as five individual candidates (Electoral Commission, 2009, 2). Alongside the Euro candidates, just under 9,000 candidates stood in local elections in England, ensuring that in many parts of the country there were local and European level campaigns, fought on the basis of differing policy platforms. Yet, as a post-election survey for the Electoral Commission

Table 10.3a EP election results in Great Britain: 1979–1994

Great Britain	1979			1984			1989			1994		
	Votes	% vote	MEPs	Votes	% vote	MEPS	Votes	% vote	MEPs	Votes	% vote	MEPs
Conservative	6,508,492	48.4	60	5,426,866	38.8	45	5,331,077	33.0	32	4,248,531	27.0	18
Labour	4,253,247	31.6	17	4,865,224	34.7	32	6,153,640	39.0	45	6,753,863	42.6	62
Liberal Democrat	1,690,638	12.6	—	2,591,659	18.5	—	986,292	6.2	—	2,552,730	16.1	2
Green	—	—	—	—	—	—	2,292,705	14.5	—	494,561	3.1	0
Scottish National Party	247,836	1.9	1	230,594	1.7	1	406,686	2.6	1	487,239	3.0	2
Plaid Cymru	83,399	0.6	—	103,031	0.7	—	115,062	0.7	—	162,478	1.0	—
Total (incl. Northern Ireland)[1]	13,132,789		81	13,998,215		81	15,827,417		81	15,827,417		87
Turnout	**31.6%**			**32.6%**			**36.2%**			**36.4%**		

Source: UK Office of the European Parliament, 2009.

Note: Northern Ireland elects 3 MEPs by proportional representation, using the single transferable vote system.

Table 10.3b EP election results in Northern Ireland: 1979–1994

Political party	1979		1984		1989		1994	
Democratic Unionist	170,688	1	230,251	1	160,110	1	163,246	1
SDLP	140,622	1	151,399	1	136,335	1	161,992	1
Ulster Unionist	125,169	1	147,169	1	118,785	1	133,459	1

Source: UK Office of the European Parliament, 2009.

Table 10.3c EP election results in Great Britain: 1999–2009

Political party	1999			2004			2009		
	Votes	% vote	MEPs	Votes	% vote	MEPs	Votes	% vote	MEPs
Conservative	3,578,218	35.8	36	4,397,087	26.7	27	4,198,664	27.7	25
Labour	2,803,821	28.0	29	3,718,683	22.6	19	2,381,760	15.7	13
Liberal Democrat	1,266,549	12.7	10	2,342,327	14.9	12	2,080,613	13.7	11
UK Independence Party	696,057	7.0	3	2,660,768	16.2	12	2,498,226	16.5	13
Greens	625,378	6.2	2	1,028,283	6.2	2	1,303,745	8.6	2
Scottish National Party	268,528	2.4	2	231,505	1.4	2	321,007	2.1	2
Plaid Cymru	185,235	1.56	2	159,888	1.0	1	126, 702	0.8	1
British National Party	102,644	1.0	–	808,201	4.9	0	943,598	6.2	2
Total	10,681,080		87	16,458,603		78	15,827,417		72
Turnout	**24%**			**38.4%**			**36.2%**		

Source: UK Office of the European Parliament, 2009.

Table 10.3d EP election results in Northern Ireland: 1999–2009

Political party	1999		2004		2009	
Democratic Unionist	192,762	1	175,761	1	88,346	1
SDLP	190,731	1	78,489	0	78,489	0
Ulster Unionist	119,507	1	91,164	1	82,893	1
Sinn Féin	117,643	0	144,541	1	126,184	1
Greens	—	—	4,810	0	15,764	0

Source: UK Office of the European Parliament, 2009.

indicated, voters were not always clear which elections were being held, with 71 per cent in areas without local elections erroneously believing that there were local elections taking place (Electoral Commission, 2009, 28–9).

The three main parties, Labour, Conservatives, and Liberal Democrats, as well as the two main Eurosceptic parties, the BNP and UKIP, all fielded full slates of candidates in all nine English regions as well as Scotland and Wales, as did the Socialist Labour Party. The Greens went one

Table 10.4 EP electoral lists in the United Kingdom: 2009

Alliance Party (Northern Ireland only)
Animals Count
British National Party (BNP)
Christian Party Proclaiming Christ's Lordship
Conservative Party (Cons.)
Democratic Unionist Party – DUP (Northern Ireland only)
English Democrats Party (EngD)
Labour Party (Lab.)
Liberal Democrats (LD)
Mebyon Kernow – The Party for Cornwall (MK) (Cornwall only)
No2EU: Yes to Democracy (No2EU)
Peace Party – Non-violence, Justice, Environment (PP)
Pensioners' Party
Plaid Cymru – The Party of Wales (Plaid) (Wales only)
Pro Democracy: Libertas.eu (Libertas)
Roman Party. Ave!
Scottish Green Party (SGP) (Scotland only)
Scottish National Party (SNP) (Scotland only)
Scottish Socialist Party (SSP) (Scotland only)
Sinn Féin (SF) (Northern Ireland and the Republic of Ireland)
Social Democratic and Labour Party (SDLP) (Northern Ireland only)
Socialist Labour Party
Socialist Party of Great Britain
Traditional Unionist Voice (TUV) (Northern Ireland only)
Ulster Conservatives and Unionists – New Force (UUP)
United Kingdom First (UKFP)
United Kingdom Independence Party (UKIP)
WAI D (registered as Your Decision)
Yes 2 Europe

---

better and fielded a candidate in Northern Ireland as well. More surprisingly, a range of other parties also fielded full or nearly full slates across Great Britain, including several new parties: No2 EU: Yes to Democracy; the Christian Party 'Proclaiming Christ's Lordship'; and the Jury Team. The last of these had a novel approach of recruiting candidates, through a system of open primaries, including via the internet, as a way of moving beyond what they felt were unaccountable party politics (Jury Team 2009). Yet, if the Jury Team moved beyond party politics they were also rather less representative than those of most parties: across the country it fielded only 7 women and 2 black and minority ethnic candidates out of 72.

The transnational Libertas party of Declan Ganley, a British businessman who claimed to be pro-European but anti-Lisbon, and sought to present lists across the whole of the EU, fielded candidates in England, but not Scotland or Wales, under the title 'Pro Democracy: Libertas.eu'. Reflecting the rise of regions and nations in Europe, SNP and *Plaid Cymru* put forward lists in Scotland and Wales respectively, while *Mebyon Kernow*, the Party for Cornwall, fielded candidates in Cornwall; in the simultaneous local election it was successful in gaining seats for the first time. Several other parties/groups presented candidates in a smaller number of regions, including the United Kingdom First and Animals Count.

The EP contest coincided with county council and unitary authority elections in much of England, thanks to the decision to move the local elections to June rather than May, as was usual. This move was always likely to reduce the emphasis on European issues, but was also expected to increase turnout and campaign activity. Most parties fielded candidates in both local and European elections and the campaigns ran in parallel. The parties did produce manifestos explicitly for the EP elections, although the weight each devoted to British – Welsh, Irish or Scottish – versus European matters differed.

The Labour, Liberal Democrat, and Green parties are all full and active members of transnational parties and party groups within the European Parliament: Labour in the Party of European Socialists (PES) and the associated Group of the Progressive Alliance of Socialists and Democrats (PASD); the Liberal Democrats in the European Liberal Democrat and Reform Party (ELDR), now Alliance of Liberals and Democrats for Europe (ALDE) Party and Group; and the Greens as part of the United Green Parties of Europe. Both Labour and the Greens adopted the transnational manifestos of their respective party families, which they supplemented with national manifestos. In the latter's case, however, the language of the UK programme was strongly reflective of the European manifesto, stressing the idea of a 'Green deal' but rejecting the aspects of capitalist Europe. Recognizing how little attention was paid to transnational manifestos, ELDR initially decided not to have one for 2009, producing instead a set of 15 key policies, although it inevitably came to be called a manifesto. The pro-European Liberal Democrats cast their own manifesto as supportive of the EU, but recognized that some further reforms might be necessary. They took the opportunity to criticize both main parties' approaches to Europe, asserting that, 'Conservatives and Labour have messed up Britain's relationship with other European countries' (Lib Dems, 2009, 3). Labour's manifesto was in line with that of the PES and explicitly pro-European, but focussed also on domestic issues, as its title – 'Winning the fight for Britain's future' – implied, and concluded with two pages on 'the Conservative threat'.

By contrast to the other three parties, the Conservatives have always refused to join a transnational party, although prior to the 2009 elections their MEPs had sat with the Group of the European People's Party since 1992. Their 2009 manifesto was entirely separate, highlighting the intention of the party to form a new group in the European Parliament after the elections, in line with David Cameron's pledge when he stood for the party leadership. All the parties, including the Nationalists, stressed their commitment to getting the best deal for the UK from Europe, although the Scottish and Welsh Nationalists respectively expressed their determination of getting the best deal for Scotland and Wales and their desire for full representation in the central EU institutions, noting that smaller states that enjoyed membership were represented in the Council and Commission as of right, which was not the case for any component state of the UK. The BNP and UKIP, both committed to taking Britain out of the Union, highlighted their concerns about immigration. The Eurosceptic BNP reiterated its desire for British jobs for British workers but rather damaged its own credibility by putting a picture of a Polish rather than British WWII spitfire on its campaign literature.

9.2 Electoral campaign

The hostility towards European integration shown in much of the UK print media, owned as it is by North American proprietors, has ensured that successive governments have been reluctant to accept EU funding and there was only a limited EP information campaign in 2009. The UK office of the EP ran 'roadshows' in different parts of the UK, but there were no large scale national events and the role overall was low-key. The fact that county elections in England coincided with European elections ensured that European issues were never likely to dominate media coverage in the run-up to the elections, despite the fact that most political parties produced separate manifestos for the two sets of elections. Yet, if the UK media are normally wont to ignore European matters or to portray the EU and its Parliament in a negative light, in 2009 they were almost entirely absent in the run-up to polling day as the media focussed on domestic issues. After years of criticizing the Brussels 'gravy train', the media focussed instead on a political landscape transformed by an expenses scandal relating to national parliamentarians. The *Sunday Times* ran a series of articles about members of the House of Lords, whom they asserted had abused the parliamentary expenses system. While significant, since some of the peers named were found guilty of various crimes associated with their expense claims and sent to gaol, these articles alone did not seem to capture public interest. By contrast, a series of strategically placed articles in the *Daily Telegraph* that implicated large numbers of parliamentarians from all three main parties over spending, including trying to avoid paying taxes on the sale of second homes, led to a protracted debate about the apparent corruption in the UK political system. For once, even the expenses of the Members of the European Parliament were subject to rather less scrutiny than those of national parliamentarians, although the *Daily Telegraph* had raised concerns about at least one British MEP's expenses in 2008. This focus ensured that key issues, such as holding referenda on European issues and the financial crisis were fairly unimportant in the British European elections in 2009, regardless of the intentions of the parties' campaign organizers.

As so often in European Parliament elections, the key issues and key actors in the 2009 elections were predominantly national, not European. Yet on this occasion the choice of topic was not that of the main political parties, candidates or voters, but of the media, determined as they were to keep the scandal of parliamentary expenses alive. Thus the talk was of 'duck houses' not the Common Agricultural Policy, of houses being 'flipped' rather than the need for adequate housing for all, and of tax avoidance rather than any common European taxation. In contrast to many previous European elections, Labour and the Liberal Democrats had planned to campaign on the basis of European issues, at least in part. Yet while all parties had devoted considerable space to European issues in their manifestos, as noted above, Europe played an even smaller role than usual in the 2009 elections. Nor were the Tories, implicated as they were in the expenses scandal, able to campaign as they had planned to make the election a referendum on Gordon Brown's Labour government, not least over what they felt was its broken promise to hold a referendum on EU treaty reform. Election expenses dominated the news, print, audio, and televisual, throughout the weeks leading up to 4 June, even featuring on a children's news programme, on the grounds that children like cheating no more than adults do.

The expenses scandal led to the first resignation of the Speaker of the House of Commons in over 300 years. All the main parties recognized that change was required but Speaker Michael Martin appeared to be impeding the process. Conservative leader David Cameron also took the opportunity to call for a general election so that voters could 'pass judgment on their politicians' (Porter, 2009). This was particularly pertinent since the 2009 EP contest took place in the shadow of a such a general election: although Parliament finally ran until spring 2010, there had been speculation that Gordon Brown would call an early election ever since he had taken over as Prime Minister in July 2007. The BNP was also keen to highlight the expenses scandal, attacking the 'stale old parties' (BNP, 2009) and portraying mainstream politicians as pigs with their snouts in a trough, safe in the knowledge that they had no parliamentarians of their own and thus could not face similar allegations.

The future of European integration was raised in public debate and in the manifestos as result of the Irish 'No' vote to the Lisbon Treaty. The Conservatives accused Labour of reneging on their commitment to hold a referendum on the earlier Constitutional Treaty. Labour asserted that the Lisbon Treaty did not necessitate a referendum precisely because it fell short of being a constitutional document. The Liberal Democrats were committed to a referendum on whether or not the UK should remain in the EU, hoping that this approach would avert party splits and ensure a 'Yes' vote, which was unlikely to be achieved in referenda for either the Constitutional or Lisbon Treaty. Meanwhile, if the latter went too far for the Conservatives, it did not go far enough for the Greens, who argued for a proper EU Constitution, which they argued 'should be subject to a referendum in every Member State where that is legally possible, including the UK' (Green Party, 2009a, 29).

Key international and European issues featured in manifestos but less clearly in the wider campaigns. Immigration and its connection with the fundamental freedoms enshrined in the European Union caused particular concern to UKIP and the far-right BNP, both of which put forward anti-immigrant, anti-EU proposals in their manifestos, stressing a preference for looser ties with the EU, a position favoured by the Conservatives. While the Liberal Democrats were broadly in favour of integration, they argued that the EU should be reformed and also rejected the idea of a common European immigration policy. By contrast, Labour and the Greens both articulated more positive approaches to European immigration policy, with the Greens stressing, 'we do not support creating a Fortress Europe' (Green Party, 2009a, 30). Despite the parties' conflicting rhetoric, immigration did not become a major issue in the campaigns, although it was to play a vital role in the general election the following year.

The financial crisis was raised in manifestos, with the Greens in particular making it the key issue in a manifesto entitled 'It's the economy, stupid' (Greens, 2009a) and some of their literature highlighting 'jobs, jobs, jobs' in an approach reminiscent of German Social Democrat Gerhardt Schröder's campaign in 1998 (Greens, 2009b). Overall, however, the economy was far less significant in the elections than might have been expected, in part because the crises had not hit the UK as markedly as some other Member States, in part because of the dominance of expenses. Nor was the euro a major campaigning point, although there was little support for Britain to accede to common currency, with the Tories, Greens, UKIP, and the BNP calling for the pound to be retained. Labour reaffirmed their intention to join, as did the Liberal Democrats, albeit using the more measured commitment to join only 'when the economic conditions [were] right' (Lib Dems, 2009, 14).

EU enlargement has not been a salient issue in the UK, with the parties generally in favour of enlargement, including Turkey; while this proposition does not find the same level of support amongst voters as amongst the elite, it has not risen up the political agenda and thus did not feature significantly in the election.

9.3 *Electoral results*

Turnout fell compared with the previous EP elections and was lower than in the local elections held on the same day: 34.5 per cent versus 39.2 per cent (Electoral Commission, 2009, 26). In a post-election ICM survey, 9 per cent of those who did vote indicated that they would not have bothered to vote in the European elections had they not coincided with the local elections, with just 2 per cent saying they only voted in the local elections because they coincided with the European elections, suggesting that European elections were still deemed less important than domestic elections (ibid., 29). The difference between 2004 and 2009 may be explained in part by the fact that four English regions that had trialled the use of all-postal ballots in 2004 reverted to normal voting at polling stations, with postal or proxy voting the exception rather than the rule. Whereas expenses formed a major part of the pre-electoral coverage, only 6 per cent told ICM that this was a reason for their not voting. However, 19 per cent said they 'disliked the candidates or political parties' (ibid., 27), a considerable indictment of the political process, particularly given the proliferation of political parties which offered voters considerable choice over European issues, in contrast to the early experience of European elections. In 2009, 72 seats were up for election in the UK, compared with 78 in 2004.

Table 10.5 Allocation of EP seats to regions in the UK

Region	MEP seats 2009	MEP seats 2004	Change
East Midlands	5	6	−1
East of England	7	7	0
London	8	9	−1
North East	3	3	0
North West	8	9	−1
South East	10	10	0
South West	6	7	−1
West Midlands	6	7	−1
Yorkshire and the Humber	6	6	0
Scotland	6	7	−1
Wales	4	4	0
Northern Ireland	3	3	0
Total	72	78	−6

Source: The Electoral Commission, 2009, 10.

Ten seats were at stake in the largest region, the South East of England, compared with just 3 in the smallest: the North East of England and Northern Ireland. London and the North West had 8 seats apiece, the East of England 7, the South West, which since 2004 includes the otherwise autonomous Overseas Territory of Gibraltar for the purposes of EP elections, like Yorkshire and the Humber, and Scotland had 6 seats on offer, the East Midlands had 5 and Wales had 4. Six MEPs were elected to represent the West Midlands in June 2009, although according to the complex allocation rules, it gained an additional seat when the provisions of the Lisbon Treaty came into effect in December 2009, bringing the UK total to 73 MEPs.

As in previous European elections, the ruling party saw its support fall in the 2009 European elections. Labour won just 13 seats compared to 19 in 2004, admittedly in a smaller Parliament, but its vote share was also down from 22.6 per cent to 15.7 per cent. While the

Table 10.6 British MEPs according to electoral constituencies§

East of England	South West
1. Geoffrey van Orden, Conservative	1. Giles Chichester, Conservative
2. *David Campbell Bannerman*, UKIP★	2. Bernard Trevor Colman, UKIP
3. Robert Sturdy, Conservative	3. Graham Watson, Liberal Democrat
4. Andrew Duff, Liberal Democrat	4. *Julie McCulloch Girling*, Conservative
5. Richard Howitt, Labour	5. *William Dartmouth*, UKIP
6. *Vicky Ford*, Conservative	6. *Ashley Peter Fox*, Conservative
7. *John Agnew*, UKIP	
★Since defected to the Conservatives	

East Midlands	West Midlands
1. Roger Helmer, Conservative	1. Philip Bradbourn, Conservative
2. Glenis Willmott, Labour	2. Mike Nattrass, UKIP
3. Derek Roland Clark, UKIP	3. Michael Cashman, Labour
4. *Emma McClarkin*, Conservative	4. Malcolm Harbour, Conservative
5. William Francis Newton Dunn, Liberal Democrat	5. Liz Lynne, Liberal Democrat
	6. *Nicole Sinclaire*, UKIP★★★
	7. Anthea McIntyre, Conservative (since 1 December 2011)

London
1. Charles Tannock, Conservative
2. Claude Moraes, Labour
3. Sarah Ludford, Liberal Democrat
4. Syed Salah Kamall, Conservative
5. Jean Lambert, Green Party
6. Gerard Batten, UKIP
7. Mary Honeyball, Labour
8. *Marina Yannakoudakis*, Conservative

North East
1. Stephen Hughes, Labour
2. Martin Callanan, Conservative
3. Fiona Hall, Liberal Democrat

North West
1. Rt Hon Sir Robert James Atkins, Conservative
2. Arlene McCarthy, Labour
3. *Paul Nuttall*, UKIP
4. Chris Davies, Liberal Democrat
5. Sajjad Haider Karim, Conservative
6. Brian Simpson, Labour
7. *Jacqueline Foster*, Conservative
8. *Nick Griffin*, British National Party

South East
1. Daniel Hannan, Conservative
2. Nigel Farage, UKIP
3. Richard Ashworth, Conservative
4. Sharon Bowles, Liberal Democrat
5. Caroline Lucas, Green Party**
6. Nirj Deva, Conservative
7. *Marta Andreasen*, UKIP★
8. James Elles, Conservative
9. Peter Skinner, Labour
10. *Catherine Zena Bearder*, Liberal Democrat

Yorkshire and the Humber
1. Edward McMillan-Scott, Conservative★★★★
2. Linda McAvan, Labour
3. Godfrey Bloom, UKIP
4. Diana Wallis, Liberal Democrat
5. Timothy Kirkhope, Conservative
6. *Andrew Henry William Brons*, British National Party

Wales
1. *Kay Swinburne*, Conservative
2. *Derek Vaughan*, Labour
3. Jill Evans, Plaid Cymru
4. *John Andreas Bufton*, UKIP

Scotland
1. Ian Hudghton, Scottish National Party
2. David Martin, Labour
3. Struan Stevenson, Conservative
4. Alyn Smith, Scottish National Party
5. *George Lyon*, Liberal Democrat
6. Catherine Stihler, Labour

Northern Ireland
1. Bairbre de Brún, *Sinn Féin*
2. Jim Nicholson, Ulster Conservatives and Unionists
3. *Diane Dodds*, Democratic Unionist Party – DUP

Notes:
§ 73 MEPs: 52 incumbents, 21 newly elected (indicated by italics).
★ Since defected to the Conservatives.
★★ Elected to House of Commons as Member of Parliament for Brighton Pavilion in May 2010.
★★★ Expelled from UKIP, now Independent.
★★★★ Since defected to the Liberal Democrats.

Source: UK Office of the European Parliament (2009); www.europarl.org.uk/section/european-elections/results-2009-european-elections-uk.

main opposition Conservative party came first in the European polls, with 25 seats and 27.7 per cent of the vote, they performed far less well than they might have wished in the run-up to a general election in which they sought to wrest power from Labour. However, as in 2004 many of their natural supporters switched to the UKIP, which now came second for the first time in a national poll, securing 16.5 per cent of the vote and 13 seats. The Liberal Democrats, who came second in local elections on the same day, came a poor fourth in the

EP vote, winning 13.7 per cent of the vote, down from 2004, but retaining 11 seats. The Greens saw their vote rise to 8.6 per cent but they still won just 2 seats, as did the Scottish Nationalists on 2.1 per cent of the vote, though of course a much larger percentage of the Scottish vote.

The Welsh Nationalists retained their single seat while the far-right British National Party secured parliamentary representation for the first time, winning 2 seats on 6.2 per cent of the vote. Overall, minority, Eurosceptic, and right-wing parties all performed well and large opposition parties did rather less well than small ones.

The proportion of women elected in 2009 was somewhat higher than in Westminster at one third: 24 women compared with 48 men. The election of a woman in the additional West Midlands seat in December that year improved the figures further. At 34.2 per cent female representation, the UK was thus above the EU average.

Table 10.7 EP detailed election results in the UK: 2009

National party	Number of votes	Percentage of votes	Seats	Political group
Conservatives	4,198,664	27.7	25	European Conservatives and Reformists Group
United Kingdom Independence Party	2,498,226	16.5	13	Europe of Freedom and Democracy Group
Labour	2,381,760	15.7	13	Group of the Progressive Alliance of Socialists and Democrats in the European Parliament
Liberal Democrats	2,080,613	13.7	11	Group of the Alliance of Liberals and Democrats for Europe
Greens	1,303,745	8.6	2	Group of the Greens/European Free Alliance
British National Party	943,598	6.2	2	Non-attached
Scottish National Party	321,007	2.1	2	Group of the Greens/European Free Alliance
Plaid Cymru	126,702	0.8	1	Group of the Greens/European Free Alliance
Others	1,282,887	8.5	0	
Total	15,137,202		69	
Northern Ireland				
Sinn Féin	126,184	26.0	1	Confederal Group of the European United Left/Nordic Green Left
Democratic Unionist Party	88,346	18.2	1	Non-attached
Ulster Conservatives and Unionists	82,893	17.1	1	European Conservatives and Reformists
Others	187, 149	38.7	0	
Total	484, 572		3	
Total UK			72	
Turnout	**34.5 %**			

Source: UK Office of the European Parliament, 2009; House of Commons Library, 2009.

Table 10.8 List of British MEPs: seventh legislature

East Midlands

Name	National party	Political group	Chair	Professional background	Date of birth	Gender	First elected
Derek Clark	UKIP	EFD		Science teacher, UKIP regional and national roles	10/10/1933	Male	2004
Roger Helmer	Conservative Party	ECR		Marketing and management	25/01/1944	Male	1999
Emma McClarkin	Conservative Party	ECR		Political advisor and government relations	09/10/1978	Female	2009
Bill Newton Dunn	Liberal Democrat	ALDE		Industry, author	03/10/1941	Male	1979
Glenis Willmott	Labour Party	S&D	Leader of Labour MEPs	Medical scientist, county councillor	04/03/1951	Female	2006

(continued)

Table 10.8 (continued)

East of England

Name	National party	Political group	Chair	Professional background	Date of birth	Gender	First elected
John Stuart Agnew	UKIP	EFD		Farmer and farm manager	30/10/1949	Male	2009
David Campbell Bannerman	UKIP	EFD	Deputy leader of UKIP	Communications, public relations	28/05/1960	Male	2009
Andrew Duff	Liberal Democrat	ALDE		Director, federal trust, county councillor	25/12/1950	Male	1999
Vicky Ford	Conservative Party	ECR		Finance manager, District councillor	21/09/1967	Female	2009
Richard Howitt	Labour Party	S&D	Chair, Disability Intergroup (1994-); Vice-Chair Human Rights sub-committe	Community care worker, Local councillor	05/04/1961	Male	1994
Robert Sturdy	Conservative Party	ECR	Vice-Chair on INTA	Accountant, farmer	22/06/1944	Male	1994
Geoffrey van Orden MBE	Conservative Party	ECR		British army	10/04/1945	Male	1999

London

Name	National party	Political group	Chair	Professional background	Date of birth	Gender	First elected
Gerard Batten	UKIP	EFD		Bookbinder and salesman	27/03/1954	Male	2004
Mary Honeyball	Labour Party	S&D		Civil society positions, London borough councillor	12/11/1952	Female	2000
Syed Kamall	Conservative Party	ECR	Vice-Chair, Committee on AFCO	Marketing, strategy and public affairs consultant	15/02/1967	Male	2005
Jean Lambert	Green Party	G/EFA	Chair, Delegation for Relations with the Countries of South Asia	Teacher	01/06/1950	Female	1999
[Baroness] Sarah Ludford	Liberal Democrats Party	ALDE	Vice-Chair, Delegation for Relations with the United States	Barrister, consultant on European affairs, London Borough councillor, Member of House of Lords (special leave granted)	14/03/1951	Female	1999
Claude Moraes	Labour Party	S&D	Chair of the Anti-Racism and Diversity Intergroup (2004–); Co-Chair of the Intergroup on Ageing (2004–)	Political advisor, director of a migration NGO	22/10/1965	Male	1999
Charles Tannock	Conservative Party	ECR	Vice-Chair, Delegation for relations with the NATO Parliamentary Assembly	Psychiatrist and senior lecturer, London Borough councilor	25/09/1957	Male	1999
Marina Yannakoudakis	Conservative Party	ECR		Financial director of own travel company, London Borough councillor	16/04/1956	Female	2009

North East

Name	National party	Political group	Chair	Professional background	Date of birth	Gender	First elected
Martin Callanan	Conservative Party	ECR	Leader of the Conservatives in the EP	Project engineer, councillor	08/08/1961	Male	1999
Fiona Hall	Liberal Democrat	ALDE	Leader, Lib Dems MEPs in EP	Teacher	15/07/1955	Female	2004
Stephen Hughes	Labour Party	S&D	S&D Deputy Leader	Local government officer	19/08/1952	Male	1984

(continued)

Table 10.8 (continued)

North West

Name	National party	Political group	Chair	Professional background	Date of birth	Gender	First elected
Sir Robert Atkins	Conservative Party	ECR		Member of Parliament, Parliamentary private secretary to minister	05/02/1946	Male	1999
Chris Davies	Liberal Democrat	ALDE		Consultancy, local councillor, Member of Parliament	07/07/1954	Male	1999
Jacqueline Foster	Conservative Party	ECR		British Airways worker, consultant in areas of aviation, aerospace and defence	30/12/1947	Female	2009
Nick Griffin	British National Party	Non-attached		Political worker and speaker, Leader of British National Party	01/03/1959	Male	2009
Sajjad Karim	Conservative Party	ECR	Chair, European Parliament Friends of Pakistan Group; Vice-Chair, European Parliament Friends of the Commonwealth Group) Vice-Chair: EMAC	Solicitor, local councillor	11/07/1970	Male	2004 (originally elected as a Liberal Democrat)
Arlene McCarthy	Labour Party	S&D		Lecturer, European Liasion Officer, author	10/10/1960	Female	1994
Paul Nuttall	UKIP	EFD		History lecturer, UKIP chairman	30/11/1976	Male	2009
Brian Simpson	Labour Party	S&D	Chair, Committee on TRAN	Teacher; local councillor, Private Secretary to the Deputy Prime Minister	06/02/1953	Male	1989

Northern Ireland

Name	National party	Political group	Chair	Professional background	Date of birth	Gender	First elected
Bairbre de Brun	Sinn Féin	EUL/NGL		Teacher, community worker, Member of Northern Ireland Assembly	10/01/1954	Female	2009
Diane Dodds	Democratic Unionist Party	Non-attached		Teacher, member Regional Assembly, Belfast City Council	16/08/1958	Female	2009
James Nicholson	Ulster Conservatives and Unionists	ECR	Vice-Chair, Delegation to the ACP-EU Joint Parliamentary Assembly	Farmer, Member of Northern Ireland Assembly, Member of the House of Commons	29/01/1945	Male	1989

Scotland

Name	National party	Political group	Chair	Professional background	Date of birth	Gender	First elected
Ian Hudghton	Scottish National Party	G/EFA		Small Business entrepreneur	19/09/1951	Male	1998
George Lyon	Liberal Democrat	ALDE		Farmer, Member of the Scottish Parliament and Deputy Finance Minster in Scotland, European Committee of the Regions	16/07/1956	Male	2009
David Martin	Labour Party	S&D	Former Vice-President of the European Parliament;	Regional Councillor, author	26/08/1954	Male	1984
Alyn Smith	Scottish National Party	G/EFA	Chair, Delegation for relations with Iraq; Vice-Chair: Committee on PECH	Solicitor, Scottish Parliamentary Advisor	15/09/1973	Male	2004
Struan Stevenson	Conservative Party	ECR		Director of think tanks and public affairs consultants, Conservative Party roles	04/04/1948	Male	1999
Catherine Stihler	Labour Party	S&D		Political advisor to an MP	30/07/1973	Female	1999

(continued)

Table 10.8 (continued)

South East

Name	National party	Political group	Chair	Professional background	Date of birth	Gender	First elected
Marta Andreasen	UKIP	EFD		Accountant, economist and auditor	26/11/1954	Female	2009
Richard Ashworth	Conservative Party	ECR		Farmer, entrepreneur, Conservative Regional Executive	17/09/1947	Male	2004
Catherine Bearder	Liberal Democrat	ALDE		Development officer in civil society organizations, county councillor	14/01/1949	Female	2009
Sharon Bowles	Liberal Democrat	ALDE	Chair: ECON Committee	Material and devices research, UK and European Patent and Trademark Attorney	12/06/1953	Female	2005 (following resignation of colleague)
Nirj Deva	Conservative Party	ECR	Vice-Chair, Committee on DEVE	Scientific advisor, political advisor, Member of Parliament.	11/05/1948	Male	1999
James Elles	Conservative Party	ECR		European Commission, Founder of Transatlantic Policy Network	03/09/1949	Male	1984
Nigel Farage	UKIP	EFD	Co-Chair of EFD	Commodity markets, UKIP leader	03/04/1964	Male	1999
Daniel Hannan	Conservative Party	ECR	Secretary General of ECR	Journalist, European Research Group, Special Advisor to MP, European Young Conservatives Executive	01/09/1971	Male	1999
Caroline Lucas* Stepped down on election to House of Commons on 6th May 2010	Green Party	G/EFA	Vice-Chair: Delegation for relations with the Palestinian Legislative Council	Press, communications and policy officer with Green Party and in civil society organizations, Green Party leader	09/12/1960	Female	1999
Peter Skinner	Labour	S&D		Lecturer in business studies and economics, training events organizer	1/06/1969	Male	1994

Wales

Name	National party	Political group	Chair	Professional background	Date of birth	Gender	First elected
John Bufton	UKIP	EFD		Health and social care manager, town and country councillor	31/08/1962	Male	2009
Jill Evans	*Plaid Cymru* – Party of Wales	G/EFA	Vice-Chair of Group of the Greens–European Free Alliance; President of *Plaid Cymru*	Public affairs officer, local councillor	8/05/1959	Female	1999
Kay Swinburne	Conservative Party	ECR		Medical research, international business and finance healthcare advisor. Corporate and government advisor on biotechnology. County councillor and town mayor	08/06/1967	Female	2009
Derek Vaughan	Labour Party	S&D		Valuation office agency officer, public and commerical services trade union, county councillor and mayor	02/05/1961	Male	2009

(continued)

Table 10.8 (continued)

West Midlands

Name	National party	Political group	Chair	Professional background	Date of birth	Gender	First elected
Anthea McIntyre	Conservative Party	ECR		Businesswoman	29/06/1954	Female	2011
Philip Bradbourn	Conservative Party	ECR	Chair, Delegation for relations with Canada	Research officer, political advisor. Conservative Party chairmanships	09/08/1951	Male	1999
Michael Cashman	Labour Party	S&D	Chair, Delegation for relations with South Africa	Actor and director, Labour Party National Executive Committee, local councillor	17/12/1950	Male	1999
Malcolm Harbour	Conservative Party	ECR	Chair, Committee on the IMCO	Design, product planning, marketing, consultant and project director	19/02/1947	Male	1999
Elizabeth (Liz) Lynne	Liberal Democrat	ALDE	Vice-Chair, Committee on EMPL	Actor, speech consultant, Member of Parliament	22/01/1948	Female	1999
Mike Nattrass	UKIP	EFD		Surveyor, entrepreneur and company director	14/12/1945	Male	2004
Nicole (Nikki) Sinclaire	UKIP	Non-attached		Political advisor	26/07/1968	Female	2009

Yorkshire and the Humber

Name	National party	Political group	Chair	Professional background	Date of birth	Gender	First elected
Godfrey Bloom	UKIP	EFD		Financial Economist	22/11/1949	Male	2004
Andrew Henry William Brons	British National Party	Non-attached		Lecturer (A Level), National Front leader	16/06/1947	Male	2009
Timothy Kirkhope	Conservative Party	ECR	Deputy Chair, ECR	Solicitor, county councillor, Member of Parliament	29/04/1945	Male	1999
Linda McAvan	Labour Party	S&D	Vice-Chair, Delegation to the ACP-EU Joint Parliamentary Assembly	Civil society and public administration positions	02/12/1962	Female	1998
Edward McMillan-Scott	Conservative Party (now a Liberal Democrat)	ECR (subsequently ALDE)	Vice-President of European Parliament	Parliamentary and political consultant	15/08/1949	Male	1984
Diana Wallis	Liberal Democrat	ALDE	Vice-President of European Parliament	Solicitor	28/06/1954	Female	1999

Source: www.europarl.europa.eu-meps-en-search.html?country=GB.

9.4 Campaign finance

The Political Parties, Elections and Referendums Act 2000 (PPERA) introduced strict rules on the financing of election campaigns in the UK, with expenditure and donations overseen by the Electoral Commission. For the purposes of the 2009 EP elections, the relevant period for expenses was the four months leading to polling day. Because the elections were fought on the basis of regional lists, party expenditure was capped at a multiple of £45,000 times the number of MEPs to be elected in each region, or a total of £3,375,000 for a party fielding a full complement of 72 seats. In practice, no party reached the national spending limit and the combined expenditure for the 33 parties registered in 2009 was £9.78 million, down from 2004 spending levels, except in Wales (Electoral Commission, 2010a, 4). The highest spenders, accounting for 70 per cent of total expenditure in 2009, were the Conservatives at £2,482,536, albeit down from their 2004 spending, Labour at £2,302,444, and UKIP at £1,270,855 (ibid., 5). Labour and the British National Party both increased their expenditure compared with 2004, as did the Scottish Nationalists and *Plaid Cymru*. UKIP halved its expenditure, while the Liberal Democrats' spending remained broadly constant although the balance shifted from England to Scotland and Wales. Although the 2009 EP elections coincided with important local elections in England, the two sets of elections were subject to separate financial arrangements, both regulated through PPERA. Parties could, however, produce literature relating to both local and EP elections, with proportions of the cost split between the two campaigns.

Aside from party funding, eight other bodies declared total election expenditure of £366,048 to the Electoral Commission in respect to the 2009 EP elections, the largest being Searchlight Information Services, a body that campaigns against Fascism and the BNP under the banner of 'hope not hate', which declared £137,409 in expenses.

10 Theoretical interpretations of Euro-elections

10.1 Second-Order Election theory

Traditionally deemed an 'awkward partner' in the EU, Britain consistently had the lowest turnout in EP elections until the arrival of the Central and East European members in 2004, and fitted the Second-Order Election theory very well, at least until the introduction of PR in the 1999 elections. Parties, politicians, and the media all focussed more on national than European issues during EP elections and little attention was paid to European manifestos, as is to be expected in elections in a second-order arena. This altered somewhat with the emergence of Eurosceptic parties, notably UKIP, but the main focus of attention nonetheless remained domestic.

In addition, the UK fits the theory's expectations about impact of the national electoral cycle on outcomes, as the Labour and the Conservative parties saw their fortunes rise and fall in the opposite direction to their respective positions in national politics. The Tory government enjoyed a honeymoon period in the very first European elections of June 1979, just a month after it had taken office, but saw its support fall repeatedly at subsequent EP elections, while Labour's vote increased steadily to the point in 1994 when the results were a mirror image of those in 1979: 63 Labour MEPs and 18 Conservatives in a slightly enlarged delegation of 87 up from 81, compared with 60 Tories and 17 Labour in 1979. The rise in support for Labour in EP elections over the years was not matched by success in national general elections, giving some credence to the hypothesis that governments perform badly mid-term but that this might reflect voters' desire to 'voice' their opposition without being indicative of the results for the subsequent general election. Only in 1997 did the Tories finally leave office. At that point the electoral fortunes of the two parties shifted again: Labour saw a steady decline in votes and seats from 1999, while the Tory vote went up. And yet the former managed to secure a solid majority in the subsequent general election.

The assumption that governing parties lose is thus upheld in the UK case. How badly their support declines depends on the point in the electoral cycle and does not provide much by way of indication about the governing party's likely success at the subsequent elections.

The hypothesis that small and new parties do well in SOEs was less clear-cut in the first four sets of EP competition, as the FPTP system ensured that minor parties struggled to gain election even when, like the Greens in 1989, they obtained 15 per cent of the popular vote. Until 1994, only Labour and the Conservatives secured representation in England, although the Nationalists achieved success in the rest of the UK. Two Liberal Democrats managed to break through in 1994 under the FPTP, but it was only in 1999 with the introduction of a system of proportional representation that smaller parties regularly gained seats in the European Parliament. New parties did not seem to flourish either until the emergence of UKIP, which won 3 seats in 1999, rising to 13 in 2009. The Greens won 2 seats when PR was introduced but were not able to rise above this level in the subsequent electoral waves.

10.2 Europe Salience theory

If the focus of European elections has been on national issues, national politicians, and national manifestos in the UK, the European dimension has not been wholly absent. Since the introduction of PR, the right-wing Eurosceptic UK Independence Party has gained a foothold both in votes and seats in the European contests. While its key policy plank of withdrawal from the EU might seem more appropriate for general elections, since national governments make such constitutional decisions, UKIP's rise at the European level has not been matched with success in national or, indeed, local elections. Similarly, in 2004 and 2009 the far-right anti-EU British National Party secured a large number of votes, which delivered them 2 seats in the 2009 elections. An anti-European stance seemed to deliver results in the UK. Both of these Eurosceptic parties are on the right/far-right of the political spectrum and thus the far right also appeared to do well in the UK. However, there was no similar support for the far left, which has been almost absent, at least since the shift of Labour to a mainstream centre-left party after the 1983 national election, when it sought to pull out of the EU.

In the elections from 1984 to 1994 inclusive, Labour did extremely well, again because the governing party was losing. However, it is important to note that large parties do not necessarily lose in the UK, where single-party government and alternance have been the rule since 1945, at least until 2010. The Green vote has been somewhat mixed in the UK. It was high in 1989 at the time of the 'green tide' across Europe, but this also coincided with a very poor performance from the Liberal Democrats, who had only just emerged from a painful merger of the Social Democrat and Liberal parties. The Greens' support subsequently ebbed and flowed, although they have two MEPs since 1999 compared to one MP in Westminster only since 2010, as a result of the differing electoral systems.

The Conservatives, divided over Europe at least since the early 1990s, have seen their support in European elections diminish as UKIP has grown. This ensured that the party did not benefit from Labour's period in government as much as it might have expected, winning only 25 seats in 2009 compared to UKIP's 13. The party's response was to adopt an increasingly Eurosceptic line, but this failed to stem the rise of UKIP. Moreover, the importance of the European dimension could be seen most distinctly in 2009 when the EP elections coincided with county council elections in much of England. Whereas the Tories topped both polls, they were the clear victors in local elections, while the Liberal Democrats came a strong second, with Labour third; in the EP poll, UKIP came second, closely followed by Labour, with the Liberal Democrats fourth. The local election results proved a good predictor for the general election the following year while the EP contest indicated the depth of Euroscepticism in the UK.

EP elections have rarely excited much interest in the UK amongst either elites or the public. While the very low turnout in 1979 could be attributed to voter and activist fatigue after a hard-fought general election barely a month earlier, as well as the novelty of the elections, persistent low turnout suggests that these were not the key issues. After 30 years and seven sets of elections, it seems fair to conclude that Britain views them predominantly as second-order national elections. The point in the national electoral cycle is a good predictor of how the governing party will fare, and governing parties typically do badly. However, there is a European dimension to voters' decisions and parties advocating a Eurosceptic agenda performed increasingly well in the 20 years after the Maastricht Treaty, which was intended to make the Union more democratic through expanding the powers of the European Parliament, yet paradoxically seemed to result in divided parties and increasingly sceptical voters and media.

References

Primary sources

Animals Count (2009) *European Parliament Elections 2009 Eastern Region,* London, Animals Count, www.animalscount.org/backup/files/manifesto_2009.pdf (accessed on 6 February 2012).
British National Party (BNP) (2009) Manifesto for the European Elections, www.archive.org/details/Bnp2009EuropeanElectionsManifesto (accessed on 6 February 2012).
Conservative Party (2009) 'Vote for Change'– European Election Manifesto, www.ecrgroup.eu/download/publications/euro-election-manifesto.pdf (accessed on 6 February 2012).
Electoral Commission (2009) *The European Parliamentary and Local Government Elections June 2009 – Report on the Administration of the 4 June 2009 Elections,* London.
Electoral Commission (2010a) *Report on Campaign Spending at the 2009 European Parliamentary Elections in the UK and Local Elections in England,* London.
European Commission (2009) *The 2009 European Elections Report,* Special Eurobarometer 303/Wave 70.1.
European Parliament (2009) 'European Elections 2009 – Pre-electoral Survey – First Wave, First Results: European Average and Major National Trends', EP Directorate General for Communication, 25 May 2009.
European Parliament website, www.europarl.europa.eu/ (accessed on 13 December 2013).
European Parliament Information Office in the UK (2009) *Previous Election Results.* Online. Avaialble at:www.europarl.org.uk/section/european-elections/previous-election-results (accessed on 31 May 2011).
European Parliament Information Office in the UK (2011) *Media Guide 2011* London, European Parliament Office
Eurostat (2013, 2014) http://epp.eurostat.ec.europa.eu/ (accessed on 5 June 2015).
Green Party (2009a) 'It's the Economy, Stupid' – The Green Party Manifesto for the European Parliament Elections 2009.
Green Party (2009b) *Green View,* Spring Issue, London, Eastern Green Party.
House of Commons Library (1999a) *European Parliament Elections – 1979 to 1994,* Research Paper 99/57. Online. Available at: www.parliament.uk/briefing-papers/RP99-57.pdf (accessed on 7 February 2012).
House of Commons Library (1999b) *Elections to the European Parliament – June 1999.* Online. Available at: www.parliament.uk/documents/commons/lib/research/rp99/rp99-064.pdf (accessed on 7 February 2012).
House of Commons Library (2001) *UK Election Statistics,* Research Paper 01/37. Online. Available at: www.parliament.uk/commons/lib/research/rp2001/rp01-037.pdf (accessed on 7 February 2012).
House of Commons Library (2004) *European Parliament elections 2004,* Research Paper 04/50. Online. Available at: www.parliament.uk/documents/commons/lib/research/rp2004/rp04-050.pdf (accessed on 7 February 2012).

House of Commons Library (2006) *General Election 2005*, Research Paper 05/33. Online. Available at: www.parliament.uk/commons/lib/research/rp2005/RP05-033.pdf (accessed on 6 February 2012).

House of Commons Library (2009) *European Parliament Elections 2009*, Research Paper 09/53. Online. Available at: www.parliament.uk/commons/lib/research/rp2009/rp09-053.pdf (accessed on 31 May 2011).

House of Commons Library (2011) *General Election 2010, Final Edition*, Research Paper 10/36, London, House of Commons.

Jury Team (2009) www.juryteam.org/ (accessed on 12 May 2009).

Labour (2009) 'Winning the Fight for Britain's Future' – European Elections 2009: www.labour.org.uk/uploads/e0e9e2d5-1437-8734-6d4e-8084302a2346.pdf (accessed on 6 February 2012).

Liberal Democrats (2009) 'Stronger Together, Poorer Apart' – The Liberal Democrat Manifesto for the 2009 Elections to the European Parliament.

Office for National Statistics(2011) 'Rural Quality of Life Can Rely on Links with Urban Areas', *News Release*, 8 June.

Plaid Cymru (2009) European Manifesto, 'Plaid – On Your Side in Wales and in Europe'.

Scottish National Party (2009) 'We've Got What it Takes' – Manifesto 2009.

UK Office of the European Parliament (2009) http://www.europarl.org.uk.

Secondary sources

Hearl, D. (1986) 'The United Kingdom', in Lodge, J. (ed.) *Direct Elections to the European Parliament 1984*, Basingstoke, Macmillan, 228–49.

Hix, S. and Marsh, M. (2007) 'Punishment or Protest? Understanding European Parliament Elections', *The Journal of Politics*, 69(2), 495–510.

Mather, J. (2001) 'The United Kingdom', in Lodge, J. (ed.) *The 1999 Elections to the European Parliament*, Basingstoke, Palgrave, 214–28.

Pateman, T. (2011) 'Rural and Urban Areas: Comparing Lives Using Rural/Urban Classifications', *Regional Trends*, 43(1), 11–86.

Porter, A. (2009) 'MPs' expenses: Michael Martin Becomes first Commons Speaker to Quit in 300 Years', *Daily Telegraph*, 19 May. Online. Available at: www.telegraph.co.uk/news/newstopics/mps-expenses/5352311/MPs-expenses-Michael-Martin-becomes-first-Commons-Speaker-to-quit-in-300-years.html (accessed on 3 June 2011).

Smith, J. (1994) *Citizens' Europe? The European Elections and the Role of the European Parliament*, London, Royal Institute of International Affairs.

Smith, J. (1995a) *Voice of the People: The European Parliament in the 1990s*, London, Royal Institute of International Affairs.

Smith, J. (1995b) *Direct Elections to the European Parliament*, Oxford, unpublished DPhil thesis.

Smith, J. (2005a)*Reinvigorating European Elections: The Implications of Electing the European Commission* London, Royal Institute of International Affairs.

Smith, J. (2005b) 'A Missed Opportunity? New Labour's European Policy 1997 – 2005', *International Affairs*, 81(4), July, 703–21.

11
IRELAND

Richard Dunphy

Figure 11.1 Map of Ireland

Table 11.1 Ireland profile

EU entry year	1973 ECSC, EEC and Euratom
Schengen entry year	Non-member
MEPs elected in 2009	12
MEPs under Lisbon Treaty	12
Capital	Dublin
Total area★	69,797 km²
Population	4,605,501
	90.0% Irish, 7.5% other White, 1.3% Asian, 1.1% Black, 1.1% mixed, 1.6% unspecified
Population density★★	67.2/km²
Median age of population	36
Political system	Parliamentary Republic
Head of state	Mary McAleese (*Fianna Fáil*), (November 1997–November 2011) Michael D. Higgins (Labour) (November 2011–)
Head of government	Brian Cowen (*Fianna Fáil*) (May 2008–March 2011); Enda Kenny (*Fine Gael*) (March 2011–)
Political majority	*Fianna Fáil* (Soldiers of Destiny) Greens and Independents Government Coalition (May 2008–March 2011); *Fine Gael* (Family of the Gael) Labour Government Coalition, (March 2011–)
Currency	Euro (€) since 1999
Prohead GDP in PPS	40,200 €

Source: Eurostat, 2013, 2014, http://epp.eurostat.ec.europa.eu/.

Notes:
★ Total area including inland waters.
★★ Population density: the ratio of the annual average population of a region to the land area of the region.

1 Geographical position

Located in the north-western part of Europe, the Republic of Ireland belongs geographically to the so-called British Isles. With an area of 70,000 square kilometres, it shares the island's territory with Northern Ireland, which belongs to the United Kingdom. The Irish Republic has a population of over 4.5 million people with a low density of 65.2 inhabitants per square kilometre. Its population is quite homogenous and does not entail the presence of any major ethnic group.

2 Historical background

The Republic of Ireland gained its independence from British rule in 1922, following an Anglo-Irish Treaty signed on 6 December 1921, that ended several years of conflict between the British government and the Irish independence movement. A crucial aspect of this treaty was the division of the island into Northern Ireland, which remained part of the United Kingdom, and the Southern Irish State, later renamed as the Republic of Ireland in 1949. The treaty, which was supported by moderate Nationalists and opposed by 'hard-line' Republicans, triggered a civil war and eventually led to the establishment of the two main parties that have dominated Irish politics ever since: the pro-treaty *Fine Gael*, Family or Clan of the Gaels, founded in 1933, and the anti-treaty *Fianna Fáil*, Soldiers of Destiny, founded in 1926. Such a division over the treaty remained a source of contention throughout the interwar period. In 1932, the leader of *Fianna Fáil* Eamon De Valera became *Taoiseach* (Prime Minister) and abolished the oath of allegiance to the British monarchy, which had been an important condition for the Anglo-Irish Treaty. He also severed ties to the United Kingdom and the Commonwealth with a new Constitution in 1937 that made Southern Ireland a Republic in all but name. The official declaration arrived only after the Republic of Ireland Act 1948 (No. 22 of 1948) was signed into law by the *Oireachtas* (Parliament) on 21 December 1948 and came into force on Easter Monday, 18 April 1949. During WWII, De Valera kept Ireland neutral; he was replaced as *Taoiseach* by *Fine Gael* leader John A. Costello in 1948. Costello introduced the Republic of Ireland Act that ended membership of the Commonwealth. The UK government, which reluctantly accepted the Act, offered reassurance to the pro-British majority living in the North of the island by declaring that this territory would join the Republic of Ireland only if this was agreed by the Northern Ireland Assembly. De Valera remained in politics as *Taoiseach* from 1951 to 1954 and later from 1957 to 1959 and as President of Ireland for two seven-year terms until 1973.

Throughout the 1960s, the objective of the various governments was to improve the economy of the country, still lagging behind in relation to most industrialized western European democracies. Despite its entry to the European Economic Community in 1973, alongside the UK and Denmark, economic recession and stagnation characterized most of the decade in Ireland. Only in the mid-1980s did its economy begin to recover. Throughout the 1990s and early 2000s, Ireland, known as the 'Celtic Tiger', undertook major transformations, thanks to massive inward investment and EU structural funds, which led to an economic boom.

However, over-reliance on foreign capital and on an artificially-inflated housing market, massive and unsustainable borrowing, and a relative failure to invest in health and education, made Ireland vulnerable to the full onslaught of the 2008 financial crisis. In November 2010, the country was left with no alternative but to take a loan from the European Financial Stability Fund (EFSF), which led to the introduction of major austerity measures in order to bring down a budget deficit that reached 32.4 per cent of gross domestic product.

Between 1997 and 2008, during Bertie Ahern's premiership, the Irish and British governments worked closely to resolve the conflict in Northern Ireland. The so-called 'Good Friday Agreement', signed on 10 April 1998, was an important milestone towards peace which was finally achieved with the restoration of the Northern Ireland Assembly and a devolved Northern Irish government. This new situation also allowed the rise of living standards for local people.

3 Geopolitical profile

Ireland is well integrated into global governance institutions. However, one major feature of Ireland's political profile has been its neutrality since WWII, which prevented its membership of the North Atlantic Treaty Organization. And yet, Irish troops have been engaged in humanitarian missions under United Nations' auspices. After the lengthy and thorny ratification process of the Treaty of the European Union, several Irish governments began to reconsider the question of neutrality within the Common Foreign and Security Policy. The introduction of the battle groups model has led to the inclusion of Irish troops, a policy which has been opposed by smaller parties, particularly the Greens. Finally, Ireland has been involved in NATO's Partnership for Peace programme since 2000.

4 Overview of the political landscape

The Republic of Ireland, or *Éire* in Irish, is a parliamentary democracy based on the bicameral *Oireachtas,* consisting of a Lower Chamber, the 166-member *Dáil* and an Upper Chamber, the 60-member *Seanad*. The former dominates the legislative process while the latter may be able to delay, but not reject, legislation. The members of the *Dáil* are elected every five years by a Single Transferable Voting (STV) system. Ireland is one of the few countries in Europe using such a system. Given that it is difficult to achieve an absolute majority within the Parliament, the two main political parties *Fine Gael* and *Fianna Fáil* usually have to form coalitions with smaller parties. The head of state is the President of the Republic, who is directly elected by the population for a seven-year period and is the Guardian of the Constitution. Between 2008 and 2011, Prime Minister Brian Cowen of *Fianna Fáil* led the country with the Progressive Democrats and the Greens.

However, the management of the financial crisis created a catastrophic loss of confidence in Cowen's government, which was replaced after early elections in January 2011 by a *Fine Gael/* Labour coalition government under the premiership of Enda Kenny. Mary McAleese, an independent candidate supported by *Fianna Fáil*, served two terms as President between 1997 and 2011, and was followed by Labour's Michael D. Higgins in November 2011.

5 A brief account of political parties

The centre-right Nationalist *Fianna Fáil* is the biggest party in Ireland, with a level of popular support that has averaged above 40 per cent in general elections since 1932. The party had been leading a minority coalition government, with the Green Party and the support of five independent parliamentary deputies, which lasted from 1997 until early 2011 when it suffered a disastrous defeat in early elections. The centre-right *Fine Gael* is the second largest party in Ireland and has occupied this position since 1932. Sometimes seen as an alliance of moderate Social Liberals and Christian Democrats, the party is more strongly tied to fiscal rectitude and is less Nationalistic than its main rival. Labour is Ireland's third political party, belonging to the moderate, social democratic tradition. Since Irish independence was attained in 1921, Labour has been in government for 19 years on six occasions in coalition with *Fine Gael*, with or without smaller parties and once with *Fianna Fáil*. In 1999, Labour merged with the small, ex-Marxist Democratic Left party, from whose ranks Labour leader Eamon Gilmore, and his immediate predecessor, Pat Rabbitte, were both drawn. However, the merger did not lead to any discernible move to the left on the political spectrum.

Amongst the smaller parties, *Sinn Féin* (Ourselves) is an ultra-Nationalist party that acted as the political wing of the Irish Republican Army (IRA), which fought in order to secure the British withdrawal from Northern Ireland and the reunification of Ireland. Both the IRA and *Sinn Féin* have played a central role in the Northern Ireland peace process; the Republican party has participated in the government of Northern Ireland alongside pro-British Unionists, effectively abandoning its 'armed struggle' and even its hard-line Republican principles in favour of much greater pragmatism. *Sinn Féin* is difficult to locate on a left–right *continuum* and its membership and support base also contain both far-left and far-right elements, whilst its leadership increasingly gravitates towards the political centre and makes no secret of its ambition to enter a coalition government.

As for other small parties, the Socialist Party was founded by Trotskyists who were expelled from the Labour Party in the early 1990s. Headed by Joe Higgins, it gained a reputation for activist politics at a local level and a trenchant defence of workers' rights. The

Table 11.2 List of Irish political parties and their European alignments

National party	Leader	Seats in Dáil 2011	Ideological orientation	Political group
Fianna Fáil	Micheál Martin (2011)	20	Centre-right, nationalist, populist, pragmatic	ALDE
Fine Gael	Enda Kenny (2002)	76	Centre-right, liberal, pro-EU	EPP
Labour Party	Eamon Gilmore (2007)	37	Social democratic, centre-left	S&D
Sinn Féin	Gerry Adams (1983)	14	Ultra-nationalist, populist, growing pragmatism	EUL/NGL
Socialist Party	Joe Higgins (1996)	2	Trotskyist, Marxist, radical left	EUL/NGL
People Before Profit	Collective leadership	2	Trotskyist, Marxist, radical left	EUL/NGL
Green Party	John Gormley (2007)	0	Moderate Green	Greens/EFA
Libertas	Declan Ganley (2008)	0	Eurosceptic neo-liberal right	n/a

Source: Electoral resources, www.electoralresources.org.ie/2011.php?constituency.

Green Party emerged in 1981 and took its present name in 1987. It entered Parliament in 1989 and won six deputies in 2002, and again in 2007. Its coalition with *Fianna Fáil* in the period 2007–2011 proved disastrous, and the Greens lost all of their seats in 2011. Finally, Libertas was founded by millionaire businessman Declan Ganley in 2006 and developed into a transnational Eurosceptic party of the neo-liberal right in 2008. It has proven short-lived, however.

5.1 Party attitudes towards the European Union

The Republic of Ireland has long been regarded as one of the most 'pro-European' member states. The two main political parties, *Fianna Fáil* and *Fine Gael*, and from the 1980s onwards Labour also, share a consensus in favour of EU membership, development and expansion.

In particular, *Fianna Fáil*'s pro-European stance has essentially pragmatic roots, being couched in terms of what Ireland can gain from EU membership and from backing further integration. It harbours many citizens whose attitudes towards EU policy are essentially cold-blooded and certainly devoid of federalist idealism. Above all, the party has tied its reputation and credibility to the strength of the Irish economy and is both deeply sceptical about ceding to the EU strong fiscal powers and highly vulnerable to electoral fluctuations when the economy is in difficulty (Hayward and Fallon, 2009, 493–4).

Fine Gael has long been described as the most pro-EU party in Ireland. However, this remains more true of *Fine Gael* party elites, who continue to exhibit a strong ideological commitment to European integration and see this allegiance as a core part of their political identity, than it does of party members and supporters, amongst whom a more pragmatic and even critical attitude has been growing in recent years. Traditionally, *Fine Gael* has drawn a sizeable proportion of its members and supporters from the farming community and it is this rural heartland that has moved from enthusiastic pragmatic support for the EU to a more detached stance since the Fischler Reforms to the Common Agricultural Policy (CAP). The Labour Party has moved from an initial position of opposition to the EU to enthusiastic support and active involvement in the Party of European Socialists (PES). However, such 'Europeanization' of its politics has affected party elites more than ordinary members (Holmes, 2009b, 538–9).

Initially strongly opposed to Ireland's membership of the EU, *Sinn Féin* has later undergone what Agnes Maillot describes as 'partial Europeanization', leading the party towards a soft Eurosceptic position (Maillot, 2009, 559). As a result, it no longer calls for Irish withdrawal from the European Union, but for reforming the EU organization from within. The motivation for this change in policy emphasis is two-fold: first, the party has come to see the EU as an opportunity, another terrain of struggle upon which to advance its goal of securing a British retreat from Northern Ireland and reuniting the country. Thus, it has enthusiastically embraced an agenda, hitherto associated with moderate Nationalists, of advocating Irish unity by stealth within the European Union, for example by urging EU institutions to treat Ireland as a single economic unit and by advocating the adoption of the Euro in Northern Ireland. Second, it has come to recognize the centrality of EU funding to Irish and Northern Irish economic regeneration.

As to the Greens' attitude towards European integration, it has evolved from outright dismissal of the EU as a centralized super state, destructive of Irish democracy, to mild support of the European Union as an opportunity structure (Bolleyer and Panke, 2009). This Europeanization involved both the downgrading of the Greens' own emphasis on participatory democracy and citizens' initiatives after 1997, and a closer alignment with EU policy after the 2003 EU Convention on the Future of Europe. After 2003, the party hardly ever applied the old, simplistic frame of the EU as a centralized super state, which it had previously deemed incompatible with local democracy. Their criticisms became less structural and much more refined in subsequent years (Bolleyer and Panke, 2009, 552). The more pro-EU policy stance facilitated the Greens' participation in coalition government with *Fianna Fáil* in 2007, and this in turn produced further moderation of its EU policies. In January 2008, the party leader, John Gormley, succeeded in winning an internal referendum of party members in favour of the Lisbon Treaty by 63 per cent to 37 per cent. However, this fell short of the two-thirds majority necessary to change the party's constitution to allow the party to support the new treaty in view of the first referendum. In fact, its members campaigned on both sides, with the Green Party officially remaining neutral.

Overall, the conduct of Irish referenda on European Union Treaties shows the emergence of a dynamic of elite withdrawal from the political field, permitting the capture of supporters by non-mainstream populist groups on both the far left and far right (O'Mahony, 2009). In particular, in June 2008, the referendum on the Lisbon Treaty was held in circumstances that favoured the emergence of Euroscepticism. Such popular consultation had itself been postponed for months as the then *Taoiseach*, Bertie Ahern, was diverted from the business of government by revelations at a judicial tribunal of enquiry into allegations of corruption (ibid., 438). Between Ahern's announcement of his pending resignation on 2 April and the election of Brian Cowen as new leader of the *Fianna Fáil* party and later as *Taoiseach* on 8 May, there was a political vacuum which was filled by populist 'No' vote campaigners. The mainstream parties failed to mount an effective debate on the subsequent referendum, relying on vague pro-European slogans and appeals for trust.

The problem they faced was that the electorate was in no mood to trust mainstream politicians. The whiff of corruption that hung over the *Fianna Fáil*-led government may not have been enough in itself to lead to widespread alienation. However, Ireland's hitherto booming economy had come to a staggering halt by the time of Lisbon I. Indeed, in September 2008, the country became the first euro-zone state to enter recession, with GDP expected to contract by 14 per cent by 2010, unemployment predicted to rise by 17 per cent in the same period, and the perilous state of government debt necessitating painful cuts in public spending. Both the incoming *Taoiseach* and the Minister for Foreign Affairs admitted to not having read the full treaty, which they were appealing to voters to support. The 'populist capture' of the Lisbon I referendum campaign comprised a number of strands. On the left, a number of small Trotskyist parties, the Socialist Party and the Socialist Workers' Party, and 'neo-Stalinist' parties, such as the Workers' Party of Ireland, were joined by trade unionists, left-Nationalists and groups such as the People's Movement in arguing that the Lisbon vote provided an opportunity to vote against policies of economic cut-backs, privatizations and reductions in welfare, assaults on workers' rights, and the undermining of Irish neutrality and sovereignty. The ultra-Nationalist *Sinn Féin*, the only party represented in Parliament to join the 'No' campaign, since the Greens reversed their position as part of the price of sharing government office with *Fianna Fáil*, called for a 'No' vote largely on grounds of national sovereignty and social justice. A National Platform guided by the prominent left-Nationalist, Anthony Coughlan, echoed these arguments together with the argument that Lisbon was detrimental to small countries such as Ireland. Left groups calling for a 'No' vote tended to use the opportunity to call on Irish voters to punish elites that were 'out of touch' with the 'true' feelings of 'the people'. On the right, a group of populist Catholic 'Ultras', led by Justin Barrett, called for a 'No' vote on the grounds that the Charter of Fundamental Rights would force Ireland to legalise abortion, gay marriage, euthanasia and prostitution (O'Mahony, 2009, 441), and again appealed to anti-elite sentiment with slogans such as 'Don't be Bullied, Vote No.'

All of these groups had been active during the Nice referenda in 2001–2002. This time, however, they were joined by a well-financed Conservative movement on the right, founded and financed by an Irish millionaire businessman with strong ties to the US military-industrial complex, Declan Ganley. He launched the Libertas movement as a lobby campaign against any EU Constitutional Treaty in 2006. During the Lisbon I Referendum, Libertas developed what were to be Ganley's key themes of support for neo-liberalism and entrepreneurship, allegations that Lisbon was *de facto* a new European Constitution and as such would hold business back by drowning it in red tape and new regulations, and attacks on the political elites as being contemptuous of democracy. Given the conservative nature of Irish political culture, Ganley's movement probably mobilized many voters that the populist left and the ultra-Catholic right alone could not have reached (Fitzgibbon, 2009, 20). Subsequently in 2008, the millionaire businessman turned Libertas into a transnational right-wing Eurosceptic political party, holding its first official Congress in Rome in May 2009 and fielding candidates in many countries in the forthcoming European elections.

6 Public opinion on the European Union

Over time, political parties' consensus towards the EU was joined by major interest groups including the powerful farmers' lobby and the main trade unions. EU membership brought very considerable economic benefits, including large-scale investment in infrastructure: Ireland received over €20 billion in funding from the Structural and Cohesion Funds since joining in 1973, facilitating an impressive modernization of roads, tunnels, bridges and telecommunications (Benoit, 2009, 447). Above all, the farming community experienced unprecedented prosperity thanks to the support of the European Agricultural Guidance and Guarantee Fund (EAGGF) which led to the transformation of Irish rural life (O'Toole, 2003, 20). European Union membership became firmly linked in the Irish popular imagination with the economic miracle which transformed a country accustomed to poverty, unemployment, and emigration into the 'Celtic Tiger' phenomenon of the 1990s, with some of the highest growth rates in the developed capitalist world. Finally, it must be noted that mainstream Irish nationalism, in sharp contrast to British nationalism, worked firmly *in favour* of positive engagement with deeper European integration. This is because the political elite had successfully 'sold' the EU project to most Irish voters as a way of shaking off economic, political, and cultural dependence on the 'old enemy', Britain, and of asserting a new and more heavyweight role for Ireland on the European and world stage.

Yet, as Table 11.3. shows, a more sceptical view of the EU and the whole process of 'deepening' started to emerge even before the Irish economy plunged into difficulties in the second half of the first decade of the twentieth-first century.

The Irish electorate's rejection of the Nice Treaty in the first ratification referendum held in June 2001 came as a shock to the political elite. This could be explained as an atypical 'blip' caused by the failure of a complacent political elite to mobilise voters and to its reluctance to invest on this campaign in view of the 2002 national election. Moreover, the relatively low turnout meant that 'No' voters were not more numerous than in the referenda on the Maastricht and Amsterdam Treaties, although 'Yes' voters had fallen considerably. The political elite's success in securing ratification with a second referendum in October 2002 – after a much more organized and coherent campaign – seemed to confirm this hypothesis. However, the Irish electorate's rejection of the Lisbon Treaty in June 2008 shattered such a comforting view. This time, the turnout was higher than in either of the Nice Treaty referenda, and the 'No' vote was marginally higher than in Nice I; indeed, as an overall percentage of the total electorate, 'No' voters had risen markedly from an average of 19 per cent in the previous four EU referenda to 28 per cent. A new era loomed on the Irish political horizon, that of Euroscepticism.

Amid a growing climate of financial fear, it became clear that the days when Ireland benefited from massive EU subsidies were over and that the country, one of the most open and globalized economies in the world, had become extraordinarily vulnerable. Not surprisingly perhaps, many Irish voters blamed the governing parties for what was perceived as a missed opportunity for growth, and for the painful disillusionment that accompanied 'boom and bust'. Irish support for European integration, which tended towards the pragmatic, started to wane and many Irish voters professed a low level of knowledge of EU matters (Laffen and O'Mahony, 2008). Polls suggested little in the way of awareness of what the Lisbon Treaty was actually about.

Despite this development, Irish public opinion remains pro-EU in general, although its support tends to be more pragmatic and closely connected to the effectiveness of the political elite in responding to the new challenges. Finally, as a result of a better organized and coordinated 'Yes' campaign, the second referendum on the Lisbon Treaty was approved in October 2009.

Table 11.3 European referendum results: 1972–2009 (%)

Date	Issue	Yes	No	Turnout	Spoilt or blank ballots
10/05/1972	EEC Accession	83.1	16.9	70.9	0.8
26/05/1987	Single European Act	69.9	30.1	44.1	0.5
18/06/1992	Maastricht Treaty	69.1	30.9	57.3	0.5
22/05/1998	Amsterdam Treaty	61.7	38.3	56.2	2.2
07/06/2001	Nice Treaty (first time)	46.1	53.9	34.8	1.5
20/10/2002	Nice Treaty (second time)	62.9	37.1	48.5	0.4
12/06/2008	Lisbon Treaty (first time)	46.6	53.4	53.1	0.4
02/10/2009	Lisbon Treaty (second time)	67.1	32.9	59.0	0.4

Source: Adapted from O'Mahony, 2009, 431.

Ireland

7 National and EP electoral systems

In Ireland, all local, national and European elections are based on the Single Transferable Vote (STV) system of proportional representation with multi-member constituencies, as enshrined in the 1937 Constitution.

For the national elections, the 166 members of the lower House of Parliament are elected in 43 multi-seat constituencies, 12 constituencies elect up to 5 members of Parliament, 13 up to 4 and 18 up to 3 representatives.

Over the years, the size of the Irish delegation in the EP has changed, in particular in 2009 it dropped from 13 to 12 with Dublin losing 1 seat. For this election, Ireland was divided into

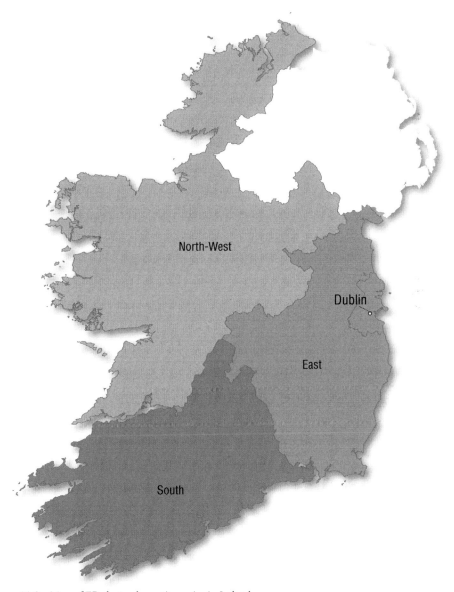

Figure 11.2   Map of EP electoral constituencies in Ireland

four constituencies, South, East, North-West and Dublin, each returning three MEPs. Moreover, in an effort to achieve a fair balance of voters in each Euro-constituency, the central Ireland counties of Longford and Westmeath were moved from the East to the thinly-populated North-West constituency.

Parties present up to three candidates for each constituency and voters are then free to distribute their first, second, third, and fourth preferences amongst all of the candidates on the ballot paper. There is no obligation to choose all candidates within the same list; voters can award preferences across party lines. A high premium is thus placed on the personal popularity of candidates, who must effectively compete, not only with candidates of other parties, but also with their own party colleagues. Personalism, combined with another strong feature of Irish political culture, localism, helps explain the relative success of independent members who are often candidates that have fallen out with one or other of the mainstream parties but can still count on a reservoir of strong local loyalty. The electoral system and the political culture together tend to maximize the seat-winning capacity of any party that can achieve the unity and discipline of its candidates and its voters, can avoid too many cross-party transfers before all of its own candidates have been voted for by its supporters, can successfully 'ride the wave' of localism by selecting candidates who appeal to all geographic parts of what are fairly large European constituencies, and can maximize transfers from candidates of the other parties.

8 A glance at national and EP elections

National and EP elections have a different outlook in the Republic of Ireland. Normally, *Fianna Fáil*, the dominant party of the political system, loses votes in EP elections in relation to previous national elections. In the midst of an economic crisis and the continuing IRA attacks in Northern Ireland, the *Fine Gael* and Labour coalition government had to call for early elections in 1977. Prime Minister Liam Cosgrave and his government had major difficulties in dealing with the worldwide recession that also affected Ireland considerably. *Fianna Fáil* won the elections after a strong campaign against the economic policies of the incumbent government, achieving an outright absolute majority of over 50 per cent. In 1979, the Irish population took part in the first direct election to the EP, registering a turnout of 61.99 per cent, lower than the 76.3 per cent turnout at the national elections. Yet, at the EP elections in 1989, turnout reached 68.3 per cent, the highest rate in the past two decades, mainly due to the fact that Irish legislative elections were held on the same day. In 1994 turnout declined to 44 per cent to recover in 1999, 2004, and 2009 to above 50 per cent due to the concurrence of local elections or sometimes referenda. Although, turnout in EP elections is lower than in national elections, it is substantially higher than in other countries if we exclude the 1984 and 1994 elections.

In the late 1970s, the stagnating economy represented a major problem for the Irish government. As a result, inflation, taxation, and disillusionment with the *Fianna Fáil* government were the main issues of the campaign of the first EP elections. The importance of this vote was not so much the contents discussed in the campaign, but the fact that Irish identity was now intrinsically linked to the European integration process (Collins, 1985, 105–6).

Fianna Fáil, Fine Gael, Labour, the Workers' Party and the Community of Democrats in Ireland – along with three independents – ran in the election, but as in Irish legislative elections, the three main parties dominated. The results saw *Fianna Fáil* with 34.7 per cent and 5 seats, *Fine Gael* with 33.1 per cent and 4 seats and Labour with 14.5 per cent and 4 seats. Moreover, two independent candidates, Maher and Blaney, were elected due to the high number of preference voting in the respective constituencies. This meant a considerable loss of voting share for the ruling Fianna Fáil of almost 16 per cent, with a 3 per cent improvement for *Fine Gael*. The big winner was Labour which, due to preference voting, secured 4 seats like *Fine Gail*, despite achieving only 14.5 per cent of the vote.

In December 1979, the economic crisis led to the resignation of *Taoiseach* Jack Lynch and his replacement with the charismatic but controversial Charles Haughey who, in spite of scandals, managed to win the election in 1981. *Fianna Fáil* achieved 45.3 per cent and 78 seats but this was not enough for an absolute majority. *Fine Gael* got 36.5 per cent and 75 seats, an improvement of 22 seats over the general election of 1977, and Labour got 9.9 per cent and 15 seats. The Workers' Party got one seat and six independents were also able to get representation. It led to a minority coalition government under the premiership *Fine Gael*'s Garrett Fitzgerald, which was defeated on budget by one vote. The early elections convened in February 1982 resulted in a hung Parliament since neither of the two big parties, *Fianna Fáil* and *Fine Gael* were able to achieve an absolute majority. Negotiations with the other parties and the independents led to the formation of a *Fianna Fáil* government, under *Taoiseach* Charles Haughey, which was defeated by two votes in a motion of confidence on 4 November 1982. Therefore, early elections were called again in which *Fianna Fáil* achieved 45.2 per cent and 75 seats (−6 in comparison to the February 1982 election), while *Fine Gael* achieved 39.2 per cent and 71 seats (+6 in comparison to the February 1982 election) while Labour got 9.4 per cent and 16 seats (+1 in comparison to the February 1982 election). The consequence was the formation of another *Fine Gael*–Labour coalition government under *Taoiseach* Garrett Fitzgerald.

The 1984 European elections represent a normalization of this kind of event. First of all turnout went down to 46.7 per cent (Collins, 1986). A major factor that may explain the decline of the turnout is that local elections were not held on the same day.

As in the 1979 elections, the three main parties dominated the elections. The two main parties were the big winners, while Labour was not able to return any MEP. The campaign was dominated by national economic issues. The government parties could present a positive balance

Table 11.4 EP election results in Ireland: 1979–2004 (%)*

Political party	1979	1984	1989	1994	1999	2004
Fianna Fáil	34.7 (5)	39.2 (8)	31.5 (6)	35.0 (7)	38.6 (6)	29.5 (4)
Fine Gael	33.1 (4)	32.2 (6)	21.6 (4)	24.3 (4)	24.6 (4)	27.8 (5)
Labour	14.5 (4)	8.4 (1)	9.5 (1)	11.0 (1)	8.7 (1)	10.6 (1)
Sinn Féin	—	—	2.2 (0)	3.0 (0)	6.3 (0)	11.1 (1)
Greens	—	—	3.7 (0)	7.9 (2)	6.7 (2)	4.3 (0)
Socialist Party	—	—	—	—	0.8 (0)	1.3 (0)
Progressive Democrats			12.0 (1)	6.5 (0)	—	—
Libertas	—	—	—	—	—	—
Workers' Party	3.3 (0)	4.3 (0)	7.6 (1)	1.9 (0)	—	—
Democratic Left	—	—	—	3.5 (0)	—	—
Christian Solidarity Party	—	—	—	—	0.7 (0)	0.3 (0)
Independents	14.4 (2)	10.6 (1)	11.8 (2)	6.9 (1)	14.3 (2)	15.5 (2)
Total MEPs	15.0	15.0	15.0	15.0	15.0	13.0
Turnout	63.6	47.6	68.3	44.0	50.2	59.7

Source: European Parliament Elections in the Republic of Ireland, http://en.wikipedia.org/wiki/Category: European_Parliament_elections_in_the_Republic_of_Ireland.

Note: *Votes as percentages and number of seats in brackets.

of membership of the EU, particularly for the farming community. As a result, *Fianna Fáil* got 39.2 per cent and 8 seats and *Fine Gael* got 32.2 per cent and 6 seats, whilst Labour with its 8.4 per cent did not secure any seats. Moreover, one independent was elected to Strasbourg (Collins, 1986, 141–3).

Ten months before the end of the five-year legislature period, Fitzgerald's *Fine Gael*–Labour government collapsed, after refusal of the junior partner to support spending cuts in order to reduce the budget deficit. Moreover, there was also a general opposition of Labour against the free-market policies of the senior partner. New early elections were called in 1987, which led to the victory of *Fianna Fáil* with 44.1 and 81 seats against *Fine Gael's* 29.3 per cent (−10.1 per cent in comparison to November 1982) and 51 seats (−10 in comparison to November 1982). New *Taoiseach* Charles Haughey formed a single majority government supported by one vote in Parliament. In early 1989, the government decided to resign after the defeat of a private bill motion on funding for AIDS victims. Although the resignation was unnecessary, Haughey's minority government, encouraged by very good opinion polls, hoped to achieve an absolute majority by calling early elections to be held on 15 June 1989 in concurrence with EP elections. *Fianna Fáil* lost seats in National Parliament in relation to 1987, but *Fine Gael* did not profit substantially from the defeat of its main rival. The Progressive Democrats, a new party that emerged in 1987, after a split within *Fianna Fáil*, got 5.5 per cent. The Workers' Party and the Greens made gains. A long period of negotiations opened the way to a new *Fianna Fáil*–Progressive Democrats government guided by Charles Haughey.

Despite the concurrence of the events, turnout at the EP election was 58.98 per cent, about 10 per cent less than that registered at the general election, with double the number of spoiled votes (Marsh, 1994, 170).

The share of the vote was far more fragmented since the two main parties got about 9–10 per cent less in European elections than national elections, while the smaller parties and independents were able to get a higher consensus. European issues were not prominent in the campaign, except for the issue of European common defence that, due to the neutrality of the country, represented an important part of Irish identity (ibid., 178–9). The final results were: *Fianna Fáil* 31.5 per cent and 6 seats, *Fine Gael* 21.6 per cent and 4 seats, and Labour 9.5 per cent and one seat, Progressive Democrats 12 per cent and one seat, Workers' Party 7.6 per cent and one seat. Moreover, the independent Neil Blaney managed to get through. This shows a fragmentation of representation towards the smaller parties in comparison to the previous EP election in 1984. Another interesting difference was the bad performance of the Progressive Democrats in the general election, but with quite a respectable share of the vote in the EP elections.

In early 1992, after a series of political scandals which discredited the coalition government, *Taoiseach* Charles Haughey resigned. At the early general elections which followed, *Fianna Fáil* and *Fine Gail* lost respectively five percentage points in relation to the 1989 elections, whilst Labour was able to improve its performance from 9.5 per cent in 1989 to 19.3 per cent in 1992. The Progressive Democrats declined even further from 5.5 to 4.7 per cent and the Workers' Party fell from 5 to 2.8 per cent. Finally, the Greens got 1.4 per cent and *Sinn Féin* 1.6 per cent. With a large absolute majority, *Fianna Fáil* formed a coalition government with Labour under the premiership of Albert Reynolds.

The 1994 EP election was an important mid-term test for the governing party. Apart from the traditional parties *Fianna Fáil*, *Fine Gael* and Labour, several small parties took part in the electoral race: Greens, the Progressive Democrats, and the Democratic Left, which had split from the Workers' Party. Although issues related to Nordic enlargement, structural funds, the common agricultural policy, and institutional reform of the European Union were discussed during the campaign, there were no major differences between the political parties. According to Edward Moxon Browne, the government used 'European issues as a camouflage to conceal serious underlying tensions between, and especially within, political parties' (Moxon Browne, 1996, 123). An important question discussed during the campaign related to the dual mandate of Irish MEPs, with some candidates arguing in its favour, whilst others were prepared to give up the national one (Moxon Browne, 1996).

In terms of results, all main three parties were able to improve on the voting share achieved in the 1994 European elections. More specifically, the government party *Fianna Fáil* got 35 per cent (+3.5 per cent) and 7 seats (+1), *Fine Gael* 24.3 per cent (+2.7 per cent) and 4 seats (no change) and Labour 11 per cent (+1.5 per cent) and one seat (no change). The biggest surprise was the excellent results achieved by the Greens, with 3.7 per cent and 2 seats. Only one independent was able to achieve representation in the EP.

By the end of 1994, Labour left the coalition government and formed a rainbow coalition with *Fine Gael* and the Democratic Left, guided by John Bruton. The reason Labour left the coalition was the emergence of several political scandals related to *Fianna Fáil*, most prominently in the beef industry. The elections of 6 June 1997 led to a victory of *Fianna Fáil* under the premiership of Bertie Ahern. *Fianna Fáil* got 39.3 per cent and 77 seats, while *Fine Gael* achieved 27.9 per cent and 54 seats; both parties improved, each by 9 seats. Labour suffered the biggest defeat, seemingly reflecting public disillusionment with its decision to change senior coalition partners in late 1994. The Progressive Democrats parliamentary group was reduced from ten to four MPs. The Greens got 2 seats, one more than previously. *Sinn Féin* got one seat, while the Democratic Left received 4 seats.

The subsequent European Parliament elections took place on 11 June 1999, during the mid-term of Ahern's coalition government and in concurrence with local elections. As such, this was a key indicator for the overall popularity of the ruling party. The government clearly pushed forward European issues and how well they had managed questions like enlargement and EU reform by highlighting the need to negotiate structural and CAP funds. The Kosovo War played an important role in the campaign, due to the debate on the watering down of Irish neutrality. In particular, small parties like the Greens opposed any Irish engagement in the NATO Partnership for Peace programme. The overall results led to a victory for *Fianna Fáil*, which was able to improve by 3.6 per cent its previous performance; it achieved 38.6 per cent of the votes by securing 6 seats, one less than in 1994. *Fine Gael* improved slightly to 24.6 per cent (+0.3 per cent) of the vote and 4 seats, whilst Labour declined to 8.7 per cent (−2.3 per cent) and the Greens lost their voting share with 6.7 per cent (−1.2 per cent), but were able to keep their 2 seats. Finally, two independent members gained access to the Strasbourg arena (Moxon-Brown, 2010)

In the 2002 Elections, *Fianna Fáil* was reconfirmed in office, again in coalition with the Progressive Democrats. *Fianna Fáil* was able to improve to 41.5 per cent (+2.2 per cent) and 81 seats. *Fine Gael* achieved just 22.5 per cent (−5.4 per cent) and 31 seats (−23 seats). Labour was able to improve slightly on the results of 1997 by achieving 10.8 per cent (+0.4 per cent) and 20 seats (−1 seat). However, in reality, this reflected a further loss for Labour, as that party had by then absorbed the smaller Democratic Left. The Progressive Democrats slightly decreased their share of the vote, getting 4 per cent (−0.7 per cent), but improved on seats to 8 (+4 seats). The Greens were able to improve to 3.8 per cent (+1 per cent) and 2 seats (+1 seat). *Sinn Féin* got 2.5 per cent and one seat, seeing little change from the previous election.

Again the 2004 EP elections were scheduled during the mid-term of Ahern's government. Local elections and a constitutional referendum on citizenship regulations were held on the same day. The 2004 elections were particularly interesting because Ireland had rejected the Nice Treaty in a referendum in 2001, which however was overturned by a follow-up referendum in

2002. It clearly gave a new image of Ireland to the outside world (Holmes, 2004, 2–3). European issues were important in the campaign, particularly ones related to common policies such as Immigration and Asylum and the Common Foreign and Security Policy. The political parties did not differ very much in their support for European policies, however the smaller Green and *Sinn Féin* parties were more Eurocritical. The three main parties claimed to be the real advocate of Europe (ibid., 3–6). In terms of results, voters punished the main ruling party *Fianna Fáil*, which got just 29.5 per cent and 4 seats, with a reduction of 9.1 per cent and two fewer seats in relation to the 1999 election. *Fine Gael* was able to improve to 27.6, increasing by 3.8 per cent and 5 seats (+1 seat) with Labour increasing to 10.8 per cent (+2.3 per cent) and one seat with no change. *Sinn Féin* got its best ever result, improving to 11 per cent (+5.2 per cent), but not in terms of seats, because it achieved only one seat with no change. The Greens were the big losers, declining from 6.5 to 4.4 per cent and losing both seats in the EP.

In the 2007 legislative elections, *Fianna Fáil* was able to repeat its 2002 victory, achieving almost the same share of the vote – 41.6 per cent. However, the Progressive Democrats' voting share and seats collapsed, so that it had to look for additional partners in order to attain a working majority. Hence, the Green party, which had achieved 4.7 per cent and 6 seats, became part of the coalition. *Fine Gael* also improved by almost 5 per cent to 27.3 per cent and 51 seats.

In sum, differences can be detected between national and EP elections. Apart from the lower turnout in EP elections, both main political parties, *Fianna Fáil* and *Fine Gael*, lost in terms of popular consensus. Smaller parties – along with independent candidates – were more likely to succeed in EP elections.

9 The 2009 European Parliament election

9.1 Party lists and manifestos

The 2009 European elections were dominated by the discussion about the Treaty of Lisbon and the growing difficult economic situation due to the bursting of the housing bubble. The party manifestos of the main political parties were quite pragmatic and pro-European, yet more Eurosceptic tunes came from smaller parties.

Table 11.5 National election results in Ireland: 1977–2011 (%)

Political party	1977	1981	1982 (Feb)	1982 (Nov)	1987	1989	1992	1997	2002	2007	2011
Fianna Fáil	50.6	45.3	47.3	45.2	44.1	44.1	39.1	39.3	41.5	41.6	17.4
Fine Gael	30.5	36.5	37.3	39.2	29.3	29.3	24.5	27.9	22.5	27.3	36.1
Labour	11.6	9.9	9.1	9.4	9.5	9.5	19.3	10.4	10.8	10.1	19.4
Sinn Féin	1.7	0.0	1.0	0.0	1.9	1.2	1.6	2.6	2.5	6.9	9.9
Greens	—	—	—	—	0.4	1.5	1.4	2.8	3.8	4.7	1.8
Socialist Party	—	—	—	—	—	—	—	—	0.8	—	1.2
Progressive Democrats	—	—	—	—	11.8	5.5	4.7	4.7	4.0	2.7	—
Workers' Party	—	1.7	2.2	3.1	3.8	5.0	2.8	2.5	—	—	—
People Before Profit Alliance	—	—	—	—	—	—	—	—	—	—	1.0
Turnout	76.3	76.7	73.8	72.9	73.4	68.5	68.5	66.1	62.6	67.7	70.0

Source: www.parties-and-elections.de/ireland2.html.

Given the perilous state of the Irish economy by June 2009, *Fianna Fáil* fought the campaign from a very defensive position whilst reiterating its deep commitment to the European Union for its great ideals and for enabling Irish sovereignty (*Fianna Fáil*, 2009, 4). The manifesto cited the pragmatic advantages to the Irish economy of access to European markets and of EU investment in developing the Irish energy market and pledged to fight to obtain maximum aid from the EU Globalization Fund and to use this money to counter job losses (ibid., 6–9). It defended the party's support for a second referendum on a revised Lisbon Treaty in which the party and the Government would campaign for a 'yes' vote (ibid., 10). In a detailed, 32-page manifesto the party covered a wide range of EU policies with which it wished to be associated, but avoided mention of its projected European Parliament alignment with the Liberal ALDE group. The *Taoiseach* and party leader, Brian Cowen, had confirmed the party's intention to leave the Union for Europe of the Nations (UEN) group after the 2009 election and join the ALDE group, despite the fact that by no stretch of the imagination could *Fianna Fáil* be considered a Liberal party. This had been publicly criticized by the party's most popular MEP, the poll-topping Brian Crowley, who has risen to be President of the UEN group. The issue continued to be a source of some friction within the party, leading Crowley to resign from it in 2014.

During the campaign, *Fianna Fáil* found itself fighting the election, not so much on the basis of its manifesto as on the basis of its record in government and the personal popularity of some of its candidates. The *Taoiseach*, Brian Cowen, defended his government's handling of the economic crisis, accusing the opposition parties of being incapable of offering an alternative coalition government because of the mutual incompatibility of *Fine Gael* calls for tighter financial rectitude with Labour calls for greater public spending (*The Irish Times*, 15 May 2009). Unfortunately for *Fianna Fáil*, by accusing the other parties of misrepresenting the state of the economy as worse than it actually was, Cowen may have played into his opponents' hands by appearing out of touch with the public mood and complacent (*The Irish Times*, 29 May 2009). Although *Fianna Fáil* appealed to its supporters to transfer their votes to Green party candidates this arrangement was decisively not reciprocated by the Greens, further placing the government on the defensive (*The Irish Times*, 8 May 2009).

Fine Gael's 20-page European election manifesto was keen to boast its pro-EU credentials, hailing its support of the Lisbon Treaty as 'good for Europe, vital for Ireland' and its membership of the Christian Democratic EPP group as proof that it was part of 'the strongest team in Europe' (*Fine Gael*, 2009, 2). The party called for an end to the government's opt-out from the Lisbon Treaty's provisions on home affairs and crime and pledged to fight to give Irish agriculture a strong voice in Brussels. It saw a central role for the EU in generating Ireland's economic recovery and vigorously defended Ireland's adoption of the euro, arguing that 'our position would have been all the worse if we still had our own small currency' (ibid.,13). Coordinated European policies on fiscal and banking issues and a stronger role in generating growth were advocated.

The party leader, Enda Kenny, tapped into a theme which would dominate the campaign, arguing that 'the mood of the electorate was one of unprecedented anger at the Government for the way it has been running the country' (*The Irish Times*, 4 May 2009). *Fine Gael* returned to this theme constantly, called on voters to use the election to punish the government and showed its desire to change the regime. However, it did also campaign on the basis of policies that highlighted its self-image as a strongly pro-EU party. It attacked the Eurosceptic view that 80 per cent of Irish legislation emanated from Brussels, arguing that the true figure was closer to 30 per cent. *Fine Gael* called for a change to the Irish Constitution to avoid the need for automatic recourse to referenda to approve EU treaties. Instead, the party proposed that treaties might be sent to the Supreme Court, which would rule on whether elements of such a text needed to be put to a popular vote or not.

At the 2009 election campaign, Labour whole-heartedly embraced the PES agenda, and its 22-page manifesto incorporated many common policies of PES. Labour highlighted two goals above all in its manifesto: jobs creation and social fairness. The party declared itself in favour of 'better regulation of global finance' and named its 'number one priority' as being 'to safeguard jobs, create new ones, and promote smart, environmentally friendly growth'. While blaming the *Fianna Fáil*-led government for the extent of the Irish economic crisis, it argued that 'This is a global crisis in global capitalism. It demands a response at European level, where countries can come together'(Labour, 2009, 3). The party called for a European Pact for the Future of Employment with greater spending on education and training; increased spending through the European Investment Bank; completion of the single market with the elimination of red tape and a reduction in bureaucracy; and reform of the banking and financial sectors with a new European system of supervision, measures against tax havens, tax avoidance and money-laundering, and an extension of workers' rights and protection of pension funds (ibid., 8–9). Labour also called for a European Social Progress Pact, 'with goals and standards for national, social, health and education policy to contribute to the fight against poverty, as well as Europe's continued social and economic development' (ibid., 10).

Like *Fine Gael*, Labour saw its membership of one of the two biggest groups in the EP as a positive 'selling point', which enabled Ireland to increase its influence. Throughout the election campaign, Labour turned its fire on *Fianna Fáil*, accusing the party of being despised by the Irish electorate and calling for an early general election (*The Irish Times*, 25 May 2009). The Labour leader, Eamon Gilmore, whose personal approval ratings were the highest of any party leader throughout the campaign, also attacked the Green party for allegedly betraying its values and principles and propping up *Fianna Fáil* in government. In what may have been a successful attempt to embarrass *Fianna Fáil* and attract that party's disillusioned voters, Labour offered the party's nomination in the East constituency to Nessa Childers, who comes from a well-known *Fianna Fáil* family. Her grandfather was one of the party's icons and her father, the late President Erskine Childers, was a long-time party leader and cabinet minister before serving as head of state. Nessa Childers herself had been a Green party city councillor before accepting Labour's invitation to stand as its candidate, dealing a further blow to the Greens.

Sinn Féin's manifesto for the 2009 European elections emphasized three themes. First, the party mobilized voters on the basis of populist nationalism rather than class-based socialism, highlighting its presence in the European Parliament in order to 'build support in Europe for Irish reunification' and to make the Irish language an official and working language of the EU. Second, the party called for institutional reform of the EU, although this, too, was couched in terms of 'national interest' as much as democratic terms. Thus, the party described any revised Lisbon Treaty referendum as 'anti-democratic and a bad deal for Ireland', called for a new treaty 'reflecting the concerns of the Irish people', demanded a strengthening of national Parliaments and local councils, and called for people in Northern Ireland to have a vote in any future Irish referenda on EU treaties. Third, the party supported an agenda of strengthening workers' rights, opposing further privatizations, and EU action to tackle unemployment and end poverty. Again, however, this was given a distinctly Nationalist flavour. For example, *Sinn Féin* pledged to be 'the strongest advocates of Irish economic sovereignty and all-Ireland tax harmonization' and to fight to ensure that health and education policy 'remain the exclusive responsibility of Member States' (*Sinn Féin*, 2009).

Interestingly, the manifesto contained no mention whatsoever of the party's membership of the EUL/NGL group in the EP – perhaps a tacit acknowledgement that an overt association with Communist parties might repel some of the party's electoral base – and no mention of 'socialism'. *Sinn Féin* had hoped to build upon its leading role in the first Lisbon Treaty referendum and upon the strong public backlash against the government parties. In theory, the party should have been pushing at an open door in 2009. Yet, its share of the vote remained as it was in 2004 and its best chance of winning a European Parliament seat, securing the re-election of Mary Lou McDonald in Dublin, fell victim to a resurgent Socialist Party, whose class-based appeal to disenchanted Dublin workers was undiluted by Nationalist rhetoric.

The Greens fought the 2009 European elections on the basis of a strongly pro-EU platform. They sought to portray the EU 'Green New Deal' as 'an exciting, EU-wide, economic stimulus plan to create millions of new green jobs'. Indeed, the European Union was central to efforts to create jobs and protect the environment. The party also called for measures to make the Union more democratic, to counter the power of lobbyists within the EU, and to increase EU support for climate protection and renewable energy schemes. The Greens also portrayed themselves as pro-business, claiming that:

> many people believe that the Irish Government sets the bar very high when it comes to implementing certain EU regulations, compared to some of our fellow EU Member States. This can place Irish businesses at a competitive disadvantage in relation to their overseas competitors.
>
> *(Greens, 2009)*

Intriguingly, this last sentence reads as if the Greens were a party of opposition not of government, which of course was the case. Indeed, they tried throughout the campaign to keep their distance from *Fianna Fáil*, refusing to recommend to their supporters that they transfer their votes to the larger government party, leading to speculation that the Greens were considering abandoning the government. It is fair to say that this 'in government but not responsible for the Government's policy failures' stance failed to convince many voters. The Greens had a wretchedly disappointing election campaign. The party only managed to field candidates in two of the four constituencies, Dublin and South, and suffered every bit as much from the anti-government backlash as *Fianna Fáil*; indeed, in proportionate terms, it suffered much more. We have already seen how former Green Councillor Nessa Childers defected to Labour to be that party's successful candidate in the East constituency. In Dublin, a bedrock of Green support, the party saw the defection of former Green MEP Patricia McKenna, an arch-Eurosceptic, who had been defeated by John Gormley in the party leadership race in July 2007, polling 263 votes to his 478. In 2008, disillusioned by the party's support for the Lisbon Treaty, she joined the anti-EU People's Movement and contested the 2009 European election in Dublin for this organization. The party had to spend a considerable part of its time, including at its manifesto launch, trying to distance itself in the public eye from McKenna's outspoken attacks on the EU. It was also savaged by the other opposition parties for the compromise it had made to stay in government, which included compromises on gas development, on US military use of the Irish air base at Shannon, and the construction of a new motorway close to the famous historic site of Tara.

The Socialist Party fought the election on a platform of all-out opposition to the EU, arguing that it was a bastion of neo-liberalism and of attacks on working-class living standards and jobs. The party sought to build on its outright rejection of the Lisbon Treaty, echoing many of the criticisms levelled at this by the parties of the European anti-capitalist left. The party only fielded one candidate, the charismatic party leader and former parliamentary deputy, Joe Higgins, who stood in the Dublin constituency. A miniscule budget of just €28,000 supported both its European campaign in Dublin and that of ten local government candidates, making its subsequent success all the more impressive (*The Irish Times*, 13 June 2009). The party appealed strongly to Dublin workers disaffected by the Government's economic policies and worried by unemployment.

Libertas, the right-wing Eurosceptic party founded by Declan Ganley, hoped to build upon its role in the Lisbon I referendum. It campaigned largely on the basis of its opposition to the Lisbon Treaty, emphasizing however that it supported Ireland's membership of the EU. It adopted a stridently populist tone, accusing the other parties' MEPs of keeping their expense 'secret and hidden' (Libertas, 2009). However, the Libertas campaign also became mired in controversy. Its candidate in the East constituency, Raymond O'Malley, called for Ireland to close its borders to workers from fellow EU Member States while its Dublin candidate, Caroline Simons, called for migrants from other EU Member States to be limited to a two-year stay and to be prevented from claiming benefits (*The Irish Times*, 15 May 2009). This led to Labour branding the party 'fascist' and other parties accusing it of playing the 'race card' (*The Irish Times*, 16 May 2009). The party gave further evidence of its right-wing credentials by accusing one of its opponents of being 'soft' on abortion rights. And party leader Declan Ganley gave a hostage to fortune by stating that he would not play a major role in the second Lisbon Treaty referendum unless he secured election as an MEP (*The Irish Times*, 23 May 2009). This may have simply furnished the three main parties and their supporters with an added incentive to ensure that he was not elected.

9.2 Electoral campaign

The 2009 European election campaign in Ireland was fought against the background of severe economic recession, which hit Ireland exceptionally hard. Just as Ireland had experienced a greater economic boom than many other EU Member States during the preceding 15 years, so too did its downturn tend to surpass that of most of its partners. The management of the Irish economy by *Fianna Fáil*-led governments had involved 'particularly loose systems of financial regulation and the inflation of a huge property bubble'. The financial crisis plunged the country into economic gloom, with rapidly rising unemployment and collapsing public finances. Not surprisingly, then, the economy totally dominated the election campaign with all parties competing to argue that they had the best policies to promote growth and jobs creation. The right-of-centre parties, including *Fine Gael* and *Fianna Fáil*, tended to argue over which was best-placed to cut public spending, lower regulation of business, and return the country to the days of the 'Celtic Tiger' economic boom, whilst the left-of-centre parties, including Labour, the Socialist Party, and *Sinn Féin*, were more critical of what they saw as a 'gung-ho' approach to capitalism which had led to the recession in the first place, and they tended to place the emphasis on greater regulation and state and/or EU initiatives to promote jobs creation and social justice. However, for all parties, the economy was central. Some of the minor parties, in particular, tried to introduce other themes and issues. *Sinn Féin* repeatedly raised the issue of national sovereignty; the Greens naturally campaigned in support of stronger EU environmental policies; and Libertas tried to raise the immigration issue and to attack opponents for allegedly supporting abortion rights. But, on the whole, these issues failed to make much of an impact in a campaign thoroughly dominated by the economy.

Of course, another issue that resonated throughout the campaign was the mounting public backlash against the governing parties, *Fianna Fáil* and the Greens. Even before the start of the campaign it was clear that public support for the government was at an all-time low and that support for *Fianna Fáil* in particular was likely to be the lowest since the party was founded in 1926. Public opinion never seriously deviated from this mood throughout the campaign; the Government's defeat was a foregone conclusion. Hardly surprising, then, that the opposition parties should seek to present the European election as something of a referendum on the popularity of a government that seemed destined to a dry and harsh defeat.

9.3 Electoral results

The outcome of the 2009 European election in Ireland reveals two clear trends. First, the electorate undoubtedly used the elections to punish the governing parties, *Fianna Fáil* and the Greens. *Fianna Fáil* polled its lowest share of the vote in a nationwide election since the 1920s and lost one of its MEPs. The loss of a single MEP might not seem so disastrous unless one bears in mind that the party had already reached a new low in terms of popular support in the 2004 European elections. The party's bad performance in local elections held on the same day led to renewed internal criticism of the leadership. *Fine Gael* was certainly the main beneficiary of *Fianna Fáil*'s disastrous performance, overtaking the latter in both European and local elections and establishing itself as a contender for the post of the biggest party. However, due to the vagaries of the Irish electoral system, *Fine Gael* still managed to lose one European seat on an increased vote.

The Greens had a devastatingly bad election, failing to recapture either of the seats in the EP they held between 1994 and 2004 and falling to less than 2 per cent of the popular vote. In their urban stronghold of Dublin, the Greens polled just 1,500 votes more than the former Green MEP turned arch-critic of the party, Patricia McKenna, standing as a candidate for the anti-EU People's Movement. The Greens faced an almost total wipeout in Dublin, losing all ten of their city councillors in the local elections. In 2010, their Dublin European election candidate, Deirdre de Burca, compounded the Greens' problems by resigning from the party amid public criticism of the leadership. It is uncertain whether the Greens will survive as a significant force in Irish politics.

The second trend that is apparent is that Ireland defied the general European move to the right. In Ireland in 2009, only the left-of-centre parties, Labour and the Socialist Party, increased both their share of the popular vote and their number of MEPs. Labour's share of 13.9 per cent of votes was certainly not as impressive as its opinion poll ratings of 20–25 per cent, but it still represented a definite success; moreover, benefitting from transfers from other parties on both its right and left, Labour secured three MEPs, up from just one in 2004. The tiny Trotskyist Socialist Party only contested the Dublin constituency, where its popular and respected leader, Joe Higgins, polled in excess of 12 per cent, cementing Dublin's reputation for delivering a strong left-wing vote. Dublin thus returned two left-of-centre MEPs with no seat in the Irish capital for *Fianna Fáil*, the third Dublin seat went to *Fine Gael*. The Socialist Party success in Dublin proves that *Sinn Féin* does not have a monopoly of the working-class protest vote, nor is *Sinn Féin* necessarily the most coherent voice of left-wing Euroscepticism. Although *Sinn Féin* substantially held its vote in the European election, its failure to retain its Dublin MEP was a bitter disappointment. This underlines two factors: *Sinn Féin*'s continued isolation within the democratic party system of the Republic, with a marked reluctance of other parties' supporters to transfer their votes to its candidates; and the party's growing ideological confusion as a party that is nominally of the radical left, yet includes within its support base many voters who are typical of the radical right, and is led by a leadership that increasingly looks towards the centre. These contradictions led in the immediate aftermath of the election to renewed friction within *Sinn Féin*; its longest serving Dublin councillor, Christy Burke, was amongst those who resigned in protest at the leadership. One might add that the victorious Socialist Party MEP in Dublin would join the Confederal Group of the United European Left/Nordic Green Left (EUL/NGL), the same group to which the ousted *Sinn Féin* MEP had belonged.

For Libertas, a national vote share of 5.4 per cent would normally be encouraging for a new political party. But Ganley's failure to win election in the North-West constituency was a disappointment to him and whether he will continue to bankroll the party, or whether it has a future at all, remains to be seen.

As Table 11.6. shows, the combined vote for the 'Eurosceptic' parties, *Sinn Féin,* the Socialist Party and Libertas, came to 19.3 per cent.

Table 11.6 EP election results in Ireland: 2009

Political party	1st Pref votes	% Votes	Seats
Fianna Fáil	440,562	24.1	3
Fine Gael	532,889	29.1	4
Labour Party	254,669	13.9	3
Sinn Féin	205,613	11.2	0
Green Party	34,585	1.9	0
Socialist Party	50,510	2.7	1
Libertas	99,709	5.4	0
Others	210,776	11.5	1
Total	1,829,313	100.0	12

Source: http://electionsireland.org/results/europe/2009euro.cfm.

When one adds to this the 2.0 per cent polled by the anti-EU People's Movement and the 3.0 per cent of the national vote polled by the Eurosceptic outgoing MEP and anti-Lisbon campaigner Kathy Sinnott, who failed, however, to be re-elected, then one can say that around one quarter of the Irish electorate voted for Eurosceptic and anti-Lisbon candidates. This relatively high vote share only produced one Eurosceptic MEP, however, reflecting the fragmented nature of the EU-critical movement in Ireland.

Finally, for reasons explained earlier, non-party independents usually perform well in Irish elections although in 2009 there was one independent MEP less than in the two previous European elections. As Table 11.7 indicates, one independent candidate, Marian Harkin, a community and voluntary sector activist and a liberal by inclination was elected in the North-West constituency and joined the ALDE group in the European Parliament.

Eleven of the 13 outgoing Irish MEPs sought re-election in 2009 and seven of them were successful. With the total number of Irish representatives reduced to 12, this meant that 4 Irish MEPs were elected for the first time. *Fianna Fáil's* Pat 'The Cope' Gallagher was not an outgoing MEP but had served previously as an MEP. The four new Irish members were Labour's Nessa Childers and Alan Kelly, the Socialist Party's Joe Higgins and *Fine Gael's* Seán Kelly.

The overall number of Irish MEPs, equivalent to 12, as agreed in Nice, did not vary after the ratification of the Lisbon Treaty.

9.4 Campaign finance

Campaign finance has so far been a grey area in the Irish political system. And yet, given that there is no real public funding, political parties have to raise money in order to conduct their campaigns, which have to be individually tailored due to the importance of the STV electoral system. It means that each individual is allowed to spend about €30,150–45,000 depending on the number of seats available in the constituency. Citizens are allowed to donate up to €600 to political parties anonymously, whilst corporations can contribute up to €5,000, although there are always opportunities to circumvent the system. Parties have to report any donations and expenditures received to the Standards in Public Office Commission.

For the 2007 general election political parties spent about €11 million, but just €1.6 million was disclosed. This clearly makes it difficult to find exact spending figures (OSCE, 2011, 8).

Table 11.7 List of Irish MEPs: seventh legislature

Name	Year of birth	Gender	Professional background	Constituency	National party	Political group	Committee
Liam Aylward★	1952	Male	Laboratory technician	East	Fianna Fáil	ALDE	Agriculture and Rural Development, Culture and Education (substitute)
Nessa Childers	1956	Female	Psychoanalyst	East	Labour	S&D	Environment, Public Health and Food Safety, Culture and Education (substitute)
Brian Crowley★	1964	Male	Legal advisor	South	Fianna Fáil	ALDE	Industry, Research and Energy, Legal Affairs (substitute)
Proinsias De Rossa★	1940	Male	Postman and salesman	Dublin	Labour	S&D	Employment and Social Affairs, Development (substitute)
Pat Gallagher	1948	Male	Fish exporter	North-West	Fianna Fáil	ALDE	Fisheries, Regional Development (substitute)
Marian Harkin★	1953	Female	Teacher and voluntary sector worker	North-West	Independent	ALDE	Employment and Social Affairs, petitions (substitute), Agriculture and Rural Development (substitute)
Jim Higgins★	1945	Male	Teacher	North-West	Fine Gael	EPP	Transport and Tourism, Fisheries (substitute), Petitions (substitute)
Joe Higgins	1949	Male	Catholic priest and teacher	Dublin	Socialist Party	EUL/NGL	International Trade, Petitions (substitute), Employment and Social Affairs (substitute)
Alan Kelly	1975	Male	Manager	South	Labour	S&D	Internal Market and Consumer Protection, Agriculture and Rural Development (substitute), Petitions (substitute)
Seán Kelly	1952	Male	Teacher	South	Fine Gael	EPP	Culture and Education, Regional Development (substitute)
Mairead McGuinness★	1959	Female	Journalist	East	Fine Gael	EPP	Agriculture and Rural Development, Petitions (substitute), Environment, Public health and Food Safety (substitute)
Gay Mitchell★	1951	Male	Accountant	Dublin	Fine Gael	EPP	Development, Financial, Economic and Social Crisis, Economic and Monetary Affairs (substitute)

Source: www.europarl.europa.eu/mepr/en/search.html?country=IE.

Note:
★ denotes an outgoing MEP re-elected in 2009.

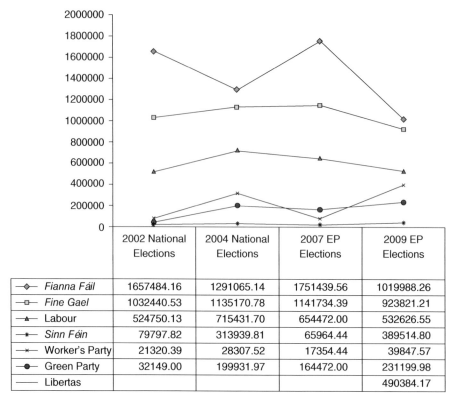

Figure 11.3 National and EP election campaign expenditure in Ireland

Source: Reports of General Elections 2002 and 2007; Reports of EP elections 2004 and 2009, the Standards in Public Office Commission, www.sipo.gov.ie/en/Reports/Elections/

10 Theoretical interpretation of Euro-elections

10.1 Second-Order Election theory

The hypothesis that governments, if they do not perform well, can be punished by voters in European elections seems to be confirmed in the Irish case. More specifically, the 2009 Euro-election represents a good test for such an assumption, since the *Fianna Fáil*-Progressive Democrats coalition government was not able to address the financial crisis properly and was thus penalized. However, by looking at all seven waves of Euro-elections, it is possible to detect a more complex pattern. The two main parties always lost more than 10 per cent of the vote in relation to previous general elections, although Labour retained the same level of support.

Smaller parties and independent candidates benefitted most from this decline in the two major parties. A timing factor also appeared quite relevant. When EP elections fell during mid-term and citizens were dissatisfied with the government's performance, these elections would become a tool to castigate its members. On the contrary, if voters were happy with the executive, this electoral contest would turn into an experiment which privileged smaller parties.

Overall, European elections in Ireland provided strong support for SOE theory, given that turnout was noticeably lower than in general elections, campaigns were not focussed on

European issues, and a very strong anti-government vote emerged to the benefit of smaller parties and independents.

10.2 Europe Salience theory

European matters were discussed during the EP electoral campaigns in Ireland, but all parties had more or less the same positive approach to the European Union. The three main parties, in particular *Fianna Fáil* and *Fine Gael*, presented themselves as the real champions of Europe. By contrast, smaller left-wing parties, like *Sinn Féin* and the Workers' Party, put forward rather Euro-critical positions, although EU membership was never contested, except by the Socialists. Also the Greens have come to be more supportive of the EU, being well integrated within the European Green group. No right-wing extreme parties tried to profit from opposition to European integration. The attempts of Libertas to capitalize on Eurosceptic views in the 2009 EP election did not work out, despite a €500,000 campaign sponsored by magnate Declan Ganley.

Over the years, there has been indeed an increase of soft Euroscepticism, which can be mostly seen as Euro-criticism within the context of ongoing support for EU membership. Irish political parties are all more or less pro-European. Ireland's involvement in the European integration project has been a core aspect of its politics, overwhelmingly supported by public opinion, and an integral part of Irish identity. All this explains why the Europe Salience theory can only marginally interpret EP elections in Ireland.

Elections in the Republic of Ireland are quite personalized through the so-called STV electoral method. This means that candidates have to campaign quite intensively and keep in touch with their respective constituencies throughout the respective legislative period. This is also one of the reasons why Ireland, despite being a small country, has decided to create four constituencies for the 12 MEPs that it elected to the EP in 2009, retaining three constituencies for the 11 MEPs it elected in 2014. This creates quite a different electoral dynamic than in most other small countries, with just one constituency from which all MEPs are elected.

References

Primary sources

http://electionsireland.org/results/europe/2009euro.cfm (accessed on 15 February 2015).
www.parties and elections.de/ireland2.html (accessed on 15 February 2015).
Electoral resources, www.electoralresources.org.ie/2011.php?constituency.
Eurobarometer (2008) National Report, Ireland, Eurobarometer 69 (2).
European Parliament Elections in the Republic of Ireland, http://en.wikipedia.org/wiki/Category: European_Parliament_elections_in_the_Republic_of_Ireland (accessed on 18 August 2013).
European Parliament website, www.europarl.europa.eu/(accessed on 7 December 2013).
Eurostat (2013, 2014) http://epp.eurostat.ec.europa.eu/ (accessed on 5 June 2015).
Fianna Fáil (2009) 'Europe: We are Better Working Together,' European Election Manifesto 2009, Dublin.
Fine Gael (2009) 'Securing Ireland's Future in Europe', European Election Manifesto' 2009, Dublin.
Greens (2009) *Focus on Europe*, European Election Manifes to 2009, Dublin.
Labour Party (Ireland) (2009) 'Putting People, Jobs and Fairness at the Heart of Europe', European Election Manifesto 2009.
Libertas (2009) *European Election Manifesto*, Dublin.
Organization for Security and Cooperation in Europe (OSCE, 2011) Ireland: Early Parliamentary Elections. 25 February 2011, OSCE/ODHIR Needs Assessment Mission Report, 7–10 February, OSCE report, www.osce.org/odihr/elections/75725 (accessed on 5 February 2012).

Sinn Féin (2009) European Election Manifesto 2009, Dublin.
Standards in Public Office Commission (2012) www.sipo.gov.ie/en/Reports/Elections (accessed on 5 February 2012).

Secondary sources

Benoit, K. (2009) 'Irish Political Parties and Policy Stances on European Integration', *Irish Political Studies*, 24(4), 447–66.
Bolleyer, N. and Panke, D. (2009) 'The Irish Green Party and Europe: An Unhappy Marriage?' *Irish Political Studies*, 24(4), 543–57.
Collins, N. (1985) 'Ireland', in Reif, K. H. (ed.) *Ten European Elections. Campaigns and Results of the 1979/81. First Direct Elections to the European Parliamen*, Aldershot, Gower, 105–17.
Collins, N. (1986) 'Ireland', in Lodge, J. (ed.) *Direct Elections to the European Parliament 1984*, Basingstoke, Macmillan, 138–54.
Collins, S. (2009) 'FF Fighting Hard And Not Expecting Bad Election Result, Says Cowen', *The Irish Times*, 15 May, 7.
Collins, S. and Gartland F. (2009) 'Kenny Says Euro Poll will be Most Crucial Ever for Ireland', *The Irish Times*, 4 May, 1.
Collins, S. and Smyth, J. (2009) 'Cowen Calls for Transfer of FF votes to Greens', *The Irish Times*, 8 May, 21.
De Bréadún, D. (2009) 'Opposition Misleading on Economy – Cowen', *The Irish Times*, 29 May, 10.
Fitzgibbon, J. (2009) 'Ireland's No to Lisbon: Learning the Lessons from the Failure of the Yes and the Success of the No Side', *Sussex European Institute Working Paper*, 110, University of Sussex.
Hayward, K. and Fallon, J. (2009) 'Fianna Fáil: Tenacious Localism, Tenuous Europeanism', *Irish Political Studies*, 24(4), 491–509.
Hennessy, M. and De Bréadún, D. (2009) 'Ganley to Forgo Major Lisbon Role if He Loses Poll', *The Irish Times*, 23 May, 8.
Holmes, M. (2004) 'The European Parliament Election in Ireland, 11 June 2004, *Sussex European Institute European Parliament Election Briefing*, 2, University of Sussex.
Holmes, M. (2009b) 'The Irish Labour Party: The Advantages, Disadvantages and Irrelevance of Europeanization?' *Irish Political Studies*, 24(4), 527–41.
Kavanagh, B. (2009) 'East Candidate Seeks Block on Immigrants', *The Irish Times*, 15 May, 7.
Laffan, B. and O'Mahony, J. (2008) *Ireland and EU Membership*, Basingstoke, Palgrave.
McGee, H. (2009) 'Libertas accused of being "fascist" over migrant plan', *The Irish Times*, 16 May, 8.
Maillot, A. (2009) 'Sinn Féin's Approach to the EU: Still More "Critical" than "Engaged"?' *Irish Political Studies*, 24(4), 559–74.
Marsh, M. (1994) 'Ireland: An Electorate with its Mind on Lower Things', in van der Eijk, C. and Franklin, M. N. (eds) *Choosing Europe? The European Electorate and National Politics in the Face of Union*, Ann Arbor, University of Michigan Press, 166–85.
Moxon-Browne, E. (1996) 'Ireland', in Lodge, J. (ed.) *The 1994 Elections to the European Parliament*, London, Pinter, 122–33.
Moxon-Browne, E. (2010) 'Ireland', in Lodge, J. (ed.) *The 2009 Elections to the European Parliament*, Basingstoke, Palgrave, 150–59.
O'Mahoney, J. (2009) 'Ireland's EU Referendum Experience', *Irish Political Studies*, 24(4), 429–46.
O'Regan, M. (2009) 'Show FF the Red Card, Says Labour', *The Irish Times*, 25 May, 7.
O'Toole, F. (2003) *After the Ball*, Dublin, New Island Books.
Sheridan, K. (2009) 'Mr Higgins Goes to Brussels', *The Irish Times*, 13 June, Weekend Review, 1.

12
DENMARK

Carina Bischoff and Marlene Wind

Figure 12.1 Map of Denmark

Table 12.1 Denmark profile

EU entry year	1973 ECSC, EEC and Euratom
Schengen entry year	1996
MEPs elected in 2009	13
MEPs under Lisbon Treaty	13
Capital	Copenhagen
Total area★	42,921 km^2
Population	5,627,235
Population density★★	130.8/km^2
Median age of population	41.3
Political system	Constitutional Monarchy
Head of state	Queen Margrethe II (January 1972–)
Head of government	Lars Løkke Rasmussen, Liberal Party (V) (April 2009–October 2011); Helle Thorning Schmidt, the Social Democrats (S) (October 2011–)
Political majority	Liberal Party (V) and Conservative People's Party (K) (April 2009–October 2011); Socialdemocratic Party (S), Social Liberal Party (R) and Socialist People's Party (SF) Government Coalition supported by the Red–Green Alliance (October 2011–)
Currency	Danish Krone (DKK)
Prohead GDP in PPS	45,600 €

Source: Eurostat, 2013, 2014, http://epp.eurostat.ec.europa.eu/.

Notes:
★ Total area including inland waters
★★ Population density: the ratio of the annual average population of a region to the land area of the region.

1 Geographical position

Located in northern Europe, Denmark occupies a strategically important geographical position between its Scandinavian neighbours and Continental Europe, in the narrow straits connecting the Baltic Sea to the North Sea. The country covers an area of 42,894 square kilometres, and has a population of over 5.5 million, largely concentrated in the cities, with an urbanization rate of 87 per cent. In religious, ethnic, and cultural terms, Denmark is highly homogenous compared to many other European countries. In recent decades, however, there has been a growing population of immigrants with different ethnic and religious backgrounds. Some 10 per cent of the population today descends from immigrants and of these 67 per cent are of non-Western origin. The Kingdom of Denmark also includes the Faroe Islands and Greenland in the North Atlantic, both of which enjoy the status of autonomous territories.

2 Historical background

The official history of Denmark dates back to the ninth and tenth centuries, when the Vikings established the first political structures. In 1397 Denmark, Norway, and Sweden formed a union under a common crown, known as the Union of Kalmar.

During WWI, the country maintained its neutrality and, as a result of Germany's defeat, it regained territory to the south. In 1940 Denmark was occupied by the Nazis. Initially the government remained in place, but it resigned in 1943.

In 1973 Denmark entered the EEC and was hit by the international oil crisis at the same time. Years of prosperity were replaced by an economic slump and higher unemployment, which lasted through the 1980s.

3 Geopolitical profile

As one of the founding members, Denmark has been well integrated in the North Atlantic Treaty Organization (NATO) since 1949. Although allied with some reservations and a relatively small defence budget for most of the Cold War period, the country has generally had a strong pro-American position in terms of its security policy. Moreover, Denmark is well integrated into the civil, yet not the military, part of the Common Foreign and Security Policy of the European Union.

Like other Scandinavian countries, Denmark has one of the most generous development aid policies in the world. It is a founding member of the United Nations, a member of the International Monetary Fund (IMF), the Organization for Economic Development and Cooperation (OECD), and the Organization for Security and Cooperation in Europe (OSCE).

4 Overview of the political landscape

Denmark is a constitutional monarchy in which the head of state plays a non-political ceremonial role. It is a unitary state, with two tiers of political representation below the national level consisting of 98 municipalities and 5 regions. The system of government is parliamentary democracy. It has a unicameral Parliament, called *Folketinget*, which consists of 179 members, including two representatives from Greenland and two representatives from the Faroe Islands, elected by a proportional electoral system. The courts do not play an active role in the political life of the country and the legality of parliamentary decisions has only rarely been challenged.

No single party has won a majority of seats since 1909, thus the most common form of government has been of minority coalitions that have initiated a tradition of broad collaboration between parties in Parliament.

At the time of the 2009 European election, eight parties were represented in Parliament. The centre-right coalition government was led by Prime Minister Lars Løkke Rasmussen from the Liberal Party (*Venstre*). Since 2001, the Conservative and Liberal Parties were in power, but were replaced by a centre-left coalition guided by the leader of the Social Democratic Party and first female Prime Minister, Helle Thorning-Schmidt.

5 Brief account of the political parties

Since October 2011, eight parties have been represented in the *Folketinget,* and a few more contest elections. In addition to these, two parties have emerged that only participate in elections to the European Parliament.

The *Socialdemokraterne* (Social Democratic Party) is the main party on the left of the political spectrum in Denmark. It was founded in 1871 to represent the interests of the working class and by 1924, it had become the largest party with the support of more than a third of the electorate. It formed a government for the first time in 1924 and in the six succeeding decades. From 1924 to 1982, the Social Democrats were almost permanently in office, except for 13 years, forming a government alone or in coalition with the *Radikale Venstre* (the Social Liberal Party). The pattern changed in 1982 when the Social Democrats lost power to a coalition of the centre-right that stayed in power until 1993. From 2001 to 2011 the Social Democrats were out of office once more, but in 2011 they won the elections and formed a coalition government with the Social Liberals and the *Socialistisk Folkeparti* (the Socialist People's Party).

The Social Democratic Party has ideological roots in socialism and has historically been closely affiliated with the working-class movement and the unions. In the post-war period, the party advocated social and economic changes through reform and supported the expansion of the welfare state with high growth and employment, a strong public sector, and redistribution policies as a means of diminishing social and economic inequalities. Due to its strong influence on government in the twentieth century, the party has played a key role in the construction and expansion of the generous welfare state and the large public sector in Denmark. Partly as a result of social and economic changes, its strength as the primary representative of the working class has eroded. On the one hand, it appeals to a broader constituency and, on the other hand, the working-class vote is shared more broadly across the parties in the system.

Socialistisk Folkeparti, SF (Socialist People's Party), founded in 1959, emerged as a splinter party from the former Communist Party. Its original programme emphasized commitment to the introduction of socialism by democratic means, public ownership of the means of production, neutrality, disarmament, and solidarity with the Third World. Today, the Socialist profile is toned down and the party advocates social and economic equality through redistribution within a controlled market economy. At the heart of its politics lies a commitment to the 'green agenda' as well as the promotion of human rights, feminism, and increasing democratic participation in the workplace. Since its inception, it has received on average 8 per cent of the votes, with 9.6 per cent at the 2011 elections, it is the second largest party on the left. After 50 years as an opposition party, it entered into government for the first time in 2011 in a coalition with the Social Democrats and the Social Liberal Party. Until then, it had only served as a supporting party to Social Democratic governments in the mid-1960s, which caused severe internal rifts over compromises made, and again in the 1990s. As part of its preparation for, and participation in, the government coalition, the party chose a more

Table 12.2 List of political parties in Denmark

Original name	Abbreviation	English translation
Socialdemokraterne	S	Social Democrats
Venstre	V	Liberal Party
Socialistisk Folkeparti	SF	Socialist People's Party
Dansk Folkeparti	DF	Danish People's Party
Det Konservative Folkeparti	K	Conservative People's Party
Folkebevægelsen mod EU	N	People's Movement Against the EU
Det Radikale Venstre	R	Social Liberal Party
Junibevægelsen	J	June Movement
Enhedslisten	Ø	Unity List
Liberal Alliance/New Alliance	LA	Liberal Alliance/New Alliance
Centrum Demokraterne	CD	Centre Democrats
Retsforbundet	E	Justice Party
Kristendemokraterne	K	Christian Democrats
Venstre Socialisterne	VS	Left Socialist Party
Fremskridtspartiet	Z	Progressive Party
Danmarks Kommunistiske Parti	DKP	Denmark's Communist Party
Fælles Kurs	P	Common Course
De Grønne	G	Green Party
Minoritetspartiet	M	Minority Party

pragmatic route for winning influence and had to compromise on a number of issues, including its advocacy for an open immigration policy.

Founded in 1989, *Enhedslisten* (Unity List), also known as the Red–Green Alliance, represents the fusion of several small parties on the extreme left that were unable to win representation on their own. Until the election in 2011, where it won 6.7 per cent of the vote, its support had been fluctuating at around 2–3 per cent. The compromises made by the SF combined with the economic crises and a hugely popular party leader undoubtedly contributed to this result. Its programme reflects a commitment to democratic socialism, with the long-term aim of attaining a classless society and the collective ownership of the means of production. It strongly opposes social inequalities and refuses to support political agreements that entail a reduction in welfare provisions. As its name indicates, it has a strong Green profile, and also supports global solidarity, disarmament, and an open immigration policy. It currently supports the centre-left coalition in government.

Det Radikale Venstre (the Social Liberal Party) was founded in 1905, as a result of internal dissension in *Venstre* (the Liberal Party), mainly over matters of defence where it took an anti-military position. It is ideologically centrist in opposing both socialism as well as pure capitalism and has pursued an agenda promoting social welfare in balance with a liberal concern for individual rights. Opposed to the advocacy of special interests, it has argued for a 'reasoned' approach to politics and has favoured broad collaboration among the parties. The promotion of education is a core issue for the party that, among others, also supports a Green agenda, generous international aid, and a liberal approach to immigration. It is also the *Folketinget*'s most pro-European party. Before 2001, it had a pivotal role as 'king-maker' in the Danish party system and even when it was not in government, it was typically an essential part of the political majorities behind agreements. Under the 2001–2011 right-wing government, it lost this key role, but it is now back in power. It has been closely associated with the Social Democrats as a coalition partner in government, but on a few occasions, in 1968–1971 and 1988–1990, it has also entered into coalitions with the parties on the centre–right. At the 2011 election, it obtained 9.5 per cent of the votes and became a very influential partner in the centre-left government.

Venstre (the Liberal Party) was founded in 1870 by different groups who shared their commitment to liberalism, advocacy for agrarian interests, as well as opposition to the existing regime. *Venstre* became the majority party in Parliament in 1872 and played a leading role in constitutional battles for the introduction of parliamentary democracy. It formed a government for the first time in 1901 and dominated governments, alternating with the Social Liberal Party, until 1924. Apart from its participation in the broad unity government during the German Occupation in WWII and as leader of a coalition government with the Conservative Party from 1950 to 1953, it did not re-enter government before 1968 as part of a three-party coalition. After two short-lived governments in the 1970s, one in an odd alliance with the Social Democrats, it participated in the stable coalition of centre-right parties that governed from 1982 to 1993. In 2001, it became the largest party and led the right-wing government that was in power until 2011.

Following the decline of agriculture and the depopulation of the countryside from the 1950s, its original platform of defending agrarian interests was transformed into that of a broader liberal party. Its electoral support had ranged from 20 to 30 per cent in the decades immediately after the war, but was reduced to a mere 10 per cent by the late 1980s. In the 1990s, the party developed a sharper ideological profile emphasizing a downsizing of the public sector, increased reliance on market forces and privatization, as well as individual freedoms. Growing in electoral support, but failing to win government power in 1998, it changed strategy to appeal to parties and voters in the political centre. It formed a government in a minority coalition with the Conservative party in 2001–2011, with the Danish People's Party as its stable parliamentary support.

Det Konservative Folkeparti (the Conservative People's Party) was founded in 1915 representing a re-organization of conservative groups that supported the Danish king in the constitutional battles leading up to parliamentary democracy. Like other Conservative parties, it has emphasized the importance of the nation, its history, culture and community, and stressed the importance of a strong national defence. Economically, it emphasizes the importance of private property and advocates pro-business policies without committing to a strong ideology of free market forces. In relation to the public sector, it has emphasized the importance of modernization and downscaling as well as decentralization to the local level. With the support of around 20 per cent of the electorate for most of the post-war period, with a drastic but short-lived dip in the 1970s, the party's electoral support started sliding in the 1990s and has been stable at 10 per cent until it hit a low 5.9 per cent in 2011. In addition to being challenged by parties both on the left and on the right, the party has suffered from internal conflicts over leadership. In the post-war period, the Conservative party was the second party in three coalition governments with centre-right parties, (1950–1953; 1968–1971; 2001–2011) and held the post of Prime Minister in the coalition that ruled from 1982 to 1993.

Dansk Folkeparti (Danish People's Party) was established in 1995 by four prominent members of the 'Progress Party', which burst onto the political scene in 1973 with a radical agenda of drastic tax-cuts, anti-defence spending and strong Euroscepticism. Defeated electorally after the emergence of the Danish People's Party, the Progress Party soon disappeared. The Danish People's Party is typically described as a party on the right due to its highly Nationalisticic values, its emphasis on law and order, and its strong anti-immigration policies. Its role as a stable parliamentary supporter of the centre-right government from 2001 to 2011 underlines this classification. However, rather than continuing the minimal state rhetoric of its predecessor, it has adopted a platform of supporting social welfare with an emphasis on care for the elderly. In its socio-economic policies, it can be regarded as a party on the centre-left. Its advocacy for restricting immigration, and even reversing it, has played a significant role in Danish politics. On the one hand, it has struck a cord with segments of the population and the party has the stable support of 12–14 per cent of voters. On the other hand, it has been able to put pressure on the other parties that in many cases have moved closer to the Danish People's Party on the issue, and as the supporting party of the late government it effectively put its mark on policy.

Liberal Alliance (Liberal Alliance) is a new party, which represents a reformed continuation of the New Alliance Party that emerged in the 2007 elections. It advocates economic liberalism and promotes tax reductions and cut-backs in welfare services. In accordance with its Liberal views, it is opposed to state regulation of the personal lives of citizens and restrictions on immigration, provided immigrants 'pay for themselves'. It is also critical of the EU, which it considers to be too detailed in its regulation. While supporting the return of a right-wing government, it is critical of the levels of taxes and public spending that were endorsed by a government of the Liberal and Conservative parties from 2001 to 2011. At the election in 2011, it won 5 per cent of the votes.

In addition to the parties represented in Parliament, two other parties run in the European Parliament elections on Eurosceptic platforms. The two parties are not regular parties as they do not hold policies on most issues. These include first, the non-partisan *Folkebevægelsen mod EU* (People's Movement Against the EU) that formed in connection with the debate on Danish accession in 1972. It started as a weak network, bringing together local committees, organizations, and party members united by their Euroscepticism and had a strong impact on the public referendum debate. It was the only non-parliamentary party that made a bid for participating in the EP elections in 1979 and it has participated in every election since then.

Junibevægelsen (June Movement) emerged after the referendum in 1993 in opposition to further integration into the EU, but was not opposed to membership as such. After its failure to obtain a seat in the 2009 EP elections, the party dissolved itself.

5.1 Party attitudes towards the European Union

The parties currently represented in the *Folketinget* or in the EP European Parliament can roughly be divided into three groups based on their positions on European issues:

- Pro-EU: the Social Liberal, the Social Democratic, the Liberal and the Conservative parties. They are in favour of membership and also for abolishing the opt-outs so that Denmark can regain its status as full member of the EU.
- Pro-EU membership, but with reservations regarding the areas covered by the opt-outs: the Socialist People's Party, a main architect of the Danish opt-outs, has changed its position in recent years. It now favours joining the Common Security and Defence Policy as well as Justice and Home Affairs, but does not want to enter into the euro-zone mainly due to the lack of a social aspect in the EMU. The Liberal Alliance is also against joining the EMU due to both the current economic situation in Europe and an increasing sceptical attitude towards the EU in general.
- Eurosceptics: leaving the European Union is the ultimate goal of the People's Movement Against the EU, which opposes the EU's infringement on national self-determination and would like Denmark to have its own voice in international fora. The Danish People's Party is also EU-sceptic due to concerns about the loss of national sovereignty. The Unity List opposes EU membership because of its market driven pro-business policies and lack of democracy.

Over the past four decades, there have been signs of tension between popular opinion and political parties' positions on Europe. Differences in the support given to the parties in the national *Folketinget* elections and the EP elections give evidence of this phenomenon. Figure 12.2 shows the gap between the share of votes of hard Eurosceptic parties at the *Folketinget* and European elections respectively.

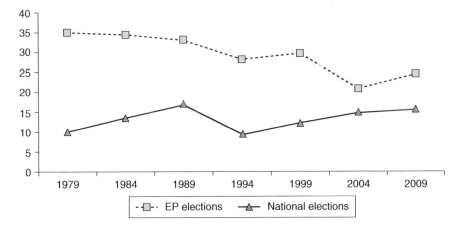

Figure 12.2 Eurosceptic party performance at EP and national elections in Denmark: 1979–2009

Source: Danmarks Statistik, Election Years: 1979–2009, www.dst.dk; DanishParliament EU information web-page: www.euo.dk/spsv/off/alle/valgtilEP/.

As seen in the figure, there has been a persistent gap between the support for Eurosceptic parties at EP and national elections, albeit that it has clearly waned over time. The highest, 25 per cent gap was registered in the late 1970s, and a 20 per cent difference was reached in the mid-1990s. The narrowing of the gap is a result of both declining support for hard Eurosceptics at EP elections as well as increasing support for Eurosceptics at national elections over the last decade. In the 2009 EP election, 25 per cent of the voters still supported Eurosceptic parties compared to 15 per cent at the preceding national election in 2007. The difference between the two party systems has been able to subsist, due to the low salience of EU issues in domestic elections on the one hand, and the participation of two additional parties with Eurosceptic profiles in the EP elections, on the other. The two additional parties have provided Eurosceptic voters with an opportunity to vote for parties they agreed with in EP elections and arguably eased some of the pressure on the parties in domestic politics. The two types of elections have therefore maintained a stronger degree of separation than has been seen elsewhere in Europe.

With the exception of the Socialist People's Party, which had received 5–10 per cent of the vote in the elections prior to the referendum on accession, all of the established parties, recommended a positive vote. The vast majority of the 36.7 per cent voting 'No' thus did so in opposition to their party's recommendations. There was a sense of disharmony between the attitudes of the elite and the general population, and the gap would not close quickly. Generally, the parties in the *Folketinget* have held a more positive view on Denmark's involvement in Europe than the general population has. The tension has traditionally been strongest on the left, where Euroscepticism has always been strongest. In fact, until the mid and late 1990s Euroscepticism in Denmark was largely a left-wing phenomenon fuelled by an antipathy towards Conservative, capitalist, and Catholic Europe. Europe was perceived as a danger to the Danish welfare state and was the preserver of an unjust global order which created a 'Fortress Europe' to the detriment of Third World countries; it was also seen as a threat to national democracy and identity. Of the parties represented in Parliament, only the Socialist People's Party held a Eurosceptic position the first two decades following Denmark's accession, but at the EP elections it was joined by the Popular Movement against the EEC/EU. After the referendum on Maastricht in the early 1990s, the Progress Party – no longer in Parliament – on the right distanced itself from its previously pro-European stance and its successful 'successor', the Danish People's Party, arrived on the stage in 1995 with a clear Eurosceptic agenda. Unlike the sceptics on the left, the new right-wing critique focusses on the threat of open borders in Europe. In their view, the EU results in an influx of immigrants and criminals to Denmark. Moreover, the EU is seen as a threat to national identity, democracy, and sovereignty. The issue of immigration has been very important in Danish politics from the 1990s onwards and creating a link between attitudes to the EU and immigration could have undermined the separation of attitudes on the EU and domestic politics that has been maintained in Denmark. Until now, the EU has not been a salient issue in connection with national elections.

With regard to the representation of voters' opinions, there was hardly any discrepancy on the centre-right on the question of membership of the EEC, but voters of the centre-left parties, the Social Democrats and the Social Liberal Party, were from the beginning quite evenly split on this issue. The tension over the question of membership on the left was not confined to the relationship between voters and parties, but also manifested itself in intra-party dissension, though without leading to the formation of proper factions or splits within parties. At the first European election, four members of the Social Democratic Party obtained nomination to the list of the anti-EEC Popular Movement. The leader of the Social Democratic Party responded to this by threatening them with exclusion and one of the candidates gave up the nomination as a result. Over the years, the Social Democratic Party has had its share of internal debates and disagreements over Europe and although it played a leading role in bringing Denmark into the EEC, it has been a less enthusiastic supporter of the European project than, for instance, the Liberal Party.

The parties in Parliament have typically recommended positive votes in referenda on Europe, but their advice has gone unheeded by large sections of citizens on several occasions. In 1986, the opposite occurred when 56 per cent of voters endorsed the adoption of the Single European Act (SEA). This happened in spite of the low degree of support for the EEC observed in the early 1980s and also went against the recommendation of the majority in Parliament. It was, however, in accordance with the advice given by the popular incumbent centre-right government.

Differences in positions over the SEA also represented the first major disagreement on European policy between the Social Democratic Party and the Liberal Party. Together, the two parties had formed a majority that largely defined Danish EU policy in the first decade following Danish accession. However, after the coalition of centre-right parties took office in 1982, the Social Democrats formed a parliamentary majority on important matters of foreign policy in alliance with the Social Liberal Party that supported the government on domestic policies and thus made it possible for it to remain in office.

However, on the question of the SEA, the voters supported the government. This election was significant not only due to its outcome, but because, according to observers, it marked the end of the 'membership' discussion and the beginning of the debate on 'union' and further integration in the EU (Worre, 1989, 100). On this issue, the pro-membership parties did not see eye to eye, as evidenced by their different positions on the SEA. The Liberals, the Conservatives, and the now-defunct Centre Democrats were described as 'federalists' with their pro-integration views, while the Social Democrats, Social Liberals, as well as the Progress Party and the Christian Democrats, were characterized as 'pragmatic pro-Europeans' or 'states rights' advocates as they were sceptical of transferring further powers to Brussels and giving up the national veto.

Analysis of voters' views in the late 1980s showed that voters on the centre-right were more in line with the position of the pragmatic pro-Europeans than the 'federalist' positions taken by their own parties. The tension between party and voter attitudes on Europe has therefore not only been a problem on the left, although it was mostly over the extent of integration on the right. In the late 1980s, the 'states rights' parties dominated in the *Folketinget* with only one-sixth of the votes going to hard Eurosceptics and a third to the 'federalists' (Worre, 1989, 101).

Following the SEA election, the Social Democrats and the Socialist People's Party went through a period of adjusting their positions on Europe and common ground with the government was found. A broadly negotiated position included the inclusion of new areas in European collaboration such as education, culture, environment, and a strengthened social dimension as well as coordination on foreign policy.

Differences did not disappear, however. Although they recommended a 'Yes' to the Maastricht Treaty in 1992, the Social Democrats had reservations about collaboration on defence and a common currency, and both the Socialist People's Party and the Progress Party did not support signing the treaty. Following the Danish 'No' to the Maastricht Treaty in 1992, the government in close collaboration with the parties in Parliament, negotiated the Edinburgh Agreement, which allowed Denmark to retain its membership of the EU while 'opting out' of four areas covered by the treaty, which include: participation in the third phase of EMU (the euro); the Common Security and Defence Policy; parts of the Justice and Home Affairs Policy; and citizenship of the European Union. The so-called 'opt-outs' have been an important issue in Danish EU politics since the Edinburgh Agreement was adopted in 1993. Several of the parties behind the agreement have since argued for abolishing some or all of the opt-outs, but so far without success.

C. Bischoff and M. Wind

6 Public opinion and the European Union

Over the years, Danish public opinion on Europe has not been characterized by strong stability. When it said 'Yes' to joining the European Economic Community in a referendum held on 2 October 1972, it was not by a slim margin but with 63.4 per cent in favour, and with a turnout of 90.1 per cent. In addition, the referendum debate was described as 'the most lively public debate in modern Danish history' (Sørensen, 1979, 51). However, compared to the divisive campaign and vote in Norway that resulted in a resounding 'No' the same year, the Danish accession went smoothly.

After Denmark's entry to the EEC, popular support for membership declined, as Figure 12.2 illustrates. The proportion of the population who thought that EEC membership was 'a good thing' dropped significantly during the 1970s while more and more, instead, considered it 'a bad thing'. Subsequently, for a short period, the Eurosceptics actually outnumbered the Europhiles, but since the mid-1980s, the overall trend has been more pro-European, with a steady decline of the share of negative as well as neutral views. This trend was only broken by a dip in the first half of the 1990s, where the share in favour of membership fell below 50 per cent. Since 2003, however, the proportion of Danes supporting membership has been steady at 60–67 per cent. As shown in Table 12.3, turnout in the various referenda on Europe testifies to an engaged, yet divided population.

In the first referendum following accession, held in 1986, there were no evident signs of a large discrepancy between voter opinions and party positions. The centre-left parties recommended a 'No' to the Single European Act, while the centre-right parties of the incumbent government advocated a 'Yes'. The positive outcome meant that Denmark was one of the first EC countries to ratify the SEA. As such, the 1992 Referendum on the Maastricht Treaty was therefore a bit of a shock to the political system. It was the first defeat of an incumbent government on European issues when a slim, but nonetheless effective, majority of voters turned it down. However, the 'No' did not go only against the government, but also against the party system that endorsed a treaty that they believed Denmark had successfully helped shape in accordance with its interests. Since this potentially threatened the ongoing European integration process and Denmark's

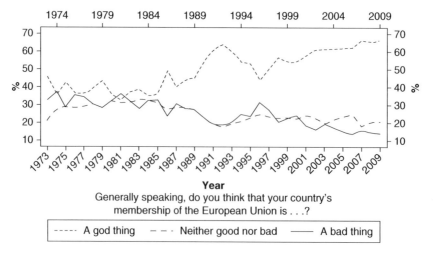

Figure 12.3 Danish attitude to the European Union: 1973–2009

Source: Eurobarometer, http://ec.europa.eu/public_opinion/index_en.htm

Table 12.3 Referenda on Europe in Denmark

Issue	Year	Turnout	'Yes'	'No'
Danish EC membership	1972	90.1%	63.4%	36.6%
Single European Act	1986	75.4%	56.2%	43.8%
Maastricht Treaty	1992	83.1%	49.3%	50.7%
Maastricht Treaty and Edinburgh Agreement	1993	86.5%	56.7%	43.3%
Amsterdam Treaty	1998	76.2%	55.1%	44.9%
The Euro Opt-out	2000	87.6%	46.8%	53.2%

Source: Folketinget, EU-oplysningen, www.eu-oplysningen.dk/dkeu/dk/afstemninger/afstemning/.

participation, the government responded by negotiating a number of 'opt-outs'. These envisaged the possibility for Denmark to sign the treaty while remaining outside certain policy areas, including defence, EMU, judicial and police cooperation, and union citizenship. The new agreement, known as the Edinburgh agreement, was approved with a comfortable, albeit not particularly enthusiastic, majority of voters in 1993. It also sparked major riots in Copenhagen, as protesters argued that the new referendum effectively represented a cancellation of the people's voice that had just been heard the year before. It also resulted in the formation of a new Eurosceptic 'party', the June Movement, which – as noted earlier – was opposed to further EU integration but not EU membership as such.

The opt-outs have widely been perceived by the political parties as a hindrance to the effective participation of Denmark in the EU, and the issue of holding a new referendum with the aim of abolishing them is a recurring theme in the Danish political debate. However, the parties are also aware that they must tread carefully. In 2000, due to favourable opinion polls, the incumbent centre-left government thought that the time was ripe to abolish the EMU opt-out and it called for a referendum on the euro. The Danes voted to remain outside of the euro-zone, despite the fact that most of the parties advocated a 'Yes' vote. Since then, no further referenda have been held although this was on the agenda of the centre-right government in power from 2001 to 2011. The image of Danes as reluctant Europeans that favour membership of the EU but are sceptical towards transferring national sovereignty has solidified in spite of the attempts by parties to pull voters in a more pro-European direction.

7 National and EP electoral systems

The 179 Danish members of the *Folketinget* are elected by a two-tier proportional representation (PR) system. The election date is set by the Prime Minister no later than four years from the previous election. One hundred and thirty-five seats are filled in multi-member electoral districts grouped into three regions that are subdivided into ten districts, which are in turn divided into 92 constituencies. Voters may cast a ballot for a district party list, or for a specific candidate. Most parties today use a type of non-ordered list that gives voters direct influence over which of the candidates get elected. In addition, 40 compensatory seats are allocated to parties that have received 2 per cent of the votes, to ensure a more proportional outcome of the election. The constituency and compensatory seats are distributed according to the d'Hondt and the Sainte-Laguës methods respectively. In practice then, the electoral system requires parties to win 2 per cent of the votes to obtain representation in the *Folketinget*. Four seats are allocated to the representatives from the Faroe Islands and Greenland.

The Danish EP elections are based on legislation dating back to 1977. All Danish parties represented in the *Folketinget* or the EP are entitled to run for EP representation. The parties must submit a list with a maximum of 20 candidates no later than four weeks prior to EP elections. Danish voters choose between individual candidates from non-ordered party lists, which means that votes for individual candidates determine who gets elected. The only exception has been the Liberal Alliance, which has used an ordered party list. The allocation of the 13 Danish seats is based on the d'Hondt method and there is only a single electoral constituency, which means that voters can vote for any of the candidates presented, unlike in *Folketinget* elections when they are restricted to voting for a candidate within one of the ten electoral districts. The 13 Danish seats amounts to one less than the 14 MEPs Denmark elected in the 2004 EP election.

In 2009 all parties, except the Danish People's Party, joined electoral alliances that generally increased their chances of obtaining a seat. The first alliance announced to voters was the Eurosceptic alliance, consisting of the June Movement and The People's Movement Against the EU. Later, the Socialist People's Party, the Social Democrats and the Social-Liberal Party announced that they would join forces, despite the fact that the Social Liberals and Socialist People's Party rarely see eye to eye on EU matters. Finally, the Liberal Alliance, the Conservatives, and the Liberals formed an alliance.

These alliances had a stronger foundation in national politics and in their prospects for gaining an electoral advantage than they had in European affairs. The fact that alliances reflect strategic concerns rather than European policy is not a new phenomenon, but goes back to the first European elections (Worre, 1989, 104).

8 A glance at the EP and national elections

As Tables 12.4 and 12.5 show, voters have a very different level of engagement in the two types of elections. Participation in national elections has fluctuated between 83 and 89 per cent, while turnout at EP elections has been consistently lower at 46–53 per cent.

Table 12.4 EP election results and turnout in Denmark: 1979–2004 (%)

Political party	1979	1984	1989	1994	1999	2004
The Social Democrats	21.9	19.5	23.3	15.8	16.5	32.6
The Social Liberal Party	3.3	3.1	2.8	8.5	9.1	6.4
The Conservative Party	14.0	20.8	13.3	17.7	8.5	11.3
The Centre Democrats	6.2	6.6	8.0	0.9	3.5	—
The Justice Party	3.4	—	—	—	—	—
The Socialist Party	4.7	9.2	9.1	8.6	7.5	7.9
The June Movement	—	—	—	15.2	16.1	9.1
The People's Movement against EC/EU	20.9	20.8	18.9	10.3	7.3	5.2
The Christian Democrats	1.8	2.7	2.7	1.1	2.0	1.3
The Liberal Party	14.5	12.5	16.6	19.0	23.4	19.4
The Left Socialist Party[1]	3.5	1.3	—	—	—	—
The Progressive Party	5.8	3.5	5.3	2.9	0.7	—
The Liberal Alliance	—	—	—	—	—	—
The Danish People's Party	—	—	—	—	5.8	6.8
Total	100.0	100.0	100.0	100.0	100.0	100.0
Turnout	**47.8**	**52.4**	**46.2**	**52.9**	**50.5**	**47.9**

Source: http://www.euo.dk/spsv/off/alle/valgtilEP/.

Note:
[1] The Left Socialist Party joined the Red–Green Alliance in 1989.

Table 12.5 National election results in Denmark: 1979–2011 (%)

Political party	1979	1981	1984	1987	1988	1990	1994	1998	2001	2005	2007	2011
Conservative People's Party (C)	12.5	14.5	23.4	20.8	19.3	16.0	15.0	8.9	9.1	10.3	10.4	4.9
Social Democratic Party (S)	38.3	32.9	31.6	29.3	29.8	37.4	34.6	36.0	29.1	25.8	25.5	24.8
Social Liberal Party (R)	5.4	5.1	5.5	6.2	5.6	3.5	4.6	3.9	5.2	9.2	5.1	9.5
Liberal Party (V)	12.5	11.3	12.1	10.5	11.8	15.8	23.3	24.0	31.2	29.0	26.3	26.7
Denmark's Communist Party (DKP)	1.9	1.1	0.7	0.9	0.8	1.7	—	—	—	—	—	—
Justice Party of Denmark (E)	2.6	1.4	1.5	0.5	—	0.5	—					—
Socialist People's Party (SF)	5.9	11.3	11.5	14.6	13.0	8.3	7.3	7.5	6.4	6.0	13.0	9.2
Left Socialist Party (VS)	3.7	2.6	2.7	1.4	0.6	—	—	—	—	—	—	—
Christian Democrats (K)	2.6	2.3	2.7	2.4	2.0	2.3	1.9	2.5	2.3	1.7	0.9	0.8
Centre Democrats (CD)	3.2	8.3	4.6	4.8	4.7	5.1	2.8	4.3	1.8	1.0	—	—
Progress Party (Z)	11.0	8.9	3.6	4.8	9.0	6.4	6.4	2.4	0.5	—	—	—
Danish People's Party (DF)	—	—	—	—	—	—	—	7.4	12.0	13.3	13.9	12.3
Common Course (P)	—	—	—	2.2	1.9	1.8	—	—	—	—	—	—
Green Party (G)	—	—	—	1.3	1.4	1.7	—	—	—	—	—	—
Unity List★ (Ø)	—	—	—	—	—	—	3.1	2.7	2.4	3.4	2.2	6.7
Minority Party (M)	—	—	—	—	—	—	—	—	—	0.3	—	—
New Alliance	—	—	—	—	—	—	—	—	—	—	2.8	—
Liberal Alliance★ (LA)	—	—	—	—	—	—	—	—	—	—	—	5.0
Total	100.0	100.0	100.0	100.0	100.0	100.0	100.0	100.0	100.0	100.0	100.0	100.0
Turnout	85.6	83.2	88.4	86.7	85.7	82.8	84.3	86.0	87.1	84.5	86.6	87.7

Source: Danmarks Statistik Befolkning og Valg (2010) www.dst.dk/valg.

Notes:
★ At the 2011 National Election New Alliance changed its name to Liberal Alliance.
★ Also known as the Red–Green Alliance.

EP election turnout has traditionally been significantly lower than in the national parliamentary elections, where the average turnout has been 85 per cent since 1979. One of the most notable differences between the two types of elections is the involvement of the two Eurosceptic parties, the Popular Movement and the June Movement, in the EP Elections.

Until 2004 these two parties gained 20–25 per cent of the votes. Their vote share has, however, been reduced at the last two elections, and only the Popular Movement has still obtained a notable vote share, while the June Movement dissolved shortly after a poor result in the 2009 election. The strongly Eurosceptic vote at EP elections is now mainly divided between the Popular Movement and the Danish People's Party. As discussed in Section 6, there have historically been more Eurosceptic voters than parties in the national party system, and at EP elections the Eurosceptic parties have received a higher vote share than in national elections.

The campaigns in connection with the European elections in 1979 and 1984 were strongly dominated by the question of Danish membership of the EEC. The 1979 election received massive coverage in the media and observers even talked of public fatigue with European issues afterwards (Sørensen, 1979, 60). Compared to the 1979 election, domestic issues appeared to play a greater role in 1984. On the one hand, the leading party in government, the Conservative Party, increased its vote share, and on the other hand turnout was higher, mainly from the voters on the right, which was interpreted as support for a government that had suffered a series of defeats in Parliament over foreign policy issues during preceding years (Elder, 1984, 82). By 1989, the membership discussion had, to a large extent, been replaced by the debate on further integration and 'union' in Europe (Worre, 1989, 100). As Torben Worre (1989) comments, 'Danish membership of the EC was no longer on the agenda of the 1989 election campaigns, and there was, for the first time ever, almost a consensus on the Danish EC policy.'

However, the effect of this consensus was to strengthen the tendency among parties to focus on domestic issues and the results also testified to the impact of domestic politics although the European cleavage was still dominant. The following EP elections were dominated by the issue of integration and the institutions of the EU rather than substantive policies. In 1999, the campaign focussed on travel costs and MEP *per diem* payments as well as on the failures of the EP to reform itself. Moreover, the focus was placed on Danish opt-outs. This was also the first election in which right-wing scepticism had to be taken seriously (Nielsen, 2001).

The 2004 election witnessed a more EU positive campaign than Denmark had experienced before. Most candidates, who were pro-European, focussed on the benefits of membership to Denmark in such areas as food safety, consumer protection and international crime. Among the parties represented in the *Folketinget*, the Danish People's Party on the political right was the only one with a sceptical message. Together with the June and Popular Movements, they warned against the Constitutional Treaty and the loss of national sovereignty it would entail. The Danish People's Party also emphasized the threat of immigration (Knudsen, 2004). The shift towards a more overall positive campaign was evident in the results where the three sceptical parties together polled 10 per cent less of the votes than they did in 1999.

9 The 2009 European election

9.1 Party lists

Denmark has no restrictions with regards to the length of EP election campaigns, but public attention usually does not turn towards the election until approximately two weeks prior to polling day. Furthermore, there are no Danish rules limiting the use of opinion or exit polls.

One hundred and two candidates were up for election, 60 per cent of whom were males. The average candidate was 44.9 years old. Compared to national elections, candidates played a much stronger and independent role whilst the parties did not bother to publish proper manifestos. The top lists included well-known politicians, such as former Conservative leader and minister Bendt Bendtsen, former Liberal spokesman Jens Rohde, former Socialist MP and MEP Margrethe Auken, former MP and MEP for the People's Movement Against the EU Søren Søndergaard, and the Danish People's Party's MP and spokesman on EU affairs Morten Messerschmidt.

Bendtsen had to contend with bad media coverage concerning several cases of travel expenses paid by influential private companies during his time in office as minister. He was also widely criticized for stating that he wished to go to Brussels in order to have more spare time. During the election campaign, both Rohde and Bendtsen ended up arguing most forcefully for clawing back powers from Brussels to the Member States. In particular, the debate about border control and cross-border crime were key issues in many of their public televised debates. Formally, Bendtsen focussed on the climate and the financial crisis, but it was the fight against cross-border crime and national self-determination that ended up dominating his campaign. Rohde also raised crucial issues such as Green job creation, less bureaucracy in Brussels, and equality and freedom, but he spoke relatively little about these compared to the issue of national sovereignty and taking back powers from Brussels.

Early in the campaign, Messerschmidt was seen as a very visible and articulate candidate. He received positive media attention for his rather detailed knowledge about the EU and because of his party's widely discussed slogan: 'Give us Denmark back.' A reintroduction of national border control was central to his campaign and he argued against Turkish EU membership and expanding the EU budget.

Social Democrat MEP Dan Jørgensen was a relatively unknown candidate, despite the fact that it was his second term. When nominated as the party's leading candidate, the press thus nicknamed him 'Dan Who?' (Quist, 2008). Representing the largest Danish party in the EP, Jørgensen nevertheless did a good job during the campaign, with a strong focus on the environment, animal welfare, and the fight against social dumping. The party managed to retain 4 of their 5 EP seats. The Social Democrats had an exceptionally good election in 2004, when former Prime Minister Poul Nyrup Rasmussen was its leading candidate. No one expected a repetition of that extraordinary result, and losing just one seat was therefore seen as a success.

Margrethe Auken was a veteran for the Socialists and was elected together with the young Emilie Turunen. Their campaign focussed on climate, the fight against social dumping, and putting an end to trans-border crime. The election generally launched a new generation of politicians, including some of the youngest leading candidates ever.

Morten Messerschmidt, from the Danish People's Party, was only 28 years old, Dan Jørgensen, from the Social Democrats' and the Social-Liberal Party's leading candidate, Sofie Carsten Nielsen, were 34. Completely unknown to the public before entering the campaign, Nielsen had to fight bad opinion polls for the Social Liberals, but was ultimately seen as the 'greatest hit' of the election due to her very clear pro-EU statements (Engell, 2009). Her main themes were more on Europe, together with a strong focus on fighting climate change, getting more well-educated immigrants to Europe, and economic aid for Eastern and Central Europe. The positive campaign evaluations did not, however, prove successful at the polls.

Another young leading candidate was 26-year-old Benjamin Dickow from the Liberal Alliance. He was on a 'mission impossible' from the outset, with polls giving the Liberal Alliance less than 0.5 per cent of the vote. MEP and leading candidate for the June Movement, Hanne Dahl, also faced a daunting challenge in defending her seat after the retirement of the June Movement's grand old man and long-standing MEP Jens-Peter Bonde. Polls gave Dahl little chance to defend the seat, which also explained why the June Movement decided to form an electoral alliance with the People's Movement against the EU.

9.2 Electoral campaign

A basic analysis of Danish news was carried out in an attempt to ascertain the most discussed issues of the EP campaign. The analysis is based on a search in Infomedia, a Danish news database, for relevant articles in the ten largest Danish newspapers – *Politiken, Berlingske Tidende, Jyllands-Posten, Information, Børsen, Weekendavisen, Erhvervsbladet, B.T., Ekstra Bladet,* and *Kristeligt Dagblad* – between 7 May and 7 June 2009.

One of the topics emerging early in the campaign was the regularly discussed question in Denmark regarding Turkish EU membership. The debate was opened by former minister and leading Conservative candidate Bendt Bendtsen, stating that Turkey should never obtain full membership. Despite the fact that this is not even a matter for the European Parliament to decide, the discussion about Turkey and Islamic values once again proved to be a hot topic in public debate.

This debate is also related somewhat to another archetypical debate in Denmark regarding the issue of immigration. The European Court of Justice's *Metock* verdict from 2008, and whether or not it undermined strict Danish immigration rules, remained an intensely debated topic in the election campaign. The Nationalisticic and EU-sceptic Danish People's Party and their popular candidate Morten Messerschmidt were particularly active in working to get this issue onto the agenda. The slogan 'Give us Denmark back' could very well be seen as a response to the *Metock* verdict and the claim that the EU has obtained jurisdiction over internal matters such as immigration.

Along the same lines, it came as a bit of a surprise when otherwise pro-European Social Democrat Dan Jørgensen suggested the reintroduction of border controls at the Danish–German border. The argument, embraced by almost all of the other candidates, except Social Liberal Sofie Carsten Nielsen, was that Denmark had lost control over the influx of criminals and immigrants due to Schengen cooperation.

A common European health system and patients' rights were among the most prominent subjects in the debate among the issues focussing on common European cooperation. Leading Social Liberal Party candidate Sofie Carsten Nielsen received attention and support from other parties when she suggested that rare diseases should be treated at centralized EU hospitals. This never became a salient topic, however, as reflected by the fact that only seven newspaper articles appeared on the matter.

With the upcoming UN Climate Summit, COP15, in December 2009 in Copenhagen, climate change and the role of the EU as an important actor attracted significant public interest. All of the parties jumped on board and attempted to label themselves 'green'. The Socialist People's Party was probably the most successful in this regard, using catchy sound bites such as 'express trains between the EU capitals' and 'the construction of 154 windmills every week in the EU'.

As a general topic underlying many of the other debates, the financial crisis and unemployment received attention from all of the parties, and solutions to the economic crisis were often suggested along with solutions to the climate crisis, such as so-called 'green growth'.

9.3 Electoral results

EP election turnout has traditionally been significantly lower than in national parliamentary elections, where the average turnout has been 85 per cent since 1979. Compared to the previous Euro-elections, the 2009 contest clearly stood out, with its unusually high turnout at 59.5 per cent.

Table 12.6 EP election results in Denmark: 2009

Political party	Votes %
The Social Democrats	21.5
The Social Liberal Party	4.3
The Conservative Party	12.7
The Socialist Party	15.9
The June Movement	2.4
The People's Movement against EC/EU	7.2
The Liberal Party	20.2
The Liberal Alliance	0.6
The Danish People's Party	15.3
Total	100.0
Turnout	59.5

Source: National Parliament EU Information Website: www.euo.dk/spsv/off/alle/valgtilEP/.

Table 12.7 List of Danish MEPs: seventh legislature

Name	National party	Political group	Professional background	Date of birth	Gender	No. of committees/ Chairs
Dan Jørgensen	S	S&D	Party employee, politician	12/06/1975	Male	1. Environment, Public Health and Food Safety
Ole Christensen	S	S&D	Ironmonger, trade unionist	07/05/1955	Male	1. Employment and Social Affairs
Christel Schaldemose	S	S&D	Consultant (education)	04/08/1967	Female	2. Budgetary Control; Internal Market and Consumer Protection
Britta Thomsen	S	S&D	Teacher, consultant (education, labour market)	23/01/1954	Female	2. Committee on Industry, Research and Energy; Women's Rights and Gender Equality
Bendt Bendtsen	C	EPP	Politician (former leader of the Conservative Party), police officer	25/03/1954	Male	1. Industry, Research and Energy
Anne E. Jensen	V	ALDE	Economist (bank), journalist, director employers' confederation	17/08/1951	Female	1. Budgets
Morten Lykkegaard	V	ALDE	Journalist	20/12/1964	Male	1. Culture and Education
Jens Rohde	V	ALDE	Journalist	18/04/1970	Male	1. Industry, Research and Energy
Magrete Auken	SF	Greens/EFA	Priest	06/01/1945	Female	2. Transport and Tourism; Petitions
Emilie Turunen	SF	Greens/EFA	Politician	13/05/1984	Female	1. Internal Market and Consumer Protection
Søren Bo Søndergaard	N	EUL/NGL	Welder and shipbuilder, teacher	16/08/1955	Male	2. Budgetary Control; Constitutional Affairs
Morten Messerschmidt	DF	EFD	Politician	13/11/1980	Male	1. Constitutional Affairs
Anna Rosbach	DF	EFD	Independent choral conductor	02/02/1947	Female	1. Environment, Public Health and Food Safety

Source: www.europarl.europa.eu/meps/en/search.html?country=DK.

This cannot plausibly be attributed to matters related to Europe alone, as a referendum on constitutional reform, namely the Act of Succession, was held simultaneously. The referendum drew a lot of attention in the media, and a prominent theme was whether a low turnout could jeopardize the ratification of the Act. It is therefore likely that this brought out more voters than otherwise had been the case. In 2009, EU supporters and sceptics went to the polls in equal numbers. While Eurosceptics were not under-represented, the young and less educated clearly were (Bhatti and Hansen, 2009).

The outcome of the 2009 EP election showed that the Eurosceptic vote was divided equally between the two strongest EU opponents, namely the Popular Movement and the Danish

People's party, while the historically stronger and more moderate Eurosceptic June Movement only won a small per cent of the vote and lost its seat. The Danish People's Party doubled its share of the vote with respect to earlier elections. It is reasonable to speculate that an effective campaign by its front-runner, combined with an increased turnout related to the simultaneous vote on the Act of Succession, contributed to such an extraordinary result.

Since its first election in 1994, the June Movement was clearly the strongest Eurosceptic movement, participating in the EP but not national elections. In a reversal of fortune, the Popular Movement doubled its vote share, a somewhat surprising outcome that was possibly indicative of a greater polarization of positions on Europe. Another reason for the increase in support for the Popular Movement could be that the political message that came from the party was much clearer than the message from the June Movement, where the former called for exiting the Union outright, whereas the June Movement had become more pro-European; it wanted to remain in the Union and work to reform it from within. Since many ordinary party candidates also proposed to reform Europe, the June Movement seemed to have lost its *raison d'être*. In any case, the poor results proved fatal, as the June Movement decided to dissolve itself shortly after the elections. The Socialist People's Party also enjoyed a remarkable success, doubling both its vote share and seats. The dramatic increase in support is most certainly a reflection of national politics, as the party's popularity soared at the time of the elections. Unsurprisingly, the Social Democrats lost ground compared to the previous election, where, as mentioned above, former Prime Minister Nyrup Rasmussen was the leading candidate and drew a historic 32 per cent for the party. Disregarding the 2004 election, however, the party had its best election since 1979 in spite of its virtually unknown front-runner. The government parties, the Liberals and the Conservatives, largely held their positions, which might have been disappointing for the Conservatives in view of the fact that their former party leader was their chief candidate and they had hoped for a stronger draw.

The only party that took an offensive pro-Europe stance, the Social Liberals, fared very poorly and lost its seat. This result most likely also relates to its dwindling support in the national arena.

9.4 Campaign finance

In Denmark, political parties have access to public funding to pursue their political activities. Virtually all parties and independent members obtaining just 1,000 votes in the latest *Folketinget* election are eligible for support . While there are no equivalent provisions for EP elections, the money allocated to the parties participating in the other national elections can be used for the Euro-campaign (http://valg.im.dk/Valg/Partistoette, 2011). Moreover, a special fund for information on the EU has been established and all parties represented in the *Folketinget* or in the European Parliament can benefit from it. The fund is used to 'promote debate and information about Europe, including development of participatory democracy' (Undervisningsministeriet BEK 192, 2011, §1). Two-thirds of the available funds, 8 million DKK or about €1.1 million in total, are granted to parties in proportion with their share of seats in the *Folketinget* and in the European Parliament (ibid., §2). The remainder is distributed equally among the parties. Precise figures for campaign spending for the 2009 EP election are not available. However, based on the official accounts of the political parties, the total expenditure of all parties can be estimated to be approximately 20 million DKK, equivalent to €2.7 million. The highest amount of spending, 6.9 million DKK, was reported by the Liberal Party (*Venstre*) on the EP election, followed by the Social Democrats with 4.4 million DKK , and the Socialist People's Party with 3.1 million DKK. The Conservative Party and the Danish People's Party appear to have spent similar amounts, but their accounts conflate EP and municipal election spending. The smaller parties, the Social Liberal Party, the Red–Green Alliance and the Popular Movement, reported spending a bit less than 0.5 million DKK, corresponding to €70,000 each. Compared to this, the estimated spending of all the parties at the previous national election was around 100 million DKK (€13.5 million).

10 Theoretical interpretation of Euro-elections

10.1 Second-Order Election theory

In Denmark, there are two sources of the discrepancy between the party system in European and national elections. First, there are parties running in the general elections that abstain from participating in the EP contest. Of the seven sets of EP elections, parties that have gained votes in the previous parliamentary election chose not to participate in the subsequent EP election on 20 occasions. These decisions were clearly related to size, as evidenced by the average electoral returns in the previous national elections obtained by the abstaining parties, which was a mere 1.6 per cent of the votes, compared to 11.6 per cent for the parties that did participate. The probability of a party winning 2 per cent of the national vote deciding to participate in the subsequent EP elections can be estimated at 30 per cent. Conversely, parties taking 4 per cent in national elections are almost 100 per cent certain to participate in the EP elections. The choice of the very small parties to decline to run can be explained by strategic concerns. The legal threshold to win seats in the Danish Parliament election is 2 per cent, while the lowest vote share for an EP seat is approximately 4.3 per cent. It is actually possible to win as much as 7 per cent of the vote and, nevertheless, fail to secure a seat. Some of the small parties, therefore, throw their weight behind some of the other parties running. The left-wing Red–Green Alliance, for example, has never run independently, instead supporting the Popular Movement against the EU. The higher thresholds have also encouraged other parties to enter into electoral alliances in an attempt to maximize their share of the seats. In the 2009 election, the Danish People's Party was the only party not to engage in such an alliance. It is worth noting that these alliances were anchored in national rather than European patterns of conflict. For example, the Social Liberals and Liberals are both members of the Alliance of Liberals and Democrats for Europe (ALDE), but did not engage in an electoral alliance together, as the former was in the opposition and the latter was part of the government on the national scene.

The low turnout clearly indicates that voters do not accord the same respect to EP elections as national elections. A simple comparison of the mean vote shares in the national and European elections reveals that parties running in national elections generally lose shares, on average 2.6 per cent, as the Eurosceptic lists that only participate in EP elections have successfully attracted some of their voters. Examination of the specific patterns of gains and losses indicates that small parties are the only parties with a small net gain. Government parties lose more than opposition parties, which is in line with the second-order hypothesis. With respect to partisan fortunes, left parties suffer more, followed by the right, while the centre parties fare best.

Party size appears to play a key role, which is somewhat strange, since the Danish electoral system and pattern of government formation are not particularly biased towards smaller parties, and there is therefore no particular reason to believe that the opportunity to vote sincerely in EP elections would make a major difference. It is possible, however, that voters tend to focus on the larger parties that are contesting for the post of Prime Minister in national elections and the absence of this focus favours the smaller parties. A multivariate analysis confirms that government parties are punished by voters. The same goes for the parties on the left, which also lose more than others parties, likely due to the stronger Euroscepticism typically among their voters. The parties on the right emerge as the relative winners, and the centre parties fall between the two blocs in terms of electoral losses. The Green motive is not included, since the time period, and thus the number of elections, is limited.

As an additional check on whether EP election results can be interpreted as a signal relevant to the domestic political situation, it is interesting to investigate whether party fortunes in the EP elections represent a harbinger of the events to follow in the national election. There is clear evidence suggesting that EP elections function as a commentary on national politics inasmuch as the results indicate how well parties will do in the upcoming national election.

Finally, Hix and Marsh (2007) suggest high volatility compared to national elections as an indicator of whether citizens vote on the basis of European issues. Volatility in EP elections is distinctly higher than in the *Folketinget* elections. However, this could also be expected due to the difference between the party system in national and European elections.

10.2 Europe Salience theory

Analyses of voter behaviour in Denmark demonstrated that the two Eurosceptic movements participating solely in EP elections attract most of their voters from the left (Bhatti and Hansen, 2009). Eurosceptic and Green parties did better than other parties, but their losses were only smaller by a slight margin. On a simple comparison of vote shares in EP elections compared to the previous national election, there is thus support for both the Second-Order Election and European Salience hypotheses.

Size and Euroscepticism are the strongest predictors of vote share differences between national and European parliamentary elections. However, the evidence is that Eurosceptic parties in the *Folketinget* obtain on average lower vote shares in EP elections than other parties do, which directly contradicts the European hypotheses. As already mentioned, the only plausible explanation for this is that the two Eurosceptic EP election 'parties', the June Movement and Popular Movement, attract many of the votes that would otherwise go to the Eurosceptic parties represented in the *Folketinget*. The result must be interpreted in this light. The mere presence of a gap between the votes cast at the EP and *Folketinget* elections indicates how voters express their views on the EU in the EP elections rather than in national elections.

References

Primary sources

http://www.euo.dk/spsv/off/alle/valgtilEP/(accessed on 7 December 2013).
Danmarks Statistik, Election Years 1979–2009, www.dst.dk (accessed on 7 December 2013).
Danmarks Statistik Befolkning og Valg (2010) www.dst.dk/valg (accessed on 7 December 2013).
Danmarks Statistik (2011) www.dst.dk/valg (accessed on 7 December 2013).
Eurobarometer (various) Brussels, European Commission, http://ec.europa.eu/public_opinion/index_en.htm (accessed on 7 December 2013).
European Parliament website, www.europarl.europa.eu/parliament/archive/elections2009/en/index_en.html (accessed on 7 December 2013).
Eurostat (2013, 2014) http://epp.eurostat.ec.europa.eu/ (accessed on 5 June 2015).
Folketinget, EU-oplysningen, www.eu-oplysningen.dk/dkeu/dk/afstemninger/afstemning/ (accessed on 7 December 2013).
National Parliament EU Information Website, www.euo.dk/spsv/off/alle/valgtilEP/ (accessed on 7 December 2013).

Secondary sources

Bhatti, Y. and Hansen, K. M. (2009) *Valg til Europa-Parlamentet, Arbejdspapir 2009/02*, Department of Political Science, University of Copenhagen.

Engel, H. (2009) *Valgets hit og nitter*, Ekstra-Bladet. Online. Available at: http://ekstrabladet.dk/nationen/article1178377.ece (accessed on 13 August 2009).

Folketinget (2011) 'De Politiske Partiers Regnskaber for 2009'. Online. Available at: www.ft.dk/Folketinget/Folketingets_administration/Tal_regnskaber/~/media/Pdf_materiale/Pdf_download_direkte/Regnskaber/Partiregnskaber/2009/Partiregnskab2009_samlet.pdf.ashx (accessed on 13 December 2013).

Hix, S. and Marsh, M. (2007) 'Punishment or Protest? Understanding European Parliament Elections', *The Journal of Politics*, 69(2), 495–510.

Knudsen, A. C. L. (2004) 'The European Parliament Election in Denmark June 13 2004', *European Parliament Election Briefing*, 11, European Parties Elections and Referendums Network. Sussex European Institute.

Nielsen, H. J. (2001) 'Denmark', in Lodge, J. (ed.) *The 1999 Elections to the European Parliament*, London, Palgrave.

Quist, S. (2008) *Nyrup efterfølges af Dan Hvem*. Ekstra-Bladet. Online. Available at: http://ekstrabladet.dk/nyheder/politik/article1016211.ece (accessed on 13 August 2009).

Sørensen, C. L. (1979)'Denmark', *Dansk udenrigspolitisk årbog*, pp. 84–111.

Worre, T. (1989) *Det politiske system i Danmark* [*The Political System in Denmark*], Copenhagen, Akademisk Forlag.

Country reviews

The Old Member States

The second and third enlargement countries

13 Greece — 291
14 Spain — 321
15 Portugal — 351

13
GREECE

Maria M. Mendrinou

Figure 13.1 Map of Greece

Table 13.1 Greece profile

EU entry year	1981 ECSC, EEC and Euratom
Schengen entry year	1992
MEPs elected in 2009	22
MEPs under Lisbon Treaty	22
Capital	Athens
Total area★	131,957 km²
Population	10,903,704
Population density★★	84.0/km²
Median age of population	43
Political system	Parliamentary Republic
Head of state	Karolos Papoulias (2nd term: February 2010–March 2015); Prokopis Pavlopoulos (March 2015–)
Head of government	Kostas Karamanlis, New Democracy (ND) (September 2007–October 2009); George Papandreou, Panhellenic Socialist Movement (PASOK) (October 2009–November 2011); Lucas Papademos, Technical Government: Panhellenic Socialist Movement (PASOK), New Democracy (ND), Popular Orthodox Rally (LAOS) Government Coalition (November 2011–February 2012); Lucas Papademos, Technocratic Government: Panhellenic Socialist Movement (PASOK), New Democracy (ND), Government Coalition (February 2012–May 2012); Panayiotis Pikrammenos, Technical Government (May 2012–June 2012); Antonis Samaras, New Democracy (ND), Panhellenic Socialist Movement (PASOK), Democratic Left (DEMAR) Government Coalition (June 2012–June 2013); Antonis Samaras (New Democracy (ND), Panhellenic Socialist Movement (PASOK) Government Coalition (June 2013–January 2015); Alexis Tsipras, Coalition of the Radical Left (SYRIZA) and Independent Greeks (ANEL) Government Coalition (January 2015–)
Political majority	New Democracy (ND) (September 2007–October 2009); Panhellenic Socialist Movement (PASOK) (October 2009–November 2011); Technocratic Government: Panhellenic Socialist Movement (PASOK), New Democracy (ND), Popular Orthodox Rally (LAOS) Coalition Government (November 2011–February 2012); Technocratic Government: Panhellenic Socialist Movement (PASOK), New Democracy (ND) Coalition Government (February 2012–May 2012); New Democracy (ND), Panhellenic Socialist Movement (PASOK), Democratic Left (DEMAR) Coalition Government (June 2012–June 2013); New Democracy (ND) and Panhellenic Socialist Movement (PASOK) Coalition Government (June 2013–January 2015); SYRIZA and ANEL (January 2015–)
Currency	Euro (€) since 2001
Prohead GDP in PPS	16,300 €

Source: Eurostat, 2013, 2014, http://epp.eurostat.ec.europa.eu/.

Notes:
★ Total area including inland waters.
★★ Population density: the ratio of the annual average population of a region to the land area of the region.

1 Geographical position

Greece is situated in south-eastern Europe, forming the southern edge of the Balkan Peninsula. The country borders Albania, the Former Yugoslav Republic of Macedonia, and Bulgaria in the north, and Turkey in the east. The main features of Greece's geographical morphology are its extensive 13,676 kilometre-long coastline and its vast archipelago of about 2,000 islands and islets in the Aegean and Ionian Seas.

As a result of an intense urbanization process during the third quarter of the twentieth century, the majority of the Greek population lives in the metropolitan area of its capital, Athens (Leontidou, 1990; Delladetsima and Leontidou, 1995). About half of the remaining Greek population lives in or around other large cities such as Piraeus, Thessaloniki and Patras. The rest of the country is relatively underpopulated, mainly due to the wave of internal and external migration in the 1960s (Hoffman, 1967). The urbanization rate is around 61 per cent. During the twentieth century, migration waves to the US, Australia, and Central and Northern Europe led to the formation of a considerable Greek diaspora (Clogg, 1999; Tziovas, 2009; McCabe et al., 2005), but towards the end of the century Greece became a 'new immigration country' (Fargues, 2004; Taylor et al., 1996; Castles and Miller, 2003; Freeman, 2004). The wave of undocumented immigration from Asia, Africa, the Balkans, and countries of the former Soviet Union has become a pressing domestic as well as an EU issue since the great majority of the immigrants who arrive in Greece seek to move to other European countries. However, the recent economic crisis has opened a new era of migration for the younger Greek generations.

2 Historical background

Greece achieved independence from the Ottoman Empire in the 1820s after the War of Independence that started in 1821; the modern state was set up in 1830 by the London Protocol. Greece has a turbulent political history, with frequent periods of political instability and political and economic crises. The common causes of political crises included cases of regime change, from republic to constitutional monarchy and vice versa, military coups and dictatorships, and economic crises. Greek involvement in all the major wars of the twentieth century, notably the Balkan Wars, WWI and WWII, had a considerable impact on its political, social, and economic life. Apart from sorting out the issue of its borders, which began with the War of Independence in 1821 and ended with the transfer of the Dodecanese Islands in 1947, the wars inflicted major ethnic tragedies, such as the wave of refugees after the Asia Minor Catastrophe in 1922 and the lengthy civil war that followed the end of WWII (Dakin, 1973; Dakin, 1972; Clogg, 1992).

The post-war period was particularly turbulent; the German occupation and the lengthy 1946–1949 civil war devastated both the country's infrastructure and its human capital, whilst the process of economic reconstruction was scanty (Varvaressos, 2002). Political strife was intense, with short-lived governments, whilst the ban on the Communists and the left had prolonged the anguish of the civil war (Meynaud, 2002a). The period ended with the military coup of 1967 (Meynaud, 2002b) that abruptly disrupted the post war development of the country. Prospects for economic recovery under a more European-oriented profile, signalled by the 1961 Association Agreement with the European Economic Community (EEC), were put on hold.

The transition to democracy in 1974 initiated a process of democratic consolidation that included mainly: the resolution of the regime question in favour of a republic; the elimination of the civil war divisions through the legalization of the Communist Party; and the completion of the country's European course by opening accession negotiations with the EC (O'Donnell et al., 1986; Pridham, 1984; Gunther et al., 1995; Featherstone, 2005; Lavdas, 1997; Kazakos, 1991; Ioakimidis, 1996). In spite of the European Commission's initial reservations about the short pre-accession period, the Council of Ministers decided in favour of accession. The decision aimed to encourage and support the consolidation of democracy and the strengthening of the country's Western ties. On May 1979, the Accession Treaty was signed, and in January 1981 the country joined the EEC as a full member.

3 Geopolitical profile

The geographical position of Greece has weighed over the country's history. Being at the crossroads of East and West, Greece has been often involved in the politics of the south-eastern Mediterranean and the Balkans. Apart from the often awkward relationships with Turkey, the new map of the Balkans after 1989 brought up new concerns with its neighbours, and particularly with the Former Yugoslav Republic of Macedoni (FYROM).

The impact of the international environment in Greek politics is prominent. Its geo-strategic position and its European profile, along with its traditional relations with Russia and the Arab world add special significance to Greek foreign policy. Moreover, the recent rapprochement with Israel and the tensions in the south-eastern Mediterranean region after the events of the Arab Spring and the situation in Egypt and Syria have added to the complexity of Greek foreign affairs. Last but not least, a close relationship with Cyprus is central to Greece's geopolitical perspectives.

Greece is a member of more than 65 international organizations, whilst a considerable number of non-governmental organizations are active in the country. As a member of the United Nations (UN), Greece participates in a number of UN organizations and missions such as the UN Educational, Scientific, and Cultural Organization (UNESCO), the UN Conference on Trade and Development (UNCTAD), the UN Interim Force in Lebanon (UNIFIL), the UN Mission in the Sudan (UNMIS), and the UN Mission for the Referendum in Western Sahara (MINURSO).

Greece is a member of most global politico-economic and financial organizations such as the World Bank, the International Monetary Fund (IMF), the International Labour Organization (ILO), the International Organization for Standardization (ISO), the Organization for Economic Cooperation and Development (OECD), the World Health Organization (WHO), and the World Trade Organization (WTO). It is also a member of various regional organizations apart from the ones that are related to the EU; such organizations concern security, economic, and political agendas and include the North Atlantic Treaty Organization (NATO), the Council of Europe (CoE), the Organization for Security and Cooperation in Europe (OSCE), the Black Sea Economic Cooperation Zone (BSEC), and the Southeast European Cooperative Initiative (SECI).

4 Overview of the political landscape

The Greek political system of the so-called 'Third Republic' was formed following a transition to democracy in 1974 (Pridham, 1984; Gunther et al., 1995; Gunther, 2005). Parliament has a four-year term, but elections are often held well before the end of the parliamentary term; the prerogative to call early elections rests with the Prime Minister. The 1985 constitutional revision considerably increased the powers of the Prime Minister compared to those of the President of the Republic; this shaped a prime ministerial governmental system. The President is elected from the Parliament for a five-year term. The election provides for multiple rounds of voting, one of which, if no President is elected, leads to the dissolution of Parliament and the call for new general elections in order for a new Parliament to elect a President.

Bipolar competitions, between the two main governmental parties, are one of the main features of the Greek political system. Until recently, the government alternations were between the two main political parties, the New Democracy (ND) and the Pan-Hellenic Socialist Movement (PASOK); their cumulative electoral percentage in general elections was often well above 80 per cent of the vote. The formation of strong one-party governments, with a considerable absolute majority in Parliament, resembled an almost two-party system. However, the polarization between the two main political parties operated in a multiparty context, with fervent electoral contests amongst all the main political parties. A considerable number of smaller parties were established; however, most of them were short-lived. A divide existed between the electoral influence of the two larger political parties and the rest, since the two parties had succeeded in mobilizing the great majority of the electorate. Regarding the third party, more often than not its percentages were around 10 per cent of the vote or lower, whilst the rest of the smaller parties registered considerably lower percentages and had limited, or no, representation in Parliament.

The sovereign debt crisis contributed to a radical change in the political landscape, as electoral results in both the 2012 general elections showed. The electoral volatility and the considerable de-alignment of the party voters suggested a change in the main features of the party system. The cumulative percentage of the two previous governing parties dropped in the May 2012 elections to 32.1 per cent of the vote compared to 77.4 per cent in the 2009 elections, which at the time was one of the lowest cumulative percentages since 1981. The previous contestants have now formed coalition governments. Nevertheless, polarization in Greek elections has remained, yet on different grounds and between different contestants. The main opposition party in both the 2012 general elections was the Coalition of the Radical Left–Uniting Social Front (SYRIZA–EKM), whose percentage rose from 4.6 per cent of the vote in the 2009 general election to 16.8 per cent in the May 2012 election and to 26.9 per cent in the June 2012 one. New political parties were established on both the left and the right of the political spectrum, some of which succeeded in electing representatives to Parliament. PASOK, the winner of the 2009 elections, registered a radical decline; its percentage dropped from 43.9 per cent in the 2009 elections to 13.2 per cent in the May 2012 elections and to 12.3 per cent in June 2012.

5 Brief account of the political parties

The current Greek party system emerged after the regime changed in 1974. The key breakthrough of the democratization process was the legalization of the Communist Party, which had been outlawed after the end of the civil war in 1949. New political parties were founded, on both the right/centre-right and the centre-left of the political spectrum: 'New Democracy' (ND) and the 'Pan-Hellenic Socialist Movement' (PASOK), respectively (Gunther, 2005). Table 13.2 provides a list of significant political parties in national and/or EP elections since 1974.

Consolidation of the post-1974 party system occurred at the 1981 general elections. The 1981 government alternation consolidated the dominance of the two main government contestants, the ND and the PASOK, with a cumulative vote total well over 80 per cent, shaping an almost two-party system. The divisions amongst the political parties of the three main political families, the left, the centre, and the right – and the intense elections – impeded cooperation between political parties and discouraged the formation of coalition governments. Moreover, the electoral system contributed to the formation of absolute majorities in Parliament (Mendrinou, 2000; Diamantopoulos, 2001; Lijphart, 1994). A further feature of the Greek party system was the nationalization of the vote that had been further facilitated by the introduction in 1990 of a 3 per cent threshold for representation.

The main party of the right and the centre-right is the ND, which was founded in 1974 by Konstantinos Karamanlis. The party has undergone considerable organizational changes since its founding, the most recent of which was the election of its leadership directly by its members. In the 2009 elections, the party suffered a severe defeat. However, a political crisis triggered by the sovereign debt crisis led the ND to participate in the Papademos government in 2011, and after the June 2012 elections, to lead the government coalitions that have been formed.

Table 13.2 List of political parties in Greece

Original name	Abbreviation	English translation
Agonistiko Socialistiko Komma Helladas (Αγωνιστικό Σοσιαλιστικό Κόμμα Ελλάδας)	ASKE	Militant Socialist Party of Greece
Amessi Democratia (Άμεση Δημοκρατία)		Direct Democracy
Anexartitoi Hellines (Ανεξάρτητοι Έλληνες)	ANEL	Independent Greeks
Antimperialistiko Metopo (Αντιμπεριαλιστικό Μέτωπο)		Anti-imperialist Front
Anticapitalistike Aristere Synergasia (Αντικαπιταλιστική Αριστερή Συνεργασία)	ANTARSYA	Anticapitalist Left Cooperation
Anticapitalistike Symmahia (Αντικαπιταλιστική Συμμαχία)		Anticapitalist Alliance
Axioprepia (Αξιοπρέπεια)		Dignity
Aristere Kinesse (Αριστερή Κίνηση)		Left Movement
Aftodynamo Kinema Epanastatikes Politikes (Αυτοδύναμο Κίνημα Επαναστατικής Πολιτικής)	AKEP	Self-reliant Movement of Revolutionary Politics
Gynekes gia mia alle Evrope (Γυναίκες για μια άλλη Ευρώπη)		Women for a different Europe
Demiourgia, xana! (Δημιουργία, ξανά!)		Creation, once again!
Democratike Anagennese (Δημοκρατική Αναγέννηση)		Democratic Revival
Democratike Ananeosse (Δημοκρατική Ανανέωση)		Democratic Renewal
Democratike Aristera (Δημοκρατική Αριστερά)	DEANA	Democratic Left
Democratike Enosse Kentrou (Δημοκρατική Ένωση Κέντρου)	DEMAR	Democratic Centre Union
Democratike Pagosmios Hellas (Δημοκρατική Παγκόσμιος Ελλάς)		Democratic Global Greece
Democratike Perferiake Enossi (Δημοκρατική Περιφερειακή Ένωση)	DPE	Democratic Regional Union
Democratike Symmahia (Δημοκρατική Συμμαχία)	DESY	Democratic Alliance
Democratiko Kinema Kinema (Δημοκρατικό Κοινωνικό Κίνημα)	DEKKI	Democratic Social Movement
Democratiko Komma (Δημοκρατικό Κόμμα)		Democratic Party
Democratiko Socialistiko Kinema (Δημοκρατικό Σοσιαλιστικό Κίνημα)		Democratic Socialist Movement
Democratiki (Δημοκρατικοί)		Republicans
Drassi (Δράση)		Action
Eleftheri (Ελεύθεροι)		Free
Ethnike Elpida (Εθνική Ελπίδα)		National Hope
Ethnike Parataxi (Εθνική Παράταξη)		National Front
Ethnike Politike Enosse (Εθνική Πολιτική Ένωση)	EPEN	National Political Union
Ethnike Symmahia (Εθνική Συμμαχία)		National Alliance
Ethnike Symparataxe (Εθνική Συμπαράταξη)		National Alignment
Ethniko Komma (Εθνικό Κόμμα)		National Party
Hellenike Enoteta (Ελληνική Ενότητα)	ELEN	Greek Unity

Helleniko Demokratiko Kinema & Kollatos (Ελληνικό Δημοκρατικό Οικολογικό Κίνημα & Κολλάτος)		Greek Democratic Ecological Movement and Kollatos
Helleniko Evropaiko Komma (Ελληνικό Ευρωπαϊκό Κόμμα)		Greek European Party
Helleniko Kinema Amesses Democratias (Ελληνικό Κίνημα Άμεσης Δημοκρατίας)		Greek Movement of Direct Democracy
Helleniko Metopo (Ελληνικό Μέτωπο)		Greek Front
Hellenikо Rizospastiko Kinema (Ελληνικό Ριζοσπαστικό Κίνημα)		Greek Radical Movement
Helleniko Socialistiko Komma (Ελληνικό Σοσιαλιστικό Κόμμα)		Greek Socialist Party
Hellenorthodoxo Kinema Soterias (Ελληνορθόδοξο Κίνημα Σωτηρίας)		Greek Orthodox Salvation Movement
Empistosyne (Εμπιστοσύνη)		Trust [Local Party]
Empistosyne/Pepromeno (Εμπιστοσύνη / Πεπρωμένο)		Trust/Destiny [Coalition of Local Parties]
Enallaktike Anticapitalistike Syspirosse (Εναλλακτική Αντικαπιταλιστική Συσπείρωση)		Alternative Anticapitalist Rally
Eniaia Socialistike Parataxe Helladas (Ενιαία Σοσιαλιστική Παράταξη Ελλάδας)	ESPE	United Socialist Front of Greece
Eniaio Ethnikistiko Kinema (Ενιαίο Εθνικιστικό Κίνημα)		United Nationalistic Movement
Enosse Democratikou Kentrou (Ένωση Δημοκρατικού Κέντρου)	EDEK	Union of the Democratic Centre
Enosse Kentrou – Nees Dynamis (Ένωση Κέντρου – Νέες Δυνάμεις)	EK-ND	Centre Union – New Forces
Enosse Kentroon (Ένωση Κεντρώων)		Union of Centrists
Enosse Ecologon & Hellenes Ecologi (Ένωση Οικολόγων & Έλληνες Οικολόγοι)		Union of Ecologists & Greek Ecologists
Enosse Paragogon, Emporon kai Katanalo on (Ένωση Παραγωγών, Εμπόρων και Καταναλωτών Ελλάδας)		Union of Producers, Tradesmen and Consumers of Greece
Enotike Anticapitalistike Aristera (Ενωτική Αντικαπιταλιστική Αριστερά)	ENANTIA	Unitary Anticapitalist Left
Epanastatike Aristera (Επαναστατική Αριστερά)		Revolutionary Left
Epanastatiko Communistiko Kinema Hellados (Επαναστατικό Κομμουνιστικό Κίνημα Ελλάδας)	EKKE	Revolutionary Communist Movement of Greece
Ergatiko Epanastatiko Komma – Trotskistes (Εργατικό Επαναστατικό Κόμμα – Τροτσκιστές)	EEK – Trotscists	Labour Revolutionary Party – Trotscists
Evropaike Economike Kinese (Ευρωπαϊκή Οικονομική Κίνηση)		European Economic Action
Evropaike Sympolitia (Ευρωπαϊκή Συμπολιτεία)		European Confederation
Evropaiko Omospondiako Orama (Ευρωπαϊκό Ορσοπονδιακό Όραμα)		European Federal Vision
Kapnistikes Omades yia ten Techne kai te Ekasti e Sygrotese (Καπνιστικές Ομάδες για την Τέχνη και την Εικαστική Συγκρότηση)	KOTES	Smoking Groups for the Arts and the Artistic Formation
Kinema den Plerono (Κίνημα δεν πληρώνω)		Movement I don't pay
Kinema Ethnikes Antistases (Κίνημα Εθνικής Αντίστασης)		National Resistance Movement
Kinema Hellenon Metarythmiston (Κίνημα Ελλήνων Μεταρρυθμιστών)		Movement of Greek Reformers
Kinese Politon (Κίνηση Πολιτών)		Citizens Movement
Kinonia, Politike Parataxe Synehiston tou Kapodistria (Κοινωνία, Πολιτική Παράταξη Συνεχιστών του Καποδίστρια)		Society, Political Front of Successors of Kapodistrias
Kinonike Symfonia (Κοινωνική Συμφωνία)		Social Alliance

(continued)

Table 13.2 (continued)

Original name	Abbreviation	English translation
Komma Anthropinon Dikeomaton (Κόμμα Ανθρωπίνων Δικαιωμάτων)		Party of Human Rights
Komma Democratikou Socialismou (Κόμμα Δημοκρατικού Σοσιαλισμού)	KODESO	Party of Democratic Socialism
Komma Ethnikon Agoniston (Κόμμα Εθνικών Αγωνιστών)		Party of National Veterans
Komma Hellenismou (Κόμμα Ελληνισμού)		Party of Hellenism
Komma Hellenon Kynegon (Κόμμα Ελλήνων Κυνηγών)		Party of Greek Hunters
Komma Neofileleftheron (Κόμμα Νεοφιλελευθέρων)		Neoliberal Party
Komma Neon (Κόμμα Νέων)		Youth Party
Komma Piraton Hellados (Κόμμα Πειρατών Ελλάδας)		Pirates Party of Greece
Komma Proodeftikon (Κόμμα Προοδευτικών)		Progressive Party
Komma Fileleftheron (Κόμμα Φιλελευθέρων)		Liberal Party
Kommounistike Aristera (Κομμουνιστική Αριστερά)		Communist Left
Kommounistiko Komma Hellados (Κομμουνιστικό Κόμμα Ελλάδος)	KKE	Communist Party of Greece
Kommounistiko Komma Hellados, essoterikou (Κομμουνιστικό Κόμμα Ελλάδος, εσωτερικού)	KKE in	Communist Party of Greece, interior
Kommounistiko Komma Hellados, essoterikou – Ananeotike Aristera (Κομμουνιστικό Κόμμα Ελλάδος, εσωτερικού, – Ανανεωτική Αριστερά)		Communist Party of Greece, interior – Renewing Left
Kommounistiko Komma Hellados, Marxistiko – Leninistiko (Κομμουνιστικό Κόμμα Ελλάδας, Μαρξιστικό – Λενινιστικό)	KKE m-l	Communist Party of Greece, Marxist – Leninist
Laikes Enosis Hyperkommatikon Koinonikon Omadon (Λαϊκές Ενώσεις Υπερκομματικών Κοινωνικών Ομάδων)	LEFKO	Populist Unions of Non-party Social Groups – LEFKO
Laikos Orthodoxos Synagermos (Λαϊκός Ορθόδοξος Συναγερμός)	LAOS	Popular Orthodox Rally
Laikos Syndesmos Crysse Avge (Λαϊκός Σύνδεσμος Χρυσή Αυγή)		Popular League Golden Dawn
Marxistiko – Leninistiko Commounistiko Komma Hellados (Μαρξιστικό – Λενινιστικό – Κομμουνιστικό Κόμμα Ελλάδος)	M-L KKE	Marxist – Leninist Communist Party of Greece
Mahomene Aristera (Μαχόμενη Αριστερά)		Militant Left
Metopo Rizospastikes Aristeras (Μέτωπο Ριζοσπαστικής Αριστεράς)	MERA	Front of Radical Left
Nea Democratia (Νέα Δημοκρατία)	ND	New Democracy
Neo Aristero Revma – Laike Antipoliteſse (Νέο Αριστερό Ρεύμα – Λαϊκή Αντιπολίτευση)		New Left Power – Popular Opposition
Neo Komma Soterias Christianike Democratia (Νέο Κόμμα Σωτηρίας Χριστιανική Δημοκρατία)		New Party of Salvation Christian Democracy
Nei Politiki (Νέοι Πολιτικοί)		New Politicians
Ecologike Anagennesse (Οικολογική Αναγέννηση)		Ecological Rebirth
Ekologi Hellados (Οικολόγοι Ελλάδος)		Greek Ecologists
Ekologi Erenistes Prassini (Οικολόγοι Ειρηνιστές Πράσινοι)		Ecologists Pacifists Greens

Ekologi Enallaktiki (Οικολόγοι Εναλλακτικοί)		Ecologist Alternative
Ekologi Prassini (Οικολόγοι Πράσινοι)		Ecologist Greens
Ekologiko Kinema – Politike Anagennese (Οικολογικό Κίνημα - Πολιτική Αναγέννηση)		Ecological Movement – Political Revival
Olympismos (Ολυμπισμός)		Olympism
Orama (Όραμα)		Vision
Organosse gia ten Anasygrotese tou Kommounistikou Kommatos Helladas (Οργάνωση για την Ανασυγκρότηση του Κομμουνιστικού Κόμματος Ελλάδας)	OAKKE	Organization for the Reconstruction of the Communist Party of Greece
Organosse Kommouniston Diethniston Helladas (Οργάνωση Κομμουνιστών Διεθνιστών Ελλάδας)	OKDE	Organization of Communists Internationalists of Greece
Uranio Toxo (Ουράνιο Τόξο)		Rainbow
Ohi, Enieo Pallaiko Metopo – Democratike Anagennesse (Όχι, Ενιαίο Παλλαϊκό Μέτωπο – Δημοκρατική Αναγέννηση)		NC United Peoples Front – Democratic Renewal
Panathenaiko Kinema (Παναθηναϊκό Κίνημα)	PANKI	Parathenaic Movement
Panhellenio Makedoniko Metopo (Πανελλήνιο Μακεδονικό Μέτωπο)	PAMME	Parhellenic Macedonian Front
Panhellenio Socialistiko Kinema (Πανελλήνιο Σοσιαλιστικό Κίνημα)	PASOK	Parhellenic Socialist Movement, PASOK
Patriotike Symmahia (Πατριωτική Συμμαχία)		Patriotic Alliance
Patriotiko Anthropistiko Kinema (Πατριωτικό Ανθρωπιστικό Κίνημα)	PANAK	Patriotic Human Movement
Pepromeno (Πεπρωμένο)		Destiny [Local Party]
Perferiake Astike Anaptyxe (Περιφερειακή Αστική Ανάπτυξη)		Regional Urban Development
Politike Anixe (Πολιτική Άνοιξη)	POLAN	Political Spring
Politike Ecologia (Πολιτική Οικολογία)		Political Ecology
Prassini (Πράσινοι)		Greens
Prote Gramme (Πρώτη Γραμμή)		First Line
Rizospastike Antiapagorefike Kinese (Ριζοσπαστική Αντιαπαγορευτική Κίνηση)	RAK	Radical Anti Prohibitive Movement
Socialistiko Ergatiko Komma (Σοσιαλιστικό Εργατικό Κόμμα)	SEK	Socialist Labour Party
Syndesmos Ethnikes Enotetas (Σύνδεσμος Εθνικής Ενότητας)		National Unity League
Synaspismos tes Aristeras kai tes Proodou (Συνασπισμός της Αριστεράς και της Προόδου)	SYN	Coalition of the Left and the Progress
Synaspismos tes Rizospastikes Aristeras (Συνασπισμός της Ριζοσπαστικής Αριστεράς)	SYRIZA	Coalition of the Radical Left
Fileleftere Symmahia (Φιλελεύθερη Συμμαχία)		Liberal Alliance
Filelefheri (Φιλελεύθεροι)		Liberals
Fos, Alethia, Dikeosyne (Φως, Αλήθεια, Δικαιοσύνη)		Light, Truth, Justice
Charizo ecopeda, … Panagrotiko Ergatiko Kinema Helladas (Χαρίζω οικόπεδα, … Παναγροτικό Εργατικό Κίνημα Ελλάδας)	PAEKE	I dcnate plots … Agricultural Labour Movement of Greece
Christianike Democratia (Χριστιανική Δημοκρατία)		Christian Democracy

Source: Greece's Ministry of Home Affairs, www.ypes.gr/el.

Relatively few new parties evolved in the right and the centre-right and most of them were short-lived. They were mainly parties founded by former ND members and centred on the personality of their leader. Democratic Renewal (DEANA) was founded by Kostis Stefanopoulos, a former member of ND and a contestant for the party's leadership. The party had elected an MEP in the 1989 Euro-elections and won a seat in the Greek Parliament in the 1990 elections. In 1995 its leader, Kostis Stefanopoulos, with the support of PASOK, was elected President of Greece. The introduction of the 3 per cent threshold in 1990 led the party to join forces with another party on the right, the Political Spring (POLAN). The latter was founded by Antonis Samaras, the current Prime Minister and leader of ND, in 1993 after his dissent from the ND along with ten more members of the ND's parliamentary group. In the 1994 Euro-elections, the party elected two MEPs, but in the subsequent national and European elections the party failed to be represented. In 2004, Antonis Samaras returned to ND along with other party members and suspended the party. More recently, the Popular Orthodox Rally (LAOS), headed by George Karatzaferis, former member of ND, had succeeded in consolidating its position in subsequent elections and in 2011 participated in the Lucas Papademos government. Nevertheless, in the 2012 elections its percentage dropped below the 3 per cent threshold. Dora Bakoyianni, a former ND member who contested the most recent ND leadership contest, along with other former ND members founded a new centre-right party, the Democratic Alliance, in 2010. In the May 2012 elections the party failed to pass the 3 per cent threshold and dissolved before the June 2012 elections. Another former ND member, Panos Kammenos, founded a new party, the Independent Greeks (ANEL) in 2012, which had been joined by a number of former ND members and other smaller political groups. In the May and the June 2012 general elections the party secured 10.6 per cent and 7.5 per cent of the vote, respectively.

Since 1974, various extreme-right Nationalist parties have been founded but they had very low electoral appeal and after some elections they tended to dissolve. In 1984 the National Political Union (EPEN) was founded, communicating its direct relationship with a jailed junta leader. In the 1984 Euro-elections the party elected one MEP with 2.3 per cent of the vote, but in the 1989 Euro-elections its vote share dropped to 1.2 per cent. Moreover, in the four general elections in which it participated, its percentages were around 0.5 per cent of the vote or less.

In the municipal elections of October 2010 the extreme-right Nationalist party Golden Dawn gained representation in the Athens Municipal Council; it also won representation to the Greek Parliament in the 2012 general elections. The party was founded in 1993 with no particular influence on the electorate until the economic crisis hit. The troika imposed austerity programme and its impact on unemployment and poverty, along with the issue of illegal immigration, appear to have triggered the nationalization of the party's appeal as the electoral results in the 2012 general elections have shown. Before 2010, the party's electoral results in both national and EP elections were well below 0.5 per cent whereas in the 2012 elections they reached 6.9 per cent.

PASOK has dominated the centre and centre-left tradition since the 1977 elections. Andreas Papandreou founded the party, drawing on the social democratic tradition, albeit of a Greek populist variety. After its notable rise to power in 1981, the party was able to secure six governmental terms in office. The 2009 PASOK government's handling of the debt crisis caused a considerable de-alignment amongst the party's supporters. In particular, in the 2012 elections, the party lost more than 70 per cent of its electoral power and came in third place.

After 1974, a number of smaller political parties in the centre and centre-left were established, yet most of them suspended their operations. In the 1974 elections there was an attempt to revive the Centre Union of the pre-1967 party system but it was short-lived, since PASOK succeeded in subsequent elections to appeal to the Centre Union's electorate. In 1995, Dimitris Tsovolas, a former member of PASOK, founded the Democratic Social Movement (DEKKI); the party had some success in the 1996 general elections, winning 9 seats in the Greek Parliament and 2 MEP seats in the 1999 Euro-elections, but since the 2000 general elections it has failed to reach the 3 per cent threshold. In the municipal elections, the party had cooperated with the Communist Party in some municipalities and joined the Coalition of the Radical Left (SYRIZA) in the general elections of 2007. In 2012, a new party, the Social Pact, was founded by Louka Katseli and other members of PASOK. The party failed to elect representatives in the May 2012 elections and did not participate in the June 2012 elections. Currently its members are in cooperation with SYRIZA.

The Communist Party of Greece (KKE), which conveys the old and purist Communist tradition, has been the main pillar of the left. The party split in 1968 and the Communist Party of Greece Interior (KKEin) was established, influenced by the Euro-Communist perception of democratic socialism. In the 1974 elections, all parties of the left participated under the United Left umbrella coalition. The KKEin often formed coalitions with other parties of the left, however they were short lived and led to splits and the founding of more parties, such as the Greek Left (EAR).

In 1989, the Coalition of the Left and Progress (SYN) was founded with the cooperation of EAR and the KKE. After the withdrawal of the KKE in 1991, SYN was transformed into a party in 2003, which was called the Coalition of the Left, of Movements and Ecology, and in 2004 it joined SYRIZA. Thirteen distinct political groups have joined forces under SYRIZA. The May 2012 election results prompted its transformation into a political party participating in the June 2012 election; after winning 26.9 per cent of the vote it became the main opposition party.

The Democratic Left (DEMAR) was founded by Fotis Kouvelis, after a split in 2010 from the SYN. The party supports a pro-European agenda and, after the June 2012 elections, participated in a coalition government with the ND and PASOK but withdrew in June 2013 over the ND's handling of the administrative reforms demanded by the troika. Apart from the aforementioned parties of the left, a considerable number of other smaller political parties of the left and the extreme left participated in the elections, yet gained no parliamentary representation. In the tradition of the left, a number of green parties have been founded; however, it was only in the 2009 Euro-elections that the Ecologist Green Party succeeded in electing an MEP. In general, all the political parties have developed green agendas.

5.1 Party attitudes towards the European Union

Most Greek political parties are generally in favour of European integration and the country's EU membership, incorporating EU affairs in their respective party platforms. However, there have been some that have suggested an anti-European stance. During the accession process, PASOK, along with the left, had argued against EEC membership and had strongly criticized the ND government's decision to apply. In the 1981 elections, PASOK had pledged to renegotiate Greece's EC membership and the holding of a referendum, however when it came into power, it modified its position. During the 1981 electoral campaign its criticism had weakened and in 1983 after the EC's acceptance of the *Greek Memorandum,* relations between the new Greek government and the EC normalized (Kazakos and Stefanou, 1987; Clogg, 1982).

The Communist Party has consistently expressed an anti-European position. On the left, the great majority of the smaller parties have projected a critical stance towards the EU, although the tradition of Euro-Communism has remained strong in political parties such as DEMAR that explicitly convey a pro-European agenda. The situation is much more complicated in the case of SYRIZA, whose umbrella structure has allowed the co-existence of both pro- and anti-European attitudes. The current economic crisis has taken its toll on Greece's pro-European sentiments; since 2010 a considerable number of political parties, covering the entire political spectrum, voice scepticism towards the EU.

6 Public opinion and the European Union

The majority of the Greek public considered EU membership as a 'good thing', as indicated in Eurobarometer surveys, however, there were periods of scepticism. In particular, from 1981 to 1985, immediately after the country's accession, only 41 per cent of the Greek public considered EU membership a 'good thing'; that percentage was considerably lower than the 55 per cent EU average. The public's stance reflected the ruling party's (PASOK) strong reservations. The shift in the government's stance in 1985 after the signing of the *Greek Memorandum* and the introduction of the Integrated Mediterranean Programmes (IMP) considerably influenced public opinion. From 1986 to 2009, 61 per cent of Greeks on average considered EU membership to be a 'good thing', well above the 56 per cent EU average. The economic crisis and its handling by the EU have led to a drop in public opinion. In particular, for the period 2010–2011, the percentage of Greeks who viewed the EU as a 'good thing' dropped to 41 per cent, compared to the 48 per cent EU average.

Greeks' attitudes towards the 'benefits' that EU membership has incurred for the country followed a similar trend. From 1983 to 1985, 46 per cent of Greeks had a positive view of the EU's benefits, compared to the 50 per cent EU average. For the period 1986–2009, it markedly increased to 70 per cent, one of the higher averages in the EU, considering that the EU average for the period was 51 per cent. However, from 2010 to 2011 the Greek average dropped to 54 per cent, which, although it was above the 52 per cent EU average, was on the decline. In Greece as well as in other Member States the EU's economic approach prompted a decline in public support and public trust in the EU and its institutions (Lavdas and Mendrinou, 2013).

Demographic differences, like education, economic and social status, affect the attitudes of survey respondents and thus there are differentiations in the concerned averages. According to Eurobarometer, those most educated, those at the top of the social scale, and those with strong political interests expressed more positive attitudes towards the EU.

7 National and EP electoral systems

The electoral system that applies to Euro-elections is proportional representation in one single constituency, with closed party lists and seat allocation by the Hare quota. The only reform concerns the 3 per cent nationwide threshold that was introduced since the 1994 EP elections (Mendrinou, 2000).

The electoral system for general elections is much more complicated and to a great extent it contributes to the formation of one-party governments with strong absolute majorities in the Greek Parliament. There have been frequent electoral reforms post-1974 (Lijphart, 1994; Mendrinou, 2000). The main features of the last three reforms were: support for the first political party in the allocation of seats, and provisions for better representation for the parties above the threshold.

The Greek Parliament has 300 seats, of which 288 are allocated in 57 electoral districts, whilst 12 are 'at large'. After the 1990 electoral reform a 3 per cent threshold was introduced. The 12 parliamentary seats, known as the seats of 'state deputies' (*epikrateias*), are allocated by the Hare quota according to closed party lists. The remaining 288 parliamentary seats are allocated in the 57 electoral districts on the basis of preference votes.

The current electoral system provides for an initial distribution of the number of seats that corresponds to each party's electoral power and then seats are allocated in the national districts. The special formula is as follows: the total number of the valid votes for a party above the threshold is multiplied by 250; the product of the multiplication is then divided by the total of the valid votes of the political parties with over 3 per cent; the result is the number of parliamentary seats that corresponds to each party. The party that gains the most seats by the above formula also gets an additional 50 bonus seats for coming in first. This is based on the 2009 revision to the formula, which increased the number of bonus seats from 40 to 50. The Hare quota is applied for the allocation of the 288 seats in the 57 electoral districts. If there are any discrepancies between the total number of allocated seats in the districts and that provided for by the electoral formula, then the political parties gain or lose seats on the basis of their remainders.

8 A glance at national and EP elections

All EP elections in Greece shared certain similar characteristics, whilst their electoral results were considerably different from results in national elections. The main feature of all elections in Greece was the polarization between the two governmental political parties. The main difference between the electoral results in the two types of elections was the decline in the cumulative percentage won by the two main political parties in Euro-elections.

Table 13.3 EP election results in Greece: 1981–2004 (%)★

Political party	1981	1984	1989	1994	1999	2004
ND	31.3 (10)	38.1 (9)	40.4 (10)	32.7 (9)	36.0 (9)	43.0 (11)
PASOK	40.1 (8)	41.6 (10)	36.0 (9)	37.6 (10)	32.9 (9)	34.0 (8)
KKE	12.8 (3)	11.6 (3)	—	6.3 (2)	8.7 (3)	9.5 (3)
KKE in	5.3 (1)	3.4 (1)	—	—	—	—
KODESO	4.3 (1)	0.8	—	—	—	—
Progressive Party	2.0 (1)	0.2	—	—	—	—
EPEN	—	2.3 (1)	1.2	0.8	—	—
SYN	—	—	14.3 (4)	6.3 (2)	5.2 (2)	—
DEANA	—	—	1.4 (1)	2.8	—	—
POLAN	—	—	—	8.7 (2)	2.3	—
SYRIZA	—	—	—	—	—	4.2 (1)
DEKKI	—	—	—	—	6.8 (2)	—
LAOS	—	—	—	—	—	4.2 (1)
Ecologists Greens	—	—	—	—	—	0.7
EDEK	1.1	0.3	0.3	—	—	—
Ecologists Alternative	—	—	1.1	—	0.2	0.0
Golden Dawn	—	—	—	0.1	0.8	—
ANTARSYA Action	—	—	—	—	—	—
Liberal Party	1.0	0.4	0.4	—	—	—
Christian Democracy	1.2	0.5	0.4	—	—	—
Liberals	—	—	—	—	1.6	—
PAMME	—	—	—	—	—	—
Greek Democratic Ecological Movement	—	—	1.1	0.7	0.7	—
Centre Union	—	—	—	1.2	0.8	0.5
Party of Greek Hunters	—	—	—	0.6	1.0	—
LEFKO	—	—	—	0.3	0.2	—
Greek Ecologists	—	—	—	—	0.5	0.5
Others	0.9	1.4	3.4	1.9	2.3	3.4
Total	100.0 (24)	100.0 (24)	100.0 (24)	100.0 (25)	100.0 (25)	100.0 (24)

Source: Greece's Ministry of Home Affairs, www.ypes.gr/el.

Note: ★ Seats in brackets.

The first Euro-elections in Greece were held along with the general elections in October 1981 that had led to the first government alternation since 1974. From that time onwards a key difference between the two types of elections emerged: the considerable decline in the electoral power of the two larger political parties in favour of the smaller parties. Although the winner in the general elections held its lead in the Euro-elections, PASOK's percentage was lower by 8 per cent.

The 1984 Euro-elections preceded the national elections of 1985 by a year. The main opposition party, ND, won the Euro-elections with a higher percentage than in the 1981 national elections. Nonetheless, in the 1985 general elections the ND remained in opposition. It may be argued that it was the main theme of the national elections that had favoured PASOK.

The June 1985 elections were held just months after the resignation of Konstantinos Karamanlis from President of the Republic. The new President had been elected in March amid great controversy and the calling of new elections, according to the Constitution, had just been averted.

The 1989 Euro-elections were held along with the national elections in June 1989. The political campaigns of both elections had been dominated by domestic political considerations and mainly by allegations of political scandals and corruption. The main opposition party, ND, succeeded in taking the lead in both elections, but did not secure an absolute majority in Parliament since the electoral reform of 1989 had introduced a considerably more proportional electoral system. All the main parties of the left, including the Communist Party, had participated in the elections under the Coalition of the Left and Progress (SYN). A period of instability began with the June 1989 elections, with short-lived coalition governments; new elections were held in November 1989 and again in April 1990. The ND's meagre absolute majority in Parliament allowed the formation of an ND government but the resignation of Antonis Samaras from the Ministry of Foreign Affairs and his dissent from the ND, along with other ND MPs, led to the fall of the government and the call for elections in October 1993.

The 1994 Euro-elections were held less than a year after the 1993 general elections that had led to a new government alternation. As in the 1993 general elections, the Communist Party participated independently from the SYN. The timing of the Euro-elections supported a looser vote that benefitted the smaller political parties, which amassed almost 30 per cent of the vote and six of the 25 seats in the EP. Their representation would have been even more extensive if the introduction of the 3 per cent threshold had not ruled out DEANA, a small right-wing party, with 2.8 per cent of the vote. Although the power of both the larger parties had declined, their ranking remained. PASOK was re-elected in the 1996 general election under its new leader, Kostas Simitis. The elections were held earlier, months after the death of its founder, Andreas Papandreou.

The 1999 Euro-elections took place a year before the 2000 national election. The main opposition party, the ND, won the Euro-elections. However, in the national elections that were held in April 2000, PASOK remained the governing party. It appeared as if the Euro-elections vote had defused the discontent, whilst the government had enough time to reverse the negative climate against its policies.

The 2004 Euro-elections followed just months after the March 2004 general elections that had led to a government alternation after ten years of PASOK governments. In addition, the EP elections were held on the eve of the Athens 2004 Olympic Games. In this context, the drop in turnout was not as disquieting as the one that was registered in the 2009 Euro-elections. The main opposition party appeared to approach the Euro-elections as an opportunity to attract attention to its new leader, George Papandreou, and to an extent to contain its losses in the preceding national elections. The mobilization of PASOK's supporters, along with the timing of the elections and the relatively low turnout, might have contributed to the limited losses of the two larger parties, although three of the smaller parties, the KKE, the SYN, and the LAOS, elected MEPs.

Table 13.4 National election results in Greece: 1981–2012 (%)*

Political party	1981	1985	6/1989	11/1989	1990	1993	1996	2000	2004	2007	2009	5/2012	6/2012
ND	35.9 (115)	40.9 (126)	44.3 (145)	46.2 (148)	46.9 (150)	39.3 (111)	38.1 (108)	42.7 (125)	45.4 (165)	41.8 (152)	33.5 (91)	18.9 (108)	29.7 (129)
PASOK	48.1 (172)	45.8 (161)	39.1 (125)	40.7 (128)	38.6 (123)	46.9 (170)	41.5 (162)	43.8 (158)	40.5 (117)	38.1 (102)	43.9 (160)	13.2 (41)	12.3 (33)
EDEK	0.4	0.1	—	—	—	—	—	—	—	—	—	—	—
KKE	10.9 (13)	9.9 (12)	—	—	—	4.5 (9)	5.6 (11)	5.5 (11)	5.9 (12)	8.2 (22)	7.5 (21)	8.5 (26)	4.5 (12)
KKE in	1.4	1.8 (1)	—	—	—	—	—	—	—	—	—	—	—
EPEN	—	0.6	0.3	—	0.1	0.1	0.2	—	—	—	—	—	—
SYN	—	—	13.1 (28)	11.0 (21)	10.3 (19)	2.9	5.1 (10)	3.2 (6)	—	—	—	—	—
Electoral Coalition of PASOK and SYN	—	—	—	—	1.0 (4)	—	—	—	—	—	—	—	—
DEANA	—	—	1.0 (1)	—	0.7	—	—	—	—	—	—	—	—
SYRIZA	—	—	—	—	—	—	—	—	3.3 (6)	5.0 (14)	4.6 (13)	16.8 (52)	26.9 (71)
POLAN	—	—	—	—	—	4.9 (10)	2.9	—	—	—	—	—	—
Trust	—	—	0.5 (1)	0.4 (1)	—	0.4	—	—	—	—	—	—	—
Trust/Destiny	—	—	—	—	0.7 (2)	—	—	—	—	—	—	—	—
DEKKI	—	—	—	—	—	—	4.4 (9)	2.7	1.8	—	—	—	—
Ecologist Alternative	—	—	—	0.6 (1)	0.8 (1)	—	0.8	0.0	—	—	—	—	—
LAOS	—	—	—	—	—	—	—	—	2.2	3.8 (10)	5.6 (15)	2.9	1.6
ANEL	—	—	—	—	—	—	—	—	—	—	—	10.6 (33)	7.5 (20)

(continued)

Table 13.4 (continued)

Political party	1981	1985	6/1989	11/1989	1990	1993	1996	2000	2004	2007	2009	5/2012	6/2012
Golden Dawn	—	—	—	—	—	—	0.1	0.2	—	—	0.3	7.0 (21)	6.9 (18)
DEMAR	—	—	—	—	—	—	—	—	—	—	—	6.1 (19)	6.3 (17)
KODESO	0.7	—	—	—	—	—	—	—	—	—	—	—	—
Ecologist Greens	—	—	—	—	—	—	—	—	—	1.1	2.5	2.9	0.9
ANTARSYA	—	—	—	—	—	—	—	—	—	—	0.4	1.2	0.3
Creation, once again!	—	—	—	—	—	—	—	—	—	—	—	2.2	1.6
Democratic Alliance	—	—	—	—	—	—	—	—	—	—	—	2.6	—
Action	—	—	—	—	—	—	—	—	—	—	—	1.8	—
Social Alliance	—	—	—	—	—	—	—	—	—	—	—	1.0	—
Independents	—	—	—	0.3 (1)	—	—	—	—	—	—	—	—	—
Others	2.6	0.9	1.7	0.8	0.9	1.0	1.3	1.9	0.9	2.0	1.7	4.3	1.5
Total	100.0	100.0	100.0	100.0	100.0	100.0	100.0	100.0	100.0	100.0	100.0	100.0	100.0

Source: Greece's Ministry of Home Affairs, www.ypes.gr/el/.

Note: * Seats in brackets

Table 13.5 Turnout at national and EP elections in Greece: 1981–2012 (%)

	EC/EU	Greece National elections	EP elections
1981	62.0	78.6	81.5
1984	59.0	—	80.6
1985	—	79.1	—
6/1989	58.4	80.3	80.1
11/1989	—	80.7	—
1990	—	79.2	—
1993	—	79.2	—
1994	56.7	—	73.2
1996	—	76.3	—
1999	49.5	—	70.3
2000	—	75.0	—
3/2004	—	76.5	—
6/2004	45.5	—	63.2
2007	—	74.1	—
6/2009	42.9	—	52.6
10/2009	—	70.9	—
5/2012	—	65.1	—
6/2012	—	62.5	—

Source: Greece's Ministry of Home Affairs, www.ypes.gr/el/.

With reference to the economy and the 2008 budget, the subsequent national elections were held months earlier – in September 2007. The elections took place on the eve of the catastrophic fires of that summer in which more than 65 people died and thousands became homeless, whilst the overall damages exceeded €4 billion. In spite of the decline in its percentage of the vote, the ND remained the governing party; PASOK renewed George Papandreou's leadership against his competitors Evangelos Venizelos, who became leader in 2012, and Kostas Skandalidis.

9 The 2009 European election

9.1 Party lists and manifestos

As shown in Table 13.6, 27 lists ran the 2009 EP race, some of which were new or had not participated in the previous Euro-election.

The contest was once again polarized, with the emphasis on domestic rather than on European politics; however, it should be noted that the evolution of EU integration has blurred the boundaries between domestic and EU politics. All political parties had incorporated in their campaigns the declarations and the political manifestos of their respective EP groups. The economic crisis, poverty, unemployment, and social policy issues were at the top of the agenda as all political parties, particularly the ones in the opposition, raised them during the electoral campaign.

PASOK, the main opposition party at the time, had launched a wide-ranging campaign against the government aiming to trigger an early general election, a prospect that materialized in October 2009. The ND, on the other hand, had focussed its campaign on enhancing

Table 13.6 EP electoral lists in Greece: 2009

PASOK
ND
KKE
LAOS
SYRIZA
Ecologist Greens
Union of Centrists
ASKE
Dimitris Vergis – Greek Ecologists
European Free Coalition Rainbow
m-l KKE
OAKKE
Liberal Alliance
PANAK
Ecologists of Greece
LEFKO
Golden Dawn
Youth Party
Party of Greek Hunters
Society
EEK Trotscists
ELEN
ANTARSYA
Greek Movement for Direct Democracy
Action
Liberal Party
PAMME

Source: Greece's Ministry of Home Affairs, www.ypes.gr/el/.

the government's profile and addressing issues regarding the economic crisis, the environment, economic development, the social dimension, security, and immigration.

European issues, such as the Lisbon Treaty and EU enlargement, did not capture the interest of the political discourse at the time. Apart from the Communist Party's traditionally-expressed Eurosceptic stance in the 2009 Euro-election, the other left party, SYRIZA, influenced by some of its constituent political groups, had articulated a more critical approach towards the EU and its policies. However, criticism of EU politics, more often than not, was directed against the Greek governments' handling of issues in the EU framework.

The environment was also at the centre of the electoral campaign and almost all the main parties had incorporated it in their agendas. This shift had been further supported by the increased influence of the Ecologists in the polls. Foreign policy was also on the agenda, particularly since a new political party, the Pan-Hellenic Macedonian Front, focussed its campaign on the issue of the name of the Former Yugoslav Republic of Macedonia (FYROM). Immigration had also evolved into a central topic of the campaign on which parties of the left, such as SYRIZA, confronted LAOS, a small right-wing party.

9.2 Electoral campaign

All national, regional, private and public television channels offered considerable coverage of the 2009 Euro-election, including the press conferences of the party leaders, discussion panels, and special programmes on the Euro-elections. The local and national press – as well as social media – also provided extensive information on Euro-elections.

In addition, the main political parties frequently broadcasted video messages and the government launched an information campaign with television spots in order to inform citizens of other EU Member States who resided in Greece about the necessary registration process for voting in Greece, as well as to promote turnout. There was a campaign against voter participation initiated by various political groups, mainly non-parliamentary ones. The 'No vote' campaign targeted mainly younger voters through posters and social media. The intensity of the No-vote campaign mobilized the main political parties, the government, and the EP to embark on a campaign in favour of participation.

The Office of the EP in Greece was also particularly active in promoting a series of initiatives in various cities. With the cooperation of Greek universities and research centres, they organized several conferences and symposia on the EP, the EU, and the Euro-elections, with speeches from EU experts. The office arranged a press conference with the leading candidates from the parliamentary parties in order to provide information on the electoral campaign in Greece and other European countries, whilst it offered live coverage through EuroparlTV on polling day.

9.3 Electoral results

The main features discerned in the previous Euro-elections were also present in the 2009 elections. The most pronounced feature was the decline of the electoral power of the two governmental parties, which was considerable in 2009. As a result the vote share of the smaller parties increased, securing them wider representation in the EP.

The novelty of the 2009 Euro-elections was the remarkably low – for Greek electoral politics – turnout of 52.6 per cent. The polarization of Greek elections had supported a relatively high voter turnout in Euro-elections compared to other EU Member States. Apart from the 'No vote' campaign, which approached abstention as a mean of protest and indicated widespread public discontent against the main governmental parties and the EU, the fact that the elections were held on a bank holiday also contributed to low voter turnout.

With an electoral result more than 10 per cent lower than the one in the 2004 Euro-elections, the ND lost its lead. The ND government at the time was confronted with widespread dissatisfaction. The poor performance of the governing party, the impact of the December 2008 riots, the allegations of political scandals, and the manifestations of the international economic crisis had created an exceptionally negative political climate for the government. In addition, the small right wing party LAOS, with an immigration agenda, had registered a considerable increase in support, inflicting losses on the main centre-right party. LAOS's percentage increased to 7.2 per cent of the vote compared to the 4.2 per cent in the 2004 Euro-elections.

The main opposition party approached a Euro-elections victory as the signal for its electoral recovery and was keen to mobilize its electorate. PASOK's vigorous campaign paid off; the party won the elections with an increased percentage compared to that in the 2004 Euro-elections. In the October 2009 national elections, just three months later, PASOK became the governing party on a platform of 'change', transparency, and accountability, along with plans for improving social benefits and pledges on the availability of necessary financial resources. The ND suffered a massive defeat that led to a leadership challenge. The party has since recovered and is at present the main government party of the coalition governments after the June 2012 national elections.

Apart from the Communist Party (KKE), whose percentage registered a decline, most of the other smaller parties had considerable increases in their electoral power. The Ecologist

Table 13.7 EP election results in Greece: 2009

Political party	% (seats)
ND	32.3 (8)
PASOK	36.6 (8)
KKE	8.6 (2)
SYRIZA	4.7 (1)
LAOS	7.2 (2)
Ecologist Greens	3.5 (1)
Golden Dawn	0.5
ANTARSYA	0.4
Action	0.8
Liberal Party	0.1
PAMME	1.3
Centre Union	0.4
Party of Greek Hunters	1.3
LEFKO	0.2
Greek Ecologists	0.7
Others	1.4
Total	100.0 (22)

Source: Greece's Ministry of Home Affairs, http://www.ypes.gr/el/.

Greens, with 3.5 per cent of the vote and one MEP, was the first Greek Green party that gained representation in the EP.

Greece was allocated 22 MEPs; the Lisbon Treaty introduced no change in the country's representation but following the entry of Croatia it was decided that from the eighth legislature the number would decrease to 21. Greek MEPs can be classified into three main categories. The first concerns established politicians in the national political arena who often swap between the national Parliament or the local level and the EP. The second category refers to new political personnel who initiate their political career as MEPs; often they are experts in their fields as counsellors, journalists and academics, have a previous governmental appointment, or are party cadres. These two categories are mainly related to the governmental parties. The third category concerns the leaders of the smaller political parties with no representation at the national level.

Table 13.8 provides detailed information regarding Greek representatives, including their membership to committees and delegations. Overall, a considerable number of the Greek MEPs had previous terms in the EP and/or wide experience in the parliamentary affairs of Greece. The October 2009 national elections led to changes in the Greek EP delegation, since four MEPs opted for the Greek political arena: George Papakonstantinou joined the PASOK government as Minister of Finance; Athanassios Pafilis, who was MEP for 1999 and 2004, was re-elected to the Greek Parliament with the KKE; Athanassios Pleuris, MEP of LAOS was also re-elected to the Greek Parliament. In addition, in the 2011 government reshuffle, an exchange of posts had been made between Stavros Lambrinidis, who became foreign minister and Dimitris Droutsas, who held that post, and became an MEP as he was next on the party's list. As Table 13.9 shows, the percentage of re-elected Greek MEPs in the 2009 Euro-elections is relatively higher than that of all other previous EP parliamentary periods.

The gender dimension is also of particular interest. Traditionally, women are under-represented in Greek politics. Even if they are elected, women rarely obtain positions with political responsibility in decision-making. In the 2009 Euro-elections, the gender distribution of the Greek MEPs approximated that of the EU average.

Table 13.8 List of Greek MEPs: seventh legislature

Name	Date of birth	Professional background	Committee Chair	Committee membership	Committee substitutes
Group of the Progressive Alliance of Socialists and Democrats in the EP					
PASOK (Panhellenic Socialist Movement)					
Arsenis, K.	3/8/1977	Studies on development		Committee on the Environment, Public Health and Food Safety; Committee on the Environment, Public Health and Food Safety; Delegation for relations with the Maghreb countries and the Arab Maghreb Union; Delegation to the Parliamentary Assembly of the Union for the Mediterranean	Committee on Development; Delegation for relations with the countries of the Andean Community
Danellis, Sp	28/01/1955	Architect, Member of the Greek Parliament (1996–2000)		Delegation for relations with the Palestinian Legislative Council	Committee on Transport and Tourism; Committee on Agriculture and Rural Development; Delegation to the EU-Croatia Joint Parliamentary Committee
Koppa, M.-E.	01/03/1963	Academic	Vice-Chair: Delegation to the EU-Turkey Joint Parliamentary Committee	Committee on Foreign Affairs; Subcommittee on Security and Defence	Committee on International Trade; Subcommittee on Human Rights; Delegation to the EU-Russia Parliamentary Cooperation Committee
Droutsas, D.	05/08/1968				
Paliadeli, Ch.	08/07/1947	Academic	Vice-Chair: Committee on Petitions	Committee on Culture and Education; Delegation for Relations with Israel	Committee on Women's Rights and Gender Equality; Delegation for relations with Albania, Bosnia and Herzegovina, Serbia, Montenegro and Kosovo
Podimata, A.	08/10/1962	Journalist	Vice-Chair: Committee on Industry, Research and Energy	Committee on Economic and Monetary Affairs; Special Committee on the Financial, Economic and Social Crisis; Delegation to the EU-Former Yugoslav Republic of Macedonia Joint Parliamentary Committee	Delegation for relations with the People's Republic of China; Delegation to the ACP-EU Joint Parliamentary Assembly

(continued)

Table 13.8 (continued)

Name	Date of birth	Professional background	Committee Chair	Committee membership	Committee substitutes
Rapti, S.	10/11/1958	Journalist, Member of the Greek Parliament (2005–2009)		Committee on Employment and Social Affairs; Delegation to the Euro-Latin American Parliamentary Assembly	Committee on the Internal Market and Consumer Protection; Committee on Petitions; Delegation to the EU–Chile Joint Parliamentary Committee; Delegation for Relations with the Mashreq Countries
Stavrakakis, G.	13/10/1954	Academic	Vice-Chair: Committee on Regional Development	Committee on Budgetary Control; Special Committee on the Policy Challenges and Budgetary Resources for a Sustainable European Union after 2013; Delegation for Relations with the People's Republic of China	Committee on Budgets; Delegation for Relations with Japan

Group of the European People's Party (Christian Democrats)

ND (New Democracy)

Name	Date of birth	Professional background	Committee Chair	Committee membership	Committee substitutes
Giannakou, M. Group Bureau Member	05/06/1951	Psychiatrist, neurologist, Member of the Greek and the EP Parliament, Ministerial Appointments		Committee on Foreign Affairs; Subcommittee on Human Rights; Special Committee on the Policy Challenges and Budgetary Resources for a Sustainable European Union after 2013; Delegation for Relations with the United States	Committee on Constitutional Affairs; Delegation for Relations with Albania, Bosnia and Herzegovina, Serbia, Montenegro and Kosovo
Koumoutsakos, G.	17/09/1961	n/a	Vice-Chair: Delegation to the EU-Turkey Joint Parliamentary Committee	Committee on Transport and Tourism	Committee on Foreign Affairs; Subcommittee on Security and Defence; Delegation to the EU–Former Yugoslav Republic of Macedonia Joint Parliamentary Committee
Kratsa-Tsagaropoulou, R. Group Bureau Member	15/04/1953	MEP since 1999	Vice-President European Parliament	Parliament's Bureau; Committee on Economic and Monetary Affairs; Committee on Women's Rights and Gender Equality; Delegation for Relations with the Mercosur countries; Delegation to the Euro-Latin American Parliamentary Assembly	Committee on Regional Development; Delegation for Relations with the Mashreq Countries; Delegation to the Parliamentary Assembly of the Union for the Mediterranean

Papanikolaou, G.	15/08/1977	Lawyer	Vice-Chair: Delegation to the EU–Chile Joint Parliamentary Committee	Committee on Civil Liberties, Justice and Home Affairs; Delegation to the Euro-Latin American Parliamentary Assembly	Committee on Culture and Education; Delegation to the ACP–EU Joint Parliamentary Assembly
Papastamkos, G.	05/03/1955	Academic, Member of the Greek Parliament, Appointments as Deputy Minister, MEP since 2004	Vice-Chair: Delegation for Relations with Australia and New Zealand	Committee on Agriculture and Rural Development	Committee on International Trade; Delegation for Relations with the Palestinian Legislative Council
Poupakis, K.	18/01/1951	n/a		Committee on Employment and Social Affairs; Delegation for relations with Albania, Bosnia and Herzegovina, Serbia, Montenegro and Kosovo	Committee on the Internal Market and Consumer Protection; Delegation to the EU–Russia Parliamentary Cooperation Committee
Skylakakis, Th.	18/10/1959	Member of the Municipality of the City of Athens		Committee on Budgetary Control; Committee on the Environment, Public Health and Food Safety; Delegation for Relations with the People's Republic of China	Committee on Industry, Research and Energy; Special Committee on the Financial, Economic and Social Crisis; Delegation for Relations with Iran
Tsoukalas, I.	03/07/1941	Academic		Committee on Industry, Research and Energy; Delegation to the EU–Armenia, EU–Azerbaijan and EU–Georgia Parliamentary Cooperation Committees; Delegation to the Euronest Parliamentary Assembly	Committee on Fisheries; Committee on Petitions; Delegation to the ACP–EU Joint Parliamentary Assembly
Confederal Group of the European United Left/Nordic Green Left					
KKE (Communist Party of Greece)					
Angourakis, Ch.	19/01/1951	Computer science, Member of the Greek Parliament (1997–2000)	Vice-Chair: Delegation for Relations with India	Committee on Regional Development	Committee on Foreign Affairs
Toussas, G. Group Bureau Member	08/09/1954	Merchant marine engineer, MEP since 2004		Committee on Transport and Tourism; Delegation for Relations with the Palestinian Legislative Council	Committee on Employment and Social Affairs; Delegation to the EU–Former Yugoslav Republic of Macedonia Joint Parliamentary Committee; Delegation to the ACP–EU Joint Parliamentary Assembly

(continued)

Table 13.8 (continued)

Name	Date of birth	Professional background	Committee Chairs	Committee membership	Committee substitutes
Syriza (Coalition of Radical Left)					
Chountis, N. Group Bureau Member	17/09/1953	Engineer		Committee on Economic and Monetary Affairs; Special Committee on the Financial, Economic and Social Crisis; Delegation for Relations with Albania, Bosnia and Herzegovina, Serbia, Montenegro and Kosovo	Committee on Foreign Affairs; Subcommittee on Security and Defence; Delegation to the EU-Russia Parliamentary Cooperation Committee; Delegation to the EU–Ukraine Parliamentary Cooperation Committee
Europe of Freedom and Democracy Group					
LAOS (Popular Orthodox Rally)					
Salavrakos, N.	15/02/1946	Lawyer	Vice-Chair: Delegation to the EU–Former Yugoslav Republic of Macedonia Joint Parliamentary Committee	Committee on Foreign Affairs; Committee on Petitions	Committee on Fisheries
Tzavela, N. Group Bureau Member	30/06/1947	N.A.	Vice-Chair: Delegation for Relations with the United States	Committee on Industry, Research and Energy; Special Committee on the Policy Challenges and Budgetary Resources for a sustainable European Union after 2013; Delegation to the EU–Turkey Joint Parliamentary Committee	Delegation for Relations with Israel; Delegation for Relations with the Mashreq countries; Delegation for Relations with the People's Republic of China; Delegation to the Parliamentary Assembly of the Union for the Mediterranean
Group of the Greens/European Free Alliance					
Oikologoi Prasinoi (Ecologist Greens)					
Tremopoulos, M.	03/03/1958	Journalist	Vice-Chair: Committee on Regional Development	Delegation for Relations with Albania, Bosnia and Herzegovina, Serbia, Montenegro and Kosovo	Committee on the Environment, Public Health and Food Safety; Delegation to the EU–Former Yugoslav Republic of Macedonia Joint Parliamentary Committee

Source: www.europarl.europa.eu/meps/en/search.html?country=GR.

Table 13.9 Re-election of Greek MEPs: 1981–2009

	1981*–2009		2009	
	No. of MEPs	No. and % of re-elected MEPs	No. of MEPs	No. and % of re-elected MEPs
PASOK	65	16 (24.6)**	8	2 (25.0)
ND	59	14 (23.7)	8	3 (37.5)
Parties of the Left	21	8 (38.1)	3	1 (3.3)
Parties of the Right	14	1 (7.1)	3	0
Total	159	39 (24.5)	22	7 (31.8)

Source: Greece's Ministry of Home Affairs, www.ypes.gr/el/.

Note:
* The numbers include the MEPs that had been indirectly elected before the first EP direct elections in Greece in 1981.
** Percentages in brackets.

Table 13.10 Greek MEPs by gender: 1981–2009 (%)

Elections	Greece		EC/EU	
	Men	Women	Men	Women
1981 (1979)	92	8	84	16
1984	92	8	82	18
1989	96	4	81	19
1994	84	16	74	26
1999	84	16	70	30
2004	71	29	69	31
2009	68	32	65	35

Source: www.europarl.europa.eu.GR.

9.4 Campaign finance

Political parties in Greece are primarily financed by the state and are exempt from taxation. Special provisions define their financing, whilst spending in electoral campaigns for both parties and their candidates is scrutinized after each election (Law 3023/2002 and its amendments).

The state finances parties represented in the Greek Parliament and/or the EP, as well as parties that participated in the previous elections with candidates in 70 per cent of the electoral constituencies and a vote share of 1.5 per cent or more nationwide. The cost of the electoral campaigns, both for national and EP elections, are covered by the state. There is also additional state financing for party research centres and for any research programmes related to the political personnel of a party. The parties can also be financed from private sources, party members, and/or donors.

Concerns about the accountability and transparency of party accounts have often been voiced. The main political parties present considerable deficits, often resorting to borrowing from the banks and/or getting advance payments from the national budget. The current economic crisis has led to considerations of cutting part of party funding.

10 Theoretical interpretation of Euro-elections

Prior to testing the two theoretical models, it is essential to take into account the main features of the Greek political system which include: (1) the intense electoral competitions between the two governmental parties that are likely to polarize the electorate; (2) the contest between the two main political parties aims at governmental office; (3) the electorate favours one-party governments, with a strong absolute majority in Parliament; (4) the low electoral volatility of the main political parties in national elections; (5) the frequent reforms of the national electoral system and the provisions that privilege the representation of the first political party; (6) the use of proportional representation in Euro-elections; and (7) the absence of a truly fixed four-year parliamentary cycle.

10.1 Second-Order Election theory

For the Second-Order Election (SOE) hypothesis, the model suggests three variables. The first aims to evaluate the effect of the Euro-elections on the party in government. It is a dummy variable, with a value of 1 for the governing party at the time of the Euro-elections and 0 for all the other parties (*Government/Opposition*). The second variable examines the influence of the size of the party on the gains and the losses in the Euro-elections. It is computed in two ways: the first as the percentage of the party in the previous national election (*Party Size 1*); and the second as the ratio of the electoral power of each party in the previous national election to the percentage of the first party of that election, thus its values range from 1, if it equals that of the first party, to 0, if it is a new party (*Party Size 2*). The third variable examines the impact of the timing of the Euro-elections in the governmental cycle (*Government Cycle*). Instead of using a dummy variable, the present model uses a composite one. This has been calculated on the basis of the actual time spans between national elections. Thus, a value of 0 is for cases that the two elections were held at the same time. For the rest, values up to 0.99 are used, according to the actual time span that elapsed between the national and EP elections. Simon Hix and Michael Marsh (2007) used a dummy variable; however, the computation proposed in the present analysis allows for short governmental cycles to be accounted for. With this calculation of the variable, the value for the timing of the 2009 Euro-elections is 0.84 rather than 0.50, if it was computed upon the constitutional provision of a four-year governmental cycle. Although, on a different basis, Jason Koepke and Nils Ringe (2006) have also suggested a calculation of a compound variable for the governmental cycle.

The main patterns of Euro-elections in Greece support the main hypotheses of the SOE model. In particular, there is a great difference in terms of results between national and EP elections, even in cases such as the 1981 and the 1989 Euro-elections that were held at the same time with the national elections. The electoral support for the two main governmental parties declined to the benefit of the smaller ones. Compared to national elections, the turnout in Euro-elections is considerably lower.

It is not uncommon in Greek politics for the main opposition party to maintain some of its gains in the subsequent national election. In this context shifts in party preferences between different types of elections are often difficult to reverse (Mendrinou, 2005). Overall, it is the party in government that suffers the greater losses compared to the main party of the opposition. In this context, the focus of Euro-election campaigns is on domestic rather than on European political issues. Last but not least, the timing of the Euro-elections in the governmental cycle appears to be particularly significant in the Greek case.

10.2 Europe Salience theory

The Europe Salience model is examined through five independent variables. The first concerns the position of a political party towards the EU. This variable uses a ten-point scale, positioning the political parties from 4.5, pro-European, to −4.5, anti-European (*Position EU*).

The second variable seeks to capture the degree of intensity of a party's positioning towards the EU. As proposed by Simon Hix and Michael Marsh (2007), it is calculated on the square value of the difference between the value of the position of a political party towards the EU, the previous variable, and the centre point of the ten-point scale (*Intensity EU*).

The third variable refers to the positioning of the political parties in the left/right scale. It is a ten-point scale, with 4.5 for the extreme right and −4.5 for the extreme left (*Left/Right*). The intensity of this positioning is accounted for as in the case of variable two.

Thus, variable four, measures left/right intensity and is computed as the square value of the difference between the value of the position of a political party in the left/right scale and its centre point (*Intensity L/R*).

Finally, the fifth variable refers to the impact on new political parties that their first participation in elections is in Euro-elections. It is a dummy variable, with a value of 1 for new parties and a value of 0 for old political parties (*New Parties*). The initial Salience theory model incorporates a further variable, that of the Greens; however, in the case of Greece, the number of observations would be so small that it would not allow for valid results.

Though not as apparent, EP elections in Greece also present some features of Europe Salience theory. When the emphasis is on the electoral agenda, the stance of the political parties towards the EU is relatively significant. The positioning of a political party on the political left/right axis considerably influences its Euro-elections results, since to a great extent the party's position influences its stance towards the EU. In the model the negative value of the *Left/Right* variable is due to the structure of the Greek party system, in which it is mainly the small political parties of the left and the centre-left that have presented more endurance and resilience through the elections.

In Greece, volatility in voter preferences in favour of smaller parties suggests elements both of strategic voting, which often concerns EU policy issues, and of protest votes against governmental policies. Hence, arguments on the sincerity of Euro-election voting and/or of elements of strategic voting and retrospective economic voting in the case of Greece seem to gain momentum, particularly if macroeconomic and policy considerations are involved (Cox, 1997; Alesina and Rosenthal, 1995; Kousser, 2004; Mendrinou, 2003; Steenbergen and Scott, 2004).

The 1994 and 2004 Euro-elections are suggestive of this kind of influence and the shift of the electorate towards smaller political parties that presented much more focussed policy-oriented agendas, without altering the first position of the governing party that had recently come into office.

The timing of Euro-elections in the governmental cycle appears to be critical in Greece. The shorter the time elapsing between the two types of elections and the more recent the governmental change, the larger the increase for smaller parties and the smaller the impact on the party in government; the case of 2004 Euro-elections was indicative. Equally, the closer the timing of the EP elections to the subsequent national elections, the more intense the polarization between the governmental parties and/or the more pronounced the decline of the party in government, suggesting voter discontent aimed at the government to modify its policy approach; the 1984 and 1999 Euro-elections were such cases where the governing party remained in power in the next national elections that took place less than a year later.

Table 13.11 Models examining the difference between EP and national election results in Greece

Variables	Model 1	Model 2
Government/opposition	−1.990 (1.080)	
Party size 1	−0.050 (0.246)	
Party size 2	−4.447 (11.128)	
Government cycle	0.096 (0.919)	
Position EU		0.569 (0.189)
Intensity EU		0.033 (0.073)
Left/Right		−0.322 (0.142)
Intensity L/R		0.477 (0.081)
New parties		2.713 (1.025)
Subsequent GE		
R	0.860	0.786
R^2	0.740	0.618
No. of observations	44	44

Note: Standard errors are provided in brackets; significance at 0.5 level; dependent variable *Divergence*.

It may be argued that the patterns discerned in the last seven Euro-elections in Greece suggest that the contests are more akin to the Second-Order Election hypothesis, mainly due to the lack of a widespread contest over the EU. However, the impact of the economic crisis in Greece is so severe that has considerably altered both the country's party system and the political agenda. There is widespread competition over EU policies and politics and considerable changes have been registered in the Greek public's attitude towards the EU.

The Euro-elections results in Greece have been linked to the features of the political system and to the timing of each of the EP contests in the governmental cycle. Depending on domestic political considerations, Euro-elections may streamline political dynamics along particular agendas and/or may diffuse discontent and dissatisfaction. Furthermore they may disseminate shifts in the voters' electoral preferences and may even be able to increase awareness of the public's concerns and preferences, enriching party platforms. Last but not least, this analysis has suggested that the difficulties in founding genuine European political parties may have led to a counter-Europeanization process, since EP competitions have been gradually embedded in national political systems.

References

Primary sources

Eurobarometer Surveys (various) Brussels, European Commission, http://ec.europa.eu//public_opinion/archives/eb_arch_en.htm (accessed on 29 January 2012); http://ec.europa.eu/public_opinion/standard_en.htm (accessed on 29 January 2012).
European Parliament website, www.europarl.europa.eu/ (accessed on 7 December 2013).
Eurostat (2013, 2014) http://epp.eurostat.ec.europa.eu/ (accessed on 5 June 2015).
Greece's Ministry of Home Affairs website, www.ypes.gr/el (accessed on 29 August 2013).
Hellenic Statistical Authority (EL.STAT.), www.statistics.gr/portal/page/portal/ESYE (accessed on 9 February 2012).
Νόμος (3023/2002) Χρηματοδότηση των πολιτικών κομμάτων από το κράτος. Έσοδα και δαπάνες, προβολή, δημοσιότητα και έλεγχος των οικονομικών των πολιτικών κομμάτων και των υποψήφιων

βουλευτών [Law 3023/2002, Financing of the political parties by the state. Revenues and expenditures, promotion, publicity and control of the finance of political parties and candidates] ΦΕΚ (146/25-6-2002, 2867–78).

Secondary sources

Alesina, A. and Rosenthal, H. (1995) *Partisan Politics, Divided Government, and the Economy*, Cambridge, Cambridge University Press.
Castles, S. and Miller, M. J. (2003) *The Age of Migration: International Population Movements in the Modern World*, New York, Guildford, 3rd edn.
Clogg, R. (1982) 'The Greek Elections of 1981', *Electoral Studies*, I, 95–106.
Clogg, R. (1992) *A Concise History of Greece*, Cambridge, Cambridge University Press, 2nd edn.
Clogg, R. (ed.) (1999) *The Greek Diaspora in the Twentieth Century*, London, Palgrave Macmillan.
Cox, G. W. (1997) *Making Votes Count. Strategic Coordination in the World's Electoral Systems*, Cambridge, Cambridge University Press.
Dakin, D. (1972) *The Unification of Greece, 1770–1923*, New York, St Martin's Press.
Dakin, D. (1973) *The Greek Struggle for Independence, 1821–1833*, Berkeley, University of California Press.
Delladetsima, P. and Leontidou, L. (1995) 'Athens', in Berry, J. and McGreal, St. (eds) *European Cities, Planning Systems and Property Markets*, London, Chapman and Hall.
Diamantopoulos, Th. (2001) *Εκλογικά Συστήματα: Θεωρία και Πρακτικές Εφαρμογές*, [Electoral Systems: Theory and Practical Applications], Athens, Patakis.
Fargues, Ph. (2004) 'Arab Migration to Europe: Trends and Policies', *International Migration Review*, 38(4), 1348–71.
Featherstone, K. (ed.) (2005) 'The Challenge of Modernization: Politics and Policy in Greece', Special Issue, *West European Politics*, 28(2).
Freeman, G. P. (2004) 'Immigrant Incorporation in Western Democracies', *International Migration Review*, 38(3), 945–69.
Gunther, R. (2005) 'Parties and Electoral Behavior in Southern Europe', *Comparative Politics*, 37(3), 253–75.
Gunther, R., Diamandouros, P. N. and Puhle, H. J. (eds) (1995) *The Politics of Democratic Consolidation: Southern Europe in Comparative Perspective*, Baltimore, The Johns Hopkins University Press.
Hix, S. and Marsh, M. (2007) 'Punishment or Protest? Understanding European Parliament Elections', *The Journal of Politics*, 69(2), 495–510.
Hoffman, G. W. (1967) 'The Problem of Underdeveloped Regions in Southeast Europe: A Comparative Analysis of Romania, Yugoslavia and Greece', *Annals of the Association of American Geographers*, 57(4), 637–66. Online. Available at: www.indexmundi.com/greece/international_organization_participation.html (accessed on 29 January 2012).
Ioakimidis, P. (1996) *Η Ελλάδα στην Ευρωπαϊκή Ένωση*, [Greece in the European Union] Athens, Papazisis.
Kazakos, P. (1991) *Η Ελλάδα ανάμεσα σε Προσαρμογή και Περιθωριοποίηση: Δοκίμια Ευρωπαϊκής και Οικονομικής Πολιτικής* [Greece between Adjustment and Marginalization: Essays of European and Economic Politics], Athens, Diatton.
Kazakos, P. and Stefanou, K. (eds) (1987) *Η Ελλάδα στην Ευρωπαϊκή Κοινότητα: Η Πρώτη Πενταετία. Τάσεις, Προβλήματα, Προοπτικές* [Greece in the European Community: The First Five Years], Athens, Ant. N. Sakkoulas.
Koepke, J. R. and Ringe, N. (2006) 'The Second-Order Election Model in an Enlarged Europe', *European Union Politics*, 7(3), 321–46.
Kousser, T. (2004) 'Retrospective Voting and Strategic Behavior in European Parliament Elections', *Electoral Studies*, 23, 1–21.
Lavdas, K. A. (1997) *The Europeanization of Greece: Interest Politics and the Crises of Integration*, London, Macmillan.
Lavdas, K. A. and Mendrinou, M. (2013) 'Contentious Europeanization and the Public Mind: Greece in Comparative Perspective', Sklias, P. and Tzifakis, N. (eds) *Greece's Horizons: Reflecting on the Country's Assets and Capabilities*, Heidelberg, Springer.
Leontidou, L. (1990) *The Mediterranean City in Transition: Social Change and Urban Development*, Cambridge, Cambridge University Press.
Lijphart, A. (1994) *Electoral Systems and Party Systems. A Study of Twenty-Seven Democracies, 1945–1990*, Oxford, Oxford University Press.

McCabe, I. B., Harlaftis, G. and Pepelasis-Minoglou, I. (eds) (2005) *Diaspora Entrepreneurial Networks. Four Centuries of History*, Oxford, Berg.
Mendrinou, M. (2000) *Η Εκλογική Πολιτική στο Ελληνικό Πολιτικό Σύστημα: Εσωτερικές και Εξωτερικές Παράμετροι, 1974–2000* [The Electoral Policy in the Greek Political System: Internal and External Parameters, 1974–2000], Athens, Papazisis.
Mendrinou, M. (2003) 'Στρατηγικές Ψήφου και Εκλογικός Ανταγωνισμός στο Ελληνικό Πολιτικό Σύστημα', [Strategic Vote and Electoral Competition in the Greek Political System], *Tetradia Politikis Epistimis*, 2, 5–31.
Mendrinou, M. (2005) 'Εκλογικοί Ανταγωνισμοί, Κομματικά Συστήματα και ο Θεσμός των Ευρωεκλογών: Συγκριτική Ανάλυση των Ευρωεκλογών του 2004', [Electoral Competitions, Political Parties and the Institution of European Elections], *Politiki Epistimi*, 1, 52–75.
Meynaud, J. (2002a) *Οι Πολιτικές Δυνάμεις στην Ελλάδα, 1946–1965* [The Political Forces in Greece, 1946–1965] vol. A, Athens, Savvalas.
Meynaud, J. (2002b) *Οι Πολιτικές Δυνάμεις στην Ελλάδα: Βασιλική Εκτροπή και Στρατιωτική Δικτατορία*, [The Political Forces in Greece: Royal coup d'etat and Military Dictatorship] vol. B, Athens, Savvalas.
O'Donnell, G., Schmitter, Ph. C. and Whitehead, L. (eds) (1986) *Transitions from Authoritarian Rule: Southern Europe*, Baltimore, The Johns Hopkins University Press.
Pridham, G. (ed.) (1984) *The New Mediterranean Democracies: Regime Transition in Spain, Greece and Portugal*, London, Frank Cass.
Steenbergen, M. R. and Scott, D. F. (2004) 'Contesting Europe? The Salience of European Integration as a Party Issue', in Marks, G. and Steenbergen, M. R. (eds) *European Integration and Political Conflict*, Cambridge, Cambridge University Press, 165–92.
Taylor, E. J., Arango, J., Hugo, G., Kouaouci, A., Massey, D. S. and Pellegrino, A. (1996) 'International Migration and National Development', *Population Index*, 62(2), 181–212.
Tziovas, D. (ed.) (2009) *Greek Diaspora and Migration since 1700*, London, Ashgate.
Varvaressos, K. (2002) *Εκθεσις επί του Οικονομικού Προβλήματος της Ελλάδος* – 1952 [Report on the Economic Problem of Greece – 1952] Lykoyiannis A. (ed.), Athens, Savvalas.

14
SPAIN

José M. Magone

Figure 14.1 Map of Spain

Table 14.1 Spain profile

EU entry year	1986 ECSC, EEC and Euratom
Schengen entry year	1991
MEPs elected in 2009	50
MEPs under Lisbon Treaty	Four additional seats since 1 December 2011 allocated to Eva Ortiz Vilella (EPP), Salvador Sedó I Alabart (EPP) Vicente Miguel Garcés Ramón (S&D), Dolores García-Hierro Caraballo (S&D)
Capital	Madrid
Total area★	505,970 km²
Population	46,512,199
	Galicians, Basques and Catalans: 10.2%; foreign population including 13.9% Romanians, 12.4% Moroccans and 8.1% Ecuadorians
Population density★★	92.9/km²
Median age of population	41.8
Political system	Constitutional Monarchy
Head of state	King Juan Carlos I (November 1975–June 2014)
Head of government	José Luis Zapatero, Spanish Socialist Workers' Party (PSOE) (March 2004–December 2011); Mariano Rajoy, People's Party (PP) (January 2012–)
Political majority	Spanish Socialist Workers' Party (PSOE) (March 2004–December 2011); People's Party (PP) (December 2011–)
Currency	Euro (€) since 1999
Prohead GDP in PPS	22,800 €

Source: Eurostat, 2013, 2014, http://epp.eurostat.ec.europa.eu/.

Notes:
★ Total area including inland waters.
★★ Population density: the ratio of the annual average population of a region to the land area of the region.

1 Geographical position

Spain is the second largest country in the European Union in terms of area. It is located on the south-western part of the Mediterranean, covering a large territory that runs from the Pyrenées in the north to Gibraltar in the south-west. Spain also includes the island archipelago of the Baleares in the Mediterranean and the Canary islands off the African coast in the Atlantic Ocean. Moreover, two enclaves called Ceuta and Melilla can be found on the northern coast of Morocco. The Moroccan government has been attempting to reclaim these two enclaves, but they so far remain an integral part of Spain. Another disputed area is Gibraltar, which is 5 kilometres long and just over 1 kilometre wide and has been an overseas territory of the United Kingdom since 1713. However, in recent years diplomacy between the two countries and Gibraltar have regained momentum, so that the around 29,000 inhabitants are able to profit from better access to Spanish infrastructure. A referendum in 2002 led to overwhelming support for the status quo, namely Gibraltar as a British overseas territory.

Spain is not a homogenous country in terms of population, it is a gathering of different 'nations': the Galicians in the north-west, the Basques in the north, and the Catalans in the north-east. Other parts of the country, like the Valencian community and the Baleares, speak similar languages to Catalan, but, unlike in Catalonia, there is no strong nationalist movement. Politically, Spain defines itself as a 'state of autonomies', meaning that it is a regionalized unitary state. Between 1979 and 1983, other regions declared their will to become autonomous as well, so that in the end this dynamic process led to the emergence of 17 autonomous regions.

The Spanish population has been growing considerably due to the influx of immigrants coming from North Africa, and in particular those from Morocco; from South America, especially Ecuador and Colombia; and from Central and Eastern Europe, particularly Romania.

2 Historical background

Before Spain was founded as a state, there were several kingdoms on the Iberian peninsula, including the Portuguese one. However, in 1469 the strategic marriage between Ferdinand II of Aragón and Isabella of Castile led to the union of their kingdoms and the building of the core of Spain. Throughout the rest of the fifteenth century, the royal couple was engaged in conquering new territories, particularly in the south, which were still dominated by Arab caliphates. Although there was a unification of the crowns, the two regions were characterized by a high level of diversity both between and inside each one of them. For example, Aragón included also Catalonia and Valencia, which had quite different cultures and also a high level of political autonomy. The so-called Catholic Monarchs (*Reyes Catolicos*) were instrumental in pushing back Arab dominance in southern Spain. In 1492, they were able to capture the important city of Granada.

After the Napoleonic Wars, Spain restored its absolutist monarchy under Ferdinand VII. However, the bourgeoisie, influenced by liberalism, tried to democratize the political system. Throughout the nineteenth century, there were several periods of civil war between Conservative and Liberal Forces, which led even to the proclamation of a short lived First Republic in 1873. After that date, a two-party constitutional monarchy with quite restricted suffrage was established. The so-called '*turno pacifico*' ('peaceful replacement in government') was based on a highly clientelistic system dominated by the political parties in power. This quite stable political system also allowed for a quite stable economic period for Spain. The whole system began to have problems in the late nineteenth and early twentieth century with the rise of other social movements, such as the Socialist Party. Therefore in 1923, Miguel Primo de Rivera introduced after a *coup d'état* a dictatorship in Spain that lasted until 1931. The Second Republic was proclaimed. In spite of many social and political hopes associated with the introduction of the Second Republic, the whole period until 1936 was characterized by political instability and a radicalization of parties on both the left and the right. In 1936, General Francisco Franco carried out a *coup d'état* against the left-wing government of the Republic. This triggered a bloody civil war until 1939 in which the Axis Powers, Germany and Italy, intervened in favour of Franco. The final defeat of the Republican forces in 1939 opened a long period of totalitarian government and austere economic autarchy.

On 20 November 1975, after the death of Franco, the 'agreed break' ('*ruptura pactada*') between old and new political elites led to a peaceful transition to democracy, which fulfilled the main condition for becoming a member of the EC. On 28 July 1977, Foreign Minister Marcelino Oreja Aguirre submitted the application for EC membership. Negotiations started at the end of 1978, but lasted almost eight years. The main reason was that the French government objected to Spanish membership due to competition coming from the agricultural sector. Only a meeting between Prime Minister Felipe González and French President François Mitterrand in 1984 allowed for a continuation of negotiations. The Treaty of Accession was signed on 10 June 1985 and Spain became member of the EC on 1 January 1986.

3 Geopolitical profile

Like all other EU countries, Spain is member of the United Nations, the International Monetary Fund, and the World Bank. And yet, in spite of being the twelfth largest economy in the world, Spain is not represented in the G20. Whereas it was a long-standing military ally of the United

States even during the Franco regime, it joined the North Atlantic Treaty Organization (NATO) only in 1982, after its democratic transition. The main geopolitical interests of Spain focus on the Mediterranean and Latin America. Spain is engaged in the Ibero-American Summits with Latin American and Portuguese leaders, which started in 1991 and subsequently developed into a more institutionalized event.

4 Overview of the political landscape

Spain is a constitutional monarchy with the head of state, currently King Juan Carlos II, holding mainly formal powers. Legislative power is exercised by a bicameral asymmetrical parliament, the so-called *Cortes*. The *Congreso de Deputados,* the Chamber of Deputies, consists of 350 MPs, whilst the *Senado,* the Senate, gathers a variable number of members according to the population in each region, reaching 263 in 2012. Whereas most of them are elected, the rest are nominated by the 17 regional chambers. The Chamber of Deputies represents the central place of decision-making, whilst the Senate just confirms, but has no power to reject legislation. The Spanish Prime Minister has quite a strong position in the political system. Moreover, the Prime Minister is protected by the so-called constructive motion of censure, which forces the opposition to present an alternative candidate, should they introduce such a parliamentary argument.

Between 2004 and 2011, Spain was ruled by a Socialist minority government under Prime Minister José Luis Zapatero. In 2008, the finance and sovereign debt crisis hit the Spanish economy severely, in particular a large part of the banking sector that had invested in the speculative housing market. Whilst in its first term, Zapatero's government tried to introduce policies to reform the political system, particularly in centre–periphery relations, and to complete the separation of church and state by reducing the power of the Catholic Church in education, the second term was characterized by economic crisis management. The financial crisis led to an increase in unemployment to over 20 per cent in 2009 and 2010.

5 Brief account of the political parties

The present Spanish party system emerged after the death of dictator Francisco Franco in 1975 and took until 1982 to consolidate itself. The consolidation of the party system took place after the 1982 general elections, when the vote of the Union of the Democratic Centre, UCD (*Unión del Centro Democratico*), a centrist party of transition which in reality was a coalition of a substantial number of Christian-Democratic, Liberal, and Social Democratic parties, collapsed and its voters either switched to the Socialists or the Conservative People's Alliance, AP (Gunther and Hopkin, 2002). Since then, there have been two main large national parties and two smaller ones, along with about ten regional parties.

Founded in 1879, the *Partido Socialista Obrero Español*, PSOE (the Spanish Socialist Workers' Party) has a long tradition that goes back to the nineteenth century. During Franco's era, the PSOE was in exile and in the 1970s one part of the PSOE, under the leadership of Felipe González and Alfonso Guerra, engaged in fighting against the dictatorship. This historical legacy allowed the PSOE to inherit some of the historical vote passed on from the older to the younger generation. Over the past three decades, the PSOE has been in power as a single-party government for 19 years, by representing the dominant party on the Spanish political stage (Mendez Lago, 2000; Mendez Lago, 2005).

The *Partido Popular,* PP (People's Party) emerged out of the more reformist wing of the former authoritarian regime around Manuel Fraga Iribarne. Its founding party conference was in 1976, after the law of political associations was approved by the *Cortes*. Originally, the party was called the People's Alliance and had major difficulties in establishing itself due to its connection to the former authoritarian regime. Manuel Fraga Iribarne, a former minister of the authoritarian regime, had difficulties in competing with the other parties due to this historical legacy. Between 1976 and 1989, AP was not able to challenge the PSOE. It achieved only about 25 per cent of the vote and this was referred as '*el techo de Fraga*' ('the ceiling of Fraga') (Hopkin, 1999, 222). However, after 1989, Manuel Fraga Iribarne rejuvenated the party through the election of José Maria Aznar as leader. The name of the party changed from AP to PP and he introduced major changes in the programme and in the party structure in order to compete with PSOE. The Aznar reforms led to a substantial increase in the vote, challenging the PSOE in 1993, and then in the 1996 general elections. In the 1996 general elections the PP surpassed the PSOE by 1 per cent. In spite of this tendency to conceptualize Spain as a unitary country, Spain had to be flexible in this position and finally accept the state of autonomies. This led to a minority, single-party government supported by the regionalist party in the *Cortes*, in particular the Catalan *Convergencia i Unió*, CiU (Party Convergence and Union). Between 2000 and 2004, Prime Minister José Maria Aznar governed with an absolute majority (Ramiro Fernandez, 2005; Balfour, 2007).

Established after 1986, the *Izquierda Unida United Left*, IU (United Left) is a Communist-led coalition including Green and other small left-wing parties. One of the reasons for the coalition was the declining fortunes of the *Partido Comunista Español*, PCE (Spanish Communist Party). From 1989 to 1996, the IU got about 9 to 10 per cent of the vote, but then, since 2000, its share of the vote declined to below 5 per cent. After the last general elections of 2008, it struggled to put a parliamentary group together. It had to create a parliamentary group with left-wing, small, regionalist parties the *Esquerra Republicana Catalana*, ERC (Catalan Republican Left) and the *Iniciativa para Cataluña-Verdes*, IC-V (Initiative for Catalonia-Greens, IC-V) (Magone, 2009a, 164–7, 187).

In the 2008 general elections, a new small political party loomed on the national horizon, called *Unión Progreso y Democracia* UPyD (Union Progress and Democracy). This centre-left party, founded by a former member of the Socialist party, Rosa Díez, opposes any form of asymmetrical 'federalism' or regionalization. To a certain extent, UPyD combines elements of the PSOE on the left–right ideological spectrum and the centre–periphery positions of the PP.

Depending on the legislature, there are ten to 12 regionalist parties represented in Parliament. In 2008, the two main parties took 80.3 per cent of the vote, whilst all regionalist parties just accounted for 10.71 per cent of the vote and 25 seats. However, they may play an important role in government formation, because none of the major parties wants to form a coalition with the IU. One also has to differentiate between regionalist-nationalist and regionalist parties. Regionalist nationalist parties can be found mainly in the historical regions of Catalonia, the Basque Country, and Galicia. They normally advocate either independence or request more competencies and a further evolution of the state of autonomies to fully-fledged federalism. Some of them are quite strong and are well represented in both houses of Parliament. The four more important regionalist-nationalist parties are the CiU, the ERC, the *Partido Nacionalista Vasco* PNV (Basque Nationalist Party) and the *Bloco Nacionalista Galego* BNG (Nationalist Galician Bloc).

Finally, there are the regionalist parties which, unlike the regionalist-nationalist ones, represent the interests of a particular region without putting the present state of autonomies into question. Amongst them, there is the *Coalición Canaria*, CC (Canary Coalition), consisting of several smaller parties from the Canary islands.

The regionalized nature of the Spanish party system led to a multilevel electoral governance system that does not include just the national and the local, but also the regional level. Over the past three decades, a regionalization of the main national parties has taken place, meaning that the PSOE, the PP, and the IU have created their respective regional political parties, giving them some degree of autonomy. Simultaneously, regionalist-nationalists have become more involved at national level, sometimes influencing the governmental constellation (Oñate and Rubalcaba, 2006, 419).

Table 14.2 List of political parties in Spain

Original name	Abbreviation	English translation
Alternativa Española	AES	Spanish Alternative
Andecha Astur	AA	The Left of Asturias
Centro Democratico y Social	CDS	Democratic Social Centre
Coalición por Europa	CpE	Coalition for Europe
Democracia Nacional	DN	National Democracy
Europa de los Pueblos–Verdes	EP–V	Europe of the Peoples–The Greens
Frente Nacional	FN	National Front
Iniciativa Feminista	IF	Feminist Initiative
Iniciativa Internacionalista–Solidariedad entre los Pueblos	II	Internationalist Initiative–Solidarity between Peoples
Izquierda Anticapitalista–Revolta Global	IZAN–RG	Anticapitalist Left–Global Revolt
Izquierda Unida–Iniciativa Per Catalunya Verds–Esquerra Unida I Alternativa-Bloque Por Asturies: La Izquierda	IU–ICV–EUIA–BA	United Left–Initiative for Catalonia–The Greens–United Left and Alternative–Bloc for Asturias: The Left
Centro Democratico Liberal	CDL	Democratic Liberal Centre
Extremadura Unida	EXTREMADURA	United Extremadura
Falange Autentica	FA	Authentic Phalanx
Falange Española de las Jons	FE de las JONS	Spanish Phalanx of the Jons
Libertas–Ciudadanos de España	LIBERTAS	Libertas–Citizens of Spain
Los Verdes–Grupo Verde Europeo	LV–GVE	The Greens–European Green Group
Movimiento Social Republicano	MSR	Social Republican Movement
Partido Antitaurino Contra el Maltrato Animal	PACMA	Anti-Bull Party Against Animal Maltreatment
Partido Comunista de Los Pueblos	PCPE	Communist Party of the Peoples of Spain
Partido Familia y Vida	PFYV	Party Family and Life
Partido Humanista	PH	Humanist Party
Partido Popular	PP	People's Party
Partido Socialista de Andalucia	PSA	Socialist Party of Andalucia
Partido Socialista Obrero Español	PSOE	Spanish Socialist Workers' Party
Partido Obrero Socialista Internacionalista	POSI	Internationalist Socialist Workers' Party
Partit Republica Catala	PRC	Republican Catalan Party
Salamanca–Zamora–León	PREPAL	Salamanca–Zamora–León
Solidaridad y Autogestion Internacionalista	SAIN	Solidarity and Internationalist Self-Management
Por Un Mundo Más Justo	PUM+J	For a More Just World
Unidá Nacionalista Asturiana	UNA	Nationalist Asturian Union
Unificacion Comunista de España	UCE	Communist Unification of Spain
Union Centrista Liberal	UCL	Centrist Liberal Union
Unión Progreso y Democracia	UPyD	Union of Progress and Democracy
Unió Valenciana	UV	Valencian Union

Whilst in the 1980s, the Spanish party system was dominated by the PSOE, which had no real competitor, since the transition period between 1993 and 2000, it has evolved to a quasi-perfect bipolarism defined by Jonathan Hopkin as an 'adulterated two-party system', dominated by the PSOE and the PP, and unchallenged by the small regionalist-nationalist and regionalist parties (Hopkin, 2005).

5.1 Party attitudes towards the European Union

Since the transition to democracy, the Spanish elite has been committed to European integration, in spite of some occasional disadvantages for the country (Alvarez-Miranda, 1996). This consensus amongst the main political parties has remained more or less intact, although today the positions between the political parties are certainly more differentiated.

The PSOE wants to be strongly involved in the European integration process and has been instrumental in supporting most of the integration initiatives, like Economic Monetary Union and the European Constitution. The party regards further European integration as intertwined with Spanish national interest, and its leaders endeavour to be at the heart of the European integration process by always supporting the efforts of the Franco-German axis. In particular, Prime Minister José Luis Zapatero was one of the strongest allies of Chancellor Angela Merkel in reviving the European Constitution, which eventually led to the signing of the Lisbon Treaty during the German presidency in the first semester of 2007.

By contrast, the PP is less pro-active in pushing European integration, therefore its leaders tend to emphasize the national interest, particularly in budgetary terms and over structural funds. This big difference over the perception of action in Europe has become more reinforced over time. Its climax became evident between 1996 and 2004, during Prime Minister José Maria Aznar's government, and in particular during the negotiations over the Constitutional Treaty in 2003 and early 2004. Within the European Parliament, the *Partido Popular* is integrated in the European People's Party. The UPyD shares a pro-European outlook, whilst the IU presents a Eurocritical approach, even if it does not reject the European Union, but wants to move more towards a social Europe. Finally, most of the small regionalist parties support the European integration project.

6 Public opinion and the European Union

Spain is one of the most Europhile countries in the European Union and its citizens have been amongst the most loyal supporters of European integration in both good and bad times.

Between 1986 and 1996, Spanish support for and perception of benefit from EU membership swung between above and below the EU average. However, since 1996, one can see a consistent trend towards support for the EU and the Spanish public's perception of membership is above the EU average.

Table 14.3 Spanish attitude to the European Union

	EB53 (2000)	EB55 (2001)	EB57 (2002)	EB59 (2003)	EB61 (2004)	EB63 (2005)	EB65 (2006)	EB67 (2007)	EB69 (2008)	EB71 (2009)	EB73 (2010)	EB75 (2011)
Spain	67	57	66	62	64	66	72	73	65	71	59	55
EU-average	49	48	53	54	48	54	55	57	52	53	49	47

Source: Eurobarometer, http://ec.europa.eu/public_opinion/index_en.htm.

Table 14.4 Perceived benefit of EU membership in Spain (%)

	EB53 (2000)	EB55 (2001)	EB57 (2002)	EB59 (2003)	EB61 (2004)	EB63 (2005)	EB65 (2006)	EB67 (2007)	EB69 (2008)	EB71 (2009)	EB73 (2010)	EB75 (2011)
Spain	66	54	63	62	69	69	71	75	66	70	60	59
EU-average	47	45	51	50	47	55	54	59	54	56	53	52

Source: Eurobarometer, http://ec.europa.eu/public_opinion/index_en.htm.
Note: * positive answers.

In spite of the economic and financial crisis, Spain remains in favour of European Union. This became quite evident in the referendum on the European Constitutional Treaty on 20 February 2005, in which 76.7 per cent voted 'Yes'.

7 National and EP electoral systems

Spanish MPs are elected by a proportional representation system using the d'Hondt method. The small size of the 50 constituencies in Continental Spain, the islands and Ceuta and Melilla, in which a very small number of seats are elected, leads to a strengthening of the larger political parties and to the disadvantage of the smaller ones. Only a highly concentrated vote in one particular part of the country can circumvent these dynamics, thus the system favours the regionalist-nationalist as well as regionalist parties. Moreover, there is no preferential voting or attachment to constituency, everything is done by closed lists selected by the political parties' central offices with some input from the regions.

The Spanish electoral system is one of the most disproportional in the European Union, just surpassed by the majoritarian ones of the United Kingdom and France. One of the features of the Spanish electoral system is that there is a high level of malapportionment, whereas in some provinces the threshold for the number of votes to elect an MP is quite low, in others it is quite high, creating inequalities across the territory (Hopkin, 2008).

As in general elections, EP contests use a similar proportional representation system based on the d'Hondt method. The only difference is that all 50 MEPs are elected in one large constituency. There are no electoral consequences for the larger parties, however the smaller parties stand a better chance if they coalesce with other smaller parties (Montero and Cordero, 2009). Such electoral coalitions happened normally amongst the regionalist-nationalist and regionalist parties. However, the IU had to coalesce with other smaller left-wing parties from Catalonia and other regions in order to increase their chances of returning representatives to the European Parliament. In accordance with the Treaty of Lisbon, the number of Spanish MEPs has increased from 50 to 54.

8 A glance at the EP and national elections

The first Spanish Members of the European Parliament were appointed soon after accession to the European Community on 1 January 1986. One and half years later, the first EP elections took place in Spain, registering a quite high electoral turnout of 68.5 per cent. In the subsequent elections of 1989, turnout declined to 54.7 per cent to rise again to 59.1 per cent and 63 per cent in 1994 and 1999, respectively. In the elections of 2004, this upward trend decreased abruptly to 45.1 per cent. In this sense, the European Parliament elections could be seen not only as second-order elections, but also as fourth-order elections in terms of their importance after national, regional, and local elections (Magone, 2009b, 176–92).

Table 14.5 Turnout at EP elections in Spain: 1987–2009 (%)

	1987	1989	1994	1999	2004	2009
Abstention	31.3	45.2	40.4	35.7	54.0	54.0
Turnout	**68.7**	**54.8**	**59.6**	**64.3**	**46.0**	**46.0**

Sources: Spain's Ministry of Home Affairs, http://www.mir.es; http://www.europarl.eu.

There are two main periods in the electoral dynamics of the European Parliament elections in Spain. In the first period, between 1987 and 1989, there is almost no dynamic in relation to the proposed working hypothesis presented in this volume. One of the main reasons is that the Socialist Party was over-dominant in the party system. The dominance of the PSOE in the party system of the 1980s was a major problem for the other political parties, particularly the second largest party, the Conservative People's Alliance, which was under the leadership of Manuel Fraga Iribarne and later on Antonio Hernández Mancha. The People's Alliance remained, as in national, regional, and local elections, from 15 to 20 percentage points behind the Socialist Party. The third largest party, the liberal *Centro Democratico y Social* CDS (Democratic Social Centre), was a major factor in undermining the position of the second largest party. The Communist left, the IU, recently set up, was never seen as an alternative to the PSOE. All other parties were smaller regionalist and regionalist-nationalist parties, so they did not affect the party system very much.

The second period since 1987 was characterized by the so-called 'adulterated bipolarized party system'. One of the main factors was that after 1989, José Maria Aznar changed the structure of the People's Alliance and renamed it the People's Party. This rejuvenation allowed for an increase in the electoral fortunes of the party. Within three years, PP was able to challenge the Socialists. Since then, we also have a highly polarized two-party system in European elections. The electoral dynamics are interdependent with the other electoral cycles and government policy.

All political parties were extremely supportive of the European integration process in the 1987 and 1989 elections. In 1987, the Socialist Party was very keen to present the EP elections as independent from national politics, whilst the other political parties clearly had campaigns addressing the policies of the government. One of the leitmotifs of the People's Alliance campaign was that the Socialist Party did not negotiate the accession of Spain into the EC well. In particular, this argument was presented by head of list Manuel Fraga Iribarne. The 1987 elections reproduced more or less the results of the 1986 general elections. The only difference was that the PSOE lost about five points in relation to the European elections, achieving 39.1 per cent of the vote and 28 seats and the People's Alliance lost 1.5 per cent, getting 24.6 per cent of the vote and 17 seats. The third largest party became the Democratic Social Centre of former Prime Minister Adolfo Suárez, with 10.3 per cent and 7 seats. The United Left, which emerged in the 1986 legislative elections and was a Communist left-wing coalition of smaller parties, came in fourth with 5.2 per cent and 3 seats. Smaller regionalist-nationalist parties were also able to achieve representation. The Catalan CiU became the fifth largest party, with 4.4 per cent of the vote and 4 seats. Furthermore, *Herri Batasuna*, the political arm of the Basque separatist organization *Euskadi ta Askatasuna*, ETA (Basque Country and Freedom) got 1.87 per cent and 1 seat, and the Coalition of Europe of the Peoples (*Coalición de Europa de los Pueblos*), which was an electoral coalition of the Basque Left, EA (*Euskadiko Askartasuna*), Catalan Republican Left, and the Nationalist Galician Party, got 1.7 per cent and 1 seat.

The context of the 1989 European Parliament elections was characterized by a growing weariness of the PSOE government and media reports of several corruption scandals involving leading Socialist Party members. The campaign and elections took place at the end of a governmental period cycle and were regarded by some parties, like the Catalan CiU, as primaries for the legislative elections that would take place in October of the same year. The campaign was more polarized between the ruling Socialist government and the opposition parties on the left and right. The People's Party was involved in a major modernization and rejuvenation process, however this process had barely started. The PP also worked closely with the liberal CDS of former Prime Minister Adolfo Suarez. Both parties were submitting anti-corruption motions at the regional and national parliaments. This was also used as part of a campaign strategy to improve their electoral fortunes in relation to the Socialist Party. On the left, the Socialist Party had to deal with a more popular United Left (IU) under the leadership of Julio Anguita. The ruling Socialist Party used a populist message to rally its supporters: if they did not vote for the PSOE, then the right would return again. By working together, the PP and CDS clearly helped to bring the message across. Amongst the regionalist-nationalist parties there was a general realignment leading to the emergence of new coalitions like the *Izquierda de los Pueblos* (Left of the Peoples) consisting of the Galician PNG, the ERC, and the *Coalición de los Pueblos* (Coalition of Peoples) consisting of the more right-centre regionalist-nationalist parties. Other groups were the *Coalición Nacionalista* Nationalist Coalition, CN – the political group around businessman José Maria Ruiz Mateos who was the owner of a major entrerprise called Rumasa, which was in financial trouble and allegedly practiced some creative accounting to disguise it. Therefore, the government nationalized the enterprise and, after a trial, he was put in jail for tax evasion and fraud. Other groups were *Herri Batasuna*, the political arm of ETA, and the Andalucian Party. In total 32 parties took part in these elections.

In spite of being in power for over six years, the Socialist Party was able to win the elections with 39.6 per cent and 27 seats, just one seat less than in the 1987 elections. In contrast, the PP lost more than three percentage points and 2 seats, achieving then 21.4 per cent and 15 seats. The CDS of former Prime Minister Adolfo Suarez also lost over three percentage points and 2 seats, getting then 7.1 per cent and 5 seats. The Communist-led United Left was able to improve and get 6.0 per cent and 4 seats. The big surprise was the electoral party centred around the businessman Ruiz-Mateos (*Agrupación Ruiz Mateos*), with 3.8 per cent of the vote and 2 seats. CiU got 4.2 per cent and 2 seats; CN got 1.9 per cent and 1 seat; the Andalucian Party won 1.9 per cent and 1 seat; the Left of the Peoples got 1.8 per cent and 1 seat; *Herri Batasuna* received 1.7 per cent and 1 seat; and For Europe of the Peoples achieved 1.5 per cent and 1 seat. The 1989 elections showed that regionalist-nationalist parties formed national electoral coalitions in order to overcome their disadvantages in relation to the single constituency for the whole of Spain. In terms of electoral dynamics, there was almost no change between the main party and the opposition, on the contrary the second largest party even lost more than the main party.

Between 1989 and 1996, the Spanish party system changed considerably. The Socialists were affected by weariness due to their longevity in government and a growing number of corruption scandals. At some stage, the party was labelled as 'Corrupsoe'.

In the June 1993 legislative elections, the party was able to win the elections by just 4 per cent in relation to the PP. New PP Leader, José Maria Aznar had rejuvenated the party and moved ideologically to the centre. Due to the new young leadership, PSOE had difficulties in connecting the PP to the authoritarian past. After the 1993 legislative elections, the PSOE was dependent on the support of the nationalist-regionalist Catalan Convergence and Union (CiU). The tension between PP and CiU was quite considerable after these elections, because CiU gave a lifeline to the ailing Socialist government. The 1994 European Parliament elections took place one year after the legislative elections.

For the first time, the EP elections became an important test for the popularity of the Socialist government. For the PP, this was an opportunity to achieve early elections if PSOE's vote declined considerably. In terms of the political campaign, PSOE clearly emphasized its pro-European credentials and its experience achieved over the years. The PP campaign combined both alternatives to the PSOE on questions related to the European Union and a permanent critique of the Socialist government. It was a very detailed 64-page programme, which clearly wanted to bring across the message that the PP was a credible alternative, with different policies than the incumbent party. For the first time, there was a Second-Order Electoral dynamic at play. The weakening of the Socialist government and the ascendancy of the PP as an alternative made these elections quite crucial for the ambitions of the second largest party. Moreover, PSOE was also under pressure from the left. The corruption scandals and the abandonment of left-wing policies were leading to a strengthening of the Communist-led United Left. Already, in the 1989 and 1993 national elections, IU had achieved almost 10 per cent of the vote. Due to voter abstention and growing discontent with the PSOE, it was possible that IU could improve on its share of the vote. The ascendancy of the PP came at the cost of the liberal CDS, which collapsed in the 1993 national elections. In this new situation, it was difficult for the smaller regionalist–nationalist parties to repeat the results of 1989. Only CiU, CN, and the Coalition of Europe of the Peoples had a realistic chance of getting representation. The results of the European Parliament elections of 1994 were a turning point for the Spanish party system. PSOE had lost heavily since 1989. It lost almost 10 percentage points and 5 seats, achieving 30.7 per cent and 22 seats. In contrast, PP increased from a low figure of 21.7 per cent to 40.2 per cent and improved from 15 to 28 seats. This was a major victory for the party. The United Left also improved considerably, from 6.2 to 13.5 per cent and from 4 to 9 seats. CiU was able to improve slightly to 4.7 per cent and 3 seats, a gain of 1 seat. Last but not least, amongst the smaller regionalist–nationalist parties only CN was able to get representation in the EP, with 2.8 per cent and 2 seats. The 1994 elections are therefore a turning point for the electoral dynamics of European Parliament elections in Spain. For the first time, a party in government was heavily punished for its policies and corruption scandals. Moreover, the EP elections confirmed the trend towards rejuvenation and the success of the People's Party. Two years later, the PP won the legislative elections by 1 per cent over the PSOE and formed a government with parliamentary support from several regionalist–nationalist parties, including the CiU. The growing importance of these small parties in the case of a lack of an absolute majority by major parties also became an important feature of party politics in Spain.

In the 1999 EP election, 36 political parties took part, but as in previous elections, just a few political formations were able to achieve representation. The political campaign was a two-horse race between PP and PSOE. Since the 1994 European Parliament elections, there had been an alternation in power. The PP was the incumbent in power and the PSOE was the main opposition party. Between 1996 and 1999, the United Left had been losing support according to the opinion polls, so that this reinforced the bipolarization of the party system even more. The PP was very keen to present the image that it professionally managed the economy and politics, both nationally as well as in Europe. The head of the list was Ignacia Loyola de Palacio, the then agriculture minister, who was well known for being a staunch defender of national interests in this sector. This was also the image that the PP was trying to bring across, that it was the party that always had the Portuguese interest at heart. The position of the PP was boosted by a booming economy and successful reforms in the labour market, which were negotiated with social partners (Sampedro, 2000).

The PSOE was in a period of transition. PSOE's new leader, Joaquin Almunia, was not very charismatic and was weakened after the party primaries that took place to elect the main candidate for Prime Minister in the legislative elections of 2000. He lost the primaries to the Catalan Josep Borrell. Up until one month before the EP elections, this dual leadership created major problems for the party and particularly for Almunia as Secretary-General. However, one month before the EP elections, Borrell had to resign due to a financial scandal involving his wife's firm. At the head of PSOE's list was Rosa Díez. Retired Prime Minister Felipe González, who was able always to rally the electorate, was a major asset during the campaigns. Rosa Diez was quite successful in bringing her message across to the young people and the abstentionists. Using the slogan 'With you' (*Contigo*), the party wanted to emphasize the different Socialist subculture and the necessity to stick together in relation to the more conservative subculture of the People's Party (Sampedro, 2000, 154). There was also a discussion going on about an eventual pact with the IU, but this was discarded as not a very good option. The opinion polls predicted a decline of the share of the vote for IU. The main issue of the IU campaign was its critique of the Kosovo War and the role that former Socialist Minister of Defence Javier Solana played as Secretary-General of NATO. He was accused of being a war criminal because he allowed the bombardment of Serbia. The position of the IU was one-sided and supportive of the Serbian regime of Slobodan Milošević against NATO (Sampedro, 2000, 156–7).

For Prime Minister Aznar, this was a test before the legislative elections scheduled for the year after. The results of the European Parliament elections in 1999 gave further evidence of a stable bipolarization between the two main parties, whilst the IU lost considerably in relation to 1994 and the legislative elections of 1996; it was the main loser of the elections. In detail, the PP was able to almost repeat its electoral success of 1994 with 39.7 per cent of the vote, but with 27 seats, one seat less, whilst the PSOE improved by five percentage points to 35.3 per cent and 24 seats, two more than in the previous elections. In contrast, IU lost two-thirds of its share of the vote and got 4.4 per cent and 3 seats. The 1999 EP elections were also quite positive for the small regionalist-nationalist parties. CiU achieved 3.2 per cent and 2 seats, CN got 2.9 per cent and 2 seats, the Nationalist Galician Bloc (BNG) received 1.6 per cent and 1 seat, and *Euskal Herritarok*, the renamed political arm of ETA, won 1.4 per cent and 1 seat.

The dominance of the PP in the party system was partly due to its moderation towards the centre-right, and also partly due to the weakness of the PSOE, which was not able to present itself as an alternative. The good economic situation clearly was an important factor in the strengthening of the PP. In the 2000 elections, the PP got an absolute majority and was then free to govern without the support of the small regionalist-nationalist parties. The new PP government's support for the Bush Administration in the US and, in particular the participation of Spanish troops in the coalition of the willing during the invasion of Iraq, considerably changed the perception of the PP government.

After the 11 March 2004 bombings in Madrid, some days before the general elections, and the misleading of public opinion about the real perpetrators, *Al Qaeda*, by the government, the new PP leader Mariano Rajoy had to acknowledge defeat. The new Socialist government did not win an absolute majority, so it was highly dependent on the left-wing Catalan parties, the ERC and IC-V. The 2004 European Parliament elections took place in June, so that the Socialists could still rely on the honeymoon period granted by the electorate. The main PSOE slogan was 'We Return to Europe' ('*Volvemos a Europa*') and was directed against the previous PP governments, which tended to put Spanish interests before European integration. The polarization between the two main parties reduced the electoral space for the IU, which formed a coalition with the eco-Socialist Initiative for Catalonia – The Greens (IC-V). Additionally the other regionalist-nationalist parties had to work together to achieve representation in the

Table 14.6 National election results in Spain: 1986–2011 (%)

Political party	1986	1989	1993	1996	2000	2004	2008	2011
PSOE	44.1	39.6	38.8	37.6	34.2	42.6	43.4	28.8
PP	26.0	25.9	34.8	38.8	44.5	37.7	40.4	44.6
CDS	9.2	7.9	—	—	—	—	—	—
IU	4.6	9.1	9.6	10.6	5.5	4.9	3.8	6.9
UPyD	—	—	—	—	—	—	1.2	4.7
CiU	5.0	5.0	5.0	4.6	4.2	3.2	3.0	4.2
PNV	1.2	1.2	1.2	1.3	1.5	1.6	1.2	1.3
BNG	—	0.2	0.5	0.9	1.3	0.8	0.8	0.8
ERC	0.4	0.4	0.8	0.8	0.8	2.5	1.2	1.1
CC	—	—	0.9	0.9	1.1	0.9	0.7	0.6
Others	9.5	10.7	8.4	4.5	6.9	5.8	4.3	7.0

Source: Spain's Ministry of Home Affairs, Elections Database, http://elecciones.mir.es/resultados2009/99PE/DPE99999TO.htm.

European Parliament. In terms of results, the PSOE won the elections with 43.5 per cent and 25 seats; this was a substantial gain of 8 per cent and 1 more seat in relation to the 1999 elections, whilst the PP also improved by 1.5 per cent but lost 3 seats. The PP got 41.2 per cent and 24 seats. Galeusca, a new coalition of regionalist-nationalist parties consisting of Catalan CiU, Basque PNV, and the Galician BNG, got 5.1 per cent and 2 seats. The IU got 4.1 per cent and 2 seats, whilst the left-wing coalition of regionalist-nationalist parties achieved 2.1 per cent and 1 seat.

Overall, Spanish European elections are now important tests for national politics. In particular, the point in time of the electoral cycle of legislative elections affects considerably the outcome of the European Parliament elections. However, the salience of European issues is less visible in the Spanish case. Both Green parties or Eurosceptic/right-wing parties are not able to capitalize on the low turnout of European elections. On the contrary, EP elections just reproduce the steady bipolarization of the Spanish party system.

Table 14.7 EP election results in Spain: 1987–2004

Political party	1987 %	1987 Seats	1989 %	1989 Seats	1994 %	1994 Seats	1999 %	1999 Seats	2004 %	2004 Seats
PP	24.7	17	21.4	15	40.1	28	39.7	27	41.2	24
PSOE	39.1	28	39.6	27	30.8	22	35.3	24	43.4	25
IU	5.3	3	6.1	4	13.4	9	5.8	4	4.1	2
CiU/Galeusca	4.4	4	4.2	2	4.7	3	4.4	3	5.1	2
Nationalist Coalition/ People's Europe/ Coalition for Europe	2.9	—	2.5	—	2.5	—	2.9	2	2.5	1
UPyD	—	—	—	—	—	—	—	—	—	—
CDS	10.3	7	7.2	5	—	—	—	—	—	—
Others	10.4	2	21.6	7	11.0	2	14.7	3	3.6	0

Source: Spain's Ministry of Home Affairs, www.mir.es.

9 The 2009 European election

9.1 Party lists and manifestos

The 2009 European Parliament election in Spain took place in the aftermath of the financial crisis that struck Spain particularly hard. Apart from a rapid increase in unemployment to four million people, equivalent to 17 per cent, Spain was hit by the collapse of the highly speculative housing market. This created major problems for the Socialist government that won the elections in March 2008. The political party programmes focussed considerably on the economic and financial crisis. There were 35 parties and electoral coalitions taking part in the elections.

The ruling Socialist Party stressed European issues and organized its campaign according to the pan-European one of the Party of European Socialists. However, it also presented its own programme which emphasized reform of the financial sector at the European level, more social rights for disadvantaged people, gender equality, a common immigration policy, the ratification of the Lisbon Treaty, and the forthcoming presidency of the EU in the first half of 2010. One priority for the Spanish presidency was to upgrade the international role of the European Union, particularly the European service for external action. In the second part of the programme, much space was devoted to foreign and security policy (PSOE, 2009). The head of the list was the experienced Juan Fernando López Aguilar, a former law professor at the University of Las Palmas in the Canary Islands. He became minister of justice in the first Zapatero Government between 2003 and 2007 and was the main candidate in the regional elections in the Canary Islands in 2007. He then became the main leader of the opposition there.

The People's Party also presented an extensive programme in which many of the policies were linked with the European People's Party. The programme's main thrust was a critique of the policies of the Socialist government. The main argument was that the Socialist government had caused harm to Spain and that the country was worse off than during the governments under the People's Party from 1996 to 2004. The programme focussed on the economic crisis, arguing that it had happened due to the wrong choices undertaken by the Socialist government. The programme addressed European issues such as the Lisbon Treaty and the Common Foreign and Security Policy, but always through a national lens, comparing the previous period of PP government with that of the then Socialist one. One particular issue emphasized throughout the programme was that the Socialist government was not able to negotiate a good deal for Spain in the last EU budgetary negotiations. In the December 2005 round, Spain got fewer structural and agricultural funds because the Socialist government did not fight for the national interest. The PP also used this critical approach during the campaign. The head of the list was the highly experienced former Minister of the Interior Jaime Mayor Oreja during the first and second Aznar governments between 1996 and 2001, who had also been the head of the PP in the Basque country before, during, and after the regional elections in 2001 (PP, 2009).

The IU–ICV–EUiA–BA parties negotiated a pre-electoral agreement in which the IU would head the list, followed by a candidate from the IC-V, the second largest group in the coalition. As defined in the pre-electoral agreement, the electoral programme would not change very much from that of 2004. Nevertheless, more emphasis was given to the consequences of the financial crisis. In terms of the Common Foreign and Security Policy, there was a general call for an autonomous foreign policy based on the de-militarization of security, cooperation, and peace. A critique of the Lisbon Treaty as a follow-up of the Constitutional Treaty was quite important. Their main criticism was that it was an elitist project, which did not take into account the opinion of the citizens and circumvented the democratic process. The crisis was regarded as an opportunity to transform the European Union into a truly democratic, social, and just space

(IU, 2009). The head of the list was the IU candidate Willy Meier, whilst IC-V presented Raúl Romeva i Rueda as its candidate.

As already mentioned, a new party was able to achieve representation in the lower house of the Spanish Parliament in the March 2008 elections. The UPyD is ideologically located between the PSOE and PP. Their overall position on the European Union is Euro-enthusiast. Although the UPyD emphasizes more democratic accountability, transparency, and the involvement of citizens, its positions are not very different from the two mainstream political parties. The UPyD's electoral programme emphasizes the need for deeper integration and more accountability in budgetary terms (UPyD, 2009). Their main candidate was the intellectual Francisco Sosa Wagner.

The regionalist-nationalist parties formed two electoral coalitions. The Coalition for Europe (*Coalición de los Pueblos*) dominated by the Basque Nationalist Party and the Catalan Convergence and Union. In the 2004 elections, this group was called Galeusca and included the Nationalist Galician Bloc, comprising the main parties of the three historical regions. BNG decided to join a more left-wing coalition of regionalist-nationalist parties called Europe of the Peoples (*Europa de los Pueblos–Verdes*). Both groups emphasized that the European Union should take into account a 'Europe of Peoples', and also those at a subnational level. The Coalition of Europe was quite supportive of the European integration process particularly emphasizing aspects related to stateless nations. This meant that the Committee of the Regions and Local Authorities and interregional cooperation through paradiplomacy were crucial aspects of the programme. Last but not least, a competitive economy was a crucial issue for all the political parties involved, particularly the PNV and the CiU. These centre-right parties in the richest regions of the country emphasize European efforts to stimulate economic growth and competitiveness paired with social policy initiatives (PNV, 2009; CiU, 2009; CC, 2009).

The Europe of Peoples-Greens consists of smaller left-wing parties of the historical regions. The main parties are the Republican Catalan Left (ERC), the Nationalist Galician Bloc (BNG), Basque Left (AA), and new Basque party Aralar. The regionalist Aragonese Junta (CHA) and some parts of the Green party took part in this coalition. The programme was similar to that of the Coalition for Europe, however it emphasized environmental issues and social cohesion. From the different programmes, one could see a strong emphasis on the Europe of the Peoples and, in the case of BNG and ERC, a criticism of the elitist nature of the European integration process. They demanded a referendum on the Lisbon Treaty in order to strengthen citizenship in the European Union. All parties were supportive of the European Union; however, like the coalition around the United Left, they were very critical of the present direction taken by the EU and suggested changes particularly in relation to democratic accountability and environmental policies (ERC, 2009; Europa de los Pueblos, 2009).

In this regard, the IU coalition and the Europe of the Peoples can be characterized as soft Eurosceptics, particularly if this term is defined as 'integration scepticism'. It means that they support the European integration process, but constructively suggest a different direction and model. Antonia María Ruiz Jiménez and Alfonso Egea de Haro (2006) have labelled this 'Eurocriticism'. It means that far from being Eurosceptic, they are engaged in shaping the process of European integration with constructive critique.

Libertas, the pan-European party set up by Irish billionaire Declan Ganley, worked with a movement called *Ciudadanos de España* (Citizens for Spain). They focussed on democratic accountability and transparency in their campaign; in particular the role of citizenship and a critique of the elitist nature of the present EU were emphasized (Libertas, 2009).

In the 2009 European Parliament elections, there were two regionalist coalitions: (1) the Coalition for Europe, CpE (*Coalición por Europa*) – consisting of the Basque Nationalist Party, Convergence and Union, the Canary Coalition, the Valencian Nationalist Bloc, the Andalucian Party and the Mallorcan Union; and (2) the Europe of the People–Greens (*Europa de los*

Pueblos–Verdes) – consisting of the Basque Left, the Greens, Aralar, the Galician Nationalist Bloc, the Catalan Republican Left, the Aragonese Junta, and the hybrid national-regional coalition IU–ICV–EUiA–BA consisting of the United Left-Initiative for Catalunya–Greens (IU–ICV), and the United Left and Alternative, Bloc for Asturias: The Left.

In addition, there were 28 political parties standing in these elections. Amongst them, there were four extreme right-wing nationalist parties, which emphasized national sovereignty and opposed the European Union. These parties were *Falange Española de las JONS* (Spanish Falange of Jons), the successor party of the authoritarian regime, the splinter group *Falange Autentica* (Authentic Falange), *Frente Nacional* (National Front), and *Movimiento Social Republicano* (Social Republican Movement).

9.2 Electoral campaign

In 2009 the European Parliament launched a pan-European campaign that also had an impact in Spain. The 'You Vote' campaign wanted to motivate people to vote, so that they expressed their opinion on the future of the European Union, and not to allow others to decide for them. Like in other countries, they used posters, television advertising, and civil society groups to motivate people to vote. Moreover, Twitter, Facebook and Myspace were used to address the young vote. According to Susana del Rio Vilar, this campaign was part of a change of strategy in the European Union, which consisted of improving its communications. All institutions regarded this as essential to achieving more legitimacy amongst the populations of the European Union (Vilar, 2009b, 8).

The actual campaign started on 22 May 2009, two weeks before polling day. All newspapers and television channels reported extensively about the elections. The main newspapers *El Pais* and *El Mundo* dedicated several pages daily to the campaign and covered all the political parties.

PSOE used the slogan 'This game is played in Europe' ('*Este partido se juega en Europa*'), which clearly wanted to direct the campaign towards European issues and away from the difficult economic crisis. PP used the slogan 'Now, solutions' ('*Ahora, soluciones!*'), which was directed against the policies of the Socialist government. PSOE used a discourse directed towards European issues, also in television advertising, whilst the PP was very keen to criticize the policies of the government, and, in defending the national interest, particularly the question of structural and common agricultural funds.

There was a television debate on the public channel RTVE between the two main candidates Juan Fernando López Aguilar of the PSOE and Jaime Mayor Oreja of PP on 25 May, and a debate by the five candidates of the political parties and coalition that had representation in the European Parliament on 3 June 2009. The two debates were dominated by the economic crisis and the position of Spain in Europe. In the debate between López Aguilar and Mayor Oreja, there were two main discourses. The Socialist López Aguilar emphasized that the economic crisis was global and not only related to domestic factors. He criticized the old neo-liberal model and proposed a new one based on sustainable growth and investment in new technologies. Mayor Oreja used the debate to criticize the policies of the Socialist government. Another topic was the emphasis on equality between men and women, the enhancement of diversity, and the expansion of social rights to minorities. The PP candidate tended to emphasize the negative economic situation, particularly the high level of unemployment, 4.1 million people, and the need to support the family as an important support mechanism in the economic crisis. In the RTVE analysis of the discourse between the two candidates, 'Spain' was the most used word, followed by 'crisis', showing really that national topics dominated this debate (RTVE, 2009).

The second debate with all five candidates concentrated mainly on the economic crisis. All issues were discussed about the policies of the Socialist government. The debate was between the number two on the lists of the PSOE and the PP, Ramón Jauregui and Luis de Grandes, respectively, and the main candidates of the smaller parties Willy Meier (IU), Ramón Tremosa (Coalition for Europe), and Oriol Junqueras (Europe of Peoples) with representation in the European Parliament. The main issues were the economic crisis and the solutions to overcome it. The Socialist government of Prime Minister José Luis Zapatero was criticized by all political parties. The positions were divided along a left–right axis. On the left, PSOE, the United Left, and the Europe of Peoples emphasized a social Europe and the protection of workers. This was particularly stressed by Willy Meier from IU. On the right, the PP and the Coalition for Europe emphasized economic growth and the role of enterprises in order to overcome the crisis. Most issues were discussed through the lens of national politics. The candidates of the regionalist coalitions highlighted the need to promote Catalan, Basque, and Galician as official languages in the European Union and in particular within the European Parliament. This was criticized by Luis de Grandes from the People's Party, who wanted Spanish to remain the only official language. Immigration was also discussed in the debate. Whilst PSOE, IU, and the Europe of Peoples were for a more humane immigration policy, the PP and the Coalition of Europe supported a stricter policy. A further liberalization abortion law was also a major issue of discussion. Here again the left-wing parties, PSOE, IU, and Europe of Peoples, were more supportive than the PP and the Coalition for Europe (RTVE, 2009). There was also a debate amongst the main candidates in Catalonia on the Catalan channel TV-3 on 29 May 2009. The candidates of the Catalan Socialist Party, the Convergence and Union, the Catalan Republican Left, and the Initiative of Catalonia–Greens united around the promotion of the Catalan language against the candidate of the Catalan People's Party who wanted the dominance of the Spanish language.

Although the economic crisis and national politics dominated the campaign of the political parties, implicitly all political parties had their proposals for the future of Europe. The PP and the Coalition for Europe pushed for a 'Europe of economic growth and support for enterprises', whilst the United Left wanted a radical overhaul of the European Union towards a stronger intervention of the state in the economy and a reinforcement of the social rights of workers. In between were the positions of the PSOE and the Europe of Peoples. The Spanish presidency of the European Union and the role for the supranational organization were not discussed at all.

9.3 Electoral results

From April 2009, the opinion polls gave a slight advantage of about four percentage points to the PP over the PSOE. However, a pre-electoral study by the Centre for Sociological Investigations published shortly before the official start of the campaign predicted a tough race between the two main parties, PP and PSOE. It was also predicted that the UPyD would be able to achieve representation in the European Parliament. Other parties and electoral coalitions would probably repeat their results in the 2004 election (CIS, 2009).

In spite of a very negative economic situation, the PSOE was able to contain its losses to 4.7 per cent, again becoming the second largest Spanish party in the European Parliament. Its success in the 2004 elections was very much influenced by the preceding legislative elections on 14 March, when the PSOE won the elections against the PP, which had been eight years in government. The EP elections took place three months later, so that the success of the PSOE has to be interpreted as being an outcome of the 'honeymoon' period (Hix and Marsh, 2007, 501). The PP's negative campaign against the policies of the Socialist government paid off, leading to the party's victory in the elections. One of the reasons for the success was the fact that the PP was able to transform the European elections into second-order national elections (Koepke and Ringe, 2006, 324) and redirect the vote towards an assessment of the Socialist government after five years in government. However, the victory was quite meagre, because in absolute terms it did not lead to a substantial increase in the vote. The PP profited more from the decline of the Socialists' overall share of the vote. Amongst the smaller parties and electoral coalitions, the only big surprise was the success of UPyD in getting representation in the European Parliament. This meant that six different groups achieved representation in the EP.

Table 14.8 EP election results in Spain: 2009

Party/electoral coalition	Percentage	Change from 2004	Seats	Change from 2004
People's Party (PP)	42.1	+0.9	25	−1
Spanish Socialist Workers' Party (PSOE)	38.8	−4.7	23	−4
Coalition for Europe (CpE)	5.1	0	3	+1
United Left–Catalan Initiative Greens (IU–ICV–EUiA)	3.7	−0.4	2	0
Unión for Progress and Democracy (UPyD)	2.9	—	1	—
Europe of the Peoples–The Greens (EDP–V)	2.5	+0.04	1	0
Internationalist Iniciative (II)	1.1	—	0	—
Greens–Green European Group (LV–GVE)	0.6	—	0	—
Anti-Bull Party Against Animal Maltreatment (PACMA)	0.3	—	0	—
For a More Just World (PUM+J)	0.2	+0.2	0	0
LIBERTAS–Citizens of Spain (LIBERTAS)	0.1	—	0	—
Anti-Capitalist Left–Global Revolt (IZAN–RG)	0.1	—	0	—
Spanish Alternative	0.1	—	0	—
Communist Party of Spanish Peoples (PCPE)	0.1	0.1	0	0
Andalucian Socialist Party (PSA)	0.1	—	0	—
Internationalist Socialist Workers' Party (POSI)	0.1	+0.04	0	0
Party of Family and Life (PFyV)	0.1	+0.03	0	0
Democratic Social Centre (CDS)	0.1	−0.02	0	0
Spanish Falange of the JONS (FE de las JONS)	0.1	+0.03	0	0
National Democracy (DN)	0.1	+0.02	0	0
Feminist Initiative (IF)	0.1	—	0	—
National Front (FN)	0.1	—	0	—
Catalan Republican Party (RC)	0.1	—	0	—
Humanist Party (PH)	0.04	+0.01	0	0
Valencian Union (UV)	0.04	—	0	—
Republican Social Movement (MSR)	0.04	—	0	—
Solidarity and Internationalist Self-Management (SAIN)	0.04	—	0	—
Democratic Liberal Centre (CDL)	0.04	—	0	—
Authentic Falange	0.03	+0.02	0	0
United Extremadura (EXTREMADURA)	0.03	—	0	—
Salamanca–Zamora–León (PREPAL)	0.03	+0.01	0	0
Communist Unification of Spain (UCE)	0.02	—	0	—
Asturian Nationalist Union (UNA)	0.02	—	0	—
Andecha Astur (AA)	0.01	—	0	—
Centrist Liberal Union (UCL)	0.01	0.0	0	0
White vote	1.4	+0.8	—	—
Nil vote	0.6	−0.4	—	—
Total	100.0	—	50	54
Participation	46.0	+0.1	—	—
Abstention	54.0	−0.1	—	—

Source: Spain's Ministry of Home Affairs, www.mir.es.

Table 14.9 List of Spanish MEPs: seventh legislature

Name	National party	Political group	Professional background	Date of birth	Gender	Committee/Chair
Jaime Mayor Oreja	PP	EPP	Agrarian engineer	12/07/1951	Male	Vice-Chairman of EPP
Luis de Grandes Pascual			Lawyer	27/01/1945	Male	Vice-Chairman Delegation to the EU–Chile Joint Parliamentary Committee
Pablo Arias Echeverria			Researcher	30/06/1970	Male	Member Committee on the Internal Market and Consumer Protection Member Delegation to the EU–Russian Parliamentary Cooperation Committee
Maria del Pilar Ayuso González			Agrarian engineer	16/06/1942	Female	Vice-Chairman Delegation to the EU–Chile Joint Parliamentary Committee Member Committee on the Environment, Public Health and Food Safety Delegation to the Euro-Latin American Parliamentary Assembly
Pilar Castillo Vera			University professor	31/07/1952	Female	Member Committee on Industry, Research and Energy Delegation for Relations with India
Agustín Díaz De Mera García Consuegra			Policeman	27/09/1947	Male	Member Committee on Civil Liberties, Justice and Home Affairs Member Special Committee on Organized Crime, Corruption and Money Laundering Member Delegation to the EU–Chile Joint Parliamentary Committee Member Delegation to the Euro-Latin American Parliamentary Assembly
Maria Rosa Estaràs i Ferragut			Lawyer	21/10/1965	Female	Member Committee on Regional Development Member Delegation to the ACP–EU Joint Parliamentary Assembly

(continued)

Table 14.9 (continued)

Name	National party	Political group	Professional background	Date of birth	Gender	Committee/Chair
Santiago Fisas Ayxelas			Lawyer	29/08/1948	Male	Vice-Chairman of Joint Parliamentary Committee EU–Mexico Member Committee on Culture and Education Member Delegation to the Cariforum–EU–Parliamentary Committee Member Delegation for Relations with the Palestinian Legislative Council Member Delegation to the Euro-Latin American Parliamentary Assembly
Maria del Carmen Fraga Estevez			Geographer	19/10/1948	Female	Member Committee on Fisheries
Maria Auxiliadora Correa Zamora			Politician	24/05/1972	Female	Member Committee on International Trade Member Delegation to the Cariforum–EU–Parliamentary Committee
Salvador Garriga-Polledo			Businessman	06/08/1957	Male	Member Committee on Budgets
Cristina Gutiérrez-Cortines Corral			Art historian	17/12/1939	Female	Member Committee on the Environment, Public Health and Food Safety Member Delegation for Relations with the Countries of Southeast Asia and the Association of Southeast Asian Nations (ASEAN) Member Delegation to the Parliamentary Assembly of the Union for the Mediterranean
Maria Esther Herranz Garcia			Environmental consultant	03/07/1969	Female	Member Committee on Agriculture and Rural Development Member Delegation for Relations with the Mercosur Countries Member Delegation to the Euro-Latin American Parliamentary Assembly

Carlos Iturgaiz Angulo	Music teacher	29/10/1965	Male	Vice-Chairman Committee on Petitions Delegation for Relations with the Countries of Central America Member Delegation to the Euro-Latin American Parliamentary Assembly
Teresa Jiménez Becerril	Enterprise manager	24/07/1951	Female	Member LIBE Committee on Civil Liberties, Justice and Home Affairs Member FEMM Committee on Women's Rights and Gender Equality Member D-JP Delegation for Relations with Japan
Antonio López-Istúriz White	University professor	01/04/1970	Male	Member Committee on Legal Affairs Member Delegation for Relations with Israel Member Delegation to the Parliamentary Assembly of the Union for the Mediterranean
Verónica Lope Fontagné	Lawyer	01/02/1952	Female	Member Committee on Employment and Social Affairs Member Delegation to the EU–Chile Joint Parliamentary Committee Member Delegation to the Euro-Latin American Parliamentary Assembly
Gabriel Mato Adrover	Lawyer	29/04/1961	Male	Chair Committee of Fisheries Member Conference of Committee Chairs Committee on Agriculture and Rural Development Delegation to the ACP–EU Joint Parliamentary Assembly
Juan Andrés Naranjo Escobar	Politician	04/01/1952	Male	Member Committee on Budget
Francisco José Millan Mon	Diplomat	08/03/1965	Male	Member Committee on Foreign Affairs Member Delegation for Relations with the United States

(continued)

Table 14.9 (continued)

Name	National party	Political group	Professional background	Date of birth	Gender	Committee/Chair
José Ignacio Salafranca Sánchez-Neyra			Lawyer	31/05/1955	Male	Chairman Delegation to the Euro-Latin American Parliamentary Assembly Member Conference of Delegation Chairs Committee on Foreign Affairs Delegation to the EU–Mexico Joint Parliamentary Committee
Alejo Vidal-Quadras Roja			University professor	20/05/1945	Male	Vice-President European Parliament Member Parliament's Bureau Committee on Industry, Research and Energy Delegation for Relations with Iraq
Pablo Zalba Bildegain			Marketing director	28/01/1975	Male	Vice-Chair Committee on Economic and Monetary Affairs Member Delegation for Relations with the People's Republic of China
Additional MEPs after Treaty of Lisbon						
Eva Ortiz Vilella	PP	EPP	Local councillor, politician	16/10/1975	Female	Member Committee on Budgetary Control Member Delegation for the Relations with the Maghreb Countries and the Arab Maghreb Union
Salvador Sedó i Alabart			Consultant in engineering	03/04/1969	Male	Member Committee on Industry, Research and Energy Member Delegation for Relations with South Africa
Juan Fernando López Aguilar	PSOE	S&D	University professor	10/06/1961	Male	Chair Committee on Civil Liberties, Justice and Home Affairs Member Conference of Committee Chairs Specialised Committee on Organized Crime, Corruption and Money Laundering Delegation to the ACP–EU Joint Parliamentary Assembly

Name	Profession	DOB	Sex	Role	Committee/Delegation
Sérgio Gutiérrez Prieto	Politician	11/07/1982	Male	Member	Committee on Agriculture and Rural Development
					Delegation to the EU–Russia Parliamentary Committee
Maria Irigoyen Perez	Politician	01/10/1962	Female	Member	Committee on Regional Development
					Delegation to the EU–Chile Joint Parliamentary Committee
					Delegation to the Euro–Latin American Parliamentary Assembly
Josefa Andrés Barrea	Nurse, health inspector	17/02/1958	Female	Member	Committee on Industry, Research and Energy
				Member	Delegation for Relations with the Mashreq Countries
Inés Ayala Sender	University professor	28/03/1957	Female	Member	Committee on Budgetary Control
					Committee on Transport and Tourism
					Delegation for Relations with the Countries of Central America
					Delegation to the Parliamentary Assembly of the Union for the Mediterranean
Maria Badia i Cutchet	School teacher	13/05/1947	Female	Member	Committee on International Trade
					Delegation for Relations with the United States
Alejandro Cercas	Civil servant	26/05/1949	Male	Member	Committee on Employment and Social Affairs
					Delegation for the Relations with Canada
Ricardo Cortés Lastra	Lawyer, manager	23/09/1969	Male	Chair	Delegation to the EU–Mexico Joint Parliamentary Committee
				Member	Conference of Delegation Chairs
					Committee on Development
					Delegation to the Euro–Latin American Parliamentary Assembly.
Iratxe Garcia Perez	Social worker	07/10/1974	Female	Member	Committee on Agriculture and Rural Development
					Committee on Human Rights and Gender Equality
					Delegations for Relations to India

(continued)

Table 14.9 (continued)

Name	National party	Political group	Professional background	Date of birth	Gender	Committee/Chair
Eider Gardiazabal Rubial			Business administrator	12/07/1975	Female	Vice-Chairman Committee on Budgets Member Delegation for Relations with India
Enrique Guerrero Salom			University teacher	28/08/1948	Male	Member Committee on Constitutional Affairs Delegation to the Cariforum–EU–Parliamentary Committee Delegation to the ACP-EU Joint Parliamentary Committee
Miguel Angel Martinez Martinez			Party functionary	30/01/1940	Male	Vice-President of European Parliament Member Parliament's Bureau Committee on Development Committee on Petitions Delegation for Relations with the Pan-African Parliament Delegation to the ACP-EU Joint Parliamentary Assembly
António Masip Hidalgo			Lawyer	03/05/1946	Male	Member Committee on Legal Affairs Delegation for Relations with Belarus
Emilio Menendez Del Valle			University teacher	20/06/1945	Male	Member Committee on Culture and Education Delegation for Relations with the People's Republic of China
Maria Paloma Muñiz De Urquiza			University teacher	05/08/1962	Female	Member Committee on Foreign Affairs Delegation for Relations with the Countries of the Andean Community Delegation to the Euro-Latin American Parliamentary Assembly
Raimon Obiols			Geologist	05/08/1940	Male	Member Committee on Foreign Affairs Subcommittee on Human Rights Delegation for Relations with the Mashreq Countries Delegation to the Parliamentary Assembly of the Union for the Mediterranean

Andres Perelló Rodriguez		Lawyer	01/07/1967	Male	Vice-Chairman Delegation to the Euro-Latin American Parliamentary Assembly Member Committee on the Environment, Public Health and Food Safety Delegation for relations with Iraq
Teresa Riera Madurelll		Researcher	13/10/1980	Female	Member Committee for Industry, Research and Energy Delegation for Relations with the countries of Southeast Asia and the Association of Southeast Asian Nations (ASEAN) Delegation for relations with the NATO Parliamentary Assembly Delegation to the Euronest Parliamentary Assembly
Carmen Romero López		School teacher	15/11/1946	Female	Member Committee on Civil Liberties, Justice and Home Affairs Delegation for Relations with the Maghreb Countries and the Arab Maghreb Union Delegation to the Parliamentary Assembly for the Union of the Mediterranean
Antolín Sanchez Presedo		Lawyer	05/04/1965	Male	Member Committee on Economic and Monetary Union Delegation for Relations with South Africa
Luiz Yañez-Barnuevo Garcia		Physician	12/04/1943	Male	Chairman of Delegation for Relations with Mercosur Member Conference of Delegation Chairs Committee on Constitutional Affairs
Two Additional MEPs after Treaty of Lisbon					
Vicente Miguel Garcés Ramón	PSOE S&D	Agricultural engineer, university professor	10/11/1946	Male	Member Committee on the Internal Market and Consumer Protection Delegation for Relations with the Arab Peninsula
Dolores García-Hierro Caraballo		Politician, trade unionist	16/05/1958	Female	Member Committee on Fisheries Delegation for Relations with Japan

(continued)

Table 14.9 (continued)

Name	National party	Political group	Professional background	Date of birth	Gender	Committee/Chair
Ramón Tremosa i Balcells	Coalition for Europe (Convergence and Union–CiU)	ALDE	University professor	30/06/1965	Male	Member Committee on Economic and Monetary Affairs Delegation for Relations with the People's Republic of China
Izaskun Bilbao Barandica	Coalition for Europe (Basque National Party–PNV)		Lawyer	27/03/1961	Female	Vice-Chairwoman Delegation for Relations with the Countries of the Andean Community Member Committee on Transport and Tourism Delegation for the Euro-Latin Americna Parliamentary Assembly
Iñaki Irazabalbeitia Fernández	Europe of Peoples	Group of the Greens/European Free Alliance	Chemist	01/08/1957	Male	Member Committee on Regional Development Committee on Petitions Delegation for Relations with the Mercosur Countries Delegation to the Euro-Latin American Parliamentary Assembly
Raúl Romeva i Rueda	IU–ICV–G–EUiA (Initiative for Catalonia–Greens)		UNESCO officer and NGO activist	12/03/1971	Male	Member Committee on Fisheries Committee on Women's Rights and Gender Equality Delegation for Relations with the Countries of Central America Delegation to the Euro-Latin American Parliamentary Assembly
Willy Meier	IU–ICV–G–EUiA (United Left–IU)	EUL/NGL	Party official	19/08/1952	Male	Vice-Chairman Committee on Foreign Affairs Committee on Petitions Delegation to the Euro-Latin American Parliamentary Assembly Member Delegation for Relations with the coutries of the Andean Community
Francisco Sosa Wagner	UPyD	NA	Jurist, writer	10/06/1946	Male	Member Committee on Industry, Research and Energy Delegation to the EU-Mexico Joint Parliamentary Committee Delegation to the EU-Latin American Parliamentary Assembly

Source: www.europarl.europa.eu-meps-en-search.html?country=ES.

Table 14.10 National and EP election campaign expenditure in Spain*

	National election 2004	EP election 2004	National election 2008	EP election 2008	National election 2011
PSOE	18.6	11.2	22.8	13.9	22.0
PP	19.2	11.2	22.9	13.3	20.6
IU	7.6	2.9	6.2	2.3	8.9
UPyD	—	—	0.7	0.8	1.7

Source: Tribunal de Cuentas, 2005 a,b.
Note: * In millions of euros

Another interesting result for Spain is that elected MEPs from the smaller United Left coalition did not join en bloc the European United Left/Green Nordic Left (EUL/NGL). The MEP of Initiative for Catalonia–Greens, Raúl Romeva i Rueda, who was placed second on the list, joined the Greens, instead of the EUL/NGL, as agreed in the pre-electoral agreement. The Coalition of Peoples agreed to rotate its MEP Oriol Junqueras, so that the second on the list from the Galician Nationalist Bloc could also be in the European Parliament.

In mid-December 2011, four additional Spanish MEPs became members of the EP. According to the electoral results, two PSOE candidates and two PP candidates became Members of the European Parliament.

9.4 Campaign finance

The level of expenditure confirmed the lesser importance of European elections within the multilevel electoral governance cycle. The main political parties tend to spend considerably more in general elections than in European elections. Although the process of reporting campaign expenditures for the European Parliament elections in 2009 to the Spanish Audit Court is still not completed, one can gain at least a good impression of the differences in investment from 2004. As shown in Table 14.10, all three main national parties spent more in the general election than in the European elections. This clearly reveals that political parties give more importance to the general election over European elections.

10 Theoretical interpretation of Euro-elections

10.1 Second-Order Election theory

Although turnout has decreased in Spain over the years, this decline has been slower than in other European countries and participation levels remain slightly above the EU average. Nevertheless, in line with the Second-Order Election approach, participation rates are much lower in European elections than in general elections.

In line with the SOE model, Spanish voters tend to castigate government parties, although only at the end of the national electoral cycle, and reward opposition parties. This was the case in the 1994 EP elections in which the People's Party in opposition was able to win against the PSOE, which had been in government since 1982. Another factor which played an important role in this election was the rejuvenation of the People's Party under the new leadership of José Maria Aznar, who was able to improve the party's competitiveness which, until the 1993 elections, lagged behind the PSOE. Certainly, multiple corruption scandals as well as the financial crisis to a great extent contributed in damaging the reputation of the Socialist government. The 2009 European elections took place at the end of the government's honeymoon period, which enabled citizens to vote sincerely. Apart from this occasion, EP elections used to lead to the victory of the incumbent party, in spite of losing slightly in comparison to the national electoral contest.

In the Spanish case, there are virtually no small parties at the national level. Most of them are regionalist parties that are strong in their respective region, but without any electoral presence in other parts of the country. Convergence and Union, the Catalan Republican Left, and the Basque Nationalist Party are such examples. However, due to the fact that the whole territory of Spain is just one constituency, these parties have to coalesce with each other to achieve representation in the EP. For a long time, *Izquierda Unida* (IU), which was the only small party at the national level, had major difficulties in achieving representation in the European Parliament. Normally, it has to coalesce with similar small left-wing parties across Spain to achieve some representation. Its share of the vote has been steadily declining. The only major exception so far has been the Union for Progress and Democracy, which achieved representation in the national Parliament in the 2008 elections and was also able to elect members to the European Parliament in 2009.

Overall, the third hypothesis can be confirmed in the Spanish case, because one year after the 2008 general elections, the PSOE's losses remained quite moderate (Hix and Marsh, 2007, 496). If we compare this to other elections, a timing effect is visible only at the end of national electoral cycles. It means that when political parties are in power too long, European elections can be an important predictor for results in the next general elections for the opposition party. This was particularly true in the 1994 and 2009 European Parliament elections in which the PP was able to do better than the PSOE, winning the 1996 and 2011 general elections and the 2009 EP election.

10.2 Europe Salience theory

The Europe Salience thesis appeared less plausible in the Spanish case, as all parliamentary parties, including the new UPyD, are pro-European (Magone, 2009b).

Extreme political parties were not able to make inroads in European elections, whilst most far right-wing parties got negligible results below 1 per cent, even if they all merged into one political party.

The Green parties were too divided in different groups, so that they did not really profit from the European elections. Amongst the political parties, the most Eurocritical is the United Left; however, its electoral results were not very different from those achieved in the general elections (Hix and Marsh, 2007).

References

Primary sources

Centro de Investigaciones Sociologicas (CIS) (2009) Preelectoral Elecciones al Parlamento Europeo, Study 2800, 29 April 2009: www.cis.es (accessed on 5 November 2009).
Coalición, C. (2009) Europa sin Escalas. Decide por Canarias, Europeas 2009, Programa Electoral: www.coalicioncanarias.org (accessed on 6 November 2009).
Convergencia i Unió (CiU) (2009) Programa Electoral, Eleccions Europees 2009, Barcelona, CiU: www.ciu.cat (accessed on 6 November 2009).
Eurobarometer (various) Brussels, European Commission, http://ec.europa.eu/public_opinion/index_en.htm (accessed on 20 October 2013).

Europa de los Pueblos (2009) Programa electoral posted on website of Green Party, www.ecoboletin.com (accessed on 6 November 2009).
European Parliament website, www.europarl.europa.eu/ (accessed on 7 December 2013).
Eurostat (2013, 2014) http://epp.eurostat.ec.europa.eu/ (accessed on 5 June 2015).
Ezquerra Republicana Catalana (ERC) (2009) Programa Electoral, Eleccions al Parlamento Europeu 2009, Barcelona.
Izquierda Unida (2009) Tu voz in Europa, Programa electoral Elecciones Europeas 2009, Madrid.
Libertas-Ciudadanos de España (2009) www.ciudadanos-cs.org (accessed on 6 November 2009).
Partido Nacional Vasco (PNV) (2009) Programa electoral, Elecciones al Parlamento Europeo.
Partido Popular (PP) (2009) *Elecciones Europeas 2009. Manifiesto del Partido Popular*. Madrid, PP.
Partido Socialista Obrero Español (PSOE) (2009) *Manifiesto. Programa Electoral PSOE Europeas*. Madrid, PSOE.
Radio Television Española (RTVE) (2009) Videos of the European Debates of 25 May and 3 June 2009, www.rtve.es (accessed on 5 November 2009).
Spain's Ministry of Home Affairs website, www.mir.es (accessed on 14 August 2013).
Spain's Ministry of Home Affairs, Elections Database, http://elecciones.mir.es/resultados2009/99PE/DPE99999TO.htm (accessed on 15 February 2015).
Tribunal de Cuentas (2005a) 'Informe de Fiscalización de las Contabilidades Electorales de las Elecciones a Cortes Generales', 14 Marzo 2004, 668, Madrid.
Tribunal de Cuentas (2005b) 'Informe de Fiscalización de las Contabilidades Electorales de las Elecciones al Parlamento Europeo', 13 Junio 2004, 669, Madrid.
Tribunal de Cuentas (2009) 'Informe de Fiscalización de las Contabilidades Electorales de las Elecciones a Cortes Generales', 9 Marzo 2008, 828, Madrid, approved on 29 March 2009.
Tribunal de Cuentas (2010) 'Informe de Fiscalización de las Contabilidades Electorales de las Elecciones al Parlamento Europeo', 7 Junio 2009, Madrid, approved on 27 May 2010.
Tribunal de Cuentas (2013) 'Informe de Fiscalización de las Contabilidades Electorales de las Elecciones a Cortes Generales', 20 Noviembre 2011, 967, Madrid, approved on 31 January 2013.
Union Progreso y Democracia (2008) www.upyd.es (accessed on 5 November 2009).

Secondary sources

Alvarez-Miranda, B. (1996) *El sur de Europa y la adhesión a la Comunidad. Los debates politicos*, Madrid, Centro de Investigaciones Sociologicas.
Balfour, S. (2007) 'El Partido Popular a la busqueda de un nuevo papel politico,' in Bernecker, W. C. and Maihold, G. (eds) *España del consenso a la polarización. Cambios en la democracia española,* Madrid/Frankfurt A M/Iberoamericana, Vervuert, 379–91.
Del Rio Vilar, S. (2009b) Comunicar, clave para aumentar la participación en las elecciones europeas de 2009: de un modelo europeo de debate a una política comunicativa europea (2a Parte), *Real Instituto Elcano,* ARI, 90.
Gallagher, M. and Mitchell, P. (eds) *The Politics of Electoral Systems*, Oxford, Oxford University Press, 374–94.
Gunther, R. and Hopkin, J. (2002) 'A Crisis of Institutionalization: the Collapse of the UCD', in Gunther, R., Montero, J. R. and Linz, J. J. (eds) *Political Parties: Old Concepts and New Challenges*, Oxford, Oxord University Press, 191–230.
Hix, S. and Marsh, M. (2007) 'Punishment or Protest? Understanding European Parliament Elections', *Journal of Politics*, 69(2), May, 495–510.
Hopkin, J. (1999) 'Political Parties in a Young Democracy', in Broughton, D. and Donovan, M. (eds) *Changing Party Systems in Western Europe,* London, Pinter, 207–31.
Hopkin, J. (2005) 'From Census to Competition: The Changing Nature of Democracy in the Spanish Transition', in Balfour, S. (ed.) *Contemporary Politics of Spain,* Basingstoke, Palgrave, 6–26.
Hopkin, J. (2008) 'Spain: Proportional Representation with Majoritarian Outcomes', in Gallagher, M. and Mitchell, P. (eds) *The Politics of Electoral Systems*, Oxford, Oxford University Press.
Magone, J. M. (2009a) *Contemporary Spanish Politics*, Basingstoke, Palgrave.
Magone, J. M. (2009b) 'European Debates and Varieties of Euroenthusiasm: The Spanish Case', in Harmsen, R. and Schild, J. (eds) *Debating Europe: The 2009 European Parliament Elections and Beyond*, Baden-Baden, Nomos, 145–63.

Mendez, M. (ed.) *Las Elecciones al Parlamento Europeo 1999*, Valencia, Tirant Lo Blanch, 91–147.
Mendez-Lago, M. (2000) *La estrategia organizativa del Partido Socialista Obrero Español (1975–1996)*, Madrid, CIS.
Mendez-Lago, M. (2005) The Socialist Party in Government and in Opposition, in Balfour, S. (ed.) *The Politics of Contemporary Spain*, London, Routledge, 169–97.
Oñate, P. R. (2006) 'Elecciones, partidos y sistemas de partidos en la España Democrática', in Murillo, F. and Garcia de la Serrana J. L. (eds) *Transformaciones y sociales en la España Democrática*, Valencia, Tirant Lo Blanch, 399–431.
Ramiro Fernandez, L. (2003) 'Electoral Incentives and Organizational Limits. The Evolution of the Communist Party (PCE) and the United Left (IU)', *Political Science Debates*, 1, 9–39.
Ruiz Jimenez, A. M. and Egea de Haro, A. (2006) 'Euroscepticism in a Pro-European Country?' *South European Society and Politics*, 16(1), 105–31.
Sampedro, V. (2000) 'Estrategias de campaña: Género, Liderazgo y Giros de Agenda', in Martinez, A. and Mendez, M. (eds) *Las Elecciones al Parlamento Europeo 1999*, Valencia, Tirant lo Blanch, 151–69.

15
PORTUGAL

José M. Magone

Figure 15.1 Map of Portugal

Table 15.1 Portugal profile

EU entry year	1986 ECSC, EEC and Euratom
Schengen entry year	1991
MEPs elected in 2009	22
MEPs under Lisbon Treaty	22
Capital	Lisbon
Total area★	92,225 km^2
Population	10,427,301
Population density★★	113.4/km^2
Median age of population	43.1
Political system	Semi-presidential Republic
Head of state	Aníbal Cavaco Silva, Social Democratic Party (PSD) (March 2006–)
Head of government	José Socrates, Socialist Party (PS) (March 2005–March 2011); Pedro Passos Coelho, Social Democratic Party (PSD) (June 2011–)
Political majority	Socialist Party (PS) (October 2009–March 2011); Social Democratic Party (PSD) and Democratic Social Centre-People's Party (CDS/PP) Government Coalition (June 2011–)
Currency	Euro (€) since 1999
Prohead GDP in PPS	16,600 €

Source: Eurostat, 2013, 2014, http://epp.eurostat.ec.europa.eu/.

Notes:
★ Total area including inland waters.
★★ Population density: the ratio of the annual average population of a region to the land area of the region.

1 Geographical position

Portugal is a small country with a population of about 10 million on the south-western coast of the European Union. Apart from continental Portugal, the ultra-peripheral islands of Madeira and the Azores in the Atlantic Ocean are an integral part of Portugal.

Despite immigration from European and Portuguese-speaking countries in Africa as well as Brazil, the Portuguese population remains quite homogenous. According to the Annual Report on Immigration of the Portuguese Service of Foreigners and Borders in 2007, there are roughly 435,736 legalized foreigners living in Portugal. They represent about 4 per cent of the population. The largest number of resident foreigners originates from Brazil, 15 per cent, the Cape Verde Islands, 15 per cent, Ukraine, 9 per cent, and Angola, 8 per cent (SEF, 2007, 23). These figures show that Portugal has remained more or less an extremely homogenous population without any significant ethnic cleavages, unlike many countries in Central and Eastern Europe, for example Latvia, Estonia, Romania, and Slovakia.

2 Historical background

Founded in 1143, Portugal is one of the oldest countries of Europe. The Golden Age of Discovery in the fifteenth and sixteenth centuries transformed Portugal into a European superpower. However, after the death of King Sebastian in North Africa in 1578, Portugal was annexed by Spain. The occupation, which lasted from 1580 to 1640, shaped the mentality of the country in relation to its neighbour.

After regaining independence, the Portuguese Empire declined in importance. Other powers, like the Netherlands and Britain, were able to establish hegemony. In the eighteenth century Portugal's power in Europe continued to decline. After the Napoleonic Wars, the country was characterized by periods of civil war between supporters of the absolutist monarchy and advocates of a liberal constitution. It was only at the end of the nineteenth century, during a highly clientelistic liberal democratic system controlled by two political parties, that the country experienced a period of relative peace. The so-called *Rotativismo* degenerated into corruption by the early twentieth century.

On 5 October 1910, Portugal became a republic. However, the new political system proved to be unstable and, in 1926, a military *coup d'état* led to the establishment of a dictatorship. Soon after, the military dictatorship was replaced by a civilian one under António Salazar. He ruled the country for almost 40 years until 1968. After suffering a stroke, Salazar was replaced by Marcelo Caetano, who ruled until 1974. On 25 April 1974, a successful *coup d'état* of the colonels led to the overthrow of the dictatorship.

After a turbulent transition to democracy between 1974 and 1976, the first constitutional government under Prime Minister Mário Soares submitted Portugal's application to the European Community on 28 March 1977. By 17 October 1978, negotiations between the EC and Portugal were started. However, it took almost eight years before Portugal joined the EC. The main reason was that the Portuguese application was linked to that of Spain. Problems with the Spanish negotiations over individual chapters led to substantial delays and frustrated the ambitions of the Portuguese political elite. Between 1976 and 1987, Portugal's political scene was characterized by considerable political and economic instability. Politically, no government was able to complete its legislative period. This led to nearly ten governments during this period. Moreover, after the excesses of the revolutionary period, Portugal suffered major economic difficulties. The International Monetary Fund's standby credits in 1978–1979 and 1983–1985 led to the introduction of two major austerity programmes by the government. The negotiation process was completed with the signing of the Accession Treaty in Lisbon on 10 June 1985. Portugal became a member of the EC on 1 January 1986. In terms of public opinion between 1981 and 1985, a majority of Portuguese supported membership. This is below the EU average for pre-accession support. The degree of knowledge about the EC/EU was also quite low in Portugal and these low levels of institutional understanding persist today. Between 1981 and 1985, two-thirds of Portuguese had no or low knowledge of the EC/EU (Magone, 2002, 224). Public opinion in Portugal towards the EC/EU has been quite instrumental after accession. In periods of economic boom and political stability, as between 1986 and 1992, public support was above the EU average, however in periods of recession, such as between 1992 and 1994, and 2001 until today, support has declined. In spite of all this, Portugal has remained one of the most supportive countries of the European integration project.

Portugal profited immensely from accession to the EC/EU. It has been one of the most important beneficiaries of the EU structural funds since 1988. Between 1989 and 2006, it received about 9 per cent of the second largest expenditure item in the EC/EU budget. This allowed for major public works programmes that upgraded infrastructures and improved the economy. In spite of these two decades of investments, two areas have been neglected: investment in human resources and research and development. In this sense, the structural problems of the Portuguese economy remained unchanged.

Successful negotiations for EU structural funds by high civil servants dedicated to EU affairs allowed Portugal to receive a significant amount of funding. EU support via structural funds remains the main priority of successive Portuguese governments. They were part of a coalition of cohesion countries led by Spain.

After 25 years of membership, the Portuguese population continues to be supportive of European integration. However, the stagnating economy has led to a decline in this support. Portugal is a member of the euro-zone, and this has been a major constraint on the Portuguese government. Due to Portugal's weak economic performance, the budget deficit in 2009 was 9.3 per cent of GDP and Portugal has been under considerable pressure to implement draconian austerity measures to reduce the budget substantially to the 3 per cent of GDP level allowed by the Growth and Stability Pact. Finally, in 2011 Portugal had to ask the EU and the International Monetary Fund (IMF) for a €76 billion credit, due to the contamination effects of the Greek crisis on Portugal's small economy. Since summer 2011, Portugal has been implementing a harsh austerity programme negotiated with the troika, consisting of representatives from the European Central Bank, the European Commission, and the IMF. This had negative effects on the social situation and the economy of the country.

3 Geopolitical profile

Portugal is part of all major international organizations. It is an active member of the United Nations. It has been member of the United Nations Security Council three times, in 1979–1980, 1997–1998, and 2011–2012. Portugal was one of the founding members of the North Atlantic Treaty Organization in 1949 and remains a strong ally of the United States. Finally, it is a member of the IMF and the World Bank.

4 Overview of the political landscape

Portugal is a semi-presidential democratic republic. The President of the republic is elected directly by the population every five years. Currently, the President is former Prime Minister Aníbal Cavaco Silva. The President of the republic has important powers to veto parliamentary legislation or send it to the Constitutional Court so that it is examined on its constitutionality. Moreover, he can dismiss a government if it has no majority in Parliament and call for new elections. Until 5 June 2011, José Socrates was the Prime Minister. He headed a Socialist minority government with variable support from other political parties in Parliament. The present sovereign debt crisis brought political parties together, in particular the main opposition party, the Social Democrats, to show solidarity and unity of purpose with the government. The Portuguese government is implementing a very austere consolidation budget, which is designed to strengthen confidence in the Portuguese economy. The relationship between the President of the republic and the Prime Minister can be characterized as one of cohabitation, due to the fact that Cavaco Silva was the candidate of the Social Democratic party. A new centre-right coalition government consisting of the Social Democrats and the Democratic Social Centre-People's Party, under Prime Minister Pedro Passos Coelho, came into power after the early elections of 5 June 2011.

5 Brief account of the political parties

The Portuguese party system emerged in the first elections of 25 April 1975 during the transition to democracy. Four main parties emerged out of these elections, which today still remain pivotal to the party system. Two are large and two are small parties. The only main cleavage is the left–right ideological one. Amongst the large parties, the Socialists, PS (*Partido Socialista*) is on the centre-left position, whilst the Social Democratic Party, PSD (*Partido democrata social*) is on a centre-right position. This is completed by the small Portuguese Communist Party, PCP (*Partido Comunista Português*), which formed a coalition with the tiny Green Party, PEV (*Partido Os Verdes*), on the left, and the Democratic Social Centre-People's Party, CDS-PP (*Centro*

Table 15.2 List of political parties in Portugal

Original name	Abbreviation	English translation
Bloco da Esquerda	BE	Bloc of the Left
Centro Democratico Social-Partido Popular	CDS-PP	Democratic Social Centre-People's Party
Coligação Democrática Unitária	CDU	Democratic Unitary Coalition
Movimento Esperança Portugal	MEP	Movement Hope Portugal
Movimento Mérito e Sociedade	MMS	Movement Party of Earth
Movimento Partido da Terra-MPT	MPT	Movement Party of Earth
Partido Comunista Portuguê-Partido Os Verdes	PCP-PEV	Communist Party-Green Party
(Partido Comunista dos Partidos Portugueses-Movimento Reorganizativo do Partido do Proletariado	PCTP-MRPP	Communist Party of the Portuguese Workers Movement for the Reorganization of the Party of the Proletariat
Partido Popular Monárquico	PPM	People's Monarchic Party
Partido Socialista	PS	Socialist Party
Partido Social Democrata	PSD	Social Democratic Party

Democratico Social-Partido Popular). The smaller parties are more radical in terms of either left-wing or right-wing policies. Since 1975, other parties have had major difficulties in joining this *quadrille bipolaire*. However, in the 1999 general elections a new party representing the legacy of the extreme left during the revolutionary process emerged and joined the *quadrille bipolaire*. Since 1999, the left-wing Left Bloc, BE (*Bloco da Esquerda*) was able to increase its share of the vote considerably. Ideologically, it is placed to the left of the Communist Party. Between the 1999 and 2009 general elections the BE increased its share of the vote from 2.4 per cent and 2 seats to 9.8 per cent and 16 seats. More surprising was that the electoral results of the PCP-PEV, which got only 7.9 per cent of the vote and 15 seats, were bypassed (Ministry of Justice, 2009).

5.1 Party attitudes towards the European Union

If we compare the Portuguese political level of intra-party cohesion over Europe with those of the United Kingdom, no major cleavages are apparent. In all main political parties, but also in the smaller parties, the official position is carried by the entire party. Most parties are pro European. This is valid particularly for the PS, the PSD, and the CDS-PP. Some Euroscepticism existed in the 1990s in the CDS-PP, but this evaporated when Paulo Portas became leader of the party between 1997 and 2004 and then again after 2006. A more pragmatic pro-European position allowed the CDS-PP to become part of a coalition government with the PSD between 2002 and 2004. The two left-wing parties, the PCP-PEV and the BE, can be characterized as soft Eurosceptic according to the categories created by Paul Taggart and Aleks Szczerbziak (2002, 11). It means that they are considerably critical of the European Union, but they propose an alternative to the present neo-liberal model. There is no call for ending membership in the European Union. Both emphasize national sovereignty against the policies of a neo-liberal Europe. One could probably characterize their posture as 'integration Euroscepticism', in that these parties regard the present direction of integration as being wrong, and they propose a different direction, which focusses more on the social rights of workers (Harmsen, 2005, 2007).

6 Public opinion and the European Union

Portugal belongs to the cluster of southern European countries that are extremely Europhile and contrast heavily with the United Kingdom and the Nordic countries. Since accession to the EC/EU in 1986, the Portuguese have always responded overwhelmingly positively to the Eurobarometer questions that EU membership is good and that the country benefitted from membership. Between 1986 and 2000, there were very few occasions when support for EU membership was slightly below the EU average; however between 1996 and 2000, it swung above the EU average to between 55 and 70 per cent (Eurobarometer 54, 2000, 47).

In the first decade of the new millennium, both support for and benefits from the EU have been decreasing. The decline in support for EU membership has been most dramatic, declining from 64 per cent in Spring 2000 to 50 per cent in Spring 2009. Since 2006, Portuguese support for the EU has been below the EU average. Similarly, we can observe a decline in the public perception of EU membership benefits from 71 per cent in Spring 2000 to 62 per cent in Spring 2009; however, this is still above the EU average.

This decline is certainly related to the economic crisis that the country has been facing since the beginning of the millennium. Economic growth has been stagnating for several years; 2003 was a negative growth year. Moreover, the crisis has led to a major budget deficit, above the 3 per cent GDP allowed by the European Union. An excessive budgetary procedure was opened against Portugal in 2002 and, despite the fact that the rules were changed after 2004–2005, Portugal still is struggling to balance its budget. The financial crisis has certainly exacerbated such efforts. However, a growth and stability programme agreed between the Portuguese government and the European Commission, which runs until 2013, is designed to make the necessary structural changes in order to achieve a balanced budget (Torres, 2009).

7 National and EP electoral systems

In Portugal, a proportional electoral system based on the d'Hondt method is used for all elections. Moreover, political parties have strong control over the candidates because the lists

Table 15.3 Portuguese attitude to the European Union (%)★

	EB53 (2000)	EB55 (2001)	EB57 (2002)	EB59 (2003)	EB61 (2004)	EB63 (2005)	EB65 (2006)	EB67 (2007)	EB69 (2008)	EB71 (2009)	EB73 (2010)	EB75 (2011)
Portugal	64	57	63	61	55	61	47	55	50	50	43	39
EU average	49	48	53	54	48	54	55	57	52	53	49	47

Source: Eurobarometer, http://ec.europa.eu/public_opinion/index_en.htm.

Note: European Union membership is a good thing.

Table 15.4 Perceived benefit of EU membership in Portugal (%)★

	EB53 (2000)	EB55 (2001)	EB57 (2002)	EB59 (2003)	EB61 (2004)	EB63 (2005)	EB65 (2006)	EB67 (2007)	EB69 (2008)	EB71 (2009)	EB73 (2010)	EB75 (2011)
Portugal	71	68	69	68	66	67	56	66	61	62	54	51
EU average	47	45	51	50	47	55	54	59	54	56	53	52

Source: Eurobarometer, http://ec.europa.eu/public_opinion/index_en.htm.

Note: Positive answers.

are closed and there is no preference voting. The MPs or MEPs do not represent a constituency, but rather the whole country, although they are elected at constituency level. This means that the central offices of political parties can select and replace MPs or MEPs during a particular legislature (Lobo, 2003, 260–5). In national elections, 230 MPs are elected in 22 multi-member constituencies and on average 11 MPs are elected in each of them. However, there are big differences between the constituencies. In 2005, 53 and 38 MPs were elected in Lisbon and Oporto, respectively. In contrast the less populated regions of inner Portugal – like Bragança and Portalegre – had just 4 and 3 elected, respectively. In Western Europe, Portugal occupies a middle-ranking place in terms of the number of MPs elected in constituencies. It is certainly more difficult in Spain, which uses the same electoral system, but there are very small constituencies leading to extremely disproportional results (Jalali, 2005, 275–7).

Although the electoral system is the same for European Parliament elections, all MEPs are elected in just one constituency. However, the number of MEPs has been declining since 1987. Originally, 25 MEPs were elected, then 24 in 2004, and 22 in 2009. This reduction in the number of Portuguese MEPs is related to the changing provisions of the EU treaties and the EU's Central and Eastern European enlargement.

8 A glance at the EP and national elections

Similar to most other countries, voter participation in European elections declined considerably after the first direct elections in 1987. In the first European Parliament elections, the participation rate was 72.4 per cent, which then declined abruptly to 51.1 per cent in 1989, and even further after 1994, with abstention figures below 40 per cent.

One of the reasons for the high turnout in the first European elections in 1987 was that it was conducted simultaneously with national elections. Prime Minister Cavaco Silva had headed a minority PSD government since 1985, but a motion of censure of all parliamentary parties led to his resignation and the call for early elections by the President of the Republic Mário Soares. Cavaco Silva and his party came out as the winner in both elections. His charismatic style and modernization agenda was boosted by Portugal's recent accession to the EU on 1 January 1986. The second largest party was undertaking a major transition, because long-standing leader Soares had become the President in 1986. In this situation, no leader of the PS was able to have the same standing and charismatic power as Soares (Magone, 2005, 505–10). The 1987 European election campaign could not be separated from the general election one, so that issues of stability and ability to govern were at the forefront of the campaign. The popularity of Cavaco Silva, particularly after the successful motion of censure by the left wing parties (PS, PCP, and PRD), led to a one-sided electoral contest. The main slogan of the PSD 'Portugal cannot stop!' ('*Portugal não pode parar!*') targeted the left-wing parties responsible for the downfall of the government. They were portrayed as major obstacles for the government's modernization and democratization programmes. The 17 July 1987 elections were a major victory for Cavaco Silva and his party in both the general as well as the European elections. In the general

Table 15.5 Turnout at EP elections in Portugal: 1987–2009 (%)

	1987	1989	1994	1999	2004	2009
Abstention	28.6	48.9	64.5	60.1	61.4	63.2
Turnout	**72.4**	**51.1**	**35.5**	**39.6**	**38.6**	**36.8**

Source: National Electoral Commission, http://www.cne.pt.

elections, the PSD got a clear electoral mandate by achieving an absolute majority, and in the European Parliament elections it obtained 37.4 per cent of the vote and 10 seats. The Socialists had catastrophic results in both elections. In the European elections they got just 22.5 per cent of the vote and 6 seats. The conservative Democratic Social Centre also did well, with 15.4 per cent and 4 seats, whilst the PCP secured 11.5 per cent and 3 seats, and the PRD, the main instigator of the censure motion, got 4.4 per cent and one seat. Probably the most salient fact of the 1987 EP elections was that the PSD got 15 percentage points less than in the general elections. In contrast, the CDS got just 4 per cent of the vote in the general elections and over 15 per cent of the vote in European elections. The main reason for this result is that the charismatic and extremely Euro-enthusiastic Francisco Lucas Pires was the head of the list in the European Parliament elections (Bacalhau, 1995, 246–7).

The 1989 EP elections were the first held simultaneously with the other EU Member States. They took place in the mid-term of the absolute majority government of Prime Minister Cavaco Silva and his PSD. Therefore, the campaign was dominated by national issues and the performance of the Cavaco Silva government. The Socialists, under new leader Jorge Sampaio, formed a coalition with the Democratic Renewal Party, PRD (*Partido Renovador Democratico*) of former President António Ramalho Eanes. Their main slogan was '*Mudar Portugal, para Ganhar Portugal*' ('Let's Change Portugal to win Portugal'), however Jorge Sampaio was not able to make an impact. The Communist Party formed a coalition with new Green Party called the Democratic Unitary Coalition, CDU (*Coligação Democrática Unitária*). The CDU targeted the alleged corruption of the government, the deterioration of the environment, and living standards. The conservative CDS, headed by Euro-enthusiast Francisco Lucas Pires, concentrated on economic issues, particularly the way the government handled the huge nationalized public sector, which had been created during the revolutionary democratic transition of 1974–1975. The Cavaco Silva government wanted to follow a Thatcherite approach towards privatization (ibid., 247).

According to Mário Bacalhau, the electorate had a low level of knowledge and the political elites did not invest considerable sums in funding in the campaign, so there was a considerable decline in abstention.

In terms of electoral results, the PSD was able to win the elections with a comfortable majority of 32.7 per cent in relation to 1987 (−5 per cent) and 9 seats (−1 seat). The PS and PSD electoral coalition did not lead to substantial gains for the two parties in comparison to 1987. The PS and PRD together got 28.5 per cent of the vote (about +1 per cent) and 8 seats (+1 seat), the Communist-Green CDU was able to improve to 14.4 per cent of the vote (+2.9 per cent) and 4 seats (+1 seat). Last but not least, the CDS was able to profit from the charismatic figure of Lucas Pires and got 14.2 per cent (−1.2 per cent) and 3 seats (−1 seat).

The 1994 elections took place at the end of the second term of Aníbal Cavaco Silva's government. In October 1991, Prime Minister Cavaco Silva had achieved an impressive second absolute majority. The main opposition party, the PS, under the leadership of Jorge Sampaio, failed to improve the electoral results of the party following the general elections of 1987. In 1992, António Guterres was elected as new PS leader and together with António Vitorino introduced a major modernization programme within the party. The 1994 European Parliament elections were a major test for the forthcoming general elections of October 1995. Between 1992 and 1994, the Portuguese economy entered a recession, so that social protests against the Cavaco Silva government increased. PS Party Leader Guterres hoped to profit from this growing unpopularity with the government. The head of the list for the PS was the well-known former Constitutional Court judge Antonio Vitorino, who was well liked by the population. In comparison to the head of list of the PSD, Eurico de Melo, he was extremely well prepared on European issues. Moreover, the PSD was quite divided in relation to the Maastricht

Treaty. The PSD government was supportive of the Maastricht Treaty, in spite of its impact on national sovereignty, however there was dissent and factionalism inside the party which led to a divided image of the party to the outside world. The PSD distanced itself from the slogan of the European parliamentary group ELDR 'My country: Europe' and presented a counter slogan 'Europe, yes, Portugal, forever' (Magone, 1996, 148 and 152). The PS could therefore present itself as the party of European integration due to the role that former Prime Minister and then President Soares played in the accession negotiations to the EC/EU.

The two other opposition parties, which had representation in the European Parliament, focussed their campaigns on the impact on national sovereignty after the ratification of the Maastricht Treaty. The Communist coalition CDU moderated their anti-EU discourse, emphasizing the need for the reinforcement of social Europe in what new party leader Carlos Carvalhas called 'Europe of the bankers and bureaucrats'. After 1993, the CDS-PP, under the new charismatic and young leader Manuel Monteiro, changed the position of the party from pro-European to Eurosceptic based on the discourse of *Europe des patries*. Monteiro wanted a national referendum on the Maastricht Treaty; the main slogan was '*Viva Portugal*' (Magone, 1996, 150). Former head of list Francisco Lucas Pires left the party, after the ideological turn and the rise of Manuel Monteiro, and joined the PSD. The CDS-PP was expelled from the EPP due to its change of position in 1993 (ibid., 150). Another ten tiny parties took part in these European Parliament elections, which clearly had Euro-manifestos targeting European integration issues.

Although opinion polls predicted a result below 30 per cent for the PSD, the results were not so bad for the government party. The PSD got 34.4 per cent (in relation to 1989, +1.7 per cent) and 9 seats (no change). The winner was the PS, which was able to improve considerably in relation to 1989. The Socialists got 34.9 per cent (+6 per cent) and 10 seats (+2 seats). The smaller parties lost to the larger parties. The Communist–Green coalition CDU got 11.5 per cent (−3.2 per cent) and 3 seats (no change) and the CDS-PP got 12.5 per cent (−1.6 per cent) and 3 seats.

In the 1994 EP elections, the smaller parties showed some resistance to the unquestioned position on European integration by both main parties, the PS and PSD. Both the CDS-PP as well as the Communist–Green CDU coalition, wanted referenda on the Maastricht Treaty due to its impact on national sovereignty. The salience of Europe allowed these smaller parties to do better in the EP elections than in general or local elections. In particular, the CDS-PP used populist language against a supranational European Union and the main political parties.

The 1999 EP elections took place at the end of the first term of the Socialist minority government of Prime Minister António Guterres. In economic terms, the Guterres government was one of considerable stability and continuity in the policies of the previous Cavaco Silva governments. Portugal was able to fulfil the Maastricht criteria to join the third phase of Economic and Monetary Union (EMU) along with ten other Member States in 1998. The PS government very much followed a 'Third Way approach' similar to that of the Labour Party in the United Kingdom. For the opposition parties, the 1999 European elections were a dress rehearsal for the general elections taking place in October. In particular, the PSD was very keen to improve on the abysmal electoral result of the last general elections in 1995, in which it lost its absolute majority and was replaced by the Socialists in power. After the departure of Prime Minister Cavaco Silva, shortly before the end of his third term, the party was characterized by infighting and factionalism. Shortly before the European Parliament elections, Manuel Durão Barroso was elected new leader. However, factionalism and divisions within the party continued before, during, and after the European Parliament elections. After the resignation of the head of the list, Leonor Beleza, Barroso appointed the polemical José Pacheco Pereira as the head of the list. The new leader pushed forward an agenda of change based on a strategy of polarization. Their campaign slogan was 'In Europe, on behalf of the Portuguese' ('*Na Europa, pelos Portugueses*').

In contrast, the Socialists were able to present as their head of the list the popular former Prime Minister and President of the Republic Mário Soares. They presented Soares as the main candidate for the presidency of the European Parliament. This annoyed people inside the Party of European Socialists and also the European People's Party. The main slogan of the party was 'Portugal in the heart of Europe' ('*Portugal no coração da Europa*'). The campaign was quite optimistic and profited from a good economic situation. There was strong campaign coordination between the Socialist Party and the Party of European Socialists.

The Communist–Green coalition had as the head of its list Ilda Figueiredo, who was part of the orthodox wing of the party and therefore a safe candidate for the European Parliament. Apart from strong criticisms about the Maastricht Treaty's impact on national sovereignty, it also condemned the Portuguese government for taking part in the Kosovo War alongside its NATO partners (Magone, 2001). After the CDS-PP's bad electoral results in the 1997 local elections, the then leader Manuel Monteiro resigned and was replaced by the charismatic former journalist Paulo Portas. The party abandoned thereafter its Eurosceptic position and moved towards the centre. Although the national interest continued to be an important aspect of their position towards the European Union, overall Portas was more flexible and ready for compromise with the other main parties, particularly the PSD. However, the opinion polls predicted a very bad result for Portas (ibid.).

The new Left Bloc, BE (*Bloco da Esquerda*), under the leadership of Francisco Louçã and Miguel Portas, was another party that was quite successful in bringing across their Socialist message, in particular through their anti-Kosovo position. Their campaign was quite different from the mainstream parties and tended to target the younger generation.

Due to the opposition parties' weak situation, the PS was able to win the elections with 43.1 per cent in relation to 1994 (+8.6 per cent) and 12 seats (+2). The PSD saw its electoral share further decline from its peak in 1987, achieving only 31.1 per cent (−3.3 per cent) and 8 seats (−1). The Green–Communist PCP-PEV coalition got 10.3 per cent (−1.5 per cent) and 2 seats (−1). The results for the CDS-PP were the big surprise of the election; opinion polls predicted that they would lose representation in the European Parliament. Paulo Portas and his party were able to achieve 8.2 per cent (−4.3 per cent) and 2 seats (−1). The Left Bloc's excellent results were quite surprising; they achieved 1.8 per cent of the vote, but no seats. This result guaranteed the public funding that could be used for the 1999 general elections. Indeed, the Left Bloc was able to improve its results and achieve representation in the Portuguese Parliament. In the general elections, the Left Bloc got 2.4 per cent and 2 seats. It was beginning of a rising movement that today achieves about 9–10 per cent of the vote in European and general elections.

Table 15.6 National election results in Portugal: 1985–2011 (%)

Political party	1985	1987	1991	1995	1999	2002	2005	2009	2011
PS	20.7	22.2	29.3	43.8	44.0	37.8	45.0	36.6	28.1
PSD	29.9	50.2	50.4	34.2	32.3	40.1	28.7	29.1	38.6
CDS-PP	9.9	4.4	4.4	9.8	8.4	8.8	7.2	10.4	11.7
PCP-PEV	15.5	12.1	8.8	8.6	9.0	7.0	7.5	7.9	7.9
PRD	17.9	4.9	—	—	—	—	—	—	—
PSN	—	1.7	0.2	—	—	—	—	—	—
BE	—	0.0	—	2.5	2.5	2.8	6.4	9.8	5.2
Others	6.1	4.6	6.9	1.1	3.5	3.6	11.6	2.8	8.5

Source: National Electoral Commission, http://www.cne.pt.

Table 15.7 EP election results in Portugal: 1987–2004

Political party	1987 Seats	%	1989 Seats	%	1994 Seats	%	1999 Seats	%	2004 Seats	%
PS	22.5	6	28.5	8	34.9	10	43.1	12	44.5	12
PSD	37.5	10	32.8	9	34.4	9	31.1	9	—	—
CDS-PP	15.4	4	14.2	3	12.5	3	8.2	2	—	—
Força Portugal (PSD+CDS/PP)	—	—	—	—	—	—	—	—	33.3	9
CDU/PCP-PEV	11.5	3	14.4	4	11.2	3	10.3	2	9.1	2
PRD	4.4	1	—	—	—	—	—	—	—	—
BE	—	—	—	—	—	—	1.8	—	4.9	1
Others	8.7	—	10.2	—	7.1	—	5.6	—	8.2	—

Source: National Electoral Commission, http://www.cne.pt.

The 2004 elections took place during the European Football Championship and in the midterm of the PSD–CDS-PP coalition government headed by Prime Minister Manuel Durão Barroso. After catastrophic local elections in December 2001, the then Prime Minister António Guterres – whose party failed by a whisker to achieve an absolute majority in the 1999 elections – decided to resign, to the surprise of his government and party colleagues. The then President Jorge Sampaio called for early elections in March 2002, which led to the victory of the PSD under the leadership of Manuel Durão Barroso. After negotiations a coalition agreement was signed between the PSD and the CDS-PP. The centre-right coalition government was under considerable European constraint due to the fact that Portugal had to deal with an excessive budgetary procedure initiated by the European Commission. Portugal had a budget deficit above the 3 per cent of GDP threshold set out by the Maastricht EMU criteria. This meant that the Barroso government had to introduce a package of austerity measures to reduce the budget deficit below 3 per cent of GDP. Major cuts in welfare provision, public administration, and the public sector reinforced the Portuguese economic recession that had already started in 2001. By 2004, the Barroso government was quite unpopular. The European Parliament elections were the first test. For the opposition parties, this was an opportunity to expose the harsh policies of the Barroso government. The government parties formed an electoral coalition under the label 'Forward Portugal' ('*Força Portugal*') similar to that of Silvio Berlusconi's party *Forza Italia*. It was a populist attempt to mobilize their constituencies in the context of the European Football Championship. The head of its list was João de Deus Pinheiro, a former member of the Jacques Delors II and Jacques Santer Commissions.

The opposition parties were quite optimistic about their performance in the EP elections, due to the unpopularity of the government. The Socialist party used the campaign to target the austerity policies of the government. They used the slogan 'We deserve a better Portugal' ('*Merecemos um Portugal melhor*'). The head of the party's list was António de Sousa Franco, the former President of the Portuguese Audit Court and also the Finance Minister during the first Guterres government. He ran a very successful campaign; however, in the northern city of Matosinhos, he collapsed due to exhaustion and died shortly thereafter before the elections on 13 June 2004. He was replaced by António Costa, a former minister of the Guterres government. There was strong coordination between the Socialist manifesto and that of the Party of European socialists.

The Green–Communist coalition also focussed their campaign against the government's austerity package. The position of the PCP–PEV coalition converged towards that of the European

United Left/Nordic Green Left (EUL/NGL), which also founded a new European Left Party in 2004. Their main slogan was 'Portugal: Another way for Portugal and Europe' ('*Portugal: Um outro caminho para Portugal e Europa*'), which focussed on social Europe and the need to change the neo-liberal priorities of the European Union and move more towards social issues. Another theme was the 'militarization of the EU' and a critique of the support that some European governments, including the Portuguese government, gave to the Iraq War. In spite of this growing convergence of the PCP to positions of the EUL/NGL parliamentary group and the European Left Party, it still did not adhere to the European Left Party.

The Left Bloc supported a supranational European Union; however, like the Communists, this party also criticized the neo-liberal outlook of European policies. The BE emphasized a peace policy against the further militarization of the EU. They also criticized the Iraq War and the involvement of the Portuguese government. Solidarity and the social dimension of the economy were important aspects of the party's manifesto. Their main slogan was 'Refounding Europe, Changing Portugal' ('*Refundar a Europa, Mudar Portugal*').

The results of the elections led to a major defeat of the government coalition. *Força Portugal* got 33.3 per cent in relation to 1999 (−7 per cent) and 9 seats (−2 seats), whilst the PS got its best electoral result ever with 44.5 per cent (+1.4 per cent) and 12 seats. The PCP-PEV got 9.1 per cent (−1.2 per cent) and 2 seats. The BE continued its successful trajectory by improving considerably on the 1999 European Parliament elections and getting representation. The BE got 4.9 per cent (+3.1 per cent) and 1 seat (+1 seat).

The Portuguese party system in European Parliament elections is quite stable. Traditionally it is a *quadrille bipolaire*: two large parties, on the left the PS and on the right the PSD, and two smaller parties, on the left the PCP-PEV and on the right the CDS-PP. After 1999, the Left Bloc, which is a merger of two small left-wing parties, was able to join the *quadrille bipolaire*.

9 The 2009 European election

9.1 Party lists and manifestos

The Portuguese Constitutional Court approved the candidacy of thirteen parties. Apart from the main five parties, the PS, PSD, CDS-PP, PCP-PEV, and BE, there were a further eight small parties taking part in the 2009 European election with 286 candidates and 77 substitutes. In this section, we will first discuss the programmes of the main five parties, and then turn to the smaller parties.

The Socialist Party closely followed the programme delineated by the Party of European Socialists (PES). There was no parallel national Euro-manifesto. The PES' very short Euro-manifesto was translated into Portuguese only, and distributed across the country. 'People First: A New Direction for Europe' was the slogan used during the campaign, which clearly was the translation of the overarching campaign of the PES. It also used the label 'Party of Europe' below the logo of the Socialist Party, emphasizing its European credentials since its foundation. Moreover, it used also the slogan 'We, Europeans' to emphasize the long tradition of the Socialist Party in terms of supporting the European integration process. The PS followed the 12 priorities set up by the PES. Amongst the aspects that they emphasized were more market regulation in order to prevent a new financial crisis, the reinforcement of social Europe through more rights for workers, the fight against climate change, and the promotion of environmental policies (PS, 2009).

The Social Democrats were less attached to the programme of the European People's Party. This has to do with the origins of the party. It has been labelled as the 'most Portuguese of all political parties' because it clearly is ideologically quite pragmatic, with both Liberal as well as Social Democratic ideological origins (Frain, 1996). It tends to be a centre-right party emphasizing the modernization of the country. It emphasized the need to establish a national platform and criticized the incumbent Socialist government in its programme. The manifesto was used strategically in order to transform the European Parliament election into what Koepke and Ringe call a 'Second-Order National Election' (Koepke and Ringe, 2006, 324) about the performance of the government in European and national issues. The main slogan was the 'European contract with the Portuguese'. The programme emphasized that the 22 candidates, if elected, would be representing the national interest. This is quite a contrast to the Socialist programme, which was quite integrated in the overall transnational campaign of the PES. Other aspects of the programme were directed against the government, such as the creation of employment through the efficient use of structural funds. They also emphasized the importance of environmental and energy policies. Support for President Manuel Durão Barroso's second term, who was a former leader of the PSD, was also quite important. They regarded this as reinforcing Portuguese leadership in the European Union. Moreover, the PSD wanted to make sure that Portuguese remained an official language of the EU. Last but not least, there was also strong support for the completion of the ratification process of the Lisbon Treaty (PSD, 2009). The PSD did not closely follow the Euro-manifesto of the European People's Party.

The CDS-PP has its origins in the Christian-Democratic movement but moved towards a more Eurosceptic position in the 1990s to return back to its roots. Its Euro-manifesto emphasized the defence of the national interest in the European Union and the importance of the European Parliament within the European Union. However, most of the manifesto was used strategically against the policies of the incumbent Socialist government. Amongst the areas that were emphasized were the 'catastrophic situation in the agricultural sector', increased taxation, and the inefficient use of structural funds especially during the finance crisis (CDS-PP, 2009). The CDS-PP did not closely follow the Euro-manifesto of the European People's Party.

The Communist Party-Greens (PCP-PEV) were quite critical of the European Union's evolution. They did not pursue a 'hard Eurosceptic' position. Rather they tended to be a soft Eurosceptic party that wanted to change the direction of the European Union towards more social policies (Taggart and Szczerbiak, 2002, 11). Their main criticism was that the EU was dominated by neo-liberal thinking and needed to move towards a more socially-oriented form of capitalism. The financial crisis was regarded as a crisis of capitalism and a unique opportunity to undertake this transformation. Moreover, the PCP-PEV emphasized the need to protect the national interest against supranational policies. The protection of national sovereignty was emphasized in this respect. The slogan of the party was 'For a Portugal of progress and peace in a Europe of peace and cooperation' (PCP-PEV, 2009). The PCP-PEV followed policies similar to those in the Euro-manifesto of the European Unitary Left/Nordic Green Left (UEL/NGL) parliamentary group.

The Left Bloc followed a similar position to the PCP-PEV, although in a more pragmatic and concrete way. Their strongholds are in the larger urban centres and amongst the younger population. They concretely addressed several issues; for example, opposition to a second Barroso term, because he was regarded as one of the reasons for the crisis in the first place, and excessive bonus payments to managers in the banking sector. The BE was also against the Lisbon Treaty because a referendum on it was not held in Portugal, which was regarded as a democratic deficit in the European Union. The discourse was similar to that of the PCP-PEV in terms of the social rights of workers. In the media, particularly on television and the internet, they used very original videos to bring their message across on health policy, labour, the Lisbon Treaty, and other issues. A quite surrealistic series called Fantasmabloco (Ghostbloc) in which real actors supporting the BE performed in horror stories about situations in Portugal was used during the campaign. In spite of this approach, the BE is certainly a moderate Eurosceptic party, due to the lack of democratic accountability and transparency in decision-making. Furthermore, similarly to the PCP-PEV, they are quite critical of the neo-liberal tendencies of the European Union, and want workers' social rights to be reinforced (BE, 2009). The BE is also integrated in the EUL/NGL and closely followed their Euro-manifesto.

Amongst the smaller parties, one has to differentiate those that were already old and those that were new in the 2009 elections. There were six old and two new parties.

The three oldest parties were the Communist Party of Portuguese Workers-Movement for the Reorganization of the Party of the Proletariate, PCTP-MRPP (*Partido Comunista dos Trabalhadores Portugueses-Movimento Reorganizativo do Partido do Proletariado*), the Workers' Socialist Unity Party, POUS (*Partido Operário de Unidade Socialista*) and the Monarchic People's Party, PPM (*Partido Monárquico Popular*).

The PCTP-MRPP and the POUS are two extreme-left parties, which were part of the revolutionary legacy. The PCTP-MRPP existed before the Portuguese 'Carnation Revolution', which took place on 25 April 1974 and is a Maoist splinter party of the PCP. It is a tiny party advocating policies similar to the PCP-PEV and the BE. The language of its programme is quite Marxist. Similarly, the POUS is even smaller than the PCTP-MRPP and emerged as a Trotskyite splinter part out of the Socialist Party. The POUS has created a separate movement called the National Commission to End Membership of the European Union, RUE (*Comissão Nacional para a Ruptura com a União Europeia*). Both emphasized that this was a crisis of capitalism and there was a need to improve the living conditions of the Portuguese population. There was some cooperation between the POUS, the PCP, and the BE, especially to stop layoffs. The POUS has major financial difficulties, which are always addressed on the website (PCTP-MRPP, 2009; POUS, 2009).

The PPM, which was founded in 1975 and was an important coalition partner of the main centre-right parties between 1979 and 1983, emphasized the defence of the Portuguese national interest in the European Union. Amongst its key issues were environment protection and more support for Portuguese agriculture and fisheries (PPM, 2009).

The Earth Party Movement, MPT (*Movimento Partido da Terra*), founded in 1994, became part of the Europe-wide coalition of parties under the Libertas banner of Irish billionaire Declan Ganley. It is a conservative green party, which emphasized not only green policies, but also the protection of the national heritage, including the culture of other Portuguese-speaking countries around the world (MPT, 2009).

The Humanist Party, PH (*Partido Humanista*) did not develop a specific European policy. It tried only to bring across its message of pacifism and non-violent conflict resolution (PH, 2009).

The last old party is the National Renewal Party, PNR (*Partido Nacional Renovador*). This party belongs to the family of extreme-right parties across Europe, such as the British National Party or the *Front National* in France. It is an anti-immigration, anti-Islamic, and hard Eurosceptic party. It emphasizes the need to protect national sovereignty, in particular through ending membership in the EU (PNR, 2009).

The two new parties seem to be influenced by events in the United States. The Movement of Hope Portugal, MEP (*Movimento da Esperança Portugal*) and the Merit and Society Movement, MMS (*Movimento Mérito e Sociedade*) emerged out of civil society. They were clearly interested in creating new citizens' movements that would challenge the main established political parties. The MEP presented a Euro-manifesto directed towards the protection of the disadvantaged in society, particularly migrants, as well as environmental policies and the accession of Turkey. Their policies were Europhile, emphasizing in particular the positive message that citizens themselves could contribute to a better Europe. The MMS clearly focussed on improving the efficiency of policies in Portugal within the European Union. The programme was well-thought out and almost like a business plan, using a SWOT analysis of the strengths and weaknesses of Portugal.

9.2 Electoral campaign

The office of the European Parliament in Portugal engaged in an ambitious information campaign targeted directly to young people in particular. It used all media, but particularly the internet, Facebook, HI5, Twitter, and YouTube to motivate people to vote. The main theme of the campaign was to emphasize that if citizens do not vote, then decisions are taken by others. The whole approach of the European Parliament was pan-European, so that the Portuguese campaign was part of an overall thrust to motivate people to vote. Prominent personalities from the entertainment sector were hired to appeal to people to vote (European Parliament, 2009a).

On 14 May 2009, there was a debate on the Portuguese public television channel RTP. The heads of the lists of all 13 parties took part in this debate. It was a two and a half hour-long debate on all issues related to the European Union, such as the financial crisis, taxation, the Lisbon Treaty, and the implementation of structural funds. Most candidates concentrated their interventions on the financial crisis. Whilst the Socialist Party was supportive of recent EU policies related to the re-launching of the economy, most of the other parties criticized the government. The BE, PCTP/MRPP, PNR, NS, and POUS criticized the policies of the EU. Vital Moreira, the PS candidate, Paulo Rangel of the PSD, and Laurinda Alves, the MEP candidate, were particularly supportive of EU policies (RTP, 2009).

Throughout election day, all major channels, in particular the public channel RTP, and the two private channels SIC and TVI, covered the election. Each one used different polling firms to get the first results from the European elections.

The most important issue during the campaign was the financial crisis and the steep rise in unemployment in Portugal. According to the National Institute of Statistics, the unemployment rate was 8.9 per cent in the first quarter of 2009, and 9.1 in the second quarter (Statistics Portugal, 2009). This was a topic that was expounded on by the parties to the left of the Socialist party.

In this context, the main opposition party, the PSD, used the European elections as a second-order national election test for the forthcoming general elections that were scheduled for 27 September 2009. Many issues related to the performance of the government were raised. The PSD used a parallel electoral website called 'Politics of Truth' ('*Politica da Verdade*') in which several policies and statements by the incumbent Socialist government were criticized. The head of the list, Paulo Rangel, was very keen to show the government's inefficient use of EU structural funds, in spite of the major crisis that the government had to deal with.

Another important topic was the Lisbon Treaty. The PS, PSD, and CDS-PP were supporters of the treaty, but they were fiercely opposed by the left-wing parties, the PCP-PEV, BE, MRPP-PCTP, and POUS. Their main criticism was that the Lisbon Treaty represented just one further step towards a neo-liberal European Union, where the social rights of workers were neglected. For the BE, a referendum on the treaty was an important issue. It characterized the treaty as lacking democratic legitimacy due to the behaviour of the EU's elites. However, one has to differentiate between the PCP-PEV and the BE, which were both members in the UEL-NGL group and represented a soft Euroscepticism as already mentioned, and the more radical PCTP-MRPP and POUS that advocated a hard Euroscepticism, which aimed at ending Portugal's membership in the European Union. Amongst the other smaller parties, only the extreme right-wing PNR was against the Treaty of the European Union and pursued a hard Eurosceptic position that included ending EU membership.

Another campaign topic was support for a second term for José Manuel Durão Barroso, the President of the European Commission. The main opposition party, PSD, particularly advocated this position, because Barroso was one of their former leaders. He was also supported by the PS and the CDS-PP. In contrast, the PCP-PEV and the BE vehemently opposed his election to a second term, because he was regarded as part of the reason for the policies.

The environment and the energy policy, were also mentioned, in particular by the smaller parties such as the MMS. The extreme right-wing PNR was the only party to voice opposition to further enlargement and especially the inclusion of Turkey. The MEP was the only party that dared to criticize the PNR's position; it was clearly supportive of further enlargement including Turkey, and for better inclusion of migrants that come to Portugal (RTP, 2009). In sum, the campaign of this second-order national election felt like a rehearsal for the forthcoming legislative elections scheduled after the EP elections on 27 September 2009. All opposition parties used the EP elections to highlight negative aspects in the government's performance. Opposition parties tended to behave as if this was a national election (Hix and Marsh, 2007, 496).

9.3 Electoral results

Throughout the campaign several opinion polls predicted a close race between the PS and the PSD. This meant that the Socialists would lose considerably after the 2004 EP elections and the 2005 legislative elections. In this sense, the opinion polls confirmed that the Socialist government would be punished heavily in the elections. Two main reasons accounted for the Socialist government's possible losses. First, Portugal was considerably affected by the financial crisis. Capital-poor enterprises had major difficulties in surviving and therefore had to close their doors. Unemployment rose steeply from 2004, but did not stop during the four years of Socialist

Table 15.8 EP election results in Portugal: 2009

National party	Vote share (%)	Seats	Political group
PSD/PPD	31.7	8	EPP
PS	26.5	7	S&D
BE	10.7	3	EUL/NGL
PCP-PEV	10.6	2	EUL/NGL
CDS-PP	8.3	2	EPP
MEP	1.5	0	—
PCTP-MRPP	1.2	0	—
MPT	0.7		—
MMS	0.6	0	—
PH	0.5	0	—
PPM	0.4	0	—
PNR	0.4	0	—
POUS	0.2	0	—
White vote	4.7	—	—
Nil vote	1.96	—	—
Total	100.0	22	—
Participation	36.8	—	—
Abstention	63.2	—	—

Source: National Electoral Commission, /www.cne.pt; European Parliament, 2009b, http://www.europarl.eu.

government. The second reason was related to the party's choice of candidate, Vital Moreira, a former Communist who became an independent and who was supported by the Socialist Party. He was a university teacher and was very knowledgeable about European affairs. However, his interaction with the public was distant and cool, so that in general terms the main candidate's lack of charisma affected the performance of the whole campaign. Moreover, he was not widely accepted within the party. In particular, Manuel Alegre, a very important leader in the party, criticized Moreira (*Expresso*, 11 May 2009).

Despite these two main factors, the main opposition party PSD/PPD had difficulties in surpassing the Socialists in the opinion polls. Amongst the reasons for this was the fact that PSD leader Manuela Ferreira Leite was not very successful in turning the party into a real alternative to the ruling Socialists. However, there was some sympathy from the public for Paulo Rangel, who clearly was able to look like an underdog in relation to the experienced Socialist candidate Vital Moreira. The inability of the PSD to achieve a convincing lead in the opinion polls led the party to campaign until the very end. The use of the internet through the parallel website 'Politics of Truth' was a major instrument used to discredit the government.

Paulo Rangel also used anti-Spanish sentiment to discredit the Socialist party. Prime Minister José Socrates opened the campaign, together with the Spanish Prime Minister José Luis Zapatero, on 23 April 2009. Both started rallies in Valencia and then in Coimbra on the same day. Prime Minister Socrates spoke Spanish at a rally in Valencia and this was interpreted as giving up on national identity. The anti-Spanish theme became an important game changer for the PSD (*Expresso*, 23 May 2009).

The electoral results were somewhat surprising. The PSD was able to achieve a victory, although it did not move very much from the predicted 30–32 per cent range. In real absolute terms they got 1,025 votes more than in the last elections. The big surprise was the Socialist vote, which clearly collapsed to 26.5 per cent. The party lost more than a half a million votes in relation to the 2004 elections. This meant that voters heavily punished the Socialist Party, in particular by voting for other parties on the left and right. Many voters either abstained or just voted for other left-wing parties as a protest.

Apart from the PSD, the big winner of the European elections was the Left Bloc. Their post-modern multimedia campaign was quite successful in mobilizing the youth vote and also probably attracted some disaffected voters from the PS. Its vote more than doubled and it increased its number of MEPs from 1 to 3. As predicted in the opinion polls, the BE surpassed the PCP-PEV and became the third largest party. The BE was able to achieve a similar result in the general elections of 27 September 2009.

Although the PCP-PEV got 70,000 more votes than in the 2004 elections, despite decreased turnout, it was one of the losers in the overall results because its main competitor on the left, the BE, was able to surpass the party.

9.4 Campaign finance

Portuguese political parties spend considerably less on European Parliament elections than on national elections, confirming the priority given by political parties to the national electoral contest. As Table 15.10 shows, all main political parties planned smaller budgets and spent less money in the European elections than in the general elections in 2009.

The major difference can be seen in the ruling Socialist Party, which had a fourfold increase in their planned budget from the European to general elections. Spending increases amongst the other parties were more modest, nevertheless leading to higher budgets for national elections than for European elections.

Table 15.9 List of Portuguese MEPS: seventh legislature

Name	National party	Political group	Professional background	Date of birth	Gender	Committee/Chair
Paulo Rangel	PSD	EPP	Lawyer	18/02/1968	Male	Member Committee on Constitutional Affairs Member Delegation for Relations with the United States
Carlos Coelho			Insurance representative	20/05/1960	Male	Member Committee on Civil Liberties, Justice and Home Affairs Member Special Committee on Organized Crime, Corruption and Money Laundering Member Delegation to the ACP–EU Joint Parliamentary Assembly
Maria da Graça Carvalho			University professor	09/04/1955	Female	Member Committee on Industry, Research and Energy Member Delegation to the ACP–EU Joint Parliamentary Assembly
Mário David			Physician	20/08/1953	Male	Chairman Delegation for Relations with the Mashreq Countries
Nuno Teixeira			Lawyer	13/01/1973	Male	Member Committee on Regional Development Member Delegation for Relations with the Mercosur Countries
Maria do Céu Patrão Neves			University professor	26/04/1959	Female	Member Committee on Fisheries Member Delegation for Relations with Canada
Regina Bastos			Lawyer	04/11/1960	Female	Member Committee on Employment and Social Affairs Member Committee on Women's Rights and Gender Equality Member Delegation for Relations with Australia and New Zealand

Name	Party	Profession	Date of Birth	Gender	Role
José Manuel Fernandes		Engineer	26/07/1967	Male	Member Committee on Budgets Member Delegation for Relations with the People's Republic of China
Nuno Melo	CDS/PP	Lawyer	19/03/1976	Male	Vice-Chairman Delegation for Relations with the Mercosur Countries
Diogo Feio		Lawyer	06/10/1970	Male	Chairman
Vital Moreira	PS	University professor	08/11/1944	Male	Committee on International Trade
Edite Estrela	S&D	School teacher	28/10/1949	Female	Vice-Chairwoman Committee on Women's Rights and Gender Equality
Luis Manuel Capoulas		Civil servant	22/08/1951	Male	Vice-Chairman Delegation to the Euro-Latin American Parliamentary Assembly
Elisa Ferreira		Diplomat	17/10/1955	Female	Chair
António Fernando Correia de Campos		University professor	14/12/1942	Male	Delegation of Relations to the EU–Chile Joint Parliamentary Committee
Luis Paulo Alves		Manager in cooperative sector	19/09/1961	Male	Member Committee on Regional Development Member Delegation to the ACP-EU Joint Parliamentary Assembly
Ana Gomes		Diplomat	09/02/1954	Female	Member Committee on Foreign Affairs Subcommittee on Human Rights Subcommittee on Security and Defence Delegation for Relations with Iraq
Marisa Matias	BE EUL/NGL	Student	20/02/1976	Female	Vice-chairman Delegation for Relations with the Mashreq Countries

(continued)

Table 15.9 (continued)

Name	National party	Political group	Professional background	Date of birth	Gender	Committee/Chair
Alda Sousa			Biologist	04/08/1953	Female	Member Committee on Budgets Member Delegation of Relations with the Maghreb Countries and the Maghreb Arab Union Delegation of Relations with Iraq
Rui Tavares	PCP-PEV		Writer	29/07/1972	Male	Vice-Chair Specialized Committee on Organised Crime, Corruption and Money Laundering
Inês Cristina Zuber			University researcher	11/03/1980	Female	Vice-Chair Committee on Employment and Social Affairs Vice-Chair Delegation for Relations with Central America
João Ferreira			Biologist	20/11/1978	Male	Member Committee on Fisheries Member Delegation to the ACP-EU Joint Parliamentary Assembly

Source: www.europarl.europa.eu/meps/en/search.html?country=PT.

Table 15.10 National and EP election campaign expenditure in Portugal: 2009*

	PSD	PS	BE	PCP-PEV	CDS-PP
EP elections 7 June 2009	2,200	1,500	725	1,200	477
National elections 27 September 2009	3,340	5,547	994	1,950	850

Source: Entidade de Contas (2009) www.tribunalconstitucional.pt/tc/contas_eleicoes-ar-2009.html#1103.
Note: * In thousands of euros.

10 Theoretical interpretation of Euro-elections

10.1 Second-Order Election theory

Overall the results of Euro-elections in Portugal confirmed the hypotheses of Second-Order Election model. As highlighted by André Freire, whereas the economic situation and the popularity of the government represent two major factors influencing the outcome of European elections, citizens tend to vote sincerely in such contests, although they change more from one ideological vote to another, and they vote strategically in general elections. One characteristic of Portuguese elections is that the level of total and inter-bloc volatility is quite high. Only small segments of the electorate use second-order elections to protest; the majority tends to vote sincerely (Freire, 2005). In this sense, the 2009 elections show that the negative economic situation may have led to the ruling party's losses in European elections, because people voted more sincerely.

The opposition usually gains votes at EP elections if these take place in the middle or at the end of the national electoral cycle, such as in 1989 and 1994 when the Socialists won by taking advantage of popular discontent with the Conservative government.

A major pattern has been the success of smaller parliamentary parties, in particular the Communist Party and the Left Bloc. One key factor is the fact that the low turnout in EP elections increases the voting share of a quite loyal constituency in both cases.

The timing really mattered in the Portuguese case, because the European Parliament elections were a general rehearsal for the subsequent general elections of 27 September 2009 (Hix and Marsh, 2007). So far, European elections have taken place at the same time as general elections just once. This was in 1987, and it led to the first absolute majority in the general elections for the PSD under Cavaco Silva's leadership.

Since then, both elections have had separate cycles due to the fact that European elections take place every five years and general elections every four years. Moreover, early elections may be called so that the four-year cycle of general elections may be interrupted, such as after Prime Minister António Guterres' resignation in December 2001, or Prime Minister Pedro Santana Lopes' dismissal by President Jorge Sampaio in 2004.

10.2 Europe Salience theory

We can also modestly interpret the results in terms of Europe Salience theory which clearly emphasizes that extreme parties attract protest votes at EP elections. Probably, the most plausible hypothesis in understanding the Portuguese case is related to the fact that the more extreme a party is on the left–right dimension, the more it will gain from national and European elections. This explains the moderate success of the Left Bloc, which was capable of developing a concrete discourse over the financial crisis, linking both the national and European levels. Manuel Durão Barroso was directly targeted as part of the crisis, not the solution (ibid., 497).

Certainly, whilst 'Europe mattered' in the Portuguese debates, issues were framed through a national lens. The financial crisis was the best vehicle to communicate all the other issues, including environment and energy policy.

It is worth pointing out that Portuguese citizens tend to vote for political parties and their personalities and less for post-materialist issues such as the environment. The low level of immigration in Portugal does not provide much of an argument for extreme right-wing parties. The fact that many Portuguese emigrated abroad during most of the twentieth century probably generates more empathy and sympathy for migrants living in the country.

One major problem in European Parliament elections in Portugal is that turnout has dropped since the country joined the EU in 1987, from 72.4 per cent in the 1987 interim elections to 36.8 per cent in 2009, reaching the lowest level of 35.5 per cent in 1994. Apart from the fact that these elections are not regarded as very important for the majority of the population, they also take place during the summer. Anecdotal evidence seems to suggest that the Portuguese preferred to go to the Algarve beaches than to vote (*Jornal de Notícias*, 7 June 2009).

References

Primary sources

Bloco da Esquerda (BE) (2009) www.bloco.org and www.esquerda.net (accessed on 2 August 2009).
Centro Democrático Social-Partido Popular (CDS-PP) (2009) *Dar Tudo por Portugal. Manifesto Eleitoral do CDS-PP*: www.cds.pt (accessed on 2 August 2009).
Comissão Nacional de Eleições (CNE) website of National Commission of Elections, www.cne.pt (accessed 2 August 2009).
Entidade de Contas website (2009) www.tribunalconstitucional.pt/tc/contas_eleicoes-ar-2009.html#1103 (accessed on 20 October 2013).
Eurobarometer (2001) Eurobarometer 54, Fieldwork November–December 2000, Brussels, European Commission, http://ec.europa.eu/public_opinion/archives/eb/eb54/eb54_en.pdf (accessed 15 February 2015).
Eurobarometer (2009) Eurobarometer 71.3, Country file Portugal fieldwork conducted between 26 January and 13 February 2009, Brussels, European Commission, www.europarl.europa.eu (accessed 30 October 2009).
European Parliament (2009a) Office in Portugal: www.parleurop.pt (accessed 2 August 2009).
European Parliament (2009b) database of MEPs: www.europarl.europa.eu (accessed on 4 August 2009).
European Parliament Database (2010) www.europarl.europa.eu/meps/eu/search.html (accessed on 4 August 2009).
Eurostat (2013, 2014) http://epp.eurostat.ec.europa.eu (accessed on 5 June 2015).
Expresso online (2009) Special file on Portugal 2009: www.aeiou.expresso.pt (accessed 7 and 8 June 2009).
Ministry of Justice (MAJ) (2009), database of electoral results: www.mj.gov.pt (accessed on 23 October 2009).
Movimento Mérito e Sociedade (MMS) (2009) www.mms.pt (accessed on 3 August 2009).
Movimento Partido da Terra (MPT) www.mpt.pt (accessed on 3 August 2009).
National Electoral Commission, www.cne.pt (accessed on 25 October 2009).
O Público online (2009) special file on European Parliament elections 2009, http://eleicoes2009.publico.pt/ (accessed on 7 and 8 June 2009 and 3 August 2009).
Partido Comunista dos Trabalhadores Portugueses-Movimento Reorganizativo do Partido do Proletariado (PCTP-MRPP) (2009) www.pctpmrpp.org (accessed on 2 August 2009).
Partido Comunista Português–Partido Os Verdes (PCP-PEV) (2009) *Declaração Programática do PCP para as Eleições Europeias 2009*, website of the PCP-PEV (accessed on 2 August 2009).
Partido Humanista (PH) (2009) www.movimentohumanista.com/ph (accessed on 2 August 2009).
Partido Nacional Renovador (PNR) (2009) www.pnr.pt (accessed on 3 August 2009).
Partido Operário de Unidade Socialista (POUS) (2009) www.pous4.no.sapo.pt (accessed on 2 August 2009).
Partido Popular Monárquico (PPM) Linhas programáticas da Candidatura do PPM ao Parlamento Europeu 2009, www.ppmeuropa2009.blogspot.com (accessed on 3 August 2009).

Partido Socialdemocrata (PSD) (2009) 'Contrato Europeu com os Portugueses. Eu assino por baixo', www.politicadaverdade.com (accessed on 2 August 2009).

Partido Socialista (PS) (2009) 'As Pessoas estão primeiro. Delegação Portuguesa do Grupo Socialista do Parlamento Europeu', www.ps.pt (accessed on 2 August 2009).

Party of European Socialists (PES) (2009) 'People First: A New Direction for Europe, PES Manifesto June', www.pes.eu (accessed on 2 August 2009).

Rádio Televisão Portuguesa (RTP) (2009), video of European debate of representatives of all 13 parties which took place on 14 May 2009, www.rtp.pt (accessed on 3 August 2009).

Serviço de estrangeiros e fronteiras (2007) 'Relatório de Actividades 2007. Imigração, Fronteiras e Asilo, Lisboa, Serviço de estrangeiros e fronteiras', website, www.sef.pt (accessed on 4 June 2009).

Statistics Portugal (2009) database on website of the National Institute of Statistics, www.ine.pt (accessed on 23 October 2009).

Secondary sources

Bacalhau, M. (1995) 'Portugal: An Ephemeral Election', in van der Eijk, C. and Franklin, M. N. (eds) *Choosing Europe? The European Electorate and National Politics in the Face of Union*, Ann Arbor, University of Michigan Press, 242–51.

Frain, M. (1996), *PPD-PSD e a consolidação do regime democrático*, Lisboa, Noticias editora.

Freire, A. (2005) 'Eleições de segunda ordem e ciclos eleitorais no Portugal Democrático, 1975–2004', *Análise Social*, XL, 2005, 815–46.

Harmsen, R. (2005) 'L'Europe et les partis politiques nationaux: Les Leçons d'un "non-clivage"', *Revue Internationale de Politique Comparée*, 12(1), 77–94.

Hix, S. and Marsh, M. (2007) 'Punishment or Protest? Understanding European Parliament Elections', *Journal of Politics*, 69(2) May, 495–510.

Jalali, C. (2005) *Partidos e Democracia em Portugal 1974–2005. Da Revolução ao Bipartidismo*, Lisboa, Instituto de Ciencias Sociais.

Koepke, R. and Ringe, N. (2006) 'The Second-Order Model in Enlarged Europe', *European Union Politics*, 7(3), 321–46

Lobo, M. C. (2003) 'Legitimizing the EU? Elections to the European Parliament in Portugal 1987–1999', in Pinto, A. C. (ed.) *Contemporary Portugal: Politics, Society and Culture*, New York, Columbia University Press, 203–26.

Magone, J. M. (1996) 'Portugal', in Lodge, J. (ed.) *The 1994 Elections to the European Parliament*, Basingstoke, Palgrave, 147–56.

Magone, J. M. (2001) 'Portugal', in Lodge, J. (ed.) The *1999 Elections to the European Parliament*, Basingstoke, Palgrave, 171–84.

Magone, J. M. (2002) 'Attitudes of Southern European Citizens towards European Integration: Before and After Accession, 1974–2000', in Pinto, A. C. and Teixeira, N. S. (eds) *Southern Europe and the Making of the European Union*, New York, Columbia University Press, 209–36.

Magone, J. M. (2005) 'The Internationalization of the Portuguese Socialist Party, 1973–2003', *Perspectives on European Politics and Society*, 6(3), 491–516.

Taggart, P. and Szczerbiak, A. (2002) *The Party Politics of Euroscepticism in EU Member States*, Sussex European Institute Working Paper, 51.

Torres, F. (2009) 'Policy Responses to the Financial Crisis in the Eurozone: the Case of Portugal', *South European Society and Politics*, 14(1), 55–70.

Country reviews

The Old Member States

The fourth enlargement countries

16	Austria	377
17	Finland	396
18	Sweden	414

16
AUSTRIA

Sylvia Kritzinger and Karin Liebhart

Figure 16.1 Map of Austria

Table 16.1 Austria profile

EU entry year	1995
Schengen entry year	1995
MEPs elected in 2009	17 MEPs
MEPs under Lisbon Treaty	19 MEPs since 1 December 2011 Two additional seats allocated to Josef Weidenholzer (SPÖ/S&D) and to Ewald Stadler (BZÖ/NA)
Capital	Vienna
Total area★	83,879 km^2
Population	8,506,889
	88.6% German-speaking, 1.6% Croatian-speaking 0.5% Hungarian speaking, 0.3% Slovenian-speaking, 0.2% Croatian-speaking – Burgenland version, 0.2% Czech-speaking, 0.1% Slovakian-speaking, 0.1% Romani-speaking
Population density★★	102.9/km^2
Median age of population	42.9
Political system	Federal Republic
Head of state	Heinz Fischer, Social Democratic Party of Austria (SPÖ) (July 2004–)
Head of government	Werner Faymann, Social Democratic Party of Austria (SPÖ) (December 2008–)
Political majority	Social Democratic Party of Austria (SPÖ) and Austrian Peoples' Party (ÖVP) Government Coalition (December 2008–)
Currency	Euro (€) since 1999
Prohead GDP in PPS	38,500 €

Source: Eurostat, 2013, 2014, http://epp.eurostat.ec.europa.eu/.

Notes:
★ Total area including inland waters.
★★ Population density: the ratio of the annual average population of a region to the land area of the region.

1 Geographical position

Located in Central Europe, Austria borders Germany, Switzerland, Lichtenstein, Italy, Slovenia, Hungary, Slovakia, and the Czech Republic. The country, extending over 83,879 square kilometres, consists of nine provinces (*Bundesländer*) with a population of 8.5 million, including small percentages of Slovenian, Croatian, Slovakian, Czech, Hungarian, and Romani language minorities. It has an urbanization rate of 68 per cent and its capital is Vienna.

2 Historical background

Austria is considered a 'belated nation' that turned from a monarchy to a republic in 1918 and was forced into independence against its will. The new nation-state was widely questioned and eventually failed, largely due to ideological conflicts between its two main political camps. The Social Democratic and Christian Socialist ruling coalition, which adopted a parliamentary form of government in accordance with the 1920 Constitutional Act, did not last long, due to the escalation of domestic political tensions. The Social Democrats' political attraction towards the democratic Weimar Republic and the resulting attachment to Germany contrasted with the hesitant Austrian patriotism felt by the Christian Socialist Party. They promoted a Catholic and dynastic-orientated Austrian patriotism and tried to turn Austria into a 'better' Germany.

In March 1933, Federal Chancellor Engelbert Dollfuss dissolved the National Assembly and, in breach of constitutional provisions, began to rule by emergency decree. The Communist Party and the Austrian National Socialist Party were banned. In May 1933 Dollfuss founded the *Vaterländische Front* (Fatherland Front) in order to unify the traditionally bourgeois parties. In February 1934, a civil war took place between the Christian Socialists, supported by the paramilitary *Heimwehr,* and the Social Democratic Party militia, the *Schutzbund*. In the process, social democracy was abolished. In May 1934, a new constitution was promulgated, ideologically rooted in political Catholicism and modelled politically according to Italian and Portuguese fascism. The corporatist state was in power between 1934 and 1938. Dollfuss was killed during a Nazi putsch attempt supported by National Socialist Germany (NS-Germany) in July 1934. His successor, Kurt Schuschnigg, continued the authoritarian political course (Wodak et al., 2009).

Although the so-called *Anschluss*, the annexation of Austria with NS-Germany in March 1938, was achieved by threat of military force, this was accompanied by euphoric celebrations by large segments of the Austrian population. Austria was integrated into the German Reich for seven years.

In the Moscow Declaration of November 1943 (Annex 6), the Allied powers – the UK, the USSR, and the US – declared the occupation of Austria by Germany null and void and expressed their intention to restore it as an independent state.

The Second Republic came into being in April 1945 and adopted the Constitution of 1920, which was amended in 1929. The political success story of the Second Republic, which, like the First Republic, emerged from the disintegration of a larger entity, was mainly based on the consensus orientation of political elites.

Between 1945 and 1955 the Allied Forces occupied Austria, but in 1955 it finally became an independent country again after signing the so-called State Treaty (*Staatsvertrag*) with the Allies. Simultaneously, Austria became a neutral country. Both neutrality and the Austrian model of neo-corporatism – based on a social partnership (*Sozialpartnerschaft*) between labour, business, and agricultural sector representations – were called pillars of Austrian national identity at least until the late 1980s.

Between 1955 and 1966, Austria was governed by the so-called Grand Coalition, consisting of the Christian Democratic Austrian People's Party, ÖVP (*Österreichische Volkspartei*) and the Socialist Party (SPÖ). Between 1966 and 1970, the ÖVP gained an absolute majority and was able to govern alone. In the early 1970s the Socialist SPÖ (later renamed the Social Democrats in 1991) became the dominant party. During Chancellor Bruno Kreisky's leadership, from 1970 to 1983, Austria emerged as a quite prosperous country, with a strong welfare system, and also gained an international reputation as a mediator in conflict situations. From 1983 to 1986 the state was governed by an SPÖ–FPÖ coalition, then the SPÖ and the ÖVP formed a coalition government again (Wodak et al., 2009).

In the 1980s, social change and the increasing mobility of voters led to the erosion of the two dominant parties and their relevant subcultures. The highly controversial and internationally debated coalition government between the right-wing populist FPÖ and the ÖVP, from 2000–2003 and 2003–2006, was again followed by a coalition between the SPÖ and ÖVP, which was renewed after the general elections of 2008 and 2013.

3 Geopolitical profile

Before the end of the bipolar bloc system, the neutral state of Austria was situated exactly between the East and the West, close to the Iron Curtain, a fact that impacted on Austrian national self-image as a bridge and a bulwark at the same time towards and against the Communist regimes. After 1989, the country was particularly challenged in redefining its position in a changed European and geopolitical landscape.

At the same time, the system change in the former Socialist single-party states and the political processes in the wake of 1989 created an opportunity for Austria to become a member of the EC/EU in 1995, after a successful referendum. Until the mid-1980s, there was a general consensus that Austrian neutrality and Austria's resulting role in international politics could not be reconciled with full membership in the EC.

Since Austria joined the EU, there has been stronger cooperation within the Common Foreign and Security Policy and also with NATO through the Partnership for Peace framework.

4 Overview of the political landscape

Austria is a federal republic, with a parliament consisting of two chambers. The first chamber (*Nationalrat*) is composed of 183 MPs, elected by Austrian citizens every five years in nine constituencies congruent with the nine federal provinces and further subdivided into 39 regional constituencies. The second, and weaker, chamber (*Bundesrat*) is the representative body of the federal provinces. It consists of nominated members of the nine regional Parliaments according to the strength that political parties have in each one of them.

With the exception of Upper Austria, where the regional government is elected every six years, the remaining eight regional governments are elected every five years. Whilst the federal government, in comparison with other political systems, has a relatively strong position, the sway of the federal provinces is considerable. The federal government, headed by the federal chancellor, is strongly accountable to parliament. Although the Austrian head of state, the federal President, is directly elected by the population for a six-year period, his or her powers are of a formal and representative nature only.

Citizens of Austria have been guaranteed basic rights and freedoms since 1867. Austria ratified the European Convention on the Protection of Human Rights and Fundamental Freedoms on 4 November 1950.

5 Brief account of the political parties

In the aftermath of WWII, three parties emerged in Austria: the Social Democratic Party (SPÖ), the Peoples' Party (ÖVP) and the Communist Party (KPÖ). The first two dominated the political landscape. In the late 1940s, a fourth party, the Alliance of the Independents (*Verband der Unabhängigen,* VdU), which was renamed the Freedom Party (FPÖ) in 1955, established itself (Pelinka and Rosenberger, 2007, 154).

During the course of the environmental social movements of the 1980s, the Green Party emerged. In 1993 the Liberal Forum (*Liberales Forum*, LIF) established itself as the first splinter party to separate itself from the Freedom Party, and in 2005 the Freedom Party split again, producing a further party called the Alliance of the Future of Austria (*Bündnis Zukunft Österreich*, BZÖ). Whilst the Liberal Forum defined the character of the party as Liberal and acted accordingly, the BZÖ can be characterized as right-wing populist (ibid., 155f).

In 2013 two new parties became important, as they were elected to the national parliament: Team Stronach and NEOS (The New Austria). Team Stronach was founded in summer 2012 by the Austrian-Canadian billionaire Frank Stronach. Meanwhile, NEOS, founded in spring 2013, can be classified as a new liberal party bringing together some former members of the LIF and the ÖVP.

Alongside these parties are two parties competing solely in the European arena: the *Liste Hans-Peter Martin* (List HPM) and the *Junge Liberale,* JuLis (Young Liberals). Hans-Peter Martin, a former journalist, was nominated as front-runner for the EP elections of 1999 by the SPÖ. During his first mandate in the EP he broke with the SPÖ. In the next EP elections in 2004

Table 16.2 List of political parties in Austria

Original name	Abbreviation	English translation
Sozialdemokratische Partei Österreichs	SPÖ	Social Democratic Party of Austria
Österreichische Volkspartei	ÖVP	Austrian Peoples' Party
Freiheitliche Partei Österreichs	FPÖ	Freedom Party of Austria
Bündnis Zukunft Österreich	BZÖ	Alliance of the Future of Austria
Die Grünen	Grüne	The Greens
Liberales Forum	LIF	Liberal Forum
Liste Hans-Peter Martin	HPM	List Hans-Peter Martin
Junge Liberale	JuLis	Young Liberals
Team Stronach	TS	Team Stronach
Das Neue Österreich	NEOS	The New Austria

he ran as an independent candidate and immediately received 14 per cent of the votes, giving him two seats in the EP. In the national elections of 2006 he also ran with this list but could not surpass the threshold of 4 per cent. Since this experience, HPM is a party running only in EP elections. In the EP elections in 2009, Martin received 17.9 per cent of the overall votes and got 3 out of the then 17 Austrian EP mandates. The second such party, JuLis, which originates from the Liberal Forum, represents economically Liberal positions. It ran in the EP elections of 2009 for the first time, but was only able to get 0.7 per cent of the vote.

The SPÖ is one of the major parties in Austria and since the 1970s, it has been in power for more than 30 years with a break between 2000 and 2006, either in a single party government in the 1970s, or in a coalition government with the ÖVP or the FPÖ (Pelinka, 2009). It is the dominant centre-left party in Austria, being particularly strong in Vienna. Meanwhile, the ÖVP is the centre-right counterpart of the SPÖ, with its strongholds in the *Länder*. Since 1986, the ÖVP has been represented in government either as junior partner of the SPÖ (from 1986 to 1999 and again since 2006) or as the senior partner, from 2000 to 2006, of the FPÖ/BZÖ. The last general elections before the EP elections in 2009 took place in September 2008, after the Grand Coalition between the SPÖ and ÖVP – in place since 2006 – collapsed in July 2008. Both government parties lost a considerable number of votes: the SPÖ obtained 29.3 per cent of the vote, losing 6.1 per cent, whilst the ÖVP received 26.0 per cent, with its support dropping by 8.3 per cent. In the last general elections in September 2013, the SPÖ and ÖVP lost again votes: the SPÖ gained 26.8 per cent and the ÖVP 24.0 per cent of the votes.

Next to the two major parties in 2008 there were three, and after 2013, four, opposition parties represented in the Austrian parliament, the *Nationalrat*. The oldest and most established party amongst these parties is the VdU/FPÖ. Up to the mid-1980s, this party was a small player on the Austrian political landscape, with electoral results ranging from 12.7 per cent in 1949 to 5.0 per cent in 1983. In 1986, with Jörg Haider taking over the party leadership and the reorientation of the party towards immigration and integration issues, the party became a major actor in Austrian politics. The FPÖ also immediately changed its performance and started acting in an explicitly populist way. This topical reorientation and the new party style attracted voters, and the FPÖ reached a first peak in 1999 where it became the second strongest party after the SPÖ, achieving 26.9 per cent of the vote. Shortly after this election, in February 2000, the FPÖ became the junior partner in an ÖVP-FPÖ government. In the following elections in 2002, it lost considerable votes due to intra-party dissent and joined the ÖVP in government as a weakened junior party.

Due to further intra-party dissent in 2005, the FPÖ split into the BZÖ and the old FPÖ, with Jörg Haider being the party leader of the newly founded BZÖ. All FPÖ ministers in the then ÖVP-FPÖ government joined the BZÖ; consequently the FPÖ lost its government party status. In the next general elections in 2006, both the FPÖ and the BZÖ managed to enter into the national parliament: between 2006 and 2013 these two parties on the right wing of the political spectrum have been represented in the Austrian Parliament. These two right-wing populist parties were the winners of the 2008 elections: the FPÖ, with its 17.5 per cent vote share, and the BZÖ, with its 10.7 per cent vote share, obtained an accumulated 28.2 per cent of the votes. The extreme right-wing populists became the second most important political group in the Austrian political system. With the unexpected death of its leader Jörg Haider in a car crash shortly after the elections in October 2008, the BZÖ lost in importance. Indeed, in the general elections of 2013 it failed to pass the threshold of 4 per cent of votes and, hence, could not enter the *Nationalrat* any longer. Meanwhile, the FPÖ gained more votes again in 2013, obtaining 20.5 per cent of the vote share.

Since 1986, the Greens have been represented in the Austrian Parliament. They have their strongholds in urban areas, in particular in Vienna. Their vote share in legislative elections has varied between 3.4 per cent in 1983 and 12.4 per cent in 2013. The vote share of the Green Party has been steadily growing since the first half of the 1980s, with the exception of the 1995 and 2008 elections. After the general election in 2013, the Greens became the fourth strongest party in the National Council. The two new parties, Team Stronach and NEOS could obtain 5.7 per cent and 5 per cent of the vote share respectively.

5.1 Party attitudes towards the European Union

Austria joined the European Union in 1995, together with Finland and Sweden. Whilst the two major parties, the SPÖ and the ÖVP, as well as the FPÖ at that time, supported EU membership, the Green Party was rather sceptic (Kritzinger and Michalowitz, 2005).

Looking at data from the Euro-manifesto project, we notice that the ÖVP can be characterized from the beginning as a Europhile party, whilst the SPÖ was much more moderate in its EU position (Lefkofridi and Kritzinger, 2008). In 2008, the SPÖ announced in an open letter to the tabloid *Neue Kronen Zeitung* that future EU treaties would be subjected to referenda, taking up a major demand by its EU-sceptic electorate and thus positioning itself as a more Eurosceptic political actor in the Austrian party landscape (Wodak et al., 2009, 243).

The FPÖ, which at the time of EU accession was positively oriented towards the EU, made a U-turn in the following years and now has to be considered a highly EU-sceptic party. The EU is blamed for the loss of national identity, high immigration rates, criminal activity, and for using Austrian taxpayers money in other regions of the EU, mostly in Eastern Europe.

The reverse applies to the Green Party: starting off with a Eurosceptic position in 1995, it developed a more balanced, positive EU position. The BZÖ, meanwhile, was rather critical of the EU, with a focus on the supposed privileges of EU politicians and representatives, the EU bureaucracy, democratic deficits within the EU, and a lack of people-oriented policy. While NEOS adopts a pro-European position, Team Stronach is rather sceptic of the European integration process and the euro in particular.

Thus, today, Austrian parties can be divided into two groups: the highly Eurosceptic and the more Euro-balanced ones. Amongst the latter group, the ÖVP shows exceptionally strong pro-EU features.

6 Public opinion and the European Union

In 1994, a 66.6 per cent majority of Austrian citizens decided in favour of EU membership in a referendum. This rather positive public outlook on the EU changed rapidly after the referendum. Already in 1995, only 39 per cent of Austrian citizens regarded their country's membership as a good thing, and over the last 15 years it even decreased to 30 per cent. Whilst

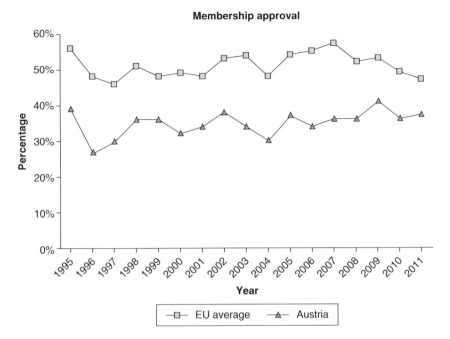

Figure 16.2 Austrian attitude to the European Union

Source: Eurobarometer, 2009, http://ec.europa.eu/public_opinion/index_en.htm (own calculation)

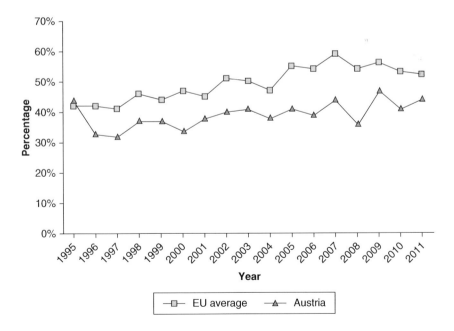

Figure 16.3 Perceived benefit of EU membership in Austria

Source: Eurobarometer, 2009, http://ec.europa.eu/public_opinion/index_en.htm (own calculation)

Table 16.3 EP and national election results in Austria: 1994–2009 (%)

Political party	EP elections				National elections						
	1996	1999	2004	2009	1994	1995	1999	2002	2006	2008	2013
ÖVP	29.7	30.7	32.7	30.0	27.7	28.3	26.9	42.3	34.3	26.0	24.0
SPÖ	29.2	31.7	33.3	23.7	34.9	38.1	33.2	36.5	35.3	29.3	26.9
FPÖ	27.5	23.4	6.3	12.7	22.5	21.9	26.9	10.0	11.0	17.5	20.5
Greens	6.8	9.3	12.9	9.9	7.3	4.8	7.4	9.5	11.1	10.4	12.4
BZÖ	—	—	—	4.6	—	—	—	—	4.1	10.7	3.5
List HPM	—	—	14.0	17.7	—	—	—	—	2.8	—	—
Team Stronach	—	—	—	—	—	—	—	—	—	—	5.7
NEOS	—	—	—	—	—	—	—	—	—	—	5.0

Source: Bundesministerium für Inneres, n.d., Wahlen und Volksbegehren: www.bmi.gv.at/cms/BMI_wahlen; Bundesministerium für Inneres, 2009, Europawahl 2009: http://wahl13.bmi.gv.at/.

positive public attitudes towards the EU average between 50 and 60 per cent in Member States, Austrian public opinion features the most negative attitudes towards EU membership amongst the old EU Member States, *surpassing*, sometimes, even the UK.

When analysing the question of whether Austria has benefitted from being a member of the EU, we can also observe that Austrians are less likely – in comparison to citizens in other Member States – to see EU membership as benefitting the country economically. Whilst in the beginning citizens still thought their country would benefit from EU membership, this attitude has changed over the years. Austrians have become more Eurosceptic, particularly after the 2004 Eastern enlargement. Only from 2009 onwards do we observe a slight upward trend, closing the gap to the EU average (Eurobarometer 75, 2011).

The loss of full national sovereignty, fear of mass-immigration especially from the new EU Member States, as well as opposition towards being a net payer in the EU led to negative attitudes towards the EU (Eurobarometer, 2009).

Overall, the Eurobarometer data reveal a slight upward trend towards EU support, although the overall majority of Austrians still have a predominantly Eurosceptic attitude towards EU membership. We could thus observe a slight discrepancy between parties' and voters' positions concerning EU stances.

7 National and EP electoral systems

In Austria, a proportional electoral system is used. It entails the possibility of preference voting, but *de facto* the Austrian system can be characterized as a closed list system. Voters rarely use the possibility of preference voting; the political parties do not use it as a competitive element in their campaigns (Müller et al., 2001). Whilst for national elections there are 39 regional constituencies, for European Parliament elections there is only one national constituency. The threshold to gain seats both in the national and European parliaments lies at 4 per cent. Finally, Austria is, as yet, the only country within the EU where citizens can already vote at the age of 16, whilst in order to stand for election they must be 18 years old.

Due to subsequent changes in EU treaties, following the accession of new Member States, the number of MEPs has decreased over the years, from 21 in 1995 to 18 in 1999, and from 17 under the Treaty of Nice, to increase again to 19 under the Treaty of Lisbon. The two new MEPs, one from the SPÖ and another from the BZÖ, took their seats in the European Parliament in mid-December 2011.

8 A glance at EP and national elections

After joining the EU in 1995, the first EP elections took place in 1996, with eight parties running the race: SPÖ, ÖVP, FPÖ, Greens and the Liberal Forum as well as three further lists, the handicap list related to people with disabilities, the citizen initiative *Die Neutralen* (The Neutrals) and the Communist Party.

The two main parties, the SPÖ and the ÖVP, achieved around 29 per cent of the vote, whilst the FPÖ obtained 27 per cent. Thus, it improved its results considerably in comparison to the national elections in 1995, when it reached 21.9 per cent (Melchior, 2001, 33–4).

Seven parties took part in the 1999 elections. Apart from the SPÖ, the ÖVP, the FPÖ, the Greens, the LIF, the Communist Party and the Conservative list *Christlich-Soziale Allianz/ Liste Karl Habsburg*, CSA (Christian-Social Alliance List Karl Habsburg) – set up by the heir to the throne of the former Austro-Hungarian monarchy – presented themselves (ibid., 34). In comparison to the 1996 elections, the established parties ÖVP and SPÖ gained votes, whilst the FPÖ lost votes, dropping to 23.5 per cent. The Greens improved their vote share from 6.8 per cent to 9.3 per cent. The LIF was not able to surpass the 4 per cent threshold and no other party was able to achieve representation in the EP.

The 1999 campaign of the SPÖ focussed on Chancellor Viktor Klima and on the EP front-runner Hans-Peter Martin, who was not a party member but was well-known to the Austrian electorate as an independent journalist who had previously written the bestseller *The Globalization Trap* (ibid., 39). The ÖVP campaign was dominated by security issues related to the potential membership of Austria in NATO. The Kosovo War also played a major role in the overall campaign of the two main political parties (ibid., 39–40). Other issues the campaign focussed upon were the Central and Eastern European enlargement, the fight against mismanagement, and transparency at the EU level. Whilst the two major parties were supporters of enlargement, the FPÖ opposed enlargement due to a potential increase in international crime, immigration, and loss of identity (ibid., 40). The FPÖ positioned itself as a Eurosceptic and protest party.

The 2004 elections differed from the former EP elections. The SPÖ won the elections and was able to improve its vote share slightly, with 33.4 per cent and 7 seats. The ÖVP came in second, with a 32.2 per cent vote share and 6 seats. The Greens were also able to slightly improve their 1999 results, surpassing for the first time the 10 per cent threshold in a nation-wide election: the party achieved 12.9 per cent of the vote share.

However, the FPÖ collapsed electorally, from 23.4 per cent and five seats to 6.3 per cent and one seat. This can partly be explained by the fact that the party was punished as a junior partner in the coalition government with the ÖVP. It had to moderate its Eurosceptic populism and support pro-European policies, resulting in a credibility loss as a protest and Eurosceptic party. Moreover, in 2004 the party was characterized by internal factionalism and a conflict of personalities and many FPO voters abstained from voting (Fallend, 2004, 7–8). Most importantly though, the new *List Hans-Peter Martin*, the former front-runner of the SPÖ in 1999, was able to capture the protest vote, pointing to mismanagement at the EP level (Fallend ibid., 5–6). List HPM obtained 14 per cent of the vote share and became the third largest party.

Table 16.4 Turnout at EP and national elections in Austria: 1994–2009 (%)

EP elections				National elections						
1996	1999	2004	2009	1994	1995	1999	2002	2006	2008	2013
67.7	49.4	42.4	46.0	81.9	86.0	80.4	84.3	78.5	78.9	74.9

Source: Bundesministerium für Inneres, n.d., Wahlen und Volksbegehren: www.bmi.gv.at/cms/BMI_wahlen.

Examining the vote share of Austrian parties in EP elections since Austria's membership in the EU, we observe some interesting dynamics. Most striking were the changes for the FPÖ. Starting out in 1996 with a 27 per cent vote share, the party dropped down to 6 per cent in 2004, only to recover slightly in 2009. Unlike in national elections, in EP elections the FPÖ faced an opponent that also presented critical but more flexible EU positions and was therefore a genuine alternative for Eurosceptic voters: the List HPM. Interestingly, the two main government parties, the SPÖ and ÖVP, were quite stable in their vote shares in EP elections until 2004; their vote shares dropped only in the elections in 2009.

Turning to turnout, we can observe that in 1995 the novelty of the first EP elections also led to a turnout of 67.7 per cent. However, in the following elections in 1999 and 2004, the turnout declined considerably. In 1999, the turnout was 49.4 per cent and in 2004 it dropped to 42.4 per cent. Thus, turnout in EP elections is considerably lower than in national elections.

9 The 2009 European election

9.1 Party lists and manifestos

In the 2009 EP elections there were eight electoral lists. Apart from the main national parliamentary parties, the SPÖ, ÖVP, FPÖ, BZÖ, and the Greens, the List HPM, the KPÖ, and the Young Liberals also entered the electoral competition.

Analysing the Austrian party programmes for the 2009 EP elections, one notices that the SPÖ was mostly concerned with its traditional policy area, growth and employment, which gained particular relevance in the context of the financial and economic crisis. In particular, the SPÖ called for a social Europe of the citizens instead of a conservative Europe of the markets. Interestingly, the SPÖ clearly assigned competences to the various levels: whilst they called for competences on issues such as immigration and access to the Austrian labour market to remain national, they called for a European-wide competence on issues such as the economic crisis, the fight against terrorism, and organized crime. Finally, typical Austrian topics such as transit policy or nuclear policy were also mentioned.

Meanwhile, the ÖVP manifesto made reference to Europe from a more global perspective. It praised European integration as a project bringing peace to the European continent. Also, the ÖVP was more eager to present itself as a successful party at the European level, resulting in higher subsidies for the Austrian economy and the implementation of Austrian interests on environmental issues. The party also pointed out measures to be taken in order to address the international economic and financial crisis. Both major parties, SPÖ and ÖVP, requested more rights for the European Parliament, greater transparency and, most interestingly, a national referendum on Turkey's entry to the EU.

Turning now to the opposition parties, the FPÖ emphasized six major topics: the reduction of EU bureaucracy, the protection of the German language and culture, the empowerment of citizens, the ending of negotiations on Turkish membership, the economy, and security issues. In particular, issues regarding corruption and bureaucracy in the EU, as well as the reduction of Austrian membership fees, were central goals. The rest of the programme was dedicated to 'national' issues and on how to maintain Austrian sovereignty. Amongst the issues raised in this context were the rejection of the Lisbon Treaty, the protection of the Austrian labour market and the Austrian banking sector, the abolishment of the Schengen Treaty and the preservation of Austria's neutrality. It is interesting to note that most issues raised problems that had already been decided upon – for example, the Lisbon Treaty – and that were not relevant or had nothing to do with the EP elections *per se*, such as Austrian neutrality. The programme of the FPÖ was therefore quite populist and focussed on EU-bashing issues.

The List HPM especially targeted EU bureaucracy and overpaid politicians as its major topics. Similar to the other parties, HPM was also in favour of national EU referenda and the preservation of Austria's neutrality, and against EU membership for Turkey. A major populist proposal was the redistribution of the potential money saved after a scaling down of the EU bureaucracy to poor people and for the creation of jobs.

Finally, the Green Party proposed a common European way to fight the economic crisis and to build up a European social policy. It argued that issues such as immigration and asylum should be regulated at the European level. Like the government parties, the Green Party was also in favour of greater EP empowerment, but, unlike any other party, it was open-minded about EU membership for Turkey and the Western Balkan states. The BZÖ did not issue an election programme.

9.2 Electoral campaign

The EP election campaign in 2009 was hardly used to convey any ideas about the future of the EU. This is true for almost all of the parties; the Green Party was somewhat of an exception. Debates and campaigns focussed more or less on issues of domestic politics or rehashed topics, which had already dominated the 2004 campaign. Amongst the latter are the rejection of Turkey's potential EU accession, which was an FPÖ issue, and the fight against the privileges of politicians, especially MEPs, which the List HPM put forward (Perlot and Zeglovits, 2010).

At the beginning of the campaign the SPÖ presented itself as a team player in Brussels, but also as a strong advocate for better social conditions in Europe, for example, with regard to employment and standardized minimum wages. The underlying reason for its social concerns was the Eastern and South-eastern enlargement of the European Union in 2004 and 2007, which brought cheaper labour to Austria. Towards the end of its campaign, it heavily condemned the xenophobic election campaign of the FPÖ, appealing to moral sentiments and the social conscience of the electorate.

The ÖVP advertised its European competence and experience, claiming to be the party that best represented Austria's interest within the EU. Its MEPs argued that the economic crisis confirmed the importance of the European Union. It emphasized the party's traditional pro-European line, drawing upon supporters of the European Union.

The List HPM promoted its fight against high wages and high pensions for EU-officials and MEPs, and emphasized the need for controlling misgovernment and corruption within the administrative bodies of the European Union. It advocated the preservation of Austrian neutrality and demanded the holding of national referenda for key European questions. Further, it acted against EU over-regulation, for instance, on energy saving lamps, a topic highly debated by the Austrian public and thus best applicable to populist campaigning. The HPM List aimed especially at Eurosceptic voters. It revealed issues that were malfunctioning in the EU and criticized the lack of clear responsibilities within the EU, the exuberant European bureaucracy, the 'culture of corruption' in Brussels, the 'privileges' granted to MEPs, and the 'waste' of taxpayer's money at the European level. Whilst supporting the principle of subsidiarity, it fiercely opposed the Lisbon Treaty and any further enlargement of the EU. The List HPM presented itself as the only defender of the people and as a fighter against those who were in political power.

The Green Party, echoing its European counterparts, advocated a European social and ecological union. This included, amongst other things, the regulation of financial markets, abandoning nuclear energy, non-genetically modified food, and the protection of the privacy of citizens, as opposed to a surveillance society. Moreover, the Greens demanded an increase in highway charges for large trucks. The Greens used a variation of the central motive of the famous painting by Eugène Delacroix, *Liberty Leading the People* (1830) as the main leitmotif for the campaign. The main reason for the use of this iconic image was to present the party as a dynamic movement to the voter.

As in any other election, the EP election campaign of the FPÖ was mainly carried out by its party leader, Heinz-Christian Strache, and not by the head of the list for the EP elections, Andreas Mölzer. The main issues were the preservation of a Christian Europe against the accession of Turkey, the closing of EU borders in order to prevent trans-border crime, the vetoing of the European directive on asylum, and the promotion of a social Europe. At the end of the campaign, the FPÖ presented itself as a victim of negative SPÖ campaigning. The SPÖ heavily attacked the FPÖ's xenophobic campaign.

The BZÖ stressed opposition against the Asylum Directive, the Treaty of Lisbon, and the accession of Turkey, on the one hand, and supported the re-introduction of border controls, a tax on speculative financial transactions, and abandoning nuclear energy and the Euratom Treaty, on the other. The head of list, Ewald Stadler, was presented as tough-minded and incorruptible.

On two instances, there were negative incidents during the electoral campaign. On the one hand, the Minister of the Interior, Maria Fekter from the ÖVP, distributed leaflets – to mobilize voters to go to the polls – that had a strong similarity to the advertising style of her own party. On the other hand, in response, the FPÖ sent party campaign material that looked like government official information brochures to young voters.

9.3 Electoral results

Voter turnout reached almost 46 per cent in 2009, which represented an increase of 3.5 per cent compared to the EP elections in 2004. However, compared to the voter turnout of 78 per cent in the previous national election in 2008, it was still relatively low. As in other countries, Austrian parties were not able to mobilize their voters. Disappointment with the EU, as well as dissatisfaction with the selection of candidates and the EU policy positions parties presented, were decisive reasons for citizens not to cast their ballots (SORA, 2009). In addition, the electoral campaigns focussed mainly on national topics and were largely neglected by the Austrian mass media. Media coverage was mostly interested in the intra-party dissents within the ÖVP and the Green Party, regarding the heads of the lists of the respective political groups. The second candidates on the candidate lists of the ÖVP, Greens, and BZÖ ran preference voting campaigns, which, at least in the case of the ÖVP, had mobilizing effects on its typical voters. The low turnout rate is already a first indication that EP elections can still be considered 'second order'.

Table 16.5 EP election results in Austria: 2009

Political party	Vote %	Change from 2004 %	Seats	Seat change from 2004
ÖVP	29.9	−2.7	6	0
SPÖ	23.7	−9.6	5	−2
List HPM	17.7	+3.7	3	1
FPÖ	12.7	+6.4	2	1
Greens	9.9	−3.0	2	0
BZÖ	4.6	+4.6	1	1
KPÖ	0.7	−0.1	0	0
JuLis	0.7	+0.7	0	0
Total	—	—	19	+2
Nil vote	2.1	−0.5	—	—
Abstention	54.0	−3.5	—	—
Turnout	**46.0**	**+3.5**	—	—

Source: Bundesministerium für Inneres, 2009, Europawahl 2009: http://wahl09.bmi.gv.at.

An examination of voter preferences shows that the predicted and expected close race between the two main parties in government: SPÖ and ÖVP, did not happen. The SPÖ lost about 10 per cent of the vote share and three seats, and was thus not successful with its newly adopted, more EU critical, position. In total the SPÖ had four MEPs, but after the ratification of the Lisbon Treaty an additional MEP joined the group after 15 December 2011. Most importantly, the SPÖ failed to mobilize its traditional constituency to participate in the EP elections (SORA, 2009). Unsurprisingly, the main reasons why voters chose the SPÖ were the economic crisis, the job market situation, and unemployment concerns, but also immigration and crime issues (Kritzinger et al., 2009).

The ÖVP also lost votes and was down 3 per cent but was, in comparison to the SPÖ, more successful in the mobilization of its traditional constituency. The intra-party dissent related to the head of list of the ÖVP campaign and the strongly personalized electoral campaign for preferential votes by the second-placed ÖVP candidate Othmar Karas, resulted in a better outcome for the junior partner in government. The ÖVP eventually became the strongest party in the EP elections and considerably distanced itself from its SPÖ coalition partner. The main reasons to vote for the ÖVP were the economic and financial crises as well as the party's support for European integration (ibid.). Both government parties benefitted substantially from the votes of their respective core voters (SORA, 2009).

The main opposition party, the FPÖ, was extremely successful in mobilizing its voters, almost doubling its share of the vote. Former voters who abstained in 2004 returned to the party in 2009 (ibid.). And yet, it lagged behind its pre-electoral expectations, failing to achieve its aim to become the largest party. It became only fourth largest party, after the ÖVP, SPÖ, and List HPM. The crucial issues explaining why voters chose the FPÖ were immigration, but also the economic crisis (Kritzinger et al., 2009). A large segment of people affected by the economic crisis voted for the FPÖ (SORA, 2009).

The second winner in the election race was the List HPM, which accumulated the protest vote that most likely would have switched to the FPÖ otherwise. The List HPM mostly benefitted from former SPÖ and FPÖ voters as well as from non-voters in 2004 (Plasser and Ulram, 2009). Its focus on issues critical of the EU, and on blaming EU institutions, proved to be a successful strategy. It attracted mainly retired persons and workers who did not agree with the 'privileges' granted to members of the EP, who were not satisfied with EU institutions and politics, who perceived that European and Austrian citizens lacked a say in European affairs, and who were in favour of greater political control over the European level (ibid., 2009). The head of List, Hans-Peter Martin, blamed the EU for its inefficiency, bureaucracy, and waste of money, and thus echoed the dissatisfaction of Austrians with the supranational organization. The unique support of the *Neue Kronen Zeitung*, Austria's top-selling tabloid – with a market share of 42 per cent – for the List HPM's electoral campaign proved to be a crucial factor towards its success. About 70 per cent of voters for the List HPM were also readers of the tabloid, or to turn the figures the other way around, nearly 30 per cent of *Kronen Zeitung* readers voted for the List HPM (ibid.).

Surprisingly, and against the European trend, the Green Party got only 10 per cent of the share of the vote, a loss of 3 per cent in comparison to 2004, and did not reach its declared targets. This might be due to leadership battles before and during the EP election. Nevertheless, the Greens were able to keep their two seats in the EP. The party did well amongst young voters and amongst voters concerned with environmental issues.

The BZÖ reached close to 5 per cent of the vote, which at the time of the election proved insufficient to gain a seat in the EP. As soon as the Lisbon Treaty came into force and Austria obtained 19 instead of 17 seats, the BZÖ gained 1 seat. In mid-December 2011, Ewald Stadler took his seat in the EP. The BZÖ received the most votes in Carinthia, the federal state, which was governed by its charismatic leader Jörg Haider until his death. Issues of importance were, once again, the economic crisis and immigration (Kritzinger et al., 2009). The Communist Party of Austria and JuLis clearly failed to gain any seats in the EP.

Austrian MEPs joined four political groups in the EP. The ÖVP members joined the European People's Party, the SPÖ MEPs the Group of the Progressive Alliance of Socialists and Democrats, and the Greens the Group of the Greens/European Free Alliance. Meanwhile, the FPÖ MEPs decided to sit in the EP as non-attached members due to their particular policy stances. In terms of representation and impact on decision-making processes these circumstances weakened a potential national Austrian position.

At the 2009 EP election, a major turnover took place: out of the then elected 17 Austrian MEPs, nine were newcomers: three from the ÖVP, two each from the SPÖ and the List HPM, and one each from the Green Party and the FPÖ, respectively. Amongst Austrian elected MEPs, 41.1 per cent were women. The Green Party had only female representatives and the FPÖ had none, the ÖVP had a clear male overbalance, whereas amongst the SPÖ and List HPM delegations gender distribution was balanced.

9.4 Campaign finance

For the 2009 EP elections, the financing of Austrian party campaigns was regulated by the so-called Political Parties Act (BKA-RIS, 2010), which specifies with further legislation how much funding each party receives for different aspects of their activities. The Austrian parties relied on a generous public funding system (Sickinger, 2009). Each party received a defined amount of funding for electoral campaigning. Public funding for EP elections was set at a lower level than for national elections. In the case of national elections in 2008, the total public funding for electoral campaigns was €2.21 multiplied by the number of persons entitled to vote and was to be allocated to the parties represented in the Parliament at the ratio of their vote share (section 2a, part G of Political Parties Act, BKA-RIS (2010)). The same rules applied to EP election campaigns, except that the total funding was 10 per cent lower (section 2b, part G; §§2a–b of Political Parties Act, BKA-RIS (2010)). However, in comparison to other countries the difference was quite small. If funding was not spent, it had to be reimbursed to the state.

Although many attempts were made to regulate non-public party funding – the latest one in 2013, which, however, is not tackled here – this is still a grey area. Again for the 2009 EP elections, Austrian political parties were able to receive voluntary contributions from anonymous donors up to a sum of €7,260. Any contribution above that level had to be disclosed to the Audit Court, but not to the public (Sickinger, 2009). However, contributions from public institutions and other

Table 16.6 Austrian MEPs' affiliation to EP political groups

Political party	%	Seats	EPP	S&D	ALDE	Greens/EFA	ECR	EUL/NGL	EFD	NA
ÖVP	30.0	6	6	—	—	—	—	—	—	—
SPÖ	23.7	5	—	5	—	—	—	—	—	—
List HPM	17.7	3	—	—	—	—	—	—	—	3
FPÖ	12.7	2	—	—	—	—	—	—	—	2
Green Party	9.9	2	—	—	—	2	—	—	—	—
BZÖ	4.6	1	—	—	—	—	—	—	—	1
KPÖ	0.7	0	—	—	—	—	—	—	—	—
JuLis	0.7	0	—	—	—	—	—	—	—	—
Total	100.0	19	6	5	0	2	0	0	0	6

Source: Bundesministerium für Inneres, 2009, Europawahl 2009: http://wahl09.bmi.gv.at; www.europarl.europa.eu/meps/.

Table 16.7 List of Austrian MEPs: seventh legislature

Name	National party	Political group	Professional background	Year of birth	Gender	Committee
Othmar Karas	ÖVP	EPP	Party official	1957	Male	Vice-President of European Parliament (since 18 Jan. 2012) Vice-Chair of EPP Committee on Economic and Monetary Affairs Subcommittee on Security and Defence, Special committee on Financial, Economic and Social Crisis (8 Oct. 2009–31 July 2011)
Elisabeth Köstinger	ÖVP	EPP	Youth politics	1978	Female	Committee on Budgetary Control (until 5 April 2011) Committee on Agriculture and Rural Development
Hella Ranner (until 31 Mar. 2011)	ÖVP	EPP	Lawyer	1951	Female	Committee on Transport and Tourism
Heinz K. Becker (since 1 Apr. 2011)	ÖVP	EPP	Managing director	1950	Male	Committee on Employment and Social Affairs Committee on Petitions
Paul Rübig	ÖVP	EPP	Businessman	1953	Male	Committee on Budgetary Control (since 6 April 2011) Committee on Industry, Research and Energy
Richard Seeber	ÖVP	EPP	Jurist, economist	1962	Male	Committee on the Environment, Public Health and Food Safety
Ernst Strasser (until 23 Mar. 2011)	ÖVP	EPP	Jurist, consultant	1956	Male	Committee on Foreign Affairs Committee on Petitions Subcommittee on Security and Defence
Hubert Pirker (since 31 Mar. 2011)	ÖVP	EPP	Management consultant	1948	Male	Committee on Transport and Tourism
Karin Kadenbach	SPÖ	S&D	Advertising and PR	1958	Female	Committee on the Environment, Public Health and Food Safety
Jörg Leichtfried	SPÖ	S&D	Jurist	1967	Male	Committee on Transport and Tourism Subcommittee on Human Rights
Evelyn Regner	SPÖ	S&D	Jurist	1966	Female	Committee on Legal Affairs (Vice-Chair)
Hannes Swoboda	SPÖ	S&D	Party functionary	1946	Male	Vice-Chair of S&D (until 17 Jan 2012) Chair of S&D (since 18 Jan 2012) Committee on Financial, Economic and Social Crisis (until 31 July 2011)
Josef Weidenholzer (since 1 Dec. 2011)	SPÖ	S&D	University professor of history	1950	Male	Committee on Civil Liberties, Justice and Home Affairs

(continued)

Table 16.7 (continued)

Name	National party	Political group	Professional background	Year of birth	Gender	Committee
Martin Ehrenhauser	List HPM	NA	Cook, business administrator	1978	Male	Committee on Budgetary Control
Hans-Peter Martin	List HPM	NA	Jurist, journalist, author	1957	Male	Committee on Economic and Monetary Affairs Special committee on Financial, Economic and Social Crisis (14 Sept. 2011)
Angelika Werthmann	List HPM	NA	Philologist	1963	Female	Committee on Budgets Women's Rights and Gender Equality
Eva Lichtenberger	Green Party	Greens/ EFA	Teacher, party official	1954	Female	Committee on Transport and Tourism
Urike Lunacek	Green Party	Greens/ EFA	Social worker, party official	1957	Female	Committee on Foreign Affairs Subcommittee on Security and Defence (until 14 Sept. 2011)
Andreas Mölzer	FPÖ	NA	Journalist	1952	Male	Committee on Foreign Affairs
Franz Obermayr	FPÖ	NA	Managing director	1952	Male	Committee on the Internal Market and Consumer Protection
Ewald Stadler (since 7 Dec. 2011)	BZÖ	NA	Jurist, party official	1961	Male	Committee on Regional Development

Source: European Parliament database, 2010, www.europarl.europa.eu/meps/en/search.html?country=AT.

major interest groups were exempt from the regulation. Moreover, any contributions from private institutions, interest groups, or enterprises given directly to the campaign were also not taken into account. Austria's campaign finance law was criticized by the Council of Europe, which strove for tighter campaign finance regulation in Austria (GRECO, 2011).

In general, Austrian parties spend less for their campaigns on EP elections than for national elections. However, we have to interpret these figures cautiously, as no detailed information on campaign expenses is available. We only know how much parties receive as campaign refunds from the state, but not how much they spend. The data show that refunds were based on the number of seats a party obtains and did not reflect their actual spending. As the ÖVP obtained more votes in the EP elections than in the national elections this might have resulted in higher campaign refunds, biasing the overall picture on campaign spending.

10 Theoretical interpretation of Euro-elections

10.1 Second-Order Election theory

The novelty of the first EP elections in 1996 led to a relative high turnout, even if it was lower than that achieved at national elections (SORA, 2006, 403f) and decreased even further in

Austria

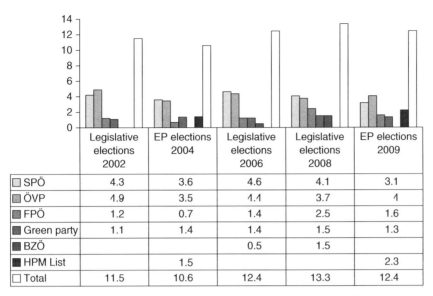

Figure 16.4 Public funding at national and EP elections in Austria: 2002–2009

Source: Bundesministerium für Inneres, Parteienförderung 2002–2010, www.bundeskanzleramt.at/Docs/2011/3/21/Parteiengesetz_2002_2010.pdf

the elections that followed. From this perspective, it can be argued that Austria partially fits in the Second-Order Election model.

Yet, the picture of the two established government parties, the ÖVP and SPÖ, concerning vote share is, instead, more blurred. Whereas the SPÖ lost considerably at the European elections, the ÖVP gained at least in the 1996, 1999, and 2009 European contests. This 'anomaly' seems to reflect that the discontent of many citizens with the SPÖ and ÖVP grand coalition government only affected negatively the senior partner, the Socialists, thus refuting the hypothesis that government parties lose votes in EP elections as a general rule in the Austrian case (Reif and Schmitt, 1980).

In general, opposition parties did not obtain substantial vote shares in EP elections. Indeed, the FPÖ won in some cases when being an opposition party but it lost quite a remarkable number of votes as a junior partner in the coalition with the ÖVP in the 2002 national elections as well as the 2004 EP elections. By contrast, the Greens did not considerably improve their results in EP elections compared to national ones. The most striking element of the 2009 Euro election was the result of the HPM List, which ran only in the European contest, and obtained the third largest share of the vote. Both the FPÖ and the HPM campaigns focussed on their party leader and their head of list respectively, confirming the important part that charismatic politicians can play at the European level.

10.2 Europe Salience theory

Although national issues seemed to dominate the Euro-election campaigns, with the emergence of the HPM List in 2004, an increase in European issues could be observed. The other parties marginally raised European topics, but domestic matters remained the focus of the electoral contest. European policy stances combined with a debate on the future of Europe were of secondary importance or did not emerge at all.

Concerning the European integration process, the more established parties, the SPÖ and ÖVP, featured very positive to more moderate stances. More specifically, the ÖVP and SPÖ tended to follow similar positions, except for social and economic policies. The SPÖ emphasized European growth and employment policies, whilst the ÖVP stressed the question of competitiveness without undermining the Austrian social market economy.

As to the opposition parties, they held substantially different positions towards the European integration process: whereas the Green Party was rather positive towards the EU, highlighting aspects connected to the European social and ecological union, the FPÖ featured the most negative stance, emphasizing the loss of national sovereignty and all kinds of immigration issues. The BZÖ was also critical of the European Union, but pointed out its economic advantages. Finally, the HPM List could be labelled as Eurosceptic, with its aim of downsizing the EU budget, reducing bureaucracy, and fighting corruption at the European level.

In brief, Austrian parties seemed unable to learn from previous experiences. The quality of communication about Europe and EU issues has not been improved since 2004. EP campaigns were fought from a national perspective and the EU is still presented as a scapegoat when it comes to unpopular political decisions, a strategy that helps EU sceptic parties and politicians on the one hand, and discourages potential Europhile voters on the other (Perlot and Zeglovits, 2010).

The EP electoral contests feature substantial aspects of the second-order election model: low turnout, loss of government parties, gain for opposition parties, and the dominance of national topics. Future elections will show whether 20 years of EU membership and changed economic conditions provoked by the financial crisis will turn EP elections into a contest in its own right.

References

Primary sources

Bundeskanzleramt – Rechtsinformationsservice (BKA-RIS) (2010) Gesamte Rechtsvorschrift für Parteiengesetz [Political Parties Act], Bundesgesetz über die Aufgaben, Finanzierung und Wahlwerbung politischer Parteien, BGBl. Nr. 404/1975, Fassung von BGBl. I Nr. 111/2010, www.ris.bka.gv.at/GeltendeFassung.wxe?Abfrage=Bundesnormen&Gesetzesnummer=10000562 (accessed on 3 February 2012).

Bundeskanzleramt – Rechtsinformationsservice (BKA-RIS) (2011) Gesamte Rechtsvorschrift für Nationalrats-Wahlordnung 1992 [Regulations on federal parliamentary elections 1992]. Bundesgesetz über die Wahl des Nationalrates, BGBl. 471/1992, Fassung von BGBl. I 43/2011, www.ris.bka.gv.at/GeltendeFassung.wxe?Abfrage=Bundesnormen&Gesetzesnummer=10001199 (accessed on 3 February 2012).

Bundesministerium für Inneres (2009) Europawahl 2009, http://wahl09.bmi.gv.at (accessed on 26 December 2011).

Bundesministerium für Inneres (n.d.) Wahlen und Volksbegehren, http://www.bmi.gv.at/cms/BMI_wahlen (accessed on 2 February 2012).

Bundesministerium für Inneres (2013) Nationalratswahl 2013: http://wahl13.bmi.gv.at/ (accessed on 21 January 2014).

Eurobarometer (2009) Standard Eurobarometer 72. Conducted October–November, published in February 2010, Brussels, European Commission, http://ec.europa.eu/public_opinion/archives/eb/eb72/eb72_vol1_fr.pdf (accessed on 30 December 2011).

Eurobarometer (2011) Standard Eurobarometer 75. Conducted May 2011, published in August 2011, Luxembourg, http://ec.europa.eu/public_opinion/archives/eb/eb75/eb75_publ_en.pdf (accessed on 15 January 2015).

European Communities (2010) *Eurostat. Europe in figures – Eurostat Yearbook 2009*, Luxembourg, Office of the Official Publications of the European Communities.

European Parliament Database (2010), www.europarl.europa.eu/meps/eu/search.html (accessed on 29 August 2013).

Eurostat (2013, 2014) http://epp.eurostat.ec.europa.eu (accessed on 5 June 2015).
Group of States against Corruption (GRECO) (2011) 'Evaluation Report on Austria: Transparency of Party Funding (Theme II)', www.coe.int/t/dghl/monitoring/greco/evaluations/round3/GrecoEval 3%282011%293_Austria_Two_EN.pdf (accessed on 2 February 2012).

Secondary sources

Bundesministerium für Inneres (BMI) (2008) 'Nationalratswahl 2008 – Wahltag, Stichtag, endgültiges Gesamtergebnis'. Online. Available at: www.bmi.gv.at/cms/BMI_wahlen/nationalrat/2008/End_Gesamt.aspx (accessed on 30 December 2011).

Bundesministerium für Inneres (BMI) (2009) 'Europawahl 2009, endgültiges Gesamtergebnis'. Online. Available at: www.bmi.gv.at/cms/BMI_wahlen/europawahl/2009/EndergebnisE.aspx (accessed on 30 December 2011).

Fischer European Commission (2011) 'Austria'. Online. Available at: http://europa.eu/aboutcu/countries/member countries/austria/index_en.htm (accessed on 30 December 2011).

Kritzinger, S. and Michalowitz, I. (2005) 'Party Position Changes through EU Membership? The (Non-) Europeanization of Austrian, Finnish and Swedish Political Parties', *Politique Européenne*, 16(2), 21–53.

Kritzinger, S., Johann, D. and Kaiser, T. (2009) 'Endbericht: European Parliament Election – Pre-Election Study', Vienna, University of Vienna. Online. Available at: http://methods.univie.ac.at/fileadmin/user_upload/fak_zentrum_methoden/Data/01European_Parliament_Elections_01.pdf (accessed on 12 December 2013).

Lefkofridi, Z. and Kritzinger, S. (2008) 'Battles Fought in the EP Arena: Developments in National Parties' Euro-Manifestos', *Österreichische Zeitschrift für Politikwissenschaft*, 37(3), 273–96.

Melchior, J. (2001) 'Austria', in Lodge, J. (ed.) *The 1999 Direct Elections to the European Parliament*, Basingstoke, Palgrave, 33–44.

Müller, W. C., Jenny, M., Steininger, B., Dolezal, M., Philipp, W. and Preisl-Westphal, S. (2001) *Die österreichischen Abgeordneten. Individuelle Präferenzen und politisches Verhalten*, Vienna, Wiener Universitätsverlag.

Pelinka, A. (2009) 'Das politische System Österreichs', Ismayr, W. (ed.), *Die politischen Systeme Westeuropas*, Wiesbaden, Verlag Sozialwissenschaften, 607–42.

Pelinka, A. and Rosenberger, S. (2007) *Österreichische Politik. Grundlagen-Strukturen-Trends*, Wien, WUV-Facultas Verlag.

Perlot, F. and Zeglovits, E. (2010) 'Die Europawahlen 2009 in Österreich', in Dialer, D., Lichtenberger, E. and Neisser, H. (eds) *Das Europäische Parlament. Institutionen. Vision und Wirklichkeit*, Europawissenschaftliche Reihe, Band 2. Innsbruck, Innsbruck University Press, 89–102.

Plasser, F. and Ulram, P. (2009) 'Analyse der Europawahl 2009: Wähler, Nichtwähler, Motive', press release by GfK Austria, Vienna, GfK. Online. Available at: www.gfk.at/imperia/md/content/gfkaustria/data/press/2009/2009-06-07_wahlanalyse_epw_2009_presseunterlage.pdf (accessed on 10 January 2012).

Reif, K. H. and Schmitt, H. (1980) 'Nine Second Order National Elections: A Conceptual Framework for the Analysis of European Election Results', *European Journal of Political Research*, 8(1), 3–44.

Sickinger, H. (2009) *Politikfinanzierung in Österreich*, Wien, Czernin Verlag.

SORA-Institute for Social Research and Consulting Ogris and Hofinger GmbH (2004) EU-Wahl 2004. Online. Available at: www.sora.at/themen/wahlverhalten/wahlanalysen/eu-wahl04.html (accessed on 30 December 2011).

SORA-Institute for Social Research and Consulting Ogris and Hofinger GmbH (2006) Nationalratswahl 2006. Online. Available at: www.sora.at/themen/wahlverhalten/wahlanalysen/nrw06.html (accessed on 3 February 2012).

SORA-Institute for Social Research and Consulting Ogris & Hofinger GmbH (2009) EU-Wahl 2009. Online. Available at: www.sora.at/themen/wahlverhalten/wahlanalysen/eu-wahl09.html (accessed on 30 December 2011).

Wodak, R., De Cillia, R., Reisigl, M. and Liebhart, K. (2009) *The Discursive Construction of National Identity*, Edinburgh, Edinburgh University Press.

17
FINLAND

Tapio Raunio

Figure 17.1 Map of Finland

Table 17.1 Finland profile

EU entry year	1995
Schengen entry year	2001
MEPs elected in 2009	13
MEPs under Lisbon Treaty	13
Total area*	338,435 km²
Population	5,451,270
	91% Finnish-speaking, 5% Swedish-speaking
Population density**	17.9/km²
Median age of population	42.4
Political system	Semi-presidential Republic
Head of state	Tarja Halonen, Social Democratic Party (SDP) (March 2000–March 2012);
	Sauli Niinistö, National Coalition (KOK) (March 2012–)
Head of government	Jyrki Katainen, National Coalition (KOK) (June 2011–)
Political majority	National Coalition (KOK), Social Democrats (SDP), Left Alliance (VAS), Green League (VIHR), Swedish People's Party (SFP) and Christian Democrats (KD) Government Coalition (June 2011–)
Currency	Euro (€) since 1999
Prohead GDP in PPS	37,400 €

Source: Eurostat, 2013, 2014, http://epp.eurostat.ec.europa.eu/.

Notes:
* Total area including inland waters.
** Population density: the ratio of the annual average population of a region to the land area of the region.

1 Geographical position

Finland is the northernmost EU Member State, sharing a land border with Norway for 727 kilometres, Sweden for 614 kilometres, and Russia for 1,313 kilometres; it has a coastline of 1,250 kilometres. The total land area is 338,435 square kilometres, and with a population of roughly 5.4 million, Finland is very scarcely inhabited. The capital Helsinki is also the northernmost national capital on the European continent, and the population is increasingly concentrated in the southern and western parts of the country.

2 Historical background

Having formed a part of the Swedish Empire since the thirteenth century, in 1809 Finland became an autonomous Grand Duchy of the Russian Empire and, in 1860, it acquired its own currency, the *markka* or Finnish mark. The Constitution adopted on 1 October 1906 made Finland the first European country to establish universal suffrage. At the same time, the old four-estate assembly was replaced by the unicameral national Parliament, the *Eduskunta*, with the first elections held in 1907. Finland declared its independence from Russia on 6 December 1917. A short but bitter civil war between the Reds and the Whites followed in 1918 and was won by the government's forces, led by General Mannerheim. The Constitution adopted on 17 July 1919 gave Finland a republican form of government, combined with strong powers for the President.

Between 1939 and 1944, Finland fought two conflicts against the Soviet Union: the 1939–1940 Winter War and the 1941–1944 Continuation War, and in accordance with the armistice agreement with the USSR, was engaged in battle against the German forces in Lapland in 1944–1945. As a result of a peace settlement, Finland was forced to concede a significant amount of its territory, mainly from the Karelia region, to the Soviet Union. This also led to close economic and political ties with its eastern neighbour, consolidated in the Treaty of Friendship, Cooperation and Mutual Assistance (FCMA) signed in 1948. In Finland, the Cold War period was characterized by cordial relations with the Soviet superpower. Whilst the direct interference of the Soviet leadership in Finnish politics has often been exaggerated, the Finnish political elite nevertheless was always forced to anticipate Moscow's reactions, and this set firm limits to Finland's cooperation with West European and Nordic countries. In 1961, Finland became an associate member of the European Free Trade Association (EFTA) and, in 1973, signed a free trade agreement with the European Economic Community (EEC). Finland became a full member of EFTA in 1986 and joined the Council of Europe in 1989.

3 Geopolitical profile

There is little doubt that, especially amongst foreign observers, the 'Western' identity of Finland was far less clear. After all, Finland shares a long border with Russia and had, during the Cold War, very close economic and political relations with the Soviet Union. The role of Finland as a frontier or bridge between East and West became accentuated during the Cold War, where the borderline between the two political blocs went along Finland's border with the Soviet Union. Finland adopted a position of military non-alignment, with the FCMA Treaty providing for the possibility of wartime military cooperation with the Soviet Union, in case Germany or one of its allies attacked the Soviet Union through Finland, but the country belonged to the West as far as the political and economic basis of its society was concerned. Finland was thus faced with the awkward challenge of balancing the two opposing blocs in a difficult international situation.

Another tenet that grew out of post-war political thinking in Finland was that of a small state, and, by the early 1990s, the Finns had become used to living in a world where state sovereignty and security formed the uncontested starting point for political life. In the Finnish case, state-centrism means that values connected with the state, such as sovereignty and territoriality, have traditionally been strongly emphasized. This has led to a very limited position given to alternative political communities, like a federal Europe or the development of a strong regional level, in Finnish political thinking. When participation in European integration started to be discussed in Finland, it first took place largely in these state-centric terms. Hence by the time Finland joined the EU, Finnish political identity was very much the identity of a small state situated on the fringes of Europe and looking for protection for its territory and people (Tiilikainen, 1998; Raunio and Tiilikainen, 2003).

4 Overview of the political landscape

Finland is by a wide margin the oldest semi-presidential country in Europe, with the semi-presidential form of government adopted in 1919, two years after the country became independent (Arter, 1999). Under the old Constitution, the President was recognized as the supreme executive power. The peak of presidential powers was reached during the reign of President Kekkonen (1956–1981), who made full use of his powers and even, arguably, overstepped the constitutional prerogatives of the presidency. However, recent constitutional reforms, enacted piecemeal since the late 1980s and culminating in the new unified Constitution that entered into force in 2000, have quite radically altered the Finnish political system, with the government and the Prime Minister emerging from the shadow of the President as the leaders of the political process (Nousiainen, 2001; Paloheimo, 2003).

Under the new Constitution the President is clearly subordinate to the government. Governments are now accountable to the *Eduskunta*, the unicameral national Parliament, and not to the President as, effectively, was the case before, and overall the President is almost completely excluded from the policy process in domestic matters. The government is responsible for EU policy, whilst foreign policy leadership is shared between the President and the government (Johansson and Raunio, 2010).

When compared with other EU countries, Finnish governments are outliers in three respects: their parliamentary support, level of fragmentation, and ideological diversity. Finland used to be characterized by short-lived and unstable cabinets living in the shadow of the President. Amongst the West European countries, only Italy had more cabinets between 1945 and 2000 than Finland. The overwhelming majority of Finnish cabinets have been cross-bloc coalitions, bringing together parties from the left and the right. Reflecting the fragmentation of the party system and the tradition of forming majority cabinets, the mean number of cabinet parties between 1945 and 2000 was as high as 3.5, the highest figure amongst West European countries (Mattila and Raunio, 2004, 269).

Recent cabinets have, as a rule, included two of the three main parties: the Social Democrats, the Centre, and the National Coalition. Since 2011, Finland has been governed by a 'six pack' coalition between the National Coalition, the Social Democrats, the Left Alliance, the Green League, the Swedish People's Party, and the Christian Democrats, commanding a comfortable majority in the *Eduskunta* with 62 per cent of the seats. Not surprisingly, the oversized coalitions that have held power since the early 1980s have ruled without much effective opposition from the *Eduskunta*. The opposition has been both numerically weak and ideologically fragmented.

5 Brief account of the political parties

Measured by the number of effective parties, the Finnish party system is the most fragmented amongst the former West European countries, with an average of 5.1 effective parties between

Table 17.2 List of political parties in Finland

Original name	Abbreviation	English translation
Suomen Keskusta	KESK	Finnish Centre Party
Kristillidemokraatit	KD	Christian Democrats
Perussuomalaiset	PS	The Finns
Suomen Kommunistinen Puolue	SKP	Communist Party
Köyhien Asialla		For the Poor
Vihreä liitto	VIHR	Green League
Itsenäisyyspuolue		Independence Party
Vasemmistoliitto	VAS	Left Alliance
Kansallinen Kokoomus	KOK	National Coalition
Suomen Sosialidemokraattinen Puolue	SDP	Finnish Social Democratic Party
Suomen Senioripuolue		Senior Citizens' Party
Suomen Työväenpuolue		Finnish Labour Party
Svenska Folkpartiet I Finland	SFP	Swedish People's Party in Finland

Source: Finland's Ministry of Justice.

1945 and 2000 (Mattila and Raunio, 2004, 269). Since the declaration of independence in 1917, no party has even come close to winning a majority of parliamentary seats, and the lack of a clearly dominant party has necessitated cooperation between the main parties. The fragmentation of the party system also facilitates consensual governance and ideological convergence between all parties aspiring to enter the government (Arter, 2009). The main cleavage has traditionally been the left–right dimension, but since the early 1990s, the rural–urban/centre–periphery divide has become the second main cleavage, partly because the EU and globalization issues have emerged on the political agenda (Paloheimo and Raunio, eds, 2008).

5.1 Party attitudes towards the European Union

The 1994 membership referendum, in which 57 per cent voted in favour of joining the EU, indicated that European integration was a problematic issue for most parties (Paloheimo, 2000). However, once the membership issue had been settled, basically all parties represented in the *Eduskunta* adjusted quickly to life in the European Union. Of the individual parties, the centre-right National Coalition and the Social Democrats have pursued broadly similar pro-integrationist policies since Finland joined the EU. The Centre Party was against EMU membership, but has since then displayed solid support for national EU policy.

The Left Alliance and the Green League were so divided over EU membership in 1994 that they chose not to adopt official positions on the issue. Joining the government in the spring of 1995 meant that both parties had to profile themselves almost overnight as pro-integrationist parties. The Greens have become solidly pro-EU, whilst the Left Alliance has, at least when in opposition, adopted a more Eurosceptic position that is also more in line with the views of its electorate. Parties that were against EU membership, the Christian Democrats (then the Christian League) and The Finns (then the Rural Party), have accepted membership but were against the EMU and are against deeper integration. The Christian Democrats' European policy could perhaps best be characterized as moderate opposition to integration.

The Finns, which achieved a major breakthrough in the 2011 *Eduskunta* elections, represent the harder variant of Euroscepticism. The party adopted its current English name, The Finns, in August 2011. Until then the party had been known as the True Finns. According to its leader Timo Soini, the new simple name was intended to emphasize the fact that the party represents ordinary citizens, whilst the old name 'True Finns' had an extremely Nationalistic slant to it. The exact translation of the Finnish name of the party, *Perussuomalaiset*, would be 'common Finns' or 'ordinary Finns'.

There was thus – at least until the 2011 national elections – a relatively broad partisan consensus about the EU in the Finnish party system. In fact, considering the divisive nature of the EU membership referendum held in 1994, the traditionally state-centric political culture, and low public support for integration, Finland would seem to possess all the key preconditions for strong party-based Euroscepticism. Indeed, as shown in the next section, the commitment to integration, which prevails amongst the parties, is not shared to the same extent by the Finnish electorate.

6 Public opinion and the European Union

The Finnish approach to integration is usually described as pragmatic and constructive, with Finnish politicians and civil servants normally portrayed as cooperative and committed to working in the EU institutions. According to the political elite, national interests can be best pursued through active and constructive participation in decision-making. Underlying this stance is a strong conviction that a strong and efficient EU can best protect the rights and interests of smaller Member States, as intergovernmental processes tend to favour larger Member States. However, according to Eurobarometer and other public opinion surveys, Finns are more sceptical of integration than the average EU citizen. In addition to the generally low levels of public support for integration, the Finnish electorate seems to be particularly concerned about the influence of small Member States in EU governance (Raunio and Tiilikainen, 2003; Tiilikainen, 2006).

There is thus a notable lack of congruence between Finnish citizens and the political parties, with most parties considerably more supportive of the EU than their electorates (Mattila and Raunio, 2005, 2006). Hence it is not surprising that, overall, the Finnish parties have kept a fairly low profile in integration matters, with the rules of the national EU coordination system, based on building broad domestic consensus, including often between the government and opposition parties, also contributing to the depoliticization of European issues (Raunio, 2005c, 2007b, 2008). Given that most parties are internally divided over the EU, it was also not surprising that the main parties showed little interest in submitting the Constitutional Treaty or the Lisbon Treaty to a referendum.

However, in the run-up to the 2011 national elections, the euro-zone crisis and the associated bailout measures triggered heated debates in the *Eduskunta*. Both the argumentation of the political parties in the 2011 election campaign and subsequent post-election developments suggest some potential changes to national integration policy. The decisions to participate in the bailout operations were justified by their positive effects on domestic economy and growth, and in general the defence of national interests was emphasized by all parties. Overall it appears that such an emphasis on national interests and on the role of smaller Member States has become more pronounced in Finland in recent years (Raunio, 2011). It can be expected that in this climate of opinion, the political elite in general will increasingly emphasize the need to defend national interests in Brussels. Indeed, since entering office in June 2011 the 'six pack' government led by the National Coalition has taken a tougher stance in EU negotiations, both in terms of demanding guarantees for its national bailout payments and in blocking, together with the Netherlands, the entry of Bulgaria and Romania into the Schengen area. Whether this signals a more long-term change in national integration policy remains to be seen, but at least in the short term the Finnish government is under considerable domestic pressure not to make too many concessions in Brussels.

7 National and EP electoral systems

The electoral system used for EP elections is essentially the same as that used for electing the *Eduskunta* (Raunio, 2005b). The only real difference is that in the national elections, the country is divided into one single-member district, the Åland Islands, and 12 multi-member electoral districts. According to the law on EP elections, candidates can be nominated by registered parties and constituency associations. Parties can form electoral alliances with one another and constituency associations can set up joint lists. The maximum number of candidates per party, or electoral alliance or joint list is 20, but a single constituency association can only put forward 1 candidate. In *Eduskunta* elections candidate selection takes place exclusively at the district level, with the national party leadership having only theoretical opportunities to influence the process. However, in EP elections it is essentially the party executive or council, the exact name of which varies between the parties, that decides who is on the final list of candidates. This does not mean that the local and district branches are totally neglected. They are consulted and asked to suggest their own candidates, but the final decision is always taken by the national party executive.

The whole country forms one single constituency, whilst voters choose between individual candidates from non-ordered party lists. Seat allocation to parties is based on the d'Hondt method. After each party, electoral alliance, and joint list has been allocated the number of seats to which it is entitled, the candidates on the lists are ranked according to the number of their preference votes. This means that within electoral alliances the distribution of seats is determined by the plurality principle, regardless of the total number of votes won by the respective parties forming the alliance.

The open list candidate-centred system impacts strongly on campaigns, with the programmes and discourses of political parties overshadowed by the campaigns of individual candidates. Under the open list electoral system the most efficient electoral strategy for the candidates is to focus on their personal qualities, international and national political experience, expertise on EU issues, or language skills. The electoral system leads to more competition within than between parties and individual candidates from the same party pursue personal campaigns, with little if any interference from the party leadership and with programmes almost completely in the background.

There has occasionally been debate about changing the electoral system. For example, before the 2004 EP elections some senior politicians argued in favour of closed lists instead of the open list system. It was suggested that the move to closed lists would improve the quality of the campaigns as the parties, rather than the individual candidates, would be forced to become the key players in contrast to the present system. There has also been discussion about dividing the country into multiple constituencies. With the whole country forming a single constituency, it is rather impossible to guarantee any degree of geographical representation. In addition, the current system favours candidates with national visibility and also makes campaigning relatively costly. However, dividing the country into several constituencies would probably also make the system less proportional.

Considering that most Finnish parties are internally divided over Europe, leaders have good cause to support the existing rules of the electoral game, as protests or dissenting opinions get channelled through individual candidates. Parties also try to make sure that these internal differences are reflected in the composition of the lists. In addition to recruiting candidates from across the country, lists thus include candidates with different views on Europe. This applies particularly to parties that are less cohesive on integration, most notably the Centre Party and the Left Alliance. Whilst this obviously causes problems for the party leaderships, it reduces tensions within the parties and probably increases their vote totals (Raunio, 2007a).

8 A glance at the EP and national elections

When comparing EP and national parliamentary elections, it is possible to notice some interesting differences concerning turnout and party competition; both have been substantially lower in EP elections.

The turnout of 40.3 per cent achieved in the 2009 EP elections was slightly below that of 41.1 per cent achieved in 2004, but 27.6 per cent less than in the 2007 national elections. The highest turnout of 60.3 per cent was achieved in the first EP elections held in October 1996, whereas the lowest turnout of 31.4 per cent was registered in the 1999 elections. However, turnout has also declined in national electoral contests. Whilst in the 1960s, on average, 85 per cent of citizens cast their votes, the figure dropped to 81 per cent in the 1970s, about 79 per cent in the 1980s, 71 per cent in the 1990s, and below 70 per cent in the first decade of the twenty-first century, reaching its lowest point at 67.9 per cent in the 2007 elections. Subsequently, the popularity of the Finns and the associated higher level of contestation and interest probably explain the rise in turnout to 70.5 per cent in the 2011 national elections.

Table 17.3 National election results in Finland: 1995–2011 (%)

Political party	1995	1999	2003	2007	2011
Centre Party	19.8	22.4	24.7	23.1	15.8
Social Democratic Party	28.3	22.9	24.5	21.4	19.1
National Coalition	17.9	21.0	18.6	22.3	20.4
Left Alliance	11.2	10.9	9.9	8.8	8.1
Green League	6.5	7.3	8.0	8.5	7.3
Swedish People's Party	5.1	5.1	4.6	4.6	4.3
Christian Democrats	3.0	4.2	5.3	4.9	4.0
Rural Party*	1.3	—	—	—	—
Young Finns**	2.8	1.0	—	—	—
The Finns	—	1.0	1.6	4.1	19.1
Others	4.1	4.2	2.8	2.3	2.0
Total	100.0	100.0	100.0	100.0	100.0
Turnout	**71.9**	**68.3**	**69.7**	**67.9**	**70.5**

Source: Finland's Ministry of Justice.

Notes:
* The Rural Party was disbanded after the 1995 elections. The Finns, established that same year, can be considered its successor.
** The right-wing Young Finns was established in 1994. The party failed to gain seats in the 1999 elections and was subsequently disbanded.

Table 17.4 EP election results in Finland: 1996–2009 (%)

Political party	1996	1999	2004	2009
Centre Party	24.4	21.3	23.4	19.0
Social Democratic Party	21.5	17.8	21.2	17.5
National Coalition	20.2	25.3	23.7	23.2
Left Alliance	10.5	9.1	9.1	5.9
Green League	7.6	13.4	10.4	12.4
Swedish People's Party	5.8	6.8	5.7	6.1
Christian Democrats	2.8	2.4	4.3	4.2
Young Finns	3.0	—	—	—
The Finns	0.7	0.8	0.5	9.8
Others	3.5	3.1	1.7	1.9
Total	100.0	100.0	100.0	100.0
Turnout	**60.3**	**31.4**	**41.1**	**40.3**

Source: Finland's Ministry of Justice.

In terms of party competition, the Finnish party system has in recent decades been remarkably stable, with the vote shares of the individual parties changing very little between *Eduskunta* elections. The three core parties, the Social Democratic Party, the Centre Party, and the National Coalition, have largely held on to their vote shares, winning collectively around 65–70 per cent of the vote. Also, the vote shares of the smaller parties display high levels of stability. The vote share of the Left Alliance has gradually decreased, whilst the Green League has become one of the most successful green parties in Europe. Hence the recent rise of The Finns has certainly enlivened the party system, adding an element of unpredictability to elections.

In all Finnish EP elections, the parties fielding candidates can be divided into two categories: those parties within the *Eduskunta* that have had realistic chances of winning seats, and minor parties without seats in the national Parliament. The first EP elections were held in October 1996. Several factors contributed to the high turnout. The contest was held in conjunction with municipal elections, main parties were able to attract high-profile candidates, and the Finnish *markka* was tied to the Exchange Rate Mechanism a week before the election, with impending EMU membership therefore high on the political agenda. Fourteen parties and one constituency association fielded a total of 207 candidates. The political parties also clearly put a lot of effort into the 1996 elections, both programmatically and particularly in terms of campaigning (Anckar, 1997; Martikainen and Pekonen, 1999).

In 1999 the busy electoral calendar, with *Eduskunta* elections held less than three months earlier in March and presidential elections forthcoming in January 2000, strained parties' resources and diverted attention from the EP elections. The Centre Party leader Esko Aho used the launch of his party's EP election campaign to announce his own presidential candidacy. The various party congresses held in May–June 1999 focussed primarily on presidential elections, with the EP contest relegated to a clear second position. Indeed, absence is overall the best word to describe the behaviour of party leaders during the campaign. Party leaders did not take part in a single televised debate, with only the leading individual candidates presenting their parties. Altogether 140 candidates were nominated by 11 parties. As in 1996, no singular issue dominated the campaign. The focus was more on looking after national interests, not on Europe. The European Commission resignation was used by most parties and individual candidates as an example of the urgent need to 'clean up' EU institutions and to increase transparency and openness. With the exception of the Green League, the record low turnout hit parties of the left especially hard.

In the 2004 elections, the political parties managed again to attract high-profile candidates, including two party leaders and prominent parliamentarians. Moreover, the reduction in the number of EP seats, from 16 to 14, meant that the election was going to be even tighter than before, with small parties in real danger of losing their seats. Altogether, 227 candidates were nominated by 14 parties. The campaign was definitely of a higher quality than the one in the elections held five years earlier. With no competing political events diverting attention away from the elections, the parties had much more time, money, and energy to spend on the campaign. This applied particularly to the party leaders, who now took part in television debates and toured the country in support of their candidates. Nevertheless, it is still fair to conclude that the party leaderships approached the election with a notable lack of enthusiasm.

Again no single issue dominated the campaign. In general, voters were far more concerned about the ability of the candidates to defend Finland's national interests in the EU than about wider questions related to European integration. Under the broad umbrella of national interests, the debate focussed on familiar themes in Finnish EU discourse: defence, agriculture, regional policy, and protecting the welfare state. The result brought few surprises, with the main parties holding on to their seat and vote shares and the Eurosceptic parties failing to gain new ground (Tiilikainen and Wass, 2004; Mattila and Raunio, 2005; Raunio, 2005a).

9 The 2009 European election

9.1 Party lists and manifestos

As the 2009 election drew closer, there was little reason to expect an interesting campaign. There had been virtually no debate on the EU since the 2004 EP election and the discussions on the Constitutional Treaty. However, there were also a number of factors that gave cause for more optimistic scenarios. The electoral calendar was empty, with the municipal elections held in the autumn of 2008 and the next *Eduskunta* elections scheduled for 2011. Nor were there any pressing domestic issues diverting attention from the EP elections, and this resulted in quite extensive media coverage of the campaigns. Whilst the main parties had serious difficulties in attracting good candidates, the reduction of seats allocated to Finland, from 14 to 13, meant that the smaller parties, in particular, needed to do well in order to maintain representation in the European Parliament.

One of the most significant factors was the candidacy of Timo Soini, the highly popular leader of the Eurosceptic party, The Finns. Soini's decision to run for a seat breathed life to the campaign, as the other parties could not ignore The Finns – whose support had more than doubled in the previous *Eduskunta* elections, from 1.6 per cent in 2003 to 4.1 per cent in 2007 – and the rise of the party had continued in the 2008 municipal elections in which it captured 5.4 per cent of the vote. Hence, the Centre and the Social Democrats particularly needed to take The Finns seriously. The Social Democrats were afraid that Soini would get votes from urban working-class suburbs, whereas the Centre feared that Soini would be popular amongst Eurosceptic rural voters.

Altogether, 241 candidates were nominated by 13 parties and one constituency association. As in the previous elections, the minor parties without *Eduskunta* seats had hardly any chance of winning a seat in the EP and they were also almost completely ignored by the media. These marginal parties were: For the Poor-party (20 candidates), *Suomen Työväenpuolue* (Labour Party, 20), Communist Party (20), *Suomen Senioripuolue* (Senior Citizens' Party, 20), and *Itsenäisyyspuolue* (Independence Party, 20). The parties represented in national Parliament all put forward 20 candidates. The exception was the electoral alliance between Christian Democrats and The Finns, where both parties fielded ten candidates.

It is probably fair to argue that, with the exception of the first EP elections held in 1996, the 2009 EP elections were in many ways more interesting and competitive than the previous rounds of elections. Most notably, the candidacy of Soini contributed to Europe, and particularly Euroscepticism, occupying a more central role in the campaigns than before. Eurosceptic parties also won more votes and seats than in previous elections. In fact, the elections would most likely have remained a low-key affair without the candidacy of Soini. But his candidacy also had the effect of focussing the spotlight very much on Soini, and not on actual issues. Other parties did their best to discredit Soini and particularly The Finns' tough line on immigration, with the consequence that their own policy agendas were often ignored or downplayed. For example, the liberal Swedish People's Party announced that it was a counterforce to The Finns. A media favourite, Soini basked in the attention and largely dominated the campaign.

Defending national interests emerged again, perhaps, as the main theme of the elections, especially as public opinion surveys showed that the citizens were again more concerned about the ability of the candidates to defend Finland's national interests in the EU than about wider questions related to Europe. This focus on 'national interests' should not necessarily be interpreted as Euroscepticism or as pitting Finland against the EU. After all, it is quite natural that the electorate would be concerned about the extent to which Finland's voice is heard at the European level, as Finland is a relatively small, geographically peripheral Member State, electing fewer than 2 per cent of all MEPs. Many candidates also based their campaigns on defending the interests of particular regions. This applied especially to candidates of the Centre Party, as this party draws most of its support from the more sparsely populated rural regions.

Otherwise, the fragmented debate focussed on a mixture of themes, with perhaps the economic and financial crisis and the environment receiving most coverage. The focus on the environment was understandable as such questions, especially the fate of the Baltic Sea, also had a prominent role in domestic debates. Agriculture and regional policy featured less in national debates, but often dominated the campaigns in the rural areas. Interestingly, quite a lot of the debate also centred on the gap or distance between Brussels and the citizens, with party leaders and candidates speaking of the need to bring the EU closer to the citizens. Overall, the leftist parties emphasized employment and the development of a social Europe, whereas the centre-right parties put more stress on the sound management of the economy, the internal market, and competitiveness.

The name of the Centre Party's programme, '*Urhoutta Eurooppaan*', at least implicitly referred to former President Urho Kekkonen, the strong leader who ruled Finland for a quarter of a century from 1956 to 1981. Whilst Kekkonen's era is the subject of quite heated national debate, most would agree that the former President was very good at defending national interests, particularly *vis-à-vis* the Soviet Union. In fact, the Centre openly acknowledged the need to look after national concerns, with agricultural and regional policy interests especially emphasized in the programme. The election programme stated that:

> the EU takes an increasing range of decisions that impact on us and our children. Hence it is essential that in elections held in June we elect to the European Parliament people that defend unconditionally the interests of Finland and Finns.
> (Centre Party, 2002, 2)

However, the programme of the Centre Party was, nonetheless, not that Eurosceptic in tone. The language of the programme was in fact quite colourful in places, stating for example that 'defending Finnish interests does not mean giving the finger to European cooperation'.

The programme of The Finns essentially mirrored a wholesale rejection of the EU. Soini clearly did not want immigration to become a key issue in the campaign, as this might have benefitted the mainstream parties. In fact, it was the National Coalition that became discredited over immigration policy when on 29 May, one of its candidates, Kai Pöntinen, published an advert on the front page of the leading national daily, *Helsingin Sanomat*, calling for a 'stop to welfare bum immigrants'. Whilst the Chair of the National Coalition, Jyrki Katainen, was quick to denounce Pöntinen's tactics and views, the episode clearly caused embarrassment to his party.

Soini based his campaign on The Finns providing a genuine alternative to the pro-EU policies of the government and the main parties, calling for an end to 'one truth' politics. As the party name implies, The Finns very much emphasize the value of 'Finnishness' and national ways of doing things, including the protection of the Nordic welfare state (Arter, 2010). The party argued against a federal Europe and enlargement mainly on account of it resulting in more immigration, and wanted to roll back integration, for example, by transferring competence in agricultural policy back to the Member States. According to The Finns, European-level democracy simply does not work and the Lisbon Treaty should have been subjected to a referendum. Interestingly, whilst the party strongly emphasized the defence of national interests, it simultaneously recognized the need to participate in EU decision-making in order to take power back from the EU. Hence the party does not call for Finland's exit from the European Union, believing instead that in the long run EU will prove unworkable and will thus, inevitably, disintegrate.

Apart from The Finns, only the Christian Democrats had a predominantly Eurosceptic campaign. The party stressed the role of national interests and was particularly concerned about the influence of small Member States; it argued in general that the EU should do less, but better. In terms of policy, Christian Democrats emphasized the virtues of the Nordic welfare state whilst stating that EU should explicitly recognize and commit itself to European Christian values and adopt a more family-oriented approach to its actions and policies.

The Social Democrats, the main opposition party in the *Eduskunta*, depicted the election as a choice between a bourgeois or a market-led Europe and a 'human' Europe:

> In the European Parliament the direction of politics is decided between the two largest party groups, the Social Democrats and the Conservatives. The main alternatives are also in Finland Social Democrats or a market-oriented right. The consequences of bourgeois politics are known here in Finland and in the majority of European countries. This is what we want to change.
> *(Social Democratic Party, 2009, 1)*

When launching its campaign, the party strongly attacked free markets and argued that the right-wing economic policy of the EU had come to its end.

Calling for more control and regulation of the market economy, the party declared the need for a more human Europe, with employment and social rights highlighted in the party programme. Whilst the discourse of the Social Democrats was solidly pro-EU, the party also stressed the importance of protecting national public services and labour market policies. Defending the welfare state, the party programme stated that:

> like the other Nordic countries, Finland has a lot to offer to the European Union. The Nordic model has provided security and well-being to citizens and has also been an economic success story. We want to make the EU also an area of well-being and economic success that is based on the needs of the people.
> *(Social Democratic Party, 2009, 1–2)*

The Green League campaigned on the basis of the programme of the European Green Party, which in general argued that the EU needs a 'new direction'. Otherwise Euro-party manifestos were again almost completely absent during the campaigns. They were available at the parties' home pages, but were not used at all in the actual election campaigns by the candidates or the parties. Nor did the Finnish parties make any real use of campaign help from the other EU countries or from their EP groups.

The Greens stressed the adoption of policies that facilitate sustainable development and a more responsible or human Europe based on solidarity, stating that economic concerns should not come before the needs and rights of people. Neo liberal policies had privileged the few at the expense of the welfare of the citizenry and the state of the environment.

The discourse of the Left Alliance reflected that of the Greens. The party stressed the need for active international and European cooperation in order to fight for an 'alternative, better Europe', which is not so dominated by business interests. Hence the party saw a need for a fundamental reform of the international and European economy, with more resources invested in improving the well-being of citizens and the environment. The party also stated that the EU should be developed as an association of independent Member States and defended the Nordic welfare state model. Like the Greens, the Left Alliance also favoured the 'civilian power' concept of EU in global politics, for example through crisis management operations, and the use of referenda in key integration matters.

As in previous rounds of elections, the National Coalition and the Social Democrats reminded the electorate that their MEPs sat in the two largest EP groups. The National Coalition was especially keen to highlight its membership in the EPP, the largest of the EP groups.

The National Coalition had a solidly pro-EU programme, with an emphasis on a 'responsible market economy'. Whilst the party continues to be against unnecessary EU-level bureaucracy and regulation, it nevertheless argued in general for a stronger and more efficient Europe. Finally, the Swedish People's Party predictably focussed on making sure that the voice of the Swedish-speaking minority in Finland was heard in Brussels, whilst emphasizing the values of linguistic and cultural diversity.

9.2 Electoral campaign

As in the previous elections, the EP information office in Helsinki was actively involved in the 2009 campaign. Its election budget was around €290,000. The main items of expenditure were outside advertisements, including about €120,000 for posters, €80,000 for radio adverts, €40,000 for organizing and participating in various events, and €25,000 for publications. The EP in Brussels also provided publications and other public relations items and, more importantly, was responsible for organizing and centrally providing most of the internet-based election material.

The media has arguably done a fairly decent job in covering EU matters between EP elections. However, during the election campaigns most of the printed and electronic media, particularly the main television channels, have focussed on selected leading candidates, giving them a lot of free nationwide exposure. Whilst this may give the electorate more information about these individual candidates, it also contributes towards the fragmentation of the debate, as party messages remain in a secondary role.

9.3 Electoral results

The 2009 EP elections were held on Sunday, 7 June. Advance voting took place from 27 May to 2 June. Turnout was 40.3 per cent, or 38.6 per cent when those enfranchised citizens residing abroad are taken into account. The collective vote share of the four government parties, the Centre, National Coalition, Green League, and Swedish People's Party, was 60.7 per cent.

This was, in fact, just over two percentage points more than the 58.5 per cent vote share of the four parties in the 2007 national elections. The leading government party, the Centre,

Table 17.5 EP election results in Finland: 2009

National party	Votes %	Seats (seat change)	Political group
National Coalition	23.2	3 (−1)	EPP
Centre Party	19.0	3 (−1)	ALDE
Social Democratic Party	17.5	2 (−1)	S&D
Green League	12.4	2 (+1)	Greens/EFA
The Finns	9.8	1 (+1)	EFD
Swedish People's Party	6.1	1	ALDE
Left Alliance	5.9	0 (−1)	—
Christian Democrats	4.2	1 (+1)	EPP
Others	1.9	0	—
Total	100.0	—	—
Turnout	**40.3**	—	—

Source: Finland's Ministry of Justice.

saw its vote share (19.0 per cent) decline by more than 4 per cent in comparison with both the 2004 EP and the 2007 legislative elections, with the resulting loss of one of its seats. However, considering the economic downturn and the low popularity ratings of Prime Minister Vanhanen, the outcome was nonetheless quite satisfactory for the party. Reflecting internal divisions within the party over integration, the attitudes of two of the three Centre MEPs, Hannu Takkula and Riikka Manner, towards the EU are more critical than the official party line.

This continues the pattern set in previous EP elections, where one or more Centre MEPs are more Eurosceptic than the party leadership. In fact, after the elections Takkula recommended to his party that the Centre should leave the ALDE group and join the ECR, but in the end it was agreed that the Centre delegation would remain with ALDE. Takkula also considered joining the European Conservatives and Reformists on a personal basis, with the other Centre MEPs staying in ALDE. However, Takkula chose to continue in the Liberal group, at least partially because he considered some of the smaller parties in the European Conservatives and Reformists as too Eurosceptic.

The National Coalition had performed well in previous EP elections, and whilst the party won 0.5 per cent fewer votes than in the 2004 EP elections, it emerged as the biggest party by a comfortable margin, winning 23.2 per cent of the vote. Nonetheless, the National Coalition lost one seat, with its three seats going to re-elected MEPs Ville Itälä, Eija-Riitta Korhola, and Sirpa Pietikäinen.

Turning to the junior partners in the coalition, the Green League has fared better in EP elections than in national parliamentary elections. This time the Greens won 12.4 per cent of the vote, 2 per cent more than in the 2004 elections and nearly 4 per cent above that achieved in the latest *Eduskunta* elections. The Greens had a very strong list, and both of their MEPs, Heidi Hautala and Satu Hassi, had previous experience in the European Parliament. The Swedish People's Party has traditionally benefitted from the higher turnout amongst Swedish-speakers, who currently comprise 5.4 per cent of the population, and this factor contributed to the party holding on to its seat with 6.1 per cent of the vote.

The main opposition party, the Social Democrats, suffered a major defeat. Capturing only 17.5 per cent of the vote, it lost one seat and nearly 4 per cent of the vote in comparison with both the 2004 EP and the 2007 national elections. The leading SDP candidate, Father Mitro, was the only 'celebrity' candidate elected to the EP from Finland. The Left Alliance finished as the seventh largest party, with 5.9 per cent of the vote, its worst election result since the party was founded in 1990. The party lost its only seat, and, three days after the elections, the election Party Chair Martti Korhonen announced his resignation. Hence with the partial exception of the Greens, who have refused to be classified as either a leftist or centre-right party, the elections were a major disappointment for the left. Much of the discussion at the European level has in recent years focussed on the need to make the EU more competitive, and when this discourse is combined with Finnish domestic measures aiming at making the public sector and the national economy in general more cost efficient and competitive, it is understandable that leftist voters may find it hard to identify themselves with European integration. In short, the left and particularly the Social Democrats may like to portray Europe as a possibility, but large sections of the leftist electorate view integration as a threat (Raunio, 2010).

The main winner of the election was undoubtedly The Finns, who won their first seat in the European Parliament. With 9.8 per cent of the vote, the party increased its vote share by just under 6 per cent compared with the 2007 national elections and by over 9 per cent compared with the 2004 EP elections. Soini was the unrivalled king of the vote in the elections, capturing 130,715 votes. It is also probable that The Finns' triumph is explained more by a combination of Soini's popularity and the electorate voting against the mainstream parties than by Euroscepticism. However, one can also argue that the voters were protesting against the broad pro-EU consensus of the political elite, and this was indeed one of the main campaign themes of The Finns. After the elections Soini faced the choice of joining either the ECR group or the EFD, but chose the latter on account of its Eurosceptic views.

Christian Democrats have benefitted from alliances in *Eduskunta* elections, and this strategy paid off again, with the party winning a seat thanks to the popularity of Soini and to Christian Democratic voters concentrating votes on their leading candidate, Sari Essayah. During the campaign, Essayah made no secret of her opposition to both further integration and the Lisbon Treaty whilst indicating that if elected she would join the EPP group. At first, the National Coalition objected to Essayah's group membership on account of her Eurosceptic views, and then prevented Essayah from sitting as a delegation on her own inside the EPP group. A compromise was found when she joined the Finnish delegation in the EPP group that also comprises three National Coalition MEPs and is led by Ville Itälä.

Six of the seven Finnish MEPs that stood for re-election won their seats. Eight of the thirteen MEPs elected in 2009 were women. This share is higher than in previous elections: in 1996, eight out of fourteen; in 1999, seven out of fourteen; and in 2004, five out of fourteen elected MEPs were women.

Table 17.6 List of Finnish MEPs: seventh legislature

Name	Date of birth	Gender	National party	Political group	Mandate	Professional background
Essayah, Sari	21/02/1967	Female	Christian Democrats	EPP	1	Economist
Haglund, Carl	29/03/1979	Male	Swedish People's Party	ALDE	1	Economist
Hassi, Satu	03/06/1951	Female	Green League	Greens/EFA	2	Engineer
Hautala, Heidi	14/11/1955	Female	Green League	Greens/EFA	3 (1995–2003, 2009)	Master's degree in agriculture and forestry
Itälä, Ville	10/05/1959	Male	National Coalition	EPP	2	Lawyer
Jaakonsaari, Liisa	02/09/1945	Female	Social Democratic Party	S&D	1	Journalist
Jäätteenmäki, Anneli	11/02/1955	Female	Centre Party	ALDE	2	Lawyer
Korhola, Eija-Riitta	15/06/1959	Female	National Coalition	EPP	3	Degree in philosophy
Manner, Riikka	24/08/1981	Female	Centre Party	ALDE	1	Economist
Pietikäinen, Sirpa	19/04/1959	Female	National Coalition	EPP	2 (2008–2009)	Economist
Repo, Mitro	03/09/1958	Male	Social Democratic Party	S&D	1	Priest
Soini, Timo	30/05/1962	Male	The Finns	EFD	1	Party official
Takkula, Hannu	20/11/1963	Male	Centre Party	ALDE	2	Teacher

Source: European Parliament database, 2010, www.europarl.europa.eu/meps/en/search.html?country=FI.

9.4 Campaign finance

There were no restrictions or upper limits concerning the budgets of the parties or the individual candidates, but according to the law on election financing, elected MEPs and those appointed as their deputies must submit within two months of the confirmation of the election result a public notification of the financing of their election campaign. According to these notifications, in the 2009 elections the average campaign expenditure of elected Finnish MEPs was €71,726. The candidates are largely responsible for funding their own campaigns, with the candidates often also investing large sums of their own money in the elections.

10 Theoretical interpretation of Euro-elections

10.1 Second-Order Election theory

The Finnish case provides mixed evidence for the Second-Order Election model. Over the years, the leading governing party has normally lost votes but the success of its coalition partners has varied. For example, in the 2009 elections the main government party, the Centre, suffered a major defeat, but its main partner in the cabinet, the National Coalition, emerged as the largest party whilst its junior partners, the Green League and the Swedish People's Party, again performed better in EP elections than in national parliamentary elections.

Moreover, the opposition parties both lost and won in the 2009 elections. The Social Democrats and the Left Alliance experienced severe defeats, whilst the Eurosceptic list of Christian Democrats and The Finns did particularly well. The Social Democrats have performed rather badly in all EP elections held so far, whilst the National Coalition has on average fared better in European than in national parliamentary elections.

10.2 Europe Salience theory

The campaigns and debates in the four EP elections held so far have focussed, to a large extent, on defending national or regional interests. However, most of this discourse cannot be labelled Eurosceptic, as the parties and individual candidates have not, at least explicitly, identified a mismatch between Finnish interests and the EU. With the exception of The Finns, the debate has therefore not been characterized by an 'us-versus-them' discourse. Instead, it is perhaps better to approach the debate as 'constituency' politics. Finland is a small, northern country, and thus its citizens have a good reason to be concerned about the influence of Finland in EU governance and whether vital national interests can realistically be defended in an enlarged European Union. The citizens and the candidates seem particularly worried about whether the EU is dominated by its larger Member States.

Overall, it appears that this emphasis on defending national interests and on the role and rights of small Member States has become more pronounced in Finland, with the government and political parties in recent years repeatedly stressing the need to pay more attention to protecting national interests in an enlarged European Union.

The dominance of 'national focus' also means that much of the debate in Finland has revolved around the relationship between Finland and the EU, or more precisely on the place of Finland in European integration. Hence there has been less debate about actual EU policies, but some common themes can nonetheless be identified. In addition to election-specific themes, such as the economic and financial turmoil in the 2009 elections, questions relating to the welfare state are always high on the Finnish political agenda. There is a relatively broad partisan and public consensus behind the welfare state regime, and hence also the centre-right parties, such as the National Coalition, the Swedish People's Party, and the Centre Party, emphasize the welfare state and the social dimension of the EU in their programmes. This socio-economic debate has been cast very much in terms of whether the Nordic welfare model can be maintained in an integrative Europe, and, as indicated above, it is plausible to argue that this debate has contributed to rising problems for the left (Raunio, 2010).

References

Primary sources

European Parliament Database (2010) www.europarl.europa.eu/meps/eu/search.html (accessed on 12 January 2015).
Eurostat (2013, 2014) http://epp.eurostat.ec.europa.eu (accessed on 5 June 2015).
The Centre Party (2009) *Urhoutta Eurooppaan: Keskustan vaaliohjelma Euroopan parlamentin vaaleissa*.
The Social Democratic Party (2009) *Euroopan parlamentin vaalien vaaliohjelma*.

Secondary sources

Anckar, D. (1997) 'The Finnish European Election of 1996', *Electoral Studies*, 16(2), 262–66.
Arter, D. (1999) 'Finland', in Elgie, R. (ed.) *Semi-Presidentialism in Europe*, Oxford, Oxford University Press.
Arter, D. (2009) 'From a Contingent Party System to Party System Convergence? Mapping Party System Change in Post-war Finland', *Scandinavian Political Studies*, 32(2), 221–39.
Arter, D. (2010) 'The Breakthrough of Another West European Populist Radical Right Party? The Case of the True Finns', *Government and Opposition*, 45(4), 484–504.
Johansson, K. M. and Raunio, T. (2010) 'Organizing the Core Executive for European Union Affairs: Comparing Finland and Sweden', *Public Administration*, 88(3), 649–64.
Martikainen, T. and Pekonen, K. (eds) (1999) *Eurovaalit Suomessa 1996: Vaalihumusta päätöksenteon arkeen*, Helsinki, Acta Politica 10, Yleisen valtio-opin laitos, Helsingin yliopisto.
Mattila, M. and Raunio, T. (2004) 'Does Winning Pay? Electoral success and government formation in 15 West European countries', *European Journal of Political Research*, 43(2), 263–85.
Mattila, M. and Raunio, T. (2005) 'Kuka edustaa EU:n vastustajia? Euroopan parlamentin vaalit 2004', *Politiikka*, 47(1), 28–41.
Mattila, M. and Raunio, T. (2006) 'Cautious Voters – Supportive Parties: Opinion Congruence between Voters and Parties on the EU Dimension', *European Union Politics*, 7(4), 427–49.
Nousiainen, J. (2001) 'From Semi-presidentialism to Parliamentary Government: Political and Constitutional Developments in Finland', *Scandinavian Political Studies*, 24(2), 95–109.
Paloheimo, H. (2000) 'Vaaliohjelmat ja ehdokkaiden mielipiteet', in Pesonen, P. (ed.) *Suomen europarlamenttivaalit*, Tampere, Tampere University Press.
Paloheimo, H. (2003) 'The Rising Power of the Prime Minister in Finland', *Scandinavian Political Studies*, 26(3), 219–43.
Paloheimo, H. and Raunio, T. (eds) (2008) *Suomen puolueet ja puoluejärjestelmä*, Helsinki, WSOY.
Raunio, T. (2005a) 'Finland', in Lodge, J. (ed.) *The 2004 Elections to the European Parliament*, Basingstoke, Palgrave.
Raunio, T. (2005b) 'Finland: One Hundred Years of Quietude', in Gallagher, M. and Mitchell P. (eds) *The Politics of Electoral Systems*, Oxford, Oxford University Press.
Raunio, T. (2005c) 'Hesitant Voters, Committed Élite: Explaining the Lack of Eurosceptic Parties in Finland', *Journal of European Integration*, 27(4), 381–95.
Raunio, T. (2007a) 'Open List, Open Mandate? Links between MEPs and Parties in Finland', *Perspectives on European Politics and Society*, 8(2), 131–46.
Raunio, T. (2007b) 'Softening but Persistent: Euroscepticism in the Nordic EU Countries', *Acta Politica*, 42(2–3), 191–210.

Raunio, T. (2008) 'The Difficult Task of Opposing Europe: The Finnish Party Politics of Euroscepticism', Szczerbiak, A. and Taggart, P. (eds) *Opposing Europe? The Comparative Party Politics of Euroscepticism: Case Studies and Country Surveys*, 1, Oxford, Oxford University Press.

Raunio, T. (2010) 'The EU and the Welfare State are Compatible: Finnish Social Democrats and European Integration', *Government and Opposition*, 45(2), 187–207.

Raunio, T. (2011) 'Debating Europe in Finland: Euroscepticism or Legitimate Concerns about National Influence?', in Harmsen, R. and Schild, J. (eds) *Debating Europe: The 2009 European Parliament Elections and Beyond*, Baden-Baden, Nomos.

Raunio, T. and Tiilikainen, T. (2003) *Finland in the European Union*, London, Frank Cass.

Tiilikainen, T. (1998) *Europe and Finland: Defining the Political Identity of Finland in Western Europe*, Aldershot, Ashgate.

Tiilikainen, T. (2006) 'Finland – An EU Member with a Small State Identity', *Journal of European Integration*, 28(1), 73–87.

Tiilikainen, T. and Wass, H. (2004) 'Puolueiden vaalikampanjat vuoden 2004 europarlamenttivaaleissa', *Politiikka*, 46(4), 250–63.

18
SWEDEN

Carina Bischoff and Marlene Wind

Figure 18.1 Map of Sweden

Table 18.1 Sweden profile

EU entry year	1995
Schengen entry year	1996
MEPs elected in 2009	18
MEPs under Lisbon Treaty	20 since 1 December 2011
	Two additional seats allocated to Amelia Andersdotter (Greens/EFA) and to Jens Nilsson (S&D)
Total area★	438,574 km²
Population	9,644,864
	92.2% Swedes, 2.5% Finns, Samit (20,000 people)
Population density★★	23.6
Median age of population	40.9
Political system	Constitutional Monarchy
	Parliamentary Democracy
Head of state	King Carl XVI Gustaf
	(September 1973–)
Head of government	Fredrik Reinfeldt, Moderate Party (M) (October 2006–);
Political majority	Moderate Party (M), Centre Party (C), Liberal People's Party (FP) and the Christian Democrats (KD) Government Coalition (October 2006–)
Currency	Swedish Krona
Prohead GDP in PPS	44,300 €

Source: Eurostat, 2013, 2014, http://epp.eurostat.ec.europa.eu/.

Notes:
★ Total area including inland waters.
★★ Population density: the ratio of the annual average population of a region to the land area of the region.

1 Geographical position

Sweden is located in northern Europe, bordering Norway to the west and Finland to the northeast. It has a long coastline to the east and south, and in the south the Øresund bridge connects the country to Denmark. About 85 per cent of the Swedish population lives in urban areas and, in particular, in the capital Stockholm, which has 1.3 million inhabitants.

Even though in geographical terms Sweden is the third largest country in Europe, it has a population below ten million, and in the context of the European Union the country is regarded as belonging to the group of small states.

2 Historical background

The history of Sweden as an independent state, which goes back to the Middle Ages, was characterized by territorial wars with its neighbours. Vast territories presently belonging to Finland and Norway were once under Swedish rule. However, cooperation with neighbouring countries was achieved for longer periods of time, and from 1397 to 1523, Sweden, Denmark, and Norway formed the Union of Kalmar.

From around the eighteenth century, and during the following centuries, the Swedish population grew rapidly and at the same time the country's agricultural production increased.

Moreover, progress was made in extracting the country's natural resources, such as wood, iron, and copper, laying the ground for the industrialization of the country. Changes in the social and economic structures that followed industrialization and urbanization during the nineteenth century resulted in a growing proletariat and the formation of the social democratic movement in the 1880s–1890s.

Sweden did not participate actively in WWII and did not suffer from the same post-war economic hardship as most of the other European countries. Instead, the country's economy flourished and after the war the Social Democratic government, led by Prime Minister Tage Erlander, introduced several welfare measures that made Sweden an excellent model of social reform. Until the 1970s, Sweden's generous welfare policies were financed by a booming economy, and the tax system was designed in order to achieve a better redistribution of the wealth. However, in the mid-1970s, the Swedish economy went into recession, the unemployment rate went up, and the public debt increased dramatically.

Despite this, Sweden did not, like Denmark, seek EC membership, as this would have compromised the country's neutral position. However, with the fall of the Berlin Wall and the collapse of the Soviet Union, Sweden's relations with the European Union changed. In light of the new geopolitical situation, and following another decline in the Swedish economy, the government increased its efforts to enter the European Union at the beginning of the 1990s.

Sweden's application for membership in the European Union was endorsed in a popular referendum held on 13 November 1994, in which 52.3 per cent of the electorate voted in favour of membership. Sweden entered the Union on 1 January 1995, and has since then been active in areas such as environmental and social policies. Sweden's entry to the EU did not automatically include accession to the EMU. The question of whether Sweden should join the euro-zone was instead decided through a referendum held on 14 September in 2003, and the result was a rejection by 55.9 per cent of the voters. According to opinion polls, this majority against joining the euro-zone has increased even further since the beginning of the financial crisis in 2008.

3 Geopolitical profile

Since the Napoleonic wars in the nineteenth century, Sweden has pursued a non-aligned foreign policy in peacetime and neutrality in wartime and, unlike Denmark and Norway, it has never been a member of NATO. More recently, however, there have been indications that its position of non-alignment is changing.

Since joining the European Union, neutrality has been watered down, and Sweden is now strongly involved in the EU's Common Foreign and Security Policy, and participates in NATO's Partnership for Peace programme. In spite of these commitments, Swedish foreign policy is still heavily influenced by its tradition of conflict resolution, peacekeeping and democracy building, and its development policy is one of the most generous in the world. In addition, Sweden joined the Council of Europe in 1949, the Organization for Economic Cooperation and Development in 1961, the Organization for Security and Cooperation in Europe, the United Nations in 1946, and the International Monetary Fund in 1951.

4 Overview of the political landscape

Sweden is a constitutional monarchy and a parliamentary democracy. An important reform of the Swedish political system came with the adoption of a new Constitution in 1975, the so-called 'Instrument of Government', which replaced the 1809 Constitution. As a result, the *Riksdag* changed from a bicameral to a unicameral system with 349 seats.

Throughout the twentieth century, Swedish politics was dominated by the Swedish Social Democratic Workers' Party (*Sveriges Socialdemokratiska Arbetarepartiet*), usually called the Social Democratic Party or Social Democrats, that governed uninterrupted from 1932 until 1976. Subsequently, for six years, the government was in the hands of the three centre-right parties: *Moderaterna* (the Moderates) – the former Conservative party – *Folkpartiet* (the Liberal People's Party), and *Centerpartiet* (the Centre Party). Differences between the parties made stable collaboration difficult and the four successive non-Socialist governments in the period represented a single-party minority government, as well as coalitions of two or three parties. In the 1982 elections the Social Democrats were able to regain office and except for a short period in opposition from 1991 to 1994, the Social Democratic Party remained in power until 2006.

Despite their dominance, the Social Democrats never succeeded in winning an absolute majority in Parliament and were therefore required to cooperate with other parties. Sweden has negative parliamentarism, which means that a government does not need a majority to support it but can rule as long as there is no majority in Parliament against it. Therefore, the Social Democrats usually ruled as a minority government, although the party shared office with centre-right parties in the 1950s. In the past, a key factor behind the Social Democrats' virtual monopoly was undoubtedly the divided nature of the opposition, with one or two parties on the left and three or four parties on the right, which struggled to form a viable alternative. In addition, the Social Democrats were for a long time regarded as the embodiment of the special Swedish concept of *Folkhemmet* (The People's Home), representing a universal welfare model with a focus on equality.

The 2006 *Riksdag* election led to a majority coalition government, consisting of four centre-right parties, the Moderate Party, the Centre Party, the Liberal People's Party, and the Christian Democratic Party. This was hardly business as usual and it seemed to open a new era in Swedish politics, one characterized by greater balance between the left and the right and a true government alternative. This change in the political landscape was more than just a short interlude, as confirmed in the 2010 parliamentary elections when the centre-right parties had to build parliamentary majorities with parties outside the ruling coalition.

5 Brief account of the political parties

The two main political parties in the Swedish political system are: the Social Democratic Party and the Moderates, which were called the Conservative Party until 1969. All other parties are small and tend to coalesce with either the Social Democrats or the Moderates.

Founded in 1889, the Swedish Social Democratic Workers' Party (Social Democrats) has dominated and shaped Swedish politics since 1932. Its main aim is to create a more egalitarian society; the expansion of the Swedish welfare state is one of its major achievements over the past 80 years. However, since the 1970s the electoral success of the party has declined, something that could be partially explained by the changes adopted in the welfare state, due to the growing pressures of globalization. Since 2006, the party has been in opposition and has suffered from a severe leadership crisis. Amongst the left-wing parties that often support or coalesce with the Social Democrats are the Green Party and the Left Party.

The Green Party (*Miljöpartiet*) was founded in 1980 and emerged out of the strong post-materialist subculture in Sweden. It advocates environmentally friendly policies combined with strong support for social engagement in society, and it gives priority to issues such as the fight

Table 18.2 List of political parties in Sweden

Original name	Abbreviation	English translation
Vänsterpartiet	V	Left Party
Socialdemokraterna	S	Social Democratic Party
Miljöpartiet	MP	Green Party
Centerpartiet	C	Centre Party
Folkpartiet	FP	Liberal Party
Kristdemokraterna	KD	Christian Democrats
Moderaterna	M	Moderate Party
Sverigedemokraterna	SD	Sweden Democrats
Junilistan	JL	June List
Feministisk Initiativ	FI	Feminist Initiative
Pirat Partiet	P	Pirate Party

against climate change, the preservation of the generous welfare state providing social security to the Swedish people, and job creation.

The Left Party (*Vänsterpartiet*) was originally named the Communist Party and was founded in 1917 as a faction that left the Social Democratic party. After being expelled from Comintern in 1929, it became the Left Party Communists and finally, in 1990, it adjusted to the new post-Soviet reality under the name of the Left Party.

On the centre-right of the political spectrum there are four parties: the Moderates, the Liberal People's Party, the Centre Party, and the Christian Democratic Party.

Founded in 1904, the Moderates are an old party, but until 1976 the party had major difficulties overcoming the dominance of the Social Democrats in Swedish politics. Tax cuts and privatization of the public sector are key issues on the political agenda of the Moderates. They underline the importance of a strong surplus economy, whilst emphasizing the need to sustain the Swedish welfare state.

The Liberal People's Party, established in 1934, advocates the traditional values of an open society, the defence of civil rights, and liberal economic principles.

Set up in 1913 as an agrarian party, the Centre Party has over the years become more of a liberal party advocating issues related to free enterprise, job creation, gender equality, and the environment.

The Christian Democratic Party (*Kristdemokraterna*), founded in 1964, focusses its political programme on Christian and traditional family values.

Finally, on the far right, it is possible to find the Swedish Democrats (*Sverigedemokraterna*), who appeared for the first time on the political stage in 1988, but had to wait until 2010 in order to gain parliamentary representation. Like most extreme right-wing parties, the Swedish Democrats have a very nationalistic and anti-immigration agenda.

5.1 Party attitudes towards the European Union

The Greens and the Left Party have been the most Eurosceptic of the political parties represented in Parliament since Sweden entered the European Union in 1995. Both have advocated Sweden's withdrawal from the EU, but in 2008 the Greens reverted this stand, whereby the Left Party became the only party against EU membership.

The Centre Party has all along been in favour of European integration, but it rejected Swedish membership of the EMU and recommended a 'No' vote in the 2003 referendum on joining the euro-zone.

Sweden

In terms of public support for the EU-sceptic parties, both the Greens and the Left Party were very successful in the first two EP elections held in Sweden in 1995 and 1999. However, in the 2004 EP election the aggregated share of the vote for the two parties dropped from 30.1 per cent in 1995 and 25.3 per cent in 1999 to 18.8 per cent in 2004, and then dropped even further to 16.7 per cent in the 2009 EP election.

The fact that for many years both parties had no prospect of entering government is congruent with a party strategy or thesis claiming that Euroscepticism is a vehicle for domestic dissent and follows the politics of opposition (Taggart, 1998; Sitter, 2001). The recent turn of the Greens on EU membership lends support to this interpretation. However, as Nicholas Aylett points out, there are also ideological roots at the base of the party positions (Aylott, 2008). The Left Party supports a model of political economy with a large public sector and sees the EU as threatening this. Conversely, the Greens' original anti-European stance might be perceived as being at odds with its ecological concerns, which favour supranational regulation, as do many other green parties in Europe. Furthermore, The Greens are strongly committed to decentralized decision-making, local democracy, and neutrality in international relations. Two of its bedrock concerns are in fundamental opposition to Europe, and even to the Greens in the European Parliament. It is, therefore, not possible to ascribe the party's history of Euroscepticism to a strategy of capitalizing on electoral dissatisfaction, or at least not to this motive alone.

Until 2004, the parties running in EP races were the same as those that competed for the *Riksdag* elections. Then *Junilistan* (the June List) was founded as an EU-sceptic popular movement. As in the case of the June Movement, a party which already existed in Denmark, the June List did not seek representation in the national Parliament, but only in the EP. The June List rejects further integration, but is not against EU membership as such.

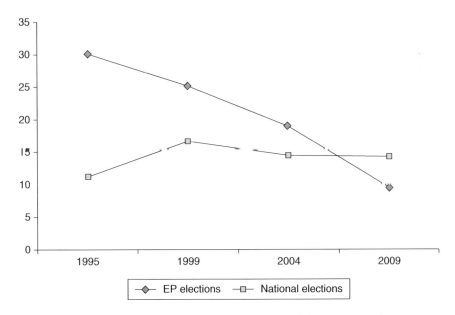

Figure 18.2 Support for hard Eurosceptic parties at EP and national elections in Sweden

Source: Statistics Sweden, www.scb.se/statistik/_publikationer/ME0111_2009A01_BR_ME09BR1101.pdf; www.scb.se/statistik/_publikationer/ME0104_2010A01p_BR_ME01BR1101.pdf

None of the parties have split as a result of disagreement on questions relating to the EU. However, although popular and elite Euroscepticism has not manifested itself clearly at the system level, this is not to say that parties have not felt its impact. Many Swedish parties can count Eurosceptics amongst their members and three of them, the Social Democrats, the Centre Party, and the Christian Democrats, even comprise organized Eurosceptic factions.

In the Social Democratic Party a Eurosceptic faction was created in 2002 in opposition to EU membership, although none of the Social Democratic MPs expressed a real wish for Sweden to leave the EU (Aylott, 2008). Instead, milder, more moderate forms of Eurosceptic attitudes, including opposition to the EMU, prevailed.

Factionalism of a harder and more persistent nature has been found in the Centre Party and amongst the Christian Democrats. In a country where party cohesion and discipline are generally high, these Eurosceptic factions have surprisingly continued to exist and a balance between candidates with pro- and anti-European profiles has been found on the party ticket. This tolerance within parties, coupled with the low salience of European issues in national elections, undoubtedly goes a long way towards explaining why EU membership has not had a significant impact on the Swedish party system.

6 Public opinion and the European Union

In the first years following accession, there was a significant drop in the number of citizens who thought that membership of the EU was 'a good thing'. In fact, by 1996, 20 per cent more Swedish respondents expressed a negative perception of EU membership. However, since then there has been a consistent downward trend in the percentage of Eurosceptics, and by 2009 the picture was completely reversed, with 35 per cent more Swedes looking positively at the European Union.

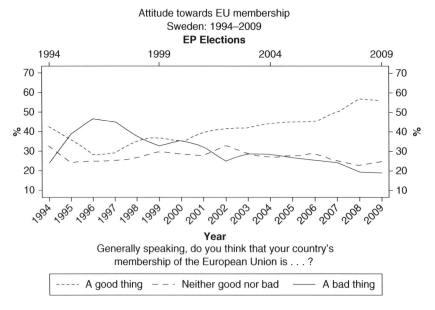

Figure 18.3 Swedish attitude to the European Union

Source: Eurobarometer Issues 1994–2009, http://ec.europa.eu/public_opinion/archives/eb_arch_en.htm.

And yet, it should not be forgotten that one out of five Swedes remains very critical, and, as Aylott puts it:

> If the term is used in a relative sense, Sweden is a Eurosceptical country. By autumn 2002, across the European Union (EU), just one in ten citizens was estimated to believe that his or her country's membership of the EU was a 'bad thing'. In Sweden, it was one in four.
>
> *(ibid., 181)*

As Figure 18.3 reveals, the rather EU-sceptical Swedes have become gradually more positive towards the EU, albeit not Euro-enthusiastic. A tension persists in the representation of popular views on Europe in Sweden, highlighting a discrepancy between party positions and public opinion.

7 National and EP electoral systems

The Swedish electoral system builds on proportional representation (PR), which guarantees a fair distribution of seats on the basis of party voting shares. The electoral period for the *Riksdag* is four years, whilst for the EP elections it is five. The 4 per cent threshold applies to both electoral contests, which precludes the smallest parties from gaining representation. One of the few differences between EP and *Riksdag* elections refers to the number of the constituencies, whilst these are 29 for *Riksdag* elections, there is only one single constituency for the EP elections. With the Lisbon Treaty, Sweden got two additional seats in the European Parliament, thus, since 1 December 2009, there have been 20 Swedish MEPs. The parties running in the EP race can list as many candidates as they wish, and Swedish voters can express their preference for individual candidates from non-ordered party lists. There are no rules limiting the use of opinion and exit polls.

8 A glance at the EP and national elections

In the 2010 parliamentary election, eight parties obtained representation. On the left of the political spectrum the parties were: the Left Party, the Green Party, and the Social Democratic Party. At the centre-right the parties were: the Centre Party, the Moderates, the Liberal People's Party, and the Christian Democratic Party. Finally, on the extreme right, *Sverigedemokraterna* (the Swedish Democrats) entered Parliament for the first time with 5.7 per cent of the vote.

One of the key differences between *Riksdag* and EP elections is turnout. Since 1998, turnout at national elections has ranged between 80.1 and 84.6 per cent, whilst that of Euro elections has oscillated between 37.9 and 45.5 per cent. Another difference is the constellation of small parties with very specific issues on their agenda that run in the EP elections. Thus in the 2009 EP election, it was not only the Eurosceptic movement, the June List, that ran, but also the Feminist Initiative and the Pirate Party, which both have a very narrow political programme.

After joining the European Union, Sweden held its first EP election in 1995. The second EP contest took place in 1999 following the normal election cycle. In the first two elections only the established parties participated, as the single-issue parties had not formed yet. Instead, Euroscepticism in Sweden was expressed by the Left Party, the Greens and, to some extent, the Social Democrats, who were split on the EU question. In the latter case, some candidates ran a somewhat more anti-European campaign than that recommended by the party leadership.

The media coverage of the 1999 EP election campaign was confusing and dealt mostly with the MEPs' allowances and salaries. The front figures in the Social Democratic Party and in the Moderate Party kept a low profile and rarely appeared in the media. Amongst some of the main

Table 18.3 National election results in Sweden: 1994–2010 (%)

Political party	1994	1998	2002	2006	2010
Vänsterpartiet	6.2	12.0	8.4	5.8	5.6
Socialdemokraterna	45.3	36.4	39.9	35.0	30.7
Miljöpartiet	5.0	4.5	4.6	5.2	7.3
Centerpartiet	77.0	5.1	6.2	7.9	6.6
Folkpartiet	7.2	4.7	13.2	7.5	7.1
Kristdemokrate	4.1	11.7	9.1	6.6	5.6
Moderaterna	22.4	22.9	15.3	26.2	30.1
Sverigedemokraterna	—	0.4	1.4	2.9	5.7
Others	2.3	2.2	1.7	2.7	1.4
Total	100.0	100.0	100.0	100.0	100.0
Turnout	**86.8**	**81.4**	**80.1**	**82.0**	**84.6**

Source: Statistics Sweden, 2011, National Elections in 2010, Part 1. Historisk statistic över valåren, 1910–2010.

European issues discussed in the election campaigns conducted by the political parties were: a European defence identity, consumer protection, including the question of hormones in beef, and issues related to the labour market and employment. The latter was not least brought up by the Social Democrats and the Moderates, whereby the parties reinvigorated the left–right approach to European affairs.

Table 18.4 EP election results in Sweden: 1995–2009

Political party	1995 %	1999 %	2004 %	2009 %	Mandates*	Difference 2004–2009 %
V	12.9	15.8	12.8	5.7	1	−7.1
S	28.1	26.0	24.6	24.4	5+1	−0.2
MP	17.2	9.5	6.0	11.0	2	+5.0
C	7.2	6.0	6.3	5.5	1	−0.8
FP	4.8	13.9	9.9	13.6	3	+3.7
KD	3.9	7.6	5.7	4.7	1	−1.0
M	23.2	20.7	18.2	18.8	4	+0.6
JL	—	—	14.5	3.5	0	−11.0
P	—	—	—	7.1	1+1	+7.1
SD	—	—	1.1	3.3	0	+2.2
FI	—	—	—	2.2	0	+2.2
Others	2.7	0.5	1.0	0.2	—	−0.8
Total	100.0	100.0	100.0	100.0	18+2	—
Turnout	**41.6**	**38.8**	**37.9**	**45.5**	—	**+7.6**
Invalid votes	**1.6**	**2.3**	**0.2**	**0.1**	—	—
Blank votes**	—	—	**2.6**	**1.7**	—	—

Source: Statistics Sweden, 2011, Democracy Statistics Report no. 10, Table 1. Valresultat vid Europaparlamentsvalen, 1995–2009.

Notes:
* With the Lisbon Treaty the number of Swedish MEPs increased from 18 to 20. The Pirate Party and the Social Democratic Party each received an additional seat.
** In 1995 and 1999 blank votes were included in the category 'invalid votes'.

The 2004 European election turned out to be a more exciting event than the previous one, as the newly formed June List entered the stage. The campaign focussed on three themes: (1) the European labour market system, which was launched by the Social Democrats who argued that the Services Directive potentially undermined the Swedish model; (2) the bureaucracy in Brussels, which was emphasized by several of the candidates who, speaking to the Eurosceptic Swedish public, talked about taking power back to the Member States; and (3) the European Union Foreign and Defence Policy was put on the agenda by the Centre Party which, to the surprise of everyone since the party had voted against joining the euro-zone, argued that qualified majority voting should be introduced over international issues. Moreover, the Moderates and the Liberals were concerned with expanding the EU's powers to fight crime (Aylott and Sundström, 2009, 5), and the Christian Democrats were concerned that Sweden's strict alcohol policy could be undermined by the EU.

9 The 2009 European election

9.1 Party lists and manifestos

The parties that ran in the 2009 EP election can be divided into two categories:

- generally pro-EU: the Social Democrats, the Moderates, the Christian Democrats, the Liberals, and the Centre Party;
- generally Eurosceptics: the June List, the Sweden Democrats, the Greens, the Left Party, and the Feminist Initiative.

All candidates running in the EP election had to be announced by the parties before 13 March 2009, and by this date approximately 500 candidates from a total of 24 parties had been listed. The leading candidates in the EP election were generally a mix of well-known personalities, although not necessarily from the world of politics, and unknown candidates, including MEPs and national politicians.

The head of the list for the Social Democrats, Party Secretary Marita Ulvskog, was a somewhat controversial candidate representing the EU-sceptical section of the party. Her scepticism was reflected in the general Social Democratic campaign, which focussed on problems in the Swedish labour market caused by the European Court of Justice's *Laval* verdict, which allows EU companies, in this case a Latvian company, to settle and work in Sweden without offering their employees the same working conditions as those required by Swedish collective agreements.

The Feminist Initiative, founded in 2004, had unsuccessfully run for the *Riksdag* elections in 2006. In the 2009 EP election, it presented as its leading candidate the former leader of the Left Party, Gudrun Schyman, who personified the focus on promoting gender equality.

The Centre Party, the Moderates, the Greens (*Carl*) and the Left Party, all nominated as the heads of their party lists former MEPs who already had experience with the European Parliament and EU politics, although they were not necessarily familiar to the broader public.

Marit Paulsen, a Liberal MEP between 1999 and 2004, returned to politics after a back injury, and she entered the campaign as one of the strongest candidates, with animal welfare as one of her key campaign issues. Her ability to speak about the EU in a manner easily understood by the general public gave talk of a 'Marit effect' with reference to the Liberals' improvements in the polls.

After all the leading candidates from the June List had backed out, former Left Party member and academic Sören Wibe entered the campaign as the main candidate for the Eurosceptic June List.

The Christian Democrats nominated the young Ella Bohlin as their leading candidate, but she soon found herself in fierce competition with the more experienced Alf Svensson, co-founder of the party and former party leader as well as minister.

One party that only ran in the 2009 EP election is the Pirate Party (*Piratpartiet*), which tends to be somewhat critical about the EU, but its position is difficult to ascertain, since it is based on single a issue: the reform of copyright laws and internet privacy. However, the party's opposition to the Lisbon Treaty indicated a certain degree of scepticism. The head of the list of the Pirate Party, Christian Angstrom, one of the founders, probably received (somewhat surprisingly) the most media attention over the course of the campaign.

The Pirate Party was able to put forward topics such as the reform of copyright legislation and internet privacy as some of the 2009 EP election's most significant issues, which ultimately also received considerable attention in the press. The government had been struggling with these issues in 2008 when it was accused of infringing upon the right to privacy when attempting to allocate further internet surveillance rights to the National Defence Radio Establishment. Along with the conviction of the Swedish founders of Pirate Bay, an online forum for sharing digital files, these events boosted the Pirate Party's electoral platform in April 2009.

Almost every party included environmental issues in their manifestos. The Greens went the furthest by suggesting that the EU, by 2020, had reduced greenhouse gas emissions by 80 per cent (Aylott and Sundström, 2009, 7). This clearly contrasted with the current goal of 20 per cent, which many already viewed to be ambitious. All of the parties were against the EU's common agricultural policy (Aylott and Sundström, 2009).

The traditional left-parties have always given priority to issues concerning employment and the labour market, but now the 'New Moderates' emphasized how they also sought to protect the Swedish labour-market model (ibid.). The traditional left–right division between the parties was shown in their position on the issue of health care. The centre-right parties thus argued that Swedish citizens should be able to seek health treatment in other EU countries, with the Swedish government paying the medical bills. The Liberals went a step further, advocating for the right to seek medical care in the EU without consulting Swedish authorities. This was in line with the European debate on the upcoming patient directive. The left-centre faction argued that the medical system ought to remain in purely national hands (ibid., 7).

The manifestos and campaign issues reveal how, even though the picture was fragmented and national topics discussed, the campaign still had a European flavour (Aylott and Sundström, 2009).

9.2 Electoral campaign

The Swedish EP Information Office ran an institutional campaign that included television spots, radio adverts, press kits, media seminars, billboards, installations, and social media. In this pan-European campaign, Member States chose amongst a variety of messages that were nationally relevant to highlight the importance of the EP elections. For its messages, Sweden chose energy, consumer protection, and border security. The EPIO in Stockholm targeted three main groups: the media, teachers, and youth (Suni, 2010).

A 'choice box', a room equipped with computers and cameras, was placed in Stockholm to encourage citizens to express themselves and leave a message for MEPs. Television spots were distributed for free: commercial TV4 aired a spot 36 times, Canal 7 aired one 152 times, and Open Channel aired a spot twice. Additionally, the EPIO in Sweden created a celebrity event that gained a lot of media attention, where a number of Swedish celebrities – together with Commissioner Margot Wallström – voted on the first day of early voting. To target younger voters, the EPIO in Stockholm used social media, such as Facebook, Twitter, and MySpace (ibid.).

Other campaign tools were used as well: billboards were put up in Stockholm, Malmö, and Gothenburg and installations on security and energy were placed in several Swedish cities. Additionally, the EPIO organized one-day training courses for about 200 young people so that they could organize election-related activities in their respective youth organizations. Swedish MEPs Göran Färm and Christofer Fjellner participated in the last training session (European Parliament, 2009).

9.3 Electoral results

An interesting feature of the 2009 Euro-election was to see how the changes that had occurred within the national government after the 2006 *Riksdag* election were reflected at the EP level. It was also the first electoral contest since the Green Party had given up its demand for Swedish withdrawal from the EU and had adopted a more soft Eurosceptic profile.

The turnout in the 2009 EP election, at 45 per cent, was higher than ever before and placed Sweden at the top compared to countries without compulsory voting. Analyses of the election have shown that the Pirate Party's ability to mobilize young voters and potential abstainers probably contributed significantly to this result (Aylott and Sundström, 2009). However, the actual turnout represents just over half of the turnout in the latest national elections, and European politics remain unable to compete with domestic politics for voters' attention.

In the 2009 EP election three parties ran on different, very narrow political programmes: the June List, the Feminist Initiative, and the Pirate Party. The most Eurosceptic parties, the Left Party and the June List, fared very poorly. The Left Party had its share of the vote halved and lost one seat, whilst the June List lost around three-quarters of its voters, and thereby lost all three seats it had won in the previous EP election. The Feminist Initiative, which also ran on a Eurosceptic platform, and was a newcomer to the European elections, had no greater success at the polls, and it failed to garner enough votes to earn a single seat.

It is difficult to interpret the results as something other than a natural consequence of the shift in popular opinion towards a more EU-positive position. The fact that the Green Party, which abandoned its hard Eurosceptic position in 2008, was not punished by the voters, but on the contrary almost doubled its support and number of EP seats, seems to support this view. However, it must be kept in mind that the Greens still have a soft Eurosceptic profile, and in that regard it was the only Eurosceptic party that actually had a good election result. The Centre Party, which traditionally has been more hesitant towards Europe, and supported a 'No' in the Euro-referendum, did not do well compared to the last election for the *Riksdag*.

Whilst the overall shift in popular views on Europe presents a background for the lack of success of the Eurosceptic parties, it is also likely that competitive pressures from both the Social Democrats and the Moderates played a certain role. As described earlier, both parties officially advocate pro-European policies, but in 2009 presented rather sceptical views on Europe to the voters. The Social Democrats even chose their leading candidate from the party's Eurosceptical faction, but their strategy did not produce better results in 2009.

As already mentioned, the winners of the 2009 EP Election were the Greens, the Liberals and the Pirate Party. Whilst the Liberals were mildly pro-European, the Pirate Party took a soft-sceptical approach by opposing the Lisbon Treaty on the grounds of democratic concerns.

9.4 Campaign finance

Financial support to political parties is a crucial issue in Sweden. Swedish regulations are rather loose and there is no limit to the amount a party can receive from a private sponsor. However,

Table 18.5 List of Swedish MEPs: seventh legislature

Name	National party	Political group	Professional background	Date of birth	Gender	Committee/Chair
Anna Maria Corazza Bildt	M	EPP	UN officer	10/03/1963	Female	Internal Market and Consumer Protection
Lena Ek	C	ALDE	County councillor	16/01/1958	Female	Industry, Research and Energy
Christian Engström	P	Greens/EFA	Computer programmer	09/02/1960	Male	Internal Market and Consumer Protection/Legal Affairs
Göran Färm	S	S&D	Member of Norrköping, own consulting company	17/10/1949	Male	1 Budgets
Christofer Fjelnner	M	EPP	Member of Enköping Municipal Council	13/12/1976	Male	1 International Trade
Gunnar Hökmark	M	EPP	Member of Swedish Parliament	19/09/1952	Male	Economic and Monetary Affairs
Anna Ibrisagic	M	EPP	Member of the Swedish Parliament, music teacher	23/05/1967	Female	1 Committee of European Affairs
Isabella Lövén	MP	Greens/EFA	Journalist	03/02/1963	Female	Committee on Fisheries
Olle Ludvigsson	S	S&D	Mechanical engineer	28/10/1948	Male	Employment and Social Affairs
Marit Paulsen	FP	ALDE	Vice-President of the Liberal People of Sweden	24/11/1939	Female	Agriculture and Rural Development
Carl Schlyter	MP	Greens/EFA	Chemical engineer in biotechnology and environment	07/01/1968	Male	Environment, Public Health and Food Safety
Olle Schmidt	FP	ALDE	Teacher, MEP, Member of the Swedish Parliament	22/07/1949	Male	Economic and Monetary Affairs
Alf Svensson	KD	EPP	Minister for Development and Cooperation, Member of Parliament	01/10/1938	Male	Committee of Development
Eva-Britt Svensson	V	EUL/NGL	Bank employee	05/12/1946	Female	Women's Rights and Gender Equality
Marita Ulvskog	S	S&D	Member of the Swedish parliament, Minister of Civil Affairs, Minister of Culture	04/09/1951	Female	Industry, Research and Energy
Åsa Westlund	S	S&D	Policy expert, Ministry of Education; Political secretary Social Democratic Party executive	19/05/1976	Female	Environment, Public Health and Food Safety
Cecilia Wikström	FP	ALDE	Member of Swedish parliament, owner and director of Wikström Consulting LTD	17/10/1965	Female	Legal Affairs
Amelia Andersdotter	P	Greens/EFA	Student, coordinator of Young Pirate Party	30/08/1987	Female	Industry, Research and Energy
Jens Nilsson	S	S&D	Politician	25/09/1948	Male	Regional Development

Source: European parliament website, 2009, www.europarl.europa.eu/meps/en/search.html?country=SE.

public support is by far the most important source of campaign finance for Swedish parties, and election campaigns are primarily financed by the state. The amount a party receives is calculated on the basis of the number of seats they hold in the *Riksdag*.

10 Theoretical interpretation of Euro-elections

10.1 Second-Order Election theory

If voters treat the EP election as second-order contests, we would expect higher returns for the opposition rather than ruling parties. In fact, they could take the opportunity to voice their dissatisfaction against the government and to show support for smaller parties compared to national elections.

Conversely, citizens may also use the EP contest to genuinely express their sentiments on Europe. If this is the case, Hix and Marsh (2007) suggest that this will lead to higher support for parties with a strong EU profile, either negative or positive, and for green parties, given that the environment has been viewed as a European issue since the late 1980s, and greater volatility in EP elections than national elections.

Lower turnout can be taken as supporting both hypotheses or none, since a failure to vote can indicate Euroscepticism or reflect factors such as a lower level of media attention.

In the case of Sweden, the smaller parties have gained more in EP elections than large parties compared to national elections. Opposition parties have gained more than those in government, and the parties with a Eurosceptic and/or Green profile have generally appeared to have a comparative advantage in Swedish EP elections.

With respect to the volatility of electoral behaviour, Swedish voters display a lack of party loyalty in Euro-elections compared to national elections. Volatility at the EP contest in the 1999–2009 period was about twice as high as the average for national elections in the same period, though in the 2004 EP, election it was only slightly higher than the norm for national elections.

The results of Swedish EP competitions support both the Second-Order Election and the Europe Salience models concerning voting behaviour. Some of the effects are difficult to distinguish from each other at this level of aggregation because without survey data, it is difficult to determine whether small parties gain votes because of 'sincere voting', because they have more green or Eurosceptic profiles, or because they belong to the opposition. The evidence of both theories in voting behaviour is congruent with a recent analysis carried out by Hobolt *et al.* (2009).

Finally, the timing of the Swedish EP elections in relation to the national cycle may play a role. The 1995 and 1999 Euro-elections in Sweden were held no more than a year after the national elections to the *Riksdag* in 1994 and 1998, respectively. Thus, according to the SOE theory, turnout could be expected to be lower and the party or parties in government have the advantage of being the winner of the previous national election (Hix and Marsh, 2007, 496). A glance at the results of the Swedish Social Democratic Party in the two national and EP contests that shortly followed shows that support for the governing party in the 1995 Euro-election was 17.2 per cent lower than in the 1994 national election, and in 1999 it was 10.4 per cent lower than in the national election to the *Riksdag* in 1998.

The 2004 EP Election was held in mid-term, when the unpopularity of the government was supposed to be at its highest and voters could use the EP election to express their dissatisfaction (Hix and Marsh, 2007). The results of the Social Democratic government in the 2004 EP election compared to the party's outcome in the 2002 national election shows a drop of 14.7 per cent in voter support, a bigger loss than in 1999, but still not as big as in 1995.

At the 2009 EP elections, the Social Democrats were out of government and the centre-right coalition led by the Moderates had won the national election in 2006 and taken office. The EP contest was held a little more than a year before the upcoming national election and, according to the SOE model, this would be reflected in the increased time and money the parties would spend on campaigning and the people's motivation to vote (ibid.).

The turnout in the 2009 EP election was rather high compared to the previous EP elections, lending support to this theory. However, as mentioned earlier, the high turnout could also be explained by the Pirate Party's ability to attract and motivate young voters. The governing coalition, which had won the 2006 national election with 48.2 per cent of the vote, received 42.6 per cent of the preferences at the Euro-elections. Thus, as predicted, ruling parties lost consensus, albeit only by 5.6 per cent, much less than what the Social Democrats lost at the European elections compared to national ones when they were in power. Finally, the hypothesis relating the timing of the EP contests within the national election cycle fits only partly with the Swedish pattern.

10.2 Europe Salience theory

The hypothesis that a party's position on Europe matters, and the more anti-European the policy position the more the party will increase its share of the vote compared to the previous national election fits well with Swedish election results. Thus, all anti-European or Eurosceptic parties experienced an increase in their voting share between national and EP elections. This was the case for the Greens and the Left Party; however, with regards to the latter, the 2009 outcome was very close to that achieved for the *Riksdag* in 2006.

The hypothesis that the more extreme a party is in terms of its distance from the political centre the more votes it will gain between the previous national election and the subsequent EP election, can be confirmed only partially in the case of Sweden. As mentioned above, until 2009 the Left Party had gained votes between the national and EP elections. As for the Sweden Democrats, they were not represented in the *Riksdag* until 2010 and although they increased their voting share at the EP elections, they have not yet managed to reach the threshold necessary to secure a seat in Strasbourg.

Since 1994, the Green Party has obtained between 4.5 and 7.3 per cent of the vote in the national elections, whilst in the EP elections it has received between 6.0 and 17.2 per cent. Whereas support for the party in EP elections has varied, the party has always gained a larger share of vote at EP elections compared to national elections, in line with the Europe Salience model.

Finally, the hypothesis that anti-European parties, whether they run in national elections or not, receive a greater increase in their vote share in EP elections compared to other parties seems to fit with the case of Sweden. However, it is difficult to evaluate the impact of different potential causal factors due to the few European electoral contests held so far.

As discussed above, the analysis of the aggregate electoral data gives support to both Second-Order Election and Europe Salience theories. Without further research using survey data, it is difficult to know whether the public votes on European or national issues. However, as already discussed, there are several indications that 'Europe' played a large role in the 2009 election campaign. This is undoubtedly a good sign in the sense that Swedes are now actually debating the future of the European Union, not merely holding 'Yes' or 'No' positions on specific European questions or simply debating national policies in the EP campaign.

References

Primary sources

Eurobarometer Issues 1994–2009, http://ec.europa.eu/public_opinion/archives/eb_arch_en.htm (accessed on 28 January 2012).

European Parliament (2009) *European Elections 2009: Institutional Campaign State of Implementation of Outdoor Elements and Complementary Activities by Member State on 16/04/2009*, Communications Directorate Coordination of Information Offices.

European Parliament website (2010) www.europarl.europa.eu/meps/eu/search.html (accessed 10 January 2015).

European Parliament Database, www.europarl.europa.eu/parliament/archive/elections2009/en/index_en.html (accessed on 7 December 2013).

Eurostat (2013, 2014) http://epp.eurostat.ec.europa.eu/ (accessed on 5 June 2015).

Statistics Sweden, General elections in 2010. Part 1. Election to the Riksdag in 2010, Table 1. Historical statistics of elections 1910–2010, p. 39, www.scb.se/statistik/_publikationer/ME0104_2010A01p_BR_ME01BR1101.pdf (accessed in November 2012).

Statistics Sweden, Democracy Statistic Report no. 10, Swedish Elections to the European Parliament, Statistiska centralbyrån (SCB), Stockholm 2011, www.scb.se/statistik/_publikationer/ME0111_2009A01_BR_ME09BR1101.pdf (accessed in November 2012).

Swedish Opinion on the Swedish Membership in the European Union in the years 1994–2009, SOM Institute, March 2010.

Secondary sources

Aylott, N. (2008) 'Softer But Strong: Euroscepticism and Party Politics in Sweden', in Taggart, P. and Szczerbiak, A. (eds) *Opposing Europe? The Comparative Party Politics of Euroscepticism. Vol.1: Case Studies and Country Surveys*, 1, Oxford, Oxford University Press, 180–200.

Hix, S. and Marsh, M. (2007) 'Punishment or Protest? Understanding European Parliament Elections', *The Journal of Politics*, 69(2), 495–510.

Hobolt, S. B., Spoon, J.-J. and Tilley, J. (2009) 'A Vote Against Europe? Explaining Defection at the 1999 and 2004 European Parliament Elections', *British Journal of Political Science*, 39(1), 93–115.

Sitter, N. (2001). 'The Politics of Opposition and European Integration in Scandinavia: Is Euro-Scepticism a Government-Opposition Dynamic?' *West European Politics*, 24(4), 22–39.

Suni, A. (2010) 'National Campaigns for a European Choice', Örebro University Political Science, Advanced Course, Independent work, Spring. Online. Available at: www.diva-portal.org/smash/get/diva2:325807/FULLTEXT01.pdf (accessed on 15 February 2015).

Taggart, P. (1998) 'A Touchstone of Dissent: Euroscepticism in Contemporary Western European Party Systems', *European Journal of Political Research*, April, 33(3), 363–88.

Country reviews

The New Member States

The fifth enlargement countries
Southern Mediterranean countries

19	Malta	433
20	Cyprus	448

19
MALTA

Roderick Pace

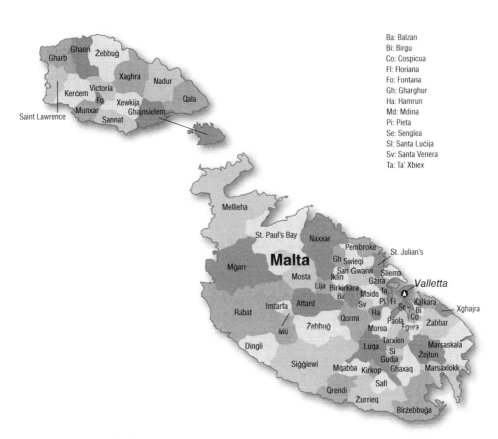

Figure 19.1 Map of Malta

Table 19.1 Malta profile

EU entry year	2004
Schengen entry year	2007
MEPs elected in 2009	5
MEPs under Lisbon Treaty	6 since 1 December 2011
	One additional seat allocated to Joseph Cuschieri (S&D)
Capital	La Valetta
Total area★	316 km²
Population	425,384
	95.3% Maltese, 1.6 % Britons
Population density ★★	1,339.8/km²
Median age of population	40.7
Political system	Parliamentary Republic
Head of state	George Abela, Labour Party (PL) (April 2009–April 2014);
	Marie Louise Coleiro Preca, Labour Party (PL) (April 2014–)
Head of government	Lawrence Gonzi, Nationalist Party (PN) (March 2008–March 2013);
	Joseph Muscat, Labour Party (PL) (March 2013–)
Political majority	Labour Party (PL) (March 2013–)
Currency	Euro (€) since 2008
Prohead GDP in PPS	18,600 €

Source: Eurostat, 2013, 2014, http://epp.eurostat.ec.europa.eu/.

Notes:
★ Total area including inland waters.
★★ Population density: the ratio of the annual average population of a region to the land area of the region.

1 Geographical position

The Maltese islands consist of three inhabited islands: Malta, where the capital Valletta is located, as well as the main airport and seaports; Gozo and Comino, and a number of smaller uninhabited islands and atolls. The total population in Malta was estimated at 425,384 as at the end of 2014, of which 5.3 per cent were foreigners (Eurostat, 2014). The population of Gozo and Comino was 31,432, with fewer than ten people actually residing in Comino. The islands' population density at 1,339.8 people per square kilometre in 2013, makes the Maltese islands one of the most densely populated countries in the world (Eurostat, 2013). There are no significant ethnic minorities in Malta.

2 Historical background

After a long period under British rule, which started in 1800, Malta became an independent country in 1964, but remained in the Commonwealth with Queen Elizabeth II as its head of state.

For most of this period, the Maltese enjoyed a limited amount of self-government in domestic affairs, a constitution, a parliamentary system, an independent judiciary and periodic free elections, whilst foreign and defence policies remained firmly in the hands of Britain. In times of political crises the constitution was usually suspended by the British authorities, only for a new one to be introduced as soon as the country returned to normality. In the nineteenth century we witness both the beginnings of a free press, the first Maltese political parties, and the initial stirrings towards self-government.

At the end of WWII, political activism intensified. In between 1955 and 1958, a government formed by the Malta Labour Party (MLP), led by Dom Mintoff, struggled to secure integration with Britain, failing which the country descended into political instability and the constitution was suspended. The restoration of a new constitutional order and the 1962 election saw the Western-oriented Nationalist Party (NP) win a wafer-thin majority in the House of Representatives and the right to form a government. One of the party's main electoral promises was to seek independence from Britain, a goal that was attained in 1964. Prior to this, the NP tried to secure Malta's membership of NATO, but its efforts were rebuffed. It also expressed a readiness to take Malta into the European Economic Community (EEC) after independence.

In 1970 a Nationalist government concluded an Association Agreement with the EEC, envisaging the eventual creation of a customs union. This agreement was expanded further between 1971 and 1987, when Malta was governed by the MLP. In March 1979, UK military bases were closed down and Malta declared itself a neutral state. In 1990, three years after the NP's return to government, Malta submitted its application to join the EU. This application was suspended in 1996, following the MLP's brief return to power, and was reactivated in 1998 by an NP government.

The MLP consistently opposed EU membership but sought the strongest relations with the EU on the basis of a free trade area agreement. The MLP described this policy as 'A Switzerland in the Mediterranean', a slogan originally coined by Dom Mintoff in 1959. After a clear majority voted for EU membership in the referendum on 8 March 2003, and subsequently returned the NP to power in the general election of 12 April of the same year, the MLP changed its policy on membership citing pragmatic reasons for doing this. In 2008, Malta joined the European Monetary Union and introduced the euro. In an election held in March of that year the NP retained a parliamentary majority of one seat and the right to form the government. That year the MLP changed its name to the Labour Party (LP) and elected Joseph Muscat as its new leader. The general election held on 9 March 2013 was won by the LP, which secured a landslide advantage of nine parliamentary seats over its rival the NP; Muscat became Prime Minister on 11 March 2013.

3 Geopolitical profile

After gaining its independence from Britain in 1964, Malta joined the United Nations (UN) and the Council of Europe in 1965. From 1973 it started participating in the Conference on Security and Cooperation in Europe (CSCE), the so-called Helsinki Process. It adopted a policy of neutrality in 1979, which was inserted into the Constitution in 1987. Malta retained neutrality when it joined the EU in 2004. Malta joined NATO's Partnership for Peace programme in 1995, left it a year later, and rejoined it in 2008. Malta is an important actor in the processes of Mediterranean cooperation such as the Euro Mediterranean Partnership and other North South Mediterranean cooperation programmes, such as the '5 + 5' in the western Mediterranean. Malta is a member of the Commonwealth.

4 Overview of the political landscape

Malta is a republic and its highest democratic institution is the unicameral Parliament, the House of Representatives, to which deputies are elected roughly every five years. Two main parties have dominated its politics for practically the whole of the post-WWII period: the Christian Democrat Nationalist Party (NP) and the left-wing Malta Labour Party (MLP), which, since 2008, has become the Labour Party (LP). The President is elected by the House of Representatives for a five-year term. His powers are formal. In contrast, the Prime Minister, moulded on the British model, is the country's executive head. From 2009, George Abela was the President of Malta, succeeded in 2014 by Marie Louise Coleiro Preca.

5 Brief account of the political parties

Since 1966, only two political parties have managed to elect deputies in the House of Representatives: the Malta Labour Party (MLP/LP since 2008), which is in government and the Nationalist Party (NP). The last time that small parties entered the House of Representatives was in 1962. All efforts since then to break the NP-LP competitive duopoly, particularly those made since 1992 by the small green party, *Alternattiva Demokratika* (AD), have been fruitless.

Ideologically, the NP is a Christian democratic party at its core but it also gathers under its wings many voters with different, non-Socialist political tendencies, such as Liberals and Conservatives, who do not have an alternative strong party to represent them. Founded in 1880, the NP initially struggled for Malta's self-government within the British Commonwealth but in the late 1950s it started demanding full independence and made this a central aim of its 1962 election manifesto. The Nationalist government elected that year secured Malta's independence from Britain in 1964.

The LP's origins go back to 1920 but it was re-founded and renamed the Malta Labour Party by Dom Mintoff after splitting in 1949. The ousted leader, Sir Paul Boffa, founded the Malta Workers Party (MWP). Between 1955 and 1958, the MLP struggled for integration with Britain. When the latter project failed, it demanded full independence and the closure of the UK and NATO military bases. In government from 1971 to 1987, it pursued non-alignment, joined the Non-Aligned Movement (NAM), developed special ties with Libya, and in 1979 declared Malta a neutral state.

5.1 Party attitudes towards the European Union

From 1993 the LP conducted a strong campaign against EU membership and in favour of a free trade area with the EU. During the membership referendum campaign, many of its supporters became active within the *Campaign for National Independence* (CNI), led by former MLP leader and Prime Minister Karmenu Mifsud Bonnici and the *Front Maltin Iqumu* (Arise Maltese Front), led by another former MLP leader and Prime Minister Dom Mintoff. The Labour Party refused to accept the result of the 8 March 2003 membership referendum and a general election was called to finally decide the issue. The LP lost the election, following which it made a pragmatic shift of policy and accepted membership.

However, members of the CNI and Eurosceptic elements continue to militate in the Party. In the 2009 European election the LP presented as one of its candidates Sharon Ellul Bonici, a prominent member of the CNI and the 'No' campaign, who had worked closely with Eurosceptic former MEP Jens-Peter Bonde and who had tried to launch a 'June Movement' in

Table 19.2 List of political parties in Malta

Original name	Abbreviation	English translation
Partit Laburista	PL	Labour Party
Partit Nazzjonalista	PN	Nationalist Party
Alternattiva Demokratika	AD	Democratic Alternative
Alleanza Liberali Demokratika	ALD	Liberal Democratic Alliance
	ALDP	Alpha Liberal Democratic Party
Azzjoni Nazzjonali	AN	National Action
Imperium Europa	IE	European Empire or better European rule or command
K.u.L. Ewropa	KULE	K.u.L. Europe
	LM	Libertas Malta
Partit tal-Ajkla	PA	Eagle's Party

Malta. Ellul Bonici was accepted as a Labour candidate only after pledging to work within the Party of European Socialists (PES) in the event of her successful election to the European Parliament. Before the 2003 membership referendum and election, Malta was the most Eurosceptic of all the candidate countries. Party Euroscepticism came to an end in 2004 (Pace, 2011).

6 Public opinion and the European Union

The success and failure of the 2009 party campaigns hung largely on the public mood and the way voters perceived the situation. Eurobarometer surveys provide a glimpse of the public mood and their findings indicate what factors are most likely to have helped shape not only voters' decisions, but also those of political campaign managers. According to the Standard Eurobarometer 70 (2008) economic optimism in Malta was ebbing. This normally hurts the governing party and helps the opposition. This survey showed that only 19 per cent of Maltese respondents stated that they expected the economic situation to improve, a decrease of 16 percentage points over the previous year; 45 per cent expected the economy to worsen, EU average 51 per cent, a substantial increase of 25 percentage points when compared to the Autumn 2007 survey. When compared to the year before, the percentage of those who said that the financial situation of their household would improve decreased by 10 points, from 23 per cent to 13 per cent, whilst respondents who stated that they were expecting it to get worse increased from 15 per cent a year earlier, to 30 per cent in autumn (Standard Eurobarometer 70, 2008).

In addition to these findings the Special Eurobarometer 303 survey on the approaching EP campaign and whose field work was carried out at the same time as the Standard Eurobarometer 70, showed how the Maltese people viewed the themes that ought to be prioritized in the European election campaign. The Maltese did not think that economic growth was to be the main theme, but 67 per cent of respondents placed immigration at the top of the list. This seems to indicate that whilst respondents had every faith in resolving their own economic problems by their own capabilities, they expected the EU to help Malta deal with illegal immigration. According to the same survey, Malta was amongst the three Member States where respondents considered themselves to be the best informed about the EP and amongst the seven countries where a majority (65 per cent) of citizens were interested in the European election and where more than six out of ten respondents (63 per cent) considered that the EP was close to their expectations.

After the European election, the spring Standard Eurobarometer 71 – field work carried out between 12 June and 6 July 2009 – reported that immigration was the main issue which 59 per cent of the Maltese wished to see emphasized by the EU, followed by energy, 39 per cent, the environment, 26 per cent, and the European education policy 23 per cent. There is no doubt that these public perceptions had been influenced by the intense election campaign, but they also indicate how the electorate viewed priorities on polling day.

7 National and EP electoral systems

The Maltese electoral system is a proportional representation one, based on the single transferable vote (STV). This system is used in the European, national, and local council elections. In national elections, the Maltese islands are divided into 13 electoral districts, with the islands of Gozo and Comino being the thirteenth and smallest one of them. Five members of Parliament are elected from each district. In the European elections the whole of the Maltese islands are merged into one district to elect five Members of the European Parliament (MEPs), six after the Lisbon Treaty provisions on the size of the European Parliament came into effect. Indeed in December 2011, Malta's sixth MEP took up his seat in Parliament.

Notwithstanding that the proportional system can lead to political fragmentation and often to government by coalition, this has not been the case in Malta.

8 A glance at the EP and national elections

Three European elections have been held in Malta since the island joined the EU on 1 May 2004. Table 19.3 summarizes the data of the first two European elections held in Malta since it joined the European Union in 2004, and those of the two national elections closest to these events, namely those of 2003 and 2008.

Table 19.4 shows that in European elections, the number of registered voters is higher than that for national elections because EU citizens residing in Malta have the right to vote and stand for election.

Table 19.3 National and EP election results in Malta: 2003–2009

Political party/electoral/list	National elections			EP elections	
	2003	2008	2013	2004	2009
NP	146,172	143,468	132,426	97,688	100,486
Percentage	51.8	49.3	43.4	39.8	40.5
LP	134,092	141,888	167,533	118,983	135,917
Percentage	47.5	48.8	54.8	48.4	54.8
AD	1,929	3,810	5,506	22,938	5,802
Percentage	0.7	1.3	1.8	9.3	2.3
AN	n/a	1,461	—	n/a	1,595
Percentage	n/a	0.5	—	n/a	0.6
IE	n/a	84	—	1,603	3,637
Percentage	n/a	0.03	—	0.65	1.5
Farrugia Carmelo (Independent)	n/a	n/a	—	3,119	n/a
Percentage	n/a	n/a	—	1.3	n/a
Others	20	88	—	1,391	732
Percentage	0	0	—	0.6	0.3
Seats won by parties					
NP	35	35	30	2	2
LP	30	34	39	3	3+1

Source: Malta Elections, University of Malta: www.um.edu.mt/projects/maltaelections.

Table 19.4 Turnout at national and EP elections in Malta: 2003–2009

	National elections			EP elections	
	2003	2008	2013	2004	2009
Registered voters*	297,9	315,3	333,1	304,3	322,4
Votes cast*	285,1	294,2	309,6	250,7	254,0
Valid votes cast	282,2	290,8	305,6	245,7	248,2
Turnout	**95.7%**	**93.3%**	**93.0%**	**82.4%**	**78.8%**

Source: Electoral Commission at: www.electoral.gov.mt.

Note:
* Votes cast/registered voters × 100.

The average turnout at EP contests was 14 per cent below the average of the last two national elections, with a fall in turnout between the first and the second one. The results show that EP elections may have become second-order ballots from their birth.

Although in raw terms more voters cast their ballots in the 2009 European election than in 2004, voter turnout in 2009 as a percentage of registered voters was 3.6 per cent below that of 2004. Notwithstanding this, in both European elections turnout in Malta was the third highest in the EU after that of Belgium and Luxembourg and well above the EU average of 45.5 per cent in 2004 and 43 per cent in 2009. However, voter participation in the Maltese European elections was markedly below that registered in national elections. Turnout in both the Maltese national and European elections shows a declining trend.

Comparative data by the International Institute for Democracy and Electoral Assistance (IDEA) shows that average turnout in Malta for all the elections between 1945 and 2001 was 88.2 per cent, placing Malta in twenty-fourth place out of the 169 countries ranked (Nohlen and Save-Soderbergh, 2002).

Several factors may account for this high voter turnout: power is overly concentrated in the government, so that the winning party wields quasi absolute domination of the decision-making process until the next election. This certainly spurs competitive behaviour between the two main parties; intense and pervasive partisanship (Baldacchino, 2002); very strong campaigning by individual candidates who compete for the parliamentary seats against other candidates of the same party as well as those from rival parties, a feature of the STV system; and strong mobilization tactics by the parties that have their own television, radio, print, and internet media (Cini, 2002; Hirczy, 2006; Pace, 2008 and 2011). The number of 'floating voters' is small, but decisive. This intense rivalry also explains the marginal difference between the winning and losing parties. The same factors with some qualifications are also at play in European elections and the fact that they do not achieve the same level of voter turnout as those of the national elections is one of the most telling signs of their second-order status.

More political parties contest the European elections than the national ones. The 2003 national election was contested by three parties, the Nationalist Party, the Labour Party, *Alternattive Demokratika*, and an independent candidate. The 2008 national election was contested by four parties that fielded candidates in all electoral districts, two parties that contested two districts, two that contested one district, and an independent candidate. The 2004 European election was contested by six parties: the NP, LP, and AD, which were joined by a number of new, much smaller parties including the Alpha Liberal Democratic Party (ALDP), the Christian Democratic Republican Party (CDRP), Imperium Europa (IE), KUL Europa, and five independents, one of whom, Carmelo Farrugia, the secretary general of the main hunting federation, polled 3,119 votes.

In the 2004 campaign, the NP capitalized on having taken Malta into the EU. At the same time it criticized the MLP for having opposed membership, only to perform a political U-turn and embrace it just a few months after the 2003 election. The NP was also struggling against the small green party AD, which enjoyed strong electoral support in view of the clear stand it had taken in favour of membership during the EU membership campaign. The NP tried to denigrate this party by claiming that it belonged to a European parliamentary group that supported abortion, but AD retorted that it informed the European Greens that it was against abortion. The MLP focussed on the domestic political issues, such as rising unemployment, which was mainly caused by the restructuring of the public sector and state-owned corporations as a result of EU membership. This diversion to national issues also suited the MLP in another way: after strongly campaigning against membership for so many years, a substantive segment of its own supporters had still not come to terms with the party's policy shift, whilst many were still opposing membership. In the election, AD's good showing, though insufficient to help it elect at least one seat, sufficiently weakened the NP's vote, which only managed to elect two of the five seats, with three going to Labour.

9 The 2009 European election

9.1 Party lists and manifestos

The 2009 European election was peculiar in a sense because it was held under pre-Lisbon rules, which meant that Malta was to elect five MEPs. However, the election was also held under the shadow of the Lisbon Treaty, since its eventual ratification would increase Malta's EP seats by one. Hence, government and opposition agreed that the runner-up in the election would eventually take up the sixth seat once this became available, as indeed happened in December 2011.

In this election, the two main parties, the NP and the LP, captured all the seats: four, including the sixth seat, went to the LP and two to the NP. The greens (AD) did not perform as well as they had done in the 2004 election, obtaining only 2.3 per cent of the valid votes cast compared to 9.3 per cent in 2004.

In all, ten parties contested the election. A handful of very small parties, fielding one or two candidates, joined the electoral fray obtaining a negligible amount of votes. Amongst these we find *Alleanza Liberali* (AL), the Alpha Liberal Democratic Party (ALDP), KUL Ewropa, Libertas Malta, and *Partit tal-Ajkla*. The right-wing *Azzjoni Nazzjonali*, which entered politics for the first time in the 2008 national election obtained 0.6 per cent of the vote, but its rival on the right, Imperium Europa, which took a markedly stronger anti-immigrant stance, outperformed it by taking 1.5 per cent of the vote. *Azzjoni Nazzjonali* tried to capitalize on hunters' disgruntlement following tighter rules on hunting introduced after membership in compliance with the EU's 'Birds' Directive'. *Alleanza Liberali* and Alpha Liberali had a single main issue, the introduction of divorce. Libertas Malta contested under Declan Ganley's 'Libertas.eu', with a single candidate who had split with *Azzjoni Nazzjonali*. The political platforms of the other small parties were obscure.

The NP's manifesto was based on four fundamental issues: employment creation, the protection of the environment, solidarity, and values. The LP capitalized on the image of its new leader Joseph Muscat, still an untried quantity in Maltese politics, and presented a manifesto with 18 main objectives: a moratorium on payments due to workers who become unemployed, more funds for retraining schemes for the unemployed, working with PES in favour of the 'Pact for Future Employment', workers retain the right to choose how much overtime they wish to work, resources for childcare centres, strengthening of consumer rights, a 20-point Action Plan to control illegal immigration, Labour MEPs to work to shorten patients' waiting time in hospital, continue legal action to return VAT overcharged on new cars to consumers, strengthen consumer rights in general, enforcement of EU regulations to compensate car owners for any damages sustained by their vehicles because of bad roads, improved opportunities for youth and students, prioritization of climate change in the European Parliament, provision of impetus to 'green economic growth', Labour MEPs to work to ensure that the EU's Climate and Energy Package benefits Malta, Labour MEPs to be bound by a code of transparency, and also to organize information sessions for the public, Labour MEPs to open a representative office in Malta and one in Gozo (Labour Party, 2009).

Both main political parties stressed the environment, which was the fulcrum of the AD's manifesto and in direct competition with it. Under the banner of a 'New Green Deal', coined by European Green Party spokesman Urlike Lunacek, AD stressed the need of a third 'voice' for Malta in the European Parliament: a European immigration policy, an ecological and social Europe, consumer rights, family values, and a stronger role for civil society.

9.2 Electoral campaign

Domestic political issues played a dominant role in both European elections. The 2009 campaign unfolded under the shadow of the international recession. Just a few months after seeing its mandate renewed as a result of the March 2008 national election, the government announced the introduction of higher utility prices, mainly water and electricity, because of the spiralling costs of petroleum in the world markets. Malta is completely dependent on petroleum as a source of energy. To compensate for these price hikes, the trade unions demanded wage increases that were fiercely resisted by the government and the main business organizations. The opposition Labour Party did not fail to capitalize on this discontent, which continued right up to and beyond the June 2009 European election. This was the most important issue, which contributed to the 'crowding out' of European issues from the campaign and which ultimately influenced voters' choice.

Indeed, as the European election campaigning started in the first quarter of 2009, Malta's economic situation was relatively uncertain both because of the global financial crisis and volatile prices in the world petroleum markets; although world oil prices declined sharply from September 2008, they resumed an upward trend in January 2009. Public finances also became a matter of concern. After reining in the public deficit within the margins of the so-called Maastricht convergence criteria, which permitted Malta to join the European Monetary Union and introduce the euro on 1 January 2008, the government seemed to lose control of spending once again, ending 2008 with a deficit of 4.7 per cent of GDP, much above the reference value of 3 per cent. The government blamed this on the international recession, but in 2008 the Maltese economy expanded by 1.6 per cent. The likelier factor contributing to the growing public deficit was an increase in government spending related to the restructuring and eventual privatization of the shipyards and unexpected delays in the payment of corporate taxes (European Commission, 2009).

Another important issue was the government's handling of illegal immigration, which was strongly criticized by the opposition. Criticism focussed on the perceived failure by the government to secure a 'burden sharing' agreement with the other Member States. This issue alone was the main factor that helped IE increase its vote tally from just 84 votes in the 2008 national election to 3,637 in the 2009 European election.

Troubled by these concerns, voters who traditionally voted for the NP grasped the opportunity presented by the 2009 European election to protest against their party either by abstaining or by switching their vote to other parties. In addition, those voters who were convinced that the result of the European election was not going to impact upon the country's governance also decided not to vote. Taken together, these factors account for the lower turnout when compared with the 2008 national election and the increased popularity of the small, single-issue parties.

In the meantime, the governing Nationalist Party unsuccessfully tried to divert the focus from domestic political issues to its record in the EU, where it could show better results. Thus, the Nationalist campaign concentrated on Malta's entry into the euro-zone and the smooth adoption of the euro on 1 January 2008, the increase in the inward flow of foreign direct investment after membership, and the fact that Malta as an 'objective one' region, had secured a substantive financial package of structural aid, €850 million at 2007 prices, for the period 2007–2013. The NP also criticized the Labour MEPs' performance in the European Parliament.

For its part, the LP responded by trying to minimize these achievements whilst strongly exploiting the domestic issues that dominated public concerns. In 2008 and in the first half of 2009, the LP carried out a campaign claiming that Malta was a net contributor and not a net beneficiary from the EU budget. This is not substantiated by facts, and the campaign may have had the aim of neutralizing any advantage that the NP could have reaped from exploiting the favourable EU structural aid package that it had negotiated.

Hence the emphasis placed by the opposition LP and other smaller parties on criticizing government on the economy and above all for mishandling illegal immigration, struck a chord with a bigger cross-section of voters than the government's campaign based on its European record.

One final issue which dogged the Nationalists both in the 2008 general election and in the 2009 European election was the ban on spring hunting. In January 2008, the European Commission took the issue of spring hunting in Malta to the European Court of Justice (ECJ). While the Maltese government rejected the Commission's position, it announced that the spring hunting season would not open (Department of Information, press release no. 0171, 31 January 2008). Hunters claimed that prior to the 2003 referendum and election they had been assured that hunting would continue to be practiced in Malta after membership in the same way as it had always been. Meanwhile, both the NP and the LP declared that they would respect the ECJ's decision. This issue also led to some vote switching from the NP to the LP, as well as some abstentions from voting.

Finally, although no Eurosceptic party contested the 2004 European election, *Azzjoni Nazzjonali* did so in 2009, obtaining 1,527 preference votes, a marginal improvement on the 1,461 preference votes it secured in the 2008 national election. This poor result also shows that amongst those who turn out to vote in the Maltese European elections, support for Euroscepticism is very low. When comparing Malta's first two European elections, it can be said that the smaller parties and independent candidates focussed on single issues, whilst the big two parties had broader agendas. AD concentrated mostly on green issues, whilst AN broached the thorny issue of identity and immigration, and tried to capitalize on the ban on spring hunting linking it to Malta's identity just as the hunters' associations do. Other small parties and independents took up other issues such as divorce and illegal immigration. In the 2004 election, Carmelo Farrugia, the Secretary General of the main hunters' federation stood as an independent representing hunters' interests and obtained 3,119 preference votes. But he did not contest the 2009 election, despite the fact that the issue was still simmering. Despite the salience of the environment, immigration, and hunting in Maltese public opinion, the smaller parties have not been able to fully capitalize on them, mostly because the two large parties have taken them over themselves.

What is also significant is that despite campaigning so strongly against EU membership and despite the fact that the NP used this to criticize it, the LP managed to do so well in both European elections. It managed to mobilize its supporters, a very difficult task in the 2004 European election, though less so in the 2009 one. The main reason behind this success is that the LP did not campaign on European issues but on the government's record in office, thus exploiting voter disgruntlement to its advantage.

9.3 Electoral results

The outcome of the 2009 EP election in Malta is summarized in Table 19.5.

This shows the number of preference votes polled by all the political parties and independents who contested the election. In Malta's STV system, parties are listed on the ballot sheet in alphabetical order and within each party section, candidates are in turn listed in alphabetical order. Voters place the numeral '1' in a box next to the name of their preferred candidate and continue

Table 19.5 EP election results in Malta: 2009

Political party	Number of candidates	First count votes	Votes (%)	EP seats
ALD	1	189	0.1	0
ALP	1	118	0.1	0
AD	2	5,802	2.3	0
AN	3	1,595	0.6	0
IE	2	3,637	1.5	0
KULE	1	47	0.0	0
Libertas	1	298	0.0	0
PA	1	80	0.0	0
PL	12	135,917	54.8	3
PN	10	100,486	40.5	2
Total	34	248,169	100.0	5 + 1 from 2011

Source: Malta's Electoral Commission: www.electoral.gov.mt.

to place their other preferences, '2', '3', next to the names of the other candidates, sometimes crossing party lines. The 'quota' or the number of votes required by a candidate to win a seat is calculated by dividing the number of valid votes by the number of seats to be filled plus one and adding one to the final answer. In the 2004 and 2009 elections, only one candidate, the Nationalist Party's Simon Busuttil, surpassed the quota and was elected on the first count. His 'extra' votes were then shared amongst other candidates according to voter preferences. In addition, with each count, half the candidates with the least number of votes are eliminated and their votes are redistributed according to voters' preferences. This process continues until all seats have been allocated. In the 2009 election all the seats were finally allocated by the twenty-ninth count:

$$\text{Quota} = \frac{\text{Valid votes cast}}{\text{Number of seats} + 1} = (n+1)$$

In the 2009 European election, the opposition Labour Party with 54.8 per cent of the vote won three seats, the remaining two seats going to the governing Nationalist Party with 40.5 per cent of the vote. In addition, as agreed by the parties before the election, the runner-up, also a Labour Party candidate, took up his seat in December 2011. In the 2009 election all of these parties except the CDRP contested, but they were also joined by some new parties, namely *Alleanza Liberali Demokratika* (ALD), *Alleanza Nazzjonali* (AN), and Libertas. In addition, two of the new parties that were launched for the 2004 European elections, namely ALDP and IE, contested the 2008 national election. It is also interesting that though none of these smaller formations managed to come within reach of electing an MEP, those that contested the national as well as European elections such as AD, IE and to a more limited extent AN, performed better in the European than in the national elections.

The main shift in voter preferences in the European elections occurred mainly from the governing NP to the smaller parties. IE, which obtained 1,603 in the 2004 European election, scraped just 84 in the 2008 national election, but then received 3,637 in the 2009 European election. AD, which fields candidates in all districts in national elections, obtained just 1,929 preference votes in the 2003 national election when the main issue was whether Malta should join the EU or not. In the European election of 2004 it secured 22,938 votes because many voters who had voted for the Nationalists the previous year to ensure EU accession switched to AD in appreciation for its support of Malta's EU membership during the membership campaign.

AD also performed better in the 2009 European election than it did in the 2008 national one. The performance of these two smaller parties is compatible with Second-Order Election theory, for it shows that in European elections there is a stronger tendency for voters to switch allegiance to the smaller parties.

Paradoxically however, whilst European issues took a back seat in both European elections, Europhile candidates managed to do better than others. NP candidate Simon Busuttil, who was the first to be elected in both European elections, surpassed the quota required to win a seat in the first count on both occasions. In 2004, he obtained 58,899 votes – the quota was 40,945 – and in the 2009 election, he improved his performance by obtaining 68,782 votes – the quota was 41,362. Busutill headed the Malta-EU Information Centre (MIC) during the membership negotiations and was the best-known public figure up to the EU referendum. The other NP MEP, David Casa, was also prominent in the 'Yes Campaign'; Casa was re-elected in 2009.

Similarly, of the three Labour MEPs elected in 2004, two were not prominent anti-EU membership campaigners; they had in fact stayed in the background whilst the LP opposed membership. The third, Joseph Muscat, who polled the highest number of preference votes amongst the Labour MPs (36,958), had taken a hard anti-membership position. His success was attributable to his popularity with the party rank-and-file, mainly due to his party loyalty, which is often richly rewarded in Maltese politics. In 2008 Muscat was also elected party leader, following which he resigned his European parliamentary seat to be co-opted into the Maltese House of Representatives. To make this possible, Joseph Cuschieri vacated his seat in the House of Representatives to clear the way for Muscat's co-option. In return Cuschieri was supported by the LP to win a seat in the EP. It is noteworthy that during the membership referendum campaign, Cuschieri took a hard Eurosceptic line.

In both European elections no woman candidate was successful, which makes Malta the only EU Member State with no woman MEP. Indeed, in the first two European elections, women fared worse than in national elections, though it must be added that female members of the House of Representatives have never surpassed the 10 per cent of parliamentary seats achieved in 1951. In both European elections, ballot positioning negatively affected the fortunes of women candidates. Since voters mark their preferences starting by giving '1' to their preferred candidate, a candidate's position on the ballot also determines his or her performance, particularly due to the widespread practice of many voters not to vote strategically, but to mark their preferences sequentially from top to bottom. This phenomenon has been studied by Carmen Ortega, who concludes that it often negatively affects women candidates.

In the 2004 election, David Casa overtook fellow NP candidate Joanna Drake largely because his name came after that of Simon Busuttil on the ballot sheet. In the 2009 election Labour candidate Marlene Mizzi was beaten by incumbent John Attard Montalto for the same reason, after the elimination of Claudette Abela Baldacchino in the twenty-sixth count.

In the EP, the NP forms part of the European People's Party (EPP), whilst the Labour Party forms part of the Group of the Progressive Alliance of Socialists and Democrats (S&D). Of the five elected MEPs, two are lawyers by profession, one is a former economics professor at the University of Malta, one is a graduate, and the fifth has no university background.

9.4 Campaign finance

There is no public financing of political parties and in February 2012 a new law aiming to regulate such financing was introduced in the House of Representatives as a private member's

Table 19.6 List of Maltese MEPs: seventh legislature

Name	National party	Political group	Profession	Date of birth	Gender	Committee Chair	Committee	Delegation	Number of mandate
Attard Montalto, John	LP	S&D	Lawyer	07/02/1953	Male		International Trade (INTA)	Vice-Chair Delegation for Relations with South Asia (DSAS)	2nd
Busuttil, Simon	NP	EPP	Lawyer	21/03/1969	Male		Civil Liberties, Justice and Home Affairs (LIBE) Petitions (PETI)	Delegation for South East Europe DSEE	2nd
Casa, David	NP	EPP	Politician	16/11/1968	Male			Delegation to the ACP-EU Joint Parliamentary Assembly DACP	2nd
Cuschieri, Joseph	LP	S&D	Politician/ journalist	20/02/1968	Male		Transport and Tourism (TRAN)	Delegation for Relations with the Arab Peninsula DARP	1st
Grech, Louis	LP	S&D	Economist	22/03/1947	Male	Vice-Chair IMCO		Delegation for Relations with Australia and New Zealand DANZ	2nd
Scicluna, Edward	LP	S&D	Economist	12/10/1946	Male	Vice-Chair ECON		Delegation to the ACP-EU Joint Parliamentary Assembly DACP	1st

Source: European Parliament website, 2010, www.europarl.europa.eu/meps/en/search.html?country=MT.

motion. The political parties raise finance from fund-raising activities, but their biggest sources are private companies, including their own, and individual wealthy donors. There is hardly any transparency on amounts spent by political parties or candidates on their political campaigns, nor is there any disclosure of where the financing comes from. There are sufficient indicators that party spending on the European election campaigns is much lower than in national ones, since the former tend to be more low-key than the latter.

10 Theoretical interpretation of Euro-elections

10.1 Second-Order Election theory

The analysis in this chapter has shown that the two European elections in Malta have so far fitted within the SOE paradigm, primarily due to lower turnout registered than in national elections, a huge loss of votes by the governing party, and small parties managing to do better than they do in national elections – though not significantly well enough to win parliamentary seats.

It must be kept in mind that the 2004 and 2009 European elections were held 14 and 15 months, respectively, from the preceding national elections of 2003 and 2008. Although this is normally considered to be the 'honeymoon' period for parties in government, historically in Malta's case this period is often the most difficult for the governing parties, for it is in this early phase of the national election cycle that they tend to implement the most unpopular reforms, with negative repercussions on their popularity. This is one of the main reasons why the NP, which led Malta into the EU, has been outperformed by the LP in the European elections. The European elections have also instigated small parties and independents who normally do not contest national elections to enter the electoral race.

10.2 Europe Salience theory

The campaigns have also focussed mainly on domestic political issues, primarily the government's record and where European issues were debated – this was usually in respect of some issue of concern to the Maltese electorate, like illegal immigration and the ban on spring hunting. Small parties and independents do not do well because of the rivalry between the two main parties and the fact that their issues are usually taken over by the former. Although the two large parties, the NP and LP, do manage to take the lion's share of the votes, the smaller parties tend to perform slightly better than in national elections. More small parties contest the European than the national elections. The smaller parties are more likely to link their campaigns to European issues than the large parties. There is also a tendency for the electorate to favour candidates who are associated with the EU. An interesting observation made in the aftermath of the 2013 national election is that the result appeared very similar to the 2009 European election. This raises a number of interesting questions related to the discussion above, which are still being assessed.

There are other signs that point to the secondary nature of the Maltese European elections. In the absence of transparency in party financing, this can be deduced from the fact that campaign advertising and mailing is appreciably lower, as is the length of the campaigns themselves. Although more work will have to be done in the future to provide more reliable data on these elections, there is little doubt that the Maltese European elections exhibit all the SOE symptoms at birth.

References

Primary sources

Alternattiva Demokratika (2009) European Election Manifesto, www.alternattiva.org/allDocs.php?catId=16 (accessed on 18 February 2012).

Demographic Review (2010) National Statistics Office, Malta, 2011.

Department of Information, Malta (2008) press release no. 0171, 31 January, www.doi-archived.gov.mt/EN/press_releases/2008/01/pr0171.asp (accessed on 28 September 2013).

Economic Survey October (2006) Economic Policy Division, Ministry of Finance, Malta, http://mfin.gov.mt/en/The-Budget/Documents/The Budget 2007/The Economic Survey 2006.pdf (accessed 28 September 2013).

Electoral Commission, www.electoral.gov.mt (accessed on 15 February 2015).

Environment Statistics (2006) Valletta, National Statistics Office, www.nso.gov.mt/statdoc/document_view.aspx?id=1649 (accessed on 28 September 2013).

European Commission Press Release (2009) IP/09/752, Brussels, 13 May, http://europa.eu/rapid/press-release_IP-09-752_en.htm (accessed on 28 September 2013).

European Parliament Database (2010) www.europarl.europa.eu/meps/eu/search.html (accessed on 10 January 2015).

Eurostat (2013, 2014) http://epp.eurostat.ec.europa.eu (accessed on 5 June 2015).

Labour Party (2009) *Success: Electoral Programme 2009 European Parliament Election*, Labour Party, 6 June, Hamrun, Malta.

Malta's Electoral Commission, www.electoral.gov.mt (accessed on 15 February 2015).

National Statistics Office, Malta (2015) *Demographic Review 2005–2012: Post-Census Review*, file:///C:/Users/user/Downloads/Demographic_Review_2005_2012.pdf

Results of the 2009 European Elections, European Parliament, www.europarl.europa.eu/parliament/archive/elections2009/en/turnout_en.html (accessed on 2 April 2010).

Standard Eurobarometer 70 and 71, and Special Eurobarometer 303, http://ec.europa.eu/public_opinion/index_en.htm;

University of Malta, Malta Elections, www.um.edu.mt/projects/maltaelections (accessed on 15 February 2015).

www.nso.gov.mt/statdoc/document_file.aspx?id=3173 (accessed on 28 September 2013).

Secondary sources

Baldacchino, G. (2002) 'A Nationless State? Malta, National Identity and the EU', *West European Politics*, 25(4), 191–206.

Cini, M. (2002) 'A Divided Nation: Polarization and the Two Party System in Malta', *South European Society and Politics*, 7(1), 6–23.

Hirczy, W. (2006) 'Explaining Near-Universal Turnout: The Case of Malta', *European Journal of Political Research*, 27(2), 255–72.

Nohlen, D. and Save Soderbergh, B. (2002) *Voting Turnout Since 1945: A Global Report*, International Institute for Democracy and Electoral Assistance (IDEA), Sweden.

Pace, R. (2008) 'Malta's 2008 Election: A Vote for Continuity and Change', *South European Society and Politics*, 13(3), 377–90.

Pace, R. (2011) 'EU-scepticism in a Polarised Polity', *South European Society and Politics*, 16(1), March, 133–58.

20
CYPRUS

Kalliope Agapiou-Josephides

Figure 20.1 Map of Cyprus

Table 20.1 Cyprus profile

EU entry year	2004
Schengen entry year	Non-member
MEPs elected in 2009	6
MEPs under Lisbon Treaty	6
Capital	Nicosia
Total area*	9,251 km²
Population	858,000
	75.9 Greek Cypriots including Armenians, Maronites and Latins; 23.4 foreigners
Population density**	93.5/km²
Median age of population	36.8
Political system	Presidential Republic
Head of state	Demetris Christophias, Progressive People's Party (AKEL) (February 2008–February 2013); Nikos Anastasiades, Democratic Rally (DISY) (February 2013–)
Head of government	Demetris Christophias, Progressive People's Party (AKEL) (February 2008–February 2013); Nikos Anastasiades, Democratic Rally (DISY) (February 2013–)
Political majority	Coalition Government: Progressive People's Party (AKEL) (February 2008–February 2013); Democratic Party (DIKO) (February 2008–August 2011); Social Democratic Movement (EDEK) (February 2008–February 2010); Coalition Government: Democratic Rally (DISY) (February 2013–); Democratic Party (DIKO) (February 2013–February 2014); European Party (EVROKO) (February 2013–)
Currency	Previously Cyprus Pound Euro (€) since 2008
Prohead GDP in PPS	20,500 €

Source: Eurostat, 2012, http://epp.eurostat.ec.europa.eu/.

Notes:
* Total area including inland waters.
** Population density: the ratio of the annual average population of a region to the land area of the region.

1 Geographical position

Located in the Eastern Mediterranean, at the crossroads of Europe, Africa, and Asia, Cyprus occupies an important geographical, geopolitical and geostrategic position. It represents the third smallest Member State of the European Union (EU), after Malta and Luxembourg and the third biggest island in the Mediterranean Sea, after Sicily and Sardinia.

2 Historical background

Cyprus gained its independence from the British Empire in 1960, in the wider context of the decolonization process, on the basis of the Zurich and London Agreements of the 11 and 19 February 1959, respectively. The country experienced a rather hazardous state-building process and remains, to this date, a divided polity and society. The conflict between its two communities in the early 1960s, the *coup d'état* by the Greek junta, and the Turkish military intervention that followed in 1974, marked the country's twisting path towards independence, peace, and security. Over the years, the centrifugal rather than centripetal dynamics of the Greek and Turkish communities led to its division and created a series of multi-fold deadlocks that have resisted time, efforts, and generations. Cyprus features among a cluster of 'intractable international conflicts' (Michael, 2007). The country is still in search of its reunification and 'une synthèse républicaine' (Agapiou-Josephides, 2010). Cyprus joined the EU in 2004, adopted the euro in 2008, and held the EU Council rotating presidency for the first time in 2012.

3 Geopolitical profile

Cyprus has a unique and strategic geopolitical location, which has greatly determined its troubled historical destiny. Based on Alain Blondy's definition, Cyprus can definitely be considered as a 'fragile historical zone' at a crossroad between East and West.

During the Cold War, it was an active member of the Non-Aligned Movement, which it left in 2004 upon joining the European Union. Cyprus participates in the multilateral political dialogues of the EU and it has been a member of the United Nations, of the Organization for Security and Cooperation in Europe (OSCE), and of the Council of Europe. It also coordinates its commercial positions with the EU within the framework of the World Trade Organization (WTO). It is an active proponent of regional cooperation in the Mediterranean basin and it strives to contribute to the regional stability in the framework of the Euro-Mediterranean Partnership. The Arab Spring of 2011 enhanced the geopolitical relevance of Cyprus, including the role of the British Sovereign Areas (SBA) in terms of the control of shipping routes for oil, and potential checkpoints. The recent discovery of hydrocarbons in the country's Exclusive Economic Zone (EEZ) has further enhanced the country's geopolitical and geostrategic position and placed Cyprus on Europe's energy map (Drevet, 2011 and 2013).

4 Overview of the political landscape

Since its foundation in the post-colonial era, the internal division of Cyprus has constantly overshadowed its political landscape (Agapiou-Josephides, 2010). The Republic of Cyprus has a presidential system. Although its constitutional and legal order is complex and difficult to describe (Rumpf, 1998), it is commonly agreed that the President stands at the apex of the executive within the political system (Ker-Lindsay, 2008; Ker-Lindsay and Faustmann, 2008).

Since 2004, popular and elite debates in Cyprus have focussed on EU membership and on the 2004 *United Nations Plan for the Settlement of the Cyprus Problem* (Palley, 2005; Hannay, 2005; Agapiou-Josephides and Rossetto, 2006). Subsequently, discourse evolved around the 2012 EU Council presidency and the discovery of hydrocarbons in the EEZ. In early 2013, the debt crisis was added to the agenda, setting the framework for a critical juncture in terms of people's attitude towards European integration. The Eurogroup's bail-in/bail-out method sparked controversies, as its flawed structure and working methods hindered national 'ownership' and compromised transparency and accountability. Nils Muižnieks, the Council of Europe's Commissioner for Human Rights, warned about the risks and threats that the debt crisis posed to human rights protection: the 'crisis affects human rights across the board, not only social and economic rights but also many civil and political rights' and that it 'affects the most vulnerable disproportionately' (*Financial Times*, 8 October 2012). Yet, forces opposing EU-imposed rigid economic policies and austerity do not necessarily oppose the EU integration process, at least to date.

5 Brief account of the political parties

Political parties play a prominent role, to the extent that the political system of Cyprus can be considered as a typical example of 'partitocracy'. Yet, in a context of general disaffection towards political institutions, political parties score extremely low on the citizens' trust scale.

Two major parties dominate the political stage in the Republic of Cyprus, while smaller parties function as coalition partners or sources of parliamentary support in order to create a working majority. Over the years, the Cypriot contemporary party system has undergone significant transformations, mainly due to internal fragmentation, strong bipolarization, and the Europeanization process (Christophorou, 2006).

Despite the fact that Cyprus enjoys a multiparty bipolar system, mainly due to its electoral system of proportional representation, over the last decades, the political stage has been dominated by three major parties: AKEL-New Powers (Progressive Party of the Working People-New Powers – Ανορθωτικό Κόμμα του Εργαζόμενου Λαού-Νέες Δυνάμεις), the Cypriot Communist party, which is the country's oldest political formation, and DISY (Democratic Rally – Δημοκρατικός Συναγερμός), the Conservative party.

Two other well-established political parties are DIKO (Democratic Party –Δημοκρατικό Κόμμα) and Movement of Social Democrats EDEK (Movement of Social Democrats EDEK Κίνημα Σοσιαλδημοκρατών ΕΔΕΚ – Ενιαία Δημοκρατική Ένωση Κέντρου). Proportional representation also allows small parties to be represented. Since the 2011 legislative election, six political parties sit in Parliament: the four parties mentioned above and two smaller ones: EVROKO (European Party – Ευρωπαϊκό Κόμμα) and the Cyprus Green Party, KOP (Movement of Ecologists and Environmentalists – Κίνημα Οικολόγων – Περιβαλλοντιστών). The Nationalist party ELAM (National Popular Front – Εθνικό Λαϊκό Μέτωπο) made its first electoral appearance in 2011, but did not win a seat, as it failed to reach the threshold of 1.8 per cent.

Table 20.2a List of Greek Cypriot political parties in Cyprus

Original name	Abbreviation	English translation
Ανορθωτικό Κόμμα Εργαζόμενου Λαού (Anorthotikó Kómma Ergazómenou Laoú)	AKEL	Progressive People's Party
Δημοκρατικό Κόμμα (Dimokratikó Kómma)	DIKO	Democratic Party
Δημοκρατικός Συναγερμός (Dimokratikós Sinayermós)	DISY	Democratic Rally
Εθνικό Λαϊκό Μέτωπο (Ethniko Laiko Metopo)	ELAM	National Popular Front
Ενωμένοι Δημοκράτες (Enomeni Dimokrate)	EDI	United Democrats
Ευρωπαϊκό Κόμμα (Evropaiko Komma)	EVROKO	European Party
Κίνημα Οικολόγων-Περιβαλλοντιστών (Oikologon Perivallontiston)	KOP	Cyprus Green Party
Κίνημα Σοσιαλδημοκρατών (Kinima Sosialdimokraton)	EDEK	Social Democratic Movement
Νέοι Ορίζοντζ (Neoi Orizontes)		New Horizons

Table 20.2b List of Turkish Cypriot political parties in Cyprus

Original name	Abbreviation	English translation
Cumhuriyetçi Türk Partisi	CTP	Republican Turkish Party
Demokrat Parti	DP	Democratic Party
Ulusal Birlik Partisi	UBP	National Unity Party
Barış ve Demokrasi Hareketi	BDH	Peace and Democracy Movement

On the Turkish Cypriot side, the main political parties, in terms of electoral strength, are the CTP (Republican Turkish Party – *Cumhuriyetçi Türk Partisi*), a left-wing party, the two Conservative parties UBP (National Unity Party – *Ulusal Birlik Partisi*) and DP (Democratic Party – *Demokrat Parti*), and BDH (Peace and Democracy Movement – *Barış ve Demokrasi Hareketi*).

The electoral system consists of a mitigated proportional representation, with an electoral barrier set at 5 per cent. As a result, many small parties emerge from time to time and then either disappear from the political landscape, or merge with other political forces.

5.1 Party attitude towards the European Union

Political parties' stance towards the European Union has evolved over time. The divided character of the country's polity and society has proved to be an idiosyncratic and decisive factor in shaping divergent Europhile and/or Eurosceptic patterns observed across political formations in each one of the island's communities. Nested opposition to the European integration of Greek Cypriot political parties is to be found on the left and that of the Turkish Cypriot on the right of the ideological spectrum. Since 2004, Euroscepticism has incrementally become more dependent on policy orientation and/or outcome, while at the same time it has operated a shift from the ideological to the strategic (Agapiou-Josephides, 2011).

At first, European integration was perceived as a positive project aimed at achieving peace and prosperity in Western Europe. As such, it has exercised a certain charm on both Greek and Turkish Cypriots, who are still in search of their own country's *unity in diversity*. After accession, a number of critical junctures are incrementally changing this perception. The EU's support to the controversial Annan Plan, for a comprehensive solution to the Cyprus problem, has contributed to the expansion of Euroscepticism/Eurocriticism, which now includes, beyond Communists, disillusioned intellectuals and active citizens among the Greek Cypriot Community. The March 2013 troika initial decision to operate a 'hair-cut' on citizens' savings, even below 100,000 euro, played an important role in enhancing Eurosceptic trends. To date, there is no call for ending EU membership, but rather a claim for a European Union that is back on track.

5.1.1 Greek Cypriot political party attitude towards the European Union

DISY (*Democratic Rally-Δημοκρατικός Συναγερμός*) is a right-wing party that, since its creation in 1976, has been strongly in favour of the EU. The party has always held a clear pro-European stance, both on ideological and strategic considerations. In 1994, DISY joined the European People's Party (EPP). Since the first European Parliament election, its MEPs have joined the EPP in the European Parliament. DISY elected two MEPs, both in 2004 and in 2009.

AKEL-New Powers (Progressive Party of the Working People-New Powers – *Ανορθωτικό Κόμμα του Εργαζόμενου Λαού-Νέες Δυνάμεις*), the Cypriot Communist party and main coalition party supporting President Vassiliou initially, displayed a somewhat hard, though rhetorical, ideological Euroscepticism. Indeed, AKEL did not prevent President Vassiliou from submitting an accession application, while keeping its Eurosceptic stance. AKEL re-evaluated its position in 1995 and accepted EU membership, on the grounds of facilitating a solution to the Cyprus problem (18th AKEL Congress, 16-19/11/1995). After the election of its Secretary General, Demetris Christofias, to the presidency of the Republic of Cyprus in 2008, the party adopted a soft or constructive Eurocriticism on ideological and strategic grounds. Its counterpart at the European Parliament is the Confederal Group of the European United Left-Nordic Green Left. AKEL managed to secure two representatives in the 2004 and 2009 EP elections.

DIKO (Democratic Party – Δημοκρατικό κόμμα) is a centre-right pro-Europe party. The party elected one MEP in 2004 and in 2009, but initially witnessed some difficulties as to which ideological family it should join within the EP. In 2004, the only DIKO MEP joined the Alliance of Liberals and Democrats for Europe Group (ALDE/ADLE) whilst in 2009 its member chose to enter the Group of the Progressive Alliance of Socialists and Democrats.

EDEK (Movement of Social Democrats EDEK – Κίνημα Σοσιαλδημοκρατών-ΕΔΕΚ) is a strong supporter of the European integration project and it has developed a close and early cooperation with the party of European Socialists. Due to its pro-European stance, it pioneered in establishing and developing close links with its counterparts in the EU well before accession. EDEK failed to elect an MEP in 2004 and succeed in electing one in 2009.

EVROKO (European Party – Ευρωπαϊκό Κόμμα) is a right-wing party with a general positive stance with regard to the European integration process, both in economic and political terms. Its counterpart at the European level is the European Democratic Party (EDP). The party has not yet managed to elect an MEP.

The Movement of Ecologists and Environmentalists, Kinima Oikologon-Perivallontiston (Κίνημα Οικολόγων-Περιβαλλοντιστών) is the Cyprus Green Party. The party has a pro-European stance and is a member of the European Greens. To this date, it has failed to obtain any representative within the EP.

ELAM (National Popular Front – Εθνικό Λαϊκό Μέτωπο) is an extreme right-wing party founded in 2008 that traditionally holds strong nationalistic positions, especially with regard to immigration issues. In the 2009 European Parliament election and in the 2011 national election it received 0.2 and 1.1 per cent of the votes respectively (Katsourides, 2013 and Ellinas, 2013).

The ratification process of EU treaties tracks political parties' attitude towards the European project. All Greek Cypriot political parties represented in the Parliament, in government or in opposition, demonstrated pro-European positions and strategies and voted in favour of the Law ratifying the Accession Treaty on the 14 July 2003 (Law N35(III)/2003). This broad political consensus was not observed in the case of subsequent EU Treaties. AKEL rejected the ratification of both the Treaty Establishing a Constitution for Europe in 2005 (Law 15(1)/2005 of 30.6.2005) and the Lisbon Treaty in 2008 (Law 17(III)/2008 of 3 July 2008). The House of Representatives ratified the Lisbon Treaty on 3 July 2008, with 31 votes in favour, 17 against and one abstention. DISY, DIKO, EDEK, and EVROKO voted in favour, while the ruling Communist party AKEL voted against and the Green Party abstained.

Empirical evidence suggests that in Cyprus the 'permissive consensus' was an operational concept until the mid-2000s. By voting against the ratification of the Treaty Establishing a Constitution for Europe in 2005 and the Lisbon Treaty in 2008, AKEL marked the end of the 'permissive consensus'. As far as the Treaty on Stability, Coordination and Governance in the Economic and Monetary Union (TSCG) is concerned, on the eve of important political events – the 2012 Cyprus EU Council presidency, the 2013 presidential election and the growing debt crisis – the ruling party AKEL avoided any parliamentary debate, leading to its depoliticization and the minimization of its scope and implications.

5.1.2 Turkish Cypriot political party attitude towards the EU

CTP (Republican Turkish Party – *Cumhuriyetçi Türk Partisi*) is a left-wing party with a clear pro-European stance.

UBP (National Unity Party – *Ulusal Birlik Partisi*) is a right-wing Conservative party that completely opposed Cyprus' entry to the EU, particularly before Turkey's accession.

DP (Democratic Party – *Demokrat Parti*) is a centre-right nationalist party with Eurosceptic positions. It also opposed EU membership and any involvement in the accession negotiations.

By contrast, BDH (Peace and Democracy Movement – *Barış ve Demokrasi Hareketi*), a coalition consisting of three parties, the Communal Liberation Party, the Cyprus Socialist Party, and the United Cyprus Party, is traditionally pro-European.

6 Public opinion and the European Union

Citizens' attitudes towards European integration, European institutions and European policies have become increasingly important. The forceful entry of public opinion into theoretical debates about the European integration project was confirmed each and every time European

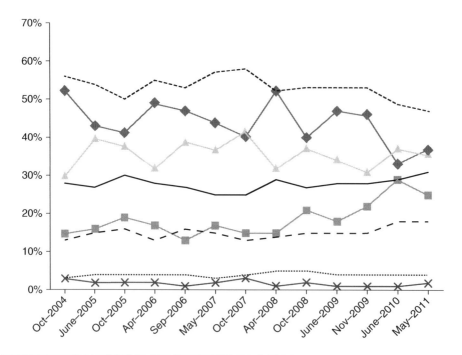

Figure 20.2 Cypriot attitude to the European Union

Source: Eurobarometer, http://ec.europa.eu/public_opinion/index_en.htm

Cyprus

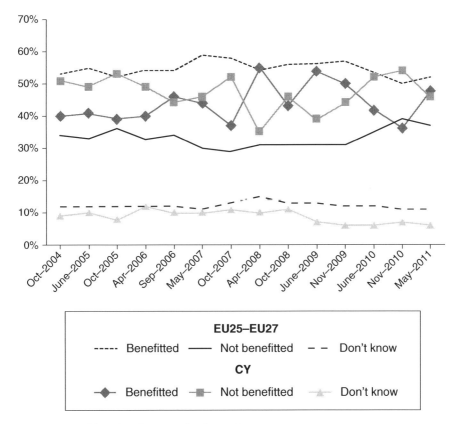

Figure 20.3 Perceived benefits of EU membership in Cyprus

Source: Eurobarometer, http://ec.europa.eu/public_opinion/index_en.htm

citizens were called upon to express their preferences. This illustrates a key and far-reaching development and highlights the incremental weakening of the implicit assumption of a 'permissive consensus' on behalf of citizens (Lindberg and Scheingold, 1970). It is clear that public opinion trends and attitudes cannot continue to be considered unimportant or be neglected without serious repercussions for the future of the European integration process itself. Needless to say, the forceful entry of public opinion is not a bad thing in itself, but it does pose a problem for a project that has been elite-driven for decades.

In October 2004, 52 per cent of Cypriot people judged the EU to be a good thing. However, this percentage fluctuated wildly over the years and fell to 37 per cent in May 2011. Over the years, the percentage of those who have expressed a negative opinion on EU membership has risen from merely 15 per cent in 2004 to 25 per cent in 2011, reaching a peak in June 2010 with 29 per cent. Respectively, the percentage of those who believe that Cyprus membership is neither good nor bad has increased by 6 per cent between 2004 and 2011.

Cypriots are divided equally between those who see Cyprus' of the EU membership as beneficial and those who reject that idea. Over the years, both the percentages fluctuated markedly, reaching approximately the same level in May 2011, 48 per cent and 49 per cent respectively.

In Cyprus, the absence of any organized opposition to the country' accession to the European Union contributed to the consolidation of a broad domestic consensus amongst all political parties, which remained unchallenged until the first couple of accession years. This led to a certain depoliticization of European issues, with some notable exceptions, as in the case of the Partnership for Peace programme.

The impact of the euro-zone crisis on Cyprus in the early 2010s seems to have laid the foundations for a turning point with regards to Cypriot public opinion dynamics towards European integration. Scholarly work tracing the patterns of Euroscepticism in Cyprus, mapping the extent and the causality of party and popular Euroscepticism in the country, has revealed a number of trends that the debt crisis has exacerbated: Cypriot Euroscepticism has undergone a shift from *ideological* to *strategic* in terms of motives and from *nested* to *mainstream* in terms of magnitude. The soft and *nested* opposition to European integration, initially confined to groups of citizens mainly on the left of the ideological spectrum for the Greek Cypriot community and on the right for the Turkish Cypriot community, acquired mainstream characteristics and can be identified across the political spectrum. Public opinion displays a decline in support and an increase in mistrust towards the EU (Agapiou-Josephides, 2011). The euro-zone crisis and the highly politicized public debates triggered by the, to this date, unprecedented combined bail-in/bail-out method applied only in the case of Cyprus, highlighted a number of issues and questions that have seriously affected public opinion.

7 National and EP electoral systems

The electoral system in the Republic of Cyprus is based on proportional representation, which favours a multiparty system. The electoral threshold is set at 1.8 per cent of valid votes cast. The country holds direct elections with open party-list proportional representation and a preferential system. Six political parties were represented in Parliament during the 2006–2011 and 2011–2016 terms.

The legal basis for the EP elections is provided by Law 10(I) of 2004, published in the *Official Journal of the Republic*, No. 3807 of 6 February 2004, which incorporates the provisions of the Council Directive 93/109/EC. The Law on the Election of the Members of the House of Representatives and the Civil Registry Law also complement the relevant legal framework.

When comparing the electoral systems for the national Parliament, *Vouli ton Antiprosopon-Βουλή των Αντιπροσώπων*, and for the European Parliament, it is possible to notice a number of similarities, but, also, and primarily, a number of meaningful and interesting differences. The key common feature is the electoral system, which is based on proportional representation. However, the interest of the comparison lies in the differences between the two sets of elections, namely the number of constituencies and the dynamics of the elections, the voter turnout and the funding of the electoral campaigns. Second-Order Election features are prominent in many respects.

For the purpose of EP elections, the whole territory of the Republic of Cyprus forms a single constituency, while it forms six for national elections. As a matter of fact, with a little bit more than half a million voters and a territory of 9,251 square kilometres, any other option can hardly be justified on objective grounds. It is worth highlighting the potential of EP elections for Cypriot citizens, as they represent the only opportunity for Greek and Turkish Cypriots to exercise their electoral rights together, even before reunification. Elected MEPs will then work together in their respective political groups in the EP on the basis of political, not national or ethnic grounds. This is indeed a new and promising political arena for the two communities.

Voting is compulsory, but without any penalties in case of abstention. This used to secure a high voter turnout. All citizens of the Republic, as well as all citizens of any EU Member State, residing in the island for a period of at least six months and aged at least 18 years, are entitled to vote in EP elections under the same conditions, but on separate electoral rolls, by virtue of a special application form. The Cypriot system does not offer alternative voting methods, such as electronic, postal, or proxy voting. Even though in 2009 the number of EU voters almost doubled following the previous

European Parliament elections in 2004, the number of those who registered to vote increased by only around 10 per cent. Cyprus was not an exception in this respect. Potential EU voters may witness best practices, such as receiving individual letters, but also face a number of obstacles in the exercise of their rights, namely concerning their registration on electoral rolls and party affiliation.

Candidates can be nominated by registered political parties, political party alliances, and constituency associations. The maximum number of candidates per political party or electoral alliance is six. Cypriot citizens and nationals of other EU Member States, who have not been deprived of their voting rights, have the right to vote from the age of 18 and to stand for election from the age of 25. Voters are entitled to choose between individual candidates from party lists presented in alphabetical order. Seat distribution is based on a combination of the Droop method and the highest remainder (Lehmann 2009, 50). Seats won by each political party or electoral alliance are allocated to the candidates that get the largest number of preferences.

As far as the funding of political campaigns is concerned, political parties receive an annual grant from the government, which is usually higher in election years. This was, though, not the case for the two sets of European Parliament elections in 2004 and 2009. Political parties received less money and, consequently, devoted less money to EP election campaigns in both the 2004 and 2009 EP elections. As a result, political campaigns received less money, less media attention, and, more importantly, less voter attention. This campaign deficit is somehow to some extent covered by the institutional campaign planned and implemented by the EP office in Cyprus.

EP elections offer *a new arena* and can make the benefits of reunification available immediately. Citizens' rights are not suspended in the areas in which the government does not exercise effective control, as is the case for the *acquis communautaire* (Act of Accession, Protocol 10, Article 1, 2003) and thus, Turkish Cypriots can indeed vote. Cypriot citizens, Greek and Turkish Cypriots alike, who reside in these areas can, therefore, exercise their electoral rights. In 2004, heavy contextual factors shadowed the opportunity offered by the EP elections. In 2009, about 1,300 Turkish Cypriots seized this opportunity.

8 A glance at the EP and national elections

A comparative look at national and EP elections enables us to detect a number of meaningful insights pertaining to key issues, such as voter participation, party competition, and political campaign funding.

In Cyprus, the substantially lower voter turnout in the 2004 and 2009 EP elections of 72.5 and 59.4 per cent respectively, as compared to 91.8 and 89 per cent reached at the 2001 and 2006 national parliamentary elections, confirms the Second-Order Election theory. Indeed, compared to the preceding parliamentary elections, the difference in terms of voter turnout was 19.3 per cent in the case of 2004 and 29.6 per cent in the case of the 2009 EP election.

Abstention in EP elections seems to have become a mainstream phenomenon. It started with a percentage of 27.5 in 2004 and grew abruptly to 40.6 in 2009. This trend increased even more dramatically to 56.03 in 2014, mainly due to the impact of the economic and financial crisis. Despite the fact that voting is compulsory in Cyprus, so far, there has been a lax approach to enforcement. Abstention in the two sets of European elections was, in both cases, significantly higher than in the previous national elections. In brief, the case of Cyprus is similar to that of most other countries, though abstention was markedly much higher in comparison with other Member States where voting is compulsory.

In terms of party competition, the case of Cyprus presents common as well as idiosyncratic features. Scholarly research has identified two dimensions that structure party competition on European integration issues: the left/right and the green/alternative/libertarian (Gal) and traditionalism/authority/nationalism (Tan) (Gal/Tan dimension) (Marks and Hooghe, 2006,

Table 20.3 National and EP election results in Cyprus: 2001–2009

Political party	National election vote % 2001	EP election vote % 2004	National election vote % 2006	EP election vote % 2009
DISY	34.0	28.2	30.3	35.6
AKEL	34.7	27.8	31.1	34.9
DIKO	14.8	17.0	17.9	12.2
For Europe		10.8		
KISOS/EDEK	6.5	10.7	8.9	9.8
EVROKO			5.7	4.1
EDI and EDI-KPE	2.6	1.9	1.5	
New Horizons	3.0	1.6		
Environmentalists	2.0	0.8	1.9	1.5
ELAM				0.2
Small Parties/Independant Candidates	2.4	1.2	2.7	1.7
Total	100.0	100.0	100.0	100.0
Turnout	**91.75**	**72.5**	**89.0**	**59.4**

Source: Cyprus' Ministry of Home Affairs, Electoral Service, http://results.elections.moi.gov.cy.

156–7). Both dimensions can be identified in the case of Cyprus, though in an uneven way, with the first one overshadowing the second one. This can be explained by the fact the left/right dimension better serves the political agenda of the two big parties at the two poles of the political spectrum, whereas, the Gal/Tan dimension serves smaller parties' political agenda.

Idiosyncratic features pertain to the country's political question. They appeared prominently among the various dimensions that structured party competition at European Parliament Election in 2004 and to a lesser extent in 2009. In the first case, they attracted almost exclusive media and citizen attention. They were by far the most prominent and discussed issues overshadowing all other 'European' subjects of the campaign, the European dimension and the real challenges and meaning of EP elections. National issues featured somehow less prominently and questions pertaining to the European political agenda started appearing timidly.

The first European Parliament elections in Cyprus were held only six weeks after its accession on 1 May 2004, and seven weeks after the crucial referendum on the Annan Plan for a comprehensive solution to the Cyprus problem held on 24 April 2004. The Annan Plan deeply divided Cypriot society, both along ethnic and political lines. It led to major divisions among political parties, both at the elite and popular level. AKEL was initially in favour and then contested it. As for DISY, whilst its leadership was quite keen on the project, not all of its members supported it. Consequently, some of them left and created a new party: For Europe, which, as a new political force, benefitted from the conducive environment favouring new parties, as well as contextual factors, and elected one MEP. The outcome of the elections revealed a decline in the voting share of both major parties in comparison to the 2001 general election, albeit less dramatically than expected. DISY won the elections, with 28.2 per cent and therefore obtained two seats in the EP, and AKEL followed closely with almost 27.9 per cent, which also secured two seats. DIKO improved its performance in relation to general elections, by rising from 14.8 per cent to almost 17.1 per cent and gained one seat. As for the Social Democrats EDEK, with a score of 10.7 per cent, they failed to secure a seat in the EP, by only 37 votes (Ker-Lindsay and Webb, 2005) to the benefit of the newcomer For Europe, the splinter party of DISY.

Table 20.4 National election results in Cyprus: 2001, 2006 and 2011

Political party	2001			2006			2011		
	Number of votes	Vote %	Number of MPs	Number of votes	Vote %	Number of MPs	Number of votes	Vote %	Number of MPs
AKEL	142,647	34.7	20	131,066	31.1	18	132,171	32.6	19
DISY	139,732	34.0	19	127,776	30.3	18	138,682	34.2	20
DIKO	60,977	14.8	9	75,458	17.9	11	63,763	15.7	8
EDEK/KISOS	26,770	6.5	4	37,533	8.9	5	36,113	8.9	5
EVROKO	—	—	—	24,196	5.8	3	15,711	3.8	2
EDI United Democrats	10,640	2.6	1	6,567	1.6	0	—	—	—
New Horizons	12,334	3.0	1	—	—	—	—	—	—
Environmentalists	8,128	2.0	1	8,193	1.9	0	8,960	2.2	1
ELAM	—	—	—	—	—	—	4,354	1.0	0
Others	9,768	2.4	0	10,310	2.5	0	4,823	1.6	—
Total	428,990	100.0	56	445,915	100.0	56	418,247	100.0	56
Turnout		**91.8**	—		**89.0**	—		**78.7**	—

Source: Cyprus' Ministry of Home Affairs, Electoral Service, http://results.elections.moi.gov.cy.

In the parliamentary election of 2006, the two biggest political parties lost in comparison to the 2001 general election, but improved slightly in relation to the 2004 EP election. AKEL received 31.1 per cent of the votes, 3.6 less than in 2001, securing 18 seats, two less compared to the previous elections. DISY obtained 30.3 per cent and 18 seats, thus 3.7 less than in 2001 and one seat less than previously. By contrast, DIKO received 17.9, thus, 3.01 more than in 2001 and gained a total of 11 seats, two more than in the previous elections. EDEK reached 8.9 per cent, increasing its voting share by 2.4 per cent compared to 2001, with five seats, one more than previously. The new political party EVROKO was also able to achieve representation by getting 5.8 per cent of the votes and three seats. The Ecologists received 1.9 per cent and one seat.

In both sets of EP elections, the voter turnout was significantly lower than in the preceding national elections. The two biggest political parties suffered losses, while smaller parties struggled to get representation, particularly in the EP, due to the low number of seats available and the high number of votes they needed to get. In terms of the government/opposition dimension, the Cypriot case offers rather mixed evidence. More empirical evidence from future sets of EP elections is needed for safe conclusions with regard to key theoretical concerns.

9 The 2009 European election

The history of the EP elections in Cyprus is definitely interwoven with the country's political destiny (Melakopides, 2005; Agapiou-Josephides, 2005). As a divided polity in a united Europe, the country presents both common and idiosyncratic features in terms of European Parliament elections. On the idiosyncratic side, one needs to bear in mind the suspension of the *acquis communautaire*, under Article 1 of Protocol 10: 'The application of the acquis shall be suspended in those areas of the Republic of Cyprus in which the Government of the Republic of Cyprus does not exercise effective control.' This is indeed a *sui generis* situation and can provide some explanation of why EP elections have never been held in these areas and why only a small number of Turkish Cypriot citizens are registered on the electoral rolls for the EP elections, despite the efforts deployed by the EP Office in Cyprus and the government of the Republic.

Although the 2009 EP election took place in a substantially different context compared to the one five years earlier, contextual factors, though not so dramatic, did play an important role once again. The timing of the contest was, indeed, not particularly helpful. But, timing on its own cannot explain the abstention rate of 40.6 per cent, the biggest ever in the country's electoral history. It was also an expression of a growing dissatisfaction with party politics and government performance.

9.1 Party lists and manifestos

Eight political formations presented 47 candidates selected amongst members of the House of Representatives, incumbent MEPs, and party officials to run for the 2009 EP election. The number of female candidates was only ten, equivalent to 21 per cent and slightly lower than the 22 per cent in 2004. The only list with more female than male candidates, four out of six, was the Ecologist-Environmentalist party that had virtually no chances of winning a single seat; AKEL and DISY nominated only one woman respectively; DIKO nominated two; and the Socialist Party and the Movement for the Reunification of Cyprus nominated one respectively.

AKEL, affiliated with the European/United Left/Nordic Green Left (EUL/NGL), as the only political party that held a Eurosceptic/Eurocritical position had major difficulties in reconciling its Eurosceptic rhetoric with its usual tactics for party mobilization in view of the 2009 EP election. The difference in the language used in the party's programme and during the actual campaign reveals this malaise. It also highlights the party's strategy to provide ordinary party members with good reasons for the need to cast their vote. Issues related to workers' rights and a differentiation between small and middle-sized enterprises dominated its agenda (Charalambous, 2009; Christophorou, 2010).

In line with the European People's Party's position, DISY was very keen to highlight the positive effects of EU membership and presented itself as the leading pro-European party, particularly against its main contender, AKEL.

DIKO also emphasized its European credentials by giving full endorsement to the economic aspects of the European integration process. The Social Democrats EDEK, who worked closely with the European Socialist Party, clearly declared their ambition to secure a seat in the EP. The right-wing European party (EVROKO), gathering former members of DISY, who did not support the Annan Plan, clearly highlighted the Cyprus question (Christophorou, 2009, 60). Finally, the Ecologists presented a programme focussed on environmental issues.

The Cyprus question was raised once again by highlighting divisions amongst political parties: AKEL and DISY were supportive of the Annan Plan, while EVROKO and DIKO opposed it. Another highly political issue that dominated the campaign was the potential membership of Cyprus to the NATO-sponsored programme Partnership for Peace. Whereas AKEL and the Ecologists rejected the text of a resolution that was debated in Parliament, DISY, EDEK, and DIKO defended it.

Concerns regarding the financial crisis emerged during the campaign and were especially highlighted by AKEL. Divisions about the merits of the liberal market economy also became associated with the 'clash of capitalisms' model in the EU. In summary, domestic as well as European issues, though seen through domestic lenses, dominated the campaign. In brief, political parties failed to attract people's interest and to mobilize citizens and party members. The 'low cost' campaign could not explain citizens' low interest, as the phenomenon was far more complex. While lip service was paid to European issues, national issues prevailed in the campaign, though in a milder way than in 2004.

9.2 Electoral campaign

Scholarly work through cross-national and longitudinal studies, as well as national case studies on political communication in EP elections consistently, suggests the 'hybrid character of these elections as both national and European' (Maier et al., 2011, 13). Empirical evidence suggests that this not only affects political parties, candidates and voters, but shapes the behaviour of all three sets of actors and their interdependent relationships.

Due to the complex matrix of political communication pertaining to EP elections, it is not possible to blame the one or the other actor without taking into account the behaviour of the other actors. The manifold deficit in political communication is nevertheless there and needs to be addressed. The EP institutional pan-European information campaign was launched during a press conference at the EU House in Nicosia on 17 March 2009, and was aimed at addressing the political communication gap by informing Cypriot citizens about EP elections. The campaign included various actions, such as talks, presentations and debates organized on different occasions. Special 3D installations were prepared and placed in Nicosia and Limassol, while the EE 2009 logo and banners were placed on the façade of the EU House, in busy locations throughout Cyprus, at trade unions' headquarters, and also on big screens at events attracting large audiences, such as football matches.

The Ministry of Interior, NGOs, mainstream media, and universities were persuaded to use the logo of the 2009 Euro-elections on their websites. Moreover, the Head and Press Attaché of the EP office visited TV and radio stations in order to persuade them to broadcast free advertising spots, to present EP websites, and to disseminate information material. In addition, a seminar was run in Brussels for the editors-in-chief of all of the major Cypriot media. In order to promote Euro-elections, interviews, statements, and articles appeared in newspapers, whilst leaflets, posters, and stickers were produced, some of which were distributed as inserts in the Sunday editions of two national newspapers. Finally, a big official reception was organized on Europe Day, also featuring the 2009 Euro-elections, which took place in Nicosia on 9 May 2009 and the beach party on EP Elections, which was held in Limassol on 31 May 2009. One of the most successful and popular initiatives was the placing of a 'choice box' in Nicosia, where citizens could address their messages to Europe.

9.3 Electoral results

In the 2009 EP election, the turnout declined to 59.4 per cent, getting closer to the EU average and equivalent to one-third less than in the 2006 national electoral contest. The big winners were actually the two main parties, which achieved a higher share of the vote than in the previous parliamentary election.

Although the opposition party DISY was the winner with 35.6 per cent of the vote and two seats, the governing AKEL was not far behind with 34.9 per cent of the share of the vote and two seats, too. AKEL even improved its performance in comparison to the 2006 elections. The other major winner was the Social Democrats (EDEK), which achieved its stated goal to get one MEP elected; EDEK received 9.8 per cent and one seat. The centrist DIKO's share declined in comparison to both the EP elections of 2004 and the general elections of 2006. It got 12.2 per cent, therefore managing to keep its only seat.

Out of the six MEPs who were elected to the EP in 2009, there were two women: Eleni Theoharous from DISY, who belongs to the EPP and Antigoni Papadopoulou from DIKO, who belongs to the S&D. This was a major breakthrough as no women MEPs were elected in 2004. Cypriot women are better represented in the European Parliament than at the national and local level. Finally, it is worth noting that four out of the six MEPs, two-thirds, were newcomers, whilst the remaining two were incumbents, notably Ioannis Kasoulides (DISY) and Kyriakos Triantaphillides (AKEL).

9.4 Campaign finance

Political parties invested limited effort and funds in a relatively short campaign in terms of intensity, scale, and resources, thus confirming the general trend at EU level, where the funds devoted to EP campaigns usually varied by 10 to 30 per cent of those spent by political parties on national elections (Gagatek, 2010, 15). The interesting revelation of the Cypriot case is not that political parties spent much less on EP elections, but rather the fact that the government itself budgeted political party grants in the relevant election years, 2004 and 2009, as if no competitions were planned.

The law sets an upper limit concerning the budget each candidate can spend on her/his campaign. A detailed report of expenses is to be submitted three weeks after the publication of the election results in the *Official Journal*. The candidates are largely responsible for funding their own campaign, except in the case of AKEL. Each party decides the budget it wishes to spend, which may vary from less than 100 to several thousands of euros.

10 Theoretical interpretation of Euro-elections

10.1 Second-Order Election theory

As a matter of fact, the two sets of EP elections in Cyprus have failed to establish what Simon Hix and Michael Marsh (2007) call 'electoral connection' between citizens and politics in the

Table 20.5 EP election results in Cyprus: 2009

National party	Number of votes	Vote %	Number of MEPs	Party family	Political group
DISY	109,209	35.6	2	Centre-right	EPP
AKEL	106,922	34.9	2	European Left	EUL/NGL
DIKO	37,625	12.2	1	European Socialists	S&D
EDEK	30,169	9.8	1	European Socialists	S&D
EVROKO	12,630	4.1	0	Centre	European Democratic Party
Environmentalists	4,602	1.5	0	Greens	European Green Party
ELAM		0.2	0	—	—
Others	5,168	1.7			
		100.0	n/a	n/a	n/a
Turnout	**312,479**	**59.4**			

Sources: Cyprus' Ministry of Home Affairs, Electoral Service, http://results.elections.moi.gov.cy; European Parliament, www.europarl.europa.eu..

Table 20.6 List of Cypriot MEPs: seventh legislature

Name	National party	Political group	Committee	Professional background	Year of birth	Gender
Takis Hadjigeorgiou	AKEL	EUL/NGL	Committee on Foreign Affairs (Member)	BA in Law	1956	Male
Ioannis Kasoulides*	DISY	EPP	Committee on Foreign Affairs (Vice-Chair)	MD in Medicine	1948	Male
Kyriakos Mavronikolas**	EDEK	S&D	Subcommittee on Security and Defence (Vice-Chair) Committee on Foreign Affairs (Member)	Medicine	1955	Male
Antigoni Papadopoulou	DIKO	S&D Member	Committee on Civil Liberties, Justice and Home Affairs (Member)	Chemistry	1954	Female
Eleni Theocharous	DISY	EPP Member of the Bureau	Committee on Foreign Affairs (Member)	Medicine	1953	Female
Kyriacos Triantafyllides	AKEL	EUL/NGL	Committee on Civil Liberties, Justice and Home Affairs (Member)	Teacher	1944	Male

Source: www.europarl.europa.eu/meps/en/search.html.?country=CY.

Notes:
* After the nomination of Ioannis Kasoulides as Minister of Foreign Affairs in 2013, Andreas Pitsillides became an MEP.
** Following the resignation of Kyriakos Mavronikolas in 2012, Sophocles Sophocleous became an MEP.

European Parliament. Cypriot voters seemed to follow the mainstream trend (Reif and Schmitt, 1980; Lodge, 2005; 2010). Briefly, they expressed national choices rather than preferences over EU-level political alternatives and voter turnout was much lower than in the previous national parliamentary elections.

After only two EP electoral contests in 2004 and 2009, it is premature to conclude safely on the robustness of the Second-Order Election (SOE) model. Having said that, we can observe that, to date, there is strong evidence on some key issues and rather mixed evidence on some others. Some of the model's key elements, such as lower voter turnout, as compared to the previous national elections, were confirmed in all sets of EP elections. However, some other elements observed in 2004, such as the big parties' performance, were not confirmed in 2009. Big parties lost votes in the 2004 EP election as compared to the 2001 parliamentary election, but they won votes in the 2009 EP election compared to the 2006 parliamentary election.

Turnout at the EP election in 2004 and especially in 2009 was lower than at national parliamentary elections. The figure recorded in 2009 was the lowest ever in the electoral history of the country and thus consistent with the SOE model. In terms of the financing of the electoral campaign, both in 2004 and 2009, it was confirmed that political parties did not invest great resources, in line with the SOE logic. The interesting revelation, in this respect, is that the government itself proceeded in a way that reflects this reality, by not granting political parties a budget for a non-electoral year.

As for the emergence of new parties, Cyprus does not provide useful evidence, bar the political party For Europe (Για την Ευρώπη) in 2004. The hypothesis regarding the punishment of governing parties by voters is validated only to some extent. Last but not least, with regard to the focus of the elections on national issues, Cyprus provides full evidence in 2004 and, to a lesser extent, in 2009.

In accordance with the SOE model, both major parties lost, whilst smaller ones did better. Nevertheless, the difference between parliamentary and European elections is negligible. The pro-European DISY did better than the Eurosceptic/Eurocritical AKEL, even though the differences between the two main parties were minimal. Indeed, to date, DISY has always been able to win and perform better than AKEL at the Euro-elections, even though only slightly.

The low number of MEPs creates problems for smaller parties, which in fact compete for two seats out of six. The emergence of the party For Europe, a splinter party of DISY over the UN Plan, in the 2004 EP election, reduced the chances for the Social Democrats, which did not gain representation by a whisker. Compared to national elections, smaller parties do better, but often not enough to achieve representation. Party size matters, as the larger political formations have more chances of gaining seats.

Timing still does not seem to be a major issue for a change of fortunes, maybe due to the fact that the presidential system in Cyprus produces a different dynamic than in the parliamentary democracies that exist in the rest of Europe. Nevertheless, they do serve as a test case for future national elections.

10.2 Europe Salience theory

In line with Europe Salience theory, political parties compete via selective issues they 'own' (Dolezal et al., 2013). However, further research is required to identify the specific conditions under which parties are more likely to adopt a strategy based on selective emphasis rather than direct confrontation. Empirical evidence from the EP elections in Cyprus suggests that political parties, by using both strategies, opted for a dual-track approach. Furthermore, the Cypriot case study highlights the interesting *rationale* behind the strategy choice. Direct confrontation seems to be clearly preferred for, nay reserved to, highly political issues that could be ideologically identified with the party and, thus, issues that could mobilize the electorate. The case of the Partnership for Peace is a prime example of confrontational approach. For other issues that do not appear so prominently on the political agenda and that are not so strong from an ideological point of view, political parties opted for the selective emphasis approach.

European issues have not dominated the campaigns and debates in the two sets of EP elections held so far in the Republic of Cyprus. Whereas they were definitely not salient in the 2004 EP elections, they started making their way in 2009.

In 2004, European issues were hardly observable on two main grounds pertaining to contextual and *new arena* factors. The United Nations Referendum on the country's reunification, held a couple of weeks before the first EP election held in 2004, overshadowed all political processes affecting each and every single item of the political agenda. It deeply divided Cypriot society across the political spectrum, as well as the Greek and Turkish Cypriot communities.

Beyond this country-specific contextual reason, the *new arena dimension* played its own role in keeping European issues off the top of the political agenda. Indeed, all key stakeholders, candidates/politicians, media, and citizens alike, tended to avoid European questions, as they were less comfortable with these than with national ones. Citizens, on their behalf, were not familiar with EU institutions, and thus could not really be interested in almost unknown institutions of a complex and atypical political system beyond the nation-state. The media took it easy and played the game as set by the key stakeholders, who are, at the same time, their recipients.

In 2009, contextual factors became less important and European issues started finding their place on the political agenda, making a shy appeal in EP election public discourse, but only through national lenses again.

Up to the 2009 election, there were no outright small Eurosceptic parties campaigning on anti-European issues. AKEL has moderated its leftist Euroscepticism towards Eurocriticism in an effort to combine both strategic and ideological considerations. Indeed, the visibility offered by EU membership to the governing party and the need to keep a high electoral score at the EP elections, especially in view of the next national elections, were better served by this newly devised smart shift. The party's announced contribution to the shaping of the European integration process towards a more social Europe as an overarching aim, illustrates the new dynamics. The European Party, EVROKO, a spin-off of DISY, has no major ideological differences with DISY, except for EVROKO's firm opposition to the 2004 UN plan.

As to the issues and topics raised in campaigns, one can identify a major gap between left and right parties. AKEL and EDEK emphasize social issues and workers' rights, while DISY, DIKO, and EVROKO focus more on economic issues. There is also a Green party, the KOP, which highlights environmental issues.

Two sets of elections can, by no means, provide sufficient evidence for cross-time analysis. More time is required and additional research is necessary in order to assess whether, in the long run, the dynamics of EP contests in Cyprus fits into main EP election theories: Second-Order Election and Europe Salience. Trends have nevertheless emerged and they seem to reveal fairly strong evidence for some key aspects of the SOE model and not for others, and rather weak evidence for the Europe Salience theory.

References

Primary sources

18th AKEL Congress, 6-19/11/1995.

Cyprus' Ministry of Home Affairs, Electoral Service, http://results.elections.moi.gov.cy (accessed on 12 July 2012).

European Commission, Report on the Election of Member of the European Parliament (1976 Act as amended by Decision 2002/772/EC, Euratom) and on the Participation of European Union Citizens

in Elections for the European Parliament in the Member State of Residence (Directive 93/109/EC), Brussels, 27 October 2010.
European Commission, Eurobarometer, http://ec.europa.eu/public_opinion/index_en.htm (accessed on 15 February 2015).
European Parliament website (2009) www.europarl.europa.eu (accessed on 12 July 2012)
Eurostat (2013, 2014) http://epp.eurostat.ec.europa.eu/ (accessed on 5 June 2015).
www.akel.org.cy/English/synedrio18politapof.html (accessed on 25 June 2012).
Law 10(I)/2004 of 6 February 2004.
Law 15(1)/2005 of 30 June 2005.
Law 17(III)/2008 of 3 July 2008.
Law N35(III)/2003 of 14 July 2003.
Protocol 10 of the 2003 Act of Accession.

Secondary sources

Agapiou-Josephides, K. (2005) 'The Challenge of European Integration in a Society Striving for Reunification: The First European Parliament Elections in Cyprus', *South European Society and Politics*, 10(1), 121–36.
Agapiou-Josephides, K. and Rossetto, J. (eds) (2006) *Chypre dans l'Union européenne*, Brussels, Bruylant.
Agapiou-Josephides, K. (2010) 'Chypre' in de Waele J.-M. and Magnette P. (eds) *Démocracies européennes*, Paris, Armand Colin, 85–100.
Agapiou-Josephides, K. (2011) 'The Changing Patterns of Euroscepticism in Cyprus: European Discourse in a Divided Polity and Society', *South European Society and Politics*, 16(1), 159–84.
Blondy, A. (1998) *Chypre*, Paris, PUF.
Charalambous, G. (2009) 'The June 2009 European Elections in the Republic of Cyprus', *European Parliament Election Briefing, no.* 34 Sussex, EPERN, 13.
Christophorou, Chr. (2006) 'Party Change and Development in Cyprus (1995–2005)', *South European Society and Politics*, 11(3–4), 513–42.
Christophorou, Chr. (2009) 'Cyprus', in Gagatek, W. (ed.) *The 2009 Elections to the European Parliament: Country Reports*, Florence, European University Institute, 59–63.
Christophorou, Chr. (2010) 'Cyprus', in Lodge, J. (ed.) *The 2009 Elections to the European Parliament*, Basingstoke, Palgrave, 68–76.
Dolezal, M., Ennser-Jedenastik, L., Müller, W. C. and Winkler, A. K. (2013) 'How parties Compete for Votes: A Test of Saliency Theory', *European Journal of Political Research*, 10.1111/1475–6765.12017, 53(1), 57–76.
Drevet, J.-F. (2011) *Chypre entre l'Europe et la Turquie*, Paris, Karthala.
Drevet, J.-F. (2013) 'Chypre et l'Union européenne (UE)', EchoGéo [En ligne], Sur le Vif, mis en ligne le 03 décembre 2013, consulté le 03 décembre 2013. Online. Available at: http://echogeo.revues.org/13658 ; DOI: 10.4000/echogeo.13658 (accessed on 10 January 2015).
Ellinas, A. (2013) 'The Rise of Golden Dawn: The New Face of the Far Right in Greece', *South European Society and Politics*, 18(4), 543–65.
Fontanella-Khan, J. (2012) 'Debt Crisis Hitting Human Rights, EU told', *The Financial Times*, 8 October.
Gagatek, W. (2010) *The 2009 Elections to the European Parliament: Country Reports*, Florence, European University Institute.
Hannay, D. (2005) *Cyprus: The Search for a Solution,* London, I.B. Tauris.
Hix, S. and Marsh, M. (2007) 'Punishment or Protest? Understanding European Parliament Elections', *The Journal of Politics*, 69(2), 495–510.
Katsourides, Y. (2013) 'Determinants of Extreme Right Reappearance in Cyprus: The National Popular Front (ELAM), Golden Dawn's Sister Party', *South European Society and Politics*, 18(4), 567–89.
Ker-Lindsay, J. (2008) 'Presidential Power and Authority', in Ker-Lindsay, J. and Faustmann, H. (eds) (2008) *The Government and Politics of Cyprus*, Vienna, Peter Lang.
Ker-Lindsay, J. and Faustmann, H. (eds) (2008) *The Government and Politics of Cyprus*, Vienna, Peter Lang.
Ker-Lindsay, J. and Webb, K. (2005) 'Cyprus', *European Journal of Political Research*, 44 (7–8), 975–98.
Lehmann, W. (2009) *The European Elections: EU Legislation, National Provisions and Civic Participation*, Brussels, European Parliament.
Lindberg, L. and Scheingold, S. (eds) (1970), *Europe's World-Be Policy: Patterns of Change in the European Community*, Englewood Cliffs, Prentice-Hall.

Lodge, J. (ed.) (2005) *The 2004 Elections to the European Parliament*, Basingstoke, Palgrave.
Lodge, J. (ed.) (2010) *The 2009 Elections to the European Parliament*, Basingstoke, Palgrave.
Maier, M. Strömbäck, J. and Kaid, L. K. (eds) (2011) *Political Communication in European Parliamentary Elections*, Aldershot, Ashgate.
Marks, G. and Hooghe, L. (2006) 'Party Competition and European Integration in the East and West: Different Structure, Same Causality', *Comparative Political Science*, 39(2), 155–75.
Melakopides, K. (2005) 'Cyprus', in Lodge, J. (ed.) *The 2004 Elections to the European Parliament*, Basingstoke, Palgrave, 73–80.
Michael, M. (2007) 'Cyprus Peace Talks: A Critical Appraisal', *Journal of Peace Research* 44(5), 585–602.
Palley, C. (2005) *An International Relations Debacle – The UN Secretary General's Mission of Good Offices in Cyprus 1999–2004*, Oxford and Portland, Oregon.
Reif, K. H. and Schmitt, H. (1980) 'Nine Second-Order National Elections: A Conceptual Framework for the Analysis of European Election Results', *European Journal of Political Research*, 8(1), 3–44.
Rumpf, Chr. (1998) 'Verfassung und Recht', in Grothusen, K.-D., Steffani, W. and Zevrakis, P., *Zypern*, Göttingen: Vandenhoeck & Ruprecht, 155–95.

Country reviews

The New Member States

The fifth enlargement countries
Central and Eastern European countries

21	Slovenia	471
22	Estonia	491
23	Latvia	507
24	Lithuania	527
25	Czech Republic	549
26	Slovakia	568
27	Hungary	589
28	Poland	608
29	Bulgaria	633
30	Romania	653

21
SLOVENIA

Danica Fink-Hafner and Tomaž Deželan

Figure 21.1   Map of Slovenia

Table 21.1 Slovenia profile

EU entry year	2004
Schengen entry year	2007
MEPs elected in 2009	7
MEPs under Lisbon Treaty	8 since 1 December 2011
	One additional seat allocated to Zofija Mazej Kukovič (EP-ED)
Capital	Ljubljana
Total area★	20,273 km²
Population	2,061,085
	79.70% Slovenes; 0.11% Italians; 0.30% Hungarians; 0.16% Roma; 1.90% Serbs; 1.74 % Croats and 1.56% Bosnian Muslims
Population density★★	102.3/km²
Median age of population	42.5
Political system	Parliamentary Republic
Head of state	Danilo Türk, Social Democrats (SD) (December 2007–December 2012); Borut Pahor, Social Democrats (SD) (December 2012–)
Head of government	Borut Pahor, Social Democrats (SD) (November 2008–February 2012); Janez Janša, Slovenian Democratic Party (SDS) (February 2012–February 2013); Alenka Bratušek, Positive Slovenia (PS) (February 2013–)
Political majority	Social Democrats (SD), Party for Real – New Politics (ZARES), Liberal Democracy of Slovenia (LDS), Democratic Party of Pensioners of Slovenia (DeSUS) (November 2008–February 2012); Slovenian Democratic Party (SDS), Gregor Virant's Civic List, Democratic Party of Slovenian Pensioners (DeSUS), Slovenian People's Party (SLS) and New Slovenia (NSi) (February 2012–March 2013); Positive Slovenia (PS), Social Democrats (SD), Civic List (DL), and Democratic Party of Pensioners of Slovenia (DeSUS) (February 2013–)
Currency	Euro (€) since 2007
Prohead GDP in PPS	18,100 €

Source: Eurostat, 2013, 2014, http://epp.eurostat.ec.europa.eu/.

Notes:
★ Total area including inland waters.
★★ Population density: the ratio of the annual average population of a region to the land area of the region.

1 Geographical position

Slovenia is situated in the heart of Europe, in the Balkan region, bordering Italy to the west, Austria to the north, Croatia to the south, and Hungary to the east. Its extremely varied territory includes large forests, mountains, fields, plains, rivers, and 46.4 kilometres of coastline along the Adriatic Sea.

2 Historical background

The first settlers settled the territory as early as 250,000 BC. The territory of current Slovenia was incorporated into the Roman Empire around 10 BC until it was invaded by the Huns and Germanic tribes in around AD 500 (Repe, 2011). The Slavic ancestors of present-day Slovenes settled in the territory at the end of the sixth century. The Duchy of Carantania flourished from about AD 600 to roughly AD 1000. Despite invasions by the Ottoman Turks from 1408 to 1415, and again from 1450 to 1550, Slovenian territory remained part of the Habsburg Empire from 1335 until 1918, with a brief interruption from 1809 to 1813, when it was incorporated into the Illyrian Provinces as one of the Napoleonic satellite states. Slovenia's national identity has gradually developed since 1550, when the Protestant priest and writer Primož Trubar penned the word 'Slovene' for the first time (ibid.). The idea of independence emerged in 1843 and the first national programme was adopted on 20 April 1848, during the revolution that swept much of Europe. In spite of political dissatisfaction, Slovenes benefitted from the broad education policies of the Habsburgs, which raised literacy rates and allowed for economic and cultural development. After the disintegration of the Habsburg Empire, Slovenia became part of the Kingdom of Serbs, Croats, and Slovenes from 1918 to 1941, renamed the Kingdom of Yugoslavia in October 1929. Although Slovenes failed to achieve political autonomy in the kingdom, they prospered economically and culturally. During WWII, Slovenian territory was occupied by German, Italian, and Hungarian forces and was finally liberated by the Yugoslav partisan movement led by the Communists.

From 1945 until 1991, Slovenia was one of the six constituent republics of the Socialist Yugoslav Federation, which were under the leadership of Marshall Josip Broz Tito until 1980. After the adoption of the 1974 Yugoslav Constitution Slovenia, enjoyed a significant degree of autonomy. By distancing itself from Moscow in 1948 as well as from the economic, military, and political organizations of the Eastern bloc, Yugoslavia contributed to the creation of the Non-Aligned Movement, forging its own Socialist self-management system open to the West.

Following Tito's death on 4 May 1980, the lack of any strong or charismatic leader, coupled with an increasing economic and political crisis, meant that discontent rose amongst the population, culminating in a series of protests, strikes and, in the Slovenian case, new social movements. Any attempts to resolve the crisis through constitutional, political, and economic reforms failed. The old political elite in Slovenia, pressured by social and political opposition, adopted several amendments to the republic's constitution in the 1988–1990 period, introducing a legal basis for a market economy, political pluralism, and legally-based secession from Socialist Yugoslavia. Amendment XCI adopted in the spring of 1990 also eliminated the word 'Socialist' from the official name of the Republic of Slovenia. On 27 September 1990, the Slovenian Parliament declared that legislation promulgated by the Yugoslav federal authorities no longer applied to the Republic. At a plebiscite held on 23 December 1990, 88.5 per cent of all registered voters in Slovenia endorsed the country's secession from the Yugoslav Federation and independence was officially proclaimed on 25 June 1991. Yet, it did not receive full recognition until mid-1992, following the so-called 'Ten-Day War' against the Yugoslav People's Army (*Jugoslovanska ljudska armada/Jugoslovenska narodna armija*) and lengthy negotiations with the international community.

3 Geopolitical profile

Slovenia, formerly Yugoslavia's border territory with rather open borders to the neighbouring Western democracies, represents an important link between Western democracies and the post-conflict Balkans. Thanks to its economic ties with Western Europe, based on a special trade agreement between the European Economic Community and the Socialist Federal Republic of Yugoslavia in 1970, Slovenia managed to survive economically after declaring its independence on 26 June 1991. The complex question of the international recognition of Slovenia as well as its foreign policy decision not to join the Visegrad group of post-Socialist countries delayed its negotiations with the EU. In June 1996, the Slovenian Republic concluded an Association Agreement with the European Union, which entered into force only on 1 February 1999; Slovenia obtained full EU membership in May 2004, and became the first new EU country from the post-Socialist world to adopt the euro on 1 January 2007 and the first to hold the EU presidency, from January to June 2008.

Due to its geographical position as well as its membership in numerous significant international organizations, such NATO, the EU, the OSCE, and the OECD, Slovenia plays an active role in the stabilization and development of the Western Balkans. This represents a policy priority for the Ljubljana government, since approximately 79 per cent of its bilateral development assistance is allocated to the region, corresponding to its second-largest market in terms of volume of trade in goods (MFA, 2011). Equipped with know-how and direct economic and security interests, Slovenia has assigned itself the role of firm supporter of the enlargement of the European Union to incorporate the countries of the Western Balkans.

4 Overview of the political landscape

In December 1991, the members of the former three-chamber Assembly of the Republic of Slovenia, democratically elected in 1990, adopted a new constitution. Having introduced a capitalist economy and a parliamentary system, and modernized its political system, Slovenia had no major problems fulfilling the EU's political criteria, with the partial exception of adapting its public administration and its temporary lagging behind in the adoption of the *acquis* due to the slowness of legislative procedures. The political elite, including all parliamentary parties except the *Slovenska nacionalna stranka*, SNS (Slovenian National Party), self-declared 'Euro-realists', and the representatives of the Hungarian and Italian minorities, supported the conclusion of an Association Agreement with the EU signed on 10 June 1996. It was only afterwards that the parliamentary parties also agreed to change the parliamentary rules in order to enable the swift adoption of the *acquis*.

The Slovenian party system has been quite fragmented since its creation, as was apparent during the first democratic elections in April 1990. Over the past 20 years, several parties have rapidly disappeared. Nevertheless, a core of political parties can be traced despite the rather dynamic changes to their organizational and ideological-political characteristics. The early elections in 2011 marked a milestone in terms of the disappearance of two parties, the *Liberalna demokracija Slovenije*, LDS (Liberal Democracy of Slovenia) and the Slovenian National Party, which had been at the parliamentary core for 20 years, whilst ushering in two completely new parliamentary parties registered just before the elections, Positive Slovenia and Gregor Virant's Civic List. These new characteristics of the Slovenian party system may affect the 2014 European elections.

A system of proportional representation was adopted in order to allow an accurate mirroring of votes to parliamentary seats. Little distortion has been evident even after the introduction of a 4 per cent threshold and the Droop formula in 2000. European elections have become opportunities for experimenting with new electoral rules. Unlike the eight constituencies for national elections, a single constituency was established for EP elections and preferential votes and gender quotas were adopted. Regardless of the type of elections and electoral system, the main axis of political competition in Slovenia has remained based on the left–right spectrum.

5 Brief account of the political parties

Since the very beginning of the new party system in 1990, there have been some parallels with the Liberal–Conservative division, which was the main division in the second half of the nineteenth century in Slovenia's political community. Today, along with classical ideological divisions, other divisions have started to emerge over the interpretation of the events that occurred during World War II: the appraisal of both the Socialist system in general and the role of the Communist Party in particular over the massacres that occurred immediately after the conflict, an evaluation of the Catholic Church's role, and, in particular, the involvement of Bishop Gregor Rožman, who was accused of collaborating with the Axis occupying forces.

The centre-left and centre-right party clusters, similar to those seen in Western Europe, express different ideological and political orientations in relation to the family, the social role of women, and the treatment of minorities. Nevertheless, empirical research reveals that it is the citizens' attitude to the former Socialist regime that primarily defines their perception of political divisions within the party system (Deželan and Sever, 2009). Whilst parties have been building their support based around this ideological division, they have also realized that most voters expect a continuation of welfare-state policies. In this sense, all political parties in Slovenia are to some extent Social Democrats. Even the more recent attempts by the 2004–2008 centre-right government led by the *Slovenska demokratska Stranka*, SDS (Slovenian Democratic Party), to introduce greater liberalization at the expense of the welfare state, was defeated before the end of the government's term by strong trade unions, backed by firm public support.

What remains quite distinct has been the various party campaigns and policy orientations relating to solutions to the social problems of social minorities, with the centre-right parties being ready not only to take a more conservative stand, but in some cases even to hold populist and extreme-right attitudes towards the Roma, and other ethnic and religious minorities, especially those with social links to the former Yugoslav republics known as the 'erased', a term used to describe the citizens of the other republics of the former Yugoslavia who lived in Slovenia at the time it became an independent state in 1991 and who did not opt for Slovenian citizenship within the time limit provided by law. They were therefore 'erased' from the electoral roll of permanent inhabitants in a controversial procedure, even though they had been living in Slovenia for a long time, leaving their status unsettled (Fink-Hafner, 2005 and 2008; Deželan, 2011). Others targeted included homosexuals or single women wishing to undertake artificial insemination.

When examining the party landscape since 1990, it can be noticed that initially the parties represented the entire European spectrum of party families, except for parties on the extreme left and extreme right, which were relatively weak. After their initial exceptional success, the Greens split. Since then, Green politics has barely survived the split between the older Green Party and the ever newly emerging small, usually mutually exclusive extra-parliamentary parties. The core parties competing in the national and European elections since 2000 have also chiefly been affiliated with their counterparts at the European level.

5.1 Party attitudes towards the European Union

Since the end of the 1980s, whilst attempting to find an acceptable model for all political actors within the former Yugoslavia, and under growing pressure from Serbian nationalism, Slovenia's newly emerging political elite – backed by public opinion – largely supported EU membership which would have brought wealth, democracy, and security. The reformed League of Communists of Slovenia even entitled its manifesto for the very first democratic elections in April 1990 'Europe now!' (*Evropa zdaj!*).

The long-term lack of politicization of EU matters in Slovenia can be explained by the consensus amongst the elite supported by a prevalent pro-European public opinion, as well as by the fact that the parties in the fragmented party system have been forced to form coalitions in order to govern. This is why they have preferred to avoid possible coalition-making barriers, whilst also pleasing their voters (Binnema, 2003).

The post-accession period has been characterized by less intense harmonization and Europeanization processes, and has seen the return of inter-party cohesion to levels seen in the mid-1990s (Deželan *et al.*, 2010). Cohesion increased dramatically during the accession period, primarily in

Table 21.2 List of Slovenian political parties

Original name	Abbreviation	English translation
Demokratična stranka upokojencev Slovenije	DeSUS	Democratic Party of Pensioners of Slovenia
Demokratska stranka	DS	Democratic Party
Državljanska lista	DL	Civic List
Liberalna demokracija Slovenije	LDS	Liberal Democracy of Slovenia (formerly Liberal Democratic Party)
Nova Slovenija – Krščansko-ljudska stranka	NSi	New Slovenia – Christian People's Party
Pozitivna Slovenija	PS	Positive Slovenia
Slovenska demokratska stranka	SDS	Slovenian Democratic Party (formerly Social Democratic Party of Slovenia)
Slovenska ljudska stranka	SLS	Slovenian People's Party
Slovenska nacionalna stranka	SNS	Slovenian National Party
Slovenska obrtniška stranka	SOS	Slovenian Craftsmen's Party
Slovenski krščanski demokrati	SKD	Slovenian Christian Democrats
Socialistična zveza delovnega ljudstva	SZDL	Socialist Alliance of the Working People
Socialni demokrati	SD	Social Democrats (formerly United List of Social Democrats)
Stranka mladih Slovenije	SMS	Party of Youth of Slovenia
Zares – nova politika	ZARES	For Real – New Politics
Zeleni Slovenije	ZS	The Greens of Slovenia GS

Source: Državna volilna komisija [State Election Commission], www.dvk-rs.si/index.php/si/arhiv-drzavni-zbor-rs.

the parliamentary term between 2000 and 2004 (ibid.). Recently, a new trend towards the selective politicization of EU issues seems to have been emerging, which has been linked to both the changing pattern of party competition, involving centre-left and centre-right party clusters, with both having a single strong leading party, and the spill-over of national to EU-related matters, as well as the links between the main Slovenian parties and their European ideological counterparts. Overall, pro-EU party unity has recently disintegrated somewhat with the emergence of more policy-specific ideological variations amongst Slovenian parties; this was already apparent in certain aspects of the 2009 European election campaign (Kustec Lipicer and Bilavčić, 2010; Krašovec, 2010).

6 Public opinion and the European Union

Overall, Slovenian politics has been characterized by a consensus amongst the economic and political elite over European integration, little Euroscepticism amongst the public, and a lack of any clearly anti-European political parties.

Slovenia's pro-European orientation was in fact both one of the triggers of its multiple economic, political, and institutional transitions as well as an important supporting factor in the country's economic and political evolution (Offe, 1991).

Over time, and due to the lengthy and slow accession process, as well as the delicate question over foreign ownership rights in Slovenia, the public's pro-European enthusiasm had started to fade. For this reason, the government decided to carry out a carefully designed campaign under the slogan, 'Slovenia at home in Europe' ('*Slovenija doma v Evropi*'). On 23 March 2003, the turnout for the referendum on Slovenia's joining the European Union was 60.4 per cent, with 89.6 per cent of the valid votes cast in favour.

Over the years, public opinion in Slovenia has remained quite pro-European by also backing the adoption of the euro, which replaced the short-lived but highly trusted national currency,

Table 21.3 List of Slovenian political parties and their European affiliations

National party	Party family	Links with European party federations	Number of MEPs (2004–2009)	Number of MEPs (2009–2014)
Socialni demokrati	Social Democratic	Party of European Socialists (PES) since 1996	1 (PES)	2 (S&D)
Demokratična stranka upokojencev Slovenije	No clear party family affiliation – party of pensioners' interest group with a social democratic orientation	—	2 common MEPs with the Liberal Democracy (ALDE)	—
Stranka mladih Slovenije	No clear family affiliation until 2003; youth and liberal issues; shift towards green issues in the 2004 campaign	European Federation of Green Parties/European Greens (EFGP/EG) since 2003	—	—
Liberalna demokracija Slovenije	Liberal	European Liberal, Democrat and Reform Party (ELDR – ALDE) since 1994	2 common MEPs with the Democratic Party of Pensioners (ALDE)	1 (ALDE)
Slovenska demokratska stranka	Conservative (previously anti-Communist Social Democratic)	European People's Party (EPP) since 2001	2 (EPP-ED)	2 (EPP)
Slovenska ljudska stranka	Conservative/Agrarian	European People's Party (EPP) since 2001	—	—
Nova Slovenija – Krščansko-ljudska stranka	Conservative/Christian democrat	European People's Party (EPP) since 2001	2 (EPP-ED)	1 (EPP)
Slovenska nacionalna stranka	Elements of Extreme Right and Left	—	—	—
Zares – nova politika	Liberal	ELDR	Party did not exist	1 (ALDE)

Sources: Državna volilna komisija [State Election Commission], www.dvk-rs.si/index.php/si/arhiv-drzavni-zbor-rs; www.dvk-rs.si/index.php/si/volitve/evropski-parlament; Socialni demokrati, www.socialnidemokrati.si/predstavitev/volilni-rezultati/; Demokratična stranka upokojencev Slovenije, http://desus.si/?cat=5; Stranka mladih Slovenije, www.sms.si/o-stranki; Liberalna demokracija Slovenije, www.lds.si/si/arhiv/zapisi/default.html; Slovenska demokratska stranka, www.sds.si/menu/42; Slovenska ljudska stranka, www.sls.si/o-stranki/zgodovina/; Nova Slovenija, www.nsi.si/zgodovina.html; Slovenska nacionalna stranka, www.sns.si/media/; Zares – Nova politika, www.zares.si/o-stranki/.

the Slovenian tolar, without any major technical problems on 1 January 2007. In a 2007 Eurobarometer survey, 65 per cent of Slovenian citizens polled trusted EU institutions and 71 per cent of them felt that their country had benefitted from EU membership, which had had a positive effect on the country's economy and security. In June 2009, when voters became aware of global economic and financial impacts on Slovenia, these figures fell to 50 per cent of Slovenian citizens trusting EU institutions and only 67 per cent trusting the euro.

7 National and EP electoral systems

The election of representatives to the European Parliament is based on a system of proportional representation. Slovenian and EU citizens vote for national party lists of candidates, since Slovenia has only one electoral constituency. MEP seats are distributed according to the d'Hondt method. There is no formal electoral threshold; however, the low number of MEP seats induces a relatively high *de facto* threshold of approximately 8 per cent to enter the chamber. Despite the district magnitude being comparatively low, the size of the unit has proved to play an important role, especially in terms of gender-balanced representation (Fink-Hafner, 2005). The latter is complemented by the gender quota system for the EP election, which has proved to be fairly effective, with three women MEPs being elected in 2004 and two in 2009. Nevertheless, a further feature of the EP electoral legislation, the institution of preferential votes, has so far prevented a more gender-balanced Slovenian contingent in the EP, since all male MEPs and only one female MEP have so far been elected by preferential votes.

The election of deputies to the Slovenian National Assembly is also based on proportional representation, although it deviates from pure proportional representation (Krašovec and Štremfel, 2007). It differs from the EP's electoral system on numerous accounts. First, there are eight electoral constituencies divided into 11 electoral districts. Therefore, the structure of voting in national elections, contrary to European elections, facilitates party lists rather than individual candidates. The seats are distributed according to the Droop formula in combination with the d'Hondt method. The threshold is defined at the national level and is set at 4 per cent. Gender quotas are applied to the national elections as well, however, with much less effect.

8 A glance at the EP and general elections

The prevalent pattern of party competition, according to Giovanni Sartori's (1976) typology, moved from an extreme pluralism towards a more moderate pluralism during the 1990s and towards a single predominant party system in 2000.

However, instead of just one dominant party, a bipolar competition between centre-left and centre-right party clusters began to emerge from 2004, moving the mechanics of the party system towards moderate pluralism, where even small parties, for example the *Demokratična stranka upokojencev Slovenije*, DeSUS (Democratic Party of Pensioners of Slovenia), and completely new parliamentary parties could enter governing coalitions.

In 2004, Slovenia was approaching the end of a period of EU euphoria associated with its accession to the EU on 1 May 2004. Political contestants paraded their European connections and their membership in European parties or party federations. The political campaign was dominated by domestic issues, whilst the EU-related debate remained marginal and narrow in scope (Krašovec *et al.*, 2004; and Krašovec and Kustec Lipicer, 2004). Several parties replaced the national practice of holding capital-intensive campaigns with television commercials, advertisements, and banners, with labour-intensive campaigning. This was due to both the lack of resources and to the approaching national elections held in October 2004 (Krašovec, 2005). Nevertheless, turnout was rather low, reaching only 28.3 per cent.

Table 21.4 EP election results in Slovenia: 2004

National party	Vote number	Vote share %
NSi	102,753	23.6
LDS–DeSUS	95,489	21.9
SDS	76,945	17.6
ZLSD	61,672	14.1
SLS	36,662	8.4
SNS	21,883	5.0
SJN	17,930	4.1
SMS–Z	10,027	2.3
GS	5,249	1.2
Turnout		28.3%

Source: Državna volilna komisija, 2004.

Table 21.5 National election results in Slovenia: 2000–2011

Party		2000[a]	2004	2008	2011
LDS	no. of votes	390,797	220,848	54,771	16,268
	% of votes	36.2	22.8	5.2	1.5
	no. of seats	34	23	5	—
	% of seats	37.8	25.6	5.6	—
SDS	no. of votes	170,541	281,710	307,735	288,719
	% of votes	15.8	29.1	29.3	26.2
	no. of seats	14	29	28	26
	% of seats	15.6	32.2	31.1	28.9
SD	no. of votes	130,268	98,527	320,248	115,952
	% of votes	12.1	10.2	30.5	10.5
	no. of seats	11	10	29	10
	% of seats	12.2	11.1	32.2	11.1
SLS★	no. of votes	102,817	66,032	54,809	75,311
	% of votes	9.5	6.8	5.2	6.8
	no. of seats	9	7	5	6
	% of seats	10.0	7.8	5.6	6.7
NSi	no. of votes	94,661	88,073	35,774	53,758
	% of votes	8.8	9.1	3.4	4.9
	no. of seats	8	9	—	4
	% of seats	8.9	10.0	—	4.4
SNS	no. of votes	47,251	60,750	56,832	19,786
	% of votes	4.4	6.3	5.4	1.8
	no. of seats	4	6	5	—
	% of seats	4.4	6.7	5.6	—
ZS	no. of votes	9,712	6,703	5,367	4,000
	% of votes	0.9	0.7	0.5	0.4
	no. of seats	—	—	—	—
	% of seats	—	—	—	—
DeSUS	no. of votes	55,696	39,150	78,353	76,853
	% of votes	5.2	4.0	7.5	7.0
	no. of seats	4	4	7	6
	% of seats	4.4	4.4	7.8	6.7

(continued)

Table 21.5 (continued)

		2000[a]	2004	2008	2011
ZARES	no. of votes	—	—	98,526	7,218
	% of votes	—	—	9.4	0.6
	no. of seats	—	—	9	—
	% of seats	—	—	10.0	—
DS	no. of votes	8,102	2,670	—	—
	% of votes	0.8	0.3	—	—
	no. of seats	—	—	—	—
	% of seats	—	—	—	—
SMS**	no. of votes	46.8	20,174	54,809	9,532
	% of votes	4.3	2.1	5.2	0.9
	no. of seats	4	—	0	—
	% of seats	4.4	—	—	—
PS	no. of votes	—	—	—	314,273
	% of votes	—	—	—	28.5
	no. of seats	—	—	—	28
	% of seats	—	—	—	31.1
DL	no. of votes	—	—	—	92,282
	% of votes	—	—	—	8.4
	no. of seats	—	—	—	8
	% of seats	—	—	—	8.9
Total	no. of valid votes	1,076,520	968,772	1,051,827	1,102,256
	% of all votes for parties passing the threshold	96.5	62.1	92.3	92.3
	no. of seats	90	90	90	90
	% of seats	100.0	100.0	100.0	100.0
Turnout%		**70.3**	**60.6**	**63.1**	**65.6**

Sources: Uradni list Republike Slovenije (The Official Gazette of the Republic of Slovenia), 98/2000; Krašovec and Boh, 2002; Državna volilna komisija, 2004; 2004a; 2008; 2009; 2011.

Notes:
* On 15 April 2000, the Slovenian People's Party and the Slovenian Christian Democrats united to form a new party, the SLS+SKD – Slovenian People's Party. Just before the 2000 parliamentary elections, a group, mostly from the former SCD, left the new party and competed in the elections as a new party: New Slovenia.
** At the 2008 National Elections, the Slovenian People's Party and the Party of Youth competed together, but no Party of Youth candidate actually gained any parliamentary seat after the joint list successfully entered parliament.
[a] At the National Elections in October 2000, a 4% threshold and the Droop formula were introduced.

The 2004 environment favoured the smaller opposition parties with more stable and mobilized support. As a result, centre-right parties ended up winning the European elections. New Slovenia and the Slovenian Democratic Party each claimed two MEP seats. The remaining three seats went to the centre-left parties: two to the Liberal Democracy of Slovenia, the main governing party at the time, and one to the Social Democrats. Four out of seven elected MEPs were elite male politicians, all elected on the basis of preferential votes. Due to special institutional innovations to raise the number of female candidates and to improve their chances of being elected, the remaining three posts had been occupied by lesser-known female candidates elected on the basis of their position on the party list. These MEPs were selected either from the lower levels of the party hierarchy or had been placed on the list due to their prior positions in fields close to politics, for example, journalism (Fink-Hafner *et al.*, 2005). The age of the seven MEPs varied considerably, but all were highly educated; the entire Slovenian delegation had obtained at least a bachelor's degree. The EP election resulted in Slovenian MEPs, all of whom were candidates representing Slovenian parliamentary parties, joining the three main EP political groups.

The results of the EP contest heralded a major change in the composition of both the national Parliament and government, as the October 2004 national elections demonstrated, for the first time since 1990. Since this time, the division between the centre-left and centre-right national clusters of parties has become more clear-cut in both national and EP elections.

9 The 2009 European election

9.1 Party lists and manifestos

Despite frequent statements about the virtually identical and superficial positions of the various political parties in the EU, there are in fact some noticeable differences. Due to the nature of the campaign and the ability of the mass media to determine the main campaign themes, the discrepancies between the parties merely remained unexposed. If we examine their election manifestos and other pre-election documents (Deželan, 2009) we can make some observations. First of all, left parties were much keener to draw on the manifestos of their corresponding European party affiliations. Compared to the other Member States, Slovenian manifestos appeared rather average, without any outstanding characteristics (Kustec Lipicer and Bilavčić, 2011). Some parties, such as the opposition *Slovenska ljudska stranka*, SLS (People's Party) and the government Democratic Party of Pensioners of Slovenia did reveal critical, but at the same time positive, stances towards the EU. The self-declared 'Euro-realism' of the Slovenian National Party was actually far from being Eurosceptic.

All political parties, barring the Slovenian National Party and the United Greens, voiced their concerns about the global economic crisis and proposed steps to ensure a more responsible and socially-oriented market economy. Parties had in more or less equal measure expressed an awareness of the importance of a clean and sustainable environment. However, foreign affairs and security issues divided the party political spectrum. The centre-left party cluster was more inclined to pursue a supranational agenda, including an enhanced European common foreign and security policy (CFSP), whilst the centre-right cluster supported an intergovernmental agenda as well as the creation of a CFSP with closer ties to NATO. As regards immigration, the parties of the left promoted greater economic mobility in line with the freedoms of the internal market, whilst the extreme right wing Slovenian National Party and the populist conservative Slovenian People's Party tended to introduce 'homeland' rhetoric.

In the field of international issues, the leftist 'environmental and progressive' agenda differed from the rightist 'peace, security, and economy' agenda (ibid.). Parties of the left also highlighted social Europe, equal opportunities, and solidarity, whilst parties of the right advocated a more socially-oriented market economy and cooperation with NATO and other relevant actors in the international community. A similar pattern is apparent in domestic issues: on the one hand, the left stressed social fairness, solidarity, and European values, on the other, the parties of the right prioritized relations with Croatia, domestic political consensus, and the market economy.

9.2 Electoral campaign

In 2009 the European Parliament faced the challenge of creating a uniform information campaign that targeted a non-existing European *demos*. However, in Slovenia it had to contend with the particularities of the national mass media, political and other elites, and the public. There were some attempts in the Slovenian mass media to emphasize a few European topics, such as an evaluation of the work of Slovenian MEPs, the institutional importance of the European parliamentary arena, the defence of Slovenian national interests through the EP, and the EU's democratic deficit. However, according to an analysis presented by the Information Bureau of the European Parliament in Slovenia, 80 per cent of the questions which Slovenian journalists posed in the campaign focussed on only one theme: MEPs' salaries and other income (Bašić Hrvatin, 2010). The EU information campaign, which was supposed to have been awarded free media space, in fact gained little visibility; very often a 'European advertisement' filled in some gaps in the usual programme.

Bašić Hrvatin argues that a double or perhaps even parallel 'cascade' activation, including the sequence of political elite-other, elites-mass, media-opinion, shapers and public, occurred during the 2009 European elections (ibid., 115). The European and national elections did not have much in common, neither in the selection of issues nor in their framing. The issues favoured by Slovenian citizens in a survey conducted in preparation for the EP campaign, inflation, decreasing purchasing power, economic growth, and growing unemployment, were ignored by the mass media. In fact, they more or less followed agendas proposed by the national political elites. In these circumstances the key issue was the test of the electoral support for the government and the opposition. Some attention was also paid to the equal opportunities agenda, along with the position of women in politics and society; however, the parties did not take up these subjects.

Viewed from the EU perspective, the EP information campaign started too late and ignored the country-specific character of the public sphere in the EU. From the Slovenian point of view, the 2009 election campaign re-affirmed the mass media's link to national political power and the rather weak role the latter played in both linking citizens and politicians as well as acting as a critical counter-power (Bašić Hrvartin, 2010).

With regard to the Slovenian political party campaigning, it mainly focussed on domestic circumstances. On the whole, the European Constitution/Lisbon Treaty, attitudes towards further EU enlargement, immigration, and related racist and xenophobic feelings were not debated. Instead, the election campaign focussed on the domestic impact of the global financial and economic crisis that had struck Slovenia with a delay, and bilateral relations with Croatia, which were marked by a border dispute and its unsuccessful EU mediation.

The campaign concluded with a major domestic political scandal similar to the 'Patria Affair' that peaked at the end of the 2008 national election campaign triggered by public revelations of dishonesty on the part of Gregor Golobič, a minister and party leader in the governing coalition. Whilst the scandal in fact mobilized both politicians and voters, who were polarized on the centre-left versus the centre-right ideological divide, it did not bring a significant increase in electoral support for the Slovenian National Party, in spite of their attempts to capitalize on it.

9.3 Electoral results

The 2009 EP election results are interesting for several reasons. Although the *Socialni demokrati*, SD (Social Democrats) as the main governing party lost a 12.1 per cent share of the vote in the previous national elections, it gained one more seat due to the effects of the electoral system. The main opposition party, the *Slovenska demokratska stranka*, SDS (Slovenian Democratic Party), acquired an equal number of seats and also a similar share of the vote compared to the national elections, with only a 2.6 per cent decrease in their share of the vote. The coalition parties overall lost a 5.7 per cent share of the vote compared to their election support in the 2008 national elections, with the prime loser being the main governing party. By contrast, *Nova*

Slovenija, NSi (New Slovenia) was particularly successful due to its front-runner, Lojze Peterle, the first Slovenian Prime Minister, who was a clear winner by preferential votes. Other extra-parliamentary parties did not play any visible role and as such did not significantly benefit from the European elections in comparison to the national elections.

The process of selecting Slovenia's MEPs is largely determined by the electoral system, the small size of Slovenia's parliamentary delegation, and party politics. In the 2009 EP elections, Slovenia's EPP-ED delegation remained the most numerous, with three MEPs, down one seat compared to the previous term. Two of these MEPs were elected from the Slovenian Democratic Party list and one from the list of New Slovenia. The two other political groups in the EP in which Slovenian MEPs are represented are PES and ALDE. The Socialist group includes two Slovenian MEPs from the Social Democrats and the ALDE group includes the remaining two MEPS, one from Liberal Democracy of Slovenia and the other from the Zares (For Real) party. The 2009 EP elections represented a shift since the parties of the left managed to acquire four of the seven possible seats; in the previous term the balance had been slightly tilted in favour of Slovenia's right-wing parties.

The incumbency level of the Slovenian EP delegation is moderate. Three out seven incumbents were re-elected in each election. The 2009–2014 delegation consists of two MEPs who hold PhDs and five who are university graduates. The majority of the elected MEPs, four out of seven, come from so-called 'brokerage occupations', lawyers, political scientists, journalists, etc. Regarding their prior occupation, we should stress that six out of the seven MEPs came to office from the public sector. The age structure of the Slovenian delegation is rather balanced. At the time of the 2009 elections, two MEPs were aged between 35 and 44, three between 45 and 54, and two were 55 or above.

Due to the specific nature of European elections and party leaders' manoeuvring amongst internal party conflicts, some candidates on the leading party lists were not publicly linked with the nominating parties. This was the case for both of the elected MEPs of the main governing party at the time.

Another idiosyncratic feature of Slovenian EP elections is the party apprenticeship status of the main contesting candidates (Norris, 1999). Five out of the seven MEPs elected in 2009, one of whom is a woman, were publicly well-known and visible members of the party that nominated them. The remaining two elected MEPs on the list of the main governing party, the

Table 21.6 EP election results in Slovenia: 2009

National party	Vote number	Vote share %
SDS	123,563	26.7
SD	**85,407**	**18.4**
NSI	76,866	16.6
LDS	**53,212**	**11.5**
ZARES	**45,238**	**9.8**
DESUS	**33,292**	**7.2**
SLS	16,601	3.6
SNS	13,227	2.9
SMS	9,093	2.0
Turnout	28.3%	

Source: Državna volilna komisija, 2009.

Note:
Government parties are marked in bold.

Social Democrats, could also be considered to be well-known public figures, although without prior links to the party. A similar pattern of diminishing party apprenticeship can be identified in the experience of MEPs in holding publicly elected offices, since, barring one re-election, female MEPs as a rule have marginal or no experience in occupying publicly elected offices. Hence, we can draw two interesting conclusions.

First, it seems that the new electoral setting took the parties by surprise. As a result, they placed their less apprenticed female candidates on the frontline due to the gender mainstreaming provisions. Second, the attitude of the main governing party in nominating two MEPs to the highest positions on its list of candidates, neither of whom had any prior party connections, gave cause for concern, since the main governing party in the 2004 EP elections behaved similarly by nominating publicly renowned individuals rather than candidates from within the party ranks.

Regardless of their term, Slovenian MEPs tend to be highly educated individuals. Six out of the seven MEPs in each term assumed office from the public sector. So far, most MEPs have been high-profile career politicians, who have served as members of government or parliament. However, their gender profile is quite specific: although the 2009 nominations represented a departure from the 2004 nominations, when all elected male MEPs were party 'big guns' and all elected female MEPs were either well-known public figures or 'anonymous' party members, the general pattern remained. None of the five women elected have been high profile politicians or occupied an office of government or legislature prior to their entering the European Parliament. Moreover, all non-party apprentices who managed to enter the Strasbourg arena were women, all were publicly recognized as non-political personas, and all were nominated by the main governing parties.

It remains unclear whether the dominant parties in the country engage with EP elections by deliberately nominating lower-profile candidates in order to assign them to potential defeat. Overall, we can argue that the post of MEP is highly regarded and considered to be a prize of sorts for the office holder. On the other hand, the fight for the remaining places falls to candidates who are second on the list, usually women due to the 'zipper' electoral rule. Politicians from the executive of the youth sections of parties frequently occupy the bottom places on the party lists.

According to Susan E. Scarrow's (1997) typology, a mixture of political personalities make the journey from Slovenia to the EP arena: some potential European careerists – mainly women and certain men who have already ascended as high as they can in national politics – a few political retirees, and a number of individuals who see the post of MEP either as a place to retreat until a better opportunity arises in the national political arena, such as a presidential race, or an open prime ministerial post, or as a stepping-stone to building a possible future role in domestic politics. This also seems to be the case with the additional eighth MEP, Zofija Mazej Kukovič, a former minister in the government led by the Slovenian Democratic Party, who, after the ratification of the Lisbon Treaty, was officially appointed by the Slovenian National Assembly on 8 December 2011, on the basis of the 2009 EP election results.

9.4 Campaign finance

Slovenia's transitional electoral legislation, from the end of 1980s until the beginning of 1990s, did not provide for the possibility of financial support for political campaigns from abroad; thus legislation had to be amended accordingly. As a result, previously banned contributions from EU citizens and legal private entities were permitted under provisions applicable for Slovenian nationals and domestic firms with the adoption of the Election of Slovenian Members to the European Parliament Act in 2004 (OJ RS 22/2004).

Table 21.7 List of Slovenian MEPs: sixth and seventh legislatures

National party EP political group	Candidate name, year of birth, gender (2004)	Professional background	Committee	Candidate name, year of birth, gender (2009)	Previous mandate	Professional profile	Committee
NSi (EPP-ED; EPP)	Lojze Peterle, 1948 (Male)	MP, ex PM	Foreign Affairs	Lojze Peterle, 1948 (Male)	✓	MP and MEP	Foreign Affairs
	Ljudmila Novak, 1959 (Female)	Mayor of small municipality	Culture and Education	—	Not re-elected	—	—
SD (PES; S&D)	Borut Pahor*, 1963 (Male)	Party leader, President of NA	Budgetary Control; Constitutional Affairs	—	Did not run	—	—
	—	—	—	Zoran Thaler, 1962 (Male)	✗	ex Minister, ex MP	Foreign Affairs
	—	—	—	Mojca Kleva, 1976 (Female)	✗	Party executive	Foreign Affairs
	—	—	—	Tanja Fajon, 1971 (Female)	✗	Journalist	Civil Liberties, Justice and Home Affairs
SDS (EPP-ED; EPP)	Mihael Brejc, 1947, (Male)	MP, ex minister	Civil Liberties, Justice and Home Affairs	—	Did not run	—	—
	Romana Jordan Cizelj, 1966 (Female)	Physicist	Industry, Research and Energy	Romana Jordan Cizelj, 1966 (Female)	✓	MEP	Industry, Research and Energy
	—	—	—	Milan Zver, 1962 (Male)	✗	ex Minister, Party Vice-President	Culture and Education
ZARES (ALDE)	**	—	—	Ivo Vajgl, 1943 (Male)	✗	Diplomat, Minister, MP	Development
LDS (ALDE)***	Jelko Kacin, 1955 (Male)	Deputy in NA, party leader, ex minister	Foreign Affairs	Jelko Kacin, 1955 (Male)	✓	MEP	Foreign Affairs
	Mojca Drčar Murko, 1942, (Female)	Journalist candidate for the presidency in former regime	Environment, Public Health and Food Safety	—	Did not run	—	—

Source: http://www.europarl.europa.eu/meps/en/search.html?country=SI.

Notes:

* Aurelio Juri replaced Borut Pahor at the end of 2008.

** The party was established in 2007.

*** In the 2004 EP elections the Liberal Democracy of Slovenia and the Democratic Party of Pensioners of Slovenia proposed a joint list of candidates, although no candidate from the pensioners' side was elected.

**** On 8 December 2011, the National Assembly named Zofija Mazej Kukovič, born in 1955 from the Slovenian Democratic Party, as the eighth MEP from Slovenia.

Barring this provision, the legislation on the financial aspects of election campaigns is the same for both national and European elections. Nevertheless, one of the hallmarks of elections to the European Parliament in Slovenia had been the unwillingness of political parties to spend a comparable amount of resources in EP campaigns to those spent financing national election campaigns. In spite of the one constituency provision for EP elections, there were no centralized media campaigns, nor any greater focus devoted to television or other forms of mass media to achieve nationwide coverage.

With the exception of the former dominant party, the Liberal Democracy of Slovenia, no political party reached the official spending threshold, whilst virtually all contenders for the government did so at the 2004 national elections (Deželan, 2007). Rather than spending campaign money, political parties tended to exploit every opportunity for 'free' media coverage, especially on national public television, which is legally obliged to provide an opportunity for lists of candidates to present their positions. So, the primary party campaign strategy was centred around four pre-election shows on the two largest television stations with nation-wide coverage. In addition, parties attempted to take advantage of everyday news reporting by preparing events that were eventually broadcast on the evening news. This second strategy drew on the positive experience of the 2004 election winners, who cruised around the country in a bus preparing small local events in order to make contact with the electorate and to make the evening news in the local and national media. In fact, street-level canvassing was a defining feature of the EP election campaigns.

Taking into account the election results, it is not possible to conclude that the greater funds allocated to the EP election campaign, capital intensive campaigning, attracted more votes than less costly campaigning methods. Rather, it seems that 'old-fashioned' campaign methods and certain campaign innovations specific to the Slovenian context outweighed the importance of funds in the campaign.

10 Theoretical interpretation of Euro-elections

10.1 Second-Order Election theory

Given the exceptionally low turnout in European Parliament elections in Slovenia, it was clear that voters did not consider them as important as national elections, thus confirming their 'second-order' status, as described by Reif and Schmitt. Political parties did not regard these electoral contests as being related to power, and therefore did not invest significant resources for the campaign.

Furthermore, candidate selection tended to take place closer to the polling day and in a more centralized manner than in the general election (Krašovec and Lajh, 2009). The campaign, mainly run by party personnel and volunteers, relied officially on allocated coverage in the national media, and the news reporting on the two main television channels, unlike the capital-intensive campaigning which characterized national elections (Deželan et al., 2010).

Clearly, parties were willing to experiment in the European elections in ways they would not dare to in national elections, the most obvious example of this being the testing of particular electoral system innovations, such as the size of the electoral unit, the preferential vote, and rules designed to enhance gender equality.

Interestingly enough, the government-opposition thesis did not hold in the Slovenian case. Although the Prime Minister's party lost in both European elections, it is not possible to see a clear pattern of voters 'punishing' the governing coalition. However, the 2004 European elections, which were held a few months prior to the national elections, did signal that the

Liberal Democracy of Slovenia's decade of primacy in the party system was over. In 2009 the governing parties received only a slightly smaller proportion of the vote than in the previous national election, which may be due to the fact that the government, in power for less than a year, was still in its 'honeymoon period'. The ruling coalition parties even gained a majority of four out of the seven seats in 2009, due to the impact of the new electoral rules. Another feature of EP elections in Slovenia was the prevalence of 'voting from the heart', which sanctioned the landslide victories of smaller parties and, in particular, that of New Slovenia.

10.2 Europe Salience theory

Public pro-European enthusiasm weakened the prospect for politicizing the question of Europe and, therefore, also the opportunities for parties to gain votes on Europe. 'Europe salience theory', which also would entail the greater success of anti-European lists and the Greens in European elections, appeared not to be relevant for Slovenia. In particular, the Party of Youth of Slovenia, which joined the European Green party family, did not manage to gain any MEPs.

The 2009 European election campaign did not focus on European issues but rather on the economic crisis, Slovene–Croat relations, and the question of political ethics. Positive attitudes towards European integration and a high level of confidence in European integration clearly are not mirrored in the public's participation in the EP elections. This may be why no major party advocates an anti-European agenda. Nevertheless, it is fair to state that parties of the left projected a more enthusiastic attitude towards European integration processes. Furthermore, parties boasting elected MEPs tried to avoid criticizing Europe, whereas some other parties openly expressed doubts about European integration processes.

The general hypothesis regarding electoral gains by extreme political parties in European elections did not seem to hold in the Slovenian context. In fact, small parties, Green parties, extra-parliamentary or extreme parties had been unable to gain any more in European elections than they had in national elections. However, exceptional individual candidates, such as Lojze Peterle of New Slovenia, were able win seats in the EP even as representatives of completely marginalized former parliamentary parties. In fact, by employing a preferential voting system, voters chose a popular individual politician.

In the case of minor extreme parties, such attempts did not appear to pay off. Due to the relatively low coverage of EU-related issues in the campaigns and the similar stances of the major parties, voters found it difficult to differentiate between parties on these grounds. Perhaps the most prominent case was the *Stranka mladih Slovenije*, SMS (Party of Youth of Slovenia), which, as a member of the European Greens, tried to advance environmental issues, but gained only marginal support. It seems that EP elections are not used by Slovenian voters to protest against the EU, but rather to demonstrate to the government that they disapprove of the conduct of the major parties. The relative success of the centre-right parties in both EP elections can be explained by the fact that both elections took place during centre-left rule. Taking this into account, the relevance of the supranational versus intergovernmental divide traced in party manifestos (Deželan, 2009) does not seem to be as plausible an explanation of the success of the centre-right parties as an explanation of the government versus opposition divide.

European elections in Slovenia have so far been embedded in the context of: (1) a rather successful democratization setting; (2) long-term, predominantly pro-European public opinion, with economic, cultural, and political elites favouring European integration processes; and (3) domestic processes in the consolidation of a young democracy.

These domestic circumstances, coupled with the European Union's still rather decentralized political system, have not encouraged Slovenian political parties to identify fully with all-EU issues and with European parties when competing for seats in the European Parliament. On the contrary, European elections in Slovenia are about domestic politics. However, the creation of a small but specialist segment of the political elite that connects national-level to EU-level politics seems to share a political culture with other MEPs rather than with domestic politicians.

Whilst the 2004 election results mirrored the major party clusters in the European Parliament, the 2009 results showed Slovenia to be more centre-left than the balance in the European Parliament. In neither 2004 nor 2009 did Slovenian representatives add to the EP ideological extremes, but the Slovenian case did contribute to 'export' the weak legitimacy of the European Parliament, based on a low electoral turnout, as well as the gender imbalance of MEPs at the expense of women. Slovenian parties did not play a significant role in promoting Euroscepticism, since only a few European issues gained public attention, and these were in any case not particularly politicized. Domestic politics still mattered most in the country.

One explanation for the above political phenomena, which was not included in any of the hypotheses that attempted to explain the idiosyncrasies of post-Communist systems, is the anti-party sentiment amongst the general public in Slovenia, which reflects the considerable low level of trust in political parties, a level that is generally lower in post-Communist democracies than in the older democracies (Rose, 2009). It remains to be seen whether the global economic and financial crisis, along with the related problems of managing the euro-zone, will impact on both citizens' future attitudes towards the EU and the responses of political parties to such developments. What is already clear is that the pre-term national elections in December 2011, together with the problems arising from the ongoing global economic and financial turmoil, have re-shaped the structure of the Slovenian party system. It remains to be seen how any new economic and political developments will spill over into the next European elections.

References

Primary sources

Državna volilna komisija (2003) 'Referendum on Accession to the EU and NATO', www.dvk.gov.si/referendum200302/index.html (accessed on 20 August 2009).

Državna volilna komisija (2004) 'Elections to the European Parliament 2004', www.dvk-rs.si/arhivi/ep2004/en/index.html (accessed on 20 August 2013).

Državna volilna komisija (2004a) 'Elections to the National Assembly 2004', http://volitve.gov.si/dz2004/ (accessed on 20 August 2009).

Državna volilna komisija (2008) 'Elections to the National Assembly 2008', http://volitve.gov.si/dz2008/ (accessed on 20 August 2009).

Državna volilna komisija (2009) 'Elections to the European Parliament 2009', http://volitve.gov.si/ep2009/ (accessed on 20 August 2009).

Election of Slovenian Members to the European Parliament Act, *Official Journal of the Republic of Slovenia*, 22, 2004.

Estonian National Electoral Committee, www.vvk.ee (accessed on 15 February 2015).

Europa.eu (2011) 'Member Countries: Slovenia': http://europa.eu/about-eu/countries/member-countries/slovenia/index_en.htm (accessed on 25 April 2011).

European Parliament Database (2010) www.europarl.europa.eu/meps/eu/search.html (accessed on 10 January 2015).

Eurostat (2013, 2014) http://epp.eurostat.ec.europa.eu (accessed on 5 June 2015).

The Government Communication Office of the Republic of Slovenia (2010) 'Slovenia in Brief':www.slovenia.si/en/slovenia/ (accessed on 25 November 2010).

The Ministry of Foreign Affairs – MFA (2011) 'Western Balkans', www.mzz.gov.si/en/foreign_policy/western_balkans (accessed on 31 November 2010).

Uradni list Republike Slovenije (The Official Gazette of the Republic of Slovenia), 1998/2000.

Secondary sources

Bašić Hrvatin, S. (2010) 'Recikliranje zdrave pameti', in Kustec Lipicer, S. (ed.) *Politične vsebine in volilna kampanja*, Ljubljana, Založba FDV, 99–119.

Binnema, H. A. (2003) 'Three Sorts of Europe. The Europeanization of Party Programmes in the Netherlands and the United Kingdom', paper presented at ECPR General Conference, Marburg, September.

Deželan, T. (2007) 'Analiza apstinencije na europskim izborima', *Politička misao*, 44(3), 23–43.

Deželan, T. (2009) 'Patterns of Competition of Slovenian Political Parties at the European Elections: Programmatic Orientations and Candidate Profiles', Research Report, Faculty of Social Sciences, University of Ljubljana.

Deželan, T. (2011) 'Citizenship in Slovenia: The Regime of a Nationalising or a Europeanising State?' *CITSEE Working Papers, 16*. Online. Available at: www.law.ed.ac.uk/file_download/series/326_citizenshipinsloveniatheregimeofanationalisingoraeuropeanisingstate.pdf (accessed on 1 April 2011).

Deželan, T. and Sever, M. (2007) 'Cohesion in the Slovenian National Assembly: A Pattern of Post-Socialist Democratic Parliament?' *Balkanistica*, 20, 29–54.

Deželan, T. and Sever, M. (2009) 'Citizen Comprehension of the Left–Right Ideological Continuum in Central and Eastern European Post-Communist Countries', Akta Fak. filoz. Západovčes, univ., 3, 15–35.

Deželan, T, Krašovec, A. and Kovačič, M. (2010) 'Volilna kampanja po slovensko', in Kustec Lipicer, S. (ed.) *Politične vsebine in volilna kampanja: slovenska izkušnja z volitev v Evropski parlament 2009*, Ljubljana, Fakulteta za družbene vede, 53–70.

Državna volilna komisija (State Election Commission): www.dvk-rs.si/index.php/si/arhiv-drzavni-zbor-rs (accessed on 15 February 2014).

European Commission (2007) 'Eurobarometer 68: Javno mnenje v Evropski uniji, jesen 2007'. Online. Available at: http://ec.europa.eu/slovenija/pdf/2008/eb68_-_porocilo_za_slovenijo_-_final-read_only.doc (accessed on 15 August 2009).

Fink-Hafner, D. (2005) 'Evropske volitve 2004 v Sloveniji – učinkovitost volilnega inženirstva v korist bolj uravnotežene zastopanosti spolov', Krašovec, A. (ed.), *Volitve v Evropski parlament: Res drugorazredne volitve?*, Ljubljana, FDV, 107–29.

Fink-Hafner, D. (2005) 'Slovenia', *Political Data Yearbook, European Journal of Political Research*, 44(7/8), 1179–87.

Fink-Hafner, D. (2008) 'Ensuring Democratic Control over National Government in European Affairs – the Slovenian Experience', in Barrett, G. (ed.) *National Parliaments in the European Union*, Dublin, Clarus Press, 393–414.

Fink-Hafner, D., Deželan, T. and Topolinjak, S. (2005) 'Kandidatke na evropskih volitvah 2004 v Sloveniji', in Kustec Lipicer, S. (ed.) *Politološki vidiki volilne kampanje: analiza volilne kampanje za volitve v Evropski parlament 2004*, Ljubljana, FDV, 128–46.

Krašovec, A. (2005) 'Financiranje volilnih kampanj', in Kustec Lipicer, S. (ed.) *Politološki vidiki volilne kampanje*, Ljubljana, Založba FDV, 173–88.

Krašovec, A. (ed.) (2010) *Volitve v evropski parlament 2009*, Ljubljana, Založba FDV.

Krašovec, A. and Boh, T. (2002) 'Podatki o preteklih volitvah', in Fink-Hafner, D. and Boh, T. (eds) *Parlamentarne volitve 2000*, Ljubljana, Založba FDV, 173–88.

Krasovec, A. and Lajh, D. (2009) *The European Parliament Elections in Slovenia 7 June 2009*. Online. Available at: www.sussex.ac.uk/sei/1-4-2-2.html (accessed on 20 August 2009).

Krašovec, A. and Štremfel, U. (2007) 'Does Institutional Context Matter for Candidate Selection? Some Evidence from Slovenia', *Politologicky časopis*, 3, 187–204.

Krašovec, A., Kustec Lipicer, S. and Lajh, D. (2005) 'Slovénie', in Déloye, Y. and Bellec, D. (eds), *Dictionnaire des élections européennes*, Paris, Economica, 606–12.

Kustec Lipicer, S. (ed.) (2010) *Politične vsebine in volilna kampanja*, Ljubljana, Založba FDV.

Kustec Lipicer, S. and Bilavčić, N. (2010) 'Volilni programi in volilne vsebine skozi volilno izkušnjo volitev v Evropski parlament 2009', in Kustec Lipicer, S. (ed.) *Politične vsebine in volilna kampanja*, Ljubljana, Založba FDV, 71–95.

Kustec Lipicer, S. and Krašovec, A. (2004) 'Party-Based Euroscepticism in Slovenia: Elections to the National and European Parliaments', in Cabada, L. and Krašovec, A. (eds) *Europeanisation of National Political Parties*, Plzeň, Vydavatelství a nakladatelství Aleš Čeněk, 219–38.

Norris, P. (1999) 'Recruitment into the European Parliament', in Katz, R. S. and Wessels, B. (eds) *The European Parliament, the National Parliaments, and European Integration*, Oxford and New York, Oxford University Press, 87–102.

Offe, C. (1991) 'Capitalism by Democratic Theory Facing the Triple Transition in East Central Europe', *Social Research*, 58(4), 865–92.

Reif, K. H. and Schmitt, H. (1980) 'Nine Second-Order National Elections – A Conceptual Framework for the Analysis of European Election Results', *European Journal of Political Research*, 8(1), 3–44.

Repe, B. (2011) 'Slovenia: History'. Online. Available at: www.slovenia.si/en/slovenia/history/ (accessed on 10 March 2011).

Rose, R. (2009) *Understanding Post-Communist Transformation. A Bottom-up Approach*, London and New York, Routledge.

Sartori, G. (1976) *Parties and Party Systems: A Framework for Analysis,* Cambridge, Cambridge University Press.

Scarrow, S. E. (1997) 'Political Career Paths and the European Parliament', *Legislative Studies Quarterly*, 22(2), 253–63.

22
ESTONIA

Piret Ehin

Figure 22.1 Map of Estonia

Table 22.1 Estonia profile

EU entry year	2004
Schengen entry year	2007
MEPs elected in 2009	6
MEPs under Lisbon Treaty	6
Capital	Tallinn
Total area★	45,227 km²
Population	1,315,819
	68.7% Estonians; 25.6% Russians; 2.1%; Ukrainians; 1.2% Belarusians; 0.8% Finns; 1.6 % others
Population density★★	30.3/km²
Median age of population	41.3
Political system	Parliamentary republic
Head of state	Toomas Hendrik Ilves, Social Democratic Party (SDE) (October 2006–)
Prime minister	Andrus Ansip, Reform Party (ER) (April 2005–March 2014); Taavi Rõivas, Reform Party (ER) (March 2014–)
Political majority	Reform Party, Pro Patria and Res Publica Union (IRL) and Social Democratic Party (SDE) Coalition Government (April 2007–April 2009); Reform Party and Pro Patria and Res Publica Union (IRL) Coalition Government (April 2009–March 2014); Reform Party (RE) and Social Democratic Party (SDE) Coalition Government (March 2014–)
Currency	Previously Estonian kroon Euro (€) since January 2011
Prohead GDP in PPS	14,800 €

Source: Eurostat, 2013, 2014, http://epp.eurostat.ec.europa.eu/.

Notes:
★ Total area including inland waters.
★★ Population density: the ratio of the annual average population of a region to the land area of the region.

1 Geographical position

The Republic of Estonia (*Eesti Vabariik*) is located in northern Europe, on the eastern shores of the Baltic Sea. Stretching 350 kilometres from east to west and 240 kilometres from north to south, the country has land borders with Latvia to the south, with Russia to the east, and a maritime border with Finland to the north. Estonia has nearly 3,800 kilometres of coastline, and over 1,500 islands and islets in the Baltic Sea.

Whilst the size of its territory is roughly comparable to that of the Netherlands or Denmark, the forested, sparsely inhabited country has a population of approximately 1,315,819 and a population density of 30.3 people per square kilometre. Almost 70 per cent of the inhabitants are urban dwellers, with a third of the population residing in the capital city, Tallinn.

2 Historical background

The Estonians speak a Finno-Ugric language closely related to Finnish. Their ancestors settled in the territory over 5,000 years ago. The local tribes remained self-governing until Danish and German crusaders conquered Estonia in the thirteenth century. Between 1558 and 1583, during the Livonian War, Russia, the Scandinavian powers, and the Union of Lithuania and Poland fought to control present-day Estonia and Latvia. Following the conflict, Estonia entered a period of relative peace and prosperity under Swedish rule. After the Great Northern War which lasted between 1700 and 1721, Estonia was incorporated into the Russian Empire. However, the Baltic-German landowning elites retained their privileges, and Lutheranism remained the dominant religion. The late nineteenth century was the period of national awakening. Amidst the chaos that followed the Bolshevik Revolution in Russia, Estonia declared independence on 24 February 1918 and secured it by defeating both the Red Army as well as Baltic-German reactionaries in the 1918–1920 War of Independence. The two decades of independence were marked by rapid economic and cultural development. The fledgling democracy, however, succumbed to authoritarian rule in the 1930s.

The Molotov–Ribbentrop Pact negotiated between the USSR and Nazi Germany in 1939 assigned Estonia to the Soviet sphere of influence. Estonia was incorporated into the USSR in 1940, an act never recognized *de jure* by the majority of Western democracies. Nazi Germany invaded in 1941; Soviet rule was re-established in 1944. Tens of thousands of Estonians were executed or deported by Soviet authorities; about 70,000 fled to the West. Agriculture was collectivized, and mass immigration from various regions of the USSR dramatically altered the ethnic composition of the country. Between 1939 and 1989 the percentage of ethnic Estonians in the country's total population fell from about 90 to 62 per cent.

In the late 1980s, Estonians demanded independence in a series of mass protests known as the 'Singing Revolution'. Independence was restored in 1991, and the last Russian troops left Estonia in 1994. Estonia's swift political transformation and rapid economic development since the early 1990s have earned it a reputation as a transition success story.

3 Geopolitical profile

Within the two decades since the collapse of the Soviet Union, Estonia's position in Europe has changed radically. In 1991, Estonia emerged from behind the Iron Curtain as a poor, peripheral, and obscure ex-Soviet republic. By 2011, Estonia had become one of the most integrated countries in northern Europe in terms of membership in major international institutions and agreements. A member of the Organization for Security and Cooperation in Europe (OSCE) since 1991 and of the European Union and NATO since 2004, Estonia acceded to the Schengen area in 2007 and to the Organization for Economic Cooperation and Development (OECD) in 2010. Having fulfilled the Maastricht convergence criteria amidst the global economic crisis, Estonia became the seventeenth member of the euro-zone on 1 January 2011.

Estonia's dedication in pursuing maximum integration with Western institutions reflects the small nation's quest to strengthen statehood in a complex international environment. The country's relations with its large neighbour, the Russian Federation, remain complicated. Moscow continues to claim that the Baltic states joined the USSR voluntarily, whilst the three Baltic states regard the half-century of Soviet rule as a period of illegal occupation. A range of contentious issues dominated the agenda of Estonian–Russian relations throughout the 1990s, including the interpretation of history, the status of the Russophone population, the question of Russian troop withdrawal, Estonia's aspirations to EU and NATO membership, trade and transit issues, the definition of borders, and the status of the Russian Orthodox Church. Whilst many policy issues have been solved, conflicts over history, identity, and political memory still loom large (Berg and Ehin, 2009). In spring 2007, the decision by the Estonian government to relocate a monument known as the Bronze Soldier dedicated to the Soviet 'liberators' of Estonia from downtown Tallinn to a military cemetery led to massive riots, mostly by Russian-speaking youth, in the Estonian capital. Tensions escalated into a major crisis in Russian–Estonian relations, involving a siege of the

Estonian embassy in Moscow, cyber attacks on Estonia's IT infrastructure, and the redirection of Russian transit shipments.

Estonia, like its Baltic neighbours, remains a vocal critic of the authoritarian regime in the Kremlin. To Moscow's irritation, the three Baltic states play an active role in the EU-Russia 'shared neighbourhood', supporting democratic reforms in the post-Soviet space, and backing the EU and NATO aspirations of countries such as Georgia, Ukraine, and Moldova.

4 Overview of the political landscape

Today's Republic of Estonia conceptualizes itself as a restored state and claims legal continuity from the Republic of Estonia that was founded in 1918 and was illegally annexed by the Soviet Union in 1940. The principle of legal continuity has far-reaching implications for legislation and policy. Notably, Estonian citizenship was automatically granted only to those who had been citizens before Soviet annexation, and to their descendants. Those who had settled in Estonia during the Soviet period, about a third of the population, could obtain citizenship by naturalization. Alternatively, they had the right to register themselves as citizens of Russia, the USSR's successor state, or to choose any other citizenship. As of 1 December 2011, 84.3 per cent of Estonia's population held Estonian citizenship, 8.8 per cent were citizens of other countries, mostly Russia, and 6.9 per cent were stateless (Ministry of Interior, 2011). The latter category consists of former Soviet citizens who have not become citizens of any country.

Under the constitution adopted in 1992, Estonia has a parliamentary system of government, with a Prime Minister as chief executive. The President, whose role is largely ceremonial, is elected by the 101-member unicameral parliament of Estonia (*Riigikogu*), with two-thirds of the votes required. If the candidate does not gain the amount of votes required, the right to elect the President goes over to a special electoral assembly. The Supreme Court is the highest court in the state, exercising constitutional review and reviewing appeals.

Whilst governments used to be short-lived in the 1990s, Estonian politics has become increasingly stable since the turn of the millennium. Centre-right parties have dominated the government since 2002. Andrus Ansip (Reform Party) is one of the longest-serving Prime Ministers in the EU. In office since 2005, he was re-elected for a third term in March 2011.

5 Brief account of the political parties

Estonia has a multiparty system in which coalition governments are the norm. The origins of the Estonian party system lie in the independence movements of the late 1980s. The *Eesti Rahvusliku Sõltumatuse Partei*, ERSP (Estonian National Independence Party), established in 1988 by leading dissidents, was the first opposition party in the entire Soviet Union. Another major political force of the era, *Rahvarinne* (the Popular Front), which played an important role in bringing down the Communist regime, fell apart soon after the restoration of independence, giving rise to a number of new political parties.

Overall, the Estonian party system has displayed many features typical of young post-Communist democracies; instability, mergers and splintering are common, and several elections have seen the success of newly founded parties, high electoral volatility, the prevalence of fuzzily focussed parties without a strong social base or civil society roots, the fragmentation of vote and seat distribution, and low levels of popular trust in parties (Rose and Munro, 2009). At the same time, there is a significant degree of continuity in the Estonian party system: all major parties currently represented in the *Riigikogu*, or their direct predecessors, have been present in politics since 1992 (Sikk, 2006, 343).

The Estonian political landscape has been dominated by centre-right actors and views. No major political actors clearly identify as 'left' and there is no real Communist successor party to speak of; the Estonian Left Party won 0.1 per cent of the vote in the 2007 general elections. Another notable feature of the Estonian party system is the absence of any significant ethnic parties, despite the fact that nearly a third of the country's population is Russian-speaking and the ethnic cleavage is strongly politicized. Whilst parties claiming to represent Estonia's Russian-speaking minority exist, they are marginal and have not been represented in the *Riigikogu* since 2003. Finally, the Estonian party system is characterized by a close relationship between parties and the state. Cartelization is evident from the institutional rules favouring established parties, patterns of party financing, an advanced system of regulation, and a 'substantial circulation of people between administrative and political echelons' (ibid., 341).

The number of parties represented in the *Riigikogu* has decreased significantly over time. Whilst nine parties or electoral alliances won enough votes to secure at least one seat in 1992, the number of parliamentary parties was reduced to six by the results of 2007 elections and to four following the 2011 vote. Table 22.2 provides an overview of the main political parties in Estonia.

The pro-market *Reformierakond* (Reform Party) has been in government continuously since 1999, usually as the leading coalition partner. The centrist *Keskerakond* (Centre Party), led by the charismatic and controversial Edgar Savisaar, has been a major force in Estonian politics since 1991. It has acquired the status of the main opposition party; whilst winning the largest share of the vote in the general elections of 2003, and placing second in both 2007 and 2011, it has been repeatedly sidelined in the process of government formation by right-wing parties. The party has been remarkably successful in appealing to Russian-speaking voters, effectively putting ethnic Russian parties out of business.

Isamaa ja Res Publica Liit, IRL (Pro Patria and Res Publica Union) was founded in 2006 when two Conservative parties merged. The first of these, *Isamaaliit* (Pro Patria Union) was the successor of *Isamaa* (Pro Patria), the party both credited and blamed for the radical reforms implemented by the Mart Laar government in the early 1990s, and the ERSP. The second of these, *Res Publica*, was created 15 months before the general elections of March 2003. Promising 'new politics' to an electorate increasingly frustrated with the self-serving ways of politicians, it took a quarter of the vote in these elections and was the leading partner in the governing coalition that lasted until 2005.

The moderately left-Liberal *Sotsiaaldemokraatlik Erakond*, SDE (Social Democratic Party) has never enjoyed the prominence that Social Democrats have experienced in the neighbouring

Table 22.2 List of political parties in Estonia

Original name	Abbreviation	English translation
Eesti Reformierakond	ER	Reform Party
Eesti Keskerakond	K	Centre Party
Isamaa ja Res Publica Liit	IRL	Pro Patria and Res Publica Union
Sotsiaaldemokraatlik erakond	SDE	Social Democratic Party
Erakond Eestimaa Rohelised	EER	Greens
Eestimaa Rahvaliit	ERL	People's Union
Erakond Eesti Kristlikud Demokraadid		Christian Democratic Party
Vene Erakond Eestis		Russian Party in Estonia
Põllumeeste kogu		Farmers' Assembly
Eestimaa Ühendatud Vasakpartei		United Left Party of Estonia
Libertas Eesti		Libertas Estonia

Scandinavian countries. It has significant coalition potential, however, as parties on both the right and left of the Estonian political spectrum regard the SDE as a suitable partner.

Erakond Eestimaa Rohelised (the Estonian Green Party) was a newcomer in the 2007 elections. Although the party was founded only in 2006, it can be considered a successor of the Green movement dating back to the late 1980s. Finally, *Rahvaliit* (the People's Union) has strong backing in rural areas. Its popularity has shrunk due to corruption scandals involving the party's leaders. Both the Greens and the People's Union failed to win seats in the 2011 *Riigikogu* elections.

5.1 Party attitudes towards the European Union

The EU integration issue has been part of a complex dynamic between the Estonian political elite and the public. Given a very strong domestic consensus on the strategic aims of democracy and a market economy, integration with the EU was largely congruent with the Estonian elite's state-building and transition strategies. In the pre-accession period, all major parties supported the objective of joining the EU.

However, dwindling levels of public support for the EU in the years just prior to accession led several parties and politicians to reconsider their strategies (Mikkel and Kasekamp, 2008). The Centre Party, the main opposition force, was torn between the conflicting incentives of seeing the accession process to a successful end and capitalizing on popular EU hesitations by criticizing the goverment's 'integration at any cost' approach. Intra-party tensions were clearly evident at the party's congress, held in August 2003, where a plurality of members voted against EU accession. Differences over European integration led a group of prominent politicians to abandon the party in 2005.

A Eurosceptic mood was strongly present in the country's first European Parliament elections, held in June 2004. Having secured a 'Yes' to accession in the referendum, political parties could safely afford to flirt with Euroscepticism in an attempt to boost their electoral appeal amongst certain segments of the electorate. All major parties, with the exception of the Social Democrats, engaged in significant EU-bashing in the 2004 election campaigns, posturing as defenders of national interests *vis-à-vis* a large, dominating, alien, and bureaucratic European Union (Sikk, 2009; Tigasson, 2009). The governing Res Publica's oversized campaign posters featured tough-looking candidates promising a 'Breakthrough'. The Conservative Pro Patria Union campaigned under the slogan 'For Estonia'. The rural People's Union vowed to 'Protect the Estonian Kroon'. The Reform Party promised to defend Estonia's pro-market policies and institutions against European over-regulation. The Centre Party sent vague and mixed signals, trying to offer something for everyone. Only the Social Democrats openly supported the deepening of integration and their leading candidate, Toomas Hendrik Ilves, argued that strong supranational institutions are in the interest of small Member States such as Estonia.

The relatively strong presence of Eurosceptic forces in Estonian politics around the time of accession seems to have been a temporary phenomenon. Public support for the EU increased rapidly in the years following accession. In this context, political parties have had few incentives to politicize Estonia's membership, and party-based Euroscepticism has once again been constrained to the fringes of the political spectrum. Amidst the economic crisis, there were virtually no attempts to scapegoat the EU for the difficulties. To the contrary, many agreed with Prime Minister Ansip that without the EU, Estonia would be worse off. Eurosceptic forces were barely visible in the European Parliament election of 2009.

6 Public opinion and the European Union

The attitudes of the Estonian public towards the EU have undergone dramatic changes over time. Roughly from 2001 to 2003, Estonia had some of the highest levels of public Euroscepticism amongst all candidate countries, as documented by Eurobarometer surveys. With the accession referendum on the horizon, the political elite feared that stubborn voters would undermine a decade of efforts by vetoing accession. The eventual referendum result was a relief: 67 per cent of those who turned out voted in favour of EU membership.

Whilst the precise reasons for Estonians' cautious attitudes towards the EU in the immediate pre-accession phase remain subject to debate, existing studies suggest that the low levels of public support in the pre-accession period reflected dwindling trust in the national government, concerns about the effects of accession for Estonia's sovereignty and culture, and a fear of price increases. Whilst the elites regarded rapid integration with the West as an unquestioned imperative ensuring 'the irreversibility of Estonia's independence', segments of the population resented elite eagerness in bending to the demands of Brussels, and argued that Estonia was heading from one union (the USSR) into another (Pettai, 2005; Ehin, 2001 and 2002; Lust, 2006; Vetik et al., 2006).

Since Estonia became a full member of the EU, however, public support has steadily increased. Since 2007, it has been well above the EU average. According to Eurobarometer surveys conducted between 2008 and 2010, some 70–80 per cent of Estonians believe that the country has benefitted from EU membership. The increase in support coincided with an economic boom that the country experienced during the first four years of EU membership. However, the EU-optimism of Estonians cannot be attributed to economic factors alone, as is evident from support rates well above the EU average in 2009, when the country was engulfed in one of the deepest recessions in the entire EU. Some observers have linked increased support to the intensified perception of external threat in the wake of the Bronze Soldier crisis of spring 2007 and the Russian-Georgian War of August 2008.

7 National and EP electoral systems

The unicameral *Riigikogu* has 101 members, each elected for a four-year term. The electoral system used in *Riigikogu* elections is proportional representation, in which each voter votes for a single candidate on a party list and the vote is counted for both the individual and the party (Ishiyama, 1996). The country is divided into 12 multi-member electoral districts. There is a complex three-stage system for distributing mandates: personal mandate, electoral list mandate, and compensation mandate. Seats unallocated based on Hare quotas on the district level are distributed at the national level according to a modified d'Hondt formula amongst parties receiving at least 5 per cent of the nationwide vote.

Estonia has six seats in the European Parliament. The elections take place in one national electoral district according to the principle of proportional representation and mandates are distributed according to the d'Hondt method. There has been an extensive debate over the use of open-list or closed-list proportional representation in EP elections, resulting in a series of amendments to the Estonian EP Election Act. Whilst all previous elections in Estonia, including the 2004 EP elections, have been open-list, the 2009 election was closed-list. The change from open- to closed-lists was criticized for increasing the influence of party backroom politics, whilst depriving citizens of a real choice amongst candidates. The reform became a prominent campaign issue and had far-reaching consequences for the results of the 2009 EP elections, contributing, in particular, to the unprecedented success of independent candidate Indrek Tarand. Dissatisfied with the results of the closed-list experiment, the major parties reinstituted open-lists shortly after the 2009 elections.

Estonia is a pioneer in e-voting and is the only country in the EU to allow internet voting in EP elections. The sophisticated internet-based voting system in which voters use government-issued ID cards fitted with computer chips has been used in national, local, and European elections since 2005. In the 2011 parliamentary elections, over 15 per cent of all eligible voters voted over the internet. The respective figure for the 2009 EP election was 6.5 per cent (Estonian National Electoral Committee, 2011).

8 A glance at the EP and national elections

Turnout in *Riigikogu* elections was 58.2 per cent in 2003, 61.9 per cent in 2007, and 63.0 per cent in 2011. In contrast, only 26.8 per cent of eligible voters went to the polls to choose their representatives in the EP election in 2004, whilst 43.9 per cent did so in 2009.

Whilst governing centre-right parties dominate national elections, they fare poorly in EP elections. In 2004, only one of the three governing parties, the Reform Party, won a seat in the European Parliament. By contrast, opposition parties and small parties performed well by obtaining the remaining five seats, as evident from the Centre Party's solid vote and the unprecedented success of the small Social Democratic Party.

Table 22.3 National election results in Estonia: 2007–2011

Party	Vote %		Seats	
	2007	2011	2007	2011
ER	27.8	28.6	31	33
K	26.1	23.3	28	26
IRL	17.9	20.5	19	23
SDE	10.6	17.1	10	19
EER	7.1	3.8	6	0
ERL	7.1	2.1	6	0

Source: Estonian National Electoral Committee, www.vvk.ee.

Table 22.4 EP election results in Estonia: 2004

Lists	Votes (%)	Seats
Sotsiaaldemokraatlik Erakond	36.8	3
Eersti Keskerakond	17.5	1
Eersti Reformierakond	12.2	1
Erakond Isamaaliit	10.5	1
Eestimaa Rahvaliit	8.0	0
Ühendus vabariigi Eest - Res Publica	6.7	0
Demokraadid - Eesti Demokraatlik Partei	1.2	0
Eesti Pensionäride Erakond	0.6	0
Eesti Sotsiaaldemokraatlik Tööpartei	0.5	0
Vene Erakond Eestis	0.3	0
Independents	5.7	0
Turnout	26.8%	

Source: Estonian National Electoral Committee, www.vvk.ee.

A third notable difference between national and European elections lies in the voters' proclivity to cast a personal vote in EP elections. In 2004, the top-ranked candidate in the list of the *Sotsiaaldemokraatlik Erakond*, Toomas Hendrik Ilves, former Foreign Minister and, since 2006 President of Estonia, won about one-third of all votes cast in the election.

9 The 2009 European election

9.1 Party lists and manifestos

One hundred and one individuals were registered as candidates for the 2009 EP contest. Eleven parties presented their electoral lists; six independent candidates also ran. The parties included the six parties represented in the national Parliament at the time. In addition, five lesser known extra-parliamentary groups contested the election. These included *Vene Erakond Eestis* (Russian Party in Estonia), *Põllumeeste Kogu* (Farmers' Assembly), *Eestimaa Ühendatud Vasakpartei* (United Left Party of Estonia), *Erakond Eesti Kristlikud Demokraadid* (Christian Democratic Party), and *Libertas Eesti* (Libertas Estonia). The six parties sitting in the *Riigikogu* fielded twelve candidates each – the maximum number allowed under the Estonian EP Elections Act – whilst extra-parliamentary parties presented between two and six candidates each. Most major parties held internal elections to draw up their electoral lists, although central party organs also had considerable say over the composition of the list (Ehin, 2009).

The lists of major parties were led by well-known politicians, such as Kristiina Ojuland, the vice-speaker of the *Riigikogu* and former Foreign Minister (Reform Party); Edgar Savisaar, the mayor of Tallinn (Centre Party); Tunne Kelam, an experienced MP and MEP (Pro Patria and Res Publica Union); Ivari Padar, a former minister of finance and leader of the Social Democrats; and Marek Strandberg, leader of the Green Party. The People's Union, in the process of reinventing itself following corruption scandals involving the party's old cadre, had listed a less well-known young politician, Ando Liivat, as their number one. Due to the fragmentation of the Estonian party system and the small number of Estonian MEPs, only the Reform Party and the Centre Party could hope to have more than one candidate elected (Sikk, 2009, 3); for most parties, all hopes focussed on the top-ranked candidate and the role of the other candidates was largely limited to embellishing the list.

The use of closed-list proportional representation encouraged the practice of including 'decoy ducks' in party lists. These were candidates with high vote-collecting potential but highly questionable intentions to become members of the EP, if elected. Edgar Savisaar, the top candidate of the Centre Party, was widely regarded as having no intention to take up a seat in the EP, which he did eventually refuse to do. Foreign Minister Urmas Paet, number two in the Reform Party's list, openly declared that he did not plan to go to Brussels but was just helping his party win votes. Whilst the enlisting of phantom candidates has been widely criticized as violating ethical standards and reducing the transparency of elections, decoy ducks continue to be routinely and unapologetically employed by the major Estonian parties in general, local, and European elections.

The independent candidates included Indrek Tarand, a former high-ranking civil servant and a popular television host; Martin Helme, an Estonian nationalist; Dimitri Klenski, a local Russian politician and an active critic of Estonia's minority policies; Yuri Zhuravlyov, a Russian rights activist; and two candidates largely unknown to the general public, Märt Õigus and Taira Aasa.

9.2 Electoral campaign

The intensity of campaigns was low. The use of closed-list PR appears to have reduced individual candidates' incentives to campaign, as only one or two top-ranked candidates in the party list stood a realistic chance of being elected. Campaigns were also rendered less visible by the ban on outdoor political advertising on streets, buildings, and public transportation during the active campaign period. The ban, enforced in 2005 with the objective of reducing campaign spending and forcing parties to focus more on 'substance', made the 2009 EP elections markedly different from the 2004 campaigns, which featured huge posters of the main candidates. Several candidates, including Tarand, successfully used internet-based communications such as blogging and YouTube to attract younger voters.

The campaign messages, to the extent that they had anything to do with the EU, were rather general. Almost no clearly identifiable focal points for political debate emerged. The campaign of the leading government party, the Reform Party, emphasized the party's EU-related competence, featuring advice from the Vice President of the European Commission Siim Kallas, a former leader of the party, and from three former and present Foreign Ministers included in the party list. The party platform emphasized rapid accession to the euro, opposition to EU-wide taxation, energy security, and the need to develop a common policy towards Russia. Notably, however, promises focussing on purely domestic matters, such as the pledge to retain generous parental benefits despite the economic crisis, received more airtime and media space than the party's visions of European integration.

The junior government partner, the Pro Patria and Res Publica Union, defended economic liberalism and fiscal conservatism, campaigning under the message 'Right decisions at a difficult time'. The platform emphasized the need to develop the single market, to retain open markets despite the economic crisis, rapid accession to the euro-zone, and the imperative of strengthening EU security and energy policies.

The Centre Party, the main opposition party, campaigned under the slogan 'Estonia needs change.' The campaign blamed the government for the economic crisis and social problems, zooming in on the hardships brought by the budget cuts. The Social Democratic Party focussed primarily on employment and social protection in the context of the economic crisis.

Whilst few observers initially paid much attention to the independent candidates, public opinion polls started to predict a mandate for Indrek Tarand a month before the elections. Tarand presented himself as a civil society candidate fighting against partocracy, determined to improve the quality of politics, and offering voters the opportunity to protest against the closed-list electoral system associated with self-serving behaviour and deal-making by political elites. Tarand had no real EU-related programme and no clear ideological position. With very limited funding, the campaign relied heavily on volunteer help, and was marked by bold and occasionally scandalous confrontations with the major political parties.

Two other independent candidates represented more extremist positions, but failed to translate these into high-visibility campaigns. The campaign of the nationalist Martin Helme was distinguished by opposition to various evils starting with the Lisbon Treaty and ending with homosexuality, immigration, and the alleged Islamization of Europe. Dimitri Klenski, charged with organizing the mass riots in Tallinn in April 2007, but declared not guilty in January 2009, took a strong stance against the Estonian state, which he described as an ethnocracy that could only be curbed with the help of various European institutions.

One of the controversies that received extensive media coverage during the week before election day concerned the erection of 20 campaign tents in Tallinn and other major cities by the Centre Party. The tents were equipped with computers and internet connections, and the party offered the opportunity to cast votes electronically during the period of advance voting. Whilst the erection of such tents did not explicitly breach electoral laws, the Electoral Committee condemned the practice, arguing that it created a fertile ground for possible violations, such as trying to influence voters or buying votes. To an extent, the concern was alleviated by the fact that the system of e-voting allows voters to replace votes cast over the internet, and to cancel an internet vote by casting a regular vote at the polling station on election day.

9.3 Electoral results

The elections were held on 7 June 2009, with advance voting taking place from 1 to 3 June. Three observations about the context of the 2009 EP elections are in order. First, the elections were genuine mid-term elections, taking place two years and three months after the national parliamentary elections were won by the pro-market Reform Party, which had formed a coalition with the centre-right Pro Patria and Res Publica Union (IRL) and the small Social Democratic Party (SDE). Second, the EP elections took place in the midst of a major economic crisis. Following a decade of high growth, the economy contracted by 15.8 per cent in the first half of 2009, and unemployment reached 14 per cent in the second quarter of 2009, up from 4.6 per cent in June 2008. Aspiring for inclusion in the euro-zone, the government had pushed through massive budget cuts to comply with the Maastricht criteria. Conflicts over the budget cuts culminated with the SDE leaving the three-member governing coalition in May 2009.

Problems with the web-based information system that was supposed to display votes in real time as they were coming in caused a delay in announcing the results on election night. The Centre Party initally appeared to have three mandates, and only with the last results coming in did it became clear that the Social Democrats had won enough votes to secure a mandate, leaving the Centre Party with two mandates.

This confusion, along with the small number of votes that separated the Centre Party from having three mandates, led to repeated requests for the recounting of votes and a close scrutiny of invalid ballots. In response to the request by the Centre Party, votes were recounted for the third time in eight out of 15 counties. The Centre Party also turned to the Estonian Supreme Court to dispute the decision of the Electoral Committee to consider as valid a few hundred ballots that did not have two stamps; according to the Estonian EP Election Act, ballots that have only one stamp are invalid. The Estonian Supreme Court abrogated three decisions of the Electoral Committee and declared 201 ballots to be invalid. Neither this decision nor the vote recount changed the distribution of mandates. Nevertheless, the Centre Party turned to the board of *Riigikogu* with a request to recall Heiki Sibul, Chairman of the National Electoral Committee, whom the party accused of failing to correctly and lawfully organize the European Parliament elections. This request was not backed by any other major political actor.

Estonia registered the greatest increase in voter turnout compared to the 2004 EP elections amongst all EU countries. Out of 909,628 eligible voters, 399,181 individuals cast their votes, yielding a turnout of 43.9 per cent (National Electoral Committee, 2009). In 2004, only 26.8 per cent of eligible voters had come to the polling booth. Turnout was highest in the capital city Tallinn with 54.1 per cent, the surrounding region, Harju county, with 48.4 per cent, and the north-east of the country, where Russian-speakers form the majority, with 46.1 per cent. Over the internet 58,669 people voted, corresponding to 6.5 per cent of eligible voters and 14.9 per

Table 22.5 EP election results in Estonia: 2009

Lists	Votes %	Seats
Eesti Keskerakond	26.1	2
Indrek Tarand (independent candidate)	25.8	1
Eesti Reformierakond	15.3	1
Isamaa ja Res Publica Liit	12.2	1
Sotsiaaldemokraatlik erakond	8.7	1
Erakond Eestimaa Rohelised	2.7	0
Martin Helme (independent candidate)	2.5	0
Eestimaa Rahvaliit	2.2	0
Dimitri Klenski (independent candidate)	1.8	0
Turnout	**43.9%**	

Source: Estonian National Electoral Committee, www.vvk.ee.

Note: Table includes parties and independent candidates receiving over 1% of the vote.

cent of all votes cast. Internet voting appears to have contributed significantly to the electoral turnout, reaching 45.4 per cent of all advance votes.

The six EP mandates were allocated between four parties and one independent candidate. The main opposition party, the Centre Party, gained the largest share of the vote of 26.1 per cent and secured two seats in the EP. The biggest surprise, however, was the unprecedented success of independent candidate Indrek Tarand, who won 25.8 per cent of the vote, only 1,046 fewer votes than the Centre Party and surpassing all other major and minor parties. Tarand gained the largest share of the vote in all 17 regions, 15 counties and two major cities, except Tallinn and Ida-Viru county, which have a high percentage of Russian speakers.

Such a spectacular performance by an independent candidate is unprecedented on many levels. First, the system used in Estonia in 2009 was closed-list proportional representation (PR), the type of electoral arrangement considered to be *least* conducive to the electoral strength of independents (Brancati, 2008). Second, to be elected to the European Parliament as an independent candidate is a rare accomplishment. Between 1999 and 2009, only eight individuals entered the EP as independents: five of them came from Ireland, which uses the single transferable vote system, and the two candidates elected from Romania, which used closed-list PR, had close ties to certain political parties. Tarand, in contrast, was a genuinely independent candidate who was not backed by any political party, significant interest group, or civil society organization. Third, Tarand's triumph is unique in the context of Estonia's electoral history, standing in sharp contrast to the negligible share of the vote (0.1 per cent) won by independents in the 2007 general election.

Political commentators unanimously attributed Tarand's victory to widespread anti-party sentiment amongst the electorate. However, a recent study that uses individual-level data from the European Elections Study to analyse the behaviour of Estonian voters suggests an alternative explanation. According to Piret Ehin and Mihkel Solvak (2012), voting for an independent candidate constituted a low-cost strategy for punishing the incumbents in a context where strong socio-political cleavages inhibited vote-switching to the opposition. The study shows that the majority of voters who voted for Tarand in 2009 had supported one of the government parties in the 2007 *Riigikogu* elections. This interpretation is entirely consistent with the Second-Order Election theory, according to which voters use secondary elections to punish or reward political incumbents.

Table 22.6 List of Estonian MEPs: seventh legislature

Name	National party	Political group	Professional background	Age in 2009	Gender	Committee
Siiri Oviir	Centre Party	ALDE	MEP since 2004; MP 1992–2004; Minister of Social Affairs in various governments; Member of Tallinn City Council 1996–2002	61	Female	Women's Rights and Gender Equality; Employment and Social Affairs
Vilja Savisaar	Centre Party	ALDE	MP 2003–2009, Municipal Politician in Tallinn	46	Female	Transport and Tourism
Indrek Tarand	Independent	Greens/EFA	Journalist; Secretary General of Ministry of Foreign Affairs 1994–2002	45	Male	Constitutional Affairs
Kristiina Ojuland	Reform Party	ALDE	Minister of Foreign Affairs 2002–2005; MP 1994–2002 and 2005–2009	42	Female	Foreign Affairs
Tunne-Väldo Kelam	Pro Patria and Res Publica Union	EPP	MEP since 2004; MP 1992–2004; Chairman of Estonian National Independence Party 1988–1995; Chairman of Pro Patria Union 2002–2005	72	Male	Foreign Affairs
Ivari Padar	Social Democratic Party	S&D	Minister of Finance 2007–2009; MP 2003–2007; Chairman of Social Democratic Party 2002–2009; Minister of Agriculture 1999–2002	44	Male	Economic and Monetary Affairs

Source: www.europarl.europa.eu/mep/it/search.html?country=EE.

The two parties of the governing coalition, the Reform Party and the Pro Patria and Res Publica Union, won 15.3 and 12.2 per cent of the vote, respectively, with one mandate each. The Social Democratic Party gained 8.7 per cent of the vote and one seat. The SDP's dramatic loss of vote share compared to the 2004 elections was expected; in 2004, the party's success was due to the extraordinary popularity of one candidate, the former Foreign Minister Toomas Hendrik Ilves. The two smaller parties represented in the *Riigikogu*, the Greens and the People's Union, remained without a mandate, receiving 2.7 and 2.2 per cent of the vote, respectively.

The six candidates elected to the European Parliament were Edgar Savisaar and Siiri Oviir (Centre Party), Indrek Tarand (independent candidate), Kristiina Ojuland (Reform Party), Tunne-Väldo Kelam (Pro Patria and Res Publica Union), and Ivari Padar (Social Democratic Party). As expected, Savisaar turned down the EP seat, passing it on to his wife, Vilja Savisaar, number three in the Centre Party's electoral list. Two of the elected members (Oviir and Kelam) had served as MEPs during the EP's previous term. Padar was also elected MEP in 2004 but he did not take up the seat in the Strasbourg arena.

9.4 Campaign finance

Under the Political Parties Act, the funding of political parties may consist of membership fees, allocations from the state budget, donations by natural persons, political party funds, and loans or credits. All of these sources of funding may be used to finance election campaigns. Independent candidates may also use donations from legal persons. In all cases, anonymous or concealed donations are prohibited. All parties that receive at least 1 per cent of the vote in general elections receive state funding. State funding to parliamentary parties is proportional to the number of seats in the *Riigikogu*. State subsidies to parties have increased consistently since the mid-1990s (Sikk, 2006), whilst significant restrictions on private financing have been introduced; notably, corporate donations were banned in 2004.

Overall, campaign spending in the 2009 EP elections was much lower than in the general elections in 2007. According to party declarations on campaign spending, the six parliamentary parties spent about 25 million kroons (€1.6 million) on EP elections, compared to 117.4 million kroons (€7.5 million) in *Riigikogu* elections. The Centre Party ran the most expensive campaign (9.5 million kroons, or about €607,000), whilst the two government parties spent over five million kroons each (€319,000). The Social Democrats spent two million kroons (€128,000), the Greens 1.8 million kroons (€115,000) and the People's Union 1.6 million kroons (€102,000) (Seaver, 2009). Tarand's campaign was by far the most cost-effective: his overall election-related spending amounted to a mere 50,000 kroons (about €3200).

10 Theoretical interpretation of Euro-elections

10.1 Second-Order Election theory

The results of EP elections in Estonia seem to corroborate most of the hypotheses associated with the Second-Order Election thesis (Reif and Schmitt, 1980). As predicted, turnout in Euro-elections, especially in 2004, was much lower than in national parliamentary elections. In addition, ruling parties were punished by voters. The leading government partner, the Reform Party, was the main loser, as its vote share dropped from 27.8 per cent in general elections to 15.3 per cent in EP elections. Another government party, the Pro Patria and Res Publica Union, also lost a significant share of the vote. The Social Democrats, a junior government partner that left the coalition shortly before the June 2009 election, suffered smaller losses, winning 8.7 per cent of the vote compared to 10.6 per cent in the general election.

However, the Estonian case deviates from the standard version of the Second-Order Election model in one important respect: the main winners were not opposition parties, large or small, but independent candidates. The main opposition party, Centre Party, repeated its election result from 2007. The smaller opposition parties, Greens, People's Union, actually lost votes. An impressive 30.4 per cent of the vote went to independent candidates, compared to 0.1 per cent in the 2007 general elections, whilst, in the 2004 EP contest, the independent candidates got 5.7 per cent of the vote. This peculiar pattern of voting behaviour could be explained by the effects of an increasingly polarized party system, where disappointed government voters find it difficult to switch to the opposition (Ehin and Solvak, 2012). Voting for an independent candidate allowed disenchanted government loyalists to punish the government without rewarding the opposition.

10.2 Europe Salience theory

The EP elections in Estonia offer very little empirical support to the alternative Europe Salience model (Hix and Marsh, 2007). There is no clear evidence that voters rewarded candidates with strong positions on Europe. Tarand's agenda focussed on domestic politics, and he expressed barely any views on European integration. Neither is there evidence of any significant success of Green, anti-European or extreme parties. As newcomers in the Estonian political arena, the Greens had established themselves in 2007, securing six seats in the *Riigikogu*. Attracting just 2.7 per cent of the vote in the EP election was a true disappointment. Eurosceptic movements appeared very weak and their campaigns were barely visible. The independent candidates with more extremist or anti-European views, such as Helme and Klenski, won 2.5 per cent and 1.8 per cent of the vote, respectively.

European integration and related issues, however, were clearly salient in 2004. Held one month after the EU's historic Eastern enlargement, in the wake of a series of high-publicity referenda on EU accession, the 2004 campaign focussed more on European issues and Estonia's position in Europe than on domestic politics, even if the debate on European matters was sometimes quite primitive (Sikk, 2009). In any case, the Estonian findings chime well with the results of comparative studies that have questioned the ability of the Second-Order Election model to explain the first EP contests in the post-Communist Member States (Koepke and Ringe, 2006; Hix and Marsh, 2007).

In a comparative perspective, Estonia's experience with EP elections lends considerable support to the familiar Second-Order Election model, whilst also suggesting that European issues can be central to EP campaigns when integration is politicized and public opinion divided. The dynamics of public and party-based Euroscepticism in Estonia challenges the conventional understanding that in forming positions on European integration, voters pick up cues from the parties. In Estonia, high levels of popular Euroscepticism preceded any significant party-based Euroscepticism. Parties began to cater to Eurosceptic voters in 2004, after a positive vote on the accession referendum had been secured and missed the mark because the public mood had already changed.

References

Primary sources

Ansip, A. (2008) Speech by Prime Minister Andrus Ansip on the Government's European Union policy in the *Riigikogu*, 9 December 2008: http://www.valitsus.ee (accessed on 5 October 2009).
Eesti Statistika: http://www.stat.ee (accessed on 12 February 2010).

Estonian National Electoral Committee (2011) 'Statistics about Internet Voting in Estonia': www.vvk.ee/voting-methods-in-estonia/engindex/statistics (accessed on 14 January 2012).
Estonian National Electoral Committee: www.vvk.ee (accessed on 1 February 2012).
European Commission (2009) Standard Eurobarometer 71, September 2009: http://ec.europa.eu/public_opinion/archives/eb/eb71/eb71_std_part1.pdf (accessed on 1 October 2009).
European Parliament Database (2010): www.europarl.europa.eu/meps/eu/search.html (accessed on 10 January 2015).
Eurostat (2013, 2014) http://epp.eurostat.ec.europa.eu (accessed on 5 June 2015).
Inter-parliamentary Union (2010) 'PARLINE Database on National Parliaments', www.ipu.org/english/home.htm (accessed on 4 April, 2010).
Ministry of the Interior, Population Register: www.siseministeerium.ee/35796/ (accessed on 15 January 2012).
Seaver, U. (2009) 'Keskerakonna eurokampaania oli ülivõimsalt kõige kallim.' *Postimees,* July 8, 2009.

Secondary sources

Berg, E. and Ehin, P. (eds) (2009) *Identity and Foreign Policy: Baltic–Russian Relations and European Integration,* Farnham, Ashgate.
Brancati, D. (2008) 'Winning Alone: The Electoral Fate of Independent Candidates Worldwide', *The Journal of Politics,* 7(3), 648–62.
Ehin, P. (2001) 'Determinants of Public Support for EU Membership: Data from the Baltic Countries', *European Journal of Political Research,* 40(1), 31–56.
Ehin, P. (2002) 'Estonian Euroscepticism: A Reflection of Domestic Politics?', *East European Constitutional Review,* 11/12(1), 96–100.
Ehin, P. (2009) 'Estonia', in Lehmann, W. (ed.) *The Selection of Candidates for the European Parliament by National Parties and the Impact of European Parties,* Brussels, Policy Department C – Citizens' Rights and Constitutional Affairs, European Parliament, 75 – 88. Online. Available at: http://www.europarl.europa.eu/studies (accessed on 1 March 2010).
Ehin, P. and Solvak, M. (2012) 'Party Voters Gone Astray: Explaining Independent Candidate Success in the 2009 European elections in Estonia', *Journal of Elections, Public Opinion and Parties,* 22(3), 269–91.
Hix, S. and Marsh, M. (2007) 'Punishment or Protest? Understanding European Parliament Elections', *The Journal of Politics,* 69(2), 495–510.
Ishiyama, J. (1996) 'Electoral Systems Experimentation in the New Eastern Europe: The Single Tranferable Vote and the Additional Member System in Estonia and Hungary', *East European Quarterly,* 29(4), 487–507.
Koepke, J. and Ringe, N. (2006) 'The Second Order Model in Enlarged Europe', *European Union Politics* 7(3), 321–46.
Lust, A. (2006) 'Westward Ho: Explaining *Estonian Euroscepticism,*' *Problems of Post-Communism,* 53(5),15–27.
Mikkel, E. and Kasekamp, A. (2008) 'Emerging Party-based Euroscepticism in Estonia', in Taggart, P. and Szczerbiak, A. (eds) *Opposing Europe: The Comparative Party Politics of Euroscepticism: Case Studies and Country Surveys,* Oxford, Oxford University Press, 295–313.
Pettai, V. (2005) '*Unfounded* Worries? Euroscepticism prior to the Referendum', in Pettai, V. and Ehin, P. (eds) *Deciding on Europe: The EU Referendum in Estonia,* Tartu, Tartu University Press, 24–38.
Reif, K. H. and Schmitt, H. (1980) 'Nine Second-Order National Elections: A Conceptual Framework for the Analysis of European Election Results', *European Journal of Political Research,* 8(1), 3–44.
Rose, R. and Munro, N. (2009) *Parties and Elections in New European Democracies,* Colchester, ECPR Press.
Sikk, A. (2006) 'From Private Organizations to Democratic Infrastructure: Political Parties and the State in Estonia,' *Journal of Communist Studies and Transition Politics,* 22(3), 341–61.
Sikk, A. (2009) 'The 2009 European Elections in Estonia', *European Parliament Election Briefing* 41, European Parties Elections and Referendums Network. Online. Available at: www.sussex.ac.uk/sei/1-4-2-2.html (accessed on 1 October 2009).
Tigasson, K.-R. (2009) 'Strategic Miscalculations: Election Campaigns to the European Parliament in Estonia 2004', *Journal of Political Marketing* 8(1), 46–58.
Vetik, R., Nimmerfelt, G. and Taru, M. (2006) 'Reactive Identity versus EU Integration', *Journal of Common Market Studies,* 44(5), 1079–1102.

23
LATVIA

Jānis Ikstens

Figure 23.1 Map of Latvia

Table 23.1 Latvia profile

EU entry year	2004
Schengen entry year	2007
MEPs elected in 2009	8
MEPs under Lisbon Treaty	9 since 1 December 2011
	One additional seat allocated to Karlis Sadurskis (EPP)
Capital	Rīga
Total area★	64,573 km²
Population	2,001,468
	59.3% Latvians; 27.8% Russians; 3.6% Belarussians 2.5%; Ukrainians; 6.8% others
Population density★★	32.4/km²
Median age of population	42.4
Political system	Parliamentary Republic
Head of state	Valdis Zatlers, Independent (July 2007–July 2011);
	Andris Bērziņš, Union of Greens and Farmers (ZZS) (July 2011–)
Head of government	Valdis Dombrovskis, New Era (JL) (March 2009–November 2010);
	Valdis Dombrovskis, Unity (V) (November 2010–January 2014);
	Laimdota Straujuma, Unity (V) (January 2014–)
Political majority	New Era (JL), Civic Union (PS), Society for Different Politics (SCP), People's Party (PT), Union of Greens and Farmers (ZZS), 'For Fatherland and Freedom' (TB)/Latvinian National Independent Movement (LNNK) Government Coalition (March 2009–November 2010);
	Unity (V), Union of Greens and Farmers (ZZS) Government Coalition (November 2010–October 2011);
	Unity (V), National Union (NA), Reform Party (RP) Government Coalition (October 2011– January 2014);
	Unity (V), National Union (NA), Reform Party (RP), Union of Greens and Farmers (ZZS) Government Coalition (January 2014–)
Currency	Previously Lats
	Euro (€) since January 2014
Prohead GDP in PPS	12,100 €

Source: Eurostat, 2013, 2014, http://epp.eurostat.ec.europa.eu/.

Notes:
★ Total area including inland waters.
★★ Population density: the ratio of the annual average population of a region to the land area of the region.

1 Geographical position

Latvia is located on the eastern rim of the Baltic Sea, bordering Estonia in the north and Lithuania in the south. The country also shares a once-disputed border with the Russian Federation and has a direct border with Belarus. Latvia has two major ice-free harbours that make it an attractive centre of logistics. The rate of urbanization in 2009 reached 67.8 per cent of the population.

2 Historical backgroud

The Republic of Latvia was established on 18 November 1918 in the territory of several provinces of the Russian Empire inhabited primarily by ethnic Latvians. The country's constitution, patterned after the Weimar Constitution, provided for universal suffrage and a parliamentary system. During WWI, the Latvian industrial sector was heavily hit and most of its equipment was transported to the inner regions of Russia. As a result, Latvia became a flourishing agrarian country. The Great Depression, along with a lack of democratic experience amongst voters, could be seen as the cause of the breakdown of democracy in Latvia in 1934. The Soviet occupation in 1940 began an extensive process of the physical extinction of Latvia's population that resulted in profound changes in the ethnic composition of Latvia and Latvians becoming a near-minority by the 1980s. As a result of WWII and targeted policies of the Soviet regime, the share of ethnic Latvians fell from 77 per cent in 1935 to 52 per cent in 1989. According to the Central Statistical Bureau of Latvia, ethnic Latvians constituted 59.2 per cent of Latvia's population whilst Eastern Slavs, including Russians, Belarusians, and Ukrainians, made up 33.9 per cent in 2009.

3 Geopolitical profile

Latvia regained its independence as a consequence of the collapse of the USSR in August 1991. The traumatic experience of Soviet occupation turned Latvia into a committed Western ally, aiming at full membership of the European Union and NATO. Both of these goals were achieved in 2004 after complex accession processes.

The withdrawal of ex-Soviet troops from Latvian soil in the first part of the 1990s was greatly facilitated by transatlantic partners. This may have contributed to the formation of a rather special relationship between the three Baltic countries and the United States, as expressed in the US-Baltic Charter signed by the Presidents of all four countries in January 1998. Furthermore, a seeming lack of internal cohesion in the EU's policy towards Russia further prompted Latvia to turn to the US for political support, since some West European countries were forging bilateral ties with Latvia's natural resource-rich neighbour.

4 Overview of the political landscape

Latvia based its struggle for independence on the principle of the legal continuity of the former republic. This approach was crucial in adopting a parliamentary system that closely resembled the institutional arrangements before the 1934 coup.

The *Saeima*, a unicameral Parliament, is solely entrusted with law-making, whilst the cabinet depends on the confidence of the Parliament. The President and all judges are chosen by the Parliament. Although the *Saeima*'s role as a law-making body has been notably diminishing, its powers of appointment make it a key political institution (Ikstens, 2008). Consequently, parliamentary elections are regarded as the most important political event during the four-year electoral cycle. Parliamentary elections are based on a party list proportional representation system. In order to prevent party proliferation, as had occurred prior to the 1934 coup, a 5 per cent electoral threshold was introduced from 1995. This has helped to reduce the number of political parties represented in the Parliament after the restoration of independence.

As of 1 October 2009, 51 political parties were officially registered, and at least 14 of them have an explicit local or regional orientation. However, only seven slates overcame the electoral threshold in the 2006 parliamentary elections. The number of relevant parties in the Parliament has oscillated between five and seven over the years.

To simplify, national parties can be placed in a two-dimensional space where the first axis of competition is related to ethnic matters, Latvians versus Eastern Slavs, and the second is linked to socio-economic issues. The former dimension grew out of the pro-/anti-independence stances of political organizations in the late 1980s and early 1990s and notably altered the ethnic structure of Latvia's population during the 50 years of Soviet occupation. The latter developed later, partly in response to hardships caused by the social and economic transition from a Soviet-style planned economy. However, linkages between parties and their supporters remained underdeveloped as bright promises by strong leaders became the cornerstone of capital-intensive election campaigns to mobilize the support of increasingly disillusioned voters who maintained openness towards new entrants into the political arena despite several spectacular failures by newcomers. Moreover, corruption, vote buying, and flagrant violations of campaign regulations led to further alienation between parties and citizens that culminated in 2007–2008 when public trust in political parties slipped into single digits and public participation in demonstrations and pickets grew palpably.

In view of both Latvia's constitutional traditions and the legal requirements for holding elections to the European Parliament (EP), a party list proportional system was introduced ahead of the 2004 EP elections, and the whole country was defined as a single electoral district. Also, the 5 per cent electoral threshold and the principle of changeable candidate lists were retained. Only registered political parties or associations thereof are allowed to field candidates. Each voter has the right to cross out any number of candidates of his preferred list or put a '+' next to the name of any candidate on his preferred list. However, a voter may not write in a candidate from a another list. Hence, voters have a profound influence over the final sequence of candidates and the composition of the elected candidates.

Each candidate hast to be at least 21 years of age on the day of EP elections. Parties have to comply with campaign spending limits that were substantially increased before the 2009 elections to reach nearly €200,000 per registered list of candidates.

5 Brief account of the political parties

At its time of establishment, a well-defined Latvian nation did not exist in the Republic of Latvia. Its population consisted of a majority of ethnic Latvians and a diversity of ethnic minorities, comprising about a quarter of local residents. A liberal citizenship law did not exclude any significant groups from the body politic, and this could be seen in the composition of the fractured Parliament. Up to 25 parties at a time had been represented in the 100-seat *Saeima* in the inter-war period, with numerous parties holding just one or two mandates. Coalition-building in those circumstances was notably challenging, despite the fact that this wealth of parties tended to cluster into five major groups: agrarian parties; Social Democratic and Communist parties; religious parties; Liberal centrist groups; and parties of ethnic minorities. The latter, holding around 20 per cent of *Saeima* seats, were not welcome coalition partners and their coalition potential was low. It is often asserted that parliamentary fragmentation between the two World

Table 23.2 Number of slates and parties at national elections in Latvia: 2002–2010

	National parliament: 2002–2006	*National parliament: 2006– 2010*
Slates	6	7
Parties	9	11

Source: Central Election Commission of Latvia, 2006; Šilde, 1982.

Table 23.3 List of political parties in Latvia

Original name	Abbreviation	English translation
Vienotība	V	Unity
Nacionālā apvienība	NA	National Union
Reformu partija	RP	Reform Party
Latvijas ceļš	LC	Latvia's Way
Latvijas Pirmā partija	LPP	First Party of Latvia
Jaunā partija	JP	New Party
Kristīgo demokrātu savienība	KDS	Christian Democratic Union
Latvijas Zemnieku savienība	LZS	Farmers' Union of Latvia
Latvijas Zaļā partija	LZP	Green Party of Latvia
Zaļo un zemnieku savienība	ZZS	Union of Greens and Farmers
Latvijai un Ventspilij	LuV	For Latvia and Ventspils
Latvijas Nacionālās neatkarības kustība	LNNK	Latvian National Independence Movement
'Tēvzemei un Brīvībai'	TB	'For Fatherland and Freedom'
'Visu Latvijai!'	VL	'All for Latvia!'
'Saskaņa Latvijai, atdzimšana tautsaimniecībai'	SLAT	'Concord for Latvia, Rebirth for Economy'
Tautas saskaņas partija	TSP	National Harmony Party
Latvijas Sociālistiskā partija	LSP	Socialist Party of Latvia
Līdztiesība	L	Equal Rights
Demokrātiskā centra partija	DCP	Democratic Centre Party
Demokrātiskā partija 'Saimnieks'	DPS	Democratic Party 'Master'
Tautas kustība 'Latvijai'	TKL	Popular Movement 'For Latvia'
Latvijas Vienības partija	LVP	Unity Party of Latvia
Tautas partija	TP	People's Party
Latvijas Sociāldemokrātiskā strādnieku partija	LSDSP	Social Democratic Workers' Party of Latvia
'Jaunais laiks'	JL	'New Era'
Pilsoniskā savienība	PS	Civic Union
'Sabiedrība citai politikai'	SCP	Society for Different Politics
'Saskaņas centrs'	SC	Harmony Centre
'Par cilvēka tiesībām vienotā Latvijā'	PCTVL	'For Human Rights in United Latvia'
'Par Dzimteni!'	PDz	'For Motherland!'
Osipova partija	OP	Osipov Party
Latvijas Atdzimšanas partija	LAP	Latvia's Rebirth Party

Wars caused short-lived governments and ultimately led to the breakdown of democracy in 1934 (Misiunas and Taagepera, 1993).

A competitive multiparty environment began to re-emerge in Latvia in 1988 as a consequence of Soviet liberalization policies. In particular, the *glasnost* policy facilitated the ascendance of the national independence issue to the top of the political agenda in Latvia. This issue swiftly divided Latvia's population into two large groups, protagonists and antagonists of independence, that gave rise to two corresponding blocs of political organizations. After the failed *coup d'état* in August 1991, this line of division transformed into an ethnic cleavage separating ethnic Latvians and representatives of Eastern Slavic minorities, Russians, Ukrainians, and Belarusians. Parties such as the National Harmony Party and the Equal Rights movement became the most prominent advocates of Slavic interests, whilst a myriad of parties claimed to represent ethnic Latvians.

Socio-economic issues rose to prominence in the mid-1990s. Whilst Slavic parties tended to profess left-of-centre values, Latvian parties offered a wide variety of economic outlooks ranging from neo-liberal platforms rooted in the so-called Washington consensus ('Latvia's Way'), to old-fashioned Social Democratic programmes (Social Democratic Workers' Party of Latvia), and populist exclamations (Siegerist Party, Unity Party). Regardless of economic problems, the socio-economic cleavage has not been as decisive in structuring voter preferences as the ethnic cleavage.

Despite a clearly pronounced cleavage structure and a 5 per cent electoral threshold, the turnover of political parties at the parliamentary level has been high. No less than a third of deputies and no less than a quarter of factions have failed to re-elect. This is likely to be related to weak linkages between parties and voters as well as high and unfulfilled expectations of economic prosperity amongst voters.

A more restrictive electoral system, introduced in 1993, has helped to reduce the number of political parties represented in the *Saeima*. It also has decisively contributed to the creation of pre-election alliances consisting of several smaller parties that otherwise would have little chance of clearing the electoral threshold.

6 Public opinion and the European Union

Although Latvia's citizens strongly supported the country's admission to the European Union in the 2003 referendum, Latvia has been one of the most Eurosceptic nations. According to Eurobarometer 71 (June 2009), only 25 per cent of Latvia's citizens called the country's membership in the European Union a good thing.

The above diagram demonstrates that an above-average amount of scepticism has been rather consistent through the years. The demographic groups that have more positive feelings about Latvia's EU membership since the early 2000s include younger people, particularly those up to 25 years old, people with a higher level of formal education, and people with higher incomes. However, it is important to note a change of mood amongst the two largest ethno-linguistic groups. Whilst Latvians displayed a more sceptical attitude towards the EU up until the latter part of the 1990s, their perception of EU membership gradually became more positive as the accession process progressed. However, the Eastern Slavs lost their initial enthusiasm about EU membership and their older and lesser-educated segments now constitute strongholds of Euroscepticism in Latvia's society. Although the Russian-language media's discourse may have contributed to the attitudinal change, no methodologically sound studies of this factor have been made public. On the other hand, ethnic Latvian concerns about the fate of their culture and identity may have receded in face of the growing international influence of Russia and the resultant concerns about the security of the country.

Whilst Latvia's membership in the European Union is decreasingly frequently seen as a good thing, the public's trust in EU institutions is higher than that in domestic institutions of government. Particularly devastating are trends of trust in political parties; the share of people trusting parties has been in the single-digit range since 2007. Similarly, trust in the national Parliament and the cabinet of ministers has fallen from 18 per cent and 20 per cent, respectively, in spring 2007, to a mere 6 per cent and 10 per cent, respectively, in summer 2009. However, trust in the less well-known European institutions is higher. In spring 2007, 47 per cent of respondents said they trusted the European Union, 43 per cent trusted the European Parliament, and 42 per cent trusted the European Commission. In summer 2009, these figures had slightly

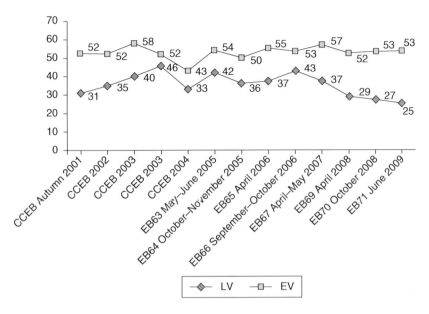

Figure 23.2 Latvian attitude to the European Union*

Source: Eurobarometer, 2001–2009, http://ec.europa.eu/public_opinion/archives/eb_arch_en.htm.

Notes:
* Positive attitude towards EU membership, %
[1] CCEB = Candidate Countries Eurobarometer.
[2] Question used in CCEB was 'Do you think EU membership will be a good/bad/neither good nor bad thing for your country?'
[3] For CCEB, EU average refers to the average in the 10 candidate countries only.
[4] Question used in EB was 'Do you think EU membership is a good/bad/neither good nor bad thing for your country?'
[5] For EB63 through EB 66, EU average refers to the average in 25 EU Member States.
[6] For EB67 through EB71, average refers to the average in 27 EU Member States.

receded to reach 44 per cent for the EU, 40 per cent for the EP, and 35 per cent for the EC (Standard Eurobarometer 67, 71).

Despite the sceptical attitude of the general public towards the European Union, party elites have been more positive about the EU and also internally more united on this issue. Regardless of cabinet composition throughout the 1990s and 2000s, government commitment to joining the EU remained firm. Although there existed pronounced differences between 'Latvian' parties and political organizations claiming to advocate the interests of Eastern Slavs on the eve of accession, those have somehow weakened and lost topicality. Only marginal political groups profess outright Euroscepticism, and they cannot be considered important by any measure. The ratification of the Lisbon Treaty by the *Saeima* was not accompanied by any significant public debate or discussions within the Parliament, which not only reflects a degree of elite cohesion but also the significance of EU-related issues in Latvian politics.

7 National and EP electoral systems

Article 6 of the Latvian Constitution stipulates that 'the *Saeima* shall be elected in general, equal and direct elections, and by secret ballot based on proportional representation'. Following this, the 1922 *Saeima* election law did not envisage any thresholds, nor did it provide any other formal hurdles to marginal political organizations. Although a refundable security deposit of 1,000 lats for each candidate slate was introduced in 1925, the number of political organizations represented in the *Saeima* decreased only gradually.

Fearing a highly fractured Parliament, the 1992 law on elections to the fifth *Saeima* was considerably more resolute, as an electoral threshold of 4 per cent of all votes was introduced. Further, a security deposit in the amount of 50 minimum wages for each registered candidate slate was to be paid to the account of the Latvian Central Election Commission. The electoral threshold was deemed insufficient in 1995 when the *Saeima* raised it to 5 per cent. The security deposit was set at 1,000 lats (about €1,500) per slate per district.

A number of marginal politicians claimed that Article 6 of the *Satversme* does not provide for any proportionality restrictions and that there were no thresholds before the breakdown of democracy in 1934 was dismissed by the Latvian Constitutional Court, stressing that electoral thresholds exist in many countries and this measure has a legitimate aim: the creation of a stable, functioning executive (*Satversmes tiesa*, 2002).

The 1922 Legislative Election Law offered a particular version of flexible party lists. Any voter was entitled to cross out any number of candidates on his favourite slate and add a corresponding number of candidates from other slates registered in the respective electoral district. This option was increasingly popular, as 20 per cent of all voters in 1922 used it, but this figure rose to 35.5 per cent in 1931 (Šilde, 1976).

The post-1991 election laws reduced the degree of flexibility but retained the opportunity for voters to indicate their personal preferences by crossing out any number of candidates on their preferred slates or giving a 'plus' to their favourites on the same slate. This has caused modest intra-party competition and individual campaigning. However, a majority of Latvia's citizens seem to underestimate the power of this system and maintain that the current electoral system should be replaced by one that provides a closer link between the voters and the elected and fosters accountability amongst parties and individual deputies. A March 2006 opinion poll showed that only 26 per cent of Latvian residents were satisfied with the current electoral system. Moreover, 37 per cent of respondents favoured a first-past-the-post system, and another 15 per cent preferred a mixed system.

Another modification aimed at electoral consolidation was related to people eligible to submit candidate slates. The 1922 election law was notably liberal and admitted any group of citizens that could provide signatures of at least 100 adult Latvian citizens along with the list of candidates. The 1992 election law retained the aforementioned liberal approach but the 1995 election law stringently provided that only registered political parties or associations thereof could submit candidate slates. An extension of the parliamentary term from three years to four years in 1997 was also seen as a move to stabilize the government.

Only adult citizens of Latvia are eligible to vote in national, municipal, or European elections. There are more restrictions for people wishing to run for an elected office. Former KGB officers, as well as people active in the Communist Party after 13 January 1991, are barred from contesting elections (Ikstens, 2008).

The Latvian Parliament notably amended the existing voting procedures to address issues related to electing Members of the European Parliament. The *Saeima* passed not only a separate law on elections to the EP, but also a law on the voter registration (VR) list and revised legislation that regulates party and campaign finance. A citizen of an EU country must be at least 18 years old to be eligible to vote and at least 21 years old to run for the European Parliament in Latvia. The *Saeima* allowed former KGB officers and people active in the Communist Party of the Soviet Union after 13 January 1991 to run in the EP elections, although they are still excluded from running in parliamentary or municipal elections. Furthermore, a citizen must be included in the voter registration list, following a set procedure, in order to be able to vote. This new register was set up for the first time to comply with 93/109/EC and enable citizens of other EU member countries to vote in Latvia. The VR is based on data compiled in the register of residents, which, in turn, aggregates information about the official place of residence of a citizen that does not necessarily match with the actual place of residence. As a consequence of this innovation, citizens had to go to a certain polling station to vote, in sharp contrast to the previous practice of walking into any polling station across the country. However, advance voting is possible, as is changing one's affiliation with a particular polling station.

Only officially registered political organizations or associations thereof have the right to submit lists of candidates for EP elections. The Latvian Central Election Commission (CEC) registers only those lists of candidates, submitters of which have transferred a deposit of 1,000 lats (about €1,500 Euros) to the CEC.

The elections are held under a proportional system and the whole country constitutes one district. Only those lists that have gained the support of at least 5 per cent of votes cast are eligible to obtain EP seats. The number of seats is calculated employing the Saint-Lague method. As the system of flexible candidate lists is used in Latvia, the list of deputies actually elected to the EP is finalized after the '+' and '–' given to each candidate by voters are counted. Parties have to comply with certain campaign spending limits and reporting requirements.

8 A glance at the EP and national elections

The 2006 parliamentary elections were the first national elections held after Latvia's accession to the European Union. Compared to the 2002 elections, the turnout dropped more than ten percentage points to reach 61 per cent. The sharp decrease was seen not only as a sign of disillusionment with party politics, but also as a consequence of economic emigration from Latvia after it became a member of the European Union; voter turnout outside Latvia was mere 22.4 per cent.

Activities associated with election campaigning started early, as some steps taken by the governing coalition in the autumn of 2005 could be regarded as electioneering. The first campaign ads were placed on the web as early as April. The main issues of the 2006 campaign were inflation and emigration from Latvia. Both received substantial media coverage and analysis, whilst parties contributed to the discussion in a modest way. Any noteworthy references to EU-wide issues were absent from the campaigns.

Most party energy seemed to have gone into advertising. The 2006 campaign saw a substantial use of third-party advertising on behalf of the People's Party and the alliance between the First Party of Latvia and 'Latvia's Way'. This innovation appears to have been closely linked to the introduction of campaign spending limits. A rather skilful negative campaign was launched against Avers Limbers, the powerful mayor of Ventspils, whose party *Latvijai un Ventspilij* allied with the Union of Farmers and Greens (ZZS) and who was the ZZS candidate to the Prime Minister's position. Heavy advertising aided the People's Party in winning the elections and helped the alliance between the First Party of Latvia and 'Latvia's Way' to gain ten seats in the *Saeima*. Russian-language television bias is believed to have helped the 'Harmony Centre' to gain the upper hand in its rivalry with the 'For Human Rights in United Latvia' bloc, a once-powerful umbrella organization of Eastern Slavic political parties.

These characteristics run in contrast to the 2009 EP campaign, where fairly limited funding was used and the campaign itself was rather peaceful and uneventful. However, the focus on domestic issues draws the two elections together.

Table 23.4 National Parliament election results in Latvia: 2002–2006

Political party	2002		2006	
	Seats	Vote %	Seats	Vote %
LC	0	4.9	10	8.6
LPP	10	9.5		
JP	—	—	—	—
KDS	—	—	—	—
LZS	12	9.4	18	16.7
LZP				
LNNK	7	5.4	8	7.0
TB				
SLAT	—	—	—	—
TSP			17	14.4
LSP	25	19.0		
L			6	6
DCP	—	—	—	—
DPS	—	—	—	—
TKL	—	—	—	—
LVP	—	—	—	—
TP	20	16.6	23	19.6
LSDSP	0	4.0	0	3.5
JL	26	23.9	18	16.4
Others	0	7.3	0	7.8
Total	100	100.0	100	100.0

Source: Central Election Commission, www.cvk.lv.

Table 23.5 Turnout in national elections in Latvia: 2002–2006

	2002	2006
Number of votes cast	997,754	901,173
Share of valid votes as % of total eligible population	71.5	62.2

Source: Central Election Commission, www.cvk.lv.

9 The 2009 European elections

European Parliament elections in Latvia were held on Saturday, 6 June 2009, concurrently with the local elections to choose representatives of the newly created municipalities. Seventeen slates were submitted and registered for the elections by the CEC to compete for eight EP mandates. Should the Lisbon Treaty be ratified, Latvia's representation in the EP would be extended to nine deputies. As these elections were held concurrently with the municipal elections, the turnout was considerably higher than in 2004 and reached 53.7 per cent of registered voters, compared to 53.8 per cent of registered voters in municipal elections, and 41.3 per cent in the 2004 EP elections. According to the official CEC data, turnout in the EP elections tended to be higher in and around major urban centres. This is a reverse trend from the 2004 elections, when turnout tended to be higher outside major urban centres, apart from the capital city of Rīga, where the turnout level was slightly above 44 per cent, signalling a slightly higher share of ethnic Latvians turning out to vote in 2004.

9.1 Party lists and manifestos

All major parties and a number of junior challengers fielded their candidate lists, offering voters a rather wide choice. Four parties quite openly targeted Eastern Slavic voters: 'Harmony Centre', 'For Human Rights in United Latvia' (FHRUL), the Osipov Party, and 'For the Motherland!' Of the four, only FHRUL had an incumbent representative in the European Parliament – Tatyana Zhdanok. The cornerstone of the FHRUL platform was the protection and further expansion of the rights of ethnic minorities, with a particular emphasis on the consolidation of the Russian diaspora in Europe which, according to the platform, was notably furthered by Zhdanok by means of creating the EU Russian-speakers Alliance. The party promised to continue its activities aimed at 'informing residents of other countries about the Russian minority in Latvia' (FHRUL, 2009). The party also set the goal of granting Latvia's non-citizens voting rights in municipal and European Parliament elections as well as the same legal requirements for employment in another EU Member State. The party pledged loyalty to the European Free Alliance and a plethora of minority organizations. It also advocated the deepening of EU integration by launching a transfer of welfare and education policies to Brussels. FHRUL also called for closer cooperation with Russia by means of setting up a joint Nordic-Russian energy market and establishing a visa-free travel regime between Russia and the EU.

The Osipov party, named after its leader, is at times seen as an extremist fringe competitor to FHRUL. This political organization tried to ride the wave generated by the deepening economic crisis by blaming both Latvia's political establishment and the EU bureaucracy for the country's problems. The party positioned itself as populist and clearly against the EU when calling for compensation for the economic and humanitarian losses suffered by Latvia during the process of EU accession. Similar to the FHRUL, the Osipov party advocated the interests of Eastern Slavic minorities and Latvia's non-citizens but went further by promising to do 'everything possible' to grant the Russian language the status of an official language in Latvia.

An even stronger strain of Eastern Slavic populism can be detected in the electoral platform of the 'For the Motherland!' party. Not only it was its platform as brief and pro-Slavic as the Osipov party, but it also promised to get the European Parliament to pass a resolution urging Latvia to grant citizenship unconditionally to all non-citizens within a three-year time frame. 'For the Motherland!' also pledged to support petitioners against Latvia in the European Court of Human Rights. Moreover, it opposed US military ambitions in Europe and the deployment of US missile shield components in Poland and the Czech Republic.

The 'Harmony Centre' (HC) party emerged as the most moderate of the four and the one that placed the highest premium on social welfare issues. Although the HC noted in its platform the eradication of all kinds of discrimination and the adoption of a binding EU-wide document on minority rights and linguistic pluralism along with granting Latvia's non-citizens voting rights in the municipal and European Parliament elections, its main focus was the strengthening of the EU's social dimension. In particular, the HC endorsed the EU-wide regulation of the minimum wage, pensions and social benefits, access to health care, and housing. This party also supported increased government regulation of the global financial markets in view of the world financial crisis. Like some of its Slavic competitors, it endorsed deeper EU integration.

The other 13 parties were not explicitly pro-Slavic and appeared to be more geared towards the ethnic Latvian vote. The right-of-centre 'New Era' party, that had become part of the governing coalition a few months before the elections and held the post of Prime Minister, fought to retain its two-deputy EP representation by offering a rather conventional platform: the accelerated economic development of Latvia by means of lower taxes and more generous EU funding for projects in Latvia. It also promised to work towards the equalization of farm subsidies between new and Old Member States and the levelling out of health care standards throughout the Union. This party advocated a joint EU energy policy aimed at increasing energy efficiency and decreasing the EU's dependence on Russian energy supplies. That coupled well with the party's stated concern for the environment and further development of a knowledge-based society.

The main rival of the 'New Era' party on the domestic political scene and its main coalition partner, the People's Party, spoke of a crisis of values and offered a package of what it recognized as Conservative values: liberty, family, solidarity amongst states, and Latvian national identity. The operationalization of these values led to something familiar: more generous EU funding, the equalization of farm subsidies, the diversification of energy supplies, and energy efficiency. However, the People's Party also emphasized stricter rules for immigration and paid more attention to measures aimed at strengthening Latvian national identity amidst the processes of globalization and Europeanization.

Another participant in the ruling coalition, the 'For Fatherland and Freedom'/LNNK union (FF/LNNK), has had a long-standing image as the most Nationalist party amongst mainstream political organizations, and it postulated the country's economic and social development as subordinated to the overall goal of protecting and strengthening Latvian national identity. It reanimated softly protectionist slogans, but heavily criticized protectionist attempts by Old Member States. The standard promises of diversification of energy sources and a swifter influx of EU funding into Latvia's economy were coupled with a rejection of the EU's federalization and the granting any voting rights to Latvia's non-citizens.

Yet, the FF/LNNK might have lost its trademark issue of fighting the consequences of Latvia's occupation to the Civic Union (CU), established by politicians who split away from the FF/LNNK and 'New Era' in early 2008. Ģirts Valdis Kristovskis and Inese Vaidere, who were at the helm of anti-occupation activities in the EP, became core members of the CU. Although the CU did emphasize the occupation issue, it also fielded the standard slogans on the diversification of energy resources, more generous EU funding, the equalization of farm subsidies, and the de-bureaucratization of the EU. However, it highlighted the need for fair competition and free markets, but stricter regulation of financial markets, the implementation of an EU Baltic Sea Region strategy, turning Rīga into *the* centre of the Baltic region, and a strong transatlantic partnership.

The 'Everything for Latvia!' party, small but youthful and quite visible on the web, consolidated the occupation issue as its *raison d'être,* but somewhat lacked the sophistication of the FF/LNNK and the CU; it oscillated between legalistic and normative statements about the obligations of Russia and EU Member States with regard to addressing the consequences of Soviet occupation. It endorsed protectionism and a tougher immigration policy, but objected to a federal EU and the Lisbon Treaty.

However, the most pronounced anti-European view was manifested in the platform of the Party of Action, a political reincarnation of 'Eurosceptics' party that suffered a miserable defeat at the polls in 2004. It heavily and extensively criticized the terms of Latvia's accession to the EU, as well as the feeble defence of Latvia's national interests in Brussels, but offered nothing more than autarchic policies that would somehow lead to the development of knowledge-intensive industry in Latvia.

An association of minor parties under the joint name of Libertas.lv and led by incumbent MEP Guntars Krasts voiced a more sophisticated Euroscepticism drawing on the Libertas platform and criticizing Brussels for excessive bureaucracy and lack of transparency and accountability. It pledged to remove obstacles to the free market and entrepreneurship within the EU and echoed familiar themes about a joint EU energy policy and the equalization of farm subsidies.

The Union of Greens and Farmers lacked innovation and spoke diplomatically about the equalization of farm subsidies, but explicitly criticized the gradual disappearance of local farm produce from the shelves of the country's grocery stores. It also called for a sustainable energy policy co-financed by EU funds, refused deeper EU integration, and showed concern for the ethnic identity of Latvians.

The union of the First Party of Latvia and 'Latvia's Way' offered a mix of strong pro-business slogans, such as an increase in export subsidies, the introduction of the euro as of 2012, the opening of labour markets in all EU countries by 2012, and an increase in emission quotas, with Conservative social values, such as family and religion, along with the standard issue of a joint energy policy.

The Social Democratic Workers' Party of Latvia drew partly on the platform of the European Socialists and called for the equalization of social welfare standards, stronger control over global financial markets, and further investment in the education system. This party also supported a joint EU foreign policy and aid to EU-aspirant countries in Eastern Europe.

The 'Society for Different Politics', which claimed to be a Social Liberal party and which was perceived as a direct competitor to the Social Democrats, spoke of solidarity and participation in EU decision-making as key to serving Latvia's national interests best. It emphasized a pro-active employment policy financed by Brussels and a reconsideration of the Lisbon strategy, along with the swift introduction of the euro in Latvia.

9.2 Electoral campaign

Elections were held in the middle of one of the deepest economic crises since Latvia regained its independence in 1991. Moreover, international organizations such as the IMF and the EU played a major role in the management of the crisis by means of requiring substantial public spending cuts and structural reforms in education and health care in return for loans totalling €7 billion. Whilst it should have been clear to voters that spending would be cut and their welfare would be affected, concrete proposals for severe wage reductions and the first round of spending cuts exceeding €700 million that had been negotiated with the above international actors were unveiled only after the elections in an obvious attempt to avoid major unrest on the eve of the two elections. However, in a conversation with the author 11 October 2011, the Prime Minister's spokesperson denied any intention of managing the electoral cycle and emphasized the desire of Prime Minister Valdis Dombrovskis to negotiate the best possible deal with international lenders that eventually ran into insurmountable obstacles.

Given the concurrence and the high importance that elections to the Rīga City Council have always had in Latvian politics, political parties focussed their attention on the municipal elections. Furthermore, these were the first municipal elections after administrative territorial reform, as a consequence of which the number of municipalities was reduced from more than 500 to 109 and the second tier of municipalities was eliminated altogether. According to Latvian election law, only registered political parties could submit candidate lists in most of the new, amalgamated municipalities.

On a par with the small number of EP deputies to be elected from Latvia, eight in total, the above factors contributed significantly to the relatively low interest that political parties showed in the EP elections. Parties launched their EP campaigns rather late, two to three weeks before polling day, and many of these were hardly visible to the wider public. A number of parties placed their second echelon of leaders in the top positions on their EP slates, but the First Party of Latvia/'Latvia's Way', in opposition since March 2009, fielded a former Prime Minister and another former member of the cabinet, whilst the Civic Union placed a former commissioner and an MEP at the helm of its list.

Most of the incumbent EP deputies ran again, but their party affiliation had at times been switched to reflect the changing party landscape in Latvia. Georgs Andrejevs (ALDE) elected on the Latvia's Way list in 2004 chose to side with the recently created 'Society for Different Politics', a political organization that called itself Social Liberal. Inese Vaidere (UEN: 'For Fatherland and Freedom'/LNNK) joined another newcomer, the right-of-the-centre Civic Union. Guntars Krasts (UEN: 'For Fatherland and Freedom'/LNNK) chose to head the Libertas list in Latvia. Ģirts Valdis Kristovskis (UEN: 'For Fatherland and Freedom'/LNNK) opted to run for the City Council of Rīga on the list of the Civic Union, whilst Aldis Kušķis (EPP-ED: 'New Era') refrained from running.

Although the platforms of many political parties running in the EP elections shared a concern for energy policy, farm subsidies, and identity issues, the actual EP election campaign lacked a clear focus and no issue could be singled out as dominant. 'For Fatherland and Freedom'/LNNK fought its arch-enemy, 'For Human Rights in United Latvia', on issues of ethnic policy. The pro-Moscow 'Harmony Centre' and the Social Democratic Workers' Party of Latvia were competing for the status of the most Social Democratic party. The Latvian branch of the Libertas movement was pushing EU transparency and accountability issues against a mildly Eurosceptic background, but hardly had any concerned interlocutors. All parties tried to address the economic problems Latvia faced, but largely limited themselves to an emphasis on accelerated and more efficient use of EU funds for sustainable economic recovery, better social protection, and the implementation of structural reforms as suggested by international lenders. European issues, including the Lisbon Treaty, further enlargement and the accession of Turkey, and foreign policy and terrorism, never reached the top of the political agenda during the campaign.

Many parties effectively merged their EP campaigns and their centrally run municipal campaigns, which largely focussed on who was the politician best suited to be Mayor of Rīga. However, this discussion turned out to be beauty contest between party leaders rather than a competition between programmes on how to deal with the severe economic crisis at the local level.

Although the campaign spending limit was notably increased before the 2009 elections and parties had an opportunity to amalgamate their spending for two concurrent elections, the 2009 campaign saw a more intensive use of the internet for political purposes in an attempt to reduce campaign costs and to tap into younger segments of society that have traditionally displayed lower levels of turnout. The most popular social networking site in Latvia, draugiem.lv, launched its elections rubric in cooperation with Jānis Domburs, one of the better-known analytical journalists, to scrutinize party platforms, involve parties in online discussions, and open them to more informal interaction with society. However, the success of this endeavor remains a topic for discussion. *Diena*, one of the most popular Latvian language dailies, overhauled its website in April 2009 and made a conscious attempt to expand its user-generated content, including blogs by politicians. As a consequence, the number of party-linked bloggers exploded but their activity has somewhat dimmed since the elections.

9.3 Electoral results

The turnout for the 2009 European Parliament elections jumped by 12 percentage points compared to the inaugural 2004 figures. However, this cannot be taken as a sign of immense growth in EP popularity or significance for voters in Latvia. The EP elections were held concurrently with municipal elections, and the turnout figure is closer to the turnout pattern in municipal elections. Therefore, it would be only reasonable to regard the increase as a function of concurrent elections.

Table 23.6 Turnout at EP elections in Latvia: 2009

Registered voters	1,484,717
Votes cast	797,219
Valid votes	791,597
Turnout	**53.7%**

Source: Central Election Commission, www.cvk.lv.

Table 23.7 EP election results in Latvia: 2009

Party/List	Votes	Seats★	Vote %
PS	192,537	2	24.3
SC	154,894	2	19.6
PCTVL	76,436	1	9.7
LPP/LC	59,326	1	7.5
TB/LNNK	58,991	1	7.4
JL	52,751	1	6.7
Libertas	34,073	0	4.3
SCP	30,444	0	3.9
LSDSP	30,004	0	3.8
ZZS	29,463	0	3.7
VL	22,240	0	2.8
TP	21,968	0	2.8
PDz	4,409	0	0.6
Party of Action	3,373	0	0.4
KDS	2,361	0	0.3
OP	2,102	0	0.3
LAP	1,712	0	0.2

Source: Central Election Commission, www.cvk.lv.

Note: ★After the ratification of the Lisbon Treaty, an additional seat was filled by a representative of the Civic Union.

Table 23.8 EP election results of major parties in Latvia: 2004–2009

Party/List	2004 vote share %	2009 vote share %	Difference
TB/LNNK	29.8	7.4	−22.4
JL	19.7	6.7	−13.0
PCTVL	10.7	9.7	−1.0
TP	6.7	2.8	−3.9
LC	6.6	7.5	−2.3
LPP	3.2		
LSDSP	4.7	3.8	−0.9
TSP	4.8	19.6	+13.1
LSP	1.7		
ZZS	4.3	3.7	−0.6
PS	n/a	24.3	+24.3
Turnout	**41.3**	**53.7**	**+12.4**

Source: Central Election Commission, www.cvk.lv.

The vote count produced some surprising and, perhaps, trailblazing results. Two members of the ruling coalition, the Union of Greens and Farmers as well as the People's Party, failed to elect any MEPs, despite the fact the latter fielded an incumbent MEP as its top candidate. The Prime Minister's party won one EP seat, whilst a junior coalition partner, the Civic Union, came out at the top, winning two seats and was poised to obtain one more seat after the ratification of the Lisbon Treaty. Parties advocating the interests of Eastern Slavic minorities, such as the 'Harmony Centre' and 'For Human Rights in United Latvia', performed considerably better than expected and won three seats in total. Ironically, a person convicted for treason against the Republic of Latvia will represent Latvia in the EP. The two big campaigners, the First Party of Latvia/'Latvia's Way' and 'For Fatherland and Freedom'/LNNK, each obtained one seat. Although Libertas was rather close to passing the electoral threshold, the charisma and reputation of former Prime Minister and incumbent MEP Guntars Krasts proved insufficient to clear the hurdle.

The number of elected women increased by one, as compared to the 2004 EP contest. One may note that two of them were incumbent EP deputies, whilst the third was a former Minister of Foreign Affairs. Moreover, all elected candidates were elected officials beforehand, apart from Alfrēds Rubiks, a former high-ranking Communist functionary who had headed the Socialist Party of Latvia for many years. Due to his close involvement in the Communist Party until the last days of the Soviet Union, Rubiks was forbidden to run in legislative or municipal elections.

9.4 Campaign finance

Given the notable impact of campaigning upon election results, as seen in a number of recent Latvian elections, particular attention was paid to campaign spending by major parties. Moreover, Latvia's Anti-corruption Bureau had recently not only acquired a new head but also a new instrument to oversee campaigning: it now had a right to suspend a party's media advertising if the party has exceeded spending limits according to the bureau's calculations, approximately €300,000 per candidate list in European elections. The First Party of Latvia/'Latvia's Way' and 'For Fatherland and Freedom'/LNNK campaigned most vigorously and the former came very close to the maximum amount (Kažoka, 2009). However, the Anti-corruption Bureau announced a few days after the elections that no violations had been detected. Total spending in 2009 for both the European and municipal elections amounted to 2.8 million lats, approximately €4 million (KNAB, 2009).

10 Theoretical interpretation of Euro-elections
10.1 Second-Order Election theory

The Latvian case offers evidence in favour of Second-Order Election theory, especially with reference to the 2009 EP contest (Reif and Schmitt, 1980). In view of the short EP campaigns of most political parties, two to three weeks before election day, and the wide presence of 'second-echelon' leaders on the EP candidate lists of most major parties, the 2009 EP election appears not to have been prioritized by political parties themselves. This ran in a stark contrast to the 2006 parliamentary election, when campaigns were launched several months before the elections, and also in contrast to the 2009 municipal campaign in the capital city, which was launched more than a month before voting day. Moreover, turnout was lower than in the last parliamentary election in 2006 by nearly eight percentage points, and might have been even lower in absence of concurrent municipal elections.

Table 23.9 List of Latvian MEPs: seventh legislature

Name	National party	Political group	Professional background	Year of birth	Gender	Committee
Ivars Godmanis	LPP/LC	ALDE	Saeima deputy, former PM	1951	Male	Budget, member; Regional Development, substitute
Sandra Kalniete	PS	EPP	Saeima deputy	1952	Female	Internal Market and Consumer Protection, member; Agriculture and Rural Development, substitute; Women's Rights and Gender Equality, substitute
Arturs Krišjānis Kariņš	JL	EPP	Saeima deputy	1964	Male	Industry, Research and Energy, member; Economic and Monetary Affairs, substitute
Aleksandrs Mirskis	TSC	S&D	Saeima deputy	1964	Male	Foreign Affairs, member
Rubiks Alfrēds	LSP	EUN/NGL	Party chairman	1935	Male	Agriculture and Rural Development, member; Transport and Tourism, substitute
Inese Vaidere	PS	EPP	MEP	1952	Female	Foreign Affairs, member; Human Rights, member; International Trade, substitute
Roberts Zīle	TB/LNNK	ECR	MEP	1958	Male	Transport and Tourism, member; Industry, Research and Energy, substitute
Tatjana Ždanoka	PCTVL	Greens/EFA	MEP	1950	Female	Civil Liberties, Justice and Home Affairs, member; Petitions, member; Employment and Social Affairs, substitute

Source: www.europarl.europa.eu/meps/en/search.html?country=LV.

Furthermore, most successful were: (1) parties that had been relatively recently established, such as the Civic Union, and were scarcely represented in the government that came into being just three months before the elections; or, (2) parties that were in opposition, such as 'Harmony Centre' and the FHRUL. Some of the more successful parties also held fewer MP positions in the *Saeima*: the Civic Union had a faction of six deputies and the 'For Fatherland and Freedom'/LNNK was also represented with six MPs. Large parties in the *Saeima*, such as the People's Party with 21 seats and the Union of Greens and Farmers with 17 seats, either failed to win any MEP positions or managed to garner enough support to win only one MEP, for example New Era with 18 seats. 'Harmony Centre' constitutes an exception here, as this party had 17 seats in the national Parliament but still won two MEP mandates.

Parties holding ministerial positions since 2006 obtained only two EP mandates. In line with the SOE model, this can be seen as a punishment of the mentioned parties for the catastrophic management of the country over the preceding few years.

The 'For Fatherland and Freedom'/LNNK suffered the greatest losses, not only because it had been in the governing coalition since the 2006 elections, but also because the party split in early 2008 and three incumbent MEPs left the party to establish the Civic Union, which was the most successful in 2009 despite the fact that only one, and perhaps less popular, incumbent ran on its list. The only party that clearly gained support was 'Harmony Centre', a long-standing opposition organization. However, one needs to take into account that, in fact, it is an amalgamation of four parties and some synergy may have taken place. Likewise in the 2004 EP elections, opposition parties and newcomers registered a victory in Latvia.

Although seven out of nine incumbents had run in the 2009 elections, only three succeeded. This can be taken as a sign of the notable general electoral volatility in Latvia and volatility in the EP elections.

10.2 Europe Salience theory

By contrast, most hypotheses of the Europe Salience model could not be corroborated in Latvia. The EP election campaign had little to do with Europe and/or the European issues of the day. Parties were often pursuing their domestic agendas and were merely using the EP campaign as another arena, a continuation of the 2004 pattern (de Vreese *et al.*, 2006). Eastern Slavic parties most often stressed issues related to the problems of Latvia's non-citizens, whilst ethnic Latvian parties reacted by advocating a strong EU policy *vis-à-vis* Russia and the need to recognize Latvia's occupation in a broader and more far-reaching fashion. Leftist parties called for EU-wide social welfare standards, whilst the right-of-centre parties advocated for the swifter consumption of EU structural funds earmarked for Latvia. All major parties were in favour of more generous EU financial support to Latvia, and many of them spoke of a revamped energy policy, indirectly aiming to weaken Russia's influence on the EU and its Member States. Parties addressed immigration and environmental issues marginally at best, and these issues were absent from public political discussions during the campaign. Hence, it is difficult to see noteworthy support for the 'Europe Salience' thesis, as proposed by Ferrara and Weishaupt (2004).

The environmentally conscious Union of Greens and Farmers lost its support, whilst the anti-immigration 'Everything for Latvia!' gained nearly 3 per cent of the vote, which was an improvement by nearly 1.5 percentage points compared to the 2006 parliamentary elections. However, this surge can hardly be attributed to the party's position on the immigration issue, given the miniscule number of immigrants and the low political salience of this issue in Latvia.

Although right-of-centre parties garnered the most votes, one has to recognize that the performance of centre-left parties improved in 2009. Parties that could be considered extremist, in relation to Latvian politics, failed to gain any noteworthy support compared to the last parliamentary elections. These observations do not provide evidence for the Europe Salience model as developed elsewhere (Hooghe et al., 2002; Hooghe and Marks, 2001; Taggart, 1998).

Another indication of the weakness of this theory was the miserable defeat of the openly anti-EU Party of Action that garnered less than 0.5 per cent of the total vote. Moreover, the equally poor showing amongst Eurosceptics was characteristic of the 2004 EP elections and the 2006 parliamentary elections as well.

Overall, the EP elections appear to have been low on the priority list of both parties and voters. This appears to stem from rational-institutional considerations: Latvia has a small representation in the European Parliament; people seem to have little credibility in MEPs' ability to make Latvia's voice heard and taken into account in this forum; other institutions, such as the Parliament and the government, may have more direct impact upon EU policy-making; and a gap between the EU's political agenda and the economically collapsing Latvian agenda appears to be wide and to contribute not only to the dominance of domestic political issues in the EP campaign, but also to voter detachment or even alienation from EU institutions on the grounds of their perceived irrelevance. Therefore, it is difficult to speak of any sense of mandate from Latvia's citizens in the absence of mass survey data attesting to the contrary, which only confirms observations by Hix and Marsh (2007) that:

> citizens do not primarily use European Parliament elections to express their preferences on the policy issues on the EU agenda or to reward or punish the MEPs or the parties in the European Parliament for their performance in the EU.

References

Primary sources

Central Election Commission of Latvia, www.cvk.lv (accessed on 15 February 2015).
European Parliament Database (2010) www.europarl.europa.eu/meps/eu/search.html (accessed on 10 January 2015).
European Parliament website, www.europarl.europa.eu/parliament/archive/elections2009/en/index_en.html (accessed on 7 December 2013).
Eurostat (2013, 2014) http://epp.eurostat.ec.europa.eu (accessed on 5 June 2015).
FHRUL (2009) 'Electoral Platform For Human Rights in United Latvia', FHRUL, www.cvk.lv/ep09/sar/eiro9.EiroKand09.programmaNR1=14 (accessed on 1 October 2009).
KNAB (2009) 'Party Finance Database of the Anti-corruption Bureau of Latvia, 30', www.knab.gov.lv/lv/finances/db (accessed on August 2010).
Latvijas Republikas Centrālā tatistikas pārvalde (2010) *Demogrāfiskās statistikas galvenie rādītāji 2009.gadā: īss informatīvais apskats*. LR Centrālā statistikas pārvalde.
Satversme (1922) http://likumi.lv/doc.php?id=57980 (accessed on 1 August 2013).
Satversmes tiesa (2002) Spriedums lietā Nr. 2002-08-01. www.satv.tiesa.gov.lv/upload/2002-08-01.rtf (accessed on 19 February 2015).
Standard Eurobarometer 67, European Commission, Brussels, http://ec.europa.eu/public_opinion/standard_en.htm (accessed on 29 August 2009).
Standard Eurobarometer 71, European Commission, Brussels, http://ec.europa.eu/public_opinion/standard_en.htm (accessed on 29 August 2009).

Secondary sources

de Vreese, C., Banducci, S. A., Semetko, H. A. and Boomgaarden, H. G. (2006) 'The news coverage of the 2004 European Parliamentary Election Campaign in 25 countries, *European Union Politics,* 7(4), 477–504.

Ferrara, F. and Weishaupt, J. T. (2004) 'Get Your Act Together: Party Performance in European Parliament Elections', *European Union Politics,* 5(3), 283–306.

Hix, S. and Marsh, M. (2007) 'Punishment or Protest? Understanding European Parliament Elections', *The Journal of Politics*, 69(2), 495–510.

Hooghe, L. and Marks, G. (2001) *Multi-level Governance and European Integration*, Oxford, Rowman & Littlefield.

Hooghe, L., Marks, G. and Wilson, C. J. (2002) 'Does Left/Right Structure Party Positions on European Integration?' *Comparative Political Studies*, 35, 965–89.

Ikstens, J. (2008) 'Political System of Latvia: Adjustment to Regained Independence', in de Waele, J-M. and Magnette, P. (eds) *European Democracies*, Free University of Brussels, Brussels, 237–52.

Kažoka, I. (2009) *Politisko partiju izdevumi pirms 2009.gada pašvaldību un Eiropas Parlamenta vēlēšanām*, Rīga, Providus.

Misiunas, R. J., and Taagepera, R. (1993) *The Baltic States: Years of Dependence*, 1940–1990, Berkley and Los Angeles, University of California Press.

Reif, K. H. and Schmitt, H. (1980) 'Nine Second-Order National Elections: A Conceptual Framework for the Analysis of European Election Results', *European Journal of Political Research,* 8(1), 3–45.

Šilde, Ā. (1976) *Latvijas vēsture 1914–1940: valsts tapšana un suverēnā valsts* (Vol. 8), Stockholm, Daugava.

Taggart, P. (1998) 'A Touchstone of Dissent: Euroscepticism in Contemporary Western European Party Systems', *European Journal of Political Research*, 33(3), 363–88.

24
LITHUANIA

Irmina Matonytė

Figure 24.1 Map of Lithuania

Table 24.1 Lithuania profile

EU entry year	2004
Schengen entry year	2007
MEPs elected in 2009	12
MEPs under Lisbon Treaty	12
Capital	Vilnius
Total area★	65,300 km²
Population	2,943,472
	84% Lithuanians, 4.9% Russians, 6.1% Poles, 1.1% Belarusians, 0.6% Ukrainians, less than 0.1% others
Population density★★	47.2/km²
Median age of population	42.4
Political system	Parliamentary Republic
Head of state	Valdas Adamkus (June 2004–July 2009); Dalia Grybauskaitė (July 2009–)
Head of government	Andrius Kubilius, Homeland Union/Lithuanian Christian Democrats (TS-LKD) (December 2008–December 2012); Algirdas Butkevičius, Lithuanian Social Democratic Party (LSDP) (December 2012–)
Political majority	Liberal-Centre Union (LiCS), Liberal Movement of the Republic of Lithuania (LRLS), Homeland Union/Lithuanian Christian Democrats (TS/LKD) and Rising Nation Party Government Coalition (December 2008–December 2012); Lithuanian Social Democratic Party (LSDP) in coalition with Party 'Order and Justice' (TTP), Labour Party (DP) and Poles' Electoral Action (LLRA) Homeland Union/Lithuanian Christian Democrats (TS/LKD), Rising Nation Party (TPP) Coalition Government (December 2012–)
Currency	Previously Litas; Euro (€) since January 2015
Prohead GDP in PPS	12,400 €

Source: Eurostat, 2013, 2014, http://epp.eurostat.ec.europa.eu/.

Notes:
★ Total area including inland waters.
★★ Population density: the ratio of the annual average population of a region to the land area of the region.

1 Geographical position

The Republic of Lithuania (*Lietuvos Respublika*) is a country in northern Europe, the southernmost of the three Baltic states. Lithuania is situated along the southeastern shore of the Baltic Sea; it borders with Latvia, Belarus, Poland, and the Russian exclave of Kaliningrad. Across the Baltic Sea to the west lie Sweden and Denmark. Vilnius is the largest city and the Lithuanian capital. According to one geographical computation method, Vilnius lies only a few kilometres south of the geographical centre of Europe. About two-thirds of the population live in urban centres.

2 Historical background

In 2009 Lithuania celebrated the millennium of its name, for the first time mentioned in European historical chronicles. During the fourteenth century, the Grand Duchy of Lithuania was the largest country in Europe and encompassed present-day Lithuania, Belarus, Ukraine, parts of Poland, Latvia, and Russia. In 1569, Poland and Lithuania signed the Lublin Union and formed a Polish-Lithuanian Commonwealth, which lasted two centuries. In 1795 the Russian Empire annexed most of Lithuania's territory.

After WWI, on 16 February 1918, Lithuania re-established itself as a sovereign state, which initially was a democratic parliamentary republic, but in 1926 after a *coup d'état* it became a Nationalist dictatorship under President Smetona's rule. In June 1940, following the secret Molotov–Ribbentrop protocols, Lithuania was occupied by the Soviet Union. In 1944, after the Nazi retreat, Lithuania, along with with Latvia and Estonia, was incorporated in the Soviet Union to form the Soviet *Pribaltika*, known for its higher levels of political consciousness and quality of life than elsewhere in the USSR. On 11 March 1990, Lithuania became the first Soviet Republic to declare its independence from Moscow although the last Soviet troops left Lithuania only in 1993. Post-Communist Lithuanian statehood is based on the principle of the legal continuity of the Republic of Lithuania from the inter-war period (1918–1940).

3 Geopolitical profile

Lithuanian citizenship was automatically granted to all residents who wished to have it. Twenty years after the breakdown of the USSR, unlike Latvia and Estonia, the population is rather homogeneous: 84 per cent Lithuanian, 6.1 per cent Polish, the biggest ethnic minority, and 4.9 per cent Russian. Lithuania is the least Russophobic of the three Baltic countries, but it is especially concerned with, and rather cautious of, Russia's political influence because of its neighbourhood, which includes the Kaliningrad exclave. Lithuania borders authoritarian Belarus and has deep historical affinities with Ukraine and Moldova; it is, therefore, particularly interested in the development of the EU's eastern neighbourhood.

In a cultural sense, Lithuania is closer to Central Europe than to northern Europe (Jacobsson, 2010, 86). Yet, in international relations, Lithuania displays both the Nordic and the Central European profiles.

Lithuania joined NATO and the EU in 2004; the latter's membership was approved by popular referendum on 10–11 May 2003, with 91 per cent voting 'Yes' and a 63.4 per cent turnout. Subsequently, on 21 December 2007, Lithuania became a full member of the Schengen Agreement.

4 Overview of the political landscape

Under the 1992 Constitution, Lithuania has a semi-presidential system of government. The President is chosen directly by the people and is active mostly in foreign affairs, appoints chief public service executives, and performs ceremonial duties. The unicameral Lithuanian Parliament (*Seimas*) consists of 141 MPs and is elected every four years. The *Seimas* was elected in October 2008, and faced a severe economic crisis. The coalition, led by Conservatives, initiated harsh budget cuts, increased VAT from 15 to 19 per cent and then to 21 per cent, started an austerity programme, and withdrew much support for small and medium enterprises. In mid-January 2009 a trade union protest rally turned into a riot and several people were injured. Riots had not occurred since January 1991, when some Lithuanians clashed with the Soviet army and the police. By spring 2009, there were no signs of financial stabilization or economic recovery in Lithuania. Public trust in Parliament and the government plummeted, whilst the President remained the most trusted person on the Lithuanian political landscape. At the time of the 2009 EP elections, the President was Valdas Adamkus, but he was replaced by Dalia Grybauskaitė in mid-July.

5 Brief account of the political parties

The origins of the Lithuanian party system lie, on one hand, in the former Communist Party, and, on the other, in the national awakening anti-Soviet movement *Sajūdis*, established in the late 1980s. Since 1990, the Lithuanian party system has been framed by the divide between the former Communist *Lietuvos social demokratu partija*, LSDP (Lithuanian Social Democrat Party), versus the *Sajūdis*-inspired Conservatives, the *Tėvynės sajunga/lietuvos krikščionys demokratai*, TS/LKD (Homeland Union/Lithuanian Christian Democrats). Although centre-right political actors and views dominated, the political left was clearly perceptible. The Polish minority, concentrated in the *Vilnius* region, has had its representatives in the *Seimas* since the first democratic elections held in 1990. The Russian minority, amounting to 5 per cent of the population and dispersed throughout all major towns, does not have autonomous parliamentary representation and, depending on political conjuncture, allies itself either with the Lithuanian Social Democrats or with the Poles.

Overall, the current Lithuanian party system is rather fragmented: party mergers and splintering are common; each election sees the success of newly founded populist parties; electoral volatility is high; charismatic personality-based parties prevail; and public trust in parties is low.

5.1 Party attitudes towards the European Union

In the mid-1990s, when the issue arose, Lithuanian political elites unanimously supported Lithuania's integration into the EU. The Association Treaty with the EU in 1995 was signed by President Algirdas Brazauskas, former leader of the Social Democrat Party, the reformed Communists. All relevant Lithuanian political parties broadly agreed that the country needed to Europeanize, i.e. to liberalize markets, promote democratic practices, respect human rights, reform its public administration, and adopt the *acquis communautaire*. The main difference amongst basically Europhile Lithuanian parties rested in their perception of the acceptable speed and depth of reforms: the centre-right parties (TS/LKD, Liberals) favoured more radical, speedy and deep reforms, whilst the left and centre-left wing parties (LSDP, NS/SL, LVLS) advocated a slower pace (Jurkynas, 2005, 129). The Polish minority (regional) party consistently voiced pro-European attitudes. Eurosceptic attitudes were expressed by extreme-right (Nationalist) parties, which were rather marginal in the *Seimas*.

Table 24.2 List of political parties in Lithuania

Original name	Abbreviation	English translation
Tėvynės sajunga/lietuvos krikščionys demokratai (Gv)★	TS-LKD	Homeland Union/Lithuanian Christian Democrats
Lietuvos social demokratų partija	LSDP	Lithuanian Social Democratic Party
Partija "Tvarka ir Teisingumas"	TTP	Party 'Order and Justice'
Tautos Prisikėlimo Partija (Gv)	TPP	Rising Nation Party
Lietuvos Respublikos Liberalų Sajūdis (Gv)	LRLS	Liberal Movement of the Republic of Lithuania
Darbo Partija	DP	Labour Party
Liberalų ir Centro Sajunga (Gv)	LiCS	Liberal-Centre Union
Lietuvos Valstiečių Liaudininkų Sajunga	LVLS	Lithuanian Peasant People Union
Lietuvos Lenkų Rinkimų Akcija	LLRA	Lithuanian Poles' Electoral Action
Naujoji Sajunga/Social Liberalai	NS/SL	New Union/Social-Liberals

Source: Lithuania's Central Electoral Commission, www.vrk.lt/.

Note:
★ Gv: parties in the Government Coalition interval 2008–2012.

Regular public opinion surveys about Lithuanian attitudes concerning the country's membership in the EU started in 1999. At that time one-third of Lithuanians did not have an opinion on the issue. Yet, the expanded information flow about the EU increased the awareness of the Lithuanian population on the topic and the number of Euro-enthusiasts increased dramatically. The increase in the pro-European camp was fuelled not only by those who had been formerly undecided, but also by those who used to oppose EU membership (Matonyte and Gaidys, 2005, 86). On the eve of the EU referendum in spring 2003, when asked the following question by a public opinion survey: If there was a referendum concerning Lithuanian integration into the EU, how would you vote: for or against?, 65.5 per cent of respondents answered 'for' and only 13 per cent 'against'. National minorities in the country also displayed pro-European attitudes: 83 per cent of Poles and 76 per cent of Russians, compared to 86 per cent of Lithuanians, said that they would vote 'for' the integration of Lithuania into the EU. None of the social or demographic groups could have been distinguished as clearly anti-European (ibid., 87). Public opinion polls in autumn 2006 showed that the majority of the Lithuanian population, 66 per cent, was in favour of the EU Constitution, which was ratified by the Lithuanian Parliament as early as 11 November 2004.

In the 2004 and 2009 European Parliament elections, all major Lithuanian parties adopted positive attitudes about European integration, and all supported the European Constitution and the Lisbon Treaty. Some minor parties, in particular, the *Tautos prisikėlimo partija*, TPP (Rising Nation Party), the *Lietuvos centro partija*, LCP (Lithuanian Centre Party), and the *Lietuvos valstiečiu liaudininku sajunga*, LVLS (Lithuanian Peasant People Union), expressed some worries about a loss of sovereignty and cultural identity, as well as the drawbacks of the cumbersome European bureaucracy. However, the political elite's support for a strong, intergovernmental Europe was rather consensual in Lithuania. Alone on the margins of public debate in 2009, the extreme left party *Frontas* advocated for a supranational Europe, which would introduce equal social rights all over the EU.

6 Public opinion and the European Union

According to Eurobarometer surveys, Lithuanian people's support for EU membership has varied in the range of 66–82 per cent throughout 2004–2009. In November 2006, Eurobarometer revealed that such positive attitudes were partly based on the belief that Lithuania would achieve higher living standards more rapidly as an EU member and thanks to EU financial assistance.

In March–May 2008, the Eurobarometer survey found that Lithuanian citizens were strongly inclined to say that EU membership was beneficial for their country – 75 per cent – whilst the EU average was 54 per cent. In addition, it appeared that Lithuanians disproportionately favoured further EU enlargement: 69 per cent versus the EU average of 47 per cent. When it comes to the question of how EU membership is beneficial to Lithuania, 49 per cent said that the EU created new job opportunities, 39 per cent thought that the EU contributed to economic growth and 29 per cent believed that membership improved relationships between Lithuania and other countries. On the negative side, 30 per cent said that Lithuania had very little influence on EU decisions and 26 per cent thought that membership negatively affected economic growth in Lithuania (Eurobarometer, 2012).

7 National and EP electoral systems

In 1992, a mixed electoral system was introduced in Lithuania, with 71 single-member constituencies, based on the number of inhabitants and administrative-territorial divisions, and one multi-member district, with 70 nationwide seats. The winners in single-member constituencies are determined by direct absolute majority vote. Elections in the single member constituencies are in two rounds. Turnout must exceed 40 per cent. Registered political parties and individuals with the support of no less than 1,000 eligible voters can contest single-seat constituencies. The 70 seats in the multi-member district are filled according to proportional rules on the basis of list votes, transferred into seats by the LR-Hare formula. Only party lists receiving at least 5 per cent, or 4 per cent until 1996, of the national vote are eligible to receive seats in Parliament. Since 1996, a 7 per cent electoral barrier was introduced for the joint electoral party lists, although until 2000, the lists of ethnic minorities used to enjoy a reduced 2 per cent threshold.

The EP electoral system in Lithuania is proportional, with preferential voting. The territory of Lithuania formed a single multi-member constituency to elect 12 MEPs in 2009 and 13 in 2004, in accordance with the law of 20 November 2003. Only political parties can nominate lists of candidates. As in national parliamentary elections, party lists gaining less than 5 per cent of the total vote are not entitled to EP representation.

8 A glance at the EP and national elections

During the 2004 EP electoral campaign, everything but EU issues was on the agenda. Populism was rampant. Candidates were liberal, when discussing business issues, and turned Socialist when appealing to the worse-off (Jurkynas, 2005, 140). Clear anti-European ideas were not voiced during the 2004 campaign. Even the Peasant Party (LVLS) did not criticize European integration. All parties promised to bring as much as possible from Brussels and Strasbourg.

The 2004 EP elections took place on 13 June concurrently with the second round of the presidential election, thus generating a relatively high turnout of 48.4 per cent. The Lithuanian representation in the 2004 EP was fragmented by encompassing members from six political parties. Yet the electoral contest produced a more centre-left oriented Lithuanian representation in the Strasbourg arena.

In the 2004 EP elections, 12 parties competed for 13 seats in Lithuania. The newly created populist DP received the greatest electoral support by securing five seats. Support for the ruling Social Democrats dwindled and they secured only two seats. The NS/SL, a minor coalition government party, failed to receive a single EP mandate. The backing for the major opposition party, the conservative TS/LKD, grew and it sent two representatives to the EP. The liberals (LiCS) won two MEP mandates. Electoral support for another newcomer populist party, the TTP, competing in national elections since 2002, decreased, but it managed to secure one seat. The peasants (LVLS) increased the number of their followers and gained one mandate. In 2004 the *Lietuvos lenku rinkimu akcija*, LLRA (Lithuanian Poles' Electoral Action), representing the Polish minority, reached their highest result ever, but the electoral formula's distribution of seats denied them a seat in the EP. The outcome was devastating for the Social Democrats LSDP, a major ruling coalition party.

The NS/SL, a minor coalition government party, was decimated in those late electoral cycle elections. In spite of controlling the position of the speaker and holding 18.4 per cent of total legislative seats, the NS/SL managed to receive only 4.8 per cent of the vote in the EP elections, and failed to secure a single EP mandate. On the contrary, the major opposition party, the conservative TS/LKD, increased its share from 8.6 per cent in the 2000 *Seimas* elections to 12.6 per cent in the 2004 EP elections and sent to the EP the best internationally known Lithuanian politician, Landsbergis, the father of national independence in 1990.

However, the biggest winner of the 2004 EP elections was the newly created populist DP, which received 30.2 per cent of valid ballots. Its leader Uspaskich decided to keep his *Seimas*

Table 24.3 National election results in Lithuania: 2000

Political party	Votes %*
Homeland Union/Lithuanian Christian Democrats **TS-LKD**	8.6
<u>Lithuanian Social Democratic Party **LDSP**</u>	31.1
Liberal-Centre Union **LiCS**	17.2
Lithuanian Peasant People Union **LVLS**	4.1
Lithuanian Poles' Electoral Action LLRA	1.9
<u>New Union/Social-Liberals **NS/SL**</u>	19.6
Lithuanian Centre Party LCP	2.9
Christian conservative social union KKSS	3.1
Lithuanian Christian Democrats LKD	4.2
Others	10.4
Total	100.0
Turnout	**58.6**

Source: www.europarl.europa.eu/parliament/archive/elections2009/en/lithuania_en.html#ancre3, accessed on 18 January 2012; Lithuania's Central Electoral Commission, http://www.vrk.lt/; the Lithuanian Parliament (Seimas), www3.lrs.lt/rinkimai/.

Notes:
[1] Parties represented in the 2004 EP are marked in bold.
[2] Table includes parties and independent candidates receiving over 1% of the vote in the EP elections;
[3] Government parties at the time of election are underlined (in spring–summer 2004 XII government, Prime Minister Algirdas Brazauskas).
* To reflect party popularity, only results from the multi-mandate district (proportional) elections are reported for *Seimas* (70 out of total 141 seats).

Table 24.4 EP election results in Lithuania: 2004

Political party	Votes %	Seats
Homeland Union/Lithuanian Conservatives TS-LKD	12.6	2
<u>Lithuanian Social Democratic Party LDSP</u>	14.4	2
Party 'Order and Justice'; Liberal Democratic Party TTP	6.8	1
Labour Party DP	30.2	5
<u>Liberal-Centre Union LiCS</u>	11.2	2
<u>Lithuanian Peasant People Union LVLS</u>	7.1	1
Lithuanian Poles' Electoral Action LLRA	5.7	0
New Union/Social Liberals NS/SL	4.8	0
Christian conservative social union KKSS	2.6	0
National Progress Party TP	1.2	0
Others	3.1	0
Total	100.0	13
Turnout	**48.4**	

Sources: Lithuania's Central Electoral Commission, www.vrk.lt; Nordsieck (2004): www.parties-and-elections.de/eu-ep2004.html.

Notes:
[1] Parties in government at the time of election are underlined.
[2] EP elections took place on the same day (13 June 2004) as the second round of the presidential election.

mandate and therefore five MEP mandates, out of the 13 allotted for Lithuania, were allocated to completely politically inexperienced people, parachuted in by the DP.

9 The 2009 European election

9.1 Party lists and manifestos

Fifteen party lists, containing 262 candidates, competed for 12 MEP seats during the 2009 EP elections in Lithuania. The longest lists, 24 names, were presented by 6 parliamentary parties. The hero of the post-Communist Lithuanian independence movement, then an MEP Vytautas Landsbergis, led the ruling coalition TS/LKD. The LiCS was led by its ambitious young leader, then an MP, Artūras Zuokas, who drew political capital from his outstanding performance as a mayor of the capital, Vilnius. A media celebrity and a public intellectual and professor of political philosophy, Leonidas Donskis, led the LRLS.

From the parliamentary opposition, the longest lists were presented by: the LSDP, led by its newly elected Vice-Chair Vilija Blinkevičiūtė, a former Minister of Labour and Social Affairs; the TTP, led by its controversial leader Rolandas Paksas, the impeached President of the state, a former Prime Minister and former mayor of Vilnius; and the Polish LLRA, which staked its high aspirations from the very beginning of the political campaign. The parliamentary DP followed closely with a 21-name-strong list headed by its controversial leader, then an MP, Viktor Uspaskich. The LVLS, led by then MEP Gintaras Didžiokas, which was represented in the *Seimas* by only three MPs elected in single-member districts, and the non-parliamentary LCP, led by then MEP Ona Juknevičienė, also had quite high electoral profiles due to the notoriety of their list leaders.

In spite of the initial media attention generated in early spring 2009 by the news that a ruling TPP might join the Libertas party of the Irish Eurosceptic Declan Ganley, the TPP finally adopted a low profile in the EP electoral campaign. Their ten-name list was led by former conservative journalist and MP Saulius Stoma, followed by another television entertainment journalist. The remaining five parties that participated in the EP elections presented rather short lists of eight to 11 names; their party programmes were fragmented and mostly concerned with issues that were resonant in the Lithuanian national scene, such as economic and energy policy, and the closure of the Ignalina nuclear power plant.

The LSDP prepared a very long and detailed programme for the 2009 EP elections, publishing it on the party's website as early as 30 March 2009. The party programme explicitly referred to the 'United Family of the European Left'. During the EP electoral campaign, the party had regular updates from the EP's PES activities and links to the Party of European Socialists (PES) manifesto on its website. The Social Democrats' electoral campaign was very active. Their candidates had numerous meetings with voters. The accent was on the global economic crisis, with its causes attributed to neo-liberal values.

The TS/LKD presented a rather brief, but quite exhaustive programme for the EP elections. The slogan of the Conservative programme was, 'For a secure future in Europe.' The programme underlined the need to stay faithful to European values, defined as Christian and pro-family values, as well as an objective evaluation of the historical past, to assure the energy independence of Lithuania via the creation of a common European energy market, and to guarantee a safe and secure future for Lithuania in the EU. During the electoral campaign, the TS/LKD only incidentally referred to the European People's Party and its programmatic stances, shared by its Lithuanian MEPs Landsbergis and Laima Liucija Andrikienė, who led the party's 2009 electoral campaign in Lithuania.

Table 24.5 EP electoral lists in Lithuania: 2009

National party	Number of candidates	Leader of the party list	Political group	Year of origin (membership)
Tautos prisikėlimo partija (Rising Nation Party) TPP	10	Saulius Stoma, MP		2008
'Fronto' partija (Political party 'Frontas') FRN	11	Algirdas Paleckis, party leader		2008
Partija Tvarka ir teisingumas (Party 'Order and Justice'; Liberal Democratic Party) TTP	24	Rolandas Paksas, party leader, the impeached president of the state, former prime minister, former mayor of Vilnius	EFD	2006
Lietuvos socialdemokratų partija (Lithuanian Social Democratic Party) LSDP	24	Vilija Blinkevičiūtė, MP, former minister of labour and social affairs	PES	1990
Žemaičių partija Žemaičių (Samogitian) party) ŽP	8	Egidijus Skarbalius, party leader		2009
Lietuvos centro partija (Lithuanian Centre Party) LCP	19	Ona Juknevičienė, MEP (ALDE)		2003
Lietuvos Respublikos liberalų sąjūdis (Liberal Movement of the Republic of Lithuania) LRLS	24	Leonidas Donskis, university professor, media celebrity	ALDE	2006
Lietuvos lenkų rinkimų akcija (Lithuanian Poles' Electoral Action) LLRA	24	Valdemar Tomaševski, MP, party leader	ECR	1994
Pilietinės demokratijos partija (Party of Civic Democracy) PDP	8	Eugenijus Maldeikis, MEP (UEN), former minister of economy		2006
Krikščionių konservatorių socialinė sąjunga (Christian conservative social union) KKSS	10	Gediminas Vagnorius, party leader, former prime minister		2000
Tėvynės sąjunga/Lietuvos krikščionys demokratai (Homeland Union/Lithuanian Christian democrats) TS/LKD	24	Vytautas Landsbergis, MEP (EPP), the first speaker of the post-Communist Parliament in Lithuania	EPP	2004/1993
Darbo partija (Labour Party) DP	21	Viktor Uspaskich, party leader, MP, former minister of economy	ALDE	2003
Tautinė partija 'Lietuvos kelias' (National Party 'Way of Lithuania') LK	9	Jonas Viesulas, NGO activist		2003
Liberalų ir centro sąjunga (Liberal-Centre Union) LiCS	24	Artūras Zuokas, party leader, MP, former mayor of Vilnius	ALDE	2003
Lietuvos valstiečių liaudininkų sąjunga (Lithuanian Peasant People Union) LVLS	22	Gintaras Didžiokas, MEP (UEN)	UEN	2005

Source: Lithuania's Central Electoral Commission, www.vrk.lt/rinkimai/404_en/KandidatuSarasai/index.html.

The TTP displayed the longest programme, with an agenda driven strictly by national concerns. It claimed that the Ignalina nuclear power plant should not be shut down by 2010, as agreed in the Lithuanian Accession Treaty, but should continue its activities until Lithuania obtained energy supply guarantees. In a populist style, the party denounced the self-seeking bureaucracy at the EU and national levels by requiring that Lithuanian MEPs should provide public accounts of their good deeds. The electoral campaign of the party was intensive, with numerous town hall meetings in various regions of the country. The party leader, the impeached President Paksas, attracted public attention, especially after addressing a complaint to the European Court of Human Rights against the State of Lithuania.

The Liberal LRLS presented voters with a rather long and sophisticated EP electoral programme. The party emphasized migration, the economic crisis, environmental protection, education, and further European integration. Led by a university professor, the party stressed the European mobility of Lithuanian students and teachers and promoted the use of modern technologies. The LRLS did not include any references to EP parties in its programme. In the electoral campaign, this Liberal party stressed human dignity, tolerance, and multicultural values. Yet the party, whose leader overtly displayed his Jewish origins, came under frequent attacks from its opponents for the latter's ethnicity and lack of political experience. The party led a campaign designed to appeal to younger voters, including a wide use of the internet, and it was active in public debates on radio and television.

The Polish LLRA, with the Alliance of Russians, presented a brief but exhaustive programme for the EP elections which, contrary to the tradition of this party, revolved around topics of concern for the general Lithuanian population, rather than issues of the Polish minority in Lithuania. The party programme first of all addressed the problem of the global economic crisis and proposed the increasing of social protection, the stimulation of consumption, the creation of new workplaces, and the use of natural energy resources, reinforced by EU-financed investments. The party clearly stated that it was in favor of prolonging the functioning of the Ignalina nuclear power plant, situated in the region where the Polish and Russian minorities are concentrated in Lithuania. In particular, the party demanded the right to use the Polish language in public spaces of the territories with Polish majorities, to improve conditions in non-Lithuanian schools, and to allow the use of non-Lithuanian characters in the official spelling of non-Lithuanian proper names.

The populist DP presented a very brief programme, emphasizing the EU as an economic union and calling for the development of its competitiveness. The party programme also underlined the need to guarantee employment and to combat poverty. The party, led by a controversial millionaire Uspaskich, who has a case pending against him in Lithuania on the grounds of alleged embezzlement of party funds, advocates the right of EU citizens to defend themselves in any court of law in all European countries. In spite of the fact that the DP has been a member of the European Democratic party since 2004, and Uspaskich is serving on the board of the Alliance of Liberals and Democrats for Europe in the EP, the DP did not make any references to any European parties or EP party groups in its 2009 EP programme and electoral campaign.

The LiCS had a concise party programme. The party's most important statement was a call to introduce the euro in Lithuania without waiting until Lithuania satisfied all Maastricht criteria. The party also underlined the importance of developing the EU's eastern neighbourhood policy through cooperative relations with Ukraine and Moldova, and the democratization of Belarus. Yet, the party's campaign was not very active and engaging.

The TTP did not have a coherent programme. The party ran in the EP elections on the general framework of its programme that it had prepared for the national elections in autumn

2008, where EU issues had been mentioned only randomly. Yet it was not very active in the EP electoral campaign and failed to gain seats in the 2009 election, precipitating a crisis amongst its parliamentary group in the *Seimas,* which resulted in the disintegration of the TPP faction.

In its 2009 EP programme, the agrarian LVLS called for the strengthening of Christian values. The party called for European agricultural policy reform and for environmental protection, as well as for a greener economy. It declared its opposition to genetically modified products. Its electoral campaign coincided with its inner leadership crisis, and was not very active.

The 2009 EP programme of the non-parliamentary Eurosceptic LCP highlighted the need to preserve Lithuanian independence, identity, and traditions. The party was led in the EP elections by then MEP Juknevičienė, who was elected in 2004 as a representative of the populist DP. She added pragmatic arguments to the party's otherwise rather philosophical electoral discourse, along with examples about EU tools that might help cushion rising unemployment in Lithuania. Even though it managed to increase its electoral success significantly, compared to the 2008 national elections, the LCP did not gain seats in the European Parliament.

The other five parties that participated in the EP elections were non-parliamentary parties, which did not manage to raise their profile in the elections. Some of them were recently marginalized from Lithuanian political life, such as the PDP and *Frontas*, which was a new splinter party on the extreme left that was formed in spring 2008 by dissenters of the then dominant coalition party of Social Democrats. Others were small parties centred on their leader, such as the *Krikščioniu konservatoriu socialinė sajunga*, KKSS (Christian Conservative Social Union) led by Gediminas Vagnorius, a former Conservative Prime Minister, or one-issue parties, such as the LK, which addressed only the question of energy supply, and the Samogitian party, *Žemaičiu partija* (ŽP), which underscored Samogitian identity and culture in Lithuania, comparable to the Breton in France. None of these parties were able to win seats in Strasbourg and Brussels.

9.2 Electoral campaign

As described above, the new law on political parties and political campaigns required that, in the course of a campaign, all mass media broadcast political advertising according to the same tariffs and conditions for all participants in the campaign. Because of this requirement, the Lithuanian EP Information Office could not contribute much to the free spread of information. Some informational activities had been carried out before the start of the electoral campaign. Since national EP information centres were not allowed to pay for television or radio broadcasts, in Lithuania commercial television and radio stations very rarely broadcast EP-related information. Yet, towards the end of the campaign, when public opinion surveys showed that turnout in Lithuania might be very low, the Brussels authorities decided to pay for some radio materials to try to increase popular interest in the EP.

The May–June 2009 EP campaign received the full blow of the new highly restrictive law on political campaigning. Several commentators observed that the unaware foreigner would not have even noticed that an electoral campaign was underway in the country. The bulk of the electoral campaign consisted of televised debates, in which party representatives responded to hosts' questions, much like school children, and could not engage in any meaningful political debate. The principle of equal access to media outlets was brought to its extreme during the public radio electoral debates, where musical melodies were played during the time allotted to parties that had failed to send their representative to the particular radio show. Some more vivid electoral debates appeared on commercial radio and television stations, but their number was truly limited. Many party lists and individual candidates put their campaign posters on the internet, in particular on the most important news sites (www.delfi.lt and www.alfa.lt) as well as on the portal of the only Lithuanian daily with a full-fledged website (www.lrytas.lt).

Political parties commissioned very few articles and photos in the press. These few campaign measures were paid for according to the predetermined egalitarian tariffs. Articles by journalists were also rather scarce and very carefully objective. The Central Electoral Commission was the main institution raising voter awareness; it hosted much of the EP and election-related information on its website (www.vrk.lt).

During the campaign, the Lithuanian media tended to present reliable information about the work experience and policy achievements of Lithuanian MEPs serving in Brussels and Strasbourg between 2004 and 2008 – ten of the thirteen Lithuanian MEPs had been running for re-election. In that respect, the Lithuanian conservative MEP, Landsbergis, received particularly good coverage. The media drew attention to the possibility of Lithuanian émigrés participating in EP elections. Only a few articles were negative; they referred mainly to the impeached President Paksas and the university professor Donskis for leading a party list without joining the party, and to the Russian-born businessman-turned-politician Uspaskich. Some articles were of the lifestyle genre and described the peculiarities of current MEPs' dress sense and communication styles. Journalists also disclosed some internal problems facing political parties, in particular problems related to fundraising and canvassing in the EP elections. Several articles questioned the Lithuanian law that allows only political parties to present their lists for EP elections.

The EP campaign material focussed largely on financial issues, concerns of small and medium businesses, and EU investment and support programmes. Many articles were written by the candidates leading parties' EP lists. The Lithuanian bishops issued a letter to believers, in which they urged them to vote for those parties and candidates who cherished family and national culture.

The Lithuanian media were not very active and did not put much effort into fulfilling the roles of civic forum, agenda-setter, and watchdog. Writing about representative democracy, Pippa Norris (2000) concluded that by transmitting political information, the media should help citizens forecast the consequences of their actions and decide how to cast their preference; the media should correspond to the specificities of the electoral system and the party system in the country, and it should be sufficiently varied, because citizens possess a different level of education and divergent cognitive capacities. In the 2009 Lithuanian EP elections, media reports were of a rather superficial nature and disengaging style. The only campaign issues that found reverberation in the media concerned the financial and organizational issues of the EP election, party finances, including the difficulty of raising money for a low-stakes election during an economic crisis, and the future lucrative salaries of the MEPs.

The EP electoral campaign in Lithuania was led by two major well-entrenched rival parties: the TS/LKD, leading the coalition government, and the LSDP in opposition. These two parties covered most topics and led political debates in the country. The debates were joined by several minor parties, none of which, however, were particularly active in the electoral campaign and did not present elaborate EP electoral programmes.

The 2009 EP electoral campaign in Lithuania generated only lukewarm political debate. For political parties in Lithuania, the EU as such mattered only slightly, and many issues were presented through Lithuanian lenses and addressed from the perspective of national interest. The two opposing major political parties led the political debates, covering all issues in a way relative to and mirroring their government and opposition positions and political-ideological stances in national politics. The smaller as well as younger parties vaguely enriched the electoral debate on several issues, including foreign affairs, environmental concerns, migration, and the danger of racist or xenophobic feelings. Eurosceptic forces and attitudes in Lithuania were, and remained, only marginally represented and lacked political saliency in 2009.

Table 24.6 EP election campaign issues in Lithuania: 2009

	TS-LKD	LSDP	TTP	DP	LiCS	LVLS	LLRA	LRLS	LCS	TPP	LK	PDP	ZP	FRN	KKSS
European integration (support or opposition to European Constitution/Treaty of Lisbon)	++	++	+	+	+	+	+	+	+	–	–	–	–	–	–
Attitude toward the new EU members and further EU enlargement	++	++	+	+	+	+	+	+	–	–	–	–	–	–	–
Immigration, danger of racist, xenophobic feelings	–	–	+	–	–	–	+	+	–	+	–	–	–	–	–
Economic crisis – unemployment, poverty	++	++	++	++	++	+	+	+	++	+	–	+	–	++	+
General environmental interest	+	+	–	+	+	++	–	+	–	+	+	–	–	–	–
Foreign affairs	++	++	++	++	+	+	+	+	+	–	–	–	–	–	–
Terrorism and security	+	+	–	–	–	–	–	–	–	–	–	–	––	–	––
Country specific issue: Energy policy and Ignalina nuclear power plant	++	++	++	++	++	++	++	++	++	++	++	++	+	++	++

Source: Author.

Notes:
Coding (by the author):
++ = elaborated statements in the programme, much of attention in the electoral campaign;
+ = issue presented in the programme and/or debated in the electoral campaign;
– = issue absent in the programme, but addressed in the electoral campaign;
–– = issue neither addressed in the programme, nor debated in the electoral campaign.

None of the Lithuanian parties directly addressed the issue of further EU enlargement, yet many parties positively evaluated the EU's Eastern Partnership initiatives and were very supportive of their enhancement. Many Lithuanian political parties underscored the economic and social progress Lithuania had achieved during its five years of EU membership. Scarce negative remarks concerning EU membership were related to the danger of losing cultural identity.

None of the parties addressed the issue of the pending EU integration of Turkey. Iceland's EU entry was considered an uncontroversial issue in Lithuania, due to her excellent political and diplomatic relationship with Lithuania, especially after the Reykjavík government's official recognition of Lithuanian independence as early as February 1991.

The issues of immigration, racism, and xenophobia received little attention in the party programmes and in the EP electoral campaign. Except for the frontal assaults on the internet against one leader of the Liberal LRLS, who did not hide his Jewish origins, racist, anti-Semitic, or xenophobic sentiments were rare. The LRLS expressed support for a common European migration policy and a common asylum system. The TTP expressed concern with illegal immigration and human trafficking.

As previously mentioned, in late 2008 to early 2009, Lithuania was hit by a severe economic and social crisis after years of economic growth. Economic concerns and issues of social guarantees dominated the EP electoral discourse in Lithuania. Even though the participants in the electoral campaign acknowledged that the EP's potential impact on the Lithuanian economy was minimal, the political party programmes and the media displayed an abundance of ideas about the economy and welfare. Practically all political parties in Lithuania addressed the problems of the economic crisis as well as unemployment and poverty.

Very few of the party platforms, including the EP electoral campaign itself, were concerned with ecological issues. No Lithuanian political party directly addressed the issue of nuclear energy as such; parties preferred to discuss the narrow theme of the Ignalina nuclear power plant. Some of the parties, such as the TTP, the LLRA, and the LVLS supported a unilateral extension of the operation of the Ignalina plant; other parties such as the TS/LKD, the LCS, and the LDSP called for the cushioning of the negative social and economic effects that would result from the closure of the plant. None of the parties directly addressed the issues of air, water, and soil pollution by industry and transport.

Foreign policy issues were overshadowed by economic concerns during the EP electoral campaign. Yet, several party programmes devoted chapters to Lithuanian as well as EU relations with Russia. The conservative TS/LKD emphasized the democratic mission of Lithuania and the EU to spread the values of human rights in the world, in other words, in Russia. The Social Democratic LSDP highlighted the need for peace and security in the world, and called for cooperation between the EU and the United States, given the new political atmosphere created by the election of President Barack Obama. The populist TTP and the DP advocated Lithuania's participation in the EU's efforts to build good relations with neighbouring countries, especially with the Russian Federation and its Kaliningrad exclave.

The view held by Lithuanian parties and civil society on issues of international terrorism and security continued to reflect the country's membership of the EU and NATO. The entire political spectrum in Lithuania stood firmly for the further enlargement of the EU and NATO. Political parties did not elaborate their views on terrorism or security matters, either in the national or the European context. Laterally, terrorism and security issues were touched upon as aspects of human rights and new global threats, which neglect traditional state borders and demand the coordination of government actions and the pooling of resources on an international scale.

9.3 Electoral results

The 2009 EP electoral contest took place at the beginning of the parliamentary cycle, since *Seimas* elections had taken place in October 2008, and three weeks after the presidential election. Turnout at the EP elections reached just 21 per cent, marking not only one of the lowest participation rates amongst EU Member States, but also the lowest in post-Communist Lithuania.

The EP contest sanctioned the success of the major coalition government party, the TS/LKD, which succeeded in increasing its electoral support from 19.7 per cent received in the 2008 *Seimas*

Table 24.7a National and EP election results: 2008–2009

Political party	Votes % 2008 NE*	Votes % 2009 EP	Difference %
Homeland Union/Lithuanian Christian Democrats **TS-LKD**	19.7	26.9	+7.2
Lithuanian Social Democratic Party **LDSP**	11.7	18.6	+6.9
Rising Nation Party TPP	15.1	1.0	−14.1
Party 'Order and Justice'; Liberal Democratic Party **TTP**	12.7	12.2	−0.5
Liberal Movement of the Republic of Lithuania **LRLS**	5.7	7.4	+1.7
Labour Party **DP**	9.0	8.8	−0.2
Liberal-Centre Union LiCS	5.3	3.5	−1.8
Lithuanian Peasant People Union LVLS**	3.7	1.9	−1.8
Lithuanian Poles' Electoral Action **LLRA****	4.7	8.4	+3.6
New Union/Social-liberals NS/SL**	3.6	Did not participate	
Lithuanian Centre Party LCP	0.7	3.1	+2.4
Christian conservative social union KKSS	Did not participate	2.9	+2.9
Political party "Frontas" FRN	3.2	2.4	−0.8
Party of Civic Democracy PDP	1.1	1.3	−0.2
Samogitian party ZP	Did not participate	1.3	+1.3
Others	8.7	0.3	−8.4
Total	100.0 (70)	100.0 (12)	
Turnout	**46.4**	**21.0**	**−25.4**

Sources: Lithuania's Central Electoral Commission, http://www.vrk.lt/, accessed on 18 January 2012; europarl.europa.eu/parliament/archive/elections2009/en/lithuania_en.html#ancre3; and www.parties-and-elections.de/eu-ep2004.html.

Notes:
[1] Parties represented in the 2009 EP are marked in bold.
[2] Table includes parties and independent candidates receiving over 1% of the vote in the EP elections.
[3] Government parties at the time of EP election are underlined (XV government, Prime Minister Andrius Kubilius, in spring–summer 2009).
* To reflect party popularity, only results from the multi-mandate district (proportional) elections are reported for *Seimas* (70 out of total 141 seats).
** These parties assured their representation in *Seimas* 2008 due to MPs elected in the single-mandate constituencies even though their party lists failed to pass the 5 per cent threshold in the multi-mandate constituency.

elections to 26.9 per cent garnered at the 2009 EP ballot. However, the major parliamentary opposition party of Social Democrats, the LSDP, also expanded its support from 11.7 per cent in the 2008 autumn national elections to 18.6 per cent in the June 2009 EP elections. Yet, the other two big opposition parties, the Order and Justice Party (TTP), and the Labour Party (DP), only succeeded in maintaining their electoral support in the EP election at similar levels as in the 2008 national election.

The most significant political accomplishment in the EP elections was the doubling of electoral support for Polish Electoral Action. Two infighting Liberal parties, both of which are minor partners in the ruling coalition, have had rather different fortunes in the EP elections. The *Lietuvos Respublikos liberalu sajūdis*, LRLS (Liberal Movement of the Republic of Lithuania) maintained its electoral success at around 7 per cent, winning one seat in the EP, whilst the *Liberalu ir centro sajunga*, LiCS (Liberal-Centre Union) lost half of its electoral support and with a meagre 3.5 per cent could not secure any seats in the EP. The other two big opposition parties, the TTP and the *Darbo partija*, DP (Labour Party) slightly increased their electoral support and secured their representation in the EP. The LVLS and the *Naujoji Sajunga/Socialliberalai*, NS/SL (New Union/Social-Liberals) were not able to pass the 5 per cent electoral threshold, much as in the 2008 parliamentary elections, where their representatives had been elected in single-seat districts, but failed miserably in the multi-member constituency.

Lithuania's representation in the EP following the 2009 election consists of well-educated, politically experienced people.

For several Lithuanians, the MEP mandate serves as a means to achieve specific goals in the national arena that have nothing to do with the EP. Such cases include Uspaskich, charged

Table 24.7b EP election results in Lithuania: 2009

Party/List	Votes %	Seats
Homeland Union/Lithuanian Christian Democrats TS-LKD	26.9	4
Lithuanian Social Democratic Party LDSP	18.6	3
Rising Nation Party TPP	1.0	0
Party 'Order and Justice'; Liberal Democratic Party TTP	12.2	2
Liberal Movement of the Republic of Lithuania LRLS	7.4	1
Labour Party DP	8.8	1
Liberal-Centre Union LiCS	3.5	0
Lithuanian Peasant People Union LVLS	1.9	0
Lithuanian Poles' Electoral Action LLRA	8.4	1
Lithuanian Center Party LCP	3.1	0
Christian Conservative Social Union KKSS	2.9	0
Political party '*Frontas*' FRN	2.4	0
Party of Civic Democracy PDP	1.3	0
Žemaičių (Samogitian) party ZP	1.3	0
Others	0.3	0
Total	100.0	12
Turnout	**21.0**	

Sources: Lithuania's Central Electoral Commission, www.vrk.lt, accessed on 18 January 2012; he European Parliament, http://cadmus.eui.eu/bitstream/handle/1814/13757/EUDO_2009-EP-Elections_CountryReports.pdf;jsessionid=D8412565D32EFC76ED30FE4759533FB4?sequence=1; www.europarl.europa.eu/parliament/archive/elections2009/en/lithuania_en.html#ancre3.

Notes:
[1] Parties in government at the time of election are underlined.

Table 24.8 List of Lithuanian MEPs: seventh legislature

Name	National party	Political group	Professional background	Age/gender	Number of mandates	Committee	Former MP (number of mandates)	Former minister	Former member of the local council
Laima Liucija Andrikienė	TS/LKD, Member of the party bureau	EPP	MEP	51/Female	2	Vice-Chairwoman: Subcommittee on Human Rights; Member: Committee on International Trade; Substitute: Committee on Foreign Affairs	Yes (3)	Yes (Industry and Commerce; European Affairs)	No
Zigmantas Balčytis	LSDP, Vice-Chair of the party, member of the party bureau	S&D	MP, Former Minister of Finance	56/Male	1	Member: Committee on Budgetary Control; Committee on Industry, Research and Energy; Substitute: Committee on Transport and Tourism	Yes (3*)	Yes (Transport; Communication; Finance)	Yes
Vilija Blinkevičiūtė	LSDP, Vice-Chair of the party, member of the party bureau	S&D	MP, former Minister of Labour and Social Affairs	49/Female	1	Member: Committee on Civil Liberties, Justice and Home Affairs; Substitute: Committee on Employment and Social Affairs; Committee on Women's Rights and Gender Equality	Yes (2*)	Yes (Social Security and Labour)	No
Leonidas Donskis	LRLS, non-affiliated	ALDE	University professor, public intellectual	47/Male	1	Member: Committee on Development; Subcommittee on Human Rights; Substitute: Committee on Civil Liberties, Justice and Home Affairs	No	No	No
Juozas Imbrasas	TTP, Vice-Chair of the party	EFD	Assistant to the MP, former mayor of Vilnius	68/Male	1	Member: Committee on Transport and Tourism Committee on Regional Development	No	No	Yes (mayor of Vilnius)
Vytautas Landsbergis	TS/LKD, Honorary President of the Party, Member of the Party Bureau	EPP, member of the bureau	MEP	77/Male	2	Member: Committee on Foreign Affairs; Subcommittee on Security and Defence; Substitute: Committee on Legal Affairs	Yes (4)	No	No
Radvile Morkūnaitė	TS/LKD, Member of the Party Bureau	EPP	Advisor to the minister for Foreign Affairs, MA student at Art academy, NGO activist	25/Female	1	Member: Committee on the Environment, Public Health and Food Safety; Substitute: Committee on Regional Development	No	No	No

(continued)

Table 24.8 (continued)

Name	National party	Political group	Professional background	Age/gender	Number of mandates	Committee	Former MP (number of mandates)	Former minister	Former member of the local council
Rolandas Paksas	TTP, Chair of the Party	EFD, group Vice-Chairman	Party leader, Vilnius city counsellor, former prime minister and President of the Lithuanian Republic	53/Male	1	Member: Committee on Economic and Monetary Affairs; Committee on Petitions Substitute: Committee on Industry, Research and Energy	Yes (1)	Yes (prime minister)	Yes (mayor of Vilnius)
Justas Vincas Paleckis	LSDP, Vice-Chair of the Party, Member of the Party Bureau	S&D	MEP	67/Male	2	Vice-Chairman: Subcommittee on Security and Defence Member: Committee on Foreign Affairs Substitute: Committee on the Environment, Public Health and Food Safety	Yes (1)	No	No
Algirdas Saudargas	TS/LKD, Member of the Party Bureau	EPP	Ambassador for special assignments, former Minister for Foreign Affairs	61/Male	1	Member: Committee on Constitutional Affairs Substitute: Committee on Industry, Research and Energy	Yes (4)	Yes (Foreign Affairs)	No
Valdemar Tomaševski	LLRA, Chair of the Party	ECR, member of the bureau	MP, party leader	44/Male	1	Member: Committee on Civil Liberties, Justice and Home Affairs	Yes (3★)	No	Yes (vice-mayor of Vilnius district)
Viktor Uspaskich★★	DP, Chair of the Party	ALDE	MP, party leader	52/Male	1	Member: Committee on Regional Development Substitute: Committee on Foreign Affairs	Yes (3★)	Yes (Economy)	No

Sources: Lithuania's Central Electoral Commission, www.vrk.lt/; www.europarl.europa.eu/meps/en/search.html?country=LT.

Notes:
★ Including elections to Seimas in autumn 2008, after election to the EP in 2009, the person ceased to have the mandate of the MP.
★★ In autumn 2012, Uspaskich was elected to Seimas and on 15 November 2012 in the EP he was replaced by Vitkauskaite–Bernard Justina.

with fraudulent accounting of party finance, and Paksas, the former President who has been impeached by the Lithuanian Constitutional Court and banned from running in national elections. This is also partially true of Landsbergis, a controversial patriarch in his own Conservative party, and Juozas Imbrasas who sacrificed his parliamentary mandate for a position as the Mayor of Vilnius, only to be voted out of that job shortly afterwards.

In terms of the EP party group affiliations, four Lithuanian MEPs belong to the leading European People's Party (EPP), three to the Progressive Alliance of Socialists and Democrats (S&D), two to the Alliance of Liberals and Democrats for Europe (ALDE), two to the minor Europe of Freedom and Democracy Group (EFD), and one to the fringe European Conservatives and Reformists (ECR).

In the summer of 2009 three (25 per cent) Lithuanian MEPs started serving their second term in the EP. All of them were entrusted with some leadership positions in the EP: Landsbergis joined the EPP bureau, Andrikiene (EPP) became a Vice-Chairwoman of the EP Subcommittee on Human Rights and Justas Vincas Paleckis (PES) became a Vice-Chairman of the Subcommittee on Security and Defence. The newcomer MEP Paksas took a position as Vice-Chairman of the EP group EFD, and the newcomer MEP Valdemar Tomaševski was appointed as a member of the ECR bureau.

As of June 2009, the age of the Lithuanian MEPs ranged from 25 to 77 years, with an average age of 54. Three out of twelve were women, whilst in 2004 there were five women MEPs from Lithuania. During both terms, the gender profile of the Lithuanian representation corresponded exactly to the overall gender distribution in the EP, which stood at 38 per cent in 2004–2009 and at 25 per cent in 2009. All twelve MEPs, elected in 2009 were Lithuanian citizens, amongst them one was of Polish origin, one of Russian origin, and one of Jewish origin.

9.4 Campaign finance

The 2009 EP elections were held under the newly adopted 'law of political parties and political campaign finance and financial control' (10 June 2008). The law was designed to reduce the cost of elections, to increase transparency in electoral campaigns and to promote rational argument-based political debate in order to counteract entertainment elements and populist appeals in audio-visual campaigns.

By law, state funding was granted for the publication of an electoral programme for each candidate list as well as for campaign broadcasts on national radio and television. In 2009, each EP candidate list was allocated one hour of airtime on public national television and one hour on public national radio during the official electoral campaign period, which was one month before polling day, beginning with the publication of the candidate lists by Lithuania's Central Electoral Committee. The law forbade any political advertising by mass media that was: (1) free of charge; (2) in any audio-visual format, such as radio and television advertisements; and (3) on the first page of a periodical. It only permitted the display of printed advertising material on specially designated boards in public spaces. The law also required that, during the course of the campaign, all mass media broadcast political advertising according to the same tariffs and conditions for all the participants in the political campaign. The state budget provided parties with subsidies, strictly following the principle of proportionality, based on votes received in previous elections and the number of candidates running in the elections. The 2009 EP campaign proved to be one of the least expensive during the entire democratic experience of post-Communist Lithuania. According to official declarations, parties spent about 3 million litas, around €900,000, on EP elections in 2009, compared to 33 million litas, around €10 million, in the 2008 parliamentary elections or 3.5 million litas, equivalent to approximately €1 million, spent in the presidential election campaign in May 2009.

10 Theoretical interpretation of Euro-elections

10.1 Second-Order Election theory

The 2004 EP elections in Lithuania seemed to corroborate the Second–Order Election thesis, by marking a decline in support for ruling parties at the end of the electoral cycle. Its results showed that this contest represented a marker-setting election, with citizens engaged in expressive voting. It could provide important cues about the relative popularity of parties in the first-order arena at the time when the markers set by the preceding first-order election had faded (Koepke and Ringe, 2006, 326). This insight was particularly relevant in the context of the political arena, with newly emerging political parties. The 2004 EP elections inaugurated the newly established DP, which succeeded in attracting 30.2 per cent of the vote.

In contrast to the SOE model, none of the Lithuanian non-parliamentary parties, which were running in the 2009 summer EP elections, were able to gain representation in the EP.

In addition, the most significant political accomplishment in the 2009 EP elections in Lithuania, the doubling of electoral support for the Polish LLRA, 8.4 per cent as compared to the 4.8 per cent obtained by the party list in the 2008 national elections, lends itself to another line of SOE reasoning. Namely, in 2009 this tremendous increase in the electoral fortunes of an ethnic minority party may be explained by an extremely low voter turnout. Our calculations show that only around 43 per cent of those citizens who cast their ballots in 2008 bothered to vote in June 2009. In this context, ethnic minorities in Lithuania appear to be much more loyal to their parties, as 65.6 per cent of those who voted for these parties in the 2008 *Seimas* election also showed up in the last EP elections.

The Lithuanian evidence supports the SOE hypothesis of a lower turnout in EP elections compared to the national election. It also confirms the early and late electoral cycle thesis, producing much bigger losses for the incumbent government parties in the late cycle of the elections than in the early cycle of the elections. However, the SOE prediction that small parties would have better electoral fortunes in the EP elections than in national parliamentary elections fails: even though some small parties received higher electoral support in the EP elections, this was not sufficient to secure their representation in the EP.

10.2 Europe Salience theory

The Lithuanian case offers very little empirical support for the Europe Salience theory, since an absolute majority of parties and candidates in the 2009 EP elections in Lithuania focussed on domestic politics and did not talk much about the European Union. For most political parties, the EU mattered little and most of the issues were presented through Lithuanian national lenses. On several issues, including foreign affairs, environmental issues, migration, racism/xenophobia, the electoral debate was vaguely enriched by smaller parties. In spite of the initial media attention generated in early spring 2009 by the news that a ruling Rising Nation Party (TPP) might join the Libertas party of the Irish Eurosceptic Declan Ganley, the TPP finally adopted a rather low profile in the EP electoral campaign and scored a flamboyantly miserable 1 per cent. The few negative remarks concerning EU membership that were voiced in the campaigns were related to the danger of losing cultural identity and political independence. Curiously, whilst philosopher Romualdas Ozolas, signatory of the Lithuanian Independence Act of 11 March 1990, had been one of the rare vocal public figures opposing Lithuania's ratification of the Lisbon Treaty, this fact was downplayed by his party, the marginal non-parliamentary LCP, during the 2009 EP elections and Ozolas himself was not even included on the candidate list.

Lithuania

In 2009 none of the parties running in the EP elections in Lithuania presented a Eurosceptic programme, and the list of the previously Eurosceptic LCP in the 2004 EP elections was led by a rather strong supporter of EU integration, then an MEP, Juknevičienė (ALDE). In retrospect, more Eurosceptic views had been voiced in the 2004 EP elections in Lithuania. In the previous election, at least two parties, the above-mentioned LCP and the TTP, were running with overtly, albeit mildly, Eurosceptic programmes, but their electoral performance was extremely poor, amounting to meager 1.5 per cent of voter support.

Like most post-Communist countries, Lithuania suffers from a distrust of politics, low political participation, and weak party penetration, combined with high voter volatility and a fragmented party system. Consensus on European issues continues to show sustainable resilience and does not polarize either voters or the political elite. Therefore, in the EP elections, populist promises and individual candidates are emphasized at the expense of party programmes and truly European issues remain largely irrelevant.

By looking at the 2004 and 2009 EP electoral results in the context of data on the national parliamentary elections and the composition of the incumbent governments in Lithuania, it is possible to find significant support for a set of hypotheses derived from the SOE model. Evidence shows that the incumbent government parties in the late cycle of national elections underwent much bigger losses in the EP elections than in the early cycle of the elections. The Europe Salience thesis is not supported in the Lithuanian case, suggesting that the Europeanization of the political game, in terms of the structure of party competition and issues addressed in the electoral campaigns, is still in its initial phase. The EP electoral campaign and electoral results in Lithuania might be fruitfully analysed through the lenses of the SOE model, but not with the help of the Europe Salience theory. The EP elections indeed mirrored major national concerns, whilst any specifically European content was fairly limited. Domestic political processes affected the June 2004 and 2009 EP election results in profound ways. In the absence of an articulated, sustained, and well thought out Europeanization of the EP campaign, the domestic popularity of parties was the crucial factor in determining voters' choices. Yet, the perceived remoteness of the EP discouraged voters from casting their ballots, so that the absolute majority of Lithuanians preferred to stay at home.

References

Primary sources

Department of Statistics to the Government of the Republic of Lithuania (Statistics Lithuania), http://db1.stat.gov.lt/statbank/default.asp?w=1280 (accessed on 18 January 2012).

European Commission, Eurobarometer Surveys, http://ec.europa.eu/public_opinion/index_en.htm (accessed on 18 January 2012).

European Parliament (2009) Database on Members of the European Parliament and Elections, www.europarl.europa.eu/members/; www.europarl.europa.eu/parliament/archive/elections2009/; and http://cadmus.eui.eu/bitstream/handle/1814/13757/EUDO_2009-EP-Elections_CountryReports.pdf;jsessionid=D8412565D32EFC76ED30FE4759533FB4?sequence=1 (accessed on 18 January 2012).

European Parliament Database (2010) www.europarl.europa.eu/meps/eu/search.html (accessed on 10 January 2015).

Eurostat (2011) *Europe in Figures. Eurostat Yearbook 2010*: http://epp.eurostat.ec.europa.eu/cache/ITY_OFFPUB/KS-CD-10-220/EN/KS-CD-10-220-EN.PDF (accessed on 18 January 2012).

Eurostat (2013, 2014) http://epp.eurostat.ec.europa.eu (accessed on 5 June 2015).

Lithuania's Central Electoral Commission, http://www.vrk.lt/ (accessed 18 January 2012).

Lithuanian Public Opinion and the EU Membership, www.euro.lt/en/lithuanias-membership-in-the-eu/lithuanian-public-opinion/ (accessed on 29 August 2009).

Nordsieck, W. (2004) 'Parties and Elections', The Database about Parliamentary Elections and Political Parties in Europe, www.parties-and-elections.de/eu-ep2004.html (accessed on 18 January 2012).
Seimas (Lithuanian Parliament) www3.lrs.lt/rinkimai/ (accessed on 18 January 2012).

Secondary sources

Jacobsson, B. (ed.) (2010) *The European Union and the Baltic States. Changing Forms of Governance*, London/New York, Routledge.

Jurkynas, M. (2005) 'Still Happy Europhiles: Europeanization and Party System in Lithuania', in Hrbek, R. (ed.) *European Parliament Elections 2005 in the Ten New EU Members States*, Baden-Baden, Nomos, 129–50.

Koepke, J. R. and Ringe, N. (2006) 'The Second-Order Election Model in an Enlarged Europe', *European Union Politics*, 7(3), 321–46.

Matonyte, I. and Gaidys, V. (2005) 'Euroreferendum in Lithuania', in de Waele, M. (ed.) *European Union Accession Referendums*, Brussels, Editions de l'Université de Bruxelles, 79–93.

Norris, P. (2000) *A Virtuous Circle*, Cambridge, Cambridge University Press.

Reif, K. H. and Schmitt, H. (1980) 'Nine Second-Order National Elections: A Conceptual Framework for the Analysis of European Election Result', *European Journal of Political Research*, 8(1), 3–44.

25
CZECH REPUBLIC

Michal Klíma

Figure 25.1 Map of Czech Republic

Table 25.1 Czech Republic profile

EU entry year	2004
Schengen entry year	2007
MEPs elected in 2009	22
MEPs under Lisbon Treaty	22
Capital	Prague
Total area★	78,867 km²
Population	10,512,419
	90.4% Czechs; 3.7% Moravians; 1.9% Slovaks; 4% others
Population density★★	136.1/km²
Median age of population	40.8
Political system	Parliamentary Republic
Head of state	Milos Zeman, Party of Civic Rights – Zemanovci (SPOZ) (March 2013–)
Head of government	Jiri Rusnok, Technical Government (June 2013–August 2013); Bohuslav Sobotka, Social Democratic Party (CSSD) (January 2014–)
Political majority	Technical Government (August 2013–August 2013); Czech Social Democratic Party (CSSD), ANO, and Christian and Democratic Union – Czechoslovak People's Party (KDU-CSL) Government Coalition (January 2014–)
Currency	Czech Koruna
Prohead GDP in PPS	14,700 €

Source: Eurostat, 2013, 2014, http://epp.eurostat.ec.europa.eu/.

Notes:
★ Total area including inland waters
★★ Population density: the ratio of the annual average population of a region to the land area of the region.

1 Geographical position

The Czech Republic is geographically located in the centre of Europe and borders four other countries: Poland to the north, Germany to the north and west, Austria to the south, and Slovakia to the east (Embassy of Czech Republic, 2012). The country consists of three historical regions: Bohemia, Moravia, and part of Silesia, collectively called the Czech Lands.

2 Historical background

In the aftermath of the Great War, the closely related Czechs and Slovaks of the former Austro-Hungarian Empire merged to form Czechoslovakia on 28 October 1918. During the inter-war period, the new country's leaders were concerned about meeting the demands of other ethnic minorities within the Republic, most notably the Sudeten Germans and the Ruthenians (Ukrainians). Following the Munich Agreement of 1939, Slovakia broke away and the Czech lands were occupied by Germany, which established the protectorate of Bohemia and Moravia (Eurostat, 2013, 2014). After WWII, a truncated Czechoslovakia, without the sub-Carpathian Ukraine, which became part of the then Soviet Union, fell within the Soviet sphere of influence. In 1968, an invasion by Warsaw Pact troops ended the efforts of the country's leaders to liberalize Communist party rule and create 'socialism with a human face'. With the collapse of Soviet authority in 1989, Czechoslovakia regained its freedom and, on 1 January 1993, the country underwent a 'velvet divorce', laying the basis for the foundation of two separate states, the Czech Republic and Slovakia.

3 Geopolitical profile

In order to address the problems related to economic and political transformation after the end of the Communist regime, the Czech Republic made efforts to enter the European political, economic, and cultural space. The Europe Agreement signed in mid-1990 by Czechoslovakia and the European Community was finally implemented. The two main tools of this agreement were to provide economic assistance through the PHARE programme and to offer Czechoslovakia access to the European Community market. After the split of Czechoslovakia, the agreement was re-negotiated in 1993 and subsequently ratified by the Czech Parliament, and entered into force on 1 February 1995. The Europe Agreement served as a key instrument to prepare the Central and Eastern European associated countries for EU membership. Following the referendum on the accession of the Czech Republic into the European Union, held in June 2003, which was supported by 77 per cent of the population, the Czech Republic became a member of the EU on 1 May 2004. The Czech Republic had joined NATO in 1999.

4 Overview of the political landscape

The current Czech political system is the result of two processes: first, a gradual transformation that has been taking place since the breakdown of the Communist regime; and second, the split of Czechoslovakia at the end of 1992.

The Czech Constitution, adopted on 16 December 1992, established a parliamentary form of government, thus entrusting political parties with a fundamental and instrumental role. This means that Parliament is conceived of as an arena in which political parties compete.

A principle of bicameralism is laid down in the Constitution, which also determines various principles of electoral systems and periods in office for both chambers. The 200 MPs of the lower house, the Chamber of Deputies, are elected for a four-year term and a method of proportional representation is applied. Elections to the Chamber of Deputies are organized in 14 regional constituencies. Votes are converted into seats by using the d'Hondt method, a highest averages method. National thresholds were set up as follows: for individual parties 5 per cent of the vote; for two-party coalitions, 10 per cent of the vote; for a three-party coalition, 15 per cent of the vote; and, for coalitions of four or more parties, 20 per cent of the vote. A partially closed party list allows for limited preferential voting, where each voter can cast two preferences. Eighty members are elected to the Senate, on a majority principle basis for a six-year period, in other words, every two years, one-third of the senators are elected by a two-ballot system in single-member districts. Should no candidate receive an absolute majority of votes on the first ballot, a second run-off ballot is held between the two best placed candidates.

The Czech Parliament is constructed as an asymmetrical bicameral body. First, the government is not responsible to the Senate, but exclusively to the lower chamber. Second, a negative vote in the legislative process on the part of the Senate may be overturned by an absolute majority of all deputies.

The political science discourse surrounding Czech political parties at the start of the twenty-first century generally concurs that the Czech Republic has a standard and stable party system that is fully comparable to those present in advanced Western democracies. Five main parties have been represented in the lower chamber of Parliament, with almost no major fluctuations for over a decade. There is one large party on the right, the Civic Democratic Party (ODS), and one large party on the left, the Czech Social Democratic Party (CSSD), and in between there is the smaller Christian Democratic Party (KDU-CSL) and the small Liberal or environmentally oriented parties. In addition, there is the Communist Party (KSCM), representing the radical left. As indicated, the Czech party system was formed predominantly along a left–right axis.

Since the 1996 parliamentary elections, a multiparty system, with two dominant parties, developed. According to ideological criteria, a party system emerged in the form of moderate pluralism where only the Communist Party on the radical left has limited coalition potential.

5 Brief account of the political parties

In comparison to many Central and Eastern European countries, the Czech party system has been quite stable. The two main political parties are the Social Democrats and the Civic Democratic Party. The *Ceska strana socialne demokraticka*, CSSD (Czech Social Democratic Party) goes back to a predecessor party that was founded in 1893, and refounded in 1990 after the end of the Communist period. It is a social democratic party and, in comparison to other reform Communist parties turned Social Democratic, it was able to keep its credentials quite intact. The CSSD is part of the European Socialist Party in the European Parliament.

The *Obcanska democraticka strana*, ODS (Civic Democratic Party) is a Conservative party advocating a free market ideology combined with Conservatism. The ODS can be regarded as a moderate Eurosceptic party, because it wants to protect national sovereignty against further Europeanization. Its former leader, Vaclav Klaus, who is presently the President of the Republic, is an admirer of Margaret Thatcher and Thatcherism. The ODS is aligned with the European Conservative Parliamentary Group in the European Parliament (Hanley, 2004).

The third traditional party is the *Komunisticka strana Cech a Moravy*, KSCM (Communist Party of Bohemia and Moravia) which is the follow-up of the former Communist Party of Czechoslovakia. It is clearly the strongest orthodox Communist Party in Central and Eastern Europe. It was re-established after the end of Communism. Its constituency consists predominantly of old members; it is an ageing party. Its main concerns are related to the protection of workers' rights, the protection of the welfare state, and the importance of the public sector in the economy. The financial and euro crises have become important topics on the Communist Party's agenda, due to their impact on people's lives.

Table 25.2 List of political parties in the Czech Republic

Original name	Abbreviation	English translation
Obcanska demokraticka strana	ODS	Civic Democratic Party
Ceska strana socialne demokraticka	CSSD	Czech Social Democratic Party
Komunisticka strana Cech a Moravy	KSCM	Communist Party of Bohemia and Moravia
Krestanska a demokraticka unie – Ceskoslovenska strana lidova	KDU-CSL	Christian and Democratic Union – Czechoslovak People's Party
Strana zelenych	SZ	Green Party
Sdruzeni nezavislych kandidatu – Evropsti demokrate	SNK-ED	Association of Independent Candidates – European Democrats
Nezavisli demokrate	NEZDEM	Independent Democrats
Veci verejne	VV	Public Affairs
ANO 2011	ANO	Yes 2011
Strana Práv Občanů Zemanovci	SPOZ	Party of Civic Rights – Zemanovci

Apart from these three traditional parties, two more parties emerged out of civil society, which have become quite important for coalition governments. They both are presently in a coalition government with ODS since summer 2010. *Veci verejne,* VV (Public Affairs) was founded in 2001 though over-run by one of the largest private security companies headed by Vit Barta. From the beginning VV focussed predominantly on the fight against political corruption and for transparency, but after entering into government it transformed into a thoroughly populist and clientelistic party. It is chaired by the former television star Radek John. An even newer party is *Tradice, Odpovednost, Prosperita,* TOP 09 (Tradition, Responsibility, Prosperity), which was founded in 2009 and is led by the charismatic and popular Karel Schwarzenberg. TOP 09 advocates free market policies and is quite pro-European. In the 2010 elections, the leaders of both parties were engaged in a fierce campaign against each other.

The emergence of these new parties has sidelined other smaller parties that are also part of the party system. On one hand, the *Krestanska a demokraticka unie – Ceskoslovenska strana lidova,* KDU-CSL (Christian and Democratic Union – Czechoslovak People's Party) which was founded in 1919 and is one of the historic parties of the Czech party system representing Christian Democracy. The party saw its electoral share, typically above 7 per cent, collapse to 4.4 per cent coupled with the loss of all its seats in the 2010 elections. Last but not least, the *Strana zelenych,* SZ (Green Party) was founded in 1990 and advocates environmental issues. In the 2006 elections, it got 6.3 per cent and six seats and became a member of the coalition government along with ODS and KDU-CSL. However, in the 2010 elections, similar to KDU-CSL, its vote collapsed and the party lost all its seats.

In sum, the Czech party system is polarized between left and right, however the right has more options for coalition scenarios than the left. The ODS and the CSSD are pivotal in the political party system. There is still a high level of electoral volatility in their choice of small parties. The 2010 elections have considerably changed the party landscape. The new parties led by charismatic leaders have replaced, at least in the short term, the Christian Democrats and the Greens, which were punished by voters after four years in government

5.1 Party attitudes towards the European Union

In the international media, the ODS is presented as a soft Eurosceptic party. Former leader and current President, Vaclav Klaus, although no longer in the party, clearly represents this current. However, the reality is that the majority of ODS voters are pro-European and also the leadership is quite pragmatic in dealing with European affairs. In a survey by the Centre for Public Opinion Research (CVVM) conducted in April 2008, about 58 per cent of ODS voters supported the ratification of the Lisbon Treaty (Hlousek and Kaniok, 2009, 5). However, there are different currents inside the party; some leaders are more pro-European, others more Eurosceptic. Importantly, hard Euroscepticism is seldom visible. Despite this, the party's position has been quite ambiguous and complicated. In contrast, the vast majority of its constituency is pro-European and seems comfortable with its soft Euroscepticism (Hlousek and Kaniok, 2009, 5, 6).

In February 2009, a more radical group under the leadership of Petr Mach, former economic advisor to Vaclav Klaus, left the ODS and created the *Strana svobodnych obcanu,* SSO (Party of Free Citizens). The party was against the Lisbon Treaty and objected to the adoption of the euro in the Czech Republic. The SSO emphasized the concept of the Europe of sovereign nations against any further supranationalism (SSO, 2009). Although the party was founded before the European Parliamentary elections, it was unable to achieve representation.

On the left, the Communist party is the main prominent representative of hard Euroscepticism. Before accession it rejected the integration of the Czech Republic into the European Union and still remains a strong opponent to its liberal economic policies. It emphasizes the protection of workers' rights and social Europe. It clearly belongs to the more hard line Communist parties of the Group of the European Left (GUE)/Nordic Green Left (NGL) in the European Parliament.

The Czech Social Democratic Party is more in line with the European mainstream. It closely follows policies of the Party of European Socialists (PES) in the European Parliament. There is no major dissent over Europe. Additionally, the Greens and the Christian Democrats are well integrated in the European mainstream following similar policies and positions on Europe to their respective party families.

The new parties, Public Affairs (VV) and TOP 09 are pro-European integration parties and focus more on domestic issues. Karel Schwarzenberg's TOP 09 is part of the European People's Party (EPP) and strongly supports European integration.

There are also other parties outside Parliament that present quite hard Eurosceptic positions such as the populist right-wing *Nezavisli demokrate*, NEZDEM (Independent Democrats) founded in 2004. NEZDEM follows positions similar to other populist right-wing parties, such as the slogan of the need to prevent the 'Islamization of society' and populist calls to end, or greatly reduce, immigration. Another group is *Suverenita-Blok Jana Bobosikova* (Sovereignty-Bloc Jana Bobosikova), which emphasizes the independence of the country. It advocates co-operation between sovereign European countries, but rejects supranationalism. *Suverenita* has been campaigning against the adoption of the common European currency, because then the country would also be involved in the problems of the present euro-zone. These parties were unable to gain more than 5 per cent in the previous elections, so that they are not represented in Parliament. Petr Kopecký developed a typology to identify the Czech political parties in terms of their position towards the European Union: 'On one hand, the CSSD, the KDU-CSL, the Greens, and I would add TOP 09, are Euro-enthusiasts; the ODS and maybe the VV are soft Eurosceptics; and the KSCM are Euro-rejectionists' (Kopecký, 2004, 236).

6 Public opinion and the European Union

The Czech population is known to be the most Eurosceptic of all Central and Eastern European countries (Kopecký, 2004). Before and after accession to the European Union, there was quite lukewarm support for membership. Since 2008 membership support has been declining to worryingly low levels, similar to those of the United Kingdom and Austria. However, one particularity is that the number of people expressing outright opposition to membership has consistently remained smaller than the segments of the population who support membership. In spite of this, a decline in support for the EU from about 51 per cent in 2006 to 31 per cent in 2010 and 2011 has led to a convergence of those who reject membership from 10 per cent in 2006 to 19 per cent in 2011. The other 50 per cent seemed either disinterested or lacked an opinion on the issue.

The public's views of the perceived benefits of the European Union are quite interesting. Although in 2004, before accession, only 46 per cent saw benefits in membership, which was below the EU average, by 2008 and 2009 this had increased to 62 per cent and was above the EU average of 58 and 57 per cent, respectively. Although after 2009 this positive perception had decreased to 57 per cent in 2010 and 53 per cent in 2011, this was higher than the EU averages of 53 and 52 per cent, respectively. There is general lukewarm support for the European Union, which could decline if the political and economic situation was not positive in Member States, for example, through poor management of the euro-crisis. However Czechs seem to think, instrumentally and pragmatically, that it is better to be within the EU than outside it, because more benefits accrue from membership.

In spite of this, one should not discount Euroscepticism in the Czech Republic, which is widespread amongst the centre-right ODS and the Communist Party. Although European integration is not a major issue in the national debate, which is typically dominated by domestic issues, it is an important source of identity for the otherness of the country in relation to Europe and the European Union. The process of enlargement played a major role in the Czechs' disenchantment with the European Union. The asymmetrical relations in the process of enlargement led to the rise of considerable Euroscepticism. It is likely that the country's recently recovered independence from the former Soviet Union produced a more distanced and lukewarm approach towards the European integration process. Another fear that may emerge in the discourse from time to time is related to the 'German question' and claims of the so-called *Sudetendeutschen*. After World War II, President Benes issued a series of laws that allowed the state to confiscate property from Germans and Hungarians in Czechoslovakia. Many Czechs feared that membership of the European Union would also lead to a reversal of these laws and a return of property to former owners. However, the Czech approach has been pragmatic and constructive as, for example, the Czech presidency of the European Union documents (Kopecký, 2004, 227–35).

7 National and EP electoral systems

Before presenting an analysis of the results, we should go over the basic rules that govern EU parliamentary elections in the Czech Republic, as set out in the Act on Elections to the European Parliament. The elections take place over two days, a Friday and a Saturday; this year, they were held on the 5–6 June respectively. Everyone aged 18 and over is entitled to vote, and the minimum age limit for candidates is 21. Elections to the European Parliament are organized in a single national electoral district, which covers the entire Czech Republic. Votes are converted to seats using the d'Hondt method, a highest averages method. In order to obtain at least one seat it is necessary to pass a 5 per cent national threshold. A partially-closed party list allows for limited preferential voting, where each voter disposes of two preferential votes.

8 A glance at the EP and national elections

A first look at the EP and national elections in the Czech Republic shows a considerable gap in turnout between the two. Whilst legislative elections have a turnout of around 60 per cent, at the European Parliament level this decreases by half. In the two elections of 2004 and 2009, turnout was slightly above 28 per cent. As already mentioned, in the Czech party system two main parties dominate, the ODS and the CSSD. They have been pivotal parties in the creation of government coalitions on the left and right. The Communist Party is the third largest, but it is ostracized from the central political system because of its orthodox ideology. In this sense, the two main parties can only coalesce with the smaller parties, the Christian Democrats and the Greens, but these did not achieve representation and were replaced as potential government partners by Public Affairs and TOP 09.

In the 2002 elections, a more intensive debate of the consequences of EU membership took place. The impact of European Union membership on the so-called 'Benes laws' was a key issue discussed. Other domestic issues were also raised, these were related to taxation, the impact of the nuclear plant in Temelin on Czech–Austrian relations, and the purchase of Gripen supersonic jets. In many ways, the main political parties used 'infotainment' strategies to attract votes. Nevertheless, the 58 per cent turnout was disappointing. The CSSD was able to become the largest party and form a coalition with the Christian Democrats and the *Unie svobody-Demokraticka Unie*, US-DEU (Freedom Union-Democratic Union) an ODS splinter party founded in 1998. Vladimir Spidla, a Social Democratic leader, became Prime Minister. The US-DEU is a pro-European and Liberal party, however after 2006 it lost its importance. The ODS lost both in the share of the vote as well as in seats. The big winners were the Communists, who improved their share of the vote and seats from 12.8 per cent to 18.5 per cent and from 24 to 41 seats (Hanley, 2006).

Therefore, the 2004 elections could be regarded as mid-term elections. European issues were important, however the domestic situation overshadowed the campaign. The Spidla government was quite unpopular due to its lack of managerial skills in dealing with the reforms in different areas such as education, the pension system, and health care. Additionally, the process of appointing its member to the European Commission after accession in 2004 was characterized by infighting amongst Social Democrats. Last but not least, its nominee for the presidency – who was elected by Parliament – Jan Sokol, was unable to win against Vaclav Klaus, the ODS candidate. The European elections led to the catastrophic defeat of the Social Democrats. Government parties received only 8.8 per cent of the vote and two seats. The US-DEU was also punished and did not gain representation. The only party to have done well was the Christian Democrats, with 9.6 per cent and two seats. Although the ODS party manifesto had a touch of dissent by presenting moderate Eurosceptic positions, it could not afford outright opposition against the EU or EU accession. The ODS mix seemed to be appealing to part of the electorate, so that it was able to win the elections and did better than in the 2002 elections in terms of vote share. It was able to win 30.0 per cent, an increase in relation to 2002 of 5.5 per cent, and nine seats. The Communist Party also did well with six seats. The election of MEPs from the Association of Independent Candidates-European Democrats (SNK-European Democrats), who were a splinter from the ODS over municipal politics and strong supporters of European integration, was surprising. They got 11.0 per cent and two seats. On the other side of the spectrum, the Independent Democrats (NEZDEM), who presented a populist right-wing programme got also 8.2 per cent and two seats (Rulikova, 2004).

Astonishingly, in the 2006 elections, the Social Democrats were able to recover from their disastrous defeat in the EP elections. In spite of major divisions within the party, under the leadership of Vladimir Spidla after the 2004 elections, the party was able to change its ways by selecting a new leader and Prime Minister, Stanislav Gross. However, the latter was replaced in 2005 due to financial scandals resulting in the emergence of Jiri Paroubek as the new Prime Minister. The Social Democrats were able to achieve 32.3 per cent and 74 seats, which was a considerable improvement over their 2002 legislative election results. However, the ODS did even better, achieving 35.4 per cent (+10 per cent in relation to 2002) and 81 seats (+23 seats in relation to 2002). New Communist leader Vojtech Filip was unable to mobilize their constituencies after former *éminence grise*, Miroslav Grebenicek, resigned from the post. Their electoral share dropped from 18.5 to 12.8 per cent and from 41 to 26 seats. The Christian Democrats got 7.2 per cent and 13 seats, whilst the Greens got 6.3 per cent and 6 seats. ODS then formed a coalition with the Christian Democrats and the Greens under Prime Minister Miroslav Topolanek (Hanley, 2006).

According to Sean Hanley, Europe was a non-issue in the campaign. The ODS avoided deploying Euroscepticism as part of their campaign. In this sense, it focussed more on their limited state programme called 'Blue Chance', promising less taxation, less state bureaucracy, and more freedom (Hanley, 2006).

In sum, the electoral behaviour of the Czech electorate remains volatile. The two main political parties have already encapsulated a substantial stable constituency, more so amongst the ODS than the CSSD. However, amongst the smaller parties there is even more volatility with some parties disappearing and new ones emerging. This makes it difficult to find clear patterns of behaviour in the two elections.

Table 25.3 National election results in the Czech Republic: 2002–2010

Political party	2002 %	Seats	2006 %	Seats	2010 %	Seats
ODS	24.5	58	35.4	81	20.2	53
CSSD	30.2	70	32.3	74	22.1	56
KCSM	18.5	41	12.8	26	11.3	26
KDU-CSL★	14.3	31	7.2	13	4.4	0
ZS	2.4	0	6.3	6	2.4	0
VV	—	—	—	—	10.9	24
TOP09	—	—	—	—	16.7	41
Others	10.1	0	6.0	0	12.0	0
Total	100.0	200	100.0	200	100.0	200
Turnout	**58**		**64.5**		**62.6**	

Source: Czech Central Statistical Office, www.volby.cz/.

Note:
★In 2002, in coalition with Freedom Union-Democratic Union (US-DEU).

9 The 2009 European election

9.1 Party lists and manifestos

Altogether 33 parties and political movements ran in the Czech elections to the European Parliament. These political subjects reflected the structure of the political cleavages in the Czech Republic. First, the primary position is occupied by class cleavage, specifically the division of the party spectrum into left and right. There are two main parties on the left, the Social Democrats (CSSD) and the Communists (KSCM), whilst the Civic Democratic Party (ODS) is the main party on the right. Second, to a lesser extent, there is also a religious cleavage on the domestic political scene, represented by the Christian-Democratic Party (KDU-CSL), and a post-material cleavage, represented by the Green Party.

Third, it is possible to observe a cleavage that directly reflected differences in attitudes towards the degree of European integration. That was why smaller political parties that defined themselves as pro-European or, conversely, as Eurosceptic, ran against each other in the elections. Pro-European parties included the European Democratic Party, the Party of Independent Candidates European Democrats, and the Liberals.cz. On the other hand, these political parties adopted a Eurosceptic profile: the Party of Free Democrats, Libertas.cz, and Sovereignty. This list shows how both supporters and critics of the EU are internally divided into little rival groups headed by ambitious leaders.

It is probably no surprise that President Vaclav Klaus not only supported all three Eurosceptic parties, but on his website also recommended that ODS voters give their preferential vote to Hynek Fajmon, who had long been a critic of European integration. Conversely, ex-President Vaclav Havel backed the 'post-material' and pro-Europe Green Party. Finally, Milos Zeman, the still-influential former leader of the Social Democratic Party, supported a small left-wing party, the Party for a Dignified Life.

Last, but not least, at the level of EU Member States, during the European elections there emerged a cleavage of opposition versus the government. In the Czech Republic however, this cleavage was absent at the time of the European Parliamentary elections, as an interim caretaker government was installed after the government fell in March, with early elections to the

Chamber of Deputies scheduled for autumn. As noted above, voters were mobilized against the parties that had toppled the government, whilst the Czech Republic held the EU presidency.

The most visible event in the pre-election contest was the 'egg-blitz', when Jiri Paroubek and other representatives of the Social Democratic Party were assaulted with eggs at a number of pre-election gatherings. Part of the reason for its visibility was of course the fact that it was a gratifying media topic, as it was an unusual occurrence accompanied by shock, emotions, and dramatic images.

Whilst, at the outset, the egg assaults were isolated occurrences, conceived of as a kind of practical joke, later towards the end of the campaign, they took on a mass scale and became exceedingly violent. Things reached a peak nine days before the elections when a pre-election gathering of Social Democrats in Prague was bombarded with eggs. These occurrences spread so widely because there was a group on Facebook called 'Eggs for Paroubek in Every Town', and within just several days more than 50,000 people joined the group. This kind of pre-election activity served, first, to activate young people, who had until then adopted a passive stance, and they reacted in their own way to public affairs by taking a stand against the fat-cat functionary style of the Chair of the Social Democratic Party, Jiri Paroubek, and against the party's empty billboard style of social populism. As the internet is regarded as a medium to which young people are drawn, in the post-Communist Czech Republic an interesting fact is that young people tend to be right-leaning, unlike their counterparts in Western Europe who tend to lean more to the left.

Although the egg assaults damaged the image of the Social Democratic Party, in the aftermath the opposite effect could also be seen. The Social Democrats tried to turn the negative action taken by these young people to their advantage by putting themselves in the role of victims of violence and the defenders of decent people. The entire country was flooded with posters featuring the faces of Social Democratic leaders with egg all over themselves beneath the heading 'Stand up to Aggression.'

Based on this experience, the CSSD acknowledged weaknesses in their internet marketing strategy and prepared to do something about it. Right after the elections, the party launched a new website and created Facebook profiles for the party leader and other members. Some parties, particularly the ODS and the Green Party, even began experimenting with microblogging on Twitter.

Prior to the European elections the CSSD's main motto was 'Security for the People and Hope for Europe', however this party, like others, essentially gave up on dealing with European topics. For the average left-wing Czech voter, European politics were too remote and sophisticated, and so there was no strong theme with which to mobilize such voters. For the European election campaign, issues that were successfully exploited in the regional elections, like opposition to the payment of fees for health care or the privatization of hospitals, were not as readily available to Social Democratic voters. Moreover, the party had lost its internal enemy in the form of the centre-right government, which the CSSD controversially toppled whilst the Czech Republic still held the presidency of the European Union. The no-confidence vote that brought down the government in March 2009 was viewed by the wider public, and even by some supporters of CSSD, as detrimental to the country's interests. Additionally, some CSSD voters showed a tendency in the European elections to experiment by voting for parties they would not usually vote for, explaining the party's surprisingly strong defeat.

Although even the right-wing ODS made little use of European themes in the pre-election period, it was still in a better position to mobilize voters, as most of its supporters were strongly pro-European in opinion. ODS's main slogan, 'Solutions not Scare Tactics', was directed against the Social Democrats, whom they blamed for the fall of the government, and for blocking health care and pension system reforms. The economy was a key issue here, as the economic crisis was also affecting the Czech Republic. It seems that, as in the majority of the EU Member States, this issue played out to the advantage of centre-right parties, who came across as the parties that were offering more rational solutions and not merely social populism.

9.2 Electoral campaign

Instead of the parliamentary parties, it was Czech Television, the public service station, which informed the public about European issues. Amongst other things, it explained the role the European Parliament had to play, for instance, in addressing the financial and economic crisis or in making decisions in matters pertaining to future subsidies for alternative energy sources. In its special pre-election programmes it also introduced viewers to the work of the incumbent MEPs and to the pre-election programmes of the political parties and their candidates.

For the first time, the head of the Catholic Church, Cardinal Miloslav Vlk, got significantly involved in the European election campaign (Kubita, 2009, 3). In the past, Cardinal Vlk had called on the public to take part in the elections, but he had never actually come out explicitly in favour of, or against, voting for a specific party. This time, on the day before the elections – through his website – he called on voters not to elect the parties that in March had brought down the government during the Czech EU presidency; by this, he was referring mainly to the Social Democrats (CSSD) and the Communists (KSCM).

An illustrative account of the character of the second elections to the European Parliament held in the Czech Republic was provided by statements that high-ranking politicians made and in the headlines of the major dailies. President Vaclav Klaus, a well-known critic of the EU, called the European electoral contest 'two-bit elections', whilst the leader of the Social Democratic Party, Jiri Paroubek, described them as of 'tertiary' significance. The day after the elections, *Lidove noviny* printed a large and negative headline on its front page that read 'Czechs Elect 22 Euro-millionaires', followed, on the next page, by the headline 'Winners Can Expect a retirement pension of 94,000' (Hympl, 2009, 1). These were allusions to the inordinately high salaries paid to MEPs, which are significantly higher than those earned by domestic politicians.

9.3 Electoral results

In the 2009 European election, the Czech vote was roughly balanced between the left and the right; out of the 22 seats the Czech Republic has in the European Parliament, half were won by parties on the left, the Social Democratic Party (CSSD) and the Communist Party of Bohemia and Moravia (KSCM), and the other half by two parties on the centre-right, the Civic Democratic Party (ODS) and the more centrist Christian Democratic Party (KDU-CSL). Unlike in a number of other EU states, none of the extreme right-wing parties in the Czech Republic were successful in the elections; of those, the party that fared best, the Workers' Party, received only 1 per cent of the vote.

Although there was a clear European context to the outcome of the European election, they played out primarily in relation to the domestic political scene. They were perceived mainly in terms of the contest between the two largest parties in the Czech Parliament, the left-wing Social Democrats (CSSD) and the right-wing Civic Democrats (ODS), which over the course of 12 months faced off in three different elections: first, in the regional and Senate elections in the autumn of 2008; second in the European elections in June 2009; and finally, four months later, in the October elections to the Chamber of Deputies. The European elections were thus something like the 'second heat' in an 'election triathlon'.

In the second EP elections held in the Czech Republic, 22 MEPs were elected, which is two MEP's less than five years ago. Turnout was relatively low, as only 28.2 per cent of the electorate turned out to vote. The Czech Republic had the fifth-lowest turnout out of the 27 EU Member States and ranked in the group of post-Communist countries with the lowest turnout.

As one public opinion poll showed (Kubik, 2009b), Czech citizens viewed the European Parliament as very remote and had no idea of how things operate in Strasbourg and Brussels. Citizens were also critical of the very high salaries and benefits that MEPs receive. The fact that the political parties themselves, and even the media, had little interest in the elections, was another reason for the low turnout. With a few exceptions, the political parties drew little on European issues and also put lower profile party figures on their ballot sheets. The prevailing opinion in the media was that news coverage of EU affairs was less interesting, so they devoted less attention to these issues.

Generally, voters who went to the polls to choose their representatives in the European Parliament belonged to the hard core of their party. In the Czech Republic, parties with a more ideological and disciplined support base, like the Communists (KSCM) and the Christian Democrats (KDU-CSL), benefitted from this. From the nature of the elections, it followed that the more dedicated supporters or opponents of European integration participated more in the elections. It was no coincidence that the biggest turnout of 36 per cent was in the capital city, where the ODS, 75 per cent of whose supporters were pro-European, won by a large margin.

The right-wing ODS had surprisingly swept the elections over the left-wing CSSD by a wide margin. The ODS won nine seats, with 31 per cent of the vote, and the CSSD only seven seats, with 22 per cent of the vote. The Communists defended their ranking in third place, with 14 per cent of the vote, which won them four seats. The last party to pass the 5 per cent national threshold was the Christian-Democratic Party, which obtained two seats, with 8 per cent of the vote. Conversely, the other parliamentary party, the Green Party, did not pass the 5 per cent threshold, nor however did any of the new and smaller non-parliamentary parties in the European elections. As a result, a large number of votes were wasted, in total 24 per cent. This is quite a large amount.

Immediately after the elections, conflict arose over how to interpret the outcome. The question was whether to compare the results to the previous European elections five years earlier or to the most recent domestic elections, which were elections to regional councils and the Senate, that took place in the autumn of the previous year. The leader of the second-place party, Jiri Paroubek, took pains to interpret the results purposefully as a CSSD success, as he related them to the results of the European elections five years earlier, when the party was routed in the elections. In an interview he said: 'We had two seats, now we have seven. We gained 320,000 more voters and the Civic Democrats gained 40,000 voters, the Communists and Christian Democrats (KDU-CSL) lost support' (Königová, 2009, 2).

However, the logical step would be to regard the Social Democrats' significant win in the previous autumn elections as the point of comparison and also take into account the long-term public opinion polls that had showed stronger support for the Social Democrats. Just one week before the European elections, preferences for ODS caught up with CSSD. Therefore, the results constituted a surprisingly high victory for the ODS over the CSSD.

In reality, the European elections represented a kind of referendum on the balance of power between the two biggest parties, a kind of dress rehearsal for the much more important parliamentary elections that were scheduled to take place four months later. To some degree the campaign before the elections to the European Parliament was conceived as an introductory or 'soft' stage in the campaign before the elections to the Chamber of Deputies. In this respect it is necessary to note a paradox: both the ODS and the CSSD were wary of a large marginal win in the European elections, as that could demobilize their voters before the autumn elections. For example, on the day of the elections, the headline emblazoned across the front page of the respected Czech daily *Hospodarske noviny* read 'ODS and CSSD are Afraid of Winning' (Valaskova, 2009, 1). It was speculated that it might be an advantage to the ODS if the Social Democrats and the Communists together won more votes than the right. In that case, before the autumn elections, the ODS would be able to mobilize voters against the 'red menace', and would be doing so right before the twentieth anniversary of the fall of the Communist regime.

The European elections were not just a contest between the two biggest parties, but also between the other three parties with representation in the lower chamber of Parliament. Of these, the Communists re-confirmed their standard third-place position and the average 15 per cent of the vote. However, there were substantial question marks hanging over the fate of the Christian Democratic Party and the Green Party. Both of these parties were experiencing internal crises and both were at risk of not reaching the 5 per cent threshold. In the end, the KDU-CSL, as a party with an ideologically clear-cut and disciplined base of support, and thanks partly to the low turnout, defended the two seats it had won in the first European elections.

Conversely, the elections ended in a great loss for the Green Party. After protracted internal conflicts and a split into two competing green parties, the smallest party in the Czech Parliament did not, as anticipated, make it past the 5 per cent threshold. But no one had expected that the party's results would be as low as just 2 per cent of the vote. The party leader, Martin Bursik, resigned as a result of this defeat; he was the only parliamentary party leader to do so.

In contrst to the previous European elections, not one non-parliamentary party won a seat in 2009. But the defeat of the Eurosceptic and extreme-right parties was much more significant. As for the Eurosceptic parties supported by President Vaclav Klaus, the Party of Free Citizens obtained only 1.3 per cent of the vote and Libertas.cz just 0.9 per cent, a Czech branch of Declan Ganley's Libertas Party. The only party appealing to Eurosceptic voters that even approached the 5 per cent threshold was *Suverenita*, headed by MEP Jana Bobosikova.

As for the defeat of the extreme-right parties, the Workers' Party (*Delnicka strana*) received 1 per cent and the National Party (*Narodni strana*) just 0.3 per cent of the vote. Despite this defeat, the media noted that the Workers' Party won 1 per cent of the vote and for the first time that entitled them to receive a state subsidy of three-quarters of a million Czech crowns (about €29,000). The Workers' Party mobilized themselves and won the most votes in areas where they organized demonstrations against socially excluded minorities, mainly Roma. Petr Uhl, a human rights activist, warned that the extreme-right was influential in those areas where the state had given up on the protection of its citizens and on defending the individual and good behaviour. He wrote: 'The extreme right thrives on nationalism and fights (. . .) against immigrants, non-adaptive citizens and rent defaulters. It also exploits the justified protest against unemployment, mafias, and criminality' (Uhl, 2009, 6).

From the defeat of the extreme right, it makes sense to turn to the subject of electoral geography. The Workers' Party made its biggest gains in the economically and socially underdeveloped Usti region, where it won 2 per cent of the vote, and in the region's two towns, where it won almost 8 per cent of the vote. It is no coincidence that it was in this region also that the most successful Eurosceptic party, *Suverenita*, won the most support, with 6 per cent of the vote. Similarly, even the Communists gained the most votes in this region, taking advantage of social tensions and the high unemployment rate there. The Communists won most of their votes in the Sudeten border regions and in rural areas rather than towns. It is consistent, too, that it was in this very region that the Christian Democratic Party on average had its weakest results and received the support of only 2.3 per cent of the electorate. Conversely, the KDU-CSL received the strongest support in areas that traditionally voted for this party, and where the

Catholic Church had strong influence, namely Moravia, 12–15 per cent, and eastern Bohemia, 6–10 per cent. As for the two biggest parties, the ODS and CSSD, the former won in 13 regions and lost in only one. The gap between these parties widened most in the capital, Prague, where the ODS won 40 per cent of the vote, whilst the CSSD received only 15 per cent. It was also in Prague that the candidate from the European Democratic Party (EDS), a pro-European party, won 7 per cent of the vote; an above-average result for the party.

Having examined the issue of electoral geography, the structure of the 22 elected MEPs will be classified from several angles. However, it should first be noted that preferential voting had practically no influence on the outcome. As mentioned above, each voter had two preferential votes, but they could only use them on one party list. The way it worked was that voters could assign a rank to two candidates on one party list, and the candidate who obtained at least 5 per cent of these preferential votes automatically moved into first position. If more than one party candidate obtained preferential votes amounting to 5 per cent, the one who obtained the most moved into the first position. Table 25.5. lists the names of all 22 newly elected MEPs from the Czech Republic grouped by party, and it clearly shows that none of the preferential votes shifted any of the candidates from an unelectable to an electable position. The only marginal change in the ranking occurred on ODS' ballot list, where Evzen Tosenovsky moved from second place in the ranking to first, as a result of receiving 14 per cent of the preferential votes.

From a gender perspective, the ratio of elected men to women in the Czech Republic is 82 to 18, with only 4 women elected as MEPs. This is the second-lowest number of women in all 27 EU Member States, after Malta. As for age, the average age of Czech MEPs is 50.

Amongst the 22 elected MEPs, 14 were incumbent members. As for the newly elected MEPs, two were originally MPs in the lower chamber of the Czech Parliament, one was a former Deputy Chair of the government and a university professor, one was a regional governor, one was Chair of the party's regional organization, one was a former deputy mayor and medical doctor, one was director of the secretariat of the Chair of the Senate, and one was a lawyer.

Table 25.4 EP election results in the Czech Republic: 2004–2009

Political party	2004		2009	
	Percentage	*Seats*	*Percentage*	*Seats*
ODS	30.0	9	31.5	9
CSSD	8.8	2	22.4	7
KCSM	20.3	6	14.2	4
SNK-ED	11.0	3	1.7	0
KDU-CSL	9.6	2	7.7	2
NEZDEM	8.2	2	0.6	0
SZ	3.2	0	2.1	0
Suverenita	—	—	4.2	0
VV	—	—	2.4	0
European Democratic Party	—	—	2.9	0
Party of Free Citizens	—	—	1.3	0
Other	8.9		9.0	0
Total	100.0	24	100.0	22
Turnout	**28.3**		**28.2**	

Source: Czech Central Statistical Office, www.volby.cz/pls/ep2004/ep11?xjazyk=EN;www.volby.cz/pls/ep2009/ep11?xjazyk=CZ.

Table 25.5 Czech elected MEPs in 2009: number of preferences

Candidate	Preferential votes Absolute	in %	Final order
Zahradil, Jan	65,731	8.9	2
Tosenovský, Evzen	104,737	14.1	1
Vlasak, Oldrich	11,744	1.6	3
Cabrnoch, Milan	7,143	1.0	4
Strejcek, Ivo	6,071	0.9	5
Ouzky, Miroslav	9,869	1.3	6
Kozusnik, Edvard	11,567	1.6	7
Fajmon, Hynek	16,041	2.2	8
Ceskova, Andrea	14,477	2.0	9
Havel, Jiri	59,818	11.3	1
Falbr, Richard	44,703	8.5	2
Roucek, Libor	19,771	3.7	3
Poc, Pavel	4,814	0.9	4
Brzobohata, Zuzana	7,736	1.5	5
Dusek, Robert	4,042	0.8	6
Sehnalova, Olga	9,386	1.8	7
Ransdorf, Miloslav	61,453	18.4	1
Remek, Vladimir	40,650	12.1	2
Mastalka, Jiri	8,181	2.4	3
Kohlicek, Jaromír	5,719	1.7	4
Roithova, Zuzana	52,503	29.1	1
Brezina, Jan	23,154	12.8	2

Source: Czech Central Statistical Office, www.volby.cz.

To sum up, influential party politicians were put at the top of the national party lists, in the first or at the very least second place on the list. Others on the list were low or non-profile politicians. As noted above, more than 60 per cent of the electable positions on the party lists were occupied by incumbent MEPs. For his 'service to the party', J. Havel ran in first place on the CSSD's party list. As an influential 'party rebel', Evzen Tosenovsky was put in second place on the ODS' party list. As a kind of 'celebrity' public figure, the former cosmonaut Vladimir Remek ran for the second time on the Communist Party's list.

It is apparent that MEPs elected for the Czech Republic have little influence on the distribution and balance of power within the European Parliament. Their influence is relatively proportional to the number of Czech MEPs out of the total number of MEPs. Given that 736 MEPs are elected in total, and 22 of them are from the Czech Republic, the Czechs hold just 3 per cent of all seats. Nevertheless, the group of nine MEPs from ODS that were elected will have the biggest impact on the work of the European Parliament. The party has arranged with the British Conservative Party and the Polish Truth and Justice Party to break away from the largest centre-right party group, the European People's Party (EPP), and form a new party group. The newly formed party group, the European Conservatives and Reformists (ECR), makes national interests, state sovereignty, and the promotion of Conservative values its priorities. As for the other MEPs, the seven from CSSD will strengthen the Progressive Alliance of Socialists and Democrats (S&D), the four Communist MEPs will again be part of the radical left-wing European United Left/Nordic Green Left (EUL/NGL), and the two Christian Democrat MEPs will continue to work with the largest party group, the centre-right EPP.

Table 25.6 List of Czech MEPs: seventh legislature

Name	National party	Political group	Committee	Professional background	Year of birth	Gender
Jan Brezina	KDU-CSL	EPP	Industry, Research and Energy	MEP	1954	Male
Zuzana Brzobohata	CSSD	S&D	Regional Development	Member of the Parliament of the CR	1962	Female
Milan Cabrnoch	ODS	ECR	Employment and Social Affairs Environment, Public Health and Food Safety	MEP	1962	Male
Andrea Ceskova	ODS	ECR	Budgetary Control Women's Rights and Gender Equality	Lawyer	1971	Female
Robert Dusek	CSSD	S&D	Agriculture and Rural Development	Member of the Parliament of the CR	1967	Male
Hynek Fajmon	ODS	ECR	Agriculture and Rural Development	MEP	1968	Male
Richard Falbr	CSSD	S&D	Employment and Social Affairs	MEP	1940	Male
Jiri Havel (died in 2012, replaced by Vojtěch Mynář)	CSSD	S&D	Budgets	former deputy prime minister and Minister for the Economy, university professor	1957	Male
Jaromir Kohlicek	KSCM	EUL/NGL	Transport and Tourism	MEP	1953	Male
Edvard Kozusnik	ODS	ECR	Internal Market and Consumer Protection	Secretariat Director of the Senate President	1971	Male
Jiri Mastalka	KSCM	EUL/NGL	Legal Affairs	MEP	1956	Male
Miroslav Ouzky	ODS	ECR	Environment, Public Health and Food Safety	MEP	1958	Male
Pavel Poc	CSSD	S&D	Environment, Public Health and Food Safety	Chairman of the party's regional organization	1964	Male
Miloslav Randsdorf	KSCM	EUL/NGL	Industry, Research and Energy	MEP	1953	Male
Vlamimir Remek	KSCM	EUL/NGL	Budgets	MEP	1948	Male
Zuzana Roithova	KDU CSL	EPP	Internal Market and Consumer Protection	MEP	1953	Female
Libor Roucek	CSSD	S&D	Foreign Affairs	MEP	1954	Male
Olga Sehnalova	CSSD	S&D	Transport and Tourism	Former deputy mayor, medical doctor	1968	Female
Ivo Strejcek	ODS	ECR	Economic and Monetary Affairs	MEP	1962	Male
Evzen Tosenovsky	ODS	ECR	Industry, Research and Energy	Governor of the Moravian-Silesian Region	1956	Male
Oldrich Vlasak	ODS	ECR	Regional Development	MEP	1955	Male
Jan Zahradil	ODS	ECR	International Trade	MEP	1963	Male

Source: www.europarl.europa.eu/meps/en/search.html?country=CZ.

9.4. Campaign finance

The financing of party electoral campaigns is largely undertaken by a generous public funding system. The main legal document regulating parties and party financing is Law 424/1991, which was updated and amended several times, most recently in 2003. Every party has to submit annual reports on their expenditure to the Chamber of Deputies. The reports are not published but are available to the public and can, if requested, be looked at in the Chamber of Deputies' library. The generous funding system consists of two forms of subsidies. The first form is a permanent contribution for parties that achieve more than a 3 per cent vote share in parliamentary elections, which may amount to up to CZK 10 Million (€400,000), whilst the second form is a mandate contribution of about CZK 855,000, equivalent to €34,200 per member per year. For legislative elections, any party that achieves more than 1.5 per cent of the vote gets CZK 100 (€4) per gained vote, whilst in European Parliamentary elections if a political party (or movement) achieves more than 1 per cent of the vote, it is entitled to CZK 30 (€1.20) (GRECO, 2011, 7).

If we look at the expenditure of the two main political parties, we get a picture of how much political parties spend in legislative elections and European Parliamentary elections. For the legislative elections of 2010, the ODS spent CZK 217 million (€8.6 million) and the CSSD spent CZK 197 million (€7.8 million) (Buehrer, 2011). In comparison to the European Parliamentary elections, each of the main parties spent about CZK 40 million (€1.6 million) (Kárniková, 2010, 68).

This shows a substantial difference, in terms of expenditure, between the two elections, which acts as a further indicator of its second-order character. In 2009, the different parties received the following public funding amounts: the ODS, CZK 197 million (€7.8 million), and the CSSD, CZK 232 million (€5.2 million). However, their expenditure claims were CZK 541 million (€21.5 million) and CZK 273 million (€10.8 million), respectively. This implies that part of the funding was provided by anonymous donors. So far, legislation has not been very clear about private funding (Heijmans, 2010). This was also highlighted by the third evaluation report of GRECO, a committee of the Council of Europe that fights corruption and the illegal financing of political parties and other institutions (GRECO, 2011, 23). After the publication of the report, the CSSD asked for caps on campaign spending for legislative elections at CZK 80 million (€3.2 million). However, rival ODS was not impressed with this suggestion (Buehrer, 2011). In sum, there is a big difference in spending between legislative and European elections, confirming the lower importance of the latter for political parties.

10 Theoretical interpretation of Euro-elections

10.1 Second-Order Election theory

In terms of turnout, both Euro-elections that have taken place in the Czech Republic clearly confirmed the validity of the classic Second-Order Election theory. In the elections to the Chamber of Deputies in 2002, which was before the first Euro-elections were held in the country, turnout was 58 per cent and in 2006 it had risen to 64 per cent. Conversely, turnout dropped in the Euro-elections in both 2004 and in 2009, to just 28 per cent, which is less than one-half of turnout in national elections.

The two Euro-elections in the Czech Republic produced different results in the distribution of votes between parties, and these differences were directly connected to the timing of the elections in the government popularity cycle. In 2004, the centre-left government was in its mid-term period in office. In the Euro-elections, the Social Democratic Party, the biggest parliamentary party and the party of government, suffered a sweeping defeat and finished in fifth place, with just under 9 per cent of the vote. This led V. Špidla, Prime Minister and party Chair, to resign. In the second Euro-elections (2009) an unusual situation had emerged in domestic politics. Just three months before the Euro-elections the centre-right government was toppled and an interim caretaker government was installed in its place, all this whilst the Czech Republic still held the EU presidency. Paradoxically, this served to mobilize voters against the opposition parties that had helped bring down the government. For this reason, there was no opposition versus government cleavage in the Czech Republic at the time of the European parliamentary elections. It is no surprise then that this time, unlike in 2004, it was the biggest parliamentary party and the main party in the centre-right government, until it was toppled in March 2009, the Civic Democratic Party, which was the biggest winner in the elections.

Small and protest parties fared very differently in each of the European parliamentary elections. In the 2004 elections they enjoyed enormous success, as two non-parliamentary parties won seats, namely the Association of Independent Candidates, European Democrats (SNK-ED; 11 per cent of the vote and three Euro-mandates) and the Independents (8 per cent of the vote and two Euro-mandates), but in 2009 they did very poorly; none of the non-parliamentary parties passed the 5 per cent threshold and they all failed to gain entry into the European Parliament. Even the smallest national parliamentary party, the Green Party, ended up well below the 5 per cent threshold, with only 2 per cent of the vote. Nevertheless, this does not mean that when compared to domestic elections, voters exhibited less of a tendency to engage in 'sincere voting' (*vote from the heart*) or to experiment. Many votes were indeed wasted, in total 24 per cent, whilst, conversely, in the domestic parliamentary elections in 2006, only 6 per cent of the vote was wasted. So, there certainly was protest voting, however, it was not concentrated, but rather dispersed amongst many parties: a total of nine parties which each gained between 1 and 5 per cent of the vote.

10.2 Europe Salience theory

It is apparent that Europe matters in the Euro-elections in the Czech Republic. However, according the election results, the fact that political parties drew little attention to European issues and put lower profile party figures on their ballot sheets, and the fact that even the media paid little attention to the elections, may all indicate that, at best, Europe remains a secondary issue.

In this regard, it is worth mentioning that parties that highlighted European issues either positively or negatively had higher gains on the whole. As noted above, in 2004 the pro-European SNK-ED party was very successful, winning 11 per cent of the vote. Conversely, even though none of the smaller parties gained entry into the European Parliament in 2009, three pro-European parties together won 4.5 per cent of the vote, whilst three Eurosceptic parties gained a total of 6.5 per cent.

In conclusion, both elections to the European Parliament that have been held in the Czech Republic confirm the validity of the classic Second-Order Election theory, but the Europe matters theory is less applicable and serves to complement the first theory.

References

Primary sources

Czech Central Statistical Office: www.volby.cz/ (accessed on 9 February 2012).
Czech Republic on Transparency of Public Funding. Third Evaluation Report Adopted by Greco at 50th Plenary Session (Strasbourg 28 May–1 April 2011).
European Parliament Database (2010) www.europarl.europa.eu/meps/eu/search.html (accessed on 10 January 2015).

European Union (2012) Portrait of the Regions Czech Republic: http://circa.europa.eu/irc/dsis/regportraits/info/data/cz_national.htm (accessed on 18 January 2012).
Eurostat (2013, 2014) http://epp.eurostat.ec.europa.eu (accessed on 5 June 2015).
Group of States Against Corruption (GRECO) (2011) 'Evaluation Report on the Strasbourg, Council of Europe: www.coe.int/t/dghl/monitoring/greco/evaluations/round3/GrecoEval3(2010)10_CzechRep_Two_EN.pdf (accessed on 10 February 2012).
SSO (2009) Volební program Strany svobodných občanů pro volby do Evropského parlamentu (5.–6. June, available at: http://www.svobodni.cz/1-nezobrazeno/37-volebni-program-do-ep/.

Secondary sources

Buehrer, J. (2011) 'ČSSD Campaign Finance Proposal Draws Criticism', *The Prague Post*, 4 May, 10, A3.
Embassy of the Czech Republic (2012) 'Geographical Location'. Online. Available at: www.mzv.cz/hague/en/general_information_on_the_czech/geographic_location/index.html (accessed on 18 January 2012).
Hanley, S. (2004) 'From Neo-liberalism to National Interests: Ideology, Strategy and Party Development of the Czech Right', *East European Politics and Society*, 18(3), 513–48.
Hanley, S. (2006) 'Europe and the Czech Parliamentary Election, 2–3 June 2006', EPERN Election Briefing nr. 27. Online. Available at: http://www.sussex.ac.uk/sei/research/ europeanpartieselections referendumsnetwork/epernelectionbriefings (accessed on 10 February 2012).
Heijmans, Ph. (2010) 'Financiers Remain Hidden', *The Prague Post*, 17 March, 23, A2.
Hlousek, V. and Kaniok, P. (2009) 'The 2009 European Parliament Election in the Czech Republic 5-6 June 2009', European Parliament Election Briefing no. 29, EPERN Network, Sussex, Sussex University. Online. Available at: www.sussex.ac.uk/sei/research/europeanpartieselectionsreferendums network/europeparliamentelections (accessed on 10 February 2012).
Hlousek, V. and Kaniok, P. (2010) 'The Absence of Europe in the Czech Parliamentary Election. May 28–29, 2009', EPERN Election Briefing, no. 57, Sussex, Sussex University. Online. Available at: www.sussex.ac.uk/sei/research/europeanpartieselectionsreferendumsnetwork/epernelectionbriefings (accessed on 10 February 2012).
Hympl, J. (2009) 'Češi zvolili 22 euromilionářů', *Lidové noviny*, 8 June, 1-2.
Kárniková, A. (2010) 'Czech Republic', in Gagatek, W. (ed.) *The 2009 Elections to the European Parliament. Country Reports,* Florence, European University Institute, 65–70.
Königová, M (2009) 'Paroubek: Já že jsem papaláš? Topolánek a Langer jsou papaláši!' *Právo*, 9, 2.
Kopecký, P. (2004) 'An Awkward Newcomer? EU Enlargement and Euroscepticism in the Czech Republic', in Harmsen R. and Spiering M. (eds) *European Studies: A Journal of European History, Culture and Politics,* Special Issue on Euroscepticism. National Identity and European Integration, 21, 225–45.
Kubik, (2009b) 'Politici, my vam nerozumime' ['We Don't Understand You Politicians'], *Mlada fronta DNES*, 8 June, A2.
Kubita, J. (2009a) 'Vlk: Nevolte ty, kdo svrhli vladu' ['Don't Vote for Those Who Brought Down the Government'], *Hospodarske noviny*, 5–7 June.
Právo (9 June 2009) Königová, M., 'Paroubek: Já že jsem papaláš? Topolánek a Langer jsou papaláši!', 2.
Rulikova, M. (2004) 'The European Parliament Elections in the Czech Republic, June 11–12, 2004'. 2004 European Parliament Election Briefing no. 9, EPERN Network, Sussex, Sussex University. Online. Available at: www.sussex.ac.uk/sei/research/europeanpartieselectionsreferendumsnetwork/europe parliamentelections (accessed on 10 February 2012).
Schmitt, H. and Mannheimer, R. (1991) 'About Voting and Non-Voting in the European Elections of 1989', *European Journal of Political Research* 19(1), 31–54.
Uhl, P. (2009) 'Bude krajne pravicove bujeni zhoubne?' ['Will a Virulent Spread of the Extreme Right be Malignant?'], *Pravo*, 9 June, 6.
Valaskova, M. (2009) 'ODS i CSSD se boji vyhry' ('ODS and CSSD Are Afraid of Winning'), *Hospodarske noviny*, 5–7 June, 1.
van der Cees, E., Franklin, M.N. and van der Brug, W. (1999) 'Policy Preference and Party Choice', in Schmitt, H. and Thomassen, J. (eds), *Political Representation and Legitimacy in the European Union*, Oxford, Oxford University Press, 161–85.

26
SLOVAKIA

Marek Rybář

Figure 26.1 Map of Slovakia

Table 26.1 Slovakia profile

EU entry year	2004
Schengen entry year	2007
MEPs elected in 2009	13
MEPs under Lisbon Treaty	13
Capital	Bratislava
Total area★	49,035 km^2
Population	5,415,949
	85.8 % Slovaks, 9.7 % Hungarians, 1.7 % Roma, 0.8% Czechs, 0.7% Ruthenians and Ukrainians, 1.3 % others and unknown
Population density★★	110.4/km^2
Median age of population	38.6
Political system	Parliamentary Republic
Head of state	President Ivan Gašparovič (June 2004–)
Head of government	Róbert Fico, Direction-Social Democracy (*Smer*-SD) (July 2006–July 2010); Iveta Radičová, Slovak Democratic and Christian Union-Democratic Party, (SDKÚ-DS), (July 2010–April 2012); Róbert Fico, Direction-Social Democracy (*Smer*-SD) (April 2012–)
Political majority	Direction-Social Democracy (*Smer*-SD), Slovak National Party (SNS), People's Party-Movement for a Democratic Slovakia (L'S-HZDS), Government Coalition (July 2006– July 2010); Slovak Democratic and Christian Union-Democratic Party (SDKÚ-DS), Freedom and Solidarity (SaS), Christian Democratic Movement (KDH), Bridge (Most-Híd) Government Coalition (July 2010–April 2012); Direction-Social Democracy (*Smer*-SD) (April 2012–)
Currency	Slovak Koruna Euro (€) since 2009
Prohead GDP in PPS	13,900 €

Source: Eurostat, 2013, 2014, http://epp.eurostat.ec.europa.eu/.

Notes:
★ Total area including inland waters.
★★ Population density: the ratio of the annual average population of a region to the land area of the region.

1 Geographical position

Slovakia is located in east Central Europe. To the east the country has common borders with Ukraine, to the southwest with Austria, to the west with the Czech Republic, to the north with Poland and to the south with Hungary. Slovakia has a population of 5.4 million inhabitants and an area of 49,036 square kilometres. About 55 per cent of the population live in urban centres. Slovakia has several minorities, including Hungarians, 9.7 per cent, Roma, 1.7 per cent, Czechs, 0.8 per cent, Ruthenians and Ukrainians, 0.7 per cent.

2 Historical background

Slovakia gained independence on 1 January 1993 following a peaceful and constitutional dissolution of the Czechoslovak federation, of which it was a constituent part. Historically, Slovakia was a part of the Czechoslovak Republic established in 1918 on the ruins of the Austro-Hungarian

(Habsburg) monarchy. With the exception of the period during WWII (1939–1945), when an independent Slovak Republic existed under the tutelage of Nazi Germany, Slovakia had no experience with independent statehood. The Communist takeover in 1948 brought about four decades of undemocratic one-party rule. Political liberalization of the Communist regime in the 1960s, also known as the Prague Spring suppressed by the Soviet Union, did not lead to free multiparty competition. In November 1989 a democratization movement swept the Communist regime in a non-violent revolution, thus paving the way for the 1990 parliamentary elections, the first free and fair elections in more than 40 years.

The new political representation initiated far-reaching political and economic reforms. At the same time, however, old issues of relations between Czechs and Slovaks emerged. Two years of negotiations between the leading national representatives of the two constituent units of Czechoslovakia failed, as no agreement on a redistribution of powers between the federal and state units was found. In 1992, a party favouring a further loosening of the relations between the two constituent parts of the state convincingly won parliamentary elections in Slovakia. In the Czech part of the federation, on the other hand, an economic liberal party supporting a more centralized federal state received a plurality of seats in the Parliament. The two parties representing the Slovak and Czech governments, respectively, embarked upon a series of negotiations to reach a constitutional solution. Eventually, however, they only agreed to disagree and decided to dissolve the Czechoslovak federation through a constitutional amendment passed by the Federal Assembly. In November 1992, both houses of the federal Parliament approved a constitutional amendment dissolving the Czechoslovak state.

Since the end of Communism, Slovakia has been a democratic state periodically organizing free and fair parliamentary elections respecting basic human and civic rights. In the period between 1994 and 1998, however, the government, led by a charismatic politician, severely circumscribed the rights of the political opposition and several of its decisions clearly contradicted the Slovak Constitution. In 1996, for example, in a reaction to his defection from the parliamentary faction supporting the government, the parliamentary majority effectively stripped a parliamentary deputy of his mandate, thus clearly violating his political rights. In addition, the Parliament refused to comply with a decision of the Slovak Constitutional Court calling for a remedy. In 1997, the government *de facto* thwarted a referendum on direct presidential elections initiated by the parliamentary opposition (Láštic, 2005). This relatively brief period of deviation from principles and practices of parliamentary democracy ended after the 1998 parliamentary elections. The then opposition parties, together with various non-governmental organizations, effectively mobilized the voters and the authoritarian-leaning government was voted out from power. The democratic backsliding of the government and the need to catch up with the neighbours on their way to EU membership had been the main electoral appeals of the opposition's successful electoral mobilization. The new broad left-to-right coalition quickly managed to re-establish the democratic credentials of the regime, and allowed Slovakia to return to the path of democratic consolidation. The new domestic political situation cleared the way for the country to start accession negotiations with the EU in 2000. The prospect of EU membership and the need to provide political stability held the heterogeneous coalition government together for the whole four-year period. The 2002 'earthquake' elections produced surprising results: whilst support for Nationalist and semi-authoritarian parties dropped considerably, and the Communist-successor left did not even manage to clear the 5 per cent electoral threshold, four centre-right parties with pro-integrationist and pro-market agendas gained a narrow majority and formed a government that successfully completed the accession negotiations. On 1 May 2004, Slovakia became a member of the European Union.

The process of Slovakia's democratic consolidation is thus intertwined with the process of EU accession. Institutionally, the constitutional changes required for the country to join the

EU were linked with amendments that modified the constitutional provisions specifying the relations between the President and the government, whose conflict before 1998 had added to political instability in the country. Behaviourally, the 2002 elections, after which four out of seven parliamentary subjects were organizationally new political parties, produced a political configuration in which the parties whose main agenda was early EU accession took control of the government. It can even be argued that the EU and NATO accession was the main theme of the 2002 parliamentary elections. Significantly, however, no relevant party was against EU membership. Quite the contrary: all parties that entered the new Parliament supported it in their election manifestos. Rather, they competed on the issue of their competence to lead the country to an early EU membership. Parties, whose reputation was damaged due to their participation in the semi-authoritarian government in 1994–1998, or whose positions on the issue of EU accession were unclear, received less then the expected share of the vote. Conversely, parties that made EU accession the key theme of their agenda clearly benefited from the time of EU expansion. As the decision about EU enlargement was expected shortly after the 2002 Slovak elections, pro-integration parties emphasized their qualities and credibility as the guarantors of integration. In addition, they may have benefitted from the EU's and NATO's political conditionality, as various representatives of these organizations and their Member States made it clear that a government with the semi-authoritarian parties, like the one before 1998, would not be acceptable as a trustworthy partner, even though the effect of such statements is difficult to assess.

Even in the 2002 elections, however, there was hardly any discussion about the desirable form of the EU that Slovakia wanted to join. Although the question of EU integration featured prominently in statements by party leaders and in election manifestos, parties rarely elaborated their positions. The question of the future shape of the EU, once Slovakia was a full member, was conspicuously absent from the election documents of all major Slovak parties in 2002 (Korba, 2002, 38-40).

3 Geopolitical profile

Slovakia is a full member of the EU and the North Atlantic Treaty Organization (NATO). It joined NATO on 29 March 2004, shortly before becoming a member of the European Union. After decades of Soviet dominance, Slovakia is strongly oriented towards the Western alliance. Slovakia is also fully integrated into the Common Foreign and Security Policy of the European Union. Moreover, Slovakia is member of the Organization for Economic Cooperation and Development, the Organization for Security and Cooperation in Europe as one of the countries emerging out of the Czechoslovak 'velvet divorce', the Council of Europe, the United Nations, the International Monetary Fund, and the World Trade Organization.

4 Overview of the political landscape

The Slovak Republic is a parliamentary democracy. Parliament consists of 150 members. Parliamentary elections take place every four years. Due to high party system fragmentation, Slovakia has so far experienced coalition governments. The Prime Minister normally comes from the largest party in the coalition. In spite of the direct election of the President for a five-year period, his or her *de facto* powers are rather limited, so that the political system performs like a classic parliamentary democracy. Before and after the 2009 EP elections, Robert Fico was the Prime Minister of a coalition government elected in 2006. The coalition government consisted of *Smer* (Direction-Social Democracy), the Slovak National Party (SNS), and the Movement for a Democratic Slovakia (HZDS). Between 2010 and 2012, Iveta Radičová was the Prime Minister of a four-party coalition government consisting of three centre-right parties and a Hungarian minority party. The government collapsed in late 2011, after a bitter dispute over whether Slovakia should ratify the expansion of the European Financial Stability Fund (EFSF) in the euro-zone. The Liberal Freedom and Solidarity Party refused to support the move and abstained in a parliamentary vote of confidence called by the Prime Minister to push through the measure, causing the automatic resignation of the cabinet. The other three governing parties negotiated with the major opposition party *Smer* for support for the EFSF expansion ratification in exchange for early elections called for March 2012.

President Ivan Gasparovic was elected in 2004 and re-elected in 2009. Like in many other new Central and Eastern European democracies, a Constitutional Court was established which has been an important player in shaping the political system.

5 Brief account of the political parties

Slovak party politics have been characterized by instability, epitomized by the frequent emergence of new political parties and the disappearance of once relevant parties. Party politics after the end of Communist regime in 1989 had been formed almost from scratch, since more than 40 years of one-party rule effectively annihilated historical political parties and previously dominant political cleavages. Behind the instability of political parties, however, one can identify four main political streams that dominate Slovak politics. These are the centre-left, the centre-right, Nationalists, and representatives of Slovakia's Hungarians, the largest ethnic minority living in the country.

Until 2002, the centre-left was primarily represented by the Communist-successor Party of the Democratic Left (SDL). Led by a reformist leadership since 1990, the party managed to

Table 26.2 List of political parties in Slovakia

Original name	Abbreviation	English translation
Smer-Sociálna demokracia	Smer-SD	Direction-Social Democracy
Slovenská demokratická a krest'anská únia-Demokratická strana	SDKÚ-DS	Slovak Democratic and Christian Union-Democratic party
Strana mad'arskej koalície	SMK	Hungarian Coalition Party
Krest'anskodemokratické hnutie	KDH	Christian Democratic Movement
L'udová strana-Hnutie za demokratické Slovensko	L'S-HZDS	Peoples Party-Movement for a Democratic Slovakia
Slovenská národná strana	SNS	Slovak National Party
Sloboda a solidarita	SaS	Freedom and Solidarity
Strana zelených	SZ	Green Party
Konzervatívni demokrati Slovenska-Občianska konzervatívna strana	KDS-OKS	Conservative Democrats of Slovakia-Civic Conservative Party
Komunistická strana Slovenska	KSS	Communist Party of Slovakia
Slobodné fórum	SF	Free Forum
Strana demokratickej l'avice	SDL'	Party of the Democratic Left
Agrárna strana vidieka	ASV	Agrarian Party of the Countryside
MISIA 21-Hnutie krest'anskej solidarity	MISIA 21	Mission 21-Movement of a Christian Solidarity
Demokratická strana	DS	Democratic Party
LIGA, občiansko-liberálna strana	LIGA	League-Civic Liberal Party

transform itself into a reasonably moderate and democratic political party. In its heyday in 1998–2000, it entered the government and occupied several key portfolios. Shortly before the 2002 parliamentary elections, however, the party broke up in a dispute over leadership style and its new policy profile, and it was replaced in the Parliament by one of its breakaway factions, *Smer* (Direction). Led by a popular leader, Róbert Fico, *Smer* gradually absorbed all relevant centre-left parties in 2004 and under the new name *Smer*-Social Democracy (*Smer*-SD) won the 2006 parliamentary elections. Slovakia's centre-right has been composed of the more conservative Christian Democratic Movement (KDH) and an economically Liberal Slovak Democratic and Christian Union-Democratic Party (SDKÚ-DS). Whilst the former has often been associated with the defence of traditional values, authority, Christianity, and family, drawing its support primarily from the rural areas, the latter represents an urban, relatively young, and educated electorate. Since its creation in 2000, the SDKÚ is the more senior of the two centre-right parties, as it received more votes and parliamentary seats in parliamentary elections, and its leader Mikuláš Dzurinda presided over two Slovak governments between 1998 and 2006.

The Nationalist-authoritarian camp has also been composed of two main parties, the Slovak National Party (SNS) and the Peoples' Party-Movement for a Democratic Slovakia (L'S-HZDS). Nationalism has been the dominant characteristic of the SNS; authoritarian tendencies, combined with appeals to national identity, were important for the electoral strategy of the L'S-HZDS until about 2002–2004. The party had been the senior member of the coalition government in 1994–98, when the country experienced problems with stability of democratic institutions and was perceived to be responsible for the authoritarian backsliding of Slovakia before 1998. Since then, however, L'S-HZDS has moderated its position and shed its association with authoritarianism and nationalism. In the 2010 parliamentary elections the party failed to clear the 5 per cent threshold of parliamentary representation and, for the first time since its inception in 1991, failed to gain parliamentary representation.

Hungarians amount to about 10 per cent of the Slovak population and their political representation has played a very important political role. Three small ethnic Hungarian political parties united in 1998 to form the Hungarian Coalition Party (SMK). The party was a member of two successive governments (1998–2006) where it controlled several important ministerial portfolios. Although the SMK's electoral appeal is primarily ethnic, the party has been a member of the European Peoples' Party and a firm ally of the centre-right parties in Slovakia. Shortly after the 2009 EP elections, a significant group of its parliamentarians and activists broke away from the party to form a more moderate party, in ethnic terms: *Most-Híd* – Slovak and Hungarian words for bridge. The new formation presented itself as a party of Slovak-Hungarian cooperation and in 2010 it entered Parliament and even joined the new government led by Iveta Radičová. The SMK, on the contrary, suffered from a flow of supporters to *Most-Híd* and did not secure parliamentary representation.

Issues of nationalism and democracy were central to Slovak politics before 2000. Whilst other themes were crucial for individual characteristics of political parties, party competition had been shaped by struggles over democracy and ethnicity. Since then, however, socio-economic themes have come to dominate Slovak politics, as exemplified primarily by the competition between the centre-left *Smer*-SD and the centre-right SDKÚ-DS. The Slovak party system is still in the making but in the 2004 and 2009 EP elections and in the 2006 national parliamentary election no new parliamentary party emerged and, thus, a discernable pattern of political cooperation and competition seems to have been established. On one side of the political competition there has been an alliance between the centre-right (SDKÚ-DS and KDH) with the ethnic Hungarian SMK. *Smer*-SD has crystallized as their main opponent, and this centre-left party has formed a strategic alliance with the Slovak national parties (SNS and L'S-HZDS).

This atypical cooperation between the centre-left and the Nationalists seems to confirm an observation that in post-Communist Europe, the main axis of competition is between the left/Nationalist/authoritarian parties and the centre-right aligned with libertarian/cosmopolitan political forces (Marks et al., 2006). These two issues, the left–right socio-economic divide and the Nationalist-ethnic minority division, have been crucial in shaping patterns of political conflict and may be seen as potential bases for a stable pattern of political party interaction.

However, contrary to this stabilization trend, in 2009–2010 two new and relevant political parties emerged that challenge the established parties of the centre-right camp. Apart from Bridge (*Most-Híd*), which effectively took over the position of the SMK in the political system, a new libertarian party called Freedom and Solidarity (SaS) emerged. The party has presented itself as a radical opponent of the Socialist-led government and has attracted primarily young, educated, and economically Liberal voters. It joined the government in 2010 and effectively caused it to break down in 2011.

5.1 Party attitudes towards the European Union

Slovakia's road to the EU has not been straightforward and exclusion from the initial phase of enlargement caused considerable shock amongst the national elite. This formative experience strongly shaped the attitudes of the political parties, because EU membership has been very popular amongst Slovak voters. Hence, even those parties that had *de facto* caused the integration failure before 1998, and had often expressed dissatisfaction with the attitudes of EU representatives, later supported EU membership. It was this experience of initial exclusion from the EU membership talks, combined with the need to catch up in the integration process after 1998, that created a peculiar legacy for Slovak political parties. The main issue in debates about the EU in Slovakia were not about elaborating detailed proposals of what the future shape of the EU should be. Rather, parties competed on who was the most competent to 'deliver'. Between 1998 and 2004, party leaders competed over their ability to bring Slovakia into the EU; after accession, the key themes revolved around the ability to 'complete' EU membership by entering the Schengen area and the euro-zone. EU integration has been a valence issue in party competition and a failure to prove one's own competence was punished by the Euro-optimist electorate.

Taggart and Szczerbiak (2004) summarized party positions towards the EU in a threefold categorization that distinguished two forms of Euroscepticism, hard and soft, alongside a supportive, Euro-enthusiastic position. The main difference between the two Eurosceptic attitudes is that the soft version involves 'contingent or qualified opposition to European integration', whilst hard Euroscepticism implies 'outright rejection of the entire project of European political and economic integration' (ibid., 3–4). Seen from this perspective, most of the relevant parties in Slovakia, including the two largest parties, *Smer*-SD and SDKÚ-DS, belong to the group of Euro-optimists.

The SDKÚ has had a positive stance towards EU integration in its pedigree: it ran in its first-ever contested national parliamentary elections of 2002 using as its main slogan the successful completion of EU and NATO accession. The party has been consistently in favour of further integration in Europe, even though it has opposed fiscal harmonization. *Smer*-SD, on the other hand, had started as a protest party in 1999, collecting votes from disillusioned leftist voters. In the 2002 parliamentary elections it registered a lower-than-expected electoral result, probably due to its somewhat lukewarm support for early EU accession. However, after it entered the government in 2006, *Smer*-SD projected itself as a true representative of what it called 'a European social model' and it supported all proposed measures taken at the EU level to further deepen European integration. Under its leadership, Slovakia also entered the Schengen zone and adopted the euro as its currency in January 2009.

The L'S-HZDS, SMK, and *Most-Híd* are also in the same category of Euro-optimistic parties. Between 1994 and 1998, the L'S-HZDS was the senior coalition party responsible for the exclusion of Slovakia from the initial wave of EU accession talks. Even though the party had paid lip service to EU integration, it effectively rejected the measures demanded by the EU in an effort to strengthen its domestic power base. However, after eight years in opposition, the party changed and became, at least rhetorically, one of the most Euro-optimistic parties, even calling for a transformation of the EU into a fully-fledged federation.

SMK and *Most-Híd*, two predominantly ethnic Hungarian parties, have supported EU membership rhetorically and also voted consistently for all key measures deepening EU integration in the national Parliament. There have been no internal rifts recorded in the two parties that could be attributed to differences over EU integration.

The Christian Democrats are the clearest representatives of soft Euroscepticism. For example, before the EU accession referendum in 2003, the party proposed a constitutional amendment that would guarantee the national veto in 'cultural and ethical issues' (Rybář, 2005). The party also proposed, again without much success, that the Constitutional Treaty and later the Lisbon Treaty should be ratified by a national referendum, and did not support the documents in parliamentary ratification. The KDH's opposition to the EU, however, is clearly qualified. It has been one of the supporters of Slovakia's EU accession and sees the benefits of cooperation between European countries. The party primarily rejects the intrusion of the EU's competences into the core of national sovereignty, moral, and cultural issues including family law harmonization, the setting up of the European prosecutor, and deeper coordination of national asylum policies.

Yet, since 2009, the KDH has also shifted away from soft Euroscepticism. The party congress in late 2009 elected Ján Figel', a member of the European Commission in the Barroso I team 2004–2009, as new party chairman. Figel' has been one of the avowed supporters of EU integration in the party and had built his 'pro-European' image as the chief Slovak negotiator with the EU during the accession talks before 2004. The shift towards an openly Euro-optimist position has been eased by the departure of several Eurosceptic and traditionally conservative parliamentarians from the party in 2008. The consensus in the party's broader leadership over its stance towards Europe has thus increased. In addition, the core source of the party's soft Euroscepticism, its insistence on the traditional conservative themes of family and religion, have been somewhat subdued in an effort to reach electorally beyond its core voters and attract economically liberal voters.

The Slovak National Party is another representative of soft Euroscepticism. However, its stances have been much less elaborated upon. Before the 2009 EP election, the party continued to dwell on the need to protect the Slovak national identity and national interests in the EU, and it criticized the tendency towards a 'European bureaucratic superstate'. It also advocated the creation of the second EP chamber representing all nation-states on a parity principle. Even though the party suffered from several splits and showdowns within its leading representatives, these were not caused by, or related to, the SNS' attitudes towards European integration. The main source of its somewhat leery stances towards European Union membership resulted from the party's self-definition as a political subject that had been advocating Slovak independence, even during the existence of the Czechoslovak Republic.

The newest candidate for the soft Eurosceptic label in Slovakia has been the Freedom and Solidarity Party. Established in 2009, the party campaigned in the 2009 EP elections on a libertarian ticket, advocating economic liberalization and voicing its support for personal freedom and alternative lifestyles. Even though it failed to enter the European Parliament, it was more successful in the national elections a year later: it gained over 12 per cent of the vote and joined the four-party coalition government. EU-related themes became the cornerstones of its identity: the party became a staunch opponent of the way in which EU leaders handled the financial crisis in the euro-zone and fiercely rejected a further expansion of the EFSF. After the Prime Minister linked parliamentary ratification of the measure with a request for a vote of confidence, the party abstained, causing the fall of the government. It is interesting to note that the soft Euroscepticism of the Freedom and Solidarity party is different from that of SNS and KDH. It is not based on old-fashioned ethnic exclusivism, as in SNS, and traditional conservatism, as in KDH. Instead, it criticizes the course of EU integration from economically liberal positions and mobilizes those groups in the electorate, such as young urban professionals, that would otherwise be inclined to vote for Euro-optimist parties. The emergence of Freedom and Solidarity as a relevant party therefore significantly changes the pattern of Euroscepticism in Slovakia.

There has been no clear-cut example of a hard Eurosceptic party in Slovakia. One possible exception is the marginal and extra-parliamentary Communist Party of Slovakia (KSS), which managed to gain parliamentary presence only in the 2002–2006 electoral term. Its overt positions towards the EU are mixed, but the party's underlying economic and political values are not compatible with the European project based on free-market and Liberal Democratic principles.

Another way to assess the position of the key political parties towards the EU is to examine their affiliations with European political parties and memberships in EP party groups. The three centre-right opposition parties, SDKÚ-DS, KDH and SMK, have been members of the European Peoples' Party. The situation of their domestic political rivals, who have been in government since the 2006 parliamentary elections, has been more complicated. Until 2009, the Ľ'S-HZDS has not been able to secure membership in any major European political party, chiefly due to its doubtful democratic credentials in the late 1990s. After the 2004 EP elections, for example, the party was denied a membership in the EPP due to the negative attitude of the Slovak membership parties. Its three MEPs thus remained unaffiliated during their 2004–2009 EP tenure. The party was eventually accepted as a member of the European Democratic Party, a centrist and Liberal European party in 2009, and the single MEP who the Ľ'S-HZDS managed to return to the EP in 2009 belongs to the ALDE faction.

The Socialist *Smer*-SD also had to face a twisted and rather complicated road to 'international acceptance'. Even though the three party MEPs elected in 2004 belonged to the PES faction in the EP, the party's status within the PES remained shaky until early 2008. The main reason for the PES' reserved attitude towards *Smer*-SD was because the party decided to invite the extreme Nationalist SNS into the Slovak government in 2006. In reaction, the PES suspended the candidate (associate member) status of the party in October 2006 and appealed to the party leadership to reconsider its choice of domestic political partners. However, after a series of interventions from the *Smer*-SD leadership aimed at presenting the SNS as a credible party that carries out the priorities of the centre-left government, the PES changed its initial decision and admitted the party as a full member in February 2008.

Finally, the SNS has maintained links with various Nationalistic political parties in several European countries and in 2002 it joined the Union for Europe of the Nations (UEN) political group in the EP. Nevertheless, this linkage had little practical meaning because the party failed to gain any EP seats in 2004. In 2009, its single MEP joined the Europe of Freedom and Democracy group and also serves as its Vice-Chairman.

6 Public opinion and the European Union

As described above, EU integration has been a valence issue in Slovak party politics. Instead of competing over various visions of Slovakia's position in the EU, Slovak voters have been offered a choice between essentially pro-European parties, who presented themselves as the most capable of securing 'the inevitable' and generally accepted goals on the way to full EU integration. The lack of contestation over Europe in Slovakia has been one of the reasons why Slovak citizens, who are amongst the most enthusiastic supporters of the EU, produced two of the lowest turnout rates in the history of EP elections. The support for EU membership has been steadily increasing even after Slovakia joined the EU. In the Eurobarometer surveys, the portion of Slovak citizens who believe that membership in the EU is beneficial for the country has increased from 62 per cent in 2004 to 80 per cent in 2009. Similarly, the share of voters who think that EU membership is a 'good thing' rose from 57 per cent in 2004 to 68 per cent in late 2009. Finally, trust in the European Parliament, conventionally understood as a level of support for supranational integration in the EU, ranged between 62 per cent and 72 per cent.

The reports of individual identities have also shown a growing number of those who consider themselves as citizens of the EU. Ol'ga Gyárfášová (2009, 84) reports that after EU entry in 2004, the Slovak population was almost evenly divided into two groups, the first considered themselves only as Slovaks, the second also considered themselves as EU citizens. After five years of EU membership, the share of those who also thought of themselves as EU citizens rose to 57 per cent (ibid.).

Support for EU integration has not been evenly distributed amongst voters of parliamentary political parties. In mid-2009, for example, the highest level of support for EU integration was displayed by supporters of the centre-right parties. Nearly 80 per cent of SDKÚ-DS and KDH voters, 79 and 78 per cent, respectively, considered EU membership to be a 'good thing', followed by 71 per cent of SMK voters (ibid., 85). Some 58 per cent of supporters of *Smer*-SD also held positive attitudes towards EU membership, whilst only 44 per cent of L'S-HZDS supporters and 43 per cent of SNS voters viewed EU membership positively. These two parties also had a near-identical share of supporters who considered it to be a 'good thing' and a 'bad thing' (ibid.).

7 National and EP electoral systems

Since the first post-Communist free and fair elections held in 1990, Slovakia has been using a list-based proportional representation system in the national parliamentary elections. There were two major modifications to this system. First, the threshold of parliamentary representation was increased from 3 per cent to 5 per cent in 1992. Second, four electoral districts were abandoned in 1998 in favour of a single nationwide electoral constituency. The same electoral system has been used for national and EP elections. The only major difference has been that the threshold of parliamentary representation for the EP elections remains the same, i.e. 5 per cent, for a single party and for an alliance of parties, whilst electoral alliances of two or three parties need to reach the increased threshold of 7 per cent, and an alliance of four or more parties requires at least 10 per cent of the vote, to gain parliamentary representation in the national elections. The largest remainders Droop method is used to distribute parliamentary seats amongst competing parties. The effective threshold in the two types of elections differs due to the fact that there are 150 seats to be distributed amongst parties in parliamentary elections, whilst only 13 (14 in 2004) seats are available in the EP for Slovak parliamentarians. It should also be mentioned that the party lists are not fully 'closed', so-called preferential voting, whereby voters may give their preference to up to two candidates from the same list, as used in the EP elections. In 2009, three incumbent MEPs used this opportunity to jump over higher-placed candidates and to secure parliamentary seats.

The elections in Slovakia provided a reliable if modest supply of MEPs to the mainstream party groups in the European Parliament. In 2004, eight MEPs went to the EPP group, three joined the PES and three remained unaffiliated. In 2009, six Slovak MEPs joined the EPP faction, five MEPs joined the Progressive Alliance of Socialists and Democrats (S&D), one parliamentarian belonged to the ALDE group, and one to the EFD.

Politically moderate Slovak EP representatives resulted from election processes that were marked by the lowest historic turnout in any EU Member State since 1979. In 2004, the turnout in Slovakia reached just 16.9 per cent, and it only slightly increased to 19.6 per cent in 2009, the two lowest rates of election participation in EP history. Two broad accounts of the low turnout were put forward after the 2004 elections. According to the electoral cycle argument, there are only a limited number of elections in which citizens can be reasonably expected to take part within a given time period. Between September 2002 and June 2004, that is 21 months, Slovak voters were mobilized to take part in the national parliamentary elections (September 2002), the local elections (December 2002), the EU accession referendum (May 2003), two rounds of presidential elections (April 2004), a referendum on early parliamentary elections (April 2004), and the EP elections in June 2004. Hence, given the timing, it was impossible to generate a great deal of interest amongst the Slovak electorate for the EP elections. The Euro-fatigue argument is a complementary one and, in a way, it is a country-specific argument. Since 1998, Slovak voters *de facto* had already voted three times on the EU-related issue: both of the parliamentary elections in 1998 and 2002, as it was argued, played the role of an informal referendum on whether the country would be invited to the EU. In the 2003 EU accession referendum voters answered the question directly (Henderson, 2004). Having secured EU membership in a series of election events, the EP elections might have been regarded as quite an unimportant episode compared to the big *sine qua non* question voters had to face regarding the geopolitical orientation of the Slovak Republic.

8 A glance at the EP and national elections

The 2004 EP elections took place in the middle of the 2002–2006 national electoral cycle. All seven parliamentary parties plus ten extra-parliamentary ones took part in the election. It was the first European Parliament election in Slovakia and it demonstrated that most of the political parties were ill-prepared for this event. Clear stances by political parties on specific policy issues were almost impossible to detect. Political parties had a hard time explaining to their voters what they stood for in the election. All vaguely argued that their candidates would represent 'the national interest' in the European Parliament, without specifying what those national interests were. Parties also tried to persuade voters on the basis of the personal qualities of their candidates. The opposition Ľ'S-HZDS, for example, claimed it had the most experienced politicians on the party list led by three former cabinet ministers. Governing parties, especially the SDKÚ-DS and the KDH, emphasized their long-term contacts with, and integration into, the European-wide party families, especially the European Peoples' Party. The ethnic-Hungarian SMK reminded their potential voters that it was the first election in which its representatives could sit in a legislative assembly together with the Hungarian politicians from Hungary, thus symbolically uniting Hungarians from the two neighbouring countries. Claims like these provoked a harsh response from the opposition, especially the Ľ'S-HZDS and *Smer*. The two parties tried to mobilize their supporters by pointing out that a low turnout of ethnic Slovaks could produce a result in a disproportionately high number of MEPs of ethnic Hungarian origin, thus suggesting that 'the Slovak national interest' would not be sufficiently represented in the EP.

Most parties also did not prepare fully fledged election manifestos. They either produced only one-page pamphlets with general and vague bullet points, or, when they did have formal manifestos, published them only a few days before the election and made little effort to let the voters know about their official positions.

All major opinion polls conducted before the vote suggested that the four-party centre-right coalition government governing the country since the 2002 elections was set to lose in the EP

Table 26.3 National election results in Slovakia: 2002 and 2006

Political party	Votes in 2002	Share of votes in 2002 %	Number of MPs in 2002	Votes in 2006	Share of votes in 2006 %	Number of MPs in 2006
Smer-SD	387,100	13.5	25	671,185	29.1	50
SDKÚ-DS	433,953	15.1	28	422,815	18.3	31
SNS	95,633	3.3	0	270,230	11.7	20
SMK	32,107	11.2	20	269,111	11.7	20
L'S-HZDS	560,691	19.5	36	202,540	8.8	15
KDH	237,202	8.2	15	191,443	8.3	14
KSS	181,872	6.3	11	89,418	3.8	—
SF	—	—	—	79,963	3.5	—
ANO	230,309	8.0	15	32,775	1.4	—
PSNS	105,084	3.6	0	—	—	—
HZD	94,324	3.3	0	—	—	—
SDA	51,649	1.8	0	—	—	—
SDL'	39,163	1.4	0	—	—	—
Others*	137,032	4.8	0	73,659	3.2	—
Turnout		**70.1**			**54.7**	

Source: Statistical Office of the Slovak Republic, www.statistics.sk.

Note:
* Includes parties that received less than 1 per cent of the votes.

Table 26.4 EP election results in Slovakia: 2004

Political party	Votes in 2004	Share of votes in 2004 %	Number of MEPs in 2004
Smer-SD	118,535	16.9	3
SDKÚ-DS	119,954	17.1	3
SMK	92,927	13.2	2
KDH	113,655	16.2	3
L'S-HZDS	119,582	17.1	3
SNS	14,150	2.0	0
SaS	—	—	—
SZ	—	—	—
KDS-OKS	7,060	1.0	0
KSS	31,908	4.5	0
SF	22,804	3.2	0
ANO	32,653	4.6	0
HZD-L'Ú	11,914	1.7	0
Others*	16,453	2.5	0
Turnout		**16.9**	

Source: Statistical Office of the Slovak Republic, www.statistics.sk.

Notes:
* Includes parties that received less than 1 per cent of the votes.

election. The government, composed of the SDKÚ-DS, KDH, SMK and the Liberal Alliance of the New Citizen (ANO), had embarked upon a series of ambitious reforms aimed at liberalizing the economy, cutting public expenditures, and introducing far-reaching reforms in taxation, pensions, and health care systems. Many of its moves were not popular amongst the public and the opposition parties, especially the L'S-HZDS and *Smer*, registered growing popular support in the polls. Nevertheless, the governing parties combined received eight EP seats, whilst the two opposition parties gained only three seats each. From amongst the parliamentary parties, only the internal-conflict-ridden ANO failed to reach the 5 per cent threshold for EP representation. With an extremely low turnout in mind, one can argue that the success of the governing SDKÚ-DS, three MEPs, resulted in its ability to mobilize a great deal of its stable voters, who perceived the party as the main guarantor of successful EU integration and rewarded its representatives for the completion of EU membership. KDH, three MEPs, and the ethnic-Hungarian SMK, two MEPs, benefitted from disciplined and faithful electorates. The opposition parties L'S-HZDS and *Smer* gained three MEPS each. Their results were lower than expected, probably due to the fact that a large portion of their supporters saw little meaning in participating in elections that did not affect domestic policies and lacked an overt political conflict.

9 The 2009 European election

9.1 Party lists and manifestos

All six parliamentary parties, plus nine extra-parliamentary ones, took part in the 2009 EP elections in Slovakia. Compared to 2004, when only three out of seven parliamentary parties elaborated a written programme for the election, in 2009 all relevant parties published their electoral manifestos. This may have been a sign of a growing importance these parties paid to EU-related themes in general and to EP elections in particular. The programmatic documents varied considerably in length as well as in their relative coverage of national and EU-related topics. One political subject, the extra-parliamentary Green Party, presented a programme entirely adopted from the European Green Party; other parties produced documents to a lesser or greater extent inspired by the European parties. An analysis of the EP manifestos of the two largest parties, *Smer*-SD and SDKÚ-DS, showed little overall differences in the extent to which these contenders identified with the goals, priorities, and electoral pledges incorporated in the election documents of their European partner parties: the Party of European Socialists for the former and the European Peoples' Party for the latter. Bátora (2009) showed that about 72 per cent of *Smer*-SD's goals and priorities could also be found in the PES document (PES 2009), and some 71 per cent of the SDKÚ-DS's manifesto pledges corresponded to the party manifesto of the EPP (EPP 2009). Interestingly, an important part of *Smer*-SD's manifesto was devoted to the protection of the national interest in the EU, a theme conventionally attributed to Nationalistic and Eurosceptic parties and absent in the PES document. This was fully in line with the trend discernable in many post-Communist countries, whereby the left has often been associated with traditional, authoritarian, and Nationalistic values. The SDKÚ-DS manifesto almost completely left out the themes of green investment and sustainable economic growth (Bátora, 2009, 48–51). A comparable analysis of the manifestos of SMK and KDH, two other Slovak member parties of the EPP, was not available. However, a cursory overview of their programmes showed that they emphasized themes and values often not present in, or even contradicted by, the EPP's manifesto. The Christian Democrats rejected the Lisbon Treaty and were much more Eurosceptic than the EPP; SMK prioritized themes of human and ethnic minority rights. The limited programmatic convergence of the parties from the same European party organization suggested that it was domestic political constituencies, and the structure of domestic political conflicts, that were more important in determining parties' programmatic orientation than membership in, and policy transfer from, the European parties.

9.2 Electoral campaign

The 2009 EP elections took part against the backdrop of two broadly unfavourable conditions with international implications that also affected the campaign of the political parties. First, as in most EU countries, the economic and financial crisis strongly impacted the Slovak economy. Slovakia is heavily dependent on international trade and decreased demand from major European economies, especially Germany, brought about a sharp decline in economic growth. Second, the dispute between Russia and Ukraine over natural gas transport tariffs to Europe, resulting in the interruption of supplies to Slovakia and other Eastern European countries for almost two weeks in early 2009, fully revealed Slovakia's vulnerability resulting from its dependence on Russian energy supplies. These two critical developments strongly affected the domestic political situation and parties reflected them in their campaign messages. However, issues of nationalism and ethnic identity impacted the campaign in its final phase and confirmed that domestic political themes dominated the public discourse in EP elections.

Probably the most significant programmatic themes of the campaign focussed around the ongoing economic crisis. As one could expect, the two largest parties presented a totally different picture of the causes of the crisis and the measures to be taken to tackle it. Both *Smer*-SD and SDKÚ-DS echoed the arguments used by the PES and EPP, respectively. The left argued that parties of the centre-right in power in most EU countries during the 2009 EP elections were not able to solve the economic crisis. *Smer*-SD went even further when it claimed that the crisis was a direct outcome of what it called the 'anti-social' policies of the right. The only way to prevent such economic turmoil, the party argued, was a victory for social democracy in the elections. SDKÚ-DS, which lost power in 2006, used the campaign to highlight the economic successes of its government in Slovakia during its tenure, and blamed *Smer*-SD for incompetence in economic and financial issues. The party argued that the *Smer*-SD-led government had proved to be unable to prevent a worsening of the economic situation and failed to take advantage of Slovakia's status as a net recipient of EU funds to compensate for declining demand in external trade. Another centre-right party, the Christian Democrats, was also critical of the government's economic policies and emphasized that lower taxes, simplification of the administrative procedures in setting up businesses, and a more effective use of EU funds would be an effective strategy to face the crisis. Amongst the relatively successful extra-parliamentary parties, the Freedom and Solidarity Party presented a well-elaborated, radically Liberal vision of the EU single market. The party criticized national protectionism in some of the big EU Member States and proposed a radical overhaul of the Common Agricultural Policy, the liberalization of the labour market, and the diversification of EU energy supplies.

The centre-right also pledged to protect the national veto in the area of direct taxation. This has long been a key plank in their party platform, since a simplified taxation system and lower taxes were at the core of their government economic programme in 2002–2006. One issue on which all parties agreed was the need to utilize EU funds to improve Slovakia's infrastructure. Party manifestos, however, were essentially vague about concrete proposals to achieve this. Structural funds thus remain a specific East European valence issue, on which all parties agree but compete on their ability to deliver the desired outcome.

A broadly conceived energy security policy was another issue of concern for the Slovak parties; however, they either did not elaborate concrete proposals or emphasized issues outside the scope of EU powers. Christian Democrats and the SDKÚ-DS called for a common energy policy at the EU level, to provide a stable and reliable supply of energy commodities for all EU Member States. They also explicitly mentioned the need for a vigorous EU position towards Russia, the key exporter of energy commodities to Slovakia. Again, no specific proposals were put forward. Parties of the centre-right also emphasized the need for a stable transatlantic partnership with the US to prevent an increase in Russian influence in the new EU Member States.

The left also acknowledged that an energy policy with an EU dimension was required to provide stable supplies from Russia. In addition, *Smer*-SD claimed that Slovakia should utilize its existing domestic capacities and orient itself more towards nuclear energy. This was not a new theme for the party; as a senior coalition partner it pressed for the completion of a nuclear power plant and it even initiated an international initiative, the so-called Nuclear Energy Forum, to increase the profile of nuclear energy in the European context. The party did not advocate an EU policy in this field; rather, it used the campaign to reiterate its preference for this kind of domestic policy.

One of the themes that had a potential bearing on the shape of the future EU was the question of further EU expansion. Most parties generally advocated EU enlargement to the countries of the Balkans, and some of them specifically mentioned Croatia, Serbia, and other ex-Yugoslav countries as future EU members. In addition, the SDKÚ-DS called for an open European perspective for Ukraine. Differences existed when it came to Turkish EU membership. The Christian Democrats and L'S-HZDS, for example, preferred what they called a 'privileged partnership' with the country, in other words close cooperation and integration between the EU and Turkey short of full membership.

These examples notwithstanding, substantial debates about 'explicitly' EU themes were scarce. Programmatic declaratory differences between parties may have existed; however, by and large they did not become the subject of discussion and political controversies that were emphasized and politicized in the campaign. Many issues, in addition, were almost completely absent from the public discourse. The Lisbon Treaty, issues of immigration, and the 'green economy' that all featured prominently in the election documents of the European political parties were sometimes mentioned in the manifestos of Slovak parties, but their visibility and importance for political debate and campaign mobilization were negligible. The KDH was the only relevant party that explicitly rejected the Lisbon Treaty in its EP manifesto. However, given the parliamentary ratification of the Lisbon Treaty by a constitutional three-fifth majority in June 2008, and a strong consensus of the parties about the benefit of EU membership, it was not an issue to provoke much debate. Occasional negative references to, and rejection of, the 'European super state' appeared in the programmes of the Slovak National Party and the Freedom and Solidarity Party, however, these notions were not further elaborated upon.

Overall, the campaign brought few programmatic confrontations between the competing parties. One country-specific issue that shaped the discussions in the campaign was Slovak-Hungarian relations and, more broadly, themes on nationalism and ethnic relations. A pretext was given at a party rally in neighbouring Hungary, where the leader of the Hungarian opposition Viktor Orbán stated that EP elections would decide how many MEPs would represent Hungarians living in the Carpathian basin (Mesežnikov, 2009, 17). *Smer*-SD and SNS interpreted this as interference in the domestic politics of Slovakia, since Orbán was referring to the Hungarians living in Hungary and in the neighbouring countries including Slovakia, apparently emphasizing ethnicity over citizenship. *Smer*-SD called a special session of the Slovak Parliament, just three days before the election. It also pointed out the close relationship between Hungarian Fidesz and the opposition SMK, the party representing the Hungarian minority in Slovakia. The opposition parties boycotted the parliamentary session but also condemned Orbán's statement. This so-called 'Hungarian card' has been regularly played in Slovak elections, including the first EP elections in 2004, even though its mobilization potential remains unclear and difficult to assess.

As far as campaign tactics were concerned, party leaders preferred to mobilize their voters at party rallies, and presented simple messages on their billboards and newspaper advertisements.

The results of Memo 98, a media monitoring project that analysed news content during the period of the official election campaign, two weeks before the election, confirm the lack of politicization of EU-related themes. A majority of broadcast statements related to the EU and EP elections had a neutral character. Most of the news tended to provide information on EU institutions and the technicalities of the elections, without coverage of contentious issues. Information on the campaign of political parties, their statements and policy preferences, was clearly marginal in the media discourse. Memo 98's analysis also showed that amongst the 'top ten' political themes covered by the four main television stations, an overwhelming majority, seven to eight depending on the television channels, had no direct connection to the EU and EP elections (Memo 98, 2009). Hence, issues relevant to the EP elections were not widely discussed, even during the peak of the campaign. This fact has been ascribed to campaign legislation that calls for balanced and fair coverage of the main political forces on television news and debates, a provision interpreted very restrictively by the broadcasters. The resulting effect was that the media either refrained from televised debates between the candidates or opted for a format of debate that discouraged direct confrontations between parties and their programmes.

Any discussion about the campaign would be incomplete without mentioning the activities of the Office of the European Parliament (OEP) in Slovakia (European Parliament, 2009). Aware of the lowest turnout Slovakia recorded in 2004, OEP representatives prepared a whole range of activities that were designed to inform voters in Slovakia about the election and the role of the EP more generally. The communications campaign lasted almost three months and ended before the official party campaign started, to avoid any interference with the party competition. The national EP office focussed its activities on both direct and indirect communications with potential voters. Its direct communication methods rested in an extensive billboard presentation of the EP's competences, open public meetings, two rock-the-vote-type concerts, television spots and radio adverts, and the participation of the head of the office in various discussions in the media. The OEP chose four motifs from the 12 broad areas defined by EP headquarters that were considered the most appealing in the Slovak context. These included consumer protection, the EU budget, energy resources, and security and individual liberties. In addition, a special European information train with six day-long stops in major Slovak towns was dispatched to supply information about the EP elections.

Indirect communication methods primarily involved organizing academic conferences, semi-public discussions, and educational quizzes for secondary schools and university students. These were targeted to influence the personal environment of potential voters, since decisions about political participation are often based on the advice and opinions of family and friends. In addition, the OEP prepared training for social workers who dealt with various socially disadvantaged citizens to provide them with basic information about the elections. These activities definitely contributed to the high visibility of the campaign – 82 per cent according to the 2009 EP Elections Eurobarometer. Gyárfášová showed that it was a complex lack of motivation to vote, and not a lack of information, that was decisive for low EP turnout in Slovakia (2009, 76–77).

9.3 Electoral results

Four issues are worth exploring with respect to the 2009 EP election results. First, compared to 2004, parties invested more effort and energy into the 2009 EP elections, as exemplified by more intense campaigning and better preparation of formal documents, especially election manifestos, related to elections. Second, voter participation remained very low, the second lowest in any EP election, despite an 'obsession' with turnout that marked the campaign (Henderson, 2009). Third, the results basically confirmed a trend towards the stabilization of the party system and were very similar to the results of the 2006 national parliamentary election. Finally, as in 2004, the election results did not have any discernable impact on the national political scene.

Even though most political parties prepared fully-fledged election manifestos in 2009, this does not mean that the campaign itself revolved around substantive issues raised in the parties' programmatic documents. As in 2004, nearly all parties campaigned on their presumed superior ability to represent 'the national interest in the European Parliament'. For some parties, especially the three governing parties *Smer*-SD, L'S-HZDS and SNS, national interests chiefly meant ethnic Slovak interests. These parties tried to mobilize their voters by pointing out that a danger of over-representation of ethnic Hungarians amongst the Slovak MEPs could somehow weaken Slovakia's standing on the international scene, especially with regard to the potential worsening of relations between Slovakia and Hungary. However, the campaigns of the individual candidates, especially the MEPs standing for re-election, were more focussed on their prospective fields of activity in the EP, emphasizing their personal qualities like experience in European and international affairs and the general 'acceptance' of their parties as trustworthy partners in the EU.

The low turnout in 2009 confirmed the importance of 'supply factors', primarily the unimaginative campaign waged by parties and candidates, the role of the media, and the limiting impact of institutional factors like campaign regulations. Most political parties nominated relatively low-profile politicians. Incumbency was an advantage, as 7 out of 14 outgoing MEPs were re-elected. However, the political importance of Slovak MEPs in their national political parties has been low from the very beginning, and a cursory overview of the squad of Slovak EP representatives suggests that EP seats either serve as 'storage' for political veterans or a training ground for young and inexperienced politicians. *Smer*-SD's Monika Beňová and SMK's Edit Bauer may be possible exceptions to this trend, but their respective positions inside their parties do not qualify them as political heavyweights.

The results of the 2009 election essentially mirrored those of the 2006 national parliamentary elections. The most successful of the individual parties was *Smer*-SD, having won five out of the thirteen seats reserved for Slovak MEPs. It received just over 32 per cent of the vote, about three percentage points more than in 2006. The centre-right opposition, composed of the SDKÚ-DS, KDH, and SMK, received a combined six MEPs; all of them belonged to the EPP group in the European Parliament. Hence, both *Smer*-SD and the opposition argued that it was more successful than its opponent. Like *Smer*-SD, each of the three opposition parties achieved about the same percentage results in 2009 as in 2006. The L'S-HZDS and SNS received one seat each, producing a final 'score' of 8:6 between government and the opposition. Nevertheless, due to very low turnout, the 2009 European election could not be considered an indicator of the overall support for political parties. Rather, it suggested that the size of the core electorate of each of the main political parties remained essentially the same for all parties.

The election results also suggested a trend towards party system stabilization. From 2002, more or less the same parties were successful in national and European elections. Three tendencies were displayed: growing support for the left-leaning *Smer*-SD, electoral stabilization of the centre-right (SDKÚ-DS, KDH and SMK) and a decline of the Nationalists (L'S-HZDS and SNS). Other than that, however, the EP elections seem to have little overall impact on the Slovak party political scene. They seemed to be more a competition for office than for power. As such, they have been treated by the party leaderships in a very cost-efficient manner: whilst symbolically important, they have been just one relatively marginal event in the permanent campaign for power at the national level.

Table 26.5 EP election results in Slovakia: 2009

Political party	Number of votes	Share of votes %	Number of MEPs	Party family	PG
Smer-SD	264,722	32.0	5	Social Democratic	S&D
SDKÚ-DS	140,426	17.0	2	Liberal/Conservative	EPP
SMK	93,750	11.3	2	Ethnic/Minority	EPP
KDH	89,905	10.9	2	Christian Democrat	EPP
L'S-HZDS	74,241	9.0	1	National/Conservative	ALDE
SNS	45,960	5.5	1	Nationalist	EFD
SaS	39,016	4.7	0	Liberal	—
SZ	17,482	2.1	0	Green	—
KDS-OKS	17,409	2.1	0	Conservative	—
KSS	13,643	1.6	0	Communist	—
SF	13,063	1.6	0	Liberal	—
Others*	17,165	2.2	0	—	—
Total	826,782	100.0	13	—	—
Turnout		**19.6**			

Source: Statistical Office of the Slovak Republic, www.statistics.sk.

Note:
* Includes parties that received less than 1 per cent of the votes.

9.4 Campaign finance

Campaign finance for EP elections remains something of a mystery. Slovak legislation does not require political parties to disclose campaign expenditures in European elections. Existing regulations hold that overall campaign expenditure must only be declared in an annual party financial report. This effectively means that, with respect to EP campaigns, parties are obliged to publish only a single number (of the total amount spent) in their official documents. This differs from the rules regulating national parliamentary elections where relatively detailed reports must be submitted to the authorities within a month after the election. Moreover, the campaign finances of individual candidates, arguably a very important share of total campaign spending, need not be disclosed at all. The flip-side of this is that political parties receive no public subsidies for their performance in the EP elections.

Official party documents suggest that Slovak political parties are heavily financially dependent on state subsidies. The share of state subsidy varied from about 60 per cent to nearly 85 per cent of the total income of parliamentary parties between 1999 and 2009 (Rybář, 2011, 121). Parties receive state subsidies on the basis of their performance in national parliamentary elections. To finance campaigns for the national Parliament, parties usually take loans from banks and repay their debts from the state subsidies. For each vote received, parties annually get a sum equivalent to 1 per cent of the average nominal wage in the national economy in the previous year. In addition, parliamentary parties also receive an annual installment tied to the number of MPs elected on their ticket to the national Parliament. Official numbers suggest that parties invest about ten times more in the national elections than in European ones. These data, however, need to be taken with caution, since they do not take into account campaigns by individual candidates and also campaigns by third parties that are only poorly regulated by Slovak legislation.

10 Theoretical interpretation of Euro-elections

10.1 Second-Order Election theory

The secondary character of the EP contest is most visible in the turnout gap between national and EP elections. The difference in turnout between the 2002 general elections and the 2004

Table 26.6 List of Slovak MEPs: seventh legislature

Name	National party	Political group	Committee	Professional background	Year of birth	Gender
Bauer, Edit	SMK–MKP	EPP (Member of the Bureau)	Employment and Social Affairs, Women's Rights and Gender Equality	Economy, sociology	1946	Female
Beňová, Monika	*Smer*-SD	S&D (Vice-Chair)	Civil Liberties, Justice and Home Affairs	Political science	1968	Female
Kozlík, Sergej	L'S-HZDS	ALDE (Member of the Bureau)	Budgets	Economy	1950	Male
Kukan, Eduard	SDKÚ-DS	EPP		Law, diplomacy, engineering	1939	Male
Maňka, Vladimír	*Smer*-SD	S&D	Budgets, Financial, Economic and Social Crisis		1959	Male
Mészáros, Alajos	SMK–MKP	EPP		Chemical engineering, university lecturer in medicine	1952	Male
Mikolášik, Miroslav	KDH	EPP	Regional Development		1952	Male
Neveďalová, Katarína	*Smer*-SD	S&D	Culture and Education	n/a	1982	Female
Paška, Jaroslav	SNS	EFD (Vice-Chair)	Industry, Research and Energy	Architecture	1954	Male
Smolková, Monika	*Smer*-SD	S&D	Regional Development	Teacher	1956	Female
Šťastný, Peter	SDKÚ-DS	EPP	International Trade	Sport (professional ice hockey player)	1956	Male
Záborská, Anna	KDH	EPP	Development, Women's Rights and Gender Equality	medicine	1948	Female
Zala, Boris	*Smer*-SD	S&D		Philosophy, university lecturer	1954	Male

Source: www.europarl.europa.eu/meps/en/search.html?country=SK.

EP elections reached an astronomic 53.1 percentage points; the gap between the 2006 national elections and the 2009 EP elections amounted to 35.1 percentage points. These electoral races are clearly secondary in voters' perceptions. However, even though the EP elections took place in the middle of the national electoral cycle, the governing parties won both in 2004 and 2009. In 2004, governing parties gained eight MEPs whilst the opposition won just six seats. Three out of four governing parties increased their share of the vote and it was only the smallest coalition partner that lost votes. Furthermore, two out of three opposition parties recorded losses in the EP elections. Similarly, governing parties were more successful than the opposition in 2009, as they received seven out of thirteen EP seats. Two out of three governing parties increased their vote share, compared to two out of three opposition parties that recorded a lower vote share compared to the 2006 national elections. These facts indicate that the Second-Order theory has not been confirmed in Slovakia. In addition, small parties were unsuccessful in both 2004 and 2009. Only parliamentary parties managed to gain EP seats. It can even be agued that the EP elections served as a stabilizing element in an otherwise unstable party system, since they provided no European parliamentary status to nationally irrelevant parties.

10.2 Europe Salience theory

The Europe Salience theory is more difficult to assess directly, but at least two facts run contrary to this explanation. Most importantly, Euro-enthusiast parties gain an overwhelming majority of votes and seats in the EP elections, and the parties with strongly critical stances of the EU, the hard Eurosceptics, remain clearly marginal. In addition, the combined vote share of the two soft Eurosceptic parties, the SNS and KDH, showed no significant increase in the EP elections. Second, EU-related themes remained secondary in the campaign and, with the possible exception of the Christian Democrats, political parties did not attempt to extensively communicate their European positions to voters.

None of the above theoretical interpretations is sufficient to explain the EP election results in Slovakia. We have argued that the key factor behind the election results in Slovakia is to be found in the extremely low turnout. This, in turn, is best explained by 'low supply' explanations that focus on the role of agency-political parties, party leaders, and the lack of politicization of EU themes. EP elections are simply a low priority for national parties in Slovakia, in which relatively low-profile candidates compete for seats in a distant representative body. More broadly, the weak mobilization capacities of political parties in the EP campaign may reflect a broader problem of representative democracy in Slovakia. Most Slovak parties are organizationally weak, top down organized and dispose of only a negligible number of activists and members (Rybář, 2006). Hence, they concentrate their resources strategically and invest primarily in national elections. The EP elections represent a low-priority event on which only limited attention and corresponding amounts of resources are spent.

References

Primary sources

European Commission, Eurobarometer 72, autumn 2009.
European Parliament (2009), European Elections 2009: Institutional Campaign State of Implementation of Outdoor Elements and Complementary Activities by Member States on 16 April 2009, Communications Directorate Coordination of Information Offices.
European Parliament website, www.europarl.europa.eu/ (accessed on 7 December 2013).

European Parliament website, www.europarl.europa.eu/parliament/archive/elections2009/en/index_en.html (accessed on 7 December 2013).
European Peoples' Party (2009) 'Strong for the People: EPP Election Document 2009'.
Eurostat (2013, 2014) http://epp.eurostat.ec.europa.eu/ (accessed on 5 June 2015).
KDH (2009) 'Volebný program KDH do Európskeho parlamentu'.
Ľ'S-HZDS (2009) Slovensko – stabilné srdce Európy. Program pre voľby do Európskeho parlamentu 2009.
Memo 98 (2009) 'Prezentácia politických subjektov a kandidátov vo voľbách do Európskeho parlamentu', www.memo98.sk/index.php?base=data/ spravy/2009//1244217231.txt (accessed on 18 April 2010).
Party of European Socialists (2009) 'People first: A New Direction for People'.
SaS (2009) 'Programové priority strany Sloboda a Solidarita (SaS) pre voľby do Európskeho parlamentu, 6 júna 2009'.
SDKÚ-DS (2009) 'Za prosperujúce Slovensko v silnej Európe'.
Smer-SD (2009) 'Sociálna Európa – Odpoveď na krízu. Volebný program strany SMER – sociálna demokracia pre voľby do Európskeho parlamentu 2009'.
SMK (2009) 'Naša budúcnosť' v Európe. Volebný program SMK k voľbám do Európskeho parlamentu'.
SNS (2009) 'Z programu SNS do Európskeho parlamentu'.
Statistical Office of the Slovak Republic: www.statistics.sk (accessed on 31 January 2012).

Secondary sources

Bátora, J. (2009) 'Vzniká európsky system politickej reprezentácie? Koordinácia strán SDKÚ-DS a Smer-SD s nadnárodnými straníckymi federáciami vo voľbách do Európskeho parlamentu', in Mesežnikov, G., Gyárfášová, O. and Kollár, M. (eds) *Slovensko volí: Európske a prezidentské voľby 2009*, Bratislava, Inštitút pre verejné otázky, 41–53.
Gyárfášová, O. (2009) 'Medzi spokojnosťou a ľahostajnosťou: Voľby do Európskeho parlamentu 2009 a voliči na Slovensku', in Mesežnikov, G.,
Henderson, K. (2004) 'The European Parliament Election in Slovakia, June 13 2004', European Parties, Elections and Referendums Network Election Briefing, no. 10.
Henderson, K. (2009) 'The European Parliament Election in Slovakia, 6 June 2009', European Parties, Elections and Referendums Network Election Briefing, no. 44.
Korba, M. (2002) 'Zahraničná, bezpečnostná a obranná politika', Mesežnikov, G. (ed.), *Analýza volebných programov politických strán a hnutí*, Bratislava: Inštitút pre verejné otázky, 35–56.
Láštic, E. (2005) 'Referendum: Absencia dohody o priamej demokracii', in Szomolányi, S. (ed.) *Spoločnosť a politika na Slovensku*, Bratislava, Univerzita Komenského, 154–80.
Marks, G., Hooghe, L., Nelson, M. and Edwards, E. (2006) 'Party Competition and European Integration in the East and West: Different Structure, Same Causality', *Comparative Political Studies*, 39(2), 155–75.
Mesežnikov, G. (2009) 'Politické strany na Slovensku vo voľbách do Európskeho parlamentu 2009', in Mesežnikov, G., Gyárfášová, O. and Kollár, M. (eds) *Slovensko volí: Európske a prezidentské voľby 2009*, Bratislava, Inštitút pre verejné otázky, 9–39.
Rybář, M. (2005) 'The 2004 EP Elections in Slovakia: Euro-Apathy in a Euro-Optimistic Country?' in Hrbek, R. (ed.) *European Parliament Elections 2004 in the Ten New EU Member States: Towards the Future European Party System*, Baden-Baden, Nomos, 201–27.
Rybář, M. (2006) 'Old Parties and New: Changing Patterns of Party Politics in Slovakia', in Jungerstam-Mulders, S. (ed.) *Post-Communist EU Member States: Parties and Party Systems*, Aldershot, Ashgate, 147–75.
Rybář, M. (2011) *Medzi štátom a spoločnosťou: Politické strany na Slovensku po roku 1989*, Bratislava, Devín.
Taggart, P. and Szczerbiak, A. (2004) 'Contemporary Euroscepticism in the Party Systems of the European Union Candidate Countries of Central and Eastern Europe', *European Journal of Political Research*, 43(1), 1–27.

27
HUNGARY

Attila Ágh and Sándor Kurtán

Figure 27.1 Map of Hungary

Table 27.1 Hungary profile

EU entry year	2004
Schengen entry year	2007
MEPs elected in 2009	22
MEPs under Lisbon Treaty	22
Capital	Budapest
Area	93,024 km²
Population	9,877,365
	Ethnic Minorities: Germans, Serbs, Croats, Slovaks, Romanians and Roma
Population density	106.4/km²
Median age of population	41.3
Political system	Parliamentary Republic
Head of state	László Sólyom, *Fidesz* – Hungarian Civic Union (*Fidesz*) (August 2005–August 2010);
	Pál Schmitt, *Fidesz* – Hungarian Civic Union (*Fidesz*) (August 2010–April 2012);
	János Áder, *Fidesz* – Hungarian Civic Union (*Fidesz*) (May 2012–)
Head of government	Gordon Bajnai, Hungarian Socialist Party (MSZP) supported (April 2009–May 2010);
	Viktor Mihály Orbán, *Fidesz* – Hungarian Civic Union (*Fidesz*) (May 2010–)
Political majority	Hungarian Socialist Party (MSZP) and Alliance of Free Democrats (SZDSZ) Government Coalition (2006–2010);
	Fidesz – Hungarian Civic Union (*Fidesz*) – Christian Democratic People's Party (KDNP) Coalition Government (April 2010–)
Currency	Hungarian Forint (HUF)
Prohead GDP in PPS	10,500 €

Source: Eurostat, 2013, 2014, http://epp.eurostat.ec.europa.eu/.

1 Geographical position

Hungary is situated in Central Europe. Its neighbouring states are Austria, Slovakia, Ukraine, Romania, Serbia, Croatia, and Slovenia. Austria, Slovakia, Romania, Slovenia, and Croatia are EU Member States, Ukraine is part of the Eastern Partnership programme, and Serbia is a candidate state. All these states have been connected into the common European Danube Strategy of the EU that promotes economic development, transport, civil society, and multiculturalism along the Danube. Hungary benefits a lot from this cooperation in the Danube Valley. It is also a priority for Hungary to intensify its relationships with Hungarian minorities living in neighbouring countries.

2 Historical background

Modern Hungary emerged through the 'Compromise' of 1867 in the Austro-Hungarian Dual Monarchy, which survived until the end of WWI. The historical kingdom of Hungary as part of the above monarchy was partitioned amongst its neighbours under the terms of the Versailles Peace Treaties after WWI. The territory of Hungary was reduced to a third of its former size with four million Hungarians still living in neighbouring countries. In the post-war period Hungary had a moderate authoritarian regime with a multiparty Parliament, but voting rights were restricted in some parliamentary elections.

After WWII, between 1945 and 1949, there was a relatively democratic system with a genuinely democratic constitution in 1946 but the Soviet occupation and the incoming Cold War turned into a repressive regime after 1949. In 1956 the Hungarians had a democratic revolution and a war of independence against Soviet rule that was brutally crushed, but due to tough resistance the János Kádár regime after 1961 was the most liberal version of state socialism. In the 1980s, economic liberalization began first, then political reforms were pushed through in the late 1980s. The *de facto* multiparty system was restored in 1987–1988 and through a negotiated transition the first fully free elections were held in the spring of 1990. The 1989 Constitution mostly relied on the 1946 Constitution and established a democratic system with a unicameral Parliament, a weak President, a strong Prime Minister, and a powerful Constitutional Court, mostly following the German and Spanish models. Since the spring of 1990 there have been six regular, free and fair parliamentary elections in Hungary, and democratic institutions have been properly Europeanized. Hungary joined NATO in 1999 and the EU in 2004, thus its Euro-Atlantic integration has been completed.

3 Geopolitical profile

Hungary has been member of the Visegrád Four (V4) organization and it has played a very active role with Poland, the Czech Republic and Slovakia. Its cooperation has also been very active in the so-called V4+, which involves Austria and Slovenia. Hungary has developed deep interests in the accession processes of the Western Balkan states, first of all in the cases of Croatia and Serbia as well as in the European Neighbourhood Policy, particularly in the Eastern Partnership with Ukraine.

4 Overview of the political landscape

Hungary has established a prime ministerial government based on the German model, in other words, on the positive non-confidence vote and the exclusive responsibility of the Prime Minister before Parliament. This system makes the Prime Minister particularly strong, but it has been balanced with a strong Constitutional Court and also with an extended system of checks and balances, including an independent national bank, the National Council of Justice, and four ombudsmen offices. In parallel with the state administration there is a full system of self-government, with regular elections at the municipal and county levels.

5 Brief account of the political parties

Hungary developed a rather stable party system in the 1990s that has recently changed drastically, as demonstrated by the 2009 EP elections and the 2010 national elections. *Magyar Demokrata Fórum*, MDF (Hungarian Democratic Forum) and *Szabad Demokraták Szövetsége*, SZDSZ (Alliance of Free Democrats) were the leading parties at the first free elections, with minor parties such as the *Magyar Szocialista Párt*, MSZP (Hungarian Socialist Party), *Fiatal Demokraták Szövetsége*, *Fidesz* (Alliance of Young Democrats), *Független Kisgazda Párt*, FKGP (Independent Smallholders Party) and *Kereszténydemokrata Néppárt*, KDNP (Christian Democratic Peoples' Party).

In the next elections the MSZP (centre-left) and *Fidesz* (centre-right) parties dominated. SZDSZ was MSZP's coalition partner in three parliamentary cycles but was fatally weakened in the late 2000s and finally could not run in the 2010 elections. MDF became a small conservative party, and did not survive the 2010 elections. FKGP has disappeared from the national political scene, and KNDP has survived only as a faction within *Fidesz* and it has not run as

Table 27.2 List of political parties in Hungary

Original name	Abbreviation	English translation
Fidesz – Magyar Polgári Szövetség	Fidesz	Fidesz – Hungarian Civic Union
Kereszténydemokrata Néppárt	KDNP	Christian Democratic People's Party
Jobbik – Magyarországért Mozgalom t	Jobbik	Jobbik – Movement for a Better Hungary
Lehet Más a Politika	LMP	Politics Can Be Different
Humanista Párt		Humanist Party
Magyar Demokrata Fórum	MDF	Hungarian Democratic Forum
Magyar Szocialista Párt	MSZP	Hungarian Socialist Party
Szabad Demokraták Szövetsége	SZDSZ	Alliance of Free Democrats
Zöldek Pártja	ZÖLDEK	Green Party
Független Kisgazda-, Földmunkás – és Polgári Párt	FKGP	Independent Smallholders, Agrarian Workers and Civic Party
Magyar Igazság és Élet Pártja	MIÉP	The Hungarian Justice and Life Party
Magyarországi Munkáspárt	Munkáspárt	Hungarian Communist Workers' Party
Magyarországi Cigán Fórum	MCF	Hungarian Roma Forum

an independent party in the latest elections. The extreme right-wing party, *Magyar Igazság és Élet Pártja*, MIÉP (Party of Hungarian Justice and Life) managed to get elected to Parliament only once, then it was marginalized by the new extreme party, *Jobbik* (Better) that had its first electoral success in the 2009 EP elections.

The 2010 general elections have basically transformed the Hungarian party system with the overwhelming victory of *Fidesz*, which received a two-thirds majority. MSZP was pushed into second place with fewer seats, whereas MDF and SZDSZ have disappeared from Parliament. *Jobbik*, an extreme-right party and the new socio-environmental protest party, *Lehet Más a Politika*, LMP (Politics Can Be Different,) have entered the new Parliament; thus the party landscape has changed beyond recognition. In the April 2010 elections, *Fidesz* won with a large, two-thirds majority. The government of Viktor Orbán took office on 29 May 2010. *Fidesz* had an electoral alliance on a joint list with KDNP, so they govern together. In the incumbent government both *Fidesz* and KDNP have deputy prime ministers.

5.1 Party attitudes towards the European Union

At the time of the 2009 EP elections, in an atmosphere of global crisis, there was no party cohesion in Hungary. All parties engaged in some degree of double-talk. The governing left-wing parties propagated 'Social Europe', but they were unable to carry it out. The opposition right-wing parties tried to combine official pro-EU rhetoric with strong anti-EU references on some particular issues to win the support of frustrated segments of society. As the results of the 2009 EP elections have also shown, the split between traditionalists and modernizers, as well as that between the winners and losers of EU accession, has been the deepest in Hungary, which has produced a quasi-bipolar party system with a protracted war over values. In Hungary this dissatisfaction with domestic democracy and, as a result, with EU membership, has generated the strongest *Kulturkampf* in East-Central Europe (ECE). Using the widespread public malaise as a political opportunity, some right-wing parties introduced the method of 'populism from above' as social-national populism in the electoral campaigns (Uitz, 2008).

In general, Hungarians, like all other EU populations, project their national problems and domestic cleavages to the EU level. They formulate their support for EU membership and for EU institutions through the prism of their domestic perceptions. Actually, Hungarians are unsatisfied above all not with the EU itself, but with the slowdown of economic growth and its short-term social consequences, i.e. with the current stagnation of living standards and increasing political tensions at home. Altogether, this is a complex system of views that can be called cognitive dissonance. Hungarians have a 'love–hate relationship' with political parties and very intensive feelings in both respects: deep disillusionment and close attachment.

Fidesz has been the strongest centre-right party in the ECE, so the usual 'double-game-double-talk' attitude can be best analysed in its case. The ECE centre-right parties have been open to the radical right, even sometimes to the militant right, therefore they have developed a double game. They have shown a European face to the EU with a balanced, moderate conservatism to the domestic audience. At the same time they have sent coded messages to the radical and extreme right to widen their electoral support. This double-talk has been greatly facilitated by the slogans of national and social populism that, as a common denominator, have also provided continuity between moderate and extreme statements. *Fidesz* refused for a long time to distinguish itself unambiguously from the anti-systemic right that rejected the democratic system. In fact, *Fidesz* echoed all excuses for the extremist mob, keeping its strategy of belittling the importance of *Jobbik* and of accusing the left of exaggerating the size, influence, and danger of the extreme right. With this strategy *Fidesz* hoped to recruit the voters of the extreme right to its own electorate, therefore it was not ready for any kind of meaningful confrontation with the extreme right. *Fidesz* just took some limited actions through a cautious distinction from *Jobbik*.

After the 2009 EP elections, however, *Fidesz* worried about *Jobbik*, since *Fidesz* had lost its former control over this party. Hungarian public opinion has been profoundly divided on this issue, since *Fidesz* supporters have at least tolerated or even welcomed the EP participation of *Jobbik*, whereas left-Liberal supporters have considered it as the biggest danger for the country.

Jobbik was born some years ago in the *Fidesz* family and it became the *enfant terrible* within this party, finally turning against its own parent party. After the September–October 2006 violent mass demonstrations against the left-wing government, *Jobbik* supporters participated at all *Fidesz* public events with their own symbols and slogans. *Fidesz* developed a Nationalistic agenda, which overlapped with many of *Jobbik*'s demands both politically and culturally; even in some municipal governments.

Jobbik has continued the *Fidesz* type of discourse and symbolism, just shouting more loudly anti-European, anti-Semitic, or anti-Roma slogans that originally stem from coded *Fidesz* messages. However, *Jobbik* has directed these slogans openly against the democratic system, demanding a new systemic change combined with a manifest expression of Hungarian chauvinism. The main slogan of *Jobbik* is 'Hungary for Hungarians', mobilizing the 'real' Hungarians against the 'traitors' and putting all the blame on Roma and Jewish minorities. *Jobbik* meetings were attended by the Hungarian Guard, a notorious paramilitary organization that was banned by the Hungarian Supreme Court on 15 December 2009. Above all, those deeply concerned by 'law and order' type security have been *Jobbik* supporters, since islands of poverty are situated in small settlements with high social tension and with a high percentage of Roma people. *Jobbik* has a close connection to Hungarian fascist traditions and this worst kind of traditionalism has been combined with 'modernity' using the instruments of internet mobilization.

6 Public opinion and the European Union

Hungarian citizens have been regularly amongst the least satisfied people in the EU. According to a Eurobarometer survey after the 2009 EP elections, only 42 per cent of Hungarians were satisfied with their lives, followed only by Bulgarians with 38 per cent, whilst the EU average was

78 per cent. Most Hungarians, 53 per cent, trust EU institutions, the EU average is 48 per cent, much fewer trust Hungarian institutions; for instance, the trust in the Hungarian Parliament is 15 per cent, in the government 14 per cent, and in the parties 9 per cent, whilst the EU average is 30 per cent, 29 per cent, and 16 per cent, respectively. In the last few years unemployment, 58 per cent, and the economic situation, 51 per cent, have been the two most important issues, followed by inflation, 30 per cent; the EU average is 51 per cent, 40 per cent, and 19 per cent, respectively. Hungarians think that the fight against terrorism, 89 per cent, foreign policy and defence, 78 per cent, research and development, 75 per cent, environment, 71 per cent, energy, 70 per cent, the fight against crime, 69 per cent, immigration, 67 per cent, and support for poor regions, 65 per cent, should be dealt with at the EU level. However, issues like taxation, education, pensions, and health care have to be decided at the national level.

The structure of Eurobarometer surveys segments public opinion into three parts: those who support EU membership, those who consider that membership is both good and bad at the same time, and those who oppose it. In Hungary the first group had a relative majority amongst citizens until 2007 but in 2007–2008, there was a turning point. In the last several years the second group has become dominant, 45 per cent, whilst the first group of supporters has declined to 34 per cent, and the third group opposing membership has increased to 21 per cent (Eurobarometer 72, 2010, 4, 6, 7, 11, 20–1).

As the Eurobarometer surveys have proven, the institutional preferences in the policy-making process are very similar in all Member States. Some basic policies, like fighting terrorism, protecting the environment, scientific research, defence and foreign affairs, support for the least developed regions, energy, immigration and fighting crime have been considered as transnational or global issues.

The overwhelming majority of EU citizens think that these issues should be dealt with jointly within the European Union. According to the majority of EU citizens, basic policies of a socio-economic character have to be pursued mostly or partly by national governments. The opinion of Hungarian citizens has been structured in the same way and their support for the bifurcation of policies falls into this general trend.

The domestic problems projected to the EU level have resulted in a number of paradoxes. First of all, Hungarians have become more and more dissatisfied with the EU but they have still maintained their preference for the EU to the domestic polity. This has also appeared as higher trust in EU institutions than in Hungarian ones, which may be called a 'democracy paradox' (Johnson, 2005, 111–13). Actually, there has been a general tendency of growing public distrust in Hungary, but it has affected national institutions much more than the EU and its institutions. Most people take EU institutions as models of mature, well-performing institutions and there has been no public debate on the EU democratic deficit. Whilst support for EU membership has steadily diminished in the last several years, a lot of data proves that Hungarians have still, in fact, been Euro-enthusiasts (Eurobarometer 72, 2010).

Public opinion surveys in 2009 indicated the shift in preferences amongst the Hungarian population to security as a basic value and to fears about a durable social crisis with increasing unemployment. The party landscape also changed beyond recognition, since pre-election surveys already showed that a slight majority of Hungarians did not consider *Jobbik* to be an extreme party, whereas the same surveys proved that this majority mostly came from *Fidesz* supporters. Hence, the biggest public debate in Hungary between left and right after the EP elections was about the party background of *Jobbik* voters. The centre-right claimed that they were disappointed Socialist voters. However, post-election surveys demonstrated convincingly that they mostly came from *Fidesz*.

In the EP elections there was still a large overlap between *Fidesz* and *Jobbik* supporters, with frequent shifts between the two parties. Most *Jobbik* voters were *Fidesz* supporters and vice versa, whereas a large number of *Jobbik* voters were recruited from young, first-time voters, and from those living in small settlements who were mostly hit by the global crisis. The April 2010 parliamentary elections showed the opposite situation, since *Jobbik* received mass support and turned against *Fidesz*.

7 National and EP electoral systems

The electoral law on national elections was passed in 1989 (Act XXXIV, 1989); it was slightly modified several times, but basically remained the same between 1990 and 2010. The electoral law on EP elections, in turn, was passed on 26 April 2004 (Act XXXII, 2004), just before the 2004 elections and the entry of Hungary into the EU. These electoral systems differ to a great extent; the national one is a mixed system, whilst the EP electoral system is proportional.

In national elections all citizens cast two votes, one for a candidate in a given district, and one for a party list. Accordingly, the electoral system has a 'majoritarian' part, with 176 individual districts, and it has also a 'proportional' part, with 210 seats, thus the number of seats in the Hungarian Parliament is 386.

In the majoritarian part, the individual candidates have to collect at least 750 signatures of local supporters to run. The winner is the candidate who has an absolute majority in the first round, or a relative majority in the second round. The proportional part is composed of the territorial lists, 152 seats, and the national list, 58 seats, and here the 5 per cent threshold is applied. There are 20 territorial lists, namely in the 19 counties and in the capital; on the territorial list the Hagenbach-Bischoff/Dropp formula is used. The national list has a compensation element, since the lost votes from the individual districts and the territorial lists are shifted to the national list; on the national list, the d'Hondt formula is used. Parties can set a national list only in the event that they have at least seven territorial lists. Due to this mixed system, both the personal dimension and the proportional approach appear in the Hungarian national electoral system. It has usually been considered a complicated system, although Hungarian citizens had no problem with its application between 1990 and 2010.

The EP electoral system is proportional. It is rather simple and similar to many other systems in EU Member States. The whole country forms one single constituency. The number of EP seats allocated for EU countries with ten million people was 24 in 2004 and 22 in 2009. The d'Hondt formula is applied in the EP elections and there is a 5 per cent threshold. Both in 2004 and 2009, eight parties ran and, due to this threshold, in both cases only four parties won seats in the EP, the other four were eliminated by the threshold. Actually, *Fidesz*, MSZP, and MDF received seats in both cases. The only difference is that in 2004, the Liberal SZDSZ was the fourth party in the EP, whereas in 2009 the extremist *Jobbik* was, which already shows the impact of the global crisis on Hungarian politics.

The main feature of the 2004 EP election was not – as could have been expected – that it was the very first EP election, but the fact that it occurred during the mid-term between two national elections in 2002 and 2006. This means that the 2004 EP elections were indeed secondary, where EU issues did not figure high on the agenda; thus the EP elections were exclusively fought over domestic issues. In general, the first EP elections were held right after EU entry in May 2004, so Hungarian citizens were not yet aware of EU issues.

On the other side, during the mid-term when the popularity of incumbent governments is usually at its lowest point, all domestic issues gain importance. It was even more so in Hungary in 2004, since *Fidesz* lost just marginally in the 2002 national elections and looked for revenge in 2004, when the popularity of the governing MSZP-SZDSZ coalition was at its lowest point. Thus, *Fidesz* wanted to turn the EP elections into a dress rehearsal for the next national elections. Although *Fidesz* won the 2004 EP elections, this model still did not work, since the governing coalition was re-elected and received even more support in 2006 than in 2002. However, the domestic political fight was so strong in the very polarized atmosphere of Hungarian political life that the European character of the 2004 EP elections was completely marginalized and the motives of national elections absolutely dominated.

The date of elections was set on 18 March 2004 for 13 June 2004, which would have indicated a three-month campaign but the parties had a long debate on the details of the EP electoral law, which finally passed in late April, so actually there was only a one-month campaign. *Fidesz* organized a very negative campaign strategy, raising no EU issues and simply attacking the government for its failures in structural reforms. The MSZP responded with its own negative campaign against *Fidesz*, so it turned out to be a sort of classic Second-Order Election.

All in all, eight parties took part in the EP elections; four parties succeeded, four parties failed, Munkáspárt and MIÉP with some support, whereas SZDP – Social Democratic Party and MNSZ – Hungarian National Alliance had almost no support. *Fidesz* emerged as a clear winner with its negative campaign, and the MSZP was the loser. The MSZP was in the midst of internal debates, since the new party programme was ready only by June 2004.

In addition, the first two leading politicians on the MSZP party list declared that they did not want to become MEPs. SZDSZ, the Liberals were markedly pro-EU, so their campaign was successful due to their party profile and they managed to get three MEPs. Finally, the MDF, the declining National-Conservative party received one seat; this was only due to the low participation rate, since it could mobilize its remaining social support.

In the 2009 EP elections the interference with national elections was the opposite compared to the situation in 2004. The EP elections on 7 June 2009 were too close to the national elections in April 2010; they indeed proved to be pre-elections for the national elections. In 2006 the MSZP-SZDSZ coalition was re-elected, for the first time in Hungarian electoral history, with a rather large majority. But right after the 2006 elections, the Hungarian government was forced to introduce an austerity programme due to high state indebtedness and it immediately lost popular support. During the whole period between 2006 and 2010, *Fidesz* had a 20 per cent lead over the MSZP, and the SZDSZ declined further after 2006. Thus, as the 2009 EP elections were the prelude to the 2010 national elections, *Fidesz* was expected to win.

In 2009 again eight parties ran for the EP elections, and four parties (*Fidesz*, MSZP, *Jobbik*, and MDF) succeeded, four parties (SZDSZ, LMP-HP, MFC-Roma Party, and Munkáspárt) failed. Thus, the basic result in party structure was the same at both elections, the only change was that *Jobbik* entered the EP instead of the SZDSZ. Beyond the defeat of the Liberals there were still two other surprises, since MSZP's loss was bigger than expected, and *Jobbik* had a very good result.

8 A glance at EP and national elections

The Hungarian case proves that interference between the EP and national elections can also play a big role in influencing both. The first ever EP elections, which took place in Hungary in 2004, were fought as a domestic battle for two reasons, first, because of the mid-term situation between two national elections, and second, because of the date was too early after EU entry. However, the second EP elections in 2009 proved that the opposite case, where EP elections were too close to the national elections, also reinforced the domestic character of EP elections. In any case, Hungarian political life is deeply polarized between left and right, and both national elections and EP elections have followed the logic of total confrontation. This sharp political confrontation, however, has produced a very high turnout in national

Table 27.3 National election results in Hungary: 2002–2010

Political party		2002	2006	2010
Fidesz	Vote share	41.1	42.0	52.7
	Seats	164	141	263
FKGP	Vote share	0.8	—	—
	Seats	—	—	—
Jobbik	Vote share	—	—	16.7
	Seats	—	—	47
KDNP	Vote share	—	—	—
	Seats	—	23	—
MDF	Vote share	—	5.0	2.7
	Seats	24	11	—
MIÉP	Vote share	4.4	2.2	0.0
	Seats	0	0	0
MSZP	Vote share	42.0	43.2	19.3
	Seats	178	190	59
SZDSZ	Vote share	5.6	6.5	—
	Seats	20	20	—
LMP	Vote share	—	—	7.48
	Seats	—	—	16
Turnout %		**73.5**	**64.4**	**64.4**

Source: Nemzeti Választási Iroda (Hungary's National Election Office), http://valasztas.hu/.

elections – around 60–70 per cent – which is much higher than in the other new democracies. However, it is logical to conclude that in Hungary there was a low turnout in the 2004 and 2009 EP elections, 38.5 and 36.3 per cent, respectively, compared to national elections, since the Hungarian case is different from the other New Member States. The participation rate is also usually high in Hungary in EP elections, the highest compared to the other New Member States. In the 2009 EP elections, the participation rate was slightly lower than in 2004, which indicated the impact of the global crisis, as in the other Member States, but the trend of the turnout in the EP elections was about 30 per cent lower than in the national elections held in Hungary.

9 The 2009 European election

In general, the media coverage of the 2009 EP elections was as large and hectic as usual but almost unconcerned with EU issues. There was a large and well-organized information network on the EU in Hungary, mostly based on the Information Department of the Foreign Affairs Ministry (www.eurovonal.hu) and the delegation of the European Commission, together with the national office of the EP. However, the only important function they could perform in this crisis-ridden situation was to try to mobilize voters. This was relatively successful compared to the other New Member States, but initiating discussions on EU issues was much less successful. The main issue for Hungarians in the first half of 2009 was the role the EU played in Hungarian crisis management. The dominant reaction was positive, but with many features of cognitive dissonance. As a typical EU-fatigue reaction, this has been seen in all Member States – the population has only paid some attention to EU affairs when a concrete EU issue has emerged in the national media that has been directly related to the home country.

9.1 Party lists and manifestos

The EU entry meant a sudden and drastic turn in EU affairs for the ECE public 'from nothing to everything', i.e. from 'under-politicization' to 'over-politicization'. Earlier, EU issues were very marginal for the public discourse, but with EU entry the change in public attention and in EU awareness was dramatic. EU issues have since then become the main controversial topics in this polarized political world, between these two divided, inimical cultural and political camps.

Far from remaining marginal, EU issues have been transformed by the parties into the most discussed topics between government and opposition in the media as well as in political fora like parliamentary debates. The real question is not whether the ECE public has turned its attention to EU affairs or not, because the change has not been initiated by, and caused by, the level of popular perception. In fact, the real situation is that after EU entry the opposing actors, the governments and opposition groups, have formulated all Hungarian domestic political issues in EU terms, with mutual accusations. Thus, they have used 'Europe' as a legitimizing or de-legitimizing device, and in such a that way the public could not manage 'not to know' about EU issues due to loud political-party quarrels every day. The public has not been simply able 'not to take part' in the discussions and deliberations of EU affairs because it has been permanently bombarded from both sides with value-laden and politically blurred EU information.

Right after taking office, in June 2006, the governing coalition of MSZP and SZDSZ introduced drastic measures to decrease the budget deficit as a convergence programme to meet the Maastricht criteria for introducing the euro. This led to a sharp drop in popular support for both parties and they did not recover from this loss of popularity in that parliamentary cycle. The governing coalition's main programme was the structural reform of taxation, health care, and education. In fact, all these drastic reforms were unpopular. They met tough resistance from the population and this resistance provided the content of the programmes for the opposition parties, first of all for *Fidesz*.

On 9 March 2008, there was a referendum on these reform issues, and all three reform items were rejected by the population by a large majority – above 80 per cent. 'We live worse than before' was the main *Fidesz* campaign slogan throughout the 2000s. *Fidesz* had lost two elections in 2002 and 2006 with this false message, but the negative campaign became successful in the late 2000s when people indeed suffered from the crisis and were looking for miracles. By the summer of 2009 *Fidesz* had a big lead over the MSZP, about 50 per cent versus 20 per cent support, and this resulted in an overwhelming victory in the 2009 EP elections.

Thus, the domestic socio-economic problems were so overwhelming in the EP electoral campaign that the transnational party federations were not at all visible and EU issues played little part in the campaign, even less than in 2004. Although *Fidesz* indicated its position on some EU issues, it still focussed on the negative campaign against the government. *Fidesz* published a long manifesto, with a wide range of vague EU policies, under the title 'Yes, Hungary could do better', but they did not use it in the campaign, given that domestic politics offered more powerful ammunition. MSZP did even less, since it mentioned only the excellence of Hungary in using EU resources with a reference to the EU's structural funds, 'What was built in your district between 2004 and 2009?', but actually with no reference to the PES Manifesto (Batory, 2009, 4–6). *Jobbik* had some sort of anti-EU campaign, although its main campaign message was that the Roma and the Jews were responsible for all the problems that had hit the real Hungarians.

9.2 Electoral campaign

The key issues raised in the EP campaign were the economic crisis, unemployment, and increasing poverty. This list basically indicated the same top-of-the-list items as the general priorities in the

EU in the Eurobarometer surveys, but Hungarians felt much more concerned about these same issues and a much larger percentage of Hungarians worried about them. This reflects a situation that I call 'the trap of materialist needs'. At the same time, Hungarians have been usually much less worried about such 'post-materialist' issues as environmental protection. All in all, Hungarians supported further European integration and there was large popular support for the Lisbon Treaty as well. Hungarians are less sensitive to old security risks and military defence than most European citizens. They think that new security risks, like international migration, have to be tackled by the EU. Hungarians have supported both the Common Foreign and Security Policy and Common Security and Defence Policy, but these issues have not been prioritized by them. Interest in foreign affairs has been centred on the Central European region and on the plight of Hungarian minorities abroad. There has been a positive attitude towards further EU enlargement, although rather selectively, first of all for the imminent accession of Croatia, followed by the Western Balkans.

Immigration has not yet been an important issue, since Hungary has mainly been a transit country. However, there has been an increasing danger of emerging or re-emerging racist sentiments towards the Roma population. Xenophobic feelings have also been nurtured by extreme right-wing movements. Anti-Semitic public events and expressions have become more pronounced. General environmental interest in this socio-economic crisis situation is not at the centre of public opinion, although environmental awareness has increased significantly in the last decade.

9.3 Electoral results

The political atmosphere of the 2009 EP elections was determined by the negative public perception of both 20 years of systemic change and the post-accession climate during Hungary's five years of EU membership. The ongoing global crisis has provoked a much deeper shock than the usual crisis cycles. The results of the 2009 EP elections have shown a widespread apathy as well as an upsurge in various kinds of extreme movements. All in all, there has been political turbulence with high government instability since the global crisis hit Hungary particularly badly.

On 20 April 2009 Ferenc Gyurcsány (MSZP) resigned as Prime Minister, and in spring 2009 the Gordon Bajnai government (MSZP) introduced a new crisis management package with austerity measures, causing further disillusionment and malaise. The growing unease and protest against this crisis management package also appeared in the results of the 2009 EP elections. There was a relatively high turnout, 36.3 per cent, slightly less than in 2004 with 38.4 per cent, and a shifting left–right balance, since the centre right *Fidesz* had an overwhelming victory, 56.4 per cent and fourteen seats, and the centre left MSZP had a decisive defeat, 17.4 per cent and four seats. A high degree of protest votes went to *Jobbik*, on the militant extreme right, 14.8 per cent and three seats. The small conservative party MDF managed to come in above the threshold, 5.3 per cent and one seat. Four other parties also ran but did not succeed in getting representation in the EP, attaining altogether 6.1 per cent.

The results of the 2009 EP elections have been outstanding in three respects and their analysis may shed a new light on the electoral fortunes of the left and right, since they have ushered in a 'golden age of populism' with the virulent protest parties.

First, electoral turnout in Hungary has been the highest amongst the New Member States. Therefore the usual lazy argument that everything can be explained in East-Central Europe by low and decreasing voter participation has to be excluded, since in Hungary, protest votes have played a big role.

Second, the Hungarian left (MSZP) suffered the biggest defeat amongst the left-wing parties, a setback from nine to four seats, with a 25.8 per cent loss compared to the latest national elections, and/or amongst the governing parties in the EU.

Table 27.4 EP election results in Hungary: 2004–2009

Parties	Political group	Votes 2004	% 2004	Seats 2004	Votes 2009	% 2009	Seats 2009	Difference
National party								
Fidesz	EPP	1,457,750	47.4	12	1,632,309	56.4	14	+2
MSZP	PES	1,054,921	34.3	9	503,140	17.4	4	−5
Jobbik	None	—	—	0	427,773	14.8	3	+3
MDF	ECR	164,025	5.3	1	153,660	5.3	1	0
LMP	None	—	—	—	75,522	2.6	0	—
SZDSZ	ELDR	237,908	7.7	2	62,527	2.2	0	−2
Munkáspárt	None	56,221	1.8	0	27,817	1.0	0	0
MCF	None	—	—	—	13,431	0.5	0	—
Total		3,075,450	100.0	24	2,896,179	100.0	22	—
Turnout			**38.5**			**36.3**		

Source: Nemzeti Választási Iroda (National Election Office), http://valasztas.hu/.

Table 27.5 List of Hungarian MEPs: seventh legislature

Name	Age	Gender	National party	Political group	Committee	Chairs	Professional background
Áder, János	51	Male	*Fidesz*–KDNP	EPP	Committee on the Environment, Public Health and Food Safety; Delegation for Relations with Switzerland, Iceland and Norway and to the European Economic Area (EEA) Joint Parliamentary Committee		Jurist
Balczó, Zoltán	62	Male	*Jobbik*	Non-attached members	Committee on the Environment, Public Health and Food Safety; Delegation to the EU-Russia Parliamentary Cooperation Committee		Engineer
Bokros, Lajos	54	Male	MDF	European Conservatives and Reformists	Committee on Budgets; Delegation for Relations with South-East Europe		Economist
Deutsch, Tamás	44	Male	*Fidesz*–KDNP	EPP	Committee on Regional Development; Delegation to the EU-Russia Parliamentary Cooperation Committee	Vice-Chair Committee on Budgetary Control	Jurist
Gál, Kinga	40	Female	*Fidesz*–KDNP	EPP	Subcommittee on Human Rights; Delegation for Relations with Albania, Bosnia and Herzegovina, Serbia, Montenegro and Kosovo	Vice-Chair Committee on Civil Liberties, Justice and Home Affairs	Jurist
Glattfelder, Béla	43	Male	*Fidesz*–KDNP	EPP	Committee on International Trade; Delegation to the EU-Moldova Parliamentary Cooperation Committee; Delegation to the Euronest Parliamentary Assembly;		Engineer
Göncz, Kinga	63	Female	MSZP	Progressive Alliance of Socialists and Democrats in the European Parliament (S&D)	Committee on Employment and Social Affairs; Committee on Petitions; Special Committee on the Financial, Economic and Social Crisis; Delegation for Relations with the countries of Southeast Asia and the Association of Southeast Asian Nations (ASEAN)	Vice-Chair Committee on Civil Liberties, Justice and Home Affairs	Psychotherapist

(continued)

Table 27.5 (continued)

Name	Age	Gender	National party	Political group	Committee	Chairs	Professional background
Gurmai, Zita	45	Female	MSZP	S&D	Committee on Women's Rights and Gender Equality; Delegation to the EU-Moldova Parliamentary Cooperation Committee	Vice-Chair Committee on Constitutional Affairs	Economist
Györi, Enikö	42	Female	Fidesz–KDNP	EPP	Committee on Economic and Monetary Affairs; Special Committee on the Financial, Economic and Social Crisis; Delegation for Relations with Japan		International relations
Gyürk, András	38	Male	Fidesz–KDNP	EPP	Committee on Development; Delegation to the EU-Armenia, EU-Azerbaijan and EU-Georgia Parliamentary Cooperation Committees; Delegation to the Euronest Parliamentary Assembly		Historian
Hankiss, Ágnes	60	Female	Fidesz–KDNP	EPP	Committee on Civil Liberties, Justice and Home Affairs; Subcommittee on Security and Defence; Delegation for Relations with Israel	Vice-Chair Committee on Petitions	Psychologist
Herczog, Edit	49	Female	MSZP	S&D	Committee on Industry, Research and Energy; Delegation to the EU-Armenia, EU-Azerbaijan and EU-Georgia Parliamentary Cooperation Committees; Delegation to the Euronest Parliamentary Assembly		Engineer
Járóka, Livia	36	Female	Fidesz–KDNP	EPP	Committee on Civil Liberties, Justice and Home Affairs; Delegation for Relations with India	Vice-Chair Committee on Women's Rights and Gender Equality	Teacher
Kósa, Ádám	35	Male	Fidesz–KDNP	EPP	Committee on Employment and Social Affairs; Delegation for Relations with Japan		Jurist
Morvai, Krisztina	47	Female	Jobbik	Non-attached members	Committee on Agriculture and Rural Development; Delegation for Relations with the United States		Jurist

Öry, Csaba	58	Male	*Fidesz*–KDNP	EPP	Committee on Employment and Social Affairs; Delegation to the EU-Kazakhstan, EU-Kyrgyzstan and EU-Uzbekistan Parliamentary Cooperation Committees, and for Relations with Tajikistan, Turkmenistan and Mongolia	Jurist
Schmitt, Pél	68	Male	*Fidesz*–KDNP	EPP	Culture and Education; Delegation to the EU–Croatia Joint Parliamentary Committee	Vice-President European Parliament Economist
Schöpflin, György	71	Male	*Fidesz*–KDNP	EPP	Committee on Constitutional Affairs; Delegation for Relations with Albania, Bosnia and Herzegovina, Serbia, Montenegro and Kosovo	
Surján, László	69	Male	*Fidesz*–KDNP	EPP Group	Committee on Budgets; Delegation to the EU–Chile; Joint Parliamentary Committee; Delegation to the Euro-Latin American Parliamentary Assembly	Physician
Szájer, József	49	Male	*Fidesz*–KDNP		Constitutional Affairs	Jurist
Szegedi, Csanád	28	Male	*Jobbik*	Non-attached members	Committee on Regional Development; Delegation to the EU-Kazakhstan, EU-Kyrgyzstan and EU-Uzbekistan; Parliamentary Cooperation Committees, and for Relations with Tajikistan, Turkmenistan and Mongolia	Student
Tabajdi, Csaba	58	Male	MSZP	S&D	Committee on Agriculture and Rural Development; Committee on Petitions; Delegation for Relations with the People's Republic of China	Economist

Source: www.europarl.europa.eu/meps/en/search.html?country=HU.

Third, the Hungarian extreme right-wing, the hard, and militant anti-EU party, *Jobbik* – like a storm emerging from the blue sky – secured the biggest victory: 14.8 per cent and three seats. The split between the winners and losers has been the deepest in Hungary, including the split between relative and absolute losers, and both camps have reacted with fear and anger.

The main result of the 2009 EP elections was the further decline of governing parties – the MSZP and SZDSZ – and the push for the basic transformation of the Hungarian party system. After the lost referendum in 2008 there was a split between the two governing parties and, from May 2008, the MSZP had a minority government. Because the public increasingly resisted the crisis management measures and the economic situation of Hungary worsened quickly, Ferenc Gyurcsány resigned as Prime Minister. Under the pressure of the global crisis, the Gordon Bajnai government introduced a very tough crisis management package. This package was successful and the budget deficit was drastically reduced, but public support for the MSZP was fatally damaged and the SZDSZ was fragmented into small groups. The final result was that MSZP suffered a drastic defeat at the last elections and SZDSZ disappeared from the political scene.

9.4 Campaign finance

Parties get state support for their budgets proportional to their election results – even those parties that get more than 1 per cent of votes cast in the elections, but less than the threshold of 5 per cent – so they do not become parliamentary parties. Parties may get a limited amount of support from private persons and firms, and they have to declare it. Party finances are controlled every year by the State Audit Office. Party financing is a very delicate issue at the time of election campaigns, since expert calculations indicate that all parties spend more than they declare.

10 Theoretical interpretation of Euro-elections

10.1 Second-Order Election theory

The 2004 and 2009 EP elections in Hungary have confirmed the Second-Order Election theory since they are secondary to the main national electoral contest, and they are 'national' contests rather than 'European' contests (Hix and Marsh, 2007, 496). This is the mainstream view on Hungarian EP elections amongst analysts as well:

> Two factors are important for explaining this outcome. One is the global economic crisis, and the other the fact that the governing party that has confronted with it had been in office for seven years. Their combined effect was to magnify the characteristic anti-incumbent bias of Second Order elections to extreme proportions.
>
> *(Batory 2009, 1)*

Altogether, the participation rate in EP contests has been about 30 per cent lower, and these elections have been fought almost completely over domestic issues.

10.2 Europe Salience theory

After the outbreak of the global crisis in 2008–2009 there have been two tendencies that have pointed towards the increasing salience of European issues. These are the politicization of European institutions and the growing pressure on Member States to create stronger economic governances. These tendencies have strengthened each other and overlapped to a great extent;

namely, the politicization of European institutions and affairs has been included in the Lisbon Treaty, with a much bigger role for the EP. The treaty presupposes the increased capacity of the European Council for urgent reactions in EU and global affairs that has also contributed to the politicization of all EU issues and policies in crisis management. This was felt in Hungary, where, since 2009, all domestic fights have been 'Europeanized' beyond recognition. The incumbent government has waged – in its own words – a 'freedom fight' against the EU on many economic policy issues, which have been sharply politicized, and as a reaction, the opposition has organized pro-EU mass demonstrations against the government.

In general, there have been many efforts to politicize the EU by suggesting EP elections with party candidates for the President of the European Commission that could present real political alternatives and could mobilize the public for participation in EP elections. Lisbet Hooghe and Gary Marks (2009) have seen an opportunity for the politicization and democratization of the EU by introducing and extending the MLG structures.

The elite-centred view of European integration survived the creation of a European Parliament and even direct elections from 1979. EP contests were popularity tests for national governments, where European integration was largely a non-issue. This view rests on three assumptions, none of which now holds. First, the public's attitude towards European integration is superficial, and therefore incapable of providing a stable structure of electoral incentives for party positioning. Second, European integration is a low salience issue for the general public, in contrast to its high salience for business groups; it therefore has little influence on party competition. And, third, the issues raised by European integration are *sui generis*, therefore unrelated to the basic conflicts that structure political competition. The experience of the past fifteen years – and the research it generated – has dismantled each of these assumptions (ibid., 2009, 2, 6–7).

The general turning point in 2009, towards Europeanization and politicization, certainly can also be observed in Hungary, which proves the validity of the Europe Salience theory as an emerging tendency in a historical approach. With further EU integration there has been an increasing emphasis on defending the national interest. Paradoxically, it best demonstrates the European salience of domestic issues, since unlike in the first years of membership before 2009, nowadays in Hungary all domestic issues have been formulated *ab ovo* in a European context and in a politicized way. The Hungarian parties have a clear position on Europe, and the left–right divide has been reformulated in this context, since the centre-right coalition has had a conflicting course with the EU and the left-Liberal opposition has supported the EU's demands against the Hungarian government. The Hungarian party structure as a whole has also been completely Europeanized because the new LMP party, which could not win seats in the EP in 2009, has been elected into the Hungarian Parliament as a 'green type' party, and *Jobbik*, the other new party, has been successful in the latest national elections by mobilizing anti-EU and Eurosceptic feelings.

Hungarian developments in the 2000s can be explained by the conceptual framework of the 'triple crisis', namely the subsequent transition, post-accession, and global crises. In the mid-2000s, there were already two generations of losers in Hungary, the first one with the socio-political transition in the early 1990s and the second one with EU entry in the mid-2000s. These waves of mass social exclusion have recently been reinforced by the global crisis and the 'golden age of populism' has begun. In an effort to compare the 2004 and 2009 EP elections, the key to understanding these results is, indeed, identifying these two kinds of the new, third generation losers: (1) the relative losers of the recession, who reacted with apathy that caused low turnout, and (2) the absolute or impoverished losers, including the young virtual losers without perspective, engaging in different kinds of extremism. There is a large body of journalism, however, on the treatment of the radical right and extreme right, since their border lines have often been blurred. These two camps are basically different, since the radical right parties are within the constitutional system, but the anti-systemic parties like *Jobbik* are against the democratic order. As a result, in Hungary, there have been large overlaps and mutual shifts between the centre-right and extreme-right parties, since even the centre-right party, *Fidesz*, has been penetrated by radical social and national populisms.

The impact of the global crisis on the EU has provoked a deep divide between the Old and New Member States, including Hungary. It has been re-enforced by a similar divide between big and small states, since the big states, above all the German-French 'engine', have played an overwhelming role in crisis management. Rightly or wrongly, the 'losers' in Hungary, about one-third of the population, already felt abandoned by the EU in the first years of membership, and this malaise has been deepened by the global crisis. Some citizens considered that EU entry was too much to the benefit of large companies located in the Old Member States, that neglected their subsidiaries during the deep crisis, causing a lot of damage to the populations of East-Central Europe. This malaise may indicate overdriven fears, but it reflects the new socio-political tension in Hungary and it demonstrates that the losers have blamed EU membership for their impoverishment.

The final conclusion is that Hungary has developed a wide gap between the winners and losers in the EU. Nonetheless, Hungary, with its deep political polarization, is still a pro-EU and pro-integration country to a great extent. As such, the current deep pessimism is transitory and the pro-EU attitude still prevails. All in all, a majority of Hungarians have a positive view on the EU's role in answering the globalization challenge, since EU membership has offered a shield against global disturbances and in the nadir of its own financial crisis, Hungary received substantial support from the EU. Most Hungarians feel that the EU is a community of values, and think that the Member States share their common basic values.

References

Primary sources

Batory, A. (2009) 'The European Parliament Election in Hungary', European Parliament Election Briefing No. 25, European Parties, Elections and Referendums Network, 18 June 2009, www.sussex.ac.uk/sei/research/europeanpartieselectionsreferendumsnetwork/europeparliamentelections (accessed on 8 December 2013).

Eurobarometer 72 (January 2010) 'National Report: Hungary', www.ec.europa.eu/public_opinion (accessed on 10 February 2010).

European Parliament Database (2010) www.europarl.europa.eu/meps/eu/search.html (accessed on 10 January 2015).

Eurostat (2013, 2014) http://epp.eurostat.ec.europa.eu (accessed on 5 June 2015).

Forsense-Századvég (2009) 'Post-election Survey 6 August 2009', www.hirek.mti.hu/cikk/393686 (accessed on 8 August 2009).

Nemzeti Választási Iroda (Hungary's National Election Office), http://valasztas.hu/ (accessed on 10 March 2011).

Publicus (2009b) 'Post-elections Survey', 10 July: www.publicus.hu/blog (accessed on 12 July 2009).

Secondary sources

Bos, E. and Dieringer, J. (eds) (2008) *Die Genese einer Union der 27: Die Europäische Union nach der Osterweiterung*, Wiesbaden: VS Verlag für Sozialwissenschaften.

Fidesz (2009) 'Igen, Magyarország többreképes! A Fidesz választási programja' ('Yes, Hungary Can Do More – The EP Electoral Program of Fidesz'), March 2009.

Galgóczi, B. (ed.) (2005) *What Price the Euro? The Social Impact Of Euro-zone Accession for the New Member States*, Brussels, European Trade Union Institute.

Hix, S. and Marsh, M. (2007) 'Punishment or Protest? Understanding European Parliamentary Elections', *The Journal of Politics*, 69(2), 495–510.

Hooghe, L. and Marks, G. (2009) 'A Postfunctionalist Theory of European Integration: From Permissive Consensus to Constraining Dissensus', *British Journal of Political Science*, (39), 1–23.

Information Department of the Foreign Affairs Ministry (www.eurovonal.hu)

Johnson, D. (2005) 'The New Outsiders of Central and Eastern Europe: With Specific Reference to Poland', *European Integration*, 27(1), 111–31.

Uitz, R. (2008) 'Hungary', in Meseznikov, G., Gyárfásová, O. and Smilov, D. (eds) (2008) *Populist Politics and Liberal Democracy in Central and Eastern Europe*, Bratislava, Institute for Public Affairs, 39–69.

28
POLAND

Jerzy Jaskiernia

Figure 28.1 Map of Poland

Table 28.1 Poland profile

EU entry year	2004
Schengen entry year	2007
MEPs elected in 2009	50
MEPs under Lisbon Treaty	51 since 1 December 2011
	One additional seat allocated to
	Arkadiusz Bratkowski (EPP)
Capital	Warsaw
Total area★	312,679 km²
Population	38,017,856
	96.74% Poles whilst the remaining includes Germans, Belarusians,
	Ukrainians, Lithuanians, Russians, Lemkos, Slovaks, Czechs, Roma and Jews
Population density★★	121.7/km²
Median age of population	39.2
Political system	Parliamentary Republic
Head of state	Lech Kaczyński, Law and Justice (PiS)
	(December 2005–April 2010);
	Bronisław Komorowski, Acting President, Civic Platform (PO)
	(April 2010–August 2010);
	Bronisław Komorowski, Civic Platform (PO)
	(August 2010–)
Head of government	Donald Tusk, Civic Platform (PO)
	(November 2007–)
Political majority	Civic Platform (PO) and Polish People's Party (PSL) Government
	Coalition (November 2007–)
Currency	Złoty (PLN)
Prohead GDP in PPS	10,700 €

Source: Eurostat, 2013, 2014, http://epp.eurostat.ec.europa.eu/.

Notes:
★ Total area including inland waters.
★★ Population density: the ratio of the annual average population of a region to the land area of the region.

1 Geographical position

Poland's territory extends across several geographical regions, bordering Germany, the Czech Republic, Slovakia, Ukraine, Belarus, Lithuania, and the Russian Federation. Poland has one of the largest number of lakes in the world. The biggest are Lake Śniardwy and Lake Mamry in Masuria. The Polish Baltic coast is approximately 528 kilometres long. Its climate is mostly moderate throughout the country, oceanic in the north with warmer and continental climates towards the south and east.

2 Historical background

The Kingdom of Poland was founded in AD 1025, and in AD 1569 it formalized a long association with the Grand Duchy of Lithuania by signing the Union of Lublin. The Polish-Lithuanian Commonwealth collapsed in 1795, and Poland's territory was partitioned amongst the Kingdom of Prussia, the Russian Empire, and Austria. Poland regained its independence as the Second Polish Republic in November 1918 at the end of the Great War. During the second world conflict, Poland was occupied by the Germans on 1 September 1939 and the Soviets on 17 September 1939. After WWII, Poland emerged as the People's Republic of Poland and resided within the Eastern bloc under Soviet influence. During the Revolutions of 1989, Communist rule was overthrown and Poland became the Third Polish Republic. Poland became the member of the Council of Europe in 1991, the OECD in 1996, NATO in 1999, and the EU in 2004. Poland was a founding member of the United Nations in 1945 and has participated in the CSCE/OSCE since 1975.

After the introduction of democratic changes in Poland in 1989, citizens supported EU membership. Yet, in the late 1990s, they began to feel the disadvantages of the accession process that came with association agreement requirements (Mayhew, 1998). Following strict regulations and the standardization of the metallurgical industry, coal mining, agriculture and environmental protection, citizens' support for Europeanization decreased. Rising unemployment and the high costs associated with meeting European standards began to weigh on the Polish economy. This was particularly important in rural areas, where a potentially substantial loss in revenues by Polish farmers due to subsidized EU farming mobilized public opinion. The question of national sovereignty in the face of increased intra-European competition and regulation became a rallying cry for those Polish citizens who preferred other cooperative scenarios to joining the EU (Jaskiernia, 2003). Opponents of the integration process spread negative myths and stereotypes (Jaskiernia, 2010b). 'Pro national' supporters came into conflict with 'pro European' supporters and the national identity crisis did not help the Polish polity to build a European identity (Skotnicka-Illasiewicz, 1997). Finally, after a successful information campaign (Orłowski, 2001) introduced by the government of Prime Minister Leszek Miller (Nikolski, 2005), as well as the crucial involvement of President Aleksander Kwaśniewski, the European referendum was approved in 2003. This vote cleared the way for Polish accession to the EU on 1 May 2004 (Jabłoński, 2007). The support of Pope John Paul II was crucial in moving Polish public opinion towards EU integration.

3 Geopolitical profile

In the aftermath of WWII, Poland was part of the Soviet Union's sphere of dominance. It was a member of the Warsaw Pact and the Council for Mutual Economic Assistance (COMECON).

In 1989, democratic reform in Poland began with round-table negotiations, known as 'Okrągły stół' Agreements between ruling Communists and their allies, and the Solidarity Democratic movement (Jabłonowski et al., 2009). Political reforms were introduced according to international democratic standards, with the support of the Council of Europe (Jaskiernia, 2010a; Machińska, 2005). Poland was the first post-Socialist country to embark on a path of democratic reform. However, it was unable to quickly adopt a modern and fully democratic constitution. The work on the democratic Polish Constitution lasted over eight years (Sarnecki et al., 1999, 5). The constitution was finally adopted by the national assembly on 2 April 1997 and the document was approved in a nationwide referendum on 25 May 1997.

After 1989, Poland followed pro-Western attitudes in foreign politics, as a member of the Council of Europe, NATO, and the European Union. Poland has treated the United States as a strategic partner for national security.

4 Overview of the political landscape

Poland is a democracy with a President as the head of state. The government structure centres on the Council of Ministers, led by a Prime Minister. The President appoints the cabinet under the advice of the Prime Minister. Officially they are typically from the majority coalition in Parliament, the *Sejm*.

Voters elect the bicameral Parliament, consisting of a 460-member lower house, the *Sejm*, and a 100-member Senate. Representatives are elected for a four-year term. Representatives in the lower house are elected under proportional representation in accordance with the d'Hondt method. The Senate is elected by a rare plurality bloc voting method, in which several candidates with the highest support are elected from each constituency according to the number of seats in their district. With the exception of ethnic minority parties, only candidates of political parties receiving at least 5 per cent of the total national vote can enter the *Sejm*. The constitution specifies that a national assembly be established through a joint session of members of the *Sejm* and the Senate. A National Assembly is formed on the following occasions: when a new President takes an oath of office; when an indictment against the President is brought to the Polish State Tribunal (*Trybunał Stanu*); or when a President's permanent incapacity to exercise his or her duties due to poor health is declared. The National Assembly approved the constitution in 1997.

The judicial branch plays a crucial role in governmental decision-making. Its major institutions include: a general court system presided over by the Supreme Court of the Republic of Poland (*Sąd Najwyższy*) and an administrative court system presided over by the Supreme Administrative Court of the Republic of Poland (*Naczelny Sąd Administracyjny*). The Constitutional Tribunal of the Republic of Poland (*Trybunał Konstytucyjny*) plays a very important role in political system, as it ensures the constitutionality of the laws passed in Parliament.

On the approval of the Senate, the *Sejm* also appoints the Ombudsman or the Commissioner for the Civil Rights Protection (*Rzecznik Praw Obywatelskich*) for a five-year term. The ombudsman has a duty to guard the observance and protection of the rights and liberties of Polish citizens and residents, the law, and the principles of community life and social justice.

Since 1 April 2010, a separation between the prosecutorial system and the Minister of Justice was established. Previously, the Minister of Justice served as general prosecutor. This reform was motivated by the desire to foster greater independence and impartiality of prosecutors.

The transition from a mono-party Communist regime to democracy and pluralism resulted in new political parties mushrooming in the early 1990s. After the first free parliamentary elections in 1991, seats in the *Sejm* were divided amongst more than a dozen different parties. The existence of so many parties in the *Sejm* was seen by many as being counterproductive to the effectiveness of the Parliament and a hindrance towards producing stable governments. This has been cited as a contributing factor to the collapse of Prime Minister Hanna Suchocka's government after his defeat in a no-confidence vote, which subsequently led to the dissolution of the *Sejm* by President Lech Wałęsa in 1993.

Consequently, electoral reforms were undertaken and an electoral threshold for the lower house was instituted prior to the 1993 elections. The set threshold required a minimum vote of 5 per cent for national parties, with the exception of ethnic minority parties, and 8 per cent for electoral coalitions. The threshold was set at the national, rather than regional, level and had the effect of preventing a large number of minor parties from winning seats in later elections. The threshold also prevented independent candidates from gaining seats in the *Sejm*. In 1993, the parliamentary election of several right-wing parties, representing almost 35 per cent of votes, did not lead to corresponding representation in the *Sejm*, because the individual parties were not able to secure 5 per cent of the vote. This opened the way for the former Communists, the SLD-Democratic Left Alliance, to return to power. Although the SLD-Democratic Left Alliance secured only 20.4 per cent of the vote, it secured significantly more representative seats due to the redistribution of seats not taken by the parties who failed to reach the 5 per cent threshold (Gebethner, 1995).

5 Brief account of the political parties

Since 1990, former Communists turned Social Democrats have dominated the leftist political scene (Waniek, 2010). The right has been largely comprised of former Solidarity activists and supporters. However, the right has experienced deep divisions from the beginning, resulting in a less cohesive bloc than the left. The right was unable to create a single bloc that could act as a lasting counterbalance to the left-wing monolith and was instead caught in a cycle of merging, splitting, and renaming itself. Despite this fractured organization, the parties of the right governed from 1989–1993 and managed to win the right to govern again from 1997–2001 with an AWS (Solidarity Election Action) umbrella. This period of governing failed to deliver successful reforms and paved the way for the SLD to return to power in 2001–2005.

Since the parliamentary elections of 2005, the right-wing parties have dominated the political scene, and appear to be in their strongest position to date (Waniek, 2006). Two important developments in the political landscape have taken place since 2005. First, the former Communist SLD party is no longer one of the major Polish political parties. Second, the main political battleground is no longer between the ex-Solidarity right versus the ex-Communist left. Instead, the political scene is characterized by the cooperation of parties such as the Democratic Party with the SLD (Left and Democrats coalition), the bitter rivalry between right-wing parties *Prawo i Sprawiedliwość*, PiS (Law and Justice Party), and Civic Platform *Platforma Obywatelska*, PO (Civic Platform) as well as the impact of several controversial parties such as *Liga Polskich Rodzin*, LPR (League of Polish Peasants) and *Samoobrona Rzeczypospolitej Polskiej*, Samoobrona (Self-Defence of the Republic of Poland) (Kowalczyk and Tomczak, 2007).

At the outset of Polish democratic politics, the party system was characterized by instability and under-institutionalization. By the end of Poland's democratic second decade, the party system had displayed strong signs of structural stabilization and some evidence of the stability of inter-party competition and party institutionalization. This implies that the Polish party system is quasi-institutionalized (Gwiazda, 2009).

It is worth noting that general public disapproval of politics and politicians as a whole has resulted in almost all major parties excluding the very word 'party' from their names, replacing it with words less associated with politics such as 'union', 'platform', 'league', or 'alliance' (Kowalczyk and Sielski 2005).

Table 28.2a List of political parties in Poland

Original name	Abbreviation	English translation
Unia Polityki Realnej	UPR	Real Politics Union
Polskie Stronnictwo Ludowe	PSL	Polish People's Party
Samoobrona RP	SoRP	Self-Defence of the Republic of Poland
Polska Partia Pracy	PPP	Polish Labour Party
Libertas Polska	LP	Libertas Poland
Sojusz Lewicy Demokratycznej-Unia Pracy	SLD-UP	Coalition Democratic Left Alliance-Labour Union
Porozumienie dla Przyszłości-Centro Lewica	PdP	Coalition Agreement for the Future – Centre-Left
Prawica Rzeczypospolitej	PRP	Right of the Republic
Platforma Obywatelska	PO	Civic Platform
Prawo i Sprawiedliwość	PiS	Law and Justice

Currently, four large major political parties dominate the Polish political system, whilst there are at least three minor parties that play a certain role on the political stage. The ruling party since 2007, *Platforma Obywatelska*, PO (Civic Platform) first entered the *Sejm* in 2001 and was re-elected in 2011. In the 2005 parliamentary elections, PO took second place but was unable to form a coalition with Law and Justice, the so-called POPiS coalition, as was expected by most observers before the election. It has been the leading party in government since 2007 under Prime Minister Donald Tusk. It formed a coalition with the Polish People's Party led by Waldemar Pawlak. The party's candidate in the presidential elections of 2010, Bronisław Komorowski, became President in 2010. In 2011, PO won the parliamentary elections and was the first party to remain in power since Poland's democratic transformation in 1989.

The second largest party is *Prawo i Sprawiedliwość*, PiS (Law and Justice). Along with PO, PiS has served as one of the two major parties since 2005 and is represented in the *Sejm* under the leadership of Jarosław Kaczyński. It was the leading party in the coalition government with the League of Polish Families and Samoobrona between 2005 and 2007, which ended after a no-confidence vote in the *Sejm*. It came in second place in the 2007 and 2011 elections, and serves as the country's largest opposition party. In the 2005 presidential elections, the Law and Justice candidate, Lech Kaczyński, brother of Jarosław Kaczyński, was voted into office. Lech Kaczyński cooperated closely with PiS between 2005 and 2007 and in 2007–2010, when PiS became the major opposition force. President Lech Kaczyński died on 10 April 2010 in an air crash catastrophe in Smoleńsk, Russia.

In the following special election, his brother Jaroslaw Kaczyński took second place. Before the 2011 elections, the PiS experienced an internal split leading to the formation of a new party, the *Polska Jest Najważniejsza* (Poland Is Most Important). However, the new party was not able to secure representation in the *Sejm*. In 2011 elections, PO once again defeated PiS. Following this defeat, the PiS experienced yet another split. The new party, led by MEP and former Justice Minister in the PiS government Zbigniew Ziobro, was called *Solidarna Polska* (Solidarity Poland). This development has influenced the political structure of Polish representation to the European Parliament and has resulted in a shift in political group affiliation.

The largest left-wing party, *Sojusz Lewicy Demokratycznej*, SLD (Democratic Left Alliance), emerged from a coalition of leftist parties and was originally called *Socjaldemokracja Rzeczypospolitej Polskiej*, SdRP (Social Democracy of the Republic of Poland). SLD was a major governmental party from 1993 until 1997 and from 2001 until 2005. In 1995 and 2000, SLD candidate Aleksander Kwaśniewski won the presidential elections. Since 2005, SLD's dominance has been successfully challenged by PO and PiS. SLD's leader Grzegorz Napieralski took third place in the 2010 presidential race. In the 2011 elections, SLD took a disappointing fifth place, losing to the new left-oriented Palikot's Movement (named after the founder Janusz Palikot, a former

Table 28.2b Parliamentary political parties in Poland

Party	Leader	Ideology
PO	Donald Tusk	Centre-right (Christian Democratic, Liberal Conservative)
PiS	Jarosław Kaczyński	Centre-right (Neo-conservative)
SLD	Grzegorz Napieralski	Centre-left (Anti-clerical, Social Democratic)
PSL	Waldemar Pawlak	Centre (Agrarian, Centrism, Christian Democratic)
PP	Jerzy Polaczek	Centre-right (Liberal conservatism)
SDPL	Wojciech Filemonowicz	Centre-left (Social democratic)
SD	Paweł Piskorski	Centre (Social liberal)

PO MP). SLD Chairman Grzegorz Napieralski resigned following this defeat and Leszek Miller, former PM and previous party leader, became a chairman of the party and parliamentary group.

Polskie Stronnictwo Ludowe, PSL (Polish People's Party) is an agrarian party founded in 1990. The PSL has been represented in the *Sejm* since its inception. Support for the PSL has been more stable than for any other Polish political party since 1989. PSL normally scores 6–9 per cent of the popular vote and achieved its best result at the 1993 legislative elections with over 15 per cent of the vote. Since 2007, the PSL has served as part of the ruling coalition with PO. Its leader, Waldemar Pawlak, is currently serving as deputy Prime Minister and minister of economy. The PO-PSL coalition has remained in power since the 2011 parliamentary elections.

Apart from these four main parties, there are three smaller political movements that may play a future role in Polish politics. *Polska Plus*, PP (Polish Plus) is a Liberal Conservative splinter from the Law and Justice party. Poland Plus was formed in 2010 by eight former PiS deputies. *Socjaldemokracja Polska*, SDPL (Social Democracy of Poland) is a splinter left-wing party that was formed in 2004 when it broke away from the larger SLD. It was represented in the *Sejm* between 2004 and 2005 and has held seats in Parliament since 2007. Between 2006 and 2008, SDPL was allied to the SLD, PD, and UP as part of the *Lewica i Demokraci,* LiD (Left and Democrats) coalition. *Partia Demokratyczna*, PD (Democratic Party) is the successor party to Freedom Union, which was formed in 2005. It was represented in the *Sejm* between 2007 and 2009. In 2007, the PD was allied to the SLD, SDPL, and UP as part of the Left and Democrats coalition

In the 2011 elections a new party arrived on the Polish political scene, Palikot's Movement. It combines the popularity of businessman and former PO deputy Janusz Palikot with a radical political message. The party's platform includes anti-Church, pro-abortion, and pro-gay rights programmes. It made Polish civil rights history, with the first openly gay and first transsexual representatives in Parliament. This movement divided left-wing votes and diminished the power of the SLD on the parliamentary scene.

5.1 Party attitudes towards the European Union

The positions of Polish political parties on European integration are strongly connected to the attitude of the Polish people (Grzesik-Robak, 2008). Using data from over 800 face-to-face interviews with Polish citizens, a recent sociological survey showed that individuals rely strongly on their social networks to decide whether they will, in fact, adopt a pro- or anti-EU stand. The results in this study indicate that one's environment, specifically interactions and discussions with other people, shape perceptions, provide information, and subsequently influence individual preferences for EU membership. This network effect is just as strong in the urban environment as it is in the rural context and, in general, generates positive influence on EU support (Radziszewski, 2005).

The parliamentary parties' attitudes after the elections of 2001 and 2005 have been analysed and compared. The aim was to identify factors that frame or change these attitudes. The change in Poland's status from candidate country to EU member forced the political parties to redefine their attitudes towards Europe. This especially applies to those parties that strongly opposed Poland's accession to the EU (Cyran, 2010). Accession was not the only factor, but was definitely one of the most important, and, in the period analysed, the European issue played a secondary role in the election behaviour of the electorate. Rather, it served as a lens on more fundamental dilemmas related to the role of state sovereignty, national identity, religion, and individual rights (Zuba, 2009).

Generally, most competing parties in the 2009 EP elections voiced pro-European attitudes. However, they differed on several issues. The Democratic Left Alliance supported deeper

European integration, as symbolized by the Lisbon Treaty, whilst Law and Justice was against the treaty. Only Libertas, the party financed by the Irish magnate Declan Ganley, presented an anti-European platform, including a challenge to the Lisbon Treaty. An important argument against the new Lisbon Treaty was that it would limit Polish sovereignty to such an extent that it might threaten Polish statehood (Jackowski, 2009, 3). However it did not influence the quality and merits of the campaign. A similar argument was presented in relation to the European Constitution in the EP elections of 2004 (Arnold and Pennings, 2009, 34).

Generally, parties adopted a pragmatic approach to campaigning in which EU issues were less important than internal issues.

6 Public opinion and the European Union

In a 2008 survey, two-thirds of Poles viewed Poland's membership in the EU as 'something good'. Three-quarters, 77 per cent, believed that Poland had benefitted from EU membership. The level of support for the EU grew from 2004. Public perception after four years of Polish EU membership was better than expected. Polish attitudes towards the EU were rationalized. Poles believed that Polish accession to the EU was as good for Poland as it was for the EU. The survey suggested that the Polish population felt like a partner in the EU. The most important advantage of EU membership was the opening of the EU labour market. Poles believed that EU accession helped to address the problem of unemployment. Sixty per cent of Poles trusted the EU, better than the EU average of 50 per cent. Trust in EU institutions was higher than the EU average: 53 per cent for the European Parliament, 54 per cent for the European Commission, and 48 per cent for the Council. Almost two-thirds of those questioned thought that things were going well in the EU. Seventy-four per cent of Poles were supporters of further EU enlargement. Poles supported extending membership to Norway and Switzerland, 84 per cent, Iceland 78 per cent, and Ukraine 73 per cent (Eurobarometer, 2008).

7 National and EP electoral systems

EP contests are the only elections not regulated in the Polish Constitution but through electoral law (Rupar, 2006). However, in case of a constitutional amendment, EP election rules would be set forth in the Polish primary act. This is especially important in the case of passive/active voting rights (Jaskiernia, 2004).

Major discussions about the best proportional electoral system for Poland took place before passing a bill (Gebethner, 2002) and there were intense discussions regarding the representational options (Rudkowski, 2002). The main controversial issue centred around whether the elections should take place at the national or regional level through a territorial division into voting districts (Sarnecki, 2003). Another disputed issue was the decision over the best method to count the votes (Sobczak, 2007). In the end, it was decided to divide the country into 13 electoral districts that had to include more than one province (*voivodship*) in order to allow the proportional representation of political powers (Dydak, 2003, 154).

In accordance with European law, the ordinance included voting rights for EU citizens (Urbaniak, 2003, 92). The electoral law enshrined basic European election rules: freedom of choice, the general character of elections, the direct nature of elections, and the confidentiality of voting.

All Polish citizens have electoral rights that are also granted to citizens of other EU countries permanently residing in Poland who are included in the register of voters. This rule was approved by the Polish Constitutional Tribunal on 31 May 2004. The right to elect is vested in persons who are at least 18 years old, have not been deprived of public rights or electoral rights

Figure 28.2 Map of EP electoral constituencies in Poland

by a judicial verdict, and are not legally incapacitated. The right to be elected is vested in persons who have not been sentenced for crimes conducted intentionally, prosecuted by public authorities, and who have been permanently residing in Poland for at least five years or in the territory of another EU country. Candidates must also be at least 21 years of age.

The right to submit candidates is vested in voters and political parties who have additionally been granted the right to establish political coalitions. Campaigns and other election-related activities are conducted by election lists. Campaigns are conducted on the basis of rules stipulated in the election ordinance to the *Sejm* and the Senate. The financing of campaigns is open and not confidential.

The voting results are determined by the State Election Commission, a body composed of judges of the Supreme Court, Superior Administrative Court, and Constitutional Tribunal. Electoral district lists that have achieved 5 per cent of valid votes in the country are allocated representative seats. As in the elections to the *Sejm*, mandates are assigned in accordance with the d'Hondt method. Afterwards, the remaining seats are allocated to nationwide constituencies and divided between the district lists by using the Hare-Niemeyer method. The state election commission prepares a protocol and publishes official election results in the *Official Journal of the Republic of Poland*. The Supreme Court reviews any challenges to the election.

On 13 February 2009, the Parliament amended the election ordinance by including, amongst other things, a two-day-long election and the ability to appoint a proxy voter for the elderly or disabled. The President did not sign the act and instead filed for review by the constitutional tribunal on 5 March 2009. Therefore, the 2009 EP elections were conducted in accordance with the 2004 ordinance.

In the *Sejm* elections, mandates are accrued in particular districts proportional to the number of people eligible to vote. Therefore, it is known prior to the elections how many MPs will be elected in each district. In EP elections, the number of seats ultimately depends on turnout. As a consequence, districts in which there is higher turnout are at a greater advantage and no district is guaranteed a seat. The 2004 and 2009 EP elections were conducted in 13 electoral districts.

8 A glance at the EP and national elections

The 2005 national election in Poland saw the defeat of the incumbent centre-left government dominated by Democratic Left Alliance (SLD).

This outcome was related to the unpopular austerity policies of the government of Prime Minister Leszek Miller. Even though this government was successful in dealing with Poland's EU accession and played a major role in the 2003 European referendum, the austerity measures introduced by the Miller government to solve the public financial crisis resulted in decreased support amongst the Polish polity, including the traditional leftist electorate. Additionally, corruption scandals, such as the so-called Rywin affair, destroyed the integrity of the left in the eyes of the public. On the other side, right-wing parties were strengthened after the creation of two dynamic parties (PO, PiS) which had learned from the negative experience of Election Action Solidarity (AWS). Anti-European forces such as *Samoobrona* and LPR have been successful in presenting anti-EU slogans and showcasing the possible negative outcomes of Poland's EU membership (Sokala et al., 2010).

Holding the parliamentary and presidential elections simultaneously made the campaigns indistinguishable and each interacted with the other. Party programmes were similar, with transition-related issues dominating the election. The Law and Justice party (PiS) was the unexpected victor with its campaign for a radical break with the trajectory of post-Communist development and a moral revolution in the new so called 'Fourth Republic'. PiS successfully appropriated the welfare mantle of the discredited Social Democrats and mobilized traditional conservative and religious values. Despite formal plans for a PiS coalition with Civic Platform (PO), the election resulted unexpectedly in a PiS coalition with two radical parties: Self-Defence (SORP) and the League of Polish Families (LPR) (Millard, 2006). This coalition collapsed in 2007, leading to early elections.

The 2007 Polish parliamentary elections are best understood as a plebiscite on the polarizing right-wing Law and Justice Party-led government and its controversial 'Fourth Republic' political project. The Liberal-Conservative Civic Platform opposition won because it was able to persuade the Polish polity that a vote for the opposition was the most effective way of removing the current government from office. The election also indicates that the 'post-Communist

Table 28.3 National election results in Poland: 2001–2007 (% and seats)

Date	PO	PiS	SLD (SLD-UP), LiD	PSL	Samoobrona	LPR	Others
2001	12.6 (65)	9.5 (44)	41.0 (216)	10.0 (42)	10.2 (53)	7.9 (38)	8.5 (0)
2005	24.1 (133)	27.0 (155)	11.3 (55)	6.7 (31)	11.4 (56)	8.0 (34)	11.2 (0)
2007	41.6 (209)	32.1 (166)	13.1 (53)	6.7 (31)		—	6.5 (0)

Source: Państwowa Komisja Wyborcza – State's Election Committee, http://pkw.gov.pl/.

divide' that dominated and provided a structural order to Polish political scene during the 1990s is losing its importance and certainly means a more consolidated Polish party system. However, Poland still has very high levels of electoral volatility and low electoral turnout, together with low levels of party institutionalization and extremely weak links between parties and their supporters.

It is too early to say whether the election also marks the emergence of a stable Polish party system based on a new bipolar divide between two big centre-right groupings, with the confinement of the left to the status of a minor actor (Szczerbiak, 2008).

Since 2005, we have witnessed the strong domination of centre-right parties (PiS, PO) with the PO's position growing after 2007. The 2010 presidential election won by Bronisław Komorowski (PO) confirms this tendency. The political picture in Poland did not change dramatically after the 2011 parliamentary election. Only the left's votes were divided between Palikot's Movement and the SLD.

Table 28.4 Turnout at national and EP elections in Poland

Dates	NE	Dates	EP
2001	46.3	2004	20.9
2005	40.6	2009	24.5
2007	53.9		

Source: Państwowa Komisja Wyborcza – State's Election Committee, http://pkw.gov.pl/.

Table 28.5 EP election results in Poland: 2004

Political party	Number of votes	Votes %	Seats
PO	1,467,775	24.1	15
LPR	969,689	15.9	10
PiS	771,858	12.7	7
SRP	656,782	10.8	6
SLD-UP	569,311	9.3	5
UW	446,549	7.3	4
PSL	386,340	6.3	4
SdPl	324,707	5.3	3
UPR	113,675	1.9	0
NKWW	94,867	1.6	0
NKIP	88,565	1.4	0
KPEiR-PLD	48,667	0.8	0
KROB	36,937	0.6	0
OKO	35,180	0.6	0
PPP	32,807	0.5	0
APP Racja	18,068	0.3	0
Zieloni 2004	16,288	0.3	0
DPL	5,513	0.1	0
RdP	2,897	0.0 (0.05)	0
NOP	2,546	0.0 (0.04)	0
PPN	2,510	0.0 (0.04)	0
Total	6,091,531	100.0	54

Source: Państwo Komisja Wyborcza – State's Election Commission, http://en.wikipedia.org/wiki/List_of_political_parties_in_Poland.

As to the Euro-elections, the first contest held in Poland in 2004 showed the growing role of the PO, which received 24.1 per cent of the vote and gained 15 seats.

It also signalled the increasing influence of Conservative parties with pro-Catholic and nationalistic messages, including the League of Polish Families (LPR), which received 15.9 per cent and ten seats. Law and Justice (PiS) came in third place with 12.7 per cent and seven seats. The biggest surprise was the success of the Eurosceptic message of *Samoobrona* (Self-Defence). *Sammobrona* received 10.8 per cent and six seats. The election also revealed the diminishing influence of the left. The coalition Democratic Left Alliance (SLD) and Labour Union (UP) received only 9.3 per cent and five seats. The remaining parties did not receive seats after receiving less than 5 per cent of the vote. Paradoxically, those parties that played a crucial role in the Polish accession process (SLD-UP) were not successful in the EP elections, whilst parties with anti-European messages such as LPR and *Samoobrona* received surprisingly strong results.

9 The 2009 European election

9.1 Party lists and manifestos

Only eight single-party tickets and two coalition tickets contested all thirteen electoral districts. The draw of the number was made by the national electoral commission. One single-party ticket, one coalition ticket, and one ticket of 'grouped independents' managed to register in at least one district.

The European Parliament election campaign was conducted on a much smaller scale and with the use of fewer financial resources compared to national election campaigns (Gagatek, 2010a). However, one must also take into consideration the fact that there is less at stake in EP elections and fewer candidates use their own resources to run a successful campaign. In spite of these considerations, Polish political parties treat EP elections very seriously and have offered detailed programmes on the EU and European integration issues. Interestingly, the differences between the manifestos of the major Polish parties for EP elections were not as pronounced as in national elections.

One of the most novel considerations in these elections is the increasing presence of and direct competition between political parties at the European level. This phenomenon has also been observed in other EU Member States. Recently, European political parties, especially the Party of European Socialists (PES), have argued that the political choices made at the European level are the same at the national level. As a consequence, the choice between the European centre-left or the European centre right at the European level is as important as it is at the national level (Gagatek, 2009, 309). This fosters the possibility for a 'greater politicization of the European Parliament elections' (Gagatek, 2010b, 24). This phenomenon led to more visible involvement by the representatives of European political parties, especially the EEP and PES, in the 2009 EP elections campaign in Poland. Additionally, many parties adopted manifestos from European political parties as an important instrument in their election campaigns.

Civic Platform (PO) has used the 'European issue' in its EP election platform. PO accepted the EPP priorities: Europe of values, Europe of economic growth and welfare, Secure Europe, and Solidarity Europe. In the election materials they stressed the achievements of PO MEPs in the 2004–2009 term (Słodkowska and Dołbakowska, 2010). An important element of the PO's electoral strategy was the congress of the European People's Party, held in Warsaw in April 2009, in which 12 Prime Ministers, the President of the European Commission, the President of the European Parliament, and several other important political figures participated. This Congress was a show of strength by European Christian-Democrats. The PO leadership stressed the importance of strong a PO showing in the EP elections to strengthen its role within the biggest and most influential political group in the EP.

Law and Justice (PiS) offered the following slogan in the EP elections: 'More for Poland'. The party's agenda included the platform that Poland should receive more support from EU and should have a privileged position within the EU due to its population and standing within the region. The party also argued that Poland should already have had a privileged position within the EU but the PO government had not been able to guarantee it. The PiS attacked the PO for its lack of ability to successfully address 'European issues'. In March 2009, it published a book on European policy issues entitled: '*Polska nowoczesna, Polska solidarna, Polska bezpieczna*' (*Modern Poland, Solidarity Poland, Secure Poland*) (Oleszowski, 2010). The PiS highlighted its contacts with British Conservatives and their leader, David Cameron. The PiS claimed that Conservatives from the Czech Republic had also contacted them for possible cooperative efforts. Their goal after the EP elections was to form a new political group in order to attract the support of the right-leaning and Eurosceptic electorate.

The electoral coalition of the Democratic Left Alliance and Labour Union (SLD/UP) expressed a pro-European platform in its campaign. The SLD held this attitude during the whole pre-accession period. It reminded the electorate that SLD's politicians, Prime Minister Leszek Miller and Foreign Affairs Minister Włodzimierz Cimoszewicz, signed the accession treaty. The SLD-UP/PSL government before EU accession played a crucial role in preparing Poland for EU integration. During the campaign, the SLD/UP electoral coalition voiced its support for the Lisbon Treaty and the further strengthening of the European integration process. It sought a more just and secure 'Social Europe' based on the free market. Characteristically, the SLD/UP took a pro-ecological stand and emphasized the role of the EU in the fight against unemployment. The SLD/UP also included in its programme the importance of improving gender equality (Słodkowska and Dołbakowska, 2010).

The Polish People's Party (PSL) tried to present itself as the party that supported European integration on behalf of Polish farmers and the agricultural industry. They proposed that by 2013 Polish agriculture should receive the same level of support through the Common Agricultural Policy as other EU countries. They promised to fight for the simplification of EU legislation. PSL stressed the importance of national sovereignty and national identity in the process of European integration (ibid.).

Libertas presented an anti-European position. In the 2009 Euro-elections this movement brought together politicians from the League of Polish Families and former members of the Polish People's Party, Self-Defence of the Republic of Poland, and Forward Poland. Libertas, was financed and strongly influenced by the Irish magnate Declan Ganley, who tried to suggest that the party presented a real alternative to Polish pro-European parties. Libertas appealed to unprivileged, Conservative, and Eurosceptic voters. Some public television and radio channels broadcast the party's message. Allegedly individuals connected to the League of Poland manipulated opinion polls, thus creating the false impression that Libertas was a growing influence on Polish politics.

9.2 Electoral campaign

An opinion poll conducted by the Centre of Public Opinion Research (OBOP) on 22 May 2009 posed the question: 'Does the campaign before the EP election encourage you to take part in this election?' Forty-three per cent of Polish voters responded 'No', 32 per cent responded that the campaign was not visible, and only 17 per cent responded 'Yes' (Olszewski, 2010).

Yet, the general attitude of the mass media towards EP elections was serious and professional. Polish electoral law provides for strict rules of media access, both public and private.

All running political parties and electoral lists were guaranteed appropriate access to public media, such as TVP1 and TV2, and especially on the Polish information channel, TVPInfo, formerly TVP3. TVPInfo held several important debates in which candidates of political parties running for EP seats participated. Private media also provided EP election coverage. The only major issue was whether such programmes were attractive enough to raise public interest and help citizens understand the European integration process and the role of the EP. Public opinion polls showed that such programmes did not have high visibility.

The public media's impartiality was an important problem. Several cases arose involving the chairman of TVP (public television) Piotr Farfał, who allegedly had connections with national right-wing forces such as the League of Polish Families and who openly supported Libertas. A visit by Libertas leader Declan Ganley was presented as a significant news story. TVP suggested that the Libertas platform would receive strong results in the EP elections, a view that contradicted opinion polls (Kublik, 2009). This was particularly evident in TVP's news coverage. The same tactic was employed in the campaign on public radio, especially in local broadcasting. Election results proved that this evident manipulation did not have any significant effects. Rather, it raised the question about the ethics and integrity of some journalists.

Civic Platform, generally in favour of the process of European integration, had an ambiguous position on the Constitutional Treaty. However, it supported the Lisbon Treaty by endorsing its ratification. Law and Justice promoted the process of European unification, but with reservations. The party was against the Constitutional Treaty and supported the Lisbon Treaty on the conditions offered by the British-Polish Protocol. Although former PiS politician President Lech Kaczyński asked Parliament to ratify the Lisbon Treaty in April, he withheld his signature, confirming the ratification only in November 2009. He claimed that the treaty was not clear following Ireland's failure to ratify it in the first referendum. The PiS argued against federalist tendencies in the EU, and that the European Union should be an 'authentic community of values'.

The SLD/UP coalition supported the European Constitution and the Lisbon Treaty, asking the President of Poland to ratify the Lisbon Treaty as soon as possible. The Polish People's Party backed the idea of a 'Europe of Fatherlands'. As part of the coalition government, it supported the ratification of the Lisbon Treaty, but it was not outspoken on this issue. Libertas campaigned fiercely against the process of European integration and voiced a strong position against the Lisbon Treaty.

This question did not play any major role in the 2009 EP elections in Poland. Generally, Polish people shared a positive attitude towards further enlargement of the EU. Ukraine's membership in the EU was strongly endorsed by the population as its neighbour was considered an important player in EU security. The PiS stated in its programme: 'EU Enlargement towards the east should occur without any further delays' (Radek, 2010, 61).

The SLD pointed out that 'process of negotiations with Turkey should be based on clear criteria and both EU and Turkey should fulfill their obligations connected with that' (Wojtasik, 2010, 75). The question of Turkey did not play a major role in the 2009 EP elections in Poland. Generally racist and xenophobic attitudes did not create an important issue, although from time to time they re-emerged in the programmes and activities of small, non-representative groups and organizations. Xenophobic and racist sentiments were generally condemned by the majority of Polish people and the media.

Civic Platform claimed in the campaign that Poland was the only EU country that continued to grow economically during the financial crisis. With the exception of Libertas, Polish people and political parties did not generally question the EU's role in Poland's economic success. In their programmes, both ruling and opposition parties argued that Poland should be more effective in its use of EU funds.

PO stressed that Europe could cope with the crisis through the reform of public finances and the regulation of financial markets. The PO stressed that the EU must support economic solidarity with those countries that were most affected by the crisis.

The PSL presented the argument that the EU, under the principles of subsidiarity and solidarity, should support Polish anti-crisis measures to minimize the consequences for Poland and other EU countries. Moreover, the PSL advocated that the EU should be more involved in providing 'economic security'.

SLD pointed out that the EU should become a leader in international negotiations to limit carbon dioxide emissions and that a new Social Democratic programme was needed to successfully combat climate change. Moreover, the SLD wanted the EU to reduce its dependence on oil and coal. The PSL noted that Poland had gained a lot from the EU in the areas of infrastructure and the environment.

Foreign affairs did not play a major role in EP elections. Generally, Polish people understood the growing role that the EU was playing in the development of a common foreign policy. The main issue for Polish political parties was Poland's controversial presence in Afghanistan. The government projected that Polish forces needed to remain in Afghanistan until 2012, but this question was not discussed during the EP elections.

Political parties in Poland agreed on the point that successful counter-terrorism measures were crucial for Polish security, especially due to the involvement of Polish troops in Iraq and Afghanistan. Generally, initiatives offered in this field by the EU were not contested.

PO stated in its programme that the 'EU should effectively protect their citizens from terrorism' (Kowalczyk, 2010, 34). PiS in its programme stated: 'Poland should support the European initiatives strengthening Polish military security, as long as they do not contradict the country's obligations to the United States' (Radek, 2000, 56). Poland should 'consider its complementary participation in the creation of the new political deal in our region' (ibid., 55).

The SLD pointed out that the :

> battle against terrorism should be a priority for the EU, but done within the rule of law and should not collide with the protection of fundamental freedoms. We should promote common a European policy in this area, including a European strategy to battle with terrorism and support a special US representative for the battle with terrorism.
> (Wojtasik, 2010, 82)

9.3 Electoral results

Following the entry into force of the Lisbon Treaty, Poland received an additional seat in the European Parliament, increasing the total number of seats from 50 to 51. In accordance with the election results, the National Election Commission offered this seat to the *Polskie Stronnictwo Ludowe*, PSL (Polish People's Party). The seat was filled, in accordance with an inter-institutional agreement between the Commission and the EP, during the mid-term of the EP elected in 2009.

When comparing the 2005 and 2009 EP elections, it is interesting to note some political changes in the political structure of the Polish EP delegation (Słodkowska and Dołbakowska, 2005, 2010).

As anticipated, Civic Platform (PO) won a significant victory, with more than 44 per cent of the vote. This resulted in the party holding half of the total available seats. PO's EP percentage was higher than the 41.5 per cent achieved at the Polish parliamentary election in 2007. To date, no other Polish party has attained as high a percentage of the vote in either the *Sejm* or the European Parliament. Civic Platform's success broke the pattern in Polish politics in which successful election campaigns were followed by a loss in the subsequent 1991–2007 election cycle (Jaskiernia, 2007, 29). PO polled strongest in the western half of Poland. The PO's success can be seen as a combination of several contributing factors: the influence of pre-election polls, an effective propaganda strategy by Prime Minister Donald Tusk's cabinet, PO's effective selection of candidates, a multitude of marketing strategies, and the failure of the PiS to mobilize undecided and centrist voters. Moreover, the political forces on the left were in disarray (Kowalczyk, 2010, 49).

Law and Justice (PiS), came second, with 27.4 per cent of the vote. Whilst it secured more than double its share of the vote and seats from the 2004 EU election, its share of the vote fell compared to the national elections of 2007. PiS scored best in the eastern half of the country, particularly the south-east. The party strengthened its position as an important political force in Poland. However, one must keep in mind that the segments of Polish society from which the PiS draws its strongest support, such as older people and rural voters, are shrinking. In this campaign season, the party experimented with partly positive, partly negative messages (Radek, 2010).

The largest alliance on the left, the Democratic Left Alliance-Labour Union (SLD-UP) came in a distant third place, with 12.3 per cent of the vote and seven seats; six for SLD and one for UP. The vote of the once largest party in Poland, the SLD, has remained static over the past five years, and the party has been unable to challenge the dominance of the PO and PiS since 2005. However, SLD leaders were satisfied that they gained an additional EP seat after the campaign, in spite of limited financial resources (Napieralski, 2009). The SLD showed that there is actually only one 'electable' leftist party and the division of left-wing forces, with two competing tickets in EP elections, limits the representation possibilities for the leftist Polish electorate (Wiatr, 2009, 12). The consolidation of the party system, specifically cooperation between the PO and PiS, and the restructuring of the parliamentary system, created major problems for the left. In this system, larger parties tend to benefit more than smaller parties (Wojtasik, 2010, 82).

Table 28.6 EP election results in Poland: 2009

National party	Political group	Votes	%	Vote change	Seats	Seat change
PO	EPP	3,271,852	44.4	+20.3	25	+10
PiS	AEN-ECR	2,017,607	27.4	+14.7	15	+8
SLD UP	PES	908,765	12.3	13.0	7	12
UPR	EPP	516,146	7.0	+0.7	3	−1
PdP	PES, ALDE	179,602	2.4	—	0	—
PRP	ID	143,966	1.9	—	0	—
SoRP	UEN	107,185	1.4	−9.3	0	−6
LP	Libertas.eu	83,754	1.1	—	0	—
UPR	*None*	81,146	1.1	−0.8	0	±0
PPP	EACL	51,872	0.7	−0.2	0	±0
Others	—	2,868	0.0 (0.04)	—	0	±0
Total	—	7,364,763	100.0	8.4	50	−4

Source: http://pe2009.pkw.gov.pl/PUE/PL/WYN/W/index.htm.

The Polish People's Party (PSL) secured 7 per cent of the vote and won three seats. PSL won an additional fourth seat after the enforcement of the Lisbon Treaty. This fourth seat was filled in the EP mid-term.

The remaining parties failed to reach the 5 per cent threshold required to win seats. Eurosceptic factions in the EP elections, such as *Samoobrona*, Libertas, *Prawica Rzeczypospolitej* (Right of the Republic), *Naprzód Polski* (Forward Poland), and *Unia Polityki Realnej* (Real Politics Union) obtained very poor results and did not manage to secure a single seat in the EP. Their defeat is all the more evident if one compares the current results with those obtained in 2004, when the *Samoobrona* (Self-Defence) and *Liga Polskich Rodzin* (League of Polish Families) had fairly good results.

The weakening of these parties' power has been the consequence of new factors. Most significant amongst these factors are: the stable and high level of popular support for Poland's membership of the EU; the lack of criticism of EU membership; the disintegration of the majority of Eurosceptic factions; financial weakness and its effect on campaign funding; as well as *Radio Maryja's*, and other media controlled by Father Tadeusz Rydzyk; support for law and justice; and the parties' use of Eurosceptic rhetoric during the campaign (Zuba, 2010).

The election results demonstrated stability in voting patterns in the country. Prior to 2005, the political environment in Poland was unpredictable, with the electorate swinging away from established parties and towards alternative parties, and with constant splits and mergers of key parties. In 2009, however, the voting pattern did not differ substantially from the 2007 elections with the large parties (PO, PiS) consolidating their positions, and smaller parties (SLD, PSL) failing to break through.

The important factor was the attitude of Catholic Church, which plays an important role in Polish society, including in political life. The Catholic Church Episcopate appealed to Catholics to vote 'for candidates who fully represent the stand of the Catholic Church in ethical and social issues, especially in defending human life and who care about marriage and family'. Individual clerics went even further. For example, Bishop Wiktor Skworc (Tarnów) advocated that the European Parliament needs Christian representatives. He argued that:

> several previous apostles of Marxism, Maoism, admirers of Che Guevara and the Red Brigades captured the Christian vision of European identity and today take a lead in the Parliament in Brussels and are active in the fronts of globalization, ecology, climatic catastrophes, help for the striving in the Third World, but simultaneously they are enemies of the family, right to life from natural birth to natural death, and even the enemies of the God.
> (Wiśniewska, 2009)

Officially, the Catholic Church did not support any specific party. However, at the grassroots level, Catholic parishes pushed potential voters towards the preferred Law and Justice Party. Although the Episcopate appealed Poles to participate in the EP election, their actions did not lead to a change in the predicted electoral results.

Following the 2009 elections, a new configuration of political groups emerged in the European Parliament.

Polish MEPs belong to only three EP political groups: the European People's Party (EPP), the European Conservatives and Reformists (ECR), and the Progressive Alliance of Socialists & Democrats (S&D). The EPP received nine MEPs from Poland, thanks in large part to the growing political position of the PO. Two additional seats went to the ECR, thanks to a good showing by PiS. Polish participation in the S&D decreased by one seat, despite the fact that the SLD/UP received better results than in the 2004 EP election. No other party received seats in the European Parliament.

Table 28.7 Polish MEPs' affiliation to EP political group: 2004–2009

EP political group	Seats 2004	Seats 2009	Seat change
European People's Party (EPP)	19	29	+10
Union for the Europe of Nations (UEN)	13	0	−13
Party of European Socialists (PES)	8	7	−1
Alliance of Liberal and Democrats in Europe (ALDE)	4	0	−4
European Conservatives and Reformist (ECR)	0	11	+11
Independence/Democracy	10	4	−6
Total	54	51	−3

Source: http://pe2009.pkw.gov.pl/PUE/PL/WYN/W/index.htm, accessed on 12 December 2009; Szczepanik, *Polacy w Parlamencie Europejskim. Podsumowanie pierwszej połowy 7. Kadencji. Raport z badań Instytutu Spraw Publicznych*, www.isp.org.pl.

Note:
During the 2009–2014 term, the Law and Justice split. Six MEPs from the Law and Justice left UEN to join ECR. Three MEPs from the Poland Comes First group, as well as two independents, Adam Bielan, Mirosław Piotrowski, joined ECR.

9.4 Campaign finance

The financing of the European Parliament election in 2009 was grounded in the 1997 Political Parties Law devoted to the financing of political parties and in the 2001 Election Law (1997 Special Division no. 11). The financial spending limit for each ticket was set at 10,351,733.84 złoty, corresponding approximately to €2.8 million. Expenditure was controlled by the Central Election Commission. All party tickets were required to report private revenues and all campaign spending publicly. The parties received public money if they reached 3 per cent in the overall vote or 6 per cent overall in the case of a coalition. The public finance model sought to root out corruption and misbehaviour in politics (Bidziński, 2011). This is still a subject of public debate (Gorgol, 2011). Every element of the campaigns, including press advertisement and campaign materials, was required to be paid through the election committee. It was forbidden to finance election campaigns from the public funds of state and local governments and from private enterprises. The National Election Commission issued several documents analysing all aspects of eligible campaign financing. Additionally, the Minister of Finance specified how election revenues and spending should be reported.

The Batory Foundation in Warsaw held a special monitoring programme on the ethics of campaign financing (*Fundacja Stefana Batorego*, 2009). Generally, the 2009 EP election was considered in Poland as 'democratic and fair'. However, several cases of irregular behaviour by campaigns were reported by the Batory Foundation. Amongst the major problems were: the declaring of election campaign expenses; the use of party offices and resources without reporting them within campaign revenues; the use of materials not reported as revenue; the over-use of local visits by members of government for campaign purposes; the dissemination of misleading advertisements; the use of national funds and resources for EP election campaigns; and the use of online campaigns without election committee approval. One of the most important findings the Batory Foundation discovered was that the spending limit was too low in many cases. Election districts in EP elections are immense projects that must be taken to all cities and small towns. This results in high overhead costs. The Batory Foundation found that this high overhead resulted in many election committees finding ways to hide expenses. This undermined the efforts of the election committee to enforce transparency in campaign financing.

Table 28.8 List of Polish MEPs: seventh legislature

Surname	First name	National party	Political group	Professional background	Date of birth	Gender	Committee/Chair
Bielan	Adam Andrzej	PiS	ECR	Politician	12/09/1974	Male	—
Borys	Piotr	PO	EPP	Lawyer	11/01/1976	Male	—
Buzek	Jerzy	PO	EPP	Professor of Technology	03/07/1940	Male	EP President
Cymański	Tadeusz	PiS	ECR	Economist	06/06/1955	Male	—
Czarnecki	Ryszard Henry	PiS	ECR	Historian	25/01/1963	Male	—
Geringer De Oedenberg	Lidia Joanna	SLD	S&D	Economist	15/09/1957	Female	—
Gierek	Adam	UP	S&D	Professor of Technology	17/04/1938	Male	—
Gräfin Von Thun Und Hohen-Stein	Róża Maria	PO	EPP	English Philologist	13/04/1954	Female	—
Gróbarczyk	Marek Józef	PiS	ECR	Mechanic Engineer	13/03/1968	Male	—
Grzyb	Andrzej Marian	PSL	EPP	Politician	23/08/1956	Male	—
Handzlik	Małgorzata Maria	PO	EPP	Politician	01/01/1965	Female	—
Hibner	Jolanta Emilia	PO	EPP	Environment Engineer	26/01/1951	Female	—
Hübner	Danuta Maria	PO	EPP	Professor of Economy	08/04/1948	Female	Chair, Regional Development
Jazłowiecka	Danuta	PO	EPP	Politician	15/05/1957	Female	—
Jędrzejewska	Sidonia Elżbieta	PO	EPP	Clerk	05/11/1975	Female	—
Kaczmarek	Filip Andrzej	PO	EPP	Politician	22/11/1966	Female	—
Kalinowski	Jarosław	PSL	EPP	Farmer	12/04/1962	Female	—
Kamiński	Michał Tomasz	PiS	ECR	Political Scientist	28/03/1972	Female	—
Kolarskabobińska	Lena Barbara	PO	EPP	Sociologist	03/12/1947	Female	—
Kowal	Paweł Robert	PiS	ECR	Politician	22/07/1975	Male	—
Kozłowski (since 4 March 2010)	Jan	PO	EPP		01/01/1946	Male	—
Kurski	Jacek Olgierd	PiS	ECR	Economist	22/02/1966	Male	—
Legutko	Ryszard Antoni		ECR	Professor	24/12/1949	Male	—
Lewandowski (until 9 February 2010)	Janusz Antoni	PO	EPP	Economist	13/06/1951	Male	—

Liberadzki	Bogusław Marian	SLD	S&D	Professor of Economy	12/09/1948	Male	Vice-Chair, Budget Control
Lisek	Krzysztof	PO	EPP	Politician	28/05/1967	Male	—
Łukacijewska	Elżbieta Katarzyna	PO	EPP	Economist	25/11/1966	Female	—
Marcinkiewicz	Bogdan Kazimierz		EPP	Businessman	21/03/1966	Male	—
Migalski	Henryk Marek		ECR	University Lecturer	14/01/1969	Male	—
Nitras	Sławomir Witold	PO	EPP	Politician	26/04/1973	Male	—
Olbrycht	Jan Marian	PO	EPP	Academic Lecturer	21/09/1952	Male	—
Olejniczak	Wojciech Michał	SLD	S&D	Economist	10/04/1974	Male	—
Piotrowski	Mirosław Mariusz		ECR	University Professor	09/01/1966	Male	—
Poręba	Tomasz Piotr	PiS	ECR	Historian	31/03/1973	Male	—
Protasiewicz	Jacek	PO	EPP	Politician	05/06/1967	Male	—
Saryuszwolski	Jacek Emil	PO	EPP	Academic Lecturer	19/09/1948	Male	—
Senyszyn	Joanna	SLD	S&D	Professor of Economics	01/02/1949	Female	—
Siekierski	Czesław	PSL	EPP	Academic Lecturer	08/10/1952	Male	—
Siwiec	Marek	SLD	S&D	Journalist	13/03/1955	Male	—
Skrzydlewska	Joanna Katarzyna	PO	EPP	Economist	17/02/1977	Female	—
Sonik	Bogusław Andrzej	PO	EPP	Lawyer	03/12/1953	Male	Vice-Chair, Environment, Public Health and Food Security
Szymański	Konrad Krzysztof	PiS	ECR	Lawyer	06/12/1969	Male	—
Trzaskowski	Rafał Kazimierz		EPP	Academic Lecturer	17/01/1972	Male	Vice-Chair Constitutional Affairs
Włosowicz	Jacek Władysław	PiS	ECR	Economist	25/01/1966	Male	—
Wałęsa	Jarosław Leszek	PO	EPP	Political Scientist	13/09/1976	Male	—
Wojciechowski	Janusz	PiS	EPP	Lawyer	06/12/1954	Male	Vice-Chair, Agriculture & Rural Development
Zalewski	Paweł Ksawery	PO	EPP	Personal Advisor	25/09/1964	Male	V-Chair, International Trade
Zasada	Artur Jarosław	PO	EPP	Manager	05/06/1969	Male	—
Zemke	Janusz Władysław	SLD	S&D	Lawyer	24/02/1949	Male	—
Ziobro	Zbigniew	PiS	ECR	Lawyer	18/08/1970	Male	—
Zwiefka	Tadeusz Antoni	PO	EPP	Lawyer	28/12/1954	Male	—

Source: www.europarl.europa.eu/meps/en/search.html?country=PL.

10 Theoretical interpretation of Euro-elections

10.1 Second-Order Election theory

In line with the SOE model, EP elections in Poland may be interpreted as an occasion to check the accuracy of public opinion surveys. If one party is losing popularity, it will be confirmed in EP ballots.

Reporting on Euro-elections was not very important, typically mirroring the secondary character of these contests (de Vreese *et al.*, 2007). In particular, the 2009 EP elections in Poland did not see news coverage on the same scale as national parliamentary and presidential elections.

In addition, the country marked the lowest voter turnout ever measured, confirming the second-order character of EP elections, without changing Polish general political tendency when comparing to national parliamentary elections. In this way, EP competitions are a mirror of general attitudes, despite their lower participation rates. The situation in the Polish political scene was stabilized after 2007 to such an extent that the position of strength held by Civic Platform was not threatened. It was clear before the 2009 EP election that the Civic Platform party would win by a great margin. The main opposition party, Law and Justice, expected that voters would give a 'yellow card' to the ruling party by voting for the opposition. However, this did not materialize and the hypothesis of voter 'punishment' of ruling parties did not occur.

Party size did not play a major role in EP elections in Poland. In 2004, the ruling SLD lost the EP elections whilst in 2009 the ruling Civic Platform easily won the electoral race. Between 2001 and 2009, no government party won the parliamentary election. This occurred for the first time in 2009 when Civil Platform (PO) remained in power. If PO's power remains stable, they may be a force to be reckoned with in the 2014 elections.

10.2 Europe Salience theory

With the Polish case, we can make several important observations related to European integration. The post-Communist Left, SLD, has been in favour of European integration at every stage; for example, with the European Constitution. Support for the European referendum in 2003 came from multiple and diverse parties, SLD, PO, PiS, PSL. It was predicted that this document would be defined in the referendum, as this occurred in France and the Netherlands. Mobilization of anti-European forces was spurred on by the idea that Poland might end up in a worse position than under the Nice Treaty (i.e. with voting power in the European Council). There was also a broad negative attitude towards the Charter of Fundamental Rights, which was especially stressed by Law and Justice (PiS). PiS provided a base of support for the British–Polish Protocol, which sought to limit the legal meaning of that document.

The Green movement does not play a major role in the Polish political scene. In the 1990s, there were several unsuccessful attempts to create a Green movement in Poland. However, environmental issues have mobilized some part of the Polish electorate and they are also debated in the context of Polish EU membership and the cost of EU-wide environmental regulation.

Samoobrona and League of Polish Families (LPR) have primarily expressed anti-European opinions within the Polish political scene. Anti-European sentiments played a role in the pre-accession period and during the debate over the European referendum in 2003. However, positive developments in rural areas increased the support for EU integration amongst farmers and people living in villages. *Samoobrona* and LPR have lost their positions in the

Polish Parliament and it appears that anti-European sentiments do not pose a major threat. There have been attempts led by the SLD to accept the Charter of Fundamental Rights as promised by Prime Minister Donald Tusk. There has also been some discussion as to how successful the Polish presidency of the EU from July to December 2012 was at allowing Poland to influence EU policy.

Voter participation is the most salient issue in European Parliament elections. In the 2009 EP election, turnout was 25.4 per cent, which whilst not impressive, was higher than the percentage of 20.9 reached in 2004. This increase in participation, which stands in contrast to a decreasing trend in 15 Western European Members in comparison to 2004 suggests that in the case of Poland, there is some hope for progress (Dowgielewicz, 2009). Despite this, voter participation remains a major problem in all elections in Poland, including parliamentary elections. It is interesting to note that a survey conducted in 2008 showed relatively high trust in the EP amongst Polish people and 65 per cent support for the EU (Wciórka, 2008). There is a dissonance between general trust in EU institutions and readiness to participate in EP elections (Smoleń, 2009). In comparison to the citizens of other countries that joined the EU in 2004, Poles displayed genuine interest in the EP's structure and political role (Olszewski, 2010).

Low turnout is a feature of electoral behaviour not only in Poland (Ronkowski, 2004), but also in New Member States. This was seen both in 2004 (Thomasson, 2005) and 2009 (Wessels and Franklin, 2009). When analysing EP elections in Poland, it is necessary to remember general Polish voting attitudes. After 1991, parliamentary election turnout never reached the 50 per cent mark and only the presidential election was able to raise public interest. In this context, low EP election turnout is nothing unexpected and stresses rather the typical general attitudes of the Polish people in favour of non-participation. Even appeals by the highly influential Catholic Church have not been able to mobilize the electorate.

In light of the EP election results in Poland, we may ask: Does Europe matter? Whilst dealing with low voter turnout and subsequent explanations, it is important to stress that people are not motivated to participate in EP contests. Euro-elections do not directly influence the Polish political scene. Additionally, the majority of Polish citizens do not understand the EP. According to surveys, 65 per cent know that the EU has a Parliament but only 23 per cent know about the activity of this body (Pankowski, 2003, 41). People do not understand what it is at stake in EP elections and, moreover, to what extent the political structure of the EP may influence the state of Polish affairs. Political parties do not view EP elections as important as national elections. It is worth noting that the growing importance of the EP has not led to an increased interest in EP elections (Wiszniowski, 2008, 18). However, once visibility and knowledge of EP achievements increase within Polish society, EP election turnout in Poland may rise in the future.

The 2009 EP elections proved that the period characterized by Euro-enthusiastic and Euro-sceptic attitudes amongst the Polish people has ended in favour of a more Euro-pragmatic approach (Fiszer, 2010, 32). Poland appears to be a stable democracy with a respectable economy that withstood the European financial crisis without significant losses. Political mechanisms, based upon the 1997 Constitution, function rather effectively. As a consequence of EU membership, there is currently some preparation to change the Constitution to introduce a European clause. Polish accession to the European Union has helped to stabilize the economic situation of the country and add value to its growth. The level of EU support is high, although the majority of Polish people prefer a 'Europe of fatherlands' rather than a federal Europe. Anti-European sentiments do not considerably influence the way the Polish population behaves electorally.

References

Primary sources

Eurobarometer (2008), racjonalny euroentuzjazm Polaków, 15 July:
European Parliament Database (2010): www.europarl.europa.eu/meps/eu/search.html (accessed on 10 January 2015).
European Parliament election, (2009) (Poland), Summary of the 7 June 2009 European Parliament elections − European party: http://pe2009.pkw.gov.pl/PUE/PL/WYN/W/index.htm (accessed on 7 February 2012).
Eurostat (2013, 2014) http://epp.eurostat.ec.europa.eu/ (accessed on 5 June 2015).
http://pe2009.pkw.gov.pl/PUE/PL/WYN/W/index.htm (accessed on 15 October 2010).
http://pe2009.pkw.gov.pl/PUE/PL/WYN/W/index.htm (accessed on 12 December 2009).
Państwowa Komisja Wyborcza − State's Election Committee: http://pkw.gov.pl/ (accessed on 5 July 2010).
Szczepanik, M. *Polacy w Parlamencie Europejskim. Podsumowanie pierwszej połowy* 7, Kadencji. Raport z badań Instytutu Spraw Publicznych, www.isp.org.pl (accessed on 22 August 2013).
www.euractiv.pl/eurowybory/artykul/eurobarometr-racjonalny, euroentuzjazm Polaków (accessed on 7 February 2012).

Secondary sources

Arnold C. and Pennings, P. (2009) 'Party Positions on the European Constitution During the European Parliaments Elections', *Journal of Contemporary European Research*, 1, 24–42.
Bidziński, M. (2011) *Finansowanie partii politycznych w Polsce. Studium porównawcze*, Warszawa, Wydawnictwo Comandor.
Cyran, A. (2010) *Partie parlamentarne w Polsce wobec integracji europejskiej w latach 1991–2007*, Kielce, PU COMPUS.
de Vreese, C. H., Lauf, E. and Peter, J. (2007) 'The Media and European Parliament Elections: Second-Rate Coverage of a Second-Order Event?', in van der Brug, W. and van der Eijk, C. (eds), *European Elections and Domestic Politics: Lessons from the Past and Scenarios for the Future*, Notre Dame, University of Notre Dame Press, 16–130.
Dowgielewicz, M. W. (2009) 'Po wyborach do Parlamentu Europejskiego w dniu 9 czerwca 2009 r.', in Barcz, J. and Janusz-Pawletta, B. (eds) *Parlament Europejski po wyborach w 2009 roku*, Warszawa, Instytut Wydawniczy EuroPrawo, 19–24.
Dydak, E. (2003) *Wybory do Parlamentu Europejskiego: Zasady i wyniki głosowania*, Warszawa, Wydawnictwo Naukowe Scholar.
Eysymontt, J. (2004), 'Polacy wybierają Parlament Europejski', *Wspólnoty Europejskie*, no. 4–5, 14–18.
Fiszer, J. M. (2010) 'Eurowybory 2009 a Traktat z Lizbony − implikacje dla Polski i Unii Europejskiej', in Słodkowska, I. and Dołbakowska, M. (eds) *Eurowybory 2009: Kandydaci i programy*, Warszawa, Instytut Studiów Politycznych Polskiej Akademii Nauk.
Fundacja Stefana Batorego (2009) *Finansowanie kampanii wyborczej do Parlamentu Europejskiego 2009 r. Wstępny raport*, Warszawa, Fundacja Stefana Batorego.
Gagatek W. (2009) 'The European People's Party and the Party of European Socialists: Government and Opposition?' *European View*, 2, 301–11.
Gagatek, W. (2010a) 'Campaigning in the European Parliament Elections' in Gagatek, W. (ed.) (2010b) *The 2009 Elections to the European Parliament. Country Reports*, Florence, European University Institute, 13–20.
Gagatek, W. (ed.) (2010b) *The 2009 Elections to the European Parliament. Country Reports*, Florence, European University Institute.
Gebethner, S. (2002) 'Przyszły polski system wyborczy do Parlamentu Europejskiego w świetle analizy prawnoporównwczej', in Zięba-Załucka, H. and Kijowski, M. (eds) *Akcesja do Unii Europejskiej a Konstytucja Rzeczypospolitej Polskiej. Materiały konferencyjne. Referaty. Dyskusja*, Rzeszów, Uniwersytet Rzeszowski, 24–31.
Gorgol, A. (2011) *Prawne aspekty finansowania partii politycznych w Polsce I na poziomie europejskim*, Lublin, Wydawnictwo Uniwersytetu Marie Curie-Skłodowskiej.
Grzesik-Robak, A. (2008) *Polskie partie polityczne wobec integracji Polski ze wspólnotami Europejskimi/Unia Europejską (1989–2004)*, Toruń, Wydawnictwo Adam Marszałek.

Gwiazda, A. (2009) 'Poland's Quasi-Institutionalized Party System: The Importance of Elites and Institutions', *Perspectives on European Politics and Society*, 10(3), 350–76.

Hobolt, S. B., Spoon, J.-J. and Tilley, J.R. (2009) 'A Vote Against Europe? Explaining Defection at 1999 and 2004 European Parliament Elections', *British Journal of Political Science*, 39 (1), 93–115.

Hrbek, R. (ed.) (2005) *European Parliament Election 2004 in the New EU Member States: Towards the Future European Party System*, Baden-Baden, Nomos.

Jabłonowski, M., Stępka, S. and Sulowski, S. (eds) (2009) *Polski rok 1989: Sukcesy, zaniechania, porażki*, Warszawa, Oficyna Wydawnicza ASPA-JR.

Jabłoński, M. (2007) *Polskie referendum akcesyjne*, Wrocław, Wydawnictwo Uniwersytetu Wrocławskiego.

Jacuński, M., Wiszniowski R. (2010) 'VII kadencja Parlamentu Europejskiego. Decyzje wyborcze, frekwencja i strategie partyjne', *Athenaeum – Polskie Studia Politologiczne*, 23, 11–30.

Jaskiernia, J. (2003) 'Główne problemy procesu integracji europejskiej w debatach publicznych poprzedzających referendum akcesyjne w Polsce', in Burlikowski, B., Rachlewicz, W. and Słomski, W. (eds) *Tradycje, przemiany, dążenia w procesie integracji europejskiej*, Kielce, Wydawnictwo Phaenomena, 15–30.

Jaskiernia, J. (2004) *Członkostwo Polski w Unii Europejskiej a problem nowelizacji Konstytucji RP*, Warszawa, Wydawnictwo Naukowe 'Scholar'.

Jaskiernia, J. (2007) 'Wybory parlamentarne 2005 roku a tendencja do cofania legitymizacji partiom rządzącym w Polsce', in Kasińska-Metryka, A. (ed.) *Polacy wobec wyborów 2005 roku*, Kielce, Wydawnictwo Uniwersytetu Humanistyczno-Przyrodniczego Jana Kochanowskiego, 29–51.

Jaskiernia, J. (ed.) (2010a) *Rada Europy a przemiany demokratyczne w państwach Europy środkowej i Wschodniej w latach 1989–2009*, Toruń, Wydawnictwo Adam Marszałek.

Jaskiernia, J. (2010b) 'Rola mitów i stereotypów w procesie integracji europejskiej', in Kasińska-Metryka, A., Gołoś, M. (eds) *Mity i stereotypy w polityce: Przeszłość i teraźniejszość*, Toruń, Wydawnictwo Adam Marszałek.

Kowalczyk, K. (2010) 'Strategia i taktyka Platformy Obywatelskiej Rzeczypospolitej Polskiej w wyborach do Parlamentu Europejskiego w 2009 roku', *Athenaeum–Polskie Studia Politologiczne*, 23, 31–50.

Kowalczyk, K. and Sielski, J. (eds) (2005) *Polskie partie i ugrupowania parlamentarne*, Toruń, Wydawnictwo Adam Marszałek.

Kowalczyk, K. and Tomczak, Ł. (eds) (2007) *Partie i system partyjny RP: Stan i perspektywy*, Toruń, Wydawnictwo Adam Marszałek.

Kublik, A. (2009) 'Nie ma już dnia bez Libertasu', *Gazeta Wyborcza*, 131, 6.

Lechmann, W. (2009) *The European Elections: EU Legislation, National Provisions and Civic Participation*, Brussels, European Parliament.

Machińska, H. (2005) *Polska i Rada Europy 1990–2005*, Warszawa, Biuro Informacji Rady Europy.

Mayhew, A. (1998) *Recreating Europe: The European Union's Policy Towards Central and Eastern Europe*, Cambridge, Cambridge University Press.

Millard, F. (2006) 'Poland's Politics and the Travails Transition after 2001: The 2005 Elections', *Europe–Asia Studies*, 58(7), 1007–31.

Napieralski, G. (2009) 'SLD po wyborach do Parlamentu Europejskiego', *Myśl Socjaldemokratyczna*, 3–4, 5–8.

Nikolski, L. (2005) *Tak, głosuję: Moja droga do referendum europejskiego*, Warszawa, Wydawnictwo Studio Emka.

Oleszowski, D. (2010) Prawo i sprawiedliwość w Parlamencie Europejskim – wybory 2004 i 2009, in Migalski, M. (ed.) *Prawo i sprawiedliwość*, Toruń, Wydawnictwo Adam Marszałek, 91–120.

Orłowski, W. M. (2001) *Przeciw stereotypom: Rozszerzenie Unii Europejskiej o Polskę*, Warszawa, Urząd Komitetu Integracji Europejskiej.

Pankowski, K. (2003) *Parlament Europejski oraz polskie i unijne instytucje w opinii Polaków*, Warszawa, Instytut Spraw Publicznych.

Piontek, D. (ed.) (2007) *Europejskie wybory Polaków: Referendum i wybory do Parlamentu Europejskiego*, Poznań, Uniwersytet Adama Mickiewicza.

Radek R. (2010a) 'Kampania wyborcza Prawa i Sprawiedliwości w wyborach do Parlamentu Europejskiego w 2009 roku', *Athenaeum. Polskie Studia Politologiczne*, 1(23), 51–68.

Radek, R. (2010b) 'Kampania wyborcza Prawa i Sprawiedliwości do Parlamentu Europejskiego w 2009 roku', *Athenaeum – Polskie Studia Politologiczne*, 23, 69–82.

Radziszewski, E. (2005) 'Social Networks, Public Opinion, and EU Membership: the Case of Poland', Paper presented at the annual meeting of the International Studies Association, Hilton Hawaiian Village, Honolulu, Hawaii. Online. Available at: http://www.allacademic.com/meta/p70806_index.html (accessed on 25 April 2009).

Ronkowski, P. (2004) 'Wybory do Parlamentu Europejskiego pod znakiem niskiej frekwencji i porażki partii rządzących', *Wspólnoty Europejskie*, 7, 5–11.
Rudkowski, D. (2002) 'Wybory do Parlamentu Europejskiego – problemy systemu wyborczego', in Kruk, M. and Popławska, E. (eds) *Parlamenty a integracja europejska*, Warszawa, Wydawnictwo Sejmowe.
Rupar, Ł. (2006) 'Tryb wyboru posłów do Parlamentu Europejskiego na terenie Rzeczypospolitej Polskiej', *Humanistyczne Zeszyty Naukowe – Prawa Człowieka*, 10, 25–36.
Sarnecki, P. (2004) 'Regulacje ustawowe dotyczące wyborów na terenie Rzeczypospolitej Polskiej posłów do Parlamentu Europejskiego', *Przegląd Sejmowy*, 3, 11–26.
Sarnecki, P., Szmyt A. and Witkowski, Z. (eds) (1999) *The Principles of Basic Institutions of the System of Government in Poland*, Warsaw, State Publishing Office.
Skotnicka-Illasiewicz, E. (1997) 'W poszukiwaniu europejskiej tożsamości Polaków', *Studia Europejskie*, 3, 130–1.
Słodkowska, I. and Dolbakowska, M. (eds) (2005) *Eurowybory 2004: Kandydaci i programy*, Warszawa, Instytut Studiów Politycznych Polskiej Akademii Nauk.
Słodkowska, I. and Dolbakowska, M. (eds) (2010) *Eurowybory 2009: Kandydaci i programy*, Warszawa, Instytut Studiów Politycznych Polskiej Akademii Nauk.
Smoleń, R. (2009) 'Kilka uwag natury politologicznej w związku z wynikami wyborów do Parlamentu Europejskiego w 2009 roku', in Barcz, J. and Janusz-Pawletta, B. (eds) *Parlament Europejski po wyborach 2009 roku*, Warszawa. Instytut Wydawniczy EuroPrawo, 47–56.
Sobczak, J. (2007) 'Prace legislacyjne nad ordynacją wyborczą do Parlamentu Europejskiego', in Piontek, D. (ed.) *Europejskie wybory Polaków: Referendum i wybory do Parlamentu Europejskiego*, Poznań, Wydawnictwo Naukowe INPiD UAM, 41–53.
Sokala, A., Michalak, B., Frydrych, A. and Zych, R. (eds) (2010) *Wybory do Parlamentu Europejskiego. Prawne, polityczne i społeczne aspekty wyborów*, Toruń, Dom Organizatora TNOiK.
Szczerbiak A. (2008) *The Birth of a Bi-Polar Party System or a Referendum on a Polarising Government? The October 2007 Polish Parliamentary Elections*, Brighton, Sussex European Institute.
Thomassen, J. J. A. (ed.) (2005) *The European Voter: A Comparative Study of Modern Democracies*, Oxford, Oxford University Press.
Urbaniak, K. (2003) 'Prawo wyborcze obywateli Unii Europejskiej w wyborach do Parlamentu Europejskiego', *Przegląd Europejski*, 2, 87–102.
van der Brug, W. and van der Eijk, C. (2007) *European Elections and Domestic Politics: Lessons from the Past and Scenarios for the Future*, Notre Dame, University of Notre Dame Press.
Waniek, D. (ed.) (2006) *Partie polityczne w wyborach 2005*, Warszawa, Alma Mer Wyższa Szkoła Ekonomiczna.
Waniek, D. (ed.) (2010) *Lewica w praktyce rządzenia*, Toruń, Adam Marszałek.
Wciórka, B. (2008) 'Zaufanie społeczne w latach 2002–2008', *Aktualne problemy i wydarzenia*, 212, Warszawa, CBOS.
Wessels, B. and Franklin, M. N. (2009) 'Turning out or Turning off: Do Mobilization and Attitudes Account for Turnout Differences between New and Established Member States at the 2004 EP Elections?', in Schmitt, H. (ed.) 'European Parliament Elections after Eastern Enlargement', *Journal of European Integration*, 5, 609–26.
Wiatr, J. J. (2009) 'Krok ku odbudowie lewicy', *Myśl Socjaldemokratyczna*, 3–4, 9–15.
Wiśniewska, K. (2009) 'Zerówka w seminarium duchownym', *Gazeta Wyborcza*, 103, 6.
Wiszniowski, R. (2008) *Europejska przestrzeń publiczna*, Wrocław, Wydawnictwo Uniwersytetu Wrocławskiego.
Wojtasik W. (2010) 'Partie polskiej lewicy w wyborach do Parlamentu Europejskiego', *Athenaeum. Polskie Studia Politologiczne*, 23(1), 69–82.
Zuba, K. (2009) 'Through the Looking Glass: The Attitudes of Political Parties towards the EU Before and After Accession', *Perspectives on European Politics and Society*, 10(3), 326–49.
Zuba, K. (2010) 'Polskie partie eurosceptyczne w wyborach do Parlamentu Europejskiego w 2009 roku', *Athenaeum – Polskie Studia Politologiczne*, 23, 83–100.

29
BULGARIA

Dobrin Kanev and Katia Hristova-Valtcheva

Figure 29.1 Map of Bulgaria

Table 29.1 Bulgaria profile

EU entry year	2007
Schengen entry year	Non-member
MEPs elected in 2009	17
MEPs under Lisbon Treaty	18 since 1 December 2011
	One additional seat allocated to Svetoslav Malinov (EPP)
Capital	Sofia
Total area★	111,002 km²
Population	7,245,677
	Ethnic minorities: Turks and Roma
Population density★★	66.7/km²
Median age of population	43.2
Political system	Parliamentary Republic
Head of state	Georgi Parvanov, Bulgarian Socialist Party (BSP) (January 2002–January 2012);
	Rosen Plevneliev, Citizens for European Development of Bulgaria (GERB) (January 2012–)
Head of government	Boyko Borisov, Citizens for European Development of Bulgaria (GERB) (July 2009–March 2013);
	Marin Raikov, Caretaker government (March 2013–May 2013);
	Plamen Oresharski, Bulgarian Socialist Party (BSP) (May 2013–)
Political majority	Citizens for European Development of Bulgaria (GERB) (July 2009–March 2013);
	Bulgarian Socialist Party (BSP) and Movement for Rights and Freedoms (DPS) Government Coalition (May 2013–)
Currency	Lev (BGN)
Prohead GDP in PPS	5,800 €

Source: Eurostat, 2013, 2014, http://epp.eurostat.ec.europa.eu/.

Notes:
★ Total area including inland waters.
★★ Population density: the ratio of the annual average population of a region to the land area of the region.

1 Geographical position

Bulgaria is a middle-sized country situated in south-east Europe, at the heart of the Balkan Peninsula, bordering Romania in the north, Serbia and FYROM in the west and Greece and Turkey in the south. It has a coastline on the Black Sea in the east. The country's territory of 111,002 square kilometres is dominated by mountains in the south-west, the Danubian plain in the north, and the Thracian plain in the southeast. Situated in the western part of the territory, the capital city of Sofia is the financial, administrative, and cultural heart of the country.

Being traditionally a unitary state, Bulgaria is divided into 27 territorial management units called *oblasts* (provinces) and the metropolitan capital province. Throughout the last two decades the population dropped from a peak of around 9 million inhabitants in 1988 to around 7.3 million in 2012, according to Eurostat data, more than 70 per cent of which reside in urban areas.

2 Historical background

Major political developments marked the rise and fall of the First Bulgarian Empire between 671 and 1018: territorial expansions, the introduction of the first written code of law, the adoption of Eastern Orthodox Christianity in 864, the introduction of the Cyrillic alphabet, and the birth and spread of the Bogomil heresy. After a period of Byzantine dominance, the state was re-established in 1185 as the Second Bulgarian Empire. For the five centuries to follow, Bulgaria formed a part of the Ottoman Empire. A national revival started in the second half of the eighteenth century and culminated in the country's liberation in 1878, with the decisive involvement of Russia. The Third Bulgarian State was set up as an autonomous principality in 1879 with the Tarnovo Constitution.

The search for national unification became a political and military priority after the 1878 Berlin Treaty left large populations of Bulgarians outside the new country. This defined the country's participation in four wars in less than half a century after liberation: in 1885 Bulgaria incorporated the semi-autonomous Ottoman territory of Eastern Rumelia after a successful war against Serbia; in 1911–1918 the country was twice severely defeated in the Second Balkan War and in WWI. Internal political life was dominated by two major factors: the Russophile sentiments of the population and of some of the important political circles on the one side, and the controversial alliances of the monarchs, who were descendants of the German dynasty on the other. During WWII, Bulgaria was a member of the Axis Pact. Authoritarian rule and the much-contested alliance with Nazi Germany led to the formation of a resistance movement.

On 9 September 1944, an uprising lead by the Communist-dominated Fatherland Front brought the monarchy to an end. A Soviet-style People's Republic was established with a Communist constitution adopted in 1947. The country's Communist rulers set up close ties with the Soviet Union, linked the development of the planned economy to the needs of the Comecon and forced the country to become a firm military ally within the Warsaw Pact. There was no internal political unrest like in Hungary, Czechoslovakia, and Poland, but by the late 1980s dissident groups started to oppose the ruling party's monopoly in *perestroika* style. Shortly after the breakdown of the Communist regime in November 1989, a new Constitution re-establishing civil and political rights as well as democratic institutions was adopted and entered into force on 12 July 1991.

3 Geopolitical profile

Bulgaria's foreign policy environment has been completely transformed since the end of the Cold War. Once the closest ally of the Soviet Union, during the early 1990s Bulgaria had to face the difficulties that came out of two parallel processes: the dissolution of the USSR itself and the USSR-led military bloc, on the one hand, and the dissolution of Yugoslavia, on the other. The first opened a space for fostering improved relations with Western European institutions and structures: Bulgaria became a member of the Council of Europe in May 1992 and signed an Association Agreement with the European Union in 1993. In the meantime Bulgarian security policy stuck to maintaining stability through non-alignment and keeping equal distances. Bulgaria has supported other regional institutions, such as the Organization for Security and Cooperation in Europe (OSCE) and the Black Sea Economic Cooperation (BSEC). The second process has pushed Bulgarian governments to adopt a balanced regional policy as a stabilizing force in the Balkans. By 1999, the ongoing conflicts in Yugoslavia had pushed Bulgaria to reconsider its security policy, and a major shift from non-alignment to guaranteeing stability through involvement was observed. Promoting regional security since then has been one of Bulgaria's major foreign policy priorities.

Bulgaria became a NATO member in March 2004 and a full EU member in January 2007. The country's well-developed energy sector and its strategic geographic location, which make it a key European energy hub, are major determinants for Bulgaria's current foreign policy.

4 Overview of the political landscape

The new Constitution of 1991 created a European-type parliamentary regime with a pluralist party system, yet with a directly elected President, aided by a Vice-President, both enjoying a five-year term of office. The (*Narodno sabranie*) is a unicameral Parliament with 240 members, each elected for four-year terms by direct popular vote. A reform of the electoral legislation that entered in force in 2009 allocates seats according to a mixed system, with predominantly a proportional system (209 seats) and a first-past-the-post system (31 seats). There is a 4 per cent threshold to be passed by political parties in order to get representation in parliament.

The Parliament is 'sovereign' in that no institution can dissolve it or terminate its mandate. Pre-term elections are a procedural outcome of three consecutive unsuccessful attempts to form a cabinet. The Bulgarian legislature is also supreme in the procedure of appointing the executive as within the process of cabinet formation the President has a very limited role as moderator. The Bulgarian model of separation of powers is a version of 'rationalized parliamentarism' (Frankowski and Paul, 1995, 158); the Bulgarian Constitutional Court has strong powers to declare acts of Parliament unconstitutional on the appeal of one-fifth of all members of the National Assembly, the President, the Council of Ministers, the Supreme Court of Cassation, the Supreme Administrative Court, and the prosecutor general.

The President has a relatively weak position in the domestic political process as he or she disposes with the authority to return a bill for further debate, although Parliament can override a presidential veto by a simple majority vote of all the members of Parliament. Between 2007 and the end of 2011 Georgi Parvanov was re-elected for a second term as President of Bulgaria. On 22 January 2012 Rosen Plevneliev was sworn in as the new President. He was the candidate of the ruling GERB party.

Proportional representation has been the predominant electoral system for almost two decades and Liberal party legislation has added to the European content of the new Bulgarian political system. Post-Communist governments in Bulgaria have displayed different trends: majoritarian cabinets were short-lived and unstable during the first years of liberalization from 1989–1997, while during the consolidation of the democracy phase consecutive full terms have been completed by a single party majoritarian cabinet (right-wing Union of Democratic Forces, 1997–2001), a single bloc Liberal coalition (National Movement for Stability and Progress and Movement for Rights and Freedoms, 2001–2005) and a cross-bloc coalition bringing together parties from the left and the centre (the Bulgarian Socialist Party, the National Movement for Stability and Progress, and the Movement for Rights and Freedoms, 2005–2009). During the past 20 years of post-Communist development, the political system in Bulgaria has displayed the major trend of majoritarian democracy.

5 Brief account of the political parties

Bulgarian political tradition, part of which is the unicameral Parliament, puts a particular emphasis on political parties. In fact, Bulgaria developed an array of reasonably developed political parties whose membership comprises about 7 to 10 per cent of voting-age Bulgarians (Tdodorov, 2010, 138).

The party system itself has proved to be relatively stable. Only four parties or election coalitions have ever won elections during the post-Communist period. Only three parties were represented in all six legislatures after 1990. The relative stability of parties and the party system

Table 29.2 List of political parties in Bulgaria

Original name	Abbreviation	English translation
Balgarska Sotsialisticheska Partiya	BSP	Bulgarian Socialist Party
Balgarski Naroden Sajuz	BNS	Bulgarian People's Union
Bulgarska Nova Demokracia	BND	Bulgarian New Democracy
Demokrati za Silna Balgariya	DSB	Democrats for Strong Bulgaria
Dvizhenie za Prava i Svobodi	DPS	Movement for Rights and Freedoms
Grazhdani za Evropeysko Razvitie na Balgaria	GERB	Citizens for European Development of Bulgaria
Lider	LIDER	The Leader Party
Natsionalno Dvizhenie za Stabilnost I Vazhod	NDSV	National Movement for Stability and Progress formerly known as *Natsionalno Dvizhenie Simeon Vtori* (National Movement Simeon II)
Partiya Ataka	PA	Party Attack
Red Zakonnost Spravedlivost	RZS	Order, Lawfulness, Justice
Sayuz na demokratichnite sili	SDS	Union of Democratic Forces
Siniata Koalicia	BC	Blue Coalition

in Bulgaria is supposed to be a noteworthy democratic asset: '[i]t is difficult to locate anything other than political parties to account for the Bulgarian advantage in democratization' (Fish and Brooks, 2000).

Major European party families, such as the Christian Democrats, the Social Democrats, Liberals and Conservatives, are represented in the Bulgarian party landscape as well. They demonstrate a certain degree of persistence and consistency in the Bulgarian national framework. There is a relatively clear division between 'left' and 'right' and between more Nationalist and more open tendencies.

On the left, the *Balgarska Sotsialisticheska Partiya*, BSP (Bulgarian Socialist Party) is the successor of the former Communist Party of Bulgaria. BSP won the grand national assembly elections in 1990 and thus has dominated the constitution-building process in Bulgaria. After an initial decade of internal ideological battles, the BSP managed to transform itself into a Social Democratic party only on the eve of the new millennium, with the substantial support of the Party of European Socialists. BSP has undergone a long process of Europeanization as well changing its initial controversial position on the country's EU accession only after Bulgaria started negotiations in 2000. Although in the early 1990s its electoral potential reached more than 40 per cent, since 1997 the party's electoral ceiling has declined to about 31 per cent. There is also considerable volatility among BSP voters. In the last elections of 2009, just 17.7 per cent voted for the party. On the other hand, the party has never faced major internal splits, even after the dramatic failure of its government in 1997, and still dominates the left part of the political spectrum in the country.

The right part of the political spectrum has undergone intense changes throughout the two decades after the breakdown of the Communist regime. Originally the right was represented by the *Sayuz na demokratichnite sili*, SDS (Union of Democratic Forces), which was founded in 1989 and consisted of 11 small anti-Communist political parties. In 1997, the SDS was transformed into a single party affiliated with the European Christian Democratic family. By the mid-1990s it was the only Reformist party with the potential to form a government. In terms of electoral strength, the party achieved over 52 per cent of the vote in the 1997 elections that then declined dramatically to about 17 per cent in 2001 and 6.4 per cent in the 2009 elections. The *Demokrati za Silna Balgaria*, DSB (Democrats for a Strong Bulgaria), which emerged after the defeat of the SDS in the 2001 general elections, is an SDS splinter party. The party follows Conservative and Liberal policies similar to the SDS. In the 2009 EP and general elections, the SDS and DSB formed the so-called Blue Coalition. The coalition got 6.4 per cent of the vote. Both parties are members of the European People's Party.

Other Conservative parties that emerged recently are the *Balgarski Naroden Sajuz*, BNS (Bulgarian People's Union), which emerged as an electoral coalition of several parties in the 2005 election only to disappear in 2009 due to growing factionalism within the party, and the *Red, Zakonnost, Spravedlivost*, RZS (Order, Lawfulness, Justice Party) founded in 2005, which was able to achieve 5.13 per cent of the vote and 13 seats in Parliament after the 2009 elections. The RZS is closer to the European Conservative Party.

At present the ruling right-wing party in Bulgaria is *Grazhdani za Evropeysko Razvitie na Balgaria*, GERB (Citizens for European Development in Bulgaria), led by the former Mayor of Sofia, Bojko Borissov. It was founded in 2006 and was able to win the EP elections of 2007 and 2009 as well as the general elections of July 2009. The party's charismatic president and current Prime Minister Boiko Borissov gained electoral support on the basis of populist Conservative language and an election programme that promised to fight against crime and corruption, and to protect Conservative values in society. GERB is a member of the European People's Party.

Two parties have dominated the Liberal political centre in Bulgaria. Founded in 1990, the *Dvizhenie za Prava i Svobodi*, DPS (Movement for Rights and Freedoms) represents the 8 per cent Turkish-Bulgarian minority. The party is an important player in government formation. Due to the lack of absolute majorities amongst the main parties, DPS became an important kingmaker three times over a period of 20 years, in 1992, 2001, and 2005, respectively. The party's ideological makeup is liberalism as far as the DPS claims to be open to any citizen, although it is predominantly the main representative of the Turkish-Bulgarian minority. Since 1990s, the party started polling about 7–8 per cent of votes, but since 2005 its electoral support has increased to 12–15 per cent.

In 2001, fatigue over the bipolar party system in Bulgaria brought to life a new Liberal, market-oriented party, *Natsionalno Dvizhenie za Stabilnost i Vazhod*, NSDV (National Movement for Stability and Progress), named after its charismatic leader Simeon II, former tsar of Bulgaria. Between 2001 and 2005, it formed a coalition with the Turkish minority party, the DPS. However, in the 2005 general elections its share of the vote declined from over 42 per cent to 19.9 per cent and in the 2009 general elections to just 3 per cent. The party is no longer represented in Parliament. After the 2009 electoral defeat, Simeon II Saxe-Coburg-Gotha resigned from the party leadership.

On the extreme right, a xenophobic, Nationalist, and populist party was founded in 2005 as a reaction to the clientelistic policy style of the 2001–2005 coalition partner DPS. The party was named *Ataka* (Attack!) and is led by Volen Siderov. The party was able to find some electoral consolidation since the 2005 elections, achieving almost the same electoral share of about 9 per cent in 2009. *Ataka* advocates national independence, protectionism of the Bulgarian economy, and the country's withdrawal from NATO, the IMF, and the World Bank. The party's principal xenophobic target is the Turkish-Bulgarian minority.

This lack of cohesion is still typical for rightist political parties in Bulgaria, which are at some stage in their development dominated by factionalism and divisions. Charismatic leaders play an important role in the foundation of new political formations, but after electoral defeats, there is a clear tendency for dissent and collapse amongst right-wing political parties.

5.1 Party attitudes towards the European Union

Although the 'European idea' has played an important role in the process of party differentiation (Todorov, 1999, 9), the European Union has never been a divisive issue among the political class in Bulgaria. As part of their quest for legitimization, political parties began to incorporate Europe as an issue into their political agendas and into party competition at a very early stage of the democratization process. There was not a single more or less influential political power in Bulgaria, with the rare exception of a few, highly marginal parties without any influence whatsoever in the political debate, which did not stress that Bulgaria's accession to EU was a matter of unquestionable first-order priority. Nevertheless, political projects for the country's accession did differ until the late 1990s as a consequence of the bipolar model of party politics that was typical for Central and Eastern European countries.

The Bulgarian Socialists started as a reformed Communist party advocating a mixed economy and pursued an agenda of generalized opposition against neo-liberal capitalism. The party's big transformation took place after its disastrous defeat in the mid-term legislative elections of 1997. The Party of European Socialists was instrumental in helping the BSP to become a mainstream social democratic party, and European integration was framed through the lens of social democracy. While in 1994 the BSP's programme was still very much framed against capitalism, in 2008 their programme resembled that of many of other social democratic parties. In the 2009 EP elections, the BSP offered the largest ever public discussion on the PES European election manifesto compared to any other political party (Spirova, 2008, 491; Dimitrov, 2000, 103; Hristova-Valtcheva, 2010).

The Union of Democratic Forces (SDS) was originally set up as an umbrella anti-Communist coalition of broad spectrum formations, including Social Democrats, as well as ecological and agricultural movements. However, after the creation of a unified party in 1997, the SDS leadership decided to affiliate with the EPP's Christian democratic profile (Todorov, 1999, 21–3; Dimitrov, 2000, 103). The SDS remained a very pro-European party with a clear outline that it had before 1997. All splinter parties remained pro-European, while the most influential ones such as Democrats for a Stronger Bulgaria (DSB), became affiliated with the mainstream EPP.

The relatively protracted accession of the country to the EU brought the collapse of the bipolar political model in 2001 and the rise of the NDSV. The party's advocacy of a free-market economy, a limited state and protection of civil rights, clearly led to strong support for European integration as well. The party soon became affiliated with the European Liberal, Democratic, and Reformist group (ELDR). Successful accession to the EU was an important part of the NDSV programme before 2007. However, its 'integration at any cost' approach while in power did not provoke any popular EU pessimism.

GERB also has strong, sometimes quite uncritical, European credentials. It clearly sees the solution to all Bulgarian problems in further European integration. However, in contrast to other right-centre parties, GERB uses populism and Nationalist rhetoric in order to attract votes. In addition, it clearly presented anti-Turkish minority positions in the 2007 EP elections that were tuned down in 2009 (Savkova, 2007, 6).

The Turkish minority Movement for Freedoms and Rights (DPS) is a strong pro-European party, and is affiliated with the ALDE. The mainstream parties, BSP, NDSV, SDS, DSB, GERB and DPS, are supportive of European integration. Probably the only major party that has remained outside this mainstream is *Ataka*. In 2005, the party became popular with a clearly populist programme, criticizing the post-Communist political class, requesting the re-nationalization of privatized assets, and calling for the re-negotiation of Bulgaria's EU accession agreement.

Nonetheless, the European Union was and is regarded as a *vincolo esterno* (external link) (Dyson and Featherstone, 1999) that is instrumentalized by the political parties to achieve the development of the country.

6 Public opinion and the European Union

Public support for Bulgaria's EU membership has constantly been positive. During the years following accession, Bulgaria retained its leading position amongst countries with the most positive image of the EU, with a high level of trust in the EU and its institutions (European Commission, 2008, European Commission, 2009, 92). Utilitarian support for the country's EU membership also displayed a steady increase in 2009 (European Commission, 2009, 92).

Bulgarian citizens did not demonstrate a particular interest in the EP elections as such, although the very objective of EU membership had for a number of years been of the highest priority on the country's political and civic agenda. Two years after accession the majority of Bulgarians still approved of EU membership. Forty-nine per cent definitely showed a positive attitude and only 14 per cent did not support membership. At the same time, they did not think that they had individually gained from EU membership. Only 9 per cent saw themselves as winners, while 15 per cent thought that they were losers. The great majority of the public, more than three-quarters, did not see any serious changes (Alpha Research, 2009).

However, this disappointment is not caused by EU institutions, but by Bulgaria's economic and political reality. It is indicative that European institutions are more trusted than domestic ones. On the eve of the EP elections in 2009, the European Parliament was trusted by 61 per cent, the highest positive shift amongst the EU 27, and the European Commission by 52 per cent (European Commission, 2009, 110), whereas the Bulgarian National Assembly and the government were trusted by only 7 per cent and 10 per cent, respectively (Alpha Research, 2009).

Finally, Bulgarian citizens were amongst the least informed in all the 27 Member States on the working principles of the EP: only 22 per cent of Bulgarians were aware that the basic principle of organizing work in the EP is based on political rather than national representation, and more than half did not have an opinion on this issue.

7 National and EP electoral systems

On 7 June 2009, Bulgarians voted for their MEPs for the second time in a two-year period. The elections were held according to slightly amended 2007 legislation. A proportional representation system with preference voting was used. Any candidate who achieved 15 per cent on the list was automatically elected. Seats were distributed in a single national constituency using the Hare-Niemayer method. Certain changes were made in order to secure better control over campaign financing and to prevent possible vote trading. The electoral law defined a three-week official period for campaigning and no day for reflection. These measures were taken to make the European elections more voter-friendly.

It was the first time that the electoral system for the EP elections differed significantly from the national election system. After an initial experiment with a mixed voting system in 1990, according to which half of the Members of Parliament (MPs) were elected through a system of proportional representation with a 4 per cent threshold, and the other half through a majority voting system in two rounds in one-mandate constituencies, a proportional voting system has been consistently applied since 1991. Only in April 2009, after continuous and heated debates, was a proposal to elect 31 out of 240 MPs through a majority system approved by Parliament.

The revised voting system provides for 209 MPs to be elected through proportional representation in 31 multi-mandate constituencies with a threshold of 4 per cent and for 31 MPs to be elected through a majority system in one round ('first-past-the-post') in the same constituencies.

8 A glance at the EP and national elections

The decision to hold the first direct although partial European elections in Bulgaria to be convened in the spring of 2007, the first 'European Year', was preceded by intense political debate. In the year before full accession to the European Union, the idea of organizing the European elections before the date of accession was tested. The idea was promoted from the ranks of the ruling coalition and political analysts suspected that it was an attempt to use technology to strengthen the electoral position of the ruling majority, after the general elections held in the summer of 2005. Options were put forward to organize the EP elections in parallel with the November 2006 presidential elections. This turned to be a rather exotic idea, given the fact that none of the other ten new EU Member States had ever convened partial elections to the European Parliament before the official date of its entry, and therefore it found no support among the political parties represented in the national Parliament. Thus, the chosen date for holding the European elections coincided with the completion of the first half of the mandate of the ruling coalition. The location of the first direct elections to the EP in the political calendar of Bulgaria is further symbolically loaded, bearing in mind the fact that in the autumn of the same year regular local elections were to be held.

Fourteen coalitions and political parties and two independent candidates took part in the June 2007 EP elections in Bulgaria. The number of candidate lists can be deemed as 'modest' compared with the practice in other Member States.

Unlike the common practice in other EU countries, where the formation of candidate lists rests on the model of a single-party presentation with a predominance of middle-echelon party leaders, the Bulgarian political parties and social elite were widely represented in the lists for elections of MEPs. The leader of the first opposition party in Bulgaria and former head of state, Petar Stoyanov, led the SDS electoral list. Another characteristic of the Bulgarian case was the involvement of the two major trade unions: the leader of the *Podkrepa* trade union led the list of candidates supported by the *Konfederatia na Nezavisimite Sindikati v Bulgaria*, KNSB (Confederation of Independent Trade Unions in Bulgaria). Both lists failed to gain seats in the assembly in Brussels and Strasbourg.

A modest presence of EU issues marked the electoral campaign in Bulgaria. The main issue for participating political parties was the struggle to mobilize support for the upcoming local elections, rather than to get involved in comprehensive discussions over the major issues of the European integration project. Indicative in this respect is the fact that only six of the 16 participating candidates, political parties, and coalitions had prepared and presented programmes directed primarily at problems of the country's EU membership (Hristova-Valtcheva, 2008, 39). Second, with a low turnout of only 28.6 per cent (Central Election Commission, 2007) Bulgaria ranked slightly above average for the ten new Member States during the 2004 EP elections, whose average level of turnout was of 26.3 per cent, This turnout is the lowest in the modern democratic history of the country and represented only 50 per cent of the voter turnout recorded in the last general elections held in June 2005.

The three ruling coalition parties received a total of 48.3 per cent of the total vote and fielded ten of the 18 Bulgarian representatives in Parliament; more specifically the BSP got five seats, the DPS won four seats, and NDSV got one seat.

The protest vote split and materialized in support of a newly established political formation: GERB obtained five seats, and remarkable support was shown to the main anti-European

Table 29.3 National election results in Bulgaria: 2005

Political party	Vote %	Seats
BSP (CB)	31.0	82
DPS	12.8	34
Ataka	8.1	21
NDSV	19.9	53
ODS	7.7	20
DSB	6.4	17
BNS	5.2	13
Others	8.9	0
Total	100.0	240

Source: Central Electoral Committee, http://pi2005.cik.bg/results.

Table 29.4 EP election results in Bulgaria: 2007

Political party	Vote %	Seats
GERB	21.7	5
BSP (CB)	21.4	5
DPS	20.3	4
Ataka	14.2	3
NDSV	6.3	1
RZS	0.5	0
Others	15.6	0
Total	100.0	18

Source: Central Electoral Committee, http://ep2007.cik.bg/results.

political opposition force, *Ataka*, which secured three seats. Unlike the Old EU Member States, where small, marginal, and extreme political parties seemed to gain support, the Bulgarian model represented a significant deviation, which is again typical of the New EU countries.

9 The 2009 European election

9.1 Party lists and manifestos

In the 2009 EP elections in Bulgaria, ten political parties and three coalitions registered their party lists of 17 nominees each. One independent candidate participated in the elections as well.

It is usual that candidates appearing in EP election party lists are not first-rank politicians. This was the case in Bulgaria in 2007, especially regarding the major opposition lists (Kanev, 2008). However, there was a change in 2009. Most of the parties nominated, at least as heads of their lists, were prominent and well-known names.

The most influential party currently in Bulgaria, Citizens for the European Development of Bulgaria (GERB), was an exception to this case. Their list was topped by MEP Rumyana Jeleva, who at that time was almost unknown by the broader public. According to a survey conducted by the National Centre for Public Opinion Research, she was trusted only by 28 per cent of Bulgarian citizens (NCIOM, 2009). However this relatively new party did not have and did not really need well-known candidates because the charisma of its leader Boyko Borisov was powerful enough.

Bulgaria

The Bulgarian Socialist Party (BSP), running in the left-wing Coalition for Bulgaria (KB), together with several minor parties, nominated the acting Foreign Minister and Deputy PM Ivailo Kalfin as the top candidate on its EP ballot. Kalfin was Foreign Minister during Bulgaria's EU accession on 1 January 2007 and his nomination was broadly approved by the electorate (38 per cent).

The Movement for Rights and Freedoms (DPS) put on the top of its ballot some recognizable names, most of which were acting MEPs: Filiz Hyusmenova at the top was followed by Vladko Panayotov and Metin Kazak. The far-right *Ataka* party list was headed by its three current MEPs: Dimitar Stoynov, Slavi Binev, and Desislav Chukulov.

Another prominent top candidate was the European Commissioner Meglena Kuneva from the National Movement for Stability and Progress (NDSV) of former PM Simeon Saxe-Coburg-Gotha. Kuneva became the first Bulgarian member of the European Commission on 1 January 2007. Before that she was EU Affairs Minister of Bulgaria, and Bulgaria's chief negotiator for EU accession. She enjoyed broad approval in the country and was placed first according the sympathies of the public (48 per cent).

The ballot of the rightist Blue Coalition (BC), an election alliance of the Union of Democratic Forces (SDS) and former PM Kostov's Democrats for Strong Bulgaria (DSB) joined by three other parties, was headed by Nadezhda Mihaylova, Bulgaria's Foreign Minister in 1997–2001, at the time that Bulgaria was invited to start EU accession negotiations.

Other parties and coalitions with ambitions to pass the 5.88 per cent threshold, like LIDER, which was founded and sponsored by the mogul Hristo Kovachki, or the Order, Law, Justice Party, also nominated relatively well-known people at the top of their lists.

An analysis of the candidates shows that most of them were either experienced European parliamentarians, or had significantly contributed to the cause of Bulgaria's EU membership. It turned out that ten of the former 18 MEPs were re-elected, and two foreign ministers as well as other well-known politicians became MEPs. This fact reduces to some extent the validity of the Second-Order Election notion for the 2009 EP elections in Bulgaria.

Respectively, most of the parties preferred not to elaborate special manifestos for the EP elections. Only five out of a total of 13 parties and coalitions presented an EP election platform. This is even fewer than in 2007, when six parties had their manifestos for the EP elections.

GERB, the party that won the highest number of votes at the elections, did not come out with such a manifesto. Moreover, in the course of the EP campaign, four days before 7 June, it presented a governmental programme designed for the parliamentary elections. The same applies to the Blue Coalition, whose representatives explained that the campaign programme of the coalition was one and the same for both elections. In this platform European issues were treated in the last chapter with the title 'Strong European policy for Bulgarian citizens'.

Ataka also did not present a concrete programme for the European Parliament, and like GERB and the Blue Coalition, it introduced its election platform for the national Parliament.

The five parties that presented separate election manifestos were the three parties from the ruling coalition, BSP, NDSV, and DPS, as well as two small parties without a chance to enter the EP: the Greens and Bulgarian Social Democracy. The general approach of the parties was to reproduce the manifestos of their respective European political parties and to add their own accents.

BSP, being a member of the Party of European Socialists (PES), adopted the basic messages of its manifesto: 'People first. A new direction for Europe.' DPS, as a member of ALDE, leaned on its election platform, developing further its ten priorities. The other member of the Liberal party family, the NDSV, came out with a concise paper of ten laconic topics on EU issues.

Party slogans and messages lacked diversity and in a number of cases did not touch upon any European issues at all. The typical approach was to choose messages that could be used for both elections in the prolonged election campaign. This was the case with some of the major actors in the campaign. For example, GERB's slogan was neutral and borrowed from Parvanov's presidential campaign in 2006: 'Bulgaria can do it.' The Blue coalition's slogan 'It's time for the good ones' sounded naive and meaningless. DPS used its abbreviation in simple general words: 'Vote confidence, get support and security.' The Order, Lawfulness, Justice party came out with one single slogan: 'No to corruption.' LIDER contented itself with the traditional 'We want change', and the *Napred* (Forward) coalition preferred the classic 'Unity is power.'

Even those slogans that emphasized European issues were simplistic and unlikely to motivate voters. BSP turned to the slogan 'We protect Bulgarian interests' and tried to connect it with specific messages to different target groups. NDSV's slogan 'Europe is hearing us' was alluding to the party's contribution in the EU integration process as well as to the capacity of its top candidate Kuneva as a European Commissioner. BND, a splinter party from the NDSV, used the unconvincing slogan 'To bring Bulgaria back to Europe'. The most clear-cut slogan belonged to the Bulgarian far-right, Nationalist, and only Eurosceptic party *Ataka*: 'Not Turkey in the EU.'

9.2 The electoral campaign

A distinct feature of the 2009 EP elections in Bulgaria was the low degree of Europeanization of the electoral campaign. Leading Bulgarian politicians almost unanimously stressed the priority of the national elections in relation to the European ones. According to Boyko Borisov, leader of the strongest party, the GERB, the EP elections were just the first half-time point of the game. PM Sergey Stanishev, from the ruling BSP, talked about a first round that would assign the pace and the tempo of the election cycle. The leader of another party in the ruling coalition, DPS's Ahmed Dogan, described both elections as the same elections in two stages. According to Ivan Kostov from the opposition Blue Coalition, the EP elections were important as a preparation for the parliamentary ones. For almost all the participants the significance of the EP elections derived mainly from the fact that they were expected to form a voting structure that would be difficult to change in a month's time.

Since the EP elections were considered by the parties as the first stage of the 'real elections', it could be expected that their campaigns would also be conceptualized as the first part of the 'real campaign'. This meant that European issues served as a background rehearsal for the national elections campaign. Some domestic topics were indeed directly connected with European ones, for example corruption and European funds. In most of the cases, however, even these issues were used in a populist manner.

This attitude became apparent at the opening of the party campaigns. From the very beginning, the major political actors accentuated aims and issues connected with the parliamentary elections, leaving aside the European ones. For example, the largest party of the governing coalition BSP started its election campaign with a claim to keep its ruling position. The leader of DPS Dogan opened the campaign stating the aims of the party and presenting some of the candidates for the parliamentary elections.

Media interest in the EP elections can be characterized as weak. According to the election law, the parties had the opportunity to broadcast one-minute introductory and final clips as well as daily election chronicles. Four 90-minute television debates were carried out on two topics: 'The role of MEPs in the effective utilization of European funds' and 'Party politics in the European Parliament, the positions of the main European parties and Bulgaria's interests.'

The European issue, however, did not become dominant as a whole, and it was often completely overshadowed by current and scandalous issues. As a whole, radio and television election programmes were broadcast in time slots that proved inconvenient for viewers or listeners, against the background of a generally low level of interest. For example, the introductory clips of the parties were broadcast at 12.30 p.m., the debates were normally broadcast at 6.30 p.m., and only the final debate between the top candidates was broadcast during prime time.

The parties conducted relatively active television advertising campaigns. This was also a certain deviation from the former EP elections and was obviously due to the upcoming national elections. The number of broadcast clips was significant. According to a GfK survey, even a small party like LIDER broadcast 579 advertisements. The leading position was occupied by the BSP and its coalition with nearly 800 clips (Web Media News, 2009).

The internet campaign was not active and intensive. None of the parties opened a special website dedicated to these elections. Most of them prepared a page linked to their official websites. The rest did not participate in any online campaign. Only a small number of all candidates for EP deputies used their own personal blogs. According to media reports, only ten of Bulgaria's 17 newly elected MEP's had Facebook profiles: three from the BSP; two from the DPS; two from the Blue Coalition; one from GERB; one from *Ataka*; and one from the NDSV. Of these, only three had fan pages. Two others had Facebook groups with a modest number of members (Sofia News Agency, 2009).

An analysis of the substance of the campaign, demonstrated in election manifestos, debates, speeches, and statements, leads to certain conclusions. First, similar to the European parties, there was a broad area of common priorities and positions between the Bulgarian political parties mainly concerning strategies and policies with regard to the world's financial and economic crisis, climate change, and the international role of the EU. Specific Bulgarian demands concerned the end of restrictions for hiring Bulgarian citizens in companies in EU Member States, the simplification of the procedures for structural and cohesion funds, membership in the Schengen Agreement, political support for the introduction of the euro, a positive approach towards the Lisbon Treaty, and EU enlargement. This can be seen as a proof of the theory that there is not sufficient potential for party differentiation at European elections.

Second, there were certain points of disagreement. For example, the BSP group emphasized the use of nuclear energy as one of the important priorities that it would support in the EP, as well as projects for energy security (Nabucco, South stream, Burgas, Alexandrupolis). It demanded additional compensation for Blocs 3 and 4 of the Kozloduy nuclear power plant, as well as support for the construction of the Belene nuclear power plant. Similar positions can be found in the position of other parties like GERB. On the contrary, other parties like the Blue Coalition did not support most of these projects, suspecting possible dependence on Russia.

Third, no real debates were carried out on these issues during the campaign. Even the debate provoked by *Ataka* namely 'In favour of or against Turkey's membership in the EU?' did not take place. Policies proposed by parties and candidates in European elections rarely had much European content. The campaign in general revolved around domestic issues following the government opposition confrontation axis. European issues were more or less ornamental or only a part of the campaign. The BSP campaigned on the performance of the party and of the coalition as a whole once in power. The opposition parties focussed negatively on governmental performance.

Fourth, there was a lot of negative campaigning or even dirty campaigning in this campaign from almost all sides. This even forced President Parvanov to warn the parties to avoid using discrediting materials and faulty practices in the campaign.

Fifth, there was a significant exception with the NDSV and its top candidate's campaign. The NDSV conducted the most EU-friendly campaign and put up positive messages. From the very beginning of the campaign, Kuneva opposed the attitude that the EP elections were a preparation for the parliamentary elections and insisted on their European character. This campaign proved very successful, since most public opinion polls showed that the NDSV would not get even one MEP and in the end it got two. This fact can be seen as a sign that the position of a party on Europe matters to the results of EP elections.

Table 29.5 Importance for Bulgarians of the 2009 EP elections

Very important	24
Important to some extent	42
Not important to some extent	15
Not important at all	12
N/A	8

Source: Institute of marketing and social researches MBMD 2009, Political Attitudes in Bulgaria May 2009, www.mbmd.net/AnonymousNewsPage.

In spite of the campaign, the majority of citizens remained uninformed about and alienated from the EP. They did not have enough reasons to consider the EP elections as something important for their everyday lives. Certainly, at a declaratory level Bulgarians acknowledged the importance of the European elections for their country, but in a two-year period this conviction decreased.

The modest information campaigns about the EP and the elections did not help to change attitudes. In contrast to 2007, the political parties in Bulgaria did nothing. The visibility and the impact of the EP information campaign itself were also weak. Only 13 per cent of Bulgarian citizens saw EP advertising materials in this campaign; 62 per cent did not see them; and 13 per cent were not sure whether they had seen any, which in fact added to the former figure (Alpha Research, 2009).

Because of all of this, citizens consider their participation in the EP elections as linked with national politics, rather than with any particular European expectations. Civic interest in specific European topics was not very high either.

9.3 Electoral results

In 2009, 2,601,677 Bulgarian citizens participated in the EP elections out of about 6.7 million registered voters on the official electoral lists. This amounted to roughly 650,000 more than in 2007. Turnout was 38.9 per cent compared to 29.2 per cent in 2007. Moreover, as far as the electoral lists are not exact, according most of the experts, the real number of Bulgarian voters is not 6.7 million but under six million, Bulgaria's participation rate falls in line with the EU average.

This does not mean, however, that the elections had attracted more Bulgarian voters because of their European character. It is surely true that after two and a half years of EU membership, knowledge and interest with regard to EU institutions had increased to some extent. On the other hand, it seems reasonable that similar to the political parties, most citizens perceived the EP elections as the first episode in the struggle for winning in the national elections. In this sense higher turnout can be interpreted as a consequence of the voters' intention to secure a better starting position for their parties.

Furthermore, while turnout was higher in the 2009 EP elections compared to the 2007 elections, it was still lower than the turnout in parliamentary or local elections in Bulgaria. The participation rate at these elections was about 55 per cent, or in absolute terms about 3.5 million votes. EP electoral activity is only coming closer to turnout in presidential elections.

Comparing the turnout at the EP and national elections, the picture becomes very clear. The parliamentary election attracted a further 1.7 million voters and the participation level was 24 per cent higher than at the EP contest. This, in a sense, is confirmation that the turnout at Euro-elections increases when they are held just before national elections.

Table 29.6 Electoral turnout in Bulgaria: 2005–2013

Elections		%
National Parliamentary Elections, June 2005	3,747,793	55.8
Presidential Elections, November 2006 (1 round)	2,848,895	42.5
Presidential Elections, November 2006 (2 round)	2,757,461	42.3
EP Elections, May 2007	1,955,296	29.2
Municipal Elections, October 2007	3,526,193	50.7
EP Elections, June 2009	2,601,677	38.9
National Parliamentary Elections, July 2009	4,323,581	62.0
National Parliamentary Elections, May 2013	3,632,174	51.3

Source: Central Electoral Committee, http://portal.cik.bg/.

Table 29.7 EP election results in Bulgaria: 2009

Political party	Vote %	Seats
GERB	24.4	5
BSP (CB)	18.5	4
DPS	14.1	3
Ataka	12.0	2
NDSV	8.0	2
Blue Coalition	8.0	1
RZS	4.7	0
LIDER	5.7	0
NAPRED	2.3	0
others	2.3	0
Total	100.0	17

Source: Central Electoral Committee, http://ep2009.cik.bg/results./.

The 2009 Euro-election results in Bulgaria did not lead to major shifts in terms of allocation to parliamentary groups. All political parties that gained seats in Brussels and Strasbourg in 2007 succeeded in 2009 as well, the only exception being the Blue Coalition. The latter was successful in gathering the support of right-wing voters and managed for the first time to secure two seats in the EP.

In the meantime, the NDSV doubled its seats within the EU parliamentary institution, while *Ataka* and the BSP lost one seat. Thus four, instead of five, Bulgarian MEPs joined the left-wing group PES; five instead of four Bulgarian MEPs joined the EP Liberal parliamentary group; seven instead of five Bulgarian MEPs joined the EPP parliamentary group; and two instead of three Bulgarian MEPs joined the far-right group in the Strasbourg and Brussels arena.

Among the elected MEPs, eight, equivalent to 47 per cent, were re-elected and five, corresponding to 29.4 per cent, were women.

9.4 Campaign finance

The financing of political campaigns in Bulgaria still needs considerable improvement in terms of implementing the legislative requirements. The first legislation that regulated campaign finance, including public funding, dates back to the round table in 1990 and then in 1991. However, it was only in 2001 that a law on political parties was adopted. The implementation of the provisions was quite difficult (Kanev, 2007).

Table 29.8 List of Bulgarian MEPs: seventh legislature

Name	National party	Political group	Professional background	Year of birth	Gender	No of mandate	Committee/Chair
Binev, Slavi	Ataka	EFD (Since December 2012)	Business	1965	Male	2	—
Hyusmenova, Filiz	DPS	ALDE	Philologist	1966	Female	2	Vice-Chairwoman REGI
Ilchev, Stanimir	NDSV	ALDE	Journalist	1953	Male	1	—
Iotova, Iliana	KB (BSP)	S&D	Journalist	1964	Female	1	Vice-Chairwoman CRIM Vice-Chairwoman D-MD
Ivanova, Iliana (until 01/01/2013)	GERB	EPP	Economic analyst	1975	Female	1	—
Borisov, Preslav (since 01/01/2013	GERB	EPP	Manager	1977	Male	1	—
Kalfin, Ivailo	KB (BSP)	S&D	Diplomat	1964	Male	1	Vice-Chairman BUDG (July 2009–January 2013)
Kazak, Metin	DPS	ALDE	Politician	1972	Male	2	Vice-Chairman DROI
Kirilov, Evgeni	KB (BSP)	S&D	Diplomat	1945	Male	2	—
Kovatchev, Andrey	GERB	EPP	Manager	1967	Male	1	Vice-Chairman AFET
Mihaylova-Neynski, Nadezhda	BC (SDS-DSB)	EPP	Philologist	1962	Female	2	—
Nedelcheva, Mariya	GERB	EPP	Political scientist	1979	Female	1	—
Panayotov, Vladko	DPS	ALDE	Engineer	1950	Male	2	—
Parvanova, Antonyia	NDSV	ALDE	Medical doctor	1962	Female	1	—
Stoyanov, Dimitar	Ataka	NA	Student	1983	Male	2	—
Stoyanov, Emil (until 06/12/2012)	GERB	EPP	Journalist	1959	Male	1	—
Panayotova, Monika (since 06/12/2012)	GERB	EPP	Politician	1983	Female	1	—
Urutchev, Vladimir	GERB	EPP	Engineer	1954	Male	1	—
Vigenin, Kristian (until 07/06/2013)	KB (BSP)	S&D	Politician	1975	Male	2	—
Lyubcheva, Marusia (since 07/06/2013)	KB (BSP)	S&D	Engineer	1949	Female	2	—

Source: www.europarl.europa.eu/meps/en/search.html?country=BG.

In 2009, the law on political parties was amended to improve the regulation of political party financing. An annual state subsidy is allocated to parliamentary parties and coalitions in proportion to the number of valid votes received. The state subsidy is also granted to all political parties that received at least 1 per cent of the vote in the last parliamentary elections. The state subsidy is based on 5 per cent of the national minimum wage. In 2011 that was €6.15 per vote. Annual reports on political party expenditures have to be submitted by 31 March of the following year to the National Audit Office. A party that fails to submit annual reports for two consecutive years faces dissolution. A list of donors and donations also has to be published. However, a specific framework was presented only in 2011 with the adoption of the electoral code. Corporate donations are forbidden. Individual donations should not exceed 10,000 BGN, equivalent to about €5,100. However, there are so far no clear sanctions if parties do not comply with financing regulations (OSCE, 2009, 12–13). In this sense, the regulatory framework is still undermined by a non-existing enforcement culture. This has been a continuous pattern in dealing with campaign and party finance. This aspect of accountability, transparency, and control has been particularly emphasized by the Group of States against Corruption Committee of the Council of Europe in its 2009 report on Bulgaria (Kanev, 2007, 49–52; GRECO, 2009, 31–32).

Political coalitions cannot spend more than 2 million BGN (€1 million) and political parties cannot spend more than 1 million BGN (€500,000) in national parliamentary election campaigns. One particular recommendation about receiving donations through bank payment (GRECO, 2009, 10) entered into force only in 2011.

There are no official figures on how much money parties spent on national and European elections. In 2009, the close timing of both European and national elections clearly showed that there was an interaction between the two kinds of elections. EP elections were used as a rehearsal for the national legislative elections.

10 Theoretical interpretation of Euro-elections

10.1 Second-Order Election theory

The outcomes of the European elections in Bulgaria in terms of party choice can be used to test some of the basic hypotheses of Second-Order Election theory.

In particular, two specific features of the 2007 EP contest have pointed out the relevance of this model: the poor relevance of European issues during the electoral campaign and the low turnout.

As to the 2009 EP elections, the government opposition hypothesis with voters using this competition to punish governing parties and to send a serious warning signal to them was confirmed in the Bulgarian case, albeit not entirely. The BSP, the leading party in the governing coalition with its 476,618 votes, did not lose votes in 2009 compared to the 2007 EP elections, but lost its relative weight in the electoral corps and got one less seat. However, the party's losses are significant if we make a comparison to the 2005 parliamentary elections. This seems natural in view of the considerably lower turnout in EP elections, as compared to that of the last parliamentary elections. However, BSP diminished its vote share between the two elections.

The other ruling coalition partner, the NDSV had an unexpected success gaining more votes and one more seat compared to the 2007 EP elections. However, the NDSV also suffered large decreases compared to the last parliamentary elections. But if we compare the NDSV's results with those at the consequent parliamentary elections, we can find certain evidence for the alternative theory of Europe Salience. As far as the issue of Europe seemed to be more salient for this party, it received better results at the EP elections than at the parliamentary ones a month after that.

The exception was the third party in the coalition cabinet, the DPS, which lost a certain number of votes and claimed one less EP mandate compared to 2007, but increased its proportional share within the electorate compared to 2005.

The election outcomes seem to prove another hypothesis: namely, that it is mainly large governing parties that are punished in European elections. Small parties in government do not lose as much. As has often happened in other EU Member States, the opposition party in Bulgaria had the best electoral performance.

A typical increase in the relative weight of smaller parties at the expense of larger parties and the breakthrough of new parties in EP elections was demonstrated in Bulgaria. Newly established parties and coalitions such as LIDER and Order, Lawfulness, and Justice have shown some surprising results, although none of them could secure parliamentary seats.

The 2009 EP elections were held just a month before the national parliamentary elections. This specific timing allows us to test all the elements of the Second-Order Election theory, including the assumption that:

> if a European Parliament election is held in the build-up to a new national general election, parties will be motivated to spend a lot of time and money in the campaign, and citizens will be motivated to vote, to try to influence the upcoming national election. In this situation, turnout should be comparatively high, and vote switching should be limited since voters are likely to behave as if this were a national election.
>
> (Hix and Marsh, 2007, 496)

The close dates of both elections created an opportunity for the EP elections to attract more attention than usual. Consequently, because of their importance, the supposed Second-Order national elections might develop a momentum of their own.

Another specific feature of an analysis of EP elections in Bulgaria is connected with the absence of a constant party system during the four years between the last parliamentary elections in 2005 and the 2009 European ones. During this period of time, several new parties were established, one of which was the expected winner in the elections and two others which had a realistic chance of entering the EP. In this sense, it might be more conclusive if the 2009 European elections in Bulgaria are compared to the subsequent national elections than compared to previous national elections.

10.2 Europe Salience theory

Some of the hypotheses of the Europe Salience theory can be tested on the electoral results of the extreme Nationalist and anti-European party *Ataka*, the only party in Bulgaria that opposed the Lisbon Treaty. With 308,052 votes, equivalent to 12 per cent of the vote, *Ataka* showed considerable stability in its electorate and even increased the absolute number of its voters compared to 2005. It has obviously occupied a niche in Bulgarian society. However, due to higher voter turnout in 2009 compared to 2007, it decreased its relative weight and sent two instead of three deputies to the extreme right of the EP spectrum. It is not possible to assess the results of the Greens, because different parties took part in different elections and this party family is rather marginal in Bulgaria at the moment.

The lack of political polarization on EU agenda issues made EP elections instrumental in the conquest of power in Bulgaria. EP elections paved the way for the rise of the present-day ruling party.

If we try to assess the relative size of the Second-Order Election theory compared to the Europe Salience theory, we can say that the Bulgarian EP elections as a whole can be seen more as second-order national elections. However, they have been not entirely of that kind, inasmuch as they included some of the characteristics of the alternative view.

References

Primary sources

Alpha Research (2009) 'Political and Economic Monitoring', www.aresearch.org/eu_election/1765.html (accessed on 26 May 2009).
Central Election Commission 2007, 'Централна избирателна комисия', www.2007izbori.org (accessed on 20 May 2009).
Central Electoral Committee, http://pi2005.cik.bg/results (accessed on 12 September 2013).
European Commission (2008) Standard Eurobarometer 70/autumn 2008. National Report on Bulgaria, http://ec.europa.eu/public_opinion/archives/eb/eb70/eb70_bg_exec.pdf , accessed on 20 May 2009 (accessed on 20 May 2009).
European Commission (2009) Standard Eurobarometer 71/spring 2009, http://ec.europa.eu/public_opinion/archives/eb/eb71/eb71_std_part1.pdf (accessed on 10 October 2009).
European Parliament Database (2010) www.europarl.europa.eu/meps/eu/search.html (accessed on 10 February 2015).
Eurostat (2013, 2014) http://epp.eurostat.ec.europa.eu (accessed on 5 June 2015).
GRECO (2009) Evaluation Report on Bulgaria: Transparency of Party Funding, http://www.coe.int/t/dghl/monitoring/greco/evaluations/round3/GrecoEval3%282009%297_Bulgaria_Two_EN.pdf (accessed on 10 October 2009).
http://www.novinite.com/view_news.php?id=104457 (accessed on 8 June 2009).
Institute of Marketing and Social Researches MBMD (2009) 'Political Attidues in Bulgaria, May 2009', www.mbmd.net/AnonymousNewsPage (accessed on 20 May 2009).
NCIOM (2009) 'Social and Political Attitudes 16–19 May 2009', www.parliament.bg/bg/search/?q=%D0%BD%D1%86%D0%B8%D0%BE%D0%BC (accessed on 20 May 2009).
OSCE (2009) Bulgaria, Parliamentary Elections, 5 July 2009, http://www.osce.org/odihr/elections/bulgaria/38933?download=true (accessed on 10 October 2009).
Sofia News Agency (2009) novinite.com 2009, 'Bulgaria's New European Parliament Members Ranked by Facebook Fans'.
The Institute of marketing and social researches MBMD 2009, Political Attitudes in Bulgaria May 2009, www.mbmd.net/AnonymousNewsPage (accessed on 20 May 2009).
Web Media Group (2009) News bg 2009 'Napred Attack the Euroelections with Greatest Number of Clips', http://news.ibox.bg/news/id_1625770075 (accessed on 16 June 2009).

Secondary sources

Dimitrov, V. (2000) 'Learning to Play the Game. Bulgaria's Relations with Multilateral Organizations', *Southeast European Politics*, 1(2), 111–14.
Dobreva, A. (2010) 'Bulgaria', in Lodge, J. (ed.) *The 2009 Elections to the European Parliament*, Basingstoke, Palgrave, 60–7.
Dyson, K. and Featherstone, K. (1999), *The Road to Maastricht: Negotiating Economic and Monetary Union*, Oxford, Oxford University Press.
Fish, S. M. and Brooks, R. S. (2000) 'Bulgarian Democracy's Organizational Weapon', *East European Constitutional Review*, 9(3) Summer, 63–71.
Frankowski, S. and Paul, S. (1995) *Legal Reform in Post-communist Europe: The View from Within*, Martinus Nijhoff Publishers.
Hristova-Valtcheva, K. (2008) 'Elections for the EP in the New Member States: A Framework for Analysis of the 2007 Elections in Bulgaria', in Krasteva, A. and Stoicova, T. (eds) *First Year of Bulgaria's EU Membership*, New Bulgarian University, 25–41 (in Bulgarian).
Hristova-Valtcheva, K. (2010) 'How Much "European" Eere the 2009 EP Elections in Bulgaria?', in Krasteva, A. and Todorov, A. (eds) *The 2009 European General and Local Elections*, New Bulgarian University, 7–17 (in Bulgarian).

Hix, S and Marsh, M. (2007) 'Punishment or Protest? Understanding European Parliament Elections', *Journal of Politics*, 69, 495–510.

Kanev, D. (2007) 'Campaign Finance in Bulgaria', in Smilov, D. and Toplak, T. (eds) *Political Finance and Corruption in Eastern Europe*, Aldershot, Ashgate, 33–52.

Kanev, D. (2008) 'European Parliament Elections as "Second Order Elections"? The Bulgarian Case of 2007', in Nikolov, K. Y. (ed.) *Adapting to Integration in an Enlarged European Union, Adapting the Enlarged Union to the Citizen*, BECSA, Sofia, 54–63 (in Bulgarian).

Savkova, L. (2005) 'Europe and the Parliamentary Elections in Bulgaria, 25th of June 2005', Election Parliament Election Briefing no. 21, EPERN Network, Sussex, Sussex University. Online. Available at: www.sussex.ac.uk/sei/research/ europeanpartieselections referendumsnetwork/epernelectionbriefings (accessed on 13 February 2012).

Savkova, L. (2007) 'The European Parliament Election in Bulgaria May, 20th, 2007', European Parliament Elections Briefing no. 23, EPERN Network, Sussex, Sussex University. Online. Available at: www.sussex.ac.uk/sei/research/ europeanpartieselections referendumsnetwork/europeparliamentelections (accessed on 13 February 2013).

Spirova, M. (2008) 'The Bulgarian Socialist Party. The Long Road to Europe', *Communist and Post-Communist Studies*, 41(4), 481–95.

Todorov, A. (1999) 'The Role of Political Parties in the Bulgaria's Accession to the EU', Center for the Study of Democracy. Online. Available at: www.csd.bg (accessed on 20 February 2012).

Todorov, A. (2010) 'Chlenstvoto v partiite seld 1989 godina' ['Membership in Political Parties in Bulgaria since 1989'] in Lubenov, M. (ed.) *Balgarskata politologia pred predizvikatelstvata na vremeto* [*Political Science in Bulgaria Facing the Challenges of the Time*], Sofia University Publishing House.

30
ROMANIA

Gabriela Borz

Figure 30.1 Map of Romania

Table 30.1 Romania profile

EU entry year	2007
Schengen entry year	Non-member
MEPs Elected in 2009	35
MEPs under Lisbon Treaty	33
Capital	Bucharest
Total area★	238,391 km²
Population	19,947,311
	89.5 % Romanians
	6.6 % Hungarians
	2.5% Roma
	0.3% Germans
	0.3% Ukrainians
	0.2 % Turks
	0.2% others
Population density★★	86.9/km²
Median age of population	40.8
Political system	Semi-presidential Republic
Head of state	Traian Băsescu
Head of government	Emil Boc, Democratic Liberal Party (PD-L) (December 2008–February 2012);
	Mihai-Răzvan Ungureanu (independent) (February–May 2012);
	Victor Ponta, Social Democratic Party (PSD) (May 2012–)
Political majority	Democratic Liberal Party (PD-L) and Democratic Union of Hungarians in Romania (UDMR) Government Coalition (December 2008–May 2012);
	Social Democratic Party (PSD), National Liberal Party (PNL), Conservative Party (PC), National Union for the Progress of Romania (UNPR) Government Coalition (May 2012–)
Currency	Romanian Leu (RON)
Prohead GDP in PPS	7,500 €

Source: Eurostat, 2013, 2014, http://epp.eurostat.ec.europa.eu/.

Notes:
★ Total area including inland waters.
★★ Population density: the ratio of the annual average population of a region to the land area of the region.

1 Geographical position

Romania is the largest country in south-eastern Europe, bordered by Ukraine in the north, Moldova in the east, Bulgaria in the south, and Hungary and Serbia in the west and south-west, respectively. The country has an exit to the Black Sea and is situated on the lower course of the Danube River. The landscape is diverse and includes the Carpathian Mountains, hills, plateaus, plains and meadows. Romania covers 238,390 square kilometres and its administrative territory is divided into 41 counties plus the Bucharest municipality, 319 towns, and 2,686 communes. It has a population of 21.4 million and 57 per cent of the population live in urban centres.

2 Historical background

The Kingdom of Romania, founded in 1859 under Alexandru Ioan Cuza and later incorporated into the Ottoman Empire, gained its independence in 1877. During World War I, Romania joined the allied side. This resulted in regaining Transylvania, Bessarabia, Bukovina, and Dobruja, which, by 1 December 1918, all (re)united with the Old Kingdom of Romania and formed the Romanian nation-state (Constantiniu, 2008). The inter-war period was marked by authoritarian King Carol II, who through his Constitution of 1938, banned political parties. During WWII, his son Michael, with the backing of the opposition parties, put an end to Ion Antonescu's fascist government and switched sides in the war.

Following the 1944 armistice, Romania became a Socialist republic and parts of its eastern territory, including Bessarabia, now the Republic of Moldova, were occupied by the Soviet Union. King Michael was forced to abdicate, and in 1947 the Communists came to power, proclaiming Romania a 'People's Republic'. After the fall of Communism with the 1989 revolution, Romania began its transition to democracy.

3 Geopolitical profile

During the era of Communism, President Nicolae Ceuşescu tried to pursue a political strategy independent from Moscow and Romania was the only Warsaw Pact country that denounced the Soviet invasion of Czechoslovakia in 1968 (Swain and Swain, 1993). He maintained diplomatic relations with Israel, West Germany, and several Arab countries. In the early 1970s, the country became member of the International Monetary Fund and the General Agreement on Trade and Tariffs. In 1975 Romania was granted most favoured nation status by the United States. Ceuşescu's autocratic policies, as well as his ambition to pay all the country's foreign debts, generated poverty and discontent, which culminated in the 1989 revolution and led to his execution. The immediate post-Communist years were focussed on democratic and economic reforms. The country joined NATO in 2004 and the European Union in 2007.

4 Overview of the political landscape

The 1991 Romanian Constitution, later amended in 2003, established a semi-presidential system of government based on the French model. The President, as head of state, and the Prime Minister, as head of government, share executive functions, although it is not clear who prevails and in practice, it resembles more a parliamentary regime with an elected president.

The President is elected by popular vote for a five-year term. The Prime Minister is appointed by the President and approved by the Parliament. The Parliament is bicameral and consists of the Senate and the Chamber of Deputies, with 137 and 334 members, respectively, which enjoy equal powers. The Constitution was amended in 2003 with the aim of complying with European regulations. The two chambers of the Romanian Parliament maintained equal powers, minority rights were strengthened, the financing of political parties became more transparent and the presidential mandate was extended from four to five years. On the basis of the latest referendum held at the time of the presidential elections in 2009, the Constitution will be further amended in order to reduce the number of MPs and the number of parliamentary chambers. If approved by two-thirds of MPs, this proposal will lead to a unicameral Parliament as opposed to the current bicameral format. Such a discussion has not taken place yet.

5 Brief account of the political parties

Post-Communist Romanian politics have been characterized by very high instability, party fragmentation, government resignation before the end of the mandate, and high electoral volatility (Stănciulescu, 2008). Furthermore, parties' changing electoral fortunes have been associated with low party identification amongst the electorate (Wyman et al. 1995; Miller et al., 1998; Rose and Mishler, 1998; Lewis, 2000).

Romania started out with a very high party replacement score of 41.7 per cent for the first two elections, which dropped to 14.7 per cent for the second and third elections, and then increased again to 32.9 per cent for the third and fourth elections (Birch, 2003, 126). This trend has, however, declined over time. After the 2008 parliamentary elections, only five parties entered Parliament. The number of parties that entered the electoral contest also decreased when compared to 2004. The decrease in political fragmentation is partly due to the fact that the electoral threshold has been raised from 3 per cent in 1990 to 5 per cent in 2000, and also partly due to the fact that parties have slowly crystallized their programmes. The number of party splits has diminished and they were compensated by a similar number of party mergers (Borz, 2009a).

The governing party in 2009, the Democratic Liberal Party (PD-L) has moved its policies towards the centre and more towards conservatism. As an early 2001 party convention stated, they favour 'a market economy but not a market society'. The current statute defines PD-L as a party of the centre-right, and a member of the European People's Party group committed to the creation of a modern society and a social market economy. Following a process of programmatic clarification, PD, before becoming PD-L at the end of 2007, changed its European Parliament membership from the European Socialists to the European People's Party.

Table 30.2a List of political parties in Romania

Original name	Abbreviation	English translation
Frontul Salvării Naționale	FSN	National Salvation Front
Partidul Social Democrat Român	PSDR	The Romanian Social Democrat Party
Alianța pentru Unitatea Românilor	A.U.R	Romanian Unity Alliance
Partidul Național Țărănesc Creștin Democrat	PNȚCD	The Christian Democrat National Peasants' Party
Partidul Ecologist Român	PER	The Romanian Ecologist Party
Mișcarea Ecologică din România	MER	The Ecological Movement
Partidul Democrat Agrar	PDAR	The Agrarian Democratic Party
Partidul Social Democrat din România	PSDR	The Romanian Social Democrat Party
Uniunea Democrată a Maghiarilor din România	UDMR	Hungarian Democratic Union
Partidul Național Liberal	PNL	The National Liberal Party
Convenția Democratică din România	CDR	Democratic Convention of Romania
Frontul Democrat al Salvării Naționale	FDSN	Democratic National Salvation Front
Partidul Unității Naționale Române	PUNR	The Romanian National Unity Party
Partidul România Mare	PRM	Greater Romania Party
Partidul Socialist al Muncii	PSM	Socialist Labour Party
Partidul Republican	PR	Republican Party
Partidul Democrat Liberal	PD-L	Democratic Liberal Party
Partidul Democrației Sociale din România	PDSR	Social Democracy Party of Romania
Uniunea Social Democrată	PD+PSDR	Social Democratic Union
Partidul Socialist	PS	The Socialist Party
Partidul Socialist al Muncii	PSM	Romanian Socialist Workers' Party

Alianța Națională Liberală	ANL	National Liberal Alliance
Partidul Pensionarilor din România	PPR	Pensioners' Party in Romania
Polul Social Democratic	PSD	Social Democratic Pole
Alianța pentru România	ApR	Alliance for Romania
Partidul Național Liberal – Radu Câmpeanu	PNL-RC	The National Liberal Party – Radu Câmpeanu
Alianța Partidul Social Democrat – Partidul Conservator	PSD+PC	Social Democratic Party – Conservative Party Alliance
Partidul Noua Generație-Creștin Democrat	PNG–CD	The Party of the New Generation-Christian Democrat
Alianța Dreptate și Adevăr	DA: PNL+PD	Justice and Truth Alliance
Uniunea Națională pentru Progresul României	UNPR	National Union for the Progress of Romania
Partidul Poporului – Dan Diaconescu	PP-DD	People's Party – Dan Diaconescu
Forța Civică	FC	The Civic Force

Source: Central Electoral Bureau, www.bec.ro; Parties and Elections in Europe, www.parties-and-elections.eu.

PD-L's close challenger is the Social Democratic Party (PSD), which entered the governing coalition in 2012. Initially, it was given guest status as the Socialist International; it received associate membership in the Party of European Socialists in 1999, which was followed by full membership thereafter. The PSD defines itself as a leftist modern and progressive party that endorses social democratic values and European policies. The Conservative Party, which formed an electoral alliance with PSD in the 2009 EP elections, is a relatively small party, committed to Conservative values. It started in 1991 with the name Humanist Party of Romania, changed its name to the Conservative Party in 2005, and has no connection to the historic Conservative Party that existed before WWI. The party is committed to European integration and to national values. It was part of the governing coalition with the Social Democrats after 2000, part of the coalition formed by DA (PD and PNL) after 2004, and part of a second alliance with PSD in 2008. This shift was also reflected in its European affiliation, which changed from ALDE in 2007 to the Alliance of Socialists and Democrats in 2009.

The third strongest party, in opposition in 2009, the Liberal Party (PNL) dates back to 1875 and has a strong commitment to Liberal values and policies as proven by its affiliation to the Liberal International, and its membership in the Alliance of Liberals and Democrats for Europe Group in the EP. They are also affiliated with the European Liberal Democrat and Reform Party, a confederation of 56 national Liberal parties across Europe.

In 2004, the Greater Romania Party (PRM) was refused membership in the European People's Party. Immediately after Romania joined the EU, the PRM Euro-observers became parliamentarians until the 2007 EP elections were organized and, together with other extreme-right parties, formed a group called 'Identity, Tradition, Sovereignty' (ITS). In this were the French National Front, Alessandra Mussolini of the Italian Social Alternative, another Italian party Tricolour Flame, the Flemish Interest (Belgium), The National Union Attack (Bulgaria), Freedom Party (Austria) and one independent MEP from the UK. Due to declarations against Romanians living in Italy by Alessandra Mussolini, declarations which were found offensive by PRM, the party withdrew from the group (Ziare online, 14 November 2007). Their action ultimately disqualified the ITS as an official group in the EP. After the 2007 elections, the PRM did not have any MEPs and currently, after the 2009 elections, its three European parliamentarians are non-affiliated.

Table 30.2b List of Romanian political parties and their European alignments

National party	Party family	Political group
PC	Conservatism	S&D
PD-L	Liberal Conservatism Christian Democracy	EPP
PNL	Liberalism	ALDE
UDMR	Liberal Conservatism Minority politics	EPP
PRM	Nationalism Far Right	—

Sources: Political Parties, www.psd.ro; www.partidulconservator.ro; www.pdl.org.ro; www.pnl.ro; www.udmr.ro; http://www.prm.org.ro; www.parties-and-elections.de.

Note:
PD (The Democratic Party) and PLD (The Liberal Democratic Party) ran as separate parties in the June 2007 European elections and at the end of December, same year, they merged and formed the PD-L (The Democratic Liberal Party).

5.1 Party attitudes towards the European Union

Across EU Member States European Union issues have been amongst those which have caused few internal party conflicts (Borz, 2009b). Likewise in Romania, the level of party programmatic cohesion was slightly affected by issues of European enlargement and integration. According to experts, parties like PRM and PC, in particular, had internal tensions over these subjects. The PRM approached the idea of the EU with caution and manifested opposition. Due to electoral reasons however, their discourse changed into a more positive one, as soon as the EP elections approached. The rest of the Romanian parliamentary parties agreed on the importance of EU membership and of complying with post-accession EU requirements.

Accession to the European Union, integration and enlargement, have not caused the deepest intra-party conflicts. More important issues stressed by parties during the campaigns were related to the state of the economy, to redistribution issues, or to the consolidation of democratic institutions. All these topics were ultimately more likely to cause dissent within parties than EU issues.

6 Public opinion and the European Union

Considering how little attention was given to the European elections, Romanians were the most supportive of the EU amongst Europeans, with 66 per cent and 67 per cent of respondents in autumn 2008 (Eurobarometer 70, 2009) and spring 2009 (Eurobarometer 71.1, 2009), respectively, supporting their country's membership in the EU. When asked to give an opinion and to describe how they perceived the EU, Romanians again were at the top of the EU-27. About 64 per cent of Romanians had a positive image of the EU, compared to an average of only 43 per cent across EU-27 Member States. A similar 63 per cent of Romanians, 7 per cent above the EU-27 average, believed in 2009 that the country benefitted from EU membership. The perception of benefits from membership – high identification with Europe, and a willingness to be part of Europe – have been constant since the collapse of Communism. Prior to the 2007 accession, 75 per cent of Romanian respondents declared in 2004 that the country would benefit from joining the EU. Public support for and positive opinions about the EU were not reflected in and did not stem from a high level of knowledge about the EU. Only 11 per cent

Table 30.3 Issue salience before and after the 2009 elections in Romania and the EU-27 (%)

Important issues	EU-27 EB70	EU-27 EB71	Romania EB70	Romania EB71	Romania EB71–EB70
Economic growth	51	52	64	65	+1
Inflation	49	40	39	43	+4
Unemployment	47	57	38	49	+9
Crime	33	29	30	27	–3
Pensions	33	32	44	40	–4
Immigration	29	24	19	10	–9
Climate change	29	26	20	16	–4
Terrorism	28	24	23	17	–6

Source: Eurobarometer 70, January–February 2009, and Eurobarometer 71, November 2009, http://ec.europa.eu/public_opinion/archives/eb_special_320_300_en.htm.

of Romanians had a high level of knowledge about the EU in 2004, and, in 2009, a high 42 per cent of respondents declared that they did not understand how the EU worked. Rather, the public's positive endorsement of the EU was the result of the overthrow of Communism and of the hope that the EU would become a means of escaping Romania's totalitarian past.

Not only was the vote preference in the EU elections predicted to be influenced by national issues, so too was the turnout. Across new Member States, and likewise in Romania, national politics related to post-Communist legacies and public perceptions of high corruption depressed turnout. Besides these issues, factors such as turnout in the last national election are all more important in influencing turnout than EU-level measures (Rose and Borz, 2010).

A Eurobarometer study (70, 2009) carried out in October–November 2009, half a year before the 2009 EP elections, revealed that the major themes likely to influence voters in the European Parliament elections all pertained to national politics. None of the European issues listed were mentioned by more than 20 per cent of respondents. The most important theme likely to influence voters' behaviour in the 2009 EP elections at the time was considered to be economic growth, which was indicated by 64 per cent of Romanian respondents. Pensions followed, with 44 per cent, then unemployment at 39 per cent, inflation at 38 per cent, crime at 30 per cent, terrorism at 23 per cent, climate change at 20 per cent, and finally immigration at 19 per cent. There was a general consensus that economic matters were the main theme for the EP elections, both in Romania and across EU-27 Member States. Eurobarometer respondents across the EU-27 perceived that the main themes on which the EP elections would be decided were economic growth, unemployment, and inflation.

A few months later, when asked the same question, 'what are the two most important issues you are facing at the moment?', the January–February 2009 Eurobarometer (71, 2009) confirmed a general European as well as Romanian interest for economic issues. Compared to the previous survey, economic growth (+1 per cent), inflation (+4 per cent), and unemployment (+9 per cent) were again considered major issues for citizens before the EP 2009 elections in Romania. This upward trend was similarly confirmed across all EU-27 Member States.

7 National and EP electoral systems

The national parliamentary elections are held under a mixed electoral system that was applied for the first time in 2008. Previously, the electoral system used proportional representation under closed lists, and for the distribution of seats, the d'Hondt method was used. Single member districts (SMDs) were introduced at the 2008 parliamentary elections to increase the responsibility and accountability of Romanian MPs. The votes are counted twice: once for the candidate in the SMDs and once for the party list in the 43 multi-member regions (Rose and Munro, 2009, 213). The seats are distributed in three stages: first, at the level of SMDs, seats are allocated to candidates who win an absolute majority of votes. Then, at the level of the multi-member region, the rest of the seats are allocated according to the Hare quota and finally, at the national level, any remaining unallocated seats are distributed according to the d'Hondt formula applied to the wasted votes in the multi-member regions.

For the European elections however, the electoral system at work is proportional representation based on closed party lists. Electoral law no. 33/2007 regulating the European elections was adopted by the Romanian Parliament immediately after accession. Party lists and independent candidates have to be supported by 200,000 and 100,000 signatures, respectively. The lists can accommodate a maximum of 43 candidates, which will enter the electoral battle for the 33 seats allocated to Romania at the European Parliament (EP) in 2009. The whole country is considered to be one electoral district and the allocation of mandates is done according to the d'Hondt method. As in the case of national elections, the electoral campaign lasts one month with a break of two days before polling day. Opinion polls are also forbidden 48 hours prior to election day. Media access, television, radio, and printed media, is granted proportionally to the number of candidates a party, political alliance, or electoral alliance has on the list. The electoral threshold is 5 per cent out of the total valid votes. An independent candidate can only be elected if he or she polls at least the national electoral coefficient. The latter is calculated by dividing the total valid votes at the national level by the number of Euro mandates, 35 in 2007 and 33 in 2009. The right to candidature in elections is given to any Romanian citizen over the age of 23.

8 A glance at EP and national elections

The electoral campaign for the 2007 EP elections included 13 parties and an independent, László Tökés. Six of the candidate parties did not have an EP group affiliation. Apart from the independent candidate, only five other parties succeeded in securing seats to the European Parliament. The Liberal Democratic Party secured thirteen seats, the Social Democrat and the Conservative Party together obtained ten seats, the National Liberal Party won six seats, and the Hungarian Democratic Union of Romania, two seats.

The focus of the campaign was mainly on national issues. However, some of the election themes revolved around the topic of how and what Romania could add to regional security. Parties also aimed to make electors aware of the fact that MEPs would contribute to decisions that would affect all 27 EU countries. They also stressed the importance of mobilizing the electorate to understand the transition from being a candidate to being a Member State of the European Union.

Party manifestos in 2007 were not focussed on key issues for Romanian citizens such as the Common Agricultural Policy or commercial policy, but mainly on energy and environmental policies or EU institutional reform. Romanian parties justified the emphasis on internal issues during the electoral campaign as a strategy used in order to attract voters to the polls. Turnout for the 2007 European elections however was only 29.4 per cent, about 10 percentage points lower than for the 2008 national elections and almost half of the turnout registered in the 2004 national elections.

Participation in the national elections organized before and after the Euro-election was higher, with 10 per cent in 2008 parliamentary elections and with almost 20 per cent in the second tour of the presidential elections. The latter were organized only six months after the European elections. Participation in the presidential elections of November 2009 was 56.9 per cent.

Table 30.4 EP election results in Romania: 2007

National party	Vote share %	No of MEPs	Political group
PD	28.8	13	EPP
PSD	23.1	10	PSE
PNL	13.4	6	ALDE
PLD	7.8	3	EPP
UDMR	5.5	2	EPP
PNG	4.8	0	
PRM	4.2	0	
Tökes L.*	3.4	1	Greens/EFA
PC	2.9	0	
PIN	2.4	0	
PNȚCD	1.4	0	
Others**	2.2	0	
Total	100	35	
Turnout	**29.5**		

Source: Central Electoral Bureau, Romanian Permanent Electoral Authority, accessed 2 June 2010; http://www.roaep.ro/bec_eu_07/wp-content/uploads/2013/10/reultate_finale_pe.pdf

Notes:
* independent candidate;
**Others include: Pro-Europe Roma Party (Partida Romilor Pro-Europa) 1.14%; Socialist Alliance Party (Partidul Alianța Socialistă) (0.55%), Green Party (Partidul Verde) 0.33%.

Table 30.5 National election results in Romania: 2004–2012 %

Political party	2004	2008	2012
FSN[a]	—	—	—
PSDR	—	—	—
A.U.R[b]	—	—	—
PNȚCD	1.8	—	ARD
PER	0.7	0.7	0.8
MER	—	—	—
PDAR	—	—	—
PSDR	—	—	—
UDMR	6.2	6.2	5.1
PNL	—	18.6	USL
CDR[c]	—	—	—
FDSN	—	—	—
PUNR[d]	0.5	—	—
PRM	12.9	3.2	1.2
PSM[e]	—	—	—
PR	—	—	—
PD-L[f]	—	32.4	ARD
PDSR[g]	—	—	—
PD+PSDR	—	—	—
PS	—	—	—
PSM	—	—	—
ANL[h]	—	—	—

(continued)

Table 30.5 (continued)

PPR	—	—	—
Social Democratic Pole[i]	—	—	—
ApR[h]	—	—	—
PNL-RC[h]	—	—	—
PSD[j]+PC	36.6	33.1	USL
PNG-CD	2.2	2.3	—
DA: PNL+PD	31.3	—	—
USL[k]			58.6
ARD[l]			16.5
PP-DD			14.0
Others	7.8	3.5	3.8
Turnout	**58.5**	**39.2**	**41.76**

Source: Romania's Central Electoral Bureau, available at www.bec.ro, accessed 1 September 2012; www.parties-and-elections.eu, accessed 1 October 2013.

Notes:
[a] In 1992 the party suffered a split; one splinter ran the 1992 elections as FDSN (future PSD) and in 1993 the other faction changed its name to PD (Democratic Party).
[b] For the 1990 elections, the A.U.R. was composed of PUNRT (which will become PUNR) and Republican Party.
[c] Consisted of FER (Romanian Ecological Federation), PDAR, PNL-CD, PNȚCD, PNL.
[d] PUNR was absorbed by PC in 2006.
[e] Partly absorbed by PSD in 2003.
[f] FSN in 1992, under the name PD from 1993 until 2007, when it merged with PLD and became PD-L.
[g] PDSR was the former FDSN merged with two other minor parties.
[h] PNL has absorbed ApR in 2002; PNL-RC in 2003 and ANL in 1998.
[i] eEectoral alliance formed by PSDR, PDSR and PUR.
[j] Merger of PSDR with PDSR in 2001.
[k] Electoral alliance for the 2012 elections USL comprised of PSD, PNL, PC, UNPR (National Union for the Romanian Progress).
[l] Electoral alliance for the 2012 elections ARD comprised of PDL, FC, PNȚCD.

9 The 2009 European election

9.1 Party lists and manifestos

Compared to the 2007 Euro-elections, fewer parties participated in the contest due to the reduction of parliamentary parties and the formation of electoral alliances. The number of candidatures decreased in 2009, when only seven parties and two independent candidates participated in the EP electoral campaign starting on 8 May 2009 The lists proposed by the Green Party and the Ecologist Party, and the candidature of one independent, were rejected by the Romanian Central Electoral Bureau after the signatures associated with the party lists and the independent candidate were verified. Also, two relatively small parties, PIN and PNG, did not run in the European elections in 2009. PNG leader George Becali signed an electoral pact with the PRM and was considered on the list of the Greater Romania Party.

PD-L's programme for the 2009 European elections called for a country without corruption, for solidarity, for joining the Schengen zone, for better status for Romanian workers in the European labour market, for measures to overcome the economic crisis, for an improved agricultural sector, and for helping Moldova with the process of joining the EU. The opposition party, PSD, focussed its discourse during the EP election campaign on the necessity of increasing pensions, salaries in the public sector, and on European funds to help the agriculture industry and other industrial sectors. The PNL electoral manifesto for the 2009 EP elections was called: 'Liberal Europe works for Romania.' The main objectives highlighted in the document were support for small- and medium-sized businesses, the necessity of subsidies for agriculture, the status of Romanians abroad and their right to work, politics towards Moldova, and perspectives on European integration. The PRM is the only Romanian party which openly speaks about the negative effects of European integration and which also has an anti-immigrant policy stance. In comparison with the other non-attached parties in the EP, they are more pro-welfare state, advocate more strongly the necessity of law and order and the role of religious values in politics, and are against permissive attitudes towards same-sex marriages or legalizing soft drugs.

Important European topics such as food security, energy, subventions and structural funds were almost missing from the electoral manifestos. Most of the topics discussed were related to unemployment, living standards, salaries and pensions, and housing for young couples. Pensions and increased salaries in the public sector were issues raised by the PSD, all associated with the message 'Choose well'. Starting with a motto 'For better or worse', the PD-L used the idea of family in order to suggest the representation of Romanian families in the big European family at the EP. Its candidates, along with those of the PSD and PNL, promised European funds and a continuing fight against corruption. The UDMR detached themselves from the forthcoming presidential campaign and promoted themselves as the ambassadors of Transylvania in relation to Europe. The Greater Romania Party had an expected and unsurprising anti-corruption and justice-oriented campaign, with the motto 'Down with the mafia and up with the country.' After losing their national parliamentary seats in 2008, the party leader, Vadim managed to revitalize the party by bringing in businessman George Becali, the former President of PNG, on their list of Euro-candidates. When compared to other members inside their European party group, in the ALDE group for example, the PNL did not put too much emphasis on green issues, did not oppose immigration, and was about average with its position towards European integration. Whilst PSD MEPs were about average in their S&D group, although slightly less permissive, the PD-L was more pro-immigration than the vast majority of parties forming the EPP group.

9.2 Electoral campaign

Although they had a low impact on turnout, efforts to publicize the EP elections came from both the European and the national side. The European Parliament launched a campaign aimed at informing the public and at stimulating their interest in the European elections. The campaign targeted several methods of communication, such as television adverts on the national television channel TVR1, one radio advertisement, banners and big advertising posters, multimedia cabins with messages addressed to Romanian voters, webpages, seminars for journalists, as well as social networking sites such as Facebook, MySpace, and Flicker. The multimedia cabin was placed in tourist areas in the capital Bucharest and in Cluj-Napoca. The advertising posters were launched on 1 April 2009 and were active for about one month.

In 2009, the mass media's interest in the electoral campaign was lower. Radio and television debates were organized, as designated by law, but several local experts noted that the campaign prepared by the parties was not as aggressive as in previous national elections. Non-governmental organizations organized a common front under the name Coalition for a Clean Parliament-European Elections (CPC-AE) and monitored 100 candidates for the EP. At the end of the process, the coalition made public a list of 11 names, two representatives of PSD, PNL, PD, three candidates of PRM, and one candidate of PNG and UDMR, who, according to them, did not fulfil the integrity criteria for becoming an MEP.

In order to mobilize citizens, the Romanian government also publicized the elections for one week at the end of the electoral campaign. Civil society was involved in monitoring the electoral campaign in various ways. The foundation Civil Society for Moral Reform made public a black list of candidates for the European Parliament. The list included 17 names of people who, according to the foundation, could not ethically and morally represent the interests of Romanians and of the European Parliament. *Academia Caţavencu*, a well-known satirical magazine, also made public a list of names drawn from amongst the Euro candidates which the publication did not believe should represent Romania in the EP. Besides these actions, the non-governmental association Pro Democracy ran a project in partnership with the Ministry of Education which involved 45 high schools to inform and stimulate the pupils to participate in the June EP elections.

Romanian parties promoted their candidates to the European Parliament more than their party programmes on European issues. Their campaigning included banners, posters, calendars, hats, T-shirts, lighters, and balloons with the name of the candidate or of the party and less specific EU-related slogans. The electoral campaigning included some social issues not necessarily related to the specifics of the EP elections. The European dimension of the elections, and in particular their impact on the political future of Romania, were almost absent from the video messages of the Romanian candidates. As noted by the Romanian press, parties used the same populist messages (*România Liberă* 2009a, 27 May) in the EP campaign as in the national election campaign. Their main messages related to employment, salaries, increase of child benefits, modernization of transport, and housing for young couples. The campaign was a bit disconnected from the reality of the economic crisis and did not emphasize what role Romanian representatives should play in the EP. Most of the candidates did not explain in detail why they wanted to go to Brussels or what kind of projects they planned to develop once arrived in the European legislative arena. The media also affirmed the use of the June 2009 campaign for the European elections as a rehearsal for the November 2009 presidential elections (*România Liberă* 2009b, 11 May). Most parties took the opportunity to announce their candidates for the presidential election and to communicate their message against the incumbent President Băsescu.

9.3 Electoral results

A lower number of electoral competitors in 2009 had positive effects on electoral proportionality. The number of wasted votes, cast for parties with no seats, was substantially reduced from 2007 to 2009. The difference between the percentage of votes received and the percentage of seats that parties gained, as calculated by the disproportionality index, was reduced from 7.6 in 2007 to 1.9 in 2009 (Radu, 2009). Higher proportionality in 2009 means that the votes cast for party lists or independent candidates situated below the electoral threshold were much lower than in the previous Euro-election.

In 2009 the Social Democrats, who were in opposition, gained slightly more popularity, but they obtained about the same percentage of the vote as the Democratic Liberals. Whilst in 2007, the incumbent PD had thirteen MEPs, and the PSD had only ten, in 2009 their fortunes balanced and the PSD received eleven EP seats, compared to ten obtained by the PD-L. The seats won by the Liberal Party had been reduced by one, from six in 2007 to five in 2009. The Hungarian minority party gained three seats in 2009, one more as compared to 2007.

Towards the party group configuration in the EP in 2007, Romania contributed eighteen MEPs to the PPE-ED group, ten to the PSE group; six to the ALDE group and one MEP to the Greens/ALE group. This distribution was relatively the same in 2009. The only groups which received fewer MEPs were the EPP and the S&D (14 EPP, 11 S&D, five ALDE, three NA). In 2009, however, due to the mandates won by the Greater Romania Party, three of the newly-elected MEPs from PRM did not join any political group and remained non-affiliated.

Table 30.6 EP election results in Romania: 2009

National party	Abbreviation	Vote share	No of MEPs	Political group
Partidul Democrat (Democratic Party)	PD	28.8	13	Party of European Socialists (PES) (until end of 2007); European People's Party (thereafter)
Partidul Social Democrat Român (Romanian Social Democrat Party)	PSDR	23.1	10	Party of European Socialists (PES)
Partidul Național Liberal (National Liberal Party)	PNL	13.4	6	Alliance of Liberals and Democrats for Europe (ALDE)
Partidul Liberal Democrat (Liberal Democratic Party)	PLD	7.8	3	European People's Party (EPP)
Uniunea Democrată a Maghiarilor din România (Hungarian Democratic Union)	UDMR	5.5	2	European People's Party (EPP)
Partidul Noua Generație-Creștin Democrat (Party of the New Generation)	PNG	4.8	0	
Partidul România Mare (Greater Romania Party)	PRM	4.2	0	
László Tőkés (Independent)		3.4	1	Group of the Greens/European Free Alliance (Greens/EFA)
Partidul Conservator (Conservative Party)	PC	2.9	0	
Partidul Inițiativa Națională (National Initiative Party)	PIN	2.4	0	
Partidul Național Țărănesc Creștin Democrat (Christian Democrat National Peasants' Party)	PNȚCD	1.4	0	
Others★		2.2	0	
Total		100	35	

Source: Central Electoral Bureau, Romanian Permanent Electoral Authority, accessed 2 June 2010; http://www.roaep.ro/bec_eu_07/wp-content/uploads/2013/10/reultate_finale_pe.pdf.

Note:
★ Others includes: Partida Romilor Pro-Europa (Pro-Europe Roma Party) 1.14%; Partidul Alianța Socialistă (Socialist Alliance Party) 0.55%, Partidul Verde (Green Party) 0.33%.

Compared to the November 2008 national elections, the most important parties retained their supremacy in the 2009 EP elections. In the 2008 national elections, the Democratic Liberal Party (PD-L) won the most seats in both chambers, and was closely followed by the Social Democratic Party (PSD), which contested the elections in an alliance with the smaller Conservative Party (PC). The National Liberal Party in alliance with the Christian Democratic National Peasant's Party (PNȚCD), came third. The Greater Romania Party had somewhat different electoral fortunes. The party came third in the 2004 national election, following the major coalitions PSD-PC and PNL-PD. In the following 2008 national elections the party lost all seats won in 2004 and experienced a slight upward trend in the 2009 EP elections.

Romanian MEPs range from high-profile career politicians who previously have had party, governmental, or parliamentary positions, to young politicians who can use the EP mandate to enhance their national political career, and a few amateur politicians as well, who previously had little or no experience of high-profile, elected public positions. With an average age of 46, the vast majority of Romanian MEPs have previously held a party position. Some of them have been involved in politics since 1990 or earlier and some held ministerial positions in previous governments. Professionally, the predominant vocation is economist, followed by engineer or lawyer.

Although the total number of MEPs has decreased from 35 to 33, the gender gap has been reduced. The number of women MEPs has increased by 5 per cent, from 34 per cent in 2007, to 39 per cent in 2009. Compared to an average age of 43 in 2007, an increase of three years is found in 2009, mainly because of MEPs' mandate renewal. Whilst in 2007 the eldest MEP was 64 and the youngest 27, in 2009 both the maximum and minimum age went up by three years. Regarding their tenure, almost two-thirds of current MEPs are in their second mandate and some of them were also observers to the EP before 2007. This continuity is mainly due to a centralized procedure of candidate selection and to their positioning on the party lists. In order to increase their chances of being re-elected, in 2009 parties placed highly on their lists those candidates who already had experience with the EP (Central Electoral Bureau website, 2010). Three UDMR candidates had already been MEPs in 2007 and they occupied the first three positions on the party list. Of the PNL's candidates, four already had been MEPs in 2007 and were placed in between the second and fifth places on the list. Likewise, eight of the PDL candidates had already represented Romania in the EP from 2007–2009. They were placed in between the first and fourteenth places on the party list. The electoral alliance PSD-PC had 43 candidates on their list like all the other parties, out of which nine, former MEPs in 2007, have been placed in between the first and sixteenth position on the list.

The MEPs' committee memberships are mostly assigned according to their professions. In terms of the allocation of committee chairs, Romania was given five Vice-Chair positions in the Committees Development, the Subcommittee on Security and Defence, the Delegation for relations with the countries of the Andean Community, the Committee on Economic and Monetary Affairs, and the Committee on Transport and Tourism. The Chair position was given for the delegation to the EU-Moldova Parliamentary Cooperation Committee.

9.4 Campaign finance

Total spending involved in the 2009 EP campaign was around €3.1 million (13,184,407 lei) out of which 46.1 per cent were donations. Total party spending declared in the 2009 EP elections (€5 million, 21,121,893 lei) was close to the 2007 figures and much lower compared to the resources invested in the 2008 national election campaign. Low EP campaign spending was visible on the electoral posters. The graphic concepts characterizing the 2008 national elections were slightly modified and used again in the 2009 Euro elections. In the electoral campaign for the 2007 EP

Table 30.7 List of Romanian MEPs: seventh legislature

Name	National party	Political group	Committee	Professional background	Year of birth	Gender	Second mandate
Elena Oana Antonescu	PD-L	EPP	Environment, Public Health and Food Safety	Lawyer	1979	Female	no
Elena Băsescu	PD-L	EPP	Petitions	Economist	1980	Female	no
George Becali	PRM	NA	Agriculture and Rural Development	Administrator	1958	Male	no
Sebastian Valentin Bodu	PD-L	EPP	Legal Affairs	Barrister	1970	Male	yes
Victor Boştinaru	PSD	S&D	Regional Development, Petitions	Teacher	1952	Male	yes
Cristian Silviu Buşoi	PNL	ALDE	Budgets, Environment, Public Health and Food Safety	Doctor	1978	Male	yes
Corina Creţu	PSD	S&D	Development (Vice-Chair), Financial, Economic and Social Crisis	Economist	1967	Female	yes
George Sabin Cutaş	PC	S&D	Economic and Monetary Affairs	Engineer	1968	Male	no
Vasilica Viorica Dăncilă	PSD	S&D	Agriculture and Rural Development	Engineer	1963	Female	no
Ioan Enciu	PSD	S&D	Industry, Research and Energy	Engineer, economist	1953	Male	no
Cătălin Sorin Ivan	PSD	S&D	Budgetary Control, Culture and Education	Economist	1978	Male	no
Petru Constantin Luhan	PD-L	EPP	Regional Development	Financial manager	1977	Male	no

(continued)

Table 30.7 (continued)

Name	National party	Political group	Committee	Professional background	Year of birth	Gender	Second mandate
Monica Luisa Macovei	PD-L	EPP	Delegation to the EU-Moldova Parliamentary Cooperation (Chair)	Prosecutor	1959	Female	no
Ramona Nicole Mănescu	PNL	ALDE	Regional Development	Lawyer	1972	Female	yes
Marian-Jean Marinescu	PD-L	EPP	Transport and Tourism	Engineer	1952	Male	yes
Iosif Matula	PD-L	EPP	Regional Development	Engineer	1958	Male	no
Norica Nicolai	PNL	ALDE	Foreign Affairs, Subcommittee on Security and Defence (Vice-Chair)	Lawyer/lecturer	1958	Female	no
Rareş-Lucian Niculescu	PD-L	EPP	Agriculture and Rural Development	Political scientist	1976	Male	yes
Ioan Mircea Paşcu	PSD	S&D	Foreign Affairs	Economist/political scientist	1949	Male	yes
Rovana Plumb	PSD	S&D	Employment and Social Affairs	Economist	1960	Female	yes
Cristian Dan Preda	PD-L	EPP	Foreign Affairs	Political scientist	1966	Female	no
Daciana Octavia Sârbu	PSD	S&D	Delegation for relations with the countries of the Andean Community (Vice-Chair), Committee on the Environment, Public Health and Food Safety	Lawyer	1977	Female	yes

Name	Party	Group	Committee	Profession	Birth	Gender	Re-elected
Adrian Severin	PSD	S&D	Foreign Affairs	Lawyer/professor, reformed pastor	1958	Male	yes
Csaba Sógor	UDMR	EFP	Civil Liberties, Justice and Home Affairs		1964	Male	yes
Theodor Dumitru Stolojan	PD-L	EFP	(Vice-chair) Economic and Monetary Affairs, Special Committee on the Financial, Economic and Social Crisis	Professor of economics	1943	Male	yes
Claudiu Ciprian Tănăsescu	PRM	NA	Environment, Public Health and Food Safety	Economist	1965	Male	no
Silvia-Adriana Țicău	PSD	S&D	(Vice-chair) Committee on Transport and Tourism	Software engineer	1970	Female	yes
László Tőkés	UDMR	EFP	Culture and Education	Pastor	1952	Male	yes
Traian Ungureanu	PD-L	EFP	Employment and Social Affairs	Foreign policy analyst	1958	Male	no
Corneliu Vadim Tudor	PRM	NA	Culture and Education	Sociologist	1949	Male	no
Adina-Ioana Vălean	PNL	AIDE	Industry, Research and Energy, Petitions	Teacher	1968	Female	yes
Renate Weber	PNL	AIDE	Civil Liberties, Justice and Home Affairs	Lawyer/lecturer	1955	Female	yes
Iuliu Winkler	UDMR	EFP	International Trade	Engineer	1964	Male	yes

Source: www.europarl.europa.eu/members/public/geoSearch/search.do?country=RO.

elections, only five parties (Greater Romania Party, Green Party, Socialist Alliance, National Christian Democrat Party, and National Alliance Party) out of 13 limited their spending and ended the campaign within budget, but none of these parties managed to get an EP seat. Total campaign spending in the 2008 national election however, involved almost four times more resources when compared to the 2007 EP election. The different importance attributed to elections was reflected proportionally in the level of donations received. Total campaign financing for 2007 was around € 5.5 million (22,908,144 lei), whilst total party revenue for the campaign was € 3.4 million (14,178,388 lei). The difference (38.2 per cent) was attributed to donations. By comparison, according to the report of the Romanian permanent electoral authority, total campaign spending for the national parliamentary elections in 2008 was about the equivalent of €17 million (70,371,819 lei) out of which 45 per cent came from the parties' budgets and 55 per cent came from donations.

10 Theoretical interpretation of Euro-elections

10.1 Second-Order Election theory

When testing the Second-Order Election model, Koepke and Ringe (2006) found that in CEECs, government parties do not lose systematically in EP Elections and that citizens do not really express a protest vote. A party's relationship with the collapse of Communism, together with the economic situation, can affect its vote share. Parties that evolved from the Communist era are more successful when the economy suffers and parties that evolved from anti-Communist movements are more successful when the economy is doing well (Tucker, 2006). After only two electoral contests organized so far, from the point of view of low turnout, EP elections can be considered secondary in Romania. However, not all the implications of SOE theory apply to the Romanian case. As it will be outlined in this section, second-order elections status does not equally imply large losses for government parties. In Romania, they did not suffer a great decline in electoral support when compared to smaller parties or even in comparison to the previous first-order election.

In a context so supportive of the EU, Romanian turnout in the European elections was quite low. Only 29.5 per cent of Romanians turned out to vote in 2007 and even fewer, 27.7 per cent, turned out in 2009. Romanian participation in the Euro-elections was well below 45.4 and 43 per cent, which were the European means in 2007 and 2009, respectively. Low participation in Euro-elections went hand in hand with the low interest shown in these elections. Eurobarometer figures from autumn 2008 show that only 19 per cent of Romanians knew that the next EP elections would take place in 2009. A majority of 53 per cent, however, declared themselves interested in these elections. In January–February 2009, the percentage of Romanians who knew about the 2009 EP elections rose to 30 per cent, and so did their interest, to 56 per cent. The intention not to vote in elections was under-reported, 7 per cent in autumn 2008 and of 8 per cent in January–February 2009. The percentage of those who definitely intended to vote was 20 per cent in autumn 2008 and 26 per cent in January–February 2009, figures that were very close to the actual turnout.

There is an obvious gap between Euro-elections and national elections, which confirms the supremacy of first-order elections. Compared to the latest national elections, turnout in the first European elections was almost 30 per cent lower. Political parties gave higher priority to national elections and did not make similar efforts to mobilize the electorate for their EP candidates. Participation in the national elections organized before and after the Euro-election was higher, with 10 per cent in 2008 parliamentary elections and with almost 20 per cent in the second tour of the presidential elections. The latter were organized only six months after the European elections. Participation in the presidential elections of November 2009 was 56.9 per cent.

When one compares the 2009 Euro-elections to the 2008 national election results, the governing parties (PD-L and UDMR) did not lose votes to the opposition parties and the PD-L vote share was almost identical with that of PSD-PC. The independent candidate Elena Băsescu, daughter of President Traian Băsescu, re-joined the PD-L after the election, which established equality between the EP mandates won by the Social Democrats and the Democratic Liberals. Lower turnout in European elections did not necessarily affect the supporters of parties in government more as opposed to those in opposition. The vast majority of those who voted for the opposition or the incumbent parties in the 2008 national elections, also voted in the 2009 European elections. Out of the PSD voters in 2008, 70 per cent of them voted in the EP elections as well, against 30 per cent who did not vote. Similar participation was registered from amongst the PD-L voters, 66 per cent of them participated in the EP elections against 34 per cent who did not; and from the PNL voters as well, 71 per cent against 29 per cent. The most mobilized and constant voters are those of the UDMR; 78 per cent of its voters in the national elections also voted in the European elections.

Large parties did not lose a large percentage of votes to smaller parties. The Hungarian minority party maintained a constant vote share across all the national and European elections. Because of the high mobilization of the Hungarian minority and given the low turnout of the Romanian population, compared to the 2008 national elections, the UDMR increased their vote share by 2 per cent. There is no strong Green Party on the Romanian political landscape. The vote share of other small parties such as the Green Party at the 2007 European elections was very low, below 1 per cent, and they did not participate in the 2009 elections. The far-right, Greater Romania Party did not gain national parliamentary representation in 2008, but won three MEPs seats in the 2009 EP elections.

The results and the turnout did not appear to be influenced by electoral timing. Whilst the 2007 EP elections came towards the end of the election cycle, with the 2008 parliamentary elections approaching, the 2009 EP elections took place at the beginning of the electoral cycle, with the next parliamentary elections held at the end of 2012 and the turnout in both elections was very similar – 29.5 per cent and 27.7 per cent in 2007 and 2009 respectively.

10.2 Europe Salience theory

The complementary Europe Salience theory does not find support for the majority of its predictions in the Romanian case. The theory posits that Europe matters in European elections through party policy positioning, low turnout should go hand in hand with declining support for European integration, and, as a consequence, extreme parties should do better in European elections than in national elections (Hix and Marsh, 2007). In the case of the 2007 and 2009 EP elections in Romania, low turnout did not go hand in hand with low support for European unification. A large majority of Romanians who did not vote in the Euro-elections still thought that EU membership was a good thing.

The far-right Greater Romania Party won three seats in the European Parliament in the 2009 Euro elections. The party opposed the country's accession to the European Union in the 1990s, then changed its discourse due to electoral reasons, and in 2009 went back to an anti-EU integration stance (Borz and Rose, 2010, 1). Two-thirds of its party's voters were, however, pro-integration, suggesting that the party's position on the EU was not decisive when they cast their vote. There was no strong Green Party on the Romanian political landscape. The vote share of the Green Party in the 2007 European elections was very low, below 1 per cent, and their lists were not accepted in the 2009 elections due to a lack of sufficient signatures.

Another indication of the lack of focus on EU policy issues and the EU elections was their overlap with other important national political issues. In 2007, the EU elections were postponed until November and overlapped with the referendum for the uninominal vote. The second European ballot in June 2009 was coloured by messages about the forthcoming presidential contest organized later in November that year. In 2009 the media and national parties used the EP electoral contest to signal the approach of the presidential elections, especially given the fragile relations between the incumbent Romanian President Traian Băsescu and Parliament. During his 2004–2009 mandate, a referendum was held in May 2007 after a joint session of the legislature voted to suspend the President from office on account of unconstitutional conduct. Almost 75 per cent of voters backed Băsescu and he was formally reinstated as a President on 23 May (Borz, 2009a, 480). The move against the President was caused by his active role in politics, especially his strong stance against corruption. This created political tensions, especially in the context of a lack of a majority to back him in the national Parliament.

References

Primary sources

Autoritatea electorală permanentă (Romanian Permanent Electoral Authority) 2009: www.roaep.ro/ro/section.php?id=11&termen=alegeri+2009&filtru=t2&page=5 (accessed on December 2011).
Biroul Electoral Central (Central Electoral Bureau) (2009): www.bec.ro (accessed on 27 December 2011).
European Commision, Eurobarometer (2008) Public Opinion in the EU, 70: http://ec.europa.eu/public_opinion/archives/eb/eb70/eb70_full_en.pdf (accessed on 8 January 2012).
European Commission, Eurobarometer (2009) Public Opinion in the EU, 71: http://ec.europa.eu/public_opinion/archives/eb/eb71/eb71_std_part1.pdf (accessed on 8 January 2012).
European Parliament Database (2010): www.europarl.europa.eu/meps/eu/search.html (accessed on 10 January 2015).
Eurostat (2013, 2014) http://epp.eurostat.ec.europa.eu (accessed on 5 June 2015).
Political Parties, www.psd.ro; www.partidulconservator.ro; www.pdl.org.ro; www.pnl.ro; www.udmr.ro; www.prm.org.ro; www.parties-and-elections.de (accessed on 2 April 2010).
România Liberă (2009a) http://www.romanialibera.ro (accessed on 27 May 2009).
România Liberă (2009b) http://www.romanialibera.ro (accessed on 11 May 2009).
Romanian National Institute of Statistics (2005) 'Romanian Statistical Yearbook': www.insse.ro/cms/files/pdf/ro/cap1.pdf (accessed on July 2011).
Ziare (2007) www.ziare-online.com/ (accessed on 14 November 2007).

Secondary sources

Birch, S. (2003) *Electoral Systems and Political Transformation in Post-Communist Europe*, London, Palgrave Macmillan.
Borz, G. (2009a) 'Romania' *Political Parties of the World*, London, John Harper Publishing, 478–84.
Borz, G. (2009b) *Determinants of Party Unity in Europe. A Comparative Study of Parliamentary Parties in 23 Countries*, Budapest, Central European University, unpublished PhD dissertation.
Borz, G. and Rose, R. (2010) *Mapping Parties across Europe with Profiler Data*, Aberdeen, CSPP Studies in Public Policy, 470.
Constantiniu, F. (2008) *O istorie sinceră a poporului roman*, București, Editura Univers enciclopedic.
Hix, S. and Marsh, M. (2007) 'Punishment or Protest? Understanding European Parliament Elections', *Journal of Politics*, 69(2), 495–510.
Koepke, J. R. and Ringe, N. (2006) 'The Second-Order Election Model in Enlarged Europe', *European Union Politics*, 7(3), 321–46.
Lewis, P. G. (2000) *Political Parties in Post-Communist Eastern Europe*, London/ New York, Routledge.
Miller, W. L., White, S. and Heywood, P. (1998) 'Political Values Underlying Partisan Cleavages in Former Communist Countries', *Electoral Studies*, 17(2), 197–216.

Radu, A. (2009) 'Alegeri europarlamentare, experiența romanească' ['European Elections, the Romanian Experience'], *Sfera Politicii (Political Sphere)*, 136.

Rose, R. and Borz, G. (2010) 'Variability in European Parliament Turnout: Political Causes and Implications', Aberdeen, CSPP Studies in Public Policy, 466.

Rose, R. and Mishler, W. (1998) 'Negative and Positive Identification in Post-communist Countries', *Electoral Studies*, 17(2), 217–34.

Rose, R. and Munro, N. (2013) *Parties and Elections in New European Democracies*, Colchester, ECPR press.

Stănciulescu, A. (2008) 'Electoral Accountability in Central Eastern Europe: Bulgaria, Czech Republic, Hungary and Romania', Florence, University of Florence, unpublished PhD dissertation.

Swain, G. and Swain, N. (1993) *Eastern Europe Since 1945*, London, Macmillan.

Tucker, J. A. (2006) *Regional Economic Voting: Russia, Poland, Hungary, Slovakia and the Czech Republic, 1990–99*, New York, Cambridge University Press.

Wyman, M., White,S., Miller B., and Heywood, P. (1995) 'The Place of "Party" in Post-communist Europe', *Party Politics,* 1(4), 535–48.

31
FINAL REMARKS
Comparative analysis of European elections

Donatella M. Viola

1 Introduction

Prior to concluding our exploratory journey into the European Parliament (EP) elections across the European Union, it seems appropriate to present the comparative findings of this collaborative project and raise some general observations in order to catch the essence of this relatively recent expression of popular representation.

It is widely acknowledged that electoral systems stand as core factors of democracy, since they influence not only Parliament's composition but, most importantly, the nature of the relationship between representatives and voters. In fact, the primary scope of politics within a representative democracy is rooted to the crucial function of elections whereby citizens may choose 'to throw the scoundrels out', hence causing the collapse of the government (Weiler, 1999, 350). Paradoxically, such a fundamental democratic prerogative does not exist within the European Union, in view of the fact that there is no government to nominate and thus to reject. Neither the European Parliament nor national Parliaments are entitled to fulfil this function at the EU level and, undeniably, the EP's privilege to dismiss the European Commission cannot be comparable to the sacrosanct right of bringing a government down (Weiler, 1999). Even if this evident shortcoming has not been fully redressed, some initial steps have been made in order to establish a closer link between the European Parliament, the European Council, and the European Commission. Further to the ratification of the Treaty of Lisbon on 1 December 2009, the EU government leaders have to 'take into account' the results of the Euro-elections when deciding on the Head of the Commission. Albeit indirectly, this connection may therefore open the way to a sort of transnational electoral accountability and control (EP, 2010).

As such, on the eve of the 2014 EP contest, the main European political families put forward their nominations to the Commission presidency so that the candidate indicated by the largest political group in the newly elected assembly would be proposed by the European Council and later endorsed by the plenary. For this purpose, parliamentary pressure was successfully exerted on the EU national governments. In fact, all the heads of state or governments of the 28 EU Member States, except for British Prime Minister David Cameron, decided to support Jean-Claude Juncker as Commission President rather than submitting an alternative candidature by building a majority-winning coalition amongst the main political alignments.

Final remarks

The comparative analysis that we are going to undertake here is based on the investigation conducted in Part II of this volume, which focuses on the first seven sets of the EP elections, held in 27 EU countries within a 30-year period from 1979 until 2009. The most recent EP contest which took place in May 2014 will be, instead, assessed separately in the Epilogue. Accordingly, in more than half the cases, referring to the Old Member States, the relevant conclusions are based on a fairly long electoral sequence. Conversely, for the New Member States that joined the EU in 2004 and 2007, such an evaluation is inevitably framed within a decidedly narrower time span, encompassing only two sets of EP voting. As a result, whereas any explanations arising from the former can be considered more definite and reliable, any interpretation regarding the latter is inevitably less rigorous and exhaustive, thus requiring further evidence to see whether it may be borne out.

By taking into account such an asymmetrical background, we will attempt to sketch out an overall picture of Euro-elections. To this avail, Table 31.1 offers a useful prospectus of the key features of EU Member States by highlighting several types of differentiations. After indicating their respective dates of entry to the European Community/Union, a distinction is made between small and big countries, not simply according to their geographical size or their number of inhabitants, but also considering their geopolitical, historical and economic peculiarities.

Stemming from Samuel P. Huntington's classification, another dichotomy is drawn between old and new democracies, set prior to or after 1974. The American scholar has aptly detected three waves of democracy in modern history. The first wave occurred between 1776 and 1914, sanctioning the transition from absolute monarchies to representative regimes, through an evolutionary process in Great Britain and a revolutionary movement in France.

The second wave took place in the aftermath of World War II, sanctioning the defeat of Fascism in Italy and of Social-Nazism in Germany as well as inspiring and favouring the European unification project. The third wave began in the mid-1970s with the peaceful *coup d'état* in Portugal, known as '*Revolução dos cravos*' ('Carnation Revolution'), the collapse of the Dictatorship of the Colonels in Greece, and the end of Francisco Franco's era in Spain. Subsequently, this wave was extended to incorporate the radical, political, and social transformations which swept away Communism in Central and Eastern Europe, after the fall of the Berlin Wall on the night of 9 November 1989 (Huntington, 1991).

Finally, two divisions are outlined between pro- and anti-European Members as well as between pro- and anti-euro countries. These are based on the answers given in spring 2013 by a sample of citizens, weighted socio-demographically and politically to ensure its representativeness, across the 27 Member States, to the following questions:

> In general, does the EU conjure up for you a very positive, fairly positive, neutral, fairly negative or very negative image?
>
> What is your opinion on European economic and monetary union with one single currency, the euro? For or Against?
>
> *(Eurobarometer 79, spring 2013)*

Inevitably, this classification bears the strong limits typical of polls that cannot take into account the manifold aspects that influence and shape popular attitude to the European Union. The survey has indicated a positive approach in 17 out of 27 cases, notably in Bulgaria, which marked the top percentage of 54, and then, in decreasing order, in Malta, Poland, Romania, Luxembourg, Lithuania, Belgium, Denmark, Slovakia, France, Ireland, Estonia, Italy, Germany, Slovenia, Hungary, and Latvia.

Table 31.1 EU Member State key features

Country	EU Membership F	I	II	III	IV	V	Pro-EU	Anti-EU	Pro-euro	Anti-euro	Big	Small	Old democracy pre-1974	New democracy post-1974
France	X	—	—	—	—	—	X	—	X	—	X	—	X	—
Germany	X	—	—	—	—	—	X	—	X	—	X	—	X BRD	X (End of DDR 1990)
Italy	X	—	—	—	—	—	X	—	X	—	X	—	X	—
Belgium	X	—	—	—	—	—	X	—	X	—	—	X	X	—
Netherlands	X	—	—	—	—	—	—	X	X	—	—	X	X	—
Luxembourg	X	—	—	—	—	—	X	—	X	—	—	X	X	—
UK	—	X	—	—	—	—	X	X	—	X	X	—	X	—
Ireland	—	X	—	—	—	—	X	X	—	—	—	X	X	—
Denmark	—	X	—	—	—	—	—	X	—	X	—	X	X	—
Greece	—	—	X	—	—	—	—	X	X	—	X	—	—	X 1981
Spain	—	—	—	X	—	—	—	X	X	—	X	—	—	X
Portugal	—	—	—	X	—	—	—	X	X	—	—	X	—	X
Austria	—	—	—	—	X	—	—	X	X	—	—	X	X	—
Finland	—	—	—	—	X	—	—	X	X	—	—	X	X	—
Sweden	—	—	—	—	X	—	—	X	X	—	—	X	X	—
Malta	—	—	—	—	—	Xa	X	—	X	—	—	X	X	—
Cyprus	—	—	—	—	—	Xa	X	—	X	—	—	X	X	—
Slovenia	—	—	—	—	—	Xa	X	—	X	—	—	X	—	X
Estonia	—	—	—	—	—	Xa	X	—	X	—	—	X	—	X
Latvia	—	—	—	—	—	Xa	X	—	—	X	—	X	—	X
Lithuania	—	—	—	—	—	Xa	X	—	—	X	—	X	—	X
Czech Republic	—	—	—	—	—	Xa	—	X	—	—	—	X	—	X
Slovakia	—	—	—	—	—	Xa	X	—	X	—	—	X	—	X
Hungary	—	—	—	—	—	Xa	X	—	X	—	X	—	—	X
Poland	—	—	—	—	—	Xa	X	—	—	X	X	—	—	X
Bulgaria	—	—	—	—	—	Xb	X	—	X	—	—	X	—	X
Romania	—	—	—	—	—	Xb	X	—	X	—	—	X	—	X

Notes:

F = Founding Member 1952–1958;
I = First Enlargement 1973;
II = Second Enlargement 1981;
III = Third Enlargement 1986;
IV = Fourth Enlargement 1995;
V = Xa: Fifth Enlargement 2004;
Xb: Fifth Enlargement 2007.

'In general, does the EU conjure up for you a very positive, fairly positive, neutral, fairly negative or very negative image?'
'What is your opinion on European economic and monetary union with one single currency, the euro? For or Against?' Eurobarometer EB79, Spring 2013.

By contrast, a critical stance to EU policies emerged in the remaining ten countries led by Cyprus, with 59 per cent, followed by Greece, the UK, Portugal, Spain, the Czech Republic, the Netherlands, Austria, Finland, and Sweden. Unexpectedly, this group includes three countries – the Netherlands, Greece, and Spain – that have reversed their traditionally pro-European trend, albeit remaining in favour of European economic and monetary union (Eurobarometer 73, spring 2013). Certainly, this change of attitude may be interpreted as a temporary reaction to the global financial crisis that has severely hit the Greek and Spanish economies, thus compelling people to look at the European Union under a different light. By reflecting this 'seemingly contagious spread of anti-Europeanism' at national level, a welter of Eurosceptic parties has flourished over the years, as will be illustrated further (Weiler, 2012, 831).

2 Theoretical interpretation of Euro-elections

In the light of the theoretical framework outlined in Chapter 3 of this book, and on the basis of the rich source of national data, accurately gathered in the country reviews, we will seek to uncover some of the major themes of the EP electoral contests, supported by a few comparative tables. More precisely, we will try to ascertain which of the tenets of the Second-Order Election (SOE) and Europe Salience (ES) models may be applied to EP contests in all EU Member States and to what extent such assumptions have been consistent since 1979 (Hix and Marsh, 2007).

2.1 Second-Order Election theory

2.1.1 The electoral campaign

The classical SOE theory posits that EP elections embody 'mid-term tests' or 'dress rehearsals' for subsequent general electoral competitions. As such, they are based on domestic political cleavages rather than policies originating in the European Community and later the European Union (Reif and Schmitt, 1980). In other words, they could be defined as second-degree national elections 'à prétexte européen' (with a European pretext) (Bibes et al., 1979, 986).

As clearly emerged in the original expert surveys, Euro-elections in the 27 EU countries have been dominated by tensions between governing and opposition parties, mainly over domestic issues. Questions inherent to the European Union have not so far characterized EP electoral debates. When, occasionally, European concerns have been raised, these have been mainly geared toward retaining national political control over EU decision-making or focussed on advantages or disadvantages of such a membership.

Rightly or wrongly, Brussels has been blamed for the aggravated economic and social conditions arising from the euro-crisis, especially in Greece, Ireland, Portugal, Spain, Cyprus, and Italy. The European Union has turned into an 'emblem of austerity', whilst its institutions have become the natural scapegoat for the most contentious and disliked political choices, a strategy often adopted by Eurosceptic parties to attract votes (Weiler, 2012, 831).

As Peter Mair has cunningly observed, 'through Europe, [. . .] politicians [have gradually divested] themselves of responsibility for potentially unpopular policy decisions and so [have] cushion[ed] themselves against possible voter discontent' (Mair, 2005, 20).

Based on the interpretations of the national experts who contributed to this volume, Table 31.2 summarizes the impact of national and European issues by indicating a range of numbers from '1' to '5'. More specifically, '1' and '2' imply respectively that domestic concerns have been addressed in an exclusive or predominant manner, '3' attributes an equal importance to both matters, '4' confirms that the campaigns have dealt predominantly with European policies, whilst '5' suggests that Europe has been the core of public debate.

In line with the hypothesis underpinning that 'Europe matters more', where public support for the EU project is low, the highest aggregate scores, based respectively on seven and four electoral rounds, have been reached in Denmark and Sweden. In fact, in these two Nordic countries, notoriously adverse to 'Brussels' bureaucracy' and to the adoption of the euro, intense and heated discussions have been recurrent. In 2009, the traditional pro-/anti-EU dispute once again echoed in Denmark, albeit undertaken in a less inflammatory fashion. Likewise, in Sweden the campaign strongly focussed on European issues, featuring EU-critical lists along with Europhile candidates.

By regularly combining both national and European elements, the Finnish EP campaign can be located, instead, in the middle of the range, under mark '3'. In accordance with

Table 31.2 European Parliament election campaign issues: 1979–2009

Country	1979	1984	1989	1994	1999	2004	2009
France	2	1	2	2	2	2	2
Germany	2	2	2	2	2	1-2	2
Italy	2	2	3	2	2	2	2
Belgium	3	3	3	3	2	2	2
Netherlands	2	1	1	1	1-2	2	2
Luxembourg	2	2	2	2	2	2	2
UK	2	2	2	—	2	2	1
Ireland	1	1	1	1	1	1	2
Denmark	5	4	2	5	5	3	3
Greece	2 (1981)	2	2	2	2	2	2
Spain	—	2 (1987)	3	3	3	3	3
Portugal	—	3 (1987)	2	3	3	3	2
Austria	—	—	—	2 (1996)	2	2	2
Finland	—	—	—	3 (1996)	3	3	3
Sweden	—	—	—	4 (1995)	3	3	3
Malta	—	—	—	—	—	2	2
Cyprus	—	—	—	—	—	1	2
Slovenia	—	—	—	—	—	2	2
Estonia	—	—	—	—	—	4	2
Latvia	—	—	—	—	—	2	2
Lithuania	—	—	—	—	—	2	2
Czech Republic	—	—	—	—	—	2	2
Slovakia	—	—	—	—	—	2	1
Hungary	—	—	—	—	—	1	1
Poland	—	—	—	—	—	2	2
Bulgaria	—	—	—	—	—	2 (2007)	2
Romania	—	—	—	—	—	1 (2007)	2

Source: Table based on information provided by the authors of the country chapters.

Note:
1 = Exclusively national issues.
2 = Predominantly national issues.
3 = Equal importance of national and European issues.
4 = Predominantly European issues.
5 = Exclusively European issues.

the realist theory of European integration, the core of the debate centred on the need to safeguard domestic interests within the European Union, by maintaining, for instance, the Nordic welfare model or even extending it to the EU level. Lastly, the lowest values were attained in Hungary whereby, despite a critical approach to the EU construct, European discourse was disregarded in 2004 and 2009. These mixed results, arising from diverse national political settings and relating to specific temporal circumstances, have made it extremely hard to unearth a precise and direct nexus between EU-driven campaigns and anti-European attitudes.

On the other hand, a comparison with first-order elections unveils shorter and lacklustre EP campaigns, marked by lower expense ceilings, which focus on domestic issues falling outside the realm of competences of future MEPs. European electoral contests do not elicit public interest, mostly due to uninspiring political debates featuring scarce antagonism between the main parties over the European Union. This may stem from the absence of a common European identity as well as from the fact that the European Union is 'policy without politics'.

In Peter Mair's words:

> The efforts to displace conflict dimension into arenas where democratic authority is lacking, as well as the efforts to depolitici[z]e issues that relate to European integration, has led to the development of a distinct political system in which the exercise of popular control and electoral accountability proves very difficult.
>
> (Mair, 2004, 339)

Until now, European citizens have been unable to perform a true civic act affecting the outcome of EU policy, whilst parties have hardly offered distinctive programmes and alternative manifestos (Weiler, 1999). Most specifically, the 2009 campaigns in the UK and Italy were overshadowed respectively by corruption scandals and controversial news about the private life of the Italian Prime Minister. In Austria, the Czech Republic and Romania, extreme right-wing anti-establishment movements and anti-integrationist parties also displaying xenophobic tendencies attracted great popular attention. In several Eurosceptic countries, the campaign raised lingering questions over the value of EU membership that had also characterized the pre-accession period. Unequivocally, the seventh EP contest was affected by past legacies and persistent doubts, coupled with concerns about the potential accession of new partners. In Slovenia, the upcoming entry of Croatia to the EU dominated the pre-electoral debate, especially because of an unresolved frontier dispute.

Meanwhile, a few attempts at opening a cross-border debate were made in order to reach out to co-nationals or members of the same language group. For instance, in Hungary Viktor Orbán, the leader of the *Fiatal Demokraták Szövetsége-Magyar Polgári Szövetség*, FIDESZ-MPSZ (Federation of Young Democrats-Hungarian Civic Alliance), and in Slovakia Pál Csáky, the chairman of the *Strana mad'arskej koalície-Magyar Koalíció Pártja*, SMK-MPK (Party of the Hungarian Coalition), carried out a joint campaign mostly geared towards defending the interests of the Hungarian minority in the Carpathian Basin. As witnessed five years earlier, when the Basque Nationalist political party named *Herritarren Zerrenda*, HZ (List of Fellow Citizens) was created in Spain and France to run in the EP elections, in 2009 in both countries the Basque parties cooperated actively. Overall, high-ranking personalities of national political parties rather than the actual candidates dominated the 2009 Euro-election campaign in most Member States. With the exception of Malta, where the atmosphere was flamboyant with public debates, rallies, meetings, canvassing, and media advertising combined with an extensive use of billboards and brochures, the climate surrounding EP elections across the European Union was less vibrant than that usually preceding national presidential or parliamentary contests (OSCE/ODIHR, 2009).

Throughout the years, the quality of communication on Europe has not truly improved. As such, in order to raise voters' awareness, the European Parliament has gradually promoted an EU-wide information campaign through the media and the internet. In particular, in 2009, the common slogan 'It's your choice' was adopted by most Member States. The same advertising material, including posters, banners, billboards as well as outdoor installations, was translated into all 23 official languages, along with additional regional languages, and distributed across the European Union. The local offices of the EP selected four out of the ten themes that were most suitable to the specific circumstances of the countries concerned, or more tuned to their national audience. Special websites were designed for the event, whilst internet and social networks — including MySpace, YouTube, Facebook, and Flickr — were used together with photo and video applications for the purpose of grabbing the attention of young voters especially (EP Information Office, 2009).

General features of the seventh EP campaign also consisted of TV and radio spots, mainly aired free by broadcasters, seminars with journalists from public and private media, lectures to school and university students, lunchtime conferences, and articles on European topics and interviews. In some cases, prior to the opening of national political party campaigns, MEPs intervened in public meetings in order to explain the role of the European Parliament in EU decision-making and to highlight the impact of such policies in European citizens' lives (ibid.).

In Bulgaria, Denmark, the Czech Republic, and the United Kingdom, election banners were put on buses, taxis, railway carriages and underground trains. In Bulgaria, the electoral contest was advertised during sporting events, whilst debates took place in universities in order to reach first-time voters and young people. The logo and a neon light sign marking EE2009 were placed on the front of the building of the EP Information Offices in Sofia and in Nicosia. In France, with the aim of encouraging female electoral participation, advertisements were introduced in women's magazines, which even opened a contest to win a visit to the European Parliament accompanied by a journalist. In Estonia, an EP Supplement was published in one of the most well-known and popular national newspapers. The Dublin Office produced a guide targeted at non-Irish EU citizens living in the country in order to alert them to the election date and to encourage them to vote. In addition, a double-decker bus toured across Ireland to conduct an information campaign.

In Luxembourg, a special stamp was issued; flags bearing the EE09 logo were displayed on the streets. On 9 May, during the celebrations for Europe's Day, a big wheel was erected displaying such a logo in all the 23 European official languages and Luxembourgish in order to promote EP electoral races, together with multilingualism. In the UK and Portugal, roadshows were arranged with the purpose of publicizing both forthcoming election dates and existing Euro-parliamentary powers. Lastly, events and training sessions were organized especially for young people in Sweden and Romania, whilst in Finland letters were mailed to first-time voters to remind them to go to the polls (ibid.).

2.1.2 Performance of government and opposition parties

By looking at the cross-time trends of Euro-elections held since 1979, it is possible to notice the recurrent defeat of ruling parties, to the benefit of opposition movements, except for Spain and Romania, along with the Netherlands up to 1994. Furthermore, mixed evidence has been found in Finland, with the loss of the major ruling party often counterbalanced by the victory of its political allies in government. Likewise, this thesis did not hold in Slovenia

Final remarks

in 2009, since voters decided to punish the Prime Minister's party, the Social Democrats, but not the whole government coalition, and even rewarded the Liberal Democrats by improving their vote share by 6 per cent, in comparison to the 2008 national election. In Slovakia, the 2009 EP contest took place three years after the legislative ballot and exactly one year prior to the subsequent one, therefore occurring towards the end of the national electoral cycle. Yet, contrary to the prediction of the SOE model, the Slovak ruling party gained about 3 per cent more of the votes achieved in the 2006 national parliamentary election and 15 per cent more of the votes attained in the 2004 EP contest, albeit combined with an exceptionally high abstention rate.

Yet, arguably, most citizens in CEECs did not cast protest votes against ruling parties during Euro-elections, but rather their party choices stemmed from 'sincere voting' (Koepke and Ringe, 2006). Lastly, it is worth mentioning the unique case of Luxembourg where, apart from the 2009 EP ballot, when greater governmental losses were registered, voters did not have to resort to the EP race for sanctioning ruling parties on national issues, as they could castigate incumbents directly in the simultaneous first-order election. In sum, anti-government effects increased significantly across the European Community/Union in the first four sets of elections from 1979 until 1999, falling instead slightly in the fifth to rise again in 2004 until 2009 (Hix and Marsh, 2007, 2011).

2.1.3 Performance of big and small parties

The SOE hypothesis underlying the loss of big parties to the benefit of small political movements in Euro-elections has held strong in seven of the Old EU Member States and three of the New EU partners, where citizens voted 'following their heart'. Now and then, some

Table 31.3a Second-Order Election theory: Old EU Member States

Country	Loss of government parties	Loss of big parties	Impact of timing
France	2 (except 1979)	2	0
Germany	2	2	1
Italy	2	1	2
Belgium	1	2	1
NL	1 (not until 1994)	1 (not until 1994)	1 (not until 1994)
Luxembourg	1 (2009)	0	0
UK	2	1	2
Ireland	2	2	2
Denmark	2	1	1
Greece	1	2	2
Spain	0	0	2
Portugal	1	2	2
Austria	1	1	0
Finland	1	1	1
Sweden	2	2	1

Source: Table based on information provided by the authors of the country chapters.

Note:
0 = Not relevant.
1 = Occasionally/partly fits in.
2 = Fits in completely.

Table 31.3b Second-Order Election theory: New EU Member States

Country	Loss of government parties	Loss of big parties	Impact of timing
Malta	2	1	2
Cyprus	1	1	1
Slovenia	0	1	1
Estonia	2	2	2
Latvia	1	1	0
Lithuania	1	1	2
Czech Republic	1	1	2
Slovakia	0	0	0
Hungary	2	0	2
Poland	1	0	1
Bulgaria	1	2	2
Romania	0	0	0

Source: Table based on information provided by the authors of the country chapters.

Note:
0 = Not relevant.
1 = Occasionally/partly fits in.
2 = Fits in completely.

of these minor parties have successfully maintained their impetus, but this positive trend has been generally reversed in the subsequent national election, confirming that volatility in EP contests is temporary and does not alter the inner structure of the party system (Tóka and Gosselin, 2010).

Moreover, this hypothesis was refuted amongst the veteran members, Luxembourg and Spain, along with the neophytes, Slovakia, Hungary, Poland, and Romania. In the case of Malta, it played a negligible role, with small parties performing better than in general elections, but still failing to get representation in the EP assembly. In the UK, this tenet could not be truly tested between 1979 and 1994, since the application of the first-past-the-post (FPTP) system prevented minor parties from entering the Euro-parliamentary arena. In fact, up to the fourth European legislature, only the Labour and Tory parties in England managed to send their representatives to Strasbourg, whilst Nationalists were successful in Scotland and Wales. Since 1999, with the introduction of a system of proportional representation, it has been possible for members of British smaller parties to regularly obtain seats in the European Parliament. Additionally, this assumption could not be applied to the Danish case, due to the discrepancy in its political system at the national and EU levels, with minor parties running in general but not in EP elections. Such a decision could be explained by strategic concerns connected to the higher electoral threshold to win seats in the European Assembly. In brief, party size mattered in the EP races, but more amongst established democracies featuring consolidated party systems than amongst post-Communist countries (Schmitt, 2005).

2.1.4 Electoral timing

In the SOE perspective, when the EP competition occurs after a general election, government parties, which are still on their honeymoon, are likely to gather a large number of votes. Conversely, when the EP contest is held in the middle of the national election cycle, when ruling parties are engaged to carry out key policy decisions that may be unpopular, they are expected to lose votes in favour of opposition and/or small political parties. Lastly, when the EP race takes place in the build-up to a general election, governing parties seek to regain voters' trust through intense and expensive campaigning, with the twofold scope of winning both competitions.

The extent of vote switching from government to opposition parties, as well as from big to minor parties, may be closely connected to the timing of the EP contest within the national electoral cycle. This temporal factor is deemed crucial for bolstering, weakening, or even invalidating SOE hypotheses. Unfortunately, its overall impact is very hard to evaluate, due to the different duration of the national legislatures in the 27 EU countries and, above all, to the unpredictable length of their governments. It is well known that EP and national electoral races usually follow separate cycles in the various countries. Whereas the European Parliament enjoys a regular five-year life span, Member State national parliaments generally do not have a fixed minimum but just a maximum term, currently ranging from four to five years (Gallagher, 2014, 168). Early legislative elections may be convened after the resignation of the cabinet or the dismissal of the government, as a result of a negative confidence vote that interrupts the natural domestic electoral cycle.

Bearing all this in mind, we have noticed that, in the wake of general elections, government parties have effectively enjoyed the so-called 'honeymoon' effect, thus maintaining their political dominance in the often labelled 'throw-away' elections, particularly in France, the Netherlands, and Austria. Timing also affected the EP electoral outcome in the UK in 1979, in Greece in 2004, as well as in Italy in 1994 and, less strikingly, in 2009. Another case occurred in Spain in 2004, when the Socialist government party even managed to increase its vote share by roughly 1 per cent (ibid.). Luxembourg stands out as *sui generis* due to the long-established conventional concomitance of national and EP contests, which makes this variable null and void.

Timing mattered in Malta, where the 2004 and 2009 EP contests took place respectively just one year after the 2003 and 2008 general competitions, and therefore at the beginning of the national electoral cycle during what is commonly referred to as 'government's honeymoon'. Then again, this period represents the most arduous and contentious in the Maltese political tradition, when severe policy reforms were introduced, inevitably causing a dramatic fall in popular support for the ruling party. Elsewhere across the European Union, instead, as already highlighted, this effect tends to surface in the middle of the national election cycle, when disenchanted government supporters switch their vote in favour of opposition or small political movements (Marsh, 1998).

Admittedly until now, Euro-elections have been secondary, but findings, especially in post-Communist countries, have questioned the 'infallibility' of the SOE theoretical framework (Koepke and Ringe, 2006; Hix and Marsh, 2007). More specifically, Estonia deviates from the standard version of the Second-Order Election model, considering that the main winners were none of the political parties, but independent politicians. Such a peculiar voting behaviour may be ascribed to the effects of an increasingly polarized party system, where disappointed government voters find it inconceivable to switch to the opposition. By supporting an independent candidate, they can still punish the ruling party or coalition without, however, rewarding their traditional political rivals.

2.2 Europe Salience theory

Against this backdrop, little by little, a new conceptual framework, known as Europe Salience (ES) theory, has loomed on the horizon. Its main tenet rests on the belief that EP elections, voters' choices and European Union issues are not entirely unrelated. Indeed, party attitude to the EU politics and policies, whether negative or positive, seems to gradually influence citizens' voting behaviour, whilst growing anti-European sentiments may favour a low turnout, although a systematic empirical link has never been fully established.

According to Hix and Marsh (2007), the ES model entails the following three core postulates:

1. Green movements tend to increase their voting share compared to the previous national elections.
2. Extreme parties on the left–right scale get relatively more votes.
3. Anti-European parties perform better because of their ability to mobilize voters dissatisfied with the European Union.

Undeniably, some of the SOE and ES hypotheses look transversal, bearing in mind that small, opposition, ecologist, extreme, and anti-European movements every so often coincide. In fact, these political actors are often deemed to score better than their rivals, encompassing large, government, traditional, mainstream, and pro-European parties that are also likely to overlap each other.

2.2.1 Performance of Green parties

The hypothesis entailing a better performance of the Greens in EP electoral races has been endorsed in most of the Old Member States, especially Germany, whilst it has been confuted in Austria and Portugal. Also in Spain, *los Verdes* have remained a negligible force, presumably since small left-wing regional parties have devoted great attention to environmental issues.

Amongst the New Member States, some progress has been registered in Malta and Latvia, compared to their preceding national contests. As a matter of fact, it has not been possible to detect an overall Green expansion across the European Union and in particular in CEECs, where this party family still remains at the margin of their national political landscape.

Table 31.3c Europe Salience theory: Old EU Member States

Country	Gain of Greens	Gain of extreme parties	Gain of anti-European parties
Germany	2	1	0
Italy	1	1	1
Belgium	2	2	2
NL	1	1 (since 1999)	1 (2009)
Luxembourg	2	1	0
UK	1	1	1
Ireland	1	0	1
Denmark	2	2 fading	2
Greece	2	1	2
Spain	1	1	0
Portugal	0	2	1
Austria	0	1	2
Finland	2	1	1
Sweden	2	1	2

Source: Table based on information provided by the authors of the country chapters.

Note:
0 = Not relevant.
1 = Occasionally/partly fits in.
2 = Fits in completely.

Final remarks

Table 31.3d Europe Salience theory: New EU Member States

Country	Gain of Greens	Gain of extreme parties	Gain of anti-European parties
Malta	2	2	0
Cyprus	0	1	1
Slovenia	0	0	0
Estonia	0	0	0
Latvia	1	0	0
Lithuania	0	0	0
Czech Republic	0	1	1
Slovakia	0	0	0
Hungary	0	1	1
Poland	0	1	1
Bulgaria	0	1	1
Romania	0	1	1

Source: Table based on information provided by the authors of the country chapters.

Note:
0 = Not relevant.
1 = Occasionally/partly fits in.
2 = Fits in completely.

2.2.2 Performance of extreme parties

The ES hypothesis underpinning gains by extreme political parties at the European level, often hard to disambiguate from the SOE tenet referring to the better performance of minor and opposition parties, has been reliably confirmed in the Old Member States, except in Ireland.

Contrary to the British traditional political culture, hardly conciliable with any form of extremism, the far-right British National Party (BNP) has started to attract electoral support since 2004, eventually securing representation for the first time in the seventh European legislature. Yet, the entry of this party into the EP arena has not been matched with its official access to Westminster, in accordance with the hypothesis that fringe parties are more successful in European rather than national electoral contests.

Conversely, in the New Member States this assumption could not be held true and, at times, it could not even be tested due to the lack of available data within such a narrow time frame. However, in Bulgaria and Romania, the performance of their respective far-right ultra-Nationalist movements, *Ataka* and *Partidul România Mare* (Greater Romania Party), improved sensibly in 2007 for the former and in 2009 for the latter, if compared to their previous national parliament elections.

2.2.3 Performance of Eurosceptic parties

Whereas the advance of Eurosceptic parties in EP elections is strictly connected to their ability to convey popular discontent against Brussels, which occasionally goes as far as wishing to dismantle the whole EU project, it cannot be ignored that governing parties tend to be more pro-European than their political rivals in opposition. As a result, it is difficult to distinguish whether vote-switching in EP races may be due to either SOE or ES effects. Furthermore, as already suggested, a close correlation is recognized between right-wing or left-wing extremism and hard-core Euroscepticism (Hartleb, 2012).

Increasingly through the years, this final hypothesis of the Europe Salience model, which refers to the progress of Eurosceptic movements, has been validated in Old EU countries, except for Spain, Germany, and Luxembourg.

In contrast, often owing to the presence of different actors in the national and European electoral platforms, this assumption has been hardly tested in New Member States and endorsed only sporadically in Cyprus, the Czech Republic, Hungary, Poland, Bulgaria, and Romania. In the case of Latvia, albeit portraying a truly negative attitude towards the European integration, anti-EU movements have not fared well. The reason behind this apparent contradiction may be easily found in the unanimous critical stance towards the European Union, expressed by all political alignments, which has prevented any imaginable competition on this ground. Lastly, since the outbreak of the financial turmoil, there has been an upward anti-EU trend, albeit with considerable variation across the continent. Regardless of their pro-European tradition, the countries most severely hit by the crisis have registered a prominent surge of Euroscepticism, to the extent of matching or even exceeding the EU average (Serricchio et al., 2013).

2.2.4 The evolution of Eurosceptic parties

The 'Question of Europe', long regarded as an English *malaise*, which contagiously, though temporarily, swept through Denmark, has later spread slowly and unevenly to the rest of the Old Continent. Far from undertaking an in-depth and accurate analysis of this phenomenon, which goes well beyond the purpose of this volume, the following section intends to offer some basic understanding of its main aspects by looking at the rise and development of Eurosceptic parties across the European Union and their official admission into the European Parliament's arena in 2009.

The term 'Euroscepticism', coined in the UK to indicate 'a sense of "awkwardness" or "otherness" in relation to a continental European project of political and economic integration', first appeared in the daily newspaper *The Times* on 11 November 1985 (Harmsen and Spiering, 2004, 13, Spiering, 2004). Over time, this concept has evolved to the extent that a distinction has emerged between 'hard' and 'soft' variants of Euroscepticism, with parties often moving between these two poles. Hard Eurosceptics strongly reject European integration by identifying it as their true 'enemy': capitalism for Communists, socialism for the right, bureaucracy for populists, supranationalism for Nationalists and neo-liberalism for Socialists, thus proposing the dismantling of the EU (Taggart and Szczerbiak, 2002). Conversely, soft Eurosceptics perceive the European Union as an 'obstacle' or a 'danger' only when and to the extent that its development may threaten their political interests or challenge national sovereignty, therefore opposing further European integration across the board (ibid.).

In order to trace the evolution and impact of anti-European parties in the EP political spectrum, we have sketched out some tables that display the percentages of their votes and the number of their seats, respectively in the original six members, in the nine countries that entered the European Community between 1973 and 1995 and, ultimately, in the 15 states that joined the European Union in 2005 and 2007.

Within the first category, the cosmopolitan Netherlands, once at the heart of the cause of European project, displays a plethora of anti-EU parties and movements. Amongst them, the *Partej voor de Vrijhed* PVV (Freedom Party) stands out as the most popular hard Eurosceptic party that calls for the withdrawal of the country from the European Union. In 2009, the right-wing populist PVV, led by Geert Wilders, seized four seats in the Strasbourg arena; this increased to five following the modification of national quotas of MEPs according to the Lisbon Treaty.

Paradoxically, France, which launched the European integration process following the Schuman Declaration of 9 May 1950, depicts a wide range of parties and movements that may

Table 31.4a Eurosceptic/Eurocritical parties in the original six countries: 1979–2009

Country	Party*	Origin	1979 %	1979 Seats	1984 %	1984 Seats	1989 %	1989 Seats	1994 %	1994 Seats	1999 %	1999 Seats	2004 %	2004 Seats	2009 %	2009 Seats
France	LO-LCR	1968–1969	3.1	0	2.1	0	1.4	0	2.3	0	5.2	5	3.3	0	4.8	0
	PCF	1920	20.6	19	11.2	10	7.8	7	6.9	7	6.8	6	5.2	2	6.0	4
	MDC	1992	—	—	—	—	—	—	2.5	0	—	—	—	—	—	—
	RPR	1976	16.1	15	—	—	—	—	—	—	—	—	—	—	—	—
	FN	1972	—	—	11.1	10	11.8	10	10.6	11	5.7	5	9.8	7	6.3	3
	DVD	—	1.4	0	—	—	—	—	—	—	—	—	—	—	1.8	0
	MPF	1994–	—	—	—	—	—	—	12.4	13	13.1	13	6.8	3	4.8	1
	DED	—	1.3	0	—	—	—	—	—	—	3.3	0	—	—	0.5	0
	CPNT	1989	—	—	—	—	4.2	0	4.0	0	6.9	6	1.7	0	—	—
Germany	NPD	1964	—	—	0.8	0	—	—	0.2	0	0.4	0	0.9	0	1.3	0
	Republikaner	1983	—	—	—	—	7.1	6	3.9	0	1.7	0	1.9	0	0.4	0
	DVU	1987–2010	—	—	—	—	1.6	0	—	—	—	—	—	—	—	—
	SED-DS/PDS/Linke	1989 SED-DS 1990 PDS 2007 Linke	—	—	—	—	—	—	4.7	0	5.8	6	6.1	7	7.5	8
Italy	DKP	1968	0.4	0	—	—	0.2	0	—	—	—	—	0.1	0	0.1	0
	LL-LV/LN	1984/1980–1989	—	—	0.5	0	1.8	2	6.6	6	4.5	4	5.0	4	10.2	9
	PRC-RC	1991	—	—	—	—	—	—	6.1	5	4.3	4	6.1	5	3.4	0
	AN	1994	—	—	—	—	—	—	12.5	11	10.3	9	11.5	9	—	—
Belgium	VB	1978	—	—	1.3	0	4.1	1	7.8	2	9.4	2	14.3	3	9.8	2
	LDD_	2007	—	—	—	—	—	—	—	—	—	—	—	—	4.5	1
Netherlands	Orthodox Protestants:															
	SGP	1918	3.3	0	5.2	1	5.9	1	7.8	2	8.7	3	5.9	2	6.8	2
	GPV	1948														
	RPF	1975														
	CU	2000														

(continued)

Table 31.4a (continued)

Country	Party*	Origin	1979 %	1979 Seats	1984 %	1984 Seats	1989 %	1989 Seats	1994 %	1994 Seats	1999 %	1999 Seats	2004 %	2004 Seats	2009 %	2009 Seats
	Extreme left:															
	CPN	1909	5.1	0	5.6	2	7	2	—	—	—	—	—	—	—	—
	PSP	1957														
	PPR	1968														
	EVP	1981														
	GL	1990														
	CD	1984	—	—	2.5	0	0.8	0	1.1	0	—	—	—	—	—	—
	SP	1971	—	—	—	—	0.6	0	1.3	0	5.1	1	7.0	2	7.1	2
	LPF/ PVV	2002–2006	—	—	—	—	—	—	—	—	—	—	2.5	0	17.0	4 (5)
	ET	2004	—	—	—	—	—	—	—	—	—	—	7.3	2	3.5	0
	PvdD	2002	—	—	—	—	—	—	—	—	—	—	3.2	0	1.5	0
Luxembourg	KPL	1921	—	0	4.1	0	4.7	0	1.6	0	—	—	1.2	0	3.4	0
	Déi Lenk	1999	—	—	—	—	—	—	—	—	2.8	0	1.7	0	7.4	0
	ADR	1987	—	—	—	—	—	—	6.9	0	9	0	8.0	0	1.4	0
	BL	2009	—	—	—	—	—	—	—	—	—	—	—	—		

Source: Table based on information provided by the authors of the country chapters.

Note:
* The list of Eurosceptic/Eurocritical parties with full names is provided in Table 32.2 of the Appendix.

be located in the anti-EU quadrant of the political landscape. Founded in 1972 by Jean-Marie Le Pen, the extreme right-wing *Front National*, FN (National Front) registered its first electoral success in the 1984 EP contest, when it received 11 per cent of the votes and obtained ten MEPs. Subsequently, FN succeeded to match this fair result in 1989 and 1994, but it saw a significant decline in consensus during the three last EP competitions.

Even the historically pro-European countries, Italy and Belgium, have started to witness the surge of Eurosceptic movements. In 2009, the Italian secessionist *Lega Nord*, LN (Northern League) doubled its voting share from 5 to 10.2 per cent by increasing the number of its seats from four to nine. In Belgium, the far-right Nationalist *Vlaams Belang*, VB (Flemish interest) and the *Lijst Dedecker* (Dedecker List), after the name of its founder, reached the percentages of 9.8 and 4.3 respectively, with the former confirming two of its three seats conquered in 2004 and the latter sending one representative to Strasbourg.

Within the second category, embracing the first four EC/EU enlargement countries, stands out the UK, the home of Euroscepticism that has affected, albeit in different stages, its two major political parties: Conservative and Labour (Spiering, 2004). The former, which negotiated and signed the Accession Treaty to the European Economic Community under the premiership of Sir Edward Heath, gradually acquired anti-European tones during Margaret Thatcher's era. Nowadays, an increasing number of Tory members advocate British exit from the European Union, commonly referred to under the acronym *Brexit*, so that the party could be defined as genuinely Eurosceptic (Kaletsky, 2014). Conversely, the Labour Party, at first hostile to the capitalist project of the Common Market, since 1983 has become more accommodating about European integration, under the leadership of Neil Kinnock. Yet, the party's real pro-European turn occurred only in 1997, under New Labour, guided by the charismatic Prime Minister Tony Blair, adamant supporter of European integration (Smith, 2005).

Meanwhile, two hard Eurosceptic movements have materialized, notably the UK Independence Party (UKIP) and the British National Party (BNP), which obtained for the first time their representation in the EP forum in 2009, mainly at the expense of the Conservatives.

Another partner that has never concealed its mistrust of the European Community is Denmark. Famous for convening six popular referenda on various EU issues, it boasts a large number of conventional parties that direct stern attacks against the European Union, including the *Socialistisk Folkeparti*, SF (Socialist People's Party) and *Dansk Folkeparti*, DF (Danish People's Party). Beyond these traditional political forces, other anti-EU lists have surfaced that run only EP electoral competitions: *Folkebevægelsen mod EF/EU* (People's Movement against the EC/EU) and the *Junibevægelsen* (June Movement). Amongst the countries of the first enlargement, Ireland is by far the most Europhile, having largely benefitted from its membership to the EC/EU. However, in 2009, an intense and expensive campaign sponsored by the Irish magnate Declan Ganley attempted in vain to capitalize on a new Eurosceptic wave. His pan-European list, called *Libertas*, did not meet with the expected popular consensus and failed to grab even just one seat in the Strasbourg Assembly.

In Greece, the imposition of harsh austerity by the EU troika, the European Central Bank and the International Monetary Fund has resulted in enormous economic difficulties and societal conflicts. Undeniably, this background has favoured the surge from obscurity of the far-right, hard Eurosceptic *Crysse Avge*, CA (Golden Dawn). What is alarming is that such a political organization is able to attract citizens' support by calling for Greek withdrawal from the European Union whilst exalting neo-Nazi ideology and culture. Although up to 2009, no CA member sits in the EP arena, the situation is likely to change after the 2014 Euro-election.

By turning our attention to those EU Member States admitted in 1995, Austria represents the country with the largest number of parties that are against further deepening and enlargement of

Table 31.4b Eurosceptic/Eurocritical parties in Old EU enlargement countries: 1979–2009

Country	Party*	Origin	1979 (1981) %	Seats	1984 (1987) %	Seats	1989 %	Seats	1994 (1995–1996) %	Seats	1999 %	Seats	2004 %	Seats	2009 %	Seats
UK	CON	1832	48.4	60	38.8	45	33.0	32	27.0	18	35.8	36	26.7	27	27.7	25
	LAB	1900	31.6	17	34.7	32	39.0	45	42.6	62	28.0	29	22.6	19	15.7	13
	UKIP	1993	—	—	—	—	—	—	—	—	7.0	3	16.2	12	16.5	13
	BNP	1982	—	—	—	—	—	—	1.0	0	4.9	0	4.9	0	6.2	2
Ireland	SF	1905	—	—	—	—	—	—	—	—	—	—	11.1	1	11.2	0
	SP	1996	—	—	—	—	—	—	—	—	—	—	1.3	0	2.7	1
	Libertas	2009	—	—	—	—	—	—	—	—	—	—	—	—	5.4	0
Denmark	Folkebevægelsen mod EF/EU	1972	2.0	4	20.8	4	18.9	4	10.3	2	7.3	1	5.2	1	7.2	1
	Junibevægelsen	1992	—	—	—	—	—	—	15.2	2	16.1	3	9.1	1	2.4	0
	SF	1959	5.0	1	9.2	1	9.1	1	8.6	1	7.1	1	7.9	1	15.9	2
	RF	1919	3.4	0	—	—	—	—	—	—	—	—	—	—	—	—
	VS	1967	3.5	0	1.3	0	—	—	—	—	—	—	—	—	—	—
	FrP	1972	5.8	1	3.5	0	5.3	0	2.9	0	0.7	0	—	—	—	—
	DF	1995	—	—	—	—	—	—	—	—	5.8	1	6.8	1	15.3	2
Greece	KKE	1918	12.8 (1981)	3	11.6	3	—	—	6.3	2	8.7	3	9.5	3	8.6	2
Portugal	CA	1993	—	—	—	—	—	—	0.1	0	0.8	0	—	—	0.5	0
	PC	1921	—	—	11.5 (1987)	3	14.4	4	11.2	3	10.3	2	9.1	2	10.6	2
Austria	FPÖ	1955	—	—	—	—	—	—	27.5 (1996)	6	23.4	5	6.3	1	12.7	2
	BZÖ	2005	—	—	—	—	—	—	—	—	—	—	—	—	4.7	0
	HPM	2004	—	—	—	—	—	—	—	—	—	—	14.0	2	17.7	3
Finland	PS	1995	—	—	—	—	—	—	0.7 (1996)	0	0.8	0	0.5	0	9.8	1
	KD	1958	—	—	—	—	—	—	2.8 (1995)	0	2.4	1	4.3	0	4.2	1
Sweden	V	1917	—	—	—	—	—	—	12.9	3	15.8	3	12.8	2	5.7	1
	MP	1981	—	—	—	—	—	—	17.2	4	9.5	2	6.0	1	11	2
	JL	2004	—	—	—	—	—	—	—	—	—	—	14.5	3	3.5	0
	SD	1988	—	—	—	—	—	—	—	—	—	—	1.1	0	3.3	0

Source: Table based on information provided by the authors of the country chapters.

Note:
* The list of Eurosceptic/Eurocritical parties with the full names is provided in Table 32.2 of the Appendix.

Final remarks

the European Union. Amongst these, the Hans Peter Martin List, founded in 2004 by former correspondent of *Der Spiegel* and bearing his name, obtained 14 per cent of the vote and two seats in 2004, rising to 17.7 per cent and three seats in 2009. In Finland, the hard-core Eurosceptic party The Finns, founded and guided by the folksy politician Timo Soini, managed for the first time in 2009 to secure representation in the EP arena, thanks to an electoral percentage of 9.8.

By and large, an intense anti-European party wave has swept over the EU Member States, with the only exception being Spain, where no hard Eurosceptic movement has emerged up to now. Nevertheless, since 2004, the attitude of the *Partido Popular*, PP (People's Party) has become more 'Euroexigente' (Euro-demanding), as stated by former Minister and MEP Jaime Mayor Oreja (Marcos, 2004).

Amid all anti-European political platforms across the European Union, the record of popular consensus was conquered by the Cypriot *Anorthotikó Kómma Ergazómenou Laoú*, AKEL (Progressive People's Party), which seized an exceptional percentage of 34.9. Yet, it is worth noting that this party has turned from a hard to a soft Eurosceptic position, gradually

Table 31.4c Eurosceptic/Eurocritical parties in New EU enlargement countries: 2004–2009

Country	Party*	Origin	2004 (2007) %	2004 (2007) Seats	2009 %	2009 Seats
Malta	AN	2007	—	—	0.6	0
	Libertas	2009	—	—	0.1	0
Cyprus	AKEL	1941	27.9	2	34.9	2
Slovenia	SNS	1991	5.0	0	2.8	0
Estonia	LEE	2009	—	—	0.6	0
	PK	1992	—	—	0.1	0
	EDE	2001	1.2	0	—	0
	ESDTP	1992	0.5	0	—	—
Latvia	*Libertas.lv*	2009	—	—	4.3	0
	RP	2009	—	—	0.4	0
	OP	2008	—	—	0.3	0
	Eiroskeptiķi	2003	0.9	0	—	—
Lithuania	TPP	1994	1.2	0	—	—
	LCP	2003 (2005)	—	—	3.1	0
Czech Republic	KSCM	1990	20.3	6	14.2	4
	NEZDEM	2005	8.2	2	0.5	0
	SBB	2009	—	—	4.3	0
	SSO	2009	—	—	1.3	0
Slovakia	SaS	2009	—	—	4.7	0
	KSS	1993	4.5	0	1.6	0
	SNS	1989	2.0	0	5.5	1
Hungary	*Jobbik*	2003	—	—	14.8	3
Poland	SRP	1992	10.8	6	1.5	0
	LPR	2001	15.9	10	0	0
	Libertas	2009	—	—	1.1	0
Bulgaria	ATAKA	2005	14.2 (2007)	3	12.0	2
Romania	PRM	1991	4.1 (2007)	0	8.7	3

Source: Table based on information provided by the authors of the country chapters.

Note:
* The list of Eurosceptic/Eurocritical parties with full names is provided in Table 32.2 of the Appendix.

abandoning its adamant opposition to the whole project of European integration and adopting more moderate Eurocritical tones.

By looking at post-Communist countries, within the third category of EU Member States, it is possible to envisage a widespread Eurosceptic trend, except for Bulgaria, thus suggesting that such new memberships to the European Union have been veritable 'marriages of convenience'. More specifically in Hungary, the extreme right-wing populist, anti-European *Jobbik Magyarországért Mozgalom,* (Jobbik Movement for a Better Hungary) stood up successfully to its baptism of fire in 2009. The party, which rejects any conventional ideological label, defining itself as purely patriotic, attracted a remarkable voting share of 14.8 per cent by securing three of the twenty-two seats reserved to Hungarian representatives in the EP assembly.

In the Czech political setting, it has been possible to capture evident signs of hard and soft Euroscepticism in all its variants, often combined with anti-German feelings rooted in the belief that the European Union has been driven too much by Chancellor Angela Merkel's decisions (Hartleb, 2012). Interestingly in 2009, the hard Euro-rejectionist *Komunistická strana Čech a Moravy, KSČM* (Czech Communist Party of Bohemia and Moravia) fared well, grabbing 14.2 per cent of the popular backing and four seats, but losing 6 per cent of the votes and two MEPs compared to 2004.

Finally, within the Bulgarian party landscape, overall supportive of European integration, an extreme far-right anti-EU party, *Ataka* (Attack) has also emerged. Surprisingly, it managed to get 12 per cent of votes and two seats in 2009, marking a 2 per cent decline and the loss of one seat in relation to the 2007 EP contest. An opposite upward trend could be seen in the case of the Nationalist, right-wing *Partidul România Mare* (Greater Romania Party), which amassed 8.6 per cent of votes in 2009, with an astonishing four-point percentage increase in relation to 2004.

Overall, the phenomenon of Euroscepticism has affected, albeit to differing degrees, virtually all EU partners, with a broad range of parties displaying firm opposition or, simply, hesitancy to proceed with the European unification project. As a result, within the seventh legislature, three anti-European political groups have gathered, notably the hard Eurosceptic *Europe of Freedom and Democracy* (EFD), and the two soft Eurosceptic or Euro-realist, as they prefer to describe themselves, *European Conservatives and Reformists* (ECR) and *European United Left/Nordic Green Left* (EUL/NGL), along with non-attached members who are staunchly hostile to the European integration process or just critical of the existing EU design (Corbett et al., 2011). Their aggregate number, consisting of approximately 20 per cent of the EP seats, was not remotely close to a clear majority and remained unable to win votes. Nevertheless, these groups stood for an influential bloc within the Assembly and, as foreseen, their weight has increased after the eighth EP election in May 2014 (Hix, 2013).

3 Electoral participation

Besides the above-mentioned hypotheses falling within the SOE and ES frameworks, there is a crucial aspect of the EP contests, referring to low electoral participation, that has been ascribed in the past to both competing theories and that has been, therefore, dealt with separately.

In the former, failure to vote can indicate the lack of popular and media attention due to the marginal importance still attributed to the EP contest. In the latter, abstention may arise from anti-European sentiments, mirroring a critical approach to European Union policies or even a total rejection of the European integration process. In this perspective, the decreasing turnout registered over a period of three decades could be interpreted as a true reflection of a declining popular backing of the European project, although their definitive connection has been confuted by Franklin and Hobolt (2011).

In any case, what cannot be denied is that, until now, the EP has not accomplished the ultimate goal of breaking the downward trend in electoral participation and that this failure clearly

Final remarks

reflects the inability of the political elite to provide citizens with a real alternative and lay the foundations for a civil society within the European Union (Franklin, 2004). Table 31.5a unmistakably highlights this drop in voters' turnout from the zenith of 62 in the first direct election held in 1979, to a nadir of 43 in 2009.

As Joseph H.H. Weiler has insightfully observed, 'What is striking about these figures is that the decline coincides with a continuous shift in powers to the European Parliament, which today is a veritable co-legislator along with the Council' (Weiler, 2012, 830).

Indeed, it is all the more paradoxical to realize that such a remarkable expansion of EP competencies seems directly proportional to the growth of popular indifference towards European elections, thus uncovering the fact that '[t]he major challenge for the European Parliament is an increase not of its power but of its legitimacy' (Steunenberg and Thomassen, 2002, 10).

Nonetheless, closer scrutiny enables us to recognize a slowing down of the sharp decline in electoral engagement and, at the same time, to spot some differences amongst the various EU countries. First of all, it is worth pointing out that the question of turnout effect is bound not to materialize in the case of Belgium and Luxembourg, owing to compulsory voting and

Table 31.5a Turnout at EP elections in all EU Member States: 1979–2009

Country	1979	1981	1984	1987	1989	1994	1995	1996	1999	2004	2007	2009
France	60.7	—	56.7	—	48.8	52.7	—	—	46.8	42.8	—	40.6
Germany	65.7	—	56.8	—	62.2	60.0	—	—	45.2	43.0	—	43.3
Italy	85.6	—	82.4	—	81.1	73.6	—	—	69.8	71.7	—	65.0
Belgium	91.4	—	**92.1**	—	90.7	90.7	—	—	91.0	90.8	—	90.4
NL	58.1	—	50.9	—	47.5	35.7	—	—	30.0	39.3	—	36.7
Luxembourg	88.9	—	88.8	—	87.4	88.5	—	—	87.3	91.3	—	90.7
UK	32.3	—	32.6	—	36.4	36.4	—	—	24.0	38.5	—	34.7
Ireland	63.6	—	47.6	—	68.3	44.0	—	—	50.2	58.6	—	58.6
DK	47.8	—	52.4	—	46.2	53.0	—	—	50.5	47.9	—	59.5
Greece	—	81.5	80.6	—	80.0	73.2	—	—	70.2	63.2	—	52.6
Spain	—	—	—	68.5	54.7	59.1	—	—	63.0	45.1	—	44.9
Portugal	—	—	—	72.4	51.1	35.5	—	—	39.9	38.6	—	36.8
Austria	—	—	—	—	—	—	67.7	—	49.4	42.4	—	46.0
Finland	—	—	—	—	—	—	—	57.6	30.1	39.4	—	40.3
Sweden	—	—	—	—	—	—	41.6	—	38.8	37.8	—	45.5
Malta	—	—	—	—	—	—	—	—	—	82.4	—	78.8
Cyprus	—	—	—	—	—	—	—	—	—	72.5	—	59.4
Slovenia	—	—	—	—	—	—	—	—	—	28.4	—	28.3
Estonia	—	—	—	—	—	—	—	—	—	26.8	—	43.9
Latvia	—	—	—	—	—	—	—	—	—	41.3	—	53.7
Lithuania	—	—	—	—	—	—	—	—	—	48.4	—	21.0
Czech Republic	—	—	—	—	—	—	—	—	—	28.3	—	28.2
Slovakia	—	—	—	—	—	—	—	—	—	**17.0**	—	19.6
Hungary	—	—	—	—	—	—	—	—	—	38.5	—	36.3
Poland	—	—	—	—	—	—	—	—	—	20.9	—	24.5
Bulgaria	—	—	—	—	—	—	—	—	—	—	29.2	39.0
Romania	—	—	—	—	—	—	—	—	—	—	29.5	27.7
EU	62.0	—	59.0	—	58.4	56.7	—	—	49.5	45.5	—	43.0

Source: Author's table adapted from data drawn from www.europarl.europa.eu/aboutparliament/en/000cdcd9d4/Turnout-(1979-2009).html.

simultaneity of elections. Their respective participation rates have generally oscillated around 90 per cent in both national and European elections, as shown in Tables 31.5a and 31.5b.

In 2009, turnout fell in 11 cases, with the most remarkable drop of approximately 28 percentage points from 48.4 to 21 in Lithuania. Furthermore, Italy, Malta, the Netherlands, the United Kingdom, France, Portugal, Hungary, and Romania registered a decrease of 2.7 percentage points. In sum, a declining average turnout could be detected at the seventh EP election, mainly due to the New EU countries, since the level of participation in the Old EU states did not vary to a great extent.

Furthermore, by dividing the EU Member States between established democracies and post-Communist countries, thus moving Malta and Cyprus to the first group, it is possible to notice an even more striking difference, confirming a 32 per cent participation in the second group, 11 points below the EU average (Kohler-Koch and Larat, 2009). The higher electoral participation of Maltese and Cypriot nationals, equivalent to 78.7 and 59.4 per cent, suggests that the true gap was not between Old and New EU states, but rather between West and East European electoral traditions, or even better between pre- and post-1989 democracies. In fact, turnout rates in all post-Communist republics, except Latvia and Estonia, fell below the EU level confirming a mere 32 per cent average participation. Such a bleak picture reveals that, despite the remarkable progress achieved, CEECs cannot be deemed as fully consolidated democracies yet, owing to a variety of factors including economic instability, continued elite dominance of politics, and absence of a fully-fledged, multiparty structure and organization. As a matter of fact, Euro-elections in these countries seemed to lack mobilization and habitual support for established parties (Wessels and Franklin, 2009).

On the other hand, it is worth emphasizing that in 2009, people's electoral attendance improved in ten Member States, notably Austria, Finland, Bulgaria, Poland, Slovakia, Denmark, Sweden, Latvia and, to a remarkable extent, Estonia, whilst it remained virtually unchanged in six other countries: Belgium, Germany, Luxembourg, Spain, Slovenia, and the Czech Republic. Fifteen Member States managed to exceed the EU average of 43 per cent, whilst the remaining twelve failed to reach it and amongst them, six fell even below 30 per cent. In particular, the Slovak electoral participation plummeted to the dismal percentage of 19.6, though this was three points higher than in 2004, when the lowest ever rate of 17 per cent in the history of all EP elections across the European Union was touched.

Moreover, by comparing the turnout data illustrated in Tables 31.5a, 31.5b and 31.5c, it becomes evident that citizens' involvement was lower at EP contests than at their previous first-order elections.

Amongst all the EU countries, Luxembourg and Belgium stood out as exceptions, since turnout was very high in both countries, sometimes even exceeding the levels achieved in national elections. This could be ascribed to the enforcement of compulsory voting in these

Table 31.5b National election turnout in Old EU Member States: 1973–2009

Country	National elections years/turnouts											
France	1978	1981	1986	1988	1993	1997	2002	2007	—	—	—	—
	71.6	70.9	78.5	66.2	68.9	68.0	62.4	60.2	—	—	—	—
Germany	1976	1980	1983	1987	1990	1994	1998	2002	2005	—	2009	—
	90.7	88.6	89.1	84.3	77.8	79.0	82.2	79.1	77.7	—	70.8	—
Italy	1976	1979	1983	1987	1992	1994	1996	2001	2006	—	2008	—
	93.4	90.4	89.0	88.9	87.4	86.3	82.9	81.4	83.6	—	80.5	—
Belgium	1978	1981	1985	1987	1991	1995	1999	2003	2007	—	—	—
	94.8	94.5	93.6	94.1	92.7	91.2	90.6	91.6	91.3	—	—	—
Netherlands	1977	1981	1982	1986	1989	1994	1998	2002	2003	—	2006	—
	88.0	87.0	81.0	85.8	80.3	78.7	73.3	79.0	79.9	—	80.4	—

Luxembourg	*1974*	*1979*	*1984*	*1989*	*1994*	*1999*	*2004*	*2009*	—	—	—	—
	90.1	88.9	88.8	87.4	88.3	86.5	91.7	90.8	—	—	—	—
UK	*1974*	*1979*	*1983*	*1987*	*1992*	*1997*	*2001*	*2005*	—	—	—	—
	72.8	76.0	72.7	75.3	77.7	71.3	**59.4**	61.3	—	—	—	—
Ireland	*1977*	*1981*	*1982*	*1982*	*1987*	*1989*	*1992*	*1997*	*2002*	—	*2007*	—
	76.3	76.7	73.8	72.9	73.4	68.5	68.5	66.1	62.6	—	67.0	—
Denmark	*1977*	*1979*	*1981*	*1984*	*1987*	*1988*	*1990*	*1994*	*1998*	—	*2001*	—
	88.7	85.6	87.8	88.4	86.7	85.7	82.9	84.3	86.0	—	87.2	—
Greece	*1974*	*1977*	*1981*	*1985*	*1989*	*1989*	*1990*	*1993*	*1996*	*2000*	*2007*	*2009*
	79.6	81.3	78.6	79.1	79.9	84.5	84.4	83	76.3	75.0	74.1	70.9
Spain	*1977*	*1979*	*1982*	*1986*	*1989*	*1993*	*1996*	*2000*	*2004*	—	*2008*	—
	78.8	68.3	79.9	70.5	69.7	76.4	77.4	68.7	75.7	—	73.9	—
Portugal	*1975*	*1976*	*1979*	*1980*	*1983*	*1985*	*1987*	*1991*	*1995*		*1999*	—
	91.7	83.3	87.5	85.5	78.6	75.4	72.6	68.2	66.3	—	61.1	—
Austria	*1975*	1979	1983	1986	1990	1994	1995	1999	2002	—	2006	—
	92.9	92.2	92.6	90.5	86.1	81.9	86.0	80.4	84.3	—	78.5	—
Finland	*1975*	*1979*	*1983*	*1987*	*1991*	*1995*	*1999*	*2003*	*2007*	—	—	—
	73.8	75.3	75.7	72.1	68.4	68.6	65.3	66.7	67.9	—	—	—
Sweden	*1976*	*1979*	*1982*	*1985*	*1988*	*1991*	*1994*	*1998*	*2002*	—	*2006*	—
	91.8	90.7	91.5	89.9	86.0	86.7	86.8	81.4	80.1	—	82.0	—

Source: Author's table based on data drawn from www.parties-and-elections.eu.

Table 31.5c National election turnout in New EU Member States: 2000–2010

Country	National elections years/turnouts		
Malta	2003	2008	—
	95.7	93.3	—
Cyprus	*2001*	*2006*	—
	91.8	89.0	—
Slovenia	2000	2004	2008
	70.3	60.6	63.1
Estonia	*2003*	*2007*	—
	58.2	61.0	—
Latvia	*2002*	*2006*	—
	71.2	62.3	—
Lithuania	*2004*	*2008*	—
	45.9	48.6	—
Czech Republic	*2002*	*2006*	—
	58.0	64.5	—
Slovakia	2002	2006	2010
	70.0	54.7	58.8
Hungary	*2002*	*2006*	—
	50.5	67.8	—
Poland	2001	2005	2007
	46.2	40.6	53.8
Bulgaria	2001	2005	2009
	66.8	55.8	60.2
Romania	*2004*	*2008*	—
	58.5	**39.2**	—

Source: Author's table based on data drawn from www.parties-and-elections.eu.

countries, although this hypothesis did not prove to be valid in 2009 in Greece and Cyprus, where voters' participation dropped by 11 and 12 per cent, hence barely reaching 52 and 59.4 per cent, presumably due to the fact that penalties or sanctions are no longer inflicted on abstainers. In Greece in the past, failing to vote would mean in the case of young conscripts, for instance, extending their military service for an extra six months.

Another element favouring people's participation has been attributed to the concurrence of national and European elections, such as in the Irish Republic in 1989. An unusually higher percentage of 48.4 was also registered in Lithuania in 2004, most ostensibly due to the simultaneous convening of presidential elections. In Greece, popular enthusiasm about EU membership led to an impressive turnout at the first EP contest, which took place on 18 October 1981, on the same day as the general election. Indeed, 81.5 per cent of Hellenic citizens went to the polls in the former election, 3 per cent more than in the latter. This exceptional pattern was reiterated at the two subsequent Euro-elections held in 1984 and 1989, when enhanced turnout rates were achieved in comparison with the preceding first-order electoral races.

Turnout has been much lower at the EP ballots, at times reaching even less than half of the rates achieved in previous national elections. For instance, at the 1999 EP contest in Finland, only 30 per cent of people cast their ballot, although just three months earlier over 65.3 of the Finns had gone to the polls to choose their representatives in the *Eduskunta*.

Conclusion

The comparative analysis of the seven EP electoral competitions, held over the last three decades, has highlighted a welter of distinctive features encompassing Old and New Member States that no single theoretical model may capture in all their complexity. To a large extent, this could be ascribed to the varied idiosyncrasies of national political environments and party systems coupled with the erratic timing of their respective national election cycles.

Nonetheless, it is fair to conclude that Euro-elections have lent considerable support to the traditional SOE framework without excluding the fact that the 'Question of Europe' has slowly gained impetus on voters' preferences. Surprisingly, the core postulates of the Second-Order Election theory continue to be upheld, even following the subsequent treaty changes that have gradually expanded the role of the European Parliament. Overall, European elections seem to endorse the victory of opposition and small political forces to the detriment of governing and large parties, being either pro- or anti-European and indifferently located on the left or right side of the political spectrum. Such party competitions offer voters the opportunity to express their dissatisfaction and frustration against the ruling majority and, at the same time, represent the chance for the opposition to communicate its alternative government proposals.

On the other hand, Europe Salience theory has gained some ground, since voters' choices have slowly been directed to movements that confer an increasing relevance to Europe, in either a positive or negative way. In this perspective, the rise of Green, extreme and Eurosceptic parties confirms that Europe is not an entirely negligible factor in Euro-elections.

Compared to national elections, EP contests present a lower turnout, a higher degree of electoral volatility, a less intense polarization, mostly at the expense of government, big and mainstream parties. By and large, the utility of both theoretical models has been higher in the Old rather than the New partners, especially in the post-Communist democracies. For instance, in Romania, none of the above characterizations has truly succeeded in explaining Euro-electoral dynamics.

Euro-elections have rarely drawn much attention amongst public opinion and the political elite, as clearly reflected in common listlessness and low party activism surrounding EP campaigns. Whilst the poor turnout achieved in 1979 could be attributed to various local and temporal factors and, above all, to the obscure novelty of the first direct elections to the European Parliament, its persistence and aggravation across time unveils a far more complex scenario. According to Eurobarometer surveys, unfamiliarity with the European Parliament and the cumbersome EU policy-making procedures represents one of the main causes of poor electoral participation. In particular, a factor discouraging people in Northern Europe from attending the polling booth up until 2009 was the custom of calling Euro-elections in June, coinciding with the beginning of school summer holidays.

Eastern enlargement could be considered as one of the reasons for the falling participation in EP elections, carrying the message that indifference to this event runs deeper amongst the New Member States. Nonetheless, the general apathy towards the 2009 EP contest should also be seen as the natural reaction to the global crisis that has aggravated economic problems in virtually all EU countries.

Moreover, it should not be overlooked that abstention is not just a recent phenomenon, confined to EP elections and originating from the weak link between European citizens and MEPs, but may be the reflection of a wider phenomenon arising from popular disaffection with politics. Even in ancient Athens, the application of the Aristotelian ideal of participation met with some practical hurdles. As described by the Greek playwright Aristophanes, the phenomenon of 'escaping citizens' who preferred to shirk their duties was rather common. In order to urge people to take part in the activities of the governing assembly, known as 'the ecclesia', the authorities used to lay a rope with fresh red paint around it; marking those who tended to linger behind it and charging them with a fine (Malkopoulou, 2007). Although the Athenian system of direct participation differs from that introduced in modern representative democracies as well as in the European Union, it seems that in all cases the idea of public involvement in politics has not met with universal enthusiasm among the citizens themselves.

This crucial question risks undermining the democratic legitimacy not only of Euro-elections, but also of the European Parliament and, more widely, of the European Union. Against this background, a series of reforms should be introduced concerning the organization of EP contests with a closer involvement of the European political parties. Electoral campaigns should be shaped in a way that voters, when casting their ballot, may express real and conscious choices about the direction of the EU polity. In this sense, the quest for a uniform voting system across the European Union should be pursued in order to remove some of the internal distorting mechanisms that overtly contradict the EP mission and are irreconcilable with the ideas of a supranational federation by reinforcing the connection between MEPs and citizens. Indeed, in order to defeat the 'ever yawning democratic deficit' of the European Union, political leaders should agree to match any transfer of power from the national to the European level by genuine accountability and citizen impact (Weiler, 2012, 825). This would mean reducing their own powers, a bullet that they have steadfastly refused to bite so far (Franklin, 2014).

Since their introduction in 1979, elections to the European Parliament by direct universal suffrage have offered the opportunity of involving the 'man in the street' in the construction of Europe (Colombo, 1977). Yet, incontrovertibly, this process is far from being accomplished, with the European Parliament still embodying a somewhat unknown and rather distant political labyrinth in the eyes of European citizens.

Given that the so-called 'permissive consensus', representing the first stage of European integration, no longer generates sufficient public commitment to the EU project nor high turnout at European elections, the EP seems to have no strong civic support and, therefore, no real mandate to enact reforms that would improve its democratic credentials. In J.H.H. Weiler's words, '[t]he question whether the undoubtedly noble [EC/EU] project enjoys popular legitimacy has always been the Achilles Heel of European construct' and will have to be duly raised in order to guarantee its survival (Weiler, 2012, 826).

Bringing Europe close to citizens means fostering democratic legitimization: this is the ultimate scope of the European Parliament, which might be achieved through new and enhanced communication and information channels. Irrefutably, an effective way has to be found in order to attract the attention of European people to the activities undertaken by the European Parliament and, more widely, to elicit public interest on European issues by making such news less dull, less obscure, and less technocratic. Only in this way is the directly elected EP likely to become 'a living reality for European citizens, not only in economic but in political, social and cultural spheres. For young persons [sic] in particular this will be an education in itself and a guarantee of freedom and effective democratic development' (Andreotti, 1975, 127).

The enduring democratic deficit of the European Union may be truly overcome if European integration is interpreted as a 'politically messianic venture *par excellence*, where its mobilizing force, along with its core legitimating features, are engrained in the 'vision offered' as well as the 'dream dreamt' of 'a promised land' of peace, justice and welfare (Weiler, 2012, 832). Alas, such an ambitious prospect seems now more than ever remote and utopian, eclipsed by recent troubles and woes arising from the economic crisis.

References

Primary sources

Andreotti, G. (1975) 'Convention Introducing Elections to the European Parliament by Direct Universal Suffrage', Debate on a Report drawn up by Patijn on Behalf of the Political Affairs Committee, *Debates of the European Parliament*, 14 January, (Doc. 368/74).
EP Information Office (2009) 'European Election Institutional Campaign, State of Implementation of Outdoor Elements and Complementary Activities by Member State 16/04/2009'.
European Commission, Eurobarometer 79, Spring 2013, Luxembourg.
European Parliament, Elections to the European Parliament by Direct Universal Suffrage, Secretariat, Directorate-General for Research and Documentation, Office For Official Publications of the European Parliament website, www.europarl.europa.eu/aboutparliament/en/000cdcd9d4/Turnout-(1979-2009).html.
Political parties, www.parties-and-elections.eu (accessed on 15 February 2015).

Secondary sources

Bibes, G., de Laserre, F., Menudier, H. and Smouts, M.-C. (1979) 'Une élection nationale à prétexte européen', *Revue Française de Science Politique*, 29(6), 986–1014.
Colombo, E. (1977) 'Preface', in European Parliament, Elections to the European Parliament by Direct Universal Suffrage, Secretariat, Directorate-General for Research and Documentation, Office For Official Publications of the European Communities, Luxembourg.
Corbett, R., Jacobs, F. and Shackleton, M. (2011) *The European Parliament*, London, John Harper Publishing, 8th ed.
European Parliament (2010) *How to Create a Transnational Party System*, Study by the Directorate General for Internal Policies Policy Department C: Citizens' Rights and Constitutional Affairs, PE 425.623, Brussels.
Franklin, M.N. (2004) *Voter Turnout and the Dynamics of Electoral Competition in Established Democracies since 1945*, Oxford, Oxford University Press.
Franklin, M.N. (2014) 'Why Vote at an Election with No Apparent Purpose? Voter Turnout at Elections to the European Parliament', *European Policy Analyst*, April, 1–12.
Gallagher, M. (2014) 'Elections and Referendums,' in Caramani, D. (ed.) *Comparative Politics*, Oxford, Oxford University Press, 166–80.

Gowan, P. (1997) 'British Euro-solipsism', in Gowan, P. and Anderson, P. (eds) *The Question of Europe*, London, Verso, 91–103.

Harsen, R. and Spiering, M. (2004) 'Introduction Euroscepticism and the Evolution of the European Political Debate' in Harsen, R. and Spiering, M. (eds) 'Euroscepticism: Party Politics, National Identity and European Integration', *European Studies*, 20, January, 13–35.

Hartleb, F. (2012) 'European Project in Danger? Understanding Precisely the Phenomena "Euroscepticsm, Populism and Extremism" in Times of Crisis', *Review of European Studies*, 4 (5), 45–63.

Hix, S. (2013) 'Why the 2014 European Elections Matter: Ten Key Votes in the 2009–2013 European Parliament', *European Policy Analysis*, September, 15, 1–16.

Hix, S. and Marsh, M. (2007) 'Punishment or Protest? Understanding European Parliament Elections', *Journal of Politics*, 69(2), 495–510.

Hix, S. and Marsh, M. (2011) 'Second-Order Effects plus Pan-European Political wings: An Analysis of European Parliament Elections across Time', *Electoral Studies*, 30, 4–15.

Huntington, S. P. (1991) *Third Wave: Democratization in the Late Twentieth Century*, Norman, OK, University of Oklahoma Press.

Kaletsky, A. (2014), 'Will Britain really leave the European Union?' *Reuters*, 16 January. Online. Available at: http://blogs.reuters.com/anatole-kaletsky/2014/01/16/will-britain-really-leave-the-european-union/ (accessed on 10 Janiary 2015).

Koepke, J. R. and Ringe, N. (2006) 'The Second-Order Election Model in an Enlarged Europe', *European Union Politics*, 7 (3), 321–46.

Mair, P. (2004) 'The Europeanization Dimension', *Journal of European Public Policy*, 11(2), 337–48.

Mair, P. (2005) 'Popular Democracy and the European Union Polity', European Governance Papers, C-05-03.

Malkopoulou, A. (2007), 'Compulsory Voting in Greece: A History of Concepts in Motion', Paper prepared for the ECPR Workshop Compulsory Voting: Principles and Practice, 7–12 May, University of Helsinki, Finland.

Marcos, P. (2004) 'El candidato del PP afirma que sobran las "hipotecas nacionalistas" y promete ser "euro-exigente"', *El País*, 3 June.

Marsh, M. (1998) 'Testing the Second-Order Election Model after Four European Elections', *British Journal of Political Science*, 28(4), 591–607.

Marsh, M. (2009) 'Efficient and Democratic Governance in the European Union', OSCE/ODIHR (2009) Office for Democratic Institutions and Human Rights, Elections to the European Parliament, 4–7 June 2009, Expert Group Report, 11–30 May 2009, Warsaw, 22 September.

Reif, K. H. and Schmitt, H. (1980) 'Nine Second-Order National Elections – A Conceptual Framework for the Analysis of European Election Results', *European Journal of Political Research*, 8(1), 3–44.

Schmitt, H. (2005) 'The European Parliament Elections of June 2004: Still Second-Order?' *West European Politics*, 28(3), 650–79.

Serricchio, F., Tsakatika, M. and Quaglia, L. (2013) 'Euroscepticism and the Global Financial Crisis', *Journal of Common Market Studies*, 51(1), 51–64.

Smith, J. (2005) 'A Missed Opportunity? New Labour's European Policy 1997–2005', *International Affairs*, 81(4),703–21

Spiering, M. (2004) 'British Euroscepticism', in Harsen, R. and Spiering, M. (eds) *Euroscepticism: Party Politics, National Identity and European Integration, European Studies*, 20, January, 127–49.

Steunenberg, B. and Thomassen, J. (2002) 'Introduction', in Steunenberg, B. and Thomassen, J. (eds) *The European Parliament. Moving toward Democracy in the EU*, Lanham, Rowman & Littlefield, 1–12.

Taggart, P. and Szczerbiak, A. (2004) 'Contemporary Euroskepticism in the Party Systems of European Union Candidate States of Central and Eastern Europe', *European Journal of Political Research*, 43, 1–27.

Tóka, G. and Gosselin, T. (2010) 'Persistent Political Divides, Electoral Volatility and Citizen Involvement: The Freezing Hypothesis in the 2004 European Election', *West European Politics*, 33(3), 608–33.

Weiler, J. H. H. (1999) 'To be a European Citizen: Eros and Civilization', *The Constitution of Europe: "Do the New Clothes have an Emperor?" And Other Essays on European Integration*, Cambridge, Cambridge University Press, 324–57.

Weiler, J. H. H. (2012) 'In the Face of Crisis: Input Legitimacy, Output Legitimacy and the Political Messianism of European Integration', *European Integration*, 34(7), 825–41.

Wessels, B., Franklin, M.N. (2009) 'Turning Out or Turning Off – Do Mobilization and Attitudes Account for Turnout Differences between New and Established Member States at the 2004 EP elections?' *Journal of European Integration*, Special Issue (5), 609–26.

32
EPILOGUE
Old and new trends in the 2014 European election

Donatella M. Viola

In the aftermath of the 2014 EP vote, it is worth undertaking a brief investigation on this set of country-by-country elections held across the European Union, for the first time, under the legal framework of the Treaty of Lisbon. On the basis of the polling results reached by national political parties among all the 28 EU Member States, we will map out, in the final section of this volume, the novel composition of the European Parliament by trying to highlight old and new trends.

As such, this additional chapter can be regarded as a preliminary attempt to explore whether or not the 2014 election was truly 'different', as formally announced in the EP information campaign.

The EP contest was the eighth opportunity for the citizens of ten states – including the original six along with the UK, Ireland, Denmark and Greece – to choose their own representatives to send to Brussels and Strasbourg. It was the seventh time for the Spanish and Portuguese people, the fifth for the Austrian, Finnish, and Swedish voters, the third for nationals from the CEECs as well as from Malta and Cyprus. Lastly, for the second time, the Croats were called upon to select their own MEPs, since their accession to the European Union on 1 July 2013.

The electoral race took place in the wake of the Eurozone sovereign debt crisis, triggered by the global financial meltdown set off in July 2007 by a speculative bubble in the US housing market. Most specifically, Greece, Ireland, and Portugal along with Italy, Spain and, subsequently, Cyprus, all embodying weak links in the euro chain, were dramatically hit by the negative effects of such an economic turmoil. The first five countries mentioned above were often referred to in the media by the unflattering acronym PIIGS or the more acceptable abbreviation GIPSI, later modified to GIPSIC in order to accommodate Cyprus.

The conjunction of economic recession and strict austerity measures imposed by the EU institutions and the International Monetary Fund (IMF) contributed to amplifying popular concerns and raise public protests around unemployment and migration in several corners of the Old Continent. And yet, inevitably, the financial muddle affected the dimension of political engagement and citizens' representation, thus unveiling another aspect of the democratic deficit of the European Union.

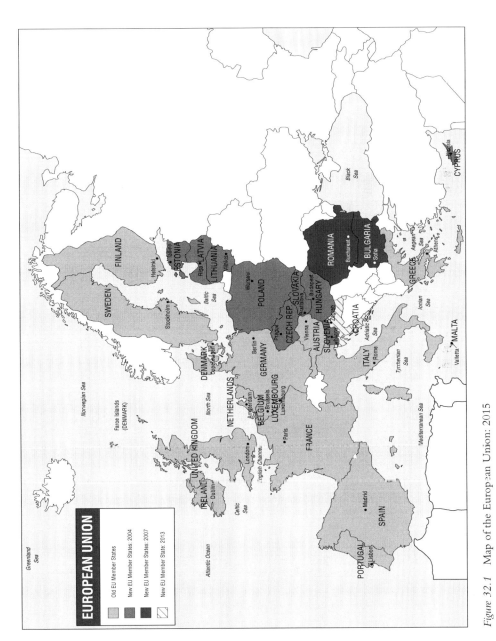

Figure 32.1 Map of the European Union: 2015

D.M. Viola

Figure 32.2 Map of the European Union with EP electoral constituencies: May 2014

1 The 2014 European election: campaign and turnout

'*This time it's different: act, react, impact*' was the official EP campaign slogan launched in the run-up to the May 2014 event.

As the European Parliament itself emphasized in its resolution of 4 July 2013,

> The 2014 elections will be the first to take place after the entry into force of the Lisbon Treaty – which widens significantly the powers of the European Parliament, including its role in the election of the President of the Commission – and, accordingly, will provide a key opportunity to increase the transparency of the elections and strengthen their European dimension.
>
> *(EP Resolution 4/7/2013, E)*

One of its novelties was, therefore, to connect the EP contest to the selection of the head of the European Commission, previously undertaken by national leaders in a rather exclusive and independent manner. This was aimed at challenging the traditional second-order character of European elections by marking a shift in the way people perceive the European Parliament, its image and its function, as well as the European Union in its entirety (van den Berge, 2014).

Epilogue

In compliance with Article 17 of the Lisbon Treaty:

Taking into account the elections of the European Parliament and after having held the appropriate consultations, the European Council, acting by a qualified majority, shall propose to the European Parliament a candidate for President of the Commission. This candidate shall be elected by the European Parliament by a majority of its component members.
(Article 17, §7 TEU, 2007, italics added)

Subsequently, the House called on the pan-European political parties to play a crucial role in the EP electoral campaign and to field their nominees to the Commission presidency, the so-called *Spitzenkandidaten,* ahead of the popular vote as well as the European Council's proposal. The candidates were expected to make themselves known to European citizens and to present personally their programmes in all EU countries. Unquestionably, linking these two elections more directly to citizens' choices would reinforce the political legitimacy of both the European Parliament and the European Commission (EP Resolution, 22/11/2012). In other words, granting voters a collective decisional power over the shaping of the European Parliament and, to a lesser extent, of the European Commission was meant to foster democracy at the EU level.

As suggested by the European Parliament itself, such a democratization process could be effectively achieved by turning Euro-elections into a genuine race over competing political agendas through the direct involvement of European political families and their active cooperation with their national counterparts. As a result, EU decision-making would become more politicized in reply to the criticism that a multi-levelled European Union offers just an enlightened and pluralist 'policy without politics' (Schmidt, 2006, Chapter 4).

Specifically, party competition over the Commission leadership was deemed to alter the EU inter-institutional dynamics and favour the politicization of the debate over European integration by swinging the pendulum towards the realization of a federal Union: 'The hope behind this proposal [was] that politici[z]ation, even at the cost of polari[z]ation, [would] prove the royal road to legitimacy' (Müller, 2014, 37). In order to realize this objective, Olli Rehn, the Finnish Former EU Commissioner for economic and monetary affairs and the euro, went even further by calling for an 'emotionalization' process of European elections (Müller, 2014).

And yet, it should not be overlooked that, although the long-awaited setting up of a closer 'legislative-executive' connection between the European Parliament and the European Commission may be highly desirable, the latter's perspective loss of neutrality does not look utterly engaging or useful at all times. According to Heather Grabbe and Stefan Lehne, a President of the Commission 'who is blatantly beholden to one party will lack the credibility to impose sanctions or take other measures against national governments who are of another political stripe'. In their view, the head of the executive could perform his/her function properly by maintaining a *super partes* role, as an impartial arbiter and 'Guardian of the Treaties', therefore pursuing broad European interests (Grabbe and Lehne, 2013, 2).

Whatever might be people's opinion regarding this matter, there were reasons to assume that in 2014, as never before in the history of the European Union, the EP political campaigns would finally focus more on European rather than national issues. As a matter of fact, this occurred in Sweden, Denmark, Luxembourg, the Netherlands, Germany, and Estonia, but not elsewhere. Domestic concerns continued to prevail in most countries, especially in Belgium, Ireland, and Lithuania where the European contest coincided with other national or regional elections (van den Berge, 2014). Television debates as well as newspaper articles addressed only marginally subjects strictly related to EU politics and policies. Nevertheless, it should not be ignored that national and European levels have become more and more intertwined and that, undeniably, topics such as unemployment or migration could be easily framed in either contexts in terms of causes as well as remedies.

Overall, the atmosphere was dominated by a deep sense of frustration over economic stagnation, combined with a feeling of genuine disaffection towards the political elite, especially in the Old Member States.

In the light of the widespread public discontent arising out of the prism of the crisis, over 395 million people from 28 countries were called to go to the polling booths with the purpose of choosing their representatives in Strasbourg and Brussels. Such a large democratic event, second only to the Indian parliamentary elections, carried the great potential of breathing new life into a decadent European Union.

The contest took place between 22 and 25 May 2014, on the day of the week designated by national authorities, in accordance with their respective traditions. Whereas in 21 Member States Euro-elections were convened simultaneously on the last day, in seven cases the race occurred earlier, setting off in the Netherlands and the UK on Thursday 22 May, followed by Ireland on Friday 23 May, by the Czech Republic on Friday 23 May, from 2 p.m. to 10 p.m., and on Saturday 24 May from 8 a.m. to 2 p.m., as well as by Latvia, Malta and Slovakia over the whole day of Saturday 24 May.

This four-day-long electoral marathon, scattered across the European Union, inevitably raised doubts about the feasibility of preventing leakages of information that could influence later voters' choices. After the unfortunate episode that occurred in June 2009 in the Netherlands, where provisional results were published prior to the opening of voting booths in most EU countries, the European Commission issued an official statement in order to prohibit Member States from making any public announcement before the official closing of the last polling stations in Italy at 11 p.m. on Sunday 25 May 2014. Although competent national government authorities upheld this rule, it was impossible to preclude the circulation of exit polls that could affect voting behaviour elsewhere.

Although it was foreseen, or at least hoped, that the new electoral provisions combined with the increased powers of the European Parliament would automatically generate higher public involvement, abstention was once more the real and absolute winner of this contest. Regretfully, notwithstanding the EP and national governments' endeavours to raise awareness and draw the interest of European citizens, a further but slim 0.55 per cent decrease, from 42.99 to 42.44, was registered, which meant that approximately 168 to 396 million eligible voters actually showed up at the ballot box.

Even if, at the eighth EP election, the EU average voter turnout dipped to its lowest ebb – presenting European elections as a sad story of scanty and waning participation – a closer look brings to light some degree of heterogeneity among the various Member States.

Table 32.1a shows the turnout rates registered all over the European Union in the last two rounds of elections and, in particular, in nine distinct country clusters:

1. The Old EU-15, consisting of the six founding members, along with the nine countries joining the EC/EU in the 1970s, 1980s, and 1990s.
2. The EU-17, referring to the so-called Old European democracies, including the above-mentioned fifteen along with Malta and Cyprus.
3. The New EU-10, embracing the Central and Eastern European countries that accessed the European Union in 2004 and 2007.
4. The New EU-11, which besides the ten post-Communist republics, includes Croatia, which entered in 2013.

Table 32.1a Turnout at EP elections in aggregate countries: 2009/2013–2014

Aggregate countries	2009/2013			2014			2009–2014 (2009/2013–2014)
	%	Total votes	Electorate	%	Total votes	Electorate	% Change
Old EU-15	46.94	142,062,524	302,661,985	46.76	144,125,368	308,216,293	–0.18
EU-17 (including Malta and Cyprus)	46.99	142,629,042	303,510,456	46.79	144,649,847	309,167,641	–0.20
New EU-10 (post-Communist countries)	28.33	23,521,430	83,014,354	27.02	22,388,888	82,870,089	–1.31
New EU-11 (post-Communist countries including Croatia)	28.01	24,087,948	83,862,825	26.94	23,365,751	86,719,648	–1.07
New EU-13 (including Croatia)	28.39	24,868,928	87,611,640	27.25	23,864,347	87,588,704	–1.14
PIIGS/GIPSI*	54.60	59,383,322	108,757,070	50.82	55,917,147	110,032,544	–3.78
GIPSIC**	54.62	59,695,801	109,283,130	50.78	56,184,038	110,639,460	–3.84
Southern EU countries***	54.58	58,073,920	106,406,252	50.81	54,739,684	107,738,468	–3.77
Nordic EU countries****	47.83	7,307,739	15,277,230	49.75	7,819,775	15,719,37	1.92
EU-27 (2009) – EU-28 (2014)	42.99	166,150,471	386,524,810	42.44	167,989,715	395,805,057	–0.55
EU-28 (2009/2013–2014)	42.77	166,931,452	390,273,625	42.44	167,989,715	395,805,057	–0.33

Sources: Author's table based on own calculations from data drawn from EU Member States national government websites and from the EP website: www.europarl.europa.eu/pdf/elections_results/review.pdf.

Notes:
* Portugal, Italy, Ireland, Greece, and Spain.
** Greece, Italy, Portugal, Spain, Ireland, and Cyprus.
*** Portugal, Italy, Greece, Spain, Malta, and Cyprus.
**** Denmark, Finland, and Sweden.

5. The New EU-13, comprising all the aforesaid CEECs and the two Mediterranean islands that obtained full EU membership in three subsequent stages in the 2000s.
6. The PIIGS/GIPSI caucus, refering to those countries mostly hit by the euro-debt crisis, notably Portugal, Italy, Ireland, Greece, and Spain.
7. Subsequently, with Cyprus joining the other 'bailout countries', the acronym turned into GIPSIC.
8. The Southern EU countries, comprising Portugal, Italy, Greece, Spain, Malta, and Cyprus.
9. Finally, the Nordic EU countries, encompassing Denmark, Finland, and Sweden.

In May 2014, a 20 per cent turnout gap emerged between the Old EU-15 and the New EU-13, which scored 46.76 and 27.25 per cent. Yet, considering the higher average attendance of the EU-17 also encompassing Cyprus and Malta, it is possible to confirm that the true rift was rather between West and East Europe or, more precisely, between pre- and post-1989 democracies.

Indeed, whilst the EU-17 touched the average of 46.79 per cent, thus losing 0.20 per cent in relation to 2009, the new EU-11 barely reached 26.94, marking a 1.07 per cent decrease compared to the previous EP competition. This proved 'just as a matter of arithmetic' that Central and Eastern European countries have sensibly lowered active public involvement in Euro-elections (Franklin, 2014, 2001). This phenomenon could be easily ascribed to the recent foundation of their political parties that are still unable to evoke people's loyalties. Nevertheless, it should not be ignored that this phenomenon is common to EP and national electoral contests.

As to the PIIGS/GIPSI and GIPSIC clusters, despite the enforcement of strict measures by the 'Brussels-Berlin-Frankfurt Triangle' in order to arrest the sovereign debt crisis, public abstention only fell by nearly 4 percentage points compared to 2009. In fact, their rates ranging between 50.82 and 50.78 remained more than eight points above the EU average.

This result was mainly due to the substantial 7.43 per cent increase in turnout in Greece, which went up from 52.54 to 59.97 per cent. The impact of the austerity regime, rather than deterring electoral mobilization, drove a higher number of Greek voters to the polling stations with the aim of calling for radical changes at national and EU level. Not least, the candidature of the leader of *Synaspismos tes Rizospastikes Aristeras*, *Syriza* (Coalition of the Radical Left), Alexis Tsipras, to the presidency of the European Commission elicited people's interest in the contest. Amongst the nine groups, only the Nordic countries registered a higher turnout compared to 2009, thanks to a larger share of Swedish voters.

In order to provide a full picture of EP electoral participation, besides drawing parallels between these nine clusters, we have compared the trend of individual countries. In fact, 13 out of 28 Member States exceeded the EU average, with Belgium and Luxembourg scoring, as usual, the top rates of 89.64 and 85.55 per cent. On the opposite side, most of the CEECs marked a further compression in turnout, with Slovakia falling below the all-time nadir of 13.05 per cent. Among them, the only three exceptions were Lithuania, Romania, and Croatia. Whilst the first country recorded a striking upswing of 26.37 per cent, by attaining the higher than average percentage of 47.35, the other two states increased more modestly by 4.77 and 4.41 per cent, therefore stretching their levels of mobilization to 32.44 and 25.24 per cent, respectively.

The May 2014 Euro-election in Croatia was convened in closer temporal proximity to its first special EP contest, which took place in April 2013 before entering the European Union. Contrary to the assumption that 'founding elections' kindle greater interest, naturally deemed to dwindle over time, the second electoral competition brought, instead, a small but net improvement compared to the previous abysmal record. The hypothesis underlying an initial top participation, attributed to a temporary 'euphoria' or 'first election boost' (Kostadinova, 2003), could not be validated in Croatia in 2013 or in the ten CEECs, given that their EP electoral debuts in 2004 and 2007 produced derisory attendance rates. Such a negative attitude stemmed from the broad perception spread in post-Communist democracies, that EU membership was a 'No option', embodying the only real opportunity or inevitable remedy to promote economic, political, and institutional development. Indeed, seen from this perspective, European integration represented nothing else but a genuinely technocratic project with limited societal engagement, which would confer a truly minor role to CEECs (Hanley, 2014). Against this backdrop, it is possible to understand the overwhelming apathy among East Europeans that reached alarming records in Slovakia and the Czech Republic in May 2014.

On the whole, the average turnout at the EU level concealed highly different levels of mobilization in each country compared to 2009. Turnout fell in 18 cases with a staggering 23.45 per cent drop in Latvia, which had previously reached the top record of 53.69 among the CEECs in 2009. This was presumably connected to the concomitance of local elections directed to choose representatives of the newly created municipalities. Five years later, following a reverse trend, only 30.24 per cent of Latvians attended the polls, albeit this figure was still above the New EU-11 average. In addition, a fall of over 5 per cent could be seen in Italy, Luxembourg, Ireland, Cyprus, Estonia, Czech Republic, Slovakia, and Hungary.

By contrast, an upward trend emerged in the ten remaining countries, with turnout soaring by 26.37 percentage points in Lithuania, from the dismal figure of 20.98 in 2009, to 47.35 in 2014, presumably on the positive trail of the second round of the presidential elections.

Yet, it is worth noticing that participation remained virtually stable in eight cases, going down by less than 1 per cent in Austria, Belgium, and Poland whilst going up by less than one percentage point in France, Belgium, Netherlands, the UK, and Finland.

No doubt, in order to tackle the steady decline in voter mobilization, it is crucial to investigate the logic behind this phenomenon. In Mark N. Franklin's view, the secondary nature of European elections could help us to understand why this contest failed to catch the public's attention, therefore perpetuating what is commonly referred to as the democratic deficit in EU affairs (Franklin, 2014).

With regard to post-Communist countries, the reason for their very disappointing turnout in Euro-elections may be connected to the absence of an old democratic tradition. Unlike Western nations, where citizens have been usually eager to go to the polling booths with the twofold intention of expressing their own ideological views and supporting their favourite candidates, in CEECs such a sense of partisan attachment and loyalty has not yet developed due to the recent origin of political parties (Franklin, 2014). In this perspective, decreasing turnout in the Old EU Member States could be interpreted as a direct consequence of the overall decline of parties in the West, with people and politicians alike sharing an 'anti-political sentiment', to use Peter Mair's expression (Mair, 2013, quoted by Müller, 2014).

Over the last 35 years, there has been a sustained and progressive slump in the EP's electoral attendance throughout the European Union, in most cases running parallel with a weaker involvement in national elections. As a result, this negative trend can not be seen exclusively as a sign of the disenchantment with or alienation from the European integration project. Furthermore, whether in the past poor electoral attendance, by mirroring the EP's institutional weakness, was regarded as a supportive evidence of the need to expand and enhance its tasks, paradoxically a greater parliamentary role has not so far matched a higher electoral turnout. This may be due to the fact that these additional EP competencies have not helped voters solve their dilemma over which party to support or clarify how they might influence the implementation of these new functions by casting their ballot. Unquestionably, deprived of this prerogative, people continue to perceive the act of showing up at the ballot box as utterly pointless, hence perpetuating the plague of abstention (Franklin, 2014).

During the May 2014 campaign, another attempt was undertaken to raise the EP's electoral profile by calling on pan-European political parties to nominate their favourite candidate to lead

Table 32.1b Turnout at EP elections in EU Member States: 2009/2013–2014

Country	2009/2013 %	Total votes	Electorate	2014 %	Total votes	Electorate	% change
France	40.63	17,992,161	44,282,823	40.73	18,955,761	46,544,712	+0.10
Germany	43.27	26,923,614	62,222,873	48.14	29,843,798	61,998,824	+4.87
Italy	65.05	32,749,004	50,342,153	57.22	28,991,258	50,662,460	−7.83
Belgium	90.39	7,014,415	7,760,436	89.64	7,125,161	7,948,854	−0.75
NL	36.75	4,573,743	12,445,497	37.32	4,782,251	12,815,496	+0.57
Luxembourg	90.76	218,423	240,669	85.55	226,217	264,433	−5.21
UK	34.70	15,723,975	45,312,626	35.60	16,545,761	46,481,532	+0.90
Ireland	58.64	1,875,920	3,199,289	52.44	1,701,942	3,245,348	−6.20
DK	59.54	2,415,568	4,057,100	56.32	2,332,217	4,141,329	−3.22
Greece	52.54	5,261,749	10,014,795	59.97	5,942,196	9,907,995	+7.43
Spain	44.87	15,935,147	35,516,119	43.81	15,998,141	36,514,084	−1.06
Portugal	36.77	3,561,502	9,684,714	33.84	3,283,610	9,702,657	−2.93
Austria	45.97	2,925,132	6,362,761	45.39	2,909,497	6,410,602	−0.58
Finland	40.29	1,664,610	4,131,827	40.98	1,728,607	4,218,081	+0.69
Sweden	45.53	3,227,561	7,088,303	51.07	3,758,951	7,359,962	+5.54
Malta	78.79	254,039	322,411	74.80	257,588	344,356	−3.99
Cyprus	59.40	312,479	526,060	43.97	266,891	606,916	−15.43
Slovenia	28.37	482,136	1,699,755	24.53	419,661	1,710,856	−3.84
Estonia	43.90	399,181	909,326	36.52	329,766	902,873	−7.38
Latvia	53.69	797,219	1,484,781	30.24	445,225	1,472,462	−23.45
Lithuania	20.98	564,803	2,692,397	47.35	1,211,279	2,557,950	+26.37
Czech Republic	28.20	2,369,137	8,401,374	18.20	1,528,250	8,395,132	−10.00
Slovakia	19.64	853,533	4,345,773	13.05	575,876	4,414,433	−6.59
Hungary	36.31	2,921,779	8,046,086	28.97	2,329,304	8,041,386	−7.34
Poland	24.53	7,497,296	30,565,272	23.83	7,301,650	30,636,537	−0.70
Bulgaria	38.99	2,601,687	6,672,274	35.84	2,336,083	6,517,383	−3.15
Romania	27.67	5,034,659	18,197,316	32.44	5,911,794	18,221,061	+4.77
Croatia	(2013) 20.83	(2013) 780,980	(2013) 3,748,815	25.24	950,980	3,767,343	+4.41
EU-27–EU-28	42.99	166,150,471	386,524,810	42.44	167,989,715	395,805,057	−0.55
EU-28	42.77	166,931,452	390,273,625	42.44	167,989,715	395,805,057	−0.33

Sources: Author's table based on own calculations from data drawn from EU Member States' national government websites and from the EP website: www.europarl.europa.eu/pdf/elections_results/review.pdf.

the executive, in order to link the shaping of both Parliament and Commission. Regretfully, this reform was unable to mend the disconnect between voters and the exercise of power as long as the aforesaid European political parties were not actively involved in the EP campaign which continued to be a '*domaine réservé*' of their national counterparts (Franklin, 2014). However, abiding by the terms of the Lisbon Treaty, the electoral results were duly taken into consideration for the appointment of the Commission President. Indeed, after a contentious process, and regardless of British opposition, the candidate of the largest political group, the European People's Party, the former Prime Minister of Luxembourg Jean-Claude Juncker, was officially proposed by the European Council and later, at the July 2014 session, approved by the European Parliament with 422 votes out of a total of 729, 46 more than the absolute majority required.

Irrefutably, the May EP contest remained essentially second-order and tailored for a protest vote by even acting as a catalyzing factor to socialize European citizens into abstention. To quote Mark N. Franklin, 'while the [Lisbon] changes appear[ed] to address th[is] problem, [. . .] in practice they seem[ed] fatally flawed' (Franklin, 2014, 10). Low participation could be also due to simple voter fatigue, given that since 1979, besides their other electoral commitments, EU citizens have been asked to choose their MEPs every five years. Overall, Euro-elections continue to depress turnout by fatally instilling habits of non-voting that may bear serious political repercussions. Intrinsically, the only antidote would be to give citizens a good reason to go to the polls and something real to vote about (Franklin and Hobolt 2011; Franklin, 2014).

Undoubtedly, the nomination of the *Spitzenkandidaten* and the subsequent election of the Commission President did not suddenly transform the European Parliament's contest from a lacklustre affair into a first-order political event, but indicated the right direction to take in the future in order to arouse motivation for voting.

2 The 2014 European Parliament's composition

2.1 Political groups

The eighth Euro-election saw the implementation of the Lisbon provisions regarding the size of the European Parliament as well as its seat apportionment among Member States. Under Article 14.2 of the Treaty on European Union (TEU), the number of representatives could not exceed 751 and no country could have less than 6 or more than 96 MEPs. Seats would be allocated on the basis of the principle of 'degressive proportionality', which takes the population of each Member State into account, although this advantage decreases the larger the population. This criterion was strongly criticized by the *Bundesverfassungsgericht* (German Federal Constitutional Court), on the grounds of its over representation of small countries.

On 30 June 2009, the Court highlighted that: '[T]he weight of the vote of a citizen from a Member State with a small population may be about twelve times the weight of the vote of a citizen from a Member State with a large population' (Bundesverfassungsgericht, 2009) [German Federal Constitutional Court] (2009, 284).

At the June 2009 EP contest, in line with the Nice Treaty which was still in force, 736 members were elected. Subsequently, in accordance with the Lisbon Treaty, 12 countries were to be given eighteen additional seats while Germany would lose three. Hence, in December 2011, by virtue of a transitional provision, the total number was increased from 751 to 754, allowing new MEPs to take up their seats and, at the same time, all German representatives to continue their mandate to the end of the legislature. On 1 July 2013, after Croatia's accession to the European Union and the arrival of 12 additional representatives, the Chamber was temporarily expanded to accommodate 766 Euro-deputies. As such, the May 2014 EP election required a fifteen-seat reduction, more precisely three from Germany and one from each of the

D.M. Viola

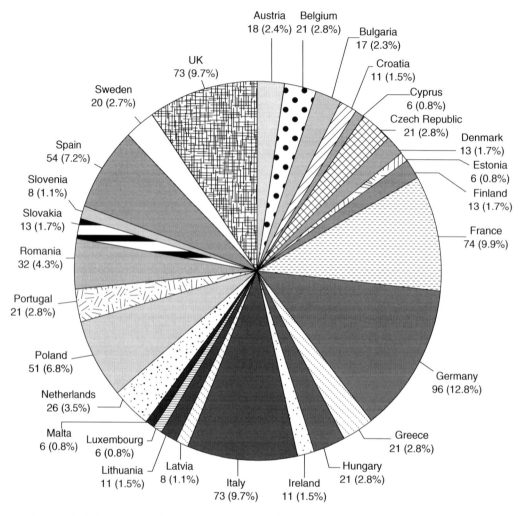

Figure 32.3 EP composition by nationality: May 2014 ★

Source: Author's figure drawn from data on the EP website, www.europarl.europa.eu.

Note: ★ Number of seats with percentages in brackets.

following countries: Belgium, Ireland, Greece, Portugal, Austria, Latvia, Lithuania, Czech Republic, Hungary, Bulgaria, Romania, and Croatia.

Finally, in July 2014, when its internal organization was finalized, the novel European Parliament presented seven political groups along with non-attached members, as depicted in Figure 32.4.

In order to gauge more consistently the extent of the changes that occurred between 2009 and 2014 among the political groups in the European Parliament with reference to their size, we have preferred to draw a comparison based on percentages rather than numbers of their respective members in the light of the different EP seat thresholds fixed in the last quinquennium.

In addition, it is worth recalling that, under the EP Rules of Procedures, in order to build a political group, members must identify a political affinity and reach a minimum number of 25 deputies from at least one-quarter of the EU countries, at present corresponding to seven.

Epilogue

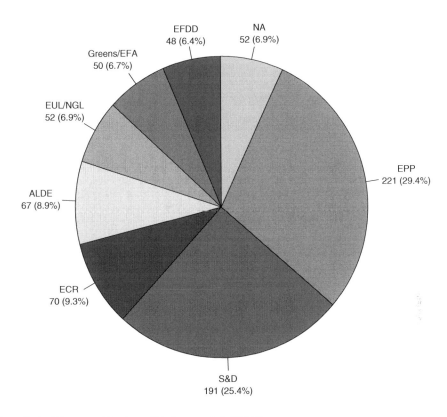

Figure 32.4 EP composition by political group: July 2014 ★

Source: Author's figure drawn from data on the EP website, www.europarl.europa.eu.

Note: ★ Number of seats with percentages in brackets.

MEPs' influence depends, to a great extent, on their ability to join big political groups benefitting from more EP funds and more speaking time at the plenary. On the basis of their relative dimension, political groups play a more incisive role in EU decision-making and obtain for their members key positions, committee Chairs or membership.

On 22–25 May 2014, the centre-right won, albeit in a subdued manner, the battle of credibility across the European Union, since it was still perceived as the most competent political force to rise to the challenge facing European society. Nonetheless, the European People's Party (EPP), dominated by Chancellor Angela Merkel's *Christlich Demokratische Union*, CDU (Christian Democratic Union), suffered a major setback, especially in those countries most deeply affected by the crisis, since the German leader was considered responsible for the adoption of strict and unfair austerity policies. Notwithstanding a tangible underperformance, the EPP retained its position as the major political alignment in the European Assembly, under the chairmanship of the German MEP Manfred Weber. The Christian Democratic group, which was backed up by 221 deputies from all over the European Union, except for Britain, diminished in strength by 6.4 per cent in comparison to 2009, mainly due to the escalation of Conservative and Eurosceptic parties.

The German delegation, made up of 29 representatives from the CDU and five from its Bavarian sister party *Christlich-Soziale Union*, CSU (Christian-Social Union), remained the most

Table 32.2a EP composition by political group: 2009, 2011, 2013 and 2014

Political group	2009 Number	2009 %	2011 Number	2011 %	2013 Number	2013 %	2014 Number	2014 %	Change % 2009–2014	Change % 2011–2014	Change % 2013–2014
Group of the European People's Party (EPP)	265	36.0	270	35.8	275	35.9	221	29.4	-6.6	-6.4	-6.5
Group of the Progressive Alliance of Socialists and Democrats in the European Parliament (S&D)	184	25.0	191	25.3	194	25.3	191	25.4	0.4	0.1	0.1
Alliance of Liberals and Democrats for Europe (ALDE)	84	11.4	85	11.3	85	11.1	67	8.9	-2.5	-2.4	-2.2
The Greens/European Free Alliances (Greens/EFA)	55	7.5	58	7.7	58	7.6	50	6.7	-0.8	-1.0	-0.9
European Conservatives and Reformists (ECR)	54	7.3	53	7.0	56	7.3	70	9.3	2.0	2.3	2.0
European United Left/Nordic Green Left (EUL/NGL)	35	4.8	35	4.6	35	4.6	52	6.9	2.1	2.3	2.3
Europe of Freedom and Democracy (EFD)	32	4.3	34	4.5	32	4.2	52	6.4	2.1	1.9	2.2
Europe of Freedom and Direct Democracy (EFDD)							48				
Non-attached	27	3.7	28	3.7	31	4.0	52	6.9	3.2	3.2	2.9
EP	736	100	754	100	766	100	751	100	+15 seats	-3 seats	-15 seats

Source: Author's table based on own calculations of data drawn from the EP website, www.europarl.europa.eu.

numerous within the EPP. In fact, despite losing popular consensus, the two parties reached jointly a remarkable 35.3 per cent of the votes, eight points ahead of their main political rival and ally at the federal level, the *Sozialdemokratische Partei Deutschlands*, SPD (Social Democratic Party of Germany). Poland boasted the second largest national contingent, caucusing 23 members from the two government partners, in particular 19 from the *Platforma Obywatelska*, PO (Civic Platform) and 4 from the *Polskie Stronnictwo Ludowe*, PSL (Polish Peasant Party). The Gaullist *Union pour un Mouvement Populaire*, UMP (Union for a Popular Movement) followed next with 20 seats, after slipping into second position at the 2014 EP contest in France. Another key component of the Christian Democratic group consisted of the *Partido Popular*, PP (People's Party), led by the Spanish Prime Minister Mariano Rajoy. By grabbing 26.1 per cent of votes, the PP was able to send 16 representatives to Strasbourg, one-third less than in the previous term. Finally, *Forza Italia*, FI (Forward Italy) run by former Premier Silvio Berlusconi, garnered a fair 16.82 per cent voting share and 13 seats which, nevertheless, marked its worst result ever (European Parliament, 2014).

Paradoxically, rival political forces competing at the national level converged within the EPP group. For instance, in the Italian emblematic case of the dissolved *Popolo della Libertà*, PdL (People's Freedom), members from the resulting split parties, the refounded FI and the novel party *Nuovo Centrodestra*, NCD (New Centre Right), guided by Interior Minister Angelino Alfano, found themselves uneasily sitting close in the European Chamber even after, and regardless of, their national political divorce.

With regard to Central and Eastern European countries, the EPP echoed the success attained in the previous Euro-elections by accounting for 87 seats, equivalent to nearly two-fifths of the total. This outcome was heavily influenced by the tragic events in Ukraine, which revived old fears about Russia's potential threat. In Latvia, the Liberal-Conservative party *Vienotība*, V (Unity), led by Premier Laimdota Straujuima, obtained 46.19 per cent of the votes by securing four mandates. Likewise, in Hungary Prime Minister Viktor Orbán's *Fidesz-Magyar Polgári Szövetség* (*Fidesz*-Hungarian Civic Union) replicated its exceptional performance carried out at the General elections held two months earlier (www.robert-schuman.eu, May 2014).

Its overall victory at the EP contest allowed the EPP to claim two top positions at the EU level, with the election of Former Luxembourg Prime Minister Jean-Claude Juncker as head of the European Commission on 15 July 2014 and the appointment of Polish Premier Donald Tusk as President of the European Council a month and half later, on 30 August.

Still lagging behind its centre-right political rival, the Progressive Alliance of Socialists and Democrats (S&D) embodies the second but, at the same time, the most transnational group in the European Parliament. Its current official name was coined in June 2009 to reflect the heterogeneous composition of the group after the adhesion of new political movements only partially belonging to the Socialist and Social Democratic tradition, such as Italy's *Partito Democratico*, PD (Democratic Party) and Cyprus' *Kinima Sosialdimokraton*, EDEK (Movement for Social Democracy).

In the aftermath of the Euro-election, the S&D gained an extra 0.4 percentage points, therefore covering 25.4 per cent of the hemicycle with its 191 representatives from all 28 EU countries. Moreover, the internal group balance varied with the most notable change coming from Italy. Under the premiership of Matteo Renzi, known as the '*rottamatore*' ('scrapper') after calling for the entire demolition of the higher echelons of Italy's political establishment, the governing PD topped the polls by touching 40.8 per cent and seizing 31 seats in the Strasbourg arena (Ministero dell'Interno, 2014).

This exceptional score, almost 15 percentage points up from 26.12 conquered five years earlier, was the best in the Italian history since 1958, when *Democrazia Cristiana*, DC (Christian Democracy) reached 42.35 per cent of the consensus in the general election (Ministero dell'Interno, 2014). Such a stunning record made the PD, which since 28 February 2014 had become full member of the Party of European Socialists and Democrats (PES), the largest national unit of the S&D in the Strasbourg arena (PES, 2014).

The slight group increase was also attributable to the recovery of the German *Sozialdemokratische Partei Deutschlands*, SPD (Social Democratic Party) and the British Labour Party, which garnered respectively 27 and 20 seats. Lastly, it is worth taking into consideration the landslide victory of the Romanian Coalition, rallying *Partidul Social Democrat*, PSD (Social Democratic Party), *Partidul Conservator*, PC (Conservative Party), and *Uniunea Nationala pentru Progresul Romaniei*, UNPR (National Union for the Advancement of Romania), which enabled 16 MEPs, exactly half of the whole Romanian cohort, to enter the S&D.

At the Rome Congress, held in March 2014, the Party of European Socialists proposed the German CDU Member, Martin Schulz, as its official candidate to the Commission presidency. Although his nomination was eventually cast aside, in July 2014 Schulz was instead elected, by an absolute majority of 409 votes out of 612, as President of the European Parliament for the first half of the eighth legislature. This was a memorable event given that, for the very first time since 1979, the same politician has been designated to cover this role for two consecutive half-terms. Consequently, the Socialists and Democrats assigned the group's top post to the former EP Vice-President, the Italian Euro-deputy Gianni Pittella.

At a great distance from the EPP and S&D, the Alliance for European Conservatives and Reformists (ECR) lies in third position in the incoming 2014–2019 European Chamber. Indeed, as a result of a 2 per cent increase which raised their number to 70, they succeeded in bypassing the Liberals.

The group was established on the eve of the seventh European Election, following the decision of the British Conservative Party and the Czech *Občanská demokratická strana*, ODS (Civic Democratic Party) to leave the EPP, due to their disagreement over the Lisbon Treaty and, more generally, over a federal European Union (Phillips, 2009).

By functioning more like a political association, the group, guided by the Tory MEP Syed Kamall, rallied a variety of Euro-realist Conservative and right-wing parties from eight Old EU Member States and from seven New ones.

In particular, the ECR is dominated numerically by the British Conservative Party, notwithstanding its 3.69 per cent loss in the last election, and by the Polish *Prawo i Sprawiedliwość* PiS (Law and Justice Party), subsequent to its 4.38 per cent rise in relation to 2009.

In May 2014, for the first time in the history of British politics since 1918, a party other than the Conservatives or Labour won an electoral contest. As never before, the Tories' hegemony was eclipsed by an insurgent party, the avowedly anti-EU United Kingdom Independence Party (UKIP). In fact, despite Prime Minister David Cameron's promise of convening a referendum about Britain's membership to the European Union, the Conservative party underwent the humiliation of sinking from first to third place by scoring only 23.31 per cent of the votes (www.robert-schuman.eu, May 2014).

Notwithstanding such a substantial erosion of the British popular mandate, the ECR was able to attract MEPs from other right-wing parties or movements moderately critical towards the European establishment. The European Conservatives and Reformists performed well in Germany, where the recently founded anti-Euro Party *Alternative für Deutschland*, AfD (Alternative for Germany) got an impressive 7 per cent of votes by grasping seven seats. Another new group component is the anti-immigration *Dansk Folkeparti*, DF (Danish People's Party), previously a member of Europe of Freedom and Democracy (EFD). By achieving a leap of almost 12 points in comparison with 2009, the DF attained a historic score of 26.6 per cent, thus doubling the number of its representatives from two to four. Ultimately, the *Nieuw-Vlaamse Alliantie*, N-VA (New Flemish Alliance) decided to join the ECR after quitting the Greens/EFA, owing to strong divergences at the domestic level with its

Epilogue

Dutch Green adversaries, *Groen!*. By coming out ahead in the 2014 European election, the Flemish separatist N-VA markedly increased the number of its representatives from one to four, turning into the largest Belgian party in the European Parliament (www.robert-schuman.eu, May 2014).

In spite of the Lisbon reforms, the ECR members of the out-going Parliament preferred not to submit any candidature to the presidency of the European Commission, on the grounds that no European political space truly existed whereby citizens or representatives could claim similar sovereignty to that existing at national level (www.robert-schuman.eu, May 2014).

Whilst ranking third in the seventh legislature, the Alliance of Liberals and Democrats for Europe (ALDE) plunged down into fourth in 2014, losing 2.5 per cent of the total number of seats. The British Liberal Democrats, LD and the German *Freie Demokratische Partei*, FDP (Free Democratic Party), being previously the two main political components of the group, suffered an overwhelming defeat due to their record unpopularity in their home countries.

In the UK, in a huge blow to the authority of its leader Nick Clegg, deputy Prime Minister in Cameron's cabinet, the LD appeared as shadow of its former self. The party almost halved its voting share to 6.68 per cent, losing all but one of the eleven seats acquired in Strasbourg at the last election. Such a dismal performance, worse than in the 1994 EP race when the LD captured just two mandates under the old first-past-the-post system, even prompted renewed calls for Clegg to resign.

Similarly, the once-grand FDP got a mere 3.4 per cent of the votes, thus retaining just one fourth of its representatives, whose number therefore plummeted from twelve to three. The other German MEP, who joined the ALDE, came from *Freie Wähler* (Free Voters), a party that, whilst scoring a scarce 1.56 per cent, was able to gain representation in the EP arena, following the abolition of the 3 per cent electoral threshold by the German Federal Constitutional Court on 26 February 2014 (Euractiv, 2014).

However, by embracing 67 Euro-deputies from 21 countries, the Liberals and Democrats continued to be the third most transnational alignment within the EP. Among the 15 Old Member States, Spain led, with eight seats assigned to representatives of *Unión Progreso y Democracia*, UPyD (Union Progress and Democracy), *Ciudadanos-Partido de la Ciudadanía*, C'S (Citizens, Citizens' Party), *Coalición por Europa* (Coalition for Europe), followed by France and the Netherlands, with one seat less. Notably, the French electoral alliance *Alternative* consisted of the centrist political party *Union des démocrates et indépendants*, UDI (Union of Democrats and Independents) and the pro-European *Mouvement Démocratique*, MoDem (Democratic Movement). As to the Dutch contingent, four seats belonged to the Social-Liberal opposition party *Democraten 66*, D66 (Democrats 66) whilst the remaining three went to the *Volkspartij voor Vrijheid en Democratie*, VVD (People's Party for Freedom and Democracy), acting as senior government partner in the second Mark Rutte cabinet since November 2012. In Belgium, the two Liberal parties, the *Open Vlaamse Liberal en Democraten*, Open VLD (Open Flemish Liberals and Democrats) and the *Mouvement Réformateur*, MR (Reformist Movement) each won three seats. In brief, within this first cluster of Member States, only Italy and Greece did not account for any ALDE representatives in the Strasbourg arena.

As to all those countries that entered the EU after 2004, eight of them elected Liberal MEPs, excluding Poland, Hungary, and Latvia along with the two Mediterranean islands, Malta and Cyprus. The Czech political movement *Akce nespokojených občanů 2011*, ANO 2011 (Action of Dissatisfied Citizens 2011), founded by the Finance Minister, the billionaire Andrej Babiš, and the Bulgarian *Dvizhenie za prava i svobodi*, DPS (Movement for Rights and Freedoms), aimed at safeguarding the interests of the Muslims and, in particular, of the Turkish minority, won respectively four seats each (European Parliament, 2014). The Liberal government party *Eesti Reformierakond*, ER (Estonian Reform Party), under the premiership of Taavi Roivas, came out victorious with 24.30 per cent, thus claiming two out of the six seats allocated to Estonia in the EP Assembly. Also the centrist, Social-Liberal opposition party *Eesti Keskerakon*, EK (Estonian

Centre Party), traditionally more popular among the Russian minority, succeeded in sending one representative to Strasbourg.

On the eve of the new term, the former Belgian Prime Minister Guy Verhofstadt from the Open VLD, who was the unsuccessful ALDE contender for the European Commission presidency, was instead confirmed as group leader.

Next in line, the European United Left/Nordic Green Left (EUL/NGL) represents, along with the Independents, the fifth largest faction in the EP arena. In relation to the 2009–2014 term, the group's share increased by 2.1 per cent, occupying 6.9 per cent of the hemicycle, the highest rate it ever achieved in the history of European elections. However, this progress was rather asymmetric, being concentrated mainly in Southern Europe: in Greece, with the victory of *Syriza* led by Alexis Tsipras, and in Spain, with the unexpected breakthrough of the newborn movement guided by Pablo Iglesias Turrión, *Por la Democracia Social, Podemos* (For the Social Democracy, We can). Furthermore, after years of parliamentary marginalization at both national and EU levels, the Italian radical left founded an electoral list called *L'Altra Europa con Tsipras* (Another Europe with Tsipras) that managed to cross the infamous 4 per cent barrier and secure three representatives in the European Parliament.

Guided by the German MEP Gabriele Zimmer, the EUL/NGL gathered 52 representatives of 14 nationalities and 19 party delegations, the biggest ones being the seven-member German *Die Linke* and the six-member Greek *Syriza*, corresponding to roughly one-quarter of the whole group. Its internal composition appears rather heterogeneous, with just a few remaining orthodox Communist elements, especially after the defection of the two MEPs from the *Kommunistikó Komma Elladas*, KKE (Communist Party of Greece). Indeed, the new group also accommodated politicians not traditionally originating from the radical left but keen to develop the bases of participative democracy or to address social, economic, and regional problems. Among them, there were deputies from the Spanish anti-establishment movement *Podemos*, from the Basque and Irish Nationalist left and from the Dutch and German parties defending animal rights. Hence, the EUL/NGL resembles a confederal body, where each component unit retains a large autonomy, but cooperates in pursuit of common political objectives. For instance, its official stance is not Europhobic, but fiercely critical of current EU neo-liberal policies. At the Fourth Congress held in Madrid in December 2013, the Party of the European Left (EL) nominated Alexis Tsipras as its candidate to the Commission presidency (EL, 2013).

On the outset of the eighth term, the number of independents reached 52, rising by 3.2 per cent in relation to the 2009 election. Many of these members came from anti-European parties, notably *Front National*, FN (National Front), *Partij voor de Vrijheid*, PVV (Party for Freedom), *Lega Nord*, LN (Northern League), *Vlaams Belang*, VB (Flemish Interest) and *Freiheitliche Partei Österreichs*, FPÖ (Freedom Party of Austria). In fact, short of the seven-nation representation required under EP rules of procedure, the French FN leader Marine Le Pen and her Dutch, Italian, Belgian, and Austrian allies failed to set up an alternative Eurosceptic political alignment and had no choice but to sit together as non-attached MEPs. The option of joining the existing anti-European political group the Europe of Freedom and Democracy, EFD, was discarded, mainly due to the refusal of the leader of the United Kingdom Independence Party, UKIP, on the grounds of the FN's anti-Semitic principles. According to Marine Le Pen, these 'insulting accusations', which were promptly bounced back, were to be attributed, instead, to the UKIP's fear that the FN would challenge its leadership within the EFD. And yet, in an interview published by the German newspaper *Die Spiegel* on 3 June 2014, Le Pen claimed to be willing to consider a possible cooperation with UKIP given their shared approach to Europe (von Rohr, 2014).

Undeniably, behind her failure to form a far-right Eurosceptic political group, there was a deep-rooted isolation and even a long-standing ostracism of the *Front National* within the European

Parliament, especially under the previous, historic leadership of her father, Jean-Marie Le Pen (www.robert-schuman.eu, May 2014). Despite its relegation to 'non-attached' status, it cannot be ignored that in May 2014 the FN, under its official electoral motto *'Non à Bruxelles, oui à la France'* ('No to Brussels, yes to France'), topped the French polls, scoring an exceptional 24.86 per cent, the best result ever achieved in both a national and European election (Calvet and Bouchet-Petersen, 2014).

The *Front National* beat its historical rival *Union pour un Mouvement Populaire*, UMP, the centre-right opposition party of former President of the Republic Nicolas Sarkozy, which captured only 20.81 per cent of the votes. Besides, Le Pen shocked the French political stage by humiliating President François Hollande's ruling Socialists, who fell to third place with a record low 13.98 per cent (European Parliament, 2014). After all, by quadrupling its 2009 score, the FN obtained twenty-three seats, becoming the biggest French delegation and the fifth largest party group in the Strasbourg arena behind the German CDU-CSU, the Italian PD, the German SDP, and UKIP.

As already mentioned, the closer allies of the French representatives from the *Front National* are the Italian MEPs from the resurgent *Lega Nord*, guided by the new leader Matteo Salvini who, under the fortunate electoral slogan *'Basta €uro'* ('Stop €uro'), doubled their vote share compared to 2009, thus securing five seats. Finally, among the non-attached, stand out the representatives of the Dutch anti-Islam and anti-immigrant *Partij voor de Vrijheid*. Conducted by the populist Geert Wilders, the party managed to confirm four places despite a 3.5 per cent loss of votes in relation to the previous EP contest.

After the success attained five years earlier and the involvement of several ecologist parties in unpopular national governments, the Greens could hardly aim to poll well in the May 2014 EP contest. Indeed, following a reverse trend, environmental and regionalist movements managed to get fifty seats, thus losing 0.8. per cent of their own representatives. This minor decline could be attributed to the poor performance of the French, German, Dutch, and Finnish Ecologists as well as the departure of the Flemish NV-A MEPs, only partially compensated by the gains achieved by their Austrian, Swedish, and Spanish partners. In addition, it is worth noting an interesting turn in the EP race with the slow spread of the Green family from its traditional Western bastions to Eastern Europe. In fact, further to their electoral breakthrough, the Hungarian Green Liberal parties *Lehet Más a Politika*, LMP (Politics Can Be Different) and *Párbeszéd Magyarországért*, PM (Dialogue Hungary) as well as the Croatian Green left-wing *Održivi razvoj Hrvatske*, ORaH (Croatian Sustainable Development) secured representation in the EP arena.

The second political family of the group, the European Free Alliance, EFA, headed by the Catalan MEP Josep Maria Terricabras, consisted of parties representing regionalist and minority interests. It rallied seven MEPs, among whom two from the Scottish National Party, SNP, one from the *Plaid Cymru* or Party of Wales and two from the Catalan electoral alliance *L'Esquerra pel Dret a Decidir* (Left for the Right to Decide) – specifically one from *Catalunya Sí* (Yes Catalonia) and one from *Esquerra Republicana de Catalunya*, ERC (Republican Left of Catalonia). The last two representatives were from the Valencian *Primavera Europea/Compromis* (European Spring/Compromise) and from the Latvian *Par Cilveka Tiesibam Vieneta*, PCTV (For Human Rights in United Latvia).

The group of the Greens/European Free Alliance (Greens/EFA), assembling representatives of 17 EU Member States, has been customarily co-chaired by two deputies of different nationality and gender. Accordingly, at the beginning of the new parliamentary term, the German MEP Rebecca Harms, along with the Belgian MEP Philippe Lambert, were elected to lead the group. The Greens also chose to continue this tradition by nominating two *Spitzenkandidaten*. For this purpose, they held a public primary election, open to anyone in the EU aged 16 or over who supported Green values. Although this initiative was marred by low public participation, it introduced an innovative and democratic selection method which led to the nomination of the French MEP José Bové and the German MEP Ska Keller (Keating, 2014).

At the bottom of the list lies the anti-European group *par excellence*, Europe of Freedom and Democracy (EFD), which, on 24 June 2014, upon the proposal of its new affiliate party, the Italian anti-establishment *Movimento 5 Stelle*, M5S (5-Star-Movement), changed its official title into Europe of Freedom and Direct Democracy (EFDD).

Despite his triumphal march at the Euro-elections in Britain, the leader of the United Kingdom Independence Party (UKIP), Nigel Farage, struggled to re-establish the group within the European Parliament after the defection of *Lega Nord*, LN (Northern League), *Dansk Folkeparti*, DF (Danish People's Party) and *Peruss*, PS (The Finns) as well as the missed re-election of some other EFD members (Watt, 2014). In fact, with only two units outliving the old group, notably UKIP and the Lithuanian *Tvarka ir teisingumas*, TT (Order and Justice), the EFD risked disappearing due to the failure to reach the seven-nation threshold. Its survival was guaranteed by the entry of Italy's maverick M5S, founded by the former comedian Beppe Grillo, and by the membership of a handful of deputies from France, Sweden, Latvia, and the Czech Republic who joined their British and Lithuanian partners.

By considering Brussels as a common enemy, a formal alliance with the French far-right *Front National* would have appeared sensible. Nonetheless, as pointed out earlier, such a prospect was vehemently rejected by UKIP, officially on ideological grounds, but in reality it was made impossible by Farage's and Le Pen's strong personal ambition and unwillingness to 'hold the sceptre together'.

Shortly afterwards, the British politician, who had ardently pledged to avoid partnership with the extreme right in the European Parliament, joined forces with *Sverigedemokraterna*, SD (Sweden Democrats), founded by white supremacists, and invited a French independent, ex-*Front National* member to enter the group. In order to explain his apparently incoherent behaviour, Farage argued that the two Swedish MEPs had officially distanced themselves from their national party's dark past, whilst the French Member Joëlle Bergeron had left FN over disagreements with the official party's opposition to grant electoral rights to migrants (Watt, 2014).

Eventually, the renamed EFDD succeeded and went on to caucus 48 members, thus boosting its size by 2.1 percentage points, with UKIP and M5S embodying the two main party delegations – with twenty-four and seventeen seats respectively. As a result, Farage remained undisputed group leader, sided, as Co-Chair, by the Italian MEP David Borrelli from *Movimento 5 Stelle*. Lastly, even more than the ECR, the hard Eurosceptics belonging to the EFDD did not deem it worthwhile to nominate their *Spitzenkandidat*.

At the opening of the eighth term, as in the whole history of the European Parliament, no single political group achieved an absolute majority of members. The 2014 EP election confirmed once again the hegemony of the traditional centre-right and centre-left poles. Yet, the contest also witnessed the rise of the far right and radical left along with the European *début* of a plethora of anti-establishment movements.

Moreover, within the newly shaped Assembly, the Europhile majority now appears to be challenged by the highest number of Eurosceptics than ever before. The mainstream pro-European bloc rallies the EPP, the S&D, the ALDE and, more recently, the Greens, thereby covering 70.4 per cent of the whole Assembly. Conversely, the Europhobic composite galaxy, embracing the EFDD, the ECR, and the independents, merely exceeds 23 per cent.

In comparison with 2009, the Europhile alliance lost 9.4 per cent – of which 6.6 per cent was achieved only by its top group, the Christian Democrats – whilst Eurosceptics and Euro-realists, by accounting for 22.6 per cent, increased by nearly 7.3 per cent their aggregate score. Between these two blocs stands the EUL/NGL, previously divided over the crucial question of Europe, but that, under the charismatic leadership of Alexis Tsipras, seems to have found a common '*alter*-European' approach, aimed at reviving the original federal principles of the integration process whilst rejecting Brussels' neo-liberal technocratic interpretation. Accordingly, the EUL/

Epilogue

Table 32.2b EP composition by nationality and political group: July 2014

Country	EPP	S&D	ECR	ALDE	EUL/NGL	Greens/EFA	EFDD	NA	Total seats	% seats
Austria	5	5	0	1	0	3	0	4	18	2.4
Belgium	4	4	4	6	0	2	0	1	21	2.8
Bulgaria	7	4	2	4	0	0	0	0	17	2.3
Croatia	5	2	1	2	0	1	0	0	11	1.5
Cyprus	2	2	0	0	2	0	0	0	6	0.8
Czech Republic	7	4	2	4	3	0	1	0	21	2.8
Denmark	1	3	4	3	1	1	0	0	13	1.7
Estonia	1	1	0	3	0	1	0	0	6	0.8
Finland	3	2	2	4	1	1	0	0	13	1.7
France	20	13	0	7	4	6	1	23	74	9.9
Germany	34	27	8	4	8	13	0	2	96	12.8
Greece	5	4	1	0	6	0	0	5	21	2.8
Hungary	12	4	0	0	0	2	0	3	21	2.8
Ireland	4	1	1	1	4	0	0	0	11	1.5
Italy	17	31	0	0	3	0	17	5	73	9.7
Latvia	4	1	1	0	0	1	1	0	8	1.1
Lithuania	2	2	1	3	0	1	2	0	11	1.5
Luxembourg	3	1	0	1	0	1	0	0	6	0.8
Malta	3	3	0	0	0	0	0	0	6	0.8
Netherlands	5	3	2	7	3	2	0	4	26	3.5
Poland	23	5	19	0	0	0	0	4	51	6.8
Portugal	7	8	0	2	4	0	0	0	21	2.8
Romania	15	16	0	1	0	0	0	0	32	4.3
Slovakia	6	4	2	1	0	0	0	0	13	1.7
Slovenia	5	1	0	1	0	1	0	0	8	1.1
Spain	17	14	0	8	11	4	0	0	54	7.2
Sweden	4	6	0	3	1	4	2	0	20	2.7
UK	0	20	20	1	1	6	24	1	73	9.7
EU	221	191	70	67	52	50	48	52	751	—

Source: Author's table based on data drawn from the EP website: www.europarl.europa.eu

NGL share at 6.9, recording a 2.2 per cent rise compared to its 4.8 percentage attained in 2009, may therefore strategically swing either way.

The real test ahead for the European Parliament is how to work efficiently in the light of the increased heterogeneity among its representatives. Over the years, in order to pass legislation, the EPP and the S&D forged a sort of informal cross-ideological partnership. This Grand Coalition, as it was usually referred to, was extended, whenever possible, to other political forces, therefore bestowing upon Parliament a greater institutional force and authority.

During the 2014–2019 term, mainstream political families are likely to embark on coalition-building more often than in the past in order to circumvent the obstructionism expected from the enlarged anti-EU front. Indeed, the presence of further opponents and severe critics to European integration, albeit inferior to the number of Europhiles, may affect somehow the balance of power in the Strasbourg Assembly, impact on the functioning of the EP, and consequently influence EU decision-making.

On the other hand, it is worth pointing out that, despite flying high on the EU firmament, Eurosceptics are not as strong and powerful as they would have been if they had converged into a single, larger political group.

Apart from their collective hostility to the European project, they do not seem to share other socio-political values or economic principles. For instance, the far-right *Front National* and the separatist *Lega Nord* hardly look similar to Farage's feisty, yet democratic UKIP, to Grillo's protest party M5S or to the neo-Nazi Hungarian movement *Jobbik* (Ignazi, 2014). Due to their different ideological roots and political outlooks, Eurosceptics are unlikely to easily find a common platform from which to defy the traditional pro-European oligarchy. Nonetheless, their larger presence in the EP arena is expected to spark off three subtler effects. First, it is likely to make it harder for European politicians to invoke 'a supranational Europe' as a *panacea* for every problem. Second, it might induce mainstream political groups to resort to a permanent alliance in order to pass legislation, by making European Union politics stale and thus aggravating the democratic deficit. Third, it could weaken and terrify Member State national governments, by compelling them to adopt more anti-European stances (Charlemagne, 2014).

In sum, the newly shaped and multifarious European Parliament is faced with the arduous task of pursuing and implementing radical reforms which are necessary in order to guarantee the survival and development of the European Union. To this avail, as Alberto Alemanno suggests, mainstream PGs should not ostracize Eurosceptics, but 'rather seize this opportunity to engage with them, address their discontent and possibly question some of their own pro-integration biases' (Alemanno, 2014).

3 European elections through gender lenses

Although women stand for more than half of the EU population, they have been generally under-represented in the Strasbourg Assembly. On several occasions, in order to favour a suitable solution to this problem, the European Parliament has called upon the Member States and the political parties to promote the participation of female candidates in Euro-elections without, nevertheless, requiring gender quotas (EP Resolution, 4/7/2013).

More women in Parliament are necessary in order to enhance the level of democratic representation in the European Union and to implement gender mainstreaming. At the May 2014 contest, 275 female candidates were elected, the highest number ever recorded in the history of the European Union. This means that the EP universe is now populated by 36.6 per cent of women, making up nearly three-eighths of the whole House. If compared to the outcome conquered in 2009, this marked a 1.6 percentage progress that might contribute towards mitigating, to some degree, sex imbalance at the parliamentary level. However, the new Assembly once again failed to attain gender parity and even the 40 per cent female threshold agreed by the Member States of the Council of Europe.

At the eighth EP contest, the performance of women differed significantly across the European continent. By looking at Table 32.3a, it is possible to notice small and large discrepancies in terms of female representation between the nine clusters of countries.

First of all, it is worth pointing out that the proportion of elected women was 11.4 per cent lower in the New EU-13 than in the Old EU-15. This gap widened to 12.2 per cent between the 17 Old democracies, including Malta and Cyprus, and the 11 post-Communist newcomers. Moreover, the infamous North–South divide extended to women's access to the European Parliament, with the Nordic countries outperforming by 9.1 per cent the Southern ones. Indeed, whilst the first category, including Denmark, Sweden, and Finland, marked a rate of 47.8 per cent, the second one, embracing Spain, Portugal, Greece, Italy, Malta, and Cyprus, touched 38.7 per cent.

Beyond doubt, within the nine categories, it is possible to detect substantial differences between the individual countries. As indicated in Table 32.3b, in eight national delegations women's presence did not even achieve 30 per cent, with Lithuania registering the worst rate of 9.1 per cent, followed by Cyprus with 16.7 and Hungary with 19 per cent. Conversely, in the other nine cases,

Table 32.3a Gender MEP ratio in aggregate countries: 2014

Aggregate countries	Male MEPs		Female MEPs	
	Number	%	Number	%
Old EU-15	325	60.19	215	39.81
EU-17	332	60.14	220	39.86
New EU-11(Post-Communist countries including Croatia)	144	72.36	55	27.64
New EU-13 (including Croatia)	151	71.56	60	28.44
PIIGS/GIPSI*	109	60.56	71	39.44
GIPSIC**	114	61.29	72	38.71
Southern EU Countries***	111	61.33	70	38.67
Nordic EU Countries****	24	52.17	22	47.83
EU-28	**476**	**63.38**	**275**	**36.62**

Source: Author's table based on own calculations of data drawn from the EP website: www.europarl.europa.eu and from EU Member States' national government websites.

Notes:
* Portugal, Italy, Ireland, Greece, and Spain.
** Greece, Italy, Portugal, Spain, Ireland, and Cyprus.
*** Portugal, Italy, Greece, Spain, Malta, and Cyprus.
**** Denmark, Sweden, and Finland.

the level of female representation within the EP arena stood at between 30 and 40 per cent, with five of them, Germany, Italy, Latvia, Portugal, and Slovenia, even crossing the 35 per cent threshold.

Women's percentage exceeded 40 per cent in the remaining 11 countries: France, Netherlands, UK, Ireland, Spain, Austria, Finland, Sweden, Estonia, Malta, and Croatia. Remarkably, female Euro-deputies outnumbered their male colleagues in Sweden, Finland, Ireland, and Malta. Whereas the first two cases, reaching 55 and 53.85 per cent respectively, could be easily framed within their Nordic political and cultural tradition underlying the embedded gender equality within their society, the outstanding Irish rate of 54.55 per cent and the all-time high Maltese score of 66.7 per cent stemmed from a more recent active campaign to drive women into politics. In particular, the magnitude of this event in the small Mediterranean island could be better understood when considering that not a single seat was occupied by a Maltese lady in the two previous parliamentary terms. Overall, the 2014 EP race indicated a growing female trend in 12 countries, with Malta heading with a prominent 66.7 per cent increase, followed in sequence by Ireland, Italy, and Luxembourg with a noteworthy 29.5, 17.5 and 16.7 per cent rise, respectively. On the other hand, the contest revealed an ebbing proportion of women MEPs in 13 cases, most dramatically in Hungary by 17.3 per cent, then in Cyprus by 16.7, in Lithuania by 15.9 and, surprisingly, even in Denmark by 15.4 per cent.

In order to complete this survey of the EP results in 2014, it seems appropriate to look more closely at the gender composition of the political groups and the non-aligned MEPs. As displayed in Table 32.3c, the S&D marked the top female record of 86 MEPs, equivalent to 11.45 per cent of the total number of representatives sitting in the Strasbourg arena. This meant a 4.81 percentage rise compared to 2009, leading to a nearly perfect male–female ratio of 55 and 45. Interestingly, the Italian PD boldly came forward as the largest 14-member 'pink' cohort, corresponding to 16.3 per cent of all the Socialist women.

Next, the EPP political family followed with 69 women, covering 9.2 per cent of the total number of Euro-deputies. Yet, despite this relatively high figure, the female proportion within the group was rather disappointing, as it barely touched 31.2 per cent, hence denoting even

Table 32.3b European Parliament composition by nationality and gender: July 2014

Country	Number of seats	% seats	Number male MEPs	% Male MEPs	% Men of total male MEPs	% Men of total MEPs	Number female MEPs	% female MEPs	% Women of total female MEPs	% Women of total MEPs
Austria	18	2.40	10	55.56	2.10	1.33	8	44.44	2.92	1.07
Belgium	21	2.80	15	71.43	3.14	2.00	6	28.57	2.19	0.80
Bulgaria	17	2.26	12	70.59	2.52	1.60	5	29.41	1.82	0.67
Croatia	11	1.46	6	54.55	1.26	0.80	5	45.45	1.82	0.67
Cyprus	6	0.80	5	83.33	1.05	0.67	1	16.67	0.36	0.13
Czech Republic	21	2.80	16	76.19	3.35	2.13	5	23.81	1.82	0.67
Denmark	13	1.73	9	69.23	1.89	1.20	4	30.77	1.46	0.53
Estonia	6	0.80	3	50.00	0.63	0.40	3	50.00	1.09	0.40
Finland	13	1.73	6	46.15	1.26	0.80	7	53.85	2.55	0.93
France	74	9.85	43	58.11	9.01	5.73	31	41.89	11.31	4.13
Germany	96	12.78	62	64.58	13.00	8.26	34	35.42	12.41	4.53
Greece	21	2.80	16	76.19	3.35	2.13	5	23.81	1.82	0.67
Hungary	21	2.80	17	80.95	3.56	2.26	4	19.05	1.46	0.53
Ireland	11	1.46	5	45.45	1.05	0.67	6	54.55	2.19	0.80
Italy	73	9.72	44	60.27	9.22	5.86	29	39.73	10.58	3.86
Latvia	8	1.07	5	62.50	1.05	0.67	3	37.50	1.09	0.40
Lithuania	11	1.46	10	90.91	2.10	1.33	1	9.09	0.36	0.13
Luxembourg	6	0.80	4	66.67	0.84	0.53	2	33.33	0.73	0.27
Malta	6	0.80	2	33.33	0.42	0.27	4	66.67	1.46	0.53
Netherlands	26	3.46	15	57.69	3.14	2.00	11	42.31	4.01	1.46
Poland	51	6.79	39	76.47	8.18	5.19	12	23.53	4.38	1.60
Portugal	21	2.80	13	61.90	2.73	1.73	8	38.10	2.92	1.07
Romania	32	4.26	22	68.75	4.61	2.93	10	31.25	3.65	1.33
Slovakia	13	1.73	9	69.23	1.89	1.20	4	30.77	1.46	0.53
Slovenia	8	1.07	5	62.50	1.05	0.67	3	37.50	1.09	0.40
Spain	54	7.19	31	57.41	6.51	4.13	23	42.59	8.36	3.06
Sweden	20	2.66	9	45.00	1.89	1.20	11	55.00	4.01	1.46
UK	73	9.72	43	58.90	9.01	5.73	30	41.10	10.95	3.99
EU	751	100	476	—	100	63.38	275	—	100	36.62

Source: Author's table based on own calculations of data drawn from the EP website: www.europarl.europa.eu and from EU Member States' national government websites.

Table 32.3c EP composition by political group, nationality and gender: July 2014

Source: Author's table based on data drawn from the EP website, www.europarl.europa.eu.

a 2.4 per cent drop in relation to 2009. By encompassing nine out of 69 female Christian Democrats, equivalent to 13 per cent, the French UMP delegation presented the highest figure of women. In addition, since nine of the 20 Gaullist members were female, it also represented the best gender-balanced national component within the EPP.

By accounting for 27 women, the European United Left/Nordic Green Left (EUL/NGL) came third, along with the ALDE, in terms of sheer female numbers, dominating 3.60 per cent of the House. The Spanish unit, embracing three *compañeras* from the *Izquierda Unida* IU (United Left) and one from the *Alternativa galega de esquerda en Europa* along with three *indignadas* from the newborn *Podemos* movement, topped up to 25.9 per cent with its seven out 27 EUL/NGL women. Most significantly, at 51.9 per cent, the EUL/NGL boasted a gender balance slightly in favour of women, thanks to an impressive 23.3 per cent increase compared to the previous legislature. Finally, it is worth emphasizing that within the EP Assembly, only the Communists were headed by a lady, the German MEP from the *Linke*, Gabriele Zimmer, following her re-election in July 2014.

Sequentially, ALDE women grabbed twenty-six seats, equivalent to 3.46 per cent of the Strasbourg hemicycle, but the female proportion within the group itself slipped to the rate of 38.8, marking a 6.4 per cent shrinkage between 2009 and 2014. The French, Dutch, and Spanish Liberal cohorts alike, each gathering three ladies and grasping 11.5 per cent, were the most successful in terms of fielding female representation.

In 2014, the Greens/EFA alliance sent 21 women to Strasbourg, among whom were 19 ecologists and two regionalists. As such, the group took up 2.8 per cent of the hemicycle, split between 2.5 and 0.3 per cent respectively for the two political components. In spite of their continued support for equal rights and equal opportunities, the Greens lost, jointly with their regionalist partners, the largest share of women representatives, equivalent to 12.5 per cent. Their rate plummeted from the historic top record of 54.5 per cent registered in 2009 to that of 42 per cent in 2014. Nevertheless, this score could be still considered fairly satisfactory as it exceeded by far the average female quota within the EP Assembly. Interestingly, the German delegation enjoyed the highest female profile within the whole Greens/EFA alignment, with seven out of 21, equal to 33.3 per cent of all the women converging into the group.

In line with this, the EFDD marked the second lowest female percentage of 2.4 by rallying 18 women, of whom 8 were affiliates to the Italian M5S, 7 representatives from UKIP, 1 a French dissident from the *Front National*, another a Euro-deputy from the *Sverigedemokraterna* (Sweden Democrats), and 1 a member from the *Latvijas Zemnieku savienība*, LZS (Latvian Farmers' Union). Between the 2009 and 2014 elections, the EFDD recorded an astonishing 21.9 female upswing, going from a dismal 15.6 per cent to a sound 37.5 per cent. By seizing 8 of the 18 EFDD female seats, corresponding to 44.4 per cent, the Italian M5S cohort grew into the second biggest female delegation among all the political groups.

Within the EP spectrum, the European Conservatives and Reformists encompassed just 15 women, equivalent to 2 per cent of the total number of Euro-parliamentarians. Hence, the ECR female proportion curved up to a bleak 21.4 per cent. This represented the worst record among all the PGs and even the non-attached, despite the 8.4 per cent progress if compared to 2009. On the other hand, it should not be overlooked that British Conservative ladies conquered 6 out 15 places, becoming the third largest national female delegation.

At the bottom of the gender parity ranking lie the independents, with barely 14 women, occupying 1.9 per cent of the Strasbourg hemicycle. Among them, the nine *Front National* female representatives embodied the biggest national party contingent, reaching 64.3 per cent.

Oddly enough, in comparison with 2009, despite a positive trend in terms of female participation, the number of women heading a political group has fallen from three Co-Chairs to one

Table 32.3d Political group breakdown by gender in aggregate countries: July 2014

	EPP Men	EPP Women	S&D Men	S&D Women	ECR Men	ECR Women	ALDE Men	ALDE Women	EUL/NGL Men	EUL/NGL Women	GREENS/EFA Men	GREENS/EFA Women	EFDD Men	EFDD Women	NA Men	NA Women	EP Men	EP Women
Old EU-15	88	41	73	69	32	10	28	20	21	26	23	20	27	17	32	13	325	215
EU-17	90	44	76	71	32	10	28	20	23	26	23	20	27	17	32	13	332	220
New EU-11	62	25	29	15	23	5	13	6	2	1	6	1	3	1	6	1	144	55
New EU-13	64	28	32	17	23	5	13	6	4	1	6	1	3	1	3	1	151	60
PIIGS/GIPSI	34	16	31	27	2	0	7	4	13	15	4	0	9	8	9	1	109	71
GIPSIC	35	17	33	27	2	0	7	4	15	15	4	0	9	8	9	1	114	72
Southern EU countries	34	17	34	28	1	0	7	3	13	13	4	0	9	8	9	1	111	70
Nordic EU countries	5	3	4	7	5	1	6	4	0	3	2	4	1	1	0	0	24	22
EU-28	152	69	105	86	55	15	41	26	25	27	29	21	30	18	38	14	476	275
%	68.78	31.22	54.97	45.03	78.57	21.43	61.19	38.81	48.08	51.92	58.00	42.00	62.50	37.50	73.08	26.92	63.38	36.62

Sources: Author's table based on own calculations of data drawn from the EP website and Member States' national government websites.

Chair and one Co-Chair, respectively Gabriele Zimmer for the EUL/NGL and Rebecca Harms for the Greens/EFA, both of them from Germany.

Unexpectedly, EPP women were by 5.68 per cent more successful in the New rather than in the Old EU countries. A reversed trend was registered, instead, by the Socialists, who managed to secure the highest scores of 15.47 and 15.22 per cent amongst the Southern and Nordic EU countries, respectively, whilst their share nearly halved to 7.54 among the 11 post-Communist newcomers. With the exception of the Greek independent MEP Notis Marias, no male or female representatives of any national parties from the GIPSI, GIPSIC and Southern countries converged into the ECR. By contrast, Conservative women conquered their top, albeit unpretentious, rate of 2.51 per cent in the 11 CEECs.

Liberal female candidates were supported mainly in the Nordic EU Member States, where they reached their 8.70 per cent peak, whilst they did not find a large consensus in Southern countries, where they secured a mere 1.66 per cent of seats.

Due to their deep-rooted political tradition and their renowned gender equality policy, Communist women were popular in the GIPSI countries, where they attained a percentage of 8.33. On the contrary, in CEECs, with the exception of the Czech Republic, the dark experience of the totalitarian regime and Soviet occupation fed into people's unwillingness to support Communist representatives, be they male or female, in any political contests. In fact, in most of these young democracies Communist parties were even outlawed.

The Ecologists obtained their better share of female representation of 8.70 in the Nordic EU countries, followed by 3.7 per cent in the Old Member States, whilst, by contrast, they performed extremely badly in the New Member States, where the percentage of 'pink' seats dipped to a dismal 0.47.

Lastly, the EFDD women garnered their top score of 4.44 in GIPSI countries, thanks to the success of the Italian anti-establishment 5-Star Movement, whilst their consensus sank to 0.47 per cent in the New EU-13.

On the whole, between 2009 and 2014, the gender distribution ratio in the European arena recorded a slight increase. However, it cannot be denied that progress in terms of female parliamentary representation and empowerment of women in the field of politics since 1979 has been lower than hoped and wished for. This disappointing result has, therefore, induced Joanna Maycock, the European Women's Lobby (EWL) Secretary-General, to assert bitterly that 'with this snail's pace it will [take] another half a century before the European Parliament (...) reach[es] gender parity' (Fronteddu, 2014).

4 Theoretical interpretation of Euro-elections

Prior to winding up this investigation, we shall endeavour to sketch a brief theoretical interpretation of the eighth EP contest, in the light of the Second-Order Election and Europe Salience models.

Evidence from testing the 2014 Euro-election against the various hypotheses of both SOE and ES frameworks appears to be rather mixed. More precisely, an increasing overlapping, or better cross-cutting, between the different tenets seems to have emerged, although its extent varies among individual as well as aggregate countries.

First of all, by sanctioning the second-order character of the EP race, the EU average turnout was the lowest since the introduction of direct elections in 1979. On the other hand, this phenomenon could either be ascribed to voters' indifference or even hostility to the European Union, fitting in better with the ES theoretical approach.

As a Second-Order Election corollary, the EP campaign was largely pervaded by concerns arising out of domestic political arenas. Nevertheless, on this occasion, 'Europe' played a more

Table 32.3e Female representation by political group in aggregate countries: July 2014

	EPP		S&D		ECR		ALDE		EUL/NGL		GREENS/EFA		EFDD		NA		Total	
	Number	%	Number	%	Number	%	Number	%	Number	%	Number	%	Number	%	Number	%	Number	%
Old EU-15	41	7.59	69	12.78	10	1.85	20	3.70	26	4.81	20	3.70	17	3.15	13	2.41	215	39.81
EU-17	44	7.97	71	12.86	10	1.81	20	3.62	26	4.71	20	3.62	17	3.08	13	2.36	220	39.86
New EU-11	25	12.56	15	7.54	5	2.51	6	3.02	1	0.50	1	0.50	1	0.50	1	0.50	55	27.64
New EU-13	28	13.27	17	8.06	5	2.37	6	2.84	1	0.47	1	0.47	1	0.47	1	0.47	60	28.44
PIIGS/GIPSI	16	8.89	27	15.00	0	0	4	2.22	15	8.33	0	0	8	4.44	1	0.56	71	39.44
GIPSIC	17	9.14	27	14.52	0	0	4	2.15	15	8.06	0	0	8	4.30	1	0.54	72	38.71
Southern EU countries*	17	9.39	28	15.47	0	0	3	1.66	13	7.18	0	0	8	4.42	1	0.55	70	38.67
Nordic EU countries	3	6.52	7	15.22	1	0.19	4	8.70	3	6.52	4	8.70	1	2.17	0	0	22	47.82
EU-28	69	9.19	86	11.45	15	2.00	26	3.46	27	3.60	21	2.80	18	2.40	14	1.86	275	36.62

Source: Author's table based on own calculations of data drawn from the EP website: www.europarl.europa.eu and from EU Member States' national government websites.

Note:
* Portugal, Italy, Greece, Spain, Malta, and Cyprus.

prominent role in citizens' voting choices by reflecting their attitudes towards European unification and, more specifically, their perception of EU leaders' ability or failure to tackle the woefully ongoing financial and economic crisis.

Echoing one of the core predicaments of the SOE theory, the 2014 Euro-election represented as yet another snapshot of the popularity, or the unpopularity, of sitting governments across Europe. As may be seen in Table 32.4a, among the Old EU countries, ruling parties were the main casualties of this competition, losing in ten out of 15 cases, with Germany and Italy embodying the most notable exceptions.

In fact, if compared to the previous EP contest, the German CDU-CSU suffered a tangible reduction of popular consensus, but still topped the national polls. More astoundingly, the new Italian PD came through with flying colours, even doubling its votes in relation to the previous General and EP elections. Consequently, as predicted by the SOE model, in most of the Old EU countries, opposition movements increased their voting share by exploiting widespread discontent over government austerity policies and public budget cuts.

By contrast, Table 32.4b shows a reverse trend among the 13 New Member States, with government parties winning the EP contest in all but two countries: Slovenia and Bulgaria.

Such an unexpected and atypical development, contrary to any SOE and ES predictions, may stem from the fact that Central and Eastern Europeans had already cast their protest votes against their ruling parties in national elections – ahead of the EP process – by turning to new, extreme, opposition, and anti-establishment movements. This unusual event could also help

Table 32.4a EP election winners in Old EU Member States: May 2014

Country	Victory of government	Victory of opposition
France	—	Front National (FN): 24.86%
Germany	Christian Democratic Union & Christian Social Union in Bavaria e. V (CDU/CSU): 35.3%	—
Italy	Democratic Party (PD): 40.81%	—
Belgium	—	New Flemish Alliance (N-VA): 16.35%
NL	—	Democrats 66 (D66):15.48%
Luxembourg	—	Christian Social People's Party (CSV/PCS): 37.65%
UK	—	United Kingdom Independence Party (UKIP): 26.77%
Ireland	—	Independents: 25.70%
Denmark	—	Danish People's Party (DF): 26.6%
Greece	—	Syriza: 26.6%
Spain	Popular Party(PP): 26.06%	—
Portugal	—	Socialist Party (PS): 31.49%
Austria*	Austrian People's Party (ÖVP): 26.98%	—
Finland	National Coalition (KOK): 22.6%	—
Sweden	—	Social Democratic Party(S): 24.4%

Sources: Author's table based on data drawn from EP website: www.europarl.europa.eu and from EU Member States' national government websites.

Note:
* In Austria the Social Democratic Party (SPO), which is the leading party of the government coalition scored 24.1% of votes.

Table 32.4b EP election winners in New EU Member States: May 2014

Country	Victory of government	Victory of opposition
Malta	Malta Labour Party (LP/MLP): 53.39%	—
Cyprus	Democratic Rally (DISY): 37.75%	—
Slovenia	—	Slovenian Democratic Party (SDS): 24.88%
Estonia	Estonian Reform Party (ER): 24.3%	—
Latvia	Unity (V): 46.19%	—
Lithuania*	Homeland Union/Lithuanian Christian Democrats TS/LKD: 17.43%	—
Czech Republic**	ANO 2011: 16.13%	—
Slovakia	Direction Social Democracy (SMER-SD): 24.09%	—
Hungary	Hungarian Civic Union (FIDESZ) & Christian Democratic People's Party (KDNP): 51.48%	—
Poland	Civic Platform (PO): 32.13%	—
Bulgaria	—	Citizens for European Development of Bulgaria (GERB): 30.4%
Romania	Social Democratic Party (PSD), Conservative Party (PC) & National Union for the Progress of Romania (UNPR): 37.6%	—
Croatia	Croatian Democratic Union (HDZ), Croatian Party of Rights Ante Starčević (HSP AS) & Croatian Peasant Party (HSS): 41.42%	—

Sources: Author's table based on data drawn from the EP and EU Member States' national government websites.

Notes:
* The Lithuanian Socialist Democratic Party (LSDP), which leads the coalition government, scored 17.26%. The TS/LKD is the first party in the country but lost 9.43% of votes in comparison with 2009.
** The Czech Social Democratic Party (CSSD), leading the coalition government, scored 14.17% but it lost 8.17% of the 2009 votes.

us understand the reasons for the mass abstention at European elections in post-Communist countries, amounting to the shocking average of 73 per cent. In reality, after playing their 'ace card' of 'kicking the villain out of government' in national competitions, most citizens preferred to turn the page by simply switching off or disengaging from the EP election game altogether, as shown in the sinisterly upward No-vote curve (Hanley, 2014).

Subsequently, another postulate of the SOE thesis, envisaging the gain of small and new political movements, could be generally upheld. As a matter of fact, these novel political actors became chief recipients of protest votes by offering shelter to disillusioned and disaffected citizens. In Cees van der Eijk and Mark Franklin's vivid metaphor, EP contests played the role of 'midwives' (van der Eijk and Franklin 1996), favouring the birth of a variety of alternative political movements which indelibly 'stamped themselves on the electoral map' (Hanley, 2014).

Moreover, by validating one of the ES hypotheses, the 2014 EP election witnessed the trend towards a more polarized Europe, thus reviving the traditional left–right cleavage (White, 2014). Interestingly, this phenomenon seems to have run parallel with an anti-European wave sweeping over the Old Continent. In particular, the far right – wearing a Eurosceptic mask – managed at times to impose itself by shaking Brussels' foundations. Four parties, the British UKIP, the French *Front National*, the *Dansk Folkeparti* (Danish People's Party), and the *Fiatal Demokraták Szövetsége-Magyar Polgári Szövetség* FIDESZ-MPSZ (Federation of Young Democrats-Hungarian Civic Alliance) got the highest score in their respective countries. Concurrently, three new extreme right-wing movements, often labelled as neo-Nazi organizations, entered the EP for the first time: the Greek *Xrysi Avgi* (Golden Dawn), the *Sverigedemokraterna* (Sweden Democrats), and the *Nationaldemokratische Partei Deutschlands* (National Democratic Party of Germany).

This switching to the far right would have acquired an even more ominously macroscopic dimension if other parties had not failed to renew their representation in the Strasbourg and Brussels arena, such as the British National Party in the UK, the *Laikos Ortodoxos Siunagermos*, LAOS (Popular Orthodox Rally) in Greece, the *Slovenská národná strana*, SNS (Slovak National Party) in Slovakia, the *Partidul România Mare*, PRM (Greater Romania Party) in Romania, and *Ataka* in Bulgaria. In effect, as Cas Mudde has sharply noticed, no far right turn took place in post-Communist countries despite offering 'a fertile breeding ground, including broadly shared prejudices towards minorities, high levels of corruption, a large reservoir of so-called "losers of the transition"'. This event was precluded by the preemptive strategy of mainstream right-wing parties that cunningly occupied the ideal political space of radical movements, by espousing ever more extreme, authoritarian, nativist, and populist discourses (Mudde, 2014).

In the Old EU Member States, by combining SOE and ES features, opposition parties, either on the extreme right or left of the political spectrum, maximized their 'relative advantage', under a sort of 'multiplier effect', by advocating anti-European messages.

In the aftermath of the eighth EP race, the Eurosceptic map covered virtually all 28 countries, with only few of them unable to send to Strasbourg representatives ready to challenge the existing political and institutional organization or even to 'declare war' on the European Union (Calabresi, 2014).

In 2014, after six years of social and economic upheaval, far-right Europhobic and anti-immigration movements gained new ground in Northern and Western Europe with the UK Independent Party and the *Front National* achieving the most spectacular victory. Conversely, anti-austerity left-wing movements, such as the Greek *Syriza* and the Spanish *Podemos,* emerged in Southern countries with the scope of offering an alternative path to the blindly bureaucratic, technocratic, and capitalist Europe.

The eighth EP election witnessed the rise of Eurosceptic parties that, in realist conceptual terms, may be justified by people's perception that the European Union epitomizes 'the other' or even 'the enemy', thus representing the perilous existential challenge to national sovereignty. Nevertheless, there are still different caveats to the picture of cosmic Euroscepticism and even if pro-European mainstream parties have been visibly weakened, they still retain a fair majority in the European Parliament arena.

As predicted by the ES model, albeit to a lesser degree than expected, anti-European movements dominated the EP contest, revealing the flaws and limits of the current European setting. The extent of their success, irrespective of their left or right ideological roots, unveiled the fragility of traditional West European politics, even in countries featuring well-established party systems that were deemed immune to populist surges (Hanley, 2014).

Overall, the findings of the eighth Euro-election seemed to corroborate most of the SOE assumptions, at times inextricably interwoven with ES hypotheses, except in Central and Eastern European Member States. As highlighted by Simon Hix and Michael Marsh in 2007, this may be still partly due to the 'fundamental differences in the semantics and bases of party competition in post-Communist [regimes]', conducive to high electoral volatility (Hix and Marsh, 2007, 497). In fact, an East–West Europe cleavage arises from the absence of a stable pluralist system and institutionalized parties capable of generating true partisan loyalty in the former geopolitical region.

Epilogue

Conclusion

This analysis of the 2014 European election, far from being exhaustive, has uncovered important similarities and differences in terms of voter turnout and party performance across the European Union. Only rarely did the contest mark a significant improvement in public engagement. Instead, every so often, it did signal further contractions in relation to the previous competition held five years earlier. Whereas the EP and Member States' efforts to raise people's participation failed miserably, the prophecy of catastrophic voter desertion fortunately remained unfulfilled. However, since 1979, political and electoral participation has undergone a brutal and linear decline, which may have been further exacerbated by the difficult socio-political conditions arising from the financial turmoil and which may delegitimize the EP race and even challenge European unification.

The European Parliament and the European Commission have tried to tackle this crucial problem through greater transparency, by allowing better access to information, and through a double popular consultation as a way of counterbalancing the lack of fully-fledged democratic governance (Greenwood, 2007).

The new appointment procedure for the Commission presidency was set in this perspective, given that it hinged on European political parties' choices, eventually endorsed by the EU citizens through the ballot box.

Such a transparent and democratic nomination of the head of the executive, aimed at prompting the participation of European party federations and shaking the apathy of European citizens, could be enhanced in the future by selecting famous high-calibre politicians. As Roberto Baldoli, Stefan Gänzle, and Michael Shackleton have aptly observed, despite its limits and shortcomings, the *Spitzenkandidaten* experiment changed Euro-elections irreversibly, by 'let[ting] the genie out of the bottle' (Baldoli *et al.*, 2014, 3).

Under this new light, the EP contest looked truly 'different', being explicitly linked to the selection of the President of the European Commission. For the first time, five cross-European Political Parties – European Peoples' Party (EPP), Party of European Socialists (PES), the Alliance of Liberals and Democrats for Europe (ALDE), the European Green Party (Greens), the Party of the European Left (EF) – fielded their preferred candidate for this institutional role. Eventually, bearing in mind the electoral outcome, the EPP, as the main winner, was best positioned to influence the decision of the EU Member States on the Commission President.

This process may be considered as the first step in order to elicit higher public attention and stimulate the active involvement of European political families facing, along with their constituent national components, the great challenge posed by the passing of the 'age of party democracy' (Mair quoted in Müller, 2014). Indeed, as Peter Mair has warned, modern democracy simply cannot work without political parties, and if, for any reason, they ceased to play their proper role, democracy itself would be at stake (Mair quoted in Müller, 2014, 37).

After all, this was the message of the eighth EP election, imparted on a dark night of growing abstention and resounding dissent. In May 2014, a welter of populist, anti-establishment, extreme and, rarely, even racist parties easily rode peoples' fears behind the long waves of the crisis. Since the enforcement of severe austerity measures, partisan loyalties were seriously challenged by reducing further citizens' trust in politics. Unprecedented results emerged in a few Member States, such as France, the UK, Spain, and Greece, by witnessing the historic victory of the above-mentioned parties. As a tribute to widespread public disaffection with the 'politics of expertise', these movements have tried to reach people's sensitivity by raising key questions of justice and fairness in society (White, 2014). Common fears and concerns regarding the serious socio-economic downturn became fertile ground for contentious radical and xenophobic policies, but did not lead, as anticipated, to a rocketing abstention and to an unrestrained Eurosceptic spiral. The EP race, besieged by a severe economic collapse, social disarray, and creeping regionally differentiated impact, revealed a more polarized political landscape, with MEPs from a far-right populist bloc, on the one hand, and representatives from alternative left-wing movements, on the other.

It remains to be seen how such extreme movements, along with Eurosceptics, may coexist in the Strasbourg arena and to what extent they are going to impinge on EP activities. And yet, it should not be forgotten that the 2014–2019 Assembly remains under the control of a traditional pro-European majority, embracing the Christian Democrats, the Socialists, the Liberal Democrats and, occasionally, the Greens.

Above and beyond the risk that the continued success of radical Europhobic political forces may jeopardize the integration process altogether, it should not be ignored that if politicians fail to meet voters' expectations over the solution of major economic and political issues, the No-vote 'virus' is likely to spread throughout the European Union. Henceforth, abstention, rather than populist and extremist voting, could prove the real long-term threat to European elections, thus affecting the democratic representation of the European Parliament and, ultimately, the authority and legitimacy of the European Union (Hanley, 2014).

If low turnout reflects people's lack of motivation to go to the polls, due to the absence of evident and salient choices, party failures have to be recognized and politicians held accountable for the distortion of democratic representation arising from this pernicious phenomenon, rather than letting voters be blamed for indifference and irresponsibility.

From the outset, most party leaders were surely aware of the deficiencies in the system they were crafting and complicit in sabotaging each attempt to fix the problem. The reason behind their ambivalence was illustrated by Jean-Marie Le Pen on the eve of the French referendum on the Maastricht Treaty in 1992, when he warned against the risks of endowing the European Union with powers that would undermine the role of the President of the French Republic who would then become 'no more important than the governor of Texas in USA' (Franklin *et al.*, 1994, 464).

By capturing the ebb and the flow of Euro-elections, it is possible to conclude that, whilst some of their features could be easily framed within the SOE model and others can be better read through the lenses of the ES theory, such a distinction has become gradually more blurred. More especially, as Franklin and Hobolt have argued, the application of ES theory to EP election turnout, previously immensely influential, seems to have been erroneous (Franklin and Hobolt, 2011).

Mirroring the biblical image reproduced on the front cover of this volume, the EP vote resulted into a metaphoric 'Tower of Babel', emphasizing the vulnerability of the European unification process. Unable to climb to the top, which had been fatefully burnt and, at the same time, debarred from going back to the bottom – being all of the sudden the base of the Tower swallowed up by the earth – political elites have been left dangerously hanging in the middle. Undeniably, this extraordinary dramatic situation could only be overcome by reviving the ideals of the original European integration project so that a durable, solid, and impressively high tower may be erected at last.

References

Primary sources

DIP (2014) Državno izborno povjerenstvo, Rezultati izbora za Europski parlament 2014.
DIP (2013) Državno izborno povjerenstvo, Rezultati izbora za Europski parlament 2013.
EU Member State national governments' websites (accessed on 18 August 2014):

Epilogue

Austria
www.bmi.gv.at/cms/BMI_wahlen/europawahl/2014/Gesamtergebnis.aspx.
Belgium
http://polling2014.belgium.be/en/eur/results/results_tab_EUR00000.html.
Bulgaria
http://results.cik.bg/ep2014/rezultati/.
Croatia
www.izbori.hr/izbori/dip_ws,nsf/0/215178D4F9D8588FC1257B60002BCE83/$file/rjesenje_konacno_20130430_final.pdf.
www.izbori.hr/2014EUParlament/ws/index.html.
www.izbori.hr/2014EUParlament/rezult/pdf/EUP2014_konacni_rezultati.pdf.
Cyprus
www. results.elections.moi.gov.cy
www.ekloges.gov.cy/English/EUROPEAN_ELECTIONS_2014/Islandwide.
Czech Republic
www.volby.cz/pls/ep2014/ep11?xjazyk=CZ.
Denmark
http://dst.dk/valg/Valg1475795/valgopg/valgopgHL.htm.
Estonia
http://ep2014.vvk.ee/voting-results-en.html.
Finland
http://tulospalvelu.vaalit.fi/EPV2014/fi/tulos_kokomaa.html.
http://tulospalvelu.vaalit.fi/EP2009/e/aanaktiivisuus/aanestys1.htm.
France
http://elections.interieur.gouv.fr/ER2014/FE.html.
www.france-politique.fr/elections-europeennes-2014.htm.
Germany
www.bundeswahlleiter.de/en/europawahlen/EU_BUND_14/ergebnisse/bundesergebnisse/.
Greece
http://ekloges.ypes.gr/may2014/e/public/index.html?lang=en#{"cls":"level","params":{"level":"epik","id":1}}.
Hungary
www.valasztas.hu/hu/ep2014/877/877_0_index.html.
Ireland
www.electionsireland.org/results/europe/2014euro.cfm.
www.environ.ie/en/Publications/LocalGovernment/.
Voting/FileDownLoad.21513.en.pdf.
Italy
http://elezioni.interno.it/europee/scrutini/20140525/index.html.
http://elezionistorico.interno.it.
Ministero dell'Interno (Italian Ministry of Interior), 2014, 'Elezioni europee 2014', http://elezioni.interno.it/europee/scrutini/20140525/E0000000000.htm.
PES (2014)'Italian Partito Democratico officially welcomed into the PES family', 28 February, http://www.pes.eu/italian_partito_democratico_officially_welcomed_into_the_pes_family.
Latvia
http://ep2014.cvk.lv/.
Lithuania
www.2013.vrk.lt/2014_ep_rinkimai/output_lt/rinkimu_diena/index.html.
Luxembourg
www.elections.public.lu/fr/index.html.
Malta
www.gov.mt/en/Government/Government%20of%20Malta/Election%20Results/EP%20elections%202014/Pages/EP-Elections%20Ct%2021-30.aspx.
Netherlands
www.kiesraad.nl/en/'new's/results-elections-members-european-parliament-22-may-2014.
www.verkiezingsuitslagen.nl/.
Poland
http://pe2009.pkw.gov.pl/PUE/EN/WYN/M/index.htm.
http://pe2014.pkw.gov.pl/pl/.

Portugal
www.europeias2014.mai.gov.pt/.
Romania
www.bec2014.ro/wp-content/uploads/2014/05/SIAEP2014_PAR_Raport-Situatie-Prezenta-la-urne.pdf.
http://www.bec2014.ro/wp-content/uploads/2014/05/PV-BEC.pdf.
Slovakia
www.minv.sk/?ep-vysledky.
Slovenia
www.dvk-rs.si/index.php/si/arhiv-evropski-parlament/volitve-v-evropski-parlament-2014.
Spain
www.juntaelectoralcentral.es/jelect/PEuropeo_2014_Resultados.pdf.
Sweden
www.val.se/val/ep2014/slutresultat/E/rike/index.html.
United Kingdom
www.europarl.org.uk/en/european_elections/results.html.

Bundesverfassungsgericht [German Federal Constitutional Court] (2009), BvE Judgment 2/08, 'Act Approving the Treaty of Lisbon compatible with the Basic Law', 30/6/2009, Absatz Nr. 284, http://www.bundesverfassungsgericht.de/SharedDocs/Entscheidungen/EN/2009/06/es20090630_2bve000208en.html.

EL (2013) 'Tsipras, Nominated by the European Left, as the Voice to Denounce the Policies of the Troika in the European Commission', 4th Congress, Madrid, December, http://www.european-left.org/4th-el-congress/tsipras-nominated-european-left-voice-denounce-policies-troika-european-commission.

Euractiv (2014) 'Germany's top court annuls 3% threshold in EU Election', European Elections 2014, www.euractiv.com/sections/eu-elections-2014/germanys-top-court-annuls-3-threshold-eu-election-300927.

European Parliament (2014) 'Election Results 2014', http://www.europarl.europa.eu/elections2014-results/en/election-results-2014.html (accessed on 15 February 2015).

European Parliament DG Communication, *Public Opinion Review: European Elections 1979-2009,* Public Opinion Monitoring Unit, Special Edition Outgoing Parliament, 7 May 2014, www.europarl.europa.eu/pdf/elections_results/review.pdf (accessed on 10 January 2015).

European Parliament Resolution on the Elections to the European Parliament in 2014, 22 November 2012, B7-0520/2012.

European Parliament Resolution on improving the Practical Arrangements for the holding of the European Elections in 2014, 4 July 2013, A7-0219/2013.

European Parliament website, www.europarl.europa.eu (accessed on 5 September 2014).

German Federal Constitutional Court, Judgment of the Second Senate of 30 June 2009, - 2 BvE 2/08, www.bverfg.de/entscheidungen/es20090630_2bve000208en.html (accessed on 10 January 2015).

'Italian Partito Democratico Officially Welcomed into the PES Family', 28 February 2014, www.pes.eu/italian_partito_democratico_officially_(accessed on 3 June 2014).

'PES congratulates "new" S&D Group President Gianni Pittella', www.pes.eu/pes_congratulates_'new'_s_d_group_president_gianni_pittella (accessed on 6 August 2014).

The 2014 European Parliament election results, website, www.results-elections2014.eu/en/election-results-2014.html (accessed on 10 January 2015).

Treaty of Lisbon, 2007, *Official Journal of the European Union,* C 306, 17 December 2007.

'Tsipras nominated European Left voice denounce policies Troika European-Commission', www.european-left.org/fr/4th-el-congress/tsipras-nominated-european-left-voice-denounce-policies-troika-european-commission#sthash.Tv5YSdCs.dpuf- (accessed on 3 July 2014).

Secondary sources

Alemanno, A. (2014) 'European Parliament Election 2014: This Time was Not Different, But Next Time it Will Be', *Friends of Europe,* 25 May.

Baldoli, R., Gänzle, S. and Shackleton, M. (2014) 'Overthrowing Secrecy: The *Spitzenkandidaten* Experiment and a "new" Chance for a European Party System', CEPS Commentary, 4 August.

Calabresi, G. (2014) 'Europarlamento: la Mappa degli Euroscettici Paese per Paese', *L'Indipendenza Nuova,* 31 March.

Calvet, C. and Bouchet-Petersen, J. (2014) 'Beaucoup de partis d'extrême droite vont se révéler aux européennes', *Libération*, 2 May.

Charlemagne (2014), 'Why This Month's European Election Matters More Than Most', *The Economist*, 5 May.

Franklin, M. N. (2014) 'Why Vote at an Election with no Apparent Purpose? Voter Turnout at Elections to the European Parliament', *European Policy Analysis*, April, 1–12.

Franklin, M. N. and Hobolt S. B. (2011) 'The Legacy of Lethargy: How Elections to the European Parliament Depress Turnout', *Electoral Studies*, 30 (1), 67–76.

Franklin, M. N., Marsh, M. and Maclaren, L. (1994) 'Uncorking the Bottle: Popular Opposition to European Unification in the Wake of Maastricht', *Journal of Common Market Studies*, 32(4), 455-72.

Fronteddu, C. (2014), 'European Elections through the Lens of Gender', *Gender Equality, 'news'*, 9 June. Online. Available at: http://timeforequality.org/'new's/2014-european-elections-through-the-lens-of-gender/(accessed on 25 August 2014).

Grabbe H. and Lehne S. (2013) *The 2014 European Elections: Why a Partisan Commission President Would be Bad for the EU*, Centre for European Reform CER.

Greenwood, J. (2007) 'Organized Civil Society and Democratic Legitimacy in the European Union', *British Journal of Political Science*, 37(2), 333–57.

Hanley, S. (2014) 'When Anger Masks Apathy', UCL European Institute. Online. Available at: www.ucl.ac.uk/european-institute/highlights/2013-14/ep2014-cee (accessed on 10 January 2015).

Hix, S. and Marsh, M. (2007) 'Punishment or Protest? Understanding European Parliament Elections', *Journal of Politics*, 69(2), 495–510.

Ignazi, P. (2014) 'Euroscettici: una scossa salutare?' *Eutopia*, 21 May.

Keating, D. (2014) 'Greens Elect Bové and Keller to Head Campaign', *European Voice*, 29 January.

Kostadinova, T. (2003) 'Voter Turnout Dynamics in Post-Communist Europe', *European Journal of Political Research*, 42(6), 741–59.

Mudde, C. (2014) 'The Far Right in the 2014 European Elections: Of Earthquakes, Cartels and Designer Fascists', *The Washington Post*, 30 May.

Müller, J.-W. (2014) 'The Party's Over', *London Review of Books*, 22 May. Commentary to Mair, P. (2013), *Ruling the Void: The Hollowing of Western Democracy*', London, Verso.

Phillips, L. (2009) 'UK Tories confirm they are to leave the EPP', *EUObserver*, 12 March.

Robert Schuman Foundation (2014) 'Political Families in the European Elections May 2014: An Assessment', *Robert Schuman Foundation, European Issue*, no. 319, 30 June. Online. Available at: www.robert-schuman.eu/en/european-issues/0319-political-families-in-the-european-elections-may-2014-an-assessment (accessed on 10 August 2014).

Schmidt, V. A. (2006) *Democracy in Europe: The EU and National Polities*, Oxford, Oxford University Press.

van den Berge, M. (2014) 'The 2014 EP Election Campaign in the Member States: National Debates, European Elections', Brussels, TEPSA.

van der Eijk, C. and Franklin, M. N. (1996) *Choosing Europe? The European Electorate and National Politics in the Face of Union*. Ann Arbor, MI, University of Michigan Press.

von Rohr, M. (2014) 'Interview with Marine Le Pen: "I Don't Want this European Soviet Union"', *Die Spiegel*, 3 June.

Watt, N. (2014) 'Nigel Farage joins forces with far-right Swedish and French MEPs', *The Guardian*, 18 June.

White, J. (2014) 'The Real Story in the European Elections Wasn't the Rise of "populists and extremists", but the Return of the Left–Right Divide', *London School of Economics*, 28 May.

APPENDIX

Table 33.1 EP electoral systems in EU Member States

Country	Eligible voters (age)	Elegible candidates (age)	Compulsory voting	Preference	Electoral system	Seat allocation	Threshold	Female quota	Constituency
Austria	16	18	NO	YES	Proportional	D'Hondt	4%	YES	1
Belgium	18	21	YES	YES	Proportional	D'Hondt	NO	YES	4
Bulgaria	18	21	NO	YES	Proportional	Hare	NO	NO	1
Croatia	18	18	NO	YES	Proportional	D'Hondt	5%	YES	1
Cyprus	18	25	YES	YES	Proportional	Hare-Niemeyer	1.8%	YES	1
Czech Republic	18	21	NO	YES	Proportional	D'Hondt	5%	NO	1
Denmark	18	18	NO	YES	Proportional	D'Hondt	NO	NO	1
Estonia	18	21	NO	YES	Proportional	D'Hondt	NO	NO	1
Finland	18	18	NO	NO	Proportional	D'Hondt	NO	YES	1
France	18	18	NO	NO	Proportional	D'Hondt	5%	YES	8
Germany	18	18	NO	NO	Proportional	Sainte-Laguë/Schepers	NO	NO	1
Greece	18	25	YES	NO	Proportional	Droop	3%	NO	1
Hungary	18	18	NO	NO	Proportional decreasing	D'Hondt	5%	YES	1
Ireland	18	21	NO	YES	Single Transferable vote	STV	NO	YES	4
Italy	18	25	NO	YES	Proportional	Hare	4%	NO	5
Latvia	18	21	NO	YES	Proportional	Sainte-Laguë	5%	NO	1
Lithuania	18	21	NO	NO	Proportional	Hagenbach-Bischoff	5%	YES	1
Luxembourg	18	18	YES	YES	Pure proportional	D'Hondt	NO	YES	1
Malta	18	18	NO	YES	Single Transferable vote	STV	NO	YES	1
Netherlands	18	18	NO	YES	Proportional on national basis	D'Hondt	NO	YES	1
Poland	18	21	NO	YES	Proportional	D'Hondt	5%	YES	13
Portugal	18	18	NO	NO	Proportional	D'Hondt	NO	YES	1
Romania	18	23	NO	NO	Proportional	D'Hondt	5%	NO	1
Slovakia	18	21	NO	YES	Proportional	Hare-Niemeyer	5%	NO	1
Slovenia	18	18	NO	YES	Proportional decreasing	D'Hondt	4%	YES	1
Spain	18	18	NO	YES	Proportional	D'Hondt	NO	YES	1
Sweden	18	18	NO	YES	Proportional	Sainte-Laguë	4%	NO	1
United Kingdom	18	18	NO	NO	Pure majority	D'Hondt (GB) STV (NI)	NO	NO	12

Table 33.2a EP composition by nationality, political group, and political party: 1979

		BE		DK		FR		GER		IR		IT		LUX		NL		UK		EP
SOC		PS	7	S	4	PS	21	SPD	35	Lab	4	PSI	13	LSAP	1	PvdA	9	Lab.	18	112
		SP	4	Siumut	3	MRG	19		35		4	PSDI	9		1		9	SDLP	17	
			3		1		2						4						1	
EPP		CVP-EVP	10		0	UFE	9	CDU	42	FG	4	DC	30	CSV	3	CDA	10		0	108
		PSC-PPE	7				9	CSU	34		4	SVP	29		3		10			
			3						8				1							
ED			0	KF	2		0		0		0		0		0		0	Cons.	61	63
					2													UUP	60	
																			1	
COM			0	SF	1	PCF	19		0		0	PCI	24		0		0		0	44
					1		19					Ind. Sin.	19							
													5							
LIB		PRL	4	V	3	UFE	17	FDP	4	Ind	1	PLI	5	DP	2	VVD	4		0	40
		PVV-ELD	2		3	PR	16		4		1	PRI	3		2		4			
			2				1						2							
DEP			0	FRP	1	DIFE	15		0	FF	5		0		0		0	SNP	1	22
					1		15				5								1	
CDI		VU	1	FolkB	4		0		0	Ind	1	PR	5		0		0		0	11
			1		4						1	DP	3							
												PDUP	1							
													1							
NA		FRF-RW	2	CD	1		0		0		0	MSI-DN	4		0	D66	2	DUP	1	10
			2		1								4				2		1	
Total			24		16		81		81		15		81		6		25		81	410

Source: European Parliament – Public Opinion Review European Elections 1979–2009: Public Opinion Monitoring Unit, Special Issue, February 2009.

Table 33.2b EP composition by nationality, political group, and political party: 1984

	BE		DK		FR		G		GR		IR		IT		LUX		NL		UK		EP
SOC	PS	7	S	4	PS	20	SPD	33	PASOK	10		0	PSI	12	LSAP	2	PvdA	9	Lab.	33	130
	SP	4	Siumut	3		20		33		10			PSDI	9		2		9	SDLP	32	
		3		1										3						1	
EPP	CVP-EVP	6	CD	1	UDF	9	CDU	41	PPE	9	FG	6	DC	27	CSV	3	CDA	8		0	110
	PSC-PPE	4		1		7		34		9		6		26		3		8			
		2			CDS	2	CSU	7					SVP	1							
ED		0	KF	4		0		0		0		0		0		0		0	Cons.	46	50
				4															UUP	45	
																				1	
COM		0	SF	1	PCF	10		0	KKE	4		0	PCI	26		0		0		0	41
				1		10				4			Ind. Sin.	23							
														3							
LIB	PRL	5	V	2	PR	12		0		0	FF	1	PRI	5	DP	1	VVD	5		0	31
	PVV-ELD	3		2	UDF	7						1	PLI	3		1		5			
		2				5								2							
RDE		0		0	RPR	20		0		0	FF	8		0		0		0	SNP	1	29
					CNIP	16						8								1	
					DCF	2															
					PR	1															
RB	VU	4	FolkB	4		0	Grüne	7		0		0	PCI	3		0	PSP	2		0	20
	Agalev	2		4				7					DP	1				2			
	Ecolo-V	1											UV-PSdA	1							
		1												1							
ER		0		0	DR	10		0	E.P.EN	1		0	MSI-DN	5		0		0		0	16
						10				1				5							
										0				3							
NA	SP	2		0		0		0		0		0	PR	3		0	SGP	1	DUP	1	7
	PS	1																1		1	
		1																			
Total		24		16		81		81		24		15		81		6		25		81	434

Source: European Parliament – Public Opinion Review European Elections 1979–2009: Public Opinion Monitoring Unit, Special Issue, February 2009.

Table 33.2c EP composition by nationality, political group, and political party: 1989

	BE		DK		FR		G		GR		IR		IT		LUX		NL		PT		SP		UK		EP
SOC		8		4		22		31		9		1		14		2		8		8		27		46	180
	PS	5	S	4	PS	18	SPD	31	PASOK	9	Lab.	1	PSI	12	LSAP	2	PvdA	8	PS	8	PSOE	24	Lab.	45	
	SP	3			App.-PS	2							PSDI	2							PSC	3	SDLP	1	
					MRG	1																			
					s.e.	1																			
EPP		7		2		6		32		10		4		27		3		10		3		16		1	121
	CVP	5	CD	2	CDS	4	CDU	25	N.D.	10	FG	4	DC	26	CSV	3	CDA	10	CDS	3	PP	15	UUP	1	
	PSC	2			s.e.	1	CSU	7					SVP	1							CiU	1			
					UDF	1																			
LDR		4		3		13		4		0		2		3		1		4		9		6		0	49
	PRL	2	V	3	PR	5	FDP	4			Ind.	1	PRI	2	DP	1	VVD	3	PSD	9	CDS	5			
	PVV	2			UDF	3					PD	1	PRI-PLI-Fed	1			D66	1			CiU	1			
					Rad	2																			
					CNI	1																			
					UDF-	1																			
					Clubs P.																				
					UDF-PSD	1																			
ED		0		2		0		0		0		0		0		0		0		0		0		32	34
			KF	2																			Cons.	32	
Greens		3		0		8		8		0		0		7		0		2		1		1		0	30
	Ecolo-V	2			Verts	8	Grüne	8					Verdi	3			Regenboog/	1	Verdes	1	IP	1			
	Agalev	1											ARCOB	2			CPN								
													DP	1			Regenboog/	1							
													LA.DROGA	1			PPR								
EUL		0		1		0		0		1		0		22		0		0		0		4		0	28
			SF	1					SYN	1			PCI	22							IU	4			

(continued)

Table 33.2c (continued)

	BE		DK		FR		G		GR		IR		IT		LUX	NL		PT		SP		UK		EP
RDE		0		0	RPR	13		0	DIANA	1	FF	6		0	0		0	0		0		0		0	20
					CNI	12				1		6													
						1																			
ER	Vl. Blok	1		0	DR	10	REP	6		0		0		0	0		0		0		0		0	17
		1				10		6																	
LU		0		0	PCF	7		0	SYN	3	WP	1	PR	0	0		0	CDU-	3		0		0	14
						7				3		1						PCP	3					
RB	VU	1	FolkB.	4	Verts UPC	1		0		0	Ind.	1	LL	3	0		0		0	EA	2	SNP	1	13
		1		4		1						1	UV-PSdA	2							1		1	
														1						PA	1			
NA		0		0	s.e.	1		0		0		0	MSI-DN	5	0	SGP	1		1	Agr.	4	DUP	1	12
						1								4			1		1	Ruiz-	2		1	
													PRI-PLI-Fed	1						Mateos	1			
																				HB	1			
																				CN				
Total		24		16		81		81		24		15		81	6		25		24		60		81	518

Source: European Parliament – Public Opinion Review European Elections 1979–2009: Public Opinion Monitoring Unit, Special Issue, February 2009.

Table 33.2d EP composition by nationality, political group, and political party: 1994

		BE		DK		FR		G		GR		IR		IT		LUX		NL		PT		SP		UK		EP
SOC			6		3		15		40		10		1		18		2		8		10		22		63	198
	PS		3	A	3	PS	14	SPD	40	PASOK	10	Lab	1	PDS	15	LSAP	2	PvdA	8	FS	10	PSOE	22	Lab	62	
	SP		3			PS (APP)	1							PSI	2									SDLP	1	
														Ind. Sin.	1											
EPP			7		3		13		47		9		4		12		2		10		0		30		19	156
	CVP		4	C	3	UDF-FR	4	CDU	38	N.D.	9	FG	4	PPI	8	CSV	2	CDA	10			PP	28	Cons.	18	
	PSC		2			UDF-CDS-	4	CSU	9					Patto	3							PNV		UUP	1	
	CSP-EVPE		1			UDF-Clubs	2		8					Segni	1							UDC	1			
						PSD	1							SVP									1			
						UDF-AD	1																			
						UDF-Rad.	1																			
ELDR			6		5		1		0		0		1		7		1		10		9		2		2	44
	VLD		3	V	4	UDF-Rad	1					Non-Party	1	LN	6	DP	1	VVD	6	FSD	9	CDC	2	LD	2	
	PRL		2	B	1									PRI	1			D66	4							
	PRL/FDF		1																							
EUL			0		0		7		0		4		0		5		0		0		3		9		0	28
						PCF	7			KKE	2			RC	5					FCP	3	IU	5			
										SYN	2											IU-IPC	4			
FE			0		0		0		0		0		0		27		0		0		0		0		0	27

(continued)

Table 33.2d (continued)

	BE		DK		FR		G		GR		IR		IT		LUX		NL		PT		SP		UK		EP
RDE		0		0	RPR	14 14		0	POLAN	2 2	FF	7 7	FI CCD	25 2		0		0	CDS-PP	3 3		0		0	26
Greens	Agalev Ecolo	2 1 1	F	1 1		0	Grüne	12 12		0	GP	2 2	Fed. Verdi RETE	4 3 1	GLEI- GAP	1 1	GroenLinks	1 1		0		0		0	23
ARE	VU	1 1		0	MRG Energie Rad.	13 7 6		0		0		0	Pannella- Riformato	2 2		0		0		0	CN-CC	1 1	SNP	2 2	19
EDN		0	J N	4 2 2	L'autre EU RPR UDF-PR	13 11 1 1		0		0		0		0		0	SGP/GPV/ RPF	2 2		0		0		0	19
NA	Vl Blok FN	3 2 1		0	FN	11 11		0		0		0	AN MSI PSDI	12 10 1 1		0		0	CDU-PCP			0	DUP	1 1	27
Total		25		16		87		99		25		15		87		6		31		25		64		87	567

Source: European Parliament – Public Opinion Review European Elections 1979–2009: Public Opinion Monitoring Unit, Special Issue, February 2009.

Table 33.2e EP composition by nationality, political group, and political party: 1999

	AU		BE		DK		FI		FR		G		GR		IR		IT		LUX		NL		PT		SP		SW		UK		EP
EPP/ED	ÖVP	7	CVP PSC MCC CSP	6 3 1 1	Kons	1	KOK SKL	4 1	UDF RPR DL SC GE	9 6 4 1 1	CDU CSU	43 10	N.D.	9	FI PPI UDEUR CCD CDU RI/Dini SVP Pens	22 4 1 2 2 1 1 1	CSV	2	CDA	9	PPD- PSD	9	PP UDC	27 1	M KD	5 2	Cons. UUP	36 1	233
	7			5		1		5		21		53		9		5		34		2		9		9		28		7		37		
PES	SPÖ	7	SP PS	2 3	Soc	3	SDP	3	PS PRG MDC	18 2 2	SPD	33	PASOK	9	DS SDI	15 2	LSAP	2	PvdA	6	PS	6	PSOE PDNI	22 2	S	6	Lab. SDLP	29 1	180
	7			5		3		3		22		33		9		17		2		6		6		24		6		30		
ELDR		0	VLD PRL+FDF	5 2	V RV	6 1	KESK SFP	4 1		0		0		0	Ind.	1	PRI/LIB Democratici	1 6	DP	1	VVD D66	6 2		8	CDC CC	2 1	CP FPL	1 3	LD	10	50
				5		5		5										7		1					3		4		10		
Greens	Grüne	2	Ecolo Agalev VU-ID21	3 2 2		0	VIHR	2	Verts	9	Grüne	7	GP	2	Fed. Verdi	2	Gréng	1	Groen Links	4		4	PA EA BNG PNV	1 1 1 1	MP	2	Greens SNP Plaid Cymru	2 2 2	48
	2			7				2		9		7		2		2		2		1		4		4		2		6		
EUL/ NGL		0		0		1		1		11		6		0		6		0		1		2		4		3		0		42

(continued)

Table 33.2e (continued)

	AU	BE	DK	FI	FR		G	GR		IR		IT		LUX	NL		PT		SP		SW		UK		EP
UEN			SF 1	VAS 1	PCF Ind LO/ LCR	4 2 5	PDS 4	KKE SYN DIKKI	3 2 2			RC CI	4 2		SP		PCP	1	IU	2	V	4		3	
	0																								
		0	DF 1	0	RPFIE	12 12	0		0	FF	6 6	AN/Segni	9 9	0		0	CDS-PP	2 2		0		0		0	30
TDI																									
	0	Vl. Blok	2 2	0	FN	5 5	0		0		0	Bonino LN MSI	11 7 3 1	0		0		0		0		0		0	18
EDD																									
	0	0	Juni.B Folk.B	4 3 1	0	CPNT	6 6	0		0		0		0		Rpf/Sgp/ Gvp	3 3		0		0		0	UK Ind.	3 3	16
NA	FPÖ	5 5		0	0	Ind	1 1	0		0		0	LN	1 1	0		0	EH	0 1	1		0	DUP	1 1	9
Total	21		25	16	16		87	99		25		15		87	6		31		25		64		22		87	626

Source: European Parliament – Public Opinion Review European Elections 1979–2009: Public Opinion Monitoring Unit, Special Issue, February 2009.

Table 33.2f EP composition by nationality, political group, and political party: 2004

	EPP/ED		PES		ALDE		Greens/EFA		EUL/NGL		IND/DEM		UEN		NA		EP
Austria	ÖVP	6	SPÖ	7		0	Grüne	2		0		0		0	Martin	3	18
		6		7				2							FPÖ	2	
																1	
Belgium	CD&V-	6	PS	7	VLD/	6	Groen	2		0		0		0	Vl.Blok	3	24
	N-VA	4	Spa-	4	Vivant	3	Ecolo	1								3	
	CDH	1	spirit	3	MR (prl)	2		1									
	CSP-EVP	1			MR	1											
					(mcc)												
Cyprus	DISY	3		0	DYKO	1		0	AKEL	2		0		0		0	6
	G.T.Evropi	2				1				2							
		1															
Czech Rep	ODS	14	ČSSD	2		0		0	KSČM	6	Nezavisli	1		0	Nezavisli	1	24
	SN/ED	9		2						6		1				1	
	KDU-ČSL	3															
		2															
Denmark	KF	1	SD	5	V	4	SF	1	FolkB.	1	JuniB.	1	DF	1		0	14
		1		5	RV	3		1		1		1		1			
						1											
Estonia	IL	1	SDE	3	K	2		0		0		0		0		0	6
		1		3	ER	1											
						1											
Finland	KOK	4	SDP	3	KESK	5	VIHR	1	VAS	1		0		0		0	14
		4		3	SFP	4		1		1							
						1											
France	UMP	17	PS	31	UDF	11	Verts	6	PC	3	MPF	3		0	FN	7	78
		17		31		11		6	PCR	2		3				7	
										1							
										7							
Germany		49		23		7		13		0		0		0		0	99

(continued)

Table 33.2f (continued)

	EPP/ED		PES		ALDE		Greens/EFA		EUL/NGL		IND/DEM		UEN		NA		EP
Greece	CDU	40	SPD	23	FDP	7	B.90/Grüne	13	PDS	7							
	CSU	9															
	ND	11	PASOK	8		0		0	KKE	4	LAOS	1		0		0	24
		11		8					SYN	3		1					
										1							
Hungary	FIDESZ-	13	MSZP	9	SZDSZ	2		0		0		0		0		0	24
	MPSZ	12		9		2											
	MDF	1															
Ireland	FG	5	Lab.	1	Ind.	1		0	Sinn Féin	1	Ind.	1	FF	4		0	13
		5		1		1				1		1		4			
Italy	FI	24	DS	16	DL	12	Fed. Verdi	2	RC	7	LN	4	AN	9	NPSI	4	78
	UDC	16	SDI	14	Margh	7		2	PdCI	5		4		9	US	1	
	AP-UDEUR	5	Ind.	1	SCDP	2				2					Alt.sociale	1	
	P. Pensionati	1			(IdV)	2									Fiamma	1	
	SVP	1			L. Bonino	1									Tric.		
					MRE												
Latvia	JL	3		0	LC	1	PCTVL	1		0		0	TB/LNNK	4		0	9
	TP	2				1		1						4			
		1															
Lithuania	TS	2	LSDP	2	DP	7		0		0		0	LDP	2		0	13
		2		2	LCS	5							VNDPS	1			
						2								1			
Luxembourg	CSV	3	LSAP	1	DP	1	Gréng	1		0		0		0		0	6
		3		1		1		1									
Malta	PN	2	MLP	3		0		0		0		0		0		0	5
		2		3													
NL		7		7		5		4		2		2		0		0	27

	CDA	7	PvdA	7	VVD D66	4 1	Groen Links EurTrans Parent	2 2	SP	2	CU/ SGP	2	
Poland	PO PSL	19 15 4	SLD SdPL UP	8 4 3 1	UW	4 4		0		0	LPR	10 10	PiS	7 7		6 6	54
Portugal	PPD-PSD CDS-PP	9 7 2	PS	12 12		0		0	CDU- PCP/ PEV BE	3 2 1		0		0		0	24
Slovakia	SDKU KDH SMK	8 3 3 2	SMER SDL	3 2 1		0		0		0		0		0	LS-HZDS	3 3	14
Slovenia	SDS NSi	4 2 2	ZLSD	1 1	LDS	2 2		0		0		0		0		0	7
Spain	PP	24 24	PSOE	24 24	CiU PNV	2 1 1	Verdes IU E.dePueblos (ERC)	3 1 1 1	IU	1 1		0		0		0	54
Sweden	M KD	5 4 1	S	5 5	FP C	3 2 1	MP	1 1	V	2 2	Junilistan	3 3		0		0	19
UK	Cons. UUP	28 27 1	Lab	19 19	LD	12 12	Greens SNP Plaid Cymru	5 2 2 1	Sinn Féin	1 1	UKIP	11 11		0	DUP UKIP	2 1 1	78
Total		268		200		88		42		41		37		27		29	732

Source: European Parliament – Public Opinion Review European Elections 1979–2009: Public Opinion Monitoring Unit, Special Issue, February 2009.

Table 33.2g EP composition by nationality, political group, and political party: 2009

	EPP/ED		S&D		ALDE		Greens/EFA		ECR		EUL/NGL		EFD		NA		EP
Austria	ÖVP	6	SPÖ	4		0	Grüne	2		0		0		0	Martin	5	17
		6		4				2							FPÖ	3	
Belgium	CD&V	5	PS	5	Open VLD	5	Ecolo	4	LDD	1		0		0	Vl.Belang	2	22
	CSP	3	Sp.a	3	MR	3	Groen	2		1						2	
	CDH	1		2		2	N-VA	1									
		1						0									
Bulgaria	GERB	6	BSP	4	DPS	5		0		0		0		0	ATAKA	2	17
	SDS	5		4	NDSV	3										2	
		1				2											
						0											
Cyprus	DISY	2	EDEK	2		0		0		0	AKEL	2		0		0	6
		2	DYKO	1								2					
				1													
Czech Rep	KDU-CSL	2	CSSD	7		0		0	ODS	9	KSCM	4		0		0	22
		2		7						9		4					
Denmark	KF	1	S	4	V	3	SF	2		0	N	1	DF	2		0	13
		1		4		3		2				1		2			
Estonia	IRL	1	SDE	1	KE	3	I. Tarand	1		0		0		0		0	6
		1		1	ER	2	(Ind.)	1									
						1											
Finland	KOK	4	SDP	2	KESK	4	VIHR	2		0		0	PS	1		0	13
	KD	3	M. Repo	1	SFP (RKP)	3		2						1			
		1	(Ind.)	1		1											
France	UMP	29	PS	14	MoDem	6	Europe	14		0	PCF	5	MPF	1	FN	3	72
	NC	26		14		6	Ecologie	14			PCR	2		1		3	
	GM	2									PG	1					
		1									M.C. Vergiat	1					
											(Ind.)						
Germany		42		23		12		14		0		8		0		0	99

Greece	CDU CSU	34 8 8	SDP	23 8 8	FDP	12 0	Grüne	14 1 1		0	Linke	8 3 2	KKE SYRIZA	2 2	LAOS	2 2		0		22
	ND	8	PASOK	8		0	OP	1		0		1		0		0			22
Hungary	FIDESZ KDNP A.Kosa (Ind.)	14 12 1	MSZP	4 4		0		0	MDF	1 1		0		0	JOBBIK	3 3		12
Ireland	FG	4 4	Lab	3 3	FF M. Harkin (Ind.)	4 3 1		0		0	SP	1 1		0		0		72
Italy	PdL UDC SVP	35 29 5 1	PD	21 21	IdV	7 7		0		0		0	LN	9 9		0		8
Latvia	PS JL	3 2 1	TSP	1 1	LPP/LC	1 1	PCTVL	1 1	TB/ LNKK	1 1	LSP	1 1		0		0		12
Lithuania	TS-LKD	4	LSDP	3	LRLS DP	2 1 1		0	LLRA	1 1		0	TT	2 2		0		6
Luxembourg	CSV	3 3	LSAP	1 1	DP	1 1	Gréng	1 1		0		0		0		0		5
Malta	PN	2 2	PL	3 3		0		0		0		0		0		0		25
NL	CDA	5 5	PvdA	3 3	VVD D66	6 3 3	Groen Links	3 3	Christen Unie	1 1	SP	2 2	SGP	1 1	PVV	4 4		50
Poland	PO PSL	28 25 3	SLD UP	7 6 1		0		0	PS	15 15		0		0		0	

(continued)

Table 33.2g (continued)

	EPP/ED		S&D		ALDE		Greens/EFA		ECR		EUL/NGL		EFD		NA		EP
Portugal	PPD/PSD	10	PS	7		0		0		0	BE	5		0		0	22
	CDS-PP	8		7								3					
		2									PCP	2					
Romania	PD-L	14	PSD	11	PNL	5		0		0		0		0	PRM	3	33
	UDMR	1	PC	10		5									PNG-CD	2	
		3		1												1	
Slovakia	KDH	6	SMER	5	LS-HZDS	1		0		0		0	SNS	1		0	13
	SDKU-DS	2		5		1								1			
	SMK-MPK	2															
		2															
Slovenia	SDS	3	SD	2	Zares	2		0		0		0		0		0	7
	N.Si	2		2	LDS	1											
		1															
Spain	PP	23	PSOE	21	CDC	2	ICV	2		0	IU	1		0	UpyD	1	50
		23	PSC	20	PNV	1	ERC	1				1				1	
				1		1		1									
Sweden	M	5	SAP	5	FP	4	MP	3		0	V	1		0		0	18
	KD	4		5	C	3	PP	2				1					
		1				1		1									
UK		0	Lab	13	LD	11	SNP	5	Cons.	25	SP	1	UKIP	13	BNP	4	72
				13		11	Greens	2	UUP	24		1		13	Cons.	2	
							Plaid Cymru	2		1					DUP	1	
								1								1	
Total		265		184		84		55		54		35		32		27	736

Source: European Parliament – Public Opinion Review European Elections 1979–2009: Public Opinion Monitoring Unit, Special Edition, November 2009.

Table 33.2h EP composition by nationality, political group, and political party: 2014

	EPP		S&D		ECR		ALDE		EUL/NGL		Greens/EFA		EFDD		NA		EP
Austria	ÖVP	5	SPÖ	5		0	NEOS	1		0	Grüne	3		0		0	18
	ÖVP	5	SPÖ	5			NEOS	1		0	Grüne	3		0	FPÖ	4	18
Belgium	CD&V	4	PS	4	N-VA	4	Open VLD	6		0	Ecolo	2		0		0	21
	CD&V	2	PS	3	N-VA	4	Open VLD	3		0	Groen	1		0	Vlaams Belang	1	21
	CSP	1	SP.a	1			MR	3									
	CDH	1															
Bulgaria	GERB	7	BSP	4	BMPO	2	DPS	4		0		0		0		0	17
	GERB	6	BSP	4	BMPO	2	DPS	4		0		0		0		0	17
	RB	1															
Croatia	HDZ+HSP AS	5	SDP+HNS− HSU+SDSS+ IDS	2	HDZ+ HSP AS	1	SDP+HNS+ HSU+SDSS+ IDS	2		0	ORaH	1		0		0	11
	HDZ+HSP AS	5		2		1		2		0		1		0		0	11
Cyprus	DISY	2	EDEK DYKO	2		0			AKEL	2		0		0		0	6
	DISY	2		2		0				2		0		0		0	6
Czech Rep	CSL	7	CSSD	4	ODS	2	ANO 2011	4	KSCM	3		0	Svobodni	1		1	21
	TOP 09+STAN	3	CSSD	4	ODS	2	ANO 2011	4	KSCM	3		0	Svobodni	1		1	21
		4															
Denmark	KF	1	A.(S)	3	DF	4	B.RV	3		1	SF	1		0		0	13
	KF	1	A.(S)	3	DF	4	V.(V)	1		1	SF	1		0		0	13
								2									
Estonia	IRL	1	SDE	1		0	KE	1		0	I. Tarand (Ind.)	1		1		0	6
	IRL	1	SDE	1		0	ER	2		0		1		1		0	6
Finland	KOK	3	SDP	2	PS	2	KESK	4	VAS	1	VIHR	1		0		0	13
	KOK	3	SDP	2	PS	2	KESK	3	VAS	1	VIHR	1		0		0	13
							SFP (RKP)	1									
France		20		13		0		7		4		6		1		23	74

(continued)

Table 33.2h (continued)

		EPP		S&D		ECR		ALDE		EUL/NGL		Greens/EFA		EFDD		NA		EP
		UMP	20	PS- PRG	13		0	Alternative (UDI+ MO-DEM)	7	UOM	1	Europe Ecologie	6	Ind.	1	FN	23	74
Germany		CDU	34	SPD	27	Familie	8	FDP	4	FG : (PCF+PG+ENS+ET+A)	3	Piraten	13		0	PARTEI	2	96
		CSU	29		27		1		3	Linke	8		1		0		1	96
			5			AfD	7	Freie Wähler	1	Tierschutzpartei	7	Grüne	11			NPD	1	
											1	ODP	1					
Greece		ND	5	TO POTAMI	4	ANEL	1		0	Syriza	6		0		0	KKE	5	21
			5	ELIA DA	2		1		0		6		0		0	X.A.	2	21
																	3	
Hungary		FIDESZ- KDNP	12	MSZP	4		0		0		0	LMP	2		0	JOBBIK	3	21
			12	DK	2		0		0		0	Együtt–PM	1		0		3	21
					2								1					
Ireland		FG	4	Ind.+ Others	1		1		0	SF	4		0		0		0	11
			4		1	FF	1	Ind. + Others	1	Ind. + Others	3		0		0		0	11
											1							
Italy		SVP	17	PD	31		0		0	L'altra Europa con Tsipras	3		0	M5S	17	LN	5	73
			1		31		0		0		3		0		17		5	73
		NCD+UDC+PPI	3															
		FI	13															
Latvia		V.	4	SASKANA	1	TB/ LNNK K+VL!	1		0		0	LKS (PCTV)	1	ZZS (LZS+LZP)	1		0	8
			4	SDP	1		1		0		0		1		1		0	8
Lithuania		TS-LKD	2	LSDP	2	LLRA	1	LRLS	3		0	LVZS	1	TT	2		0	11
			2		2		1		2		0		1		2		0	11

Luxembourg	3			1		DP	1			0	0			0	6
	3	LSAP	1			DP	1	Gréng	1	0			0	6
Malta	3	PN/NP	3				1		1	0			0	6
	3		3				0		0	0			0	6
Netherlands	5	CDA	3			VVD	0		0	3			0	26
	5	CDA	3	CU-SGP		VVD	7		2	2	PVV		4	26
						D66	3	Groen Links	2	1			4	
Poland	23			(AWPL)	0		4		0	0			0	51
	19	PO	5		19		0		0	0	KNP		4	51
	4	PSL	5	PiS	19		0		0	0			4	
Portugal	7	PSD+CDS-PP	8		0	B.E	2		0	0			0	21
	7	PS	8		0	CDU (PCP+PEV)	2		0	0			0	21
Romania	15	PMP	16		0		1		0	0			0	32
	2	PSD+PC+UNPR	16		0	M. Diaconou (Ind.)	1		0	0			0	32
	2	UDMR												
	5	PDL												
	6	PNL												
Slovakia	6	MOST-HID	4	NOVA	2	SAS	1		0	0			0	13
	1	SMER-SD	4	OL'ANO	1		1		0	0			0	13
	1	SMK-MPK												
	2	KDH												
	2	SDKU-DS												
Slovenia	5				0	DESUS	1	VERJAMEM	1	0			0	8
	3	SD	1		0		1		1	0			0	8

(continued)

Table 33.2h (continued)

	EPP	S&D	ECR	ALDE	EUL/NGL	Greens/EFA	EFDD	NA	EP
Spain	NSI+ SLS 2								
	17							0	54
	CpE 1 (CDC+UDC+EAJ -PNV+CCA- PNC+ CXG)	PSOE/PSC 14		CpE 8 (CDC+UDC+ EAJ-PNV+ CCA-PNC+ CXG)	IP 11 (IU+ICV+ANOVA)	Primavera Europea 4 IP(IU+IC V+ANO VA) 1		0	54
	PP 16			CCA-PNC+ 2 CXG	Podemos 5 LPD (BNG+EH 1 BILDU)				
				UPyD 4		EPDD 2 (ERC+NECAT+I ND)			
Sweden	M 4	S 6		C'S 2					
	KD 1	FI 5 1		C 3 FP 1	V 1	MP 4	SD 4	2	20
	0							2	20
UK		LAB 20	Cons. 20 UUP 1	LD 19 1	SF 1	Plaid Cymru 1 SNP 2 Greens 3	UKIP 24 1	24 DUP	73 73
Total	221	191	70	67	52	50	48	52	751

Source: Author's table based on the information taken from www.elections2014.eu/en/new-parliament/towards-a-new-parliament, accessed on 27 June 2014.

Table 33.3 Political group Chair and Co-Chair: July 2014

Political group	Chair/co-chairs	Nationality	National party	Gender
European People's Party (EPP)	Manfred Weber	German	Christlich-Soziale Union in Bayern e.V – CSU (Christian Social Union in Bavaria)	Male
Progressive Alliance of Socialists and Democrats in the European Parliament (S&D)	Gianni Pittella	Italian	Partito Democratico – PD (Democratic Party)	Male
European Conservatives and Reformists (ECR)	Syed Kamall	British	Conservative Party Cons.	Male
Alliance of Liberals and Democrats for Europe (ALDE)	Guy Verhofstadt	Belgian	Open Vlaamse Liberalen en Democraten - VLD (Open Flemish Liberals and Democrats)	Male
European United Left/Nordic Green Left (EUL/NGL)	Gabriele Zimmer	German	Die Linke (The Left)	Female
The Greens/European Free Alliance (Greens/EFA)	Rebecca Harms	German	Bündnis 90/Die Grünen – Grünen (Alliance '90/The Greens)	Female
	Philippe Lamberts	Belgian	Ecologistes Confédérés pour l'Organisation de Luttes Originales – Ecolo (Confederated ecologists for the organization of original struggles)	Male
European Free Alliance (EFA)	Josep Maria Terricabras	Spanish (Catalan)	L'Esquerra pel Dret a Decidir (Left for the Right to Decide)	Male
Europe of Freedom and Direct Democracy (EFDD)	Nigel Farage	British	United Kingdom Independence Party – UKIP	Male
	David Borrelli	Italian	Movimento 5 Stelle – M5S (5 Star Movement)	Male

Source: Author's table based on data drawn from the EP website: www.europarl.europa.eu, accessed on 13 July 2014.

Table 33.4 List of Eurosceptic/Eurocritical parties in EU Member States: 1979–2009

France
Lutte ouvrière, LO (Workers' Struggle)
Ligue communiste révolutionnaire, LCR (The Revolutionary Communist Ligue)
Parti communiste français, PCF (French Communist Party)
Mouvement des Citoyens, MDC (Citizens' Movement)
Rassemblement pour la République, RPR (The Rally for the Republic)
Front National, FN (National Front)
Divers Droite, DVD (Miscellaneous Right)
De Villiers - Mouvement pour la France, 1994 (Movement for France)
Divers Extreme Droite (Miscellaneous Extreme-Right)
Chasse Pêche Nature et Tradition, CPNT (Hunting, Fishing, Nature and Tradition)

Germany
NationaldemokratischePartei Deutschland, NPD (National Democratic Party of Germany)
Die Republikaner (The Republicans)
Deutsche Volksunion, DVU (German People's Union)
Sozialistische Einheitspartei Deutschlands-Partei des Demokratischen Sozialismus SED-PDS- Die Linke (Party of Democratic Socialism/The Left)
Deutsche Kommunistische Partei, DKP (German Communist Party)

Italy
Lega Autonomista Lombarda/Liga Veneta (Lombard, Venetian Autonomy League)
Lega Nord, LN (Northern League)
Partito di Rifondazione Comunista, PRC/*Rifondazione Comunista*, RC (Communist Refoundation Party/Communist Refoundation)
Alleanza Nazionale, AN (National Alliance)

Belgium
Vlaams Blok/Vlaams Belang, VB (Flemish Block/Flemish Interest)
Lijst Dedecker (The Dedecker List)

Netherlands
Orthodox Protestants:
Staatkundig Gereformeerde Partij, SGP (Reformed – Calvinist-State Party)
Gereformeerd Politiek Verbond, GPV (Reformed Political League)
Reformatorische Politieke Federatie, RPF (Reformed Political Federation)
Christen Unie, CU (Christian Union)
Extreme Left:
Communistische Partij Nederland, CPN (Communist Party of the Netherlands)
Pacifistische Socialistische Partij, PSP (Pacifist Socialist Party)
Politieke Partij Radikalen, PPR (Political Radical Party)
Evangelische Volkspartij, EVP (Evangelical People's Party)
GroenLinks, GL (GreenLeft)
Centrum Democraten, CD (Centre Democrats)
Socialistische Partij, SP (Socialist Party)
Lijst Pim Fortuyn, LPF (Pim Fortuyn List)
Partij Voor de Vrijheid, PVV (Freedom Party)
Europa Transparant, ET (Europe Transparent)
Partij voor de Dieren, PvdD (Animal Rights Party)

Luxembourg
Kommunistische Partei Luxembourg, KPL (Luxembourg Communist Party)
Déi Lenk (The Left)

Alternative Demokratesch Reformpartei, ADR (Alternative Democratic Reform Party)
Biergerlëscht, BL (Citizens' List)

Ireland
Sinn Féin, SF
Socialist Party, SP
Libertas

United Kingdom
British Conservative Party, Cons.
British Labour Party, LAB
UK Independence Party, UKIP
British National Party, BNP

Denmark
Folkebevægelsen mod EF/EU (Popular Movement against the EC/EU)
Junibevægelsen (June Movement)
Socialistisk Folkeparti, SF (Socialist People's Party)
Retsforbundet, RF (Justice Party)
Venstresocialisterne, VS (Left Socialists)
Fremskridtspartiet, FrP (Progress Party)
Dansk Folkeparti, DF (Danish People's Party)

Greece
Kommounistikó Kómma Elládas, KKE (Communist Party of Greece)
Laikos Syndesmos Crysse Avge, CA (Popular League – Golden Dawn) or *Crysse Avge* (Golden Dawn)

Portugal
Partido Comunista Português PCP (Portuguese Communist Party)

Austria
Freiheitliche Partei Österreichs, FPÖ (Freedom Party of Austria)
Bündnis Zukunft Österreich, BZÖ (Alliance for the Future of Austria)
Liste Hans-Peter Martin, HPM (Hans-Peter Martin List)

Finland
Peruss, PS (The Finns) - previously *Perussuomalaiset*, PS (True Finns)
Suomen Kristillisdemokraatit, KD (Christian Democrats)

Sweden
Vänsterpartiet, V (The Left Party)
Miljöpartiet, MP (The Green Party)
Junilistan, JL (The June List)
Sverigedemokraterna, SD (Sweden's Democrats)

Malta
Azzjoni Nazzjonali AN (National Action)
Libertas Malta

Cyprus
Anorthotikó Kómma Ergazómenou Laoú, AKEL (Progressive People's Party)

Slovenia
Slovenska nacionalna stranka, SNS (Slovenian National Party)

(continued)

Table 33.4 (continued)

Estonia
Libertas Eesti Erakond, LEE (Libertas Estonia Party)
Põllumeeste Kogu, PK (Farmers' Council)
Eesti Demokraatlik Erakond, EDE (Democratic Party of Estonia)
Eesti Sotsiaaldemokraatlik Tööpartei, ESDTP (Social Democratic Labour Party of Estonia)

Latvia
Libertas.lv
Rīcības partija, RP (Action Party)
Osipova partija, OP (Osipov Party)
Eiroskeptiķi (Eurosceptics)

Lithuania
Tautos pažangos partija, TPP (National Progress Party)
Lietuvos centro partija, LCP (Lithuanian Centre Party)

Czech Republic
Komunistická strana Čech a Moravy, KSCM (Communist Party of Bohemia and Moravia)
Nezávislí demokraté, NEZDEM (Independent Democrats)
Suverenita - blok Jany Bobošíkové, SBB (Sovereignty – Jana Bobošíková Bloc)
Strana svobodných občanů – Svobodní, SSO (Party of Free Citizens – The Free)

Slovakia
Sloboda a solidarita, SaS (Freedom and Solidarity)
Komunistická strana Slovenska, KSS (Communist Party of Slovakia)
Slovenská národná strana, SNS (Slovak National Party)

Hungary
Jobbik Magyarországért Mozgalom, Jobbik, (Jobbik Movement for a Better Hungary)

Poland
Samoobrona RP, SRP (Self-Defence of Republic of Poland)
Liga Polskich Rodzin, LPR (League of Polish Families)
Libertas

Bulgaria
Politicheska partiya Ataka, ATAKA (Attack Political Party)

Romania
Partidul România Mare, PRM (Greater Romania Party)

Source: Table based on information provided by the authors of the country chapters.

Table 33.5a List of political parties in Croatia

Original name	Abbreviation	English translation
Hrvatska Demokratska Zajednica	HDZ	Croatian Democratic Union
Blok Umirovljenici Zajedno	BUZ	Party of United Pensioners
SocijalDemokratska Partija	SDP	Social Democratic Party
Hrvatska Narodna Stranka	HNS	Croatian People's Party
Hrvatska Stranka Umirovljenika	HSU	Croatian Party of Pensioners
Hrvatski Laburisti-Stranka Rada	HL-SR	Croatian Labourists-Labour Party
Hrvatska Stranka Prava Ante Starčević	HSP AS	Croatian Party of Rights Ante Starčević

Table 33.5b List of Croatian MEPs: seventh legislature

Name	National party	Political group	Professional background	Date of birth	Gender	Committee
Dubravka Šuica	HDZ	EPP	Faculty of humanities and social sciences	20/05/1957	Female	Committee on the Environment, Public Health and Food Safety
Andrej Plenković	HDZ	EPP	Lawyer	08/04/1970	Male	Committee on Constitutional Affairs
Davor Ivo Stier	HDZ	EPP	Political scientist	06/01/1972	Male	Committee on Foreign Affairs
Ivana Maletić	HDZ	EPP	Economist	12/10/1973	Female	Committee on Economic and Monetary Affairs
Zdravka Bušić	HDZ	EPP	Political scientist/ information manager	06/09/1950	Female	Committee on Constitutional Affairs
Ruža Tomašić	HSP AS	ECR	Police officer	10/05/1958	Female	Committee on Employment and Social Affairs
Tonino Picula	SDP/HNS/HSU	S&D	Sociologist	31/08/1961	Male	Committee on Foreign Affairs
Biljana Borzan	SDP/HNS/HSU	S&D	School of medicine	29/11/1971	Female	Committee on the Environment, Public Health and Food Safety
Marino Baldini	SDP/HNS/HSU	S&D	Master of social services, archaeology and art	12/07/1963	Male	Committee of Economic and Monetary Affairs
Oleg Valjalo	SDP/HNS/HSU	S&D	Economist	19/11/1970	Male	Committee on Budgets
Sandra Petrović Jakovina	SDP/HNS/HSU	S&D	Jurist	21/03/1985	Female	Committee on Constitutional Affairs
Nikola Vuljanić	HL-SR	EUL/NGL	Philology/English language	25/06/1949	Male	Committee on Foreign Affairs

Source: www.europarl.europa.eu/meps/en/search.html?country=HR (accessed on 13 July 2014).

INDEX

(*Italic* page numbers indicate figures and tables)

Abela, George, *434,* 435
Abela Baldacchino, Claudette 444
Abélès, Marc 17
Abruzzo earthquake 129, 130, 131
absolute-majority two round system (TRS) 83
Afghanistan *39,* 79, 82, 131, 170, 622
Ahern, Bertie 245, 248, 255
Albert II, King *148*
Albertini, Gabriele 136, *137*
Alliance of Liberals and Democrats for Europe (ALDE) 28, *29, 30, 31, 32,* 34, *70* 71, *72,* 98, *102,* 134, *135, 136, 137, 138,* 152, *160, 161, 183,* 225, 230, *231, 232, 233, 234, 235, 236, 238,* 247, 257, 262, *263, 283,* 285, *345, 390, 408,* 409, *410, 426,* 453, *477, 483, 485, 503, 520, 523, 535,* 536, *543, 544,* 545, 547, *576, 577, 585, 586, 623, 625,* 639, *643, 648,* 657, *658,* 663, 664, *665, 667, 668, 669, 711, 712,* 715, 718, *719, 723,* 724, *725, 727,* 731, *745, 746, 748, 750, 751, 752, 754, 755*
Almunia, Joaquin 331–2
Al Qaeda 332
Amato, Giuliano 12, 127
American National Election Study (ANES) 40
Amsterdam Treaty (ToA) 5, 11, 18, 173, 250, *250, 277*
Anastasiades, Nikos 449
Anastassopoulos Report (1998) 6
Andreotti, Giulio 124, 698Angelilli, Roberta 136, *137*
Anguita, Julio 330
Annan Plan 452, 458, 461Ansip, Andrus *492,* 494, 496
Arab Spring 112, 294, 450

armed forces *see* defence; security, 13, 34, 65, 83, 92, 169, 172, 181, 256, 269, 308, 334, 334, 385, 386, 424, 481, 512, 539, 540, 540, 599, 621, 622, 635
Aristophanes 697
Atomic Energy Community (Euratom) Treaty 8, 53, 149, 191, 388
Attard Montalto, John 444
Attinà, Fulvio 5
Auken, Margrethe 280, 281, *283*
Austria 377–94, *377;* allocation of EP seats 23, 24, 25, *31, 32;* EP and national elections 385–6; geographical position 378; geopolitical profile 379–80; historical background 378–9; national and EP electoral systems 384; overview of the political landscape 380; profile *378*
Ayrault, Jean-Marc 52
Aznar, José Maria 325, 327, 329, 330, 332, 334, 347

Bacalhau, Mário 358
Bajnai, Gordon *590,* 599, 604
Balkans 293, 294, 473, 582, 599, 635
Balkenende, Jan Peter *168,* 170, 181
Balladur, Edouard 59
Barnier, Michel 63, 65, *69,* 73
Barroso, José Manuel xxxii, 65, 96, 575
Barroso, Manuel Durão 359, 361, 363, 366, 371
Băsescu, Elena *665, 667,* 671
Băsescu, Traian *654,* 664, 672
Bašić Hrvatin, Sandra 482
Bavaria (Germany) 77, *81,* 82, 85, 86, 87, 89, 90, *92, 93,* 95, *728, 755*
Bayrou, François 55, 61, 63, 67
Beatrix, Queen *168*
Belgium 147–65, *147;* allocation of EP seats 22, 23, *24, 25, 31, 32;* compulsory voting

Index

133, 158, 159; Constitution 149; electoral constituencies *154,* EP and national elections 154–7; geographical position 148; geopolitical profile 149; historical background 149; linguistic diversity 149, 150, 154; Lisbon Treaty *148,* 152, 158; national and EP electoral systems 153–4; overview of the political landscape 149–50; profile*148;* media coverage 158; Flanders 149, 150, 151, *154,* 156, 157, 159
Bendtsen, Bendt 280, 280, *283*
Bennett Stephen E. 45
Benoit, Kenneth 33
Berlinguer, Enrico 122
Berlusconi, Silvio *110,* 113, 116, 125, 127, 128, 129, 131, 132, 133, 136, 361, 712
Bertinotti, Fausto 127
Bērziņš, Andris *508*
Besancenot, Olivier 61, 63
Bettel, Xavier *190*
Bisky, Lothar 30, 96, *102*
Black Sea Economic Cooperation Zone (BSEC) 294, 635
Blair, Tony 6, 217, 689
Blondel, Jean 44 Boc, Emil *654*
Bocklet Report 5
Bolkestein, Frits 172, 173, 177, 179
Bonde, Jens-Peter 281, 436
Bonino, Emma 129, *133,* 134, *744, 746*
border control 280, 281, 282, 388
Borisov, Boyko *634,* 642, 644
Borrell, Josep 332
Borrelli, David 718, *755*
Boselli, Enrico 127
Bossi, Umberto 116. 129, 132, 133 Brandt, Willy 86
Bratkowski, Arkadiusz *609*
Bratušek, Alenka *472*
Brexit 689
Britain *see* United Kingdom
British Empire 169
Brown, Gordon *214,* 217, 226
Bruegel, Pieter xxxv
Brugmans, Henrik 4
Brussels Treaty 112
Budget Committee 19, 136
Bulgaria 633–51; *633;* allocation of EP seats 23, *24, 25, 31, 32;* EP and national elections 641–2; geographical position 634; geopolitical profile 635; historical background 634–5; national and EP electoral systems 640–1; overview of the political landscape 636; profile *634*
Bundesländer (Germany) 79, 80, 85, 86, 87, 89
  Bundesländer (Austria) 378
Busuttil, Simon 443, 444, *445*

Calderoli, Roberto 119
Cameron, David xxxi, *214,* 217, 225, 226, 620, 714, 715

Carrubba, Cliff 44
Carvalhas, Carlos 359
Casa, David 444,
Casini, Carlo 136, *136, 137*
Cavaco Silva, Aníbal *352,* 354, 357, 358, 359, 371
Cavaliere see Berlusconi, Silvio
Celtic Tiger (Ireland) 245, 249, 260
Chabod, Federico 114
Childers, Nessa 258, 259, 262, *263*
Chirac, Jacques 53, 54, 55, 59, 60
Christophias, Demetris, 449
Ciampi, Carlo Azeglio 124
civil society 12, 19, 22, 62, 195, 336, 364, 441, 494, 500, 502, 540, 553, 590, 692
Civil Society (Foundation) 664
climate change 92, 129, *130,* 157, 179, 199–200, 281, 282, 362, 418, 440, 622, 645, 659, *659*
codecision 11, 13
Cohn-Bendit, Daniel 28, 61, 62, 63, 67, *69, 70,* 204
Cold War 78, 79, 112, 169, 193, 269, 398, 450, 591, 635
Colombo, Emilio 4, 10
Colony/ies 53, 149, 169
committees 18, 34, 35, *35, 36,* 37
Common Agricultural Policy (CAP) 88, 91, 247, 254, 255, 620
Common Assembly 4, 7, 17, 21, 27, 34
Common Foreign and *Security* Policy (CFSP) 10, 11, 12, 79, 245, 269, 334, 380, 416, 481, 751, 599
Common Security and Defence Policy (CSDP) 273, 275, 599
Confederation of Socialist Parties 27
Conference on Political Union 10; establishment of electoral procedures 3–7
Conference on Security and Cooperation in Europe (CSCE) 112, 435, 610
CONNEX network 39
Constitutional Affairs Committee 6, 19, 23, 136,
Conti, Nicolò 117
Copenhagen Summit 282
Corbett, Richard 17
corruption/fraud 34, 62, 119, 113, 124, 139, 140, 193, 198, 226, 248, 304, 329, 330, 331, 347, 353, 358, 386, 387, 394, 496, 499, 510, 522, 553, 565, 617, 625, 638, 644, 659, 663, 672, 679, 730
Cosgrave, Liam 252
Costa, António 361
Coughlan, Anthony 249
Council of Europe (CoE) 7, 17, 53, 112, 294, 392, 398, 416, 435, 450, 565, 571, 610, 635, 649, 720; Consultative Assembly 4, 21
Council of Ministers/Council of the European Union 4, 8, 13, 42, 132
Cowen, Brian *244,* 246, 248, 257

Crespy, Amandine 158
crime, organized 34, 118, 386
Croatia 23, 31; allocation of EP seats 23, *24*, *25*; list of political parties 758; women MEPs 26, *722*, *723*
Curtice, John 44
Cuschieri, Joseph *434*, 444
customs duties 8
Cyprus 448–66, *448;* allocation of EP seats *24*, *25*, *31*, *32*; EP and national elections 457–60; geographical position 449; geopolitical profile 450; historical background 449; national and EP electoral systems 456–7; overview of the political landscape 450, profile *449*
Czech Republic 549–66, *549;* allocation of EP seats 23, *24*, *25*, *31*, *32*; EP and national elections 555–7; geographical position 550; geopolitical profile 551; historical background 550–1; national and EP electoral systems 555; overview of the political landscape 551–2; profile *550*

Dahl, Hanne 281
Dati, Rachida 62, 63, 73, *70*
Daul, Joseph 19, *68*, *70*
de Clercq, Willy 27
decolonization 53, 449
de Gaulle, Charles 53
de Grandes, Luis 336, 337, *339*
De Gucht, Karel 5
Delacroix, Eugène 387
de la Malène, Christian 40
de Sousa Franco, António 361
De Valera, Eamon 245
de Villiers, Philippe 61, 63, 67, *68, 74, 71, 756*
de Vreese, Claes 45
debates, allocation of speaking time 33, 34
defence 10, 12, 34, 63, 80, 88, 112, 169, 254, 269, 271, 272, 275, 277, 404, 434, 594, 599
degressive proportionality/degressively proportional 23, 24, 132, 709
Dehaene, Jean-Luc 12, 155, 158, *160*, 162
Dehousse, Renaud xxx
Dehousse, Fernand 5
Dehousse Report 4
delegations 21, 30, 34, 35, *36, 37*, 69; four types 35–7; inter-parliamentary 35, 37
Delors, Jacques 217, 361
democratic accountability xxix, xxx, 309, 335, 364, 450, 514, 518, 520, 649, 660, 697
democratic deficit xxix, xviii, 14, 27, 45, 157, 363, 382, 482, 594, 697–8, 700, 707, 720
democratic legitimacy 4, 14, 20, 21, 22, 46
Denmark 267–86, *267;* allocation of EP seats *24*, *25*, *31*, *32*; EP and national elections 278–80; geographical position 268; geopolitical profile 269; historical background 268–9; national and EP electoral systems 277–8; overview of the political landscape 269; profile *268;* ECJ *Metock* verdict 282; Maastricht Treaty 274, 275, 276, 277; opt-outs 273, 275, 277, 280; *referenda* 9, 11, 275, 276; SEA 275, 276
d'Hondt formula/method/system 5, 58, 119, 153, 175, 277, 278, 328, 356, 402, 478, 497, 551, 555, 595, 611, 616, 659, 660, *736*; Austria 382–4; Belgium 152–3; Bulgaria 640; Cyprus 454–6; Czech Republic 554; Denmark 276–7; Estonia 496–7; Finland 400–1; France 56, 56; Germany 82–3, 84; Greece 302; Hungary 593–4; Ireland 249–50; Italy 117–18; Latvia 512–13; Lithuania 531; Luxembourg 194–5; Malta 437; Netherlands 174–5; Poland 615; Portugal 356, 356; Romania 658–9; Slovakia 576; Slovenia 476–7; Spain 327, 328, 328; Sweden 421; United Kingdom 218
del Rio Vilar, Susana 336
Dickow, Benjamin 281
Díez, Rosa 325, 332
direct election xxviii, xxxiii, xxxiv, 3, 4, 5, 15, 21, 22, 27, 28, 34, 40, 132, 164, 196, 252, 315, 357, 456, 513, 571, 605, 693, 696, 726
direct universal suffrage 4, 6, 7, 56, 58, 697
Dombrovskis, Valdis *508*, 519
Di Rupo, Elio *148*
Drake, Joanna 444
Droop formula/method 457, 474, 478, *480*, 577, *736*
dual mandate 22, 207, 255
Duff Report I, II 6–7
Duff, Andrew 6, 12, *228*, *232*
Dumont, Patrick 199
Dux see Mussolini, Benitoeconomic/financial crisis (2008–2009) xxxv, 19, 62, 63, 64, 65, 83, 91, 95, 96, 104, 113, 118, 129, *130*, 153, 158, 191, 200, 203, 208, 226, 227, 245, 246, 257, 258, 260, 264, 280, 282, 293, 307, 308, 309, 315, 318, 324, 328, 334, 336, 337, 347, 356, 362, 363, 365, 371, 372, 386, 387, 389, 405, 416, 441, 457, 461, 481, 487, 488, 496, 500, 501, 517, 520, 529, 534, 536, 538, *539*, 540, 554, 559, 575, 581, 598, 599, 604, 606, 621, 629, 645, 663, 664, 686, 697, 726

Economic and Monetary Union 10, 112, 173, *345*, 359, 454, 675, *676*, 677
Edinburgh Summit/Agreement 10, 18, 275, 277
Eduskunta (Finnish Parliament) 397, 399, 400, 401, 403, 404, 405, 407, 409, 410, 696
Egea de Haro, Alfonso 335
Egypt 294
Ehin, Piret 502
electoral cycles 329, 348
Elizabeth II, Queen *214*
Ellul Bonici, Sharon 436, 437

Index

energy policy 366, 372, 518, 519, 520, 524, 534, 581, 582
English language *759*
enhanced cooperation 11–13
environmental issues/groups 44, 104, 152, 157, 335, 386, 389, 424, 461, 466, 487, 524, 546, 553, 628, 684
Estonia 491–505; *491*; allocation of EP seats *24, 25, 31, 32*; EP and national elections 498–9; geographical position 492; geopolitical profile 493; historical background 492; national and EP electoral systems 493; overview of the political landscape 494; profile *492*euro: Austria *378*; Belgium *148*; Cyprus *449*; Estonia *492*; Finland *397*; France *52*; Germany *77*; Greece *292*; Ireland *244*; Italy *110*; Latvia *508*; Lithuania *528*; Luxembourg *190*; Malta *434*; the Netherlands *168*; Portugal *352*; Slovakia *569*; Slovenia *472*; Spain *322*
Eurobarometer xxviii, 56, 65, 83, 84, 118, 152, 153, 194, 217, *276*, 302, *327, 328*, 356, *383*, 384, 401, *421,* 437, *454, 455,* 478, 497, 512, 513
euro-crisis xxviii, 19, 62, 63, 64, 65, 83, 91, 95, 96, 104, 113, 118, 129, 153, 158, 191, 200, 203, 208, 226, 227, 245, 246, 252, 253, 257, 258, 260, 264, 280, 282, 293, 300, 301, 302, 307, 308, 309, 315, 318, 324, 328, 334, 336, 337, 347, 356, 362, 363, 365, 366, 371, 372, 386, 387, 389, 405, 416, 441, 457, 461, 481, 487, 488, 493, 496, 500, 501, 517, 520, 529, 534, 536, 538, 540, 554, 559, 575, 581, 598, 599, 604, 606, 617, 621, 629, 645, 663, 664, 677, 686, 698, 726; *see also* economic/financial crisis
Eurocriticism 92, 335, 453; *see also* Euroscepticism
euro-debt crisis *see* economic/financial crisis and euro-crisis
Europe of Democracies and Diversities Group EDD 29
Europe Salience (ES) theory 39, 43–6; Belgium 164–5; Denmark 286; France 74; Germany 104–5; Greece 317–18; Ireland 265; Italy 142–3; Luxembourg 207–9; Netherlands 185–6; New EU Member States *685*; Old EU Member States *684*; Portugal 371–2; Spain 348; UK 240–1
European Agricultural Guidance and Guarantee Fund-EAGGF 249
European Atomic Energy Community (Euratom) 8, 53, 149, 191, 388
European Central Bank (ECB) 11, 129, 130, 200, 354, 689
European Citizens initiative 18
European citizenship/citizenship of the European Union 10, 194, 198, 275, 277, 335
European Coal and Steel Community (ECSC) 4, 7, 8, 14, 17, 21, 27, *52*, 53, *77*, 78, *110, 148, 149, 168,* 169, *190,* 191, *244*

European Commission (EC) xxii, xxiv, xxxii, xxxiii, xxxiv, 6, 9, 11, 15, 16, 20, 21, 22, 31, 39, 65, 75, 89, 117, 122, 127, 142, 165, 174, 175, 183, 187, 193, 194, 197, 198, 199, 200, 217, 217, *236,* 241, 242, 276, 286, 293, 301, 318, 329, 348, 353, 354, 356, 359, 361, 366, 372, 380, 394, 395, 404, 441, 442, 447, 456, 466, 467, 489, 500, 506, 512, 515, 525, 547, 556, 575, 587, 597, 605, 615, 619, 640, 643, 651, 672, 674, 689, 697, 698, 702, 703, 704, 706, 713, 714, 715, 731, 734; President of xxx, 18, 28, 34, 113, 136, *160,* 509
European Community (EC)/European Union (EU) i, xx, xxxiii, 3, 6, 14, 15, 20, 21, 28, 34, 39, 40, 48, 53, 78, 123, 217, 220, 319, 328, 353, 467, 551, 675, 677, 681, 686, 689; enlargement 20, 22, 27, 49, 63, 65, 82, 83, 129, *130,* 152, 153, 173, 174, 175, 178, 179, 194, 197, 198, 211, 218, 227, 289, 308, 357, 366, 375, 384, 385, 387, 406, 474, 482, 505, 520, 531, *539,* 540, 555, 571, 574, 582, 599, 615, 621, 645, 658, 689, *690, 691,* 697
European Conservatives and Reformists (ECR) 29, *29,* 30, *31, 32, 98, 159, 160,* 182, *184, 214,* 230, *230, 231, 232, 233, 234, 235, 236, 237, 238, 390, 409,* 410, 523, 535, 544, *545, 563, 564, 600, 601,* 624, *625, 626, 627,* 692, *711, 712,* 715, 718, *719, 723,* 724, *725,* 726, *727, 732, 748, 750, 751, 752, 754, 755, 759*
European Constitution/European Constitutional Treaty xxv, 12, 62, 64, 67, 83, 173, 174, 177, 180, 186, 194, 195, 199, 249, 327, 328, 331, 482, 531, *539,* 615, 621, 628
European Council xxx, xxxi, 10, 12, 13, 19, 23, 24, 38, 58, 65, 174, 605, 628, 674, 702, 709, 713
European Court of Auditors 8, 11, 191
European Court of Justice (ECJ) 9, 12, 19, 20, 38, 191, 282, 442 European *demos* xxxiii, 481
European Democrat Party 55
European Development Fund (EDF) 14
European Economic Community (EEC) 4, 8, 15, *52,* 53, 77, 83, 110, 112, 148, 149, 168, 169, 172, *190,* 191, 215, *244,* 245, 250, 269, 274, 275, 276, 279, 293, 301, 398, 435, 473, 689
European Elections Studies (EES) xx, 39, 47
European Financial Stability Fund (EFSF) 245, 572, 576
European Food Safety Authority (EFSA) 11
European Green Party 62, 179, 407, 440, *463,* 580, 731
European identity 14, 45, 200, 610, 624, 679
European integration xxxiii, xxxiv, xxxv, 3, 4, 7, 9, 14, 28. 30, 37, 43, 44, 45, 46, 53, 55, 63, 65, 78, 82, 83, 86, 88, 91, *93,* 104, 105, 115, 118, *130,* 143, 152, 158, 172, 173, 174, 175, 176, 177, 179, 180, 186, 193, 194, 200, 208,

763

Index

216, 217, 225, 226, 227, 228, 250, 252, 265, 277, 301, 327, 329, 332, 335, 353, 359, 362, 382, 386, 389, 394, 398, 400, 404, 409. 411, 418, 450, 452, 453, 454, 455, 456, 458, 461, 466, 476, 487, 496, 500, 505, 531, 532, 536, *4539*,554, 555, 556, 557, 560, 574, 575, 599, 605, 614, 615, 619, 620, 621, 628, 639, 641, 657, 663, 671, 678, 679, 686, 689, 691, 692, 697. 698, 703, 706, 707, 720, 732

European Investment Bank EIB 191, 258

European Left Party xix, 362

European Liberal Democrat and Reform Party (ELDR) 65, 179, *183,* 225, 359, *477, 600, 639, 657, 741, 743*

European Monetary Union (EMU) 10, 112, 118, 126, 127, 194, 215, 227, 273, 275, 277, 359, 361, 400, 404, 416, 418, 420, 435, 441, 450, 452, 474, 476, 478, 500, 519, 536, 552, 553, 574, 598, 645, 675, *676, 678,* 700

European Parliament (EP) 3–14; Act for direct elections 5, 6; and budgets/finance 8, 13; composition 17, 21–37; by political group 27–34, *29, 30, 31, 32–3*; by nationality *31, 32, 33*; costs 19, 21, 34; genesis 3–14; languages 17, 20–1; location 14, 17–20; modification 6–7; right of assent 9; Rules of Procedures of 28, 710; Secretariat 9, 17, 18, 20; three-site arrangement 18–20

European Parliament composition 17, 21–37; **by gender ratio of MEPs 2014** – in aggregate countries: Old EU 15, EU 17, New EU 10, New EU 11, New EU 13, PIIGS/GIPSI, GIPSIC, Southern EU Countries, Nordic EU Countries, EU28 *721* in all EU Member States: Austria, Belgium, Bulgaria, Croatia, Cyprus, Czech Republic, Denmark, Estonia, Finland, France, Germany, Greece, Hungary, Ireland, Italy, Latvia, Lithuania, Luxembourg, Malta, Netherlands, Poland, Portugal, Romania, Slovakia, Slovenia, Spain, Sweden, UK; **by nationality 2009–2013** – Austria, Belgium, Bulgaria, Croatia (2013), Cyprus, Czech Republic, Denmark, Estonia, Finland, France, Germany, Greece, Hungary, Ireland, Italy, Latvia, Lithuania, Luxembourg, Malta, Netherlands, Poland, Portugal, Romania, Slovakia, Slovenia, Spain, Sweden, UK 708; **by nationality 2014** – Austria, Belgium, Bulgaria, Croatia, Cyprus, Czech Republic, Denmark, Estonia, Finland, France, Germany, Greece, Hungary, Ireland, Italy, Latvia, Lithuania, Luxembourg, Malta, Netherlands, Poland, Portugal, Romania, Slovakia, Slovenia, Spain, Sweden, UK *708;* **by nationality and political group 2014** *719, 751–3;* **by nationality, political groups and political party** – 1979 *737;* 1984 *738;* 1989 *739–40;* 1994 *741–2;* 1999 *743–4;* 2004 *745–7;* 2009 *748–50;* 2014 *751–4;* **by political group 2009–2011–2013** – Group of the European People's Party (EPP), Group of the Progressive Alliance of Socialists and Democrats in the European Parliament (S&D), Alliance of Liberals and Democrats for Europe (ALDE), The Greens/European Free Alliances (Greens/EFA), European Conservatives and Reformists (ECR), European United Left/Nordic Green Left (EUL/NGL), Europe of Freedom andt Democracy (EFD), Non-Attached *712;* **by Political Group 2014** – Group of the European People's Party (EPP), Group of the Progressive Alliance of Socialists and Democrats in the European Parliament (S&D), Alliance of Liberals and Democrats for Europe (ALDE), The Greens/European Free Alliances (Greens/EFA), European Conservatives and Reformists (ECR), European United Left/Nordic Green Left (EUL/NGL), Europe of Freedom and Direct Democracy (EFDD), Non-Attached *710, 712;* **by political group, nationality and gender 2014** *722;* **by political group breakdown by gender 2014** – in aggregate Countries: Old EU 15, EU 17, New EU 10, New EU 11, New EU 13, PIIGS/GIPSI, GIPSIC, Southern EU Countries, Nordic EU Countries, EU28 *725;* female representation by political group in aggregate countries in aggregate countries: Old EU 15, EU 17, New EU 10, New EU 11, New EU 13, PIIGS/GIPSI, GIPSIC, Southern EU Countries, Nordic EU countries, EU28 *727;* **by political group breakdown by gender in aggregate countries** – Old EU 15, EU 17, New EU 10, New EU 11, New EU 13, PIIGS/GIPSI, GIPSIC, Southern EU Countries, Nordic EU countries, EU28 *725*

European Parliament election: timing 39, 41, 42; turnout 40, 41, 43, 45, 46

European Parliament election 2009:
Austria 386–95; campaign finance 390–2; electoral campaign 387–8, *388;* electoral results 388–90; list of MEPs 391–2; party lists/manifestos 386–7; turnout 385; women MEPs *26, 722, 723*

Belgium 157–66; campaign finance 163; electoral campaign 158; electoral results 158–63, *159, 162, 163;* media coverage 158; list of MEPs *160–1;* party lists/manifestos 157–8; turnout 153, 155, *155,* 158, 159, 164; women MEPs *26, 722, 723*

Bulgaria 642–52; campaign finance 647–9; electoral campaign 644–6; electoral results 646–647; list of MEPs 648; party lists/

Index

manifestos 642–4; turnout 641, 646, *647*, 649, 650; women MEPs *26, 722, 723*

Cyprus 460–8; campaign finance 462; electoral campaign 456, 461–2, 465; electoral results 462; list of MEPs 464; party lists/manifestos 457, 460–1; turnout 456, 457, *458*, *459*, 460, 462, *463*, 465; women MEPs *26, 722, 723*

Czech Republic 557–67; campaign finance 565; electoral campaign 559; electoral results 559–64, *562;* list of MEPs *564;* party lists/manifestos 557–9, 563; turnout 555, *557*, 560, 561, *562*, 565 women MEPs *26, 722, 723*

Denmark 280–7; campaign finance 284–285; electoral campaign 281–2; electoral results 282–4, *282;* media coverage 280; party lists 278, 280–1; turnout 276, *277*, 278, *278*, 279, *279*, 280, 282, *282*, 284, 285; women MEPs *26, 722, 723*

Estonia 499–506; campaign finance 504; electoral campaign 500–1; electoral results 501–4; list of MEPs *503;* party lists/manifestos 499; turnout 498, *498*, 501, *502*, 504; women MEPs *26, 722, 723*

Finland 396–413; campaign finance 411; electoral campaign 408; electoral results 408–410, *408;* list of MEPs 410; party lists/manifestos 402, 404–8; turnout 402, *403*, 404, 408, *408*, 409; women MEPs *26, 722, 723*

France 61–75; campaign finance 73; electoral campaign 61, 63–6; electoral results 63, 66–73, *66, 68–9, 74;* media coverage 63, 64; list of MEPs *70–2;* party lists/manifestos 58, 61–3, 65; television debates 61, 64; turnout 66, *68*, 73; women MEPs *26, 722, 723*

Germany 91–108; campaign finance 98; electoral campaign 87, 95–6; electoral results *88*, 90, 96–8, *97, 98;* list of MEPs *99–102;* party lists/manifestos 85, 91–4, *93–4*, women MEPs *26, 722, 723*

Greece 307–20; campaign finance 315; electoral campaign 301, 307, 308–9; electoral results 295, 300, 303, 309–15, *318, 310;* environmental issues 308; media coverage 308–9; list of MEPs *311–14;* Office of the EP 309; party lists/manifestos 302, 307–8, *308;* turnout 304, *307*, 309, 316; women MEPs *26, 296, 311, 312, 315, 722, 723*

Hungary 597–607; campaign finance 604; electoral campaign 592, 598–9; electoral results 599–604, *600*, 604; list of MEPs *601–3;* party lists/manifestos 598; turnout 596, 597, *597*, 599, *600*, 605; women MEPs *27, 722, 723*

Ireland 256–6; campaign finance 262–4, *264;* electoral campaign 260; electoral results 261–2, *262;* list of MEPs *263;* party lists/manifestos 256–60; women MEPs *27, 722, 723*

Italy 128–46; campaign finance 139–40, *139, 140;* electoral campaign 118, 127, *130*, 131–2, 139; media 128, 131, 132, 145; electoral results 132–8, *133, 135, 136, 137–8*, 141; list of MEPs *137–8;* party lists/manifestos 121, 125, 126, 128–31, 134; pre-election survey 118; turnout 127, *128*, 132, 142, 143; women MEPs *27, 722, 723*

Latvia 516–26; campaign finance 514, 522; electoral campaign 519–20; electoral results *516*, 520–2, *521*, 522, 526; list of MEPs *523;* party lists/manifestos 514, 517–19; turnout 515, 516, *516*, 520, *521*, 522; women MEPs *27, 722, 723*

Lithuania 534–48; campaign finance 545; electoral campaign 532, 534, 536, 537, 537–40, *539*, 540, 545, 546, 547; electoral results *533, 541*, 541–5, *542*, 547; list of MEPs 543–4; party lists/manifestos 532, 534–7, *541;* turnout 529, 532, *533*, 537, 541, *541, 542*, 546; women MEPs *27, 722, 723*

Luxembourg 199–210; age/gender/nationality of candidates *190*, 196, 199, 200–1, 205, *206;* electoral campaign 197, 200, 201–4, *203;* electoral results 197, 204–5, *204, 205* media coverage 201, 208; list of MEPs *206;* party lists/manifestos 195, 199–201; turnout/abstention 201, *205*, 207; women MEPs *27, 722, 723*

Malta 440–7; campaign finance 444–5; electoral campaign 441–2; electoral results *438*, 442–4, *443;* list of MEPs *445;* party lists/manifestos 440–1; turnout *438*, 439, 441, 446, 447; women MEPs *27, 722, 723*

The Netherlands 178–88; campaign finance 184–5; electoral campaign 180–1; 184; electoral results 181–4, *176, 177, 182*, 185; list of MEPs *183–4;* party lists/manifestos 176, 178–80; turnout 174, 176, *176, 177, 177*, 181, *182*, 185, 186; women MEPs *27, 722, 723*

Poland 619–32; campaign finance 625; electoral campaign 620–2; electoral results 616, *617, 618*, 621, 622–5, *623*, 629; list of MEPs *626–7;* party lists/manifestos 619–20; turnout 617, 618, *618*, 628, 629, 632; women MEPs *27, 722, 723*

Portugal 362–73; campaign finance 367; electoral campaign 365–366; electoral results 355, 358, 360, *361*, 366–7, *367;*

media coverage 365; list of MEPs *368–70*; party lists/manifestos 362–5; turnout 357, *357*, 367, 371, 372; women MEPs 27, 722, 723

Romania 662–73; campaign finance 666–70; electoral campaign 660, 662, 663–664, 666; electoral results *661*, 664–66, *665*, 671; list of MEPs *367–69*; party lists/manifestos 660, 662–63, 664, 666; turnout 659, 660, *661*, 663, 670, 671, 672; women MEPs 27, 722, 723

Slovakia 580–8; campaign finance 585; electoral campaign 581–3; electoral results *579*, 583–5, *585*, 587; list of MEPs *586*; party lists/manifestos 577, 580; turnout 577, 578, *579*, 580, 583, 584, *585*, 585, 587; women MEPs 27, 722, 723

Slovenia 480–90; campaign finance 484–6; electoral campaign 481–2; electoral results *479*, 482–4, *483*, 486, 488, 490; list of MEPs *476*; party lists/manifestos 478, 481, 483, 484; turnout 476, 478, *480*, *479*, *483*, 486, 488; women MEPs 27, 722, 723

Spain 334–50; campaign finance 347; electoral campaign 336–7; electoral results *333*, 337–47, 348, *338*; list of MEPs *339–46*; Media coverage 336, party lists/manifestos 334–6; turnout 328, *329*, 333, 347; women MEPs 27, 722, 723

Sweden 423–9; campaign finance 425–7; electoral campaign 424–5; electoral results *422*, 425, 428; list of MEPs *426*; party lists/manifestos 421, 423–4; turnout 421, *422*, 425, 427, 428 women MEPs 27, 722, 723

United Kingdom 213–42; campaign finance 239; electoral campaign 225–7; electoral results *221, 222, 223*, 227–39, *230*, 241, 242; list of MEPs *231–8*; media coverage 225; party lists/manifestos 221–225; turnout 218, 221, *221, 222, 223*, 225, 227, *230*, 239, 241; women MEPs 27, 722, 723

European Parliament election theories 39–46; Europe Salience (ES) model 39, 43–6; and 'marker-setting' throw-away'/'elections 42–43; Second-Order Election (SOE) model/theory 40–3, 73, 98, 104, 105, 140, 141, 164, 185, 207, 208, 239, 264, 285, 316, 347, 371, 392, 393, 411, 427, 428, 444, 446, 456, 457, 462, 465, 466, 486, 502, 504, 505, 522, 546, 565, 585, 596, 604, 628, 646, 649, 650, 670–1, 677, *681, 682,* 696; and 'sincere'/'protest' voting 42; studies/surveys of 39–40, 43, 44–5

European Parliament election turnout 40, 41, 43, 45, 46; turnout in aggregate countries: Old EU 15, EU 17, New EU 10, New EU 11, New EU 13, PIIGS/GIPSI, GIPSIC, Southern EU Countries, EU27(2009) - EU28 (2013) *705*; in all EU Member States: Austria, Belgium, Bulgaria, Croatia (2013), Cyprus, Czech Republic, Denmark, Estonia, Finland, France, Germany, Greece, Hungary, Ireland, Italy, Latvia, Lithuania, Luxembourg, Malta, Netherlands, Poland, Portugal, Romania, Slovakia, Slovenia, Spain, Sweden, UK *708*

European Parliament election turnout 2014: turnout in aggregate countries: Old EU 15, EU 17, New EU 10, New EU 11, New EU 13, PIIGS/GIPSI, GIPSIC, Southern EU Countries, EU28 *705;* in all EU Member States: Austria, Belgium, Bulgaria, Croatia, Cyprus, Czech Republic, Denmark, Estonia, Finland, France, Germany, Greece, Hungary, Ireland, Italy, Latvia, Lithuania, Luxembourg, Malta, Netherlands, Poland, Portugal, Romania, Slovakia, Slovenia, Spain, Sweden, UK *708*

European Parliament election winners in Old EU Member States 728

European Parliament election winners in New EU Member States 729

European Parliament electoral systems in EU Member States *736*

European Parliament political groups: Alliance of Liberals and Democrats for Europe (ALDE) 28, 29, 30, 31, 32, 34, 71 72, 73, 98, 102, 134, 135, 136, 137, 138, 152, 160, 161, 183, 225, 230, 231, 232, 233, 234, 235, 236, 238, 247, 257, 262, 263, 284, 285, 345, 390, 408, 409, 410, 426, 453, 477, 483, 485, 503, 520, 523, 535, 536, 543, 544, 545, 547, 576, 577, 585, 586, 623, 625, 639, 643, 648, 657, 658, 663, 664, 665, 667, 668, 669, 711, 712, 714, 715, 718, 719, 723, 724, 725, 727, 731, 745, 746, 748, 750, 751, 752, 754, 755; European Conservatives and Reformists (ECR) 29, 29, 30, 31, 32, 98, 159, 160, 182, 184, 214, 230, 230, 231, 232, 233, 234, 235, 236, 237, 238, 390, 409, 410, 523, 535, 544, 545, 563, 564, 600, 601, 624, 625, 626, 627, 692, 711, 712, 714, 718, 719, 723, 724, 725, 726, 727, 732, 748, 750, 751, 752, 754, 755, 759; Europe of Democracies and Diversities Group EDD 29; Europe of Freedom and Democracy (EFD) 29, *29*, 30, *30*, *31, 32–3*, 72, *98,* 134, *135, 136, 137, 138,* 184, *230, 283, 314, 390, 408,* 410, *535, 543, 544,* 545, 576, 577, 585, *586, 648,* 692, *712,* 714, 716, 717, 718, *748, 750*; Europe of Freedom and Direct Democracy (EFDD) *711, 712,* 718, *719, 723,* 724, *725,* 726, 727, *751, 752, 754, 755*; European People's Party (EPP) xxxii, 6, 19, 27, 28, *29, 30, 31, 32,* 34; European Liberal Democrat and Reform Party (ELDR) 65, 179, 183, 225, 359, 477, 600, 639, 657, 741, 743; European People's Party (EPP)

Index

xxxii, 6, 19, 27, 28, *29, 30, 31, 32,* 34, *71–3; 90–102, 137–8;* 160; *183–4; 206; 263;* 284; *312, 339–46, 368–70, 391,* 410, *426, 445, 464, 485, 503,* 523, *543–44, 564, 586, 601–3, 626–7, 648, 667–9;* Greens/European Free Alliance (EFA) 28, *29, 30, 31, 32,* 34, *98, 101,* 152, *159, 160, 161, 183, 184, 206, 230, 235, 236, 237, 247, 284, 314, 346,* 390, *390, 392, 408, 410, 415, 426, 503,* 517, *523,* 711, 712, 714, 717, *719, 723,* 724, *725,* 727, *745, 746, 748, 750, 751, 752, 754, 755;* Independence and Democracy Group (IND/DEM) 29, 180, 745, 746; Party of European Socialists (PES) 34, 55, 65, 91, *179, 183,* 220, 225, 248, 258, 334, 360, 362, 363, 437, 440, 477, 483, *485, 503,* 534, *535, 543, 544,* 545, 554, 576, 577, 580, 581, 598, *600,* 619, *623, 625,* 637, 639, 643, 647, 657, 714, 731; Progressive Alliance of Socialists and Democrats (S&D) 28, *29, 30, 31, 32,* 70, *71, 72, 98, 100,* 134, *135, 136, 137, 138, 159, 160, 161,* 206, 225, 230, 247, *263, 283, 311, 322, 342, 345, 367, 367, 378, 390,* 390, *391, 392, 408, 410, 415, 426, 434,* 444, 453, 462, *463, 464,* 477, 485, 563, *564,* 577, *585, 586, 601, 602, 603,* 624, *626, 627, 648, 658,* 663, 664, *665,* 667, *668, 669,* 711, 712, 713, 714, 718, *719,* 721, *723, 725, 727, 748, 750, 751, 752, 754, 755, 759;* Union for Europe of the Nations (UEN) 257, 520, *535,* 576, *623, 625, 744, 745, 746;* United Left/Nordic Green Left (EUL/NGL) *29,* 30, *31, 32,* 70, *71, 72, 98, 102,* 180, *235, 247, 263, 283, 347, 367, 390, 426, 564,* 692, 711, 712, 716, 718, *719, 723,* 724, *725, 727, 743, 745, 746, 748, 750, 751, 752, 754, 755, 759;*
European Parliamentary Assembly 8, 15, 21
European Political Cooperation (EPC) 9
European Social Progress Pact 258
European Union (Treaty) 10–14, budget 13, 14, 18, 19, 62, 91, 281, 353, 394, 442, 583; bureaucracy 92, 152, 157, 173, 175, 382, 386, 387, 389, 394, 408, 517, 531, 536, Draft Treaty 8, 9, 14; Presidents/Vice-Presidents xxx, 136; Spanish presidency of 337; symbol/anthem 174
European Union Member States: Old *684;* New *685*
European unification xxxv, 18, 174, 621, 675, 692, 726, 731, 732
European Union Solidarity Fund (EUSF) 129
European United Left/Nordic Green Left, EUL/NGL *29,* 30, *30, 31, 32–3,* 70, 72, *72, 98, 102, 184,* 180, *247, 263, 283, 390, 426, 564,* 711, 712, *719, 723, 725, 727, 743, 751, 752, 754, 755, 759*
Europeanization xviii, xix, xx, xxii, xxiii, 208, 248, 318, 451, 475, 518, 547, 552, 605, 610, 637, 644
Euro-realism 152, 481

Eurosceptic 10, 45, 61, 104, 117, 118, 134, 143, 152, 157, 158, 178, 179, 180, 181, 182, 186, 203, 205, 208, 216, 217, 218, 220, 221, 225, 230, 239, 240, 241, 247, 248, 249, 256, 257, 259, 260, 261, 262, 265, 272, 273, 274, 277, 278, 279, 283, 284, 285, 286, 308, 333, 335, 355, 359, 360, 363, 364, 365, 384, 385, 387, 394, 400, 404, 405, 406, 409, 410, 411, 418, *419,* 420–1, 421, 423, 425, 427, 428, 436, 437, 442, 444, 452, 453, 460, 465, 466, 481, 496, 505, 512, 520, 530, 534, 537, 538, 546, 547, 552, 553, 554, 556, 557, 561, 566, 574, 575, 576, 580, 587, 605, 619, 620, 624, 629, 644, 677, 679, 685, 686, *687–88,* 689, *690,* 691, *691,* 692, 696, 711, 716, 729, 730, 732, *756*
Eurosceptic/Eurocritical parties in EU Member States 756–8; in New Enlargement countries *691;* in Original Six countries *687–8;* in Old EU enlargement countries *69*
Euroscepticism 117, 157, 217, 220, 241, 248, 261, 265, 272, 274, 286, 355, 365, 400, 405, 410, 419, 420–1, 427, 437, 442, 476, 488, 553, 555, 556, 574, 575, 576
euro-zone 79, 114, 126, 220, 248, 273, 277, 353, 401, 416, 418, 423, 441, 456, 488, 293, 500, 501, 554, 572, 574, 576, 700
Evans, Jill 28, *229, 237*
Exclusive Economic Zone (EEZ) 450
Extreme parties 22, 31, 44, 74, 80, 85, 92, 104, 129, 133, 165, 265, 364, 371, 487, 531, 559, 561, 592, 606, 671

Facebook 95, 131, 202, *203,* 336, 365, 424, 558, 645, 663, 680Farage, Nigel 30, *229, 236,* 718, 720, *755*
farmers 87, 249, 610, 620, 628
federalism 172, 173, 179, 180;
Federation of the European Liberal, Democrat, and Reformist Parties 27
Ferrara, Federico 41, 44, 45, 524
Fico, Róbert, *569,* 571, 573
Fillon, François *52*
Finland 396–412, *396;* allocation of EP seats *24, 25, 31, 32;* EP and national elections 402–4; geographical position 397; geopolitical profile 398; national and EP electoral systems 401–2; overview of the political landscape 398–9; profile *398;* historical background 397–8
First-past-the-post (FPTP) system 218, 240, 682
Fischer, Joschka 79
Fitzgerald, Garrett 253, 254
Flanders (Belgium) 149, 150, 151, *154,* 156, 157, 159
Flickinger, Richard S. 45
Folketinget (Danish Parliament) 269, 271, 273, 274, 275, 277, 278, 280, 284, 285, 286
Food and Agriculture Organization FAO 112

Foreign Affairs Committee 34, *35*, 136
foreign ministries 9
Former Yugoslav Republic of Macedonia FYROM *36*, 79, 292, 294, 308, *312, 313, 314*
Fox, Ashley Peter 19, 20, *228*
Fraga Iribarne, Manuel 324, 325, 329
France 51–74, *51;* allocation of EP seats 22, 23, *24, 25, 31, 32;* Constitution 53, 54, 58; electoral constituencies *57,* 58 ; EP and national elections 59–61; geographical position 52; geopolitical profile 53; historical background 52–3; national and EP electoral systems 56–59; overview of the political landscape 53–4; profile *52;* Lisbon Treaty *52,* 63, 64; Maastricht Treaty 10; referendum on Constitutional Treaty 62, 64, 67
France versus Parliament (C-237–11) 19
Franco, Francisco 111, 323, 324, 675
Franklin, Mark 39, 42, 43, 44, 45, 707, 708, 709, 729
Freire, André 371
Frieden, Luc 204
Friedenspolitik 79

G8 countries 53, 112, 132
Gallagher, Pat 262, *263*
Ganley, Declan 63, 92, 180, 224, 247, *247,* 249, 260, 261, 262, 263, 265, 335, 364, 440, 546, 561, 615, 620, 621, 689
Gargani, Giuseppe *110, 137*
General Agreement on Tariffs and Trade (GATT) 112, 655
Gašparovič; Ivan *569,* 572
gauche plurielle 60
Gauck, Joachim 77, 79
GDR (East Germany) 78, 79, 80
Geißler, Heiner 88
gender quotas 34
Genscher, Hans-Dietrich 87, 89
Germany 76–108, *76;* allocation of EP seats 22, 23, *24, 25, 31, 32;* EP and national elections 85–90; geographical position 77–8; geopolitical profile 79 ; historical background 78; national and EP electoral systems 83–5; overview of the political landscape 79–80; profile *77;* Basic Law (*Grundgesetz*) 78; electoral systems 83–5; *Bundestag* seats 83, 85; employment/unemployment 82, 83, 88, 91; Federal Constitutional Court 10, 80, 85; Lisbon Treaty 80, 92; Nazi period 80, 83, 86, 293, 323; peace approach to foreign policy 79, 83, 92; Presidential powers/role 79; Maastricht Treaty 10; (re)unification 34, 78, 79, 83; Weimar Republic 80, 83, 85, 378;
Giscard d'Estaing, Valéry 5, 10, 12, 53, 60
globalization 14, 118, 170, 172, 199, 200, 385, 400, 417, 518, 606, 624
Globalization Fund 257

Goerens, Charles 200, 204
González, Felipe 323, 324, 332
Good Friday Agreement (Ireland-UK) 245
Gormley, John *247,* 248, 259
Grabbe, Heather 703
Greece 291–318, *291;* allocation of EP seats 22, 23, *24, 25, 31, 32, 33,* 310; EP and national elections 303–7; geographical position 292–3; geopolitical profile 294; historical background 293, national and EP electoral systems 302–303, overview of the political landscape 294–5; profile *292;* Macedonia 292, 294, 308, *311, 312, 313, 314; Memorandum* of (1983) 301, 302; political instability 293, 304; Turkey 294, *311, 312, 314*
Greens/EFA group *29, 30, 31, 32, 98,* 152, *159, 160, 161, 183, 184, 283, 408, 415, 426, 711, 712, 719, 745, 746, 748, 750, 751, 752, 754, 755*
Grillo, Beppe 113, 718, 720
Gualtieri and Trzaskowski Report 23
Guevara, Che 624
Guterres, António 358, 359, 361, 371
Gyárfášová, Ol'ga 577–83, 473, 570

Häfner, Gerald 19, *101*
The Hague Conference/Summit 4
Hague, William 220
Hare-Niemeyer method 85, 616, 640, *736*
Harms, Rebecca 28, 92, *101*
Haughey, Charles 253, 254
Heath, sir Edward 216, 689
Hemingway, Ernest xxxv
Henri, Grand Duke *190*
Hernández Mancha, Antonio 329
Higgins, Joe 246, *247,* 259, 261, 262, *263*
Higgins, Michael D. *244,* 246
Hirschman, Albert O. 143
Hix, Simon 44, 104, 286, 316, 317, 427, 525
Hobolt, Sara B. 40, 43, 45
Hooghe, Lisbet, 605
Hollande, François *52,* 54, 717
Hopkin, Jonathan 327
Hortefeux, Brice 63, 73
human rights 34, 79, 96, 112, 129, 130, 134, *161,* 169, 199, 270, 450, 530, 540, 561
Hungary 589–606, *589;* allocation of EP seats 23, *24, 25, 31, 32, 33;* EP and national elections 596–7; geographical position 590; geopolitical profile 591; historical background 590–1; national and EP electoral systems 595–6; overview of the political landscape 591; profile *590*

Ilves, Toomas Hendrik *492,* 496, 504
immigration xxv, 13, 42, 55, 63, 78, 89, 118, 129, 130, 131, 132, 151, 152, 157, 180, 195, 197,

225, 227, 256, 260, 271, 272, 274, 280, 282, 293, 300, 308, 309, 334, 337, 352, 364, 372, 381, 382, 384, 385, 386, 387, 389, 394, 405, 406, 418, 437, 440, 441, 442, 446, 453, 481, 493, 500, 518, 524, 540, 554, 582, 594, 659, 663, 714
Independence and Democracy Group (IND/DEM) 29, 180, *745, 746*
Integrated Mediterranean Programme (IMP) 302
Inter-institutional Agreement on Budgetary Discipline (1988) 10
Intergovernmental Conference on European Monetary Union and Political Union 10
internal market 11, 406, 481
International Democrat Union 54
International Labour Organization (ILO) 294
international law 79, 169
International Monetary Fund (IMF) 79, 269, 294, 323, 354, 416, 519, 571, 638, 655, 689, 700
internet 64, 65, 131, 163, 181, 184, 201, 202, 224, 363, 365, 367, 408, 424, 439, 498, 500, 501, 520, 536, 538, 540, 558, 593, 645, 680
Iraq, invasion/occupation 79, 127, 131, 177, 332
Ireland 243–65, *243*; allocation of EP seats 22, 23, *24, 25, 31, 32, 33*; Constitution 245, 246, 251, 257; economy of 245, 248–50, 252, 257, 258, 260; electoral constituencies *251;* EP and national elections 252–6; geographical position 244; geopolitical profile 245; historical background 244–5; national and EP electoral systems 251–2 ; overview of the political landscape 246; profile *244;* Lisbon Treaty referendum 248–9, 250, *250*, 256, 257, 258–60, 262; Nice Treaty 249, 250, 255–6; opt-outs 12, 257; Republic of Ireland Act (1948) 245; UK/Northern Ireland 244–5, 252, 258
Islamization 170, 180, 500, 554
Israel 36, 294, *311, 314, 341, 388, 602,* 655
Italy 109–46, *46;* Abruzzo earthquake 130; allocation of EP seats 23, *24, 25, 31, 32, 33*; Constitution 112–113, 121; corruption 119, 125, 139, 140; electoral constituencies 120; EP and national elections 121–8; geographical position 110–111; geopolitical profile 111–12; historical background 111; overview of the political landscape 112–14; profile *110;* Lisbon/Maastricht Treaties 137; *Pentapartito* 122; *Ulivo* coalition *115,* 125, 127, 133, 142; Valle d'Aosta region *109,* 119, 128; *Piccoli* Bill 139; *Porcellum* Bill 118, 119, 146; referenda 121

Jacobs, Francis 17
Juknevičienė, Ona 534, *535*
Jauregui, Ramón 336
joint parliamentary committees JPCs 35, *36*
Jørgensen, Dan 38, 281, 282, *283*
Jospin, Lionel 59

Juan Carlos, King *322,* 324
Juncker, Jean-Claude xxxii, *190,* 193, 195, 198, 199, 204, 708, 713
Junqueras, Oriol 337, 347
Justice and Home Affairs (JHA) 10, 13, *35, 136, 161,* 179, 273, 275, *313, 339, 341, 342, 345, 368, 392, 445, 464, 485, 523, 543, 544, 586, 601, 602, 609*

Kaczyński, Lech
Kallas, Siim 500
Kammenos, Panos 300
Karamanlis, Konstantinos 295, 304
Karamanlis, Kostas *292*
Karatzaferis, George 300
Katzenstein, P. J. 78, 83, 107
Kenny, Edna *244,* 246, *247,* 257, 266
Koch-Mehrin, Silvana 90, ,95, 96, 97, *102*
Koepke, Jason R. 42, 43, 47, 316, 319, 337, 363, 373, 505, 506, 546, 548, 670, 672, 681, 683, 699
Kohl, Helmut 87, 88, 89
Köhler, Horst 77, 79
Komorowski, Bronisław 609, 613, 618
Kosovo War 79, 90, 255, 332, 360, 385
Krivine, Alain 204

labour reform 82
Laeken European Council 12
Lafontaine, Oskar 80, 82, 92
Lamassoure-Séverin Report 23, 132
Latvia 507–25, *507;* allocation of EP seats 23, *24, 25, 31, 32, 33*; EP and national elections 515–16; geographical position 508; geopolitical profile 509; historical background 509; national and EP electoral systems 513; overview of the political landscape 509–10; profile *508*
Le Pen, Jean-Marie 55, 59, 60, 63, *68, 72,* 686, 717, 718
Le Pen, Marine 61, 63, *68, 72* , 716, 718, 735
League of Nations 149
Lefevere, Jonas 155, 158, 166
Lehne, Stefan 703
Løkke Rasmussen, Lars *268,* 269
Leopold I (King) 149
Leopold II (King) 149
Leopold III (King) 149
Leterme, Yves *148*
Letta, Enrico *110,* 113
Libya 111, 112, 436
Lindberg, Leon N. 117, 145, 455, 467
Lisbon Treaty or Treaty of Lisbon (ToL): xxix, 18, 23, 31, 52, 63, 64, 77, 80, 92, 96, *110,* 137, *148,* 152, 158, *168,* 174, 175, 177, 178, 179, 180, 182, 186, *190,* 199, 200, *214,* 218, 226, 227, 228, *244,* 248, 250, *250,* 257, 258, 259, 260, 262, *268, 292,* 308, 310, *322,* 327, 334,

335, *352*, 363, 365, *378*, 386, 387, 389, *397*, 401, 406, 410, *415*, 421, 422, 424, 425, *434*, 437, 440, *449*, 453, 454, *472*, 482, 484, *492*, 500, *508*, 513, 516, 518, 520, 521, 522, *528*, 531, 546, *550*, 553, *569*, 575, 580, 582, *590*, 599, 605, *609*, 615, 620, 621, 622, 624, *634*, 645, 650, *654*, 686, 702, 708, 709, 715
Louçã, Francisco 360
Loyola de Palacio, Ignacia 331
Lucas Pires, Francisco 358, 359
Luxembourg 189–209, *189*; allocation of EP seats 25; EP and national elections 196–9; geographical position 190; geopolitical profile 191; historical background 190–1; national and EP electoral systems 195–6; overview of the political landscape 191; profile *190*; Constitution 191

McAleese, Mary *244*, 246
McElroy, Gail 33
McKenna, Patricia 259, 261
Maillot, Agnes 248
Major, John 10
Malmström, Cecilia 18
Malta 433–46, *433*; allocation of EP seats 23, *24*, 25, *31*, *32*, *33*; EP and national elections 438; geographical position 434; geopolitical profile 435; historical background 434–5; national and EP electoral systems 437; overview of the political landscape 435; profile *434*
manifestos 44
Mannheimer, Renato 39, 123
Margrethe II, Queen *268*
Marks, Gary 605
'marker-setting'/'throw-away' elections 42, 43
Marsh, Michael 44, 286, 316, 317, 427, 462, 525, 684, 730
Martens, Wilfried 27
Martin, David *229*, *235*
Mattarella, Sergio *110*
Mattila, Mikko 40
Mauro, Mario 136, 138
Mayor Oreja, Jaime 334, 336, 691
Meier, Willy 335, 337, 346
Mélenchon, Jean-Luc 55, 61, 68, *72*
Memoli, Vincenzo 117
Merkel, Angela 63, 77, 80, 83, 95, 96, 327, 692, 711
Messerschmidt, Morten 280, 281, 282, *283*
Milošević, Slobodan 332
Mitterrand, François 10, 53, 55, 59, 61, 323
Mizzi, Marlene 444
mixed member proportional (MMP) system 83
money laundering 34, 203
Monteiro, Manuel 359, 360
Monti, Mario *110*, 113
Moreira, Vital 365, 367, *369*

Moxon Browne, Edward 255
multiculturalism, multicultural 172, 178, 536, 590
multilingualism, multilingual 20–1, 680
Mussolini, Alessandra 657
Mussolini, Benito 111, 114
MySpace 131, 336, 424, 663, 680

Napieralski, Grzegorz 613, *613*, 614
Napolitano, Giorgio *110*
Nasiriyah 127
national electoral cycle xxxiv, 42, 88, 104, 105, 127, 141, 239, 241, 347, 348, 371, 578, 587, 681, 683
national identity 129, 175, 179, 194, 198, 199, 200, 274, 367, 370, 382, 473, 518, 573, 575, 610, 614, 620
neo-liberal policies 716
The Netherlands 167–86, *167*; allocation of EP seats 22, 23, *24*, 25, *31*, *32*, *33*; Constitution 169, 174; European Constitutional Treaty 173–4, 177, 180; EP and national elections 175–8; geographical position 168; geopolitical profile 169–70; historical background 169; Lisbon Treaty 174, 175, 82; national and EP electoral systems 175; overview of the political landscape 170; profile *168*
NGOs (non-governmental organizations) 19, 294, 461, 570
Nice Treaty (2001) 250, *250*, 255, 628, 709
Nordic Council 21
North Atlantic Assembly 21
North Atlantic Treaty Organization (NATO) 21, *36*, 37, 53, 79, 88, 112, 131, 149, 169, 172, 191, 215, *233*, 245, 255, 269, 294, 324, 332, *345*, 354, 360, 380, 385, 416, 435, 436, 461, 474, 481, 488, 493, 494, 509, 529, 540, 551, 571, 574, 591, 610, 635, 638, 655; NATO Partnership for Peac1e programme 245, 255, 435
Northern Ireland *xiii*, 214, 215, 216, 218, *219*, *222*, *223*, 224, *224*, 228, *228*, *229*, 230, *235*, 244, 245, 246, 248, 252, 258
Norway *36*, 112, 268, 276, 397, 415, 416, *601*, 615
nuclear energy/technology 96, 130, 387, 388, 540, 582, 645
Nyrup Rasmussen, Poul 65, 281, 284

Oblast, province (Bulgaria) 634
Oireachtas (Irish Parliament) 245, 246
Ombudsman 11, 191, 611
Oppenhuis, Erik 39, 42
Orbán, Viktor Mihály 582, *590*, 592, 679, 713
Oreja Aguirre, Marcelino 323
Organization for Economic Cooperation and Development (OECD) 86, 112, 149, 191, 203, 269, 294, 474, 493, 610, 203

Organization for Security and Cooperation in Europe (OSCE) 149, 262, 269, 294, 416, 450, 474, 493, 571, 610, 635
Oresharski, Plamen *634*

Pacheco Pereira, José 359
panachage, inter-party 195
Pannella, Marco 125, 129, *133*, 134, *742*
Papademos, Lucas *292*, 295, 300
Papandreou, Andreas 300, 304
Papandreou, George *292*, 300, 304
Papoulias, Karolos *292*
Paris Agreements 112
Paris Summit/Treaty 5
Partnership for Peace programme 245, 255, 435
Parvanov, Georgi *634*, 636, 643, 645
Pasqua, Charles 61, 74
Passos Coelho, Pedro *352*, 354
Patijn, Schelto 3, 5
Pavlopoulos, Prokopis *292*
Plevneliev, Rosen *634*, 636
Ponta, Victor *654*
pension(s) 94, 118, 130, 177, 193, 198, 258, 387, 517, 556, 559, 579, 594, 663
'permissive consensus' 56, 117, 454, 455, 697
Perestroika 635
Philippe VI, King *148*
Pikrammenos, Panayiotis *292*
PIREDEU project 39
Pittella, Gianni 136, *138*, 714,755
Poland 608–28, *608*; allocation of EP seats 23, *24*, *25*, *31*, *32*, *33*; electoral constituencies *616*; EP and national elections 617–19; geographical position 609; geopolitical profile 610; historical background 609–10; national and EP electoral systems 615–17; overview of the political landscape 610–11; profile *610*; political union 10, 14
Political parties:
  Austria
    Political parties 380–2, *381*
    Bündnis Zukunft Österreich, BZÖ (Alliance of the Future of Austria), 380, *381*, 381, 382, *384*, 386, 387, 388, *388*, 389, *390*, *392*, 392, *393*, 394, *690*, 757
    Das Neue Österreich, NEOS (The New Austria) 380, *381*, 382, *384*, *751*
    Die Grünen (The Greens) *381*
    Freiheitliche Partei Österreichs, FPÖ (Freedom Party of Austria) *381*, 716, 757
    Junge Liberale, JuLis (Young Liberals) 380, *381*, *388*, 389, *390*
    Liberales Forum, LIF (Liberal Forum) 380, *381*, 381, 385
    Liste Hans-Peter Martin, HPM (Hans-Peter Martin List) 380, *381*, 385, 389, 390, *390*, *392*, 393, *393*, 394, *690*, *757*

Österreichische Volkspartei, ÖVP (Austrian Peoples' Party) 378, 379, 380, *381*, 381, 382, *384*, 385, 386, 387, 388, *388*, 389, *390*, *391*, 392, *393*, 393, 394, *728*, *743*, *745*, *748*, *751*
Sozialdemokratische Partei Österreichs, SPÖ (Social Democratic Party of Austria) 378, 379, 380, 381, *381*, 382, *384*, *384*, 385, 386, 387, 388, *388*, 389, *390*, *390*, *391*–*2*, 393, *393*, 394, *728*, *743*, *745*, *748*, *751*
Team Stronach Frank, TS (Team Stronach Frank) *381*
Belgium
  political parties 150–2, *151*
  Centre Démocrate Humaniste, CDH (Humanist Democratic Centre) *148*, *151*, 151, 152, *156*, 157, *162*, 163, 165, *745*, *748*, *751*
  Christlich Soziale Partei, CSP (Christian Social Party) *151*,*161*, *741*, *743*, *745*, *748*, *751*
  Écologistes Confédérés pour l'Organisation de Luttes Originales, Ecolo (Confederated ecologists for the Organization of original struggles) 151, *151*, 152, *156*, 157, *161*, *162*, 163, *163*, 165, *738*, *739*, *742*, *745*, *748*, *751*, *755*
  Groen! (Green!) (Walloon/Flemish Greens) *151*, *162*, 165
  Front National, FN (National Front) *151*, 151, *156*, 157, *162*, 165, *742*
  Lijst Dedecker, LDD (Dedecker List) *151*, 151, 157, 158, *160*, 164, 165, *687*, 689, *748*, *756*
  Mouvement réformateur, MR (Reformist Movement) *148*, *151*, *156*, 156, 157, *161*, 162, *162*, 165, 715, *745*, *748*, *751*
  Nieuw-Vlaamse Alliantie, N-VA (New Flemish Alliance) *151*, 151, 152, 155, 158, *162*, *162*, 165, 714, *728*, *743*, *748*, *751*
  Partei für Freiheit und Fortschritt, PFF (Party for Freedom and Progress-Reformist Movement) *151*, 151, *163*
  Parti socialiste, PS (Socialist Party); *148*, *151*, 151, 152, 155, 156, *156*, 157, *161*, 163, 166, *737*, *738*, *739*, *741*, *743*, *745*, *748*, *751*
  Socialistische Partij Anders, SPA (Socialist Party Different) *148*, *151*, 151, 152, 155, *160*, 162, *162*, 166
  Vlaams Belang, VB (Flemish Interest) *151*, 151, 155, *155*, *156*, 161, 162, *162*, 165, 166, 657, *687*, 689, 716, *751*, *756*

Vlaamse Liberalen en Democraten, Open VLD (Flemish Liberal and Democratic Party), *148, 151,* 151, 152, *155, 156,* 157, *160,* 162, *162,* 166, 715, 716, *748, 751, 755*

Bulgaria
Political parties 636–9, *637*
Balgarska Sotsialisticheska Partiya, BSP (Bulgarian Socialist Party) *634,* 636, 637, *637,* 639, 641, 642, *642,* 643, 644, 645, 647, *647, 648,* 649, *748, 751,* 652
Balgarski Naroden Sajuz, BNS (Bulgarian People's Union) *637,* 638, *642*
Bulgarska Nova Demokracia, BND (Bulgarian New Democracy) *637,* 644
Demokrati za Silna Balgariya, DSB (Democrats for Strong Bulgaria) *637,* 638, 639, 643, *648*
Dvizhenie za Prava i Svobodi, DPS (Movement for Rights and Freedoms) *634,* 636, *637,* 638, 639, 641, *642,* 643, 644, 645, *647, 648,* 650, 715, *748, 751*
Grazhdani za Evropeysko Razvitie na Balgaria, GERB (Citizens for European Development of Bulgaria) *634,* 636, *637,* 638, 639, 641, 642, *642,* 643, 644, 645, *647, 648,* 729, *748, 751*
Lider (Leader Party) *637*
Natsionalno Dvizhenie za Stabilnost I Vazhod, NDSV (National Movement for Stability and Progress) 636, *637,* 638, 639, 641, *642,* 643, 644, 645, *647, 647, 648,* 649, *748*
Partiya Ataka, PA (Party Attack) *637,* 640, 643
Red Zakonnost Spravedlivost, RZS (Order, Lawfulness, Justice) *637,* 638, 639, 641, *642,* 643, *647*
Sayuz na demokratichnite sili SDS (Union of Democratic Forces) 636, *637, 637,* 638, 639, 641, 643, *648, 748*
Siniata Koalicia BC (Blue Coalition) *637,* 638, 643, 644, 645, 647, *648*

Croatia
Political parties *758*
Blok Umirovljenici Zajedno BUZ Party of United Pensioners *758*
Hrvatska Demokratska Zajednica HDZ Croatian Democratic Union *729, 751, 758, 759,*
Hrvatska Narodna Stranka HNS Croatian People's Party *751, 758, 759*
Hrvatska Stranka Prava 'Ante Starčević' HSP AS Croatian Party of Rights 'Ante Starčević' *729, 751, 758, 759*

Hrvatska Stranka Umirovljenika HSU Croatian Party of Pensioners *751, 758, 759*
Hrvatski Laburisti- Stranka Rada HL-SR Croatian Labourists - Labour Party *758, 759*
SocijalDemokratska Partija SDP Social Democratic Party *758, 759*

Cyprus
Political parties 451–4, *451, 452*
Anorthotikó Kómma Ergazómenou Laoú, AKEL (Progressive People's Party) *449, 451,* 462, *463, 464,* 465, 466, 691, *691,* 745, *748, 751,* 757
Dimokratikó Kómma, DIKO (Democratic Party) *449, 451,* 451, 452, *452,* 453, 454, *458,* 458, *459,* 460, 461, 462, *463, 464,* 466
Dimokratikós Sinayermós, DISY (Democratic Rally) *449, 451,* 451, 452, 454, *458,* 458, *459,* 460, 461, 462, *463, 464,* 465, 466, 729, 745, *748, 751*
Ethniko Laiko Metopo, ELAM (National Popular Front) *451,* 451, 453, *458, 459, 463,* 467
Enomeni Dimokrate, EDI (United Democrats) *451, 458, 459*
Evropaiko Komma, EVROKO (European Party) *449, 451,* 451, 453, 466
Oikologon Perivallontiston, KOP (Cyprus Green Party) *451,* 451, 453, 466
Kinima Sosialdimokraton EDEK Social-Democratic Movement *449, 451,* 451, 453, 454, *458,* 458, *459,* 460, 461, 462, *463, 464,* 466, 713, *748, 751*
New Horizons *451, 458, 459*

Czech Republic
Political parties 552–4, *552*
Obcanska demokraticka strana, ODS (Civic Democratic Party) 29, *552,* 552, 553, 554, 555, 556, 557, *557,* 558, 559, 560, 561, 562, *562,* 563, *564,* 565, 566, 567, 714, *745, 748, 751*
Ceska strana socialne demokraticka, CSSD (Czech Social Democratic Party) *550, 552, 552,* 553, 554, 555, 556, 557, *557,* 558, 559, 560, 561, 562, *562, 563, 564,* 565, 567, 729, *745, 748, 751*
Komunisticka strana Cech a Moravy KSCM (Communist Party of Bohemia and Moravia) *552, 552,* 554, 557, 559, 560, *564,* 691, 692, *745, 748, 751, 758*
Krestanska a demokraticka unie – Ceskoslovenska strana lidova, KDU-CSL(Christian and Democratic

Index

Union – Czechoslovak People's Party) *550*, 552, *552*, 553, 554, 557, *557*, 559, 560, 561, *562*, *745*, *748*
Strana zelenych, SZ (Green Party) *552*, 553, 557, 558, 560, 561, *562*, 566
Sdruzeni nezavislych kandidatu – Evropsti demokrate, SNK-ED (Association of Independent Candidates – European Democrats) *552*, *562*, 566
Nezavisli demokrate, NEZDEM (Independent Democrats) *552*, 554, 556, *562*, *691*, *758*
Veci verejne VV (Public Affairs) *552*, 553, 554, 555, *557*, *562*

Denmark
Political parties 269–75, *270*
Centrum Demokraterne, CD (Centre Democrats) *270*, 275, *278*, *279*, *738*, *739*
Dansk Folkeparti, DF (Danish People's Party) *270*, 271, 272, 273, 274, *278*, *278*, 279, *279*, 280, 281, *282*, *282*, 284–85, 689, *690*, 714, 718, *728*, 729, *744*, *745*, *748*, *751*, *757*
Danmarks Kommunistiske Parti, DKP (Denmark's Communist Party) *270*, *279*
Det Konservative Folkeparti, K (Conservative People's Party) 268, *270*, 272, *278*, *279*, 280, *282*, 284–285;
Enhedslisten, Ø (Red Green Alliance) 268, *270*, 271, *279*, *279*, 285
Folkebevægelsen mod EU, N (People's Movement Against the EU) *270*, 272, 273, *278*, 280, *283*, 689, *690*, *757*
De Grønne, G (Green Party), *270*, *279*,
Junibevægelsen, J (June Movement) *270*, 273, 277, *278*, *278*, *279*, 281, *282*, 284, 286, 689, *690*, *757*
Liberal Alliance, LA (Liberal Alliance) *270*, 272, 273, *278*, *278*, *279*, 281, *282*
Radikale Venstre, R (*Social Liberal Party*) *268*, 269, *270*, *270*, 271, *274*, *275*, *278*, *278*, *279*, 282, 285
Socialdemokraterne, S (Social Democrats) *268*, *269*, *270*, 271, 274, 275, *278*, *278*, *279*, 281, *282*, 284
Socialistisk Folkeparti SF (Socialist People's Party) 268, *270*, *270*, 273, 274, 275, *278*, 279, *282*, 284, 689, *737*, *738*, *739*, 744 , *745*, *748*, *751*, *757*
Venstre, V (Liberal Party) 268, 269, *270*, 271, 275, *278*, *278*, *279*, 282, 284, 285.

Estonia
Political parties 494–6, *495*
Eersti Reformierakond, ER (Reform Party) *492*, 494, *495*, 496, *498*, 498, 499,
500, 501, *502*, *503*, 504, 715, *729*, *745*, *748*, *751*
Eestimaa Rahvaliit, ER (People's Union) *492*,*495*, 496, *498*, 499, *502*, 504, 505, 715, *729*, *745*, *748*, *751*
Eestimaa Ühendatud Vasakpartei (United Left Party of Estonia) *495*, *498*, 499
Erakond Eesti Kristlikud Demokraadid (Christian Democratic Party) *495*, *498*, 499
Erakond Eestimaa Rohelised, EER (Greens) *495*, 496, *498*, *502*, *503*, 504, 505
Isamaa ja Res Publica Liit IRL Pro Patria and Res Publica Union *492*, *495*, *495*, *498*, 499, 500, 501, *502*, *503*, 504, *748*, *751*
Keskerakond, K (Centre Party) *495*, *495*, 496, *498*, 499, 500, 501, 502, *502*, *503*, 504, 505, 715, *745*, *758*
Libertas Eesti , Libertas Estonia *495*, *498*, 499, *758*
Põllumeeste kogu (Farmers' Assembly) *495*, *498*, 499
Sotsiaaldemokraatlik erakond, SDE (Social Democratic Party) *492*, *495*, *495*, *498*, 501, *502*, *503*, 504, *745*, *748*, *751*
Vene Erakond Eestis (Russian Party in Estonia) *495*, *498*, 499

Finland
Political parties 399–400, *400*
Itsenäisyyspuolue (Independence Party) *400*, 405
Kansallinen Kokoomus, KOK (National Coalition) *397*, 399, *400*, 401, 403, *403*, 406, 407, 408, *408*, 409, 410, *410*, 411, 412, *728*, *743*, *745*, *748*, *751*
Köyhien Asialla (For the Poor) *400*, 405
Kristillidemokraatit Perussuomalaiset, KD PS (Christian Democrats; The Finns) *397*, 399, *400*, 400, *403*, 405, 406, *408*, 410, *410*, 411
Suomen Keskusta, KESK (Finnish Centre Party) *400*, *743*, *745*, *748*, *751*
Suomen Kommunistinen Puolue, SKP (Finnish Communist Party) *400*
Suomen Senioripuolue (Senior Citizens' Party) *400*, 405
Suomen Sosialidemokraattinen Puolue, SDP (Finnish Social Democratic Party) *397*, *400*, 409, *743*, *745*, *748*, *751*
Suomen Työväenpuolue (Finnish Labour Party) *400*, 405
Svenska Folkpartiet, SFP (Swedish People's Party) *397*, 399, *400*, 403, *403*, 405, 408, *408*, 409, *410*, 411, 412, *743*, *745*, *748*, *751*

Vasemmistoliitto, VAS (Left Alliance) *397*, 399, *400*, 400, 402, 403, *403*, 407, *408*, 409, 411, *744*, *745*, *751*
Vihreä liitto, VIHR (Green League) *397*, 399, 400, *400*, 403, *403*, 404, 407, 408, *408*, 409, *410*, 411, *743*, *745*, *748*, *751*

France
Political parties 54–6, *54*
Chasse, Pêche, Nature, Traditions (CPNT) Hunting, Fishing, Nature and Traditions) *54*, 63, 64, *66*, 67, *68–9*, 74, *744*, *756*
Debout La République DLR (Arise The Republic) *54*, 55, 55, *74*
Front National, FN (National Front) *54*, 55, 56, 60, 61, 63, 64, *66*, 67, *68*, 69, *74*, *71*, 71, *72*, *74*, 74, 686, 716, 717, 718, 720, 724, 728, 729, *744*, *745*, *748*, *752*, *756*
La Gauche modern, LGM (Modern Left) *54*,
Le Nouveau Centre, NC (The New Centre) *54*, 55, *70*, *748*
Lutte Ouvrière, LO (Workers' Struggle) *54*, 56, *66*, 67, *687*, *744*, *757*,
Mouvement démocrate, MoDem (Democratic Movement) *54*, 55, 56, 61, 62, 63, 64, 65, *66*, 67, *68*, *69*, 715, *748*
Mouvement pour la France, MPF (Movement for France) *54*, 55, 61, 63, *66*, 67, 68, *69*, *74*, *71*, *687*, *745*, *748*, 756
Mouvement Républicain et Citoyen, MRC (Citizen and Republican Movement) *54*, 55
Nouveau Parti Anticapitaliste, NPA, (New Anticapitalist Party) *54*, 56, 61, 62, 63, *66*, 67, 68, 69
Parti Communiste Français, PCF (French Communist Party) *54*, 55, *59*, 60, 64, *66*, *70*, 71, *72*, *687*, *737*, *738*, *740*, *741*, *744*, *748*, *752*, *756*
Parti Communiste Réunionnais, PCR (Communist Party of Réunion) *54*, *71*, *745*, *748*
Parti de Gauche, PG (Left Party) *54*, 55, 62, *748*, *752*
Parti Radical de Gauche, PRG (Left Radical Party) *52*, *54*, 55, 64, *743*, *752*
Parti Socialiste, PS (Socialist Party) *52*, *54*, 55, *59*, 60, 60, 61, 62, 64, *66*, 67, *68*, *69*, *70*, 71, *72*, *737*, *738*, *739*, *741*, *743*, *745*, *748*, *752*
Partitu di a Nazione Corsa, PNC (Party of the Corsican Nation) *54*, *72*

Union pour la Democratie Française, UDF (Union for the French Democracy) 55, 56, 59, *59*, 60, *60*, 61, *66*, 73, *738*, *739*, *741*, *742*, *743*, *745*
Union pour un Mouvement Populaire, UMP (Union for a Popular Movement) 28, *52*, 54, *54*, 55, 56, 59, *59*, 60, 61, 62, 63, 64, 65, *66*, 67, *68*, *69*, *70*, 71, *72*, 712, 716, 722, *745*, *748*, *752*
Verts, Greens *31*, *32*, *52*,*54*, 55, 59, 60, 61, 62, 67, 74, *74*, *70*, *71*, *72*, 74, *739*, *740*, *743*, *745*

Germany
Political parties 80–2, *81*
Bayernpartei, BP (Bavaria Party) *81*, *93*, *94*, *97*
Bündnis 90/Die Grünen, Grüne (Alliance '90/Greens) *31*, *32*, 80, *81*, 86, 87, *87*, 88, *88*, 89, 90, 91, 92, 95, 96, 97, *97*, 98, *98*, *101*, 104, 105, *738*, *739*, *742*, *743*, *746*, *749*, *752*, *755*
Christlich Demokratische Union Deutschlands, CDU (Christian Democrats) 28, 77, 80, *81*, 82, 85, 86, 87, *87*, 88, *88*, 89, 90, 91, 92, 95, 96, 97, 98, *98*, *99*, *103*, 104, 105, 107, 717, 728, *728*, *737*, *738*, *739*, *741*, *743*, *746*, *749*, *752*
Christlich-Soziale Union in Bayern, CSU (Christian Social Union) 28, 77, 80, *81*, 82, 85, 86, 87, *87*, 88, *88*, 89, 90, 91, 95, 96, *97*, *98*, 98, *100*, *103*, 105, 107, 711, 717, 728, *728*, *737*, *738*, *739*, *741*, *743*, *746*, *749*, *752*, *755*
Die Linke, (Linke) (The Left) 30, *81*, *87*, *88*, 91, 92, 96, 97, *97*, 98, *98*, *102*, *103*, 104, 107, *687*, 716, 755, 756
Freie Demokratische Partei FDP (Free Democratic Party) 28, 77, 80, *81*, 82, 86, 87, *87*, 88, *88*, 89, 90, 91, 92, 95, 96, 97, *97*, 98, *98*, *102*, *103*, 104, 106, 715, *737*, *739*, *746*, *749*, *752*
Das Generationen-Bündnis 50 Plus, 50 Plus (Alliance of Generations 50 Plus) *81*, *93*
Nationaldemokratische Partei Deutschlands, NPD (National Democratic Party of Germany) *81*, *87*, *787*, 730, *752*, 756
Partei Des Demokratischen Sozialismus, PDS (Party of Democratic Socialism) 80, *81*, 82, *87*, *88*, 89, 90, *103*, *687*, *744*, *746*, *756*
Piratenpartei Deutschland, Piraten, (German Pirate Party) *81*, *93*, *94*, *97*, 106, *752*
(Die) Republikaner REP (The Republicans) *81*, *88*, *88*, 89, 90, 92, *94*, *97*, 98, 104, *687*, *740*, *756*

774

*Sozialdemokratische Partei (Deutschlands), SPD, (*Social Democratic Party (of Germany)/Social Democrats*)* 77, 80, *81*, 82, 86, 87, *88*, *87*, *88*, 89, 90, 91, 92, 95, 96, *97*, 98, *98*, *100*, *103*, 104, 106, 107, 711, 713, *737*, *738*, *739*, *741*, *743*, *746*, *752*
Arbeit und soziale Gerechtigkeit – Die Wahlalternative, WASG (Labour and Social Justice – The Electoral Alternative) 80, *81*, 82, ,
Deutsche Kommunistische Partei, DKP (German Communist Party) 80, *81*, *87*, *94*, *97*, *687*, *756*
Kommunistische Partei Deutschlands, KPD (Communist Party of Germany) *81*, *87*
Nationaldemokratische Partei Deutschlands, NPD (National Democratic Party of Germany) *81*, *87*, *687*, 730, *752*, *756*

Greece
Political parties 295–301, *296–9*
Anexartitoi Hellines, ANEL (Independent Greeks) 292, *296*, 300, *306*, *752*
Agonistiko Socialistiko Komma Helladas, ASKE (Militant Socialist Party of Greece) *296*, *308*
Anticapitalistike Aristere Synergasia, ANTARSYA (Anticapitalist Left Cooperation) *296*, *303*, *306*, *308*, *310*
Enosse Kentrou – Nees Dynamis, EK-ND, (Centre Union – New Forces) *297*, 300, *303*, *305*, *310*
Democratike Ananeosse, DEANA (Democratic Renewal) *296*, *299*, 300, *303*, 304, *305*
Democratike Aristera, DEMAR (Democratic Left) 292, *296*, 301, *306*
Democratike Periferiake Enossi, DPE (Democratic Regional Union) *296*
Democratike Symmahia, DESY (Democratic Alliance); *296*, 300, *306*
Democratiko Kinoniko Kinema Democratic Social Movement (DEKKI) *296*, 300, *303*, *306*
Ethnike Democratike Enosse, EDE (National Democratic Union); *296*, *306*
Ekologi Prassini, Ecologists Greens *298*, *299*, *303*, *306*, *308*, *308*, 310, *310*
Ethnike Politike Enosse, EPEN (National Political Union) *296*, 300, *303*, *305*;
Nea Democratia, ND (New Democracy) 292, 294, 295, *298*, 300, 301, *303*, 304, *305*, 307, *308*, 309, *310*, 312, *315*, *746*, *749*, *752*
Kommounistiko Komma Hellados , KKE (Communist Party of Greece) 293, 295, *298*, 301, *303*, 304, *305*, *308*, 309, 310, *310*, 313, *690*, 716, *738*, *741*, *744*, *746*, *749*, *752*, *757*
Laikos Orthodoxos Synagermos, LAOS (Popular Orthodox Rally) 292, *298*, 300, *303*, 304, *306*, 308, *308*, 309, 310, *310*, *314*, 730, *746*, *749*
Laikos Syndesmos Crysse Avge, Popular League Golden Dawn, Golden Dawn *298*, 300, *303*, *306*, *308*, *310*, *689*, *757*
Panhellenio Socialistiko Kinema, PASOK(Pan-hellenic Socialist Movement), *292*, 294, 295, *299*, 300, 301, 302, *303*, 304, *305*, 307, *308*, 309, 310, *310*, *315*, *738*, *739*,*741*,*743*, *746*, *749*
Politike Anixe, POLAN (Political Spring) *299*, 300, *303*, *305*, *742*
Synaspismos tes Aristeras kai tes Proodou, SYN (Coalition of the Left and the Progress); *292*, 295, *299*, 301, *303*, 304, *305*, *739*, *740*,*741*, *744*, *746*
Synaspismos tes Rizospastikes Aristeras, SYRIZA (Coalition of the Radical Left) 292, 295, *299*, 301, *303*, *305*, *308*, *308*, *310*, *314*, *706*, *749*

Hungary
Political parties 591–3, *592*
Fidesz – Magyar Polgári Szövetség (Fidesz–Hungarian Civic Union) 582, 590, 591, *592*, *592*, 593, 594, 595, 596, *597*, 598, 599, *601*, *602*, *603*, 606, 713
Független Kisgazda-, Földmunkás- és Polgári Pár, FKGP (Independent Smallholders, Agrarian Workers and Civic Party) 591, *592*, *597*
Humanista Párt, Humanist Party *592*
Jobbik – Magyarországért Mozgalom (Jobbik – Movement for a Better Hungary) *592*, *592*, 593, 594, 595, *596*, *597*, *598*, *599*, *601*, *602*, *603*, 604, 605, 606, *691*, *692*, 720, *758*
Kereszténydemokrata Néppárt, KDNP (Christian Democratic People's Party) *590*, 591, *592*, *592*, *597*, *601*, *602*, *603*, *629*, *649*, *652*
Lehet Más a Politika, LMP (Politics Can Be Different) *592*, *592*, *596*, *597*, *600*, 605, *717*, *752*
Magyar Demokrata Fórum, MDF (Hungarian Democratic Forum) 591, *592*, *592*, 595, 596, *597*, *599*, *600*, *601*, *746*, *749*
Magyar Igazság és Élet Pártja, MIÉP (The Hungarian Justice and Life Party) *592*, *592*, 596, *597*

Magyar Szocialista Párt, MSZP (Hungarian Socialist Party) *590*, 591, 592, *592*, 595, 596, *597*, 598, 599, *600*, *601*, *602*, *603*, 604, 746, 749, 752

Magyarországi Cigán Fórum, MCF (Hungarian Roma Forum) *592*, *600*,

Magyarországi Munkáspárt (Hungarian Communist Workers' Party) *592*, *591*, 592, *592*, 595, 596, *597*, 598, *600*, 604, 746

Zöldek Pártja, ZOLDEK (Green Party) *592*

Ireland

Political parties 246–9, *247*

Fianna Fáil 28, *244*, 245, 246, *247*, *247*, 248, 249, 252, 253, *253*, 254, 255, 256, *256*, 257, 258, 259, 260, 261, *262*, *263*, 264, *264*, 265, 266

Fine Gael *244*, 245, 246, *247*, *247*, 252, 253, *253*, 254, 255, 256, *256*, 257, 258, 260, 261, *262*, *263*, *264*, 265

Greens *244*, 245, 246, *247*, *247*, 248, 249, *253*, 254, 255, 256, *256*, 257, 258, 259, 260, 261, *262*, *264*, 265

Labour *244*, 246, *247*, *247*, 252, 253, *253*, 254 255, 256, *256*, 257, 258, 259, 260, 261, *262*, *263*, 264, *264*, *265*, *266*

Libertas 247, *247*, 249, *253*, 260, 261, *262*, *264*, 265, 266

People's Movement 249, 259, 261, 262

Progressive Democrats 246, *247*, *253*, 254, 255, 256, *256*, 264

Sinn Féin 30, 246, *247*, 248, 249, *253*, 254, 255, 256, *256*, 258, 260, 261, *262*, *264*, 265, 746, *747*, *757*

Socialist Party 246, *247*, 249, *253*, *256*, 259, 260, 261, *262*, *263*, 757

Workers' Party 249, 252, 253, *253*, 254, *256*, 265

Italy

Political parties 114–17, *115*

Alleanza Nazionale, AN (National Alliance) *115*, 116, 117, 125, *124*, 125, *126*, 127, 133, 136, *742*, *744*, *746*, 756

Centro Cristiano Democratico, CCD (Christian Democratic Centre) *115*, 125, *124*, 126, *126*, 127, *138*, *742*, *743*

Cristiani Democratici Uniti, CDU (United Christian Democrats) *115*, *124*, 126, *126*, 127, *743*

Democrazia Cristiana, DC (Christian Democracy) 114; *115*, 117, 116, 121, 122, *123*, 125, 141, 713, *737*, *738*, *739*

Democrazia europea, DE (European Democracy) *115*, *125*

Democrazia è Libertà - La Margherita, DL (Democracy is Freedom-The Daisy) *115*, 116, *124*, *125*, 746

Democratici di Sinistra/Partito Democratico della Sinistra PDS/DS/PDS (Democrats of the Left/Democratic Party of the Left) *110*, *115*, 116, *123*, 125, *125*, 126, *126*, *741*, *743*, *746*

Democrazia Proletaria, DP (Proletarian Democracy) *115*, *123*, *737*, *738*, *739*,

Forza Italia, FI (Forward Italy) *115*, 116, 125, *124*, 125, 126, *126*, 127, 133, 141, 142, 361, 712, 713, *746*, *752*

Fiamma Tricolore (Movimento Sociale-Fiamma Tricolore) FT (MSFT)Tricolour Flame (Social Movement-Tricolour Flame) *115*, *124*, *126*, 126, 129, *133*

Fratelli d'Italia, FdI (Brothers of Italy) *115*,

Futuro e Libertà per l'Italia, FLI (Future and Freedom for Italy) *115*, 116, *138*

Italia dei Valori, IdV (Italy of Values) *115*, *124*, *130*, 130, 133, *133*, 134, 135, *135*, 136, *136*, *137*, *138*, 139, *139*, *140*, *746*, 749

Lega d'Azione meridionale, LAM (Southern Action League) *115*, *125*,

La Destra, LD (The Right) *115*, *124*, 127, 129, *133*

Lega Nord, LN (Northern League) 29, *110*, 113, *115*, 116, 117, 119, *123*, 125, *124*, 125, *126*, 127, 129, 130, *130*, 132, 133, *133*, 134, 135, 136, *136*, *137*, *138*, 139, *139*, *140*, 143, 687, 689, 716, 717, 718, 720, *641*, *744*, *746*, 749, *752*, 756

Liberal Democratici, LD (Liberal Democrats) *115*, *124*, *133*

Movimento per l'Autonomia, MPA (Movement for Autonomy) *115*, *124*, 129, *133*

Movimento Repubblicani Europei, MRE (European Republicans Movement) *115*, *125*, *746*

Movimento Cinque Stelle, M5S (Five-Star Movement) *115*, 718, 720, 724, *752*, 755

Movimento Sociale Italiano/Destra Nazionale, MSI/DN (Italian Social Movement/ National Right) 22, *115*, 116, *123*, 142, *737*, *738*, *740*, *742*, *744*

Nuovo Partito Socialista Italiano, NPSI (New Italian Socialist Party); *115*, 116, *125*, 127, *746*

Partito Comunista Italiano, PCI (Italian Communist Party) 114, *115*, 116, 117, 122, 123, *123*, 141, 142, *737*, *738*, *739*

Partito Democratico, PD (Democratic Party) 28, *110,* 113, *115,* 116, 121, *124, 126,* 128, 129, *130,* 133, *133,* 134, 135, *135,* 136, *136, 137, 138,* 139, *139, 140,* 142, 713, 717, 721, 728, *728,* 734, *749, 752, 755*

Partito dei Comunisti italiani, PDCI (Party of the Italian Communists) *115, 124*

Popolo della Libertà, PdL (Party of Freedom) 28, *110,* 113, *115,* 116, 117, 121, *126,* 129, *130,* 133, *133,* 134, 135, *135,* 136, *136, 137, 138,* 139, *140, 140,* 142, 713, *749*

Partito Liberale Italiano, PLI (Italian Liberal Party) *115,* 117, 122, *123,* 142, *737, 738, 739, 740*

Partito Popolare Italiano, PPI (Italian Popular Party) 114, *115,* 125, *125, 126, 126,* 741, *743, 752*

Partito di Rifondazione Comunista (P)RC (Party of) Communist Refoundation *115,* 125, *131, 133,* 134, 687, *741, 744, 746, 756*

Partito Socialista Democratico Italiano, PSDI (Italian Socialist Democratic Party) *115,* 117, 122, *123, 126,* 142, *737, 738, 739, 742*

Partito Socialista Italiano, PSI (Italian Socialist Party)114, *115,* 122, 123, *123,* 125, *124, 126,* 142, *737, 738, 739, 741*

Partito Radicale, PR (*Radical* Party Radicals) *115, 123, 124, 126, 737, 738, 740*

Rinnovamento Italiano, RI (Italian Renewal) *115, 125, 743*

Scelta Civica, SC (Civic Choice) *110,* 113, *115*

Sinistra Arcobaleno, SA (Rainbow Left); *115, 124*

Sinistra Ecologia e Libertà, SEL (Left, Ecology and Freedom) *115,* 117, *126, 129, 133*

Südtirolervolkspartei, SVP (South Tyrol People's Party) *115, 123, 124, 126, 133, 135, 137,* 139, *139, 140, 737, 738, 739, 741, 743, 746, 749, 752*

Ulivo (Olive) *115, 125, 127, 133, 142*

Unione Democratica, UD (Democratic Union) *115, 125*

Unione di Centro Unione dei Democratici Cristiani e di Centro, UDC (Union of Christian Democrats and Centrists) *115, 124, 126,* 130, *130, 133, 135, 136, 137, 138, 741, 743, 746, 749, 752*

Unione Democratici per l'Europa, UDEUR (Democrats' Union for Europe) *115, 124, 126, 126, 127, 138, 743, 746,*

Union Valdotaine, UV (Valdotanian Union) *115, 123, 126, 738, 740*

Verdi, V (Greens) *115, 123, 126,* 125, *739, 742, 743, 746*

Verdi Arcobaleno, V-ARC (Rainbow Greens) *115,* 123, *123*

Latvia
Political parties 510–12, *511*

Demokrātiskā centra partija, DCP (Democratic Centre Party) *511,* 516

Demokrātiskā partija Saimnieks, DPS (Democratic Party Master) *511, 516*

Jaunā partija JP (New Party) *511, 516*

Jaunais laiks, JL (New Era) 508, *511, 516, 521, 523, 746, 749*

Kristīgo demokrātu savienība, KDS (Christian Democratic Union) *511, 516, 521*

Latvijas Atdzimšanas partija, LAP (Latvia's Rebirth Party): *511, 521*

Latvijas ceļš, LC (Latvia's Way) *511, 516, 521*

Latvijas Nacionālās neatkarības kustība, LNNK (Latvian National Independence Movement) 508, *511, 516,* 518, 520, *521,* 522, *523,* 524, *746, 752*

Latvijas Pirmā partija, LPP (First Party of Latvia) *511, 516, 521, 523, 749*

Latvijas Sociāldemokrātiskā strādnieku partija, LSDSP (Social Democratic Workers' Party of Latvia) *511, 516, 521*

Latvijas Sociālistiskā partija, LSP (Socialist Party of Latvia) *511, 516, 521, 749*

Latvijas Vienības partija, LVP (Unity Party of Latvia) *511, 516*

Latvijas Zaļā partija, LZP (Green Party of Latvia) *511, 516, 752*

Latvijas Zemnieku savienība, LZS (Farmers' Union of Latvia) *511, 516,* 724, *752*

Līdztiesība, L (Equal Rights) *511,* 512, *516*

Osipova partija, OP (Osipov Party) *511,* 517, *758*

Par cilvēka tiesībām vienotā Latvijā, PCTVL (For Human Rights in United Latvia) *511, 521, 523, 746, 749*

Par Dzimteni!, PDz (For Motherland!) *511, 521*

Pilsoniskā savienība, PS (Civic Union) 508, *511,* 518, 519, 520, 521, 522, 524

Sabiedrība citai politikai, SCP (Society for Different Politics) *511, 521*

Saskaņa Latvijai, atdzimšana tautsaimniecībai, SLAT (Concord for Latvia, Rebirth for Economy) *511, 516*

Saskaņas centrs, SC (Harmony Centre) *511,* 515, 517, 520, 522, 524

Index

Tautas kustība Latvijai, TKL (Popular Movement For Latvia) *511, 516*
Tautas partija,TP (People's Party) *511, 516, 521*
Tautas saskaņas partija TSP (National Harmony Party) *511, 516, 521, 749*
Tēvzemei un Brīvībai, TB (For Fatherland and Freedom) *508, 511,* 518, 520, *522,* 524
Visu Latvijai!, VL (All for Latvia!) *511, 521*
Zaļoun zemnieku savienība, ZZS (Union of Greens and Farmers) *508, 511,* 515, *521, 752*

Lithuania
Political parties 529–31, *530*
Darbo Partija, DP (Labour Party) *528, 530,* 532, *533,* 534, *535,* 536, 537, *539,* 540, *541,* 542, *542,* 544, 546, 746, 749, 753
Liberalų ir Centro Sąjunga, LiCS (Liberal-Centre Union) *528, 530,* 532, *533,* 534, *535,* 536, *539, 541, 542, 542*
Lietuvos Lenkų Rinkimų Akcija, LLRA (Lithuanian Poles' Electoral Action) *528, 530,* 532, *533,* 534, *535,* 536, *539,* 540, *541, 542,* 544, 546, 749,
Lietuvos Respublikos Liberalų Sąjūdis, LRLS (Liberal Movement of the Republic of Lithuania) *528, 530,* 534, *535,* 536, *539,* 540, *541, 542, 542, 543,* 749, 752
Lietuvos SocialDemokratų Partija, LSDP (Lithuanian Social Democratic Party) *528, 530,* 530, 532, *533,* 534, *535,* 538, *539,* 540, *541, 542,* 542, *543, 729,* 746, 749, 752
Lietuvos Valstiečių Liaudininkų Sąjunga, LVLS (Lithuanian Peasant People Union) 530, *530,* 531, 532, *533,* 534, *535,* 537, *539,* 540, *541, 542, 542,*
Naujoji Sąjunga/Social-Liberalai, NS/SL (New Union/ Social-Liberals) 530, *530,* 532, *533, 541,* 542
Partija "Tvarka ir Teisingumas", TTP (Party "Order and Justice") 542, *528, 530,* 532, *533,* 534, *535,* 536, 536, *539,* 540, *541, 542, 542, 543,* 547
Tautos Prisikėlimo Partija, TPP (Rising Nation Party) *528, 530,* 531, 534, *535,* 537, *539, 541, 542,* 546, *691, 758*
Tėvynės Sąjunga – Lietuvos Krikščionys Demokratai, TS-LKD (Homeland Union-Lithuanian Christian Democrats) *528, 530, 533, 539, 541, 542,* 749, *752*

Luxembourg
Political parties 192–4, *193;*
Alternativ Demokratesch Reformpartei, ADR (Alternative Democratic Reform) 192, *193,* 193, 195, *197,* 198, 199, 203, 204, 205, *205, 688* 757
BiergerLëscht (Citizens' List) 199, 757
Chrëschtlech Sozial Vollekspartei ,CSV (Christian Democrats) 190, 192, 193, *193,* 195, 196, *197,* 198, 200, 203, 204, *204,* 205, *205, 206,* 207, 208, *728, 743, 746,* 749, *753*
Déi Lénk; Lénk (The Left) 193, *193,* 194, 195, *197,* 199, 204, *204,* 205, *205, 756*
Demokratesch Partei DP (Democratic Party) 190, 192, 193, *193, 197, 197,* 198, 200, 203, 204, *204, 205, 737, 738, 739, 741, 743, 746,* 749, *753*
Déi Gréng, Gréng (Greens) 190, 192, 193, *193,* 196, 198, 199, 200, 204, *204,* 205, *205, 206,* 207, *746,* 749, *753*
Kommunistesch Partei Lëtzebuerg, KPL (Communist Party of Luxembourg) 193, *193,* 194, 197, *197,* 199, 204, 205, *205, 688, 756*
Lëtzebuerger Sozialistesch Arbechterpartei, LSAP (Luxembourg Socialist Workers Party) /Socialists 190, 192, 193, *193,* 197, *197,* 198, 200, 203, 204, *204, 205,* 206, *743, 746,* 749, *753*

Malta
Political parties 436–7, *436*
Alpha Liberal Democratic Party, ALDP *436,* 439, 440, 443
Alleanza LiberaliDemokratika, ALD (Liberal Democratic Alliance) *436, 443, 443*
Alternattiva Demokratika, AD (Democratic Alternative) 436, *436, 438,* 439, 440, 442, 443, *443,* 447
Azzjoni Nazzjonali, AN (National Action) *436,* 438, 440, 442, 443, *443, 691,* 757
Imperium Europa, IE (European Empire or better European rule or command) *436,* 439, 440, 441, 443, *443,*
K.u.L. Europa, KULE (K.u.L. Europe) *436, 443*
Libertas Malta, LM *436,* 440, 757
Partit Laburista, PL (Labour Party) *434,* 435, 436, *436,* 439, *440,* 441, 443, *443,* 444, 447, *729,* 749, *753*
Partit Nazzjonalista, PN (Nationalist Party) *434,* 435, 436, *436,* 439, 441, 443, *443, 746,* 749, *753*
Partit tal-Ajkla, PA (Eagle's Party) *436,* 440, *443*

Index

The Netherlands
  Political parties 170–4, *171*
  Christen-Democratisch Appèl, CDA (Christian Democratic Appeal) *168*, 170, 171, *171*, 172, *176*, 177, 179, 181, 182, *182*, *183*, 185, 186, *737*, *738*, *739*, *741*, *743*, *747*, *749*, *753*
  ChristenUnie, CU (Christian Union) *168*, *171*, 173, 174, 175, *176*, *177*, 180, 182, *184*, *687*, *747*, *753*, *756*
  Democraten 66, D66 (Democrats 66) 170, 171, *171*, 172, 173, 174, *176*, 177, *177*, 178, 179, 180, 181, 182, *182*, 183, 185, 186, 187, *715*, *728*, *737*, *739*, *741*, *743*, *747*, *749*, *753*
  GroenLinks, GL, Green Left 170, 171, *171*, 172, 173, 174, 175, *176*, *177*, 178, 179, 180, 181, 182, *182*, 183, 186, 187, *688*, *742*, *756*
  Lijst Pim Fortuyn, LPF (Pim Fortuyn List) 171, 173, *176*, 179, *688*, *756*
  Partij van de Arbeid, PvdA (Labour Party) *168*, 170, 171, *171*, 172, *176*, *176*, 177, *177*, 179, 181, *182*, *183*, 187, *737*,*738*, *739*, *741*, *743*, *747*, *749*, *753*
  Partij voor de Dieren, PvdD (Animal Rights Party) 170, *171*, 172, 174, *176*, 180, 181, *182*, 187, *688*, *753*, *756*
  Partij voor de Vrijheid, PVV (Freedom Party) 170, 171, *171*, 172, *176*, *177*, 178, 180, 181, 182, *182*, 183, 187, 686, 688, 716, 717, *749*, *753*, *756*
  Partij voor de Vrijheid, SGP (Protestant Reform Party) 170, *171*, 173, *176*, *177*, 180, 182, *182*, *184*, *184*, *186*, 187, *687*, 716, 717, *738*, *740*, *742*, *747*, *750*
  Socialistische Partij, SP (Socialist Party) 170, 171, *171*, 172, 173, *176*, *177*, 178, 180, 181, *182*, *184*, 185, 186, 187, *688*, 744, *747*, *749*, *753*, *756*
  Volksparty voor Vrijheid en Democratie, VVD (People's Party for Freedom and Democracy) *168*, 170, 171, *171*, 172, 173, *176*, *176*, 177, *177*, 179, 180, 181, *182*, 183, 187, *715*, *737*, *738*, *739*, *741*, *743*, *747*, *749*, *753*
  Staatkundig Gereformeerde Partij, SGP (Political Reformed Party) 170, *171*,173, *176*, *177*, 180, 182, *182*, *184*, 186, *687*, *738*, *740*, *742*, *747*, *749*, *753*, *756*
  50PLUS partij (50PLUS Party) *171*,
Poland
  Political parties 612–15, *612*, *613*
  Libertas Polska, LP (Libertas Poland) *612*, *623*, *729*

Platforma Obywatelska, PO (Civic Platform) 28, *609*, 612, *612*, 613, *613*, 614, 617, *617*, 618, *618*, 619, 620, 621, 622, 623, *623*, 624, *626*, *627*, 628, *712*, *729*, *747*, *749*, *753*
Polska Partia Pracy, PPP, (Polish Labour) *612*, *618*, *623*
Party Polskie Stronnictwo Ludowe, PSL (Polish People's Party) *609*, *612*, *613*, *613*, 614, *617*, *618*, 620, 621, 622, 624, *626*, 628, *712*, *747*, *749*, *753*
Porozumienie dla Przyszłości, CentroLewica, PdP (Coalition Agreement for the Future – Centre-Left) *612*, *623*
Prawica Rzeczypospolitej, PRP (Right of the Republic) *612*, *623*, 624,
Prawo i Sprawiedliwość, PiS (Law and Justice); 29, *609*, 612, *612*, 613, *613*, 614, 615, 617, *617*, 618, *618*, 619, 620, 621, 622, 623, *623*, 624, 625, *626*, *627*, 628, *714*, *747*, *753*
Samoobrona RP, SoRP (Self-Defence of the Republic of Poland) 612, *612*, 620, *623*, *758*
Sojusz Lewicy Demokratycznej – Unia Pracy SLD-UP (Coalition Democratic Left Alliance-Labour Union) *612*, *617*, *618*, 619, 620, *623*, *623*
Unia Polityki Realnej, UPR (Real Politics Union) *612*, *618*, *623*, 624
Portugal
  Political parties 354–5, *355*
  Bloco da Esquerda BE (Left Bloc) 355, *355*, 360, *360*, *361*, 362, 363, 364, 365, 366, 367, *367*, *369*, 371, *371*, 372, *747*, *750*
  Centro Democratico Social-Partido Popular, CDS-PP (Democratic Social Centre-People's Party) *352*, 354, 355, *355*, 358, 359, 360, *360*, 361, *361*, 362, 363, 365, 366, *367*, *371*, 372, *742*, *744*, *747*, *750*, *753*
  Coligação Democrática Unitária, CDU (Democratic Unitary Coalition) *355*, 358, 359, *361*, *740*, *742*, *747*, *753*
  Movimento Partido da Terra, MPT (Earth Party Movement) *355*, 364, *367*, 372, *753*
  Partido Communista Português PCP (Portuguese Communist Party) 354, 355, *355*, 357, 358, 360, *360*, 361, 362, *361*, 362, 363, 364, 365, 366, 367, *367*, *370*, *371*, 372, *740*, *741*, *742*, *744*, *747*, *750*, *753*, *757*
  Partido Comunista dos Trabalhadores Portugueses-Movimonto Reorganizativo do Pardito do Proletariado, PCTP-MRPP

779

Index

(Communist Party of the Portuguese Workers-Movement for the Reorganization of the Party of the Proletariat) *355*, 364, 365, *367*, 372

Partido Os Verdes, PEV (Green Party) 354, 355, *355*, 360, *360*, 361, 362, *361*, 363, 364, 365, 366, 367, *367*, *370*, 371, 372, 747, 753

Partido Nacional Renovador PNR (National Renewal Party) 364, 365, 366, *367*, 372

Partido Operário de Unidade Socialista, POUS (Workers' Socialist Unity Party) 364, 365, *367*, 372

Partido Popular Monárquico, PPM (People's Monarchic Party) *355*, 364, *367*, 372

Partido Renovador Democratico PRD (Democratic Renewal Party) 357, 358, *360*, 361

Partido Socialista, PS (Socialist Party) 352, 354, 355, *355*, 357, 358, 359, 360, *360*, 361, 362, 364, 365, 366, 367, *367*, 369, *371*, 372, 373, 728, 739, 741, 743, 747, 750, 753

Partido democrata social, PSD (Social-Democratic Party) 352, 354, 355, *355*, 357, 358, 359, 360, *360*, 361, *361*, 362, 363, 365, 366, 367, *368*, 371, *371*, 372, 373, 739, 741, 743, 747, 750, 753

Romania
Political parties 656–8, *656–7*
Alianța Dreptate și Adevăr, DA: PNL+ PD (Justice and Truth Alliance) 657, 662
Alianța Națională Liberală, ANL (National Liberal Alliance) 657, 652
Alianța Partidul, Social Democrat-Partidul Conservator, PSD-PC (Social Democratic Party–Conservative Party Alliance) 657, *665*, 665, 666, 671
Alianța pentru România, ApR (Alliance for Romania) 657, 662
Alianța pentru Unitatea Românilor, AUR (Romanian Unity Alliance) 656, 662
Convenția Democratică din România, CDR (Democratic Convention of Romania) 656
Forța Civică, FC (Civic Force) 657, 662, 665
Frontul Democrat al Salvării Naționale, FDSN (Democratic National Salvation Front) 656, 661, 662
Frontul Salvării Naționale FSN (National Salvation Front) 656, 662
Mișcarea Ecologică din România MER (The Ecological Movement of Romania) 656, 661

Partidul Democrat Agrar, PDAR (The Agrarian Democratic Party) 656, 661, 662
Partidul Democrat Liberal, PD-L (Democratic Liberal Party) 654, 656, *656*, 658, 658, *662*, 663, 665, *665*, 667, 668, 669, 671, 750,
Partidul Ecologist Român, PER (The Romanian Ecologist Party) 656, 661
Partidul Național Liberal – Radu Câmpeanu, PNL-RC (The National Liberal Party–Radu Câmpeanu) 657, 662
Partidul Național Liberal, PNL (The National Liberal Party) 654, 656, 657, 658, 661, 662, 663, 665, 667, 668, 669, 671, 750, 753
Partidul Național țărănesc Creștin Democrat, PNȚCD (The Christian Democrat National Peasants' Party) 656
Partidul Noua Generație-Creștin Democrat, PNG–CD (The Party of the New Generation-Christian Democrat) 657, 662, 750,
Partidul Pensionarilor din România, PPR (Pensioners' Party in Romania) 657, 662
Partidul Poporului – Dan Diaconescu, PP-DD (People's Party – Dan Diaconescu) 657, 662
Partidul Republican, PR (Republican Party) 656, 661
Partidul România Mare, PRM (Greater Romania Party) 656, 657, 658, *658*, 661, 663, 665, *665*, 667, *667*, 669, 671, 685, 691, 692, 730, 750, 758
Partidul Social Democrat din România, PSDR (The Romanian Social Democratic Party) 656, 661, 662
Partidul Socialist, PS (The Socialist Party) 656, 662, 713, 729
Partidul Socialist al Muncii, PSM (Socialist Labour Party) 656, 662
Partidul Unității Naționale Române, PUNR (The Romanian National Unity Party) 656, 662
Polul Social Democratic, PSD (Social Democratic Pole) 654, 657, *657*, 663, 665, *665*, 667, 668, 669, 671, 750, 753
Uniunea Democrată a Maghiarilor din România, UDMR (Hungarian Democratic Union) 654, 656, 658, 660, 661, 663, 665, 666, 669, 671, 750, 753
Uniunea Națională pentru Progresul României, UNPR (National Union for the Progress of Romania) 654, 657, 662, 714, 729, 753

780

Uniunea Social Democrată, PD PSDR (Social Democratic Union) *656, 662*

Slovakia
Political parties 572–6, *572*
Agrárna strana vidieka, ASV (Agrarian Party of the Countryside) *572*
Demokratická strana, DS (Democratic Party) *572*
Komunistická strana Slovenska, KSS (Communist Party of Slovakia *572, 576, 579, 585, 691, 758*
Konzervatívni demokrati Slovenska – Občianska konzervatívna strana, KDS-OKS (Conservative Democrats of Slovakia – Civic Conservative Party) *572, 579, 585*
Krest'anskodemokratické hnutie, KDH (Christian Democratic Movement) *569, 572, 573, 575, 576, 576, 577, 578, 579, 579, 580, 582, 584, 585, 586*, 587, 588, *747, 750, 753*
LIGA, občiansko-liberálna strana, LIGA (League – Civic Liberal Party) *572*
L'udová strana – Hnutie za demokratické Slovensko, LS-HZDS (Peoples Party – Movement for a Democratic Slovakia) *572, 747, 750*
MISIA 21 – Hnutie krest'anskej solidarity, MISIA 21 (Mission 21 – Movement of a Christian Solidarity) *572*
Sloboda a solidarita, SaS (Freedom and Solidarity) *569, 572, 572*, 574, 575, 576, *579*, 581, 582, *585*, 588, *691, 758*
Slobodné forum, SF (Free Forum) *572, 579, 585*
Slovenská demokratická a krest'anská únia – Demokratická strana, SDKÚ-DS (Slovak Democratic and Christian Union – Democratic party) *569, 572, 573, 574, 576, 577, 578, 579, 579, 580, 581*, 582, 584, *585, 586*, 588, *750, 753*
Slovenská národná strana, SNS (Slovak National Party) *569*, 571, *752, 753, 755*, 576, 577, *579*, 582, 584, *585, 586*, 587, 588, *691, 730, 750, 758*
Smer – Sociálna demokracia, Smer-SD (Direction – Social Democracy) *569, 572, 573, 574, 576, 577, 579, 580, 581, 582, 584, 585, 586, 588, 729, 753*
Strana demokratickej L'avice, SDL' (Party of the Democratic Left) 572, *572, 579, 747*
Strana mad'arskej koalície, SMK (Hungarian Coalition Party) *572, 573, 574, 575, 576, 577, 578, 579*, 580, 582, 584, *585, 586*, 588, *679, 747, 750, 753*
Strana zelených, SZ (Green Party); *572, 579, 580, 585*

Slovenia
Political parties 474–6, *476*
Demokratična stranka upokojencev Slovenije, DeSUS (Democratic Party of Pensioners of Slovenia) *472, 476, 477, 478, 479, 479, 481, 485*
Demokratska stranka, DS (Democratic Party) *476, 480*
Državljanska lista, DL (Civic List) *472, 476, 480*
Liberalna demokracija Slovenije, LDS (Liberal Democracy of Slovenia) *472, 474, 476, 477, 479, 480, 479, 483, 483, 485, 486, 747, 750*
Nova Slovenija – Krščansko-ljudska stranka, NSi (New Slovenia – Christian People's Party) *472, 476, 479, 479, 485, 747*
Pozitivna Slovenija, PS (Positive Slovenia) *472, 474, 476, 480*
Slovenska demokratska stranka, SDS (Slovenian Democratic Party) *472, 475, 476, 477, 479, 480, 479, 482, 483, 484, 485, 729, 747, 750, 753*
Slovenska ljudska stranka, SLS (Slovenian People's Party) *472, 476, 477, 479, 480, 479, 481, 383, 754*
Slovenska nacionalna stranka, SNS (Slovenian National Party) *474, 476, 477, 479, 479, 482, 483, 691, 757*
Slovenska obrtniška stranka, SOS (Slovenian Craftsmen's Party) *476*
Slovenski krščanski demokrati, SKD (Slovenian Christian Democrats) *476, 480*
Socialistična zveza delovnega ljudstva, SZDL (Socialist Alliance of the Working People) *476*

Spain
Political parties 324–7, *326*
Bloco Nacionalista Galego, BNG (Nationalist Galician Bloc) 325, 332, 333, *333*, 335, 336, *743, 754*
Centro Democratico y Social, CDS (Democratic Social Centre) *326*, 329, 330, 331, *333, 338, 739*
Coalición por Europa, CpE (Coalition for Europe) *326, 333*, 335, 337, *338, 345, 346, 715*
Convergencia i Unió, CiU (Party Convergence and Union) 325, 329, 330, 331, 332, 333, *333*, 335, *345*, 348, *739, 747*

Coalición Nacionalista, CN (Nationalist Coalition) 330, 331, 332, *333,* 740, 742
Europa de los Pueblos EP-V (Europe of the Peoples) *326,* 329, 330, 331, 335, *338,* 349
Esquerra Republicana Catalana, ERC (Catalan Republican Left) 325, 329, 330, 332, *333,* 335, 336, 337, 348, 349, 717, *747, 750, 754*
Euskadi ta Askatasuna, ETA (Basque separatists) 329, 330, 332
extreme right-wing 336
Galeusca 333, *333,* 335
Iniciativa para Cataluña-Verdes, I-CV (Initiative for Catalonia-the Greens) 325, *326,* 332, *346,* 347
Izquierda Unida, IU (United Left) 325, *326,* 327, 328, 329, 330, 331, 332, 333, *333,* 334, 335, 336, 337, *338, 346, 347,* 347, 348, 349, 350, 724, *739, 741, 744, 747, 750, 754*
Partido Popular, PP (People's Party) 28, *322,* 324, *326,* 327, 329, 330, 331, 332, 333, *333,* 334, 335, 336, 337, *338, 338, 339, 342, 347, 347,* 348, 349, 691, 355, *355,*691, 699, 712, *728, 739, 741, 743, 747, 750, 754*
Partido Socialista Obrero Español, PSOE (Spanish Socialist Workers' Party) *322,* 324, 325, *326,* 327, 329, 330, 331, 332, 333, *333,* 334, 335, 336, 337, *338, 342, 345, 347, 347, 348,* 349, 350,*739, 741, 743, 747, 750, 754*
regionalist/nationalist 322, 325, 326, 327, 328, 329, 330, 331, 332, 333, 335, 336, 337, 348
Unión Progreso y Democracia, UPyD (Union Progress and Democracy) 325, *326,* 327, *333,* 335, 337, 338, *338, 346, 347,* 348, 349, 715, *754*

Sweden
Political parties 417–20, *418*
Centerpartiet, C (Centre Party) 417, *418, 422, 426, 747, 750*
Feministisk Initiativ, FI (Feminist Initiative) *418,* 421, *422,* 423, 425, *754,*
Folkpartiet FP (Liberal Party) *415,* 417, *418, 422, 426, 747, 750, 754*
Junilistan, JL (June List) *418,* 419, 421, *422,* 423, 425, *690, 747, 757*
Kristdemokraterna, KD (Christian Democrats) *415,* 418, *418,* 420, *422,* 423, 424, *426, 743, 747, 750, 754*
Miljöpartiet, MP (Green Party) 417, *418,* 421, *422,* 425, *426,* 428, *743, 747, 750, 754, 757*
Moderaterna, M (Moderate Party) *415,* 417, *418,* 421, *422, 426, 743, 747, 750, 754*
Pirat Partiet, P (Pirate Party) *418,* 421, *422,* 424, 425, *426*
Socialdemokraterna, S, Social Democratic Party 417, *418,* 420, 421, *422, 426,* 427, *728*
Sverigedemokraterna, SD (Sweden Democrats) 418, *418,* 421, *422,* 423, *426,* 428, *690,* 718, 724, 730, *754,* 757
Vänsterpartiet, V (Left Party) 417, 418, *418,* 419, 421, *422,* 423, 425, *426,* 428, *744, 750, 754, 757*

United Kingdom
Political parties 216, 217, *224*
British National Party, BNP 216, *223,* 224, *224,* 225, 226, 227, 229, 230, 234, *234, 238,* 239, 240, 241, 364, 685, 689, *690,* 730, *750, 757*
Conservative, Cons, 10, 19, 29, 182, *214,* 216, 217, 220, *221, 223, 224,* 225, 226, *228,* 229, *229,* 231, *232, 233, 234, 235, 236, 237, 238,* 239, 241, 690, 714, 724, *755, 757*
Democratic Unionist, DUP, 216, *223,* 224, 229, 230, *737, 738,* 740, 742, 744, *747, 750, 754*
Greens 216, 220, *222, 223,* 224, *224,* 225, 227, 229, *230, 233, 236,* 240, 241, 242
Labour, Lab, *214,* 216, 217, 220, *221, 222, 223,* 224, *224,* 225, 226, 227, *228,* 229, *229,* 230, *231–238,* 239, 240, 241, *737, 738, 739, 741, 743, 747, 750, 757,;*
Liberal Democrats/Liberal Democrat Party, LD , *214,* 216, 217, 220, *222, 223, 224, 224,* 225, 226, 227, *228,*229, 230, *230, 233, 238,* 239, 240, 241, 715, *741, 743, 747, 750, 754*
Plaid Cymru (Party of Wales) 28, 216, *222, 223, 224, 224, 229, 230,* 237, 239, 241, *717, 743, 747, 750, 754*
Social Democratic and Labour Party, SDLP 216, *223, 224, 737, 738, 739, 741, 743*
Sinn Féin, SF 216, *223, 224,* 229, 230, *235, 747, 754*
Scottish National Party, SNP 216, *222, 223,* 224, *224, 229, 230, 235,* 241, 717, *737, 738,* 740, 742, *743, 747, 750, 754*
UK Independence Party, UKIP 29, 216, 217, 220, *223, 224, 224,* 225, 227, *228,* 229, *229,* 230, *231, 232, 233, 234, 236, 237, 238,* 239, 240, 241,

689, *690,* 714, 716, 717, 718, 720, 724, *728,* 729, *747, 750, 754, 755, 757*
Ulster Unionist Party, UUP, 29, *224, 737, 738, 739, 741, 743, 747, 750, 754*
Pompidou, Georges 53
Porcellum Bill 118–19
Portas, Miguel 360
Portas, Paulo 355, 360
Portugal 351–72, *351*; allocation of EP seats 22, 23, *24, 25, 31, 32, 33*; EP and national elections 357–62; geographical position 352; geopolitical profile 354; historical background 352–4; national and EP electoral systems 356–7; overview of the political landscape 354; profile *352;* Lisbon Treaty 363, 365; unemployment issue 365, 366
Pöttering, Hans-Gert 95, 96, *99*
preferential voting 5, 6, 58, 120, 175, 328, 487, 532, 551, 555, 562, 577
Pridham, Geoffrey 117
Prodi, Romano 116, *124,* 125, *125,* 126, 127
Prokopis, Pavlopoulos 292
proportional representation (PR) 5, 83, 119, 124, 125, 153, 169, 220
public health 11, 13

Quaglia, Lucia 117
qualified majority (QM) 11, 12, 423, 702

Radaelli, Claudio 117
Radičová, Iveta *569,* 572, 573
Raikov, Marin *634*
Rajoy, Mariano 332, 712
Ramalho Eanes, António 358
Rangel, Paulo 365, 367, *368*
Reding, Viviane 198, 204, 205
refugees/asylum seekers 112, 131, 195, 293
Rehn, Olli, 703
Reif, Karlheinz 39, 40, 41, 42, 486
Renzi, Matteo *110,* 114, 713
'*Revolução dos cravos*' ('Carnation Revolution') 364, 675
Reynolds, Albert 254
right-wing parties 55, 92, *94,* 230, 333, 348, 372, 418, 483, 495, 554, 559, 592, 611, 612, 617, 714, 730
Riigikogu (Estonian Parliament) 494, 495, 496, 497, 498, 499, 501, 502, 504
Ringe, Nils 42, 43, 316, 363, 670
Risorgimento (Italy) 111
Rogers, Richard xxxv
Rohde, Jens 280, *283*
Roma people 593
Romania 653–72, *653*; allocation of EP seats 22, 23, *24, 25, 31, 32, 33*; EP and national elections 660–2; geographical position 654; geopolitical profile 655; historical background 655; national and EP electoral systems 659–60; overview of the political landscape 655; profile *654*
Rome, Treaty of 8, 18, 27
Romeva i Rueda, Raúl 335, *346,* 347
Ronchi, Andrea 131
'*rottamatore*' ('scrapper') *see* Renzi, Matteo
Rotativismo (Portugal) 353
Ruiz-Mateos, José María 330
Ruiz Jiménez, Antonia María 335
Rusnok, Jiri 550
Russia 36, 55, 102, 129, 294, 311, 313, 314, 343, 397, 398, 492, 493, 494, 500, 509, 512, 517, 518, 524, 528, 540, 581, 582, 601, 613, 635, 645
Rutte, Mark *168,* 181, 715

Sainte-Laguë/Schepers method 85, *736,*
Samaras, Antonis *292,* 300, 304
Sampaio, Jorge 358, 361, 371
Santer, Jacques 8, 193, 198
Sarkozy, Nicolas *52,* 54, 61, 62, 63, 64, 65, 717
Sartori, Giovanni 119, 478
Scarrow, Susan E. 484
Scheingold, Stuart A. 117, 455
Schengen Area 401, 493, 574; Agreement/Treaty 91, 386, 529, 645; Entry Year: Austria *378;* Belgium *148;* Czech Republic *550;* Denmark *268;* Estonia *492;* Finland *397;* France *52;* Germany *77;* Greece *292;* Hungary *590;* Italy *110;* Latvia *508;* Lithuania *528;* Luxembourg *190;* Malta *434;* The Netherlands *168,* Poland *609;* Portugal *352;* Slovakia *569;* Slovenia *472;* Spain *322;* Sweden *415*
Schmidt, Helle Thorning *268,* 269
Schmidt, Helmut 86
Schmitt, Hermann 39, 40, 41, 42, 393, 465, 486, 504, 522, 677, 682,
Schröder, Gerhard 80, 90, 95, 104
Schulz, Martin 95, 96, *101,* 204, 714
Schuman, Robert xxv, xxxvi, 7, 78, 735,
Scotland xxvi, 214, 215, 216, 217, 218, *219,* 224, 225, *228, 228, 235,* 239, 682
seat allotment 17
Second-Order Election (SOE) theory 39, 40–3, 46; Belgium 164; Denmark 285–6; France 73–4; Germany 98–104; Greece 316; Ireland 264–5; Italy 141–2; Luxembourg 207; Netherlands 185; New EU Member States *682;* Old EU Member States *681;* Portugal 363, 365, 371; Spain 331, 337, 347–8; UK 239–40; Old EU Member States *681;* in New EU Member States *682*
security 12, 13, 34, 65, 83, 92, 149, 149, *160,* 169, 172, 175, 181, 256, 269, 294, 308, 334, 385,

386, 398, 407, 418, 424, 425, 450, 474, 475, 478, 481, 500, 512, 514, 539, 540, 553, 581, 583, 593, 594, 599, 610, 621, 622, 635, 644, 645, 660, 663
Seimas (Lithuanian Parliament) 529, 530, 532, *533*, 534, 537, 541, *541, 544,* 546
Sejm (Lower House of Polish Parliament) 610, 611, 613, 614, 616, 617, 622
Shackleton, Michael 17
Simitis, Kostas 304
Single European Act (SEA) 9–10, 15, 27, *250, 275, 276, 277*
Single Market 9
single transferable voting (STV) 6, 246, 251, 262, 265, 437, 439, 442, *736*
single-issue parties 92, 421, 441
Sinnot, Richard 44, 46, 48
Sinnott, Kathy 262
Seitlinger Report (1982) 5
Slovakia 568–87, *568*; allocation of EP seats *24, 25, 31, 32, 33*; EP and national elections 578–80; geographical position 569; geopolitical profile 571; historical background 569–71; national and EP electoral systems 577–8; overview of the political landscape 571–2; profile *569*
Slovenia 471–88, *471*; allocation of EP seats 23, *24, 25, 31, 32, 33*; EP and national elections 478–81; geographical position 472; geopolitical profile 473–4; historical background 472; national and EP electoral systems 478; overview of the political landscape 474; profile *472*
Soares, Mário 353, 357, 359, 360
social justice xxxv, 90, 92, 249, 260, 611
social media 181, 309,
social networks 95, 424, 624, 680; *see also* Facebook, MySpace, YouTube and Twitter
social policy 10, 11, 90, 91, 92, 172, 179, 307, 335, 387
Socialist International 55, 657
Socrates, José *352*, 354, 367
Soini, Timo 400, 405, 406, 409, 410, *410*, 691
Solana, Javier 332
Solvak, Mihkel 502
Sólyom, László *590*
Somalia 79, 111
Somer-Topcu, Zeynep 43, 44
Sosa Wagner, Francisco 335
sovereignty 67, 78, 80, 108, 172, 173, 178, 179, 180, 181, 194, 197, 198, 249, 257, 258, 260, 273, 274, 277, 280, 281, 336, 355, 358, 359, 360, 363, 364, 384, 386, 394, 398, 497, 531, 552, 563, 575, 610, 614, 615, 620, 686, 714, 730
Soviet Union 79, 111, 397, 406, 416, 493, 494, 514, 522, 529, 550, 555, 570, 635, 655; former 293

Spaak, Paul-Henri 18 398
Spain 321–48, *321*; allocation of EP seats 23, *24, 25, 31, 32, 33*; EP and national elections 328–33; geographical position 322–3; geopolitical profile 323–4; historical background 323; national and EP electoral systems 328–33; overview of the political landscape 324; profile *322;* corruption scandals 329–30, 331, 347–8; financial crisis 324, 334, 336–7, 347–8
Special Committee on the Financial, Economic and Social Crisis 34, *102, 206, 311, 313, 314, 601, 602, 669*
Special Committee on Policy Challenges 34
Speroni, Francesco Enrico 30, 134, *138*
Spinelli, Altiero xxxv, 4, 9, 14, 18
Spitaels, Guy 27
Spitzenkandidat(en) xxxi, xxxii, 95, 703, 709, 717, 718, 731
Spoon, Jae-Jae 40, 43, 427
Spreitzer, Astrid 199
Stability and Growth Pact 186
Steed, Michael 40
Stefanopoulos, Kostis 300
Stoiber, Edmund 86, 95
Strasbourg (France) xxxiii, xxxv, 17, 18, 19, 20, 22, 23, 24, 28, 34, 39, 42, 53, 59, 61, 67, 69, 73, 86, 88, 89, 90, 92, 96, 126, 128, 132, 133, 134, 137, 162, 163, 181, 182, 196, 197, 209, 254, 255, 428, 484, 504, 532, 537, 538, 560, 641, 647, 675, 682, 686, 689, 703, 712, 713, 715, 717, 719, 720, 721, 724, 730, 732
Strauß, Franz Joseph 86, 88
Structural and Cohesion Funds 249
Studlar, Donley 45
Suarez, Adolfo 329, 330
subsidiarity principle 129, 152, 157, 198
supranationalism 152, 172, 553, 554, 686
Svensson, Alf 424, *426*
Svensson, Palle 44
Sweden 414–29, *414,* allocation of EP seats 23, *24, 25, 31, 32, 33*; EP and national elections 421–3; geographical position 415; geopolitical profile 416; historical background 415–16; national and EP electoral systems 421; overview of the political landscape 416–17; profile *415*
Swoboda, Hannes 28, *391*
Syria 112, 294
Szczerbziak, Aleks 355

Taggart, Paul 355, 574
Tangentopoli 116
Taoiseach (Irish Pime Minister) 245, 248, 249, 253, 254, 257
Tapie, Bernard 60, *60*

784

Tarand, Indrek 497, *498,* 499, 500, 502, *502, 503,* 504, 505, 748, 751
taxation 12, 151, 169, 226, 252, 315, 363, 365, 500, 555, 556, 579, 581, 594, 598
terrorism 118, *130,* 169, 332, 386, 520, 540, 594, 622
Tito, Josip Broz 473
Thatcher, Margaret 10, 218, 552, 689
theoretical interpretation of Euro-elections in Austria 392; Belgium 164–5; Bulgaria 649; Cyprus 462; Czech Republic 565; Denmark 285; Estonia 504; Finland 411; France 73–4; Germany 98–105; Greece 316–18; Hungary 604; Ireland 264–5; Italy 140–3; Latvia 522; Lithuania 565; Luxembourg 207–9; Malta 446; Poland 628; Portugal 371–2; Romania 670; Slovakia 585; Slovenia 486; Spain 347–8; Sweden 427; The Netherlands 185–6; The United Kingdom 239–41
Thorn, Gaston 197, 198
Tilley, James R. 40
Tillman, Erik R. 43, 48
Timpone, Richard 44
Tower of Babel xxxv, 732
trade 63, 89, 136, 148, 168, 169, 172, 215, 398, 435, 436, 473, 474, 493, 581
trade agreements 9
trade unions 80, 114, 128, 192, 193, 198, *206, 237,* 249, *283, 345,* 441, 461, 475, 529, 641
transport 11, 92, 199, 540, 581, 590, 664
Treaty xxix, 4, 5, 6, 7, 8, 9, 10, 11, 12, 13, 14, 15, 16, 18, 23, 31, 38, *59,* 56, 58, 62, 63, 64, 67, *77,* 79, 80, 89, 91, 92, 96, *110, 111,* 112, 117, 137, *148,* 152, 158, *168,* 169, 173, 174, 175, 177, 178, 179, 180, 182, 186, *196,* 194, 198, 199, 200, *214,* 215, 217, 217, 218, 226, 227, 228, 241, 244, *244,* 245, 248, 249, 250, *250,* 255, 256, 257, 258, 259, 260, 262, *268,* 269, 275, 276, *277,* 280, *290,* 293, 294, 308, 310, *322,* 323, 324, 327, 328, 334, *335,* 342, *345, 352,* 353, 354, 358, 359, 363, 365, *378,* 379, 384, 386, 387, 388, 389, *397,* 398, 401, 405, 406, 410, 415, 421, 422, 424, 425, *434,* 437, 440, *449,* 453, 454, *472,* 482, 484, *492,* 500, *508,* 513, 516, 518, 520, 521, 522, *528,* 530, 531, 536, *539,* 546, *550,* 553, *569, 571,* 575, 580, 582, *590,* 599, 605, *609,* 615, 620, 621, 622, 624, 628, *634,* 635, 645, 650, *654,* 674, 686, 689, 700, 702, 708, 709, 714, 734
Treaty Establishing a Constitution for Europe (TECE) 12, 453, 454
Trematerra, Gino *110,* 137, *138*
Tremosa, Ramón 337, *345*
Tsebelis, George 9, 11

Tsipras, Alexis *292,* 706, 716, 718, *752*
Tsovolas, Dimitris 300
Turkey 12, 36, 65, 82, *94,* 179, 180, 199, 227, 281, 294, 364, 366, 387, 388, 520, 540, 582, 621, 644; and Greece 22, 319, 634, 675, 715, 731
Tusk, Donald 609, 613, *613,* 623, 629, 713
Twitter 336, 365, 424, 558
Two round system (TRS) 83

unemployment 64, 83, 88, 118, 130, 194, 195, 199, 203, 248, 249, 258, 259, 260, 269, 282, 300, 307, 324, 334, 336, 365, 389, 416, 439, 482, 501, 537, 540, 561, 594, 598, 610, 615, 620, 659, 663, 700, 703
Ungureanu, Mihai-Răzvan *654*
Uniform electoral procedure 3, 4, 5, 6, 15
United Green Parties of Europe 225
United Kingdom (UK) 213–41, *213;* allocation of EP seats 22, 23, *24, 25, 31, 32, 33;* electoral constituencies 218–20, *219,* 240; EP and national elections 218–21; geographical position 214; geopolitical profile 215; historical background 214; national and EP electoral systems 218–20; overview of the political landscape 215; profile *214;* Lisbon Treaty 218, 226–7, 228; MPs expenses scandal 226; opt-outs 10, 12; Maastricht Treaty 217
United Nations (UN) 79, 111, 169, 191, 245, 269, 294, 323, 416, 435, 450, 466, 571, 610; FAO 112; General Assembly 20, 21; Security Council 53, 79, 131, 149, 215, 354

Vaclav, Klaus 552, 553, 556, 557, 559, 561
Valle d'Aosta (Italy) *109,* 119, 128
Valls, Manuel *52*
Van Aelst, Peter 155
van der Eijk, Cees 39, 42, 43, 208, 729
van der Stoep, Daniel *168,* 182, *184*
van Spanje, Joost 45
VAT (value added tax) 8, 440, 529
Vedel, George 4
Vendola, Nichi 129
Verhofstadt, Guy 28, 65, 155, 158, *160,* 162, 716, *755*
Vidal-Quadras, Alejo 20, *342*
Virant, Gregor (Civic List) *472,* 474
Vitorino, António 358
Vittorio Emanuele II, King 111
Vlk, Miloslav 559
Voivodship, province (Poland) 615
voter apathy xxxiii, 45, 118, 186, 599, 605, 697, 706, 731
voting abstentions 6, 7, 19, 61, *66,* 442; and cognitive deficit 74
Voting Advice Applications VAAs 184, 202

Wales 214, 215, 216, 217, 218, *219*, 224, 225, 228, *228, 229, 237,* 239, 682, 717
Wałęsa, Lech 611
Wallonia (Belgium) 149, 150, 154, 158
Wallström, Margot 424
Watson, Graham/Watson Lord 40, 228,
Weber, Max 114
Weber, Til 42
Weiler, J.H.H v, xxv, xxxii, xxxv, 10, 674, 677, 679, 693, 697, 698,
Weishaupt, Timo J. 41, 44, 45, 47, 524, 526
welfare state 82, 91, 151, 170, 171, 172, 173, 175, 270, 274, 404, 406, 407, 411, 412, 417, 418, 475, 552, 663
Werner, Pierre 193, 197
Western European Union (WEU) 112
Western Union Assembly 21
Wilders, Geert 173, 178, 184, 686, 717
Wilkens, Andreas 83
Willem, King *168*
wine industry 65
Wiseler, Claude 20
Wittrock, Jill 43, 47

women MEPs 24, *26, 27*, 34, 69, 134, *135*, 159, 205, 310, 315, 330, 390, 410, 444, 462, 478, 484, 522, 545, 562, 647, 666, 720–726
World Bank 79, 294, 323, 354, 638
World Trade Organization WTO 112, 294, 450, 571
World War I 149, 655
World War II 78, 79, 111, 169, 474, 555, 675; reconstruction after 111, 112
Wulff, Christian 77, 79

xenophobia xxvii, *130*, 172, 540, 546

YouTube 95, 131, 365, 500, 680
Yugoslav People's Army *(Jugoslovanska ljudska armada/Jugoslovenska narodna armija)* 473

Zagrebelsky, Gustavo 119
Zapatero, José Luis *322*, 324, 327, 334, 337, 367
Zar, Michelle E. 43, 44
Zatlers, Valdis *508*
Zeman, Milos 550, 557
Zincone, Giovanna 143